PREFACE

THIS book is the result of an invitation from the publishers to prepare for their well-known series of collected plays a volume to cover the period lying before that represented in Professor Neilson's *Chief Elizabethan Dramatists*. I have aimed to tell, as clearly as may be in selections, the story of the origin and development of the English drama, to render the plays as intelligible and as vivid to college students as I could, and to make the texts so accurate as to be of genuine service to scholars. In order clearly to illustrate the origin of the drama, I have necessarily had to include a few liturgical plays from the Continent, since the corresponding English plays, though known to have existed, have not survived; here my procedure is justified by the fact that the early drama, as a part of the service of the Roman Church, was international in its development. In order to render the plays intelligible to college students, I have furnished translations of the mediæval Latin texts, have modernized the punctuation, have added, in brackets, stage-directions, and have explained in footnotes all words that seemed to offer difficulty. Finally, in order to make the texts accurate and serviceable, I have tried to print from the most authoritative sources, and have spared no pains in collating the proofs with the originals. In general, the proofs have been compared at least twice with the indicated sources; and the result, I hope, will gain for the volume the confidence of scholars.

I wish to acknowledge, as of right due, my indebtedness to the excellent collection of a similar nature, *Specimens of the Pre-Shakespearean Drama*, issued by my former teacher, Professor John M. Manly, to whose instruction and abiding inspiration I owe more than I can well express. Without his earlier labors in charting the sea, the present volume would have been more difficult to prepare, and not nearly so effective. Some of my detailed indebtedness I have been able to indicate in the footnotes, but not all; and hence I here wish to make this general acknowledgment.

To various friends and colleagues I am also under obligation for assistance generously rendered. In translating the very bad Latin of some of the liturgical texts, I have had valuable aid from Professor George Lincoln Burr and Professor Charles Love Durham; in elucidating difficult words in the Middle

English texts, I have had no less valuable aid from Professor William
Strunk, Jr.; and in collating the proofs with the originals, I have been
assisted by Mr. Horace Mack. To all these I wish to express my sincere
gratitude.

J. Q. A

CONTENTS

CHIEF PRE–SHAKESPEAREAN DRAMAS

I

SOURCES OF THE LITURGICAL DRAMA

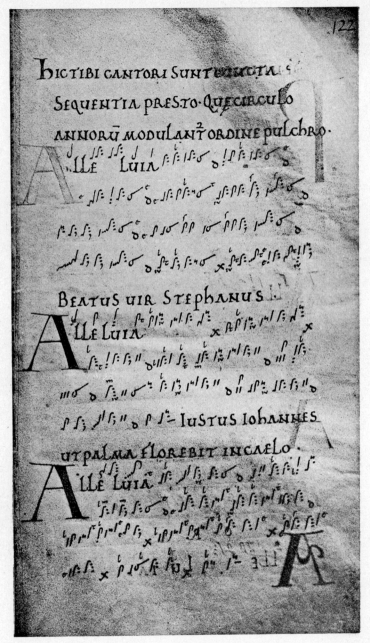

THE ALLELUIA WORDLESS SEQUENCE
From the Winchester Troper (Bodleian M.S. 775) of the year 979

THE *QUEM-QUÆRITIS* TROPE[1]

DE RESURRECTIONE DOMINI	OF THE LORD'S RESURRECTION
Int[errogatio]:	Question [of the angels]:
Quem quæritis in sepulchro, [o] Christicolæ?	*Whom seek ye in the sepulchre, O followers of Christ?*
R[esponsio]:	Answer [of the Marys]:
Jesum Nazarenum crucifixum, o cælicolæ.	*Jesus of Nazareth, which was crucified, O celestial ones.*
[Angeli:]	[The angels:]
Non est hic; surrexit, sicut prædixerat.	*He is not here; he is risen, just as he foretold.*
Ite, nuntiate quia surrexit de sepulchro.	*Go, announce that he is risen from the sepulchre.*

[1] In the ninth century, words were set to the wordless sequences, thus making "tropes." The one printed above, commonly referred to as *Quem quæritis*, and belonging to the Introit of the Mass at Easter, is from the St. Gall MS. 484, of the ninth century (see the facsimile in Léon Gautier, *Histoire de la Poésie liturgique au Moyen Age*, 1886, p. 216). The text is the earliest we have, and doubtless represents the original form of this particular trope. The lines were sung in the manner of dialogue between the angels and the three Marys at the sepulchre on Easter morning (see St. Mark, xvi, 1–8). From this simple dialogued song of the Easter Mass service the modern drama developed.

THE EASTER SEPULCHRE[1]

I

DEPOSITIO CRUCIS

[Good Friday.]

Within the Abbye Church of Durham, uppon Good Friday, theire was marvelous solemne service, in the which service time, after the Passion was sung, two of the eldest Monkes did take a goodly large CRUCIFIX, all of gold, of the picture of our Saviour Christ nailed uppon the crosse, lyinge uppon a velvett cushion, havinge St. Cuthbert's armes uppon it all imbroydered with gold, bringinge that betwixt them uppon the said cushion to the lowest greeces in the Quire; and there betwixt them did hold the said picture of our Saviour, sittinge of every side, on ther knees, of that, and then one of the said Monkes did rise and went a pretty way from it, sittinge downe uppon his knees, with his shooes put of, and verye reverently did creepe away uppon his knees unto the said Crosse, and most reverently did kisse it. And after him the other Monke did so likewise; and then they did sitt them downe on every side of the Crosse, and holdinge it betwixt them; and after that the Prior came forth of his stall, and did sitt him downe of his knees, with his shooes off, and in like sort did creepe also unto the said Crosse; and all the Monkes after him, one after another, in the same order; and in the mean time all the whole quire singinge an himne. The service beinge ended, the two Monkes did carrye it to the SEPULCHRE with great reverence, which Sepulchre was sett upp in the morninge on the north side of the Quire, nigh to the High Altar, before the service time; and there lay it within the said SEPULCHRE with great devotion, with another picture of our Saviour Christ, in whose breast they did enclose, with great reverence, the most holy and blessed Sacrament of the Altar, senceinge it, and prayinge unto it upon theire knees, a great space, settinge two tapers lighted before it, which tapers did burne unto Easter day in the morninge, that it was taken forth.

II

ELEVATIO CRUCIS

[Easter Day.]

There was in the Abbye Church of Duresme[1] verye solemne service uppon Easter Day, betweene three and four of the clocke in the morninge, in honour of the RESURRECTION, where two of the oldest Monkes of the Quire came to the Sepulchre, being sett upp upon Good Friday, after the Passion, all covered with red velvett and embroidered with gold, and then did sence it, either Monke with a pair of silver sencers sittinge on theire knees before the Sepulchre. Then they both rising came to the Sepulchre, out of which, with great devotion and reverence, they tooke a marvelous beautifull IMAGE OF OUR SAVIOUR, representing the resurrection, with a crosse in his hand, in the breast wherof was enclosed in bright christall the holy Sacrament of the Altar, throughe the which christall the Blessed Host was conspicuous to the behoulders. Then, after the elevation of the said picture, carryed by the said two Monkes upon a faire velvett cushion, all embrodered, singinge the anthem of Christus resurgens, they brought it to the High Altar, settinge that on the midst therof, whereon it stood, the two Monkes kneelinge on theire knees before the Altar, and senceing it all the time that the rest of the whole quire was in singinge the foresaid

[1] Durham.

---

[1] From A Description or Brief Declaration of all the Ancient Monuments, Rites and Customes belonginge or beinge within the Monastical Church of Durham before the Suppression, edited by J. Raine, in the Surtees Society, xv. For a more primitive form of the Depositio Crucis and the Elevatio Crucis, see the Latin text from the Regularis Concordia of St. Ethelwold, printed by E. K. Chambers, The Mediæval Stage, ii, 306.

anthem of *Christus resurgens*. The which anthem beinge ended, the two Monkes tooke up the cushions and the picture from the Altar, supportinge it betwixt them, proceeding, in procession, from the High Altar to the south Quire dore, where there was four antient Gentlemen, belonginge to the Prior, appointed to attend theire cominge, holdinge upp a most rich CANNOPYE of purple velvett, tached round about with redd silke and gold fringe; and at everye corner did stand one of theise ancient Gentlemen, to beare it over the said image, with the Holy Sacrament, carried by two Monkes round about the church, the whole quire waitinge uppon it with goodly torches and great store of other lights, all singinge, rejoyceinge, and praising God most devoutly, till they came to the High Altar againe, whereon they did place the said image, there to remaine untill the Ascension day.

SEMI–DRAMATIC TROPE [1]

[Easter.]

Post hæc [tert. resp.] duo pueri in albis, unus ad dextram altaris, alius ad sinistram, cantant:

> Quem quæritis [in sepulchro, o Christicole]?

Tres capellani cum dalmaticis albis, coopertis capitibus, ante altare respondent:

> Jesum Nazarenum [crucifixum, o celicole].

Item pueri:

> Non est hic; [surrexit sicut predixerat.
>
> Ite, nuntiate quia surrexit a mortuis].

Deinde illi tres accedentes ad altare, et intro aspicientes, versi ad chorum dicunt alta voce:

> Alleluia, surrexit Dominus!

Post hæc cantor incipit:

> Te Deum [laudamus].

After this [the third responsory] let two boys, in albs,[1] one at the right of the altar, the other at the left, sing:

> Whom seek ye in the sepulchre, O followers of Christ?

Let three chaplains, garbed in white dalmatics,[2] with covered heads,[3] standing before the altar, reply:

> Jesus of Nazareth, which was crucified, O celestial ones.

Then the boys:

> He is not here; he is risen, just as he foretold.
> Go, announce that he is risen from the dead.

Then those three, approaching the altar and looking within, turning towards the choir, say in a loud voice:

> Alleluia, the Lord is risen!

After this the cantor [4] begins:

> We praise thee, O God.

[1] A full-length vestment of white linen.
[2] A vestment resembling the alb, but with slits in the side.
[3] Probably in order that they might the better represent women.
[4] The leader of the choir, who regularly sang the Te Deum marking the end of the Matin service.

[1] Performed at Tours, in France. I have reproduced the text from Carl Lange's Die lateinischen Osterfeiern, 1887, p. 24. Under the influence of the "Easter Sepulchre" just described, as well as because of the more appropriate time, the Quem quæritis trope has been transferred from the Mass to the Matin service, and rendered partly dramatic by having the lines of the angels sung by two choir boys standing at the altar, and the lines of the Marys by three chaplains who advance up to the altar. Since the Te Deum laudamus closed the Matin, it is obvious that the song was inserted just before the conclusion of the service.

II
LITURGICAL PLAYS DEALING WITH
THE STORY OF CHRIST

SEPULCHRUM [1]

[Easter.]

Dum tertia recitatur lectio, quatuor fratres induant se, quorum unus alba indutus ac si ad aliud agendum ingrediatur, atque latenter sepulchri locum adeat, ibique manu tenens palmam, quietus sedeat. Dumque tertium percelebratur responsorium, residui tres succedant, omnes quidem cappis induti, turribula cum incensu manibus gestantes ac pedetemptim ad similitudinem querentium quid, ueniant ante locum sepulchri. Aguntur enim hæc ad imitationem angeli sedentis in monumento atque mulierum cum aromatibus uenientium ut ungerent corpus Ihesu. Cum ergo ille residens tres uelut erraneos ac aliquid querentes uiderit sibi adproximare, incipiat mediocri uoce dulcisono cantare:

Quem queritis [in sepulchro, o Christicole]?

Quo decantato fine tenus, respondeant hi tres uno ore:

Ihesum Nazarenum [crucifixum, o celicola].

Quibus ille:

Non est hic; surrexit, sicut prædixerat:

Ite, nuntiate quia surrexit a mortuis.

Cujus iussionis uoce uertant se illi tres ad chorum dicentes:

Alleluia! resurrexit Dominus [hodie, Leo fortis, Christus filius Dei. Deo gratias dicite, eia!]

While the third lesson is being chanted, let four brethren vest themselves; of whom let one, vested in an alb, enter as if to take part in the service, and let him without being observed approach the place of the sepulchre, and there, holding a palm in his hand, let him sit down quietly. While the third responsory is being sung, let the remaining three follow, all of them vested in copes, and carrying in their hands censers filled with incense; and slowly, in the manner of seeking something, let them come before the place of the sepulchre. These things are done in imitation of the angel seated in the monument, and of the women coming with spices to anoint the body of Jesus. When therefore that one seated shall see the three, as if straying about and seeking something, approach him, let him begin in a dulcet voice of medium pitch to sing:

Whom seek ye in the sepulchre, O followers of Christ?

When he has sung this to the end, let the three respond in unison:

Jesus of Nazareth, which was crucified, O celestial one.

To whom that one:

He is not here; he is risen, just as he foretold.

Go, announce that he is risen from the dead.

At the word of this command let those three turn themselves to the choir, saying:

Alleluia! The Lord is risen to-day, The strong lion, the Christ, the Son of God. Give thanks to God, huzza!

---

[1] From the *Regularis Concordia* of St. Ethelwold, written between 965 and 975. According to the *Proœmium* of the document, it was prepared by the bishops, abbots, and abbesses of England at the request of King Edgar at a Council of Winchester. I have reproduced the text from that printed by W. S. Logeman in *Anglia* (1891), xiii, 365 ff., and have followed Manly in expanding the songs from the cues given; the expansion of the second song of the Marys I have based on the text of the Winchester Troper, Bodleian MS. 775, dating from 979. Lines in italic type were intended to be sung. See St. Mark, xvi, 1–8.

Dicto hoc, rursus ille residens, uelut reuocans illos dicat antiphonam:

Uenite, et uidete locum [ubi positus erat Dominus, alleluia! alleluia!]

Hæc uero dicens surgat, et erigat uelum, ostendatque eis locum cruce nudatum, sed tantum linteamina posita quibus crux inuoluta erat. Quo uiso, deponant turribula quæ gestauerant in eodem sepulchro, sumantque linteum et extendant contra clerum, ac, ueluti ostendentes quod surrexerit Dominus et iam non sit illo inuolutus, hanc canant antiphonam:

Surrexit Dominus de sepulchro,
[Qui pro nobis pependit in ligno].

Superponantque linteum altari. Finita antiphona, Prior congaudens pro triumpho Regis nostri, quod, deuicta morte, surrexit, incipiat hymnum:

Te, Deum, laudamus.

Quo incepto, una pulsantur omnia signa.

This said, let the former, again seating himself, as if recalling them, sing the anthem:

Come, and see the place where the Lord was laid. Alleluia! Alleluia!

And saying this, let him rise, and let him lift the veil and show them the place bare of the cross, but only the cloths laid there with which the cross was wrapped. Seeing which, let them set down the censers which they carried into the same sepulchre, and let them take up the cloth and spread it out before the eyes of the clergy; and, as if making known that the Lord had risen and was not now therein wrapped, let them sing this anthem:

The Lord is risen from the sepulchre,
Who for us hung upon the cross.

And let them place the cloth upon the altar. The anthem being ended, let the Prior, rejoicing with them at the triumph of our King, in that, having conquered death, he arose, begin the hymn:

We praise thee, O God.

This begun, all the bells chime out together.

SEPULCHRUM [1]

[Easter.]

Finito iij Responsorium cum suo $\bar{V}$ et Gloria Patri, uenient tres persone in superpelliceis et in capis sericis capitibus uelatis quasi tres Marie querentes Ihesum, singule portantes pixidem in manibus quasi aromatibus, quarum prima ad ingressum chori usque sepulcrum procedat per se quasi lamentando dicat:

At the end of the third responsory with its verse and the *Gloria Patri*, let three persons enter, in surplices and with their heads covered with silk copes, as if they were the three Marys seeking Jesus, each one carrying in her hands a censer as if it were filled with spices; of whom let the first proceed alone from the entrance of the choir up to the sepulchre, and say as if lamenting:

> *Heu! pius pastor occiditur,*
> *Quem nulla culpa infecit:*
> *O mors lugenda!*

> *Alas! the good shepherd is killed,*
> *Whom no guilt stained.*
> *O lamentable death!*

Factoque modico interuallo, intret secunda Maria consimili modo et dicat:

After a short interval of time, let the second Mary enter in like manner and say:

> *Heu! nequam gens Iudaica,*
> *Quam dira frendet uesania,*
> *Plebs execranda!*

> *Alas! vile race of Jews,*
> *Whom a dire madness makes frenzied,*
> *Detestable people!*

Deinde iij Maria consimili modo dicat:

Then let the third Mary in like manner say:

> *Heu! uerus doctor obijt,*
> *Qui uitam functis contulit:*
> *O res plangenda!*

> *Alas! the true teacher is dead*
> *Who gave life to the dead.*
> *O lamentable fact!*

Ad huc paululum procedendo prima Maria dicat:

At this let the first Mary, advancing a little, say:

> *Heu! misere cur contigit*
> *Uidere mortem Saluatoris?*

> *Alas! why has it pitiably befallen us*
> *To see the death of the Saviour?*

Deinde secunda Maria dicat:

Then let the second Mary say:

> *Heu! Consolacio nostra,*
> *Ut quid mortem sustinuit?*

> *Alas! our Consolation,*
> *Why did he suffer death?*

Tunc iij Maria:

Then the third Mary:

> *Heu! Redempcio nostra,*
> *Ut quid taliter agere uoluit?*

> *Alas! our Redeemer,*
> *Why did he choose to pursue such a course?*

---

[1] Printed by E. K. Chambers, *The Mediæval Stage*, ii, 315, from Bodleian MS. 15,846, described as " a Sarum processional written in the fourteenth century, and belonging in the fifteenth century to the church of St. John the Evangelist, Dublin." Another, and somewhat inferior text, is reproduced in facsimile by W. H. Frere, *Winchester Troper*, 1894, from which it is printed by Manly, *Specimens*, i, xxii. The play is of interest as illustrating textual expansion by the introduction of new tropes, and dramatic expansion by the introduction of a new scene, the Race of Peter and John. Lines in italic type were chanted or sung; in the manuscript they are accompanied by musical notation. See St. Mark, xvi, 1-8, St. John, xx, 1-10.

Tunc se coniungant et procedant ad gradum chori ante altare simul dicentes:

Iam, iam, ecce, iam properemus ad tumulum
Unguentes Delecti corpus sanctissimum!

Deinde procedant similiter prope sepulchrum, et prima Maria dicat per se:

Condumentis aromatum
Ungamus corpus sanctissimum,
Quo preciosa.

Tunc secunda Maria dicat per se:

Nardi uetet commixtio,
Ne putrescat in tumulo
Caro beata!

Deinde iij Maria dicat per se:

Sed nequimus hoc patrare sine adiutorio.
Quis nam saxum reuoluet a monumenti ostio?

Facto interuallo, angelus nixus sepulcrum apparuit eis et dicat hoc modo:

Quem queritis ad sepulcrum, o Cristicole?

Deinde respondeant tres Marie simul dicentes:

Ihesum Nazarenum crucifixum, o celicola!

Tunc angelus dicet:

Surrexit, non est hic, sicut dixit;
Uenite et uidete locum ubi positus fuerat.

Deinde predicte Marie sepulcrum intrent et inclinantes se et prospicientes undique intra sepulcrum, alta uoce quasi gaudentes et admirantes et parum a sepulcro recedentes simul dicant:

Then let them join together, and advance to the steps of the choir before the altar, saying in unison:

Now, now, behold, now let us hasten to the tomb
To anoint the most sacred body of the Beloved One!

Then let them advance in similar fashion almost up to the sepulchre, and let the first Mary say alone:

With preservatives of spices
Let us anoint the most sacred body, —
With the most costly ones possible.

Then let the second Mary say alone:

Let a mixture of spikenard hinder
Lest in the tomb putrefy
The Blessed Flesh!

Then let the third Mary say alone:

But this we cannot accomplish without assistance.
Who shall roll us away the stone from the door of the sepulchre?

After an interval, an angel, leaning on the tomb, appears to them; and let him speak in this manner:

Whom seek ye at the sepulchre, O followers of Christ?

Then let the three Marys answer, saying in unison:

Jesus of Nazareth, which was crucified, O celestial one!

Then let the angel say:

He is risen; he is not here, just as he said.
Come and see the place where he was laid.

Then let the aforesaid Marys enter the sepulchre; and, bowing themselves and looking on all sides within the sepulchre, in a loud voice as if rejoicing and wondering, and withdrawing a little distance from the sepulchre, let them say in unison:

Alleluya! resurrexit Dominus!
Alleluya! resurrexit Dominus hodie!
Resurrexit potens, fortis, Christus, Filius
Dei!

Deinde angelus ad eas:

Et euntes dicite discipulis eius et Petro
quia surrexit.

In quo reuertant ad angelum quasi mandatum suum ad implendum parate simul dicentes:

Eya! pergamus propere
Mandatum hoc perficere!

Interim ueniant ad ingressum chori due persone nude pedes sub personis apostolorum Iohannis et Petri indute albis sine paruris cum tunicis, quorum Iohannes amictus tunica alba palmam in manu gestans, Petrus uero rubea tunica indutus claues in manu ferens; et predicte mulieres de sepulcro reuertentes et quasi de choro simul exeuntes, dicat prima Maria per se sequentiam:

Victime paschali laudes
Immolant Christiani.
Agnus redemit oues:
Christus innocens Patri
Reconsiliauit peccatores.
Mors et uita duello
Conflixere mirando:
Dux uite mortuis
Regnat uiuus.

Tunc obuiantes eis in medio chori predicti discipuli, interrogantes simul dicant:

Dic nobis, Maria,
Quid uidisti in uia?

Tunc prima Maria respondeat quasi monstrando:

Sepulcrum Christi uiuentis,
Et gloriam uidi resurgentis.

Alleluia! the Lord is risen!
Alleluia! the Lord is risen to-day!
He is risen, the powerful, the strong, the
Christ, the Son of God!

Then the angel to them:

And, going, tell his disciples and Peter that
he is risen.

Whereupon, let them turn towards the angel as if ready to execute his command, saying in unison:

Come on!   Let us go quickly
To perform this command!

Meanwhile let there come to the entrance of the choir two persons barefooted, impersonating the apostles John and Peter, clad in albs without ornaments, with tunics, of whom John clothed in a white tunic, carrying a palm in his hand, Peter clad in a red tunic, carrying the keys in his hand;[1] and the above-mentioned women returning from the sepulchre, and as if going forth from the choir together, let the first Mary say alone the sequence:

Let Christians offer the sacrifice of praises
To the Paschal Victim.
The Lamb has redeemed the sheep:
The innocent Christ, to the Father
Has reconciled the sinners.
Death and Life have fought
In a wonderful duel:
The Prince of Life, having died,
Reigns living.

Then let the above-mentioned disciples, meeting them in the middle of the choir, questioning them, say in unison:

Tell us, Mary,
What hast thou seen on the way?

Then let the first Mary answer as if pointing:

The sepulchre of the living Christ,
And the glory of the Resurrected One, I
saw!

[1] The keys to heaven and hell, symbolical of papal authority.

Tunc ij Maria responde[a]t similiter monstrando:

> *Angelicos iestes,*
> *Sudarium et uestes.*

Tunc iij Maria respondeat:

> *Surrexit Christus, spes nostr⌣,*
> *Precedet uos in Galileam.*

Et sic procedant simul ad ostium chori; interim currant duo ad monumentum; uerumptamen ille discipulus quem diligebat Ihesus uenit prior ad monumentum, iuxta euangelium: "Currebant autem duo simul et ille alius discipulus precucurrit cicius Petro et uenit prior ad monumentum, non tamen introiuit." Uidentes discipuli predicti sepulcrum uacuum et uerbis Marie credentes reuertant se ad chorum dicentes:

> *Credendum est magis soli Marie ueraci*
> *Quam Iudeorum turbe fallaci!*

Tunc audita Christi resurreccione, cnorus prosequatur alta uoce quasi gaudentes et exultantes sic dicentes:

> *Scimus Christum surrexisse*
> *A mortuis uere.*
> *Tu nobis, uictor Rex, miserere!*

Qua finita, executor officii incipiat:

> *Te, Deum, laudamus.*

Tunc recedant sanctae Marie, apostoli, et angelus.

Then let the second Mary answer, likewise pointing:

> *Angelic witnesses,*
> *The sudarium and the vestments!*

Then let the third Mary answer:

> *Christ, our hope, is risen!*
> *He will go before you into Galilee.*

And so let them [i.e. the three Marys] proceed together to the door of the choir; meanwhile let the two [i.e. John and Peter] run to the tomb; but that disciple whom Jesus loved [i.e. John] comes first to the tomb, according to the evangelist: "Moreover they ran both of them together, and that other disciple outran Peter, and came first to the tomb; yet he did not enter." Let the above-mentioned disciples, seeing the sepulchre empty, and believing the words of the Marys, turn themselves toward the choir, saying:

> *It is better to believe a single truthful Mary*
> *Than all the lying host of the Jews.*

Then, having heard of the resurrection of Christ, let the choir follow after, in a loud voice, as if rejoicing and exulting, saying thus:

> *We know that Christ is risen*
> *From the dead in very truth!*
> *Do thou, O Victor King, have mercy on us!*

This having been finished, let the manager of the office begin:

> *We praise thee, O God.*

Then let the holy Marys, the apostles, and the angel withdraw.

SEPULCHRUM [1]

[Easter.]

Ad faciendam similitudinem Domini sepulchri, primum procedant tres fratres præparati et vestiti in similitudinem trium Mariarum, pedetentim, et quasi tristes, alternantes hos versus cantantes:

PRIMA eorum dicat:

Heu! pius pastor occidit,
Quem culpa nulla infecit! [1]
O res plangenda!

SECUNDA.

Heu! verus pastor obiit,
Qui vitam sanctis contulit!
O mors lugenda!

TERTIA.

Heu! nequam gens Judaica,
Quam dira frendens vesania!
Plebs execranda!

PRIMA.

Cur nece pium impia
Dampnasti sava invida?
O ira nefanda!

SECUNDA.

Quid justus hic promeruit
Quod crucifigi debuit?
O gens dampnanda!

TERTIA.

Heu! quid agemus misere
Dulci magistro orbate?
Heu! sors lacrymanda!

To make the representation of the Lord's sepulchre, first let three brothers, prepared beforehand and clothed in the likeness of the three Marys, advance slowly and as if sad, alternately singing these verses: the first of them shall say:

Alas! the good shepherd is killed,
Whom no guilt stained.
O lamentable occurrence!

The second:

Alas! the true shepherd is dead
Who gave life to the upright!
O lamentable death!

The third:

Alas! vile race of Jews,
Whom a dire madness makes frenzied!
Detestable people!

The first:

Why condemned ye to an impious death
The Holy One with savage hate?
O direful rage!

The second:

How has this righteous man deserved
To be crucified?
O race accursed!

The third:

Alas! what are we wretched ones to do,
Bereft of our sweet Master?
Alas! lamentable chance!

---

[1] Lange prints *occidit*, apparently an error derived from the preceding line.

---

[1] The manuscript, of the thirteenth century, is from Orléans, France. It shows the development of the *Sepulchrum* into a play of three episodes, the Visit of the Three Marys, the Race of Peter and John, and the Appearance of Christ to Mary Magdalene. I have reproduced the text from Carl Lange, *Die lateinischen Osterfeiern*, 1887, p. 160. The lines in italic type were sung or chanted. See St. Mark, xvi, 1-8, St. John, xx, 1-18, St. Luke, xxiv, 1-12.

PRIMA.

Eamus ergo propere,
Quod solum quimus facere,
Mente devota.

SECUNDA.

Condimentis aromatum
Ungamus corpus sanctissimum,
Quo preciosa.

TERTIA.

Nardi vetet commixcio,
Ne putrescat in tumulo
Caro beata.

Cum autem venerint in chorum, eant ad monumentum quasi quærentes, et cantantes omnes simul hunc versum:

Sed nequimus hoc patere sine adiutorio.
Quisnam saxum hoc revolvet ab monumenti hostio?

Quibus respondeat Angelus sedens foris, ad caput sepulchri, vestitus alba deaurata, mitra tectus caput, etsi deinfulatus, palmam in sinistra, ramum candelarum plenam tenens in manu dextra, et dicat moderata et admodum gravi voce:

Quem quæritis in sepulchro, O Christicolæ?

MULIERES.

Jesum Nazarenum crucifixum, O celicola.

Quibus respondeat Angelus:

Quid, Christicolæ, viventem quæritis cum mortuis?
Non est hic; surrexit, prædixit ut discipulis.
Mementote quid iam vobis locutus in Galilea,
Quod Christum opportebat pati, atque die tertia
Resurgere cum gloria.

The first:

Let us therefore go quickly,
To do the only thing we can do,
With mind devout.

The second:

With preservatives of spices
Let us anoint the most sacred body, —
With the most costly ones possible.

The third:

Let a mixture of spikenard hinder
Lest in the tomb putrefy
The Blessed Flesh.

When they have entered the choir, let them go towards the sepulchre as if seeking, and all singing together this verse:

But we cannot open this without assistance.
Who shall roll us away the stone from the door of the sepulchre?

To whom let the angel respond, seated without at the head of the tomb, clothed in an alb gilded over, his head covered with a coif, yet unadorned with the *infula,* holding in his left hand a palm, in his right hand a candelabrum full of candles, and let him say in a modulated and very grave voice:

Whom seek ye in the sepulchre, O followers of Christ?

The women:

Jesus of Nazareth, which was crucified, O celestial one.

To whom let the angel respond:

Why, O followers of Christ, seek ye the living among the dead?
He is not here; he is risen, as he foretold to his disciples.
Remember now what he said to you in Galilee,
That it behoved the Christ to suffer, and on the third day
To rise with glory.

Mulieres, conversæ ad populum, cantent:

Ad monumentum Domini venimus
Gementes; angelum Dei sedentem vidimus
Et dicentem quia surrexit a morte.

Post hæc Maria Magdalene, relictis duabus aliis, accedat ad sepulchrum, in quod sepe aspiciens, dicat:

Heu dolor! heu! quam dira doloris angustia
Quod dilecti sum orbata magistri præsencia!
Heu! quis corpus tam dilectum sustulit e tumulo?

Deinde pergat velociter ad illos qui in similitudine Petri et Johannis præstare debent erecti,[1] stansque ante eos quasi tristis, dicat:

Tulerunt Dominum meum,
Et nescio ubi posuerunt eum.
Et monumentum vacuum est inventum,
Et sudarium cum sindone intus est repositum.

Illi autem hoc audientes velociter pergant ad sepulchrum ac si currentes; sed junior, S. Johannes, perveniens stet extra sepulchrum, senior vero, S. Petrus, sequens eum, statim intret; postquam et Johannes intret; cum inde exierint, Johannes quasi mirans dicat:

Miranda sunt quæ vidimus!
An furtim sublatus est Dominus?

Cui [2] Petrus:

Imo, ut prædixit vivus,
Surrexit, credo, Dominus.

JOHANNES.

Sed cur liquit in sepulchro
Sudarium cum lintheo?

---

[1] *Erecti* is omitted by Lange, but appears in Milchsack.
[2] Omitted by Lange; supplied from Milchsack.

Let the women, turned about towards the people, say:

To the sepulchre of the Lord we have come
Lamenting; we have seen the angel of God seated
And saying that he is risen from the dead.

After this let Mary Magdalene, having left the other two, draw near to the sepulchre, into which looking many times, let her say:

Alas the grief! alas! how dire the anguish of grief
That I am bereft of the presence of my beloved Master!
Alas! who bore away the body, so dear, from the tomb?

Then let her go swiftly to those who in the likeness of Peter and John should present themselves with heads erect; and standing before them as if sad, let her say:

They have taken away my Lord,
And I know not where they have laid him;
And the tomb is found empty,
And the sudarium with the muslin cloth lying within.

Then let these, upon hearing this, proceed swiftly to the sepulchre as if running; but let the younger, Saint John, upon arriving, stand without the sepulchre, but let the elder, Saint Peter, following him, immediately enter in; after which John also enters; when they have come out, let John, as if wondering, say:

Marvelous are the things we have seen!
Hath the Lord been taken away by stealth?

To whom Peter:

Nay, as he predicted while alive,
The Lord, I believe, is risen.

John:

But why did he leave in the sepulchre
The sudarium with the linen cloth?

PETRUS.

Ista quia resurgenti[s]
Non erant necessaria,
Imo resurrectionis
Restant hæc indicia.

Illis autem abeuntibus, accedat Maria ad sepulchrum, et prius dicat:

Heu dolor! heu! quam dira doloris an-
gustia!
Quod dilecti sum orbata magistri præ-
sencia.
Heu! quis corpus tam dilectum sustulit e
tumulo?

Quam alloquantur duo angeli sedentes infra sepulchrum dicentes:

Mulier, quid ploras?

MARIA.

Quia tulerunt Dominum meum,
Et nescio ubi posuerunt eum.

ANGELUS.

Noli flere, Maria; resurrexit Dominus.
Alleluia!

MARIA.

Ardens est cor meum desiderio
Videre Dominum meum;
Quæro et non invenio
Ubi posuerunt eum.
Alleluia!

Interim veniat quidam præparatus in similitudinem hortolani, stansque ad caput sepulchri, dicat:

Mulier, quid ploras? quem quæris?

MARIA.

Domine, si tu sustulisti eum, dicito mihi
ubi posuisti eum, et ego eum tollam.

Peter:

Because to one rising from the dead
These things were not necessary;
Nay, they remain here
As tokens of his resurrection.

Then, as they are going out, let Mary approach the sepulchre, and let her first say:

Alas the grief! alas! how dire the anguish
of grief,
That I am bereft of the presence of my be-
loved Master!
Alas! who bore away the body, so dear,
from the tomb?

To whom let two angels sitting inside the sepulchre speak, saying:

Woman, why weepest thou?

Mary:

Because they have taken away my Lord,
And I know not where they have laid him.

Angel:

Weep not, Mary; the Lord is risen.
Alleluia!

Mary:

My heart is burning with desire
To see my Lord;
I seek, and I do not find
Where they have laid him.
Alleluia!

In the meanwhile let one come, prepared beforehand in the likeness of a gardner; and standing at the head of the sepulchre, let him say:

Woman, why weepest thou? whom seekest
thou?

Mary:

Sir, if thou hast borne him hence, tell me
where thou hast laid him, and I will
take him away.

Et Ille.

Maria!

Atque procidens ad pedes ejus, Maria dicat:

Rabboni!

At ille subtrahat se, et quasi tactum ejus devitans, dicat:

Noli me tangere, nondum enim ascendi ad Patrem meum et Patrem vestrum, Dominum meum et Dominum vestrum.

Sic discedat Hortolanus, Maria vero, conversa ad populum, dicat:

Congratulamini mihi omnes qui diligitis Dominum, quia quem quærebam apparuit mihi, et dum flerem ad monumentum vidi Dominum meum. Alleluia!

Tunc duo angeli exeant ad ostium sepulchri, ita ut appareant foris, et dicant:

Venite et videte locum ubi positus erat Dominus.
Alleluia!
Nolite timere vos:
Vultum tristem jam mutate:
Jesum vivum nuntiate.
Galileam jam adite:
Si placet videre, festinate:
Cito euntes dicite discipulis quia surrexit Dominus.
Alleluia!

Tunc mulieres discedentes a sepulchro dicant ad plebem:

Surrexit Dominus de sepulchro,
Qui pro nobis pependit in ligno.
Alleluia!

Hoc facto, expandeant sindonem, dicentes ad plebem:

Cernite vos, socii, sunt corporis ista beati Lintea, quæ vacuo iacuere relicta sepulchro.

And he:

Mary!

And falling prostrate at his feet, let Mary say:

Rabboni!

And let him draw himself back; and as if avoiding her touch, let him say:

Touch me not, for I am not yet ascended to my Father and your Father, to my Lord and your Lord.

Thus let the Gardner go out; but let Mary, having turned toward the people, say:

Rejoice with me, all ye who love the Lord, for he whom I sought has appeared to me, and while I was weeping at the tomb I saw my Lord. Alleluia!

Then let the two angels come to the door of the sepulchre in such a way that they are visible without, and let them say:

Come and see the place where the Lord was laid.
Alleluia!
Be not affrighted:
Change now your sad countenance!
Proclaim Jesus living!
Go now into Galilee.
If it please you to see, hasten!
Go quickly, and tell his disciples that the Lord is risen from the dead.
Alleluia!

Then let the women, going away from the sepulchre, say to the people:

The Lord is risen from the sepulchre,
Who for us hung upon the cross!
Alleluia!

Having done this, let them unfold the muslin cloth, saying to the people:

Look you, friends, these are the cloths of the blessed body
Which lay abandoned in the empty tomb.

Postea ponant sindonem super altare, atque revertentes alternent hos versus:

Then let them place the cloth upon the altar; and turning themselves about, let them sing alternately these verses: let the first say:

PRIMA dicat:

Resurrexit hodie Deus Deorum!

The God of Gods has arisen to-day!

SECUNDA.

Frustra signas lapidem, plebs Judeorum!

The second:

In vain do ye seal the stone, O race of Jews!

TERTIA.

Jungere jam populo Christianorum!

The third:

Join now with the people of Christ!

Item PRIMA dicat:

Resurrexit hodie Rex angelorum!

Likewise let the first say:

The King of the angels has arisen to-day!

SECUNDA.

Ducitur de tenebris turba piorum!

The second:

The throng of the righteous is led out of hell!

TERTIA.

Reseratur aditus regni celorum!

The third:

The door of the kingdom of heaven is opened!

Interea is qui ante fuit Hortulanus, in similitudinem Domini veniat, dalmaticatus candida dalmatica, candida infula infulatus, phylacteria pretiosa in capite, crucem cum labaro in dextra, textum auro paratorium in sinistra habens, et dicat mulieribus:

In the meantime let him who had previously been the Gardner come in the likeness of the Lord, clothed in a dazzling-white robe, adorned with a white infula, with a precious phylacterium on his head, holding in his right hand a cross with the labarum, in his left hand a paratorium [1] woven of gold, and let him say to the women:

Nolite timere vos; ite, nuntiate fratribus meis ut eant in Galileam, ibi me videbunt sicut prædixi eis.

Be not affrighted: go, tell my brethren that they shall go into Galilee; there they shall see me, just as I foretold to them.

CHORUS.

Alleluia! Resurrexit hodie Dominus!

The choir:

Alleluia! The Lord is risen to-day!

Qui finito, dicant omnes insimul:

Leo fortis, Christus, filius Dei!

Which being ended, let all say in unison:

The strong Lion, the Christ, the Son of God!

Et Chorus dicat:

Te Deum laudamus, etc.

And let the choir say:

We praise thee, O God! etc.

[1] The pall used to cover the sacramental chalice before and after the celebration of Mass.

PEREGRINI [1]

[Monday of Passion Week.]

Nota, fili: Officium Peregrinorum debet hic fieri hoc modo.

Duo de ij sede, qui sint scripti in tabula ad placitum scriptoris, induti tunicis et desuper cappis transversum [eant], portantes baculos et peras in similitudinem Peregrinorum, et habeant capellos super capita et sint barbati. Exeant a vestiario, cantantes hymnum:

Observe, son: The office of the Wayfarers [to Emmaus] [1] should at this point be performed in the following manner.

Let two of the lower row,[2] whose names may be written on the bulletin-board at the pleasure of the scribe, clothed in tunics and copes, go across, carrying staffs and wallets in the likeness of travelers; and let them have caps upon their heads and be bearded. Let them advance from the vestry singing the hymn:

Jhesu, nostra redemptio,
[Amor et desiderium,
Deus creator omnium,
Homo in fine temporum,

Jesus, our Redeemer,
Love and Ardent Desire,
God, Creator of all things,
Man in these final times,

Quæ te vicit clementia
Ut ferres nostra crimina,
Crudelem mortem patiens
Ut nos a morte tolleres,

What mercy has o'erwhelmed thee
That thou shouldst bear our sins,
Enduring a cruel death
In order to free us from death,

Inferni claustra penetrans,
Tuos captivos redimens,
Victor triumpho nobili
Ad dextram Patris residens.

Entering the gates of Hell,
Releasing thy captives,
Conqueror in a glorious triumph,
Sitting at the right hand of the Father!

Ipsa te cogat pietas
Ut mala nostra superes
Parcendo, et voti compotes
Nos tuo vultu saties.

Let sheer compassion impel thee
To overcome our wrong-doing
With forbearance, and to satisfy us,
Our desire thereby fulfilled, with thy countenance.

Tu esto nostrum gaudium,
Qui es futurus præmium;

Be thou our joy,
Who wilt be our reward!

[1] See St. Luke, xxiv, 13–35; cf. St. Mark, xvi, 12–13. I have retained, in so far as possible, the language of the King James' version.

[2] Who sat in the lower stalls of the choir; of the lower rank, here petty-canons.

---

[1] The *Peregrini*, in existence by the twelfth century, was performed, we know, in England; but no English text has come down to us save the late and transitional fragment reproduced on page 73 to illustrate the introduction of the vernacular. I have selected the Rouen text (printed from A. Gasté, *Les Drames liturgiques de la Cathédrale de Rouen*, 1893, p. 65) as being the most interesting one available. The Saintes text (see *Bibliothèque de l'École des Chartes*, 1873, xxxiv, 314) is more primitive in form, but is almost entirely devoid of descriptive matter relating to its method of performance. It contains only the single scene of the appearance of Christ to the two disciples, and ends with the supper at Emmaus. The Rouen text, it will be observed, adds the interview with Mary Magdalene. The Benedictbeuern text, from Germany, introduces all three Marys; and the Beauvais and Fleury texts, as well as the Benedictbeuern text, are expanded by an additional scene, the incredulity of Thomas, a suggestion of which appears in the English fragment mentioned above. The lines in italic type were sung. See St. Luke, xxiv, 13–35.

Sit nostra in te gloria
Per cuncta semper sæcula!]

In thee be our glory
Through all ages, forever!

venientes lento pede per dextram alam ecclesie usque ad portas occidentales, et subsistentes in capite processionis.   Et cum cantaverint hymnum usque ad eum locum *Nos tuo voltu sacies,* tunc quidam sacerdos de majori sede, scriptus in tabula, indutus alba et amictu, nudus pedes, ferens crucem super dextrum humerum, voltu demisso, veniens usque ad eos per dextram alam ecclesie, et subito stet inter illos et dicat:

coming at a slow pace, through the right aisle of the church, as far as the western doors, and taking their stand at the head of the procession.   And when they shall have sung the [above-quoted] hymn to the line "Our desire thereby fulfilled, with thy countenance," then let a priest from the upper row, whose name has been written on the bulletin-board, clothed in an alb and an amice, barefooted, bearing the cross upon his right shoulder, with a downcast countenance, come up to them through the right aisle of the church, and let him suddenly stand with them and say:

Qui sunt hii sermones [quos confertis ad invicem ambulantes, et estis tristes?]

What manner of communications are these that ye have one to another as ye walk and are sad?

Peregrini quasi admirantes, et eum respicientes, dicant:

Let the wayfarers, as if in wonder, and gazing at him, say:

Tu solus peregrinus [es in Jerusalem, et non cognovisti quæ facta sunt in illa his diebus?]

Art thou only a stranger in Jerusalem, and hast not known the things which are come to pass there in these days?

Sacerdos interroget:

Let the priest inquire:

Que?

What things?

Peregrini respondeant:

Let the wayfarers reply:

De Jhesu Nazareno [qui fuit vir propheta, potens in opere coram Deo et omni populo, quomodo tradiderunt eum summi Sacerdotes et Principes nostri in damnationem mortis et crucifixerunt eum; et super omnia, tertia dies est quod hec facta sunt.]

Concerning Jesus of Nazareth, which was a prophet, mighty in deed before God and all the people, how the chief priests and our rulers delivered him up to be condemned to death, and have crucified him; and beside all this, to-day is the third day since these things were done.

Sacerdos, utrimque respiciens, dicat:

Let the priest, looking fixedly at both, say:

O stulti! et tardi corde [ad credendum omnibus quæ locuti sunt Prophetæ!   Nonne sic oportuit pati Christum et intrare in gloriam suam?]

O fools! and slow of heart to believe all that the prophets have spoken!   Ought not Christ to have suffered these things, and to enter into his glory?

Quibus dictis, statim recedens Sacerdos, fingens se longius ire, et Peregrini, festinantes, prosequentes, eum detineant quasi ad

With these words, immediately let the priest walk away, making as though he would go further, and let the wayfarers, hastening, following after him, detain him

hospicium invitantes et trahentes, baculis ostendentes castellum, et dicentes:

Mane nobiscum [quoniam advesperascit, et inclinata est jam dies. Sol vergens ad occasum suadet ut nostrum velis hospicium; placet enim nobis sermones tuos, quos confers de ressurrectione magistri nostri.]

Et ita cantantes, ducant eum usque ad tabernaculum, in medio navis ecclesie, in similitudinem castelli Emaux preparatum. Quo cum ascenderint, et ad mensam ibi paratam sederint, et Dominus inter eos sedens panem eis fregerit, [et] fractione panis agnitus ab illis, subito recedens ab oculis eorum evanescat. Illi autem, quasi stupefacti surgentes, versis vultibus inter ipsos, cantent lamentabiliter:

Alleluia!

cum versu:

Nonne cor nostrum [ardens erat in nobis, dom loqueretur in via, et aperiret nobis scripturas? Heu! miseri! ubi erat sensus noster quando intellectus abierat?]

Quo reiterato, vertent se versus pu[l]pitum, et cantent hunc versum:

Dic nobis, Maria,
[Quid vidisti in via?]

Tunc quidam de majori sede, indutus dalmatica et amictu, in modum mulieris caput circumligatus, respondeat:

Sepulchrum Christi [viventis
Et gloriam vidi resurgentis;

Angelicos testes,
Sudarium et vestes.]

Tunc ostendat et explicet unam syn-

---

as if inviting and urging him to be their guest, pointing to the village with their staffs, and saying:

Abide with us, for it is toward evening, and the day is now far spent. The sun declining towards the west urges that thou accept our hospiiality; for we are pleased with what thou sayest to us concerning the resurrection of our Master.

And thus singing, let them lead him to the structure in the middle of the nave of the church, prepared in the likeness of the village of Emmaus. When they have ascended into it, and are seated at the table ready there, and the Lord, sitting between them, has broken bread unto them, and has been recognized by them through his breaking of the bread, then let him suddenly vanish out of their sight. Moreover, let them, rising up as if dumfounded, with faces turned towards each other, mournfully sing:

Alleluia!

with the verse:

Was not our heart burning within us while he was talking by the way, and while he opened to us the scriptures? Alas! wretched we! where were our senses when we did not comprehend?

Having repeated this, let them turn themselves toward the pulpit and sing this verse:

Tell us, Mary,
What hast thou seen on the way?

Then let one from the upper row, clothed in a dalmatic and an amice, his head bound about after the fashion of a woman, answer:

The sepulchre of the living Christ,
And the glory of the Resurrected One, saw!
Angelic witnesses,
The sudarium and the vestments!

Then let him hold up to view and unfold a

donem ex una parte, loco sudarii, et aliam
ex alia parte, loco vestium, et projiciat ante
magnum hostium chori.   Deinde dicat:

Surrexit Christus [spes mea!
Præcedit suos in Galilæam.]

Chorus cantet duos versus sequentes re-
siduos:

[Credendum est magis soli Mariæ veraci
Quam Judæorum turbæ fallaci.

Scimus Christum surrexisse
A mortuis vere.
Tu nobis, victor Rex, miserere!]

Et interim recedant Maria et Peregrini.

muslin cloth from one side, to represent the
sudarium, and another muslin cloth from
the other side, to represent the vestments;
and let him cast them before the main entrance to the choir.   Then let him say:

Christ is risen, my hope!
He goes before his disciples into Galilee!

Then let the choir sing the remaining two
verses, which follow:

It is better to believe a single truthful Mary
Than all the lying host of the Jews!

We know that Christ is risen
From the dead in very truth!
Do thou, O Victor King, have mercy on us!

And, in the meanwhile, let Mary and the
Wayfarers withdraw.

PASTORES [1]

[Christmas.]

Finito *Te Deum laudamus*, peragatur Officium Pastorum hoc modo secundum Rothomagensem usum.

Presepe sit paratum retro altare et ymago sancte Marie sit in eo posita. In primis quidam puer ante chorum in excelso in similitudinem angeli nativitatem Domini annuncians ad quinque canonicos quindecim marcharum et librarum vel ad eorum vicarios de ij sede, pastores intrantes per magnum hostium chori per medium chorum transeuntes, tunicis et amictis indutos, hunc versum ita dicens: [1]

Nolite timere: ecce enim evangelizo vobis gaudium magnum quod erit omni populo: quia natus est vobis hodie Salvator, qui est Christus Dominus, in civitate David. Et hoc vobis signum: Invenietis infantem pannis involutum, et positum in præsepio.

Sint plures pueri in voltis ecclesie quasi angeli qui alta voce incipiant:

Gloria in excelsis Deo, et in terra pax hominibus bone voluntatis.

Hoc audientes, pastores ad locum in quo paratum est præsepe accedant, cantantes hunc versum:

The *Te Deum laudamus* being ended, let the Office of the Shepherds be performed in this manner, according to the usage of Rouen.

Let a manger be prepared at the back of the altar, and let a figure representing the Holy Mary be placed in it. First let a boy, dressed like an angel, from a lofty place in front of the choir announce the birth of the Lord to the five canons of fifteen marks and pounds,[1] or to their proxies of the second row;[2] and let the shepherds, entering through the main door of the choir, and crossing through the middle of the choir, vested in tunics and amices, say this verse: [3]

Fear not: for behold I bring you good tidings of great joy, which shall be to all people; for unto you is born this day in the city of David a Saviour, which is Christ the Lord. And this shall be a sign unto you: Ye shall find the babe wrapped in swaddling clothes, and lying in a manger.

Let there be many boys, as if they were angels, in the roof of the church, who in a loud voice shall begin:

Glory to God in the highest, and on earth peace, good will to men!

Hearing this, let the shepherds draw near to the place in which the manger has been prepared, singing this verse:

---

[1] The MS. reads: "*Nolite timere, ecce enim,* usque *in præsepio.*" I have replaced this with the full text; and have followed the same procedure throughout the play.

[1] So called because they received annual stipends from two special endowments; four canons received fifteen marks annually, others shared in a bequest yielding £15 annually.
[2] The second row of choir stalls, occupied by canons of inferior rank.
[3] St. Luke, ii, 10–11. I have retained, in so far as possible, the language of the King James' version.

---

[1] Printed from A. Gasté, *Les Drames liturgiques de la Cathédrale de Rouen*, 1893, p. 25. The text is found in two manuscripts (Rouen MSS. y.110 and y.108) of the fourteenth and fifteenth centuries respectively. The play, which probably came into existence not later than the eleventh century, existed in England (there are allusions to it in the twelfth-century Statutes of Lichfield), but no English text, so far as we know, has been preserved. The lines here printed in italic type are set to music in the manuscript. See St. Luke, ii, 1–20.

Pax in terris nuntiatur,
  In excelsis gloria!
Cœlo [1] terra federatur,
  Mediante gratia.

Let peace be proclaimed on earth,
  Glory in the highest!
Earth is leagued with heaven,
  By means of grace.

Mediator homo Deus
  Descendit in propria,
Ut ascendat homo reus
  Ad admissa gaudia.   Eya!   Eya!

The God-Man as mediator
  Comes down to his own,
That condemned man may ascend
  To the admitted joys.   Huzza!   Huzza!

Transeamus, videamus
  Verbum hoc quod factum est;
Transeamus ut sciamus
  Quod hic [2] nuntiatum est.

Let us go, let us see
  This thing which is come to pass.
Let us go that we may know
  What has here been announced.

In Judea puer vagit,
  Puer salus populi,
Quo bellandum se presagit
  Vetus hospes seculi.

In Judea a boy is crying,
  A boy-saviour of the people,
For whom that he would wage war
  The ancient heathen stranger foretold.

Accedamus, accedamus
  Ad presepe Domini,
Et congaudentes [2] dicamus:
  Laus fecundæ Virgini!

Let us draw nigh, let us draw nigh
  To the manger of the Lord,
And rejoicing together, let us say:
  "Glory to the fecund Virgin!"

Quod dum intraverint, duo presbyteri dalmaticati, de majori sede, quasi obstetrices quid ad præsepe fecerint, dicant:

When they enter this [the place of the manger], let two clerics of the upper row, clothed in dalmatics, as if they were the midwives who had served at the manger, say:

Quem quæritis in præsepe, pastores, dicite.

Whom seek ye in the manger, O shepherds?
  Tell us.

Pastores respondeant:

Let the shepherds reply:

Salvatorem Christum Dominum infantem, pannis involutum, secundum sermonem angelicum.

The Saviour, the Christ, the infant Lord, wrapped in swaddling clothes, according to the words of the angel.

Item obstetrices, cortinam aperientes, puerum demonstrent, dicentes:

Whereupon let the midwives, drawing aside the curtain, show the boy, saying:

Adest hic parvulus cum Maria matre sua, de qua dudum, vaticinando, Isayas dixerat propheta:

The little one is here with Mary his mother, of whom long ago in prophecy the prophet Isaiah spoke:

hic ostendant matrem pueri dicentes:

here let them expose to view the mother of the boy, saying:

---

[1] Added by Tougard.   Du Méril proposes *Namque.*
[2] Added by Du Méril.

"Ecce virgo concipiet et pariet filium."
Et nunc euntes dicite quia natus est.

"Behold, a virgin shall conceive and bear a son." *And now, as ye go forth, announce that he is born.*

Tunc, eo viso, inclinatis cervicibus, adorent ɔuerum et salutent, dicentes:

And having seen him, with bowed heads let them worship the boy, and salute him, saying:

Salve, virgo singularis;
Virgo manens, Deus paris!
Ante sæcla generatum
   Corde patris,
Adoremus nunc creatum
   Carne matris.

Hail, virgin unparalleled!
Remaining a virgin, the bride of God!
Before the ages he was generated
   In the heart of the Father,
Let us worship him now embodied
   In the flesh of his mother.

Nos, Maria, tua prece
A peccati purga fæce;
Nostri cursum incolatus
   Sic dispone
Ut det sua frui Natus
   Visione.

O Mary, with thy prayers
Cleanse us from the impurities of sin;
Our life of exile
   So fashion
That thy son may allow us
   To see his face.

Deinde vertant se ad chorum redeuntes et dicentes:

Then let them turn themselves about, returning into the choir, and saying:

Alleluia! Alleluia! Jam vere scimus Christum natum in terris; de quo canite omnes, cum propheta dicentes.

Alleluia! Alleluia! Now we know in very truth that the Christ is born into the world; of whom let all sing, saying with the prophet: . . .[1]

Hoc finito, incipiatur Missa, et Pastores regant chorum.

This ended, the Mass is begun, and the Shepherds rule the choir.

[1] Apparently a song, in which the choir was invited to join, is omitted.

MAGI [1]

[Twelfth Day.]

Officium regum trium secundum usum Rothomagensem. Die Epyphanie, tercia cantata, tres de majori sede more regum induti, — et debent esse scripti in tabula, — ex tribus partibus ante altare conveniant, cum suis famulis portantibus regum oblaciones, induti[s] tunicis et amictis, — et debent esse de secunda sede, scripti in tabula ad placitum scriptoris.

Ex tribus regibus medius ab Oriente veniens, Stellam cum baculo ostendens, dicat alte:

Stella fulgore nimio [rutilat].

Secundus rex a dextra parte respondeat:

Que regem regum [natum demonstrat].

Tertius rex a sinistra parte dicat:

Quem venturum olim [prophetiæ signaverant].

Tunc Magi ante altare sese osculentur, et simul cantent:

Eamus ergo et inquiramus [eum, offerentes ei munera: aurum, thus, et myrrham].

Hoc finito cantor incipiat R̸:

Magi veniunt [ab Oriente Jerosolimam, quærentes et dicentes: Ubi est qui natus est? Cujus stellam vidimus, et venimus adorare Dominum].

The office of the Three Kings, according to the usage of Rouen. On the day of Epiphany, after Tierce, let three, of the upper row, clothed in the manner of kings — their names should be written on the bulletin-board — come from three parts of the church up before the altar, with their servants bearing the offerings of the kings, clothed in tunics and amices — and they should be from the second row, their names written on the bulletin-board at the pleasure of the scribe.

Let the middle one of the three kings, coming from the east, pointing with his staff at the star, say in a loud voice:

This star blazes with an exceeding brightness.

Let the second king, from the right side, reply:

That shows that the King of Kings is born.

Let the third king, from the left side, say:

Whose coming long ago the prophets foretold.

Then let the Magi greet each other with a kiss before the altar, and sing together:

Let us go, then, and seek him, offering to him gifts: gold, frankincense, and myrrh.

This being ended, let the cantor begin the response:

From the East the Magi are come to Jerusalem, seeking, and saying: "Where is he who is born? We see his star, and come to worship the Lord."

---

[1] Acted at Rouen in France. The text comes from a manuscript of the fourteenth century entitled *Ordinarium seu liber ordinarius Ecclesiæ Rothomagensis* (reproduced by Armand Gasté, *Les Drames liturgiques de la Cathédrale de Rouen*, 1893, p. 49). The play of the Magi, which was developed before the end of the eleventh century, appears in its simplest form in the Limoges version (printed by E. Du Méril, *Origines latines du Théâtre moderne*, 1849, p. 151), but I have chosen to reproduce the Rouen version as being more interesting. The lines here printed in italic type were sung or chanted. See St. Matthew, ii, 1–18.

Et moveat processio.

℣: *Cum natus [esset Jesus in Bethleem Judæ, in diebus Herodis regis, ecce Magi ab Oriente venerunt Jerosolimam, dicentes: Ubi est qui natus est rex? Cujus stellam vidimus, et venimus adorare Dominum].*

And let the procession move. Verse:

When Jesus was born in Bethlehem of Judea, in the days of King Herod, behold the Magi came from the East to Jerusalem, saying: "Where is he who is born king? We see his star, and come to worship the Lord."

Sequatur aliud ℟, si necesse fuerit:

Let there follow another response, if it shall be necessary:

Interrogat Magos [dicens ipsis: Quodnam vidistis signum de rege genito? Dicite mihi. Et dixerunt illi Magi: Stella ejus nata est magna et illuxit super stallas cœli].

He inquires of the Magi, saying to them: "What sign do you see of the king who is born? Tell me." And those Magi said: "His great star has arisen, and shines above all the stars of heaven."

Processio in navi ecclesiæ constituta stationem faciat. Dum autem processio navem ecclesiæ intrare ceperit, corona ante crucem pendens in modum stelle accendatur, et Magi, stellam ostendentes, ad ymaginem sancte Marie super altare Crucis prius positam cantantes pergant:

Let the procession, having been drawn up in the nave of the church, make a stand. Moreover, when the procession begins to enter the nave of the church, let the *corona*[1] hanging before the cross be raised in the fashion of the star, and let the Magi, pointing to the star, proceed up to the image of the Holy Mary previously placed upon the altar of the cross, singing:

Ecce stella in Oriente [prævisa iterum præcedit nos lucida. Hæc inquam stella natum demonstrat, de quo Balaam cecinerat dicens: Oritur stella ex Jacob, et exsurget homo de Israel, et confringet omnes duces alienigenarum, et erit omnis terra possessio ejus].

Behold the star, already seen in the East, again leads us on, brightly shining. This star indicates the birth of him whom Balaam foretold, saying: "There shall come a star out of Jacob, and a man shall arise out of Israel, and he shall break to pieces all the leaders of the gentiles, and all the earth shall be his possession."

Hoc finito, duo de majori sede cum dalmaticis, ex utraque altaris parte stantes, suaviter respondeant:

This being ended, let two of the upper row, vested in dalmatics, standing on either side of the altar [impersonating the midwives], reply in courteous tones:

Qui sunt hii qui, stella [duce], nos adeuntes, inaudita ferunt?

Who are these, who, star-led, approaching us, bear strange things?

Magi respondeant:

Let the Magi answer:

Nos sumus, quos cernitis [reges Tharsis, et Arabum, et Saba, dona ferentes Christo,

We, whom ye see, are the Kings of Tharsis, and of Arabia, and of Saba, bearing gifts to the Christ, the new-born king,

---

[1] A chandelier in the shape of a crown, illuminated with candles, and hanging from the ceiling above or slightly in front of the altar.

*regi nato, Domino, quem, stella dedu-
cente, adorare venimus*].

Tunc duo dalmaticati, aperientes cortinam,
dicant:

*Ecce, puer adest [quem quæritis. Jam pro-
perate adorare, quia ipse est redemptio
mundi*].

Tunc procidentes reges ad terram, simul
salutent puerum, ita dicentes:

Salve, princeps seculorum!

Tunc unus a suo famulo aurum accipiat et
dicat:

Suscipe, rex, aurum [regis signum].

Et offerat.   Secundus ita dicat, et offerat:

Tolle thus, tu vere Deus.

Tercius ita dicat et offerat:

Mirram, signum sepulture.

Interim fiant oblaciones a clero et populo, et dividatur oblacio predictis duobus
canonicis.

Tunc, Magis orantibus et quasi sompno
sopitis, quidam puer, alba indutus, quasi
angelus, illis ante altare dicat:

*Impleta sunt omnia que prophetice [dicta
sunt: ite viam remeantes aliam, nec
delatores tanti regis puniendi eritis*].

Hoc finito, cantor incipiat ad introitum
chori. ℞:

*Tria sunt munera [pretiosa quæ obtulerunt
Magi Domino in die illa, et habent in se
divina mysteria. In auro, ut ostendatur
Regis potentia; in thure sacerdotem
magnum considera, et in myrrha domi-
nicam sepulturam*].

---

*the Lord, whom we, led by a star, are
come to worship.*

Then let the two in dalmatics, drawing
aside the curtain, say:

*See, here is the boy whom ye seek.   Now
hasten to worship him, for he is the redeemer of the world.*

Then let the kings, falling prostrate on the
ground, salute the boy together, saying
thus:

Hail, prince of the ages!

Then let one take from his servant gold,
and say:

Receive, O King, gold, the sign of a king.

And let him offer it.   Let the second in like
manner speak and offer:

Accept frankincense, thou very God.

Let the third in like manner speak and
offer:

Myrrh, the sign of thy sepulture.

Meanwhile let offerings be made by the
clergy and the people, and let the offering
be divided by the two above-mentioned
canons.

Then, after the Magi have prayed and,
as it were, have fallen into slumber, let a
boy, clothed in an alb, as if he were an
angel, say to them before the altar:

*All things are fulfilled which were spoken
of the prophets.   Returning, go another
way, and ye will not be informers to
bring punishment on so great a king.*

This being ended, let the cantor, at the
entrance to the choir, begin the response:

*Three are the precious gifts which the Magi
brought to the Lord on that day, and they
have in them divine mysteries: in the
gold, that the power of a king shall be
manifested; in the frankincense think of
the High Priest; and in the myrrh, of the
sepulture of the Lord.*

Verse:

℣ *Salutis nostre autorem [Magi venerati sunt in cunabulis, et de thesauris suis mysticas ei munerum species obtulerunt. In auro, etc.].*

The Magi worshipped in the cradle the author of our salvation, and from their treasure offered him the mystic sort of gifts: in gold, etc.

Ad missam tres reges chorum regant.

In the Mass [which immediately follows], let the three kings rule the choir.

HERODES [1]

[Twelfth Day.]

Tunc incipit ordo ad representandum Herodem.

Parato Herode et ceteris personis, tunc quidam Angelus cum multitudine in excelsis appareat. Quo viso, pastores perterriti; salutem annuntiet eis (Angelus) de ceteris adhuc tacentibus:

Nolite timere vos, ecce enim evangelizo vobis gaudium magnum quod erit omni populo, quia natus vobis [1] hodie Salvator mundi in civitate David, et hoc vobis signum: Invenietis infantem pannis involutum et positum in presepio, in medio duum animalium.

Et subito omnis multitudo cum Angelo dicat:

Gloria in excelsis Deo et in terra pax hominibus bone voluntatis. Alleluia! Alleluia!

Tunc demum surgentes (Pastores) cantent intra se:

Transeamus usque Bethleem, et videamus hoc verbum quod factum est, quod fecit Dominus et ostendit nobis.

Et sic procedant usque ad presepe, quod ad januas monasterii paratum erit. Tunc due Mulieres custodientes presepe, interrogent pastores, dicentes:

Quem queritis [in presepe], pastores, dicite?

Respondeant Pastores:

[1] The MS. apparently reads *nobis*.

Then begins the order for the representing of Herod.

Herod and the other persons being ready, let an Angel appear aloft, accompanied by a multitude [of angels]. At the sight of this the shepherds are frightened; let the Angel, the other [angels] still remaining silent, proclaim to them safety:

Fear not; for behold I bring you good tidings of great joy, which shall be to all people; for unto you there is born this day in the city of David a Saviour of the world. And this shall be a sign unto you: Ye shall find the babe wrapped in swaddling-clothes and lying in a manger between two beasts.

And suddenly let all the multitude with the Angel say:

Glory to God in the highest, and on earth peace, good will to men! Alleluia! Alleluia!

Then let the shepherds, rising up, sing among themselves:

Let us now go unto Bethlehem and see this thing which is come to pass, which the Lord hath done and hath made known unto us.

And so let them advance up to the manger, which shall have been prepared at the doors of the monastery. Then let two women, the guardians of the manger, inquire of the shepherds, saying:

Whom seek ye in the manger, O shepherds? Tell us.

Let the shepherds answer:

---

[1] From a twelfth-century manuscript of the Abbey Saint-Benoît-sur-Loire, preserved in the library at Orléans. The play is of interest as showing the fusion of the *Pastores* and the *Magi*, and also the dramatic development of the rôle of Herod, who already gives promise of tearing a passion to tatters. I have reproduced the text from E. de Coussemaker, *Drames liturgiques du Moyen Age*, 1861, p. 143. The lines here printed in italics are set to music (the music is reproduced by Coussemaker). See St. Matthew, ii, 1-18.

Salvatorem Christum Dominum infantem, pannis involutum secundum sermonem angelicum.

Mulieres:

Adest parvulus cum Maria matre ejus, de qua dudum vaticinando Isaias propheta dixerat: "Ecce virgo concipiet et pariet filium."

Tunc Pastores procidentes, adorent infantem, dicentes:

Salve, Rex seculorum!

Postea surgentes, invitent populum circumstantem ad adorandum infantem, dicentes turbis vicinis:

Venite, venite, venite, adoremus Deum, quia ipse est salvator noster.

Interim Magi prodeuntes, quisque de angulo suo quasi de regione sua, conveniant ante altare vel ad ortum stelle, et dum appropinquant, Primus dicat:

Stella fulgore nimio rutilat.

Secundus:

Quem venturum olim propheta signaverat.

Tunc stantes collaterales, dicat dexter ad medium:

Pax tibi, frater!

Et ille respondeat:

Pax quoque tibi!

Et osculentur sese; sic medius ad sinistrum et sinister ad dextrum. Salutatio cuique. Tunc ostendant sibi mutuo et dicant:

Ecce stella! Ecce stella! Ecce stella!

The Saviour, the Christ, the infant Lord, wrapped in swaddling clothes, according to the words of the angel.

The women:

The little one is here with Mary his mother, of whom long ago in prophecy the prophet Isaiah said: "Behold, a virgin shall conceive and bear a son."

Then let the shepherds, falling prostrate, worship the babe, saying:

Hail, King of the ages!

Afterwards, rising up, let them invite the people standing about to worship the babe, saying to the adjacent throng:

Come! Come! Come! Let us worship the God, since he alone is our Saviour.

Meanwhile let the Magi, each coming forward from his corner as if from his own land, meet before the altar, or at the rising-place of the star; and while they are drawing near, let the first say:

This star blazes with an exceeding brightness!

The second:

Whose coming long ago the prophet foretold.

Then, standing side by side, let the one at the right say to the one in the middle:

Peace to you, brother!

And let that one reply:

Peace also to you!

And let them greet each other with a kiss; in a similar way the one in the middle to the one at the left, and the one at the left to the one at the right — a greeting to each one. Then let them point out [the star] to each other in turn, and say:

Behold the star! Behold the star! Behold the star!

Procedente autem stella, sequentur et ipsi precedentem stellam, dicentes:

> *Eamus ergo et inquiramus eum, offerentes ei munera: aurum, thus et myrrham. Quia scriptum didicimus: Adorabunt eum omnes reges, omnes gentes servient ei.*

Venientes ad ostium chori, interrogent adstantes:

> *Dicite nobis O Jerosolimitani cives: Ubi est expectatio gentium, ubi est qui natus est rex Judeorum, quem signis celestibus agnitum venimus adorare?*

Quibus visis, Herodes mittat ad eos Armigerum, dicens:

> *Que rerum novitas, aut que causa vos subegit, vos, ignotas temptare vias? Quo tenditis ergo? Quod genus? Unde domo? Pacem ne huc fertis an arma?*

Responsio Magorum:

> *Chaldei sumus; pacem ferimus; Regem regum querimus, Quem natum esse stella indicat, Que fulgore ceteris clarior rutilat.*

Armiger reversus salutat Regem; flexo genu dicat:

> *Vivat Rex in eternum!*

Herodes:

> *Salvet te gratia mea!*

Armiger ad Regem:

> *Adsunt nobis, Domine, tres viri ignoti, ab oriente venientes, noviter natum quemdam regem queritantes.*

Tunc mittat Herodes oratores vel interpretes suos ad Magos, dicens:

Then, the star moving forward, let them follow after and the star leading them, saying:

> Let us go, then, and seek him, offering to him gifts: gold, frankincense, and myrrh. For we are familiar with that which is written: "All kings shall worship him, all nations shall serve him."

Coming to the entrance of the choir, let them ask of those standing by:

> Tell us, O citizens of Jerusalem: Where is the one expected of the peoples? Where is he who is born king of the Jews, whom, recognized by celestial signs, we have come to worship?

Let Herod, having seen them, send a soldier, saying:

> What strange things, or what motive has impelled ye, ye, to try unknown roads? Whither, therefore, are ye going? Of what nation are ye? Where is your home? Do ye bring peace or war?

The answer of the Magi:

> We are Chaldeans; we bring peace; We are seeking the King of Kings, Whose birth is shown by the star Which shines clearer than all others in brightness.

Let the soldier, returning, salute the king; and on bended knee let him say:

> Live, O king, forever!

Herod:

> Let my grace welcome thee!

The soldier to the king:

> There are present among us, Lord, three unknown men, coming from the East in search of a certain newly-born king.

Then let Herod send his envoys, or interpreters, to the Magi, saying:

Lecti quaestores,[1] *qui sunt inquirite reges,*
affore quos nostris jam fama revolvit in
oris.

Interpres ad Magos:

Principis edictu, reges, prescire venimus
quo sit profectus hic vester et unde pro-
fectus.

Magi:

Regem quesitum duce stella significatum;
munere proviso, properamus eum ve-
nerando.

Oratores reversi ad Herodem:

Reges sunt Arabum; cum trino munere
natum querunt infantem, quem mon-
strant sidera regem.

Herodes mittens Armigerum pro Magis:

Ante venire jube, quo possim singula scire:
qui sunt, cur veniant, quo nos rumore
requirant?

Armiger:

Quod mandas, cilius, rex inclyte, profici-
etur.

Armiger ad Magos:

Regia vos mandata vocant: non segniter ite!

Armiger adducens Magos ad Herodem:

En Magi veniunt, et regem natum stella
duce requirunt.

Herodes ad Magos:

Que sit causa vie? Qui vos, vel unde veni-
tis? dicite.

Magi:

Rex est causa vie; Reges sumus ex Arabitis.

---

[1] The manuscript gives *Leti inquisitores;* but on
the score of both metre and sense this reading seems
to be corrupt. I have therefore adopted the emendation proposed by Du Méril.

Excellent quaestors, examine into who
these kings are; accost those of whose
presence rumor already is running on
our shore.

The interpreter to the Magi:

By command of our sovereign, O kings, we
come to learn for what purpose ye jour-
ney hither, and whence ye come.

The Magi:

Star-led, in search of the betokened king;
furnished with gifts, we hasten to wor-
ship him.

The envoys, returning to Herod:

They are kings of the Arabs; with a triple
gift they are seeking a babe new-born,
whom the stars show to be a king.

Herod, sending the soldier for the Magi:

Bid them come before me that I may learn
each of the following things: Who are
they, Why do they come, Because of
what rumor do they seek us?

The soldier [to Herod]:

What thou commandest, renowned king,
shall speedily be performed.

The Soldier to the Magi:

Royal orders summon ye: come with speed!

The soldier, leading the Magi to Herod:

Behold, the Magi come, and, star-led, they
seek a newly-born king.

Herod to the Magi:

What may be the cause of your journey?
Who are ye? or whence come ye? Speak.

The Magi:

A king is the cause of our journey. We
are kings from Aiabia. Coming hither,

Huc venientes querimus en regem regnantibus imperitantem, quem natum mundo lactat judaica virgo.

Herodes ad Magos:

Regem, quem queritis, natum esse quo signo didicistis?

Magi:

Illum natum esse didicimus in Oriente, stella monstrante.

Herodes:

Illum regnare creditis, dicite nobis?

Magi:

Illum regnare fatentes, cum mysticis muneribus de terra longinqua adorare venimus, ternum Deum venerantes tribus cum muneribus.

Tunc ostendant munera. Primus dicat:

Auro regem.

Secundus:

Thure Deum.

Tertius:

Myrrha mortalem.

Tunc Herodes imperet Symistis qui cum eo sedent in habitu juvenili, ut adducant Scribas qui in diversorio parati sunt barbati:

Vos, mei Symiste, legis-peritos ascite ut dicant in Prophetis quid sentiant ex his.

Symiste ad Scribas, et adducant eos cum libris Prophetarum:

Vos, legis-periti, ad regem vocati, cum Prophetarum libris properando venite.

---

we seek, lo, a king reigning over the rulers, whom, newly-born into the world, a Jewish virgin is suckling.

Herod to the Magi:

By what sign did you learn that the king whom ye seek was born?

The Magi:

We learned in the East that he was born, by the evidence of the star.

Herod:

Do ye believe that he reigns? Tell us.

The Magi:

Confessing that he reigns, we are come with mystic gifts from a far country to worship him, paying homage to the Triune God with three gifts.

Then let them show the gifts. Let the first say:

By gold a king [is meant].

The second:

By frankincense, a God.

The third:

By myrrh, a mortal.

Then let Herod order the companions who are sitting with him in the garb of young gallants to bring the scribes, who, with beards on, are ready in a room.

You, my companions, order the men learned in the law to tell us what they find in the Prophets concerning these things.

The companions, to the scribes; and let them bring them with the books of the Prophets:

Ye men learned in the law, summoned before the king, come in haste, with the books of the Prophets.

Postea Herodes interroget Scribas, dicens:

O vos, Scribe interrogati, dicite, si quid de hoc Puero scriptum videritis in libro.

Tunc Scribe Duo revolvant librum, et tandem, inventa quasi prophetica, dicant:

Vidimus, domine, in Prophetarum ∨neis, nasci Christum in Bethleem Jude, civitate David; Propheta sic vaticinante.

Et ostendentes cum digito, Regi incredulo tradant librum.

Chorus:

Bethleem non es minima, [etc.]

Tunc Herodes, visa prophetica, furore accensus, projiciat librum; at Filius ejus, audito tumultu, procedat pacificaturus patrem, et stans salutet eum:

*Salve, pater inclyte;
Salve, Rex egregie,
Qui ubique imperas,
Sceptra tenens regia.*

Herodes:

*Fili amantissime,
Digne laudis munere,
Laudis pompam regie
Tuo gerens nomine,*

*Rex est natus fortior
Nobis et potentior.
Vereor ne solio
Nos extrahet regio.*

Tunc Filius despective loquens de Christo, offe.at se ad vindictam, dicens:

*Contra illum regulum,
Contra natum parvulum,
Jube, pater, filium
Hoc inire prelium.*

Then let Herod inquire of the scribes, saying:

O ye scribes, being asked, tell me if ye see anything concerning this boy written in the book.

Then let two scribes turn over the leaves of the book, and at last, as if having found the prophecy, let them say:

We see, lord, in the lines of the Prophets, that the Christ is born in Bethlehem of Judea, in the city of David; the Prophet foretells thus.

And pointing with the finger, let them hand over the book to the incredulous king.

The choir:

Thou, Bethlehem, art not the least, etc.[1]

Then let Herod, having seen the prophecy, kindled with rage, hurl the book to the floor; but let his son, hearing the tumult, advance to calm his father, and, standing, salute him:

*Hail, renowned father!
Hail, illustrious king,
Who rulest everywhere,
Holding the royal sceptre!*

Herod:

*Most beloved son,
Worthy of the tribute of praise,
Bearing in thy name
The pomp of regal glory.*

*A king is born stronger
Than we, and more powerful
I fear lest he shall drag us
From our royal throne.*

Then let the son, speaking contemptuously of Christ, offer himself as a champion, saying:

*Against that petty king,
Against the new-born babe,
Bid, O father, thy son
To begin this combat.*

[1] See St. Matthew, ii, 6.

Tunc demum dimittat Herodes Magos ut inquirant de Puero, et coram eis spondeat regi nato, dicens:

> Ite, et de Puero diligenter investigate; et, invento, redeuntes michi renunciate, ut et ego veniens adorem eum.

Magis egredientibus, precedat stella eos, que nondum in conspectu Herodis apparuit. Quam ipsi sibi mutuo ostendentes, procedant. Qua visa, Herodes et Filius minentur cum gladiis.

Magi:

> Ecce stella in Oriente previsa;
> Iterum precedit nos lucida.

Interim Pastores, redeuntes a presepe, veniant gaudentes et cantantes in eundo:

> O Regem celi! [etc.]

Ad quos Magi:

> Quem vidistis?

Pastores:

> Secundum quod dictum est nobis ab Angelo de Puero isto, invenimus infantem pannis involutum et positum in presepio, in medio duum animalium.

Postea Pastoribus abeuntibus, Magi procedant post stellam usque ad presepe, cantantes:

> Quem non prevalent propria magnitudine
> Celum, terra atque maria lata capere
> De virgineo natus utero,
> Ponitur in presepio.
> Sermo cecinit quem vatidicus,
> Stat simul bos et asinus.
> Sed oritur stella lucida,
> Prebitum Domino obsequia
> Quem Balaam ex judaica
> Nasciturum dixerat prosapia.
> Hec nostrorum oculos fulguranti lumine
> prestinxit lucida,

Then at last let Herod send forth the Magi that they may seek out the boy; and let him, before them, vow allegiance to the new-born king, saying:

> Go ye, and search out carefully concerning the boy; and when ye have found him, bring me word as ye return, that I also may come and worship him.

As the Magi are departing, let the star go before them, which has not yet appeared in the sight of Herod. Let them proceed, pointing it out to each other in turn. Having seen this, let Herod and his son menace with their swords.

The Magi:

> Behold, the star already seen in the East
> Again leads us on, shining brightly.

Meanwhile let the shepherds, returning from the manger, come rejoicing and singing on their way:

> O king of heaven! etc.

To whom the Magi:

> Whom have ye seen?

The shepherds:

> According to what was told us by the Angel concerning that boy, we found the babe wrapped in swaddling-clothes and lying in a manger between two beasts.

Then, the shepherds having gone out, let the Magi proceed on their way following the star up to the manger, singing:

> He whom heaven, earth, and the wide seas
> Could not contain in their own magnitude,
> Born from the womb of a virgin,
> Is lying in a manger.
> He whom prophetic speech foretold
> Stands together with an ox and an ass.
> But the bright star arises
> To offer homage to the Lord,
> Who, Balaam said,
> Would be born of Jewish stock.
> This bright star has blinded our eyes with
> its dazzling light,

Et nos ipsos provide ducens ad cunabula resplendens fulgida.	*The gleaming brilliance prudently leading us to the cradle.*

Tunc Obstetrices, videntes Magos, alloquantur:

Qui sunt hii qui, stella duce, nos adeuntes, inaudita ferunt?

Then let the midwives, seeing the Magi, say:

Who are these, who, star-led, approaching us, bear strange things?

Magi:

Nos sumus quos cernitis, reges Tharsis et Arabum et Saba, dona ferentes Christo nato, Regi, Domino, quem, stella ducente, adorare venimus.

The Magi:

We whom ye see are the Kings of Tharsis, and of Arabia, and of Saba, bearing gifts to the new-born Christ, the king, the Lord, whom we, led by a star, are come to worship.

Obstetrices ostendentes Puerum:

Ecce, puer adest quem queritis. Jam properate ei adorate, quia ipse est redemptio mundi.

The midwives, showing the boy:

See, here is the boy whom ye seek. Now hasten and adore him, for he is the redeemer of the world.

Magi:

Salve, Rex seculorum!
Salve, Deus deorum!
Salve, salus mortuorum!

The Magi:

Hail, king of the ages!
Hail, God of gods!
Hail, salvation of the dead!

Tunc procidentes Magi adorent Puerum et offerant. Primus dicat:

Suscipe, Rex, aurum, regis signum.

Then let the Magi, falling prostrate on the ground, worship the boy, and make their offerings. Let the first say:

Receive, O king, gold, the sign of a king

Secundus:

Suscipe myrrham, signum sepulture.

The second:

Receive myrrh, the sign of thy sepulture.

Tertius:

Suscipe thus, tu vere Deus.

The third:

Receive frankincense, thou very God.

Istis factis, Magi incipiant dormire ibi, ante presepe, donec Angelus desuper apparens, moneat in somnis ut redeant in regionem suam per aliam viam. Angelus dicat:

Impleta sunt omnia que prophetice scripta sunt. Ite, viam remeantes aliam, nec delatores tanti regis puniendi eritis.

These things having been done, let the Magi fall asleep there before the manger while an angel, appearing from above, advises them in dreams to return to their country by another way. Let the angel say:

All things are fulfilled which were written by the prophets. Returning, go another way, and ye will not be informers to bring punishment on so great a king.

Magi evigilantes:

> *Deo gratias! Surgamus ergo, visione
> moniti angelica, et, calle mutato, lateant
> Herodem que vidimus de Puero.*

The Magi, awakening:

> *Praise be to God! Let us arise, then,
> warned by the vision of the angel, and,
> by changing our road, let us keep hidden
> from Herod what we have seen concern-
> ing the boy.*

Tunc Magi abeuntes per aliam viam, non
vidente Herode, cantent:

> *O admirabile commercium!
> Creator omnium.*

Then let the Magi, departing by another
way without being seen of Herod, sing:

> *O wonderful meeting!
> The creator of all things.*

Venientes choro dicentes:

> *Gaudete, fratres, Christus nobis natus est:
> Deus homo factus est.*

Coming to the choir, let them say:

> *Rejoice, brethren! Christ is born to us!
> God is made man!*

Tunc Cantor incipiat:

> *Te Deum.*

Then let the cantor begin:

> *Te Deum.*[1]

Sic finit.

Thus it ends.

[1] The presence of the *Te Deum* shows that the
play was acted immediately before the conclusion
of the Matin service.

PROPHETÆ [1]

[Christmas.]

ORDO PROPHETARUM:

Ysaias, barbatus, dalmatica indutus, stola rubea per medium verticis ante et retro dependente.[1]
Jheremias, similiter absque stola.

Daniel, adolescens, veste splendida indutus.
Moyses, cum dalmatica, barbatus, tabulas legis ferens.
David, regio habitu.
Abacuc, barbatus, curvus, gibosus.

Elisabeth, femineo habitu, pregnans.
Johannes Baptista, pilosa veste et longis capillis, barbatus, palmam tenens.

Virgilius, cum cornu et calamo, edera coronatus, scriptorium tenens.

Nabugodonosor, regio habitu, superbo incessu.
Sibilla, veste feminea, decapillata, edera coronata, insanienti simillima.

Symeon, barbatus, capa serica indutus, palmam tenens.
Balaam, super asinam, curvus, barbatus, palmam tenens, calcaribus urgens.

[Tercia cantata, paratis Prophetis juxta suum ordinem ... processio moveat de claustro, et duo clerici de secunda sede, in cappis, processionem regant, hos versus canentes:] [2]

THE ORDER OF THE PROPHETS:

Isaiah, bearded, clothed in a dalmatic, with a red stole hanging halfway down before and behind.[1]
Jeremiah, in like fashion, except for the stole.

Daniel, a young man, wearing gorgeous clothes.
Moses, with a dalmatic, bearded, bearing the tables of the law.
David, in royal habit.
Habakkuk, bearded, stooping, hunchbacked.

Elizabeth, in female attire; pregnant.
John the Baptist, with a shaggy cloak and with long hair, bearded, holding a palm.

Virgil, with an ink-horn and a candlestick, crowned with ivy, holding a quill pen.

Nebuchadnezzar, in royal habit, with a proud mien.
Sibyl, in female dress, shorn of hair, crowned with ivy, very much like one insane.

Simeon, bearded, wearing a silken cape, holding a palm.
Balaam, upon an ass, bent, bearded, holding a palm, plying his spurs.

[After Tierce, the Prophets having been arranged in their order ...[1] let the procession advance from the door, and let two clerics of the lower row, in copes, lead the procession, singing these verses:]

---

[1] MS. *dependens*.
[2] I have inserted this direction from the very similar play at Rouen, which thus introduces the same hymn, *Gloriosi et famosi*.

[1] The words omitted from this stage direction of the Rouen text are: "a furnace having been set up in the middle of the nave of the church, with linen and flax." The furnace was used in connection with a little play which grew up about Nebuchadnezzar. The play does not appear in the present text, although a parallel may be found in the case of Simeon.

---

[1] Printed by U. Chevalier, *Ordinaires de l'Église Cathédrale de Laon*, 1897, p. 385, from a manuscript of the thirteenth century. A somewhat more dramatic, but longer, version may be found in the Rouen text, Gasté, *op. cit.*, p. 4; and a simpler and less dramatic version, in the Limoges text, printed by E. de Coussemaker, *Drames liturgiques du Moyen Age*, 1861, p. 11, with the music. The *Prophetæ* is of interest in connection with the development of the Old Testament plays

Gloriosi
Et famosi
Regis festum
Celebrantes,
Gaudeamus,
Cujus ortum
Vite portum
Nobis datum
Predicantes,
Aveamus.[1]
Ecce regem
Novam legem
Dantem orbis circuitu
Predicamus.

[Tunc processio in medio ecclesie stet, et sex Judei sint ibi parati, et ex altera parte sex Gentiles.][2]

Duo Cantores:

Omnes gentes
Congaudentes
Dent cantus letitie!
Deus homo
Fit de domo
David, natus hodie.

Ad Judeos:

O Judei,
Verbum Dei
Qui negastis hominem,
Vestre legis
Testes regis
Audite per ordinem.

Ad Paganos:

Et vos, Gentes,
Non credentes
Peperisse Virginem,
Vestre legis
Documentis
Pellite caliginem.

[Duo] Appellatores:

Isaias, verum qui scis,
Veritatem cur non dicis?

Celebrating
The festival
Of the glorious
And renowned king,
Let us rejoice!
Proclaiming his advent,
As the port of life
Given to us
Let us hail him!
Lo the king
Giving to the whole world
A new law,
Let us tell forth!

[Then let the procession stand in the middle of the church, and let six Jews be ready there, and on the other side six Gentiles.]

The two singers:

Let all races,
Rejoicing together,
Sing songs of gladness!
A God-man,
Sprung from the house of David,
Is born to-day.

To the Jews:

O Jews,
Who denied the "Word" of God
Become man,
Hear in succession
The testimonies of your law
And of your king.

To the Gentiles:

And you, O Gentiles,
Not believing
That the Virgin had given birth,
Banish the darkness
On the evidences
Of your own law.

The two summoners:

Isaiah, thou who knowest the truth,
Why dost thou not declare truth?

[1] The manuscript as reproduced by Chevalier has habeamus; I have changed this to aveamus on the authority of another text of the hymn. The uses of the initial h, and of b for v, are common.
[2] Added from the Rouen text.

Isaias:

> Est necesse
> Virgam Jesse
> De radice provehi,
> Flos deinde
> Surget inde,
> Qui est Filius Dei.

[Duo] Appellatores:

> Iste cetus
> Psallat letus,
> Error vetus
> Condempnetur.

Omnis Chorus:

> Quod Judea
> Perit rea
> Hec chorea
> Gratulatur.

[Duo] Appellatores:

> Huc accede, Jheremias;
> Dic de Christo prophetias.

Hieremias:

> Sic est,
> Hic est
> Deus noster.

Duo Appellatores:

> Iste cetus, etc.

Item Chorus:

> Quod Judea, etc.

Duo Appellatores:

> Daniel, indica
> Voce prophetica
> Facta dominica.

Daniel:

> Sanctus sanctorum veniet,
> Et unctio defitiet.

Duo Appellatores:

> Iste cetus, etc.

Isaiah:

> It is necessary
> That a scion from the root of Jesse
> Be exalted;
> A flower, then,
> Will spring thence,
> Who is the Son of God.

The two summoners:

> Let this gathering
> Chant in gladness!
> Let ancient error
> Be condemned!

The whole choir:

> That Judea, the guilty,
> Is destroyed,
> This choir
> Is rejoiced.

The two summoners:

> Approach, Jeremiah,
> Speak thy prophecies of the Christ.

Jeremiah:

> Thus it is:
> This is
> Our God.

The two summoners:

> Let this gathering, etc.

Next, the choir:

> That Judea, etc.

The two summoners:

> Daniel, declare
> With prophetic voice
> The deeds of the Lord.

Daniel:

> The Saint of Saints shall come,
> And the oil of anointing will be wanting.

The two summoners:

> Let this gathering, etc.

Chorus:
> Quod Judea, etc.

[Duo] Appellatores:
> Dic tu, Moyses legislator,
> Quis sit Christus et Salvator.

Moises:
> Prophetam accipietis
> Tanquam me hunc audietis.

Duo Appellatores:
> Iste cetus, etc.

Chorus:
> Quod Judea, etc.

[Duo] Appellatores:
> Dic, tu David, de nepote
>
> Causas que sunt tibi note.

David:
> Universus
> Rex conversus
> Adorabit Dominum,
> Cui futurum
> Serviturum
> Omne genus hominum.

Duo Appellatores:
> Iste cetus, etc.

Chorus:
> Quod Judea, etc.

[Duo] Appellatores:
> Abacuc, regis celestis
> Nunc ostende quod sis testis.

Abacuc:
> Opus tuum
> Inter duum
> Latus animalium
> Ut cognovi,
> Mox expavi
> Metu mirabilium.

The choir:
> That Judea, etc.

The two summoners:
> Say thou, Moses, the law-giver,
> Who this Christ and Savior is.

Moses:
> Ye will receive a Prophet;
> And ye will hear him just as ye hear me.[1]

The two summoners:
> Let this gathering, etc.

The choir:
> That Judea, etc.

The two summoners:
> Declare thou, David, concerning thy descendant
> The things which are known unto thee.

David:
> Every king,
> Converted,
> Shall worship the Lord,
> To whom
> Shall be subject
> The whole race of man.

The two summoners:
> Let this gathering, etc.

The choir:
> That Judea, etc.

The two summoners:
> Habakkuk, now show that thou
> Art a witness of the heavenly king.

Habakkuk:
> When I perceived
> Thy deed [of incarnation?]
> Between the flanks
> Of two beasts,[2]
> I was straightway terrified
> With fear of thy wondrous works.

[1] See Deuteronomy, xviii, 15, 18, 19.
[2] See Habakkuk, iii, 2. Saint Jerome gives the reading: "Domine, opus tuum; in medio annorum vivifica illud," and this is followed in the authorized version; but the Alexandrian text has: Ἐν μέζῳ δυὸ ζωῶν γνωσθήσῃ, which is obviously the source of the hymn quoted above.

Duo [Appellatores]:

Iste cetus, etc.

Chorus:

Quod Judea, etc.

[Duo] Appellatores:

Illud, Elisabeth, in medium
De Domino profer eloquium.

Elisabeth:

Quid est rei
Quod me mei
Mater regis visitat?
Nam ex eo
Ventre meo
Letus infans palpitat.

Duo [Appellatores]:

Iste cetus, etc.

Chorus:

Quod Judea, etc.

Item Duo [Appellatores]:

Da, Baptista,
Ventris cista
Clausus,
Quos dedisti
Causa Christi
Plausus.
Cui dedisti gaudium
Profer et testimonium.

Johannes:

Venit talis
Sotularis
Cujus non sum etiam
Tam benignus
Ut sim dignus
Solvere corrigiam.

Duo [Appellatores]:

Iste cetus, etc.

Chorus:

Quod Judea, etc.

The two summoners:

Let this gathering, etc.

The choir:

That Judea, etc.

The two summoners:

Elizabeth, now recite in public
That declaration concerning the Lord.

Elizabeth:

What is the reason
That the mother
Of my king visits me?
For, upon that,
Within my womb
The babe leaps joyfully.

The two summoners:

Let this gathering, etc.

The choir:

That Judea, etc.

Next, the two summoners:

O Baptist
Shut up within the chest
Of that womb,
Repeat the eulogy
Which thou utteredest
On account of Christ.
To him, for whom thou once ex-
pressed joy,
Offer now also testimony.

John:

There comes one, such that,
Of his shoes,
I am not even
So good
As to be worthy
To unloose the latchet.

The two summoners:

Let this gathering, etc.

The choir:

That Judea, etc.

Duo [Appellatores]:

> Maro, vates gentilium,
> Da Christo testimonium.

Maro:

> Ecce polo dimissa sola nova progenies est.

Duo Appellatores:

> Iste cetus, etc.

Chorus:

> Quod Judea, etc.

Appellatores reducunt Danielem et dicunt ad regem:

> Puerum cum pueris,
> Nabugodonosor,
> Cum in igne videris,
> Quid dixisti?

Nabugodonosor:

> Tres in igne positi pueri
> Quarto gaudent comite liberi.

Duo [Appellatores]:

> Iste cetus, etc.

Chorus:

> Quod Judea, etc.

[Duo] Appellatores:

> Tu, Sibilla,
> Vates illa,
> Dic adventum judicis,
> Dic signum judicii.

Sibilla:

> Judicii signum: Tellus sudore madescet;
>
> E celo rex adveniet per secla futurus,

The two summoners:

> Virgil, seer of the gentiles,
> Give thy testimony to Christ.

Virgil:

> Behold, from the heavens has been sent
> down a single new offspring.

The two summoners:

> Let this gathering, etc.

The choir:

> That Judea, etc.

The two summoners lead forward Daniel
again, and say to the king [i.e. Nebuchad-
nezzar]:

> O Nebuchadnezzar, when
> Thou sawest in the fire
> A young man along with the young men,
> What didst thou say?

Nebuchadnezzar:

> The three young men who were placed in
> the fire
> Rejoiced when liberated by a fourth com-
> panion.

The two summoners:

> Let this gathering, etc.

The choir:

> That Judea, etc.

The two summoners:

> Thou, O Sibyl,
> That prophetess,
> Tell of the coming of the Judge,
> Tell of the sign of the Judgment.

The Sibyl:

> The sign of the Judgment: The earth shall
> become moist with sweat;
> Down from heaven shall come the King,
> who is to rule through the ages,

Scilicet in carne presens, ut judicet or-
bem,
Unde Deum cernent incredulus atque
fidelis
Celsum cum sanctis evi jam termino in
ipso.

Verily present in the flesh, that he may
judge the world,
Whence the unbelieving and the faithful
shall see
God aloft with his saints, now at the very
end of time.

Duo [Appellatores]:

    Iste cetus, etc.

The two summoners:

    Let this gathering, etc.

Chorus:

    Quod Judea, etc.

The choir:

    That Judea, etc.

[Duo] Appellatores:

    Symeon, inter prophetas
    Pande nobis quid expectas.

The two summoners:

    Simeon, reveal to us
    What thou waitest for among the prophets.

Symeon:

    Vite non spero terminum,
    Donec videam Dominum.

Simeon:

    I hope not to see death
    Until I see the Lord.

Duo [Appellatores]:

    Iste cetus, etc.

The two summoners:

    Let this gathering, etc.

Chorus:

    Quod Judea, etc.

The choir:

    That Judea, etc.

Symeon, accipiens puerum, dicit:

    Tuum sub pacis tegmine
    Servum dimittis, Domine.

Simeon, taking a boy in his arms, says:

    Dismiss thy servant
    Under the shelter of peace, O Lord.[1]

[Duo] Appellatores:

    Dic, Balaam, ex Judaica
    Oriturum Dominum prosapia.

The two summoners:

    Declare, O Balaam, the descent of the Lord
    From Jewish stock.

Balaam:

    Exibit de Jacob rutilans nova stella,
    Et confringet ducum agmina
    Regionis Moab maxima potentia.

Balaam:

    There shall come forth out of Jacob a new
    star shining,
    And he shall break down the hosts of the
    leaders,
    With greatest power in the land of Moab.

Hic veniat Angelus cum gladio. Balaam
tangit asinam, et illa non procedente dicit
iratus:

Here let an angel come with a sword.
Balaam beats the ass, and when it fails to
go forward, he says in anger:

[1] We observe here the tendency to dramatize the
episodes with which the prophecies were connected.

Quid moraris, asina,
Obstinata bestia?
Jam scindent calcaria
Costas et precordia.

Why do you stand still, ass?
Obstinate beast!
Now the spurs shall tear
Your ribs and entrails.

Puer sub asina respondet:

A boy underneath the ass answers:

Angelus cum gladio,
Quem adstare video,
Prohibet ne transeam;
Timeo ne peream.[1]

An angel with a sword
Whom I see standing in the way
Keeps me from going on;
I fear lest I be killed.[1]

Vocatores:

Iste cetus, etc.

[The summoners:

Let this gathering, etc.

Chorus:

Quod Judea, etc.

The choir:

That Judea, etc.

Quo finito, omnes prophete et ministri in pulpito cantent hos versus:

Ortum predestinacio, etc.][2]

Which being ended, let all the prophets and the clerics in the pulpit sing these verses:

The predestination of his coming, etc.]

[1] In the Rouen version this little play appears as follows:

Tunc Balaam, ornatus, sedens super asinam, habens calcaria, retineat lora et calcaribus percuciat asinam; et quidam juvenis habens alas, tenens gladium, obstet asine. Quidam sub asina dicat:

Cur me cum calcaribus miseram sic leditis!

Hoc dicto, Angelus ei dicat:
Desine regis Balac preceptum perficere.

Vocacio Balaam:
Balaam, esto vaticinans.

Tunc Balaam respondeat:
Exibit ex Jacob rutilans, etc.

Vocatores:
Iste cetus, etc.

Chorus:
Quod Judea, etc.

[2] The conclusion I have added from the Rouen text. The celebration of the Mass immediately followed.

[1] In the Rouen version this little play appears as follows:

Then let Balaam, adorned, seated upon an ass, having spurs, pull on the reins and pierce the ass with the spurs; and let a certain youth having wings on, holding a sword, stand in the way of the ass. Let some one under the ass say:
Why do you thus wound wretched me with spurs?

This spoken, let the angel say to him:
Cease to carry out the commands of King Balak.

The summons to Balaam:
Balaam, be prophetic.

Then let Balaam answer:
There shall come forth out of Jacob, etc.

The summoners:
Let this gathering, etc.

The choir:
That Judea, etc.

III

LITURGICAL PLAYS DEALING WITH MISCELLANEOUS BIBLICAL STORIES, AND WITH THE LEGENDS OF THE SAINTS

CONVERSIO BEATI PAULI APOSTOLI [1]

[Festival of the Convertion of St. Paul.]

Ad representandam Conversionem beati Pauli apostoli, paretur in competenti loco, quasi Jerusalem, quedam sedes, et super eam Princeps sacerdotum. Paretur et alia sedes, et super eam juvenis quidam in similitudine Sauli; habeatque secum ministros armatos. Ex alia vero parte, aliquantulum longe ab his sedibus, sint parate quasi in Damasco due sedes; in altera quarum sedeat vir quidam nomine Judas, t in altera Princeps Synagoge Damasci. Et inter has duas sedes sit paratus lectus, in quo jaceat vir quidam in similitudine Ananie.

His ita paratis, dicat Saulus ministris suis:

Propalare vobis non valeo
Quam ingenti michi sunt odio
Christicole, qui per fallaciam
Totam istam seducunt patriam.

Ite ergo, ne tardaveritis,
Et quoscunque tales poteritis
Invenire, vi comprehendite;
Comprehensos vinctos adducite.

For representing the conversion of the blessed apostle Paul, let there be prepared in a suitable place, as if it were Jerusalem, a seat,[1] and upon it the High Priest. Let there be prepared also another seat, and upon it a young man in the likeness of Saul; and let him have with him armed attendants. On the other side, somewhat removed from these seats, let there be, as it were in Damascus, two seats prepared; in one of which let there be seated a man called Judas, and in the other, the High Priest of the Synagogue of Damascus. And between these two seats let there be a bed prepared, in which let a man lie impersonating Ananias.

These things thus made ready, let Saul say to his attendants:

I am quite unable to reveal to you
How monstrously odious to me are the
Christians,
Who by means of deceit
Are seducing this entire nation

Go, therefore, delay not,
And all such persons ye can find
Seize by force.
Those whom ye have seized, bring hither
bound.

[1] It is not easy to understand exactly what is meant here by *sedes.* The "seats" may have been on platforms, or may have been merely set in cleared spaces. Early illustrations represent some *sedes* as on platforms, others as lofty thrones.

---

[1] In addition to the liturgical plays dealing with the story of Christ (the plan and history of man's salvation) there grew up in the church miscellaneous plays on Biblical themes acted by the clerics between the services. Doubtless they arose in imitation of the *Sepulchrum,* the *Pastores,* and the *Magi,* for in general form and style they follow these earlier plays. Hilarius (fl. 1125) is known to be the author of a *Suscitatio Lazari* and a *Daniel.* We have an allusion in the eleventh century to a *Convivium Herodis* (dealing, probably, with John the Baptist and Herod), and to an *Elisaeus.* From Limoges comes a twelfth-century *sponsus* dealing with the wise and foolish virgins; and from Kloster Vorau in Styria a twelfth-century fragment of an *Isaac and Rebecca.* In a thirteenth-century Fleury manuscript we have a *Lazarus* and a *Daniel,* as well as the *Conversio Beati Pauli Apostoli* here printed. In England, unfortunately, we have no early Latin texts preserved; but we do have the later developments from these in such plays as *The Conversion of Saint Paul* and *Saint Mary Magdalen.* I have based the text of the *Conversio* on that of E. de Coussemaker, *Drames liturgiques du Moyen Age,* 1861, p. 210, who gives the music as well. In the present reprint, all the lines that appear in italic type were set to music in the manuscript. See The Acts of the Apostles, ix, 1–31. The play was doubtless acted on the Festival of The Conversion of St. Paul, January 25.

Hoc audientes Ministri abeant, et, cum redierint, duos sumptos ad Dominum suum conducant, dicentes:

> Christicolas multos invenimus,
> Et ex illis retinuimus;
> In Damascum fugerunt alii
> Seductores hujus consortii.

Tunc Saulus quasi iratus surgat, et ad Principem Sacerdotum eat; cumque ad eum veniat, dicat:

> Vestre michi dentur epistole
> In Damascum, ubi Christicole
> Blandis verbis sue fallacie
> Gentem hujus seducunt patrie.

Tunc Princeps Sacerdotum det ei aliquid breve sigillatum et dicat:

> Trado vobis meas epistolas
> In Damascum contra Christicolas:
> Evadere ne dimiseritis
> Christicolas quos invenietis.

(Tunc vox ex alto:)

> Saule! Saule! quid me persequeris?
> Vidi mala que meis feceris.
> Quem dilexi cur noces populo?
> Recalcitres nequaquam stimulo.

Hoc audito, Saulus, quasi semi-mortuus in terram cadat, et jam non cadens, dicat:

> Quid sic faris? Quis es tu, Domine?
> Cur me meo privasti lumine?
> Quando tuum afflixi populum?
> Quis es, et quod tibi vocabulum?

Dominus:

> Jesus vocor, quem tu persequeris,
> Cujus sepe servos afflixeris.

Upon hearing this, let the attendants go out; and when they have returned, let them bring to their lord two whom they have taken, saying:

> We have found many Christians,
> And some of them we have bound.
> To Damascus have fled other seducers
> Belonging to this fellowship.

Then let Saul rise up as in anger, and let him go towards the High Priest; and having come to him, let him say:

> Let letters of thine be given me
> To Damascus, where the Christians
> With the enticing words of their false doc-
> trine
> Are beguiling the people of this nation.

Then let the High Priest give him some brief letter, and let him say:

> I deliver to thee my letters
> To Damascus against the Christians.
> Suffer not to escape
> The Christians whom thou shalt find.

(Then a voice from aloft:)

> Saul! Saul! why persecutest thou me?
> I have seen the evil which thou hast done
>   my disciples,
> Why dost thou afflict the people which I
>   have chosen?
> In nowise canst thou kick against the
>   pricks!

Having heard this, let Saul, as if half-dead, fall to the ground; and when he has done falling,[1] let him say:

> Why speakest thou thus? Who art thou,
>   Lord?
> Why hast thou deprived me of my sight?
> When have I afflicted thy people?
> Who art thou? And what is thy name?

The Lord:

> I am called Jesus, whom thou persecutest,
> Whose disciples thou hast often afflicted.

---

[1] So I have translated et jam non cadens (literally "and now not falling"). I assume that the actor staggered, with his arms protecting his eyes, before finally falling to the ground.

Surgens tamen urbem ingredere
Et audies quid debes facere.

Tunc resurgat Saulus, cumque homines sui viderint eum excecatum, apprehendant eum et ducant in Damascum ad domum Jude. Tunc veniat Dominus ad Ananiam, et dicat:

Anania, surge quam propere,
Atque Jude domum ingredere.
Te expectat vir, Saulus nomine;
Dices ei que debet facere.

Ananias:

De hoc Saulo audivi plurima;
Fecit tuis mala quam maxima;
Si quem videt qui tibi serviat,
Semper furit ut eum destruat.

Hic princeps habet epistolas
Ut occidat omnes Christicolas:
His de causis hunc Saulum timeo,
Ad hunc Saulum ire non audeo.

Tunc Dominus:

Anania, surge velociter;
Quere Saulum fiducialiter:
Ecce enim orat ut venias,
Et ut eum videre facias.

Hunc elegi meo servicio;
Hunc elegi nostro consortio;
Hunc elegi ut de me predicet
Et nomen meum clarificet.

Tunc surgens Ananias domum Jude introeat, et, cum viderit Saulum, dicat:

Ad te, Saule, me misit Dominus
Jhesus, Patris excelsi Filius,
Qui in via tibi apparuit:
Ut venirem ad te me monuit.

Predicabis coram principibus
Nomen ejus et coram gentibus;
Ut sis civis celestis patrie,
Multa feres pro Christi nomine.

But arise, go into the city,
And it shall be told thee what thou must do.

Then let Saul arise; and when his men have seen that he has been stricken blind, let them take him by the hand and lead him into Damascus to the house of Judas. Then let the Lord come to Ananias and say:

Ananias, arise with all haste,
And go into the house of Judas.
There awaits thee a man called Saul.
Thou shalt tell him what he must do.

Ananias:

I have heard many things of this Saul.
To thy disciples he hath done the utmost harm;
If he sees any one that serves thee,
Ever he rages to destroy him;

This lord hath letters
To put to death all Christians.
For these reasons I fear this Saul.
To this Saul I dare not go.

Then the Lord:

Ananias, arise quickly;
Seek Saul without fear.
Lo, indeed, he prays that thou come,
And that thou mayest make him see.

Him have I chosen for my service;
Him have I chosen for our fellowship;
Him have I chosen to preach concerning me,
And to make my name illustrious.

Then let Ananias arise and enter the house of Judas; and having seen Saul, let him say:

To thee, O Saul, the Lord Jesus,
The Son of the Heavenly Father,
Who appeared to thee on the way, hath sent me.
He hath instructed me to come to thee.

Thou shalt preach his name
Before kings and before the gentiles.
That thou mayest be a citizen of the heavenly kingdom
Many things shalt thou suffer for the name of Christ.

Tunc surgat Saulus et quasi jam credens, et predicans alta voce, dicat:

> Cur, Judei, non resipiscitis?
> Veritati cur contradicitis?
> Cur negatis Mariam virginem
> Peperisse Deum et hominem?
>
> Jhesus Christus, Marie Filius,
> Ei Deus est, et homo carneus,
> Deitatem a Patre retinens
> Et a matre carnem suscipiens.

Hec audiens, Princeps Synagoge Damasci ministris suis armatis dicat:

> Custodite urbis introitus,
> Conservate viarum exitus,
> Et, quam cito Saulum videritis,
> Mortem ejus ne distuleritis.

Tunc Ministri eant et querant Saulum. Quo comperto, Saulus cum discipulis suis, in sporta ab aliquo alto loco, quasi a muro, ad terram demittatur. Cum autem venerit in Jerusalem, occurrat ei vir unus, in similitudine Barnabe, qui, cum viderit Saulum, ei dicat:

> Te elegit Marie Filius,
> Ut sis fratrum nostrorum socius:
> Nunc, ut laudes nobiscum Dominum,
> Veni; vide nostrum collegium.

Ad Apostolos:

> Gaudeamus, fratres, in Domino;
> Colletemur de tanto socio;
> Qui nunc erat lupus sevissimus,
> Nunc est agnus mansuetissimus.

Omnes Apostoli incipiant:

> Te Deum laudamus.

Then let Saul rise up; and, as if now believing, and preaching in a loud voice, let him say:

> Why, O Jews, come ye not to your senses?
> Why do ye oppose the truth?
> Why do ye deny that Mary, a virgin,
> Brought forth the God and man?
>
> Jesus Christ, the son of Mary,
> Is both God and man of flesh,
> Retaining divinity from his Father,
> And receiving flesh from his mother.

Hearing this, let the High Priest of the Synagogue of Damascus say to his armed attendants:

> Guard the entrances of the city;
> Keep watch over the ways of egress;
> And as soon as ye shall have seen Saul,
> Delay not his death.

Then let the attendants go and seek Saul. Having learned of this, let Saul with his disciples, from some high place, as if from the wall, be let down in a basket to the ground. And when he shall have come into Jerusalem, let a man run up to him, impersonating Barnabas, who, when he has seen Saul, shall say to him:

> Thee hath the Son of Mary chosen
> To be a comrade in our brotherhood.
> Now, that thou mayest praise the Lord with us,
> Come; see our fellowship.

To the Apostles:

> Brothers, let us rejoice in the Lord!
> Let us rejoice together over so excellent a comrade!
> He who lately was a most ferocious wolf,
> Is now a most gentle lamb!

Let all the Apostles begin:

> We praise thee, O God.[1]

---

[1] The conclusion of the text with the *Te Deum laudamus* shows that the play was designed for performance at the end of the Matin service.

LUDUS SUPER ICONIA SANCTI NICOLAI [1]

[St. Nicholas' Day.]

Ad quem he persone sunt necessarie: persona Barbari qui conmisit ei tesaurum; persona iconie; iiii or *vel sex latronum; Sancti Nicholai.*

In primis Barbarus, rebus suis congregatis, ad ichoniam [Sancti Nicolai] veniet, et ei res suas commendans dicet:

For which these actors are necessary: the impersonator of Barbarus [1] who entrusted to it [i.e. the statue] his treasure; the impersonator of the statue; of four or six robbers; and of Saint Nicholas.

First let Barbarus, having gathered together his goods, come to the statue; and committing to it the care of his effects, he shall say:

Nicholae, quidquid possideo,
Hoc in meo misi teloneo:
Te custodem rebus adibeo,
 Serva que sunt ibi.
Meis, precor, adtende precibus;
Vide nullus sit locus furibus;
Preciosis aurum cum vestibus
 Ego trado tibi.

O Nicholas, all that I possess
I have put in this my chest;
To thee I bring it as guardian of my
 wealth.
Protect what things are there.
Give heed, I beseech thee, to my prayers.
See to it that this be no place for thieves!
Gold and precious garments
 I entrust to thee.

Proficisci foras disposui:
Te custodem rebus imposui.
Revertenti redde quæ posui
 Tua sub tutela.
Jam sum magis securus solito,
Te custode rebus inposito;
Revertenti vide ne merito
 Mihi sit querela.

I have arranged to travel abroad;
I have laid upon thee the custody of my
 wealth;
On my return deliver back what I have
 placed
Under thy protection.
I feel now more secure than usual,
Having set thee as guard over my effects.
See to it that on my return I have no
 Worthy cause for complaint!

Illo autem profecto, fures transeuntes cum

But upon his departure, let the thieves,

[1] A foreigner; here used of one who is not a Christian.

[1] Of the liturgical, or semi-liturgical plays that arose in imitation of the earlier *Sepulchrum* and its immediate followers, a specially popular type dealt with the stories of the saints. The earliest examples preserved were connected with the great scholastic festival held on the Eve or on the Day of St. Nicholas, December 6; indeed, we have a large group of plays dealing with this famous patron of scholars. The two earliest texts of the St. Nicholas play, very primitive in form, are contained in an eleventh-century manuscript from Hildesheim, Germany; another text is found in a twelfth-century manuscript from Einsiedeln, Germany; a thirteenth-century manuscript from Fleury furnishes us with no fewer than four. Records show that plays dealing with the stories of the saints — their lives and martyrdom, or their miraculous deeds — were very common in England; unfortunately, however, no texts have been preserved. The text of the play here printed is based on that in J. J. Champollion-Figeac, *Hilarii Versus et Ludi*, 1838, p. 34, from Bib. Nat. Latin MS. 11331, of the twelfth century. The author, Hilarius, is generally believed to have been an Englishman by birth, though he seems to have spent much of his life in France. Most of his verses are addressed to Englishmen; and since Barbarus, a foreigner, is made to use French, the present play may have been designed for an English rather than a French audience. At the end of the two other plays by Hilarius, contained in the same manuscript, the author directs that in case the play is performed at the Matin service the *Te Deum* is immediately to follow, if, however, at the Vesper service, then the *Magnificat* (see *Hilarii Versus et Ludi*, pp. 33, 60). We may assume that the St. Nicholas play was likewise intended for presentation at the Matin or at the Vesper service on the Day or the Eve of St. Nicholas.

*viderint hostium apertum et nullum custodem,
omnia diripient, Barbarus vero rediens, non
invento tesauro, dicet:*

> Gravis sors et dura!
> Hic reliqui plura,
> Sed sub mala cura.
> *Des! quel domage!*
> *Qui pert la sue chose purque n'enrage.*

> Hic res plusquam centum
> Misi et argentum;
> Sed non est inventum.
> *Des! quel domage!*
> *Qui pert la sue chose purque n'enrage.*

> Hic reliqui mea;
> Sed hic non sunt ea.
> Est imago rea.
> *Des! quel domage!*
> *Qui pert la sue chose purque n'enrage.*

Deinde accedens ad imaginem, dicet ei:

> Mea congregavi,
> Tibi commendavi;
> Sed in hoc erravi.
> *Ha! Nicholax!*
> *Si ne me rent ma chose, tu ol comparras.*

> Hic res meas misi
> Quas tibi commisi;
> Sed eas amisi.
> *Ha! Nicholax!*
> *Si ne me rent ma chose, tu ol comparras.*

Sumto flagello, dicet:

> Ego tibi multum
> Inpendebam cultum;
> Nun feres inultum.
> *Hore t'enci,*
> *Qu'are me rent ma chose que g'ei mis ci.*

> Tuum testor deum,
> Te, ni reddas meum,
> Flagellabo reum.
> *Hore t'enci,*
> *Qu'are me rent ma chose que g'ei mis ci.*

*passing by, when they see the door open and
no guard, plunder everything. Then let
Barbarus, returning, and not finding his
treasure, say:*

> O heavy and cruel chance!
> Here have I left many things,
> But under bad guardianship.
> *Des! quel domage!*
> *Qui pert la sue chose, purque n'enrage?* [1]

> Here I placed more than a hundred
> Valuables, as well as money;
> But they are not to be found.
> *Des! quel domage!*
> *Qui pert la sue chose, purque n'enrage?* [1]

> Here I left my treasures;
> But here they are not.
> The image is to blame!
> *Des! quel domage!*
> *Qui pert la sue chose, purque n'enrage?* [1]

Then approaching the statue, he shall say to it.

> I assembled my riches,
> I entrusted them to thee;
> But in this I erred.
> *Ha! Nicholas!*
> *Si ne me rent ma chose, tu ol comparras.* [2]

> Here I placed my goods,
> Which I committed to thy care;
> But I have lost them.
> *Ha! Nicholas!*
> *Si ne me rent ma chose, tu ol comparras.* [2]

Taking up a whip he shall say:

> I expended much
> Adoration upon thee;
> Thou shall not go unpunished.
> *Hore ten ci,*
> *Quare me rent ma chose que g'ei mis ci.* [3]

> I call thy god to witness,
> Unless thou return my property
> I shall scourge thee, culprit!
> *Hore ten ci,*
> *Quare me rent ma chose que g'ei mis ci.* [3]

[1] "God! what a loss! He who loses his wealth,
why should he not be angry?"
[2] "If you do not return to me my property, you
shall pay for it."
[3] "Now I've got you here, so return to me my
property which I placed here."

Tunc Sanctus Nicholaus, veniens ad lat-
rones, dicet eis:

> Miseri, quid facitis?
> Non longua de perditis
>   Erunt vobis gaudia.
> Custos eram positus
> Vosque sum intuitus,
>   Cum porta[s]tis omnia.

> Flagella sustinui,
> Cum ea non potui,
>   Ut debebam, reddere:
> Verba passus aspera
> Cumque verbis verbera;
>   Ad vos veni propere.

> Reportate perdita;
> Erant enim omnia
> Sub mea custodia,
> Que portasti, posita.

> Quod si non feceritis,
> Suspensi cras eritis
>   Crucis in patibulo.
> Vestra namque turpia
> Vestra latrocinia
>   Nunciabo populo.

Latrones timentes omnia reportabunt.
Quibis inventis Barbarus dicet:

> Nisi visus fallitur,
>   Jo en ai.
> Tesaurus hic cernitur.
> De si grant merveile en ai.

> Rediere perdita,
>   Jo en ai.
> Nec per mea merita,
> De si grant mervegle en ai.

> Quam bona custodia
>   Jo en ai
> Qua redduntur omnia'
> De si grant mervegle en ai.

Tunc accedens ad imaginem et suplicans,
dicet:

Then Saint Nicholas, coming to the robbers,
shall say to them:

> Wretches, what are ye doing?
> Not long to you rascals
>   Shall be your joys!
> I was placed as custodian,
> And I was watching you
>   When ye bore all away!

> I suffered a scourging
> When I could not restore the things
>   As I should have done.
> Having endured harsh words,
> And, with the words, blows,
>   I have come swiftly to you.

> Carry back the lost things;
> For they were all placed
> Under my guard
> Which ye stole away.

> If this ye fail to do,
> Ye shall be hanged to-morrow
>   On the beam of a gibbet:
> For, your base deeds
> And your robberies
>   I shall proclaim to the people.

The frightened robbers shall carry back all;
and Barbarus, having found them, shall say:

> Unless my eyesight fails,
>   Jo en ai.[1]
> Here is seen my treasure!
> De si grant merveile en ai.[2]

> The lost things have returned,
>   Jo en ai,[1]
> And not by my efforts.[3]
> De si grant merveile en ai.[2]

> What an excellent guardian,
>   Jo en ai,
> By whom all the things are returned!
> De si grant merveile en ai.

Then approaching the statue and kneeling,
let him say:

[1] "I have them."
[2] "By so great a miracle I have them." But perhaps we should read: "By some great miracle I have
them."
[3] Literally "deserts."

Suplex ad te venio,
      Nicholax,
Nam per te recipio
Tut icei que tu gardas.

Sum profectus peregre,
      Nicholax
Sed recepi integre
Tut ice[i] que tu gardas.

Mens mea convaluit,
      Nicholax;
Nichil enim defuit
De tut cei que tu gardas.

Postea ap[p]arens ei beatus Nicholaus, dicet:

Sup[p]licare mihi noli,
Frater; inmo Deo soli,
Ipse namque factor poli,
Factor maris atque soli,
      Restauravit perditum.
Ne sis ultra quod fuisti.
Solum laudes nomen Christi;
Soli Deo credas isti
Per quem tua recepisti.
      Mihi nullum meritum.

Cui respondens Barbarus, dicet:

Hic nulla consultacio,
Nulla erit dilacio,
Quin ab erroris vicio
      Jam recedam.
In Christum Dei filium,
Factorem mirabilium,
Ritum linquens gentilium,
      Ego credam.

Ipse creavit omnia,
Celum, terram, et maria;
Per quem erroris venia
      Mihi detur.
Ipse potens et dominus
Meum delebit facinus,
Cujus regnum ne terminus
      Consequetur.

A suppliant, I come to thee,
      Nicholas;
For by thy means I receive
Tut icei que tu gardas.[1]

I went traveling abroad,
      Nicholas,
But I have received intact
Tut icei que tu gardas.

My mind has become eased,
      Nicholas;
For nothing is lacking
De tut cei que tu gardas.[2]

Then the Blessed Nicholas, appearing to him, shall say:

Do not pray to me,
Brother, but rather to the only God,
For he himself, the maker of the heavens,
The maker of the sea and of the earth,
      Restored what was lost.
Be no longer what thou hast been.
Praise the name of Christ alone.
Only in that God believe,
By whom thou received thy goods.
      No merit belongs to me.

Answering him, Barbarus shall say:

Here shall be no deliberation,
Nor shall there be any delay!
But from the vice of error
      I shall now withdraw.
Leaving the religion of the heathen,
In Christ, the Son of God,
The performer of miracles,
      I will believe.

He alone created all things,
Heaven, earth, and the seas.
Through him forgiveness of my error
      Will be granted unto me!
He himself the Mighty One and the
      Lord
Will blot out my sin,
Whose kingdom shall have
      No end!

---

[1] " All those things which you guarded."
[2] "Of all," etc.

TRES CLERICI [1]

[St. Nicholas' Day.]

[SCENE I.]

[*Enter three scholars on their way to the university.*]

I. CLERICUS:

Nos quos causa discendi literas
Apud gentes transmisit exteras,
Dum sol adhuc extendit radium,
Perquiramus nobis hospicium.

I. SCHOLAR:

Let us, whom the motive of acquiring scholarship
Has transported among foreign peoples,
Seek for ourselves a lodging
While the sun still spreads its rays.

II. CLERICUS:

Jam sol equos tenet in littore,
Quos ad praesens merget sub equore;
Nec est nota nobis hec patria:
Ergo quaeri debent hospicia.

II. SCHOLAR:

The sun now holds his horses upon the shore
Which presently he will plunge beneath the sea;
Nor is this land known to us:
Therefore lodgings should be sought.

[*They approach the house of the* OLD MAN.]

III. CLERICUS:

Senem quemdam maturum moribus
Hic habemus coram luminibus;
Forsan, nostris compulsus precibus,
Erit hospes nobis hospitibus.

III. SCHOLAR:

A certain old man, sober in manners,
We have here before our eyes.
Perhaps, moved by our prayers,
He will be host to us as his guests.

Insimul Omnes ad SENEM *dicant:*

Hospes care, querendo studia
Huc relicta venimus patria;
Nobis ergo prestes hospicium,
Dum durabit hoc noctis spacium.

Let all say together to the OLD MAN:

Dear host, in search of schools,
Having left our own land, we have come hither;
Therefore give to us lodging
While this night shall last.

SENEX:

Hospitetur vos factor omnium!
Nam non dabo vobis hospicium;
Nam nec mea in hoc utilitas,
Nec est ad hoc nunc oportunitas.

THE OLD MAN:

Let the Maker of all be your host!
For I will not give you lodging;
For there is in this no benefit to me,
Nor is it now convenient.

---

[1] The text reproduces that in E. de Coussemaker, *Drames liturgiques du Moyen Age*, 1861, p. 100, from a twelfth-century manuscript of the Abbey Saint-Benoît-sur-Loire. The lines were all sung or chanted, and Coussemaker gives the music from the original manuscript.

CLERICI *ad* VETULAM:

Per te, cara, sit impetrabile
Quod rogamus, etsi non utile:
Forsan, propter hoc beneficium
Vobis Deus donabit puerum.

MULIER *ad* SENEM:

Nos his dare, conjux, hospicium,
Qui sic vagant querendo studium,
Sola saltem compellat karitas:
Nec est damnum, nec est utilitas.

SENEX:

Acquiescam tuo consilio,
Et dignabor istos hospicio.

SENEX *ad* CLERICOS:

Accedatis, scolares, igitur;
Quod rogastis vobis conceditur.

SENEX, CLERICIS *dormientibus:*

Nonne vides quanta marsupia?
Est in illis argenti copia:
Hec a nobis absque infamia
Possideri posset pecunia.

VETULA:

Paupertatis onus sustulimus,
Mi marite, quamdiu viximus;
Hos si morti donare volumus,
Paupertatem vitare possumus.

Evagines ergo jam gladium;
Namque potes morte jacentium,
Esse dives quamdiu vixeris;
Atque sciet nemo quod feceris.

The SCHOLARS *to the* OLD WOMAN:

Through thee, dear woman, may what we
  ask
Be attainable, even though not profitable
  to thee.
Perchance, because of this kindness
God will give to thee a son.

The WOMAN *to the* OLD MAN:

Mere charity at least, husband, compels us
To give lodging to these scholars
Who thus wander seeking a school;
To us it means neither loss nor profit.

THE OLD MAN:

I acquiesce in thy advice,
And will deem them worthy of lodging.

The OLD MAN *to the* SCHOLARS:

Draw near, therefore, scholars;
What ye have asked for is granted to you.

[*The scholars enter the house, lie down,
  and go to sleep.*]

[SCENE II.]

The OLD MAN, *while the scholars are sleeping:*

Seest thou not how great their purses are?
There is a large quantity of money in them.
Were it not for the infamy involved
We might take possession of this wealth.

THE OLD WOMAN:

We have borne the load of poverty,
My husband, as long as we have lived;
If we are willing to put these to death,
We shall be able to escape penury.

Therefore now unsheath thy sword;
For by the death of these lying here
Thou canst be rich as long as thou livest,
And no man will know what thou hast
  done.

[*The* OLD MAN *and* OLD WOMAN *murder the three scholars, and conceal the
  bodies.*]

NICOLAUS:

Peregrinus, fessus itinere,
Ultra modo non possum tendere;
Hujus ergo per noctis spacium
Michi prestes, precor, hospicium.

SENEX *ad* MULIEREM:

An dignabor istum hospicio,
Cara conjux, tuo consilio?

VETULA:

Hunc persona commendat nimium
Et est dignum ut des hospicium.

SENEX:

Peregrine, accede propius;

Vir videris nimis egregius:
Si vis, dabo tibi comedere;
Quicquam voles temptabo querere.

NICOLAUS, *ad mensam:*

Nichil ex his possum comedere;
Carnem vellem rescentem edere.

SENEX:

Dabo tibi carnem quam habeo,
Namque carne rescente careo.

NICOLAUS:

Nunc dixisti plane mendacium;
Carnem habes rescentem nimium,
Et hanc habes magna nequicia;
Quam mactari fecit pecunia.

SENEX *et* MULIER *simul:*

Misereri nostri, te petimus;
Nam te sanctum Dei cognovimus:
Nostrum scelus abominabile,
Non est tamen incondonabile.

[SCENE III.]

[*Enter* SAINT NICHOLAS *dressed as a traveler; he salutes the* OLD MAN *and* OLD WOMAN.]

NICHOLAS:

A traveler, weary of his journey,
I cannot proceed any farther.
Therefore, for the duration of this night,
Give to me, I beg, lodging.

The OLD MAN *to the* WOMAN:

Shall I deem this one worthy of lodging,
Dear wife, on thy advice?

THE OLD WOMAN:

Great rank commends this man very much,
And it is fitting that thou give him lodging.

THE OLD MAN:

Traveler, draw near.

[SAINT NICHOLAS *enters the house.*]

Thou seemest to be a very eminent man.
If thou wisheth, I will give thee something to eat.
Whatsoever thou desirest I will try to obtain.

NICHOLAS, *at the table:*

I can eat none of these things.
Fresh meat would I eat.

THE OLD MAN:

I will give thee such meat as I have,
For with fresh meat I am unprovided.

NICHOLAS:

Now thou hast plainly told a lie!
Fresh meat thou hast in too great quantity,
And this thou hast by grand villainy,
Which money caused to be slaughtered.

The OLD MAN *and the* OLD WOMAN *together:*

Have mercy on us, we pray thee!
For we know thee to be a saint of God.
Our crime, though detestable,
Is, nevertheless, not unpardonable.

NICOLAUS:

Mortuorum afferte corpora,
Et contrita sint vestra pectora!
Hi resurgent per Dei gratiam;
Et vos flendo queratis veniam!

Oratio SANCTI NICOLAI:

Pie Deus, cujus sunt omnia,
Celum, tellus, aer et maria,
Ut resurgant isti precipias,
Et hos ad te clamantes audias!

Et post Omnis Chorus dicat:

Te Deum laudamus.

NICHOLAS:

Bring forth the bodies of the slain;
And penitent be your hearts!
These shall rise from the dead, through the
grace of God;
And ye, through weeping, may obtain
pardon.

[*The dead bodies are brought forth and
placed before* SAINT NICHOLAS.]

The Prayer of SAINT NICHOLAS:

Holy God, to whom belong all things,
Heaven, earth, the air, and the seas,
Command those to rise from the dead,
And pardon these crying out to thee!

[*The* SCHOLARS *come to life,* SAINT
NICHOLAS *disappears, and the* OLD
MAN *and* OLD WOMAN *are forgiven.*]

And afterwards, let the whole choir sing:

Te Deum laudamus.[1]

[1] The presence of this hymn shows that the play
was intended for performance in the Matin service.

ADEODATUS [1]

[St. Nicholas' Day.]

Ad representandum quomodo Sanctus Nicolaus Getron filium de manu Marmorini, regis Agarenorum, liberavit, paretur in competenti loco cum ministris suis armatis, Rex Marmorinus in alta sede, quasi in regno suo, sedens. Paretur et in alio loco Excoranda, Getronis civitas, et in ea Getron, cum consolatoribus suis, uxor ejus Euphrosina et filius eorum Adeodatus; sitque ab orientali parte civitatis Excorande, ecclesia Sancti Nicolai in qua puer rapietur.

His itaque paratis, veniant ministri Marmorini regis coram eo et dicant Omnes vel Primus ex eis:

Salve, princeps! salve, Rex optime!
Que sit tue voluntas anime
Servis tuis ne tardes dicere;
Sumus que vis parati facere.

Rex dicet:

Ite ergo, ne tardaveritis,
Et quascunque gentes poteritis
Imperio meo subicite:
Resistentes vobis occidite.

Interim Getron et Euphrosina, cum multitudine clericorum, ad ecclesiam Sancti Nicolai, quasi ad ejus solemnitatem celebrandam, filium suum secum ducentes, eant. Cumque ministros regis armatos illuc venire viderint, filio suo pro timore oblito, ad civitatem suam confugiant. Ministri vero regis, Puerum rapientes, coram regem veniant, et dicant Omnes vel Secundus ex eis:

Quod jussisti, Rex bone, fecimus;

For representing how Saint Nicholas delivered the son of Getron from the hands of Marmorinus, King of the Agareni, let there be prepared in a suitable place King Marmorinus sitting upon a high seat with his armed attendants, as though in his own kingdom. And in another place let there be prepared Excoranda, the city of Getron, and in it Getron, with his comforters, his wife Euphrosina, and their son Adeodatus; and let there be in the eastern part of the city of Excoranda the church of Saint Nicholas, in which the boy is to be seized.

And so, these things being ready, let the attendants of King Marmorinus come before him, and let them all, or the First of them, say:

Hail, sovereign! Hail, noblest king!
Whatever may be the desire of thy heart
Delay not to inform thy servants.
We are ready to do whatsoever thou wishest.

Let the King say:

Go, then, without delay,
And whatsoever peoples ye can,
Bring under my rule:
Those who resist thee, kill.

In the meanwhile let Getron and Euphrosina, leading with them their son, together with a throng of clerics, go to the church of Saint Nicholas as if for the celebration of his festival. And when they see the armed attendants of the King coming thither, let them, forgetting their son in their fear, flee together to their city. Let the attendants of the King, dragging away the boy, come into the presence of the King, and let all, or the Second of them, say:

What thou didst command, noble King, we have done.

---

[1] The text is based on that in E. de Coussemaker, *Drames liturgiques du Moyen Age,* 1861, p. 123, from a twelfth-century manuscript of the Abbey Saint-Benoît-sur-Loire. The lines here printed in italic type are set to music in the original, and the music is carefully reproduced by Coussemaker. That the play was designed for performance on St. Nicholas' Day is shown by the anthem, *Copiose caritatis,* at the end.

Gentes multas vobis subegimus,
Et de rebus quas adquisivimus
Hunc Puerum vobis adducimus.

Many peoples we have made subject unto
thee;
And from the spoils we have acquired
We bring to thee this boy.

Omnes dicant vel Tercius:

Puer iste, vultu laudabilis,
Sensu prudens, genere nobilis,
Bene debet, nostro judicio,
Subjacere vestro servicio.

Let all, or the Third, say:

This boy, beautiful of face,
Knowing of mind, high-born of race,
Well deserves, in our opinion,
To be taken into thy service.

Rex:

Apolloni qui regit omnia
Semper sit laus, vobisque gracia
Qui fecistis michi tot patrias
Subjugatas et tributarias!

The King:

Now to Apollo, who governs all things,
Be praise forever! And to you, thanks,
Who have for me made so many lands
Subject and tributary.

Rex puero:

Puer bone, nobis edissere
De qua terra, de quo sis genere,
Cujus ritu gens tue patrie
Sunt gentiles, sive christicole?

The King to the boy:

Good boy, declare to us
Of what land, of what family thou art,
Of what religion the people of thy country;
Are they pagans, or Christians?

Puer:

Excorande principans populo,
Pater meus, Getron vocabulo,
Deum colit cujus sunt maria,
Qui fecit nos et vos et omnia.

The boy:

My father, Getron by name,
Ruling the people of Excoranda,
Serves the God to whom belong the seas,
Who made us, and you, and all things.

Rex:

Deus meus Apollo; Deus est
Qui me fecit; verax et bonus est;
Regit terras, regnat in ethere,
Illi soli debemus credere.

The King:

Apollo is my god; he is the god
Who made me; true and good he is;
He rules over the lands, he reigns in the
firmament.
In him alone ought we to believe.

Puer:

Deus tuus mendax et malus est;
Stultus, cecus, surdus et mutus est;
Talem Deum non debes colere,
Qui non potest seipsum regere.

The boy:

Thy god is false and evil;
Foolish, blind, deaf, and mute he is!
Such a god thou ought not to worship,
Who is unable to rule himself.

Rex:

Noli, Puer, talia dicere;
Deum meum noli despicere:
Nam si eum iratum feceris,
Evadere nequaquam poteris.

The King:

Boy, do not say such things;
Do not despise my god:
For, if thou makest him angry,
In no wise canst thou escape.

Interea Euphrosina, comperta oblivione filii, ad ecclesiam Sancti Nicolai redit; cumque filium suum quesitum non invenerit, lamentabili voce:

> Heu! Heu! Heu! michi misere!
> Quid agam? quid queam dicere?
> Quo peccato merui perdere
> Natum meum, et ultra vivere?

> Cur me pater infelix genuit?
> Cur me mater infelix abluit?
> Cur me nutrix lactare debuit?
> Mortem michi quare non prebuit?

Consolatrices exeant et dicant:

> Quid te juvat hec desolatio?
> Noli flere pro tuo filio;
> Summi Patris exora Filium,
> Qui conferat ei consilium.

Euphrosina, quasi non curans consolationem earum:

> Fili care, fili carissime,
> Fili, mee magna pars anime,
> Nunc es nobis causa tristitie
> Quibus eras causa letitie!

Consolatrices:

> Ne desperes de Dei gracia,
> Cujus magna misericordia
> Istum tibi donavit puerum;
> Tibi reddet aut hunc aut alium.

Euphrosina:

> Anxiatus est in me spiritus;
> Cur moratur meus interitus?
> Cum te, fili, non possum cernere
> Mallem mori quam diu vivere.

Consolatrices:

> Luctus, dolor et desperacio
> Tibi nocent nec prosunt filio;
> Sed pro eo de tuis opibus
> Da clericis atque pauperibus.

In the meanwhile Euphrosina, having discovered that they had forgotten their son, returns to the church of Saint Nicholas; and when, after searching for her son, she fails to find him, let her say in a lamenting voice:

> Alas! Alas! Alas! O wretched me!
> What shall I do? What can I say?
> For what sin have I deserved to lose
> My son, and yet live after.

> Why did my hapless father beget me?
> Why did my hapless mother bear me?
> Why should my nurse have suckled me?
> Why did she not grant death to me?

Let the comforters go out [to her] and say:

> In what does this grief avail thee?
> Weep not for thy son:
> Pray to the Son of the Heavenly Father,
> That he bring succor to him.

Euphrosina, as if not regarding their consolation:

> O dear son! most dear son!
> O son, the greatest part of my soul!
> Now thou art the cause of grief to us
> To whom thou wert the cause of joy!

The comforters:

> Despair not of God's grace,
> Whose great mercy
> Hath given to thee this boy;
> He will restore to thee either this one or
>   another.

Euphrosina:

> My spirit is troubled within me.
> Why does my death delay?
> If, O son, I cannot see thee
> I could prefer death to long life.

The comforters:

> Sorrow, grief, and despair
> Injure thee, and do not aid thy son.
> But for him give of thy means
> To the clerics and to the poor.

Nicolai roga clemenciam
Ut exoret misericordiam
Summi Patris pro tuo filio,
Nec falletur tua peticio.

Ask the mercy of Nicholas,
That he may, by petition, obtain the pity
Of the Heavenly Father for thy son;
And thy prayer will not fail.

.Euphrosina:

Nicolae, pater sanctissime,
Nicolae, Deo carissime,
Si vis ut te colam diucius,
Fac ut meus redeat filius!

Qui salvasti multos in pelago
Et tres viros a mortis vinculo,
Preces mei precantis audias,
Et ex illo me certam facias!

Non comedam carnem diucius
Neque vino fruar ulterius,
Nullo mero letabor amplius,
Donec meus redibit filius.

Getron:

Cara soror, lugere desine;
Tue tibi nil prosunt lacrime;
Sed oretur pro nostro filio
Summi Patris propitiacio.

In crastino erit festivitas
Nicolai, quem christianitas
Tota debet devote colere,
Venerari et benedicere.

Audi ergo mea consilia:
Adeamus ejus solemnia;
Conlaudemus ejus magnalia;
Deprecemur ejus suffragia!

Dei forsan est inspiracio
Que me monet pro nostro filio;
Est oranda cum Dei gracia,
Nicolai magna clemencia.

Euphrosina:

O Nicholas, most holy father!
O Nicholas, most dear to God!
If thou dost wish that I cherish thee longer,
Bring it about that my son may return!

O thou, who hast saved many on the sea,
And delivered three men from the bond of
　　death,[1]
Hear the prayers of me imploring,
And give me tidings of him.

I will no longer eat meat,
Neither will I take delight in wine further,
I will rejoice no more in unmixed wine,
Until my son shall return.

Getron:

Dear wife, cease to grieve;
Thy tears avail thee nought;
But let there be sought for our son
The propitiation of the Heavenly Father.

On the morrow will be the festival
Of Nicholas, whom all Christianity
Ought devotedly to worship,
To revere, and to praise.

Hear, therefore, my plan:
Let us go to his feast;
Let us together highly extol his wonderful
　　deeds;
Let us beseech his assistance!

Perchance it is the inspiration of God
Which advises me on behalf of our son;
The great mercy of Nicholas
Must be sought with the grace of God.

Tunc resurgant, ad ecclesiam Sancti Nico-
lai eant; in quam cum introierint, tendat
manus suas ad celum Euphrosina, et dicat:

Then let them rise up and go to the church
of St. Nicholas; when they have entered
it, let Euphrosina lift her hands towards
heaven, and say:

---

[1] Apparently an allusion to the miracle by which
Nicholas restored the three scholars to life; see
pp. 59–62.

Summe regum Rex omnium,
Rex unicorum remorientium,
Nostrum nobis fac redi filium,
Vite nostre solum solacium!

Audi preces ad te clamantium,
Qui in mundum misisti Filium
Qui nos cives celorum faceret
Et inferni claustris eriperet!

Deus Pater, cujus potencia
Bona bonis ministrat omnia,
Peccatricem me noli spernere,
Sed me meum natum fac cernere!

Nicolae, quem Sanctum dicimus,
Si sunt vera que de te credimus,
Tua nobis et nostro filio
Erga Deum prosit oracio!

Supreme King of all kings,
King of the only ones who die a second
death,[1]
Effect for us the return of our son,
The only solace of our lives!

Hear our prayers as we cry unto thee,
Who sent into the world thy Son
That he should make us citizens of heaven
And should snatch us from the gates of Hell.

O God the Father, whose power
Provides to good men all things good,
Do not spurn me, a sinner,
But make me to see my son.

O Nicholas, whom we call Saint,
If those things are true which we believe of
thee,
May thy prayer to God be of benefit
To us and to our son.

His dictis, exeat ab ecclesia et eat in domum suam, et paret mensam, et super mensam panem et vinum, unde clerici et pauperes reficiantur. Quibus vocatis et comedere incipientibus, dicat Marmorinus ministris suis:

With these words, let her go out from the church and go to her home, and prepare a table, and on the table bread and wine, from which the clerics and the poor may refresh themselves. When they have been summoned and are beginning to eat, let King Marmorinus say to his attendants:

Dico vobis, mei carissimi,
Quod ante hanc diem non habui
Famem tantam quantam nunc habeo;
Famem istam ferre non valeo.

Vos igitur quo vesci debeam
Preparate, ne mortem subeam.
Quid tardatis? Ite velocius;
Quod manducem parate cicius.

I declare unto you, my most beloved,
That before this day I have not had
So great a hunger as now I have;
This hunger I am unable to endure!

Therefore prepare ye what I should eat,
Lest I suffer death.
Why are ye slow? Go more swiftly!
Quickly provide something that I may devour.

Ministri euntes afferant cibos et dicant Regi:

Let the attendants, going, bring food, and let them say to the King:

Ad preceptum tuum paravimus
Cibos tuos, et hic adtulimus;
Nunc, si velis poteris propere
Qua gravaris famem extinguere.

According to thy command we have prepared
Thy food, and have brought it here.
Now, if thou wilt, thou canst speedily
Banish the hunger with which thou art annoyed.

[1] If the Latin is correct, the allusion may be to such persons as Lazarus who were raised from the dead by divine power. But possibly the line is a corruption of *Rex vivorum et morientium.*

His dictis, afferatur aqua, et lavet manus suas Rex, et incipiens comedere, dicat:

> Esurivi et modo sitio;
> Vinum michi dari precipio;
> Quod afferat michi quam cicius
> Meus Getronis filius.

Puer itaque, hoc audiens, suspiret graviter et secum dicat:

> Heu! Heu! Heu! michi misero!
> Vite mee finem desidero;
> Vivus enim quamdiu fuero,
> Liberari nequaquam potero.

Rex puero:

> Pro qua causa suspiras taliter?
> Suspirare te vidi fortiter.
> Quid est pro quo sic suspiraveris?
> Quid te nocet, aut unde quereris?

Puer:

> Recordatus mee miserie,
> Mei patris et mee patrie
> Suspirare cepi et gemere,
> Et intra me talia dicere:

> Annus unus expletus hodie,
> Postquam servus factus miserie,
> Potestati subjectus regie,
> Fines hujus intravi patrie.

> Heu! miselle, quid ita cogitas?
> Quid te juvat cordis anxietas?
> Nemo potest te michi tollere
> Quamdiu te non velim perdere.

Interea veniat aliquis in similitudine Nicolai; Puerum, scyphum cum recentario vino tenentem, apprehendat, apprehensumque ante fores componat, et quasi non compertus, recedat. Tunc vero unus de civibus ad Puerum dicat:

> Puer, quis es, et quo vis pergere?

Having said this, let water be brought, and let the King wash his hands; and, as he begins to eat, let him say:

> I have hungered, and now I thirst!
> I command that wine be given me;
> And this let my son of Getron
> Bring to me as quickly as possible.

And so let the boy, hearing this, sigh deeply, and say to himself:

> Alas! Alas! Alas! O wretched me!
> I wish for the end of my life;
> For, however long I shall live,
> In no wise can I gain my freedom.

The King to the boy:

> For what cause sighest thou thus?
> I saw thee sigh heavily.
> What is it that has made thee sigh in this
>   wise?
> What harms thee? or for what reason dost
>   thou lament?

The boy:

> Thinking in my mind of my wretchedness,
> Of my father, and of my native country,
> I began to sigh and to groan,
> And within myself to say such things:

> To-day one year is completed
> Since, made slave to misery,
> A vassal to kingly power,
> I entered the confines of this country.

The King:

> Alas! poor boy, why dost thou ponder thus?
> What will sadness of heart avail thee?
> No one can take thee away from me
> So long as I do not wish to lose thee.

In the meanwhile let some one come in the likeness of Nicholas; let him take up the boy, holding the goblet of fresh wine; and having seized him, let him restore him to his place before the doors of his home; and, as if not recognized, let him withdraw. Then let one of the citizens say to the boy:

> Boy, who art thou? and where wouldst thou
>   go?

Cujus tibi dedit largicio
Scyphym istum cum recentario?

Puer:

Huc venio, non ibo longius;
Sum Getronis unicus filius.
Nicolao sit laus et gloria,
Cujus hic me reduxit gracia!

Quo audito, currat civis ille ad Getronem et dicat:

Gaude, Getron, nec fleas amplius;
Extra fores stat tuus filius.
Nicolai laudat magnalia,
Cujus eum reduxit gracia.

Cumque hujus modi nuntium audierit Euphrosina, ad filium suum currat; quem sepius deosculatum amplexetur et dicat:

Deo nostro sit laus et gloria,
Cujus magna misericordia,
Luctus nostros vertens in gaudium,
Nostrum nobis reduxit filium!

Sintque patri nostro perpetue
Nicolao laudes et gracie,
Cujus erga Deum oracio
Nos adjuvit in hoc negocio.

Chorus Omnis:

Copiose caritatis, etc.[1]

Whose largess gave to thee
That goblet filled with fresh wine?

The boy:

I am come to this place; I will go no further;
I am the only son of Getron.
To Nicholas be praise and glory,
Whose kindness has brought me back here.

Having heard this, let that citizen run to Getron and say:

Rejoice, Getron!   Weep no more!
Without the doors stands thy son!
He praises the wonderful deeds of Nicholas,
Whose kindness brought him back again.

And when Euphrosina hears the message of this kind, let her run to her son; and, kissing him many times, let her embrace him and say:

To our God be praise and glory,
Whose great compassion,
Turning our sorrows into joy,
Has restored to us our son!

And to our father Nicholas
Be praises and thanks forever,
Whose prayer to God
Helped us in this affair.

The whole choir [sings the anthem]:

Of abundant love, etc.

[1] The anthem used at Lauds on St. Nicholas' Day.

IV
THE INTRODUCTION OF THE VERNACULAR

I

THE SEPULCHRE [1]

[Easter.]

Hic incipit Officium Resurreccionis in die Pasche.

[*The three Marys come in separately, each walking towards the entrance of the choir.*]

[I. MARIA.[1] *Heu!* . . . .

. . . .

II. MARIA. *Heu!* . . . .

. . . .]

III. MARIA. *Heu! Redemcio Israel,*
Ut quid mortem sustinuit?

[I. MARIA. Alas! . . . .

. . . .

II. MARIA. Alas! . . . . . .

. . . .] payne.[2]

III. MARIA. Allas! he that men wend
schuld by [3]
All Israel, bothe knyght and knaue,
Why suffred he so forto dy,
Sithe [4] he may all sekenes saue?

[I. MARIA. *Heu!* . . . .

. . . .

II. MARIA. *Heu!* . . . .

. . . . ?

III. MARIA. *Heu! cur ligno fixus clauis*
Fuit doctor tam suauis?
Heu! cur fuit ille natus
Qui perfodit eius latus?

[I. MARIA. Alas! . . . .

. . . .

II. MARIA. Alas! . . . .

. . . .] is oght.

III. MARIA. Allas, that we suche bale
schuld bide [1]
That sodayn sight so forto see,
The best techer in world wide
With nayles be tacched to a tre!
Allas, that euer so schuld betyde,
Or that so bold mon born schuld be
For to assay oure Saueour side
And open hit with-oute pite!

[*They come together at the entrance to the choir,*[2] *and sing in unison:*]

Iam, iam, ecce, iam properemus ad tumulum,
Vngentes Dilecti corpus sanctissimum! [3]

Et appropriantes sepulcro cantent:

<hr/>

[1] For the probable lines spoken by the first two Marys see p. 11. It will be observed that the actors spoke first in Latin, and then paraphrased their lines in the vernacular.
[2] The cue for the actor assuming the part of the Third Mary.
[3] Thought should redeem.
[4] Since.

[1] Such grief should endure.
[2] Cf. p. 12.
[3] These lines are accompanied by musical notation.

<hr/>

[1] The manuscript was discovered by W. W. Skeat and published by him in *The Academy*, 1890; its real significance, however, was first pointed out by Manly. We have here not full plays, but merely the actor-parts, with cues, used by some cleric who was a speaker in three separate plays, assuming on different days the rôles of the Third Mary in the *Sepulchrum*, of one of the Wayfarers in the *Peregrini*, and of the Third Shepherd in the *Pastores*. As a dramatic curiosity the fragment is unique. Its chief importance, however, is the evidence it affords of the way in which the vernacular was gradually introduced. In the course of time the vernacular entirely displaced the Latin; here we find the transitional stage clearly illustrated. By means of bracketed insertions I have attempted to give some general indication of the plays as wholes, in order that the reader may better understand the manuscript. I have also changed the order of the plays. The text is based on that in Osborn Waterhouse's *The Non-Cycle Mystery Plays*, re-edited from the manuscripts for the Early English Text Society, 1909.

O Deus, quis reuoluet nobis lapidem
Ab hostis monumenti? [1]

[I. MARIA. . . . .
. . . .

II. MARIA. . . . .
. . . .] him leid.

III. MARIA.   He that thus kyndely vs has
    kend [2]
Vn-to the hole where he was hid,
Sum socoure sone he wil vs send,
    At help to lift away this lid.

[At this point there is apparently a lacuna in the manuscript. The three Marys
find the stone rolled away; the angel sings
"*Quem queritis*," etc.; and the Marys enter
the sepulchre and display the sudarium and
burial cloths to the audience. Leaving the
sepulchre, they sing joyfully:]

[I. MARIA. Alleluia! . . . .
. . . .

II. MARIA. Alleluia! . . . .
. . . .]

III. MARIA.   Alleluya schal be oure song,
    Sithen Crist, oure Lord, by angellus
    steuen,[3]
Schewus him as mon here vs among,
    And is Goddis Son, heghest in heuen.

[A red line in the manuscript, probably
to indicate a new scene. As the Marys

---

[1] These lines are accompanied by musical notation.
    [2] Directed.   [3] Voice.

reach the door of the choir they meet
Peter and John.]

[PETER AND JOHN.   *Dic nobis, Maria,*
              Quid uidisti in uia?

I. MARIA.   *Sepulcrum Christi uiuentis,*
    Et gloriam uidi resurgentis.
        [translating:]
. . . .

II. MARIA.   *Angelicos testes,*
    Sudarium et uestes.
        [translating:]
. . . .
. . . .] was gon.

III. MARIA.[1] *Surrexit Christus, spes nostra,*
    Precedet vos in Galileam!
Crist is rysen, wittenes we
    By tokenes that we haue sen this morn!
Oure hope, oure help, oure hele,[2] is he,
    And hase bene best, sithe we were born!
Yf we wil seke him for to se,
    Lettes noght this lesson be for-lorn:
"But gose euen vnto Galilee;
    There schal ye fynd him yow beforn!"

[Another red line in the manuscript indicates the conclusion of the Third Mary's
part in the play. Probably after the
Marys left the choir, the scene of the Race
of Peter and John to the Sepulchre, and
possibly the scene of Appearance of Christ
to Mary Magdalene, followed.]

---

[1] The name is prefixed to the English verses that
follow, but it is clear that the Latin lines were
also spoken by the Third Mary.
    [2] Health, salvation.

II

THE WAYFARERS

[Monday of Passion Week.]

Feria secunda in ebdomada Pasche dis-
    cipuli insimul cantent:[1]

[DISCIPLES.]   *Infidelis incursum populi*

[1] "On the second day in Passion Week, the disciples sing in unison."

Fugiamus, Ihesu discipuli!
Suspenderunt Ihesum pati-
    bulo;
Nulli parcent eius discipulo.[1]

[1] These lines are set to music.

[*The disciples separate; Luke and Cleo-
phas go together towards Emmaus.*]

[LUKE.[1] . . . . . .] fast to fle.

[CLEOPAS.] But if we flee, thai wil vs fang,[2]
  And full felly thai wil vs flay;[3]
Agayn to Emause wil we gang,[4]
  And fonde [5] to get the gaynest [6] way.
And make in mynd euer vs amang
Of oure gode Maister, as we may,
How he was put to paynes strang, —
  On that he tristed con him be-tray![7]

[Here a red line in the manuscript, possibly
to indicate a new scene with the entrance
of Jesus.]

[JESUS. . . . .
  . . . .

LUKE. . . . .
  . . . .] but agayn.

[CLEOPAS.] By wymmen wordis wele
    wit [8] may we
  Christ is risen vp in gode aray;
For to oure-self the sothe [9] say[d] he,
  Where we went in this world away,
That he schuld dye and doluen be, [10]
  And rise fro the dethe the thrid day.
And that we myght that sight now se,
  He wisse [11] vs, Lord, as he well may!

[JESUS. . . . .

  . . . .

LUKE. . . . .
  . . . . . .] resoun right.

[CLEOPAS.] [12] *Et quoniam tradiderunt eum*

  [1] The manuscript fails to give the names of the
actors in this play. One of them was Cleopas (see St.
Luke, xxiv, 18), the other probably Luke. I have
followed Skeat in assigning the actor-parts to Cleopas.
  [2] Seize.
  [3] And full cruelly they will us flay.   (Manly
queries *slay*).
  [4] Go.   [5] Try.   [6] Nearest.
  [7] One whom he trusted did him betray!
  [8] Well know.   [9] Truth.
  [10] Buried be.   [11] Direct, show.
  [12] Skeat leaves these Latin lines unassigned, though
he prefixes the name of Cleopas to the English translation that follows; corrected by Manly.

*summi sacerdotes et principes nostri in
dampnacione[m] mortis et crucifixerunt
eum.*

Right is that we reherce by raw [1]
  The maters that we may on mene, [2]
How prestis and princes of oure lawe
  Ful tenely [3] toke him hom [4] be-twen,
And dampned him, with-outen awe,
  For to be dede with dole, [5] be-dene;[6]
Thai crucified him, wele we knaw,
  At Caluary, with caris kene.

[LUKE.[7] . . . .
  . . . .]

[CLEOPAS.] *Dixerunt etiam se visionem angelorum vidisse, qui dicunt eum uiuere.*

[JESUS. . . . .
  . . . .

LUKE. . . . .
  . . . .] wraist.

[CLEOPAS.] The wymmen gret,[8] for he
      was gon;
  But yet thai told of meruales mo:
Thai saw angellus stondyng on the ston,
  And sayn [9] how he was farne hom fro.[10]
Sithen of oures went ful gode wone [11]
  To se that sight, and said right so.
Herfore we murne and makis this mon;[12]
  Now wot [13] thou wele of all oure wo.

[JESUS. . . . .
  . . . .
  . . . .] in pese.

[CLEOPAS AND LUKE.] *Mane nobiscum,
quoniam aduesperascit et inclinata est iam
dies. Alleluya!* [14]

  [1] In due order.   [2] Recall.   [3] Cruelly.
  [4] Them.
  [5] Skeat has *dele;* corrected by Manly.   Deceit,
craft.
  [6] Indeed (often a meaningless rhyme-word).
  [7] What Luke probably said may be found in St.
Luke, xxiv, 21–22.
  [8] Wept.   [9] Say.   [10] Gone from them.
  [11] Afterwards full many of us went.
  [12] Lamentation.   [13] Knowest.
  [14] Accompanied by musical notation for singing.

[*Jesus agrees to remain with them, and they walk together towards Emmaus.*]

[JESUS. . . . .] wight.

[CLEOPAS.]   Amend oure mournyng, maister dere,
And fond [1] oure freylnes for to fell! [2]
Herk, brother! help to hold him here,
   Ful nobel talis wil he us tell!

[LUKE. . . . .] lent.

[CLEOPAS.]   And gode wyne schal vs wont non,
   For ther-to schal I take entent.

[*Jesus seats himself at the table with them, and breaks the bread. After blessing it and giving it to them, he suddenly vanished.*]

[LUKE. . . . .
      . . . .] he went!

[CLEOPAS.]   Went he is, and we ne wot [3] how,
   For here is noght left in his sted!
Allas! where were oure wittis now?
   With wo now walk we, wil of red! [4]

[LUKE. . . . .
      . . . .] oure bred.

[CLEOPAS.]   Oure bred he brak and blessed hit;
   On mold [5] were neuer so mased [6] men,
When that we saw him by vs sit,
   That we couthe [7] noght consayue [8] him then.

[LUKE. . . . .
      . . . .] ay.

[*Luke and Cleopas start back to Jerusalem, singing:*]

Quid agamus vel dicamus,
Ignorantes quo eamus,
Qui Doctorem sciencie
Et patrem consolacionis
Amisimus? [1]

[LUKE. . . . .
      . . . .] gode state.

[CLEOPAS.]   We schal home [2] tell, with-outen trayn, [3]
   Bothe word and werk, how [that] hit was,
I se hom sitt samyn in a plain. [4]
   Forthe in apert [5] dar I not pas!

[*They meet the other disciples, and narrate their experience.*]

[LUKE. . . . .
      . . . .] and wife.

[CLEOPAS.]   We saw him holl, hide and hewe; [6]
Therfore be still, and stint youre strife!
That hit was Crist ful wele we knewe,
   He cutt oure bred with-outen knyfe.

[*Believing that Christ has arisen, they all sing in unison:*]

Gloria tibi, Domine,
Qui surrexisti a mortuis,
Cum Patre et Sancto Spiritu,
In sempiterna secula; Amen! [7]

[*Thomas enters, and refuses to believe. Christ reappears and convinces him. The disciples sing in unison:*]

Frater Thoma, causa tristicie
Nobis tulit summa leticie!

[1] Accompanied by musical notation for singing.
[2] Them (the other disciples).
[3] Delay.
[4] I see them sitting together in an open place.
[5] Openly, in public view.
[6] Hue, complexion.
[7] Accompanied by musical notation.

[1] Try.   [2] Destroy.   [3] Know not.
[4] Bewildered in mind.   [5] Earth.
[6] Dumfounded, stupefied.
[7] Could.   [8] Recognize.

III

THE SHEPHERDS

[Christmas.]

[The three shepherds enter, singing:]

*Pastores erant in regione eadem uigilantes
et custodientes gregem suum. Et ecce
angelus Domini astitit iuxta illos et timu-
erunt timore magno.* [1]

[I. PASTOR. . . . .
. . . .

II. PASTOR.] We, Tib. [2]

III. PASTOR.   Telle on!

[I. PASTOR. . . . .
. . . .

II. PASTOR. . . . .
. . . .] the nyght.

[The star appears above.]

III. PASTOR.   Brether, what may this be,
Thus bright to man and best?

[I. PASTOR. . . . .
. . . .

II. PASTOR.   . . . .
. . . .] at hand.

III. PASTOR.   Whi say ye so?

[II. PASTOR.   . . . .
. . . . . .] warand.

III. PASTOR.   Suche sight was neuer sene
Before in oure Iewery;
Sum merueles wil hit mene
That mun be here in hy. [3]

[The angel appears and sings.]

Accompanied by musical notation.
Tib is the name of the First Shepherd.
That must be here aloft.

[I. PASTOR. . . . .
. . . .

II. PASTOR. . . . .
. . . .] a sang.

III. PASTOR.   Ye lye, bothe, by this light,
And raues as recheles royes! [1]
Hit was an angel bright
That made this nobulle noyes. [2]

[I. PASTOR. . . . .
. . . .

II. PASTOR. . . . .
. . . .] of prophecy.

III. PASTOR.   He said a barn [3] schuld be
In the burgh of Bedlem born;
And of this, mynnes me, [4]
Oure fadres fond beforn. [5]

[I. PASTOR. . . . .
. . . .

II. PASTOR. . . . .
. . . . .] Iewus kyng.

III. PASTOR.   Now may we se the same
Euen in oure pase puruayed; [6]
The angel nemed his name, —
"Crist, Saueour," he saied.

[I. PASTOR. . . . .
. . . .

II. PASTOR. . . . .
. . . .] not raue.

III. PASTOR.   Yone brightnes wil vs bring
Vnto that blisful boure; [7]

[1] Reckless boasters.   [2] Noise.
[3] Child.   [4] I remember.
[5] Found, or discovered, long ago.
[6] In our way provided.   [7] Bower.

For solace schal we syng
 To seke oure Saueour.

[*Following the star, they walk towards the manger, singing:*]

Transeamus usque Bethelem, et uideamus hoc verbum quod factum est, quod fecit Dominus et ostendit nobis.[1]

[I. PASTOR. . . . .
  . . . .

II. PASTOR. . . . .
  . . . .] to knawe.

III. PASTOR. For no-thing thar vs drede,[2]
 But thank God of all gode;
This light euer wil vs lede
 To fynde that frely fode.[3]

[*They reach the manger, and worship the babe. Each in turn presents a gift.*]

[1] Accompanied with musical notation.
[2] Need we fear.   [3] Noble child.

[I. PASTOR. . . . .
  . . . .

II. PASTOR. . . . .
  . . . .] I mene.

III. PASTOR. A! loke to me, my Lord dere,
 All if I put me noght in prese![1]
To suche a prince without[en] pere
 Haue I no presand that may piese.
But lo! a horn-spone haue I here
 That may herbar an hundrith pese:
This gift I gif the with gode chere, —
 Suche dayntese wil do no disese.[2]

Fare-wele now, swete swayn,
 God graunt the lifyng lang!

[I. PASTOR. And go we hame agayn,
 And mak mirth as we gang!][3]

[*The shepherds go out, singing joyfully.*]

[1] Although I do not value myself highly.
[2] Harm.
[3] The last two lines supplied by Skeat from the York mysteries.

V
THE CRAFT CYCLES

BANNS [1]

[Advertising the Performance of the N. towne Plays.[2]]

PRIMUS VEXILLAT[OR].   Now, gracyous
    God, groundyd of alle goodnesse,
  As thi grete glorie nevyr be-gynnyng
    had,
So thou socour and saue alle tho that sytt
    and sese,[1]
  And lystenyth to oure talkyng with
    sylens stylle and sad;
For we purpose us pertly [2] stylle in this
    prese,
  The pepyl to plese with pleys ful glad. 6
Now lystenyth us, louely, bothe more and
    lesse,
  Gentyllys and yemanry [3] of goodly lyff
    lad,
    This tyde.
We xal you shewe, as that we kan,
How that this werd [4] ffyrst be-gan,
And how God made bothe molde [5] and man,
    Iff that ye wyl a[byde].   13

SECUNDUS VEXILLA[TOR].   In the ffyrst
    pagent, we thenke to play
  How God dede make, thurowe his owyn
    myth,[6]
Hevyn so clere upon the fyrst day,
  And ther in he sett angelle fful bryth.

[1] See.   [2] Openly.   [3] Yeomanry.
[4] World.   [5] Earth.   [6] Might.

Than angelle with songe — this is no nay—
  Xal worchep God, as it is ryth;   19
But Lucyfer, that angelle so gay,
  In suche pompe than is he pyth,[1]
  And set in so grete pride,
That Goddys sete [2] he gynnyth to take,
Hese [3] lordys pere hym self to make,
But than he ffallyth a ffend [4] ful blake,
  From hevyn in helle to a[byde.]   26

TERTIUS VEXILL[ATOR].   In the secunde
    pagent, by Godys myth,
  We thenke to shewe and pley, be-dene,[5]
In the other sex days, by opyn syth,
  What thenge was wrought ther xal be
    sene;
How best was made and foule of flyth,[6]
  And last was man made, as I wene;   32
Of mannys o ryb, as I yow plyth,
  Was woman wrougth mannys make [7] to
    bene,
  And put in paradyse.
Ther were flourys bothe blew and blake,
Of alle frutys thei myth ther take,
Saff frute of cunnyng [8] thei xulde for-sake,
  And towche it no wyse.   39

[1] Placed.   [2] Seat, throne.   [3] His.
[4] Fiend.
[5] Indeed (a more or less meaningless rhyme-tag).
[6] Flight.   [7] Mate.   [8] Knowledge.

[1] Banns were public announcements of the performance of plays made usually by vexillatores (banner-bearers) in the neighboring towns and hamlets several days in advance; compare the Banns of *The Play of the Sacrament*.

[2] The manuscript (Brit. Mus. Cotton MS. Vespasian D. viii) of this cycle contains forty-two plays, and bears on folio 100 verso the date 1468. Where the plays were acted is not known. The librarian of Sir Robert Cotton, who purchased the manuscript about 1629, wrote on the fly-leaf: "*vulgo dicitur hic liber Ludus Coventriae, sive ludus Corporis Christi.*" From this brief notation it was for a time inferred that the plays were acted at Coventry; but the term "Coventry plays" was a vulgar designation for Corpus Christi plays in general; and there seems to be no good reason to connect this large cycle with the town of Coventry; it certainly was not the famous cycle performed there by the craft organizations. How to label the collection has puzzled scholars. Professor Manly calls the cycle the *Hegge Plays*, after an early owner of the manu-script; others refer to it as the *So-Called Coventry Plays*, or as the *Ludus Coventriæ*. It seems, however, un-desirable to associate the plays with the name of Coventry at all; and since the Banns clearly state that they were to be performed at "N. towne," I have designated them simply as the "N. towne Plays." Linguistic authorities assign the manuscript to the northeast Midlands. "N. towne" might be an abbreviation for "Northamptowne," but we cannot prove that Northampton had a cycle of plays. Possibly the Banns were originally written to describe a processional performance on waggons; but the manuscript in its present state, as well as the revised Banns, shows the plays as arranged for continuous presentation on a group of fixed platforms about a *platea*. I have based the text on the edition by K. S. Block, *Ludus Coventriæ*, edited for the Early English Text Society, 1922, and have compared this with Halliwell's careful edition of 1841. The punctuation, and the use of capital letters I have modernized. And since the Banns are very long, I have omitted some of the description of certain "pageants"; the extent of the omissions can be observed from the line-numbering.

The serpent toke Eve an appyl to byte,
  And Eve toke Adam a mursel of the
    same;
Whan thei had do thus a-gens the rewle of
    ryte,
  Than was oure Lord wrothe and grevyd
    al with grame.[1]
Oure Lord gan appose [2] them of ther gret
    delyte, [3]
  Bothe to askuse [4] hem of that synful
    blame;   45
And than Almyghty God, ffor that gret
    dyspite,
  Assygned hem grevous peyn, as ye xal se
    in game,
  In dede.
Seraphyn, an angelle gay,
With brennyng swerd — this is verray —
From paradise bete hem a-way,
  In Bybyl as we rede.   52

PRIMUS VEXILLATOR.   We purpose to
    shewe in the thryd pagent,
  The story of Caym and of hese brother
    Abelle . . .

SECUNDUS VEXILATOR.   The iij.de pagent
    is now yow tolde.
The ffourte pagent of Noe xal be,
How God was wrothe with man on molde,[5]
  Because fro synne man dede not fle . . . 69

TERTIUS VEXIL[LATOR].   Of Abraham is
    the fyfte pagent,
  And of Ysaac his sone so fre,
How that he xulde with fere be brent,
  And slayn with swerd, as ye xal se . . .

PRIMUS VEXIL[LATOR].   The sexte pagent
    is of Moyses,   92
  And of tweyn tabelys that God hym
    took,
In the whiche were wrete, with-out les, [6]
  The lawes of God to lerne and lok . . .

SECUNDUS VEXILLATOR.   Off the gentyl
    Jesse rote,   105
  The sefnt pagent forsothe xal ben,

Out of the whiche doth sprynge oure
    bote,[1]
  As in prophecye we redyn and sen;
Kyngys and prophetys with wordys fful
    sote,[2]
  Schulle prophesye al of a qwene,
The whiche xal staunche oure stryff and
    moote,[3]
  And wynnen us welthe with-outyn wene,[4]
    In hevyn to abyde.   113
They xal prophecye of a mayde,
Alle ffendys of here xal be affrayde,
Here sone xal saue us, be not dismayde,
  With hese woundys wyde.

TERTIUS VEXILLATOR.   Of the grete
    bushop Abyacar,   118
  The viii.[5] pagent xal be with-out
    lesyng [6] . . .

PRIMUS VEXILLATOR.   In the ix.[7] pagent,
    sothe to say,   144
  A masangere fforthe is sent;
Dauydis kynrede with-out de-lay
  They come fful sone with good entent.
Whan Joseph offeryd his yerde [8] that day,
  Anon ryth fforth in present
The ded styk do floure fful gay;
  And than Joseph to wedlok went,
    Ryth as the angel bad . . .

SECUNDUS VEXILLATOR.   In the x.[9] pagent
    goth Gabryelle,   157
  And doth salute Oure Lady ffre,
Than grett with chylde, as I yow telle . . .

TERTIUS VEXILLATOR.   In the xi.[10] pagent,
    as I yow telle,   170
  Joseph comyth hom fro fer countre;
Oure Ladyes wombe with chylde doth
    swelle,
  And than Joseph ful hevy is he . . .

PRIMUS VEXILLATOR.   The xii.[11] pagent, I
    sey yow, be-dene,   183

---

[1] Salvation.   [2] Sweet.   [3] Disputation.
[4] Doubt.
[5] MS. *tende*, a later addition over an erased word.
For the significance of these changes, see Block,
Ludus Coventriæ, pp. xix–xxv.
[6] Lying.
[7] MS. x^{te}, changed from an original ix^{te}.   [8] Rod.
[9] MS. xj.^{de}, changed from an original x^{de}.
[10] MS. xij, changed from an original *hellenthe*.
[11] MS. xiiij.^{te}, changed from an original xii^{te}.

[1] Anger.   [2] Interrogate.
[3] The MS. is not clear; Block reads *debyte*, Halliwell *delyte*.
[4] Excuse.   [5] On the earth.   [6] Lie.

Xal be of Joseph and mylde Mary,
How they were sclawndryd with trey and
    tene,[1]
And to here purgacion thei must hem hy.

SECUNDUS VEXILLATOR. In the xiii.[2]
    pagent shewe we xal,   187
How Joseph went with-oute varyauns,
For mydwyuys to helpe Oure Lady at alle,
Of childe that she had delyuerauns.

TERTIUS VEXILLATOR. In the xiv.[3] pagent
    Cryst xal be born.   191
Of that joy aungelys xul synge,
And telle the shepherdys in that morn
The blysseful byrth of that kyng.
The shepherdys xal come hym be-fforn,
With reuerens and with worchepyng . . .

PRIMUS VEXILLATOR. The xv.[te] pagent
    come kyngys iij.,   204
With gold, myrre, and ffrankynsens;
Kyng Herowdys styward[4] hem doth se,
And bryngyth alle to his presens . . .

SECUNDUS VEXILLATOR. In the xvi.
    pagent as wroth as wynde   217
Is kyng Herownde, the sothe to say,
And cruel knytys[5] and vn-kende
To sle male chylderyn he sendyth that
    day . . .

TERTIUS VEXILLATOR. In the xvii. pagent
    the knythtys, be-dene,   230
Shulle brynge dede childeryn be-for the
    kyng;
Whan kyng Herownde that syth[6] hath
    sene,
Ful glad he is of here kyllyng . . .

PRIMUS VEXILLATOR. In the xviii. pagent
    we must purpose,   243
To shewe whan Cryst was xij. yer of age,
How in the Temple he dede appose
And answerd doctoris ryth wyse and
    sage . . .

SECUNDUS VEXILLATOR. In the xix.
    pagent xal seynt Jhone   256

Baptyse Cryst, as I yow say,
In the watyr of flom[1] Jordone,
With which devys, as we best may,
The Holy Gost xal ouyr[2] hym on . . .

TERTIUS VEXILLATOR. In the xx.[ti]
    pagent alle the deuelys of helle, 269
They gadere a parlement, as ye xal se,
They have gret doute the trewth to telle,
Of Cryst Jhesu whath he xulde be.
They sende Sathan, that ffynde so ffelle,
Cryst for to tempte in fele degre . . .

PRIMUS VEXILLATOR. The xxi.[ti] pagent
    of a woman xal be,   282
The whiche was take in adultrye . . .

SECUNDUS VEXILLATOR. The grettest
    meracle that evyr Jhesus   295
In erthe wrouth be-forn his passyon,
In xxii.[ti] pagent we purpose vs
To shewe in dede the declaracion.
That pagent xal be of Lazarus . . .

TERTIUS VEXILLATOR. In the xxiij.[ti]
    pagent, Palme Sunday,   308
In pley we purpose ffor to shewe,
How chylderyn of Ebrew with flowrys ful
    gay,
The wey that Cryst went thei gun to
    strewe.

PRIMUS VEXILLATOR. In the xxiiij.[ti]
    pagent, as that we may,
Cryst and his apostelys, alle on rewe,[3]
The mawnde[4] of God ther xal they play,
And sone declare it with wordys
    ffewe.   315
    And than
Judas, that fals traytour,
For xxx.[ti] platys of werdly tresour,
Xal be-tray oure Savyour
    To the Jewys certan.

SECUNDUS VEXILLATOR. For grevous
    peyn, this is no les, [5]   321
In the xxv.[ti] pagent, Cryst xal pray
To the Fadyr of hevyn that peyn for to ses
His shamful deth to put away.

---

1 Slandered with trouble and injury.
2 MS. xv, changed from an original xiii.
3 MS. xvj, changed from an original xiv.
4 Steward.   5 Knights, soldiers.   6 Sight.

1 River.   2 Hover.   3 Row.
4 Feast, the Lord's Supper.   5 Lie.

Judas that traytour, befor gret pres,[1]
Xal kys his mouthe and hym betray. . .

TERTIUS VEX[ILLATOR].   Than in the
        xxvj.[ti] pagent,   334
To Cayphas Cryst xal be brouth;
Tho Jewys fful redy ther xul be bent
Cryst to acuse with worde and thouth.
Seynt Petyr doth folwe with good intent,
To se with Cryst what xuld be wrouth;
For Crystys dyscyple whan he is hent,[2]
    Thryes [3] he doth swere he knew hym
        nowth, —
    A kok xal crowe and crye;
Than doth Petyr gret sorwe make . . .

PRIMUS VEXILLATOR.   In the xxvij. pagent,
        sere [4] Pylat   347
Is sett in sete as hy justyce . . .

SECUNDUS VEXILLATOR.   In the xxviij.[ti]
        pagent xal Judas,   360
    That was to Cryst a ffals traytour,
With wepyng sore evyr crye, alas,
    That evyr he solde oure Savyour.
He xal be sory ffor his trespas,
    And brynge a-gen alle his tresour,
Alle xxx. pens, to sere Cayphas,   366
    He xal them brynge with gret dolowre,[5]
For the whiche Cryst was bowth.[6]
For gret whanhope,[7] as ye xal se,
He hangyth hym self vpon a tre;
For he noth [8] trostyth in Godys pete, [9]
    To helle his sowle is browth.

TERTIUS VEXILLATOR.   In the xxix.
        pagent, to Pylatus wyff   373
In slepe aperyth the devyl of helle,
For to savyn Crystys lyff . . .

PRIMUS VEXILLATOR.   In the xxx.[ti] pagent
        thei bete out Crystys blood,   386
And nayle hym al nakyd upon a rode
        tre,
Betwen ij. thevys; i-wys [10] they were to
        wood; [11]
    They hyng Cryst Jhesu, gret shame it is
        to se . . .

1 Crowd.   2 Taken.   3 Thrice.
4 Sir.   5 Grief.   6 Bought.
7 Despair.   8 Not.   9 Pity.
10 Truly.   11 Mad.

SECUNDUS VEXILLATOR.   We purpose to
        shewe in oure pleyn place, [1]   399
In the xxxj.[ti] pagent, thorwe Godys
        mythe,
How to Crystys herte a spere gan pace,[2]
    And rent oure Lordys bryst in ruly
        plyth [3] . . .

TERTIUS VEXILLATOR.   Joseph and Nyco-
        demus, to Cryst trew servaunt, 412
In the xxxij. page[nt] the body thei aske
        to haue.
Pylat ful redyly the body doth hem graunt;
    Than thei with reverens do put it in
        grave . . .

PRIMUS VEXILLATOR.   In the [x]xxiij.
        pagent the soule of Cryst Jhesu 425
Xal brynge alle his ffrendys ffrom helle
        to paradyse . . .

SECUNDUS VEXILLATOR.   In the xxxiiii.[ti]
        pagent xal Maryes thre   438
Seke Cryst Jhesu in his grave so coolde;
An aungel hem tellyth that aresyn is he;
And whan that this tale to them is tolde,
To Crystys dyscyplis, with wurdys fful fre,
    They telle these tydyngys with brest ful
        bolde.
Than Petyr and Johan, as ye xal se,
    Down rennyn in hast ouer lond and
        wolde,   445
    The trewth of this to haue.
Whan thei ther comyn, as I yow say,
He is gon ffrom vndyr clay;
Than thai wytnesse a-noon that day,
    He lyth not in his grave.

TERTIUS VEXILLATOR.   Onto Mary Maw-
        delyn, as we haue bent,   451
Cryst Jhesu xal than apere,
In the xxxv.[ti] pagent,
    And she wenyth [4] he be a gardenere . . .

PRIMUS VEXILLATOR.   In the xxxvj.[ti]
        pagent xal Cleophas   464
And Sent Luke to a castel go;
Of Crystys deth as thei fforth pas
They make gret mornyng and be ful wo;
Than Cryst them ovyr-tok, as his wyl was,

1 Playing place?   2 Pass.
3 Rueful plight.   4 Thinketh.

And walkyd in felachep [1] fforth with
　　hem too.
To them he doth expowne bothe more and
　　las   470
　　Alle that prophetys spakad of hym self
　　　also;
　　　That nyth in fay,
Whan thei be set within the castelle,
In brekyng of bred thei know Cryst welle,
Than sodeynly, as I yow telle,
　　　Cryste is gon his way.

SECUNDUS VEXILLATOR.　　In the xxxvij.[ti]
　　pagent than purpos we,   477
　　To Thomas of Ynde Cryst xal apere;
And Thomas euyn ther, as ye xal se,
　　Xal put his hand in his woundys dere.

TERTIUS VEXILLATOR.　　In the xxxviij.[ti]
　　pagent up stye [2] xal he   481
　　Into hefne that is so clere . . .

PRIMUS VEXILLATOR.　　Than ffolwyth next,
　　sekyrly, [3]   490
　　Of Wyttsunday that solempne ffest;
Whyche pagent xal be ix. and thretty.
　　To the apostelys to apere be Crystys
　　　hest, [4]
In Hierusalem were gaderyd xij. opynly,
　　To the Cenacle comyng ffrom West and
　　　Est;   495
The Holy Gost apperyd fful veruently,
　　With brennyng ffere thyrlyng [5] here
　　　brest,
　　Procedyng from hevyn trone [6]. . .

| [1] Fellowship. | [2] Mount, ascend. | [3] Truly. |
| [4] Command. | [5] Piercing. | [6] Throne. |

SECUNDUS VEXILLATOR.　　The xl.[ti] pagent
　　xal be the last,   403
　　And Domysday that pagent xal hyth. [1]
Who se that pagent may be agast
　　To grevyne his Lord God eyther day or
　　　nyth.
The erthe xal qwake, bothe breke and
　　　brast, [2]
　　Beryelys [3] and gravys xul ope ful tyth, [4]
Ded men xul rysyn and that ther in hast,
　　And ffast to here ansuere thei xul hem
　　　dyth, [5]   510
　　　Beffore Godys fface.
But prente wyl this in your mende:
Who so to God hath be vnkende,
Frenchep ther xal he non ffynde,
　　　Ne ther get he no grace.

TERTIUS VEXILLATOR.　　Now haue we told
　　yow alle, be-dene,   516
　　The hool mater that we thynke to play;
Whan that ye come, ther xal ye sene
　　This game wel pleyd in good a-ray.
Of Holy Wrytte this game xal bene,
　　And of no fablys be no way.   521
Now God them save from trey and tene,
　　For us that prayth upon that day,
　　And qwyte [6] them wel ther mede. [7]
A Sunday next, yf that we may,
At vj. of the belle [8] we gynne oure play,
In N. towne; wherfore we pray,   527
　　　That God now be youre spede.
　　　　　Amen.

[1] Be called.	[2] Break and burst.
[3] Tombs.	[4] Quickly.	[5] Prepare.
[6] Requite.	[7] Reward.
[8] The bell of the clock, six o'clock.

THE FALL OF LUCIFER [1]

[Acted at N. towne.]

[*Deus upon his throne.*]

DEUS.   *Ego sum alpha et Ω, principium et finis.*
My name is knowyn, God and Kynge.
My werk for to make now wyl I wende.[1]

[*Deus rises.*]

In my self restyth my reynenge; [2]
    It hath no gynnyng ne non ende;   5
And alle that evyr xal haue beynge,
    It is closyd in my mende;
Whan it is made at my lykynge,
    I may it saue, I may it shende,[3]
        After my plesawns.[4]   10
So gret of myth is my pouste,[5]
Alle thyng xal be wrowth [6] be me.
I am oo [7] God, in personys thre,
    Knyt in oo substawns.   14

I am the trewe Trenyte,
    Here walkyng in this wone; [8]
Thre personys myself I se,
    Lokyn [9] in me, God alone.   18
I am the Fadyr of powste,[5]
    My Sone with me gynnyth gon,
My Gost is grace in mageste,
    Weldyth welthe up in hevyn tron,   22
    O [7] God thre I calle,
I a Fadyr of myth,[10]
My Sone kepyth ryth,
My Gost hath lyth,
    And grace with-alle.   27

My-self begynnyng nevyr dyd take,
    And endeles I am thorw [11] myn own myth.
Now wole I be-gynne my werke to make.
    Fyrst I make hevyn with sterrys of lyth   31
In myrth and joy euermore to wake;
    In hevyn I bylde [12] angelle fful bryth,

My servauntys to be, and for my sake,
    With merth and melody worchepe my myth;   35
    I belde them in my blysse.
Aungelle in hevyn evyr-more xal be,
In lyth ful clere bryth as ble,[1]
With myrth and song to worchip me,
    Of joye thei may not mys.   40

[*Deus withdraws.*]

Hic cantent angeli in celo: "*Tibi omnes angeli, tibi celi et vniuerse potestates, Tibi cherubyn et seraphyn incessabili voce proclamant — Sanctus! Sanctus! Sanctus! Dominus Deus Sabaoth.*" [2]

LUCIFERE.   To whos wurchipe synge ye this songe?
    To wurchip God, or reverens me?
But [3] ye me wurchipe ye do me wronge,
    For I am the wurthyest that evyr may be.   44
ANGELI BONI.[4]   We wurchipe God, of myth most stronge,
    Whiche hath fformyd bothe vs and the;
We may nevyr wurchyp hym to longe,
    For he is most worthy of mageste.   48
    On knes to God we ffalle,
Oure Lorde God wurchyp we,
And in no wyse honowre we the.
A gretter lord may nevyr non be,
    Than he that made us alle!   53

LUCIFERE.   A wurthyer lord, forsothe, am I;
    And worthyer than he euyr wyl I be!
In evydens that I am more wurthy,
    I wyl go syttyn in Goddys se.[5]   57

[1] Bright as color; *qy.* of countenance.
[2] Here let the angels in heaven sing: "To thee all the angels, to thee the powers of heaven and of the universe, to thee the cherubim and seraphim with unceasing voice cry out: 'Holy! Holy! Holy! Lord God of Sabaoth!'"
[3] Unless.   [4] The Good Angels.   [5] Seat.

[6] Wrought, created.   [7] One.
[8] Dwelling, place.   [9] Locked.   [10] Might.
[11] Through.   [12] Make.
[1] Go.   [2] Reigning, sovereignty.
[3] Destroy.   [4] Pleasure.   [5] Power.

---

[1] For a discussion of the N. towne Plays, and for the source of the text, see page 81, note 2.

[Seats himself in God's throne.]

Above sunne and mone and sterrys on sky
  I am now set, as ye may se.
Now wurchyp me ffor most mythy,
  And for your Lord honowre now me, 61
  Syttyng in my sete.
ANGELI MALI.[1] Goddys myth we for-sake,
And for more wurthy we the take;
The to wurchep honowre we make,
  And ffalle downe at thi ffete. 66

[Deus advances.]

DEUS. Thu Lucyfere, ffor thi mekyl
    pryde,
  I bydde the ffalle from hefne to helle;
And alle tho[2] that holdyn on thi syde,
  In my blysse nevyr more to dwelle. 70

  [1] The Bad Angels.   [2] Those.

At my comawndement anoon down thou
    slyde,
  With merthe and joye nevyr more to
    melle. [1]
In myschyf and manas[2] evyr xalt thou
    abyde,
  In byttyr brennyng and fyer so felle, 74
  In peyn evyr to be pyht.[3]
LUCYFERE. At thy byddyng thi wyl I werke,
And pas fro joy to peyne smerte.
Now I am a devyl ful derke,
  That was an aungelle bryht. 79

Now to helle the wey I take,
  In endeles peyn ther to be pyht.
For fere of fyre a fart I crake; 82
  In helle donjoone myn dene[4] is dyth.[5]

  [1] Mix.   [2] Danger.   [3] Fixed.
  [4] Den.   [5] Prepared.

THE CREATION OF EVE, WITH THE EXPELLING OF ADAM AND EVE OUT OF PARADISE [1]

[Acted by the Grocers of Norwich.]

The Storye of the Temptacion of Man in Paradyce, being therin placyd, and the expellynge of man and woman from thence, newely renvid [1] and accordynge unto the Skripture, begon thys yere, Anno 1565, Anno 7. Eliz.

ITEM. *Yt ys to be notyd that when the Grocers Pageant is played withowte eny other goenge befor yt,[2] then doth the Prolocutor say in this wise:*

[THE FIRST ALTERNATIVE PROLOGUE.]

Lyke as yt chancyd, befor this season,
  Owte of Godes Scripture revealid, in
    playes
Was dyvers stories sett furth, by reason
  Of pageantes apparellyd in Wittson
    dayes; [3]
  And lately be fal[l]en into decayes;
Which stories dependyd in theyr orders
    sett
By severall devices, much knowledge to
  gett;   7

Begynny[n]g in Genesis, that story repleate,

Of God his creacion of ech lyvynge
  thynge,
Of heaven, and of erth, of fysh smalle and
  great,
  Of fowles, herbe, and tre, and of alle
    bestes crepynge,
  Of angell, of man, which of erth hath
    beynge,
And of the fall of angell[s], in the Apocalips
  to se;
Which stories with the Skriptures most
    justly agree.   14

Then followed this ower pageant; which
  sheweth to be
  The Garden of Eden, which God dyd
    plante,
As in the seconde chapter of Genesis ye
  se;
  Wherin of frutes pleasant no kynde
    therof shulde wante;
  In which God dyd putt man to cherish
    tre and plante,
To dresse and kepe the grounde, and eate
  what frute hym lyste, —
Ex[c]ept the tre of knoweledge, Godes high
  wytt to resyste.   21

The story sheweth further, that, after man
  was blyste,
  The Lord did create woman owte of a
    ribbe of man;
Which woman was deceyvyd with the Ser-
  pentes darkned myste;
  By whose synn ower nature is so weake
    no good we can;
Wherfor they were dejectyd, and caste
  from thence than
Unto dolloure and myseri, and to traveyle
  and payne,

---

[1] Renewed. An earlier version of the play dating from 1533, though not complete, is found in the transcript noted above, and is reproduced by Fitch, Manly, and Waterhouse.

[2] At this date the mystery plays were falling into decay, and the grocers anticipated the possibility of there being no preceding pageants. Shortly afterwards the grocers themselves gave up their performance; in 1570 their splendid waggon was broken to pieces, having stood for six years in a "Gate howse," and later "at ye Black Fryers brydge in open street" where it had become "so weather beaten yt ye cheif parte was rotton." (See E. K. Chambers, *The Mediæval Stage*, ii, 388–89.)

[3] At an earlier date the plays were given on Corpus Christi Day. (See E. K. Chambers, *op. cit.*, ii, 386, 388.)

---

[1] Printed, with many inaccuracies, by Robert Fitch, from an eighteenth-century transcript of certain portions of the lost Grocers' Book of Norwich, in *Norfolk Archæology* (1856), v, 8 (also separately issued), whence it was reprinted by Manly, *Specimens of the Pre-Shaksperean Drama*, 1897, with some valuable emendations. In 1909 the play was more accurately reproduced for the Early English Text Society by O. Waterhouse. I have based the present text on Waterhouse's edition, with certain emendations from Fitch and Manly.

Untyll Godes spright renvid.   And so we
ende certayne.   28

*Note that yf ther goeth eny other pageantes
before yt, the Prolocutor sayeth as ys on
the other syde and leaveth owte this.*

[THE SECOND ALTERNATIVE PROLOGUE.]

THE PROLOCUTOR.   As in theyr former
pageantes is semblably declared
Of Godes mighty creacion in every
lyvyng thynge,
As in the fyrst of Genesis to such it is prepared
As lust they have to reade to memory to
brynge,
Of pride and fawle of angells that in hell
hath beinge;
In the seconde of Genesis of mankynde hys
creacion
Unto this Garden Eden is made full prepa-
racion.   7

And here begynneth ower pageant to make
the declaracion,
From the letter C in the chapter before
saide,
How God putt man in Paradyse to dresse
yt in best fassion,
And that no frute therof from hym shuld
be denayed,
Butt of the tre of lyffe that man shuld be
afraide
To eat of, least that daye he eat that he
shuld dye;
And of womanes creacion appering by and
bye;   14

And of the Deavilles temptacion deseaiv-
inge with a lye
The woman, beinge weakest, that
cawsed man to tast.
That God dyd so offende, that even con-
tynentlye [1]
Owte of the place of joye was man and
woman caste,
And into so great dolloure and misery
browght at last;
Butt that by God his spright was com-
forted ageyne.

[1] Instantly.

This is of this ower pagent the some and
effect playne.   21

[THE CREATION OF EVE, WITH THE
EXPELLING OF ADAM AND EVE
FROM PARADISE]

[*On the upper part of the pageant, representing Paradise.[1]*]

GOD THE FATHER.   I am Alpha et Ho-
mega, my Apocalyps doth testyfye,
That made all of nothinge for man his
sustentacion.
And of this pleasante garden, that I have
plant most goodlye,
I wyll hym make the dresser for his good
recreacion.
Therfor, Man, I gyve yt the, to have thy
delectacion.
In eatyng thou shalt eate of every growenge
tre,
Ex[c]epte the tre of knowledge, the which
I forbydd the;   7

For in what daye soever thou eatest thou
shallt be
Even as the childe of death.   Take hede!
And thus I saye:

[1] The play-waggon was obviously in two divisions,
the upper representing Paradise, the lower, Earth
(see the stage direction following line 103).   Possibly the wainscoted section below was used for
Hell.   The records of the Grocers' Guild at Norwich
supply us with the following information about the
pageant and its properties:

*Inventory of ye p'ticulars appartaynyng to ye Company
of ye Grocers, a.d. 1565.*

A Pageant, yt is to saye, a Howse of Waynskott
paynted and buylded on a Carte wt fowre whelys.
A square topp to sett over ye sayde Howse.
A Gryffon, gylte, wt a fane to sett on ye sayde toppe.
A bygger Iron fane to sett on ye ende of ye Pageante.
iiijxx iij [i.e. 83] small Fanes belongyng to ye same
Pageante.
A Rybbe colleryd Red.
A cote & hosen wt a bagg & capp for Dolor, steyned.
2 cotes & a payre hosen for Eve, stayned.
A cote & hosen for Adam, Steyned.
A cote wt hosen & tayle for ye serpente, steyned, wt
a wt heare [=white wig].
A cote of yellow buckram wt ye Grocers' arms for
ye Pendon bearer.
An Angell's Cote & over hoses of Apis Skynns.
3 paynted clothes to hang abowte ye Pageant.
A face [i.e. mask] & heare [i.e. wig] for ye Father.
2 hearys for Adam & Eve.
4 head stallis of brode Inkle wth knopps & tassells.
6 Horsse Clothes, stayned, wt knopps & tassells.
Item, Weights, &c.

I wyll the make an helper, to comforte
the allwaye.
Beholde, therfore, a slepe I bryng this daye
on the,   11

[*Man lies down and falls asleep.*]

And owte of this thy ribbe, that here I
do owte take,

[*God lifts "a rybbe colleryd red."*]

A creature for thy help behold I do the
make.

[*Eve rises from below.*]

Aryse, and from thy slepe I wyll the
nowe awake,

[*Man awakes and rises.*]

And take hyr unto the, that you both be as
one
To comfort one thother when from you I
am gone.   16

And, as I saide before when that thou wert
alone,
In eatying thow mayst eate of every tre
here is,
Butt of the tre of knowledge of good and
evyll eate non,
Lest that thou dye the deth by doenge
so amysse!   20
I wyll departe now wher myne habytacion
is.
. leave you here........................¹
Se that ye have my woordes in most high
estymacion.

Then Man and Woman speke bothe.

[MAN AND WOMAN.]   We thanke the,
mighty God, and gyve the honor-
acion.   [*Exit God.*]   24

Man spekethe.

[MAN.]   Oh bone of my bones and flesh of
my flesh eke,²
Thou shalte be called Woman, bycaus
thow art of me.
Oh gyfte of God most goodlye, that hast us
made so lyke!
Most lovynge spowse, I muche do here
rejoyce of the.

¹ Lacuna in the MS.   ² Also.

WOMAN.   And I lykewyse, swete lover, do
much reioyce of the.
God therefore be praised, such comforte
have us gyve
That ech of us with other thus pleasantly
do lyve.   31

MAN.   To walke abowt this garden my
fantasye me meve;
I wyll the leave alone tyll that I turne
ageyne.
Farewell, myn owne swete spouse!   I
leave the to remayne.
WOMAN.   And farewell, my dere lover,
whom my hart doth conteyn.   35

[*Man walks to another part of Paradise.*]

The Serpent speketh.

[THE SERPENT.]   Nowe, nowe, of my
purpos I dowght nott to atteyne;
I can yt nott abyde, in theis joyes they
shulde be.
Naye, I wyll attempt them to syn unto
theyr payne;
By subtyllty to catch them the waye I
do well se;
Unto this, angell of lyght I shew my-
sylfe to be,
With hyr for to dyscemble; I fear yt nott at
all,
Butt that unto my haight some waye I
shall hyr call.   42

[*The Serpent approaches Eve.*]

Oh lady of felicite, beholde my voice so
small!
Why have God sayde to you, "Eate nott
of every tre
That is within this garden"?   Therein
now awnswere me.   45

WOMAN.   We eate of all the frutte that in
the grounde we se,
Ex[c]epte that in the myddest, wherof
we may nott taste,
For God hath yt forbydd; therfor yt may
not be,
Lest that we dye the deth, and from this
place be caste.   49
THE SERPENT.   Ye shall not dye the deth.
He made you butt agaste.

Butt God doth know full well that when
   you eate of yt
Your eys shall then be openyd, and you
   shall [be] at the last
As God; both good and evyll to knowe ye
   shall be fytt.   53

WOMAN.   To be as God, indede, and in his
   place to sytt,
Thereto for to agre my lust conceyve
   somewhatt;
Besydes, the tre is pleasante to gett wysedome and wytt,
And nothyng is to be comparyd unto
   that.
THE SERPENT.   Then take at my request,
   and eate, and fere yt natt.   58

Here she takyth and eatyth, and Man
cumyth in and sayeth unto hyr:

MAN.   My love, for my solace I have here
   walkyd longe.
Howe ys yt nowe with you? I pray you
   do declare.
WOMAN.   In-dede, lovely lover, the
   Heavenly Kyng most stronge
To eate of this apple his angell hath
   prepare.
Take therof at my hande thother frutes
   emonge,
For yt shall make you wyse, and even as
   God to fare.[1]   64

Then Man taketh and eatyth and sayethe:

[MAN.]   Alack! alacke! my spouse, now se
   I nakid we ar;
The presence of ower God we can yt nott
   abyde.
We have broke his precepte, he gave us of
   to care;
From God therfor in secrete in some
   place lett us hide.
WOMAN.   With fygge leavis lett us cover
   us, of God we be nott spyede.   69

[Adam and Eve hide themselves. Enter
God.]

THE FATHER.   Adam! I saye, Adam!
   Wher art thou nowe this tyde,
That here before my presence thou dost
   nott nowe apere?

[1] Go, to be.

ADAM.   I herde thy voyce, oh Lorde, but
   yett I dyd me hide;
For that which I am naked I more
   greatly dyd feare.   73

THE FATHER.   Why art thou then nakyd?
   Who so hath cawsyd the?
MAN.   This woman, Lord and God, which
   thou hast gyven to me.
THE FATHER.   Hast thou eat of the frute
   that I forbyd yt the?
Thow Woman, why hast thou done unto
   him thys trespace?
WOMAN.   The Serpente diseayvyd me with
   that his fayer face.   78

THE FATHER.   Thow Serpente, why
   dydst thou this wise prevente my
   grace,
My creatures and servantes in this
   maner to begyle?
THE SERPENTE.   My kind[1] is so, thou
   knowest, and that in every case,
Clene oute of this place theis persons to
   exile.   82

THE FATHER.   Cursed art, for causynge
   my commandement to defyle,
Above all cattell and beastes. Remayne
   thou in the fylde;
Crepe on thy belly and eate duste for this
   thy subtyll wyle;
The womans sede shall overcome the;
   thus that have I wylde.[2]
Thou, Woman, bryngyng chyldren with
   payne shall be dystylde,[3]
And be subiect to thy husbonde, and thy
   lust shall pertayne
To hym. I hav determynyd this ever to
   remayne.   89
And to the, Man, for that my voyce thou
   didst disdayne,
Cursed is the erth for ever for thy
   sake;
Thy lyvyng shall thou gett with swett unto
   thy payne,
Tyll thou departe unto the erth [wherof][4]
   I dyd the make.
Beholde, theis letherin aprons unto
   yourselves now take.   94

[1] Nature.   [2] Decreed.
[3] Dissolved (as in tears).   [4] *Added by Manly.*

Lo! Man as one of us hathe bene,[1] good
    and evyll to knowe;
Therfor I wyll exempt hym from this
    place to aslake,[2]
Lest of the tre of lyfe he eate and ever
    growe.
  Myne angell, now cum furth and kepe
    the waye and porte,
  Unto the tre of lyffe that they do not
    resorte.   99

[Enter the Angel; exit God.]

THE AUNGELL. Departe from hence at
    onys from this place of comforte,
  No more to have axcesse, or elles for to
    apere.
From this place I exile you, that you no
    more resorte,
  Nor even do presume ageyne for to com
    here.   103

*Then Man and Woman departyth to the
nether parte of the pageant, and Man
sayeth:*

[MAN.] Alack! myn owne sweteharte, how
    am I stroke with feare,
  That from God am exiled and browght
    to payne and woo!
Oh! what have we lost! Why dyd we no
    more care?
  And to what kynde of place shall we re-
    sort and goo?
WOMAN. Indede, into the worlde now
    must we to and fro,
And where or how to rest I can nott say at
    all.
I am even as ye ar, what so ever me
    befall.   110

*Then cumeth Dolor and Myserye and
taketh Man by both armys, and Dolor
sayeth:*

[DOLOR.] Cum furth, O Man, take hold of
    me!
  Through envy hast lost thy heavenly
    lyght
By eatinge; in bondage from hence shall
    be.
  Now must thou me, Dolor, have allways
    in sight.   114

MYSERYE. And also of me, Myserye.
  Thou must taste and byte
Of hardenes and of colde, and eke of
    infirmitie;
Accordinge to desarte thy portion is, of
    right,
  To enjoye that in me that is withoute
    certentye.   118

ADAM. Thus troublyd, nowe I enter into
    dolor and miserie.
  Nowe, Woman, must we lerne ower
    lyvynges to gett
With labor and with travell; ther is no
    remedye,
  Nor eny thyng therfrom we se that maye
    us lett.   122

*Then cumyth in the Holy Ghost comforting
Man, and sayeth:*

[THE HOLY GHOST.] Be of good cheare,
    Man, and sorowe no more.
  This dolor and miserie that thou hast
    taste
Is nott in respect,[1] layd up in store,
  To the joyes for the that ever shall last.
Thy God doth nott this the away to cast,
But to try the as gold is tryed in the fyer;
In the end, premonyshed, shalt have thy
    desyre.   129

Take owte of the Gospell that yt the
    requyre,
  Fayth in Chryst Ihesu, and grace shall
    ensewe.
I wyl be thy guyde, and pay the thy hyer
  For all thy good dylygence and doenge
    thy dewe.
Gyve eare unto me, Man, and than yt ys
    trewe,
Thou shalt kyll affectes that by lust in the
    reygne,
And put Dolor and Mysery and Envy to
    payne.   136

Theis armors ar preparyd, yf thou wylt
    turne ageyne
  To fyght wyth — take to the, and reach
    Woman the same:
The brest plate of rightousnes Saynte Paüle
    wyll the retayne;

---

1 Been.
2 Slacken, **abate.**

1 Nothing in respect to.

The shylde of faythe to quench, thy
    fyrye dartes to tame;
The hellmett of salvacion the devyles
    wrath shall lame;
And the sworde of the spright, which is the
    worde of God.
All theis ar nowe the offred to ease thy
    payne and rodd.[1]   143

[Exit the Holy Ghost.]

ADAM.   Oh! prayse to the, Most Holye,
    that hast with me abode,
  In mysery premonyshynge by this thy
    Holy Spright.
Howe fele I such great comforte, my syns
    they be unlode
And layde on Chrystes back, which is
    my joye and lyght.
This dolor and this mysery I fele to me no
    wight;[2]
  No!   Deth is overcum by forepredes-
    tinacion,

[1] Cross, suffering.   [2] Weight.

And we attayned wyth Chryst in
    heavenly consolacion.   150

Therfor, myne owne swett spous, withouten
    cavylacion
  Together lett us synge, and lett our
    hartes reioyse
And gloryfye ower God wyth mynde,
    powre and voyse.   153
    Amen.

Old musick, Triplex, Tenor, Medius, Bass:

With hart and voyce
Let us reioyce
  And prayse the Lord alwaye
  For this our joyfull daye,
To se of this our God his maiestie,
Who the hath given himsellfe over us to
    raygne and to governe us.[1]
  Lett all our harte[s] reioyce together,
  And lett us all lifte up our voyce, on of us
    with another.   161

[1] The stanza is apparently corrupt.

THE KILLING OF ABEL[1]

[Acted by the Glovers of Wakefield.]

Mactacio Abel. Secunda Pagina. Glover Pag.

[*Enter Pikeharness, Cain's boy.*]

GARCIO. All hayll! all hayll! both blithe
    and glad!
For here com I, a mery lad!
Be peasse [1] youre dyn, my master bad,
    Or els the dwill [2] you spede.   4
Wote ye not I com before?
Bot who that ianglis [3] any more
He must blaw my blak hoill [4] bore,
Both behynd and before,
    Till his tethe blede.   9
Felows, here I you forbede
To make nother nose [5] ne cry;
    Who so is so hardy to do that dede,
The dwill hang hym vp to dry!   13

Gedlyngis,[6] I am a fulle grete wat.[7]
A good yoman my master hat,[8]
    Full well ye all hym ken.   16
Begyn he with you for to stryfe,
Certis, then mon [9] ye neuer thryfe.
Bot I trow, bi god on life,
    Som of you ar his men.   20
    Bot let youre lippis couer youre ten,[10]
Harlottis, euerichon! [11]
    For if my master com, welcom hym then.
Farewell, for I am gone.   24

[*Exit Garcio. Enter Cain, ploughing and shouting to his team.*]

CAYN. Io furth, Greyn-horne! and war
    oute, Gryme!
Drawes on! God gif you ill to tyme! [12]
Ye stand as ye were fallen in swyme.[13]
    What! will ye no forther, mare?   28
War! Let me se how Down will draw.

Yit, shrew, yit! pull on a thraw! [1]
What! it semys for me ye stand none aw!
    I say, Donnyng, go fare!   32
    A, ha! God gif the soro and care!
Lo! now hard [2] she what I saide.
    Now yit art thou the warst mare
In plogh that euer I haide.   36

How! Pike-harnes, how! com heder be-
    life! [3]

[*Enter Garcio.*]

GARCIO. I fend,[4] Godis forbot, that euer
    thou thrife!
CAYN. What, boy, shal I both hold and
    drife?   39
    Heris thou not how I cry?

[*Garcio drives the team.*]

GARCIO. Say, Mall and Stott, will ye not
    go?
Lemyng, Morell, White-horne, Io!
    Now will ye not se how thay hy?   43

CAYN. Gog gif the sorow, boy. Want of
    mete it gars.[5]
GARCIO. Thare prouand, [6] sir, for-thi, I
lay behynd thare ars,
And tyes them fast bi the nekis,
With many stanys [7] in thare hekis.[8]
CAYN. That shall bi [9] thi fals chekis.   48

[*Strikes him.*]

GARCIO. And haue agane as right.

[*Strikes back.*]

CAYN. I am thi master; wilt thou fight?
GARCIO. Yai, with the same mesure and
weght

---

[1] Silence.   [2] Devil.   [3] Chatters.
[4] Hole.   [5] Noise.   [6] Fellows.
[7] Man.   [8] Is called.   [9] May.
[10] Teeth.   [11] Rascals every one.
[12] Befall.   [13] Dizziness.

[1] Short while.   [2] Heard.   [3] Quickly.
[4] Forbid.   [5] Causes it.   [6] Provender.
[7] Stones.   [8] Hay-racks?   [9] Pay for.

---

[1] From *The Towneley Plays*, edited for the Early English Text Society by George England and Alfred W. Pollard, 1897. I have modernized the punctuation and the use of capitals, and have added stage directions. The manuscript, which is assigned to the latter half of the fifteenth century, was long preserved in the library of the Towneley family at Towneley Hall, Lancashire, hence the name "Towneley Plays." There is little doubt that they were performed by the crafts of Wakefield.

That I boro will I qwite.[1]   52
CAYN.   We![2] now, no thyng, bot call on
    tyte,[3]
That we had ployde this land.
GARCIO.   Harrer, Morell, iofurth! hyte![4]
And let the plogh stand.   56

[Enter Abel.]

ABELL.   God, as he both may and can,
Spede the, brother, and thi man.
CAYN.   Com kis . . . .,[5] me list not
    ban,[6]
    As welcom standis ther oute.   60
Thou shuld haue bide til thou were cald;
Com nar,[7] and other drife or hald,
    And kys . . . .
. . . .
For that is the moste lefe.[8]
ABELL.   Broder, ther is none here aboute
That wold the any grefe.   67

Bot, leif[9] brother, here my sawe[10] —
It is the custom of oure law,
All that wyrk as the wise
Shall worship God with sacrifice.   71
Oure fader vs bad, oure fader vs kend,[11]
That oure tend[12] shuld be brend.[13]
Com furth, brothere, and let vs gang[14]
To worship God.   We dwell full lang.
Gif we hym parte of oure fee,
Corne or catall, wheder it be.   77

And therfor, brother, let vs weynd;[14]
And first clens vs from the feynd
    Or[15] we make sacrifice:
Then blis withoutten end
    Get we for oure seruyce,   82

Of hym that is oure saulis leche.[16]
CAYN.   How! let furth youre geyse, the fox
    will preche!
How long wilt thou me appech[17]
    With thi sermonyng?   86
Hold thi tong, yit I say,
Euen ther the good wife strokid the hay;

Or sit downe in the dwill way,
    With thi vayn carpyng.[1]   90

Shuld I leife[2] my plogh and all thyng
And go with the to make offeryng?
Nay! thou fyndys me not so mad!
Go to the dwill, and say I bad!
What gifys God the to rose[3] hym so?
Me gifys he noght bot soro and wo.   96

ABELL.   Caym, leife this vayn carpyng,
For God giffys the all thi lifyng.
CAYN.   Yit boroed I neuer a farthyng
Of hym — here my hend.
ABELL.   Brother, as elders haue vs kend,
First shuld we tend[4] with oure hend,
And to his lofyng[5] sithen[6] be brend.   103

CAYN.   My farthyng is in the preest hand
Syn last tyme I offyrd.
ABELL.   Leif brother, let vs be walkand;
I wold oure tend were profyrd.   107

CAYN.   We! wherof shuld I tend, leif
    brothere?
For I am ich yere wars then othere, —
Here my trouth it is none othere.
    My wynnyngis ar bot meyn,
    No wonder if that I be leyn.
    Full long till hym I may me meyn,[7]
For bi hym that me dere boght,
I traw that he will leyn[8] me noght.   115

ABELL.   Yis, all the good thou has in
    wone[9]
Of Godis grace is bot a lone.
CAYN.   Lenys he me, as com thrift apon
    the so?
For he has euer yit beyn my fo;   119
For had he my freynd beyn,
Other-gatis[10] it had beyn seyn.
When all mens corn was fayre in feld
Then was myne not worth a neld;[11]   123
When I shuld saw,[12] and wantyd seyde,
And of corn had full grete neyde,
Then gaf he me none of his;
No more will I gif hym of this.   127
Hardely hold me to blame
Bot if I serue hym of the same.

---

[1] Requite.   [2] An exclamation of anger.
[3] Quickly shout to the team.
[4] A word of encouragement given to horses.
[5] Here, and in several places below, the language
is too offensive to be reproduced.
[6] Curse.   [7] Nearer.   [8] Dearest to thee.
[9] Dear.   [10] Speech .   [11] Taught.   [12] Tenth.
[13] Burned.   [14] Go.   [15] Ere.
[16] Physician.   [17] Cast imputations upon.

[1] Chattering.   [2] Leave.   [3] Praise.
[4] Tithe.   [5] Praise.   [6] Afterwards.
[7] Complain.   [8] Lend.   [9] Habitually.
[10] Otherwise.   [11] Needle.   [12] Sow.

ABELL.   Leif brother, say not so,
Bot let vs furth togeder go.   131
Good brother, let vs weynd [1] sone;
No longer here, I rede, we hone.[2]
CAYN.   Yei, yei, thou iangyls waste! [3]
The dwill me spede if I haue hast,   135
As long as I may lif,
To dele [4] my good or gif,
Ather to God or yit to man,
Of any good that euer I wan;   139
For had I giffen away my goode,
Then myght I go with a ryffen [5] hood;
And it is better hold that I haue
Then go from doore to doore and craue.[6]
ABELL.   Brother, com furth, in Godis
    name;   144
I am full ferd [7] that we get blame.
Hy we fast that we were thore.[8]
CAYN.   We! ryn on, in the dwills nayme
    before!   147
Wemay,[9] man! I hold the mad!
Wenys [10] thou now that I list gad [11]
To gif away my warldis aght? [12]
The dwill hym spede that me so taght! 151
What nede had I my trauell [13] to lose,
To were my shoyn [14] and ryfe my hose?
ABELL.   Dere brother, hit were grete
    wonder
That I and thou shuld go in sonder;   155
Then wold oure fader haue grete ferly.[15]
Ar we not brether, thou and I?
CAYN.   No, bot cry on! cry, whyls the
    thynk good!
Here my trowth, I hold the woode.[16] 159
Wheder that he be blithe or wroth,
To dele my good is me full lothe.
I haue gone oft on softer wise
Ther I trowed som prow [17] wold rise. 163
Bot well I se go must I nede.
Now weynd [18] before, ill myght thou
    spede!
Syn that we shall algatis [19] go.
ABELL.   Leif brother, whi sais thou so? 167
Bot go we furth both togeder.
Blissid be God we haue fare weder.

---

 [1] Go.   [2] I advise, we delay.
[3] You waste words.   [4] Divide.
[5] Torn.   [6] Beg.   [7] Afraid.
[8] There.   [9] An exclamation.
[10] Thinkest.   [11] Gad about.
[12] Possessions.   [13] Labor.
[14] Shoes.   [15] Wonder.
[16] Mad.   [17] Profit.
[18] Go.   [19] At all events.

[*They cross to the place of sacrifice.*]

CAYN.   Lay downe thi trussell [1] apon this
    hill.
ABELL.   Forsoth broder, so I will.   171
Gog of heuen, take it to good.
CAYN.   Thou shall tend [2] first, if thou were
    wood.
ABELL.   [*Kneeling.*] God, that shope both
    erth and heuen,
I pray to the thou here my steven,[3]   175
And take in thank, if thi will be,
The tend that I offre here to the;
For I gif it in good entent
To the, my Lord, that all has sent.   179
I bren [4] it now, with stedfast thoght,
In worship of hym that all has wroght.

[*Abel sets fire to his tithes, which burn
    brightly.*]

CAYN.   Ryse! Let me, now, syn thou has
    done.
Lord of heuen, thou here my boyne! [5] 183
And, ouer Godis forbot,[6] be to the
Thank or thew to kun me; [7]
For, as browke I thise two shankys,
It is full sore, myne vnthankys,[8]   187
The teynd that I here gif to the,
Of corn, or thyng, that newys [9] me.
Bot now begyn will I then,
Syn I must nede my tend to bren.   191
Oone shefe, oone,[10] and this makys two, —
Bot nawder of thise may I forgo.[11]
Two, two, now this is thre, —
Yei, this also shall leif [12] with me,   195
For I will chose, and best haue;
This hold I thrift of all this thrafe.[13]
Wemo,[14] wemo, foure; lo, here!
Better groved [15] me no this yere.   199
At yere tyme I sew fayre corn,
Yit was it sich when it was shorne,
Thystyls and brerys, yei grete plente,
And all kyn wedis that myght be.   203
Foure shefis, foure, lo, this makis fyfe
(Deyll I fast thus long or I thrife).

---

[1] Bundle.   [2] Tithe.   [3] Voice.
[4] Burn.   [5] Prayer.   [6] And, God forbid.
[7] To show me gratitude or favor.
[8] Unwillingness.   [9] Renews.
[10] The repetition indicates that he selects the
largest sheaves or possibly that he weighs them in
his hand.
[11] Part with.   [12] Remain.   [13] Sheaf.
[14] Oh!   [15] Grew.

Fyfe and sex, now this is sevyn, —
Bot this gettis neuer God of heuen; 207
Nor none of thise foure, at my myght,
Shall neuer com in Godis sight.
Sevyn, sevyn, now this is aght, —
ABELL. Cain, brother, thou art not God
    betaght.[1] 211
CAYN. We! therfor is it that I say,
For I will not deyle my good away:
Bot had I gyffen hym this to teynd
Then wold thou say he were my freynd; 215
Bot I thynk not, bi my hode,
To departe so lightly fro my goode.
We! aght, aght, and neyn, and ten is this;

[Selecting the smallest sheaf.]

We! this may we best mys. 219
Gif hym that that ligis thore?
It goyse agans myn hart full sore. 221

ABELL. Cam! teynd right of all, bedeyn.[2]
CAYN. We! lo twelve, fyfteyn, sexteyn —

[Hurling sheafs rapidly.]

ABELL. Caym, thou tendis wrang, and of
    the warst.
CAYN. We! com nar, and hide myne een![3]
    In the wenyand[4] wist ye now at last,
Or els will thou that I wynk?[5]
Then shall I doy no wrong, me thynk. 228

Let me se now how it is.
    Lo, yit I hold me paide.
I teyndyd wonder well bi ges,[6]
    And so euen I laide. 232

ABELL. Came, of God me thynke thou has
    no drede.
CAME. Now, and he get more, the dwill
    me spede!
As mych as oone reepe,[7]
For that cam hym full light chepe; 236
Not as mekill, grete ne small,
As he myght ...... with all.
For that, and this that lyys here,
Haue cost me full dere; 240
Or it was shorne, and broght in stak,
Had I many a wery bak;
Therfor aske me no more of this,

For I haue giffen that my will is. 244
ABELL. Cam, I rede thou tend right
For drede of hym that sittis on hight.
CAYN. How that I tend, rek the neuer a
    deill,[1]
Bot tend thi skabbid[2] shepe wele; 248
For if thou to my teynd tent take,[3]
It bese the wars for thi sake.
Thou wold I gaf hym this shefe? or this
    sheyfe?
Na, nawder of thise two wil I leife; 252
Bot take this; now has he two,
And for my saull now mot it go.
Bot it gos sore agans my will,
And shal he like full ill. 256
ABELL. Cam, I reyde thou so teynd
That God of heuen be thi freynd.
CAYN. My freynd? na, not bot if he will!
I did hym neuer yit bot skill.[4] 260
If he be neuer so my fo,
I am avisid gif hym no mo.
Bot chaunge thi conscience, as I do myn.
Yit teynd thou not thi mesel[5] swyne? 264
ABELL. If thou teynd right thou mon it
    fynde.
CAYN. Yei, ... behynde!
The dwill hang the bi the nek!
How that I teynd, neuer thou rek. 268
Will thou not yit hold thi peasse?
Of this ianglyng I reyde[6] thou seasse.
And teynd I well, or tend I ill,
Bere the euen and speke bot skill. 272
Bot now syn thou has teyndid thyne,
Now will I set fyr on myne.

*[He sets fire to his offering, which refuses
to burn.]*

We! out! haro! Help to blaw!
It will not bren for me, I traw. 276
Puf! this smoke dos me mych shame —
Now bren in the dwillys name!
A! what dwill of hell is it?
Almost had myne breth beyn dit.[7] 280
Had I blawen oone blast more
I had beyn choked right thore;[8]
It stank like the dwill in hell,
That longer ther myght I not dwell. 284
ABELL. Cam, this is not worth oone leke;[9]
Thy tend shuld bren withoutten smeke.

---

[1] Devoted to. [2] Right through. [3] Eyes.
[4] In the waning of the moon (an unlucky time).
[5] Shut my eyes. [6] Guess. [7] Sheaf.

[1] Bit. [2] Scabbed. [3] Give attention.
[4] That which is reasonable.
[5] Leprous, diseased.
[6] Advise. [7] Stopped. [8] There. [9] Leek.

CAYM. Com kys the dwill ......,
For the it brens bot the wars;   288
I wold that it were in thi throte,
Fyr, and shefe, and ich a [1] sprote.

[*God speaks above.*]

DEUS. Cam, whi art thou so rebell
Agans thi brother Abell?   292
Thar thou nowther flyte [2] ne chyde.
If thou tend right thou gettis thi mede;
And be thou sekir,[3] if thou teynd fals,
Thou bese alowed ther after als.   296

CAYM. Whi, who is that hob-ouer-the-
      wall?
We! who was that that piped so small?
Com go we hens, for perels all.
      God is out of hys wit!   300
Com furth, Abell, and let vs weynd;
Me thynk that God is not my freynd;
      On land then will I flyt.[4]   303

ABELL. A, Caym, brother, that is ill done.
CAYN. No, bot go we hens sone;
And if I may, I shall be
Ther as God shall not me see.   307
ABELL. Dere brother, I will fayre [5]
On feld ther oure bestis ar,
To looke if thay be holgh [6] or full.
CAYM. Na, na, abide; we haue a craw [7] to
      pull.   311
Hark, speke with me or thou go.
What! wenys [8] thou to skape so?
We! na! I aght [9] the a fowll dispyte,
And now is tyme that I hit qwite.[10]   315
ABEL. Brother, whi art thou so to me in
      ire?
CAYM. We! theyf, whi brend thi tend so
      shyre,[11]
Ther myne did bot smoked
Right as it wold vs both haue choked? 319
ABEL. Godis will I trow it were
That myn brened so clere;
If thyne smoked am I to wite? [12]
CAYM. We! yei! That shal thou sore
      abite.   323
With cheke bon,[13] or that I blyn,
Shal I the and thi life twyn.[14]

[*Cain strikes Abel with a jawbone.*]

So, lig down ther and take thi rest;
Thus shall shrewes be chastysed best. 327
ABELL. Veniance, veniance, Lord, I cry!
For I am slayn, and not gilty.   [*Dies.*]
CAYN. Yei, ly ther, old shrew! ly ther,
      ly!   330

[*To the audience.*]

And if any of you thynk I did amys
I shal it amend wars then it is,
      That all men may it se:
Well wars then it is
      Right so shall it be.   335

Bot now, syn he is broght on slepe,
Into som hole fayn wold I crepe.
For ferd I qwake, and can no rede,[1]
For be I taken, I be bot dede.   339
Here will I lig [2] thise fourty dayes,
And I shrew [3] hym that me fyrst rayse!

[*God speaks above.*]

DEUS. Caym, Caym!
CAYM.   Who is that that callis me?
I am yonder, may thou not se?   343
DEUS. Caym, where is thi brother Abell?
CAYM. What askis thou me? I trow at
      hell.
At hell I trow he be —
Who so were ther then myght he se — 347
Or somwhere fallen on slepyng.
When was he in my kepyng?
DEUS. Caym, Caym, thou was wode.[4]
The voyce of thi brotheris blode,   351
That thou has slayn on fals wise,
From erth to heuen venyance cryse.
And, for thou has broght thi brother downe,
Here I gif the my malison.[5]   355
CAYM. Yei, dele aboute the! for I will
      none;
Or take it the, when I am gone!
Syn I haue done so mekill syn,
That I may not thi mercy wyn,   359
And thou thus dos me from thi grace,
I shall hyde me fro thi face;
And where so any man may fynd me,
Let hym slo me hardely;[6]   363
And where so any man may me meyte,

---

[1] Every.   [2] You need neither quarrel.
[3] Sure.   [4] Depart.   [5] Go.
[6] Hollow.   [7] Crow.   [8] Thinkest.
[9] Owe.   [10] Requite.   [11] Clear.
[12] Blame.   [13] Jaw-bone.   [14] Divide.

---

[1] Know no plan.   [2] Lie.   [3] Curse.
[4] Mad.   [5] Curse.   [6] Slay me boldly·

Ayther bi sty,[1] or yit bi strete;
And hardely, when I am dede,
Bery me in Gudeboure at the Quarell
    Hede;[2]   367
For, may I pas this place in quarte,[3]
Bi all men set I not a fart.
DEUS. Nay, Caym, it bese not so;
I will that no man other slo.   371
For he that sloys yong or old
It shall be punyshid sevenfold.
CAYM. No force,[4] I wote, wheder I shall;
In hell, I wote, mon [5] be my stall.   375
It is no boyte [6] mercy to craue,
For if I do I mon none haue.   377
Bot this cors [7] I wold were hid,
    For som man myght com at vngayn:[8]
"Fle, fals shrew," wold he bid,
    And weyn [9] I had my brother slayn. 381
Bot were Pike-harnes, my knafe, here,
We shuld bery hym both in fere.[10]
How, Pyke-harnes! scape-thryft! how,
    Pike-harnes! how!

[Enter Garcio.]

GARCIO. Master, master!   385
CAYN. Harstow,[11] boy? Ther is a podyng
    in the pot.
Take the that, boy! tak the that!

[Strikes him.]

GARCIO. I shrew thi ball vnder thi hode,
If thou were my syre of flesh and
    blode!   389
All the day to ryn and trott,
    And euer amang [12] thou strykeand;
Thus am I comen bofettis [13] to fott.
CAYN. Peas, man; I did it bot to vse [14] my
    hand.   393

Bot harke, boy, I haue a counsell to the to
    say —
I slogh my brother this same day.
I pray the, good boy, and thou may,
To ryn away with the bayn.[15]   397
GARCIO. We! out apon the, thefe!
Has thou thi brother slayn?
CAYM. Peasse, man, for Godis payn! 400

I saide it for a skaunce.[1]
GARCIO. Yey, bot for ferde [2] of grevance
Here I the forsake.
    We mon haue a mekill myschaunce
And the bayles [3] vs take.   405

CAYM. A, sir, I cry you mercy; seasse!
And I shall make you a releasse.
GARCIO. What, wilt thou cry my
    peasse [4]   408
Throughout this land?
CAYN. Yey, that I gif God a vow, belife.
GARCIO. How will thou do, long or thou
    thrife?
CAYM. Stand vp, my good boy, belife,
And thaym [5] peasse [6] both man and
    [w]life;   412
And who so will do after me
Full slape [7] of thrift then shal he be.
Bot thou must be my good boy,
And cry "Oyes, oyes, oy!"
GARCIO. Browes,[8] browes, to thi boy. 417

*[Garcio gets up to cry the proclamation, and
wilfully miscries each line.]*

CAYM. I commaund you in the kyngis
    nayme,
GARCIO. And in my masteres, fals Cayme,
CAYM. That no man at thame [9] fynd
    fawt ne blame,
GARCIO. Yey, cold rost is at my masteres
    hame.   421
CAYM. Nowther with hym nor with his
    knafe,
GARCIO. What, I hope my master rafe.[10]
CAYM. For thay ar trew, full many fold.
GARCIO. My master suppys no coyle [11] bot
    cold.
CAYM. The kyng wrytis you vntill.[12]
GARCIO. Yit ete I neuer half my fill. 427
CAYM. The kyng will that thay be safe.
GARCIO. Yey, a draght of drynke fayne
    wold I hayfe.
CAYM. At thare awne will let tham wafe.[13]
GARCIO. My stomak is redy to receyfe. 431
CAYM. Loke no man say to theym, on nor
    other.
GARCIO. This same is he that slo his
    brother.

1 Lane.   2 At the quarry head.
3 Safety.   4 No matter.   5 Must.
6 Boot, use.   7 Corpse.
8 Inconveniently.   9 Think.
10 Together. 11 Hearest thou. 12 Constantly.
13 Buffets.   14 Practise.   15 Quickly.

1 Joke.   2 Fear.   3 Bailiffs.   4 Peace.
5 Them.   6 Silence.   7 Crafty.
8 Broth.   9 Them.   10 Raves.
11 Pottage.   12 Unto.   13 Wander

CAYM. Byd euery man thaym luf and
     lowt,[1]

GARCIO. Yey, ill spon weft [2] ay comes
     foule out.

CAYM. .... [3]

GARCIO. Long or thou get thi hoyse and [4]
     thou go thus aboute.   436

CAYM. Byd euery man theym pleasse to
     pay.

GARCIO. Yey, gif Don, thyne hors, a wisp
     of hay.

CAYM. We! com downe in twenty dwill
     way!
   The dwill I the betake;
For bot it were Abell, my brothere,
   Yit knew I neuer thi make.   442

[*Garcio continues to address the audience.*]

GARCIO. Now, old and yong, or that ye
     weynd,[5]
The same blissyng, withoutten end,
   All sam then shall ye haue,
That God of heuen my master has giffen.
Browke [6] it well, whils that ye liffen;
   He vowche it full well safe.   448

CAYM. Com downe yit, in the dwillis way!
   And angre me no more.

[1] Honor.
[2] Woof (an old proverb).
[3] A line missing in MS.
[4] Hose if.   [5] Go.   [6] Use.

[*Garcio comes down.*]

Atnd take yond plogh, I say,
   And weynd the furth fast before;   452
And I shall, if I may,
   Tech the another lore.[1]
I warn the, lad, for ay,
Fro now furth, euermore,
   That thou greue me noght;   457
For, bi Godis sydis, if thou do,
I shall hang the apon this plo,[2]
With this rope, lo, lad, lo!
   By hym that me dere boght.   461

[*Exit Garcio. Cain addresses the audience.*]

Now fayre well, felows all,
   For I must nedis weynd,
And to the dwill be thrall,
   Warld withoutten end.   465
Ordand ther is my stall,
   With Sathanas the feynd.
Euer ill myght hym befall
   That theder me commend,
     This tyde.   470
Fare well les, and fare well more!
For now, and euer more,
   I will go me to hyde.   [*Exit Cain.*] 473

     Explicit Mactacio Abell.
     Sequitur Noe.

[1] Lesson.   [2] Plow.

NOAH [1]

[Acted at Wakefield.]

Processus Noe cum Filiis.   Wakefeld.

[*God on the upper stage, Noah and his family below.*]

NOE.   Myghtfull God veray, / maker of
all that is,
Thre persons withoutten nay, / oone God
in endles blis,
Thou maide both nyght and day, / beest,
fowle, and fysh;
All creatures that lif may / wroght thou at
thi wish,
 As thou wel myght.   5
The son, the moyne, verament,[1]
Thou maide; the firmament;
The sternes also full feruent
 To shyne thou maide ful bright.   9

Angels thou maide ful euen, / all orders
that is,
To haue the blis in heuen./   This did thou,
more and les.
Full mervelus to neuen,[2] / yit was ther
vnkyndnes,
More bi foldis seuen [3] / then I can well ex-
pres;
 For whi   14
Of all angels in brightnes
God gaf Lucifer most lightnes,
Yit prowdly he flyt his des,[4]
 And set hym euen hym by.   18

He thoght hymself as worthi / as hym that
hym made.
In brightnes, in bewty, / therfor he hym
degrade;
Put hym in a low degre / soyn after, in a
brade,[5]
Hym and all his menye,[6] / wher he may be
vnglad
 For euer.   23

¹ Truly.   ² Relate.
³ By seven-fold.   ⁴ Left his daïs.
⁵ Jiffy.   ⁶ Followers.

Shall thay neuer wyn [1] away
Hence vnto domysday,
Bot burne in bayle for ay;
 Shall thay neuer dysseuer.[2]   27

Soyne after, that gracyous Lord / to his
liknes maide man,
That place to be restord / euen as he be-
gan,
Of the Trinite bi accord, / Adam, and Eue
that woman.
To multiplie without discord / in paradise
put he thaym;
 And sithen [3] to both   32
Gaf in commaundement
On the tre of life to lay no hend.
Bot yit the fals feynd
 Made hym with man wroth,   36

Entysyd man to glotony, / styrd him to
syn in pride.
Bot in paradise, securly, / myght no syn
abide;
And therfor man full hastely / was put out,
in that tyde,
In wo and wandreth [4] for to be; / paynes [5]
full vnrid [6]
 To knawe,   41
Fyrst in erth, sythen [7] in hell,
With feyndis for to dwell.
Bot he his mercy mell [8]
 To those that will hym trawe.[9]   45

Oyle of mercy he hus hight,[10] / as I haue
hard red,
To euery lifyng wight / that wold luf hym
and dred.
Bot now before his sight / euery liffyng
leyde [11]

¹ Go.   ² Depart.
³ Afterwards.   ⁴ Misfortune.
⁵ MS. In paynes, *corr. by Manly*.   ⁶ Cruel.
⁷ Afterwards. MS. in sythen in.
⁸ Speaks of.   ⁹ Believe.
¹⁰ Us promised.   ¹¹ Man.

¹ For the source of the text see page 94, note 1. I have availed myself of certain textual emendations
from Manly's reprint, as the footnotes will indicate.

Most party day and nyght / syn in word
    and dede
Full bold, —   50
Som in pride, ire, and enuy,
Som in couetyse [1] and glotyny,
Som in sloth and lechery,
    And other wise many-fold.   54

Therfor I drede lest God / on vs will take
    veniance,
For syn is now alod [2] / without any repent-
    ance.
Sex hundreth yeris and od / haue I, with-
    out distance,[3]
In erth, as any sod, / liffyd with grete
    grevance
All-way;   59
And now I wax old,
Seke, sory, and cold;
As muk apon mold
    I widder away.   63

Bot yit will I cry / for mercy, and call.

[Kneels in prayer.]

Noe, thi seruant, am I, / Lord ouer-all!
Therfor me and my fry [4] / shal with me
    fall.
Saue from velany / and bryng to thi hall
    In heuen;   68
And kepe me from syn
This warld within.
Comly Kyng of mankyn,
    I pray the here my stevyn! [5]   72

[God speaks above.]

DEUS. Syn I haue maide all thyng / that
    is liffand,
Duke, emperour, and kyng / with myne
    awne hand,
For to haue thare likyng / bi see and bi
    sand,
Euery man to my bydyng / shuld be
    bowand [6]
Full feruent,   77
That maide man sich a creatoure,
Farest of favoure.
Man must luf me paramoure
    By reson, and repent.   81

Me thoght I shewed man luf / when I
    made hym to be
All angels abuf, / like to the Trynyte;
And now in grete reprufe / full low ligis [1]
    he,
In erth hymself to stuf / with syn that dis-
    pleasse me
Most of all.   86
Veniance will I take
In erth for syn sake.
My grame [2] thus will I wake
    Both of grete and small.   90

I repente full sore / that euer maide I man.
Bi me he settis no store, / and I am his
    soferan.
I will distroy therfor / both beest, man,
    and woman;
All shall perish, les and more. / That bar-
    gan may thay ban [3]
    That ill has done.   95
In erth I se right noght
Bot syn that is vnsoght; [4]
Of those that well has wroght
    Fynd I bot a fone.[5]   99

Therfor shall I fordo [6] / all this medill-erd
With floodis that shall flo / and ryn with
    hidous rerd.[7]
I haue good cause therto; / ffor me no man
    is ferd.[8]
As I say shal I do, / of veniance draw my
    swerd,
    And make end   104
Of all that beris life —
Sayf Noe and his wife,
For thay wold neuer stryfe
    With me ne [9] me offend.   108

Hym to mekill wyn [10] / hastly will I go,
To Noe my seruand, or I blyn,[11] / to warn
    hym of his wo.
In erth I se bot syn, / reynand to and fro,
Emang both more and myn;[12] / ichon [13]
    other fo
    With all thare entent.   113
All shall I fordo
With floodis that shall floo;

---

[1] MS. Couetous.   [2] Allowed.
[3] Dispute.   [4] Children.
[5] Voice.   [6] Obedient.

[1] Lies.   [2] Anger.   [3] Curse.
[4] Unatoned for.   [5] Few.   [6] Destroy.
[7] Sound.   [8] Afraid.   [9] MS. then.
[10] Joy.   [11] Stop.
[12] Less.   [13] Each one.

Wirk shall I thaym wo,
  That will not repent.   117

[*God descends and addresses Noah.*]

Noe, my freend, I thee commaund, / from
  cares the to keyle,[1]
A ship that thou ordand / of nayle and
  bord ful wele.
Thou was alway well wirkand, / to me
  trew as stele,
To my bydyng obediand; / frendship shal
  thou fele
  To mede.[2]   122
Of lennthe thi ship be
Thre hundreth cubettis, warn I the;
Of heght euen thirte;[3]
  Of fyfty als in brede.   126

Anoynt thi ship with pik and tar / without
  and als within,
The water out to spar.[4] / This is a noble
  gyn.[5]
Look no man the mar.[6] / Thre chese[7]
  chambres begyn;
Thou must spend many a spar[8] / this
  wark or thou wyn
  To end fully.   131
Make in thi ship also
Parloures oone or two,
And houses of offyce mo
  For beestis that ther must be.   135

Oone cubite on hight / a wyndo shal thou
  make;
On the syde a doore with slyght[9] / be-
  neyth shal thou take.
With the shal no man fyght / nor do the no
  kyn wrake.[10]
When all is doyne thus right, / thi wife,
  that is thi make,
  Take in to the;   140
Thi sonnes of good fame,
Sem, Iaphet, and Came,
Take in also [t]hame,
  Thare wifis also thre.   144

For all shal be fordone / that lif in land bot
  ye,

---

[1] Cool.   [2] Reward.
[3] MS. thrirte.   [4] Keep.
[5] Contrivance.   [6] Hinder.
[7] Tiers; one above the other. [8] Beam.
[9] Skill.   [10] Injury.

With floodis that from abone / shal fall,
  and that plente.
It shall begyn full sone / to rayn vnces-
  santle,
After dayes seuen be done, / and induyr
  dayes fourty,
  Withoutten fayll.   149
Take to thi ship also
Of ich kynd beestis two,
Mayll and femayll, bot no mo,
  Or thou pull vp thi sayll,   153

For thay may the avayll / when al this
  thyng is wroght.
Stuf thi ship with vitayll, / ffor hungre
  that ye perish noght;
Of beestis, foull, and catayll, / ffor thaym
  haue thou in thoght;
For thaym is my counsayll / that som
  socour be soght
  In hast;   158
Thay must haue corn and hay,
And oder mete[1] alway.
Do now as I the say,
  In the name of the Holy Gast.   162

NOE. A! benedicite! / what art thou that
  thus
Tellys afore that shall be? / Thou art full
  mervelus!
Tell me, for charite, / thi name so gracius.
DEUS. My name is of dignyte, / and also
  full glorius
  To knawe: 167
I am God most myghty,
Oone God in Trynyty,
Made the and ich man to be.
  To luf me well thou awe.[2]   171

NOE. I thank the, Lord so dere, / that
  wold vowch-sayf
Thus low to appere / to a symple knafe.
Blis vs, Lord, here; / for charite I hit
  crafe;
The better may we stere / the ship that we
  shall hafe,
  Certayn.   176
DEUS. Noe, to the, and to thi fry,
My blyssyng graunt I.
Ye shall wax and multiply,
  And fill the erth agane,   180

---

[1] Food.   [2] Owest.

When all thise floodis ar past / and fully
   gone away.

       [*God ascends.*]

NOE.   Lord! homward will I hast / as fast
   as that I may;
My [wife] will I frast [1] / what she will say.
And I am agast / that we get som fray
   Betwixt vs both,   185
For she is full tethee,[2]
For litill oft angre;
If any-thyng wrang be,
   Soyne is she wroth.   189

Then he shall cross over to his wife.[3]

God spede, dere wife! / How fayre ye?
VXOR.   Now, as euer myght I thryfe, / the
   wars I thee see!
Do tell me belife, / where has thou thus
   long be?
To dede may we dryfe, / or lif, for the,
   For want.   194
When we swete or swynk,[4]
Thou dos what thou thynk;
Yit of mete and of drynk
   Haue we veray skant.   198

NOE.   Wife, we ar hard sted / with tyth-
   yngis new—
VXOR.   Bot thou were worthi be cled / in
   Stafford blew![5]
For thou art alway adred, / be it fals or
   trew.
Bot, God knowes, I am led; / and that may
   I rew
   Full ill;   203
For I dar be thi borow,[6]
From euen vnto morow
Thou spekis euer of sorow.
   God send the onys thi fill!   207

       [*Addressing the audience.*]

We women may wary / all ill husbandis.
I have oone, bi Mary / that lowsyd me of
   my bandis!
If he teyn,[7] I must tary, / how-so-euer it
   standis,
With seymland [8] full sory, / wryngand both
   my handis

       For drede.   212
Bot yit other while,
What with gam and with gyle,
I shall smyte and smyle, ,
   And qwite hym his mede.   216

NOE.   We! hold thi tong, ram-skyt, / or I
   shall the still!
VXOR.   By my thryft, if thou smyte, / I
   shal turne the vntill.
NOE.   We shall assay as tyte.[1] / Haue at
   the, Gill!
Apon the bone shal it byte. / [*Strikes her.*]
VXOR.   A, so! Mary! thou smytis ill!
   Bot I suppose   221
I shal not in thi det
Flyt of this flett! [2]
Take the ther a langett [3]
   To tye vp thi hose! [*Strikes him.*]   225

NOE.   A! wilt thou so? / Mary, that is
   myne.   [*Strikes her.*]
VXOR.   Thou shal [have] thre for two, / I
   swere bi Godis pyne.[4] [*Striking back.*]
NOE.   And I shall qwyte the tho, / in
   fayth, or syne.[5] [*Strikes her down.*]
VXOR.   Out apon the, ho! /
NOE.   Thou can both byte and whyne
   With a rerd! [6]   230

       [*To the audience.*]

For all if she stryke,
Yit fast will she skryke.[7]
In fayth, I hold none slyke [8]
   In all medill-erd!   234

Bot I will kepe charyte, / ffor I haue at do.[9]
VXOR.   Here shal no man tary the; / I
   pray the go to!
Full well may we mys the, / as euer haue I
   ro.[10]
To spyn will I dres me. /

       [*Seats herself at her spinning.*]

NOE.   We! fare well, lo.
   Bot, wife,   239
Pray for me besele
To eft [11] I com vnto the.

---

1 At once.   2 Leave this floor.
3 Thong.   4 Christ's passion.
4 Toil.   5 To be beaten blue with a staff?
6 Pledge.   7 Be vexed.
5 Afterwards.   6 Noise.   7 Screech.
8 Such.   9 Business in hand.
10 Quiet.   11 Until again.
8 Semblance, countenance.

Vxor. Euen as thou prays for me,
  As euer myght I thrife!   243
Noe. I tary full lang / fro my warke, I
  traw;[1]
Now my gere[2] will I fang[3] / and theder-
  ward draw.

[*Crossing to the other end of the pageant.*]

I may full ill gang, / the soth for to knaw.
Bot if God help amang, / I may sit downe
  daw[4]
  To ken.   248
Now assay will I
How I can of wrightry.[5]
In nomine Patris, et Filii,
  Et Spiritus Sancti, Amen.[6]   252

To begyn of this tree / my bonys will I
  bend;
I traw from the Trynyte / socoure will be
  send.
It fayres full fayre, thynk me, / this wark
  to my hend;
Now blissid be he / that this can amend.

[*Takes his measuring rod.*]

  Lo, here the lenght,   257
Thre hundreth cubettis euenly;
Of breed, lo! is it fyfty;
  The heght is euen thyrty
  Cubettis full strenght.   261

[*Takes off his gown.*]

Now my gowne will I cast, / and wyrk in
  my cote.
Make will I the mast, / or I flyt oone foote.
A! my bak, I traw, will brast! / This is a
  sory note!
Hit is wonder that I last, / sich an old
  dote,[7]
  All dold,[8]   266
To begyn sich a wark.
My bonys ar so stark,[9]
No wonder if thay wark,[10]
  For I am full old.   270

The top and the sayll / both will I make;

The helm and the castell / also will I take;
To drife ich a nayll / will I not forsake;
This gere[1] may neuer fayll, / that dar I
  vndertake
  Onone.[2]   275
This is a nobull gyn.[3]
Thise nayles so thay ryn
Thoro more and myn,
  Thise bordis ichon.   279

[*He views the completed Ark.*]

Wyndow and doore, / euen as he saide;
Thre ches-chambre, / thay ar well maide;
Pyk and tar full sure / ther-apon laide;
This will euer endure, / therof am I paide;
  For why   284
It is better wroght
Then I coude haif thoght.
Hym that maide all of noght
  I thank oonly.   288

Now will I hy me, / and no-thyng be leder,[4]
My wife and my meneye[5] / to bryng euen
  heder.

[*Approaches his wife.*]

Tent hedir tydely,[6] / wife, and consider;
Hens must vs fle / all sam togeder
  In hast.   293
Vxor. Whi, syr, what alis you?
Who is that asalis you?
To fle it avalis you
  And ye be agast.   297

Noe. Ther is garn[7] on the reyll / other,
  my dame.
Vxor. Tell me that ich a deyll,[8] / els get
  ye blame.
Noe. He that cares may keill,[9] — / blissid
  be his name! —
He has [spokyn][10] for oure seyll,[11] / to sheld
  vs fro shame,
  And sayd,   302
All this warld aboute
With floodis so stoute,
That shall ryn on a route,[12]
  Shall be ouerlaide.   306

---

[1] Trow.   [2] Tools.   [3] Take.
[4] Melancholy?   [5] Carpentry.
[6] In the name of the Father, and of the Son, and
of the Holy Ghost, amen.
[7] Dotard.   [8] Dulled (with age).
[9] Stiff.   [10] Ache.

[1] Affair.   [2] At once.
[3] Contrivance.   [4] Lazy, slow.
[5] Household.   [6] Quickly.
[7] Yarn.   [8] Every bit.
[9] Cool.   [10] *Supplied by Manly.*
[11] Happiness.   [12] Roaring noise.

He saide all shall be slayn / bot oonely we,
Oure barnes,[1] that ar bayn,[2] / and thare
  wifis thre;
A ship he bad me ordayn / to safe vs and
  oure fee.[3]
Therfor with all oure mayn / thank we
  that fre,[4]
Beytter of bayll.[5]   311
Hy vs fast, go we thedir!
Vxor.   I wote neuer whedir.
I dase and I dedir[6]
For ferd of that tayll.   315

Noe.   Be not aferd. Haue done. / Trus[7]
  sam oure gere,
That we be ther or none,[8] / without more
  dere.[9]
I. Filius.   It shall be done full sone. /
  Brether, help to bere.
II. Filius.   Full long shall I not hoyne[10] /
  to do my devere,
Brether Sam.   319
III. Filius.   Without any yelp,
At my myght shall I help.
Vxor.   Yit for drede of a skelp[11]
Help well thi dam!   324

[They cross over with their stuff to the Ark.]

Noe.   Now ar we there / as we shuld be.
Do get in oure gere, / oure catall and fe,
In-to this vessell here, / my chylder fre.

[They enter the Ark.]

Vxor.   I was neuer bard ere,[12] / as euer
  myght I the,[13]
In sich an oostre[14] as this!   329
In fa[i]th, I can not fynd,
Which is before, which is behynd!
Bot shall we here be pynd,
Noe, as haue thou blis?   333

[Exit from the Ark.]

Noe.   Dame, as it is skill,[15] / here must vs
  abide grace;

[1] Children.   [2] Ready.
[3] Possessions.   [4] Generous one (God).
[5] Healer of sorrow.
[6] I am dazed and I tremble.
[7] Pack up.   [8] Noon.
[9] Harm.   [10] Delay.   [11] Blow.
[12] Shut up before.   [13] Thrive.
[14] Lodging.   [15] Reason.

Therfor, wife, with good will / com into
  this place.
Vxor.   Sir, for Iak nor for Gill / will I
  turne my face,
Till I haue on this hill / spon a space
  On my rok.[1]   338
Well were[2] he, myght get me!
Now will I downe set me.
Yit reede I no man let me,
For drede of a knok.   342

[Seats herself to spin. Noah appeals to her.]

Noe.   Behold to the heuen; / the cate-
  ractes all,
That are open full euen, / grete and small,
And the planettis seuen / left has thare
  stall;[3]
Thise thoners and levyn[4] / downe gar fall[5]
  Full stout   347
Both halles and bowers,
Castels and towres;
Full sharp ar thise showers
  That renys aboute;   351

Therfor, wife, haue done; / com into ship
  fast.
Vxor.   Yei, Noe, go cloute thi shone![6] /
  The better will thai last.
I. Mulier.   Good moder, com in sone, /
  ffor all is ouer-cast,
Both the son and the mone. /
II. Mulier.   And many wynd blast
  Full sharp;   356
Thise floodis so thay ryn;
Therfor, moder, come in.
Vxor.   In fayth, yit will I spyn.
All in vayn ye carp.[7]   360

III. Mulier.   If ye like ye may spyn, /
  moder, in the ship.
Noe.   Now is this twyys: com in, / dame,
  on my frenship.
Vxor.   Wheder I lose or I wyn, / in fayth,
  thi felowship,
Set I not at a pyn. /   This spyndill will I
  slip
  Apon this hill   365
Or I styr oone fote.
Noe.   Peter! I traw we dote!

[1] Distaff.   [2] Guard himself.
[3] Station.   [4] Lightning.
[5] Make fall down.
[6] Mend thy shoes.   [7] Talk.

Without any more note,
Come in if ye will. 369

VXOR. Yei, water nyghys so nere / that I
sit not dry;
Into ship with a byr,[1] / therfor, will I hy
For drede that I drone here./

[Rushes into the ship.] [2]

NOE. Dame, securly,
It bees boght full dere / ye abode so long by
Out of ship. 374
VXOR. I will not, for thi bydyng,
Go from doore to mydyng.[3]
NOE. In fayth, and for youre long tary-
yng,
Ye shall lik on [4] the whyp. 378

VXOR. Spare me not, I pray the; / bot
euen as thou thynk,
Thise grete wordis shall not flay me. /
NOE. Abide, dame, and drynk,
For betyn shall thou be / with this staf to
thou stynk.
Ar strokis good? say me. / *[Striking her.]*
VXOR. What say ye, Wat Wynk?
[Striking back.]
NOE. Speke! 383
Cry me mercy, I say!
VXOR. Therto say I nay.
NOE. Bot thou do, bi this day,
Thi hede shall I breke! 387

[Wife, addressing the audience.]

VXOR. Lord, I were at ese, / and hertely
full hoylle,
Might I onys haue a measse [5] / of wedows
coyll; [6]
For thi saull, without lese,[7] / shuld I dele
penny doyll.[8]
So wold mo, no frese,[9] / that I se on this
sole [10]
Of wifis that ar here, 392
For the life that thay leyd,
Wold thare husbandis were dede;
For, as euer ete I brede,
So wold I oure syre were! 396

[Noah, addressing the audience.]

NOE. Yee men that has wifis, / whyls
they ar yong,
If ye luf youre lifis, / chastice thare tong.
Me thynk my hert ryfis,[1] / both levyr and
long,
To se sich stryfis / wedmen emong.
Bot I, 401
As haue I blys,
Shall chastyse this!
VXOR. Yit may ye mys,
Nicholl Nedy! 405

NOE. I shall make the still as stone, /
begynnar of blunder!
I shall bete the, bak and bone, / and breke
all in sonder.

*[Fighting ad lib., with Noah finally
victorious.]*

VXOR. Out, alas, I am gone! / Oute
apon the, mans wonder!
NOE. Se how she can grone / and I lig [2]
vnder!
Bot, wife, 410
In this hast [3] let vs ho,[4]
For my bak is nere in two.
VXOR. And I am bet so blo
That I may not thryfe. 414

I. FILIUS. A! whi fare ye thus, / ffader and
moder both?
II. FILIUS. Ye shuld not be so spitus, /
standyng in sich a woth.[5]
III. FILIUS. Thise [strifis] [6] ar so hidus, /
with many a cold coth.[7]
NOE. We will do as ye bid vs; / we will no
more be wroth,
Dere barnes! 419
Now to the helme will I hent, [8]
And to my ship tent.[9]
VXOR. I se on the firmament,
Me thynk, the seven starnes. 423

NOE. This is a grete flood; / wife, take
hede.
VXOR. So me thoght, as I stode; / we ar
in grete drede;

---

[1] Rush. [2] *Supplied by Manly.*
[3] Dunghill. [4] Have a taste of.
[5] Mess. [6] Pottage.
[7] Lie. [8] Dole.
[9] Fear [10] Hall, place.

---

[1] Splits. [2] Lie. [3] Haste, rashness.
[4] Stop. [5] Peril.
[6] *Supplied by Manly.* [7] Disease.
[8] Seize. [9] Attend.

Thise wawghes [1] ar so wode.[2] /
NOE.   Help, God, in this nede!
As thou art stere-man good, / and best, as
    I rede,
Of all,   428
Thou rewle vs in this rase,[3]
As thou me behete [4] hase.
VXOR.   This is a perlous case.
    Help, God, when we call!   432

NOE.   Wife, tent the stere-tre,[5] / and I
    shall asay
The depnes of the see / that we bere, if I
    may.
VXOR.   That shall I do ful wysely; / now
    go thi way,
For apon this flood haue we / flett many
    day
    With pyne.   437
NOE.   Now the water will I sownd.

[He lowers a plummet.]

A! it is far to the grownd.
This trauell,[6] I expownd,
    Had I to tyne.[7]   441

Aboue all hillys bedeyn[8] / the water is
    rysen late
Cubettis fyfteyn. /   Bot in a higher [9]
    state
It may not be, I weyn; / for this well I
    wate,
This forty dayes has rayn beyn, / it will
    therfor abate
    Full lele.[10]   446
This water in hast
Eft will I tast.[11]

[He lowers the plummet again.]

Now am I agast,
    It is wanyd a grete dele.   450

Now are the weders cest / and cateractes
    knyt,
Both the most and the leest. /
VXOR.   Me thynk, bi my wit,
The son shynes in the eest. /   Lo, is not
    yond it?

1 Waves.   2 Mad, wild.   3 Voyage.
4 Promised.   5 Tiller.   6 Labor.
7 Lose.   8 Completely.
9 MS. highter, *corr. by Manly.*
10 Loyal.   11 Try.

We shuld haue a good feest, / were thise
    floodis flyt,
So spytus.   455
NOE.   We haue been here, all we,
Thre hundreth dayes and fyfty.
VXOR.   Yei, now wanys the see.
    Lord, well is vs!   459

NOE.   The thryd tyme will I prufe / what
    depnes we bere.

[He again lowers the plummet.]

VXOR.   How [1] long shall thou hufe? [2]/
    Lay in thy lyne there.
NOE.   I may towch with my lufe [3] the
    grownd evyn here.
VXOR.   Then begynnys to grufe [4] / to vs
    mery chere.
    Bot, husband,   463
What grownd may this be?
NOE.   The hyllys of Armonye. [5]
VXOR.   Now blissid be he
    That thus for vs can ordand!   468

NOE.   I see the toppys of hyllys he,[6] /
    many at a syght;
No thyng to let me, / the wedir is so bright.
VXOR.   Thise ar of mercy / tokyns full
    right.
NOE.   Dame, thou [7] counsell me: / what
    fowll best myght
    And cowth [8]   473
With flight of wyng
Bryng, without taryying,
Of mercy som tokynyng,
    Ayther bi north or southe?   477

For this is the fyrst day / of the tent
    moyne.
VXOR.   The ravyn, durst I lay, / will
    come agane sone.
As fast as thou may, / cast hym furth;
    haue done.

[He sends out a raven.]

He may happyn to-day / com agane or
    none
    With grath.[9]   482

1 MS. Now, *corr. by Child.*   2 Heave.
3 Hand.   4 Grow.
5 Armenia.   6 High.
7 MS. thi, *corr. by Kittredge.* 8 Could.
9 Readiness? Growth (i.e. branch)?

NOE. I will cast out also
Dowfys oone or two.
Go youre way, go; [*He sends out the
      doves.*]
   God send you som wathe![1]   486

Now ar thise fowles flone / into seyr [2]
      countre.
Pray we fast ichon, / kneland on our kne,
To hym that is alone / worthiest of
      degre,
That he wold send anone / oure fowles som
      fee
   To glad vs.   491
VXOR. Thai may not fayll of land,
The water is so wanand.
NOE. Thank we God all-weldand,[3]
   That Lord that made vs.   495

It is a wonder thyng, / me thynk sothle,[4]
Thai ar so long taryyng, / the fowles that
      we
Cast out in the mornyng. /
VXOR.   Syr, it may be
Thai tary to [5] thay bryng. /
NOE.   The ravyn is a-hungrye
   All-way;   500
He is without any reson;
And he fynd any caryon,
As peraventure may befon,[6]
   He will not away.   504

The dowfe is more gentill, — / her trust I
      vntew, —
Like vnto the turtill, / for she is ay trew.
VXOR. Hence bot a litill / she commys.
      Lew, lew!
She bryngys in her bill / som novels [7] new.
   Behald!   509
It is of an olif tre
A branch, thynkys me.
NOE. It is soth, perde;
   Right so is it cald.   513

Doufe, byrd full blist, / ffayre myght the
      befall!
Thou art trew for to trist / as ston in the
      wall;
Full well I it wist, / thou wold com to thi
      hall.

[1] Hunting.   [2] Various.   [3] All-ruling.
[4] Truly.   [5] Until.   [6] Befall.   [7] News.

VXOR. A trew tokyn ist, / we shall be
      sauyd all;
   For whi [1]   518
The water, syn she com,
Of depnes plom
Is fallen a fathom
   And more, hardely.   522

I. FILIUS. Thise floodis ar gone, / fader,
      behold.
II. FILIUS. Ther is left right none, / and
      that be ye bold.
III. FILIUS. As still as a stone / oure ship
      is stold.[2]
NOE. Apon land here anone / that we
      were, fayn I wold.
   My childer dere,   527
Sem, Japhet and Cam,
With gle and with gam
Com go we all sam;
   We will no longer abide here.   531

VXOR. Here haue we beyn, / Noy, long
      enogh,
With tray and with teyn / and dreed mekill
      wogh.

[*They leave the Ark.*]

NOE. Behald, on this greyn / nowder [3]
      cart ne plogh
Is left, as I weyn, / nowder tre then
      bogh,
   Ne other thyng,   536
Bot all is away;
Many castels, I say,
Grete townes of aray,
   Flitt has this flowyng.   540

VXOR. Thise floodis not afright / all this
      warld so wide
Has mevid with myght / on se and bi
      side.
NOE. To dede ar thai dyght,[4] / prowdist
      of pryde,
Euer ich a wyght / that euer was spyde
   With syn;   545
All ar thai slayn,
And put vnto payn.
VXOR. From thens agayn
   May thai neuer wyn?   549

[1] For that reason.   [2] Fixed.
[3] Neither.   [4] Done.

Noe. Wyn? No, i-wis, / bot [1] he that
    myght hase
Wold myn [2] of thare mys / and admytte
    thaym to grace.
As he in bayll is blis, / I pray hym in this
    space,
In heven hye with his / to purvaye vs a
    place,

    [1] Unless.   [2] Take thought.

      That we,   554
With his santis [1] in sight
And his angels bright,
May com to his light.
    Amen, for charite.   558

Explicit processus Noe, sequitur Abraham.

    [1] Saints.

THE DELUGE [1]

[Acted by the Waterleaders and Drawers in Dye of Chester.]

Pagina Tertia de Deluvio Noe [1]

The waterleaders and drawers in dye.

And first in some high place, or in the cloudes yf it may be, God speaketh vnto Noe standing with-out the Arke with all his familye. [2]

DEUS.   I, God, that all the world have wrought,
Heaven and earth, and all of nought,
I see my people, in deede and thought,
Are sett fowle in sinne.

My ghost shall not lenge [3] in man,
That through fleshlie liking is my fone,
But till six skore yeares be gone,
To loke if they will blynne. [4]   8

Manne that I made I will destroy,
Beast, worme, and fowle to flie;
For on earthe they doe me nye, [5]
The folke that are theron.

Hit harmes me so hartfullie, [6]
The malyce now that can [7] multeply,
That sore it greueth me inwardlie
That ever I made manne.   16

Therfore, Noe, my servant free,
That righteous man art, as I see,
A shipp sone thou shalt make the
Of trees drye and lighte.

Little chambers therein thou make;
And bynding slich [8] also thou take,
With-in and -out thou ne slake [9]
To anoynte it through all thy mighte.   24

300 Cubytes it shall be long,
And 50 of breadeth, to mak it stronge,
Of heighte 50.   The mete [1] thou fonge, [2]
Thus measure it about.

One wyndow worch through thy wytte,
One cubyte of length and breadeth make it.
Vpon the side a dore shall sit
For to come in and out.   32

Eating places thou make also;
Three-roofed chambers, one or two;
For with water I thinke to flow [3]
Man that I can make.

Destroyed all the world shalbe,
Save thou; thy wife, thy sonnes three,
And all there wives also with thee
Shall saved be, for thy sake.   40

NOE.   Ah! Lord, I thanke the lowd and still,
That to me art in such will,
And spares me and my house to spill, [4]
As now I sothlie fynde.

Thy bydding, Lord, I shall fulfill,
And never more the greeve ne grill, [5]
That suche grace hast sent me till
Among all mankinde.   48

[*Noah calls to his family.*]

Haue done, yow men and women all!
Helpe, for ought that may befall,
To worke this shipp, chamber and hall,
As God hath bydden vs doe.

SEM.   Father, I am already bowne. [6]
Anne axe I haue, by my crowne,
As sharpe as any in all this towne,
For to goe there-to.   56

HAM.   I haue a hatchet wonder-kene

---

[1] The third pageant of Noah's Flood.
[2] MS. *Et primo in aliquo supremo loco sive in nubibus, si fieri poterit, loquatur Deus ad Noe extra Archam existentem cum tota familia sua.*   I have inserted the English form of this stage-direction as found in two other MSS.
[3] Linger.   [4] Cease.
[5] Annoy.   [6] Grievously.
[7] Does.
[8] Slime, pitch.   [9] Slack.

[1] Measure.   [2] Take.   [3] Deluge.
[4] Destroy.   [5] Vex.   [6] Ready, prepared.

[1] The text here reproduced is that of British Museum Harleian MS. 2124, as printed in *The Chester Plays*, Part I, edited for the Early English Text Society by H. Deimling, 1892.   I have modernized the punctuation, and have added, in brackets, some stage-directions.

To byte well, as may be seene;
A better grownden,[1] as I weene,
Is not in all this towne.

IAPHET.   And I can well make a pyn,
And with this hammer knock yt in;
Goe and worche without more dynne,
And I am ready bowne.   64

UXOR NOE.   And we shall bring tymber
        to,
For wee mon nothing els doe;
Women be weake to vnderfoe [2]
Any great travayle.[3]

VXOR SEM.   Here is a good hackstock; [4]
On this yow maye hew and knock;
Shall non be idle in this flock,
Ne now may no man fayle.   72

VXOR HAM.   And I will goe to gather
        sliche,[5]
The ship for to caulke [6] and piche;
Anoynted yt must be every stich,
Board, tree, and pyn.

VXOR IAPHET.   And I will gather chippes
        here
To make a fire for yow in feere,[7]
And for to dight your dynner,
Against yow come in.   80

*Then they make signs as if laboring with
        divers tools.[8]*

NOE.   Now in the name of God I will begin
To make the shippe that we shall in,
That we be ready for to swym
At the cominge of the flood.

These bordes I ioyne here together,
To kepe vs safe from the wedder,
That we may row both hither and thider,
And safe be from this floode.   88

Of this tree will I make the mast
Tyde with gables that will last,
With a sayle-yarde for each blast,
And each thinge in ther kinde.

With topcastle and bewsprytt,
With coardes and ropes I haue all meete,
To sayle forth at the next weete.[1]
This shipp is at an ende.   96

*Then Noah with all his family again make
signs of laboring with divers tools.[2]*

Wife, in this castle we shall be keped,[3]
My childer and thou, I wold, in leaped.
VXOR NOE.   In faith, Noe, I had as lief
        thou sleppit.[4]
For all thy frankish fare [5]

I will not doe after thy red.[6]
NOE.   Good wife, doe now as I the bydd.
VXOR NOE.   By Christ! not or I see more
        neede,
Though thou stand all the day and
        stare.   104

NO[E].   Lord, that women be crabbed aye,
And never are meke, that dare I saye.
This is well sene by me to daye,
In witnes of yow each one.

Good wife, let be all this beere [7]
That thou makes in this place here;
For all they wene [8] thou art master, —
And so thou art, by St. John!   112

[*God speaks above.*]

DEUS.   Noe, take thou thy meanye,[9]
And in the shippe hye that yow be;
For none so righteous man to me
Is now on earth lyvinge.

Of cleane beastes with thee thou take
Seaven and seaven, or thou slake,[10]
Hee and shee, make to make,[11]
Be-lyve in that thou bringe;   120

Of beastes vncleane two and two,
Male and female, without moe;
Of cleane fowles seaven alsoe,
The hee and shee together;

Of fowles vncleane two and no more,
As I of beastes said before;
That shalbe saved throughe my lore,
Against I send the wedder.   128

---

[1] Sharpened.   [2] Undertake.   [3] Labor.
[4] Chopping-block.   [5] Slime, pitch.
[6] MS. clean; *I take* caulke *from two other MSS. A
fourth MS. reads* clam.
[7] Likewise.
[8] MS. *Tunc faciunt signa quasi laborarent cum
diversis instrumentis.*

[1] Flood.
[2] MS. *Tunc Noe iterum cum tota familia faciunt
signa laborandi cum diversis instrumentis.*
[3] Preserved.   [4] Slept.   [5] Frantic behavior.
[6] Advice.   [7] Tumult.   [8] Think.
[9] Household.   [10] Slacken, stop.   [11] Mate.

Of all meates [1] that must be eaten
Into the ship loke there be getten;
For that no way may be foryeten,
And doe all this bydeene,

To sustayne man and beast therein,
Aye till the water cease and blyn.
This world is filled full of synne,
And that is now well sene.   136

Seaven dayes be yet coming,
You shall haue space them in to bringe;
After that is my lyking
Mankinde for to n[o]ye. [2]

40 dayes and 40 nightes
Rayne shall fall for ther vnrightes;
And that I haue made through my mightes
Now think I to destroye.   144

NOE. Lord, at your byddinge I am
bayne. [3]
Sith non other grace will gayne,
Hit will I fulfill fayne,
For gratious I thee fynde.

A 100 wynters and 20
This shipp making taried haue I,
If through amendment any mercye
Wolde fall vnto mankinde.   152

[*Noah calls to his family.*]

Haue done, you men and women all!
Hye you lest this water fall,
That each beast were in his stall,
And into the ship broughte.

Of cleane beastes seaven shalbe,
Of vncleane two; this God bade me.
This floode is nye, well may we see,
Therfore tary you noughte.   160

*Then Noye shall goe into the Arke with all
his family, his wief except, and the Arke
must be borded rounde about, and one the
bordes all the beastes and fowles receaved
must be painted that thes wordes may agree
with the pictures.* [4]

SEM. Syr, here are lyons, libardes [1] in;
Horses, mares, oxen, and swyne,
Geates, calves, sheepe and kine
Here sitten thou may see.

HAM. Camels, asses men may finde,
Bucke, doe, harte, and hynde,
And beastes of all manner kinde
Here bene, as thinkes mee.   168

IAPHET. Take here cattes and doggs to,
Otter, fox, fulmart [2] also;
Hares hopping gaylie can goe
Have cowle [3] here for to eate.

VXOR NOE. And here are beares, wolfes
sett,
Apes, owles, marmoset,
Weesells, squirrels, and firret;
Here they eaten their meate.   176

VXOR SEM. Yet more beastes are in this
howse:
Here cattis maken it full crowse,
Here a rotten,[4] here a mowse,
They stand nye together.

VXOR HAM. And here are fowles, les and
more:
Hearnes, cranes and byttour,
Swans, peacockes; and them before
Meate for this wedder.   184

VXOR IAPHET. Here are cockes, kites,
crowes,
Rookes, ravens, many rowes,
Duckes, curlewes. Who euer knowes
Eache one in his kinde?

And here are doves, diggs, drakes,
Redshankes runninge through the lakes;
And each fowle that ledden [5] makes
In this shipp men may finde.   192

[*Noah approaches his wife, who has joined
her gossips at the other end of the pageant.*]

NOE. Wife, come in! Why standes thou
here?
Thou art ever froward, that dare I sweare.
Come in, on Gods half! Tyme yt were,
For feare lest that we drowne.

VXOR NOE.   Yea, sir, set vp your sayle
And rowe forth with evill heale! [1]
For, without any fayle,
I will not out of this towne.   200

But [2] I haue my gossips everichon,
One foote further I will not gone;
They shall not drowne, by St. John,
And [3] I may save their lyfe!

They loved me full well, by Christ;
But [2] thou wilt let them in thy chist,
Els rowe forth, Noe, whether thou list,
And get thee a new wife!   208

[Noah returns to the Ark.]

NOE.   Sem, sonne, loe, thy mother is wraw.[4]
For sooth such another I do not know.
SEM.   Father, I shall fett her in, I trow,
Without any fayle.

[He crosses over to his mother.]

Mother, my father after thee send,
And bydds the into yonder ship wend.
Loke vp and se the wynde,
For we be readye to sayle.   216

VXOR NOE.   Sonne, goe again to him and
          say:
I will not come therein to daye.

[Noah and his sons go to her.]

NOE.   Come in, wife, in 20 devills waye!
Or els stand there without.

HAM.   Shall wee all fet her in?
NOE.   Yea, sonnes, in Christs blessinge
          and myne:
I would yow hyde yow betyme,
For of this flood I am in doubte.   224

*[Noah returns to the Ark.   The Wife's
"Good Gossips" enter with a pottle of
malmsey.]*

THE GOOD GOSSOPES.   The flood comes in,
          full fleetinge fast,
On every side it spredeth full fare.
For feare of drowning I am agast;
Good gossip, let us draw neare.   228

And let vs drinke or we depart,
For often tymes we have done soe;

---
[1] Success.   [2] Unless.   [3] If.   [4] Angry.

For at a draught thou drinkes a quarte,
And so will I doe, or I goe.   232

[They sing.]

*[Here is a pottell of malmesy, good
          and stronge,
It will reioyce both hart and tong;
Though Noy thinke vs neuer so long
Yet wee will drinke alyke.]* [1]

IAPHET.   Mother, we praye you alto-
          gether —
For we are here your owne childer —
Come into the ship for feare of the wed-
          der,
For His love that you boughte.

VXOR NOE.   That will I not for all your
          call,
But I haue my gossopes all.
SEM.   In feith, mother, yet you shall,
Whether you will or not.   240

[They drag her towards the Ark.]
          Then she shall go. [2]

NOE.   Welcome, wife, into this boate.
VXOR NOE.   And haue thou that for thy
          mote!

          And she gives him a lively blow. [3]

NOE.   A! ha! mary! this is hote!
It is good to be still.

A! children, me thinkes my boate re-
          meves;
Our tarying here hugelie me greves.
Over the lande the water spredes.
God doe as he will.   248

Ah! great God that art so good!
That worchis not thie will is wood.[4]
Now all this world is on a flood,
As I see well in sighte.

This window I will shut anon,
And into my chamber will I gone
Till this water, so greate one,
Be slaked throughe thy mighte.   256

---
[1] I have inserted the song from other MSS.
[2] MS. *Tunc ibit.*
[3] MS. *Et dat alapam vita.*
[4] Mad.

Then Noah shall close the window of the
Ark, and for a short while within let them
sing the Psalm "Save me, O God"; and
opening the window and looking around,
Noah says: [1]

Now 40 dayes are fullie gone.
Send a raven I will anone
If ought-where earth, tree, or stone
Be drye in any place.

And if this foule come not againe,
It is a signe, soth to sayne,
That drye it is on hill or playne,
And God hath done some grace.   264

Then he shall send out the raven; and taking a
dove in his hand let him say: [2]

Ah! Lord, wherever this raven be,
Somewhere is drye, well I see.
But yet a dove, by my lewtye,[3]
After I will sende.

Thou wilt turne againe to me
. . . .

For of all fowles that may flye,
Thou art most meke and hend.[4]   272

Then he shall send out the dove; and there
shalt be in the ship another dove bearing
an olive branch in its mouth, which Noah
shall let down from the mast by a string in
his hand; and afterwards let Noah say: [5]

Ah! Lord, blessed be thou aye,
That me hast comfort thus to-day;
By this sight I may well saye
This flood beginnes to cease.

My sweete dove to me brought hase
A branch of olyve from some place;
This betokeneth God has done vs some
grace,
And is a signe of peace.   280

[1] MS. *Tunc Noe claudet fenestram Archæ, et per mo-*
dicum spatium infra tectum cantent psalmum "Save
mee, O God"; et aperiens fenestram, et respiciens. Another MS. has the stage-direction: "Then Noye
shall shut the windowe of the Arke, and for a little
space within bord he shalbe silent, and afterwardes
opening the windowe and lookinge round about, saying."

[2] MS. *Tunc dimittet corvum; et capiens columbam in*
manibus dicat.

[3] Loyalty.   [4] Obedient.

[5] MS. *Tunc emittet columbam, et erit in nave alia col-*
umba ferens olivam in ore, quam dimittet ex malo per
funem in manus Noe, et postea dicat Noe.

Ah! Lord, honoured most thou be!
All earthe dryes now, I see,
But yet, tyll thou comaunde me,
Hence will I not hye.

All this water is awaye,
Therfore as sone as I maye
Sacryfice I shall doe in faye
To thee devoutlye.   288

[*God speaks above.*]

DEUS.   Noe, take thy wife anone,
And thy children every one;
Out of the shippe thou shalt gone,
And they all with thee.

Beastes and all that can flie
Out anone they shall hye,
On earth to grow and multeplye.
I will that yt be soe.   296

NOE.   Lord, I thanke the through thy
mighte;
Thy bidding shall be done in height.[1]
And as fast as I may dighte [2]
I will doe the honoure,

And to thee offer sacrifice;
Therfore comes in all wise,
For of these beastes that bene hise,[3]
Offer I will this stower.[4]   304

Then going out of the Ark with all his
family he shall take his animals and birds,
and shall offer them and make sacrifice. [5]

Lord, God in maiestye,
That such grace hast graunted me,
Where all was lorne,[6] save to be,
Therfore now I am bowne,

My wife, my Childer, my meanye [7]
With sacrifice to honoure thee
With beastes, fowles, as thou may see,
I offer here right sone.   312

[*God speaks above.*]

DEUS.   Noe, to me thou arte full able,
And thy sacrifice acceptable.
For I have fownd thee trew and stable,

[1] With speed.   [2] Get ready.
[3] His.   [4] Store.
[5] MS. *Tunc egrediens archam cum tota familia sua,*
accipiet animalia sua et volucres, et offeret ea, et -nacta-
bit.

[6] Lost.   [7] Family.

On the now must I myn:[1]

Warry[2] Earth will I no more
For mans synne that greves me sore;
For of youth man full yore
Has byn enclyned to syne.   320

You shall now grow and multeply,
And earth againe you edefie;
Each beast and fowle that may flie,
Shall be afrayd of you.

And fishe in sea that may flytte
Shall susteyne yow, I yow behite;[3]
To eate of them yow ne lett,
That cleane bene you may knowe.   328

Thereas you have eaten before
Grasse and rootes, sith you were bore,[4]
Of cleane beastes now, les and more,
I geve you leave to eate;

Safe bloode and flesh bothe in feare
Of wrong-dead carren that is here,
Eates not of that in no manere;
For that aye you shall let.   336

Manslaughter also you shall flee;
For that is not pleasant to me.
That shedes bloode, he or shee,
Ought-where amongst mankinde,

That blood foule sheede shalbe,
And vengence have, that men shall se;
Therfore beware now, all yee,
You fall not in that synne.   344

[1] Remember, be mindful of.
[2] Curse, destroy.
[3] Promise.   [4] Born.

A forwarde[1] now with thie I make,
And all thy seede for thy sake,
Of suche vengeance for to slake,
For now I haue my will.

Here I behet the a heaste,[2]
That man, woman, fowle ne beaste,
With water, while the world shall last,
I will no more spill.   352

My bowe betwene you and me
In the firmament shall bee,
By verey token that you may see
That such vengeance shall cease,

That man ne woman shall never more
Be wasted by water as is before;
But for syn that greveth me sore,
Therfore this vengeance was.   360

Where cloudes in the welkin bene,
That ilke bowe shall be sene
In tokeninge that my wrath and tene[3]
Shall never this wroken be.

The stringe is turned toward you,
And toward me is bent the bowe,
That such wedder shall never showe;
And this behett I thee.   368

My blessing now I geue the here,
To thee, Noe, my servant dere,
For vengeance shall no more appeare.
And now, fare well, my darling deere. 372

Finis paginæ Tertiæ.

[1] Covenant.   [2] Promise.   [3] Vexation.

Messenger, God, Angel (handwritten)

THE SACRIFICE OF ISAAC [1]

[On the upper stage God with his angels; on the lower stage Abraham and his young son Isaac. Abraham kneels in prayer.]

ABRAHAM.   Fader of heuyn omnipotent,
  With all my hart to the I call.
Thow hast goffe me both lond and rent;
And my lyvelod thow hast me sent.
  I thanke the heyly euer-more of all.   5

Fyrst off the erth thou madyst Adam,
  And Eue also to be hys wyffe;
All other creatures of them too cam.
And now thow hast grant to me, Abra-
  ham,
  Her in thys lond to lede my lyffe.   10

In my age thou hast grantyd me thys,
  That thys yowng chyld with me shall
  wone.[1]
I love no-thyng so myche, i-wysse,
Except thin owyne selffe, der Fader of
  blysse,
  As Ysaac her, my owyne swete sone.   15

I haue dyuerse chyldryn moo,
  The wych I loue not halffe so wyll;
Thys fayer swet chyld he schereys [2] me soo
In euery place wer that I goo,
  That noo dessece [3] her may I fell.   20

And therfor, Fadyr of heuyn, I the prey
  For hys helth and also for hys grace;
Now, Lord, kepe hym both nyght and
  day,
That neuer dessese nor noo fray [4]
  Cume to my chyld in noo place.   25

  [1] Dwell.   [2] Cheers.
  [3] Discomfort, trouble.   [4] Harm, terror.

[Rises.]

Now cum on, Ysaac, my owyne swete
  chyld;
  Goo we hom and take owr rest.
ISAAC.   Abraham, myne owyne fader so
  myld,
  To folowe yow I am full prest,[1]
  Bothe erly and late.
ABRAHAM.   Cume on, swete chyld.   I love
  the best   31
  Of all the chyldryn that ever I be-
  gat.

[They cross to another place.   God speaks above.]

DEUS.   Myn angell, fast hey the thy
  wey,
  And on-to medyll-erth anon thou goo;
Abrams hart now wyll I asay,[2]
  Wether that he be stedfast or noo.   36

Sey I commaw[n]dyd hym for to take
  Ysaac, hys yowng sonne, that he love so
  wyll,
And with hys blood sacryfyce he make,
  Yffe ony off my freynchepe he wyll
  ffell.   40

Schow hym the wey on-to the hylle
  Wer that hys sacryffyce schall be.
I schall asay, now, hys good wyll,
  Whether he lovyth better hys chyld or
  me.
All men schall take exampyll be hym
  My commawmentes how they schall
  kepe.   46

  [1] Ready.   MS. glad, *corr. by Manly.*
  [2] Try, test.

---

[1] This play, as Miss Lucy Toulmin Smith observes, is superior to the five other extant plays on the same theme.   It has often been printed, for it is justly regarded as the best example of pathos in the early religious drama.   I have based the text on *The Non-Cycle Mystery Plays*, re-edited from the manuscripts for the Early English Text Society by O. Waterhouse, 1909, but have adopted some emendations made by other editors. The manuscript is preserved at Brome Manor, Suffolk, in a commonplace-book of 1470–80; the original, however, of which this is a transcript must be dated as early as the fourteenth century.   Waterhouse suggests that the play was not a part of a cycle, but was designed for representation by itself.   We cannot be certain.   In form and language it is closely akin to the *Abraham and Isaac* of the Chester Cycle, and it differs in no essential way from the ordinary craft play.   And, even if acted separately, "it is to be supposed," says Waterhouse, "that the stage was the usual pageant, and the mode of performance practically identical with" that of the regular cycle plays.

[*The angel descends.   Abraham, returning,*
        kneels in prayer.]

ABRAHAM.   Now, Fader of heuyn, that
        formyd all thyng,
My preyeres I make to the a-geyn,
For thys day my tender-offryng [1]
    Here mvst I geve to the, certeyn.
A! Lord God, allmyty Kyng,   51
    Wat maner best woll make the most
        fayn? [2]
Yff I had ther-of very knoyng,
    Yt schuld be don with all my mayne,
        Full sone anone.
To don thy plesyng on an hyll,
    Verely yt ys my wyll,
        Dere Fader, God in Trinyte.   58

THE ANGELL.   Abraham! Abraham! wyll
        thou rest!
Owre Lord comandyth the for to take
Ysaac, thy yowng sone that thow lovyst
        best,
    And with hys blod sacryfyce that thow
        make.   62

In-to the Lond of V[i]syon thow goo,
    And offer thy chyld on-to thy Lord;
I schall the lede and schow all-soo.
    Vnto Goddes hest,[3] Abraham, a-cord, 66

And folow me vp-on thys grene.
ABRAHAM.   Wolle-com to me be my
        Lordes sond,[4]
    And hys hest I wyll not with-stond.
Yit Ysaac, my yowng sonne in lond,
A full dere chyld to me haue byn.   71

I had lever,[5] yf God had be plesyd,
    For to a-for-bore all the good [6] that I
        haue,
Than Ysaac my sone schuld a be desessyd,[7]
    So God in heuyn my sowll mot saue! 75

I lovyd neuer thyng soo mych in erde,[8]
    And now I mvst the chyld goo kyll.
A! Lord God, my conseons ys stronly
        steryd!

<hr/>

[1] Burnt-offering.   [2] Pleased.
[3] Decree.   [4] Messenger.
[5] Rather.   [6] Goods, possessions.
[7] Injured.   [8] MS. erthe, *corr. by Manly.*

And yit, my dere Lord, I am sore a-ferd
    To groche ony thyng a-gens yowre
        wyll.   80

I love my chyld as my lyffe;
    But yit I love my God myche more.
For thow my hart woold make ony stryffe,
Yit wyll I not spare for chyld nor wyffe,
    But don after my Lordes lore.[1]   85

Thow I love my sonne neuer so wyll,
    Yit smythe [2] of hys hed sone I schall.
A! Fader of heuyn, to the I knell;
An hard dethe my son schall fell
    For to honor the, Lord, with-ali.   90

THE ANGELL.   Abraham! Abraham! thys
        ys wyll seyd!
    And all thys comamentes loke that thou
        kepe.
But in thy hart be no-thyng dysmayd.
ABRAHAM.   Nay, nay, for-soth, I hold me
        wyll a-payd [3]
    To plesse my God to the best that I
        haue.[4]   95

For thow my hart be heuely sett
    To see the blood of my owyn dere sone,
Yit for all thys I wyll not lett,
But Ysaac, my son, I wyll goo fett,
    And cum asse fast as euer we can.   100

[*Abraham crosses to the end of the pageant,*
        where Isaac is kneeling in prayer.]

Now, Ysaac, my owyne son dere,
    Wer art thow, chyld? Speke to me.
YSAAC.   My fader, swet fader, I am here,
    And make my preyrys to the Tren-
        yte.   104

ABRAHAM.   Rysse vp, my chyld, and fast
        cum heder,
My gentyll barn [5] that art so wysse,
For we to, chyld, must goo to-geder
And on-to my Lord make sacryffyce. 108

YSAAC.   I am full redy, my fader, loo!
    Yevyn at yowr handes I stand rygth
        here;

<hr/>

[1] Precept.   [2] Smite.
[3] MS. plesyd: *Manly suggests* a-payd.
[4] *Manly suggests* may.
[5] Child.

And wat-so-euer ye byd me doo,
  Yt schall be don with glad cher,
    Full wyll and fyne.
ABRAHAM.   A! Ysaac, my owyn son soo
    dere,
  Godes blyssyng I gyffe the, and
    myn.   115

Hold thys fagot vpon thi bake,
  And her myselffe fyer schall bryng.
YSAAC.   Fader, all thys her wyll I packe;
  I am full fayn to do yowr bedyng.
ABRAHAM.   [Aside.]   A! Lord of heuyn,
    my handes I wryng,
  Thys chyldes wordes all to-wond my
    harte.   121

Now, Ysaac [s]on,[1] goo we owr wey
  On-to yon mownte, with all owr mayn.
YSAAC.   Gowe we, my dere fader, as fast
    I as may;
  To folow yow I am full fayn,
    Allthow I be slendyr.
ABRAHAM.   [Aside.]   A! Lord, my hart
    brekyth on tweyn,
  Thys chyldes wordes, they be so
    tender.   128

    [They arrive at the Mount.]

A! Ysaac, son, anon ley yt down;
  No lenger vpon thi backe yt hold,[2]
For I mvst make redy bon [3]
  To honowr my Lord God as I schuld. 132

YSAAC.   Loo, my dere fader, wer yt ys!

    [Lays down the fagot.]

To cher yow all-wey I draw me nere.
But, fader, I mervell sore of thys,
  Wy that ye make thys heuy chere.   136

And also, fader, euer-more dred I:
  Wer ys yowr qweke [4] best that ye schuld
    kyll?
Both fyer and wood we haue redy,
  But queke best haue we non on this
    hyll.   140

A qwyke best, I wot wyll,[5] must be ded [6]

Yowr sacryfyce for to make.
ABRAHAM.   Dred the nowgth, my chyld, I
    the red,[1]
Owr Lord wyll send me on-to thys sted [2]
  Summ maner a best for to take,
    Throw hys swet sond.[3]
YSAAC.   Ya, fader, but my hart begynnyth
    to quake
  To se that scharpe sword in yowr
    hond.   148

Wy bere ye yowr sword drawyn soo?
  Off yowre conwnauns [4] I haue mych
    wonder.
ABRAHAM.   [Aside.]   A! Fader of heuyn,
    so I am woo!
  Thys chyld her brekys my harte on-
    sonder.[5]   152

YSAAC.   Tell me, my dere fader, or that ye
    ses,[6]
  Ber ye yowr sword draw[yn] [7] for me?
ABRAHAM.   A! Ysaac, swet son, pes! pes!
  For, i-wys, thow breke my harte on
    thre.   156

YSAAC.   Now trewly, sum-what, fader, ye
    thynke,
  That ye morne thus more and more.
ABRAHAM.   [Aside.]   A! Lord of heuyn,
    thy grace let synke,
  For my hart was neuer halffe so sore. 160

YSAAC.   I preye yow, fader, that ye wyll
    let me that wyt,[8]
  Wyther schall I haue ony harme or
    noo.
ABRAHAM.   I-wys, swet son, I may not tell
    the yit,
  My hart ys now soo full of woo.   164

YSAAC.   Dere fader, I prey yow, hyd yt [9]
    not fro me,
But sum of yowr thowt that ye tell me.
ABRAHAM.   A! Ysaac, Ysaac, I must kyll
    the!
YSAAC.   Kyll me, fader?   Alasse! wat
    haue I done?   168

---

[1] MS. on; I have adopted Manly's emendation.
[2] MS. bere, corr. by Kittredge.
[3] Quickly ready.   [4] Live.
[5] Well.   [6] Killed.

[1] Advise.   [2] Place.
[3] Messenger.   [4] Countenance.
[5] MS. on-too, corr. by Holthausen.
[6] Cease.   [7] Added by Holthausen.
[8] Know.   [9] Manly's reading for MS. hydygth.

Yff I haue trespassyd a-gens yow owt,
  With a yard [1] ye may make me full myld;
And with yowr scharp sword kyll me nogth,
  For, i-wys, fader, I am but a chyld.   172

ABRAHAM.   I am full sory, son, thy blood
    for to spyll,
YSAAC.   Now I wold to God my moder
    were her on this hyll!
  Sche woold knele for me on both hyr
    kneys
    To save my lyffe.
And sythyn [2] that my moder ys not here,
I prey yow, fader, schonge [3] yowr chere,   179
    And kyll me not with yowyr knyffe.

ABRAHAM.   For-sothe, son, but yf [4] I the
    kyll,
  I schuld greve God rygth sore, I drede.
Yt ys hys commawment, and also hys
    wyll,
    That I schuld do thys same dede.   184

He commawdyd me, son, for serteyn,
  To make my sacryfyce with thy blood.
YSAAC.   And ys yt Goddes wyll that I
    schuld be slayn?
ABRAHAM.   Ya, truly, Ysaac, my son soo
    good;
    And ther-for my handes I wryng.   189

YSAAC.   Now, fader, agens my Lordes wyll
I wyll neuer groche, lowd nor styll.
He mygth a sent me a better desteny
Yf yt had a be hys plecer. [5]   193

ABRAHAM.   For-sothe, son, but yf I ded
    this dede,
    Grevosly dysplessyd owr Lord wyll be.
YSAAC.   Nay, nay, fader, God for-bede
    That euer ye schuld greve hym for
    me.   197

Ye haue other chyldryn, on or too,
  The wyche ye schuld love wyll be kynd. [6]
I prey yow, fader, make ye no woo;
For, be I onys ded, and fro yow goo,
  I schall be sone owt of yowre mynd.   202

Ther-for doo owre Lordes byddyng,
  And wan I am ded, than prey for me.
But, good fader, tell ye my moder no-
    thyng;
Sey that I am in a-nother cuntre dwellyng.
ABRAHAM.   A! Ysaac, Ysaac, blyssyd
    mot thow be!   207

My hart be-gynnyth [1] stronly to rysse,
  To see the blood off thy blyssyd body.
YSAAC.   Fader, syn yt may be noo other
    wysse,
    Let yt passe ouer as wyll as I.   211

But, fader, or I goo on-to my deth,
  I prey yow blysse me with yowr hand.

[*Isaac kneels.*]

ABRAHAM.   Now, Ysaac, with all my breth
  My blyssyng I geve the upon thys lond,
  And Godes also ther-to, i-wys.
Ysaac, sone, up thow stond,
  Thy fayer swete mowthe that I may
    kys.   218

YSAAC.   Now for-wyll, my owyne fader so
    fyn;
  And grete wyll my moder in erde. [2]
But I prey yow, fader, to hyd my eyne,
  That I se not the stroke of yowr scharpe
    swerd, [2]
    That my fleysse schall defyle.   223
ABRAHAM.   Sone, thy wordes make me to
    weep full sore;
Now, my dere son Ysaac, speke no more.
YSAAC.   A! my owyne dere fader, were-
    fore?
    We schall speke to-gedyr her but a
    wylle.   227

And sythyn that I must nedysse be ded,
  Yit, my dere fader, to yow I prey,
Smythe but fewe [3] strokes at my hed,
  And make an end as sone as ye may,
    And tery not to longe.
ABRAHAM.   Thy meke wordes, child,
    make me afray;
  So, "welawey!" may be my songe,   234

---

1 Rod.   2 Since.
3 Change.   4 Unless.
5 Pleasure.   6 Well by nature.

1 MS. begynnyd, *corr. by Manly. Miss Smith
and Waterhouse prefer* begynnys.
2 *Here, and elsewhere, MS. has* erthe *and* sword,
which Manly alters for the sake of the rhyme.
3 MS. feve, *spelling altered by Manly.*

Excepe alonly Godes wyll.
> A! Ysaac, my owyn swete chyld,
Yit kysse me a-gen vp-on thys hyll!
> In all thys war[l]d ys non soo myld. 238

YSAAC. Now truly, fader, all thys tery[y]ng
> Yt doth my hart but harme;
I prey yow, fader, make an enddyng.
ABRAHAM. Cume vp, swet son, on-to my
> arme. 242

[Starts to bind him.]

I must bynd thy hand[e]s too,
> All-thow thow be neuer soo myld.
YSAAC. A! mercy, fader! wy schuld ye do
soo?
ABRAHAM. That thow schuldyst not let [1]
[me], my chyld. 246

YSAAC. Nay, i-wysse, fader, I wyll not let
yow.
> Do on, for me, yowre wyll;
And on the purpos that ye haue set
> yow,
> For Godes love kepe yt for the styll. 250

I am full sory thys day to dey,
> But yit I kepe [2] not my God to greve.
Do on yowre lyst for me hardly;
> My fayer swete fader, I geffe yow
> leve. 254

But, fader, I prey yow euermore,
> Tell ye my moder no dell; [3]
Yffe sche wost [4] yt, sche wold wepe full
sore,
> For i-wysse, fader, sche lovyt me full
wyll.
> Goddes blyssyng mot sche haue! 259

Now for-wyll, my moder so swete!
> We too be leke [5] no mor to mete.
ABRAHAM. A! Ysaac, Ysaac! son, thou
makyst me to gret,
> And with thy wordes thow dystempurst
me. 263

YSAAC. I-wysse, swete fader, I am sory to
greve yow.
I cry yow mercy of that I haue donne,

And of all trespasse that euer I ded meve
> yow;
> Now, dere fader, for-gyffe me that I haue
donne.
> God of heuyn be with me! 268

ABRAHAM. A! dere chyld, lefe of thy
monys;
In all thy lyffe thow grevyd me neuer onys.
Now blyssyd be thow, body and bonys,
> That euer thow were bred and born!
Thow hast be to me chyld full good.
> But i-wysse, child, thow I morne neuer
so fast,
> Yit must I nedes here at the last
In thys place sched all thy blood. 276

Ther-for, my dere son, here schall thou lye.

[Places him on the altar.]
> On-to my warke I must me stede.[1]
I-wysse I had as leve my-selffe to dey,
> Yff God wyll [be] plecyd wyth my dede,
> And myn owyn body for to offer.
YSAAC. A! mercy, fader, morne ye no
more!
> Yowr wepyng maketh [2] my hart sore,
> As my owyn deth that I schall suf-
fer. 284

Yowr kerche, fader, a-bowt my eyn ye
wynd.
ABRAHAM. So I schall, my swettest chyld
in erde.
YSAAC. Now yit, good fader, haue thys in
mynd,
> And smyth me not oftyn with yowr
scharp swerd,
> But hastely that yt be sped.

*Here Abraham leyd a cloth on Ysaaces face,
thus seyyng:*

ABRAHAM. Now fore-wyll, my chyld, so
full of grace.
YSAAC. A! fader, fader, torne downgward
my face,
> For of yowre scharpe sword I am euer
a-dred. 292

ABRAHAM. *[Aside.]* To don thys dede I
am full sory,

---

[1] Hinder.   [2] Desire.
[3] Bit.   [4] Knew.   [5] Like.

[1] Set myself.   [2] MS. makes; *corr. by Holthausen.*

But, Lord, thyn hest [1] I wyll not with-
  stond.
YSAAC. A! Fader of heuyn, to the I crye;
  Lord, reseyve me into thy hand.   296

ABRAHAM. [Aside.] Loo! now ys the
  tyme cum, certeyn,
  That my sword in hys necke schall bite.[2]
A! Lord, my hart reysyth the[r]-ageyn;
  I may not fynd yt [3] in my harte to
    smygth;
    My hart wyll not now ther-too.   301
Yit fayn I woold warke my Lordes wyll.
But thys yowng innosent lygth so styll,
I may not fynd yt [3] in my hart hym to kyll.
    O! Fader of heuyn, what schall I
    do?   305

YSAAC. A! mercy, fader, wy tery ye so,
  And let me ley thus longe on this heth?
Now I wold to God the stroke were doo!
Fader, I prey yow hartely, schorte me of
  my woo,
  And let me not loke [thus] after my
    degth.   310

ABRAHAM. Now, hart, wy wolddyst not
  thow breke on thre?
  Yit schall thou not make me to my God
    onmyld.
I wyll no lenger let for the,
For that my God a-grevyd wold be.
  Now hoold [4] tha stroke, my owyn dere
    chyld.   315

*Her Abraham drew hys stroke and the angel
toke the sword in hys hond soddenly.*

THE ANGELL. I am an angell, thow may-
  ist se blythe,
  That fro heuyn to the ys senth.
Owr Lord thanke the an C [5] sythe [6]
  For the kepyng of hys commawment. 319

He knowyt thi wyll, and also thy harte,
  That thow dredyst [7] hym above all
    thyng;
And sum of thy hevynes for to departe
  A fayr ram yinder I gan brynge;   323

He standyth teyed, loo! a-mong the
  breres.[1]
Now, Abraham, amend thy mood,
For Ysaac, thy yowng son that her ys,
  Thys day schall not sched hys blood. 327

Goo, make thy sacryfece with yon rame.
Now forwyll, blyssyd Abraham,
  For onto heuyn I goo now hom;
    The way ys full gayn.[2]
      Take vp thy son soo free.   332
                       [*Exit.*]

ABRAHAM. A! Lord, I thanke the of thy
  gret grace,
  Now am I yeyed [3] on dyuers wysse.
  Arysse vp, Ysaac, my dere sunne,
    arysse;
    Arysse vp, swete chyld, and cum to
    me.   336

YSAAC. A! mercy, fader, wy smygth ye
  nowt? [4]
  A! smygth on, fader, onys with yowr
    knyffe.
ABRAHAM. Pesse, my swet son,[5] and take
  no thowt,
  For owr Lord of heuyn hath grant thi
    lyffe
    Be hys angell now,   341

That thou schalt not dey this day, sunne,
  truly.
YSAAC. A! fader, full glad than wer I, —
  I-wys, — fader, — I sey, — i-wys, —
    Yf thys tale wer trew.
ABRAHAM. An hundyrd tymys, my son
  fayer of hew,
  For joy thi mowt[h] now wyll I kys. 347

YSAAC. A! my dere fader, Abraham,
  Wyll not God be wroth that we do thus?
ABRAHAM. Noo, noo! har[de]ly, my swyt
  son,
  For yin same rame he hath vs sent
  Hether down to vs.   352

Yin best schall dey here in thi sted,
  In the worthschup of owr Lord alon.

---

[1] Command.
[2] MS. synke; *corr. by Holthausen.*
[3] *Manly's reading for* MS. fyndyg⁺h.
[4] Receive.   [5] Hundred.
[6] Times.   [7] Reverest.

[1] Briars.   [2] Direct.   [3] Eased.
[4] MS. not yit; *corr. by Holthausen.*
[5] MS. sir; *Manly changes to* son.

Goo, fet hym hethyr, my chyld, in-ded.

YSAAC.   Fader, I wyll goo hent [1] hym be
    the hed,
    And bryng yon best with me anon. 357

[Isaac, untying the ram.]

A! scheppe, scheppe, blyssyd mot thou be,
    That euer thow were sent down heder!
Thow schall thys day dey for me
In the worchup of the Holy Trynyte. 361
    Now cum fast and goo we to-geder
    To my Fader of heuyn.
Thow thou be neuer so jentyll and good,
Yit had I leuer thow schedyst thi blood,
    Iwysse, scheppe, than I.   366

[He leads the ram to his father.]

Loo! fader, I haue browt here full smerte
    Thys jentyll scheppe, and hym to yow I
    gyffe.
But, Lord God, I thanke the with all my
    hart,
    For I am glad that I schall leve,[2]
    And kys onys my dere moder.

ABRAHAM.   Now be rygth myry, my swete
    chylld,
    For thys qwyke best, that ys so myld,
      Here I schall present before all
      other.   374

YSAAC.   And I wyll fast begynne to
    blowe;
    Thys fyere schall brene a full good spyd.
But, fader, wyll I stowppe downe lowe,
Ye wyll not kyll me with yowr sword, I
    trowe?
ABRAHAM.   Noo, har[de]lly, swet son; haue
    no dred;
    My mornyng ys past.
YSAAC.   Ya! but I woold that sword wer
    in a gled,[3]
    For, iwys, fader, yt make me full yll
    agast.   382

*Here Abraham mad hys offryng, knelyng and
seyyng thus:*

ABRAHAM.   Now, Lord God of heuen in
    Trynyte,
    Allmyty God omnipotent,
My offeryng I make in the worchope of the,
And with thys qweke best I the present.

    [1] Seize.   [2] Live.   [3] Fire.

Lord, reseyve thow myn intent,
    As [thow] art God and grownd of owr
    grace.   388

[God speaks above.]

DEUS.   Abraham, Abraham, wyll mot
    thow sped,
    And Ysaac, thi yowng son the by!
Trvly, Abraham, for thys dede
I schall mvltyplye yowres botheres [1] sede
    As thyke as sterres be in the skye, 393
    Bothe more and lesse;
    And as thyke as gravell in the see,
    So thyke mvltyplyed yowre sede schall
    be.
    · Thys grant I yow for yowre good-
    nesse.   397

Off yow schall cume frowte gret [won],[2]
    And euer be in blysse withowt yend,
For ye drede me as God a-lon
And kepe my commawmentes eueryschon;
    My blyssyng I geffe, wersoeuer ye
    wend.[3]   402

ABRAHAM.   Loo! Ysaac, my son, how
    thynke ye
    Be thys warke that we haue wrogth?
Full glad and blythe we may be,
    Agens the wyll of God that we grocched
    nott,
    Vpon thys fayer hetth.
YSAAC.   A! fader, I thanke owr Lord euery
    dell,[4]
That my wyt servyd me so wyll
    For to drede God more than my
    detth.   410

ABRAHAM.   Why! derewordy son, wer
    thow adred?
Hardely,[5] chyld, tell me thy lore.[6]
YSAAC.   Ya! be my feyth, fader, now
    haue [7] I red,
I wos neuer soo afrayd before
    As I haue byn at yin hyll.
But, be my feth, fader, I swere
I wyll neuermore cume there
    But yt be a-gens my wyll.   418

    [1] Both your.
    [2] Number.   *Added by Manly.*
    [3] MS. goo; corr *by Holthausen.*
    [4] Part.   [5] Boldly.
    [6] Thinking.   [7] MS. hath; *corr. by Manly.*

ABRAHAM.   Ya! cum on with me, my
 owyn swet sonn,
And hom-ward fast now let vs goon.
YSAAC.   Be my feyth, fader, therto I
 grant;
I had neuer so good wyll to gon hom,
 And to speke with my dere moder. 423
ABRAHAM.   A! Lord of heuyn, I thanke
 the,
 For now may I led hom with me
 Ysaac, my yownge sonn soo fre,
  The gentyllest chyld a-bove all other,
  Thys may I wyll a-voee.   428

Now goo we forthe, my blyssyd sonn.
YSAAC.   I grant, fader, and let vs gon;
 For, be my trowthe, wer I at home,
 I wold neuer gon owt vnder that forme.[1]
  I pray God geffe vs grace euermo,
  And all thow [2] that we be holdyng
  to.[3]   [*Exeunt.*]   434

[*Enter Doctor.*]

DOCTOR.   Lo! sovereyns and sorys,[4] now
 haue we schowyd
Thys solom story to grete and smale.
It ys good lernyng to lernd and lewyd,[5]
 And the wysest of vs all,
  Wythowtyn ony berryng.[6]
For thys story schoyt[7] yowe [her][8]
How we schuld kepe, to owr po[we]re,[8]
  Goddes   commawmentes   withowt
  grochyng.   442

Trowe ye, sores, and God sent an angell

And commawndyd yow yowr chyld to
 slayn,[1]
Be yowr trowthe, ys ther ony of yow
 That eyther wold groche or stryve ther-
 ageyn?
How thyngke ye now, sorys, ther-by? 447

I trow ther be iij or iiij or moo.
And thys women, that wepe so sorowfully
 Whan that hyr chyldryn dey them froo,[2]
  As nater woll and kynd,   451
 Yt ys but folly, I may well awooe, [3]
 To groche a-gens God or to greve yow,
 For ye schall neuer se hym myschevyd,
  wyll I knowe,
  Be lond nor watyr, haue thys in
  mynd;   455

And groche not a-gens owr Lord God
 In welth or woo, wether that he yow send,
Thow ye be neuer so hard bestad;
 For when he wyll, he may yt a-mend,
Hys commawmentes treuly yf ye kepe with
 goo[d] hart,
 As thys story hath now schowyd you
 be-for[n]e,   461
And feytheffully serve hym qwyll ye be
 qvart, [4]
 That ye may plece God bothe euyn and
 morne.
 Now Jesu, that weryt the crown of
 thorne,
  Bryng vs all to heuyn blysse!   465

Finis.

---

[1] Condition? [2] Those. [3] Beholden to.
[4] Sirs. [5] Ignorant. [6] Barring.
[7] Showeth. [8] *Added by Manly.*

[1] MS. to smygth of your chyldes hed; *emended by
Holthausen*
[2] From. [3] Avow. [4] Safe and sound.

PHARAOH [1]

[Acted by the Litsters [2] of Wakefield.]

Incipit Pharao. Litsters pagonn.

PHARAO. Peas, of payn that no man pas;
  Bot kepe the course that I commaunde;
And take good hede of hym that has
  Youre helth all holy [1] in hys hande!
For Kyng Pharro my fader was,
  And led [2] thys lordshyp of thys land;
I am hys hayre, as age wyll has,
  Euer in stede [3] to styr or stand.   8

All Egypt is myne awne
  To leede aftyr my law.
I wold my myght were knawne [4]
  And honoryd, as hyt awe.[5]
Full low he shall be thrawne
  That harkyns not my sawe,
Hanged hy and drawne, —
  Therfor no boste ye blaw! [6]   16

Bot as for kyng I commaund peasse,
  To all the people of thys empyre.
Looke no man put hym self in preaase,[7]
  Bot that wyll do as I desyre;
And of youre wordis look that ye seasse!
  Take tent [8] to me, youre soferand syre,
That may youre comfort most increasse,
  And to my lyst [9] bowe lyfe and lyre.[10] 24

I. MILES. My lord, if any here were
  That wold not wyrk youre wyll,
If we myght com thaym nere,
  Full soyn we shuld theym spyll.[11]   28

PHARAO. Thrugh out my kyngdom wold I
    ken,
  And kun [12] hym thank that wold me tell,
If any were so waryd [13] men
  That wold my fors downe fell. [14]
II. MILES. My lord, ye haue a maner of
    men

That make great mastres vs emell,[1]
The Iues, that won in Gersen; [2]
  Thay ar callyd Chyldyr of Israel.   36

Thay multyplye full fast,
  And sothly we suppose
That shall euer last,
  Oure lordshyp for to lose.[3]   40

PHARAO. Why, how haue thay sych
    gawdis [4] begun?
  Ar thay of myght to make sych frayes?
I. MILES. Yei, lord, full fell [5] folk ther
    was fun [6]
In Kyng Pharao, youre fader dayes.
Thay cam of Ioseph, was Iacob son —
  He was a prince worthy to prayse —
In sythen [7] in ryst [8] haue thay ay ron;
  Thus ar thay lyke to lose youre layse, [9] 48

Thay wyll confound you cleyn,
  Bot if thay soner sesse.
PHARAO. What deuyll is that thay meyn
  That thay so fast incresse?   52

II. MILES. How thay incres full well we
    ken,
  As oure faders dyd vnderstand.
Thay were bot sexty and ten
  When thay fyrst cam in to thys land;
Sythen haue soierned in Gersen
  Fower hundreth [10] wynter, I dar war-
    and;[11]
Now ar thay nowmbred of myghty men
  Moo then thre hundreth [12] thousand, 60

Wyth outen wyfe and chyld,
  Or hyrdis [13] that kepe thare fee.
PHARAO. How thus myght, we be begyld?
  Bot shall it not be;   64

---

[1] Wholly.   [2] Ruled.   [3] Place.
[4] MS. Knowne.   [5] Ought.   [6] Blow.
[7] Throng.   [8] Give attention.
[9] Pleasure.   [10] Submit life and flesh.
[11] Destroy.   [12] Give.   [13] Cursed.   [14] Throw.

[1] Superiority among us.   [2] Dwell in Goshen.
[3] Destroy.   [4] Tricks.   [5] Many.
[6] Found.   [7] Afterwards.
[8] Insurrection.   [9] Destroy your laws.
[10] MS. iiijc.   [11] Warrant.
[12] MS. ccc.   [13] Shepherds.

---

[1] From the Towneley Plays; see page 94, note 1.   [2] Dyers.

For wyth quantyse [1] we shall thaym quell,
So that thay shall not far sprede.

I. MILES. My lord, we haue hard oure
faders tell,
And clerkis that well couth rede,
 Ther shuld a man walk vs amell [2]
That shuld fordo [3] vs and oure dede. [4]

PHARAO. Fy on hym, to the deuyll of
hell!
Sych destyny wyll we not drede; 72

We shal make mydwyfis to spyll them
 Where any Ebrew is borne,
And all menkynde [5] to kyll them;
 So shall thay soyn be lorne. [6] 76

And as for elder [7] haue I none awe,
 Sych bondage shall I to thaym beyde, [8]
To dyke [9] and delf, bere and draw,
 And to do all vnhonest deyde;

So shall these laddis be halden law, [10]
 In thraldom euer thare lyfe to leyde.

II. MILES. Now, certis, thys was a sotell
saw!
Thus shall these folk no farthere sprede. 84

PHARAO. Now help to hald theym downe;
Look I no fayntnes fynde.

I. MILES. All redy, lord, we shall be
bowne, [11]
In bondage thaym to bynde. 88

Then Moses enters with a rod in his hand. [12]

MOYSES. Gret God, that all thys warld
began,
 And growndyd it in good degre,
Thou mayde me, Moyses, vnto man;
 And sythen [13] thou sauyd me from the se;
Kyng Pharao had commawndyd than
Ther shuld no man-chyld sauyd be;
Agans hys wyll away I wan. [14]
 Thus has God shewed hys myght for
me. 96

Now am I sett to kepe,
 Vnder thys montayn syde,

Byshope Iettyr shepe,
 To [1] better may be-tyde. 100

A, Lord, grete is thy myght!

[He spies the burning bush.]

What man may of yond meruell meyn?
Yonder I se a selcowth [2] syght;
 Sych on in warld was neuer seyn;
A bush I se burnand full bryght,
 And euer elyke [3] the leyfes are greyn.
If it be wark of warldly wyght, [4]
 I wyll go wyt wythoutyn weyn. [5] 108

[God from above calls him.]

DEUS. Moyses, Moyses!

*Here he hurries to the bush, and God says to
him:* [6]

[DEUS.] Moyses, com not to nere,
Bot styll in that stede [7] thou dwell,
And harkyn vnto me here;
 Take tent what I the tell.
Do of thy shoyes in-fere, [8]
 Wyth mowth [9] as I the mell.
The place thou standis in there
 Forsothe, is halowd well. 117

I am thy Lord, wythouten lak,
 To lengthe thi lyfe euen as I lyst;
I am God that som tyme spake
 To thyn elders, as thay wyst.
To Abraam, and Isaac,
 And Iacob, I sayde shuld be blyst,
And multytude of them to make,
 So that thare seyde [10] shuld not be
myst. 125

Bot now thys Kyng Pharao,
 He hurtys my folk so fast,
If that I suffre hym so,
 Thare seyde shuld soyne be past.
Bot I wyll not so do,
 In me if thay wyll trast,
Bondage to bryng thaym fro.
 Therfor thou go in hast, 133

To do my message haue in mynde,

---

[1] Skill. [2] Among. [3] Destroy.
[4] Deeds. [5] Males.
[6] Lost, destroyed. [7] The grown-ups.
[8] Order, command. [9] Dig, ditch.
[10] Low. [11] Prepared.
[12] MS. *Tunc intrat Moyses cum virga in manu, etc.*
[13] Afterwards. [14] Won.

---

[1] Until. [2] Strange. [3] Every single one.
[4] Human being. [5] Know without doubt.
[6] MS. *Hic properat ad rubum, et dicit ei Deus, etc.*
[7] Place. [8] Put off thy shoes likewise.
[9] Mouth. [10] Seed, offspring.

To hym that me sych harme mase.[1]
Thou speke to hym wyth wordis heynde,[2]
  So that he let my people pas,
To wyldernes that thay may weynde,
  To worshyp me as I wyll asse.[3]
Agans my wyll if that thay leynd,[4]
  Ful soyn hys song shall be "Alas!" 141

Moyses.   A, Lord! pardon me, wyth thy
    leyf.
  That lynage [5] luffis me noght.
Gladly thay wold me greyf,
  If I sych bodworde [6] broght.   145

Good Lord, lett som othere frast,[7]
That has more fors the folke to fere.
Deus.   Moyses, be thou nott abast.
My bydyng shall thou boldly bere;
  If thay with wrong away wold wrast,[8]
Outt of the way I shall the were.[9]
Moyses.   Good Lord, thay wyll not me
    trast
For all the othes that I can swere.   153

To neuen sych noytis [10] newe
  To folk of wykyd wyll,
Wyth-outen tokyn trew,
  Thay wyll not tent ther tyll.[11]   157

Deus.   If that he wyll not vnderstand
Thys tokyn trew that I shall sent,
Afore the Kyng cast downe thy wand,
  And it shall turne to a serpent;
Then take the tayll agane in hand —
  Boldly vp look thou it hent [12] —
And in the state that thou it fand,
  Then shal it turne by myne intent.[13]165

Sythen [14] hald thy hand soyn in thy barme,[15]
  And as a lepre it shal be lyke,
And hole agane with outen harme.
  Lo, my tokyns shal be slyke.[16]   169

And if he wyll not suffre then
  My people for to pas in peasse,
I shall send venyance neyn [17] or ten,
  Shall sowe [18] full sore, or I seasse.

Bot the Ebrewes, won [1] in Iessen,[2]   174
  Shall not be merkyd with that measse; [3]
As long as thay my lawes wyll ken
  Thare comforth shall euer increasse. 177

Moyses.   A, Lord, to luf the aght [4] vs
    well,
  That makis thy folk thus free.
I shall vnto thaym tell
  As thou has told to me.   181

Bot to the Kyng, Lord, when I com,
  If he aske what is thy [5] name,
And I stand styll, both deyf and dom,
  How shuld I skape [6] withoutten blame?
Deus.   I say the thus: "*Ego sum qui sum,*"
  I am he that is the same;
If thou can nother muf [7] nor mom,[8]
  I shall sheld the from shame.   189

Moyses.   I vnderstand full well thys
    thyng.
I go, Lord, with all the myght in me.
Deus.   Be bold in my blyssyng;
  Thi socoure shall I be.   [*Deus retires.*] 193

Moyses.   A, Lord of luf, leyn me thy lare,[9]
  That I may truly talys tell.
To my freyndis now wyll I fare,
  The chosyn Childre of Israell,
To tell theym comforth of thare care,
  In dawngere ther as thay dwell.

[*Moses accosts the Children of Israel.*]

God manteyn you euermare,
  And mekyll myrth be you emell! [10] 201

I. Puer.   A, master Moyses, dere!
Oure myrth is all mowrnyng;
  Full hard halden ar we here,
As carls [11] vnder the kyng.   205

II. Puer.   We may mowrn, both more and
    myn;[12]
Ther is no man that oure myrth mase.[13]
  Bot syn we ar all of a kyn,
God send vs comforth in thys case.

---

[1] Does.	[2] Gracious.	[3] Ask.
[4] Linger.	[5] Lineage.	[6] Message.
[7] Try.	[8] Wrest.	[9] Defend.
[10] Name such things.		[11] Attend thereto.
[12] Seize.	[13] Purpose, design.	
[14] Afterwards.	[15] Bosom.	
[16] Such.	[17] MS. ix.	[18] Pain.

[1] That dwell.	[2] Goshen.
[3] Shall not be stricken.	[4] Ought.
[5] MS. my.	[6] MS. shake.
[7] Speak indistinctly.	[8] Mutter.
[9] Lend me thy learning, instruct me.	
[10] Among.	[11] Serfs.
[12] Less.	[13] Makes.

MOYSES.   Brethere, of youre mowrnyng
    blyn.[1]
God wyll delyuer you thrugh his grace;
    Out of this wo he wyll you wyn,
And put you to youre pleassyng place; 213

For I shall carp [2] vnto the Kyng,
And fownd [3] full soyn to make you free.
1. PUER.   God graunt you good weyndyng,
And euermore with you be!   217

[*Moses crosses over to Pharaoh.*]

MOYSES.   Kyng Pharao, to me take
    tent.[4]
PHARAO.   Why, boy, what tythyngis can
    thou tell?
MOYSES.   From God hym-self hydder am
    I sent
To foche the Chyldre of Israell;
To wyldernes he wold thay went.
PHARAO.   Yei, weynd the to the devyll of
    hell!
I gyf no force what he has ment!
    In my dangere, herst [5] thou, shall thay
    dwell.   225

And, fature,[6] for thy sake,
Thay shalbe put to pyne.
MOYSES.   Then wyll God venyance take
Of the, and of all thyn.   229

PHARAO.   On me?   Fy on the, lad! out of
    my land!
Wenys thou thus to loyse oure lay? [7]

[*To the soldiers.*]

Say, whence is yond warlow [8] with his
    wand
That thus wold wyle [9] oure folk away?
1. MILES.   Yond is Moyses, I dar warand,
Agans all Egypt has beyn ay.
    Greatt defawte [10] with hym youre fader
    fand;
Now wyll he mar you, if he may.   237

PHARAO.   Fy on hym!   Nay, nay, that
    dawnce [11] is done.
Lurdan,[12] thou leryd [13] to late!

¹ Cease.   ² Talk.   ³ Seek.
⁴ Pay attention.   ⁵ Hearest.
⁶ Traitor.   ⁷ Destroy our law.   ⁸ Sorcerer.
⁹ Lure.   ¹⁰ Fault.   ¹¹ Dance.
¹² Lowt.   ¹³ Learned.

MOYSES.   God bydis the graunt my bone,[1]
And let me go my gate.[2]   241

PHARAO.   Bydis God me?   Fals losell,[3]
    thou lyse!
What tokyn told he?   Take thou tent.
MOYSES.   He sayd thou shuld dyspyse
Both me, and hys commaundement.
    Forthy, apon thys wyse,
My wand he bad, in thi present,
    I shuld lay downe, and the avyse
How it shuld turne to oone serpent.   249

And, in hys holy name,
    Here I lay it downe.
Lo, syr, here may thou se the same!
PHARAO.   A, ha, dog! the devyll the
    drowne!   253

MOYSES.   He bad me take it by the tayll,
For to prefe [4] hys powere playn;
    Then, he sayde, wythouten fayll
Hyt shuld turne to a wand agayn.
    Lo, sir, behold!
PHARAO.   Wyth ylahayll! [5]
Certis this is a sotell swayn!
    Bot thyse boyes shall abyde in bayll;
All thi gawdis shall thaym not gayn;   261

Bot wars, both morn and none,
Shall thay fare, for thi sake.
MOYSES.   I pray God send us venyange
    sone,
And on thi warkis take wrake.   265

[*Moses departs.*]

[*After an interval the soldiers go to Pharaoh.*]
1. MILES.   Alas, alas! this land is lorn! [6]
On lyfe we may [no] longer leynd; [7]
    Sych myschefe is fallen syn morn,
Ther may no medsyn [8] it amend!
PHARAO.   Why cry ye so, laddis? lyst ye
    skorn?
II. MILES.   Syr Kyng, sych care was neuer
    kend,[9]
In no mans tyme that euer was borne!
PHARAO.   Tell on, belyfe,[10] and make an
    end.   273

¹ Boon, request.   ² Way.   ³ Rascal.
⁴ Prove.   ⁵ Bad luck to you!
⁶ Lost.   ⁷ Remain.   ⁸ Medicine.
⁹ Known.   ¹⁰ With speed.

I. MILES.   Syr, the waters that were
        ordand
For men and bestis foyde,[1]
    Thrugh outt all Egypt land,
Ar turnyd into reede bloyde;   **277**

Full vgly and full yll is hytt,
That both fresh and fayre was before.
PHARAO. O, ho! this is a wonderfull thyng
        to wytt,
Of all the warkis that euer wore!
II. MILES.   Nay, lord, ther is anothere yit,
That sodanly sowys [2] vs full sore;
    For todis and froskis [3] may no man flyt,[4]
Thay venom vs so, both les and more. 285

I. MILES.   Greatte mystis,[5] sir, ther is
        both morn and noyn,
Byte vs full bytterly.
    We trow that it be doyn
Thrugh Moyses, oure greatte enmy.   **289**

II. MILES.   My lord, bot if this menye [6]
        may remefe,
Mon neuer myrth be vs amang.
PHARAO. Go, say to hym we wyll not
        grefe. —
Bot thay shall neuer the tytter [7] gang.

[The First Soldier goes to Moses.]

I. MILES.   Moyses, my lord gyffys leyfe [8]
To leyd thi folk to lykyng lang,
    So that we mend of oure myschefe.
MOYSES. Full well I wote, thyse wordis ar
        wrang;   **297**

But hardely all that I heytt [9]
    Full sodanly it shall be seyn;
Vncowth [10] meruels shalbe mevt [11]
    And he of malyce meyn.[12]   **301**

[After an interval the soldiers go to Pharaoh.]

II. MILES. A, lord, alas! for doyll [13] we dy!
We dar look oute at no dowre!
PHARAO. What, the ragyd [14] dwyll of hell,
        alys you so to cry?
I. MILES.   For we fare wars then euer we
        fowre! [15]

Grete loppys [1] ouer all this land thay fly,
    And where thay byte thay make grete
        blowre; [2]
And in euery place oure bestis dede ly. **308**

II. MILES.   Hors, ox, and asse,
Thay fall downe dede, syr, sodanly.
PHORAO. We! lo, ther is no man that has
Half as mych harme as I!   **312**

I. MILES.   Yis, sir, poore folk haue mekyll
        wo,
To se thare catall thus out cast.
    The Iues in Gessen [3] fayre not so;
Thay haue lykyng for to last.
PHARAO. Then shall we gyf theym leyf to
        go,
To tyme this perell be on past; —
    Bot, or thay flytt oght far vs fro,
We shall them bond twyse as fast.   **320**

[The Second Soldier goes to Moses.]

II. MILES.   Moyses, my lord gyffis leyf
Thi meneye [4] to remeue.
MOYSES. Ye mon hafe more myschefe
Bot if [5] thyse talys be trew.   **324**

[After an interval the soldiers go to Pharaoh.]

I. MILES.   A, lord, we may not leyde thyse
        lyfys!
PHARAO.   What, dwyll! is grevance
        grofen [6] agayn?
II. MILES.   Ye, sir, sich powder apon vs
        dryfys,
Where it abidys it makys a blayn; [7]
    Mesell [8] makys it man and wyfe.
Thus ar we hurt with hayll and rayn,
    Syr, v[y]nys [9] in montanse may not
        thryfe,
So has frost and thoner thaym slayn.   **332**

PHARAO.   Yei, bot how do thay in Gessen,
The Iues, can ye me say?
I. MILES.   Of all thyse cares no thyng thay
        ken;
Thay feyll noght of our afray.   **336**

PHARAO.   No? the ragyd! the dwyll! sytt
        thay in peasse?

---

[1] Food.	[2] Pains.	[3] Frogs. [4] Go.
[5] Gnats.	[6] Crowd (the Jews).	[7] Quicker.
[8] Permission.	[9] Promised.	[10] Wonderful.
[11] Met.	[12] Complain.	[13] Grief.
[14] MS. ragyd the; *cf. l. 414.*		[15] Fared.

---

[1] Insects.	[2] Blisters.	[3] Goshen.
[4] Crowd.	[5] Unless.	
[6] Grown.	[7] Swelling, boil.	
[8] Leprous.	[9] Vines.	

And we euery day in doute and drede?
II. MILES.   My lord, this care wyll euer
    encrese,
To [1] Moyses haue his folk to leyd;
    Els be we lorn, it is no lesse.
Yit were it better that thai yede.[2]   342

PHARAO.   Thes folk shall flyt no far,
If he go welland wode! [3]
I. MILES.   Then will it sone be war.[4]
It were better thay yode.   346

II. MILES.   My lord, new harme is comyn
    in hand.
PHARAO.   Yei, dwill, will it no better be?
I. MILES.   Wyld wormes [5] ar layd ouer all
    this land;
Thai leyf no floure, nor leyf on tre.
II. MILES.   Agans that storme may no man
    stand;
And mekyll more meruell, thynk me,
    That thise thre dayes has bene durand
Sich myst, that no man may other se.
I. MILES.   A, my lord!
PHARAO.   Hagh!   355

II. MILES.   Grete pestilence is comyn;
It is like ful long to last.
PHARAO.   Pestilence! [6] in the dwilys name!
Then is oure pride ouer past.   359

I. MILES.   My lord, this care lastis lang,
And will, to [1] Moyses haue his bone.[7]
    Let hym go, els wyrk we wrang;
It may not help to houer ne hone.[8]
PHARAO.   Then will we gif theym leyf to
    gang,
Syn it must nedis be doyn;
    Perchauns we sall thaym fang [9]
And mar them or to morn at none.   367

[The Second Soldier goes to Moses.]
II. MILES.   Moyses, my lord he says
Thou shall haue passage playn.

[Moses addresses the Children of Israel.]
MOYSES.   Now haue we lefe to pas,
My freyndis, now be ye fayn.   371

Com furth; now sall ye weynd
To land of lykyng you to pay.
I. PUER.   Bot Kyng Pharao, that fals
    feynd,
He will vs eft [1] betray;
    Full soyn he will shape vs to sheynd,[2]
And after vs send his garray.[3]
MOYSES.   Be not abast; God is oure
    freynd,
And all oure foes will slay.   379

Therfor com on with me;
Haue done and drede you noght.
II. PUER.   That Lord blyst might he be,
That vs from bayll has broght.   383

[They arrive at the Red Sea.] [4]
I. PUER.   Sich frenship neuer we fand.
Bot yit I drede for perels all;
    The Reede See is here at hand,
Ther shal we byde to [5] we be thrall.
MOYSES.   I shall make way ther with my
    wand,
As God has sayde, to sayf vs all;
    On ayther syde the see mon stand,
To we be gone, right as a wall.   391

[Moses parts the Red Sea.]
Com on wyth me; leyf none behynde.
Lo fownd ye now youre God to pleasse.

Here they pass through the Sea.[6]
II. PUER.   O, Lord! this way is heynd.[7]
Now weynd we all at easse.   395

[The soldiers go to Pharaoh.]
I. MILES.   Kyng Pharao! thyse folk ar
    gone.
PHARAO.   Say, ar ther any noyes [8] new?
II. MILES.   Thise Ebrews ar gone, lord,
    euer-ichon.[9]
PHARAO.   How says thou that?
I. MILES.   Lord, that tayll is trew.
PHARAO.   We! out tyte,[10] that they were
    tayn;
That ryett radly [11] shall thay rew!

[1] Until.   [2] Went.
[3] Boiling mad.
[4] Worse.   [5] I.e., locusts.
[6] MS. pentilence.   [7] Request.
[8] Tarry nor delay.   [9] Seize.

[1] Again.   [2] Destroy.   [3] Armed force.
[4] Some notion of how this was represented may be gained from the following entry in the guild accounts of Coventry: "Item, paid for halfe a yard of Rede Sea"; Sharp, A Dissertation, p. 64.
[5] Until.   [6] MS. Hic pertransient mare.
[7] Gracious.   [8] Annoyances.
[9] Every one.   [10] Quick.   [11] Speedily.

We shall not seasse to thay be slayn,
For to the see we shall thaym sew.[1]   403

So charge youre chariottis swythe,[2]
And fersly [3] look ye folow me.
II. MILES.   All redy, lord, we ar full
    blyth [4]
At youre byddyng to be.   407

I. MILES.   Lord, at youre byddyng ar we
    bowne [5]
Oure bodys boldly for to beyd;
    We shall not seasse, bot dyng all
    downe,
To all be dede withouten drede.
PHARAO.   Heyf vp youre hertis vnto
    Mahowne; [6]
He will be nere vs in oure nede.

[*They attempt to pass through the Red Sea.*]

    Help! the raggyd dwyll! we drowne!
Now mon we dy for all oure dede.   415

---

    1 Pursue.   2 Quickly.
    3 Fiercely, valiantly. 4 Glad.
    5 Ready.   6 Mahomet.

Then the Sea shall overwhelm them.[1]

MOYSES.   Now ar we won from all oure wo,
And sauyd out of the see!
    Louyng gyf we God vnto.
Go we to land now merely.   419

I. PUER.   Lofe we may that Lord on hyght,
And euer tell on this meruell;
    Drownyd he has Kyng Pharao myght.
Louyd be that Lord Emanuell!
MOYSES.   Heuen, thou attend, I say, in
    syght,
And erth my wordys; here what I tell:
    As rayn or dew on erth doys lyght
And waters herbys and trees full well, 427

Gyf louyng to Goddys mageste;
    Hys dedys ar done, hys ways ar trew.
Honowred be he in Trynyte;
    To hym be honowre and vertew!   431
        Amen.

Explicit pharao.
1 MS. *Tunc merget eos mare.*

THE PROPHETS [1]

[Acted by the Cappers of Chester.]

Pagina Quinta de Mose et Rege Balaak et
Balaam Propheta. The Cappers.

DEUS.   Moyses, my servaunte life [1] and
 dere,
And all the people that be here,
You wott in Egipte when you were,
 Out of thralldome I you broughte.
I wyll, you honour no God saue me;
Ne mawmentrye [2] none make yee;
My name in vayne nam [3] not yee,
 For that me lykes naughte.   8

I will, you hold your holy daye;
And worshipp also, by all waye,
Fa.her and mother all that you maye;
 And slaye no man no-where.
Fornication you shall flee;
No mens goods steale yee;
Ne in no place abyde ne bee
 Falce wytnes for to beare.   16

Your neighboures wyves covettes noughte,
Servant ne good that he hath boughte,
Oxe ne asse, in deede ne thoughte,
 Nor any-thinge that is his,
Ne wrongefullie to haue his thinge
Agayne his will and his lykinge.
In all these doe my byddinge,
 That you doe not amisse.   24

*Then let the High Priest stand up, and as
if for the people let him speak to God and
Moses.* [4]

PRINCEPS SINAGOGÆ.   Ah! good Lord,
 much of mighte,
Thou comes with so great lighte,
We bene so afraide of this sighte,

[1] Beloved. [2] Idols. [3] Take.
[4] MS. *Tunc princeps Sinagogæ statuet eum in
loco, et quasi pro populo, loquatur ad Dominum et
Moysen.*

No man dare speake ne see! [1]
God is so grym with us to deale,
But Moyses, master, with us thou mele; [2]
Els we dyen, many and feele, [3]
 So afrayde bene all wee.   32

*Then let Moses, standing on the mount, speak
to the people.* [4]

MOYSES.   Gods folke, drede you noughte.
To prove you with, God hath this wrought,
To make you afrayd in deede and thoughte,
 Aye for to avoyde synne.
By this sight you may now see
That he is pereles of postye; [5]
Therfore his teaching look done yee,
 Thereof that you not blyn. [6]   40

PRINCEPS SINAGOGÆ.   Ah! highe Lord,
 God almighte,
That Moyses shynes wondrous bright!
I may no way for great lighte
 Now looke upon hym.
And horned he semes in our sighte! [7]
Sith he came to the hyll, dight [8]
Our lawe he hase, I hope, aright,
 For was he never so grym.   48

MOYSES.   You, Gods folke of Israell,
Harkens to me that loven heale; [9]
God bade you sholde doe, everye deale,
 As that I shall saye.
Six dayes boldelye worches [10] all,
The seaventh Sabaoth you shall call;
That daye for ought that may befall
 Hallowed shalbe aye.   59

[1] MS. looke; *corr. by Deimling.* [2] Speak. [3] Many.
[4] MS. *Tunc Moyses stans super montem loquatur ad
populum.*
[5] Power.   [6] Cease.
[7] Through a misconception of the text Moses was
formerly supposed to have appeared with horns on
his head.
[8] Prepared. [9] Health, salvation. [10] Work.

[1] The Chester *Prophets* can hardly be omitted from any book of selected plays designed to illustrate the origin and growth of the drama, for it shows in a primitive form the dramatization of the *Sermo contra Iudaeos, Paganos et Arianos de Symbolo* which ultimately led to the group of Old Testament Plays (see E. K. Chambers, *The Mediæval Stage*, pp. 52 seq.).   In the York Cycle this residual play is entirely lacking; in the Wakefield Cycle it exists only as a fragment; and in the N. towne Cycle the episode of Moses and the Two Tables has been developed into a separate play.   I have reproduced the text from *The Chester Plays*, Part I, edited by H. Deimling for the Early English Text Society; see page 111, note 1.

That doth not this deede deade shall be.
In houses fire shall no man see.
First fruytes to God offer yee, —
  For so hym-selfe bade.
Gould and silver offers also,
Purple, bisse,[1] and other moe,
To hym that shall save you from woe
  And helpe you in your neede.   64

[The Expositor advances.]

EXPOSITOR.   Lordinges, this comaund-
    ment
Was of the Old Testamente,
And yet is used with good entent
  With all that good bene.
This storye all if we shold fong,[2]
To playe this moneth it were to longe;
Wherfore most frutefull there amonge
  We taken, as shall be sene.   72

Also we read in this storie,
God in the Mownt of Synai
Toke[3] Moises these comaundmentis, vere-
    lye,
  Wrytten with his owne hande
In tables of ston, as reade I;
But when men honoured mawmentry,[4]
He brake them in anger hastelye,
  For that he wold not wonde.[5]   80

But afterward sone — leeve[6] ye me —
Other tables of stone made he,
In which God bade wrytten shold be
  His wordes that were before;
The which tables shryned were
After as God can Moyses leare;[7]
And that shryne to them was deare
  Thereafter evermore.   88

[The Expositor retires.]

*Then Moses shall descend from the
mount, and from another part of the
mount King Balaack shall speak, riding.*[8]

BALAACK REX.   I, Balaack, King of Moab
    land,
All Israell, had I it in my hand,
I am so wroth I wold not wond[9]

To slaye them, ech wighte;
For their God helpes them stiflye
Of other landes to haue mastrye,
That it is bootles, witterlie,[1]
  Against them for to fighte.   96

What nation soever dose them noye,[2]
Moyses prayes anone in hye,
Therefore haue they sone the victorie
  And other men they haue the worse.
Therfore how will I wroken[3] be?
I am bethought, as mot I the!
Balaam I will shall come to me
  That people for to curse;   104

For sworde ne knife may not avayle
These ilke shroes[4] for to assaile;
That fowndes[5] to fight he shall faile,
  For sicker[6] is hym no boote.
All nations they doe any,[7]
And my-selfe they can destroie,
As ox that gnawes biselie
  The grasse right to the roote.   112

Who-so Balaam blesses, i-wis,
Blessed, sickerlie, that man is;
Who-so he curses, fareth amisse:
  Such loos[8] over all hase he.
Therfore goe fetch hym, bach[e]ller,[9]
That he may curse the people here;
For, sicker, on them in no manner
  Mon we not wroken[10] be.   120

MILES.   Syr, on your errand I will gone;
Yt shall be well done, and that anone,
For he shall wreak[11] you on your fone,[12]
  The people of Israell.
BALAACK.   Yea, looke thou het[13] hym
    gold gret wone,[14]
And riches for to lyve upon,
To destroy them if he can,
  The freakes[15] that be so fell.   128

Then he shall go to Balaam.[16]

MILES.   Balaam, my lorde greetes well
    thee,

---

[1] Precious stuff.   [2] Take.   [3] Delivered.
[4] Idols.   [5] Refrain.   [6] Believe.
[7] Gave Moses instruction.
[8] MS. *Tunc Moyses descendet de monte, et ex altera
parte montis dicet rex Balaac, equitando.*
[9] Hesitate.

[1] Truly.   [2] Annoy.   [3] Avenged.
[4] Shrews.   [5] Endeavors.
[6] Surely, truly.   [7] Annoy.
[8] Power.   [9] Knight, soldier.
[10] Avenged.   [11] Avenge.   [12] Foes.
[13] Promise.   [14] Quantity.
[15] Warriors, men.
[16] MS. *Tunc ibit ad Balaam.*

And prayes the right sone at hym to be,
To curse the people of Iudy,
    That do hym great anoye.
BALAAM. Forsooth, I tell the, bacheler,
That I may haue no power
But if Gods will were.
    That shall I witt in hye.[1]   136

[*Balaam prayeth to God one his knees.*][2]

DEUS (*in supremo loco*).[3]   Balaam, I
        comaund the
King Balaak his bydding that thou flee;
That people that is blessed of me
    Curse thou not by no waye.
BALAAM. Lord, I must doe thy byddinge,
Thoughe it be to me unlykeing;
For truly much wynninge
    I might haue had to-daye.   144

DEUS. Thoughe the folke be my foe,
Thou shalt haue ieaue thydder to goe;
But looke that thou doe right soe
    As I haue thee taughte!
BALAAM. Lord, it shall be done in height.
This asse shall beare me aright.
Goe we together anone, sir knight,
    For now leave I haue coughte.   152

*Then they shall ride towards the King, and
        going let Balaam say:* [4]

Now, by the law I leve upon,
Sith I haue leaue for to gone,
They shalbe cursed every one,
    And [5] I ought wyn maye.
If Balaak hold that he has heighte [6]
Gods hest [7] I set at light.
Warryed [8] they shalbe this night
    Or that I wend awaye!   160

*Then the angel shall stand before Balaam
with a sword drawn in hand, and the ass
shall halt.* [9]

Goe forth, Burnell! Goe forth, goe!

What the dyvell! my asse will not goe!
Served me she never soe.
    What sorrow so her dose nye? [1]
Rise up, Burnell! make thee bowne,[2]
And helpe to beare me out the towne;
Or, as brok I my crowne,
    Thou shalt full sore abye! [3]   168

*Then he shall beat the ass, and some one in
        the ass shall speak.* [4]

ASINA. Maister, thou dost evell, witterly,
So good an ass as me to nye!
Now hast thou beaten me thry,[5]
    That beare the thus aboute.
BALAAM. Burnell, whye begiles thou me,
When I haue most nede to the?
ASINA. That sight that I before me see
    Makes me downe to lowte.[6]   176

Am I not, master, thyne owne ass,
That ever before ready was
To beare the whether thou woldest pas?
    To smyte me now yt is shame.
Thou wottest [7] well, master, pardy,[8]
Thou haddest never ass like to me,
Ne never yet thus served I thee.
    Now, I am not to blame.   184

*Then let Balaam, seeing the angel with the
drawn sword, say, falling upon his knees:* [9]

BALAAM. Ah! Lord, to thee I make a vowe,
I had no sight of thee erre now.
Lyttle wist I it was thou
    That feared my asse soe.
ANGELUS. Why hast thou beaten thy ass
        thry?
Now I am comen thee to nye,
That changes thy purpose falcelye,
    And woldest be my foe.   192

And the ass had not downe gone,
I wold haue slayne the here anone.
BALAAM. Lord, haue pittye me upon,
    For sinned I haue sore!
Is it thy will that I forth goe?
ANGELUS. Yea; but looke thou doe this
        folk no woe

---

[1] Know at once.
[2] Added by Manly from the other MSS., with the preceding Latin sentence: "Tunc ibit Balaam ad consulendum Dominum in oratione, et scedens dicat Deus."
[3] "In the uppermost place."
[4] MS. *Tunc equitabunt versus regem, et eundo dicat Balaam.*
[5] If.   [6] Promised.   [7] Command.   [8] Cursed.
[9] MS. *Tunc angelus obuiabit Balaam cum gladio extracto in manu, et stabit asina.* Possibly the ass stopped so suddenly as to throw Balaam off; see line 167.

[1] Annoy.   [2] Ready.   [3] Pay for it.
[4] MS. *Tunc percutiet asinam, et loquetur aliquis in asina.*
[5] Thrice.   [6] Fall, stoop.
[7] Knowest.   [8] Par Dieu.
[9] MS. *Tunc Balaam videns angelum evaginatum gladium habentem, adorans dicat.*

Otherwise then God bade thee tho [1]
   And saide to thee before.   200

Then Balaam and the soldier shall proceed,
*   and Balaack meets them.* [2]

BALAACK.   Ah! welcome, Balaam, my
   frend!
For all myne anguish thou shalt end,
If that thy will be to wend,
   And wreake [3] me of my foe.
BALAAM. Nought may I speake, so haue I
   win,
But as God puttes me in,
To forby [4] all and my kin; —
   Therfore, sure, me is woe!   208

BALAACK. Come forth, Balaam, come
   with me!
For on this hill, so mot I thee,
The folke of Israell thou shalt see.
   And curse them, I thee praye!
Thou shalt haue riches, golde and fee,
And I shall aduance thy dignytye,
To curse men, — cursed they may be! —
   That thou shalt see to-day.   216

Then leading Balaam with him upon the
mount, and looking towards the south, let
him speak as follows: [5]

[BALAACK. [6] Lo! Balaam, now thou seest here
Godis people all in feare, [7]
   Cittie, castell, and riuer.
   Looke now how likes thie.
Curse them now at my prayer,
As thou wilte be to me full dere,
And in my realme most of power
   And greatest under me.]

BALAAM. How may I curse them in this
   place,
The people that God blessed hase?
In them is both might and grace,
   And that is alwayes seene.
Wytnes I may none beare
Against God that this can were [8]

His people that no man may deare [1]
   Ne troble with no teene. [2]   224

I saye these folkes shall haue their will;
That no nation shall them gryll; [3]
The goodnes that they shall fulfill
   Nombred may not be;
Their God shall them kepe and save.
No other repreve may I not [4] have,
But such death as they shall haue
   I praye God send me.   232

BALAACK. What the devilles eyles the,
   poplart? [5]
Thy speach is not worth a fart!
Doted [6] I wot well thou art,
   For woodlie [7] thou has wrougt.
I bade thee curse them, every one,
And thou blest them, blood and bone!
To this north syde thou shalt anon,
   For here thy deed is nought.   240

Then he shall lead him to the north side. [8]

BALAAM. Herken, Balaack, what I say:
God may not gibb [9] by no waye;
That he saith, is veray,
   For he may not lye.
To bless his folk he me sent;
Therfore I saie, as I am kent: [10]
That in this land, verament,
   Is used no mawmentry;   248

To Iacobs blood and Israell
God shall send ioy and heale;
And as a lyon in his weale [11]
   Christ shalbe haunsed [12] hye,
And rise also in noble araye
As a prynce to wyn great paye,
Overcome his enemyes, as I say,
   And them bowndly bye. [13]   256

BALAACK. What the devill is this! Thou
   cursest them naught,
Nor blessest them nether, as me thought.
BALAAM. Syr kinge, this I thee beheight [14]

---

[1] Then.   [2] MS. *Tunc Balaam et miles ibunt, Balaack venit*
in obuiam.
[3] Avenge.   [4] Purchase, save.
[5] MS. *Tunc adducens secum Balaam in montem,*
et ad australem partem respiciens, dicat ut sequitur.
[6] Lacuna in MS. I have supplied the missing
stanza from the other MSS.
[7] Together.   [8] Defend.

[1] Injure.   [2] Vexation.   [3] Vex.
[4] *Manly prefers the reading of the other MSS.:* shall
they none.
[5] A term of abuse.   [6] Crazy, a dotard.
[7] Madly, in a crazy way.
[8] MS. *Tunc adducet eum ad borealem partem.*
[9] Turn, waver.   [10] Instructed.
[11] Weald, woodland.   [12] Exalted.
[13] Graciously save.   [14] Promised, foretold.

Or that I come here.

BALAACK.   Yet shalt thou to an-other
    place,
Ther Gods power for to embrace.[1]
The dyvell geve the hard grace,
    But thou doe my prayer!   264

To the west part.[2]

BALAAM.   Ah! Lord, that here is fayre
    wonning![3]
Halls, chambers of great lyking,
Valleyes, woodes, grass springing,
    Fayre yordes,[4] and eke river!
I wot well God made all this
His folke to lyue in ioye and blisse.
That warryeth[5] them, warried is;
    That blessest them, to God is deare. 272

BALAACK.   Popelard! thou preachest as a
    pie![6]
The deuill of hell thee destroy!
I bade thee curse myne enemye;
    Therfore[7] thou came me to.
Now hast thou blessed them here, thry,[8]
For thou meanes me to nye.
BALAAM.   So tould I the before twye,
    I might none other doe.   280

BALAACK.   Out! alas! what dyvell ayles thee?
I haue het thee gold and fee
To speake but wordes two or three,
    And thou makes much distance.[9]
Yet once I will assay thee,
If any boote of bale[10] will be;
And if thou falcely now faile me,
    Mahound[11] geue thee mischance!   288

Then Balaam looking at the sky, in
    prophecy.[12]

BALAAM.   *Orietur Stella ex Iacob, et exurget*
    Homo de Israell, et confringet omnes
    duces alie[ni]ginarum, et erit omnis
    terra possessio eius.

Now one thinge I will tell you all,
Hereafter what shall befall:

¹ Undertake.
² MS. *Ad occidentalem partem.*
³ Dwelling, living.   ⁴ Fields.
⁵ Curseth.   ⁶ Magpie.
⁷ To that end.   ⁸ Thrice.   ⁹ Dispute.
¹⁰ Redress of injury.   ¹¹ Mahomet.
¹² MS. *Tunc Balaam ad cælum respiciens prophe-
tando.*

A starre of Iacob springe shall,
    A man of Israell;
He shall overcome and haue in band
All kinges, dukes of strang land,
And all the world haue in his hand,
    As lord to dight and deale.   296

*[The Expositor advances with the other
    prophets.]*

ESAYAS.   I saye a mayden meeke and
    mylde
Shall conceave and beare a childe,
Cleane, without workes wilde,
    To wyn mankinde to wayle;[1]
Butter and hony shall be his meate,
That he may all evill forgeat,
Our soules out of hell to get,
    And called Emanuell.   304

EXPOSITOR.   Lordinges, these wordes are
    so veray
That exposition, in good faye,
None needes. But you know may
    This word Emanuell:
Emanuell is as much to saye
As "God with us night and day";
Therfore that name for ever and aye
    To his Sonne cordes wondrous well. 312

EZECHIELL.   *Vidi portam in domo Domini
    clausam, et dixit angelus ad me,
    "Porta hæc non aperietur sed clausa
    erit" et ct. Ezechiel capitulo 2.*

I, Ezechiell, sothlie see
A gate in Gods house on hye.
Closed it was; no man came nye.
    Then told an angell me:
"This gate shall no man open, i-wis,
For God will come and goe by this;
For him-self it reserved is,
    None shall come there but hee."   320

EXPOSITOR.   By this gate, lords, verament,
I understand in my intent
That way the Holy Ghost in went
    When God tooke flesh and bloode
In that sweet mayden Mary.
She was that gate, witterly,
For in her he light[2] graciouslie
    Mankind to doe good.   328

¹ Weal, happiness.   ² Alighted.

IHEREMIA. *Deducunt oculi mei lacrimas per diem et noctem, et non taceant; contritione magna contrita est virgo filia populi mei et plaga, et çt.*

My eyes must run and sorrow aye
Without ceasing, night and daye,
For my daughter, soth to saye,
 Shall suffer great anye;
And my folke shall doe, in faye,
Thinges that they ne know may
To that mayden, by many waye,
 And her sonne, sickerlie.[1]   336

EXPOSITOR. Lordinges, this prophesie,
  i-wis,
Touches the Passion nothing amisse.
For the prophet see well this
 What shall come, as I reade:
That a childe borne of a maye[2]
Shall suffer death, sooth to saye;
And they that mayden shall afray,
 Haue vengeance for that deede.   344

IONAS. *Clamaui de tribulacione mea ad Dominum et exaudiuit; de ventre inferi clamavi et exaudisti vocem meam et proiecisti me.*

I, Ionas, in full great any
To God I prayed inwardlie,
And he me hard through his mercy,
 And on me did his grace.
In myddes the sea cast was I,
For I wrought inobedyentlie;
But in a whalles bellye
 Three dayes saved I was.   352

EXPOSITOR. Lordinges, what this may
  signifie
Christ expoundes apertelie,[3]
As we reade in the Evangely
 That Christ him-self can saie:
Right as Ionas was dayes three
In wombe of whall, so shall he be
In earth lyinge, as was he,
 And rise the third daye.   360

DAUID. *De summo cœlo egressio eius, et occursus eius ad sum[m]um eius. Psal.*

I, Davyd, saie that God almighte
From the highest heaven to earth will light,

And thidder againe with full might,
 Both God and man in feare;[1]
And after come to deeme[2] the righte.
May no man shape them[3] of his sight,
Ne deeme that to mankind is dighte,
 But all then must apeare.   368

EXPOSITOR. Lordes, this speach is so
  veray
That to expound it to your pay[4]
It needes nothing in good faye,
 This speach is so expresse.
Each man by it knowe may
That of the Ascension, soth to saie,
David prophesied in his daye,
 As yt rehearsed was.   376

IOELL. *Effundam de spiritu meo super omnem carnem, et prophetabunt filij vestri.*

I, Ioell, saie this sickerlye:
That my Ghost send will I
Upon mankinde merciably
 From heaven, sitting in see;[5]
Then shold [y]our childre prophesie,
Ould men meet swevens,[6] wytterly,
Yong se sightes that therby
 Many wise shall be.   384

EXPOSITOR. Lordinges, this prophet
  speakes here
In Gods person, as it were,
And prophesies that he will apeare
 Ghostlie to mankinde.
This signes non other, in good faye,
But of his deede on Whitson-day,
Sending his Ghost, that we ever may
 On hym haue sadlie mynd.   392

MICHEAS. *Tu, Bethlem, terra Iuda, nequaquam minima es in principibus Iuda; ex te enim exiet Dux qui reget populum meum Israell.*

I, Micheal, through my mynde
Will saye that man shall sothlie[7] finde
That a childe of kinges kinde
 In Bethlem shall be borne,

---

[1] Truly.   [2] Maid.   [3] Clearly.

[1] Together, combined.   [2] Judge.
[3] *Kittredge:* scape then.
[4] Satisfaction.   [5] Throne.
[6] Dreams. MS. sweens; *corr. by Deimling.*
[7] Truly.

That shall be duke to dight and deale,
And rule the folke of Israell,
Also wyn againe mankindes heale [1]
    That through Adam was lorne.   400

EXPOSITOR. Lordinges, two thinges apert-
    lie
You may see in this prophesie:
The place certifies thee sothlie
    Where Christ borne will be;
And after his ending, sickerlie,
Of his deedes of great mercy,
That he shold sit soveraynly
    In heauen, thereas is he.   408

Moe prophetis, lordinges, we might play,
But yt wold tary much the daye;
Therfore six, sothe to say,
    Are played in this place.
Twoo speakes of his Incarnation;
An-other of Christe[s] Passion;
The fourth of the Resurrection.
                416

The fifte speakes expreslie
How he from the highest heavenlye
Light into earth us to forby,[3]
    And after thydder steigh [4]
With oure kinde to heaven-blisse.
More loue might he not shew, i-wis,
But right there-as hym-selfe is
    He haunshed [5] our kinde on high.   424

[1] Salvation, happiness.
[2] Line missing in all MSS.
[3] Redeem.   [4] Ascended.   [5] Exalted.

The sixt shewes, you may see,
His Goste to man send will he,
More stidfast that they shalbe
    To loue God evermore.
Thus that beleve [1] that leven we
Of Gods deedes that had pittye
One man, when that he made them
    free,
    Is prophesied here before.   432

BALAACK. Goe we forth! It is no
    boote
Longer with this man to moote; [2]
For God of Iewes is crop and roote,
    And lord of heaven and hell.
Now see I well no man on lyue
Gaynes with him for to stryve;
Therefore here, as mot I thryue,
    I will no longer dwell.   440

[Exeunt the Prophets, led by Balaack.]

EXPOSITOR. Lordinges, much more mat-
    ter
Is in this story then you see here;
But the substance, without were,[3]
    Is played you beforne.
And by these prophesies, leav [4] you me,
Three kinges, as you shall played see,
Presented at his Nativitye
    Christ, when he was borne.   448

    Finis paginæ quintæ.

[1] Belief. MS. beleven; *corr. by Manly.*
[2] Argue.   [3] Doubt.   [4] Believe.

THE SALUTATION AND CONCEPTION [1]

[Acted at N. towne.]

[On the upper stage God, his Son, the Holy Spirit, Gabriel, and others; on the lower stage Mary.]

PATER.   From vs, God, aungel Gabryel, thou xalt be sende
In to the countre of Galyle
(The name of the cyte Nazareth is kende) [1]
To a mayd.   W[e]ddyd to a man is she,
Of whom the name is Joseph, se,
Of the hous of Davyd bore;
The name of the mayd ffre
Is Mary, that xal al restore.   196

FILIUS.   Say that she is with-owte wo, and ful of grace;
And that I, the Son of the Godhed, of here xal be bore. [2]
Hyghe the thou were there a pace,
Ellys we xal be there the be-ffore,
I haue so grett hast to be man thore
In that mekest and purest virgyne.
Sey here, she xal restore
Of yow aungellys the grett ruyne.   204

SPIRITUS SANCTUS.   And if she aske the how it myth be,
Telle here, I, the Holy Gost, xal werke al this;
Sche xal be savyd thorwe oure vnyte.
In tokyn, here bareyn cosyn Elyzabeth is
Qwyk with childe in here grett age, i-wys.
Sey here, to vs is no thynge impossyble.
Here body xal be so ful-fylt with blys
That she xal sone thynke this sonde [3] credyble.   212

GABRIEL.   In thyn hey inbassett, [4] Lord, I xal go;

It xal be do with a thought.
Be-holde now, Lord, I go here to,
I take my fflyth, and byde nowth.   216

[Gabriel descends, and approaches Mary.]
Ave, Maria, gratia plena, Dominus tecum!
Heyl, fful of grace!   God is with the!
Amonge alle women blyssyd art thu.
Here this name "Eva" is turnyd "Aue";
That is to say, with-owte sorwe ar ye now.   220

Thow sorwe in yow hath no place,
Yett of joy, lady, ye nede more;
Therfore I adde and sey "fful of grace,"
For so ful of grace was nevyr non bore.
Yett who hath grace, he nedyth kepyng sore;
Therfore I sey "God is with the,"
Whiche xal kepe yow endlesly thore.
So amonge alle women blyssyd are ye!   228

MARIA.   A! mercy, God! this is a mervelyous herynge!
In the aungelys wordys I am trobelyd her;
I thynk, "How may be this gretynge?"
Aungelys dayly to me doth aper,
But not in the lyknes of man; that is my fer.
And also thus hyghly to comendyd be,
I [1] am most vn-wuthry.   I can-not answere.
Grett shamfastnes and grett dred is in me.   236

GABYREL.   Mary, in this take ye no drede,
For at God grace ffownde haue ye.
Ye xal conceyve in your wombe, in dede,
A childe, the sone of the Trynyte.
His name of yow Jhesu clepyd [2] xal be;

[1] Known.   [2] Born.
[3] Message.   (MS. sownde.)   [4] Embassy.
[1] MS. &.   [2] Called.

[1] For an account of the N. towne Plays see page 81, note 2.   I have based the present text on the editions by Block and Halliwell, compared with the edition by Manly (whose stanzaic form I have adopted).   I have omitted the long prologue of 188 lines, entitled by Block "The Parliament of Heaven," in which Contemplation, the Virtues, Veritas, Misericordia, Justicia, Pax, Pater, Filius, and Spiritus Sanctus discuss the salvation of man.   The prologue is of some interest as showing the influence of allegory on the Corpus Christi plays; but this influence has already been illustrated in the Norwich *Creation* printed on page 88.

He xal be grett, the son of the hyest clepyd
    of kende; [1]
And of his ffadyr, Davyd, the Lord xal
    geve hym the se, [2]
Reynyng in the hous of Jacob, of whiche
    regne xal be no ende.   244

MARIA.   Aungel, I sey to yow,
    In what manere of wyse xal this be?
For knowyng of man I haue non now;
    I haue evyr more kept, and xal, my vir-
      ginyte.
I dowte not the wordys ye han seyd to me,
But I aske how it xal be do.
    GABRYEL.   The Holy Gost xal come fro
    a-bove to the,
And the vertu of hym Hyest xal schadu the
    so;   252
Ther fore that Holy Gost of the xal be bore;
    He xal be clepyd the Son of God sage.
And se, Elyzabeth, your cosyn thore,
    She hath conseyvid a son in hyre age;
This is the sexte monyth of here passage,
Of here that clepyd was bareyn.
    No thynge is impossyble to Goddys
      vsage.
They thynkyth longe to here what ye wyl
    seyn.   260

*Here the aungel makyth a lytyl restynge,
and Mary be-holdyth hym; and the aungel
seythe:*

Mary, com of, and haste the,
    And take hede in thyn entent
How [3] the Holy Gost, — blyssyd he be! —
    A-bydyth thin answere and thin assent.
Thorwe wyse werke of dyvinyte
    The Secunde Persone, verament,
Is mad man by fraternyte
    With-inne thi self, in place present. 268

Ferther more, take hede this space
    How [3] alle the blyssyd spyrytys of vertu
That are in hefne by-ffore Goddys face,
    And alle the gode levers and trew
That are here in this erthely place,
    Thyn owyn kynrede, the sothe ho [4] knew,
And the chosyn sowlys this tyme of grace
    That are in helle and byde [ther]
    rescu, —   276

As Adam, Abraham and Davyd, in fere, [1]
    And many othere of good reputacion, —
That thin answere desyre to here
    And thin assent to the Incarnacion,
In whiche thou standyst as preserver, [2]
    Of alle man-kende savacion.
Gyff me myn answere now, lady dere, 283
    To alle these creaturys comfortacion.

MARIA.   With alle mekenes I clyne [3] to
    this a-corde,
Bowynge downe my face with alle be-
      nyngnyte.
Se here the hand-mayden of oure Lorde.
    Aftyr thi worde be it don to me.
GABRYEL.   Gramercy, my lady ffre;
Gramercy of your answere on hyght;
    Gramercy of your grett humylyte;
Gramercy, ye lanterne off lyght!   292

*Here the Holy Gost discendit with iij
bemys to Our Lady; the Sone of the Godhed next [4] with iij bemys to the Holy Gost;
the Fadyr Godly with iij bemys to the Sone:
and so entre alle thre to here bosom; and
Mary seyth:*

MARIA.   A! now I ffele in my body be
    Parfyte God and parfyte man,
Havyng al schappe of chyldly carnalyte.
    Evyn al at onys, thus God be-gan; 296

Nott takynge ffyrst o [5] membyr and sythe [6]
    a-nother,
But parfyte childhod ye haue a-non.
Of your hand-mayden now ye haue mad
    your modyr,
With-owte peyne, in fflesche and bon.
Thus conceyved nevyr woman non
That evyr was beynge in this lyff.
    O, myn hyest Fadyr, in your trone,
It is worthy your Son — now my son —
    haue a prerogatyff!   304

I can not telle what joy, what blysse,
    Now I fele in my body!
Aungel Gabryel, I thank yow for thys.
    Most mekely recomende me to my
    Faderys mercy.

----

[1] Kind.   [2] Throne.
[3] MS. whow.   [4] Who.

[1] Likewise.
[2] MS. persevere, *corr. by Manly.*
[3] Incline.
[4] MS. nest, *corr. by Manly.*
[5] One.   [6] Then.

To haue be the modyr of God fful lytyl
   wend [1] I.
Now myn cosyn Elyzabeth ffayn wold I se,
   How sohe hath conseyvid as ye dede
   specyfy.
Now blyssyd be the hygh Trynyte!   312

GABRYEL.   Fare weyl, turtyl, Goddys
   dowtere dere!
Fare wel, Goddys modyr! I the honowre!
Fare wel, Goddys sustyr and his pleynge
   fere! [2]
   Fare wel, Goddys chawmere [3] and his
     bowre!   316

MARIA.   Fare wel, Gabryel, specyalye!
Fare wel, Goddys masangere expresse!
I thank yow for your traveyl hye;
   Gramercy of your grett goodnes,   320

And namely of your comfortabyl massage.
For I vndyrstande, by inspyracion,
That ye knowe by syngulere preuylage [4]
   Most of my sonys Incarnacion.
I pray yow take it in to vsage,
   Be a custom ocupacion,
To vesyte me ofte be mene passage;
   Your presence is my comfortacion.   328

      [1] Thought.   [2] Companion.
      [3] Chamber.   [4] Privilege.

GABRIEL.   At your wyl, lady, so xal it be.
Ye gentyllest of blood and hyest of kyn-
   rede
That reynyth in earth in ony degre,
   Be pryncypal incheson [1] of the God-
     hede,   332

I comende me on to yow, thou trone of
   the Trinyte.
   O mekest mayde, now the modyr of
     Jhesu!
Qwen of Hefne, Lady of Erth, and Empres
   of Helle be ye;
   Socour to alle synful that wole to yow
     sew; [2]
   Thour your body beryth the babe oure
     blysse xal renew.
To yow, modyr of mercy, most mekely I
   recomende.
   And, as I began, I ende, with an "Ave!"
     new,
Enjonyd hefne and erth. With that I as-
   cende.   [Exit.] 340

    Angels singing this hymn: [3]

    Ave, Maria, gratia plena!
    Dominus tecum, uirgo serena!

  [1] Cause.
  [2] Sue, petition.
  [3] MS. *Angeli cantando istam sequenciam.*

THE BIRTH OF JESUS [1]

[Acted by the Tile Thatchers of York.]

[Joseph and Mary, in a cattle-shed at Bethlehem.]

JOSEPH.   All-weldand [1] God in Trinite,
I praye the, Lord, for thy grete myght,
Vnto thy symple seruand see,
Here in this place where we are pight,[2]   4
   Oure self allone.
Lord, graunte vs gode herberow [3] this nyght
   Within this wone.[4]   7

For we haue sought both vppe and doune,
Thurgh diuerse stretis in this cite,
So mekill pepull is comen to towne
That we can nowhare herbered be,
   Ther is slike [5] prees.   12
For-suthe I can no socoure see
But belde [6] vs with there bestes.

And yf we here all nyght abide,
We shall be stormed [7] in this steede: [8]   16
The walles are doune on ilke a side,
The ruffe is rayned [9] aboven oure hede,
   Als haue I roo. [10]
Say, Marie doughtir, what is thy rede? [11]   20
   How sall we doo?

For in grete nede nowe are we stedde,
As thou thy selffe the soth may see;
For here is nowthir cloth ne bedde,   24
And we are weyke and all werie,
   And fayne wolde rest.
Now, gracious God, for thy mercie
   Wisse [12] vs the best.   28

MARY.   God will vs wisse, full wele witt ye;
Ther-fore, Joseph, be of gud chere,
For in this place borne will he be

That sall vs saue fro sorowes sere,[1]   32
   Bothe even and morne.
Sir, witt ye wele the tyme is nere
   Hee will be borne.

JOSEPH.   Than behoves vs bide here stille   36
Here in this same place all this nyght.
MARY.   Ya, sir, forsuth, it is Goddis will.
JOSEPH.   Than wolde I fayne we had sum light,
   What so befall.   40
It waxis right myrke [2] vnto my sight,
   And colde withall.

I will go gete vs light for-thy,   43
And fewell [3] fande with me to bryng.
MARY.   All-weldand God yow gouerne and gy [4]
As he is sufferayne of all thyng
   Fo[r] his grete myght,
And lende me grace to his louyng   48
   That I me dight.[5]

[Exit Joseph.]

Now in my sawle grete ioie haue I!
I am all cladde in comforte clere!
Now will be borne of my body   52
Both God and man to-gedir in feere.[6]
   Blist mott he be!
Jesu, my son that is so dere,
   Nowe borne is he.   56

[Mary worships the babe.]

Hayle, my Lord God!   Hayle, prince of pees!
Hayle, my fadir! and hayle, my sone!
Hayle, souereyne sege [7] all synnes to sesse! [8]   59
Hayle, God and man in erth to wonne! [9]

---

¹ All-ruling.   ² Pitched, set.
³ Harborage, lodging.   ⁴ Dwelling, house.
⁵ Such.   ⁶ Shelter.
⁷ Subject to the storms.   ⁸ Place.
⁹ Rain-soaked? Ruined?
¹⁰ As have I peace (a mild oath).
¹¹ Advice.   ¹² Direct, guide.

¹ Many.   ² Dark.
³ Fuel.   ⁴ Guide.
⁵ Make ready.   ⁶ In company, united.
⁷ Warrior (against Satan).
⁸ Put an end to.   ⁹ Dwell.

---

¹ Printed from *York Plays*, edited by Lucy Toulmin Smith, 1885. I have expanded abbreviations, altered the punctuation, and added stage directions.

Hayle! thurgh whos myht
All this worlde was first be-gonne,
  Merknes and light.
Sone, as I am sympill sugett [1] of thyne,
Vowchesaffe, swete sone, I pray the,   65
That I myght the take in the[r] armys of
  myne,
And in this poure wede [2] to arraie the.
  Graunte me thi blisse!   68
As I am thy modir chosen to be
  In sothfastness.

[*Joseph speaks without.*]

JOSEPH.   A! Lorde, what the wedir is
  colde!
The fellest freese that euere I felyd!
I pray God helpe tham that is alde,   73
And namely tham that is vnwelde,[3]
  So may I saie.
Now, gud God, thou be my belde
  As thou best may.   77

[*The star blazes above.*]

A! Lord God! what light is this
That comes shynyng thus sodenly?
I can not saie, als haue I blisse.   80
When I come home vn-to Marie
  Than sall I spirre.[4]
A! here be God, for now come I.

[*Enters the shed.*]

MARY.   Ye ar welcum, sirre.   84
JOSEPH.   Say, Marie doghtir, what chere
  with the?
MARIE.   Right goode, Joseph, as has been
  ay.
JOSEPH.   O Marie! what swete thyng is
  that on thy kne?   87
MARY.   It is my sone, the soth to saye,
  That is so gud.
JOSEPH.   Wele is me I bade this day
  To se this foode! [5]

Me merueles mekill of this light   92
That thus-gates shynes in this place.
For-suth it is a selcouth [6] sight!
MARY.   This has he ordand of his grace,
  My sone so ying,   96
A starne to be schynyng a space
  At his bering.[7]

For Balam told ful longe be-forne
How that a sterne shuld rise full hye; 100
And of a maiden shulde be borne
A sonne that sall oure saffyng [1] be
  Fro caris kene.
For-suth it is my sone so free   104
  Be whame Balam gon meene.

JOSEPH.   Now welcome, floure fairest of
  hewe!
I shall the menske [2] with mayne and myght.
Hayle, my maker! Hayle, Crist Jesu!
Hayle, riall kyng, roote of all right!
  Hayle, saueour!
Hayle, my Lord, lemer [3] of light!
  Hayle, blessid floure!   112

MARY.   Now, Lord, that all this worlde
  schall wynne
(To the, my sone, is that I saye),
Here is no bedde to laye the inne;
Therfore, my dere sone, I the praye,   116
  Sen it is soo,
Here in this cribbe I myght the lay
  Betwene ther bestis two.

And I sall happe [4] the, myn owne dere
  childe,   120
With such clothes as we haue here.
JOSEPH.   O Marie, beholde thes beestis
  mylde!
They make louyng in ther manere
  As thei wer men.   124
For-sothe it semes wele be ther chere
  Thare Lord thei ken.

MARY.   Ther Lorde thai kenne, that wote
  I wele;
They worshippe hym with myght and
  mayne.   128
The wedir is colde, as ye may feele;
To halde hym warme thei are full fayne
  With thare warme breth,
And oondis [5] on hym, is noght to layne, [6]
  To warm hym with.   133

O, nowe slepis my sone! Blist mot he be!

---

[1] Saving, salvation. MS. saffyne.
[2] Honor, worship.
[3] Beamer (shedder of light).
[4] Wrap up.   [5] Breathe.
[6] Is nought to conceal, obviously (see N.E.D.,
Lain, *v. trans.*).

---

[1] Subject.   [2] Garment.   [3] Infirm.   [4] Inquire.
[5] Creature, child.   [6] Wonderful.   [7] Birth.

And lyes full warme ther bestis by-twene.
JOSEPH.   O, now is fulfilled, for-suth I see,
That Abacuc in mynde gon mene   137
   And preched by prophicie:
He saide oure sauyoure shall be sene
   Betwene bestis lye.   140

And nowe I see the same in sight.
MARY.   Ya, sir, for-suth, the same is he.
JOSEPH.   Honnoure and worshippe both
   day and nyght,
Ay-lastand Lorde, be done to the   144

   All way, as is worthy.
And, Lord, to thy seruice I oblissh [1] me
   With all myn herte holy.
MARY.   Thou mercyfull maker, most
   myghty,   148
My God, my Lord, my sone so free,
Thy hande-mayden, for-soth, am I,
And to thi seruice I oblissh me
   With all myn herte entere.   152
Thy blissing, beseke I thee,
   Thou graunte vs all in feere!

     [1] Oblige, bind.

THE SHEPHERDS [1]

[Acted at Wakefield.]

[*At one end of the pageant, the open fields
where the three Shepherds tend their sheep;
at the other end, the home of Mak and his
wife Gill. Enter the First Shepherd, half
frozen with the cold.*]

1. PASTOR. Lord, what these weders ar
    cold! / And I am yll happyd.[1]
I am nere-hande dold,[2] / so long haue I
    nappyd.
My legys thay fold, / my fyngers ar
    chappyd;
It is not as I wold, / for I am al lappyd
    In sorow.   5
In stormes and tempest,
Now in the eest, now in the west,
Wo is hym has neuer rest
    Myd-day nor morow!   9

Bot we sely [3] shepardes / that walkys on
    the moore,
In fayth, we are nere-handys / outt of the
    doore!
No wonder, as it standys, / if we be poore,
For the tylthe of oure landys / lyys falow
    as the floore,
    As ye ken.   14
We ar so hamyd,[4]
For-taxed, and ramyd,[5]
We ar mayde hand-tamyd
    With thyse gentlery men.   18

Thus thay refe [6] vs oure reste   / — Oure
    Lady theym wary![7]
These men that ar lord-fest [8] / thay cause
    the ploghe tary.
That, men say, is for the best; / we fynde it
    contrary.

Thus ar husbandys opprest / in po[i]nte to
    myscary
    On lyfe.   23
Thus hold thay vs hunder;
Thus thay bryng vs in blonder!
It were greatte wonder
    And euer shuld we thryfe.   27

Ther shall com a swane [1] / as prowde as a
    po, [2]
He must borow my wane,[3] / my ploghe
    also;
Then I am full fane / to graunt or he go.
Thus lyf we in payne, / anger, and wo,
    By nyght and day.   32
He must haue if he langyd,
If I shuld forgang [4] it.
I were better be hangyd
    Then oones say hym nay.[5]   36

For may he gett a paynt slefe,[6] / or a
    broche, now on dayes,
Wo is hym that hym grefe / or onys agane
    says!
Dar noman hym reprefe / what mastry he
    mays.
And yit may noman lefe [7] / oone word that
    he says,
    No letter.   41
He can make purveance,
With boste and bragance;
And all is thrugh mantenance
    Of men that are gretter.   45

It dos me good, as I walk / thus by myn
    oone,[8]
Of this warld for to talk / in maner of mone.

[1] Clothed.   [2] Nearly numb.
[3] Poor, miserable.   [4] Crippled.
[5] Over-taxed and crushed.   [6] Rob.
[7] Curse.   [8] Lord-fast, bound to a lord.

[1] Swain, gallant.   [2] Peacock.
[3] Wagon.   [4] Have to do without it.
[5] This and the following stanza are transposed in
the MS.
[6] Sleeve.   [7] Believe.   [8] Self.

[1] For an account of the Towneley Plays, and the source of the present text, see page 94, note 1.   This play,
which Mr. Pollard describes as "perfect as a work of art," is generally regarded as the finest example of comedy in the early religious drama.   In the Towneley manuscript there are two plays dealing with the visit of
the Shepherds to the manger, labeled respectively *Incipit Pagina Pastorum* and *Incipit Alia Eorundum*.   Mr.
Pollard suggests that in the *Prima Pastorum* the author was "only feeling his way," and that in the *Secunda
Pastorum* he has achieved his masterpiece.   As the footnotes will indicate, I am frequently indebted to Manly
for textual emendations.

To my shepe wyll I stalk / and herkyn
    anone;
Ther abyde on a balk,[1] / or sytt on a stone,
    Full soyne.   50
For I trowe, perde,
Trew men if thay be,
We gett more compane
    Or it be noyne.[2]   54

    [*Enter the Second Shepherd. He does not
    see the First Shepherd.*]

II.   PASTOR.   Benste and Dominus! /
    What may this bemeyne?
Why fares this warld thus?   / Oft haue
    we not sene!
Lord, thyse weders are spytus, / and the
    winds[3] full kene;
And the frostys so hydus / thay water myn
    eeyne;
    No ly.   59
Now in dry, now in wete,
Now in snaw, now in slete,
When my shone freys to my fete,
    It is not all esy.   63

Bot, as far as I ken, / or yit as I go,
We sely wedmen / dre mekyll wo;
We haue sorow then and then,[4] / it fallys
    oft so.
Sely Capyle, oure hen, / both to and fro
    She kakyls;   68
Bot begyn she to crok,
To groyne or [to clo]k,
Wo is hym[5] oure cok,
    For he is in the shekyls.[6]   72

These men that ar wed / haue not all thare
    wyll.
When they ar full hard sted,[7] / thay sygh
    full styll.
God wayte[8] thay ar led / full hard and full
    yll;
In bower nor in bed / thay say noght ther-
    tll.[9]
    This tyde,   77
My parte haue I fun —
I know my lesson! —

[1] Ridge.   [2] Noon.
[3] MS. weders; *suggested by Manly.*
[4] Continually.
[5] MS. hym is of; *corr. by Manly.*
[6] Shackles.   [7] Situated.
[8] Knows.   [9] Thereto.

Wo is hym that is bun,[1]
    For he must abyde.   81

Bot now late in oure lyfys — / a meruell to
    me,
That I thynk my hart ryfys / sich wonders
    to see,
What that destany dryfys, / it shuld so
    be! —
Som men wyll have two wyfys, / and som
    men thre
    In store.   86
Som ar wo that has any!
Bot so far can I, —
Wo is hym that has many,
    For he felys sore.   90

    [*Addressing the audience.*]

Bot, yong men, of wowyng, / for God that
    you boght,
Be well war of wedyng, / and thynk in
    youre thoght,
"Had I wyst" is a thyng / it seruys of
    noght.
Mekyll[2] styll mowrnyng / has wedyng
    home broght,
    And grefys,   95
With many a sharp showre;
For thou may cach in an owre
That shall [savour] fulle sowre
    As long as thou lyffys.   99

For, as euer red I pystyll,[3] / I haue oone to
    my fere,[4]
As sharp as a thystyll, / as rugh as a
    brere;
She is browyd lyke a brystyll, / with a
    sowre-lotcn chere;
Had she oones wett hyr whystyll, / she
    couth syng full clere
    Hyr Pater Noster.   104
She is as greatt as a whall;
She has a galon of gall;
By hym that dyed for vs all,
    I wald I had ryn to I had lost hir!   108

    [*The First Shepherd interrupts him.*]

I.   PASTOR.   God! looke ouer the raw![5] /
    Full defly ye stand.

[1] Bound.   [2] Much.
[3] Epistle, i.e. in the New Testament.
[4] Companion.   [5] Row.

II. PASTOR.   Yee, the dewill in thi maw, /
so tariand!
Sagh thou awro [1] of Daw? /
I. PASTOR.   Yee, on a ley-land
Hard I hym blaw. / He commys here at
hand
Not far.   113
Stand styll.
II. PASTOR.   Qwhy?
I. PASTOR.   For he commys, hope I.
II. PASTOR.   He wyll make vs both a ly
Bot if we be war.[2]   117

[Enter the Third Shepherd, a boy.]

III. PASTOR.   Crystys crosse me spede, /
and Sant Nycholas!
Ther-of had I nede; / it is wars then it was.
Whose couthe take hede / and lett the
warld pas,
It is euer in drede / and brekyll as glas,
    And slythys.[3]   122
This warld fowre [4] neuer so,
With meruels mo and mo,
Now in weyll, now in wo,
    And all thyng wrythys.[5]   126

Was neuer syn Noe floode / sich floodys
seyn,
Wyndys and ranys so rude, / and stormes
so keyn!
Som stamerd, som stod / in dowte, as I
weyn.
Now God turne all to good! / I say as I
mene,
    For ponder.   131
These floodys so thay drowne,
Both in feyldys and in towne,
And berys all downe;
    And that is a wonder.   135

We that walk on the nyghtys / oure catell to kepe,
We se sodan syghtys / when othere men
slepe. [Spying the others.]
Yit me-thynk my hart lyghtys;[6] / I se
shrewys pepe.
Ye ar two [t]all [7] wyghtys! / I wyll gyf my
shepe

A turne.   140
Bot full yll haue I ment;
As I walk on this bent,
I may lyghtly repent,
    My toes if I spurne.   144

[The other two advance.]

A, sir, God you saue! / and master
myne!
A drynk fayn wold I haue, / and somwhat
to dyne.
I. PASTOR.   Crystys curs, my knaue, / thou
art a ledyr hyne! [1]
II. PASTOR.   What! the boy lyst rave! /
Abyde vnto syne [2]
We haue mayde it.   149
Yll thryft on thy pate!
Though the shrew cam late,
Yit is he in state
    To dyne — if he had it.   153

III. PASTOR.   Sich seruandys as I, / that
swettys and swynkys,[3]
Etys oure brede full dry; / and that me
forthynkys.[4]
We ar oft weytt and wery / when master-
men wynkys; [5]
Yit commys full lately / both dyners and
drynkys.
    Bot nately   158
Both oure dame and oure syre,
When we haue ryn in the myre,
Thay can nyp at oure hyre,
    And pay vs full lately.   162

Bot here my trouth, master: / for the fayr
that ye make,[6]
I shall do therafter, — / wyrk as I take; [7]
I shall do a lytyll, sir, / and emang euer
lake; [8]
For yit lay my soper / neuer on my
stomake
    In feyldys.   167
Wherto shuld I threpe? [9]
With my staf can I lepe;
And men say "Lyght chepe [10]
    Letherly [11] for-yeldys." 171

---

[1] Anywhere.   [2] Wary.
[3] Slides.   [4] Fared, went.
[5] Writhes.   [6] Lightens.
[7] Fine. MS. all; em. by Kittredge.

[1] Worthless hind.   [2] Until after.
[3] Toil.   [4] Displeases.   [5] Sleep.
[6] Food that you supply.   [7] Receive.
[8] Play, sport.   [9] Argue.
[10] Cheap bargain.   [11] Badly.

I. Pastor.   Thou were an yll lad / to ryde
on wowyng
With a man that had / bot lytyll of spend-
yng.
II. Pastor.   Peasse, boy, I bad! /   No
more iangling,
Or I shall make the full rad,[1] / by the heu-
ens kyng,
    With thy gawdys.[2]   176
Wher ar oure shepe, boy?   We skorne.
III. Pastor.   Sir, this same day at morne
I thaym left in the corne,
    When thay rang lawdys.[3]   180

They haue pasture good, / thay can not go
    wrong.
I. Pastor.   That is right.   By the roode,
    / thyse nyghtys ar long!
Yit I wold, or we yode,[4] / oone gaf vs a
    song.
II. Pastor.   So I thoght as I stode, / to
myrth vs emong.
    III. Pastor.   I grauntt.   185
I. Pastor.   Lett me syng the tenory.
II. Pastor.   And I the tryble so hye.
III. Pastor.   Then the meyne fallys to
me.   188
    Lett se how ye chauntt.   [They sing.]

*Then Mak enters with a cloak drawn over his
tunic.[5]*

Mak.   Now, Lord, for thy naymes sevyn,
    / that made both moyn and starnes
Well mo then I can neuen,[6] / thi will,
    Lorde, of me tharnys.[7]
I am all vneuen; / that moves oft my
    harnes.[8]
Now wold God I were in heuen, / for
    the[re] wepe no barnes[9]
So styll.[10]   194
I. Pastor.   Who is that pypys so poore?
Mak.   Wold God ye wyst how I foore!
Lo, a man that walkys on the moore,
And has not all his wyll!   198

II. Pastor.   Mak, where has thou gon? /
    tell vs tythyng.

III. Pastor.   Is he commen?   Then
    ylkon[1] / take hede to his thyng.

He takes the cloak from him.[2]

Mak.   What! ich[3] be a yoman, / I[ch] tell
    you, of the king;
The self and the same, / sond from a greatt
    lordyng,
    And sich.   203
Fy on you! Goyth hence!
Out of my presence!
I[ch] must haue reuerence.
    Why, who be ich?   207

I. Pastor.   Why make ye it so qwaynt?[4]
    Mak, ye do wrang.
II. Pastor.   Bot, Mak, lyst ye saynt?[5] / I
    trow that ye lang.[6]
III. Pastor.   I trow the shrew can paynt![7]
    / The dewyll myght hym hang!
Mak.   Ich shall make complaynt, / and
    make you all to thwang[8]
At a worde;   212
And tell euyn how ye doth.
I. Pastor.   Bot, Mak, is that sothe?
Now take outt that sothren tothe,
    And sett in a torde!   216

II. Pastor.   Mak, the dewill in youre ee! /
    A stroke wold I leyne[9] you.
                                 [Strikes him.]
III. Pastor.   Mak, know ye not me? / By
    God, I couthe teyn[10] you.
                        [Drawing back to strike him.]
Mak.   God, looke you all thre! / Me
    thoght I had sene you.
Ye ar a fare compane. /
I. Pastor.   Can ye now mene[11] you?
    II. Pastor.   Shrew[d] iape![12]   221
Thus late as thou goys,
What wyll men suppos?
And thou has an yll noys[13]
    Of stelyng of shepe.   225

Mak.   And I am trew as steyll; / all men
    waytt![14]

---

[1] Afraid.   [2] Tricks.
[3] Lauds, the first of the day hours of the Church.
[4] Went.
[5] MS. *Tunc intrat Mak in clamide se super togam
-estitus.*
[6] Name.   [7] Lacks.   [8] Brains.
[9] Children, babes.   [10] Continuously.

[1] Every one.   [2] MS. *Et accipit clamidem ab ipso.*
[3] I. Mak, in his attempt to deceive the shepherds,
adopts the Southern pronunciation (cf. l. 215).
[4] Strange.   [5] *Qy.*: faynt, feint, deceive.
[6] Long to do so.   [7] Act, deceive.
[8] Be flogged.   [9] Lend.
[10] Injure.   [11] Remember yourself (*qy.*: demean).
[12] Shrewd jest.   [13] Reputation.   [14] Know.

Bot a sekenes I feyll / that haldys me full
    haytt; [1]
My belly farys not weyll, / it is out of
    astate.
III. PASTOR. Seldom lyys the dewyll /
    dede by the gate! [2]
MAK. Therfor   230
Full sore am I and yll;
If I stande stone styll,
I ete not an nedyll
    Thys moneth and more.   234

I. PASTOR. How farys thi wyff? by my
    hoode, / how farys sho?
MAK. Lyys walteryng, [3] by the roode, /
    by the fyere, lo!
And a howse full of brude. [4] / She drynkys
    well, to;
Yll spede othere good / that she wyll do
    Bot so!   239
Etys as fast as she can;
And ilk [5] yere that commys to man
She bryngys furth a lakan, [6] —
    And som yeres two.   243

Bot were I not more gracyus / and rychere
    be far,
I were eten outt of howse / and of harbar.
Yit is she a fowll dowse [7] / if ye com nar;
Ther is none that trowse / nor knowys a
    war [8]
    Then ken I.   248
Now wyll ye se what I profer?
To gyf all in my cofer
To-morne at next [9] to offer
    Hyr hed-mas penny. [10]   252

II. PASTOR. I wote so forwakyd [11] / is
    none in this shyre.
I wold slepe, if I takyd / les to my hyere.
III. PASTOR. I am cold and nakyd, / and
    wold haue a fyere.
I. PASTOR. I am wery, for-rakyd, [11] / and
    run in the myre. [12]
    Wake thou!   257
II. PASTOR. Nay, I wyll lyg downe by,
For I must slepe, truly.

III. PASTOR. As good a mans son was I
As any of you.   261

Bot, Mak, com heder! Betwene / shall
    thou lyg downe.
MAK. Then myght I lett [1] you, bedene, [2] /
    of that ye wold rowne, [3]
....
..................................[4]

[They lie down.]

[MAK.] No dred.
Fro my top to my too,
Manus tuas commendo,
Poncio Pilato,
    Cryst crosse me spede!   268

Then he rises up, the shepherds being asleep,
and says: [5]

Now were tyme for a man / that lakkys
    what he wold
To stalk preuely than / vnto a fold,
And neemly [6] to wyrk than, / and be not to
    bold,
For he might aby the bargan, / if it were
    told,
    At the endyng.   273
Now were tyme for to reyll; [7]
Bot he nedys good counsell
That fayn wold fare weyll,
    And has bot lytyll spendyng.   277

[Pretends to be a magician.]

Bot abowte you a serkyll [8] / as rownde as
    a moyn, [9]
To I haue done that I wyll, / tyll that it be
    noyn, [10]
That ye lyg stone styll / to that I haue
    doyne.
And I shall say thertyll / of good wordys a
    foyne [11]
    On hight.   282
Ouer youre heydys my hand I lyft:
Outt go youre een! Fordo your syght! —
Bot yit I must make better shyft
    And it be right.   286

---

[1] Hot.   [2] Road.   [3] Lolling.
[4] Children.   [5] Every.   [6] Baby.
[7] Slut.   [8] Worse.
[9] The following morning.
[10] For her funeral.
[11] Worn out, tired.   [12] Tired.

[1] Hinder.   [2] Indeed.
[3] Whisper.   [4] A lacuna in the MS.
[5] MS. *Tunc surgit, pastoribus dormientibus, et dicit.*
[6] Nimbly.   [7] Set about it.
[8] Circle.   [9] Moon.
[10] Noon.   [11] Few.

[The shepherds begin to snore.]

Lord, what! thay slepe hard! / that may ye
  all here.
Was I neuer a shepard, / bot now wyll I
  lere.[1]
If the flok be skard, / yit shall I nyp nere.

[He approaches the sheep.]

How! Drawes hederward! / Now mendys
  oure chere
  From sorow.   291
A fatt shepe I dar say!
A good flese dar I lay!
Eft-whyte [2] when I may,
  Bot this will I borow.   295

[Takes the sheep, and crosses to his home.]

How, Gyll, art thou in? / Gett vs som
  lyght.
Vxor eius. Who makys sich dyn / this
  tyme of the nyght?
I am sett for to spyn; / I hope not I myght
Ryse a penny to wyn. / I shrew them on
  hight
  So farys!   300
A huswyff that has bene
To be rasyd [3] thus betwene!
Here may no note [4] be sene
  For sich small charys.[5]   304

Mak. Good wyff, open the hek! [6] / Seys
  thou not what I bryng?
Vxor. I may thole [7] the dray the snek.[8] /
  A, com in, my swetyng!
Mak. Yee, thou thar not rek [9] / of my
  long standyng.
Vxor. By the nakyd nek / art thou lyke
  for to hyng.
Mak. Do way!   309
I am worthy my mete;
For in a strate can I gett
More then thay that swynke and swette
  All the long day.   313

Thus it fell to my lott, / Gyll! I had sich
  grace.

[1] Learn.   [2] Repay.
[3] Has to be aroused.
[4] Work.   [5] Chores.
[6] Door.   [7] Suffer.
[8] Draw the latch.
[9] Took no thought.

[He shows her the sheep.]

Vxor. It were a fowll blott / to be hanged
  for the case.
Mak. I haue skapyd, Ielott, / oft as hard
  a glase.[1]
Vxor. Bot so long goys the pott / to the
  water, men says,
  At last   318
Comys it home broken.
Mak. Well knowe I the token;
Bot let it neuer be spoken,
  Bot com and help fast.   322

I wold he were slayn; / I lyst well ete.
This twelmo[n]the was I not so fayn / of
  oone shepe mete.
Vxor. Com thay or he be slayn / and
  here the shepe blete —
Mak. Then myght I be tane! / That were
  a cold swette!

[He begins to tremble.]

Go spar [2]   327
The gaytt doore.[3]
Vxor.   Yis, Mak,
For and thay com at thy bak —
Mak. Then myght I by for all the pak!
  The dewill of the war!   331

Vxor. A good bowrde [4] haue I spied, / —
  syn thou can none.
Here shall we hym hyde / to thay be
  gone, —
In my credyll abyde, — / lett me alone,
And I shall lyg besyde / in chylbed, and
  grone.
Mak. Thou red!
And I shall say thou was lyght [5]   336
Of a knaue [6] childe this nyght.
Vxor. Now well is me day bright,
  That euer was I bred!   340

This is a good gyse [7] / and a far cast!
Yit a woman avyse / helpys at the last!
I wote neuer who spyse. / Agane go thou fast.
Mak. Bot I com or thay ryse, / els
  blawes a cold blast!
I wyll go slepe.   345

[1] Blow.   [2] Fasten.   [3] Front door.
[4] Trick, jest.   [5] Delivered.
[6] Male.   [7] Guise, disguise.

[*Mak returns to the shepherds, and resumes
his place.*]

Yit slepys all this meneye;
And I shall go stalk preuely,
As it had neuer bene I
  That caryed thare shepe.   349

[*The First and Second Shepherds awake.*]

I. PASTOR.   *Resurrex a mortruis!* / Haue
  hald my hand.
Iudas carnas dominus! / I may not well
  stand:
My foytt slepys, by Ihesus; / and I water
  fastand.[1]
I thoght that we layd vs / full nere Yng-
  land.
  II. PASTOR.   A ye!   354
Lord, what I haue slept weyll.
As fresh as an eyll,
As lyght I me feyll
  As leyfe on a tre.   358

[*The Third Shepherd awakes.*]

III. PASTOR.   Benste be here-in! / so my
  [body][2] qwakys,
My hart is outt of skyn, / what-so it
  makys.
Who makys all this dyn? / So my browes
  blakys.[3]
To the dowore[4] wyll I wyn. / Harke, fel-
  ows, wakys!
  We were fowre: 363
Se ye awre of Mak now?
I. PASTOR.   We were vp or thou.
II. PASTOR.   Man, I gyf God a-vowe,
  Yit yede he nawre.[5]   367

III. PASTOR.   Me thoght he was lapt / in a
  wolfe skyn.
I. PASTOR.   So are many hapt / now —
  namely, within.
III. PASTOR.   When we had long napt, /
  me thoght with a gyn[6]
A fatt shepe he trapt; / bot he mayde no
  dyn.
  II. PASTOR.   Be styll!   372

[1] Fasting; thirsting for water?
[2] *Supplied by Kittredge.*
[3] Grows black.   [4] Door.   [5] Went he nowhere.
[6] Quaint device. In the MS. this speech is attributed to the Second Shepherd, and the following
speech to the Third Shepherd; corrected by Manly.

Thi dreme makys the woode;[1]
It is bot fantom, by the roode.
I. PASTOR.   Now God turne all to good,
  If it be his wyll!   376

[*They awaken Mak.*]

II. PASTOR.   Ryse, Mak! For shame! /
  thou lygys right lang.
MAK.   Now Crystys holy name / be vs
  emang!
What is this, for Sant Iame? / I may not
  well gang![2]
I trow I be the same. / A! my nek has
  lygen wrang
  Enoghe.   381

[*They help him to his feet.*]

Mekill thank! Syn yister euen,
Now, by Sant Strevyn,
I was flayd with a swevyn,[3]
  My hart out of-sloghe.[4]   385

I thoght Gyll began to crok / and trauell
  full sad,
Welner at the fyrst cok, / of a yong lad
For to mend oure flok. / Then be I neuer
  glad;
I haue tow on my rok[5] / more then euer I
  had.
  A, my heede!   390
A house full of yong tharnes![6]
The dewill knok outt thare harnes![7]
Wo is hym has many barnes,
  And therto lytyll brede!   394

I must go home, by youre lefe, / to Gyll, as
  I thoght.
I pray you looke my slefe / that I steyll
  noght;
I am loth you to grefe / or from you take
  oght.

[*Mak leaves them.*]

III. PASTOR.   Go furth; yll myght thou
  chefe! / Now wold I we soght,
  This morne,   399
That we had all oure store.

[1] Mad.   [2] Go, walk.
[3] Dream, nightmare.
[4] That slew my heart.   [5] Distaff.
[6] Bellies, i.e., children. (MS. tharmes; *corr. by
Manly*.)
[7] Brains.

I. PASTOR.   Bot I will go before;
Let vs mete.
II. PASTOR.   Whore?
   III. PASTOR.   At the crokyd thorne.
                        [*Exeunt.*]

[Mak arrives at his home.]

MAK.   Vndo this doore! Who is here? /
   How long shall I stand?   404
VXOR EIUS.   Who makys sich a bere? [1] /
   Now walk in the wenyand! [2]
MAK.   A, Gyll, what chere? / It is I,
   Mak, youre husbande.
VXOR.   Then may we se [3] here / the dewill
   in a bande,
Syr Gyle.   408
Lo, he commys with a lote [4]
As he were holden in the throte.
I may not syt at my note [5]
   A hand-lang while.   412

MAK.   Wyll ye here what fare she makys /
   to gett hir a glose? [6]
And dos noght bot lakys,[7] / and clowse hir
   toose.[8]
VXOR.   Why, who wanders? who wakys?
   / who commys? who gose?
Who brewys? who bakys? / who [9] makys
   me thus hose?
   And than,   417
It is rewthe to beholde,
Now in hote, now in colde,
Full wofull is the householde
   That wantys a woman.   421

Bot what ende has thou mayde / with the
   hyrdys,[10] Mak?
MAK.   The last worde that thay sayde, /
   when I turnyd my bak,
Thay wold looke that thay hade / thare
   shepe all the pak.
I hope thay wyll nott be well payde / when
   thay thare shepe lak,
Perde.   426
Bot how-so the gam gose,
To me thay wyll suppose,

And make a fowll noyse,
   And cry outt apon me.   430

Bot thou must do as thou hyght.[1] /
VXOR.   I accorde me thertyll;
I shall swedyll [2] hym right / in my credyll.
If it were a gretter slyght, / yit couthe I
   help tyll.
I wyll lyg downe stright. / Com hap [3] me.
MAK.   I wyll.

[He tucks her in bed.]

VXOR.   Behynde!   435
Com Coll and his maroo,[4]
Thay will nyp vs full naroo.
MAK.   Bot I may cry "Out haroo!"
   The shepe if thay fynde.   439

VXOR.   Harken ay when thay call; / thay
   will com onone.
Com and make redy all; / and syng by
   thyn oone;
Syng lullay thou shall, / for I must grone
And cry outt by the wall / on Mary and
   Iohn,
   For sore.   444
Syng lullay on fast
When thou heris at the last;
And bot I play a fals cast,
   Trust me no more!   448

*[The Shepherds return, and speak at the other
end of the pageant.]*

III. PASTOR.   A, Coll, good morne! / Why
   slepys thou nott?
I. PASTOR.   Alas, that euer was I borne! /
   we haue a fowll blott.
A fat wedir [5] haue we lorne. /
III. PASTOR.   Mary, Godys forbott!
II. PASTOR.   Who shuld do vs that
   skorne? / That were a fowll spott.
   I. PASTOR.   Som shrewe.   453
I haue soght with my dogys
All Horbery Shrogys,[6]
And of fefteyn hogys
   Fond I bot oone ewe.   457

III. PASTOR.   Now trow [7] me, if ye will; ,
   by Sant Thomas of Kent,

---

[1] Noise.
[2] In the waning of the moon (an unlucky time).
[3] MS. be; *corr. by Kittredge.*
[4] Noise (the allusion is to hanging).
[5] Work.   [6] Pretext, excuse.
[7] Plays.   [8] Scratches her toes.
[9] MS. What.   [10] Herdsmen.

[1] Promised.   [2] Swaddle.
[3] Cover me up.   [4] Mate.   [5] Sheep.
[6] Horbury thickets, four miles from Wakefield.
[7] Believe.

Ayther Mak or Gyll / was at that assent.

I. PASTOR. Peasse, man! Be still! / I
    sagh when he went.
Thou sklanders hym yll. / Thou aght to
    repent
    Goode spede. 462

II. PASTOR. Now as euer myght I the,[1]
If I shuld euyn here de,
I wold say it were he
    That dyd that same dede. 466

III. PASTOR. Go we theder, I rede, / and
    ryn on oure feete.
Shall I neuer ete brede / the sothe to I
    wytt.[2]
I. PASTOR. Nor drynk in my heede / with
    hym tyll I mete.
II. PASTOR. I wyll rest in no stede / tyll
    that I hym grete,
    My brothere. 471
Oone I will hight:[3]
Tyll I se hym in sight
Shall I neuer slepe one nyght
    Ther I do anothere. 475

[*As the shepherds approach, Mak's wife
begins to groan, and Mak, sitting by the
cradle, to sing a lullaby.*]

III. PASTOR. Will ye here how thay hak?[4]
    / Oure syre lyst croyne.[5]
I. PASTOR. Hard I neuer none crak[6] / so
    clere out of toyne!
Call on hym.
II. PASTOR. Mak! / vndo youre doore
    soyne.
MAK. Who is that spak / as it were noyne
    On loft? 480
Who is that, I say?
III. PASTOR. Goode felowse, were it day.
MAK. [*Opening the door.*] As far as ye
    may,
    Good, spekys soft, 484

Ouer a seke womans heede / that is at mayll-
    easse;
I had leuer be dede / or she had any dys-
    easse.[7]
VXOR. Go to an othere stede! / I may not
    well qweasse.[8]

Ich fote that ye trede / goys thorow my
    nese [1]
    So hee! 489
I. PASTOR. Tell vs, Mak, if ye may,
How fare ye, I say?
MAK. Bot ar ye in this towne to-day?
    Now how fare ye? 493

Ye haue ryn in the myre, / and ar weytt
    yit.
I shall make you a fyre / if ye will syt.
A nores [2] wold I hyre, / thynk ye on yit.
Well qwytt is my hyre; / my dreme — this
    is itt, [*Points to the cradle.*]
    A seson. 498
I haue barnes, if ye knew,
Well mo then enewe.
Bot we must drynk as we brew,
    And that is bot reson. 502

I wold ye dynyd or ye yode. / Me thynk
    that ye swette.
II. PASTOR. Nay, nawther mendys oure
    mode / drynke nor mette.
MAK. Why, sir, alys you oght bot goode?
III. PASTOR. Yee, oure shepe that we gett
Ar stollyn as thay yode. / Oure los is
    grette.
MAK. Syrs, drynkys! 507
Had I bene thore,
Som shuld haue boght it full sore.
I. PASTOR. Mary, som men trowes that ye
    wore;
    And that vs forthynkys.[3] 511
II. PASTOR. Mak, som men trowys / that
    it shuld be ye.
III. PASTOR. Ayther ye or youre spouse, /
    so say we.
MAK. Now, if ye haue suspowse / to Gill,
    or to me,
Com and rype oure howse, / and then may
    ye se
    Who had hir. 516
If I any shepe fott,[4]
Aythor cow or stott,[5]
And Gyll, my wyfe, rose nott
    Here syn she lade hir, 520

As I am true and lele, / to God here I pray

---

[1] Thrive.   [2] Until I know the truth.
[3] One thing will I swear.   [4] Sing.
[5] Croon.   [6] Bawl.
[7] Annoyance.   [8] Breathe.

[1] Nose.   [2] Nurse.   [3] Troubles.
[4] Fetched.   [5] Bullock.

That this be the fyrst mele / that I shall ete
this day.   [*Points to the cradle.*]
I. PASTOR.   Mak, as haue I ceyll,[1] / avyse
the, I say;
He lernyd tymely to steyll / that couth
not say nay.

[*The shepherds begin the search.*]

VXOR.   I swelt![2]   525
Outt, thefys, fro my wonys![3]
Ye com to rob vs, for the nonys.
MAK.   Here ye not how she gronys?
Youre hartys shuld melt.   529

VXOR.   Outt, thefys, fro my barne! /
Negh hym not thor!
MAK.   Wyst ye how she had farne,[4] /
youre hartys wold be sore.
Ye do wrang, I you warne, / that thus
commys before
To a woman that has farne. / Bot I say no
more!
VXOR.   A, my medyll!   534
I pray to God so my!de,
If euer I you begyld,
That I ete this chylde
That lygys in this credyll.   538

MAK.   Peasse, woman, for Godys payn! /
and cry not so!
Thou spyllys thy brane, / and makys me
full wo.
II. PASTOR.   I trow oure shepe be slayn. /
What finde ye two?
II:. PASTOR.   All wyrk we in vayn; / as
well may we go.
Bot, hatters,[5]   543
I can fynde no flesh,
Hard nor nesh,
Salt nor fresh,
Bot two tome [6] platers.   547

Whik [7] catell bot this, / tame nor wylde,
None, as haue I blys, / as lowde as he
smylde.[8]
VXOR.   No, so God me blys, / and gyf me
ioy of my chylde!
I. PASTOR.   We haue merkyd amys; / I
hold vs begyld.

<hr>

[1] Bliss.   [2] Become faint.   [3] Dwelling
[4] Laboured (with child-birth).
[5] Plague take it.   [6] Empty.
[7] Living.   [8] Smelled?

II. PASTOR.   Syr, don.   552

[*Addressing Mak at the cradle.*]

Syr, Oure Lady hym saue!
Is youre chyld a knaue? [1]
MAK.   Any lord myght hym haue,
This chyld to his son.   556

When he wakyns he kyppys [2] / that ioy is
to se.
III. PASTOR.   In good tyme to hys hyp-
pys [3]/ and in cele! [4]
Bot who was his gossyppys [5] / so sone
rede?
MAK.   So fare fall thare lyppys! /
I. PASTOR.   [*Aside.*] Hark now, a le!
MAK.   So God thaym thank,   561
Parkyn, and Gybon Waller, I say,
And gentill Iohn Horne, in good fay,
He made all the garray,[6]
With the greatt shank.   565

II. PASTOR.   Mak, freyndys will we be, /
ffor we ar all oone.
MAK.   We! now I hald for me, / for mendys gett I none.
Fare-well all thre! / All glad were ye gone!

[*Exeunt the shepherds.*]

III. PASTOR.   Fare wordys may ther be, /
bot luf is ther none
This yere.   570
I. PASTOR.   Gaf ye the chyld any-thyng?
II. PASTOR.   I trow, not oone farthyng!
III. PASTOR.   Fast agane will I flyng;
Abyde ye me there.   574

[*The Third Shepherd returns.*]

Mak, take it to no grefe, / if I com to thi
barne.
MAK.   Nay, thou dos me greatt represe, /
and fowll has thou farne.
III. PASTOR.   The child will it not grefe, /
that lytyll day-starne.[7]
Mak, with youre leyfe, / let me gyf youre
barne
Bot sex pence.   579
MAK.   Nay, do way! He slepys.
III. PASTOR.   Me thynk he pepys.

<hr>

[1] Boy.   [2] Snatches.   [3] Hips.
[4] Happiness.   [5] Sponsors at baptism.
[6] Commotion.   [7] Day-star.

Mak.   When he wakyns he wepys!
I pray you go hence!   583

III. Pastor.   Gyf me lefe hym to kys, /
and lyft vp the clowtt.[1]

[*Lifts the cloth, thinks the baby deformed.*]

What the dewill is this?   / he has a long
snowte!

[*The other shepherds, pressing forward, look
at the baby.*]

I. Pastor.   He is merkyd amys.[2] / We
wate ill abowte.

II. Pastor.   Ill spon weft,[3] iwys, / ay
commys foull owte.

[*Suddenly, realizing that it is a sheep.*]

Ay, so!   588
He is lyke to oure shepe!
III. Pastor.   How, Gyb! may I pepe?
I. Pastor.   I trow, kynde[4] will crepe
Where it may not go!   592

[*They lift the sheep out of the cradle.*]

II. Pastor.   This was a qwantt gawde,[5] /
and a far cast!
It was a hee frawde! /
III. Pastor.   Yee, syrs, wast.[6]
Lett bren[7] this bawde, / and bynd hir fast.
A! fals skawde, / hang at the last!
So shall thou.   597
Wyll ye se how thay swedyll
His foure feytt in the medyll?
Sagh I neuer in a credyll
A hornyd lad or now!   601

Mak.   Peasse byd I! What! / Lett be
youre fare!
I am he that hym gatt, / and yond woman
hym bare.
I. Pastor.   What dewill shall he hatt?[8] /
"Mak?"   Lo, God, Makys ayre!
II. Pastor.   Lett be all that. / Now God
gyf hym care,
I sagh.   606
Vxor.   A pratty childe is he

As syttys on a womans kne;
A dyllydowne, perde,
To gar a man laghe.   610

III. Pastor.   I know hym by the eere-
marke; / that is a good tokyn!
Mak.   I tell you, syrs, hark! / hys noyse[1]
was brokyn;
Sythen[2] told me a clerk / that he was for-
spokyn.[3]
I. Pastor.   This is a fals wark; / I wold
fayn be wrokyn.[4]
Gett wepyn!   615
Vxor.   He was takyn with an elfe,
I saw it myself;
When the clok stroke twelf
Was he forshapyn.[5]   619

II. Pastor.   Ye two ar well feft[6] / sam in
a stede.
III. Pastor.   Syn thay manteyn thare
theft, / let do thaym to dede.
Mak.   If I trespas eft, / gyrd of my
heede!
With you will I be left. /
I. Pastor.   Syrs, do my reede: 623
For this trespas
We will nawther ban ne flyte,[7]
Fyght nor chyte,[8]
Bot haue done as tyte,[9]
And cast hym in canvas.   628

[*They toss Mak in a sheet, and then return to
the fields.*]

[I. Pastor.]   Lord, what! I am sore / in
poynt for to bryst.
In fayth, I may no more; / therfor wyll I
ryst.
II. Pastor.   As a shepe of sevyn skore / he
weyd in my fyst.
For to slepe ay-whore[10] / me thynk that I
lyst.
III. Pastor.   Now I pray you,   633
Lyg downe on this grene.
I. Pastor.   On these thefys yit I mene.
III. Pastor.   Wherto shuld ye tene?[11]
Do[12] as I say you!   637

---

[1] Cloth.   [2] Deformed.
[3] An old proverb: "From an ill-spun woof ever
comes foul out."
[4] An old proverb: "Nature will walk where it may
not go."
[5] Device.   [6] Was it.
[7] Burn.   [8] Be named.

[1] Nose.   [2] Afterwards.
[3] Bewitched.   [4] Avenged.
[5] Deformed.   [6] Endowed.
[7] Curse nor quarrel.   [8] Chide.
[9] Quickly.   [10] Anywhere.
[11] Trouble.   [12] MS. so; *corr. by Manly.*

[*They lie down and fall asleep.*]

*An angel sings "Gloria in exelsis"; then let
    him say:* [1]

ANGELUS.   Ryse, hyrd-men heynd! / for
    now is he borne
That shall take fro the feynd / that Adam
    had lorne:
That warloo [2] to sheynd [3] / this nyght is
    he borne;
God is made youre freynd / now at this
    morne.
    He behestys   642
At Bedlem go se,
Ther lygys that fre
In a cryb full poorely
    Betwyx two bestys.   646

[*The angel withdraws.*]

I. PASTOR.   This was a qwant stevyn [4] /
    that euer yit I hard.
It is a meruell to neuyn, / thus to be skard.
II. PASTOR.   Of Godys son of heuyn / he
    spak vpward.
All the wod on a leuyn [5] / me thoght that
    he gard [6]
    Appere.   651
III. PASTOR.   He spake of a barne
In Bedlem, I you warne.
I. PASTOR.   That betokyns yond starne; [7]
    Let vs seke hym there.   655

II. PASTOR.   Say, what was his song? /
    Hard ye not how he crakyd it,
Thre brefes to a long? /
III. PASTOR.   Yee, mary, he hakt [8] it;
Was no crochett wrong, / nor no-thyng
    that lakt it.
I. PASTOR.   For to syng vs emong, / right
    as he knakt it,
    I can.   660
II. PASTOR.   Let se how ye croyne.
Can ye bark at the mone?
III. PASTOR.   Hold youre tonges! Haue
    done!
    I. PASTOR.   Hark after, than!   664

II. PASTOR.   To Bedlem he bad / that we
    shuld gang;

---

[1] MS. *Angelus cantat Gloria in exelsis, postea dicat.*
[2] Warlock (the devil).   [3] Destroy.
[4] Voice.   [5] Lightning.
[6] Made.   [7] Star.   [8] Sang.

I am full fard [1] / that we tary to lang.
III. PASTOR.   Be mery and not sad; / of
    myrth is oure sang;
Euer-lastyng glad / to mede [2] may we
    fang,
    Withoutt noyse.   669
I. PASTOR.   Hy we theder for-thy, [3]
If we be wete and wery,
To that chyld and that lady!
    We haue it not to lose.   673

II. PASTOR.   We fynde by the prophecy —
    / let be youre dyn! —
Of Dauid and Isay / and mo then I
    myn, [4]
Thay prophecyed by clergy / that in a
    vyrgyn
Shuld he lyght and ly, / to slokyn [5] oure
    syn
    And slake it,   678
Oure kynde from wo.
For Isay sayd so:
Ecce virgo
    Concipiet a chylde that is nakyd.   682

III. PASTOR.   Full glad may we be, / and
    abyde that day
That lufly to se, / that all myghtys may.
Lord, well were me, / for ones and for ay,
Myght I knele on my kne / som word for to
    say
    To that chylde.   687
Bot the angell sayd,
In a cryb wos he layde;
He was poorly arayd,
    Both meke [6] and mylde.   691

I. PASTOR.   Patryarkes that has bene, /
    and prophetys beforne,
Thay desyryd to haue sene / this chylde
    that is borne.
Thay ar gone full clene; / that haue thay
    lorne. [7]
We shall se hym, I weyn, / or it be morne,
    To tokyn.   696
When I se hym and fele,
Then wote I full weyll
It is true as steyll
    That prophetys haue spokyn: 700

---

[1] Afraid.   [2] Reward.   [3] Therefore.
[4] Remember.   [5] Quench.
[6] MS. mener; *corr. by Kölbing.*   [7] Lost.

To so poore as we ar / that he wold appere,
Fyrst fynd, and declare / by his messyn-
 gere.
II. PASTOR. Go we now, let vs fare; / the
 place is vs nere.
III. PASTOR. I am redy and yare; / go we
 in-fere [1]
  To that bright.   705
Lord, if thi wyll it [2] be —
We ar lewde [3] all thre —
Thou grauntt vs somkyns gle [4]
  To comforth thi wight.   709

[*They enter the stable. The First Shepherd
 kneels before the babe.*]

I. PASTOR. Hayll, comly and clene! /
 hayll, yong child!
Hayll, Maker, as I meyne! / of a madyn so
 mylde!
Thou has waryd, [5] I weyne, / the warlo [6] so
 wylde;
The fals gyler of teyn, [7] / now goys he be-
 gylde.
  Lo, he merys!   714
Lo, he laghys, my swetyng!
A welfare metyng!
I haue holden my hetyng.[8]
  Haue a bob of cherys!   718

[*The Second Shepherd kneels.*]

II. PASTOR. Hayll, sufferan Sauyoure, /
 ffor thou has vs soght!
Hayll, frely foyde [9] and floure, / that all
 thyng has wroght!
Hayll, full of fauoure, / that made all of
 noght!
Hayll! I kneyll and I cowre. / A byrd
 haue I broght
  To my barne.   723
Hayll, lytyll tyne mop! [10]
Of oure crede thou art crop.
I wold drynk on thy cop, [11]
  Lytyll day-starne!   727

[*The Third Shepherd kneels.*]

III. PASTOR. Hayll, derlyng dere, / full of
 godhede!
I pray the be nere / when that I haue nede.
Hayll! swete is thy chere! / My hart wold
 blede
To se the sytt here / in so poore wede, [1]
  With no pennys.   732
Hayll! put furth thy dall! [2]
I bryng the bot a ball:
Haue and play the with-all,
  And go to the tenys.   736

MARIA. The Fader of heuen, / God omny-
 potent,
That sett all on seuen, [3] / his Son has he sent.
My name couth he neuen [4] / and lyght [5] or
 he went.
I conceyuyd hym full euen, / thrugh myght
 as he ment;
  And now he is borne.   741
He kepe you fro wo!
I shall pray hym so.
Tell, furth as ye go,
  And myn on this morne. 745

I. PASTOR. Farewell, lady, / so fare to be-
 holde,
With thy childe on thi kne! /
II. PASTOR.   Bot he lygys full cold.
Lord, well is me! / Now we go, thou be-
 hold.
III. PASTOR. For sothe, all redy / it semys
 to be told
  Full oft.   750
I. PASTOR. What grace we haue fun!
II. PASTOR. Com furth; now ar we won! [6]
III. PASTOR. To syng ar we bun:
  Let take on loft!   754

[*They go out singing.*]

Explicit pagina Pastorum.

---

[1] Together. [2] MS. wylles: *corr. by Manly.*
[3] Unlettered. [4] Joy of some kind.
[5] Cursed. [6] The Devil.
[7] Injury. [8] Promise.
[9] Noble offspring, child. [10] Baby.
[11] Cup, of the Sacrament.

[1] Garment. [2] Fist.
[3] Usually "to venture everything"; here, possibly,
"That made all things."
[4] Name.
[5] Alighted (an allusion to the incarnation).
[6] Saved.

THE MAGI, HEROD, AND THE SLAUGHTER OF THE INNOCENTS [1]

[Acted by the Shearmen and Taylors of Coventry.]

There the profettis gothe furthe and Erod cumyth in, and the messenger.

NONCEOSE.[1] Faytes pais, dñyis, baronys de grande reynowme!

Payis, seneoris, schevaleris de nooble posance!

Pays, gentis homos, companeonys petis egrance!

Je vos command dugard treytus sylance.

Payis, tanque vottur nooble Roie syre ese presance!

Que nollis persone ese non fawis perwynt dedfferance,

Nese harde de frappas; mayis gardus to to paceance, —

Mayis gardus voter seneor to cor reyuerance;

Care lat vottur Roie to to puysance.

Anoñ de leo, pase tos! je vose cummande,

E lay Roie erott la grandeaboly vos vmport.   485

---

[1] With the help of the suggestions by Manly (some, he states, were secured from Sheldon and Kittredge), I have ventured to reconstruct the French verses which have been so sadly corrupted through oral tradition:

Faites paix, domnes [i.e. lords], barons de grand renom!
Paix, seigneurs, chevaliers de noble puissance!
Paix, gentilshommes, compagnons petits et grands!
Je vous commande de garder trestous silence.
Paix, tant que votre noble Roi sera ici présent!
Que nulle personne ici ne fasse point différends
Ni se hasarde de frapper; mais gardez toute patience —
Mais gardez votre seigneur toute révérence:
Car il est votre Roi tout puissant.
Au nom de lui, paix tous! je vous commande
Est le Roi Hérode le grand!
Le Diable vous emporte!

ERODE.   *Qui statis in Jude et Rex Iseraell,*[1]

And the myghttyst conquerowre that eyuer walkid on grownd!

For I am evyn he thatt made bothe hevin and hell;

And of my myghte powar holdith vp this world rownd.

Magog and Madroke, bothe the[m] did I confownde,

And with this bryght bronde [2] there bonis I brak on-sunder,

Thatt all the wyde worlde on those rappis did wonder.   492

I am the cawse of this grett lyght [3] and thunder;

Ytt ys throgh my fure that the[y] soche noyse dothe make.

My feyrefull contenance the clowdis so doth incumbur

That oftymis for drede ther-of the verre yerth doth quake.

Loke! when I with males [4] this bryght brond [2] doth schake,

All the whole world, from the north to the sowthe,

I ma them dystroie with won worde of my mowthe!   499

To reycownt vnto you myn innevmerabull substance,

Thatt were to moche for any tong to tell!

---

[1] Possibly this is to be read as "And King of the Israelites who dwell in Judea."
[2] Sword.   [3] Lightning.   [4] Malice.

---

[1] Reprinted from Thomas Sharp's *A Dissertation on the Pageants or Dramatic Mysteries Anciently Performed at Coventry by the Trading Companies of that City*, 1825. The manuscript, formerly in the possession of Sharp, was burned with the Shakespeare Memorial Library at Birmingham in 1879. The Shearmen and Taylors' Play, and the Weavers' Play (also burnt) are the sole remnants of the famous cycle acted at Coventry — a cycle which, it is almost certain, Shakespeare witnessed as a boy. Allusions in his works to Herod and to the slaughter of the innocents are probably recollections of the play here printed. I have omitted the first 474 lines, which include a prologue by Isaiah, the Annunciation to Mary, the Doubt of Joseph, the Journey to Bethlehem, the Nativity, the Visit of the Shepherds, and a long Dialogue between two prophets. In preparing the text I have taken advantage of the reprints by Manly, *Specimens*, 1897, and by Hardin Craig, *Two Corpus Christi Plays*, edited for the Early English Text Society, 1902, both of which necessarily reproduce Sharp's text of 1825.

For all the whole Orent ys vnder myn ob-
  beydeance,
  And Prynce am I of Purgatorre, and
    Cheff Capten of Hell!
  And those tyraneos trayturs be force ma
    I compell
Myne enmyis to vanquese, and evyn to
    dust them dryve,
And with a twynke of myn iee [1] not won to
    be lafte alyve.   506

Behold my contenance, and my colur,
  Bryghtur then the sun in the meddis of
    the dey!
Where can you haue a more grettur succur
  Then to behold my person that ys soo
    gaye,
  My fawcun [2] and my fassion, with my
    gorgis araye?
He thatt had the grace all-wey ther-on to
    thynke,
  Lyve he [3] myght all-wey with-owt othur
    meyte or drynke.   513

And thys my tryomfande fame most hylist
    dothe a-bownde
  Throgh-owt this world in all reygeons
    abrod,
Reysemelyng the fauer of thatt most
    myght Mahownd; [4]
  From Jubytor be desent, and cosyn to
    the grett God,
  And namyd the most reydowndid [5] Kyng
    Eyrodde,
Wyche thatt all pryncis hath under sub-
    jeccion,
And all there whole powar vndur my pro-
    teccion.   520

And therefore, my hareode [6] here, callid
    Calcas,
  Warne thow eyuer[e] porte thatt noo
    schyppis a-ryve,
Nor also aleond [7] stranger throg my realme
    pas,
  But the[y] for there truage [8] do pay
    markis [9] fyve.
    Now spede the forth hastele;

For the[y] thatt wyll the contrare
  Apon a galowse hangid schalbe;
And, be Mahownde, of me the[y] gett noo
    grace!   528

NONCIOS. Now, Lord and mastur, in all
    the hast,
Thy worethe [1] wyll ytt schall be wroght,
And thy ryall cuntreyis schalbe past
In asse schort tyme ase can be thoght.532
                                    [Exit.]

ERODE. Now schall owre regeons throgh-
    owt be soght
  In eyuer[e] place, bothe est and west.
Yff any katyffis to me be broght,
  Yt schalbe nothyng for there best.
  And the whyle thatt I do resst,
Trompettis, viallis, and othur armone [2]
Schall bles the wakyng of my maieste. 539

*Here Erod goth awey, and the iij Kyngis
    speykyth in the strete.*

[*Enter the First King.*]

I. REX. Now blessid be God of his swet
    sonde! [3]
For yondur a feyre, bryght star I do see!
Now ys he comon vs a-monge,
  Asse the profet [4] seyd thatt yt schuld
    be.   543

A [5] seyd there schuld a babe be borne,
  Comyng of the rote of Jesse,
To sawe [6] mankynd that wasse for-lorne.[7]
  And truly comen now ys he.   547

Reyuerence and worschip to hym woll I do
  Asse God and man, thatt all made of
    noght.
All the profettis acordid and seyd evyn soo,
  That with hys presseos [8] blod mankynd
    schuld be boght.[9]   551

He grant me grace,
  Be yonder star that I see,
And in-to thatt place
  Bryng me

---

[1] Eye.   [2] Falchion (or falcon).
[3] MS. the; *corr. by Manly.*   [4] Mahomet.
[5] Redoubtable.   [6] Herald.
[7] Alien.   [8] Toll.
[9] 13s. 4d. was the value of a mark.

[1] Worthy.   [2] Harmony, music.
[3] Messenger (or dispensation?).
[4] MS. profettis; *corr. by Manly.*
[5] He.   MS. aseyd; *corr. by Manly.*   [6] Save.
[7] Lost.   [8] Precicus.   [9] Redeemed.

Thatt I ma hym worschipe with umel-
lete [1]
And se hys gloreose face.   557

[Enter the Second King.]

II. REX.   Owt off my wey I deme [2] thatt I
am,
For toocuns [3] of thys cuntrey can I non
see.
Now, God, thatt on yorth [4] madist man,
Send me sum knoleyge where thatt I
be!   561

Yondur, me thynke, a feyre, bryght star I
see;
The wyche be-tocunyth the byrth of a
chyld
Thatt hedur ys cum to make man fre,
He borne of a mayde, and sche nothyng
defyld.   565

To worschip thatt chyld ys myn in-tent.
Forth now wyll I take my wey.
I trust sum cumpany God hathe me sent,
For yonder I se a kyng labur on the
wey.   569

To-warde hym now woll I ryde.

[Approaches the First King.]

Harke, cumly kyng! I you pray,
In-to whatt co[a]st wyll ye thys tyde,
Or weddur [5] lyis youre jurney?   573

I. REX.   To seke a chylde ys myne in-tent,
Of whom the profetis hathe ment.
The tyme ys cum, now ys he sent,
Be yondur star here ma [you] see.
II. REX.   Sir, I prey you, with your ly-
sence,
To ryde with you vnto his presence.
To hym wyll I offur frank-in-sence,
For the hed of all Whole [6] Churche schall
he be.   581

[Enter the Third King.]

III. REX.   I ryde wanderyng in veyis [7] wyde,
Ouer montens and dalis; I wot not where
I am.

Now, Kyng off all kyngis, send me soche
gyde
Thatt I myght haue knoleyge of thys
cuntreys name.   585

A! yondur I se a syght, be-semyng [1] all
afar,
The wyche be-tocuns sum nevis,[2] ase I
troo;
Asse me thynke, a chyld peryng [3] in a stare.
I trust he be cum that schall defend vs
from woo.   589

T[w]o kyngis yondur I see,
And to them woll I ryde
Forto haue there cumpane;
I trust the[y] wyll me abyde.

[He approaches the two kings.]

Hayle, cumly kyngis and gent! [4]
Good surs, I pray you, whedder ar ye
ment?   595

I. REX.   To seke a chylde ys owre in-tent,
Wyche be-tocuns yonder star, asse ye
ma see.
II. REX.   To hym I purpose thys present.
III. REX.   Surs, I pray you, and thatt
ryght vmblee,
With you thatt I ma ryde in cumpane.

[The Kings join, and say in unison:]

[ALL.]   To all-myghte God now prey we
Thatt hys pressiose persone we ma se. 602

[They retire, riding.]

*Here Erode cumyth in ageyne, and the mes-
sengere seyth:*

NUNCIOS.   Hayle, lorde most off myght!
Thy commandement ys right;
In-to thy land ys comyn thys nyght
iij kyngis, and with them a grett cum-
pany.
EROD.   Whatt make those kyngis in this
cuntrey?
NONCIOS.   To seke a kyng and a chyld,
the[y] sey.
ERODE.   Of whatt age schuld he bee?

---

[1] Humility. In this stanza, and elsewhere, I have
Ilowed Manly's line division.
[2] Judge.   [3] Tokens.   [4] Earth.
[5] Whither.   [6] Holy.   [7] Ways.

[1] Seemingly.   [2] News.   [3] Appearing.
[4] " Hail, kings, comely and noble."   MS. augent.
I have adopted Manly's suggested emendation.

NONCIOS.   Skant   twellve   deyis   old
   fulle.   610

EROD.   And wasse he soo late borne?
NONCIOS.   E, syr, soo the[y] schode me
   thys same dey in the morne.
EROD.   Now, in payne of deyth, bryng
   them me beforne! [1]
And there-fore, harrode,[2] now hy the in
   hast,
In all spede thatt thow were dyght [3]
   Or thatt those kyngis the cuntrey be
     past;
Loke thow bryng them all iij before my
   syght.   617

And in Jerusalem inquere more of that
   chyld.
But I warne the that thy wordis be mylde,
For there must thow hede [4] and crafte
   wey[lde] [5]
How to for-do [6] his powere; and those iij
   kyngis shalbe begild.   621

NONCIOS.   Lorde, I am redde att youre
   byddyng
To sarve the ase my lord and kyng.
For joye there-of, loo, how I spryng
With lyght hart and fresche gamboldyng
   Alofte here on this molde!
ERODE.   Then sped the forthe hastely,
And loke that thow beyre the eyvinly; [7]
And also I pray the hartely
Thatt thow doo comand [8] me
   Bothe to yong and olde.   631

*[The three Kings, returning, are saluted by
   the messenger.]*

NUNCIOS.   Hayle, syr kyngis, in youre
   degre!
   Erood, kyng of these cuntreyis wyde,
Desyrith to speyke with you all thre,   634
   And for youre comyng he dothe abyde.

I. REX.   Syr, att his wyll we be ryght
   bayne.[9]
Hy us, brethur, vnto thatt lordis place;
To speyke with hym we wold be fayne.

Thatt chyld thatt we seke, he grant us of
   his grace!   639

[The messenger leads them to Herod.]

NUNCIOS.   Hayle, lorde with-owt pere!
These iij kyngis here have we broght.
ERODE.   Now welcum, syr kyngis, all in-
   fere; [1]
But of my bryght ble,[2] surs, bassche [3] ye
   noght!   643

Sir kyngis, ase I vndurstand,
A star hathe gydid you into my land,
Where-in grett harting [4] ye haue fonde
Be reysun of hir beymis bryght.
Wherefore I pray you hartely
The vere truthe thatt ye wold sertefy,
How long yt ys, surely,
   Syn of that star you had furst syght. 651

I. REX.   Sir kynge, the vere truthe to sey,
And forto schoo you ase hit ys best,
This same ys evin the xij[th] dey
   Syth yt aperid to vs be [5] west.   655

ERODE.   Brethur, then ys there no more to
   sey
But with hart and wyll kepe ye your jur-
   ney,
And cum whom [6] by me this same wey,
   Of your nevis [7] thatt I myght knoo.

You schall tryomfe in this cuntre
And with grett conquorde [8] bankett with
   me;
And thatt chyld myself then woll I see,
   And honor hym also.   663

II. REX.   Sir, youre commandement we
   woll fullfyli,
And humbly abaye [9] owreself there-tyll.
He thatt weldith [10] all thyng at wyll
   The redde [11] way hus teyche,
Sir kyng, thatt we ma passe your land in
   pes!
ERODE.   Yes, and walke softely eyvin at
   your one e[a]s;   669

[1] Before.   [2] Color.
[3] Quail, be dismayed.
[4] Cheer, encouragement; MS. harie; *corr. by*
Manly.
[5] By.   [6] Home.   [7] News.
[8] Concord.   [9] Bow, subject.
[10] Ruleth.   [11] Direct.

---

   [1] Before.   [2] Herald.
   [3] Set about it.   [4] Heed, care.
   [5] *Supplied by Manly.*
   [6] Destroy.   [7] Evenly, craftily.
   [8] Commend.   [9] Ready.

Youre pase-porte for a C [1] deyis
  Here schall you haue of clere cummand;
Owre reme [2] to labur [3] any weyis
  Here schall you haue be spesschall
    grante.   673

III. REX.   Now fare-well, kyng of hy
    degre;
  Humbly of you owre leyve we take.
ERODE.   Then adev, sir kyngis all thre!
And whyle I lyve, be bold of me.
There ys nothyng in this cuntre
  But for youre one [4] ye schall yt take. 679

[*Exeunt the three kings.*]

Now these iij kyngis ar gon on ther wey;
  On-wysely and on-wyttely [5] haue the[y]
    all wroghte.
When the[y] cum ageyne, the[y] schall dy
    that same dey,
  And thus these vyle wreychis to deyth
    the[y] schalbe broght, —
Soche ys my lykyng.
He that agenst my lawis wyll hold,
Be he kyng or keysar neyuer soo bold,
I schall them cast in-to caris [6] cold,
  And to deyth I schall them bryng.   688

*There Erode goth his weyis, and the iij
    kyngis cum in ageyne.*

I. REX.   O blessid God, moche ys thy
    myght!   689
Where ys this star thatt gawe [7] vs lyght?
II. REX.   Now knele we downe here in this
    presence,
Be-sekyng that Lord of hy maugnefecens
That we ma see his hy exsellence
  Yff thatt his swet wyl[l] be.   694

III. REX.   Yondur, brothur, I see the
    star,
Where-by I kno he ys nott far;
Therefore, lordis, goo we nar
  Into this pore place.   698

*There the iij kyngis gois in to the jesen, [8]
    to Mare and hir child.*

I. REX.   Hayle, Lorde thatt all this world,
    hath wroght!

Hale, God and man to-gedur in-fere! [1]
For thow hast made all thyng of noght,
  Albe-yt thatt thow lyist porely here.
A cupe-full golde here I haue the broght
  In toconyng thow art with-owt pere. 704

II. REX.   Hayle be thow, Lorde of hy
    maugnyffecens!
  In toconyng of preste[h]od and dyngnete
    of offece,
To the I offur a cupe full off in-sence,
  For yt be-hovith the to haue soche sacre-
    fyce.   708

III. REX.   Hayle be thow, Lorde, longe
    lokid fore!
  I haue broght the myre [2] for mortalete
In to-cunyng thow schalt mankynd restore
  To lyff be thy deyth apon a tre.   712

MARE.   God haue marce, kyngis, of yowre
    goodnes!
  Be [3] the gydyng of the Godhed hidder
    ar ye sent.
The provyssion off my swete sun your
    weyis whom [4] reydres,
  And gostely reywarde you for youre
    present.   716

[*The kings withdraw from the stable.*]

I. REX.   Syr kyngis, aftur owre promes,
  Whome be Erode I mvst nedis goo.
II. REX.   Now truly, brethur,[5] we can noo
    las.
  But I am soo far-wachid [6] I wott not wat
    to do.   720
III. REX.   Ryght soo am I; where-fore I
    you pray,
  Lett all vs rest vs awhyle upon this
    grownd.
I. REX.   Brethur, youer seying ys right
    well vnto my pay.[7]
  The grace of thatt swet chylde saue vs
    all sownde!   724

[*They lie down and fall asleep.   Enter an
    angel.*]

ANGELLUS.   Kyng of Tawrus, Sir Jespar!
Kyng of Arraby, Sir Balthasar!

---

[1] Hundred.	[2] Realm.	[3] Travel.
[4] Own.	[5] Foolishly.	[6] Cares.
[7] Gave.	[8] Childbed.	

[1] United, in company.		
[2] Myrrh.	[3] By.	[4] Home.
[5] MS. berthur; *corr. by Manly.*		
[6] Tired.	[7] Liking.	

Melchor, Kyng of Aginare!
To you now am I sent.
For drede of Eyrode, goo you west whom.[1]
In-to those parties [2] when ye cum downe
Ye schalbe byrrid with gret reynowne.
The Wholle Gost thus knoleyge hath
   sent.   [*Exit Angelus.*] 732

I. Rex. Awake, sir kyngis, I you praye!
For the voise of an angell I hard in my
   dreyme.
II. Rex. Thatt ys full tru thatt ye do
   sey,   735
For he reyherssid owre names playne.

III. Rex. He bad thatt we schuld goo
   downe be west
For drede of Eyrodis fawls be-traye.
I. Rex. Soo forto do yt ys the best.
The child that we haue soght, gyde vs
   the wey!   740

Now fare-well, the feyrist of schapp soo
   swete!
And thankid be Jhesu of his sonde,[3]
Thatt we iij to-geder soo suddenly schuld
   mete,
Thatt dwell soo wyde and in straunge
   lond,   744

And here make owre presentacion
Vnto this Kyngis Son clensid soo cleyne
And to his moder for ovre saluacion.
Of moche myrth now ma we meyne,[4]
Thatt we soo well hath done this obbla-
   cion.[5]   749

II. Rex [*bowing*]. Now farewell, Sir Jaspar,
   brothur, to yoeu,
Kyng of Tawrus the most worthe!
Sir Balthasar, also to you I bow.
And I thanke you bothe of youre good
   cumpany
Thatt we togeddur haue had.
He thatt made vs to mete on hyll,
I thanke hym now, and eyuer I wyll;
For now may we goo with-owt yll,
And off owre offerynge be full glad.[6] 758

III. Rex. Now syth [1] thatt we mvst nedly
   goo
For drede of Erode thatt ys soo wrothe,
Now fare-well brothur, and brothur also;
I take my leve here at you bothe
   This dey on fete.[2]
Now he thatt made vs to mete on
   playne
And offur [3] to Mare in hir jeseyne,[4]
He geve vs grace in heyvin a-gayne
   All to-geyder to mete!   767

[*Exeunt the three kings severally. Enter the
messenger running to Herod.*]

Nuncios. Hayle, kynge, most worthist in
   wede!
Hayle, manteinar of curtese throgh all
   this world wyde!
Hayle, the most myghtyst that eyuer
   bestrod a stede!
Ha[y]ll, most monfullist mon in armor
   man to abyde!
Hayle, in thyne hoonowre!
Thesse iij kyngis that forthe were sent,
And schuld haue cum ageyne before the
   here present,
Anothur wey, lorde, whom the[y] went,
   Contrare to thyn honowre.   776

Erode. A-nothur wey? owt! owt! owtt!
Hath those fawls traytvrs done me this
   ded?
I stampe! I stare! I loke all abowtt!
Myght I them take, I schuld them bren
   at a glede! [5]
I rent! [6] I rawe! [7] and now run I wode! [8]
A! thatt these velen [9] traytvrs hath mard
   this my mode!
The[y] schalbe hangid, yf I ma cum
   them to!   783

*Here Erode ragis in the pagond and in the
strete also.*

E! and thatt kerne [10] of Bedlem, he schalbe
   ded,[11]
And thus schall I for-do his prof-
   ccc.[12]   785

---

[1] Home.   [2] Parts.
[3] Dispensation.   [4] Have in mind.
[5] Act of devotion.
[6] MS. fayne; *corr. by Manly.*

[1] Since.   [2] MS. fote; *corr. by Manly.*
[3] MS. offurde; *corr. by Manly.*
[4] Childbed.   [5] Fire.
[6] Tear (the hair, etc.).   [7] Run.
[8] Mad.   [9] Villain.   [10] Rascal.
[11] Killed.   [12] Prophecy.

How sey you, sir knyghtis, ys not this the
best red?
Thatt all yong chyldur for this schuld be
dede,
   Wyth sworde to be slayne?
Then schall I, Erod, lyve in lede,[1]
And all folke me dowt and drede,
And offur to me bothe gold, rychesse and
mede;
   Thereto wyll the[y] be full fayne. 792

I. MYLES.   My lorde, Kyng Erode be
name,
   Thy wordis agenst my wyll schalbe.
To see soo many yong chylder dy ys
schame;
   Therefore consell ther-to gettis thou non
of me!   796

II. MYLES.   Well seyd, fello, my trawth I
plyght!
Sir kyng, perseyve [2] right well you may
Soo grett a morder to see of yong frute
   Wyll make a rysyng in thi noone cun-
trey.   800

ERODE.   A rysyng?   Owt! owt! owt! 801

*There Erode ragis ageyne, and then seyth
thus:*

Owt! velen wrychis,[3] har [4] apon you I cry!
My wyll vtturly loke that yt be wroght,—
Or apon a gallowse bothe you schall dy,
   Be Mahownde most myghtyste, that me
dere hath boght!   805

I. MYLES.   Now, cruell Erode, syth we
schall do this dede —
Your wyll nedefully in this realme mvste
be wroght —
All the chylder of that age dy the[y] mvst
nede.
Now with all my myght the[y] schall be
vpsoght.[5]   809

II. MYLES.   And I woll sweyre here apon
your bryght swerde,[6]
All the chylder thatt I fynd, sclayne
the[y] schalbe;

---

[1] Leadership.   [2] Perceive.   [3] Wretches.
[4] Plague?   [5] Sought out.
[6] MS. sworde; *corr. by Manly.*

Thatt make many a moder to wepe and be
full sore aferde
In owre armor bryght when the[y] hus
see.   813

[*Herod makes them swear upon his sword.*]

ERODE.   Now you have sworne, forth
that ye goo,
And my wyll thatt ye wyrke bothe be
dey and nyght;
And then wyll I for fayne [1] trypp lyke a
doo.[2]
But whan the[y] be ded, I warne you
bryng [t]ham be-fore my syght. 817

[*Exeunt.   An angel appears and speaks to
Mary and Joseph.*]

ANGELLUS.   Mare and Josoff, to you I sey,
Swete word from the Fathur I bryng you
full ryght:
Owt of Bedlem in-to Eygype forth goo ye
the wey,
And with you take the Kyng, full of
myght,
   For drede of Eroddis rede! [3]

[*Exit Angelus.*]

JOSOFF.   A-ryse up, Mare, hastely and sone!
Owre Lordis wyll nedys mvst be done,
   Lyke ase the angell vs bad.   825

MARE.   Mekely, Josoff, my none [4] spowse,
Towarde that cuntrey let vs reypeyre;
Att Eygyp to sum cun [5] off howse,
   God grant hus grace saff to cum
there!   829

*Here the wemen cum in wythe there chyldur,
syngyng them; and Mare and Josoff goth
awey cleyne.*

[*The song.*[6]]

*Lully, lulla, thow littell tine child;
By by, lully, lullay, thow littell tyne child;
   By by, lully, lullay!*

O sisters too,
How may we do

---

[1] Joy.   [2] Doe.   [3] Design.   [4] Mine own.
[5] Kind; MS. sum tocun; *em. by Kittredge.*
[6] In the MS. the song is put at the end; I have inserted it here, though without numbering the lines.
The music may be found in Sharp, pp. 116-17.

For to preserve this day
This pore yongling
For whom we do singe
By by, lully, lullay?

Herod, the king,
In his raging,
Chargid he hath this day
His men of might
In his owne sight
All yonge children to slay, —

That wo is me,
Pore child, for thee,
And ever morne and may [1]
For thi parting
Nether say nor singe,
By by, lully, lullay.]

I. WOMON.   I lolle - my chylde wondursly
swete,
And in my narmis [3] I do hyt kepe,
Be-cawse thatt yt schuld not crye.
II. WOMAN.   Thatt babe thatt ys borne in
Bedlem, so meke,
He saue my chyld and me from vel-
any!   834

III. WOMAN.   Be styll, be styll, my lyttull
chylde!
That Lorde of lordis saue bothe the and
me!
For Erode hath sworne with wordis wyld
Thatt all yong chyldur sclayne the[y]
schalbe.   838

[Enter the soldiers.]

I. MYLES.   Sey, ye wyddurde wyvis, [4]
whydder ar ye a-wey?
What beyre you in youre armis nedis
mvst we se.
Yff the[y] be man-chyldur, dy the[y] mvst
this dey,
For at Eroddis wyll all thyng mvst
be.   842

II. MYLES.   And [5] I in handis wonys [6]
them hent, [7]
Them forto sley noght woll I spare!

1 MS. say; em. by Kittredge.   2 Lull.
3 Mine arms.   4 Married women.
5 If.   6 Once.   7 Seize.

We mvst full-fyll Erodis commandement,
Elis be we asse trayturs, and cast all in
care.   846

I. WOMAN.   Sir knyghtis, of youre curtes-
see,
Thys dey schame not youre chevaldre, [1]
But on my child haue pytte
For my sake in this styde. [2]
For a sympull sclaghtur yt were to sloo [3]
Or to wyrke soche a chyld woo,
That can noder speyke nor goo,
Nor neuer harme did.   854

II. WOMON.   He thatt sleyis my chyld in
syght,
Yff thatt my strokis on hym ma lvght,
Be he skwyar [4] or knyght,
I hold hym but lost.
Se, thow fawls losyngere, [5]
A stroke schalt thow beyre me here
And spare for no cost!   861
[Striking him.]

III. WOMAN.   Sytt he neyuer soo hy in
saddull,
But I schall make his braynis addull,
And here with my pott-ladull
With hym woll I fyght.

[Brandishing her pot-ladle.]

I schall ley on hym a[s] thog[h] [6] I wode [7]
were,
With thys same womanly geyre;
There schall noo man steyre, [8]
Wheddur thatt he be kyng or knyght. 869

[The soldiers overcome the women and
slay the children.   Exeunt the women
lamenting.]

I. MYLES.   Who hard eyuer soche a cry
Of wemen thatt there chyldur haue lost?
And grettly reybukyng chewaldry [9]
Throgh-owt this reme in eyuere co[a]st;
Wyche many a mans lyff ys lyke to cost.
For thys grett wreyche [10] that here ys done
I feyre moche wengance ther-off woll
cum.   876

1 Chivalry.   2 Place.   3 Slay.
4 Squire.   5 Rascal.
6 Though. MS. athog; corr. by Manly.
7 Mad.   8 Stir.
9 Chivalry.   10 Pain, suffering.

II. MYLES. E! brothur, soche talis may
  we not tell;
Where-fore to the kyng lett vs goo,
For he ys lyke to beyre the perell,
  Wyche wasse the cawser that we did soo.
Yett must the[y] all be broght hym to
With waynis [1] and waggyns fully fryght.[2]
I tro there wolbe a carefull syght.   883

[They take the dead children to Herod.]

I. MYLES. Loo! Eyrode, kyng, here
  mast thow see
How many M' [3] thatt we haue slayne!
II. MYLES. And nedis thy wyll full-fyllid
  must be;
There ma no mon sey there-ageyne. 887

[Enter Nuntius running.]

NUNCIOS. Eyrode, kyng, I schall the tell,
All thy dedis ys cum to noght;
This chyld ys gone in-to Eygipte to dwell.
Loo! sir, in thy none [4] land what wondurs
  byn wroght!   891

EROD. Into Eygipte? Alas, for woo!
Lengur in lande here I canot abyde.

---

[1] Carts.   [2] Frightful (or perhaps "freighted").
[3] Thousands.   [4] Thine own.

Saddull my palfrey, for in hast wyll I goo;
Aftur yondur trayturs now wyll I ryde,
  Them for to sloo!
Now all men hy fast
In-to Eygipte in hast!
All thatt cuntrey woll I tast,[1]
  Tyll I ma cum them to.   900

Fynes lude de taylars and scharmen.

T[h]ys matter
  nevly correcte be Robart Croo
  the xiiij dey of Marche,
fenysschid in the yere of our Lorde God
  MCCCCC and xxxiiij[te].
then beyng mayre mastur Palmar,
also mastris of the seyd fellyschipp Hev
  Corbett,
  Randull Pynkard, and
  John Baggeley.[2]

---

[1] Search out.
[2] Attached are three songs, sung by the shepherds
and by the women, with the following heading:
"Theise Songes belonge to the Taylors and Shearemens
Pagant. The first and the laste the shepheardes
singe, and the second, or middlemost, the women
singe. Thomas Mawdycke die decimo tertio Maij,
anno Domini millessimo quingentesimo nonagesimo
primo. Prætor fuit ciuitatis Couentriae D. Mathaeus
Richardson, tune Consules Johanes Whitehead et
Thomas Grauener."

CHRIST'S MINISTRY [1]

[Acted by the Glovers of Chester.]

Pagina Decima Tertia de Chelidonio Ceco et de Resurrectione Lazari.[1]

The Glovers.

[SCENE I.]

[Enter Jesus and his disciples.]

IESUS. *Ego sum lux mundi; qui sequitur me, non ambulat in tenebris, sed habebit lumen vitæ.*

Brethren, I am Filius Dei, the light of this world;
He that followeth me, walketh not in darknes;
But hath the light of lyfe — the scriptures so record —
As patriarchs and prophetts of me bereth witnes,
Both Abraham, Isaac, and Iacob in their sondry testimonies,
Vnto whom I was promised before the world began,
To pay ther ransome and to become man.   7

Ego et Pater vnum sumus: my Father and I are all one,
Wiche hath me sent from his throne sempiternall,
To preach and declare his will vnto man,
Because he loveth him aboue his creatures all,
As his treasure and darling most principall,
Man, I say agayne, which is his owne elect
Aboue all creaturs, peculiarly select.   14

Wherfore, dere brethren, it is my mynd and will
To goe to Bethany, that standeth hereby,
My Fathers hestes and commandementis to fulfill;
For I am the good sheapheard, that putteth his lyfe in ioperdy

To save his flocke which I loue so tenderly,
As it is written of me — the scriptures beareth witnes:
Bonus pastor ponit animam suam pro ovibus suis.   21

Go we therfore, brethren, while the day is light,
To doe my Fathers workes, as I am fully minded,
To heale the sick and restore the blynd to sight,
That the prophesy of me may be fulfilled;
For other sheep I haue, which are to me committed;
They be not of this flocke, yet will I them regarde,
That ther may be one flocke and one shepheard.   28

But, or we goe hence, print thes sayinges in your mynd and hart;
Record them, and oft keep them in memory;
Continue in my word, from it doe not depart;
Therby shall all men know most perfectly
That you are my disciples and of my familye.
Goe not before me, but let my word be your guyde;
Then in your doinges you shall allway well speede.   35

Si vos manseritis in sermone meo, veri discipuli mei eritis et cognoscetis veritatem; et veritas liberabit vos.

[Enter a boy leading Chelidonius, the blind man.[1]]

PUER. If pitty may moue your gentell hart,
Remember, good people, the pore and the blynd,
With your charitable almes this poore man to comfort,

---

[1] Pageant thirteen, of the blind Chelidonius, and of the Raising of Lazarus from the Death.

[1] MS. *Puer ducens cacum.*

[1] I have reproduced the text from *The Chester Plays*, Part II, re-edited from the MSS. by Dr. Matthews, for the Early English Text Society, 1916; but I have altered the punctuation, modernized the use of capitals, changed the stanzaic division, and added, in brackets, scene divisions and stage-directions.

That is your owne neighbour and of your
   owne kynde.   39

CHELIDONIUS.   Your almes, good people,
   for charity!
To me that am blynd and never did see,
Your neighbour, borne in this citty.
Helpe me, or I goe hence!   43
PETRUS.   Mayster, instruct us in this case,
Why this man blynd borne was.
Is it for his owne trespas,
Or ells for his parentes?   47

IOHN.   Was sinne the cause originall, —
Wherin we be conceived all, —
That this blynd man was brought in thrall,
Or his forfathers offence?   51

IESUS.   Hit was neither for his offence,
Neither the sinnes of his parentes,
Nor other fault or neglgence,
That he was blind borne.
But for this cause specially,
To set forth Gods great glory,
His power to shew manifestly,
This mans sight to reforme.   59

While the day is fayre and bright,
My Fathers workes I must worke right,
Untill the cominge of the night
That light be gone away.
In this world, when I am here,
I am the light that shyneth clear;
My light to them shall well apear
Which cleave to me alway.   67

   *Then Jesus spits upon the ground and
   makes a clay and rubs the eyes of the
   blind man with his hands: and then let
   him say:* [1]

IESUS.   Do, man, as I say to thee:
Goe to the water of Siloe
And washe thyne eyes, and thou shalt see;
And geue to God the prayse.

   *Then the blind man seeks the water, and
      Jesus went away:* [2]

CHELIDONIUS.   Lead me, good child, right
   hastely

[1] MS. *Tunc Iesus super terram spuit et lutum faciet et oculos ceci manibus fricabit, postea dicat.*
[2] MS. *Tunc cacus querit aquam, et abiit Iesus.*

Unto the water of Siloe.   73
Then he washes, and afterwards let him say: [1]

Praysed be God omnipotent,
Which now to me my sight hath sent!
I see all things now here present.
Blessed be God alwayes!   77

When I had done, as Christ me badd,
My perfect sight forth-with I hadd;
Wherfore my hart is now full gladd,
That I dowt wher I am.

[SCENE II.]

[Chelidonius meeting the neighbors.]

I. PROXIMUS.   Neighbour, if I the truth
   should say,
This is the blind man which yesterday
Asked our almes, as we came this way.
It is the very same!   85

II. VICINUS.   No, no, neighbour, it is not
   hee;
But is the likest to him that ever I see!
One man to another lyke may bee,
And so is he to him.
CHELIDONIUS.   Good men, truly I am he,
That was blynd, and now I se.
I am no other, verely;
Enquier of all my kynne.   93

I. VICINUS.   Then tell the truth, we thee
   pray,
And how this is happened, to us say,
Thou, that even yesterday
Couldst se no earthly thinge,
And now seeth so perfectly.
No want of sight in thee we see;
Declare to us therfore truly
Without more reasoninge.   101

CHELIDONIUS.   The man, which we call
   Iesus,
That worketh miracles dayly with us,
And whom we fynde so gracious,
Anoynted my eyes with clay,
And to the water of Siloei
He badd me goe immediatly,
And wash myne eyes, and I should see.
And thidder I tooke the way.   109

[1] MS. *Tunc lavat, et postea dicat.*

When the water on myne eyes light,
Immediately I had my sight!
Was ther neuer earthly wight
So joyfull in his thought.   113

II. VICINUS.   Wher is he now, we thee pray?
CHELIDONIUS.   I know not wher he is by
    this day.

II. VICINUS.   Thou shalt with us come on
    this way,
And to the pharisies these wordes say;
But if thou wouldst these thinges deny,
It shall helpe thee right nought.   119

    [They approach the Pharisees.]

Looke up, lordings and iudges of right,
We have brought you a man that had no
    sight,
And on the Sabaoth Day, throughe one
    mans might,
Was healed and restored, for-sooth.
I. VICINUS.   Declare to them, thou wicked
    wight,
Who did restore thee to thy sight,
That we may know anon right
Of this matter the truthe.   127

CHELIDONIUS.   Iesus anoynted myne eyes
    with clay,
And badd me wash in Siloe;
And before I came away
My perfect sight I hadd.
I. PHARISEUS.   This man, the truth if I
    should say,
Is not of God — my head I lay —
Which doth violate the Sabaoth Day;
I iudge him to be madd.   135

II. PHARISEUS.   It can not enter into my
    thought,
That he which hathe this marvayle
    wrought
Should be a sinner.   I leeue it nought;
It is not in my creed.   139

Say, what is he that did thee heale?
CHELIDONIUS.   A prophet he is, withe-out
    fayle.

I. PHARISEUS.   Surely, thou art a knave of
    kynd,

And faynest thy selfe for to be blynd;
Wherfor now this is my mynd,
The truth to trye, in deed: 145

His father and mother, both in feere,[1]
Shall come declare the matter here,
And then the truth shall soone apeare,
And we putt out of dowbt.
Goe forth, messenger, anon in hye,[2]
And fetch his parentis by and by.
This knave can nought but prate and
    lye;
I would his eyes were out!   153

NUNTIUS.   Your biddinge, maisters, I shall
    fulfill
And do my duty, as is good skyll;
From this day hither, I know, they will,
And I shall spy them out.

    Then he looks about, and says [3] *[to the*
    Father and Mother of the blind man]:

Sir and dame, booth in feer,
You must afore the pharisies apeare;
What ther will is, ther shall you here.
Have done, and come your way!   161

MATER.   Alas! man, what doe we here?
Must we afore the pharisies appeare?
A vengeance on them, far and neere!
The[y] neuer did poore man good.
PATER.   Dame, ther is no other way,
But ther commandement we must obay;
Or ells they would without delay
Cursse us and take our good.   169

[The messenger leads them to the Pharisees.]
NUNTIUS.   Here I haue brought, as you
    badd me,
These two persons, that aged be;
They be the parentis of him, truly,
Which sayd that he was blynde.
I. PHARISEUS.   Come near to us, bothe
    two,
And tell us truly, or that you goe,
Whether this be your sonne or no.
Looke, no deceit we fynd!   177

PATER.   Maisters, we know certaynly
Our sonne he is; we can not denye;

---

[1] Together.   [2] Hastily.
[3] MS. *Tunc circumspectat, et loquitur.*

And blynd was borne, undoubtedly.
And that we will depose. 181

But who restored him to his sight,
We be uncertayne, by God almight!
Wherfore of him, as it is right,
The truth you must enquier.
MATER. For he hath age, his tale to tell,
And his mother tonge to utter it well,
Althoughe he could never buy nor sell.
Let him speak, we desyre. 189

I. PHARISEUS. Geue prayse to God, thou crafty knave!
And looke, hereafter, thou doe not rave
And say that Iesus did thee save,
And restored thee to thy sight.
II. PHARISEUS. He is a sinner, and that we know,
Deceiving the people, too and froe.
This is most true that we thee show;
Beleev us, as is right. 197

CHELIDONIUS. If he be sinnfull, I doe not know;
But this is truth that I doe show:
When I was blynd, and in great wo,
He cured me, as you see. 201

I. PHARISEUS. What did he, thow lither swayne?
CHELIDONIUS.[1] I towld you once; will you here it agayne?
Or his desciples will you become,
Of all your sinnes to have remission? 205

II. PHARISEUS. O cursed caytafe! ill mott thou thee!
Would thou haue us his disciples to be?
No, no! Moyses disciples been all we,
For God with him dyd speak. 209

But whence this is, we never knew.
CHELIDONIUS. I marvayle of that, as I am true,

That you know not whenc he should bee,
That hath me cured that never did see,
Knowing this most certainly:
God will not sinners heare;
But he that honoureth God truly,
Him will he heare by and by,
And graunt his askinge graciously,
For that man to him is deare. 219

And to this I darr be bould:
Ther is no man that ever could
Restore a creature unto his sight
That was blynd borne and never saw light,
If he of God were not, iwis;
He could never worke such things as this! 225

I. PHARISEUS. What, sinfull knave, wilt thou teach us,
Which all the scriptures can discusse,
And of our lyving be so vertuous?
We cursse thee out of this place! 229

[SCENE III.]

[*Chelidonius, Jesus and the Jews.*]

IESUS. Beleuest thou in Gods Sonne truly?
CHELIDONIUS. Yea, gracious Lord; who is hee?

IESUS. Thou hast him seene with thine eye:
He is the same that talketh with thee.
CHELIDONIUS. Then hear I honour him with hart free,
And ever shall serve him, untill I dye. 235

I. IUDEUS. Say, man, that makes such maystery,
Or thou our soules do any anye,
Tell us here apertly,
Christ if that thou bee.
IESUS. That I speak unto you openly,
And workes that I doe verely
In my Fathers name almighty,
Beareth witnes of me. 243

But you beleve not as you seene,
For of my shepe you ne beene;
But my flock, withouten weene,[1]
Hear my voyce alway.
And I know them well echon,
For with me alway the[y] gone,
And for them I ordayned in my one[2]
Everylasting lyfe for aye. 251

[1] MS. Cæcus.

[1] Doubt. [2] Habitation.

No man shall reave my shepe from me;
For my Father in maiesty
Is gretter then bene all yee,
Or any that ever was.

II. IEW.   Thou shalt abye, by my bone, or
thou heathen [1] passe!   256

Help, fellow, and gather stones,
And beat him well, for Cockes bones!
He scorns us quintly, for the nones,
And dothe us great anye.

Then they collect stones. [2]

Yea, stones anow here I haue
For this ribauld that thus can rave.
One strock, as God me save,
He shall haue sone in hye!   264

IESUS.   Wretches, many a good deed
I haue done you in great need;
Now quite you foule my meed
To stone me on this maneer!

I. IEW.   For thy good deed that thou hast
wrought,
At this tyme stone we thee nought,
But for thy leasings, falsely wrought,
Thou shewest apeartly here.   272

Thou that art man, as well as I,
Makes thy self God here openly.
Ther thou lyest foule and falcely,
Bothe in word and thought!
IESUS.   But I do well and truly,
My Fathers biddinge by and by;
Ells you may hope well I lye,
And then leeves you me nought.   280

But sithen you will not leeven me,
Nor my deeds which you now see,
To them belevinge takes yee,
For nothing may be sother.[3]
So you may know well and veray:
In my Father that I am aye,
And he in me, [the] sothe to say,
And eyther of us in other.   288

*Then they shall collect stones, and straightway
Jesus shall disappear.* [4]

II. IEW.   Out, out, alas! wher is our fone?

Quintly that he is heathen gone!
I would haue taken him, and that anone,
And foull him all-to-frapped.[1]
Yea, make we never so much mone,
Now ther is no other wone; [2]
For he and his men everichon
Are from us clearly scaped.   296

I. IUDEUS.   Now, by the deathe I shall on
dye,
May I see him with my eye,
To sir Cayphas I shall him wry,[3]
And tell that shall him dere.[4]
Se I never none, by my fay,
When I had stones, so sone away!
But yet no force; an other day
His tabret [5] we shall fere.[6]   304

[SCENE IV.]

[Enter Mary and Martha.]

MARIA.   A Lord Iesu, that me is woo
To wit [7] my Brother sickly so.
In feble tyme Christ yode [8] me fro.
Well were we, and [9] he were heer.
MARTHA.   Yea, suster, about I will goe
And seeke Iesu, to and fro.
To help him he would be thro,
And he wist how it were.   312

Then Jesus comes [with his disciples]. [10]

A my Lord, swet Iesu, mercy!
Lazar, that thou lovest tenderly,
Lyeth sick a little hereby
And suffereth much teene.
IESUS.   Yea, woman, I tell thee witterly,
That sicknes is not deadly,
But Gods Sonne to glorify,
By him as may be seene.   320

[Jesus and his disciples depart.]

Then Martha shall go to Mary. [11]

MARIA.   A! Martha, suster, alas! alas!
My brother is dead since thou here was.
Had Iesu, my Lord, been in this place,
This case had not befalne.
MARTHA.   Yea, suster, neer is God[e]s grace.

---

[1] Hence.   [2] MS. *Tunc lapides colligunt.*
[3] Truer.
[4] MS. *Tunc colligent lapides, et statim evanescet
Iesus.*

[1] Rained blows upon.   [2] One?
[3] Betray.   [4] Injure.   [5] Tabor.
[6] Accompany? Frighten?   [7] Know.
[8] Went.   [9] If.
[10] MS. *Tunc venit Iesus.*
[11] MS. *Tunc ibit Martha ad Mariam.*

Many a man he holpen hase;
Yet may he doe for us in this case,
And him to lyfe call[en].   328

MARIA.   Here will I sitt and mourninge
    make,
Tyll that Iesu my sorrow slake.
My teene to hart, Lord, [that] thou take,
And leech [1] me of my woe.
MARTHA.   In sorrow and wo here will I
    wake,
And lament for Lazar my brothers sake;
Though I for could [2] and penance quake,
Heathen [3] will I not goe.   336

*Then they shall seat themselves near the
    sepulchre of Lazarus, lamenting.[4]*

[SCENE V.]

[Jesus and his disciples.]   And Jesus says:

IESUS.   Brethren, goe we to Iudy!
PETRUS.   Maister, right now thou might
    well see,
The Iewes would haue stoned thee,
And yet thou wilt agayne?
IESUS.   Wot you not well, this is veray,
That xij hours are in the day,
And who so walketh in that tyme his way,
Trespasseth not, the sooth to say[n].   344

He offendeth not that goeth in light;
But who so walketh about in night,
He trespasseth all against the right,
And light in him is none.
Why I say this, as I haue tight,[5]
I shall tell you sone in height;[6]
Haue mynd on it through your might,
And thinkes well therupon.   352

To the day my self may likned be,
And to the twelue howers all ye,
That lightned bene through following me
That am most lyking light.
For world[e]s light I am veray,
And who so followeth me, sooth to say,
He may goe no chester [7] way,
For light in him is dight.   360

---

[1] Heal.   [2] Cold.   [3] Hence.
[4] MS. *Tunc pariter iuxta sepulcrum Lazari, sedebunt
plorantes, et ait Iesus.*
[5] Good breeding (a rhyme-tag).
[6] At once.   [7] Chaster?

*Oportet me operari opera eius, qui misit
me, donec dies est; venit nox, quando nemo
est operari; quam diu sum in mundo, lux
sum mundi. Iohannis Cap. 10 de Lazaro
resuscitato.*

Brethren, I tell you tydinge:
Lazar my frend is slepinge.
Thider must we be goinge,
Upon him for to call.
IOHANNES EVAN.   Lord, if he sleep, safe
    he may be;
For in his sleep no peryll is he.
Therfore it is not good for thee
To goe thider for so small.   368

IESUS.   I tell you, brethren, certaynly:
Lazar is dead, and thyder will I.
Fayne I am you wott that I
Was not ther, as you may see.
THOMAS.   Follow him, brethren, to his
    anoy,
And dye with him devoutly;
For other it will not be.
Goe we thider in hye!   376

*Then Jesus shall go to the place where
    Mary and Martha are sitting.[1] [He comes
    first to Martha.]*

MARTHA.   A! Lord Iesu, hadst thou bene
    here leade,[2]
Lazar, my brother, had not bene dead.
But well I wott thou wilt us read,[3]
Now thou art with us here.
And this I leeue and hope aright:
What thing thou askest of God almight,
He will graunt it thee in height,
And graunt thee thy prayer.   384

IESUS.   Martha, thy brother shall ryse, I
    say.
MARTHA.   That leeue I, Lord, in good
    fay,
That he shall ryse the last day.
Then hope I him to see.
IESUS.   Martha, I tell thee, without nay,
I am rysinge and lyfe veray;
Which lyfe, I say, shall last for aye,
And never shall ended bee.   392

---

[1] MS. *Tunc versus locum ibit Iesus, ubi Maria et
Martha sedent.*
[2] Led here.   [3] Advise.

Whosoever leeveth stidfastly
In me, I tell the truly,
Though he dead be, and down lye,
Shall lyve and fare well.
Leevest thou, woman, that this may
  bee? 397

MARTHA. Lord, I leeue, and leeue mon,[1]
That thou art Christ, Gods Sonne,
And commen into this world to woon,[2]
Mans boot for to bee.
Thus haue I leued stidfastly;
Therfore on me thou haue mercy,
And on my suster eeke, Mary!
I will fetch her to thee. 405

Then Martha shall go and call Mary, saying:[3]

A! Mary, suster, leefe and deer,
Hye thee quickly and come neare!
My swet Lord Iesu, he is here,
And calleth thee him too.
MARIA. A! well were we, and it so were!
But had my louely Lord of leere [4]
Seene my brother lye on bere,[5]
Some boot might haue bene do.[6] 413

But now he stinketh, sooth to say;
For now this is the fourth[e] day,
Since he was buryed in the clay,
That was to me so leefe.
But yet, my Lord I will assay,
And with all my hart him will I pray,
To comfort us, if that he may,
And mend all our mischefe. 421

*Then let Mary, seeing Jesus, fall at his
  feet, saying:*[7]

A! Lord Iesu, hadst thou bene here,
Lazar, my brother, thy owne dere,
Had not bene dead in this maner.
Much sorrow is me upon.
IESUS. Wher haue you layd him? tell[e]s
  me.
MARIA. Lord, come thither and thou may
  see;
For buryed in this place is he
Four days now agon. 429

Then come the Jews, of whom let the first say:[1]

I. IEW. Se, fellow, for Cock[e]s sowle!
This freak beginneth to reem and youle,[2]
And make great dole for a gole,[3]
That he loved well befor[n]e.
II. IEW. If he had cunninge, me think he
  might
From death haue saved Lazar by right,
As well as send that man his sight,
That which so blynd was borne. 437

IESUS. Haue done, and putt away the
  stonne!
MARTHA. A, Lord! iiij dayes be now gone
Sith he was buryed, blood and bone.
He stinkes, Lord, in good fay.
IESUS. Martha, sayd I not to thee,
If that thou leeved fullye in me,
Gods grace soone shouldst thou see?
Therfore doe as I thee say. 445

*Then they shall remove the stone from the
  sepulchre; and Jesus, turning his back,
  with hands lifted up, says:*[4]

Father of heaven, I thank it thee,
That so sone hast hard me!
Well I wist, and soothly see,
Thou hearest my entent.
But for this people that stand hereby,
Speak I the more openly,
That they may leeue stidfastly
From thee that I was sent. 453

Lazar, come forth, I bydd thee!

[*Lazarus comes out of the sepulchre bound in
  burial cloths.*]

LAZARUS. A! Lord, blessed most thou be!
From death to lyfe hast raysed me
Through thy mickle might.
Lord, when I hard the voyce of thee,
All hell fayled of ther posty,[5]
So fast from them my soule can flee,
All devills were afright.[6] 461

IESUS. Loose him now, and let him goe!

---

[1] Must. [2] Dwell.
[3] MS. *Tunc Martha ibit et vocabit Mariam, dicens.*
[4] Face. [5] Bier. [6] MS. done.
[7] MS. *Tunc Maria, videns Iesum, prosternat se ad pedes, dicens:*

[1] MS. *Tunc veniunt Iudei, quorum dicat primus.*
[2] This fellow begins to weep and howl.
[3] Fellow?
[4] MS. *Tunc deponent lapidem de sepulcro; et Iesus, tergum vertens, manibus levatis dicit.*
[5] Power. [6] MS. a frayd.

[*Martha and Mary kneel before Jesus.*]

MARTHA.   A! Lord, honored be thou oo,[1]
That us hath saved from muche woe,
As thou hast ofte beforne;
For well I wit, it should be so,
When you were full far me froe.
The, Lord, I honour, and no moe,
Kneling upon my knee.   469

MARY.   A! Lord Iesu, much is thy might!
For now my hart is gladd and light,
To se my brother ryse in my sight,
Here before all thes meny.[2]
Well I hoped, that soone in height,
When thou came, it should fare aright.

     [1] Always.   [2] People, throng.

Thee, Lord, I honour with all my might,
Knelinge upon my knee.   477

MARTHA.   A! Lord Iesu, I thank thee,
That on my brother hast pitty.
By very signes now men may see
That thou art God[e]s Sonne.
Withe thee, Lord, ever will I bee,
And serue thee with hart free,
That this day hast gladded me,
And alway with thee wonne.[1]   485

IESUS.   Haue good day, my deghter deer!
Wherever you goe, farr or neer,
My blessinge I geue you here.
To Ierusalem I take the way.   489

        Finis decimæ tertiæ paginæ.

          [1] Dwell.

THE BETRAYING OF CHRIST [1]

[Acted at N. towne.]

[Jesus addresses his disciples.]

[JESUS.] Now, my dere frendys and
    bretheryn echone,[1]
Remembyr the wordys that I xal sey:
The tyme is come that I must gon
    For to fulfylle the prophesey   4
That is seyd of me that I xal dey,
    The fendys power fro yow to flem; [2]
Weche deth I wole not deney,   7
    Mannys sowle, my spovse, for to redem.

The oyle of mercy is grawntyd playn
Be this jorne that I xal take.
Be my Fadyr I am sent, sertayn,
    Be-twyx God and man an ende to
        make.   12
Man for my brother may I not for-sake,
    Nor shewe hym vn-kendenesse be no wey;
In peynys for hym my body schal schake,
    And for love of man, man xal dey.   16

*Here Jhesus and his discipulys go toward
the mount of Olyvet; and whan he comyth
a lytyl ther be-syde, in a place lyche [3] to a
park, he byddyt his dyscipulys a-byde hym
ther, and seyth to Petyr or he goth:*

Petyr, with thi felawys here xalt thou
    a-byde,
    And weche [4] tyl I come a-geyn.
I must make my prayere here you be-syde;
    My flesch qwakyth sore for fere and
        peyn.   20
PETRUS. Lord, thi request doth me
        constreyn;
    In this place I xal abyde stylle,
Not remeve tyl that thou comyst ageyn,
    In confermyng, Lord, of thi wylle.   24

*Here Jhesu goth to Olyvet and settyth hym
downe one his knes, and prayth to his
Fadyr, thus seyng:*

O, Fadyr! Fadyr! for my sake

This gret passyone thou take fro me,
Weche arn [1] ordeyned that I xal take
    Yf mannys sowle savyd may be.   28
And yf it be-hove, Fadyr, for me
    To save mannys sowle that xuld spylle,[2]
I am redy in eche degre,
    The vyl [3] of the for to fulfylle.   32

*Here Jhesus goth to his dyscipulis and
fyndyth hem sclepyng, Jhesus thus
seyng to Petyr:*

Petyr! Petyr! thou slepyst fast!
    A-wake thi felawys, and sclepe no
        more.
Of my deth ye are not agast;
    Ye take your rest, and I peyn sore.   36

*Here Cryst goth ageyn the second tyme to
Olyvet, and seyth knelyng:*

Fadyr in hevyn, I be-seche the
    Remeve my peynes be thi gret grace,
And lete me fro this deth fle,
    As I dede nevyr no trespace!   40
The watyr and blood owth of my face
    Dystyllyth for peynes that I xal take;
My flesche qwakyth in ferful case,
    As thow the joyntys a-sondre xuld
        schake.   44

*Here Jhesus goth a-gen to his discipulis
and fyndyth hem asclepe; Jhesus thus
seyng, latyng hem lyne:* [4]

Fadyr, the thrydde tyme I come a-geyn,
    Fulleche myn erdon [5] for to spede.
Delyuere me, Fadyr, fro this peyn,
    Weche is reducyd with ful gret drede. 48
On-to thi sone, Fadyr, take hede!
    Thou wotyst I dede nevyr dede but
        good!
It is not for me this peyn I lede,
    But for man I swete bothe watyr and
        blode.   52

[1] Each one.   [2] Drive, banish.
[3] Like.   [4] Watch.

[1] Is (are).   [2] Be lost.   [3] Will.
[4] Lie.   [5] Errand.

[1] For the source of the text and a discussion of the N. towne Plays see page 81, note 2.

Here an aungel descendyth to Jhesus, and
bryngyth to hym a chalys, with an host [1]
there-in.

ANGELUS.   Heyl, bothe God and man in-
        dede!
The Fadyr hath sent the this present.
He bad that thou xuldyst not drede,
    But fulfylle his intent,   56
As the parlement of hefne hath ment
    That mannys sowle xal now redemyd
        be.
From hefne to herd,[2] Lord, thou wore sent;
    That dede appendyth [3] on-to the.   60

This chalys ys thi blood, this bred is thi
        body,
    For mannys synne evyr offeryd xal be;
To the Fadyr of heffne, that is al-mythty,
    Thi dyscipulis and alle presthood xal
        offere fore the.   64

Here the aungel ascendyth a-gen sodeynly.

JHESU.   Fadyr, thi wyl ffulfyllyd xal be;
    It is nowth to say a-gens the case;
I xal fulfylle the prophesye,
    And sofre deth ffor mannys trespace. 68

Here goth Cryst a-geyn to his dyscipulys,
and fyndyth hem sclepyng stylle.

A-wake, Petyr! thi rest is ful long;
    Of sclep thou wylt make no delay.
Judas is redy, with pepyl strong,
    And doth his part me to be-tray.   72
Ryse up, serys, I you pray!
    On-close your eyne for my sake.
We xal walke in-to the way,
    And sen [4] hem come that xul me take. 76

Petyr, whan thou seyst I am for-sake
Amonge myn frendys, and stond alone,
Alle the cher that thou kanst make
    Geve to thi bretheryn every-chone.   80

Here Jhesus with his dyscipulis goth in-to
the place, and ther xal come in a x.
personys weyl be-seen [5] in white arneys,[6]
and breganderys,[7] and some dysgysed in

---

    [1] The bread consecrated in the Eucharist.
    [2] From heaven to earth.
    [3] Belongs.   [4] See.
    [5] Arrayed.   [6] Armor.
    [7] Armor worn by foot-soldiers.

odyr garmentys, with swerdys, gleyvys,[1]
and other straunge wepone, as cressettys
with feyr, and lanternys and torchis lyth; [2]
and Judas formest of al conveying hem
to Jhesu be contenawns.[3]   Jhesus thus
s[eyng]:

Serys, in your wey ye haue gret hast
    To seke hym that wyl not fle.
Of yow I am ryth nowth a-gast.
    Telle me, serys, whom seke ye?   84

LEYONE.   Whom we seke here I telle the
        now, —
    A tretour, is worthy to suffer deth.
We knowe he is here a-mong yow;
    His name is Jhesus of Nazareth.   88

JHESU.   Serys, I am here that wyl not
        fle,
    Do to me all that ye kan.
For-sothe I telle yow I am he,
    Jhesus of Nazareth, that same man. 92

Here alle the Jewys falle sodeynly to the
erde whan thei here Cryst speke, and qwan
[he] byddyth hem rysyn thei rysyn agen,
Cryst thus seyng:

A-ryse, serys! Whom seke ye?   Fast haue
        ye gone.
    Is howth [4] your comyng hedyr for
        me?
I stond be-forn yow here echone,
    That ye may me bothe knowe and se. 96

RUFYNE.   Jhesus of Nazareth we seke,
    And we myth hym here a-spye.
JHESU.   I told yow now with wordys
        meke,
    Be-forn yow alle, that it was I.   100

JUDAS.   Welcome, Jhesu, my mayster
        dere!
    I haue the sowth [5] in many a place!
I am ful glad I fynd the here,
    For I wyst nevyr wher thow wace.[6] 104

Here Judas kyssyth Jhesus, and a-noon
alle the Jewys come a-bowth hym, and ley
handys on hym, and pullyn hym as thei

---

    [1] Spears.   [2] Lighted.
    [3] Countenance.   [4] Aught.
    [5] Sought.   [6] Wast.

were wode,[1] and makyn on hym a gret cry all at-onys; and aftyr this Petyr seyth;

PETRUS. I drawe my swerd now this sel; [2]
Xal I smyte, mayster? fayn wolde I wete! [3]

And forth-with he smytyth of Malcheus here,[4] and he cryeth " Help myn here! myn here!" and Cryst blyssyth it, and tys hol.

JHESUS. Put thy swerd in the shede [5] fayr and wel,
For he that smyth with swerd, with swerd xal be smete. 108

A, Judas! this treson cowntyrfetyd [6] hast thou!
And that thou xalt ful sore repent!
Thou haddyst be bettyr a ben vn-born now; 111
Thi body and sowle thou hast shent! [7]

GAMALYEL. Lo, Jhesus, thou mayst not the cace refuse;
Bothe treson and eresye [8] in the is fownde;
Stody now fast on thin excuse,
Whylys that thou gost in cordys bownde. 116
Thou kallyst the [9] kyng of this werd [10] rownde,
Now lete me se thi gret powere!
And save thi-self here, hool and sownde,
And brynge the out of this dawngere!

LEYONE. Bryng forth this tretoure!
Spare hym nowth! 121
On-to Cayphas thi jewge [11] we xal the ledde.
In many a place we haue the sowth;
And to thi werkys take good hede! 124

RUFYNE. Com on, Jhesus, and folwe me;
I am ful glad that I the haue;
Thou xalt ben hangyn up-on a tre, —
A melyon [12] of gold xal the not save! 128

LEYONE. Lete me leyn hand on hym in heye,

On-to his deth I xal hym bryng.
Shewe forth thi wyche-crafte and nygra-mansye! [1]
What helpyth ye now al thi fals werkyng? 132

JHESU. Frendys, take hede! Ye don vn-ryth
So vn-kendely with cordys to bynd me here,
And thus to falle on me be nyth, [2]
As thow I were a thevys fere.[3] 136
Many tyme be-forn yow I dede a-pere;
With-inne the Temple sen [4] me ye have,
The lawys of God to teche and lere,[5]
To hem that wele here sowlys sawe.[6] 140

Wy dede ye not me dysprave,[7]
And herd me preche, both lowd and lowe?
But now as wood [8] men ye gynne to rave,
And do thyng that ye notwth knove.[9]

GAMALY[EL]. Serys, I charge yow not o [10] word more this nyth, 145
But on-to Cayphas in hast loke ye hym lede.
Have hym forth with gret dyspyte,
And to his wordys take ye non hede. 148

Here the Jewys lede Cryst outh of the place with gret cry and noyse, some drawyng Cryst forward and some bakwarde, and so ledyng forth, with here weponys a-lofte and lytys brennyng. And in the mene tyme Marye Magdalene xal rennyn to oure Lady, and telle here of oure Lordys takyng, thus seyng:

MARIA MAGDELENE. O, in-maculate modyr, of alle women most meke!
O devowtest, in holy medytacion evyr a-bydyng!
The cawse, Lady, that I to your person seke, 151
Is to wetyn [11] yf ye heryn ony tydyng

Of your swete sone, and my reverent lord, Jhesu,

---

[1] Mad.	[2] Occasion.	[3] Know.	[4] Ear.
[5] Sheath.	[6] Counterfeited.	[7] Destroyed.	
[8] Heresy.	[9] Callest thyself.		
[10] World.	[11] Judge.	[12] Million.	

[1] Necromancy.		[2] Night.
[3] Companion.		[4] Seen.
[5] Expound.	[6] Save.	[7] Disprove.
[8] Mad.	[9] Know not what.	
[10] One.	[11] Know.	

That was your dayly solas, your gostly
   consolacyone!
MARYA. I wold ye xuld telle me, Mawde-
   lyn, and [1] ye knew,
For to here of hym it is alle myn
   affeccyone.   156

MARIA MAGD[ALEN]. I wold fayn telle,
   Lady, and [1] I myth for wepying.
For sothe, Lady, to the Jewys he is solde;
With cordys thei haue hym bownde and
   haue hym in kepying;
Thei hym bety spetously, and haue hym
   fast in holde.   160
MARIA VIRGO. A! A! A! how myn
   hert is colde!
A! hert, hard as ston, how mayst thou lest?
Whan these sorweful tydyngys are the told,
   So wold to God, hert, that thou mytyst
   brest.   164

A! Jhesu! Jhesu! Jhesu! Jhesu!
   Why xuld ye sofere this trybulacyon and
   advercyte?
How may thei fynd in here [2] hertys yow to
   pursewe,
   That nevyr trespacyd in no maner
   degre?   168
For nevyr thyng but that was good thowth
   ye.
   Wherc-fore than xuld ye sofer this gret
   peyne?
I suppoce veryly it is for the tresspace of
   me,
   And I wyst that myn hert xuld cleve on
   tweyne.   172

For these langowrys [3] may I [not] susteyne,
   The swerd of sorwe hath so thyrlyd [4] my
   meende.

[1] If.   [2] Their.   [3] Sorrows.   [4] Piereed.

Alas! what may I do? alas! what may I
   seyne?
These prongys myn herte a-sondyr thei
   do rende.   176

O Fadyr of hefne! wher ben al thi be-
   hestys [1]
That thou promysyst me, whan a modyr
   thou me made?
Thi blyssyd Sone I bare be-twyx tweyn
   bestys,
   And now the bryth [2] colour of his face
   doth fade.   180

A, good Fadyr! why woldyst that thin
   owyn dere Sone xal sofre al this?
And dede he nevyr agens thi precept, but
   evyr was obedyent,
And to every creature most petyful, most
   jentyl, and benyng, i-wys;
   And now for alle these kendnessys is now
   most shameful schent. [3]   184

Why wolt thou, gracyous Fadyr, that it
   xal be so?
May man not ellys be savyd be non other
   kende? [4]
Yet, Lord Fadyr, than that xal comforte
   myn wo,
   Whan man is savyd be my chylde, and
   browth to a good ende.   188

Now, dere sone, syn thou hast evyr be so
   ful of mercy,
That wylt not spare thi-self for the love
   thou hast to man,
On alle man-kend now haue thou pety, —
   And also thynk on thi modyr, that hevy
   woman.   192

[1] Promises.   [2] Bright.
[3] Injured.   [4] Way.

THE TRIAL OF CHRIST [1]

[Acted at N. towne.]

*Here xal a massanger com in-to the place
rennyng and criyng, "Tydyngys! tydynges!" and so rownd abowth the place,
"Jhesus of Nazareth is take! Jhesus of
Nazareth is take!" and forth-with heylyng
the prynces, thus seyng:*

MASSANGER.   Alle heyle, my lordys,
    princys of prestys! [1]
Sere Cayphas and sere Annas, lordys of
    the lawe!
Tydyngys I brynge you! Reseyve them in
    your brestys:
Jhesus of Nazareth is take! Ther-of ye
    may be fawe! [2]   4

He xal be browth [3] hedyr to you a-non,
    I telle you trewly, with a gret rowth. [4]
Whan he was take I was hem among,   7
    And ther was I ner to kachyd a clowte. [5]

Malcus bar a lanterne, and put hym in
    pres; [6]
A-noon he had a towche [7] — and of
    went his ere! [8]
Jhesus bad his dyscyple put up his swerd
    and ces,
And sett Malcus ere ageyn as hool as it
    was ere!   12

So mot Y the, [9] methowut it was a strawnge
    syth!
Whan we cam fyrst to hym he cam vs
    a-geyne, [10]
And haskyd whom we sowth that tyme of
    nyth.
We seyd, "Jhesus of Nazareth; we wolde
    haue hym fayn."   16

And he seyd, "It is I, that am here in your
    syth."
With that word we ovyr-throwyn bak-
    ward every-chone; [1]
And some on [t]her bakkys lyeng up-ryth,
    But standyng up-on fote manly [2] ther
    was not one.   20

Cryst stode on his fete as meke as a lom, [3]
    And we loyn [4] stylle lyche ded men, tyl
    he bad us ryse.
Whan we were up, fast handys we leyd
    hym up-on;
But yet me-thought I was not plesyd
    with the newe gyse. [5]   24

Ther-fore takyth now your cowncel, and
    a-vyse you ryth [6] weyl,
And beth ryth ware that he make you
    not a-mat; [7]
For, be my thryfte, I dare sweryn at this
    seyl, [8]
Ye xal fynde hym a strawnge watt! [9] 28

*Here bryng thei Jhesus be-forn Annas and
C[ayphas], and on xal seyn thus:*

Lo! lo! lordys, here is the man
    That ye sent us fore.
ANNAS.   Therfore we cone [10] you thanke
    than,
    And reward ye xal haue the more.   32

Jhesus, thou art welcome hedyr to oure
    presens;
    Ful oftyn-tymes we han the besyly do
    sowth. [11]
We payd to thi dyscyple for the thretty
    pens,

---

[1] Priests.   [2] Glad.
[3] Brought.   [4] Crowd.
[5] Near to have caught a blow.
[6] Throng.   [7] Touch, blow.
[8] Ear.   [9] Prosper.
[10] Into our presence, face to face with us.

[1] Every one.   [2] Boldly.
[3] Lamb.   [4] Lay.
[5] Guise, fashion. [6] Right.
[7] Dismayed.   [8] Time.
[9] Fellow.   [10] Give.
[11] Had thee sought for.

---

[1] For the source of the text, and a discussion of the N. towne Plays see page 81, note 2. I have followed Halliwell's division of the play, which seems to me more logical than that indicated by the numbering in the manuscript.

And as an ox or an hors we trewly the
    bowth;   36

Ther-fore now art oure [1] as thou standyst
    us be-fore.
Sey, why thou [h]ast trobelyd us, and
    subuertyd oure lawe?
Thou hast ofte concludyd [2] us, and so thou
    hast do more;
Wher-fore it were ful nedful to bryng the
    a dawe. [3]   40

CAYPHAS.   What arn thi dysciplys that
    folwyn the a-boute?
And what is thi doctryne that thou dost
    preche?
Telle me now some-whath, and bryng us
    out of doute,
That we may to othere men thi prechyng
    forth teche.   44

JHESUS.   Al tymes that I haue prechyd,
    opyn it was done
In the synagog or in the Temple, where
    that alle Jewys come:
Aske hem what I haue seyd, and also what
    I have done;
Thei con telle the my wordys; aske hem
    everychone.   48

I. JUDEUS.   What, thou fela! to whom
    spekyst thou?
Xalt thou so speke to a buschop?
Thou xalt haue on the cheke, I make a
    vow,
And yet ther-to a knok.   52

Here he xal smyte Jhesus on the cheke.

JHESUS.   Yf I haue seyd amys,
Ther-of wytnesse thou mayst bere;
And yf I haue seyd but weyl in this,
    Thou dost amys me to dere! [4]   56

ANNAS.   Serys, takyth hed now to this
    man,
That he dystroye not oure lawe;
And brynge ye wyttnesse a-gens hym that
    ye can,
So that he may be browt of dawe.[5] 60

I. DOCTOR.   Sere, this I herd hym with his
    owyn mowth seyn:
"Brekyth down this Temple with-out
    delay,
And I xal settynt up ageyn
    As hool as it was, by the thrydde
    day."   64

II. DOCTOR.   Ya, ser, and I herd hym seyn
    also
That he was the Sone of God;
And yet many a fole wenyth [1] so,
    I durst leyn ther-on myn hod. 68

III. DOCTOR.   Ya! Ya! and I herd hym
    preche meche [2] thing,
And a-gens oure lawe every del; [3]
Of wheche it were longe to make rekenyng,
    To tellyn alle at this seel.[4]   72

CAYPHAS.   What seyst now, Jhesus?   Whi
    answeryst not?
Heryst not what is seyd a-gens the?
Spek, man! Spek! Spek, thou fop!
    Hast thou scorn to speke to me? 76

Heryst not in how many thyngys thei the
    acuse?
Now I charge the and conjure, be the
    sonne and the mone,
That thou telle us and [5] thou be Goddys
    Sone.   79

JHESUS.   Goddys Sone I am; I sey not nay
    to the!
And that ye alle xal se at Domys-day,
Whan the Sone xal come in gret powere
    and majeste,
    And deme [6] the qweke [7] and dede, as I
    the say.   83

CAYPHAS. A! Out! Out! Allas! What
    is this!
Heryth ye not how he blasfemyth
    God?
What nedyth us to haue more wytness?
    Here ye han herd alle his owyn word! 87

Thynk ye not he is worthy to dey?

---

[1] Ours.   [2] Confuted.
[3] Kill thee.
[4] Injure.   [5] Slain.

[1] Thinketh.   [2] Many.
[3] Every bit.   [4] Time.
[5] If.   [5] Judge.   [7] Living.

And all shall cry out: [1]

Yis! yis! yis! Alle we seye he is worthy
    to dey, ya! ya! ya!

ANNAS.   Takyth hym to yow and betyth
    hym some del,[2]
For hese blasfemyng at this sel.[3]   91

*Here thei xal bete Jhesus a-bout the hed and
the body, and spyttyn in his face, and
pullyn hym down, and settyn hym on a
stol, and castyn a cloth ouyr his face; and
the fyrst xal seyn:*

I. JUDEUS.   A! felawys, beware what ye
    do to this man,
For he prophecye weyl kan.

II. JUDEUS.   That xal be a-sayd [4] be this
    batte.[5]
What thou, Jhesus! ho gaff the that?   95

And he shall strike him on the head.[6]

III. JUDEUS.   Whar? whar? now wole I
Wetyn [7] how he can prophecy.
Ho was that?   [*Strikes him.*]

IV. JUDEUS.   A! and now wole I a newe
    game begynne,
That we mon pley at, alle that arn here-
    inne; [8]   100
Whele and pylle! [9] whele and pylle!
Comyth to halle ho so wylle. [*Strikes him.*]
Ho was that?   103

*Here xal the woman come to [the] Jewys and
seyn:*

I. ANCILLA.   What, serys, how take ye on
    with this man?
Se ye not on of hese dysciplys how he be-
    heldyth you than?

Here xal the tother woman seyn to Peter.

II. ANCILLE.   A! good man, me semyth be
    the
That thou on of hese dysciplys xulde
    be.

[1] MS. *Et clamabunt omnes.*
[2] Somewhat.
[3] Time.   [4] Tested.   [5] Blow.
[6] MS. *Et percuciet super caput.*
[7] Know.   [8] Here.
[9] Wheel and pillage (the name of an old game?).

PETRUS.   A! woman, I sey nevyr er this
    man   108
Syn that this werd [1] fyrst be-gan.

And the cock shall crow.[2]

I. ANCILLA.   What? thou mayst not sey
    nay!   Thou art on of hese men!
Be thi face wel we may the ken.   111

PETRUS.   Woman, thou seyst a-mys of
    me;
I knowe hym not, so mote I the.

I. JUDEUS.   A! fela myn, wel met,
For my cosynys ere thou of smet,   115
Whan we thi mayster in the yerd toke;
Than alle thi ffelawys hym for-soke,
And now thou mayst not hym for-sake,
For thou art of Galyle, I vndyr-take.   119

PETRUS.   Sere, I knowe hym not, be hym
    that made me!
And ye wole me be-leve ffor an oth,
I take record of alle this compayne,
That I sey to yow is soth.   123

And the cock shall crow.[2] *And than
Jhesus xal lokyn on Petyr, and Petyr xal
wepyn, and than he xal gon out and seyn:*

A! weel-a-way! weel-a-way! Fals hert,
    why whylt thou not brest,[3]
Syn thi maystyr so cowardly thou hast
    forsake?
Alas! qwher xal I now on erthe rest,
    Tyl he of his mercy to grace wole me
    take?   127

I haue for-sake my mayster and my lord,
    Jhesu,
Thre tymes, as he tolde me that I xulde
    do the same;
Wherfore I may not haue sorwe a-now,
    I, synful creature, am so meche to
    blame.   131

Whan I herd the cok crowyn, he kest [4] on
    me a loke,
    As who seyth, "Be-thynke the what I
    seyd be-fore!"
Alas, the tyme that I evyr hym for-soke!

[1] World.   [2] MS. *Et cantabit gallus.*
[3] Burst.   [4] Cast.

And so wyl I thynkyn from hens evyr-
more.

CAYPHAS.   Massangere! Massangere!
MASSANGERE.   Here, lord, here!   137

CAYPHAS.   Massanger, to Pylat in hast
thou xalt gon,
And sey hym we comawnde [1] us in word
and in dede;
And prey hym that he be at the mot-halle
a-noon,
For we han a gret matere that he must
nedys spede.   141
In hast now go thi way,
And loke thou tery nowth.
MASSANGER.   It xal be do, lord, be this day;
I am as whyt [2] as thought.   145

*Here Pylat syttyth in his skaffald, and the
massanger knelyth to hym, thus seyng:*

Al heyl! sere Pylat, that semly [3] is to se!
Prynce of al this Jure, and kepere of the
lawe!
My lord, busshop Cayphas, comawndyd
hym to the,
And prayd the to be at the mot-halle by
the day dawe. [4]   149

PYLAT.   Go thi way, praty masanger, and
comawnde me also.
I xal be there in hast, and so thou mayst
say:
Be the oure of prime I xal comyn hem to;
I tery no longer, no make no delay.   153

*Here the massanger comith agen and
bryngith an ansuere, thus seyng:*

MASSANGER.   Al heyl! myn lordys, and
buschoppys, and princys of the lawe!
Ser Pylat comawndyth hym to you, and
bad me to you say,
He wole be at the mot-halle in hast sone
after the day dawe,
He wold ye xuld be ther be prime with-
outh lenger de-lay.

CAYPHAS.   Now weyl mote thou fare,[5] my
good page;
Take thou this for thi massage.   159

*Here enteryth Judas on-to the Juwys, thus
seyng:*

JUDAS.   I, Judas, haue synyd, and treson
haue don,
For I haue be-trayd this rythful [1] blood;
Here is your mony a-gen, alle and some.
For sorwe and thowth [2] I am wax
wood. [3]   163

ANNAS.   What is that to us?   A-vyse the
now,
Thou dedyst with us counawnt make,
Thou soldyst hym us as hors or kow;
Therfore thin owyn dedys thou must
take!   167

*Than Judas castyth down the mony, and
goth and hangyth hym-self.*

CAYPHAS.   Now, serys, the nyth is passyd,
the day is come;
It were tyme this man had his jewge-
ment;
And Pylat abydyth in the mot-halle
alone,
Tyl we xuld this man present;   171

And ther-fore go we now forth with hym
in hast.
I. JUDEUS.   It xal be don, and that in
short spas.
II. JUDEUS.   Ya! but loke yf he be bownd
ryth wel and fast.
III. JUDEUS.   He is saff a-now!   Go we
ryth [4] a good pas!   175

*Here thei ledyn Jhesu a-bowt the place tyl
thei come to the halle.*

CAYPHAS.   Sere Pylat, takyht hede to this
thyng!
Jhesus we han be-forn the browth,
Wheche owre lawe doth down bryng,   178
And mekyl schame he hath us wrowth.

ANNAS.   From this cetye in-to the lond of
Galyle,
He hath browth oure lawys neyr [5] in-to
confusyon;
With hese craftys wrowth be nygra-
mancye,[6]

---

[1] Commend.   [2] Swift.
[3] Lovely.   [4] Dawn.   [5] Prosper.

[1] Righteous.   [2] Thought, grief.   [3] Mad.
[4] Right.   [5] Near.   [6] Necromancy

Shewyth to the pepyl be fals sym-
    ulacyon.   183

i. Doctor. Ya! Yet, ser, a-nother, and
    werst of alle!
Agens Sesare, oure Emperour that is so
    fre,
Kyng of Jewys he doth hym [1] calle,
    So oure Emperourys power nowth [2]
    xuld be!   187

ii. Doctor. Sere Pylat, we kan not telle
    half the blame
That Jhesus in oure countre hath
    wrowth;
Therfore we charge the, in the Emperorys
    name,   190
That he to the deth in hast be browth!

Pylat. What seyst to these compleyntys,
    Jhesu?
These pepyl hath the sore acusyd,
Be-cause thou bryngyst up lawys newe,
    That in oure days were not vsyd. 195

Jhesus. Of here a-cusyng, me rowth
    nowth,[3]
So that thei hurt not here soulys, ne non
    mo.
I haue nowth yet founde that I haue
    sowth,[4]   198
For my Faderys wyl fforth must I go.

Pylat. Jhesus, be this, than, I trowe
    thou art a kyng,
And the Sone of God thou art also, —
Lord of erth and of alle thing, —
    Telle me the trowth, if it be so. 203

Jhesus. In hefne is knowyn my Faderys
    intent,
And in this werlde I was born;
Be my Fadyr I was hedyr sent,
    For to seke that was for-lorn. 207

Alle that me heryn,[5] and in me belevyn,
    And kepyn here feyth stedfastly,
Thow thei weryn dede [6] I xal them recuryn,
    And xal them bryng to blysse end-
    lesly.   211

Pilate. Lo! serys, now ye an erde [1] this
    man, how thynk ye?
Thynke ye not alle, be youre reson,
But as he seyth it may wel be,
    And that xulde be be this incheson? [2] 215

I fynde in hym non obecyon [3]
    Of errour, nor treson, ne of no maner
    gylt;
The lawe wele, in no conclusyon, 218
    With-owte defawth [4] he xuld be spylt [5]

i. Doctor. Sere Pylat, the lawe restyth
    in the,
And we knowe veryly his gret trespas.
To the Emperour this mater told xal be,
    Yf thou lete Jhesus thus from the
    pas!   223

Pylat. Serys, than telle me o thyng:
What xal be his a-cusyng?

Annas. Sere, we telle the, alto-gedyr,
For his evyl werkys we browth hym
    hedyr;   227
And yf he had not an evyl doere be,
We xuld not a browth hym to the.

Pylat. Takyth hym, than, after your
    sawe,[6]
And demyth hym aftyr your lawe. 231

Cayphas. It is not lefful [7] to vs, ye seyn,
No maner man for to slen;
The cawse why we bryng hym to the,
    That he xuld not oure kyng be. 235
Weyl thou knowyst kyng we haue non,
But oure Emperour alon.

Pylat. Jhesu, thou art kyng of Jure?
Jhesus. So thou seyst now to me. 239
Pylat. Tel me than, where is thi kyng-
    ham?

Jhesus. My kyngham is not in this
    werld,
I telle the at o word.   242
Yf my kyngham here had be,
I xuld not a be delyveryd to the.

---

[1] Himself.   [4] Nought.   [3] I rue me not.
[4] Sought.   [5] Hear, obey   [6] Dead.

[1] Have heard.   [2] Reason, occasion.
[3] Obstacle.   [4] Fault.   [5] Killed.
[6] Saying, speech.   [7] Lawful.

PYLAT. Seres, a-vyse yow as ye kan.
I can fynde no defawth in this man. 246
ANNAS. Sere, here is a gret record; take
 hed ther-to!
 And knowyng gret myschef in this
  man, —
And not only in o [1] day or to,
 It is many yerys syn he began, — 250
We kan telle the tyme where and whan,
 That many a thowsand turnyd hath
  he;
As alle this pepylle record weyl kan,
 From hens in-to the lond of Galyle. 254

 And they shall cry out [2] *"Ya! Ya! Ya!"*

PILAT. Serys, of o thyng than gyf me
 relacyone,
 If Jhesus were out-born in the lond of
  Galelye;
For we han no poer,[3] ne no jurediccyone,
 Of no man of that contre. 258
Ther-fore the trewth ye telle me,
 And a-nother wey I xal provyde.
If Jhesus were born in that countre,
 The jugement of Herowdys he must
  a-byde. 262

CAYPHAS. Sere, as I am to the lawe trewly
 sworn,
 To telle the trewth I have no fer;
In Galelye I know that he was born;
 I can telle in what place and where. 266
Agens this no man may answere,
 For he was born in Bedlem Jude;
And this ye knowe, now alle I haue don
 here,
 That it stant in the lond of Galelye. 270

PYLAT. Weyl, serys, syn that I knowe
 that it is so,
 The trewth of this I must nedys se;
I vndyrstand ryth now what is to do.
 The jugement of Jhesu lyth not to
  me; 274
Herowde is kyng of that countre,
 To jewge that regyon in lenth and in
  brede;
The jurysdyccyon of Jhesu now han must
 he.
 Ther-fore Jhesu in hast to hym ye
  lede. 278

[1] One. MS. [2] *Et clamabunt.* [3] Power.

In halle [1] the hast that ye may spede,
 Lede hym to the Herownde a-non
  present,
And sey I comawnde me, with worde and
 dede,
 And Jhesu to hym that I haue sent. 282

I. DOCTOR. This erand in hast sped xal
 be,
 In alle the hast that we can do;
We xal not tary in no degre, 285
 Tyl the Herowdys presens we come to.

Here thei take Jhesu and lede hym in gret
hast to the Herowde; and the Herowdys
scafald xal vn-close, shewyng Herowdes in
astat, alle the Jewys knelyng, except Annas
and Cayphas, thei xal stondyn, etcetera.

I. DOCTOR. Heyl, Herowde, most excyllent
 kyng!
 We arn comawndyd to thin presens;
Pylat sendyth the be us gretyng, 289
 And chargyth us, be oure obedyens, —
II. DOCTOR. That we xuld do oure dylygens
 To bryng Jhesus of Nazareth on-to
  the,
And chargyth us to make no resystens,
 Be-cawse he was born in this coun-
  tre. 294

ANNAS. We knowe he hath wrowth gret
 fole [2]
 A-geyns the lawe shewyd present;
Ther-fore Pylat sent hym on-to the, 297
 That thou xuldyst gyf hym jugement.

HEROWDE REX. Now, be Mahound, my
 god of grace!
 Of Pylat this is a dede ful kende!
I for-gyf hym now his gret trespace,
 And schal be his frend with-owtyn
  ende. 302
Jhesus to me that he wole sende,
 I desyred ful sore hym for to se;
Gret ese in this Pylat xal fynde. 305
 And, Jhesus, thou art welcome to me!

I. JUDEUS. My sovereyn lord, this is the
 case:
 The gret falsnesse of Jhesus is opynly
  knawe;

[1] All. [2] Mischief.

Ther was nevyr man dede so gret trespas,
  For he hath al-most destroyd oure
    lawe. 310

II. JUDEUS.   Ya! be fals crafte of soserye,[1]
  Wrowth opynly to the pepylle alle,
And be sotyl poyntys of nygramancye,
  Many thowsandys fro oure lawe be
    falle. 314

CAYPHAS.   Most excellent kyng, ye must
    take hede!
  He wol dystroye alle this countre, bothe
    elde and ying,
Yf he ten monthis more procede.
  Be his meraclys and fals prechyng, 318
He bryngyth the pepyl in gret fonnyng,[2]
  And seyth dayly a-mong hem alle,
That he is Lord, and of the Jewys kyng;
  And the Sone of God he doth hym
    calle 322

REX HEROWDE.   Serys, alle these materys
    I haue herd sayd,
  And meche more than ye me telle;
Alle to-gedyr thei xal be layde,
  And I wyl take there-on cowncelle. 326

[*Turning to Jesus.*]

Jhesus, thou art wel-come to me!
  I kan [3] Pylat gret thank for his sendyng;
I have desyryd ful longe the to se,
  And of thi meracles to haue know-
    yng. 330
It is told me thou dost many a wondyr
    thyng, —
  Crokyd to gon, and blynd men to sen,
And thei that ben dede gevyst hem levyng,
  And makyst lepers fayre and hool to
    ben. 334

These arn wondyr werkys wrought of the,
  Be what wey I wolde knowe the trew
    sentens.
Now, Jhesu, I pray the, lete me se
  O meracle wrougth in my presens. 338
In hast, now, do thi dylygens,
  And per-aventure I wyl shew favour to
    the;
For, now thou art in my presens,
  Thyn lyf and deth here lyth in me. 342

*And here Jhesus xal not speke no word to
the Herowde.*

Jhesus, why spekyst not to thi kyng?
  What is the cawse thou standyst so stylle?
Thou nowyst I may deme [1] alle thyng.
  Thyn lyf and deth lyth at my wylle! 346

What!   Spek Jhesus, and telle me why
  This pepyl do the so here acuse?
Spare not, but telle me now, on hey,[2]
  How thou canst thi-self excuse. 350

CAYPHAS.   Loo! serys, this is of hym a
    false sotylte;
  He wyl not speke but whan he lyst.
Thus he dysceyvyth the pepyl in eche degre;
  He is ful fals, ye veryly tryst.[3] 354

REX HEROWDE.   What, thou on-hangyd
    harlot! why wylt thou not speke?
  Hast thou skorne to speke on-to thi
    kyng?
Be-cawse thou dost oure lawys breke,
  I trowe thou art a-ferd of oure talk-
    yng. 358

ANNAS.   Nay, he is not aferde, but of a fals
    wyle,[4]
  Be-cawse we xuld not hym a-cuse;
If that he answerd yow on-tylle,
  He knowyth he can not hym-self ex-
    cuse. 362

REX HEROWDE.   What!   Spek I say, thou
    foulyng!   Evyl mot thou fare!
  Loke up!   The devyl mote the cheke!
Serys, bete his body with scorgys bare,
  And a-say to make hym for to speke!

I. JUDEUS.   It xal be do with-outyn
    teryeng. 367
  Come on, thou tretour, evyl mot thou the!
Whylt thou not speke on-to oure kyng?
  A new lesson we xal lere the! 370

*Here thei pulle of Jhesus clothis, and betyn
hym with whyppys.*

II. JUDEUS.   Jhesus, thi bonys we xal not
    breke,

---

[1] Sorcery.   [2] Foolishness.   [3] Give.

[1] Judge.   [2] At once.
[3] Trust, believe.   [4] Stratagem.

But we xal make the to skyppe!
Thou hast lost thi tonge?   Thou mayst not
speke?
Thou xalt a-say now of this whippe.   374

III. JUDEUS.   Serys, take these whyppys
in your hande,
And spare not whyl thei last;
And bete this tretoure that here doth
stonde.
I trowe that he wyl speke in hast!   378

*And qwan thei han betyn hym tyl he is alle
blody, than the Herownde seyth:*

[HEROWDE.] Sees,[1] seres, I comawnde you
be name of the devyl of helle!
Jhesus, thynkyst this good game?
Thou art strong, to suffyr schame;
Thou haddyst levyr [2] be betyn lame,
Than thi defawtys for to telle.   383

But I wyl not thi body alle spyl,
Nor put it here in-to more peyne.

[1] Cease.   [2] Rather.

Serys, takyth Jhesus at your owyn wyl,
And lede hym to Pylat hom ageyne. 387
Grete hym weyl, and telle hym, serteyne,
Alle my good frenchep xal he haue.
I gyf hym powere of Jhesus, thus ye hym
seyn,   390
Whether he wole hym dampne [1] or save.

I. DOCTOR.   Sere, at your request it xal
be do;
We xal lede Jhesus at your demaw[n]de,
And delyver hym Pylat on-to,
And telle hym alle, as ye comawnde. 395

*Here enteryth Satan in-to the place in the
most orryble wyse; and qwyl that he pleyth,
thei xal don on [2] Jhesus clothis and ouerest [3]
a whyte clothe, and ledyn hym ab-owth the
place, and than to Pylat be the tyme that
hese wyf hath pleyd.[4]*

[1] Condemn.
[2] Put on.
[3] Uppermost.
[4] The play that immediately follows is *Pilate's
Wife's Dream.*

THE HARROWING OF HELL [1]

[Acted by the Cooks and Innkeepers of Chester.]

Pagina Decima Septima de Descensu
    Christi ad Inferos.

The Cookes and Inkepers.

*[The interior of Hell. A "great light" begins
to shine. Adam advances.]*

ADAMUS. A! Lord and severayne Sav-
     iour,
Our comfort and our counseler,
Of this light thou art author,
As I se well in sight.   4
This is a signe thou would succour
Thy folke that bene in great langour,
And of the Devill be conquerour,
As thou hast yore behight.[1]   8

Me thou madest, Lord, of clay,
And gaue me Paradice in to play;
But after my sinne, sooth to say,
Deprived I was therfro,   12
And from that weale [2] putt away;
And here haue lenged [3] sithen aye,
In thesternes,[4] both night and day;
And all my kynd also.   16

Now, by this light that I now se,
Ioy is commen, Lord, through thee;
And of thy people thou hast pitty,
To putt them out of payne.   20
Sicker [5] it may none other be,
But now thou hast mercy on me;
And my kynd, through thy posty,[6]
Thou wilt restore agayne.   24

[Isaiah advances.]

ESAY. Yea, sickerly, this ilke [7] light
Comes from Gods Sonne almight;
For so I prophesyed aright,
Whyle that I was lyvinge.   28
Then I to all men beheight,
As I ghostly [8] sawe in sight,

This word that I through Gods might
Shall rehearce without tariinge: 32
    *Populus qui ambulabat in tenebris vidit
      lucem magnam. Isa. lx, 3.*

The people, that tyme I sayd expresse,
That went about in thesternes,
Se a full great lightnes,
As we done now, echone.   36
Now is fulfilled my prophesy,
That I, the Prophet Esay,
Wrott in my books that will not lye,
Who so will looke theron.   40

[Simeon the Just advances.]

SIMEON IUSTUS. And I, Symeon, sooth to
     say,
Will honor God, all that I may;
For when Christ a child was, in good
     fay,
In Temple I him tooke.   44
And as the Holy Ghost that day
Taught me, or I went away,
These wordes I sayd to God[ë]s pay,
As men may fynd in booke: 48
    *Nunc dimittis servum tuum, Domine,
      secundum verbum tuum in pace. St.
      Luke ii, 29.*

Ther I prayd, with-out[ë] lesse,
That God would lett me dye in peace,
For he is Christ that commen was, —
I had both feld and seene, —   52
That he had ordayned for mans heale,
Ioy to the people of Israell.
Nowe is it wonnen, that ilk weale,[1]
To vs, withouten weene.[2]   56

[John the Baptist advances.]

IOHANNES BAPTISTA. Yea, Lord, I am
     that ilk Iohn,
That followed thee in flood Iordan,
And that in world about can gone [3]

---

[1] Promised of yore.   [2] Happiness.
[3] Tarried.   [4] Darkness.   [5] In truth.
[6] Power.   [7] Same.   [8] Spiritually.

[1] Now is it won, that very happiness.
[2] Doubt.   [3] Did go.

---

[1] For the source of the text, see page 167, note 1.

To warne of thy comminge.   60
And with my finger I shewed expresse
A meke lamb in thy lyknes,
In token that thou common was
Mankynd of bale to bringe.   64
  Ecce agnus Dei, ecce qui tollit peccata
    mundi.

[*Seth advances.*]

SETH.   And I, Sethe, Adams sonne, am
      here,
That lyvinge went, without[en] were,[1]
To aske at paradyce a prayer
At God, as I shall say.   68
That he would graunt an angell in hye,
To geue oyle of his mercy,
To anoynt my father in his nye,[2]
In sicknes when he lay.   72

Then to me appered Michaell,
And bade me travell[3] never a deale,
And sayd wepinge nor prayers fell[4]
Avayled me nothing to seckc.   76
Nay of that oyle might I haue none,
Made I neuer so much mone,
Vntill fyve thousand years were gone,
And fyve hundreth eeke.   80

All bending the knee[5] [*as King David*
      advances].

DAVID.   A! high God and king of blisse,
Worshiped be thy name, iwis!
I hope that tyme now come[n] is
To deliuer vs of danger.   84
Come, Lord! come to Hell anone,
And take out thy folk, everychon,
For those years are fully gone
Sith mankynd first came heare.   88

Then let Satan sitting on his throne say to the
      devils:[6]

SATHAN.   Hell hownds, all that be here,
Make you bowne[7] with bost and bere;[8]
For to this fellowship in feere[9]
Ther hyes a fearly freak.[10]   92
A noble morsell you haue mon:[11]
Iesu, that is Gods Sonne,

----
[1] Doubt.   [2] Annoyance, suffering.
[3] Worry, suffer.   [4] Many.
[5] MS. *Omnes genu flectantes.*
[6] MS. *Tunc Sathan sedens in cathedra dicat de-*
monibus.
[7] Ready.   [8] Clamor.   [9] Together.
[10] Terrible fellow.   [11] Must.

Comes hither with vs to wonne.[1]
On him now ye you wreake![2]   96

A man he is fullye, in faye,
For greatly death he dredd to day,
And these wordes I hard him say:
"My soule is thirste vnto death:"   100
  Tristis est anima mea vsque ad mortem.
Such as I made halt and blynd,
He hath healed into ther kynd;
Therfor that boyster[3] looke that you
      bynde
In bale of hell breath!   104

II. DEMON.   Sir Sathanas, what man is he
That should thee pryve of thy posty?
How dare he doe agaynst thee,
And dread his death to day?   108
Gretter then thou he semes to bee;
For degraded of thy degree
Thou must be soone, well I see,
And pryvëd of thy pray.[4]   112

III. DEMON.   Who is this, so stiff and
      stronge,
That maisterly comes vs amonge,
Our felowship that he would fonge?
But therof he shall fayle.   116
Wete[5] he vs with any wrong,
He shall singe a sory song.
But on the, Sathanas, it is long,
And[6] his will ought avayle.   120

SATHAN.   Against this shrew, that comes
      here,
I tempted the folke in fowle manere;
Ayesell[7] and gall to his dinner
I made them for to dight,   124
And hange him on a rood tree.
Now is he dead right so throw me;
And to Hell, as you shall se,
He comes anone in height.   128

II. DEMON.   Sathan, is not this that syre
That raysed Lazar out of the fyre?
SATHAN.   Yea, this is he that wil conspyre
Anone to reave[8] vs all.   132
III. DEMON.   Out! Out! Alas! Alas!
Hear I coniure the, Sathanas,

----
[1] Dwell.   [2] Avenge yourselves.
[3] Boaster.   [4] Prey.
[5] Blame, censure.   [6] If.
[7] Vinegar.   [8] Rob.

Thou suffer him not to come to this place,
For ought that may befall.   136

II. DEMON.   Yea, sickerly, and he come
      here,
Passed is cleane our power;
For all this fellowship in feere
He may take away when he would,   140
For all be at his commandment.
Lazar, that was with vs lent,
Mawger [1] our teeth away he went,
And him might we not howld.   144

*Then shall come Jesus, and a clamor shall be
made, or a loud sound of things striking
together, and let Jesus say: "Lift up your
heads, O ye gates, and be ye lift up, ye everlasting doors, and the King of Glory shall
come in."* [2]

IHESUS.   Open Hell gates anone!
You princes of payn, every chon!
That Gods Sonne may in gone,
And the Kinge of Blisse!   148
II. DEMON.   Goe hence, poplard, [3] from
      this place!
Or thou shalt haue a sory grace!
For all thy boste and thy manase [4]
These men thou shalt[ë] misse.   152

SATHAN.   Out! Alas! What is this?
See I never so much blisse
Toward Hell come, iwisse,
Sith I was prince here.   156
My maisterdome now fares amisse,
For yonder a stubborn fellow is,
Right as wholly Hell were his
To reve me of my power.   160

III. DEMON.   Yea, Sathanas, thy sover-
      ainty
Fayl[e]s cleane! Therfore flee,
For no longer in this see [5]
Here shalt thou not sytt.   164
Goe forth! Feight for thy degree!
Or ells our prince shall thou not be;
For now passeth thy postye,
And hence thou must flitt.   168

Then let them hurl Satan from his seat. [1]

SATHAN.   Out! Alas! I am shent!
My might fayles verament!
This princ that is now present
Will spoyle from me my pray.   172
Adam, by my intycement,
And all his bloud, through me, were blent. [2]
Now hence thy shall all be hent, [3]
And I in Hell for aye.   176

IHESUS.   Open vp Hell gates, yet I say,
You princes of pine [4] that be present,
And lett the Kinge of Bliss this way,
That he may fulfill his intent!   180

SATHAN.   Say, what is he, that Kinge of
      Blisse?
IHESUS.   That Lord the which almighty is.
Ther is no power lyke to his;
Of all ioy he is kinge.   184
And to him is none lyk, iwis,
As is soothly seene by this,
For man, that sometyme did amis,
To his blisse he will bringe.   188

Then Jesus shall take Adam by the hand. [5]

IESUS.   Peace to the, Adam, my darlinge,
And eke to all thy ofspringe,
That righteous were in airth lyvinge;
From me you shall not sever.   192
To blis[se] now I will you bringe;
Ther you shall be without endinge.
Michael, lead these men singinge
To ioy that lasteth ever.   196

MICHAELL.   Lord, your will done shall be.
Come forth, Adam! Come with me!
My Lord vpon the rood tree
Your sinn[e]s hath forbought. [6]   200
Now shall you haue lyking and lee, [7]
And be restored to your degree,
That Sathan with his subtilty
From bliss to bale hath brought.   204

*Then Michael shall lead Adam and the
saints to Paradise; and in the way shall*

---

[1] In spite of.
[2] MS. *Tunc veniet Ihesus, et fiet clamor vel sonitus
materialis magnus, et dicat Ihesus: "Attolite portas
principes vestras, et elevamini portæ æternales, et introi-
bit Rex gloriæ.*
[3] A term of abuse.   [4] Menace.   [5] Throne.

[1] MS. *Iaceant tunc Sathanam de sede sua.*
[2] Cheated.
[3] Carried away.
[4] Pain, suffering.
[5] MS. *Tunc Iesus accipiet Adam per manum.*
[6] Paid for.
[7] Happiness and protection.

come Enoc and Elias and the saved thief;
and let Satan say: [1]

SATAN.   Out, alas! Now goeth away
My prisoners and all my pray!
And I might not stirr one stray,[2]
I am so streitly dight.   208
Now comes Christ.   Sorrow I may
For me and my meny for aye.
Never sith God made the first day,
Were we so fowle of right.   212

Then Adam, seeing Enoc and Elias, says: [3]

ADAMUS.   Say, what maner men bene yee,
That bodely meten vs, as I see,
And, dead, come not to Hell as we,
Since all men damned were?   216
When I trespassed, God hett [4] me
That this place closed always should be
From earthly man to haue entry;
And yet fynd I you here.   220

ENOCH.   Sir, I am Enocke, sooth to say,
Putt into this place to Gods pay;
And here haue lyved euer since that day,
At lyking all my fill.   224
And my fellow here, in good fay,
Is Hely, the prophett, as you se may,
That ravished was in that aray,[5]
As it was God[e]s will.   228

HELIAS.   Yea, bodely death — leeue thou
me —
Yet never suffred we;
But here ordaynd we are to be,
Till Ante Christ come with his.   232
Feight against vs shall he,
And slay vs in the holy citty;
But, sickerly, with-in days three
And half one we shall ryse.   236

ADAM.   And who is this that comes
here
With crosse on shoulder in such manere?
LATRO.   I am that theefe, my fader
deere,
That honge on roode tree.   240
But for I leeved, without weere,[1]
That Christ might saue vs both in feere,
To him I made my prayer,
The which was graunted me.   244

When I see signes veray
That he was Gods Sonne, soth to say,
To him devoutly I can pray,[2]
In his realme when he come,   248
To think on me by all way.
And he aunswered and sayd: "This day
In Paradice with me thou shalt be aye."
So hither the way I noome.[3]   252

And he betooke [4] me this tokeninge,
A crosse vpon my backe hanginge,
The angell Michael for to bringe,
That I might haue entrye.   256

ADAMUS.   Goe we to blisse, then, owld
and yonge,
And worship God, alway weldinge,[5]
And afterward, I read,[6] we singe
With great solemnity: 260
   "*Te deum laudamus, te Dominum con-*
   fitemur."

And thus they shall go out glorifying God,
singing "Te Deum." [7]

Finis Paginæ Decime Septimæ. [8]

[1] Doubt.   [2] Did pray.
[3] Took.   [4] Assigned.
[5] Ruling.   [6] Counsel.
[7] MS. "*Te Deum laudamus, te Dominum confitemur.*"
Et sic ibunt glorificantes Deum, cantantes "Te Deum."
[8] The other manuscripts add sixty lines, consisting
of a lamentation by an unsaved ale-woman, and her
welcome to hell by Satan and two devils, one of
whom offers to wed her.   It seems to be an addition
to the play itself, and since it is not of any special
merit, I have omitted it.

---

[1] MS. *Tunc Michael adducet Adam et sanctos ad*
Paradisum et in obviam venient Henoc et Helias, latro
salvatus; et Sathan dicat.
[2] Straw, bit.
[3] MS. *Tunc Adam, videns Enock et Heliam, ait.*
[4] Promised, assured.
[5] Attire, dress.

THE RESURRECTION OF CHRIST [1]

[Acted at Wakefield.]

Resurreccio Domini.

PILATUS. Peasse, I warne you, woldys [1] in
    wytt!
And standys on syde, or els go sytt;
For here ar men that go not yit,
    And lordys of me[kill] myght.
We thynk to abyde, and not to flytt, [2]
    I tell you euery wyght!   6

Spare youre spech, ye brodels [3] bold!
And sesse youre cry, till I haue told
What that my worship wold
    Here in thise wonys; [4]
Whoso that wyghtly nold [5]
    Full hy bese hanged his bonys!   12

Wote ye not that I am Pilate,
That satt apon the iustyce late,
At Caluarie where I was att
    This day at morne?
I am he, that great state,
    That lad has all to-torne. [6]   18

Now sen [7] that lothly losell [8] is thus ded,
I haue great ioy in my manhede;
Therfor wold I in ilk sted [9]
    It were tayn hede,
If any felowse felow his red, [10]
    Or more his law wold lede. [11]   24

For, and I knew it, cruelly
His lyfe bees lost, and that shortly,
That he were better hyng ful hy
    On galow tre!
Therfor ye prelatys shuld aspy
    If any sich be.   30

As I am man of myghtys most,
If ther be any that blow sich bost,

With tormentys keyn bese he indost [1]
    For euermore.
The devill to hell shall harry hys goost!
    Bot I say nomore.   36

CAIPHAS. Sir, ye thar nothyng be dredand, [2]
For Centurio, I vnderstand,
Youre knyght, is left abydand [3]
    Right ther behynde;   40
We left hym ther for man most wyse,
If any rybaldys wold oght ryse, [4]
To sesse theym to the next assyse, [5]
    And then forto make ende.   44

Then shall come the Centurion like a knight,
riding. [6]

CENTURIO. A, blyssyd Lord Adonay, [7]
What may this meruell sygnyfy
That here was shewyd so openly
    Vnto oure sight,
When the rightwys man can [8] dy
    That Ihesus hight?   50

Heuen it shoke abone; [9]
Of shynyng blan [10] both son and moyne;
And dede men also rose vp sone,
    Outt of thare grafe;
And stones in wall anone
    In sonder brast and clafe.   56

Ther was seen many a full sodan sight.
Oure prynces, for sothe, dyd nothyng
    right;
And so I saide to theym on hight, [11]
    As it is trew,
That he was most of myght,
    The Son of God, Ihesu.   62

Fowlys in the ayer and fish in floode

[1] Loaded.   [2] You need dread nothing.
[3] Abiding.
[4] If any rabble would make insurrection.
[5] Session of court.
[6] MS. *Tunc veniet Centurio velut miles equitans.*
[7] One of the names given to the Supreme Being.
[8] Did.   [9] Above.
[10] Ceased.   [11] At once.

[1] Wielders, possessors of.   [2] Depart.
[3] Wretches.   [4] Dwellings, places.
[5] Quickly would not.   [6] Torn to pieces.
[7] Since.   [8] Loathsome scamp.
[9] In every place.   [10] Follow his teaching.
[11] Lead, follow.

[1] For the source of the text, and a discussion of the Towneley Plays see page 94, note 1.

That day changid thare mode,
When that he was rent on rode,[1]
  That Lord veray;
Full well thay vnderstode
That he was slayn that day.   68
Therfor, right as I meyn, / to theym fast
    will I ryde,
To wyt withoutten weyn [2] / what they
    will say this tyde
Of this enfray.[3]
I will no longer abyde,
  Bot fast ride on my way.   73

[*He approaches Pilate and the High Priests.*]

God saue you, syrs, on euery syde!
Worship and welth in warld so wyde!
PILATUS. Centurio, welcom this tyde,
  Oure comly knyght!
CENTURIO. God graunt you grace well
    forto gyde,
  And rewll you right.   79

PILATUS. Centurio, welcom; draw nere
    hand!
Tell vs som tythyngys here emang;
For ye haue gone thrughoutt oure land,
  Ye know ilk dele.
CENTURIO. Sir, I drede me ye haue done
    wrang
  And wonder yll.   85

CAYPHAS. Wonder yll! I pray the why?
Declare that to this company!
CENTURIO. So shall I, sir, full securly,
  With all my mayn;
The rightwys man, I meyn hym by,[4]
  That ye haue slayn.   91

PILATUS. Centurio, sese of sich saw![5]
Ye ar a greatt man of oure law,
And if we shuld any wytnes draw
  To vs excuse,
To mayntene vs euermore ye aw,[6]
  And noght refuse.   97

CENTURIO. To mayntene trowth is well
    worthy.
I saide, when I sagh hym dy,
That it was Godys Son almyghty

---

[1] Cross.   [2] To know without doubt.
[3] Affray.   [4] I have him in mind.
[5] Speech.   [6] Owe.

That hang thore;
So say I yit, and abydys therby
  For euermore!   103

ANNA. Yee, sir, sich resons [1] may ye
    rew![2]
Thou shuld not neuen [3] sich notes new,
Bot thou couth [4] any tokyns trew
  Vntill vs tell.
CENTURIO. Sich wonderfull case neuer ere
    ye knew
  As then befell.   109

CAYPHAS. We pray the tell vs, of what
    thyng?
CENTURIO. Of elymentys, both old and
    ying,
In thare manere maide greatt mowrnyng
  In ilka stede;[5]
Thay knew by contenaunce that thare
    Kyng
  Was done to dede.   115

The son for wo it waxed all wan;
The moyn and starnes of shynyng blan;
And erth it tremlyd, as a man
  Began to speke;
The stone, that neuer was styrryd or
    than,
  In sonder brast and breke;   121

And dede men rose vp bodely, both greatt
    and small.
PILATUS. Centurio, bewar with-all!
Ye wote the clerkys the clyppys [6] it call,
  Sich sodan sight,
That son and moyne a seson shall
  Lak of thare light.   127

CAYPHAS. Sir, and if that dede men ryse
    vp bodely,
That may be done thrugh socery;[7]
Therfor nothyng we sett therby,
  That be thou bast.[8]
CENTURIO. Sir, that I saw truly,
  That shall I euermore trast.   133

Not for that ilk warke that ye dyd wyrke,
Not oonly for the son wex myrke,

---

[1] Sayings.   [2] Repent.   [3] Name.
[4] Could.   [5] In every place.
[6] Eclipse.   [7] Sorcery.
[8] Abast, abashed, astonished.

Bot how the vayll rofe in the kyrke,[1]
 Fayn wyt I wold.
PILATUS. A, sich tayles full sone wold
  make vs yrke,[2]
 If thay were told.   139

Harlot! wherto commys thou vs emang
With sich lesyngys [3] vs to fang? [4]
Weynd furth! Hy myght thou hang,
 Vyle fatur! [5]
CAYPHAS. Weynd furth in the wenyande!
 And hold styll thy clattur! 145

CENTURIO. Sirs, sen ye set not by my saw,
 / haues now good day!
God lene you grace to knaw / the sothe all
 way.   147

ANNA. With-draw the fast, sen thou the
  dredys;
For we shall well mayntene oure dedys.

[Exit Centurio.]

PILATUS. Sich wonderfull resons [6] as now
  redys [7]
 Were neuer beforne!
CAYPHAS. To neuen this note [8] nomore vs
  nedys,
 Nawder [9] euen nor morne, 153

Bot forto be-war of more were [10]
That afterward myght do vs dere; [11]
Therfor, sir, whils ye ar here
 Vs all emang,
Avyse you of thise sawes sere [12]
 How thay will stand. 159

For Ihesus saide full openly
Vnto the men that yode [13] hym by, —
A thyng that grevys all Iury,
 And right so may, —
That he shuld ryse vp bodely
 Within the thryde day. 165

If it be so, as myght I spede,
The latter dede is more to drede
Then was the fyrst, if we take hede
 And tend therto.

---

[1] The veil split apart in the church.
[2] Feel distressed. [3] Lies. [4] Seize.
[5] Deceiver. [6] Incidents. [7] Spoken of.
[8] Affair. [9] Neither. [10] Doubt.
[11] Harm. [12] Several sayings. [13] Passed.

Avyse you, sir, for it is nede,
 The best to do. 171

ANNA. Sir, neuer-the-les if he saide so,
He hase no myght to ryse and go,
Bot his dyscypyls steyll his cors vs fro
 And bere away.
That were till vs, and othere mo,
 A fowll enfray.[1] 177

Then wold the pepyll say euerilkon
That he were rysen hym self alon;
Therfor ordan to kepe that stone
 With knyghtys heynd [2]
To thise thre dayes be commen and gone
 And broght till ende. 183

PILATUS. Now, certys, sir, full well ye say!
And for this ilk poynt to puruay
I shall, if that I may,
 He shall not ryse,
Nor none shall wyn hym thens away
 Of nokyns [3] wyse. 189

[He addresses his soldiers.]

Sir knyghtys, that ar of dedys dughty,[4]
And chosen for chefe of cheualry,
As I may me in you affy,[5]
 By day and nyght,
Ye go and kepe Ihesu body
 With all youre myght; 195

And for thyng that be may,[6]
Kepe hym well vnto the thryd day,
That no tratur steyll his cors you fray [7]
 Out of that sted;
For if ther do, truly I say,
 Ye shall be dede! 201

I. MILES. Yis, sir Pilate, in certan,
We shall hym kepe with all oure mayn;
Ther shall no tratur with no trayn [8]
 Steyll hym vs fro!
Sir knyghtys, take gere [9] that best may gayn,
 And let vs go. 207

II. MILES. Yis, certys, we are all redy
  bowne; [10]
We shall hym kepe till youre renowne.

---

[1] Affray. [2] Gracious.
[3] No kind of. [4] Doughty. [5] Trust.
[6] For anything that may happen. [7] From.
[8] Guile, deceit. [9] Weapons. [10] Prepared.

[They cross over to the sepulchre.]

On euery syde lett vs sytt downe,
  We all in fere; [1]
And I shall fownde [2] to crak his crowne
  Whoso commys here.   213

I. MILES.   Who shuld be where,[3] fayn
     wold I wytt.
II. MILES.   Euen on this syde wyll I sytt.
III. MILES.   And I shall fownde [2] his feete
     to flytt.[4]
IV. MILES.   We, ther, shrew, ther!
Now by Mahowne, fayn wold I wytt
  Who durst com here   219

This cors with treson forto take!
For if it were the burnand drake [5]
Of me styfly he gatt a strake,
  Haue here my hand.
To thise thre dayes be past,
  This cors I dar warand.[6]

*[Christ rises from the tomb; the soldiers fall
into a stupor.]*

*Then the angels shall sing "Christus resur-
gens"; and afterwards Jesus shall speak.*[7]

IHESUS.   Erthly man, that I haue wroght,
Wightly wake, and slepe thou noght!
With bytter bayll I haue the boght,
  To make the fre.
Into this dongeon depe I soght,
  And all for luf of the.   231

Behold how dere I wold the by! [8]
My woundys ar weytt and all blody!
The, synfull man, full dere boght I
  With tray and teyn; [9]   .
Thou fyle the noght eft for-thy,[10]
  Now art thou cleyn. . . .[11]   237

Bot luf, noght els, aske I of the,
And that thou fownde [2] fast syn to fle;
Pyne [12] the to lyf in charyte

---

1 Together.   2 Endeavor.
3 Where should each (of us) be?
4 Strive with.   5 Dragon.   6 Warrant.
7 MS. *Tunc cantabunt angeli "Christus resurgens";
et postea dicet Iesus.*
8 Redeem.   9 Suffering and pain.
10 Defile thyself not again, therefore.
11 At this point I omit 77 lines of Christ's long ora-
tion to man.
12 Labor, try.

Both nyght and day;
Then in my blys that neuer shall mys
  Thou shall dwell ay.   321

For I am veray Prynce of Peasse,
And synnes seyr I may releasse.
And whoso will of synnes seasse,
  And mercy cry,
I grauntt theym here a measse [1]
  In brede — myn awne body.   327

That ilk veray brede of lyfe
Becommys my fleshe in wordys fyfe;
Whoso it resaues in syn or stryfe
  Bese dede for euer;
And whoso it takys in rightwys lyfe
  Dy shall he neuer.   333

[Jesus retires, and the three Maries advance.]

MARIA MAGDALENE.   Alas! to dy with
     doyll [2] am I dyght!
In warld was neuer a wofuller wight!
I drope, I dare, [3] for seyng of sight
  That I can se!
My lord, that mekill was of myght,
  Is ded fro me.   339

Alas! that I shuld se hys pyne! [4]
Or that I shuld his lyfe tyne! [5]
For to ich [6] sore he was medecyne,
  And boytte [7] of all,
Help and hold to euer ilk hyne [8]   345
  To hym wold call.

MARIA IACOBI.   Alas! how stand I on my
     feete
When I thynk on his woundys wete!
Ihesus, that was on luf so swete,
  And neuer dyd yll,
Is dede and grafen vnder the grete,[9]
  Withoutten skyll.   351

MARIA SOLOMEE.   Withoutten skyll thise
     Iues ilkon
That lufly Lord thay haue hym slone; [10]
And trespas dyd he neuer none,
  In nokyn [11] sted.

---

1 Mess (alluding to the Sacrament).
2 Dole, sorrow.   3 Gaze fixedly.
4 Pain.   5 Suffer deprivation of.
6 Each.   7 Remedy.   8 Person.
9 Buried under the earth.
10 Slain.   11 No kind of.

To whom shall we now make oure mone?
  Oure Lord is ded.   357

MARIA MAGDALENE.   Sen he is ded, my
  systers dere,
Weynd we will with full good chere,
With oure anoyntmentys fare and clere
  That we haue broght,
For to anoyntt his woundys sere,[1]
  That Iues hym wroght.   363

MARIA IACOBI.   Go we then, my systers
  fre,
For sore me longis his cors to see.
Bot I wote neuer how best may be;
  Help haue we none;
And which shall of vs systers thre
  Remefe the stone?   369

MARIA SALOMEE.   That do we not bot we
  were mo,[2]
For it is hogh[3] and heuy also.
MARIA MAGDALENE.   Systers, we thar[4] no
  farther go
  Ne make mowrnyng;
I se two syt where we weynd to,
  In whyte clothyng.   375

MARIA IACOBI.   Certys, the sothe is not to
  hyde;
The graue stone is put besyde.
MARIA SALOMEE.   Certys, for thyng that
  may betyde,
  Now will we weynde
To late the luf,[5] and with hym byde,
  That was oure freynde.   381

[They approach the sepulchre.]

I. ANGELUS.   Ye mowrnyng women in
  youre thoght,
Here in this place whome haue ye soght?
MARIA MAGDALENE.   Ihesu that vnto ded
  was broght,
  Oure Lord so fre.
II. ANGELUS.   Certys, women, here is he
  noght;
  Com nere and se.   387

I. ANGELUS.   He is not here, the sothe to
  say;

The place is voyde ther in he lay;
The sudary[1] here se ye may
  Was on hym layde.
He is rysen and gone his way,
  As he you sayde.   393

II. ANGELES.   Euen as he saide, so done
  has he;
He is rysen thrugh his pauste;[2]
He shalbe fon in Galale,
  In fleshe and fell.[3]
To his dyscypyls now weynd ye,
  And thus thaym tell.   399

MARIA MAGDALENE.   My systers fre, sen
  it is so,
That he is resyn the deth thus fro,
As saide till vs thise angels two,
  Oure Lord and leche,[4]
As ye haue hard, where that ye go
  Loke that ye preche.   405

MARIA IACOBI.   As we haue hard so shall we
  say.
Mare, oure syster, haue good day!
MARIA MAGDALENE.   Now veray God,
  as he well may,
  Man most of myght,
He wysh you, systers, well in youre way,
  And rewle you right.   411

[Exeunt Maria Jacobi and Maria Salome;
  manet Maria Magdalene.]

Alas, what shall now worth on me?[5]
My catyf hart wyll breke in thre
When that I thynk on that ilk bodye
  How it was spylt;
Thrugh feete and handys nalyd was he
  Withoutten gylt.   417

Withoutten gylt then was he tayn,[6]
That lufly Lord; thay haue hym slayn,
And tryspas dyd he neuer nane,
  Ne yit no mys.
It was my gylt he was fortayn,[7]
  And nothing his.   423

How myght I, bot[8] I lufyd that swete
That for me suffred woundys wete,

---

[1] Many.   [2] Unless we were more.
[3] Huge.   [4] Need.   [5] To find the dear one.

[1] Sudarium.   [2] Power.   [3] Skin.
[4] Physician.   [5] Become of me.
[6] Taken.   [7] Taken away.   [8] Unless.

Sythen [1] to be grafen vnder the grete,[2]
  Sich kyndnes kythe; [3]   427
Ther is nothyng till that we mete
  May make me blythe.

*[Mary Magdalene stands aside weeping.
The soldiers awake one after the other.]*

I. MILES.   Outt, alas! what shall I say?
Where is the cors that here-in lay?
II. MILES.   What alys the man?   He is
      away
  That we shuld tent?
I. MILES.   Ryse vp and se.
II. MILES.   Harrow! thefe! for ay
  I cownte vs shent! [4]   435

III. MILES.   What devyll alys you two
Sich no[i]se and cry thus forto may?
II. MILES.   For he is gone!
III. MILES.   Alas, wha?
II. MILES.   He that here lay.
III. MILES.   Harrow! Devill! How-swa
      gat he away?   441

IV. MILES.   What! is he thus-gatys [5] from
      vs went?
The fals tratur that here was lentt,[6]
That we truly to tent [7]
  Had vndertane?
Certanly I tell vs shent [8]
  Holly, ilkane.[9]   447

I. MILES.   Alas, what shall I do this day
Sen this tratur is won away?
And safely, syrs, I dar well say
  He rose alon!
II. MILES.   Wytt sir Pilate of this enfray
  We mon be slone.[10]   453

IV. MILES.   Wote ye well, he rose in dede!
II. MILES.   I sagh [11] myself when that he
      yede.[12]
I. MILES.   When that he styrryd out of the
      steed
  None couth it ken.
IV. MILES.   Alas, hard hap was on my
      hede
  Emang all men!   459

III. MILES.   Ye, bot wyt sir Pilate of this
      dede,
That we were slepand when he yede,
We mon forfett, withoutten drede,
  All that we haue.
IV. MILES.   We must make lees,[1] for that
      is nede,
  Oure self to saue.   465

I. MILES.   That red [2] I well, so myght I go.
II. MILES.   And I assent therto also.
III. MILES.   A thowsand shall I assay,[3]
      and mo,
  Well armed ilkon,
Com and toke his cors vs fro,
  Had vs nere slone.   471

IV. MILES.   Nay, certys, I hold ther none
      so good
As say the sothe [4] right as it stude,
How that he rose with mayn and mode,[5]
  And went his way.
To sir Pilate, if he be wode,[6]
  Thus dar I say.   477

I. MILES.   Why, and dar thou to sir Pilate
      go
With thise tythyngys, and tell hym so?
II. MILES.   So red I that we do also.
  We dy bot oones.
III. MILES ET OMNES.   Now he that
      wroght vs all this wo,
  Wo worth his bones!   483

IV. MILES.   Go we sam,[7] sir knyghtys
      heynd,[8]
Sen we shall to sir Pilate weynd;
I trow that we shall parte no freynd,
  Or that we pas.

[They come to Pilate.]

I. MILES.   Now and I shall tell ilka word
      till ende,
  Right as it was.   489

Sir Pilate, prynce withoutten peyr,
Sir Cayphas and Anna both in fere,
And all the lordys aboute you there,
  To neuen [9] by name;

---

¹ Then.   ² Grit, earth.
³ Proclaim, acknowledge.   ⁴ Disgraced, ruined.
⁵ In this fashion.   ⁶ Placed.   ⁷ Watch.
⁸ I account us ruined.   ⁹ Wholly, everyone.
¹⁰ Must be slain.   ¹¹ Saw.   ¹² Went.

¹ Lies.   ² Counsel.   ³ Say?
⁴ Truth.   ⁵ Strength and courage.
⁶ Mad.   ⁷ Together.
⁸ Gracious.   ⁹ Name.

Mahowne you saue on sydys sere [1]
   Fro syn and shame!   495

PILATUS. Ye ar welcom, oure knyghtys so
   keyn!
A mekill myrth now may we meyn; [2]
Bot tell vs som talkyng vs betwene,
   How ye haue wroght.
I. MILES. Oure walkyng, lord, withoutten
   wene, [3]
   Is worth to noght. [4]   501

CAYPHAS. To noght? Alas, seasse of sich
   saw!
II. MILES. The prophete Ihesu, that ye
   well knaw,
Is rysen, and went fro vs on raw, [5]
With mayn and myght.
PILATUS. Therfor the devill the all to-
   draw! [6]
   Vyle recrayd knyght!   507

What! combred [7] cowardys I you call!
Lett ye hym pas fro you all?
III. MILES. Sir, ther was none that durst
   do bot small
   When that he yede.
IV. MILES. We were so ferde we can
   downe fall,
   And qwoke for drede.   513

I. MILES. We were so rad, [8] euerilkon,
When that he put besyde the stone,
We quoke for ferd, and durst styr none;
   And sore we were abast.
PILATUS. Whi, bot rose he bi hym self
   alone?
II. MILES. Ye, lord, that be ye trast. 519

We hard neuer, on euyn ne morne,
Nor yit oure faders vs beforne,
Sich melody, myd-day ne morne,
   As was maide thore.
PILATUS. Alas! Then ar oure lawes
   forlorne [9]
   For euer more!   525

A, devill! what shall now worth [10] of this?
This warld farys with quantys. [11]

I pray you, Cayphas, ye vs wys [1]
   Of this enfray. [2]
CAIPHAS. Sir, and I couth [3] oght, by my
   clergys,
   Fayn wold I say.   531

ANNA. To say the best, for sothe, I shall;
It shalbe profett for vs all:
Yond knyghtys behovys thare wordys
   agane call,
   How he is myst;
We wold not, for thyng that myght befall,
   That no man wyst: [4]   537

And therfor of youre curtessie
Gyf theym a rewarde for-thy.
PILATUS. Of this counsell well paide [5] am I;
   It shalbe thus.
Sir knyghtys, that ar of dedys doghty,
   Take tent till vs: 543

Herkyns now, how ye shall say,
Where so ye go, by nyght or day,
Ten thowsand men of good aray
   Cam you vntill,
And thefyshly toke his cors you fray
   Agans youre will. ·   549

Loke ye say thus in euery land;
And therto, on this couande, [6]
Ten thowsand pounds haue in youre hande
   To youre rewarde;
And my frenship, I vnderstande,
   Shall not be sparde.   555

Bot loke ye say as we haue kende! [7]
I. MILES. Yis, sir, as Mahowne me mende,
In ilk contree where-so we lende [8]
   By nyght or day,
Where-so we go, where-so we weynd,
   Thus shall we say.   561

PILATUS. The blyssyng of Mahowne be
   with you nyght and day!

[*Jesus appears at the sepulchre in the disguise
of a gardener. Mary Magdalene ad-
vances to him.*]

MARIA MAGDALENE. Say me, garthynere,
   I the pray,

---

[1] Many.   [2] Call to mind.
[3] Doubt.   [4] Come to nought.
[5] In a line, straight.   [6] Pull to pieces.
[7] Benumbed.   [8] Frightened.
[9] Lost, destroyed.   [10] Come.   [11] Craft.

---

[1] Teach, advise.   [2] Affray.
[3] Knew.   [4] Knew.   [5] Pleased.
[6] Agreement.   [7] Instructed.   [8] Come.

If thou bare oght my Lord away.
Tell me the sothe, say me not nay,
 Where that he lyys;
And I shall remeue hym, if I may,
 On any kyn wyse. 568

IHESUS. Woman, why wepys thou? Be styll!
Whome sekys thou? Say me thy wyll,
 And nyk [1] me not with nay. 571
MARIA MAGDALENE. For my Lord I
 lyke [2] full yll.
The stede thou bare his body tyll
 Tell me, I the pray;
And I shall, if I may, / his body bere with me.
Vnto myn endyng day / the better shuld I
 be. 576

IHESUS. Woman, woman, turn thi thoght!
Wyt thou well I hyd hym noght,
 Then [3] bare hym nawre [4] with me. 579
Go seke; loke if thou fynde hym oght.
MARIA MAGDALENE. In fayth I haue hym
 soght,
 Bot nawre he will fond be. 582

IHESUS. Why, what was he to the, / in
 sothfastnes to say?
MARIA MAGDALENE. A! he was to me /
 no longer dwell I may.
IHESUS. Mary, thou sekys thy God —
 and that am I. 585

[Recognizing him, Mary falls at his feet.]

MARIA MAGDALENE. Rabony! My
 Lord so dere!
Now am I hole that thou art here.
Suffer me to negh the nere,
 And kys thi feete;
Myght I do so, so well me were,
 For thou art swete. 591

IHESUS. Nay, Mary, neghe thou not me,
For to my Fader, tell I the,
 Yit stevynd [5] I noght. 594
Tell my brethere I shall be
Before theym all in Trynyte,
Whose will that I haue wroght.
To peasse now ar thay boght / that pry-
 sond were in pyne; [6]
Wherfor thou thank in thoght / God, thi
 Lord and myne. 599

Mary, thou shall weynde me fro;
Myn erand shall thou grathly [1] go,
 In no fowndyng [2] thou fall; 602
To my dyscypyls say thou so,
That wilsom [3] ar and lappyd in wo,
 That I thaym socoure shall.
By name Peter thou call, / and say that I
 shall be
Before hym and theym all / my self in
 Galyle. 607

MARIA MAGDALENE. Lord, I shall make
 my vyage [4]
 To tell theym hastely;
Fro thay here that message
 Thay will be all mery. 611

[Exit Jesus.]

This Lord was slayn, alas for-thy,
Falsly spylt, noman wyst why,
 Whore he dyd mys.
Bot with hym spake I bodely;
 For-thi commen is my blys! 616

Mi blys is commen, my care is gone!
That lufly haue I mett alone!
I am as blyth in bloode and bone
 As euer was wight!
Now is he resyn that ere [5] was slone;
 Mi hart is light! 622

I am as light as leyfe on tre,
For ioyfull sight that I can se,
For well I wote that it was he
 My Lord Ihesu!
He that betrayde that fre [6]
 Sore may he rew. 628

To Galyle now will I fare,
And his dyscyples cach from care.
I wote that thay will mowrne no mare;
 Commyn is thare blys!

[To the audience.]

That worthi childe that Mary bare,
 He amende youre mys. 634

Explicit Resurreccio Domini.

---

[1] Deny.   [2] Look.   [3] Thence.
[4] Nowhere. [5] Ascended. [6] Pain.

[1] Promptly.   [2] Temptation.
[3] Bewildered.   [4] Journey.
[5] Formerly.   [6] That noble one.

THE JUDGMENT DAY [1]

[Acted by the Mercers of York.]

Deus incipit.

[DEUS.]   Firste when I this worlde hadde
    wroght,
Woode and wynde and wateris wan,
And all-kynne thyng that nowe is oght,[1]
Fulle wele, me-thoght, that I did thanne;
Whenne thei were made, goode me thame
    thoght.
Sethen [2] to my liknes made I man;
And man to greue me gaffe he noght.
    Therfore me rewis that I the worlde
      began.[3]   8

Whanne I had made man at my will,
    I gaffe hym wittis hym-selue to wisse;[4]
And Paradise I putte hym till,
    And bad hym halde it all as his.
But of the tree of goode and ill
    I saide, "What tyme thou etis of this,
Manne, thou spedes thi-selue to spill;[5]
    Thou arte broght oute of all blisse."   16

Belyue [6] brak manne my bidding.
    He wende [7] haue bene a god therby;
He wende haue wittyne [8] of all-kynne
    thyng,
In worlde to haue bene als wise as I.
He ete the appill I badde schulde hyng;[9]
    Thus was he begilid thurgh glotony.
Sithen both hym and his ospring
    To pyne [10] I putte thame all for-thy.[11]   24

To lange and late [12] me thoghte it goode
    To catche [13] thois caitiffis oute of care.
I sente my Sone, with full blithe moode,
    Till erthe to salue thame of thare sare.[14]

For rewthe of thame he reste on roode,
    And boughte thame with his body bare;
For thame he shedde his harte and bloode.
    What kyndinesse myght I do thame
      mare?   32

Sethen, aftirwarde, he heryed [1] hell,
    And toke oute thois wrechis that ware
    thare-inne;
Ther faughte that free [2] with feendis feele [3]
    For thame that ware sounkyn for synne.
Sethen in erthe than gonne he dwelle;
    Ensaumpill he gaue thame heuene to
    wynne,
In Tempill hym-selffe to teche and tell,
    To by thame blisse that neuere may
    blynne.[4]   40

Sethen haue thei founde me full of mercye,
    Full of grace and for-giffenesse.
And thei als wrecchis, wittirly,[5]
    Has ledde ther liffe in lithirnesse; [6]
Ofte haue thei greued me greuously: —
    Thus have thei quitte me my kyndi-
    nesse.
Ther-fore no lenger, sekirlye,[7]
    Thole [8] will I thare wikkidnesse.   48

Men seis the worlde but vanite,
    Yitt will no-manne be ware ther-by;
Ilke a day ther mirroure may thei se,
    Yitt thynke thei noght that thei schall
    dye.
All that euere I saide schulde be
    Is nowe fulfillid thurgh prophicie.
Ther-fore nowe is it tyme to me
    To make endyng of mannes folie.   56

I haue tholed mankynde many a yere
    In luste and likyng for to lende;[9]
And vnethis [10] fynde I ferre or nere

---

1 Aught, anything.   2 Afterwards.
3 The metre would be improved by omitting "the
world"; but it need not be supposed that the early
writers were meticulous in such details.
4 Govern.   5 Ruin.
6 Quickly.   7 Thought to.
8 Known.   9 Hang.
10 Punishment.   11 Therefor.
12 At last?   13 Snatch.   14 Woe.

1 Harrowed, despoiled.   2 Noble one.
3 Many.   4 Cease.   5 Truly.
6 Wickedness.   7 Certainly.
8 Endure.   9 Remain.   10 Scarcely.

---

1 The *Judgment Day* of the Wakefield Cycle (which closely parallels the York play) and of the N. towne
Cycle are both incomplete; that of the Chester Cycle is far less interesting and unduly long.   For the
source of the text see page 142, note 1.

A man that will his misse amende.
In erthe I see butte synnes seere.[1]
  Therfore myne aungellis will I sende
To blawe ther bemys [2] that all may here.
  The tyme is comen I will make ende. 64

Aungellis, blawes youre bemys belyue,[3]
  Ilke a creature for to call!
Leerid and lewde,[4] both man and wiffe,
  Ressayue ther dome this day thei schall,
Ilke a leede [5] that euere hadde liffe;
  Bese none for-getyn, grete ne small.
Ther schall thei see the woundes fyve
  That my Sone suffered for them all. 72

And sounderes [6] thame be-fore my sight!
  All same in blisse schall thei not be.
My blissid childre, as I haue hight,[7]
  On my right hande I schall thame see;
Sethen schall ilke a weried wight [8]
  On my lifte side for ferdnesse [9] flee.
This day ther domys thus haue I dight,
  To ilke a man as he hath serued me. 80

I. ANG. Loued be thou, Lorde, of myghtis
    moste,
That aungell made to messengere!
Thy will schall be fulfillid in haste,
  That heuene and erthe and helle schalle
    here.

    [The angels blow their trumpets.]

[I. ANG.] Goode and ill, euery ilke a [10] gaste,
  Rise and fecche youre flessh, that was
    youre feere! [11]
For all this worlde is broght to waste.
  Drawes to youre dome! It neghes
    nere!   88

II. ANG. Ilke a creature, bothe olde and
    yhing,
Be-lyue I bidde you that ye ryse!
Body and sawle with you ye bring,
  And comes be-fore the high justise!
For I am sente fro heuene kyng
  To calle you to this grette assise.
Therfore rise vppe, and geue rekenyng
  How ye hym serued vppon sere wise.[12] 96

    [The dead arise in their shrouds.]

I. ANIMA BONA. Loued be thou, Lorde,
    that is so schene,[1]
That on this manere made vs to rise,
Body and sawle to-gedir, clene,
  To come before the high justise.
Of oure ill dedis, Lorde, thou not mene,[2]
  That we haue wroght vppon sere wise;
But graunte vs for thy grace, be-dene,[3]
  That we may wonne [4] in paradise. 104

II. AN. BONA. A! loued be thou, Lorde of
    all,
That heuene and erthe and all has
    wroght,
That with thyne aungellis wolde vs call
  Oute of oure graues, hidir to be broght.
Ofte haue we greued the, grette and small;
  Ther-aftir, Lorde, thou deme vs noght;
Ne suffir vs neuere to fendis to be thrall,
  That ofte in erthe with synne vs
    soght!   112

I. ANIMA MALA. Allas! allas! that we
    were borne!
So may we synfull kaytiffis say.
I here wele be [5] this hydous horne
  Itt drawes full nere to domesday.
Allas! we wrecchis that ar for-lorne,[6]
  That never yitt serued God to paye,
But ofte we haue his flessh for-sworne.
  Allas! allas! and welaway! 120

What schall we wrecchis do for drede?
  Or whedir for ferdnes may we flee,
When we may bringe forthe no goode dede
  Before hym that oure juge schall be?
To aske mercy vs is no nede,
  For wele I wotte dampned be we.
Allas! that we swilke [7] liffe schulde lede
  That dighte [8] vs has this destonye! 128

Oure wikkid werkis thei will vs wreye,[9]
  That we wende [10] never schuld haue bene
    weten.[11]
That we did ofte full pryuely,
  Appertely [12] may we se them wreten.

---

[1] Many.	[2] Trumpets.	[3] Quickly.
[4] Learned and unlettered.	[5] Person.	
[6] Separate.	[7] Promised.	[8] Cursed person.
[9] Terror.	[10] Every single.	
[11] Companion.	[12] In various ways.	

[1] Shining.	[2] Remember.	[3] Indeed.
[4] Dwell.	[5] By.	[6] Lost.
[7] Such.	[8] Prepared.	
[9] Destroy.	[10] Thought.	
[11] Known.	[12] Openly.	

Allas, wrecchis! dere mon we by! [1]
Full smerte with helle-fyre be we smetyn.
Nowe mon neuere saule ne body dye,
But with wikkid peynes euermore be
betyne.[2]   136

Allas! for drede sore may we quake!
Oure dedis beis oure dampnacioune.
For oure mys-menyng [3] mon we make;
Helpe may none excusacioune.
We mon be sette for our synnes sake
For-euere fro oure saluacioune,
In helle to dwelle with feendes blake,
Wher neuer schall be redempcioune. 144

II. AN. MALA.   Als carefull caitiffis may
we ryse!
Sore may we ringe oure handis and wepe!
For cursidnesse and for covetise
Dampned be we to helle full depe!
Rought we neuere of Goddis seruise;
His comaundementis wolde we noght
kepe;
But ofte than made we sacrafise
To Satanas when othir slepe.   152

Allas! now wakens all oure were! [4]
Oure wikkid werkis may we not hide,
But on oure bakkis vs muste them bere;
Thei wille vs wreye [5] on ilke a side.
I see foule feendis that wille vs feere,[6]
' And all for pompe of wikkid pride.
Wepe we may with many a teere.
Allas, that we this day schulde bide! 160

Before vs playnly bese fourth brought
The dedis that vs schall dame be-dene.
That eres has herde, or harte has thoght,
Sen any tyme that we may mene,[7]
That fote has gone, or hande has wroght,
That mouthe has spoken, or ey has sene,
This day full dere thanne bese it boght.
Allas, vnborne and we hadde bene! 168

[The angel separates the good from the bad.]
III. ANG.   Standis noght to-gedir! Parte
you in two!
All sam schall ye noght be in blisse.

Ye [1] Fadir of heuene woll it be soo,
For many of yowe has wroght amys.
The goode, on his right-hande ye goe,
The way till heuene he will you wisse; [2]
Ye weryed [3] wightis, ye flee hym froo,
On his lefte-hande, as none of his. 176

[Jesus speaks above.]
JESUS.[4]   This woffull worlde is brought till
ende;
My Fadir of heuene he woll it be.
Therfore till erthe nowe will I wende,[5]
Mi-selue to sitte in mageste.
To deme my domes I woll descende.
This body will I bere with me;
How it was dight,[6] mannes mys [7] to mende,
All mankynde there schall it see.   184

[Jesus descends to the earth and addresses
the Apostles.]
JESUS.   Mi postelis and my darlyngis dere,
The dredfull dome this day is dight.
Both heuen and erthe and hell schall here
Howe I schall holde that I haue hight,[8]
That ye schall sitte on seetis sere [9]
Be-side my-selffe, to se that sight,
And for to deme folke ferre and nere
Aftir ther werkyng wronge or right. 192

I saide also, whan I you sente
To suffre sorowe for my sake,
All tho that wolde thame right repente
Schulde with you wende and wynly
wake;[10]
And to youre tales who toke no tente
Shulde fare [11] to fyre with fendis blake.
Of mercy nowe may noght be mente;
Butt, aftir wirkyng, welth or wrake. 200

My hetyng haly [12] schall I fullfille.
Therfore comes furth and sittis me by
To here the dome of goode and ill.
I. APOSTOLUS.   I loue the, Lord God all-
myghty!
Late and herely,[13] lowde and still,
To do thy bidding bayne [14] am I.
I obbliish [15] me to do thi will

---

[1] Pay for it.   [2] Beaten.
[3] Lamentation. (Smith prints mys-meunyng; corr.
by Manly.)
[4] Doubt, confusion.   [5] Destroy.
[6] Frighten.   [7] Remember.

[1] MS. Mi.   [2] Show.   [3] Cursed.
[4] MS. Deus from here on.   [5] Go.
[6] Maltreated?   [7] Sin.
[8] Promised.   [9] Several thrones.
[10] Go and joyfully awake (from the dead).
[11] Go.   [12] Promise wholly.   [13] Early.
[14] Ready.   [15] Oblige, bind.

With all my myght, als is worthy.   208

II. Apost.   A! myghtfull God, here is it
    sene
Thou will fulfille thi forward right,
And all thi sawes thou will maynteyne.
    I loue the, Lorde, with all my myght,
    That for [1] vs that has erthely bene
        Swilke dingnitees has dressed and dight.
Jesus.   Comes fourthe! I schall sitte you
        betwene,
    And all fulfille that I haue hight.   216

*Here he goes to the seat of judgment, with the
    singing of angels.* [2]

[The Devils advance.]

I. Diabolus.   Felas, arraye vs for to fight,
    And go we faste oure fee to fange. [3]
The dredefull dome this day is dight;
    I drede me that we dwelle full longe.
II. Diab.   We schall be sene euere in ther
        sight,
    And warly [4] waite, ellis wirke we wrange;
For if the domisman do vs right,
    Full grete partie with vs schall gang.   224
III. Diab.   He schall do right to foo and
        frende,
    For nowe schall all the soth be sought.
All weried wightis with vs schall wende;
    To payne endles thei schall be broght.228

Jesus.   Ilke a creature, takes entent
    What bodworde [5] I to you bringe:
This wofull worlde away is wente,
    And I am come as crouned kynge.
Mi Fadir of heuene he has me sente
    To deme youre dedis, and make ending.
Comen is the day of jugement;
    Of sorowe may ilke a synfull synge.   236

The day is comen of kaydyfnes, [6]
    All tham to care that are vnclene,
The day of bale and bittirnes;
    Full longe abedyn has it bene!
The day of drede to more and lesse,
    Of care, of trymbelyng, and of tene, [7]
That ilke a wight that weried is
    May say, "Allas, this daye is sene!"   244

[1] MS. ther-fore; *corr. by Holthausen.*
[2] MS. *Hic ad sedem judicij cum cantu angelorum.*
[3] Seize.   [4] Watchfully.
[5] Message.   [6] Wretchedness.   [7] Sorrow.

Here may ye see my woundes wide,
    The whilke I tholed [1] for youre mysdede,
Thurgh harte and heed, foote, hande and
        hide, —
    Nought for my gilte butt for youre nede.
Beholdis both body, bak, and side,
    How dere I bought youre brotherhede!
Thes bittir peynes I wolde abide;
    To bye you blisse, thus wolde I bleede.252

Mi body was scourged with-outen skill; [2]
    As theffe full thraly [3] was [I] thrette;
On crosse thei hanged me on a hill,
    Blody and bloo, as I was bette,
With croune of thorne throsten full ill;
    This spere vnto my side was sette;
Myne harte bloode spared noght thei for to
        spill.
    Manne, for thy loue wolde I not lette.260

The Jewes spitte on me spitously;
    Thei spared me nomore than a theffe.
When thei me strake, I stode stilly;
    Agaynste tham did I no-thyng greve.
Behalde, mankynde, this ilke is I,
    That for the suffered swilke mischeue.
Thus was I dight for thy folye.
    Man, loke, thy liffe was me full leffe. [4] 268

Thus was I dight thi sorowe to slake;
    Manne, thus behoued the to borowed [5]
        be.
In all my woo toke I no wrake; [6]
    Mi will itt was for the loue of the.
Man, sore aught the for to quake,
    This dredfull day this sight to see.
All this I suffered for thi sake.
    Say, man, what suffered thou for me? 276

[Addressing the Good Souls.]

Mi blissid childre on my right hande,
    Youre dome this day ye thar [7] not drede,
For all youre comforte is command;
    Youre liffe in likyng [8] schall ye lede.
Commes to the kyngdome ay lastand
    That you is dight [9] for youre goode dede.
Full blithe may ye be where ye stande,
    For mekill in heuene schall be youre
        mede.[10]   284

[1] Suffered.   [2] Reason.
[3] Angrily, furiously.   [4] Dear.   [5] Redeemed.
[6] Vengeance.   [7] Need.
[8] Pleasure.   [9] Prepared.   [10] Reward.

Whenne I was hungery, ye me fedde;
  To slake my thirste youre harte was free;
Whanne I was clothles, ye me cledde;
  Ye wolde no sorowe vppon me see;
In harde prisoun [1] whan I was stedde,
  Of my paynes ye hadde pitee;
Full seke whan I was brought in bedde,
  Kyndely ye come to coumforte me.   292

Whanne I was wikke [2] and werieste,
  Ye herbered me full hartefully; [3]
Full gladde thanne were ye of youre geste,
  And pleyned [4] my pouerte piteuously;
Be-lyue ye brought me of the beste,
  And made my bedde full esyly.
Therfore in heuene schall be youre reste,
  In joie and blisse to be me by.   300

I. ANIMA BONA.   Whanne hadde we,
    Lorde that all has wroght,
Meete and drinke the with to feede?
Sen we in erthe hadde neuere noght
  But thurgh the grace of thy godhede.
II. AN. BONA.   Whanne waste that we the
    clothes brought?
  Or visite the in any nede?
Or in thi sikenes we the sought?
    Lorde, when did we [to] [5] the this
    dede?   308

JESUS.   Mi blissid childir, I schall you
    saye
  What tyme this dede was to me done:
When any that nede hadde, nyght or day,
  Askid you helpe and hadde it sone;
Youre fre hartis saide them neuere nay,
  Erely ne late, mydday ne none;
But als ofte sithis [6] as thei wolde praye,
  Thame thurte but bide, [7] and haue ther
    bone.   316

[Addressing the Bad Souls.]

Ye cursid caytiffis of Kaymes [8] kynne,
  That neuere me comforte in my care,
I and ye for-euer will twynne, [9]
  In dole to dwelle for-euermare.
Youre bittir bales schall neuer blynne

That ye schall haue whan ye come thare.
Thus haue ye serued [1] for youre synne,
  For derffe [2] dedis ye haue done are.   324

Whanne I had mistir [3] of mete and drynke,
  Caytiffis, ye cacched [4] me fro youre gate;
Whanne ye were sette as sirs on benke, [5]
  I stode ther-oute werie and wette;
Was none of yowe wolde on me thynke,
  Pyte to haue of my poure state:
Ther-fore till hell I schall you synke, —
  Weele are ye worthy to go that gate! [6]

Whanne I was seke and soriest,   333
  Ye visitte me noght, for I was poure;
In prisoune faste when I was feste, [7]
  Was none of you loked howe I fore; [8]
Whenne I wiste neuere where for to reste,
  With dyntes [9] ye draffe me fro your
    dore;
Butte euer to pride thanne were ye preste;
  Mi flessh, my bloode, ofte ye for-
    swore.   340

Clothles whanne I was ofte and colde,
  At nede of you, yede I full naked;
House ne herborow, helpe ne holde,
  Hadde I none of you, thof [10] I quaked;
Mi mischeffe sawe ye many-folde;
  Was none of you my sorowe slaked;
Butt euere for-soke me, yonge and alde.
  Therfore schall ye nowe be for-saked. 348

I. ANIMA MALA.   Whan had thou, Lorde,
    that all thyng has,
  Hungir or thirste, sen thou God is?
Whan was that [11] thou in prisonne was?
  Whan was thou naked or herberles?
II. AN. MALA.   Whan was it we sawe the
    seke, allas?
  Whan kid [12] we the this vnkyndinesse?
Werie or wette to late the passe,
  When did we the this wikkidnesse?   356

JESUS.   Caitiffis, als ofte als it be-tidde
  That nedfull aught askid in my name,
Ye herde them noght, youre eris ye hidde,

[1] MS. presse; the reading supplied from the Towneley play by Herttrich.
  [2] Feeble.   [3] Heartily, cordially.
  [4] Pitied.   [5] Supplied by Manly.
  [6] Times.   [7] They needed but ask.
  [8] Cain's.   [9] Separate.

[1] Deserved.   [2] Wicked.   [3] Need.
[4] Drove.   [5] Bench.   [6] Way.
[7] Bound.   [8] Fared.
[9] Blows.   [10] Though.
[11] Inserted from the Towneley play by Holthausen.
[12] Showed.

Youre helpe to thame was noght at
    hame, —
To me was that vnkyndines kyd!
    There-fore ye [1] bere this bittir blame.
To lest or most when ye it did,
    To me ye did the selue and the same. 364

[*Turning to the Good Souls.*]

Mi chosen childir, comes vnto me!
    With me to wonne nowe schall ye
    wende;
There joie and blisse schall euer be
    Youre liffe in lyking schall ye lende.

[*To the Bad Souls.*]

Ye cursed kaitiffis, fro me ye flee,
    In helle to dwelle with-outen ende.

[1] *Inserted from the Towneley play by Manly.*

Ther ye schall neuere butt sorowe see
    And sitte be Satanas the fende.   372

Nowe is fulfillid all my for-thoght,[1]
    For endid is all erthely thyng.
All worldly wightis that I haue wroght
    Aftir ther werkis haue nowe wonnyng: [2]
Thei that wolde synne and sessid noght,
    Of sorowes sere now schall thei syng;
And thei that mendid [3] thame whils thei
    moght,   379
    Schall belde [4] and bide in my blissing.

*And thus he makes an end, with the song of
    angels crossing from place to place.*[5]

[1] Design.   [2] Reward.
[3] Amended.   [4] Find shelter.
[5] MS. *Et sic facit finem cum melodia angelorum
transiens a loco ad locum.*

VI
NON–CYCLE PLAYS

DUK MORAUD [1]

[Scene I.]

[Enter Duk Moraud and his wife.]

[D]uk Moraud. Emperoures and kynges
  be kende,[1]
  Erlys and barunnys [2] bolde,
Bachelerys [3] and knytes to mende,[4]
  Sueyeres and yemen [5] to holde,
Knauys and pagys to sende,   5
  So parfyt [6] that aryn to be solde,
I prey yow, lordynges so hende,[7]
  No yangelynges [8] ye mak in this folde [9]
    To day.
Als [10] ye are louely in fas,[11]   10
Set yow alle semly in plas,
And I xal with outyn falas [12]
    Shewe resounus here to youre pay.[13]

Welthys I welde [14] at my wylle;
  In werd [15] I am knowyn ful wyde;   15
I [h]aue hert and hynd vp on hille;
  I am gay on grounde for to glyde;
Semly ther I syt vp on sille,[16]
  My wyf and my mene [17] by my syde.
I [command] yow tende me tylle, [18]   20
  Or ellys I xal bate [19] yowre pride
    Wyt dynt! [20]
And ther-for I warne you, infere,[21]
That ye mak neyther criyng ne bere! [22]
  If ye do, with outyn duere,[23]   25
    Strokes at yow xal I mynt.[24]

Duk Morawd I hot [25] be name.
  Korteyser [26] lord may be none.

Wol fer than rengnyt [1] my fame
  To be comly korownyt [2] from one.   30
I geue gode [3] gyftys with game,[4]
  And saue iche [5] lordynges fro fone.[6]
Me bowyn [7] bothe wylde and tame,
  Quethire [8] so thei rydyn, er gone,
    Ore scheppe.[9]   35
I am dowty in dede!
I am worly in wede! [10]
I am semly on stede! [11]
  No weleny [12] to me wyl I kyppe.[13]

*[His wife announces that she will make a
journey, probably to visit relatives or
friends.]*

[Moraud.] Dam, do now thi wylle,   40
Thi wyage [14] to fulfylle.
  To the wyl I be beyne.[15]
For loue, I the pray,
Rap [16] the faste in thi way,
  And cum hom sone ageyne.   45

[Wyf. . . . .]

[Moraud.] Thorow the grace of that ich
  kyngk [17]
  That formyt vs alle with winne,[18]
I xal me kepyn from fondyng,[19]
  And als from blame and synne,
    With gras.   50
Iesu, als thou me wrowtes,[20]
And with woundys sore me bowtes,[21]
Saue me fro wykyt thowtes,
  Iesu, fayr in fas!

[Wyf. . . . .]

[Moraud.] Fare wel, my worlych [22] wyf! 55

---

[1] By right of birth.   [2] Earls and barons.
[3] Knights-bachelor, knights of the lower order.
[4] To bear in mind.   [5] Squires and yeomen.
[6] Perfect.   [7] Gracious.   [8] Janglings, noises.
[9] Enclosure.   [10] As.   [11] Face.
[12] Deception.   [13] Satisfaction.
[14] Wealth I control.   [15] World.
[16] Sill, floor (i.e. in my house).   [17] Retainers.
[18] Listen to me.   [19] Abate, let down.
[20] With a blow.   [21] All together.
[22] Outcry.   [23] Doubt.   [24] Aim.
[25] Am called.   [26] A more courteous.

[1] Rangeth, extends.   [2] Crowned.   [3] Good.
[4] Delight.   [5] Each, every.   [6] Foes.
[7] To me bow.   [8] Whether.
[9] Or walk, or sail.   [10] Lovely in costume.
[11] Place.   [12] Villainy, vile deed.
[13] Embrace.   [14] Voyage.   [15] Ready, obedient.
[16] Haste.   [17] Very King.
[18] Joy.   Heuser reads *wonne*.
[19] Folly.   [20] Wrought, created.
[21] Bought, redeemed.   [22] Excellent.

---

[1] Printed by W. Heuser, in *Anglia*, xxx (1907), 180, from a manuscript in the Bodleian Library. The text, written in the fourteenth century, appears "on a margin (cut off) of an Assize Roll for Norfolk and Suffolk of the second half of the thirteenth century, a small part of which is left." We have only the speeches of the actor who took the part of Duke Moraud. I have attempted to edit his speeches in such a way as to give some suggestion of the play as a whole. Unfortunately portions of the manuscript are now illegible.

Fare wel, loue in lond!
Fare[wel], thou semlyest lyf! [1]
Fare[wel], thou happy in hond!

[Scene II.]

[Duk Moraud addresses his daughter.]

[Moraud.] Maydyn, so louely and komly
    of syte,[2]
 I prey the for loue thou wyl lystyn to
    me!   60
To here my resun I prey the wel tythe! [3]
Loue so deryn [4] me most schewe to the.
My loue to thi body is castyn so bryth [5]
 My wyl me most aue [6] of the.
Thou art louely to leykyn! [7] and brythest
    with ryth! [8]   65
 I loue the in thowt, thou semly of ble,
    Be name!
Thou maydyn that moryst [9] thi merthis
    with myth,
Derne dedys [10] me most do be day and be
    nyth.
Be the worthiest woundyn,[11] wytthest
    wyt.[12]   70
    [Th]e sothe [13] tale I telle with outyn
    ony blame.

[Daughter. . . . .]

[Moraud.] My fere [14] so graciouse in gras,
Thanc thou xalt auen of me;
For thou art louely in fas,
 And therto bryth berende of ble! [15]   75
Now wyl I makyn solas,
 For my deryn loue xalt thou be.
Kys me now, par amour, in plas,
 Als thou art worly [16] to se
    In syte.   80
Damysel, fayrest to fonde,[17]
Als thou art semly to stonde,[18]
Rap we vs to wendyn [19] in honde
    To thi chambyr that is so louely of
    lythe.

---

[1] Seemliest person.
[2] Comely of sight.
[3] Grant.   [4] Dark, secret, evil.
[5] Bright.   [6] Have.
[7] To sport with (in an amorous sense).
[8] Right.   [9] Increasest.
[10] Evil deeds.
[11] By the worthiest wounded one (i.e. Christ).
[12] Noblest being.   [13] True.
[14] Companion.
[15] Bright looking of appearance.
[16] Lovely.   [17] Be found.
[18] Stand.   [19] Let us hasten to go.

[Scene III.]

[The Wyf, having returned and discovered the incestuous relations of Moraud with his daughter, threatens to expose them publicly.]

[Scene IV.]

[Enter Duk Moraud and his daughter.]

[Moraud.] A! I am wondyn [1] in gret
    dolour!   85
With danger and tene [2] I am bownde!
To me thou geue tent, [3] par amour,
 And lystne quat I say this stounde.[4]
Th[at] traytowr xal be-wrey vs this oure,
 I telle the, semly on grownde.   90
Than xul [5] we aue no socowr,
 But carys [6] to vs xal be fownde,
    I-wys.[7]
I ne may neuer be fawe [8]
Tyl that traytowr be slaw [9]   95
That is so rebel in sawe [10] —
    Sorow mot ay to her kys!

[The daughter goes out, kills her mother, and returns.]

[Moraud.] [Have] thou now slayne, be
    thi fay,
The fo[o]l that dede vs that tene? [11]

[Daughter. . . . .]

[Moraud.] A! now am I mery this
    stound [12]   100
That che [13] is browt to that ded!
For che suld a wreyd [14] vs on grownd,
 That ilke old schrewed qued! [15]
To sorowe che xuld vs a found.
 That [had] ben to vs an ewyl red! [16]   105
In care, for-sothe, is che wownd.
 Ther-for I am mery to led,[17]
    And gay!
Damysel, louely of chere,
Mak we mery here!   110
For care with outyn duere [18]
    Is went away for ay.

---

[1] Enveloped.   [2] Harm.   [3] Give heed.
[4] Time.   [5] Shall.   [6] Cares.
[7] Indeed.   [8] Glad in mind.   [9] Slain.
[10] Speech, in her talk.   [11] Harm.   [12] Time.
[13] She.   [14] Have betrayed.
[15] That same old malignant filth.   [16] Occurrence.
[17] Lead.   [18] Doubt.

[SCENE V.]

[The daughter presents to Moraud a newly-born child.]

[MORAUD.]   [A! h]ave I be-gotyn this
    stownd [1]
  A schyld [2] so louely of the?
I am [in] sorowe wownd!   115
  For care me most fle.
I prey the in welt [3] now wownd [4]
  [This chyld?] myth I se.

[DAUGHTER. . . . .]

[MORAUD.]   [Damisel], fayr and bryt
Go out of my syt —   120
  For thowt I am ny sclawe! [5] —
[And slay] it in present. [6]
  That i[s m]ly commaundement.
    Fast bry[n]g it of dawe. [7]
For al this lond I wold nowt   125
That lordes of this lond ad [8] yt thowt
  That I ad synd be the!
For sorow and care that we xuld drywe, [9]
We xuld leden lyf ful rywe, [10]
  And ther-on ay to be.   130
Ther-for, I prey the,
For loue of me,
  Slo yt with thin hond!
[And al] we ben in pes,
With outyn ony lees, [11]   135
  And auyn merth in lond.

*[The daughter goes out, kills the child, and
returns to Moraud with the news.]*

[MORAUD.]   [   ] [12] syng!
  Ther I sytte louely in thowr! [13]
I thank the, louely thing,
  [For   ]nges this oure;   140
For that parfyt tydyng
  [I geue the allys] and bour. [14]
[For thou], with outyn lesyng, [15]
  [Pottyst m]e fro[m] scham and dolowr.

In to [   ] I wyl wend, [16]   145

---

1 Time.   2 Child.
3 A strip of cloth.   4 Wound.
5 For sadness I am nigh slain.   6 At once.
7 Quickly deprive it of life.
8 Had.   9 Endure.
10 Rueful.   11 Without any lies.
12 At this point the manuscript becomes in part
illegible.
13 Tower.   14 Halls and bower[s].
15 Lying.   16 Go.

To a place bothe fer and hend, [1]
[   ].
Thus it [   ] mend
[   ] mete with [   ] frend
    [   ]   150

Betyd me god or ille
In to [contre fle I wylle]
  [   ]
But I prey the this oure,
My der swet par amowre,   155
  [Take it to   ]
I xal no [onore stond]
But, sertes, I xal f[ond]
  With outyn [to com.]

[SCENE VI.]

*[The danger of discovery being over, Duk
Moraud returns, to greet his daughter
with joy.]*

[MORAUD.]   [Ha] godday, worlych wyth! [2]
Ha godday, louely in lyth!   161
Thou xal [sittyn] semly in syth
  [So] comly [   ].

[DAUGHTER. . . . .]

[MORAUD.]   I am mythful and mery,
    markyd in mynd!
I am flour fayrest [b]e fryt for to fare! [3]
I am fayrest in fas ferly [4] to fynd!   166
I am loueliche in lond, lyttest in lare! [5]
I am comly and curteys and crafty of
    kynd!
I am comly castyn fro knottes of care!
I am lordly to leykyn lyt [6] vndyr lynd! [7]
I am semly to syttun syttes so sare! [8]
  I wyl pres me in pride.
Quan alle tho lordes of this lond are
    gadered infere, [9]
I am flour of hem alle, with outyn duere. [10]
And ellys I were woxyd of blamys [11] ryt
    here   175
  But I be ryal in rayis [12] forto ryde.

[The church bell rings.]

A! now I here

---

1 Far and near.   2 Lovely person.
3 By frith (i.e. a wood) to go.   4 Far.
5 Countenance.   5 To sport lightly.
7 Linden.   8 To go on journeys so arduous.
9 Together.   10 Doubt.
11 Grown blameworthy.
12 (Robes of) striped cloth, gay clothes.

A bell ryngant ful nere,
  Yendyr in the kyrk.
Thether I wyl fare,[1]   180
For I am in gret care
  There sum god ded to work.

[SCENE VII.]

*[Duk Moraud returns from the church
penitent.]*

[MORAUD.]   A synful kaytyf I am!
Synfully I aue wrowt blam
  Be gret tyme of my lyfe.   185
Now, Cryst, ast thou [2] me bowt,
For-geue me that blam that I aue wrowt,
  And mak me sum-quat blythe! [3]
For in this werd [4] may be none
That ever tok lyf with flesch and bone 190
  That auyt [5] so gret blam.
But [6] I aue gras [7] and help of the,
I am lost fro[m] the so fre
  In helle to be be-nam.[8]
A prest [9] now me most aue,   195
If [I] xal be saue
  Ageynus [10] Cryst of myth,
To telle hym my blam
That I aue wrowt be nam.
  That is my thowt now ty[th] [11]   200
    To day.
Iesu, heuene flowr,[12]
Pot me from dolour,
And geue me gras this oure
  A prest to auyn, I say!   205

[Enter a priest.]

[MORAUD.]   A! blyssyd be thou ay
That thou com to-day
  To here my dedly syn!
Quylys [13] we are infere [14]
I wyl schrywe [15] me here,   210
  For now wil I be-gyn:
I aue led my lyf
In sorow and in stryf,
  With cursydnessys and care.
Yet is more in my th[o]wt.   215
Synnus I aue wrowt
  Be my douter in lare; [16]

And chyld che bar be me,
Quyk [1] was fayr and fre
  Bothe in body and fas;   220
And I myt neuer be fawe [2]
Tyl we had hym sclawe.[3]
  I sey the sothe [4] cas!
Yet more I wyl telle now.
My wyf ther che sclow   225
  Thowr egment me.[5]
And thus is my lyf spend.
Lord omnipotent,
  Grant me my synnus to fle!

[PRIEST. . . . .   ]

[MORAUD.]   I wyl blely,[6] my leue [7] frend,
Do penawns,[8] bothe fer and hend,[9]   231
  To saue my sowle fro wra[th].

[SCENE VIII.]

*[Duk Moraud returns home and greets his
daughter.]*

[MORAUD.]   Heyl, douter, louely of syt!
Heyl, louely leuende [10] to-day!
Cryst, that is mytty in myt,   235
  Saue the ermor [11] and ay!

[DAUGHTER. . . . .   ]

[MORAUD.]   Lat be, my douter dere!
Lat be, louely in lere! [12]
I aue for-sakyn here
  My blam and my syn.   240
My syn I aue forsake,
And to penawns I aue me take;
  For that wykkyd wrake [13]
    Now is time to blyn.[14]
And ther-for I prey the,   245
Sertes,[15] with herte fre,
That thou mak now me
  To falle in no mor blam.
Now wyl I don [16] away
My tresorys [17] rych and gay,   250
[And] traueylyn [18] I wyl ay
  For my wykyt fam.

---

[1] Go.   [2] Hast thou.
[3] Somewhat blithe.   [4] World.
[5] Hath.   [6] Unless.   [7] Grace.
[8] Confined.   [9] Priest.
[10] In the presence of.   [11] Quickly.
[12] Flower.   [13] While.   [14] Together.
[15] Shrive, confess.   [16] Daughter in her bed.

[1] Which.   [2] Joyful.
[3] Slain.   [4] True.
[5] Through my incitement.
[6] Willingly.   [7] Dear.
[8] Penance.   [9] Near.
[10] Living one.
[11] Evermore.
[12] Face.   [13] Sin.
[14] Cease.
[15] Certes, assuredly.   [16] Put.
[17] Treasures.   [18] Travel.

[SCENE IX.]

[*Duk Moraud, coming to his death,
addresses his daughter.*]

[MORAUD.]   Now my lyf wyl pase
Fro me this ilk stonde! [1]
I am smetyn in the fas   255
   With carful strokes and rownde.
Iesu, ful of gras,
For-geue the this trespas
   That thou ast don to me!

> [1] Time.

And geue the gras to blyn [1]   260
Of that wykyd syn
   Quylk thou ast don so fre.
My tyme comyt faste to
That I xal pas yow fro, [2]
   In othir plas to duelle.   265
In manus tuas Domine! [3]
Iesu, haue mercy on me,
   And saue my sowle fro helle! [4]

> [1] Cease.   [2] From.
> [3] "Into thy hands, O Lord."
> [4] The end of the fragment, and apparently the end
> of the play.

THE CONVERSION OF ST. PAUL [1]

[FIRST STATION. JERUSALEM.] [1]

[PROLOGUE.]

POETA. *Rex glorie,* Kyng omnipotent,
    Redemer of the world by the pouer
      diuine,
And Maria, that pure vyrgy[n], quene
      most excellent,
Wyche bare that blyssyd babe Iesu, that
      for vs sufferd pyne,[2]
Vnto whoys goodnes I do inclyne,
Besechyng that Lord, of hys pytous influ-
      ens,
To preserue and gouerne thys wyrshypfull
      audyens.   7

Honorable frendes, besechyng yow of ly-
      cens
    To procede owr processe,[3] we may, vnder
      your correccion,
[Show] [4] the conuersyon of Seynt Paule, as
      the Byble gyf experyens.[5]
Whoo lyst to rede the booke *Actum Ap-*
      postolorum,[6]
Ther shall he haue the very notycyon.[7]
But, as we can, we shall vs redres,[8]
Brefly, with yowr fauour, begynyng owr
      proces.   [*Exit.*] 14
          Daunce.[9]

---

[1] The "station" was a *platea,* or open space, surrounded by spectators (some of them seated, see line
505). There were probably a scaffold, or "mansion,"
for the High Priests Caiaphas and Anna, and a stable.
[2] F. prints *payne;* corr. by M.
[3] To proceed with our story.
[4] Supplied by M.; cf. ll. 166–67.
[5] Information.
[6] See The Acts of the Apostles ix, 1–31.
[7] Information.
[8] Address ourselves to our task.
[9] Added in a later hand. Apparently the audience found the play tiresome, and an effort was made
to render it more attractive.

Here entryth Saule, goodly besene [1] *in the
best wyse lyke an aunterous* [2] *knyth, thus
sayyng:*

SAULUS. Most dowtyd [3] man I am lyuyng
      vpon the ground!
    Goodly besene with many a riche garne-
      ment! [4]
My pere on lyue I trow ys nott found.
    Thorow the world, fro the oryent to the
      occydent,
My fame ys best knowyn vndyr the
      fyrmament.
I am most drad of pepull vnyuersall;
    They dare not dysp[l]ease me [5] most
      noble.   21

Saule ys my name, — I wyll that ye no-
      tyfy, —
    Whych conspyreth [6] the dyscyplys with
      threte and menace; [7]
Be-fore the prynces of prestes most noble
      and hye [8]
    I bring them to punyshement for ther
      trespace.
    We wyll them nott suffer to rest in no
      place,
For they go a-boughte to preche and gyff
      exemplis
To destroye our lawes, sinagoges, and
      templis.   28

---

[1] Apparelled.
[2] Adventurous.
[3] Dreaded.
[4] F. *garlement;* corr. by M.
[5] F. *my;* corr. by M.; but the line seems to be corrupt.
[6] Used in its etymological sense "to breathe together," possibly echoing Acts ix, 1: "And Saul, yet
breathing out threatenings" (*Saulus autem adhuc
spirans minarum*).
[7] F. *thretes and menaces;* corr. by M.
[8] F. *hye and noble;* corr. by M.

---

[1] From the Digby MS., which contains four (one a fragment) late fifteenth-century plays. I have based
the text on F. J. Furnivall's *The Digby Mysteries,* 1882 (F.), and have availed myself of certain valuable
emendations by Manly (M.). I have also adopted the stanzaic form employed by Manly, since Furnivall
gives no indication of the metrical scheme. The play was probably written by an East Midland author.
The method of performance shows that it was designed for presentation in a small village. Three "stations"
were used, and the audience, as well as the actors, moved in a body from one station to another. The
reader should compare the play with the liturgical *Conversio Beati Pauli Apostoli* printed on page 51. The
Festival of the Conversion of St. Paul came on January 25, and we may suppose that both these plays were
designed for performance on that day.

By the god Bellyall, I schall make progresse
  Vnto the princes, both Caypha and
    Anna,
Wher I schall aske of them, in suernes,
  To persue thorow all Dammask and
    Liba;
And thus we schall soone after than
Bryng them that so do lyff in-to Ierusalem,
Both man and child, that I fynd of them. 35

*Her cummyth Sale to Caypha and Anna,
  prestes of the tempyll.*

Nobyll prelates and princes of regalyte,
  Desyryng and askyng of your benyngne
    wurthynes
Your letters and epystolys of most sou-
    erente
  To subdue rebellyous [1] that wyll, of
    frawardnes,
A-gaynst our lawes rebell or transgresse,
Nor wyll not inclyne but mak obiecc[i]on.
To pursue all such I wyll do proteccion. [2] 42

CAYPHA. To your desyer we gyf perfyth
    sentens, [3]
  Accordyng to your petycions that ye
    make postulacion; [4]
By-cause we know your trewe delygens
  To persue all tho that do reprobacion
A-gayns owur lawes by ony redargua-
    cion. [5]
Wherefor shortly we gyf in commandment
To put down them that be dy[s]obedy-
    ent.   49

ANNA. And by thes letturs, that be most
    reuerrent —
  Take them in hand, full agre [6] ther-to —
Constreyn all rebellys by owur hole assent;
  We gyf yow full power so to doo.
Spare not, hardly, for frend nor foo!
All thos ye fynd of that lyfe in thys realme,
Bounde loke ye bryng them in-to Ierusa-
    lem.   56

Her Saule resayuyth ther letters.

SAULUS. Thys precept here I take in
    hande,

[1] F. *rebellyons;* corr. by M.; cf. ll. 135, 142.
[2] Give protection.
[3] Perfect sentence (complete authority?).
[4] Request.
[5] Reprehensible conduct.   [6] Agree.

To fullfyll after yowur wylles both;
Wher I shall spare with-in this londe
  Nother man nor woman, — to this I
    make an oth, —
  But to subdue I wyll not be loth.
Now folow me, knytys and seruantes
    trewe,
In-to Damaske as fast as ye can sewe. [1] 63

I. MILES. Vnto your commaundment I do
    obeysaunce.
  I wyll not gaynsay nor make delacion, [2]
But with good mynd and harty plesaunce
  I shall yow succede and make perambu-
    lacion
  Thorow-oute Damaske with all delecta-
    cion;
And all thoo [who] rebell and make resys-
    tens,
For to oppres I wyll do my delygens.   70

II. MILES. And in me shalbe no neclygens,
  But to thys precept my-self I shall ap-
    plye,
To do your behest [3] with all conuenyens,
  With-owt eny frowardnes or eny obsty-
    nacy, —
  Non shall appere in me; but, verely,
With all my mynd, I yow insure, [4]
To resyst tho rebelles I wyll do my cure. [5] 77

SAULUS. Truly to me yt ys grett consola-
    cion
  To here thys report that ye do avauns. [6]
For your sapyencyall wyttes I gyf com-
    mendacion;
  Euer at my nede I haue founde yow
    constant.
  But, knytes and seruuantes, that be so
    plesaunt,
I pray yow anon my palfray ye bryng,
To spede my iurney with-owt lettyng.   84

*Here goyth Sale forth a lytyll a-syde for to
  make hym redy to ryde, the seruuant thus
  seyng:*

SERUUS. How, hosteler! how! A peck of
    otys and a botell [7] of haye!
  Com of a-pase, or I wyll to a-nother inne!

[1] Follow.   [2] Delay.
[3] Command   [4] Make pledge, assure.
[5] I will apply myself diligently.
[6] Advance.   [7] Bundle.

What, hosteler! why commyst not thy way?
Hye the faster, I beshrew thi skynne!
STABULARYUS.   I am non hosteler, nor non
 hostelers kynne,
But a ientylmanys seruuant, i[f] [1] thou dost
 know!
Such crabyysh wordes do aske a blow.   91

SERUUS.   I cry yow mercy, sir! I wyst
 well sum-what ye were,
 Owther a gentylman, or a knaue, me
  thynkyth by your physnomy!
Yf on[e] loke yow in the face that neuer se
 yow ere,[2]
Wold thynk ye were at the next dore by.
In good fayth, I wenyd [3] yow had bene
 an hosteler, verely:
I sye [4] suche a-nother ientylman with yow
 a barowfull bare
Of horsdowng, and dogges tordes, and sych
 other gere.   98

And how yt happenyd, a mervelous chance
 be-tyde:
 Your felow was not suer of foote, and
  yet he went very brode,
But in a cow tord both dyd ye slyde, —
 And, as I wene, your nose ther-in rode,
 Your face was be-payntyd with sowters
  code.[5]
I sey [6] neuer sych a syght, I make God
 a vow!
Ye were so be-grymlyd and yt had bene a
 sowe.   105

STAB.   In fayth, thou neuer syest me tyll
 this day.
I haue dwellyd with my master thys vij
 yere and more;
Full well I haue pleasyd hym — he wyll
 not say nay —
And mykyll [7] he makyth of me therfore.
SERUUS.   By my trowth, than be ye
 changyd to a new lore! [8]
A seruand ye are, and that a good,
Ther ys no better lokyth owt of a hood. 112

STAB.   For soth, and a hood I vse for to
 were;

Full well yt ys lynyd with sylk and
 chamlett; [1]
Yt kepyth me fro the cold that the wynd
 doth me not dere,[2]
 Nowther frost nor snow that I therby do
 sett.
SERUUS.   Yea, yt ys a dobyll hood, and
 that a fett! [3]
He was a good man that made yt, I warant
 yow;
He was nother horse ne mare, nor yet
 yokyd sow!   119

Here commyth the fyrst knyth to the stabyl
grom, sayng:

1. MILES.   Now, stabyll grom, shortly
 bryng forth away
 The best horse, for owur lorde wyll ryde.
STAB.   I am full redy.   Here ys a palfray.
There can no man a better bestryde!
He wyll conducte owur lorde and gyde
Thorow the world; he ys sure and abyll;
To bere a gentyllman he [is] esy and proph-
 etabyll.   126

Her the knyth cummyth to Saule with a horse.

1. MILES.   Behold, sir Saule, your palfray
 ys com,
 Full goodly besene, as yt ys yowr desyer
To take yowur vyage thorow euery regyon.
 Be nott in dowt he wyll spede your
  mater.
 And we, as your seruauntes, with glad
  chere
Shall gyf attendance; we wyll nott gayn-
 say,
But folow you where ye go be nyght or
 day.   133

SAULUS.   Vnto Damask I make my pro-
 gressyon,
 To pursue all rebellyous, beyng froward
  and obstynate,
Agayns our lawes be ony transgressyon.
 With all my delygens my-self I wyl
  preparate [4]
 Concernyng my purpose to oppres and
  separate;
Non shall reioyce that doth offend,

 1 Supplied by M. 2 Saw you before.
 3 Thought. 4 Saw.
 5 Cobbler's wax. 6 Saw.
 7 Much. 8 Rule of behavior.

 1 Camlet, a beautiful and costly fabric.
 2 Harm. 3 A fine one.
 4 F. *prepare*; emend. by M.

But vtterly to reproue with mynde and intende. 140

Her Sale rydyth forth with hys seruantes a-bowt the place,[1] [and] owt of the p[lace].

CAYPHA.　Now Saule hath takyn hys wurthy wyage [2]
To pursue rebellyous, of what degre thei be.
He wyll non suffer to raygne nor haue passage
With-in all thys regyon, we be in ser-tayn[te].[3]
Wherefor I commende hys goodly dyg-nyte,
That he thus aluay takyth in hande
By hys power to gouerne thus all thys lande. 147

ANNA.　We may lyue in rest, by hys con-solacion.
He defendyth vs; where-for we be bownde
To loue hym intyrely with our harttes affeccion,
And honour hym as champyon in euery stownde.[4]
Ther ys non suche lyuyng vpon the grownde
That may be lyke hym nor be hys pere,
Be [5] est nor west, ferre nor nere. 154

　　　POETA — *si placet.*[6]

CONCLUSYON.

Daunce.[7]

[EPILOGUE.]

[POETA.] Fynally, of this stac[i]on [8] thus we mak a conclusyon,
Besechyng thys audyens to folow and succede
With all your delygens this generall proces-syon.[9]

---

[1] I.e. the *platea*, or open space surrounded by the spectators.
[2] Journey. 　　　　[3] Added by M.
[4] Continually. 　　[5] By.
[6] This refers, apparently, to the "Conclusyon" or Epilogue. "Daunce" was later inserted.
[7] Added in a later hand.
[8] F. *stacon;* corr. by M.
[9] It is clear that the audience had to walk in pro-cession to the next station.

To vnderstande this matter, wo lyst to rede
The Holy Bybyll for the better spede,
Ther shall he haue the perfyth intellygens.
And thus we comyt yow to Crystys mag-nyfycens. 161

The end of that station, and another follows: [1]

[SECOND STATION. DAMASCUS.] [2]

[PROLOGUE.]

POETA.　Honorable frendes, we beseche yow of audyens
To here our intencion and also our pros-ses.
Vpon our matter, be your fauorable lycens,
A-nother part of the story we wyll re-dres.
Here shalbe brefly shewyd with all our besynes,[3]
At thys pagent, Saynt Poullys conuercyon.
Take ye good hede and ther-to gyf affec-cion. [*Exit.*] 168

Here commyth Saule rydyng in with hys seruantes.

SAULUS.　My purpose to Damask fully I intende.
To pursewe the dyscypulys my lyfe I apply.
For to breke down the chyrchys thus I condescende,
Non I wyll suffer that [they] shall edyfey.[4]
Perchaunce owur lawes than myghte [peyre] [5] ther-by,
And the pepull also turne and conuerte;
Whych shuld be gret heuynes vnto myn hart. 175

Nay, that shall nott be butt layd a-part!
The prynces haue gouyn [6] me full potes-tacion.[7]

---

[1] MS. *Finis istius stacionis, et altera sequitur.*
[2] Again the audience is gathered about an open space, or *platea*. Within the *platea* are constructed, it seems, a "mansion" for Annanie, a "mansyon" (see lines 269–71) for Saul, and Heaven.
[3] Diligence. 　　　[4] Build.
[5] Become impaired. *Supplied by Kittredge,* in M.
[6] Given. 　　　[7] Power.

All that I fynd, thei shall nott start,[1]
  But bounde, to Ierusalem, with furyous
    vyolacion,
  Be-for Cesar, Caypha and Annas [haue] [2]
    presentacion.
Thus shalbe subduyd tho wretchys of that
    lyfe,
That non shall in-ioy, nother man, chy[l]de,
    nor wyfe.   182

Here commyth a feruent [flame] [2] with gret
tempest, and Saule faulyth down of hys
horse; that done, Godhed spekyth in heuyn.

DEUS. Saule! Saule! why dost thou me
    pursue?
Yt ys hard to pryke a-gayns the spore!
I am thi Savyour, that ys so trwe,
  Whych made heuyn and erth and eche
    creature.
  Offende nott my goodnes! I wyll the
    recure! [3]
SAULUS. O Lord, I am a-ferd! I trymble
    for fere!
What woldyst I ded? [4] Tell me here! 189

DEUS. A-ryse, and goo thou wyth glad
    chere
  In-to the cyte a lytyll be-syde,
And I shall the socor in euery dere,[5]
  That no maner of yll xal be-tyde;
And I wyll ther for the prouyde
By my grete goodnes what thou shalt
    doo.
Hy the as fast thether as thou mast goo.196

[*Deus withdraws.*]

SAULUS. O mercyfull God, what aylyth
    me?
I am lame; my legges be take me fro;
My sygth [6] lykwyse; I may nott see;
  I can nott tell whether [7] to goo.
My men hath forsake me also.
Whether shall I wynde? or whether shall I
    pas?
Lord, I beseche the, helpe me, of thy
    grace.   203

I. MILES. Syr, we be here to help the in
    thi nede

With all our affyance;[1] we wyll not seise.[2]
SAULUS. Than, in Damask, I pray yow,
    me lede,
I[n] Godes name, accordyng to my prom-
    yse.
II. MILES. To put forth yowur hand loke
    ye dresse.[3]
Cum on your way. We shall yow bryng
In-to the cyte with-owt taryng.   210

Here the knyghtes lede forth Sale in-to a
place,[4] and Cryst apperyth to Annanie,
saying:

DEUS. Ananie! Ananie! Where art
    thou, Ananie?
ANAN. Here, Lord; I am here, trwly. 212

DEUS. Go thy way and make thi curse,[5]
  As I shall assyng [6] the by myn aduysse,
Into the strete *qui dicitur rectus,*[7]
  And in a certayn house, of warantyse,[8]
  Ther shall ye fynd Saule in humble
    vyse,[9]
As a meke lambe, that a wolf before was
    namyd.
Do my behest; be nothyng a-shamyd! 219

He wantyth hys syth,[10] by my punyshment
    constrayned.
  Prayeng vnto me, I assure, thou shalt
    hym fynd.
With my stroke of pyte sore ys he paynyde,
  Wantyng hys sygth, for he ys truly
    blynyde.
ANAN. Lord, I am aferd; for aluay in my
    mind
I here so myche of hys furyous cruelte,
That for spekyng of thi name to deth he
    will put me.   226

DEUS. Nay, Ananie; nay, I assure the!
He wulbe glad of thy cummyng.
ANAN. A! Lord, but I know, of a cer-
    tayn[te],[11]
  That thy seyntes in Ierusalem to deth he
    doth bryng.

---

[1] Escape.   [2] Supplied by M.
[3] Redeem, save.   [4] Did, should do.
[5] Injury.   [6] Sight.   [7] Whither.

[1] Duty, loyalty.   [2] Cease.
[3] Address yourself.
[4] Obviously the "mansyon" or house indicated in
lines 216, 269–71.
[5] Course.   [6] Assign.
[7] "Which is called straight."
[8] Without fail.   [9] Wise, condition.
[10] Sight.   [11] Added by M.

Many yllys of hym I haue bekennyng,[1]
For he hath the pour [2] of the princes alle
To saue or spylle,[3] do which he schall. 233

DEUS. Be nothyng a-drad! He ys a
chosen wessell
To me, assyngned by my godly eleccion.
He shall bere my name be-fore the kynges
and chylder of Israell,
By many sharpe shoures [4] sufferyng cor-
reccion,
A gret doctor, of benyngne conpleccion,
The trwe precher of the hye deuynete,
A very pynacle of the fayth, I ensure
the. 240

ANAN. Lorde, thy commandment I shall
fullfyll.
Vn-to Saule I wyll take my waye.
DEUS. Be nothyng in dowte for good nor yll.
Fare-well, Ananie! Tell Saule what I do
say.

Let God depart.[5]

ANAN. Blyssyd Lord, defende me, as thou
best may!
Gretly I fere hys cruell tyranny.
But to do thi precept my-self I shall ap-
plye. 247

Here Ananias goth toward Saule.

I. MILES. I maruayle gretly what yt doth
mene,
To se owur master in thys hard stounde.[6]
The wonder grett lythtys [7] that were so
shene [8]
Smett hym doune of hys hors to the
grownde;
And me thowt that I hard a sounde
Of won spekyng with voyce delectable,
Whych was to [vs] [9] wonderfull myr-
able.[10] 254

II. MILES. Sertenly thys lyght was ferefull to see;
The sperkys of fyer were very feruent;

Yt inflamyd so greuosely about the countre
That, by my trowth, I went [1] we shuld a
ben brent.[2]
But now, serys, lett vs relente [3]
Agayne to Caypha and Anna, to tell this
chaunce
How yt be-fell to vs thys greuauns. 261

[*The two soldiers depart for Jerusalem.*]

Her Saule ys in contemplacion.

SAULUS. Lord, of thi counfort moch I
desyre,
Thou myghty Prince of Israell, Kyng of
pyte,
Whyche me hast punyshyd as thi presoner,
That nother ete nor dranke thys dayes
thre.
But, gracyos Lorde, of thi vysytacyon I
thanke the;
Thy seruant shall I be as long as I haue
breth,
Thowgh I therfor shuld suffer dethe. 268

Here commyth Anania to Saule, sayeng:

ANAN. Pease be in thys place and goodly
mansyon!
Who ys with-in? Speke, in Crystys holy
name!
SA[U]LUS. I am here, Saule. Cum in, on
Goddes benyson!
What ys your wyll? Tell, with-owten
blame.
ANAN. From Almyghty God, sertanly, to
the sent I am;
And Ananie men call me wher-as I dwell.
SAULUS. What wold ye haue, I pray yow
me tell. 275

ANAN. Gyfe me your hand for your
awayle.[4]
For, as I was commaundyd by hys gracyos sentens,
He bad [5] the be stedfast, for thou shalt be
hayle.[6]
For thys same cause he sent me to thi
presens.
Also he bad the remember hys hye
excellens,

---

[1] Knowledge. F. prints *be kennyng;* but see
N.E.D. *sub* bekenning.
[2] Power, authority.   [3] Destroy.
[4] Pangs, attacks of pain.
[5] MS. *Et exiat Deus.*
[6] Fierce attack, shock.
[7] Lights.   [8] Bright.
[9] Supplied by M.   [10] Marvellous.

[1] Thought.   [2] Burned.   [3] Return.
[4] Avail, benefit.
[5] F. & *bad.* Manly reads *I byd;* but cf. ll. 280, 289.
[6] Whole, healed.

Be the same tokyn that he dyd the
 mete [1]
Toward the cyte, when he apperyd in the
 strete. 282

Ther mayst thou know hys power celestyall,
 How he dysposyth euery thyng as hym
  lyst;
No thyng may withstand hys myghte es-
 sencyall.
 To stond vp-ryght, or els doun to
  thryste,[2]
 Thys ys hys powur; yt may not be
  myste,
For who that yt wantyth, lackyth a frende.
Thys ys the massage that he doth the
 sende. 289

SAULUS. Hys marcy to me ys ryght welcom;
 I am ryght glad that yt ys thus.

Here the Holy Spirit shall appear above him.[3]

ANAN. Be of good chere and perfyte
 iubylacion,
 Discendet super te Spirytus Sanctus,[4]
 Whych hath with hys grace illumynyd
  vs.
Put fo[r]th thi hond and goo wyth me.
A-gayne to thy syght here I restore the. 296

SAULUS. Blyssyd Lord, thankys to yow
 euer bee!
 The swame [5] ys fallyn from my eyes
  twayne!
Where I was blynyd and cowd nott see,
 Lord, thou hast sent me my syght
  agayne.
From sobbyng and wepyng I can not
 refrayne.
My pensyue hart [is] full of contryccion;
For my offences my body shal haue puny-
 cyon; [6] 303

And, where I haue vsed so gret persecucyon
Of thi descyplys thorow all Ierusalem,

I wyll [aid] and defende ther predycacyon [1]
 That th[e]y dyd tech on all this reme.[2]
Wherefor, Ananie, at the watery streme
Baptyse me, hartely I the praye,
A-mong your numbyr that I electe and
 chosen be may. 310

ANAN. On-to this well [3] of mych vertu
 We wyll vs hye with all our delygens.
SAULUS. Go yow be-fore, and after I shall
 sewe,
 Laudyng and praysyng our Lordes be-
  nevolens.
I shall neuer offend hys myghty magnyf-
 ycens,
But aluay obserue hys preceptys and
 kepe.
For my gret vnkyndnes my hart doth
 wepe. 317

[They arrive at the place of baptism.]

ANAN. Knele ye down vpon thys grownde,
 Receyuyng thys crystenyng with good
  intent,
Whyche shall make yow hole of your dedly
 wound,
 That was infecte with venom nocent.[4]
Yt purgyth synne; and fendes poures [5] so
 fraudelent
It putyth a-syde; where thys doth at-
 tayne,
In euery stede, he may not obtayne. 324

I crysten yow with mynd full perfyght,
 Reseyuyng yow in-to owur relygyon,
Euer to be stedfast and neuer to flyt,[6]
 But euer constant with-owt varyacyon.
Now ys fulfyllyd all our obseruacyon;
Concludyng, thou mayst yt ken,
In nomine Patris et Filij et Spiritus Sancti,
 Amen! 331

SAULUS. I am ryght glad as foule on flyte [7]
 That I haue receyuyd this blyssyd sacre-
  ment.
ANAN. Com on your way, Saule; for nothyng lett.[8]
 Take yow sum coumforth for your
  bodyes noryschment.

---

[1] Meet. [2] Thrust.
[3] MS. *Hic aparebit Spiritus Sanctus super eum.*
Cf. John i, 32: "I saw the Spirit descending from
heaven like a dove, and it abode upon him."
[4] "The Holy Spirit descends upon thee."
[5] Scale. [6] Punishment.

---

[1] Preaching. [2] Realm.
[3] Probably a baptismal font set in the *platea*
[4] Injurious. [5] Fiends' power.
[6] Deviate. [7] Bird on wing. [8] Delay.

Ye shall abyde with the dyscyplys, vera-
  ment,
Thys many dayes in Damask cyte,
Vn-tyll the tyme more perfyt ye may be. 338

SAULUS.   As ye commande, holy father
  Ananie;
  I full[y] [1] assent at yow[r] request,
To be gydyd and rulyd as ye wyll haue me,
  Evyn at your pleasur, as ye thynk best.
I shall not offend for most nor lest.
Go forth yowur way; I wyll succede
In-to what place ye wyll me lede.   345

          [*Exeunt.*]

          CONCLUSYO[N].

          Daunce.[2]

          [EPILOGUE.]

POETA.   Thus Saule ys conuertyd, as ye se
  expres,
The very trw seruant of our Lord Iesu.
Non may be lyke to hys perfyght holynes,
So nobyll a doctor, constant and trwe;
  Aftyr hys conuersyon neuer mutable,
    but styll insue
The lawys of God to teche euer more and
  more.
As Holy Scryptur tellyd who-so lyst to
  loke ther-fore.   352

Thus we comyte yow all to the Trynyte,
  Conkludyng thys stacion as we can or
  may,
Vnder the correccyon of them that letteryd
  be;
  How-be-yt vnable, as I dare speke or
  say,
  The compyler her-of shuld translat veray
So holy a story, but with fauorable correc-
  cyon
Of my fauorable masters of ther benygne
  supplexion.[3]   359

*The end of that second station, and the third
  follows:* [4]

[1] Added by M.
[2] In a later hand (though not so stated by F.).
[3] Supplementation.
[4] MS   *Finis istius secunde stacionis, et sequitur
  urcia.*

[THIRD STATION. JERUSALEM.] [1]

          [PROLOGUE.]

POETA.   The myght of the Fadires poten-
  ciall deite
  Preserue thys honorable and wurshyp-
  full congregacion
That here be present of hye and low degre,
  To vnderstond thys pagent at thys lytyll
  stacion,
  Whych we shall procede with all our
  delectac[i]on,
Yf yt wyll plese yow to gyf audyens fauorable.
Hark wysely ther-to; yt ys good and
  profetable.   [*Exit.*]   366

[*The two soldiers from Damascus come up to
  Caiaphas and Anna.*]

I. MILES.   Nobyll prelates, take hede to
  owur sentens!
  A wundyrfull chaunce fyll [2] and dyd be-
  tyde
Vn-to owr master Saull, when he departyd
  hens,
  In-to Damaske purposyd to ryde.
  A meruelous lyght fro thelement [3] dyd
  glyde,
Whyche smet doun hym to grunde, both
  horse and man,
With the ferfulest wether that euer I in
  cam.   373

II. MILES.   It rauysshid hym, and his
  spirites did benome.
  A swete, dulcet voyce spake hym vnto,
And askyd wherfor he made suche persecucyon
A-geynst hys dyscyplys, and why he dyd
  soo.
  He bad hym in-to Damaske to Ananie
  goo,

[1] Not without some hesitation I have labeled this
Jerusalem. All the action seems to take place there,
although the Bible represents some of this as occur-
ring in Damascus. We may suppose that the author,
or the actors, were forced by the conditions of performance to take liberties with the Biblical story.
Or it may be that the text of the play has been re-
vamped for a three-station performance. There
seems to have been on the *platea* the house of
Caiaphas and Anna, a scaffold for the devils, and a
pulpit (or possibly a house) for Saul.
[2] Fell, befell.   [3] The element, the sky.

And ther he shuld reseyue baptym, truly.
And now clene a-geyns owur lawys he ys
   trwly.   380

CAYPHA. I am sure thys tale ys not trw!
What! Saule conuertyd from our law!
He went to Damask for to pursue
   All the dyscyplys that dyd with-draw
Fro owur fayth: thys was hys sawe.[1]
How say ye, Anna, to thys mater? This ys
   a mervelos chans!
I can not beleve that thys ys of assur-
   ans!   387

ANNA. No, Caypha! My mynde trwly
   do [I] tell:
   That he wyll not turne in no maner wyse,
But rather to deth put and expell
   All myscreauntes and wretchys that
    doth aryse
Agaynst our lawes by ony enterpryse.

[*Turning to the soldiers.*]

Say the trwth with-[owt] ony cause frawd-
   elent,
Or els for your talys ye be lyke to be
   shent!   394

I. MILES. Ellys owur bodyes may [ye][2]
   put to payn![3]
All that we declare I sye yt with my nye;[4]
Nothyng offendyng, but trwly do iusty-
   fye.   397

CAYPHAS. By the gret God, I do maruayle
   gretly!
And[5] thys be trw that ye do reherse,
He shall repent hys rebellyous treytory,
   That all shalbe ware[6] of hys falsnes.
We wyll not suffer hym to obtayne[7] dowt-
   les,
For meny perellys that myght be-tyde
By hys subtyll meanys on euery syde. 404

ANNA. The law ys commyttyd to owur
   aduysment;
   Wherfor we wyll not se yt decay,

But rather vphold yt, help, and augment,
   That ony reprofe to vs fall may
Of Cesar, themprour, by nyght or day.
We shall to such maters harke and at-
   tende,
Accordyng to the lawes our wyttes to
   spende.   411

[1] [*Here to enter a dyvel with thunder and
fyre, and to avaunte [2] hym sylfe, saying as
folowyth; and, hys spech spokyn, to syt
downe in a chayre.*

BELYALL. Ho! ho! Be-holde me, the
   myghte prince of the partes in-
   fernall!
Next vnto Lucyfer I am in magestye!
By name I am nominate the god Belyall;
   Non of more myghte, nor of more excel-
    lencye!
My powre ys princypall, and now of
   most soferaynte.
In the temples and synogoges who deneyth
   me to honore,
My busshopes, thorow my motyon,[3] thei
   wyl hym sone devoure.   418

I have movyd my prelates, Cayphas and
   Anna,
   To persew and put downe by powre
    ryall,
Thorow the sytyes of Damask and Liba,
   All soch as do worship the hye God su-
    pernall.
   Ther deth ys conspyryd with-owt any
    fauoure at all.
My busshopys hathe chosyne won most
   rygorus
Them to persew, howse[4] name ys
   Saulus.   425

Ho! Thus as a god, most hye in magestye,
   I rayne and I rule ouer creatures hu-
    mayne!
With souerayne sewte sowghte to ys my
   deyte.[5]

---

[1] Saying.   [2] Supplied by M.
[3] As Manly points out, four lines seem to be missing here.
[4] Mine eye.   [5] If.
[6] Cautious in avoiding.
[7] Prevail, gain the day.

[1] At this point, and extending through the stage
direction following line 502 (I have enclosed the
scene in brackets), a later writer has inserted on three
separate leaves a comic episode between Belial and
Mercury. His purpose seems to have been to render the play more entertaining.
[2] Vaunt, brag about. (F. *avaunce*.)
[3] Suggestion.   [4] Whose.   [5] Deity.

Mans mynd ys applicant as I lyst to
ordeyne.
My law styll encreasyth; wherof I am
fayne.
Yet of late I haue hard of no newys truly;
Wherfor I long tyll I speke with my messenger Mercurye.   432

*Here shall entere a-nother devyll, callyd
Mercury, with a fyeryng,[1] commyng in
hast, cryeng and roryng, and shal say as
folowyth:*

MARCURY. Ho! owght! owght! Alas thys
sodayne chance!
Well may we bewayle this cursyd aduenture!

BELYAL.   Marcurye, what aylyse thou?
Tell me thy grevaunce!
Ys ther any that hath wrowghte vs dys-
pleasure?

MERC.   Dyspleasure i-nowgh, therof ye
may be sure!
Our law at lengthe yt wylbe clene downe
layd,
For yt decayth sore; and more wyl, I am
a-frayd.   439

BEL.   Ho! how can that be? Yt ys not
possyble!
Co[n]syder, thou foole, the long contynu-
ance!
Decaye, quod a?[2] Yt ys not credyble!
Of fals tydynges thou makyst here vt-
terance.
Behold how the peple hath no pleasaunce
But in syn and to folow our desyere,
Pryde and voluptuosyte ther hartes doth so
fyre.   446

Thowghe on[e] do swauer[3] away from our
lore,
Yet ys our powre of suche nobylyte
To have hym a-gayne, and twoo therfore
That shal preferre the prayse of owre
maiestye.
What ys the tydynges? Tell owt! Lett
vs see!
Why arte thou amasyd so? Declare afore
vs

---

[1] An explosion of powder; cf. *The Castle of Perseverance,* stage-direction after line 2199. (But *N.E.D.*
explains this as "a quantity of burning fuel.")
[2] Says he.   [3] Decline.

What fury ys fallyn that troblyth the
thus!   453

MERCURY. Ho! owght! owghte! He that
I most trustyd to,
And he that I thowghte wold haue ben
to vs most specyall,
Ys now of late turnyd, and our cruell foo!
Our specyall frynd, our chosen Saull,
Ys be-comme seruante to the hye God
eternall!
As he dyd ryde on our enemyes persecu-
tyon,
He was sodenly strykyn by the hye provy-
syon;   460

And now ys baptysyd, and promys he hath
made
Neuer to vary; and soch grace he hath
opteynyd
That ondowtyd[1] hys fayth from hym
can-not fade.
Wherfor to complayne I am con-
straynyd,
For moch by hym shuld we haue pre-
vaylyd.

BELYAL.   Ho! owght! owght! What!
haue we loste
Our darlyng most dere, whom we lovyd
moste?   467

But ys yt of trowth that thou doyst here
specyfye?
MERCURY.   Yt ys so, ondowghtyd. Why
shuld I fayne?
For thowghte I can do non other but crye!

*Here thei shal rore and crye; and then Belyal
shal saye:*

BELYAL.   Owghte! This grevyth vs
worse than hell payne!
The conuersyon of [one] synner, certayne,
Ys more payne to vs and persecutyon
Than all the furyes of the infernall don-
gyon.   474

MERCURY. Yt doyth not avayl vs thus to
lament;
But lett vs provyd for remedy shortlye.
Wherfor let vs both by on[e] assent

---

[1] Without doubt.

Go to the busshopys and moue them
pryvelye
That by some sotyl meane thei may
cause hym to dye.
Than shal he in our law make no dysturb-
aunce,
Nor here-after cause vs to haue more greuaunce. 481

BELYAL. Wel sayd, Mercurye! Thy
cowncel ys profytable.
Ho, Saul, thou shalt repent thy vnstable-
nes!
Thou hadyst ben better to haue byn con-
fyrmable
To our law; for thys deth, dowtles,
Yt ys conspyryd to reward thy falsnes.
Thowgh on[e] hath dyssayvyd [1] vs, yet
now a days
Twentie doyth gladly folow oure layes: 488

Some by Pryde, some thorowgh Envye;
Ther rayneth thorow my myght so moch
dysobedyaunce,
Ther was neuer a-mong Crystyans lesse
charyte
Than ys at this howre; and as for Con-
cupysence,
[He] [2] rayneth as a lord thorow my
violence.
Glotony and Wrath euery man doth devyse;
And most now ys praysyd my cosyn Cov-
ytyce. 495

Cum, Mercury, let vs go and do as we haue
sayd;
To delate yt any lenger yt ys not best.
MERCURY. To bryng yt a-bowght I wold
be wel apayd; [3]
Tell yt be done let vs not rest.

.   .   .   .

BELYAL. Go we than shortly, let vs departe,
Hys deth to devyse, syth he wyl not
revart. [4] 502

*Here thei shal vanyshe away with a fyrye
flame and a tempest.* [5]]

---

[1] Deceived.   [2] Supplied by M.
[3] Contented, pleased.
[4] Return (after estrangement).
[5] Probably made by pots and kettles beaten together.

Her apperyth Saule in a disciplis wede, [1]
sayng:

SAULUS. That Lord that ys shaper of see
and of sond
And hath wrowth with hys woord all
thyng at hys wyll,
Saue thys semely [2] that here syttyth or
stonde, [3]
For his meke marcy, that we do not
spyll!
Grant me, good Lord, thy pleasur to ful
fyll,
And send me suche speche that I the trwth
say,
My entencions proph[i]table to meve yf I
may. 509

Welbelouyd frendes, ther be vij mortall
synnes . . . [4]

[*From among those listening to Saul, the
servant of the High Priests speaks up.*]

SERUUS. Whate! Ys not thys Saule that
toke hys vyage
In-to Ierusalem, [5] the dyscyplys to op-
presse?
Bounde he wold bryng them, yf ony dyd
rage
Vpon Cryst, — this was hys processe.
To the princes of prestys, he sayde
dowtles:
Thorow all Damask and also Ierusalem
Subdwe all templys that he founde of
them. 579

SA[U]LUS. Yes, sertaynly, Saule ys my
proper name,
That had in powr the full dominion —
To hyde yt fro you yt were gret shame
And mortall synne, as in my opynyon, —
Vnder Cesar and pristes of the relygyon
And templys of Iues, that be very hedy-
ous
A-gayns almghty Cryst, that kyng so
precyous. 586

[1] Costume.   [2] Assembly.
[3] Possibly scaffolds were erected with seats for
some of the spectators.
[4] I have omitted Saul's long sermon on the Seven
Deadly Sins, for the same reason that impelled the
later writer to add the comic scene of Belial and Mercury. The sermon has no dramatic value.
[5] Possibly, as F. notes, an error for Damascus.

SERUUS. To Anna and Caypha ye must
  make your recurse.[1]
Com on your way, and make no delacion!
SAULUS. I wyll yow succede, for better or
  wors,
To the prynces of pristes with all delectacion.

[*The Servant leads Saul to Caiaphas and
  Anna.*]

SERUUS. Holy pristes of hye potestacion,
Here ys Saule! Lok on hym wysely!
He ys a-nother man than he was, verely.593

SAULUS. I am the seruant of Ihesu Al-
  myghty,
Creator and maker of see and sonnd,
Whiche ys kyng conctypotent [2] of heuyn
  glory,
Chef comfort and solace both to fre and
  bonde,
A-gayns whos power nothyng may
  stonde.
Emperowr he ys both of heuyn and hell,
Whoys goodnes and grace al thyng doth
  excell.   600

Saul withdraws for a little while.[3]

CAYPHA. Vn-to my hart thys ys gret ad-
  myracion,
That Saule ys thus mervelously changyd!
I trow he ys bewytchyd by sum coniura-
  cion,
Or els the devyll on hym ys auengyd.
Alas! to my hart yt ys dessendyd [4]
That he ys thus takyn fro our relygyon!
How say ye, Anna, to thys conuercyon? 607

ANNA. Full mervelously, as in my concep-
  cion,
Thys wnderfull case how yt be-fell,
To se thys chaunce so sodenly don,
Vn-to my hart yt doth grete yll.
But for hys falsnes we shall hym spyll! [5]
By myn assent to deth we wyll hym
  bryng,
Lest that more myschef of hym may
  spryng.   614

CAYPHA. Ye say very trew; we myght yt
  all rewe!
But shortly in thys we must haue ad-
  uysement,
For thus a-gayns vs he may nott con-
  tynew;
Perauentur than of Cesar we may be
  shent.[1]
ANNA. Nay, I had leuer in fyer he were
  brent
Than of Cesar we shuld haue dysp[l]easure
For sych a rebell and subtyle fals treator

CAYPHA. We wyll command the gates to
  be kept aboute   622
And the walles suerly on euery stede,
That he may not eskape no-where owghte.
For dye he shall, I ensuer yow indede.
ANNA. Thys traytour rebellyous, evyll
  mut [2] he spede,
That doth this vnhappynes a-gayns all!
Now euery costodyer kepe well hys wall!

SERUUS. The gatys be shytt, he can not
  eskape! [3]   629
Euery place ys kepte well and sure,
That in no wyse he may, tyll he be take,
Gett owt of the cyte, by ony coniecture.
Vpon that caytyf and fals traytour
Loke ye be auengyd with deth mortall,
And iudge hym as ye lyst to what end he
  shall.   635

[*An angel appears to Saul.*]

ANGELUS. Holy Saule, I gyf yow mony-
  cyon,[4]
The princes of Iues entende, sertayn,
To put yow to deth. But by Goddes pro-
  vysyon
He wyll ye shall lyue lenger, and op-
  tayn,
And after thy deth thou shalt rayng [5]
Above in heuyn, with owr Lordes grace.
Conuay yowr-self shortly in-to a-nother
  place.   642

SAULUS. That Lordes pleasur euer mut be
  down
Both in heuyn and in hell, as hys wyll ys!

---

[1] Return.   [2] All-powerful.
[3] MS. *Recedit paulisper.*
[4] Descended.   [5] Destroy.

[1] Disgraced.   [2] May.
[3] F. *note skape;* corr. by M.
[4] Warning.   [5] Reign.

In a beryng-baskett or a lepe,[1] a-non
   I shall me co[n]uay with help of the
     dyscyplys,
  For euery gate ys shett and kept with
     multytud of pepull[ys];[2]
But I trust in owr Lord, that ys my socour,
To resyst ther malyce and cruell furour. 649

CONCLUSYO[N].

[EPILOGUE.]

POETA. Thus leve we Saule with-in the
     cyte,
  The gates kep by commandment of
     Caypha and Anna;
But the dyscyplys in the nyght ouer the
     wall, truly,

---

[1] In a carrying-basket or a basket.
[2] Added by M.

As the Bybull sayeth: *dim[i]serunt eum*
   summittentes [1] *in sporta;*
And Saule after that, in Ierusalem, vera,
Ioyned hym-self and ther accompenyed
With the dyscyplys, wher thei were vn-
     fayned.[2]   656

Thys lytyll pagent thus conclud we
  As we can, lackyng lytturall scyens;[3]
Besechyng yow all, of hye and low degre,
  Owr sympylnes to hold excusyd and
     lycens,
That of retoryk haue non intellygens;
Commyttyng yow all to owr Lord Ihesus,
To whoys lawd ye syng: *Exultet celum*
   laudibus!   663

    Finis Co[n]uercionis Sancti Pauli.

---

[1] F. *summittens;* corr. by M. See the Vulgate, Actus Apostolorum ix, 25.
[2] Not feigned, unconcealed.
[3] Literary skill.

MARY MAGDALENE [1]

[*The stage of the Emperor Tiberius Cæsar, Rome. The Emperor, Serbyl, Provost, and others.*]

INPERATOR.   I command sylyns, in the peyn of forfetur,
To all myn avdyeans present general.
Of my most hyest and mytyest wolunte,[1]
I woll it be knowyn to al the word [2] vnyversal,   4
That of heven and hell chyff rewlar am I,
To w[h]os magnyfycens non stondyt egall,[3]
For I am soveren of al soverens subjugal [4]
On-to myn empere, beyng in-comparable,
Tyberyus Sesar, w[h]os power is potencyall.
I am the blod ryall [5] most of soverente;   10
Of all emperowers and kynges my byrth is best,
And all regeouns obey my myty volunte.
Lyfe and lem [6] and goodes, all be at my request.
So of all soverens, my magnyfycens most mytyest

May nat be a-gayn-sayd of frend nor of foo;   15
But all abydyn ivgment and rewle of my lyst.[1]
All grace up-on erth from my goodnes commyt fro,[2]
And that bryng-is [3] all pepell in blysse so.
For the most worthyest, woll I rest in my sete.

[*He seats himself in his throne.*]

SERYBYL.   Syr, from your person growyt [4] moch grace.   20

INPERATOR.   Now for thin answer, Belyall blysse thi face!
Mykyl presporyte [5] I gyn to porchase;
I am wonddyn [6] in welth from all woo.
Herke thou, Provost, I gyff the in commandment,
All your pepull preserve in pesabyl possesson.   25
Yff ony ther be to my goddes [dis]obedyent,
Dyssever tho[s] harlottes,[7] and make to me declaracyon,

[1] Will.	[2] World.
[3] Equal.	
[4] Subject.	[5] Royal.
[6] Limb.	

[1] Pleasure, will.	[2] From.
[3] Bringeth.	[4] Groweth.
[5] Great prosperity.	[6] Wound, wrapt.
[7] Separate out those rascals.	

[1] The text is preserved in a manuscript, Bodleian Digby MS. 133, containing four plays (three complete plays on Biblical themes, and a fragment of a morality) accidentally brought together. The manuscript is probably to be dated in the early part of the sixteenth century, but the plays themselves were composed in the latter half of the fifteenth century. The play here reproduced, dealing with the legendary history of Mary Magdalene, belongs to the midland section of England, though the exact place of its origin cannot be indicated. The text is based on the edition by F. J. Furnivall, *The Digby Mysteries*, 1882. I have, of course, modernized the punctuation and the use of capitals; and I have added in brackets a few stage-directions in order to enable the student to visualize the performance. The actors, it is clear, employed a series of "stages" or small platforms, arranged in a circle about a *platea* or unlocated region (called "the place"), and the attention of the audience was shifted from one platform to the other, or to "the place," as the necessity of the text demanded. The accompanying diagram, though not intended to be exact, will help to make the stage arrangement clear.

The play, which is of great length, was probably acted in two parts; the first part, dealing with the fall and conversion of Mary (here reprinted), was acted, we may suppose, in the forenoon, the second part, dealing with the voyage of Mary to Marcylle and her conversion of the King and Queen of Marcylle to Christianity, in the afternoon. It is true that the transcript of the play gives no indication of a break in the performance; but the second half constitutes a separate unit of action after a lapse of time, and involves an almost entirely new set of stages.

Caesar / Herod / Pilate / Cyrus / Simon / Devil / Flesh / World / Place

And I xall make all swych to dye,
Thos precharsse [1] of Crystys incarnacyon.

PROVOST. Lord of all lorddes, I xall gyff
    yow in-formacyon.   30

INPERATOR. Lo, how all the word obeyit [2]
    my domynacyon!
That person is nat born that dare me dysse-
    obey.
Syrybbe, I warne yow se that my lawys
In all your partyys [3] have dew obeysavns.
In-quere and aske, eche day that davnnes,
Yf in my pepul be fovnd ony weryouns,[4]
Contrary to me in ony chansse,   37
Or with my goldyn goddes grocth or
    grone; [5]
I woll marre swych [6] harlottes with mordor
    and myschanse!
Yff ony swyche remayn, put hem in re-
    preffe,   40
And I xall yow releff.

SERYBB. Yt xall be don, lord, with-owtyn
    ony lett [7] or with-owt doth.[8]

INPERATOR. Lord and lad, to my law
    doth lowte.[9]
Is it nat so? sey yow all with on showte.

Here answerryt all the pepul at ons,
" Ya, my lord, ya."

INPERATOR. So, the froward folkes, now
    am [I] plesyd.   45
Sett wyn and spycys to my consell full cler.
Now have I told yow my hart, I am wyll
    plesyd;
Now lett vs sett don alle, and make good
    chyr.

[*They seat themselves at the council table.*]

[*The stage of Cyrus, the Castle of Maudleyn, Bethany. Cyrus, Mary, Martha,
and Lazarus.*]

*Her entyr Syrus, the fader of Mary
Mavdlyn.*[10]

SYRUS. Emperor, and ky[n]gges, and con-
    querors kene,

Erlys, and borons, and knytes that byn [1]
    bold,   50
Berdes [2] in my bower, so semely to sene,[3]
I commav[n]d yow at onys my hestes [4] to
    hold. [5]
Be-hold my person, glysteryng in gold,
Semely be-syn of all other men!
Cyrus is my name. Be cleffys so cold, 55
I command yow all, obedyent to beyn;
W[h]o-so woll nat, in bale I hem bryng,
And knett swyche cayftyys [6] in knottes of
    care.
Thys Castell of Mavdleyn is at my wyld-
    dyng,[7]
With all the contre, bothe lesse and more,
And Lord of Ierusalem. Who agens me
    don dare?   61
Alle Beteny [8] at my beddyng be.
I am sett in solas from al syyng [9] sore;
And so xall all my posteryte,
Thus for to leuen in rest and ryalte.[10]   65
I have her a sone that is to me ful trew,
No comlyar creatur of Goddes creacyon;
T[w]o amyabyll dovctors [11] full brygth of
    ble.[12]
Ful gloryos to my syth, an[d] ful of de-
    lectacyon,
Lazarus my son, in my resspeccyon;[13]   70
Here is Mary, ful fayr, and ful of femynyte;
And Martha, ful [of] bevte and of delycyte,
Ful of womanly merrorys [14] and of be-
    nygnyte.
They haue fulfyllyd my hart with conso-
    lacyon.
Here is a coleccyon of cyrcumstance,   75
To my cognysshon [15] never swych
    a-nothyr,
As be demonstracyon knett incontynens,
Save a-lonly my lady, that was ther mother.
Now, Lazarus, my sonne, whech art ther
    brothyr,
The lordshep of Ierusalem I gyff the after
    my [16] dysses;[17]   80
And Mary, thys castell, a-lonly, an non
    othyr;
And Martha xall haue Beteny, I sey
    exprese.

---

[1] Preachers.   [2] World obeyeth.
[3] Parts, regions.   [4] Variance, disagreement.
[5] Grumble or groan; F. reads *on*, instead of *or*.
[6] Destroy such.   [7] Hindrance, delay.
[8] Doubt.   [9] Bow.   [10] Magdalene.

[1] Be.   [2] Maidens.   [3] See.
[4] Commands.   [5] Keep.   [6] Caitiffs.
[7] Command, rule.   [8] Bethany.   [9] Sighing.
[10] Royalty.   [11] Daughters.   [12] Countenance.
[13] Regard.   [14] Shining qualities.
[15] Knowledge.   [16] MS. mo.   [17] Decease.

Thes gyftes I gravnt yow with-owtyn les,[1]
Whyll that I am in good mynd.
LAZARUS. Most reuerent father, I thank
yow hartely   85
Of yower grett kyndnes shuyd on-to me!
Ye haue gravntyd swych a lyfelod,[2]
worthy
Me to restreyn from all nessesyte.
Now, good Lord, and hys wyll it be,
Gravnt me grace to lyue to thy plesow-
ans,[3]   90
And a-gens hem so to rewle me,
Thatt we may have ioye with-owtyn
weryauns.[4]

MARY MAVDLEYN. Thatt God of pes and
pryncypall covnsell,
More swetter is thi name than hony be
kynd![5]
We thank yow, fathyr, for your gyftes
ryall,   95
Owt of peynes of poverte vs to on-bynd;
Thys is a preseruatyff from streytnes,[6] we
fynd,
From worldy labors to my covmfortyng;
For thys lyfflod is abyll[7] for the dowtter[8]
of a kyng,
Thys place of plesavns, the soth to seye.

MARTHA. O, ye good fathyr of grete
degre,   101
Thus to departe with your ryches,
Consederyng ower lowlynes and humyl-
yte,
Vs to save from wordly dessetres,
Ye shew vs poyntes of grete ientylnes, 105
So mekly to meyntyn vs to your grace.
Hey in heuen a-wansyd mot[9] yow be
In blysse, to se that Lordes face,
Whan ye xal hens passe!

CYRUS. Now I reioyse with all my
mygthtes!   110
To enhanse[10] my chyldryn, it was my
delyte.
Now wyn and spycys, ye ientyll knyttes,
On-to thes ladys of ientylnes.

*Here xal they be servyd with wyn and
spycys.*

[*The stage of the Emperor Tiberius Cæsar,
Rome.*]

INPERATOR. Syr Provost, and Skrybe,
iugges of my rem,[1]
My massenger I woll send in-to ferre
cuntre,   115
On-to my sete of Ierusalem,
On-to Herowdes, that regent ther ondyr
me,
And on-to Pylat, iugges of the covntre:
Myn entent I woll hem teche.
Take hed, thou Provost, my precept
wretyn[2] be,   120
And sey I cummavnd hem, as they woll be
owght wrech,[3]
Yf ther be ony in the cuntre, ageyn[4] my
law doth prech,
Or ageyn my goddes ony trobyll telles,
That thus agens my lawys rebelles,
As he is regent, and in that reme dwelles,
And holdyth hys crovn of me be ryth, 126
Yff ther be ony harlettes that a-gens me
make replycacyon,[5]
Or ony moteryng[6] agens me make with
malynacyon.[7]

PROVOST. Syr, of all thys they xall have
in-formacyon,
So to vp-hold yower renovn and ryte.[8] 130

[INPERATOR.] Now, massenger, with-
owtyn taryyng,
Have here gold on-to thi fe.[9]
So bere thes lettyrs to Herowdes the
kyng,
And byd hem make in-quyrans in euery
cuntre,
As he is iugge in that cuntre beyng. 135

NVNCYUS. Soueren, your arend[10] it xall
be don ful redy
In alle the hast that I may;
For to fullfyll your byddyng
I woll nat spare nother be nyth nor be
day.

*Here goth the masenger to-ward
Herowdes.*

---

[1] Lie, deceit. [2] Livelihood.
[3] Pleasure. [4] Variance.
[5] By nature. [6] Hardship.
[7] Fit. [8] Daughter.
[9] Advanced may. [10] Advance.

[1] Realm. [2] Written.
[3] As they wish to be free from punishment.
[4] Against. [5] Answer.
[6] Muttering. [7] Feeling of ill-will.
[8] Right. [9] Reward, pay.
[10] Errand.

[*The Stage of Herod, Jerusalem.   Herod,*
Philosophers, Soldiers, and others.]

HEROWDES.   In the wyld wanyng word,[1]
      pes all at onys!   140
No noyse, I warne yow, for greveyng of
      me!
Yff yow do, I xal hovrle [2] of yower hedes,
      be Mahondes [3] bones,
As I am trew kyng to Mahond so fre.
Help, help, that I had a swerd!
Fall don, ye faytours,[4] flatt to the grovnd!
Heve of your hodes and hattes, I cum-
      mavnd yow alle: 146
Stond bare-hed, ye beggars! W[h]o made
      yow so bold?
I xal make yow know your kyng ryall!
Thus woll I be obeyyd thorow al the
      wor[l]d;
And who-so wol nat, he xal be had in
      hold;   150
And so to be cast in carys cold,
That werkyn ony wondyr a-gens my
      magnyfycens.
Be-hold these ryche rubyys, red as ony fyr,
With the goodly grene perle ful sett
      a-bowgth! [5]
What kyng is worthy or egall [6] to my
      power?   155
Or in thys word,[7] who is more had in dowt [8]
Than is the hey name of Herowdes, Kyng
      of Ierusalem,
Lord of Alapye,[9] Assye,[10] an Tyr,
Of Abyron,[11] Bergaby,[12] and Bedlem? [13]
All thes byn ondyr my governouns.   160
Lo, all thes I hold with-owtyn reprobacyon.
No man is to me egall, save a-lonly the
      emperower
Tyberyus, as I have in provostycacyon.[14]
How sey the, phylyssoverys, be my ryche
      reyne?
Am nat I the grettest governower?   165
Lett me ondyr-stond whatt can ye seyn.

PHELYSOFYR.   Soueren, and it plece [15]
      yow, I woll expresse:
Ye be the rewlar of this regyon,

And most worthy sovereyn of nobylnes
That euer in Iude [1] barre domyna-
      cyon!   170
Bott, syr, skreptour [2] gevytt informacyon,
And doth rehersse it werely,[3]
That chyld xal remayn of grete renovn,
And all the word [4] of hem shold magnyfy, —
Et ambulabunt gentes in lumine, et reges 175
In splendore ortus tui.

HEROWDES.   And whatt seyst thow?

II. PHY[LOSOFYR.]   The same weryfyyt [5]
      my bok; as how,
As the skryptour doth me tell,
Of a myty duke xal rese [6] and reyn,   180
Whych xall reyn and rewle all Israell.
No kyng a-gens hys worthynes xall
      opteyn; [7]
The whech in profesy hath grett elo-
      quence, —
Non avferetur septrum Iuda, et dux de
Femore eius, donec veniet Imitendus est. 185

HEROWDES.   A, owt! owt! now am [I]
      grevyd all with the worst!
Ye dastardus! ye dogges! the dylfe mote
      yow draw! [8]
With fleyyng flappes [9] I byd yow to a fest.
A swerd! a swerd! thes lordeynnes [10] wer
      slaw! [11]
Ye langbaynnes! [12] loselles! for-sake ye
      that word!   190
That caytyff xall be cawth,[13] and suer I xall
      hem flaw; [14]
For hym, many mo xal be marry [15] with
      mordor.

I. MILES.   My sovereyn lord, dyssemay
      yow ryth nowt!
They ar but folys,[16] ther eloquens wantyng,
For in sorow and care sone they xall be
      cawt;   195
A-gens vs they can mak no dysstonddyng.[17]

II. MILES.   My lord, all swych xall be
      browte before your avdyens,[18]
And leuyn [19] ondyr your domynacyon,

---

[1] Wild waning world (an imprecation).
[2] Hurl.   [3] Mahomet's.   [4] Rascals.
[5] About.   [6] Equal.   [7] World.
[8] Fear.   [9] Aleppo?   [10] Asia.
[11] Hebron.   [12] Beersheba.   [13] Bethlehem.
[14] Regency.   [15] If it please.

[1] Judea.   [2] Scripture.   [3] Verily.
[4] World.   [5] Verifyeth.   [6] Rise.   [7] Prevail.
[8] Tear in pieces.   [9] Flaying blows.
[10] Lurdans, rascals.   [11] Slain.
[12] Longbones. [13] Caught.   [14] Flay.
[15] Marred.   [16] Fools.
[17] Withstanding.
[18] Presence.   [19] Live.

Or elles dammyd to deth with mortal
    sentense,
Yf we hem gett onder ower gubernacyon.[1]

HEROWDES.   Now thys is to me a grac-
    yows exsortacyon,   201
And grettly reioysyth to my sprytes in-
    dede.
Thow thes sottes a-gens me make reply-
    cacyon,
I woll suffer non to spryng of that kenred;[2]
Some woys[3] in my lond shall sprede, 205
Prevely or pertely[4] in my lond a-bowth.
Whyle I haue swych men, I nede nat to
    drede
But that he xal be browt onder, with-
    owtyn do[w]th.

*Her commyt the Emperowers [masenger] thus
    sayyng to Herowdes:*

MASENGER.   Heyll, prynse of bovnty-
    owsnesse!
Heyll, myty lord of to magnyfy!   210
Heyll, most of worchep of to expresse!
Heyll, reytyus[5] rewlar in thi regensy!
My sofereyn, Tyberyuus, chyff of chyfalry,[6]
His soveren sond[7] hath sent to yow here:
He desyrth yow, and preyyt,[8] on eche
    party   215
To fulfyll his commavndment and desyre.

*Here he xall take[9] the lettyrs on-to the
    kyng.*

HERAWDES.   Be he sekyr[10] I woll natt
    spare
For [to] complyshe his cummavnddment,
With scharp swerddes to perce the bare,[11]
In all covntres with-in thys regent, 220
For his love, to fulfyll his in-tentt:
Non swych xall from ower handys stertt,[12]
For we woll fulfyll his ryall iuggement,
With swerd and spere to perce thorow the
    hartt.
But, masenger, reseyve thys letter wyth,[13]
And berytt[14] on-to Pylatt-ys syth. 226

MESENGER.   My lord, it xall be don ful
    wygth;[1]
In hast I woll me spede.   [*Exit.*]

*[The stage of Pilate, Jerusalem. Pilate,
    two Sergeants.]*

PYLATT.   Now ryally I reyne in robys of
    rych[e]sse,
Kyd[2] and knowyn both ny and ferre 230
For Iuge of Ierusalem, the trewth to ex-
    presse,
Ondyr the emperower Tyberius Cesar.
Therfor I rede[3] yow all, be-warre
Ye do no pregedyse[4] a-gen the law,
For, and ye do, I wyll yow natt spare 235
Tyl he haue iugment to be hangyd and
    draw;
For I am Pylat, pr[o]mmyssary and
    pres[e]dent,
Alle renogat robber inper-rowpent,[5]
To put hem to peyn, I spare for no pete.[6]
My ser-jauntes semle,[7] quat sey ye? 240
Of this rehersyd,[8] I wyll natt spare.
Plesauntly, serrys, avnswer to me,
For in my herte I xall haue the lesse care.

I. SERIUNT.   As ye haue seyd, I hold it for
    the best,
Yf ony swych a-mong vs may we know.

II. SERJAWNT.   For to gyff hem iugment I
    holdd yt best;   246
And so xall ye be dred of hye and low.

PYLAT.   A! now I am restoryd to felycyte.

*Her comyt the Emprores masenger to
    Pylat.*

MASENGER.   Heyll, ryall in rem,[9] in robis
    of rychesse!
Heyl, present thou prynsys[10] pere! 250
Heyl, Iugge of Ierusalem, the trewth to
    expresse!
Tyberyus, the Emprower, sendyt wrytyng
    herre,
And prayyt yow, as yow be his lover dere,
Of this wrytyng to take a-vysement[11]

---

[1] Governance.   [2] Kindred.
[3] Woes; *qy*, shrowys, rascals.
[4] Secretly or openly.   [5] Righteous.
[6] Chief of chivalry.   [7] Message.
[8] Prayeth.   [9] Give.   [10] Sure.
[11] The bare skin, the flesh. Professor Strunk
points out that this speech is repeated in the Digby
Killing of the Children, ll. 97–104.
[12] Escape.   [13] Quickly.   [14] Bear it.

[1] Quickly.   [2] Known.   [3] Advise.
[4] Prejudice, violence.
[5] Professor Sampson suggests the emendation *in
pressour pent*. Cf. Lydgate, *De Guil. Pilgr.*: "In a
pressour off gret peyne I kan ful offte a man dis-
treyne." (*N.E.D.*)
[6] Pity.   [7] Seemly.   [8] Foresaid.
[9] Royal in realm.   [10] Princes'.   [11] Advisement.

In strenthyng [1] of his lawys cleyr,   255
As he hath set yow in the state [2] of iugment.

*Her Pylat takyt the lettyrs with grete
reverens.*

PYLAT.   Now, be Martes [3] so mythy, I xal
     sett many a snare,
His lawys to strenth in al that I may.
I rejoyse of his renown and of his wylfare;
And for thi tydyngges, I geyff the this
     gold to-day.   260

MASENGER.   A largeys,[4] ye lord, I crye
     this day;
For this is a geft of grete degre.

PYLAT.   Masenger, on-to my sovereyn
     thou sey,
On the most specyall wyse [I] recummend
     me.

*Her a-voydyt the masengyr, and Syrus takyt
     his deth.*

[*The Stage of Cyrus, the Castle of Maudleyn,
     Bethany.*]

SYRUS.   A! help! help! I stond in drede!
Syknes is sett onder my syde!   266
A! help!   Deth wyll a-quyte me my mede! [5]
A! gret Gode!   Thou be my gyde.
How I am trobyllyd both bak and syde!
Now wythly [6] help me to my bede.   270
A! this rendyt my rybbys!   I xall never
     goo nor ryde!
The dent [7] of deth is hevyar than led.
A! Lord! Lord! what xal I doo this tyde?
A! gracyows God! have ruth on me,
In thys word [8] no lengar to a-byde.   275
I blys yow, my chyldyrn, God mot with vs
     be!

*Her a-voydyt Syrus sodenly, and than [thus]
     sayyng Lazarus:*

[LAZARUS.]   Alas, I am sett in grete
     hevynesse!
Ther is no tong my sorow may tell,
So sore I am browth in dystresse!
In feyntnes I falter for [th]is fray fell; [9]

Thys dewresse [1] wyl lett me no longar
     dwelle.   281
But God of grace sone me redresse.
A! how my peynes don me repelle!
Lord, with-stond this duresse!

MARY.   The in-wyttissymus [2] God, that
     euer xal reyne,   285
Be his help, an sowlys sokor!
To whom it is most nedfull to cumplayn,
He to bry[n]g vs owght of ower dolor.
He is most mytyest governowr,
From soroyng,[3] vs to restryne.   290

MARTHA.   A! how I am sett in sorowys
     sad,
That long my lyf Y may nat indevre!
Thes grawous [4] peynes make me ner mad!
Vndyr clower [5] is now my fathyris cure,[6]
That sumtyme was here ful mery and
     glad.   295
Ower Lordes mercy be his mesure,
And defeynd hym from peynes sad!

LAZARUS.   Now, systyrs, ower fatherys
     wyll we woll exprese:
Thys castell is owerys, with all the fee.[7]

MARTHA.   As hed and governower, as
     reson is,   300
And on this wyse abydyn with yow, wyll
     wee;
We wyll natt desevyr, [8] whatt so be-falle.

MARIA.   Now, brothyr and systyrs,
     welcum ye be.
And ther-of specyally I pray yow all.[9]

[*The stage of the World.*]

*Her xal entyr the Kyng of the word [10] [at-
tended by Pride and Covetousness]; thus
seyyng the Word:*

[WORLD.]   I am the Word, worthyest that
     euyr God wrowth! [11]   305

---

[1] Affliction.   [2] Infinitissimus (Latin).
[3] Sorrowing.   [4] Grievous.
[5] Grassy ground, turf.   [6] Care? Cover?
[7] Property, wealth.   [8] Separate.
[9] At this point in the MS. appears the general
stage-direction: "Her xal entyr the Kyng of the
word; [then on his stage the Kyng of] the Flesch; and
[then on his stage] the Dylfe; with the Seuen Dedly
Synnes [distributed on the three stages]; a Bad Angyll
an an Good Angyl: thus seyyng the Word." Since
all except the first clause is repeated later, I have
relegated this general direction to the footnotes.
[10] World.   [11] Wrought, created.

[1] Strengthening.   [2] Seat.
[3] By Mars.   [4] Reward.
[5] Meed, merited reward.
[6] Quickly.   [7] Blow.
[8] World.   [9] Conflict cruel.

And also I am the prymatt portatur [1]
Next heueyn, yf the trewth be sowth,[2] —
And that I iugge me [3] to skryptur; —
And I am he that lengest xal induer,[4]
And also most of domynacyon.   310
Yf I be hys foo, w[h]oo is abyll to re-
cure?
For the whele of fortune with me hath sett
his sentur.[5]
In me restyt [6] the ordor of the metelles
seuyn,[7]
The whych to the seuen planyttes [8] ar
knett ful sure;
Gold perteynyng to the sonne, as astron-
omer nevyn; [9]   315
Sylvyr, to the mone, whyte and pure;
Iryn, onto the Maris, that long may en-
dure;
The fegetyff [10] mercury, on-to Mercuryus;
Copyr, on-to Venus red in his merrour; [11]
The frangabyll tyn, to Iubyter, yf ye can
dyscus;   320
On this planyt Saturne, ful of rancur,
This soft metell led, nat of so gret puer-
nesse.
Lo, alle this rych tresor with the Word
doth indure —
The vij prynsys of hell of gret bowntos-
nesse.
Now, who may presume to com to my
honour?   325

PRYDE. Ye worthy Word, ye be grond-
dar [12] of gladnesse,
To them that dwellyng ondyr yower
domynacyon.

COVETYSE. And who-so wol nat, he is sone
set a-syde,
Wher-as I, Couetyse, take mynystracyon.

WORLD.[13] Of that I pray yow make no
declareracyon;   330
Make swych to know my soverreynte,
.nd than they xal be fayn to make supplycacyon
Yf that they stond in ony nesessyte.

---

[1] Chief supporter.   [2] Sought.
[3] I appeal to, or prove by.   [4] Endure.
[5] Centre.   [6] Resteth.
[7] The seven metals.   [8] Planets.
[9] Declare.   [10] Fugitive.
[11] Mirror (reflection?).
[12] Grounder, establisher.
[13] This personage is variously named "World" and
"Mundus"; I have employed "World" throughout.

[The Stage of the Flesh.]

*Her xal entyr the Kynge of Flesch with
Slowth, Gloteny, Lechery.*

FLESCH. I, Kyng of Flesch, florychyd ir
my flowers;
Of deyntys [1] delycyows I have grett domy-
nacyon.   335
So ryal a kyng was neuyr borne in bowrys,[2]
Nor hath more delyth [3] ne more delecta-
cyon;
For I haue comfortatyws [4] to my comfor-
tacyon:
Dya galonga, ambra, and also margaret-
ton,[5] —
Alle this is at my lyst [6] a-gens alle vex-
acyon;   340
Alle wykkyt [7] thynges I woll sett a-syde, —
Clary,[8] pepur long,[9] with granorum
paradysy,[10]
Gengybyr [11] and synamom at euery tyde.
Lo, alle swych deyntyys delycyus vse I;
With swyche deyntyys I have my blysse.
Who woll covett more game and gle   346
My fayer spowse Lechery to halse [12] and
kysse?
Here ys my knyth, Gloteny, as good reson
is,
With this plesavnt lady to rest be my syde.
Here is Slowth, anothyr goodly of to
expresse.   350
A more plesavnt compeny doth no-wher
a-byde.

LECHERY.[13] O ye prynse! how I am ful of
ardent lowe,[14]
With sparkylles ful of amerowsnesse!
With yow to rest fayn wold I a-prowe,
To shew plesavns [15] to your ientylnesse.

THE FLESCH. O ye bewtews byrd, I must
yow kysse!   356
I am ful of lost [16] to halse yow this tyde.

---

[1] Dainties.
[2] Bowers, dwellings.
[3] Delight.
[4] Cordials, restoratifs (cf. O. Fr. *confortatif*). MS.
has *comfortat yuys* (emendation by Strunk).
[5] Remedies made with galingale, with amber,
and also with pearls (see N.E.D., *dia*).
[6] Pleasure.   [7] Noxious.
[8] A plant with medicinal value.
[9] Long pepper.   [10] Grains of Paradise.
[11] Ginger.   [12] Embrace.
[13] The name of this speaker sometimes appears as
Luxuria. I have used throughout the English form.
[14] Love.   [15] Pleasure.   [16] Desire.

[The stage of the Devil.]

Here xal entyr the prynse of dylles [Satan, attended by Wrath and Envy] in a stage, and Helle ondyr-neth that stage, thus seyyng the dylfe:

[SATAN.] Now I, prynse pyrked,[1] prykkyd[2] in pryde,
Satan, [y]ower sovereyn, set with euery cyrcumstanse,
For I am atyred in my tower to tempt yow this tyde.   360
As a kyng ryall I sette at my plesavns,[3]
With Wroth [and] Invy at my ryall retynawns;[4]
The bolddest in bower I bryng to a-baye;
Mannis sowle to be-segyn[5] and bryng to obeysavns,[6]
Ya, [with] tyde and tyme I do that I may,
For at hem I haue dysspyte that he xold haue the ioye   366
That Lycyfer, with many a legyown,[7] lost for ther pryde.
The snares that I xal set wher never set at Troye,[8]
So I thynk to besegyn hem be every waye wyde;
I xal getyn hem from grace, wher-so-euer he abyde,   370
That body and sowle xal com to my hold,[9] Hym for to take.
Now, my knythtes so stowth,
With me ye xall ron in rowte,[10]
My consell to take for a skowte,[11]   375
Whytly[12] that we wer went for my sake.

WRATH.   With wrath orwyhylles we xal hyrre wynne.

ENVY.   Or with sum sotyllte[13] sett hur in synne.

SATAN.[14]   Com of, than, let vs be-gynne
To werkyn hur sum wrake.   380

Her xal the Deywl [attended by Wrath and Envy] go to the Word with his compeny.

---

[1] Prince made spruce.
[2] Attired.   [3] Pleasure.   [4] Retinue.
[5] Besiege.   [6] Obedience.
[7] Legion.   [8] Troy.   [9] Stronghold.
[10] In a troop. [11] A scheme.
[12] Quickly.   [13] Subtlety.
[14] This speaker's name appears variously as "Satan," "Dylfe," "Rex Diobolus," etc. I have kept the form "Satan" throughout.

[The stage of the World.]

[Satan, attended by Wrath and Envy, mount the stage of the World.]

SATAN.   Heyle, Word, worthyest of a-bowndans!
In hast we must a conseyll take:
Ye must aply yow with all your afyavns,[1]
A woman of whorshep[2] ower servant to make.

WORLD.   Satan, with my consell I wyll the a-wansse.[3]   385
I pray the cum vp on-to my tent.
Were the Kyng of Flesch her with his asemlaunvs![4]
Masenger, a-non that thu werre went Thys tyde!
Sey[5] the Kyng of Flesch with grete re-nown,   390
With his consell that to hym be bown,
In alle the hast that euer they mown,[6]
Com as fast as he may ryde.

MASENGER.   My lord, I am your servant, Sensvalyte.
Your masege to don, I am of glad chyr;[7]
Ryth sone in presens ye xal hym se,   396
Your wyl for to fulfylle her.

Her he goth to the Flesch, thus seyynge:

[The stage of the Flesch.]

[The Messenger ascends the stage.]

[MESSENGER.]   Heyl, lord in lond, led with lykyng!
Heyl, Flesch in Lust, fayyrest to be-hold!
Heyl, lord and ledar of empror and kyng!
The worthy Word, be wey and wold,[8]   401
Hath sent for yow and your consell.
Satan is sembled with his howshold,
Your covnseyl to haue, most fo[r] a-weyle.[9]

FLESCH.   Hens!   In hast, that we ther wh[e]re!   405
Lett vs make no lengar delay!

MESSENGER.[10]   Gret myrth to ther hertes shold yow arere,[11]
Be my trowth, I dare safly saye.

---

[1] Assurance.   [2] Worship.   [3] Assist.
[4] Assembly.   [5] Tell, say to.   [6] May.   [7] Cheer.
[8] By highway and country.
[9] Avail.   [10] MS. senswalite.   [11] Raise.

[*The stage of the World.*]

*Her comyt the Kynge of Flesch [attended
by Lechery, Sloth, and Gluttony] to the
Word, thus seyynge:*

[FLESCH.] Heyl be yow, soverens lefe [1]
    and dere!
Why so hastely do ye for me send? 410

WORLD. A! we ar ryth glad we haue yow
    here,
Ower covnsell to-gethyr to comprehend!
Now, Satan, sey your devyse.

SATAN. Serys, now ye be set, I xal yow
    say:
Syrus dyyd this odyr day; 415
Now Mary his dowctor, that may,[2]
Of that castel beryt the pryse.[3]

WORLD. Sertenly, serys, I yow telle,
Yf she in vertu stylle may dwelle,
She xal byn abyll to dystroye helle, 420
But yf [4] your covnseyll may othyrwyse
    devyse.

FLESCH. Now, the lady Lechery, yow
    must don your attendans,
For yow be flower fayrest of femynyte;
Yow xal go desyyr servyse, and byn at hur
    atendavns,
For ye xal sonest enter, ye beral of bewte.[5]

LECHERY. Serys, I abey your covnsell in
    eche degre; 426
Strytt waye thethyr woll I passe.

SATAN. Spirits malyngny [6] xal com to the,
Hyr to tempt in euery plase.
Now alle the vj that her be, 430
Wysely to werke, hyr fawor to wynne,
To entyr hyr person be [7] the labor of
    Lechery,
That she at the last may com to helle.
How, how, spirits malyng; thou wottyst [8]
    what I mene!
Cum owght, I sey! Heryst nat what I
    seye? 435

BAD ANGYLL. Syrrus,[9] I obey your
    covnsell in eche degree;
Strytt-waye thethyr woll I passe.

Speke soft, speke soft! I trotte hyr to
    tene.[1]
I prey the pertly make no more noyse.

[*The Castle of Maudleyn, Bethany.*]

*Her xal alle the vij Dedly Synnes be-sege
the castell tyll [Mary] a-gre to go to
Ierusalem. Lechery xall entyr the castell
with the Bad Angyl, thus seyynge Lechery.*

[LECHERY.] Heyl, lady most lavdabyll of
    alyauvns! [2] 440
Heyl, oryent as the sonne in his reflexite!
Myche [3] pepul be comfortyd be your
    benyng afyavns.[4]
Bryter than the bornyd [5] is your bemys o
    bewte;
Most debonarius with your aungelly
    delycyte!

MARYA. Qwat personne be ye that thus
    me comende ? [6] 445

LECHERY. Your servant to be, I wold
    comprehende.

MARY. Your debonarius obedyauns
    ravyssyt [7] me to trankquelyte!
Now, syth [8] ye desyre in eche de-gree,
To receyve yow I have grett delectacyon.
Ye be hartely welcum on-to me! 450
Your tong is so amyabyll devydyd with
    reson.

LECHERY. Now, good lady, wyll ye me
    expresse,
Why may ther no gladdnes to yow re-
    sort?

MARY. For my father, I haue had grett
    heuynesse;
Whan I remembyr, my mynd waxit
    mort.[9] 455

LECHERY. Ya lady, for all that, be of
    good comfort,
For swych obusyouns[10] may brede myche
    dysese; [11]
Swych desepcyouns,[12] potyt peynes to
    exsport,[13]

---

[1] Dear, beloved. [2] Maid. [3] Prize.
[4] Unless. [5] Beryl of beauty. [6] Evil.
[7] By. [8] Knowest. [9] Sirs.

[1] Injure. [2] Alliance.
[3] Much, many. [4] Benign assurance.
[5] Burnished. [6] MS. comendyde.
[7] Ravisheth. [8] Since. [9] Dead.
[10] Abuses, deceptions. [11] Distress.
[12] Such deceptions. [13] Expel pains.

Prynt [1] yow in sportes whych best doth
  yow plese.

MARY.   For-sothe ye be welcum to myn
  hawdyens! [2]   460
Ye be my hartes leche. [3]
Brother Lazarus, and it be yower plesauns,
And ye, systyr Martha, also in substawns,
Thys place I commend on-to your
  governons, [4]
And on-to God I yow be-take. [5]   465

LAZARUS.   Now, systyr, we xal do your
  intente,
In thys place to be resydent
Whyle that ye be absent,
To kepe this place from wreche. [6]

*Here takyt Mary hur wey to Ierusalem
  with Lechery.*

[The place of the Taverner, in Jerusalem.]

*And they [Mary and Lechery] xal resort
  to a taverner, thus seyy[n]g the taverner:*

[TAVERNER.]   I am a taverner, wytty and
  wyse,   470
That wynys [7] haue to sell gret plente.
Of all the taverners I bere the pryse
That be dwellyng with-inne the cete. [8]
Of wynys I haue grete plente,
Both whyte wynne and red that [ys] so
  cleyr: 475
Here ys wynne of mawt, [9] and malmeseyn,
Clary [10] wynne, and claret, and other moo,
Wyn of Gyldyr [11] and of Galles, [12] that
  made at the Grome, [13]
Wyn of Wyan [14] and Vernage, I seye also.
Ther be no better, as ferre as ye can
  goo.   480

LECHERY.   Lo, lady, the comfort and the
  sokower. [15]
Go we ner and take a tast;
Thys xal bryng your sprytes to fawor.
Taverner, bryng vs of the fynnest thou
  hast.

---

[1] Stamp, impress.   [2] Audience, presence.
[3] Physician.   [4] Rule.
[5] Commit.   As F. points out, the rhyme suggests
  "beteche."
[6] Harm, ruin.   [7] Wines.   [8] City.
[9] Malta?   [10] Claret.   [11] Guelder.
[12] France.   [13] Groine, in Spain.
[14] Guyenne.   [15] Comfort and succor thyself.

TAVERNER.   Here, lady, is wyn, a repast   485
To man and woman, a good restoratyff.
Ye xall nat thynk your mony spent in
  wast;
From stodyys [1] and hevynes it woll yow
  relyff.

MARY.   I-wys ye seye soth, ye grom [2] of
  blysse;
To me ye be covrtes and kynde.   490

*Her xal entyr a galavnt [Curiosity] thus
  seyyng:*

GALAVNT.   Hof! hof, hof! a frysch new
  galavnt!
Ware of thryst, ley that a-doune!
What! wene ye, syrrys, that I were a mar-
  chant
Be-cavse that I am new com to town?
With sum praty tasppysster [3] wold I fayne
  rown [4]   495
I haue a shert of reynnes [5] with slevys
  peneawnt, [6]
A lase [7] of sylke for my lady constant.
A! how she is bewtefull and ressplend-
  ant!
Whan I am from hyr presens, Lord, how I
  syhe!
I wol a-wye [8] sovereyns; and soiettes [9] I
  dys-deyne.   500
In wynter a stomachyr, [10] in somer non att
  al;
My dobelet and my hossys euer to-gether
  a-byde.
I woll, or euen, be shavyn, for to seme
  ying.
With her a-gen the her, [11] I love mych
  pleyyng;
That makyt me ilegant and lusty in
  lykyng.   505
Thus I lefe in this word; I do it for no
  pryde.

LECHERY.   Lady, this man is for yow, as I
  se can;
To sett yow i[n] sporttes and talkyng this
  tyde.

---

[1] Studies.   [2] Man.
[3] Pretty tapstress, barmaid.
[4] Whisper.   [5] Cloth of Raines.
[6] Hanging, loose?   (Pendeawnt?)
[7] Lace.   [8] Emulate.   [9] Subjects.
[10] Stomacher.   [11] Hair against the hair.

MARY. Cal hym in, taverner, as ye my
    loue wyll han; [1]
And we xall make ful mery yf he wolle
    a-byde   510

TAVERNER. How, how, my Mastyr
    Coryossyte!

CORYOSTE. What is your wyll, syr? what
    wyl ye with me?

TAVERNER. Her ar ientyll women dysyor [2]
    your presens to se,
And for to dryng [3] with yow thys tyde.

CORYOSTE. A dere dewchesse,[4] my
    daysyys iee! [5]   515
Splendavnt of colour, most of femynyte,
Your sofreyn coloures set with synseryte!
Conseder my loue in-to yower alye,[6]
Or elles I am smet with peynnes of per-
    plexite!

MARI. Why, sir, wene [7] ye that I were a
    kelle? [8]   520

CORIOSTE. Nay, prensses,[9] parde, ye be
    my hertes hele! [10]
So wold to God ye wold my loue fele.

MARI. Qwat cavse that ye love me so
    sodenly?

CORIOSTE. O nedys I mvst, myn own
    lady!
Your person, ittis so womanly,   525
I can nat refreyn, me swete lelly.

MARI. Sir, curtesy doth it yow lere.[11]

CORIOSTE. Now, gracyus gost,[12] with-
    owtyn pere,
Mych nortur [13] is that ye conne.[14]
But wol yow dawns, my own dere?   530

MARY. Sir, I asent in good maner;
Go ye be-fore; I sue [15] yow ner;
For a-man at alle tymys beryt [16] reverens.

CORIOSTE. Now, be my trowth, ye be with
    other ten.[17]
Felle a pese,[18] Taverner! let vs sen[19]   535
Soppes in wyne. How, love ye?

MARI. As ye don, so doth me.
I am ryth glad that met be we;
My loue in yow gynnyt to close.

CORYOSTE. Now, derlyng dere, wol yow
    do be my rede? [1]   540
We haue dronkyn and ete lytyl brede.
Wyll we walk to a-nother stede? [2]

MARI. Ewyn at your wyl, my dere
    derlyng!
Thowe ye wyl go to the wordes eynd,
I wol neuer from yow wynd,[3]   545
To dye for your sake.

Here xal Mary and the Galont a-woyd.

[*The Stage of the World, where the World, the
Flesh, and the Devil are still assembled.*]

*And the bad Angyll goth to the Word,
the Flych, and the Dylfe, thus sayyng the
Bad Angyll.*

[BAD ANGYL.] A lorges,[4] a lorges, lorddes
    alle at onys!
Ye haue a servant fayer and afyabylle,
For she is fallyn in ower grogly gromys! [5]
Ya, Pryde, callyd Corioste, to hur is ful
    lavdabyll,   550
And to hur he is most preysseabyll,[6]
For she hath gravnttyd hym al his bones; [7]
She thynkyt his person so amyabyll,
To her syte he is semelyar [8] than ony kyng
    in trones.[9]

SATAN. A! how I tremyl and trott for
    yese tydynges!   555
She is a soveryn servant that hath hur fet [10]
    in synne.
Go thow agayn, and ewer be hur gyde.
The lavdabyll lyfe of lecherry let hur neuer
    lynne,[11]
For of hur al helle xall make reioysseyng.

Here goth the Bad Angyl to Mari a-gayn.

SATAN. Fare-well, fare-well, ye t[w]o
    nobyl kynges this tyde!   560
For whom in hast I wol me dresse.

----

1 Have.   2 Desire.   3 Drink.   4 Duchess.
5 Eye.   6 Alliance.   7 Think.
8 Woman of ill fame (cf. "callet").
9 Princess.   10 Healing, cure.   11 Teach.   12 Spirit.
13 Good breeding.   14 Know.   15 Follow.
16 Beareth.   17 With other things grieved.
18 Fill a cup.   19 See.

1 Advice.   2 Place.   3 Go.
4 Largess, reward.
5 Grysly (terrible)? harms.
6 Precious.   7 Requests.
8 Seemlier.   9 Thrones.
10 Fetched.   11 Cease.

WORLD. Fare-well, Satan, prynsse of pryde!

FLESCH. Fare-well, sem[l]yest all sorowys to sesse!

Here xal Satan go hom to his stage, and Mari xal entyr in-to the place alone, save the Bad Angyl. And al the Seuen Dedly Synnes xal be conveyyd in-to the howse of Symont Leprous; they xal be a-rayyd lyke vij dylf, thus kept closse.

[The "Place," or middle region surrounded by the stages, supposed to be the city of Jerusalem. An arbour on one side.]

Mari xal be in an erbyr, thus seyynge:

MARI. A! God be with my valentynes,[1]
My byrd swetyng, my lovys so dere! 565
For they be bote for a blossum of blysse.
Me mervellyt sore they be nat here.
But I woll restyn in this erbyr
Amous thes bamys [2] precyus of prysse,
Tyll som lover wol apere,   570
That me is wont to halse and kysse.

Her xal Mary lye doun, and slepe in the erbyr.

[The stage of Simon the Leper, a house, with a table spread.]

SYMOND LEPRUS. Thys day holly [3] I pot in rememberowns
To solas my gestes to my power.
I haue ordeynnyd a dyner of substawns,[4]
My chyff freyndes therwith to chyr. 575
In-to the sete [5] I woll a-pere,
For my gestes to make porvyawns,[6]
For tyme drayt ny to go to dyner,
And my offycyrs be redy with ther ordy-
nowns.
So, wold to God, I myte have a-queyn-
towns [7]   580
Of the Profyth of trew perfytnesse,
To com to my place and porvyowns!
It wold rejoyse my hert in gret gladnesse;
For ye report of hys hye nobyll-nesse
Rennyt [8] in contreys fer and ner;   585

[1] Valentines, lovers.
[2] Fragrant garden-herbs.
[3] Wholly.   [4] A grand dinner.   [5] City.
[6] Provision.   [7] Acquaintance.   [8] Runneth.

Hys precheyng is of gret perfythnes,
Of rythwysnesse, and mercy cleyr.

Her entyr Symont in-to ye place.[1]

[The "Place." Mary's arbour at one side.]

The Good Angyll thus seyynge to Mary:

[GOOD ANGYLL.] Woman, woman, why art thou so on-stabyll?
Ful bytterly thys blysse it wol be bowth! [2]
Why art thou a-gens God so veryabyll? [3]
Wy thynkes thou nat God made the of nowth?   591
In syn and sorow thou art browth;
Fleschly lust is to ye full delectabyll.
Salue for thi sowle must be sowth;
And leve thi werkes wayn [4] and very-
abyll.   595
Remembyr, woman, for thi pore pryde,
How thi sowle xal lyyn [5] in helle fyr!
A! remembyr how sorowful ittis to a-byde
With-owtyn eynd in angur and ir[e]!
Remembyr the on mercy; make thi sowle
clyr!   600
I am the gost of goodnesse that so wold ye gydde.

MARY. A! how the speryt of goodnesse hat promtyt [6] me this tyde,
And temtyd me with tytyll of trew per-
fythnesse!
A-las! how betternesse in my hert doth a-byde!
I am wonddyd [7] with werkes of gret dystresse.   605
A! how pynsynesse [8] potyt me to oppresse,
That I haue synnyd on euery syde!
O Lord! w[h]o xall putt me from this peynfulnesse?
A! w[h]oo xal to mercy be my gostly gyde?
I xal porsue the Prophett, wherso he be,
For he is the welle of perfyth charyte; 611
Be [9] the oyle of mercy he xal me relyff.
With swete bawmys [10] I wyl sekyn hym this syth,[11]
And sadly folow his lordshep in eche degre.

[1] The *platea* surrounded by the several "stages," here supposed to be "the city."
[2] Paid for.   [3] Variable.
[4] Vain.   [5] Lie.
[6] Prompted.   [7] Enveloped.
[8] Pensiveness.   [9] By.
[10] Balms, ointments.   [11] Time.

Here xal entyr the Prophet with his desyplys [into the "Place," meeting Simon, and passing near Mary's arbour], thus seyyng Symont Leprus:

[SYMONT.] Now ye be welcom, mastyr,
  most of magnyfycens! 615
I be-seche yow benyngly ye wol be so
  gracyows,
Yf that it be lekyng on-to yower hye
  presens,
Thys daye to com dyne at my hows.

IESUS. God a mercy, Symont, that thou
  wylt me knowe!
I woll entyr thi hows with pes and vnyte;
I am glad for to rest; ther grace gynnyt
  grow; 621
For with-inne thi hows xal rest charyte,
And the bemys of grace xal byn illumynows.
But syth thou wytyst-saff [1] a dyner on me,
With pes and grace I entyr thi hows. 625

[They go to the house of Simon the Leper.]

[The stage of Simon the Leper.]

SYMOND. I thank yow, master, most
  benyng [2] and gracyus,
That yow wol of your hye soverente.
To me ittis a ioye most speceows,
With-inne my hows that I may yow se!
Now syt to the bord, mastyrs alle. 630

Her xal Mary folow a-longe, with this lamentacyon:

MARY. O I, cursyd cayftyff, that myche
  wo hath wrowth [3]
A-gens my makar, of mytes most!
I have offendyd hym with dede and thowth.
But in his grace is all my trost,
Or elles I know well I am but lost, 635
Body and sowle damdpnyd perpetuall.
Yet, good Lord of lorddes, my hope
  perhenuall, [4]
With the to stond in grace and fawour to
  se,
Thow knowyst my hart and thowt in
  especyal;
Therfor, good Lord, after my hart reward
  me. 640

Her xal Mary wasche the fett of the Prophet with the terres of hur yys,[1] whypyng hem with hur herre, and than a-noynt hym with a precyus noyttment. Iesus dicit:

[IESUS.] Symond, I thank ye speceally
For this grett r[e]past that her hath be;
But, Symond, I telle the fectually
I have thynges to seyn to the.

SYMOND. Master, qwat your wyll be, 645
And it plese yow, I well yow her;
Seyth your lykyng on-to me,
And al the plesawnt of your mynd and
  desyyr.

IESUS. Symond, ther was a man in this
  present lyf,
The wyche had t[w]o dectours [2] well
  suer, 650
The whych wher pore, and myth make no
  restoratyf,
But stylle in ther debt ded in-duour; [3]
The on[e] owght hym an hondyrd pense
  ful suer,
And the other fefty, so be-fell the chanse;
And be-cawse he cowd nat his mony re-
  cure, 655
They askyd hym forgewnesse; and he
  forgaf in substans.
But, Symont, I pray ye, answer me to this
  sentens;
Whych of thes t[w]o personnes was most
  be-holddyn to that man?

SYMOND. Master, and it plese your hey
  presens,
He that most owght hym, as my reson gef
  can. 660

IESUS. *Recte iudicasti!* [4] thou art a wyse
  man,
And this quesson hast dempte [5] trewly.
Yff thu in thi concyens remembyr can,
Ye t[w]o be ye dectours that I of specefy.
But, Symond, be-hold this woman in al
  wyse, 665
How she with teres of hyr better [6] wepyng
She wassheth my fete, and dothe me
  servyse,

---

[1] Vouchsafest. [2] Benign.
[3] Wrought. [4] Perennial.

[1] Eyes. [2] Debtors.
[3] Endure. [4] Thou hast rightly judged.
[5] Judged. [6] Bitter.

And anoy[n]tyt hem with onymentes, lowly
    knelyng,
And with her her,[1] fayer and brygth
    shynnyng,
She wypeth hem agayn with good in
    entent.   670
But, Symont, syth that I entyrd thi hows,
To wasshe my fete thou dedyst nat aplye,
Nor to wype my fete thou wer nat so
    faworus;
Wherfor in thi conscyens thou owttyst[2]
    nat to replye.
But, woman, I sey to the, werely,[3]   675
I forgeyffe the thi wrecchednesse,
And hol in sowle be thou made therby!

MARIA.   O blessyd be thou, Lord of euer-
    lastyng lyfe!
And blyssyd be thi berth of that puer
    vergynne![4]
Blyssyd be thou, repast contemplatyf, 680
A-gens my seknes, helth and medsyn!
And for that I haue synnyd in the synne of
    pryde,
I wol en-abyte[5] me with humelyte;
A-gens wrath and envy, I wyl devyde 684
Thes fayer vertuys, pacyens and charyte.

IESUS.   Woman, in contrysson thou art
    expert,
And in thi sowle hast inward mythe,[6]
That sumtyme were in desert,
And from therknesse[7] hast porchasyd
    lyth.
Thy feyth hath savyt the, and made the
    bryth;   690
Wherfor I sey to the, "vade in pace."[8]

With this word vij dyllys xall de-woyde[9]
frome the woman, and the Bad Angyll
enter into hell with thondyr.

[MARIA.]   O thou gloryus Lord!   This
    rehersyd for my sped,[10]
Sowle helth attes[11] tyme for-to recure.
Lord, for that I was in whanhope,[12] now
    stond I in dred,
But that thi gret mercy with me may
    endure;   695

My thowth thou knewyst with-owtyn ony
    dowth.
Now may I trost the techeyng of Izaye in
    scryptur,
W[h]os report of thi nobyllnesse rennyt fer
    abowt.

IESUS.   Blyssyd be they at alle tyme
That sen me nat[1] and have me in credens.
With contrysson thou hast mad a recum-
    pens,   701
Thi sowle to save from all dystresse.
Be-war, and kepe the from alle neclygens,
And after thou xal be pertener[2] of my
    blysse.

Here devodyte Iesus with his desipylles, the
Good Angyll reioysynge ofe Mawdleyn.

GOOD ANGEL.   Holy God, hyest of om-
    nipotency,   705
The astat of good governouns to the I
    recummend,
Humbylly be-secheyng thyn inperall
    glorye,
In thi devyn vertu vs to comprehend.
And, delectabyll Iesu, soverreyn sapyens,
Ower feyth we recummend on-to your
    purpete,[3]   710
Most mekely prayyng to your holy
    aparens,[4]
Illumyn ower ygnorans with your devyn-
    yte!
Ye be clepyd Redempcyon of sowlys
    defens,
Whyche shal ben obscuryd be[5] thi blessyd
    mortalyte.
O *lux vera*,[6] gravnt vs yower lucense,[7] 715
That with the spryte of errour I nat
    seduet[8] be!
And Sperytus alme,[9] to yow most benyne,
Thre persons in trenyte, and on[e] God
    eterne,
Most lowly ower feyth we consyngne,
That we may com to your blysse gloryfyed
    from malyngne,   720
And with your gostely[10] bred to fede vs, we
    desyern.

---

[1] Hair.   [2] Oughtst.
[3] Verily.   [4] Pure Virgin.
[5] Array.   [6] Might, power.
[7] Darkness.   [8] Depart in peace.
[9] Go out. See the stage-direction following line
63.
[10] Advantage.   [11] At this.   [12] Despair.

---

[1] That see me not.   [2] Partner, partaker.
[3] Proprietorship.   [4] Appearance.
[5] By.   [6] True light.   [7] Light.
[8] Misled.
[9] Reviving (the Holy Spirit).   [10] Spiritual.

[*The stage of the Devil.*]

SATAN. A, owt! owt! and harrow! I am
    hampord with hate!
In hast wyl I set on iugment to se!
With thes betyll-browyd bycheys [1] I am at
    debate.
How!   Belfagour, and Belzabub! com vp
    here to me!   725

*Here aperytte t[w]o dyvllys be-fore the
    master.*

II. DIABOLUS.   Here, lord, here! Qwat
    wol ye?

SATAN.[2] The iugment of harlottes here to
    se,
Settyng in iudycyal lyke a state.[3]
How, thow Bad Angyll! a-pere before my
    grace!

BAD ANGEL. As flat as fox, I falle before
    your face.   730

SATAN. Thow theffe, wy hast thou don
    alle this trespas,
To lett then woman thi bondes breke?

BAD ANGEL. The speryt of grace sore ded
    hyr smyth,
And temptyd so sore that ipocryte.

SATAN.   Ya! thys hard balys [4] on thi
    bottokkys xall byte!   735
In hast on the I wol be wroke.
Cum vp, ye horsons, and skore a-wey the
    yche! [5]
And with thys panne [6] ye do hym pycche! [7]
Cum of, ye harlottes, that yt wer don!

*Here xall they serva all the sewyne as they do
    the freste.*

SATAN.   Now have I a part of my
    desyer: 740
Goo in-to this howsse, ye lordeynnes,
    here,
And loke ye set yt on a feyer,
And that xall hem a-wake.

Here xall the tother deylles sette **the**
    howse [1] one a fyere, and make a sowth,[2]
    and Mari xall go to Lazar and to Martha.

SATAN.   So, now have we well afrayyd [3]
    these felons ffals!
They be blasyd [4] both body and hals! [5] 745
Now to hell lett vs synkyn als,
To ower felaws blake.

[*The Castle of Maudleyn, Bethany.*]

[*Enter Mary to Lazarus and Martha.*]

MARI.   O brother, my hartes consola-
    cyown!
O blessyd in lyffe, and solytary!
The blyssyd Prophet, my comfortacy-
    own,   750
He hathe made me clene and delectary,[6]
The wyche was to synne a subiectary.[7]
Thys kyng, Cryste, consedyryd his crea-
    cyown;
I was drynchyn [8] in synne deversarye [9]
Tyll that Lord relevyd me be his domy-
    nacyon,   755
Grace to me he wold never de-nye;
Thowe I were nevyr so synful, he seyd
    "*revertere!*" [10]
O, I synful creature, to grace I woll a-plye;
The oyle of mercy hath helyd myn in-
    fyrmyte.

MARTHA. Now worchepyd be that hey
    name Iesu,   760
The wyche in Latyn is callyd Savyower!
Fulfyllyng that word ewyn of dewe; [11]
To alle synfull and seke he is sokour.

LAZARUS. Systyr, ye be welcum on-to
    yower towere!
Glad in hart of yower obessyawnse,   765
Wheyl that I leffe, I wyl serve hym with
    honour,
That ye have forsakyn synne and vary-
    awns.[12]

MARY.   Cryst, that is the lyth and the
    cler daye,

<hr>

[1] Beetle-browed bitches.
[2] MS. tercius diabolus. Possibly something has
been dropped in the text.
[3] Judicial-like estate.
[4] Rods.
[5] Itch.
[6] Pan.
[7] Smear with pitch.

[1] Presumably the superstructure over hell.
[2] Black smoke.   [3] Frightened.
[4] Burnt.   [5] Neck.   [6] Delectable.
[7] Subject.   [8] Overwhelmed.
[9] Divers.   [10] Turn again.
[11] By right, by just title.   [12] Variance.

He hath on-curyd the therknesse [1] of the
  clowdy nyth;
Of lyth the lucens and lyth veray,   770
W[h]os prechyng to vs is a gracyows lyth.
Lord, we be-seche the, as thou art most of
  myth,
Owt of the ded slep of therknesse de-fend
  vs aye!
Gyff vs grace ewyr [2] to rest in lyth,
In quyet and in pes to serve the nyth and
  day!   775

Here xall Lazar take his deth, thus seyynge:

[LAZARUS.]   A! help, help, systyrs! for
  charyte!
A-las! dethe is sett at my hart;
A! ley on handes! Wher ar ye?
A! I faltyr and falle! I wax alle on-
  quarte! [3]
A! I bome [4] a-bove! I wax alle swertt! [5]
A, good Iesu, thow be my gyde!   781
A! no lengar now I reverte!
I yeld vp the gost! I may natt a-byde!

MARY.   O, good brother, take covmforth
  and myth,
And lett non heuynes in yower hart
  a-byde;   785
Lett a-way [6] alle this feyntnesse and
  fretth,[7]
And we xal gete yow leches,[8] yower peynes
  to devyde.

MARTHA.   A! I syth and sorow, and sey,
  a-las!
Thys sorow ys a-poynt [9] to be my con-
  fusyon.
Ientyl syster, hye we from this place,   790
For the Prophe[t] to hym hatt grett
  delectacyon.
Good brother, take somme comfortacyon,
For we woll go to seke yow cure.

*[The "Place"; Jesus walking with his
  disciples.]*

*Here goth Mary and Martha, and mett with
  Iesus, thus seyynge:*

[MARY AND MARTHA.]   O Lord Iesu, ower
  melleflueus swettnesse,

---

[1] Darkness.   [2] Ever.   [3] Dismayed.
[4] Hum, buzz (in the head).   [5] Black.
[6] Allow to pass.   [7] Fretting.
[8] Physicians.   [9] Appointed.

Thowe art grettest Lord in glorie!   795
Lover to the Lord, in all lowlynesse
Comfort thi creatur that to the crye!
Be-hold yower lover, good Lord, specyally,
How Lazar lyth seke in grett dystresse!
He ys thi lover, Lord, suerly;   800
On-bynd hym, good Lord, of his heuynesse!

IESUS.   Of all in-fyrmyte, ther is non to deth,
For of all peynnes that is inpossyble.
To vndyr-stond be reson, to know the
  werke,
The ioye that is in Ierusallem heuenly, 805
Can never be compylyd be covnnyng of
  clerke,[1] —
To se the ioyys of the Fathyr in glory,
The ioyys of the Sonne whych owth [2] to
  be magnyfyed,
And of the Therd Person, the Holy Gost
  truly,   809
And alle iij but on[e] in heuen gloryfyed.
Now, women, that arn in my presens here,
Of my wordys take a-wysement; [3]
Go hom a-gen to yower brothyr Lazere;
My grace to hym xall be sent.

MARY.   O thow gloryus Lord, here present,
We yeld to the salutacyon!   816
In ower weyys we be expedyent.
Now, Lord, vs defend from trybulacyon!

*Here goth Mary and Martha homvard, and
  Iesus devodyte.*

[The Castle of Maudleyn, Bethany.]

LAZARUS.   A! in woo I waltyr,[4] as wawys [5]
  in the wynd!
A-wey ys went all my sokour!   820
A! Deth, Deth, thou art on-kynd!
A! a! now brystyt [6] myn hartt! This is a
  sharp shower!
Fare-well, my systyrs, my bodely helth!

Mortuis est.[7]

MARY.   Iesu, my Lord, be yower sokowr,
And he mott be yower gostes welth! [8]   825

I. MILES.   Goddes grace mott be hys
  governour,
In ioy euerlastyng for to be!

---

[1] Scholar.   [2] Ought, deserveth.
[3] Advisement.   [4] Welter.
[5] Waves.   [6] Bursteth.
[7] He is dead.   [8] Spirit's welfare.

11. MILES. A-monge alle good sowlys send
    hym favour,
As thi power ys most of dygnyte!

MARTHA. Now syn the chans is fallyn
                                       soo   830
That deth hath drewyn hym don [1] this day,
We must nedys ower devyrs [2] doo,
To the erth to bryng hym with-owt delay.

MARY. As the vse is now, and hath byn
    aye,
With wepers [3] to the erth yow hym
    bryng.   835
Alle this must be donne as I yow saye,
Clad in blake, with-owtyn lesyng.[4]

1. MILES. Gracyows ladyys of grett
    honour,
Thys pepull is com here in yower syth,
Wepyng and welyng with gret dolour 840
Be-cavse of my lordes dethe.

Here the one knygth make redy the stone,[5]
and other bryng in the wepars arayyd in
blak.

1. MILES. Now, good fryndes that here
    be,
Take vp thys body with good wyll,
And ley it in his sepoltur [6] semely to se.
Good Lord, hym save from alle maner
    ille!   845

Lay hym in. Here al the pepyll resort to the
castell.

[The "Place"; Jesus walking with his
disciples.]

Thus seyynge Iesus:

[IESUS.] Tyme ys comyn, of very cognys-
    son.[7]
My dyssyplys, goth with me,
For to fulfyll possybyll peticion.
Go we to-gether in-to Iude,
Ther Lazar, my frynd, is he;   850
Gow we to-gether as chyldyurn of lyth;
And, from grevos slepe, sawen [8] heym wyll
    we.

DISSIPULUS. Lord, it plese yower myty
    volunte,[1]
Thow he slepe, he may be savyd be skyll.

IESUS. That is trew, and be possybilyte;
Therfor of my deth shew yow I wyll. 856
My Fathyr, of nemyows [2] charyte,
Sent me, his Son, to make redemcyon,
Wyche was conseyvyd be puer [3] verginyte,
And so in my mother had cler incarna-
    cyon;   860
And therfor must I suffyr grewos [4] passyon
Ondyr Povnse Pylat, with grett perplexite,
Betyn, bobbyd, skoernyd, crownnyd with
    thorne:
Alle this xall be the soferons [5] of my deite.
I, therfor, hastely folow me now,   865
For Lazar is ded verely to preve;
Whe[r]for I am ioyfull, I sey on-to yow,
That I knowledge [6] yow ther-with, that ye
    may it beleve.

Here xal Iesus com with his dissipules
[walking toward the Castel of Maudleyn];
and one Iew tellyt Martha:

[IEW.] A! Martha, Martha! be full of
    gladnesse!
For the Prophett ys comyng, I sey
    trewly,   870
With his dyssypylles in grett lowlynesse;
He shall yow comfortt with his mercy.

Here Martha xall ronne a-gene Iesus [as he
approaches the Castle of Maudleyn], thus
seyynge:

[MARTHA.] A, Lord! me, sympyl creatur,
    nat denye!
Thow I be wrappyd in wrecchydnesse!
Lord, and thou haddyst byn her,
    werely [7]   875
My brother had natt a byn ded; I know
    well thysse.

IESUS. Martha, docctor,[8] on-to the I sey,
Thy brother xall reyse agayn.

MARTHA. Yee, Lord, at the last day;
That I be-leve ful pleyn.   880

IESUS. I am the resurreccyon of lyfe, that
    euer xall reynne; [9]

---

[1] Driven him down.   [2] Duties.
[3] Weepers, mourners.   [4] Lie.
[5] The tomb was arranged in the "Place" near the
Castle of Maudleyn.
[6] Sepulchre.   [7] Knowledge.   [8] Save.

[1] Will.   [2] Exceeding.
[3] Pure.   [4] Grievous.
[5] Sufferance.   [6] Acquaint.
[7] Verily.   [8] Daughter.   [9] Reign.

And whoso be-levyt verely in me
Xall have lyfe euerlastyng, the soth to
   seyn.[1]
Martha, be-levyst thow this [truly]?

MARTHA.   Ye, forsoth, the Prynsse of
   Blysch![2]   885
I be-leve in Cryst, the Son of sapyens,
Whyche with-owt eynd ryngne[3] xall be,[4]
To redemyn vs freell[5] from ower iniquite.

Here Mary xall falle to Iesus, thus seyynge
Mary:

MARY.   O thou rythewys[6] regent, reyn-
   yng in equite!
Thou gracyows Lord!   Thou swete
   Iesus!   890
And thou haddyst byn her, my brothyr
   a-lyfe had be.
Good Lord, myn hertt doth this dyscus.

IESUS.   Wher have ye put hym? sey me
   thys.

MARY.   In his mo[nu]nent, Lord, is he.

IESUS.   To that place ye me wys;[7]   895
Thatt grave I desyre to se.

[*They lead Jesus to the tomb of Lazarus in*
the "Place" near the Castle of Maudleyn.]

Take of the ston of this monvment!
The agrement of grace her shewyn I wyll.

MARTHA.   A, Lord, yower preseptt ful-
   fyllyd xall be;
Thys ston I remeve with glad chyr.   900
Gracyows Lord, I aske the mercy,
Thy wyll mott be fullfyllyd here.

Here xal Martha put ofe the grave-stone.

IESUS.   Now, Father, I be-seche thyn hey
   paternyte,
That my prayour be resowndable to thi
   Fathyrod in glory,

[1] The truth to say.	[2] Bliss.	[3] Reigning.
[4] MS. he.	[5] Frail beings.	
[6] Righteous.	[7] Guide.	

To opyn theyn erys[1] to thi Son in hu-
   manyte!   905
Nat only for me, but for thi pepyll
   verely,
That they may be-leue, and be-take[2] to
   thi mercy.
Fathyr, for them I make supplycacyon.
Gracyows Father, gravnt me my bone![3]
Lazer!   Lazer! com hethyr to me!   910

Here xall Lazar a-ryse, trossyd[4] with
towelles, in a shete.[5]

LAZAR.   A! my makar! my Savyowr!
   blyssyd mott thou be!
Here men may know thi werkes of wondyr!
Lord, no thy[n]g ys on-possybyll to the,
For my body and my sowle was departyd
   asonder!
I xuld a-rottyt, as doth the tondyr,[6]   915
Fleysch from the bonys a-consumyd a-way.
Now is a-loft, that late was ondyr!
The goodnesse of God hath don for me
   here;
For he is bote of all balys[7] to on-bynd,
That blyssyd Lord that here ded a-pere.

Here all the pepull, and the Iewys, Mari,
and Martha with one woys sey thes wordes:
"We be-leve in yow Savyowr! Iesus! Iesus!
Iesus!"

[IESUS.]   Of yower good hertes I have ad-
   vertacyounes,[8]   921
Where-thorow,[9] in sowle holl[10] made ye be;
Be-twyx yow and me be never varyacy-
   ounes,
Wherfor I sey, "*vade in pace.*" [11]

Here devoydyt Iesus with his desypylles:
Mary and Martha and Lazcre gone home
to the castell.

[1] Ears.	[2] Commit themselves.
[3] Request.	[4] Trussed, wrapped.
[5] Sheet.	[6] Tinder.
[7] Healer of all griefs.	[8] Advertisement.
[9] By means of which.	
[10] Whole, well.	[11] Depart in peace.

THE PLAY OF THE SACRAMENT [1]

[THE BANNS.]

I. Vexillator. Now the Father and the
    Sune and the Holy Goste,
That all this wyde worlde hat[h]
    wrowg[h]t,
Save all thes semely,[1] bothe leste and
    moste,
    And bryn[g]e yow to the blysse that he
        hath yow to bowght! [2]
We be ful purposed, with hart and with
    thowght,
Off oure mater to tell the entent,
    Off the marvellis that wer wondurfely
        wrowght
Off the holi and bleyssed Sacrament.   8

II. Vexillator.[3] Sid[s]eyns,[4] and yt lyke
    yow to here the purpoos of this play
That [ys] representyd now in yower
    syght,
Whych in Aragon was doon, the sothe [5] to
    saye,
    In Eraclea, that famous cyte, aryght:
Therin wonneth [6] a merchante off mek-
    yll [7] myght, —
Syr Arystorye was called hys name, —
Kend [8] full fere with mani a wyght;[9]
Full fer in the worlde sprong hys fame. 16

I. Vexillator. Anon to hym ther cam a
    Jewe,
    With grete rychesse for the nonys,[10]
And wonneth [11] in the cyte of Surrey, —
    this [is] full trewe, —

The wyche had gret plente off precyous
    stonys.   20

Off this Cristen merchante he freyned [1] sore,
    Wane [2] he wolde haue had hys entente.
Twenti pownd, and merchandyse mor,
    He proferyd for the Holy Sacrament. 24

II. Vexillator. But the Christen mer-
    chante theroff sed nay,
    Because hys profer was of so lityll val,
    ewe;
An hundder pownd but he wolde pay,
    No lenger theron he shuld pursewe. 28

But mor off ther purpos they gun[n]e
    speke,
    The Holi Sacramente for to bye;
And all for [that] the[i] wolde be wreke,[3]
    A gret sume off gold begune down ley. 32

I. Vexillator. Thys Crysten merchante
    consentyd, the sothe to sey,
    And, in the nyght affter, made hym de-
    lyuerance.
Thes Jewes all grete joye made they.
    But off thys betyde a stranger chance: 36

They grevid our Lord gretly on grownd,[4]
    And put hym to cruell passyon —
With daggers gouen [5] hym many a grieuyos
    wound;
Nayled hym to a pyller; with pynsons [6]
    plukked hym doune.   40

II. Vexillator. And sythe [7] thay toke
    that blysed brede so sownde,[8]

---

[1] Assembly.   [2] Redeemed.
[3] From this point on the MS. has *Secundus* and
Primus alternately for the speakers' names.
[4] Citizens; emend. by Manly. But the MS., says
Waterhouse, may be *Souereyns.*
[5] Truth.   [6] Dwelleth.   [7] Great.
[8] Known.   [9] Person.
[10] A metrical tag without special meaning.
[11] Dwelleth.

[1] Enquired.   [2] When.   [3] Avenged.
[4] On the earth (a metrical tag).   [5] Gave.
[6] Pincers.   [7] Then.   [8] Good.

[1] The manuscript, now preserved in the Library of Trinity College, Dublin, was written in the latter half of
the fifteenth century, and apparently was the work of Irish scribes. The play itself, however, was unquestionably of English origin, the dialect belonging to the East Midland section. According to the Banns the
performance was designed for Croxton; there are no less than seven places of this name in England, five being
in the East Midland section. I have based the text on *The Non-Cycle Mystery Plays*, re-edited from the manuscripts for the Early English Text Society by Osborn Waterhouse, 1909; but I have carefully collated this
with the editions by Manly and Stokes, and have adopted the stanzaic divisions of Manly, which seem to me
more logical than those employed by Waterhouse. I have modernized the punctuation and have added. in
brackets, stage directions.

And in a cawdron [1] they ded hym boyle,
In a clothe full just they yt wounde,
 And so they ded hym sethe [2] in oyle; 44

And than thay putt hym to a new tor-
 mentry,
In an hoote ouyn [3] speryd [4] hym fast:
There he appyred [5] with woundis blody;
 The ovyn rofe [6] asondre and all tobrast.[7]
I. VEXILLATOR. Thus in ouer lawe they
 wer made stedfast;
The Holy Sacrament shewyd [8] them
 grette faueur;
In contrycyon th[e]yr hertis wer cast,
 And went and shewyd ther lyues to a con-
 fesour.   52

Thus, be maracle off the Kyng of Hevyn,
 And by myght and power govyn to the
 prestis mowthe,
In an howshold wer convertyd, i-wys,
 elevyn.
 At Rome this myracle ys knowen well
 kowthe.[9]
II. VEXILLATOR. Thys marycle at Rome
 was presented, for sothe,
Yn the yere of your Lord a M[l]cccclxi,
 That the Jewes that Holy Sacrament
 dyd with,
In the forest seyd of Aragon.   60

Below thus God at a tyme showyd hym
 there,
 Thorwhe hys mercy and hys mekyll
 myght;

[1] Cauldron. [2] Boil. [3] Oven.
[4] Shut. [5] Appeared out.
[6] Split, broke [7] Burst to pieces.
[8] Shewed. [9] Known.

Vnto the Jewes he gan [1] appere
 That thei shuld nat lesse [2] hys hevenly
 lyght.
I. VEXILLATOR. So therfor, frendis, with
 all your myght
Vnto youer gostly father shewe your synne;
 Beth [3] in no wanhope [4] daye nor nyght.
No maner off dowghtis [5] that Lord put
 in;   68

For that the dowgthtis the Jewys than in
 stode, —
 As ye shall se pleyd,[6] both more and
 lesse, —
Was yff the Sacrament wer flesshe and
 blode;
 Therfor they put yt to suche dystresse.
II. VEXILLATOR. And [7] yt place yow, thys
 gaderyng [8] that here ys,
At Croxston [9] on Monday yt shall be sen.
 To sen the conclusyon of this lytell proc-
 esse
Hertely welcum shall yow bene.   76

Now Jhesu yow sawe [10] from treyn and
 tene,[11]
 To send vs hys hyhe ioyes of hevyne,
There myght ys withouton mynd [12] to
 mene!
 Now, mynstrell, blow vp with a mery
 stevyn!   80
    Explicit.

[1] MS. *gayn;* corr. by Manly.   [2] Lose.
[3] Be.   [4] Despair.   [5] Doubts.
[6] Played. [7] If.   [8] Gathering.
[9] See page 243, note 1.   [10] Save.
[11] Pain and vexation.
[12] More than one can calculate (see *N.E.D.*, mind,
7c, and 20).

HERE AFTER FOLOWETH THE PLAY OF THE CONUERSYON OF SER JONATHAS
THE JEWE BY MYRACLE OF THE BLYSSED SACRAMENT.

[*The Stage of the Christian Merchant,
Aristorius. Aristorius, with his clerk,
Peter Paul, and his chaplain, Sir Isoder.*]

ARISTORIUS MERCATOR. Now Cryst, that
 ys ouer Creatour, from shame he
 cure vs;
He maynteyn vs with myrth that meve
 vpon the mold;[1]
    [1] Earth.

Vnto hys endlesse joye myghtly he restore
 vs,
 All tho [1] that in hys name in peas well
 them hold!
For of a merchante most myght therof
 my tale ys told;
In Eraclea ys non suche, woso wyll vnderstond.
 For off all Aragon I am most myghty of
 syluer and of gold, —
     [1] Those

For, and yt wer a countre to by, now wold I
    nat wond.[1]   8

Syr Arystory is my name,
    A merchante myghty, of a royall araye.
Ful wyde in this worlde spryngyth my
    fame,
    Fere kend [2] and knowen, the sothe for to
    saye.
In all maner of londis, without ony naye,
My merchandyse renneth, the sothe for to
    tell;
    In Gene, and in Jenyse, and in Gene-
    waye,
In Surrey, and in Saby, and in Salern I
    sell;   16

In Antyoche and in Almayn moch ys my
    myght,
    In Braban and in Brytayn I am full
    bold,
In Calabre and in Coleyn ther rynge [3] I full
    ryght,
    In Dordrede and in Denmark [I] [4] be the
    chyffe told,[5]
In Alysander I haue abundaunse in the
    wyde world,
In France and in Farre fresshe be my
    flower[is],
    In Gyldre and in Galys haue I bowght
    and sold,
In Hamborowhe and in Holond moche mer-
    chantdyse ys owris;   24

In Jerusalem and in Jherico among the
    Jewes jentle,
    Among the Caldeys and Cattlyngis kend
    ys my komyng;
In Raynes and in Rome to Seynt Petyrs
    temple
I am knowen certenly for bying and sell-
    yng;   28

In Mayne and in Melan full mery haue I
    be; [6]
Owt of Navern to Naples moch good ys
    that I bryng;
Pondere and in Portyngale moche ys my
    gle; [7]

In Spayne and in Spruce moche ys my
    spedyng;
    In Lombardy and in Lachborun, there
    ledde ys my lykyng;
In Taryfe and in Turkey, there told ys my
    tale;
    And in the Dukedom of Oryon moche
    have I in weldyng: [1]
And thus thorowght all this world sett ys
    my sale.   36

No man in thys world may weld more
    rychesse;
    All I thank God of hys grace, for he yt
    me sent;
And as a lordis pere thus lyve I in worthy-
    nesse.
    My curat wayteth vpon me to know myn
    entent,
    And men at my weldyng; and all ys me
    lent
My well for to worke in thys worlde so
    wyde.
    Me dare they nat dysplese by no con-
    descent,
And who-so doth, he ys not able to
    abyde.   44

PRESBYTER.   No man shall you tary ne
    toroble thys tyde,
    But every man delygently shall do yow
    plesance; [2]
And I vnto my connyng [3] to the best shall
    hem guyde
    Vnto Godis plesyng to serue to attruen-
    ance. [4]
For ye be worthy and notable in substance
    of good;
    Off merchantes of Aragon ye have no
    pere, —
And therof thank God that dyed on the
    roode,[5]
    That was your makere, and hath yow
    dere.   52

ARISTORIUS.   For soth, syr pryst, yower
    talkyng ys good;
    And therfor affter your talkyng I wyll
    atteyn

---

[1] Turn away.   [2] Known.
Reign.   [4] Supplied by Manly.
Counted.   [6] Been.   [7] Mirth.

[1] Control.   [2] Pleasure.
[3] Knowledge.   [4] Instruction.
[5] Cross.

To wourshyppe my God that dyed on the
    roode;
  Neuer whyll that I lyve ageyn that wyll I
    seyn! [1]
But, Petyr Powle, my clark, I praye the
    goo wele pleyn [2]
Thorowght all Eraclea, that thow ne
    wonde, [3]
  And wytte [4] yff ony merchante be come
    to this reyn [5]
Of Surrey or of Sabe or of Shelysdown. 60

CLERICUS. At youer wyll for to walke I
    wyl not say nay,
  Smertly to go serche at the wateris syde;
Yff ony pleasant bargyn be to your paye, [6]
  As swyftly as I can I shall hym to yow
    guyde.
Now wyll I walke by thes pathes wyde,
And seke the haven both vp and down
  To wette [7] yf ony on know[e]th shyppes
    therin do ryde,
Of Surrey or of Saby [or] of Shelysdown. 68

Now shall the merchantis man [Peter Paul]
withdrawe hym, and the Jewe Jonathas
shall make hys bost.

[The Stage of the Jewish Merchant, Jona-
thas. Jonathas with his four servants,
Jason, Jasdon, Masphat, and Malcus.]

JONATHAS. Now, almyghty Machomet,
    marke [8] in thi mageste,
Whose laws tendrely I have to fulfyll,
After my dethe bryng me to thy hyhe see, [9]
  My sowle for to save, yff yt be thy
    wyll!
For myn entent ys for to fulfyll,
As my gloryus God the to honer. [10]
  To do agen [11] thy entent, yt shuld
    gr[e]ue me yll
Or agen thyn lawe for to reporte; 76

For I thanke the hayly [12] that hast me sent
  Gold, syluer and presyous stonys;
And abu[n]ddance of spycis thou hast me
    lent,

As I shall reherse before yow onys:
  I have amatystis [1] ryche for the nonys,
And baryllis [2] that be bryght of ble,
  And saphyre semely I may show yow
    attonys,
And crystalys clere for to se; 84

I have dyamantis derewourthy so to
    dresse,
  And emerawdis, ryche I trow they be,
Onyx and achatis [3] both more and lesse,
  Topazyons, smaragdis [4] of grete degre,
    Perlys precyous grete plente;
Of rubes ryche I have grete renown;
  Crepawdis [5] and calcedonyes semely to
    se,
And curyous carbunclys here ye fynd
    moren; [6] 92

Spycis I have both grete and smale
  In my shyppes, the sothe for to saye,
Gyngere, lycoresse, and cannyngalle, [7]
  And fygis fatte to plese yow to paye, [8]
Peper, and saffyron, and spycis smale,
  And datis wole [9] dulcett for to dresse,
Almundis, and reys, [10] full euery male, [11]
  And reysones [12] both more and lesse; 100

Cloueys, grenynis, [13] and gynger grene,
  Mace, mastyk [14] that myght ys,
Synymone, [15] suger, as yow may sene,
  Long peper, and Indas lycorys,
Orengis and apples of grete apryce,
  Pungarnetis, and many other spycis, —
  To tell yow all I haue now, i wys, —
And moche other merchandyse of sundry
    spycis. 10

Jew Jonathas ys my name;
  Jazun and Jazdun thei waytyn on m
    wyll,
Masfat and Malchus they do the same,
  As ye may knowe, yt ys bothe rycht
    and skyll.
I telle yow all, bi dal and by hylle,
In Eraclea ys noon so moche of myght.

---

[1] Say.   [2] Directly.   [3] Desist.
[4] Know, learn.   [5] Realm.
[6] Satisfaction.   [7] Know.
[8] Murky, dark.   [9] Seat.
[10] This line, or line 76, seems to be corrupt.
[11] Against.   [12] Wholly.

[1] Amethysts.   [2] Beryls.   [3] Agate
[4] Emeralds.   [5] Toad-stones.
[6] The rhyme requires *mown*.
[7] Ganyngale, or galingale, an aromatic root.
[8] Gratification.   [9] Very.   [10] Rice.
[11] Sack.   [12] Raisins.
[13] Grains of paradise.   [14] Mastic.
[15] Cinnamon.   [16] Right.

Werfor ye owe tenderli to tende [1] me
tyll,
For I am chefe merchante of Jewes, I telle
yow be ryght.   116

But, Jazun and Jazdun, a mater wollde I
mene,[2] —
Mervelously yt ys ment in mynde, —
The beleve [3] of thes Crysten men ys false,
as I wene,
For the[y] beleve in a cake, — me thynk
yt ys onkynde,[4] —
And all they seye how the prest dothe yt
bynd,[5]
And be [6] the myght of hys word make yt
flesshe and blode, —
And thus be a conceyte the[y] wolde
make vs blynd, —
And how that yt shuld be he that deyed
upon the rode.   124

JASUN.   Yea, yea, master, a strawe for
talis!
That ma not fae iln my beleve!
But myt we yt gete onys [7] within our
pales,[8]
I trowe we shuld sone affter putt yt in a
preve![9]
JAZDUN.   Now, be Machomete so myghty,
that ye doon of meue,[10]
I wold I wyste how that we myght yt
gete!
I swer be my grete god, and ellys mote I
nat cheue,[11]   131
But wyghtly [12] theron wold I be wreke. [13]

MASPHAT.   Yea, I dare sey feythfulli that
ther feyth [ys fals:] [14]
That was neuer he that on Caluery was
kyld!
Or in bred for to be blode yt ys ontrewe
als; [15]
But yet with ther wyles thei wold we
were wyld.[16]
MALCUS.   Yea, I am myghty Malchus,
that boldly am byld.[17]
That brede for to bete byggly am I bent.

Onys out of ther handis and yt myght be
exyled,
To helpe castyn yt in care wold I consent.   140

JONAT[H]AS.   Well, syrse,[1] than kype
cunsel, I cummande yow all,
And no word of all thys be wyst.
But let us walke to see Arystories halle,
And affterward more consell among vs
shall caste.
With hym to bey and to sel I am of
powere prest;[2]
A bargyn with hym to make I wyll assaye;
For gold and syluer I am nothyng agast
But that we shall get that cake to ower
paye.[3]   148

[The Stage of Aristorius.]

*Her shall ser Ysodyr, the prest, speke
ont[o] ser Arystori, seyng on thys wyse to
hym; and Jonat[h]as goo don of his stage.*

PRESBITER.   Syr, be yowr leue, I may [nat]
lengere dwell.
Yt ys fer paste none;[4] yt ys tyme to go to
cherche,
There to saye myn evynsong, forsothe as I
yow tell,
And syth [5] come home ageyne, as I am
wont to werche.[6]   152

ARISTORIUS.   Sir Isydor, I praye yow
walke at yowr wylle.
For to serfe God yt ys well done;
And, syr, come agene, ye shall suppe your
fylle,
And walke then to yo[u]r chamber, as ye
are wont to doon.   156

[On the platea.]

*Her shall the marchant's man [7] mete with the
Jewes.*

JONATHAS.   A! Petre Powle, good daye,
and wele i-mett!
Wer ys thy master, as I the pray?
CLERICUS.   Lon[g] from hym haue I not
lett

---

[1] Pay heed.	[2] Mention.
[3] Belief.	[4] Unnatural.
[5] Bind (with words).	[6] By. [7] Once.
[8] Limits. [9] Proof.	[10] Move, suggest.
[11] Prosper. [12] Swiftly.	[13] Avenged.
[14] Supplied by Manly.	[15] Also.
[16] Deceived.	[17] Built.

[1] Sirs.	[2] Ready.	[3] Satisfaction.
[4] Noon.	[5] Then.	
[6] Accustomed to do.		
[7] MS. *marchant men*; corr. by Stokes.		

Syt[h] I cam from hym, the sothe for to
   saye.
W[h]at tidyng with yow, ser, I yow
   praye,
Affter my master that ye doo frayen? [1]
Haue ye ony bargen that wer to hys
   paye?
Let me haue knowlech; I shall wete [2] hym
   to seyn.[3]   164

JHONATHAS.   I haue bargenes royalle and
   ry[c]h
For a marchante with to bye and sell;
In all thys lond is ther non lyke
Off abondance of good, as I will tell. 168

[*The Stage of Aristorius.*]

Her shall the clerk goon to ser Aristori,
   saluting him thus:

CLERICUS.   All hayll, master, and wel
   mot [4] yow be!
Now tydyngis can I yow tell:
The grettest marchante in all Surre
Ys come with yow to bey and sell;

Syr Jonathas ys hys nam,
A marchant of ryght gret fame.
This tale ryght well he me told:
He wollde sell yow, without blame,
Plente of clothe of golde.   177

ARISTORIUS.   Petre Powle, I can [5] the
   thanke!
I prey the rychely araye myn hall
As owyth [6] for a marchant of the banke.
Lete non defawte [7] be fownd at all.
CLERICUS.   Sekyrly,[8] master, no more ther
   shall.
Styffly about I thynke to stere,
   Hasterli to hange your parlowr with
   pall,[9]
As longeth for a lordis pere.   185

Here shall the Jewe merchante and his men
   come to the Cristen merchante.

JONATHAS.   All haylle, syr Aristorye,
   semele [10] to se,

[1] Inquire.   [2] Know.
[3] Say, tell.   [4] May.
[5] Give.   [6] Oweth, beseemeth.
[7] Default, lack. [8] Surely.
[9] Rich cloths.   [10] Seemly.

The myghtyest merchante off Arigon!
Off yower welfare fayn wet [1] wold we,
And to bargeyn with you this day am I
   boun.   189

ARISTORIUS.   Sir Jonathas, ye be wellecum
   vnto myn hall!
I pray yow come vp and sit bi me,
And tell me wat good ye haue to sell,
   And yf ony bargeyn mad may be. 193

JONATHAS.   I haue clothe of gold, precyous
   stons, and spycis plente.
Wyth yow a bargen wold I make; —
I wold bartre wyth yow in pryvyte.
On[e] lytell thyng, ye wylle me yt take [2]
   Prevely on this stownd,
And I wolle sure yow, be thys lyght,
Neuer dystrie [3] yow daye nor nyght,
But be sworn to yow full ryght, —
   And geve yow twenti pownde. 202

ARISTORIUS.   Ser Jonathas, sey me, for my
   sake,
What maner of marchandis ys that ye
   mene?
JONATHAS.   Yowr God, that ys full my-
   theti, in a cake, —
And thys good, anoon, shall yow seen.
[ARISTORIUS.]   Nay, in feyth, that shall
   not bene.
I wollnot for an hundder pownd
   To stond in fere my Lord to tene,[4]
And for so lytell a walew [5] in conscyen[c]e
   to stond bownd.   210

JONATHAS.   Ser, the entent ys if I myght
   knowe or vndertake
Yf that he were God all-myght.
Off all my mys [6] I woll amende make,
   And doone hym wourshepe bothe day
   and nyght.   214

ARISTORIUS.   Jonathas, trowth I shall the
   tell:
I stond in gret dowght to do that dede
To yow that bere all for to sell;
I fere me that I shuld stond in drede;
For, and I vnto the chyrche yede,[7]

[1] Know.   [2] Deliver.   [3] Betray.
[4] Injure, grieve   [5] Value.
[6] Misdeeds.   [7] Went.

And preste or clerke myght me aspye,
  To the bysshope thei wolde go tell that
    dede,
And apeche me of eresye.   222

JONATHAS. Sir, as for that, good shyffte
    may ye make,
  And, for a vaylle,[1] to walkyne on a
    nyght
W[h]an prest and clerk to rest ben take;
  Than shall ye be spyde of no wyght.
ARISTORIUS. Now sey me, Jonathas, be
    this lyght!
  W[h]at payment therfor wollde yow me
    make?
JONATHAS. Forty pownd, and pay yt ful-
    ryght,
  Evyn for that Lorde sake.   230

ARISTORIUS. Nay, nay, Jonathas, there-
    agen;
  I wold not for an hundder pownd.
JONATHAS. Ser, hir ys yower askyng,
    toolde pleyn!
  I shall yt tell[2] in this stownd.   234

[Counts out the money.]

Here is a hundder pownd, neyther mor
    nor lesse,
  Of dokettis good, I dar well saye.
Tell[2] yt er yow from me passe.
  Me thynketh yt a royalle araye!   238

But fyrst, I pray yow, tell me thys:
  Off thys thyng whan shall I hafe delyu-
    erance?
ARISTORI[US]. To morowe betymes. I
    shall not myse;
  This nyght therfor I shall make pur-
    veance.   242

Syr Isodyr he ys now at chyrch,
  There seyng hys evensong,
As yt ys worshepe for to werche.
  He shall sone cum home, — he wyll nat
    be long, —
  Hys soper for to eate;
And whene he ys buskyd to[3] hys bedde,
  Ryght sone there-after he shalbe
    spedd. —

No speche among yow ther be spredd;
  To kepe your toungis ye nott lett.[1] 251
JONATHAS. Syr, almyghty Machomyght
    be with yow!
  And I shalle cume agayn ryght sone.
ARYSTORIUS. Jonathas, ye wott[2] what I
    haue sayd, and how
  I shall walke for that we haue to
    donn.   255

*Here goeth the Iewys away, and the preste
    commyth home.*

PRESBITER. Syr, almyghty God mott be
    yower gyde
  And glad yow where-soo ye rest!
ARISTORIUS. Syr, ye be welcom home thys
    tyde!
  Now, Peter, gett vs wyne of the best. 259

[Enter Peter with wine and bread.]

CLERICUS. Syr, here ys a drawte of Rom-
    ney Red, —
  Ther ys no better in Aragon, —
And a lofe of lyght bred;
  Yt ys holesame, as sayeth the fesy-
    cyoun.[3]   *[Exit Peter.]* 263

ARYSTORIUS. Drynke of[f], ser Isoder, and
    be of good chere!
  Thys Romney ys good to goo with to
    reste;
Ther ys no precyouser fer nor nere,
  For alle wykkyd metys[4] yt wylle de-
    gest.   267

PRESBITER. Syr, thys wyne ys good at a
    taste,
  And ther-of haue I drunke ryght welle.
To bed to gone thus haue I cast,
  Euyn strayt after thys mery mele.   271

Now, ser, I pray to God send yow good
    nyght,[5]
  For to my chamber now wyll I gonne.
ARISTORIUS. Ser, with yow be God al-
    myght,
  And sheld yow euer from yowr fone![6] 275

[Exit Presbiter to bed.]

---

[1] Veil, concealment.   [2] Count.
[3] Has made ready for.

[1] Forbear.   [2] Know.
[3] Physician.   [4] Indigestible foods.
[5] MS. *rest.*   [6] Foes.

Here shall Aristorius call hys clarke to hys presens.

Howe, Peter! In the ys all my trust,
  In especyall to kepe my consell:
For a lytyll waye walkyne I must;
  I wyll not be longe. Trust as I the
    telle.   279

[He enters the platea and walks toward the church.]

Now preuely wyll I perseue [1] my pace,
  My bargayn thys nyght for to fulfyll.
Ser Isoder shall nott know of thys case,
  For he hath oftyn sacred,[2] as that ys
    skyll.
The chyrche key ys at my wyll;
Ther ys no-thynge that me shall tary;
I wyll nott abyde by dale nor hyll
Tyll yt be wrowght, by Saynt Mary! 287

Here shal he enter the chyrche and take the Hoost.

Ah! now haue I all myn entent.
  Vnto Jonathas now wyll I fare.[3]
To fullfyll my bargayn haue I ment;
  For that mony wyll amend my fare,[4]
    As thynketh me.

[Exit from church to the platea.]

But nowe wyll I passe by thes pathes
    playne;
To mete with Jonathas I wold fayne.
Ah! yonder he commyth in certayne;
  Me thynkyth I hym see!   296

[Enter Jonathas.]

Welcom, Jonathas, gentyll and trew,
  For well and trewly thou kepyst thyn
    howre.
Here ys the Host, sacred newe.
  Now wyll I home to halle and bowre. 300

JONATHAS.   And I shall kepe thys trusty
    treasure
As I wold doo my gold and fee.
Now in thys clothe I shall the couer,
  That no wyght shall the see.   304

---

[1] Waterhouse prints *preue*, Manly *perseue*.
[2] Consecrated the bread.
[3] Go.
[4] Condition, welfare.

Here shall Arystory goo hys waye [and Jonethas shall return to his stage].

[The stage of the Jewish Merchant, Jonathas.]

And Jonathas and hys seruauntis shall goo to the tabylle, thus sayng:

JONATHAS.   Now, Jason and Jasdon, ye be
    Jewys jentyll,
  Masfatt and Malchus, that myghty arn
    in mynd,
Thys merchant from the Crysten temple
  Hathe gett vs thys bred that make vs
    thus blynd.
Now, Jason, as jentyll as euer was the
    lynde,[1]
Into the forsayd parlowr [2] preuely take thy
    pase;
  Sprede a clothe on the tabyll that ye
    shall there fynd,
And we shall folow after to carpe [3] of thys
    case.   312

Now the Jewys goon and lay the Ost on the tabyll, sayng:

JONATHAS.   Syris, I praye yow all, harkyn
    to my sawe! [4]
  Thes Crysten men carpyn of a mer-
    velows case;
They say that this ys Ihesu that was at-
    taynted [5] in ower lawe,
  And that thys ys he that crwcyfyed
    was.   316

On thes wordys there lawe growndyd hath
    he
  That he sayd on Sherethursday [6] at hys
    soper:
He brake the brede and sayd *Accipite*,[7]
  And gave hys dyscyplys them for to
    chere;
And more he sayd to them there,
Whyle they were all together and sum,
Syttyng at the table soo clere,
Comedite; [hoc est] corpus meum.[8]   324

---

[1] Linden, lime-tree.
[2] Dining room.
[3] Talk.   [4] Saying.
[5] Condemned.
[6] Sheer Thursday, the Thursday in Holy Week.
[7] "Take."
[8] "Eat: this is my body." The words in bracket supplied from the Vulgate, Matthaeus xxvi, 26.

And thys powre he gaue Peter to proclame,
And how the same shuld be suffycyent to
all prechors.
The bysshoppys and curatis saye the same;
And soo, as I vnderstond, do all hys
progenytors.   328

JASON. Yea, sum men in that law reherse
another:
They say of a maydyn borne was hee,
And how Joachyms dowghter shuld be hys
mother,
And how Gabrell apperyd and sayd *Aue;*
And with that worde she shuld con-
ceyuyd be,
And that in hyr shuld lyght [1] the Holy
Gost.
Ageyns ower law thys ys false heresy, —
And yett they saye he ys of myghtis
most.   336

JASDON. They saye that Ihesu to be ower
kynge,
But I wene he bowght that full dere!
But they make a royall aray of hys vprys-
yng; [2]
And that in euery place ys prechyd farre
and nere,
And how he to hys dyscyples agayn dyd
appere,
To Thomas, and to Mary Mawdelen; [3]
And syth how he styed [4] by hys own
powre.
And thys, ye know well, ys heresy full
playn.   344

MASPHAT. Yea, and also they say he sent
them wytt and wysdom
For to vnderstond euery langwage,
When the Holy Gost to them came;
They faryd [5] as dronk men of pymente [6]
or vernage; [7]
And sythen how that 'he lykenyd hym-
self a lord of perage; [8]
On hys fatherys ryght hond he hym sett.
They hold hym wyser than euer was
Syble sage,
And strenger than Alexander, that all the
worde [9] ded gett.   352

MALCHUS. Yea, yet they saye as fols, I
dare laye my hedde,
How they that be ded shall com agayn to
Judgement,
And ower dredfull Judge shalbe thys same
brede,
And how lyfe euerlastyng them shuld be
lent.
And thus they hold, all at on consent,
Because that Phylyppe sayd for a lytyll
glosse,[1] —
To turn vs from owr beleve ys ther en-
tent, —
For that he sayd, *judecare viuos et mor-
tuos.*[2]   360

JONATHAS. Now, seris, ye haue rehersyd
the substance of their [3] lawe.
But thys bred I wold myght be put in a
prefe [4]
Whether this be he that in Bosra [5] of vs
had awe.
Ther staynyd were hys clothys, this may
we belefe;
Thys may we know, there had he grefe,
For ower old bookys veryfy thus, —
Thereon he was jugett to be hangyd as a
thefe, —
Tinctis [de] [6] Bosra vestibus.[7]   368

JASON. Yff that thys be he that on Caluery was mad red,
Onto my mynd, I shall kenne [8] yow a
conceyt good:
Surely with ower daggars we shall ses on [9]
thys bredde,
And so with clowtis [10] we shall know yf
he haue eny blood.
JASDON. Now, by Machomyth so myghty,
that meuyth in my mode!
Thys ys masterly ment, thys matter thus
to meue!
And with ower strokys we shall fray [11]
hym as he was on the rode,
That he was on-don with grett repreue. 376

---

[1] Lie.
[2] "To judge the living and the dead."
[3] MS. *our.*   [4] Test, proof.   [5] Bozrah.
[6] Added by Manly, from Vulgate, Isaias lxii, 1.
[7] "With dyed garments from Bozrah" (Isaih
xlii, 1).
[8] Inform.
[9] Prick in, pierce (cf. 1. 390).
[10] Blows.   [11] Frighten.

---

[1] Alight.   [2] Rising from the dead.
[3] Magdalene.   [4] Ascended (to heaven).
[5] Behaved.   [6] A spiced drink.
[7] A white wine.   [8] High lineage.   [9] World.

MASPHAT. Yea, I pray yow, smyte ye in
    the myddys of the cake,
    And so shall we smyte theron woundys
    fyve.[1]
We wyll not spare to wyrke yt wrake,[2]
    To prove in thys brede yf ther be eny
    lyfe.   380

MALCHUS. Yea, goo we to, than, and take
    ower space;
    And looke ower daggaris be sharpe and
    kene!
And when eche man a stroke smytte
    hase,
    In the mydyll part there-of ower master
    shall bene.
JONATHAS. When ye haue all smytyn, my
    stroke shalbe sene!
With this same dagger that ys so styf and
    strong
    In the myddys of thys prynt[3] I thynke
    for to prene.[4]
On lashe I shall hyme lende or yt be
    long.   388

*Here shall the iiij Jewys pryk ther daggeris
in iiij quarters [5] thus saying:*

JASON. Haue at yt! Haue at yt, with all
    my myght!
    Thys syde I hope for to sese![6]
JASDON. And I shall with thys blade so
    bryght
    Thys other syde freshely afeze![7]
MASPHAT. And I yow plyght I shall hym
    not please,
For with thys punche I shall hym pryke.
MALCHUS. And with thys angur[8] I shall
    hym not ease;
Another buffett shall he lykke.[9]   396

JONATHAS. Now am I bold with batayle
    hym to bleyke,[10]
This mydle part alle for to prene;
A stowte stroke also for to stryke, —
    In the myddys yt shalbe sene![11]   400

Here the Ost must blede.

Ah! owt! owt! harrow! what deuyll ys
    thys?
    Of thys wyrk I am on were![1]
Yt bledyth as yt were woode,[2] i-wys!
    But yf ye helpe, I shall dyspayre.   404

JASON. A fyre! a fyre! and that in hast!
    Anoon a cawdron full of oyle!
JASDON. And I shalle helpe yt wer in cast,
    All the iij howris[3] for to boyle!   408

[Malchus goes for the oil.]

MASPHAT. Yea, here is a furneys stowte
    and strong,
And a cawdron therin dothe hong!
Malcus, wher art thow so long,
    To helpe thys dede were dyght?[4]

MALC[H]US. Loo, here ys iij[5] galons off
    oyle clere!
Haue doon fast! Blowe up the fere!
Syr, bryng that ylke[6] cake nere,
    Manly, with all yowre myghthe.   416

JONATHAS. And I shall bryng that ylke
    cak[e]
And throw yt in, I undertake.

*[He seizes the Sacrament, which clings to his
hand.]*

Out! out! yt werketh me wrake!
    I may not awoyd[7] yt owt of my hond!
I wylle goo drenche me in a lake, —
    And in woodnesse I gynne to wake![8]
    I rene! I lepe ouer this land!   423

*Her he renneth wood, with the Ost [9] in hys
hond.*

JASON. Renne, felawes, renne, for Cokkis
    peyn![10]
Fast we had ower mayster agene!

---

[1] In doubt.   [2] Mad.
[3] Apparently symbolical of the three days Christ
lay in the tomb.
[4] Done.
[5] MS. iiij. But the number "three" runs throughout the scene, with the suggestion, as pointed out, of
the three days spent in the tomb.
[6] Same.
[7] Cast.
[8] In madness I begin to toss restlessly (or come
into a condition of madness).
[9] Host, the bread.
[10] An oath (for Christ's pain).

---

[1] The five wounds of Christ.   [2] Injury.
[3] The cake.   [4] Prick.
[5] Representing the wounds in the hands and feet.
The scene repeats the crucifixion of Christ.
[6] Pierce deeply.   [7] Terrify.
[8] Hunger, dagger.
[9] Experience.   [10] Make pale.
[11] Seen. Representing the spear-thrust into Christ's
side.

[They run and catch Jonathas.]

Hold prestly [1] on thys pleyn,
And faste bynd hyme to a poste.
JASDON. Here is an hamer and naylys iij,
   I s[e]ye.
Lyffte vp hys armys, felawe, on hey,
Whyll I dryue thes nayles, I yow praye,
  With strong strokis fast.   431

[They nail the Sacrament to the post.]

MASPHAT. Now set on, felouse, with
  mayne and myght,
And pluke hys armes awey in syght!

[They attempt to pull their master from the Sacrament.]

Wat! I se he twycche, felovse, a-ryght!
  Alas, balys breweth ryght badde!

Here shall thay pluke the arme, and the hand shalle hang stylle with the Sacrament.

MALCHUS. Alas! alas! what deuyll ys
  thys?
Now hat[h] he but oon hand, i-wyse!
For sothe, mayster, ryght woo me is
  That ye this harme haue hadde.   439

JONATHAS. Ther ys no more; I must
  enduer!
Now hastely to ower chamber lete us
  gon,
Tyll I may get me sum recuer.   442
  And therfor [I] [2] charge yow euery-choon [3]
  That yt be consell that we have doon.

[They withdraw.]

[On the Platea.]

Here shall the lechys [4] man come into the place sayng:

COLLE. Aha! here ys a fayer felaw-
  shyppe!
Thewhe [5] I be nat sh[a]pyn, I lyst to
  sleppe.
I hauc a master — I wolld he had the
  pyppe! —
I tell yow in consel —
He ys a man off all syence,

But off thryfte, — I may with yow dys-
  pence.
He syttyth with sum tapstere in the
  spence; [1]
Hys hoode there wyll he sell.   452

Mayster Brendyche of Braban,
I telle yow, he ys that same man,
Called the most famous phesy[cy]an
  That euer sawe uryne.
He seeth as wele at noone as at nyght,
And sumtyme by a candelleyt
Can gyff a judgyment aryght
  As he that hathe noo eyn. [2]   460

He ys allso a boone-setter, [3] —
I knowe no man go the better;
In euery tauerne he ys detter, —
  That ys a good tokenyng.
But euer I wonder he ys so long;
I fere ther gooth sum-thyng a-wrong,
For he hath dysa[rv]yde to be hong, —
  God send neuer worse tydyng!   468

He had a lady late in cure;
I wot by this she ys full sure;
There shall neuer Crysten creature
  Here hyr tell no tale!
And I stode here tyll mydnyght,
I cowde not declare aryght
My masteris cunyng insyght —
  That he hat[h] in good ale.   476

But what deuyll delayeth hym so long to
  tarye?
A seekman myght soone myscary.
Now alle the deuyllys of hell hym wari! —
  God giue me my boon!
I trowe best, we mak a crye: [4]
Yf any man can hym aspye, [5]
Led hym to the pyllere[ye]. —
  In fayth, yt shall be don.   484

Here shalle he stond vp and make proclama-cion, seyng thys:

COLLE. Yff therbe eyther man or woman
That sawe Master Brundyche of Braban,

---

[1] Room where wines are dispensed.   [2] Eyes.
[3] Possibly with a pun on "dice player."
[4] A public proclamation. The crying of a humor-ous proclamation was a favorite device with play-wrights, even so late as the sixteenth century.
[5] Spy. The MS. apparently reads *can I aspye.*

---

[1] Quickly.   [2] Added by Manly.
[3] Every one.   [4] Physician's.   [5] Though.

Or owyht [1] of hym tel can,
Shall wele be quit hys mede. [2]
He hath a cut berd and a flatte noose,
A therde-bare gowne and a rente hoose;
He spekyt[h] neuere good matere nor pur-
  poose.
To the pyllere ye hym led[e]! 492

[*Enter behind him, and unobserved, Master
  Brundyche.*]

MASTER BRUNDYCHE. What, thu boye!
  what janglest here?
COLL[E]. A! master, master, but to your
  reuerence!
I wend [3] neuer to a seen yowr goodly
  chere, [4]
Ye tared hens so long.
MASTER BRUNDYCHE. What hast thow
  sayd in my absense?
COLL[E]. Nothyng, master, but to yowr
  reuerence,
I haue told all this audiense —
And some lyes among. 500

But, master, I pray yow, how dothe yowr
  pacyent
That ye had last vnder yowr medyca-
  mente?
MASTER BRUNDYCHE. I warant she neuer
  fele anoyment.
COLL[E]. Why, ys she in hyr graue?
MASTER BRUNDYCHE. I haue gyven hyr a
  drynke made full well
Wyth scamely, [5] and with oxennell,
Letuce, sauge, and pympernell. [6]
COLL[E]. Nay, than she ys full saue! 508

For, now ye ar cum, I dare well saye
Betwyn Douyr and Calyce the ryght
  wey [7]
Dwellth non so cunnyng, be my fey,
In my judgyment.
MASTER BRUNDYCHE. Cunnyng? Yea,
  yea! And with pratise
I haue sauid many a manys lyfe.
COLL[E]. On wydowes, maydese, and
  wy[v]se
Yowr connyng yow haue nyhe spent. 516

MASTER BRUNDYCHE. Were ys bowgtt
  with drynke profytable.

[*Takes out a bottle and drinks.*]

COLL[E]. Here, master, master, ware how
  ye tugg!
The devyll, I trowe, within shrugg,
For yt gooth rebyll-rable. [1] 520

MASTER BRUNDYCHE. Here ys a grete
  congregacyon,
And all be not hole, [2] without negacyon.
I wold haue certyfycacyon;
Stond vp and make a proclamacion.
Haue do faste, and mak no pausa[c]yon,
But wyghtly [3] mak a declaracion
To all people that helpe w[o]lde haue. 527

Hic interim proclamationem faciet. [4]

COLL[E]. All manar off men that haue any
  syknes,
To Master Brentberecly loke that yow redresse. [5]
What dyesease or syknesse that euer ye
  haue,
He wyll neuer leue yow tyll ye be in yow[r]
  graue.
Who hat[h] the canker, the colyke, or the
  laxe,
The tercyan, the quartan, or the brynn-
  y[n]g axs; [6]
For wormys, for gnawyng, gryndyng in
  the wombe or in the boldyro;
Alle maner red-eyn, bleryd-eyn, and the
  myregrym also; 535
For hedache, bonache, and therto the toth-
  ache;
The colt-euyll, and the brostyn men he
  wyll undertak,
All tho that [haue] the poose, the sneke, [7] or
  the teseke. [8]
Thowh a man w[e]re ryght heyle, [9] he cowd
  soone make hym seke.
Inquyre to the Tolkote, for ther ys hys
  loggyng,
A lytyll besyde Babwell Myll, yf ye wyll
  haue understondyng. 541

---

[1] Aught.   [2] Reward.   [3] Thought.
[4] Countenance.   [5] Scammony.
[6] Pimpernel, an herb with medicinal properties.
[7] In a straight line between Dover and Calais (all
water).

[1] Imitating the sound of a gurgling liquid.
[2] In health.   [3] Quickly.
[4] "Here he will make the proclamation."
[5] Address yourselves.   [6] Fever.
[7] Cold in the head, catarrh.
[8] Phthisis.   [9] Hale, strong.

MASTER BRUNDYCHE.   Now, yff therbe
ether man or woman
That nedethe helpe of a phesyscion —
COLL[E].   Mary, master, that I tell can,
And ye wyll vnderstond.

MASTER BRUNDYCHE.   Knoest any abut
this plase?
COLL[E].   Ye, that I do, master, so haue
[I] grase!
Here ys a Jewe, hyght [1] Jonathas,
Hath lost hys ryght hond.   549

MASTER BRUNDYCHE.   Fast to hym I wold
inquere.
COLL[E].   For God, master, the gate [2] ys
hyre.
MASTER BRUNDYCHE.   Than to hym I
wyll go nere.

[*He ascends the stage of the Jews, and salutes
Jonathas.*]

My master, wele mot yow be!
JONATHAS.   What doost here, felawe?
What woldest thu hanne? [3]
MASTER BRUNDYCHE.   Syr, yf yow nede
ony surgeon or physycyan,
Off yow[r] dysese help yow welle I cane,
What hurtis or hermes [4] so-euer they
be.   557

JONATHAS.   Syr, thu art ontawght to come
in thus [un]henly, [5]
Or to pere [6] in my presence thus mala-
pertly.
Voydeth from my syght, and that
wyghtly, [7]
For ye be mysse-a-vysed.
COLL[E].   Syr, the hurt of yowr hand ys
knowen full ryfe;
And my master have sauyd many a manes
lyfe.
JONATHAS.   I trowe ye be cum to make
sum stryfe.
Hens fast, lest that ye be chastysed. 565

COLL[E].   Syr, ye know well yt can nott
mysse,
Men that be masters of scyens be profytable.

In a pott yf yt please yow to pysse,
He can tell yf yow be curable.
[JONATHAS.]   Avoyde, fealows; I love not
yower bable!
Brushe them hens bothe, and that anon!
Gyff them ther reward that they were
gone!   572

*Here shall the iiij Jewys bett away the leche
and hys man.*

JONATHAS.   Now haue don, felawys, and
that anon,
For dowte of drede what after befall!
I am nere masyd! [1]   My wytte ys gon!
Therfor of helpe I pray yow all.   576

And take yowr pynsonys [2] that ar so
sure,
And · pluck owt the naylys won and
won; [3]
Also in a clothe [4] ye yt cure [5]
And throw yt in the cawdron, and that
anon.   580

*Here shall Jason pluck owt the naylys and
shake the hond into the cawdron.*

JASON.   And I shall rape [6] me redely anon
To plucke owt the naylys that stond so
fast,
And bear thys bred and also thys bone,
And into the cawdron I wyll yt cast. 584

JASDON.   And I shall with thys dagger so
stowte
Putt yt down that yt myght plawe, [7]
And steare [8] the clothe rounde abowte
That nothyng ther-of shalbe rawe.   588

MASPHAT.   And I shall manly, with all my
myght,
Make the fyre to blase and brenne, [9]
And sett thervnder suche a lyght
That yt shall make yt ryght thynne.

*Here shall the cawdron b[l]oyle, apperyng to
be as blood.*

MALCHAS.   Owt! and harow! what deuyll
ys here-in?
Alle thys oyle waxyth redde as blood,

[1] Named.   [2] Door.   [3] Have.
[4] Harms.   [5] Rudely.   [6] Appear.   [7] Quickly.
[1] Dazed.   [2] Pincers.   [3] One by one.
[4] MS. *cloke;* but cf. ll. 587, 622.
[5] Cover, wrap.   [6] Hasten.
[7] Boil.   [8] Stir.   [9] Burn.

And owt of the cawdron yt begynnyth to
    rinn.
I am so aferd I am nere woode! [1]   596

*Here shall Jason and hys compeny goo to ser
    Jonathas, sayng:*

JASON.   Ah! master, master, what there ys
    with yow,
I can not see owr werke wyll avayle.
I beseche yow avance [2] yow now
    Sumwhatt with yowr counsayle.   600

JONATHAS.   The best counsayle that I now
    wott,[3]
That I can deme,[4] farre and nere,
Ys to make an ovyn as redd hott
As euer yt can be made with fere;
And when ye see yt soo hott appere,
Then throw yt into the ovyn fast;
    Sone shall he stanche hys bledyng
    chere!
When ye haue done, stoppe yt; be not
    agast.   608

JASDON.   Be my fayth, yt shalbe
    wrowgh[t],
And that anon, in gret hast.
Bryng on fyryng, seris. Here ye nowght?
    To hete thys ovyn be nott agast!   612

MASPHAT.   Here ys straw and thornys
    kene.
Come on, Malchas, and bryng on fyre,
For that shall hete yt well, I wene.

Here thei kyndyll the fyre.

Blow on fast, that done yt were!
MALCHAS.   Ah, how! thys fyre gynnyth to
    brenne clere!
Thys ovyn ryght hotte I thynk to make.
    Now, Jason, to the cawdron that ye
    stere,
And fast fetche hether that ylke cake. 620

*Here shall Jason goo to the cawdron and
take owt the Ost with hys pynsonys and
cast yt in-to the ovyn.*

JASON.   I shall with thes pynsonys, with-
    owt dowt,
Shake thys cake owt of thys clothe,

And to the ovyn I shall yt rowte,[1]
    And stoppe hym there, thow he be loth.
    Thys cake I haue caught here, in good
    sothe, —
The hand ys soden,[2] the fleshe from the
    bonys, —
Now into the ovyn I wyll therwith.
Stoppe yt, Jasdon, for the nonys!   628

JASDON.   I stoppe thys ovyn, wythowtyn
    dowte;
    With clay I clome [3] yt vppe ryght fast,
That non heat shall cum owte.
    I trow there shall he hete and drye in
    hast!   632

*Here the ovyn must ryve asunder, and
blede owt at the cranys, and an image appere owt with woundis bledyng.*

MASPHAT.   Owt! owt! here is a grete won-
    der!
Thys ovyn bledyth owt on euery syde!
MALCHAS.   Yea, the ovyn on peacys gyn-
    nyth to ryve asundere!
Thys ys a mervelows case thys tyde! 636

*Here shall the image speke to the Juys, sayng
thus:*

JHESUS.   *O mirabiles Judei, attendite et
    videte
Si est dolor sicut [4] dolor meus!*   638
Oh ye merveylows Jewys,
    Why ar ye to yower kyng onkynd,
And [I] so bytterly bowt [5] yow to my
    blysse?
    Why fare [6] ye thus fule [7] with yowr
    frende?
Why peyne yow me and straytly me
    pynde,[8]
And I yower loue so derely haue bowght?
    Why are ye so vnstedfast in your mynde?
Why wrath [9] ye me?   I greve yow
    nowght.   646

Why wylle ye nott beleve that I haue
    tawght?
    And forsake your fowle neclygence?
And kepe my commandementis in yower
    thowght?

---

[1] Mad.   [2] Advance.
[2] Know.   [4] Judge.   [5] Go.

[1] Cast.   [2] Boiled.   [3] Plaster.
[4] MS. *similis.*   [5] Purchased, redeemed
[6] Behave.   [7] Foul.
[8] Tormented.   [9] Be angry with.

And vnto my godhed to take credence? 650

Why blaspheme yow me? Why do ye
thus?
Why put yow me to a newe tormentry?
And I dyed for yow on the crosse!
Why consyder not yow what I dyd crye?
Whylle that I was with yow, ye ded me
velanye.
Why remember ye nott my bitter chaunce,
How yower kynne dyd me awance [1]
For claymyng of myn enherytaunce?
I shew yow the streytenesse of my greu-
aunce,
And all to meue yow to my mercy. 660

JONATHAS. *Tu es protector vite mei; a quo*
trepidabo?
O thu, Lord, whyche art my defendowr,
For dred of the I trymble and quake!
Of thy gret mercy lett vs receyue the
showre;
And mekely I aske mercy, amendys to
make. 665

Here shall they knele down all on ther kneys,
sayng:

JASON. Ah! Lord, with sorow and care
and grete wepyng
All we felawys lett vs saye thus,
With condolent harte and grete sorowyng:
Lacrimis nostris conscienciam nostram
baptizemus! 669

JASDON. Oh, thow blyssyd Lord of mykyll
myght,
Of thy gret mercy, thow hast shewyd vs
the path,
Lord, owt of grevous slepe and owt of dyrk-
nes to lyght,
Ne grauis sompnus irruat. 673

MASPHAT. Oh Lord, I was very cursyd,
for I wold know thi crede.
I can no men[d]ys [2] make, but crye to the
thus:
O gracyows Lorde, forgyfe me my mys-
dede!
With lamentable hart: *miserere mei,*
Deus! 677

MALCHAS. Lord, I haue offendyd the in
many a sundry vyse.[1]
That styckyth at my hart as hard as a
core.
Lord, by the water of contryc[i]on lett me
aryse:
Asparges me, Domine, ysopo, et mun-
dabor. 681

JHESUS. All ye that desyryn my seru-
auntis for to be,
And to fulfyll the preceptis of my lawys,
The intent of my commandement knowe ye:
Ite et ostendite vos sacerdotibus meis.
To all yow that desyre in eny wyse
To aske mercy, to graunt yt redy I am.
Remember and lett yower wyttis suffyce,
Et tunc non auertam a vobis faciem meam. 689

Ser Jonathas, on thyn hand thow art but
lame,
And this thorow [2] thyn own cruelnesse.
For thyn hurt thou mayest thi-selfe blame;
Thow woldyst preve thy power me to
oppresse.
But now I consydre thy necesse; [3]
Thow wasshest thyn hart with grete con-
tryc[i]on;
Go to the cawdron, — thi care shalbe
the lesse, —
And towche thyn hand to thy salua-
c[i]on. 697

Here shall ser Jonathas put hys hand in-to
the cawdron, and it shalbe hole agayn; and
then say as fo[lo]wyth:

JONATHAS. Oh thow my Lord God and
Sauyouer, osanna!
Thow Kyng of Jews and of Jerusalem!
O thow myghty, strong Lyon of Juda,
Blyssyd be the tyme that thow were in
Bedlem! [4]
Oh thou myghty, strong, gloryows and
gracyows oyle streame,
Thow myghty conquerrowr of infernall
tene,[5]
I am quyt of moche combrance thor-
owgh thy meane,[6]
That euyr blyssyd mott thow bene! 705

---

[1] Lift me up (on the cross).   [2] Amends.

[1] Wise, ways.   [2] Through.
[3] Necessity.   [4] Bethlehem.
[5] Injury, suffering.   [6] Mediation.

Alas that euer I dyd agaynst thy wyll,
  In my wytt to be soo wood
That I with ongoodly wyrk shuld soo
    gryll! [1]
Agens my mys-gouernaunce thow glad-
    dyst me with good:
I was soo prowde to prove the on the
    roode,
And thou haste sent me lyghtyng [2] that
    late was lame;
  To bete the and boyll the I was myghty
    in moode,
And now thou hast put me from duresse
    and dysfame.   713

But, Lord, I take my leve at thy high
    presens,
  And put me in thy myghty mercy.
The bysshoppe wyll I goo fetche to se ower
    offens,
  And onto hym shew ower lyfe, how that
    we be gylty.   717

*Here shall the master Jew goo to the byshopp,
and hys men knele styll [before the image].*

[The Stage of the Bishop.]

[Enter Jonathas.]

JONATHAS. Hayle, father of grace! I
    knele vpon my knee
Hertely besechyng yow and interely
A swemfull [3] syght all for to see
  In my howse apperyng verely:
The Holy Sacrament, the whyche we
    haue done tormentry,
And ther we haue putt hym to a newe pas-
    syon,
  A chyld apperyng with wondys bloody:
A swemfull syght yt ys to looke vpon. 725

EPISCOPUS. Oh Jhesu, Lord, full of good-
    nesse!
  With the wyll I walke with all my
    myght.
Now, all my pepull, with me ye dresse [4]
  For to goo see that swymfull syght. 729

Now, all ye peple that here are,
  I commande yow, euery man,

On yower feet for to goo, bare,
  In the devoutest wyse that ye can. 733

[They cross over the platea to the Jew's house.]

[The Stage of Jonathas.]

*Here shall the bysshope enter into the Jewys
howse, and say:*

O Jhesu fili Dei,
  How thys paynfull passyon rancheth [1]
    myn hart!
Lord, I crye to the, *miserere mei*,
  From thys rufull syght thou wylt re-
    uerte.[2]
Lord, we all with sorowys smert;
For thys vnlefull work we lyue in langower;
  Now, good Lord, in thy grace let vs be
    grett,
And of thy souereyn marcy send vs thy
    socower;[3]   741

And for thy holy grace forgyfe vs ower
    errowr.
  Now lett thy pete [4] spryng and sprede;
Thowgh we haue be vnrygh[t]full, forgyf vs
    our rygore,
  And of ower lamentable hartis, good
    Lord, take hed[e].   745

*Here shall the im[a]ge changeag ayn onto
brede.*

Oh th[o]u largyfluent [5] Lord, most of
    lyghtnesse,
  Onto owr prayers thow hast applyed;
Th[o]u hast receyuyd them with grett
    swettnesse,
  For all ower dredfull dedys thou hast
    not so denyed.
Full mykyll owte [6] thy name for to be
    magnyfyed
  With mansuete [7] myrth and gret swett-
    nes,
And as our gracyows God for to be glory-
    fyed,
For th[o]u shewyst vs gret gladnes.   753

Now wyll I take thys Holy Sacrament
  With humble hart and gret devoc[i]on,

---

[1] Irritate, grieve.   [2] Relief.
[3] Sorrowful.   [4] Prepare.

[1] Teareth.   [2] Turn away.
[3] Succor.   [4] Pity.
[5] Bountiful.   [6] Ought.   [7] Gentle.

And all we wyll gon, with on[e] consent,
　And bear yt to chyrche with sole[m]pne
　　processyon.
Now folow me, all and sume!
And all tho that bene here, both more and
　　lesse,
　Thys holy song, *O sacrum Dominum,*
Lett vs syng all with grett swetnesse. 761

[*Singing, they bear the Host in solemn
　procession towards the Church.*]

[*The Stage of Aristorius.*]

*Here shall the pryst, ser Isoder, aske hys
　master what this menyth.*

PRESBITER.　Ser Arystory, I pray yow,
　　what menyth all thys?
　Sum myracle, I hope, ys wrowght be
　　Goddis myght;
The bysshope commyth [in] processyon
　　with a gret meny [1] of Jewys;
　I hope sum myracle ys shewyd to hys
　　syght.
　To chyrche in hast wyll I runne full
　　ryght,
For thether, me thynk, he begynnyth to
　　take hys pace.
　The Sacrament so semly is borne in
　　syght,
I hope that God hath shewyd of hys
　　grace.　　　　　　　　　　　769

ARYSTORIUS.　To tell yow the trowth I
　　wylle nott lett:
Alas that euer thys dede was dyght! [2]
An onlefull [3] bargayn I began for to beat; [4]
　I sold yon same Jewys ower Lord full
　　ryght
　For couytyse of good,[5] as a cursyd
　　wyght.
Woo the whyle that bargayn I dyd euer
　　make!
　But yow be my defensour in owr dyoce-
　　sans syght;
For an heretyke I feare he wyll me take.777

PRESBITER.　For sothe, nothyng well-
　　avysed was your wytt, —

───────
[1] Throng.　　　　　　[2] Done.
[3] Unlawful.　　　　　[4] Discuss.
[5] Goods, wealth (I see no reason to change to
gold)

Wondrely was yt wrowght of a man of
　　dyscresc[i]on
In suche perayle [1] your solle for to putt!
But I wyll labor for your absolucyon. 781

Lett vs hye vs fast that we were hens,
　And beseche hym of hys benygne grace
That he wyll shew vs hys benyvolens
　To make amendys [2] for yower tres-
　　pas.　　　　　　　　　　　785

[*The Church.*]

*Here shall the merchant and hys prest go
to the chyrche and the bysshop [attended by
the Jews] shall entre the chyrche and lay
the Os[t] u[p]on the auter,*[3] *sayng thus:*

[EPISCOPUS.]　*Estote fortes in bello et pug-
nate cum antico serpente,*
Et accipite regnum eternum, et cetera.
My chyldern, be ye strong in batayll gostly
For to fyght agayn [4] the fell serpent,
That nyght and day ys euer besy;
　To dystroy owr sollys ys hys intent.
Look ye be not slow nor neclygent
To arme yow in the vertues seuyn.
　Of synnys forgetyn take good avyse-
　　ment
And knowlege [5] them to yowr confessor full
　euyn.　　　　　　　　　　　795

For that serpent, the deuyll, ys full strong
　Meruelows myscheues for man to mene,
But that the Passyon of Cryst ys meynt vs
　　among,
And that ys in dyspyte of hys infernall
　　tene.[6]
Beseche ower Lord and Sauyower so
　　kene
To put doun that serpent, cumberer of
　　man,
　To withdraw hys furyous froward doc-
　　tryn bydene,[7]
Fulfyllyd of the fend callyd Leuyathan. 803

Gyff lawrell [8] to that Lord of myght
　That he may bryng vs to the joyous
　　fruycion
From vs to put the fend to flyght,

───────
[1] Peril.　　　　　　[2] MS. menyn.
[3] Altar.　　　　　　[4] Against.
[5] Acknowledge.　　[6] Suffering.
[7] Also.　　　　　　[8] Praise.

That neuer he dystroy vs by hys tempta-
c[i]on.   807

PRESBITER.   My father vnder God, I knele
vnto yower kne,
In yowr myhty mysericord to tak vs in
remembrance;
As ye be materyall to ower degre,
We put vs in yower moderat ordynance,
Yff yt lyke yower hyghnes to here ower
greuaunce;
We haue offenddyd sorowfully in a syn
mortall,
Wherfor we fere vs owr Lord wyll take
vengaunce
For owr synnes both grete and small. 815

EPISCOPUS.   And in fatherhed, that longyth [1] to my dygayte,
Vnto yower grefe I wyll gyf credens.
Say what ye wyll, in the name of the Trynyte,
Agayn[s]t God yf ye haue wroght eny
inconuenyence.   819

ARISTORIUS.   Holy ffather, I knele to yow
vnder benedycite.
I haue offendyd in the syn of couytys; [2]
I sold our Lordys body for lucre of mony
And delyueryd to the wyckyd with
cursyd advyce.
And for that presumpc[i]on gretly I
agryse [3]
That I presumed to go to the auter [4]
There to handylle the holy sacryfyce, —
I were worthy to be putt in brenyng
fyre.   827

But, gracyous lord, I can no more
But put me to Goddys mercy and to
yower grace.
My cursyd werkys for to restore,
I aske penaunce now in thys place. 831

EPISCOPUS.   Now for thys offence that
thou hast donne
Agens the Kyng of Hevyn and Emperour of Hell,
Euer whyll thou lyuest good dedys for to
done

And neuermore for to bye nor sell;
Chastys thy body, as I shall the tell,
With fastyng, and prayng, and other good
wyrk,
To withstond the temtacyon of fendis of
hell;
And to call to God for grace looke thou
neuer be irke.[1]   839

Also, thou preste, for thy neclygens,
That thou were no wyser on thyn office,
Thou art worthy inpresu[n]ment for thyn
offence;
But beware euer herafter, and be mor
wyse.   843

And all yow creaturys [2] and curatys that
here be,
Off thys dede yow may take example
How that your pyxys [3] lockyd ye shuld see
And be ware of the key of Goddys
temple.   847

JONATHAS.   And I aske crystendom with
great devoc[i]on,
With repentant hart in all degrees,
I aske for vs all a generall absoluc[i]on,

Here the Juys must knele al down.

For that we knele all vpon ower
knees;   851
For we haue greuyd ower Lord on grovnd,
And put hym to a new paynfull passion,
With daggars styckyd hym with greuos
wo[u]nde,
New naylyd hym to a post, and with
pynsonys pluckyd hym down. 855

JASON.   And syth [4] we toke that blyssyd
bred so sownd,
And in a cawdron we dyd hym boyle,
In a clothe fulle just we hym wounde,
And so dyd we seth hym in oyle.   859

JASDON.   And for that we myght not ouer-
com hym with tormentry,
In an hott ovyn we speryd [5] hym fast.
Ther he apperyd with wo[u]ndis all bloody;

---

[1] Belongeth.   [2] Covetousness.
[3] Am horrified.   [4] Altar.

[1] Tired.
[2] Manly suggests *vicarys*, or *prechorys*.
[3] The vessels in which the bread of the sacrament
is preserved.
[4] Then.   [5] Enclosed.

The ovyn rave asunder and all tobrast.[1] 863

MASPHAT. In hys law to make vs stedfast,
There spake he to vs woordis of grete
favor;
In contrycyon owr hartis he cast,
And bad take vs to a confessor. 867

MALCHUS. And therfor all we with on[e]
consent
Knele onto yower hygh souereynte;
For to be crystenyd ys ower intent.
Now all ower dedys to yow shewyd haue
we. 871

*Here shall the bysshope crysten the Jewys
with gret solempnyte.*

EPISCOPUS. Now the Holy Gost at thys
tyme mot yow blysse
As ye knele all now in hys name!
And with the water of baptyme I shall yow
blysse
To saue yow all from the fendis blame.
Now, that fendys powre for to make lame,
In the name of the Father, the Son, and
the Holy Gost,
To saue yow from the deuyllys flame,
I crysten yow all, both lest and most. 879

SER JONATHAS. Now owr father and bysh-
oppe that we well know,
We thank yow interly,[2] both lest and
most.
Now ar we bownd to kepe Crystis lawe
And to serue the Father, the Son, and the
Holy Gost.
Now wyll we walke by contre and cost,
Owr wyckyd lyuyng for to restore;
And trust in God, of myghtis most,
Neuer to offend as we have don before. 887

Now we take ower lea[v]e at lesse and more;
Forward on ower vyage we wyll vs
dresse.[3]
God send yow all as good welfare
As hart can thynke or towng expresse! 891

ARYSTORIUS. In-to my contre now wyll I
fare [4]

For to amende myn wyckyd lyfe;
And to kep[e] the people owt of care
I wyll teache thys lesson to man and
wyfe. 895

Now take I my leave in thys place;
I wyll go walke, my penaunce to fullfyll.
Now, God, ageyns whom I haue done thys
trespas,
Graunt me forgyfnesse, yf yt be thy
wylle! 899

PRESBITER. For joy of thys me thynke my
hart do wepe,
That yow haue gyuyn yow all Crystis
seruauntis to be,
Hym for to serue with hart full meke, —
God, full of pacyens and humylyte, — 903

And the conuersac[i]on [1] of all thes fayre
men,
With hartis stedfastly knett [2] in on[e],
Goddis lawys to kepe and hym to serue
bydene,[3]
As faythfull Crystanys euermore for to
gonne. 907

EPISCOPUS. God omnypotent euermore
looke ye serue
With deuoc[i]on and prayre whyll that
ye may;
Dowt yt not he wyll yow preserue
For eche good prayer that ye sey to hys
pay.
And therfor in euery dew tyme loke ye
not delay
For to serue the Holy Trynyte,
And also Mary, that swete may;[4]
And kepe yow in perfyte loue and char-
yte. 915

Crystis commandementis ten there bee;
Kepe welle them; doo as I yow tell.
Almyght God shall yow please in euery
degre,
And so shall ye saue yower sollys from
hell;
For there ys payn and sorow cruell,
And in heuyn ther ys both joy and blysse,

---

[1] Burst apart. [2] Entirely.
[3] Betake ourselves. [4] Go.

[1] Behavior, mode of life.
[2] Knit. [3] Also. [4] Maid.

More then eny towng can tell;
There angellys syng with grett swet-
    nesse.   923

To the whyche blysse [1] he bryng vs
  Whoys name ys callyd Jhesus,
And in wyrshyppe of thys name gloryows
  To syng to hys honor *Te Deum lauda-*
    mus.   927

FINIS.

Thus endyth the Play of the Blyssyd
Sacrament, whyche myracle was don in the

[1] Omitted by Waterhouse, but without comment
and apparently in error; I restore the word on the authority of the text as reproduced by Stokes and
Manly.

forest of Aragon, in the famous cite Eraclea, the yere of ower Lord God. M^{l}cccc.lxi.,
to whom be honower, Amen!

The namys and number of the players:

Jh[es]us.	Jason, Judeus ij^{us}.
Episcopus.	Jasdon, Judeus iij^{us}.
Aristorius, Chris-	Masphat, Judeus iiij^{us}.
tianus mercator.	
[Isoder, presbiter.]	Malchas, Judeus v^{tus}.
Clericus.	M[agister] phisicus.
Jonathas, Jude-	Colle, seruus.
us i^{mus}.	

IX may play yt at ease

R. C.

VII
MORALITIES

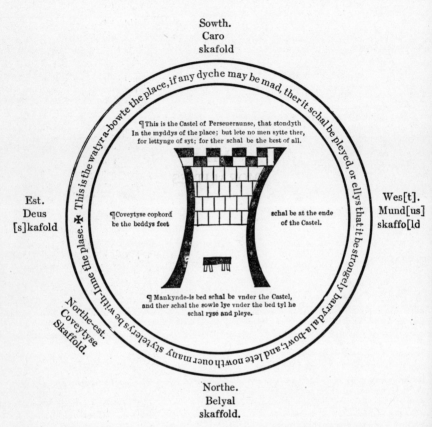

Sowth.
Caro
skafold

¶This is the Castel of Perseueraunse, that stondyth
In the myddys of the place; but lete no men sytte ther,
for lettynge of syt; for ther schal be the best of all.

This is the watyr a-bowte the place, if any dyche may be mad, ther it schal be pleyed, or ellys that it be strongely barryd a-bowt; and lete nowth ouer many stytelerys be with-inne the plase. ✠

Est.
Deus
[s]kafold

¶Coveytyse copbord
be the beddys feet

schal be at the ende
of the Castel.

Wes[t].
Mund[us]
skaffo[ld]

¶ Mankynde-is bed schal be vnder the Castel,
and ther schal the sowle lye vnder the bed tyl he
schal ryse and pleye.

Northe-est.
Coveytyse
Skaffold.

Northe.
Belyal
skaffold.

He that schal pleye Belyal, loke that he haue gunne-powder brennyn[ge] In pypys in his handis and in his eris, and in his ers, whanne he gothe to bat[tel]. The iiij dowteris schul be clad in mentelys; Merci in wyth, Rythwysnesse in red, al togedyr; Trewthe in sad grene, and Pes al in blake; and thei schal pleye in the place al togedyr tyl they brynge up the sowle.

THE CASTLE OF PERSEVERANCE [1]

THE BANNS

I. Vexil[lator]. Glorious God, in all de-
gres Lord most of myth,
That heuene and erthe made of nowth,
bothe se and londe,
The aungelys in heuene hym to serue
bryth,
And [man]-kynde in mydylerd [1] he made
with hys honde,   4
And [our lo]fly Lady, that lanterne is of
lyth,
Save our lege lord, the kynge, the leder
of this londe,
And all the ryallis of this revme,[2] and rede
hem the ryth,
And all the goode comowns [3] of this
towne that be-forn us stonde   8
In this place!
We mustyr you with menschepe,[4]
And freyne you of frely frenchepe.[5]
Cryst safe you all fro schenchepe,[6]
That knowyn wyl our case!   13

II. Vexillator. The case of our comynge,
you to declare,

[1] Middle-earth.   [2] Nobles of this realm.
[3] Commons, people.
[4] We call you together with honor.
[5] And ask of you generous friendship.
[6] Harm.

Euery man in hym self for sothe he it
may fynde.
Whon mankynde in-to this werld born is
ful bare —
And bare schal beryed be at [t]he [l]ast
ende —   17
God hym geuyth t[w]o aungelis ful yep and
ful yare,[1]
The goode aungel and the badde, to hym
for to lende.[2]
The goode techyth hym goodnesse; the
badde, synne and sare; [3]
Whanne the ton hath the victory, the
tother goth be-hende,   21
Be skyll.[4]
The goode aungel coueytyth euermore mans saluacion,
And the badde bysytyth [5] hem euere
to hys dampnacion.
And God hathe govyn man fre arbri-
tracion
Whether he wyl hymse[lf] saue or
his soule per[yll.]   26

I. Vexilla[tor]. Spylt is man spetously [6]
whanne he to synne asent!

[1] Prompt and ready.   [2] Lend.   [3] Sorrow.
[4] Reason.   [5] Attacks.   [6] Sadly.

[1] With the possible exception of *The Pride of Life*, which exists only in a fragment, *The Castle of Perseverance* is the earliest, as it is certainly the most primitive, of the extant moralities. Of the still older *Paternoster*
plays (first mentioned in 1378), acted at York, Beverley, and Lincoln — apparently the grandparents of the
type — we have only scattered records. From these records, however, we are led to believe that the plays
dealt with the struggle between the Seven Deadly Sins and the Seven Moral Virtues for the soul of man; and
we know that they were given as open-air community performances. Thus *The Castle of Perseverance*, it is obvious, is closely akin in form and spirit to the first moralities of which we have knowledge. Although its exact
date of composition cannot be determined, scholars have agreed upon the year 1425 as approximately correct.

The manuscript of *The Castle of Perseverance*, along with the manuscripts of *Mankind* and *Mind, Will, and
Understanding*, was formerly owned by the Rev. Cox Macro (b. 1688, d. 1767), from which circumstance the
plays are called "Macro Moralities." There is no real connection between the plays, however, for they were
written by different scribes at different times. Affixed to the end of *The Castle of Perseverance* is a plan of the
staging, showing the scaffolds arranged about a *platea* (called "the place"), with the Castle in the centre, and
around all an encircling ditch filled with water to keep the spectators at a proper distance. With the aid of
this plan we can readily visualize the performance.

I have based the present text on that in *The Macro Plays*, edited by F. J. Furnivall and A. W. Pollard for
the Early English Text Society, 1904, and in doubtful readings I have consulted the photographic facsimile of
the manuscript issued by J. S. Farmer. The play is far too long to be printed here in full; but by cutting
down the speeches of the personages (who have a habit of talking in stanzas) and omitting a few episodes, I
have been able to preserve the plot as a whole. The extent of the omissions can readily be discovered from
the line-numbering. The punctuation and the use of capitals are my own; and I have added, in brackets,
stage-directions designed to show how the actors moved from place to place, or how the attention of the audience was shifted from one scaffold to another. In the text the personages invariably have English names—
yet the scribe has affixed to the speeches the Latin equivalents of these names (on the same principle that he
puts the stage-directions in Latin). I have avoided the annoying inconsistency by adopting the English form
of the names throughout; the Latin forms used by the scribe may be found in his catalogue of the actors at
the end.

The bad aungel thanne bryngyth hym
iij enmys so stout:
The Werlde, the Fende, the foul Flesche so
joly and jent;[1]
Thei ledyn hym ful lustyly with synnys
al a-bowt.   30
Pyth[2] with Pride and Coueytyse, to the
Werld is he went,
To meynten his manhod; all men to hym
lout.[3]
Aftyre, Ire and Envye the Fend hath to
hym lent,
Bakbytynge and Endytynge, with all
men for to route,[4]   34
Ful evyn.
    But the fowle Flesch, homlyest of all,
    Slawth,[5] Lust and Leccherye, gun to
    hym call,
    Glotony, and other synnys, bothe
    grette and small.
    This mans soule is soylyd with
    synnys moo thanne seuyn. 39

II. Vexillator.   Grace if God wyl
graunte us of hys mykyl myth,
    These parcellis in propyrtes[6] we purpose
us to playe
This day seuenenyt be-fore you in syth,
    At ——[7] on the grene, in ryall a-ray. 134
Ye haste you thanne thedyrward, syris,
hendly in hyth,[8]
    All goode neyboris ful specyaly, we you
pray.

---

[1] Courteous.   [2] Set, furnished.
[3] Bow, make obeisance.
[4] Make trouble.   [5] Sloth.
[6] Parts (characters) in properties (costumes, etc.).
[7] Apparently to be filled in with the name of the town where the play was to be acted. The MS. does not have a dash, but curious marks which may be an abbreviation for some town.
[8] Courteous in highest degree.

And loke that ye be there be-tyme, luffely
and lyth,
For we schul be onward be vnderne[1] of
the day.   138
    Dere frendys,
    We thanke you of all good daly-
    aunce,[2]
And of all youre specyal sportaunce,[3]
And preye you of good contynnaunce
To oure lyuys endys.   143

I. Vexillator.   Deus, oure lyuys we loue
you,[4] thus takande oure leue.
Ye manly men of ——, thus Crist saue
you all!
He maynten youre myrthis and kepe you
fro greve,
    That born was of Mary myld in an ox
    stall.   147
Now, mercy be all ——, and wel mote ye
cheve![5]
All oure feythful frendys, thus fayre
mote ye fall!
Ya, and welcum be ye whanne ye com, prys
for to preve,[6]
And worthyi to be worchepyd in boure
and in hall,   151
    And in euery place.
    Fare-wel, fayre frendys,
    That lofly wyl lystyn and lendis![7]
    Cryste kepe you fro fendis!

        [*To the trumpetors.*]

    Trumpe up, and lete vs pace![8] 156

---

[1] The third hour of the day, about nine o'clock
[2] Talk.   [3] Entertainment.
[4] All our lives we praise you.
[5] Thrive
[6] Our worth (as actors) to prove.
[7] Remain   [8] March on.

[DRAMATIS PERSONÆ

World.
    Lust,
    Folly, } his attendants.
    Covetousness, his treasurer.
    Backbiter, his messenger.
    Boy, serving him.

Flesh.
    Lechery,
    Gluttony, } his attendants.
    Sloth,
Devil.
    Pride,
    Wrath, } his attendants.
    Envy,

MANKIND.
  GOOD ANGEL, } his advisors.
  BAD ANGEL,
  SOUL, of Mankind.
MEEKNESS,
CHARITY,
ABSTINENCE,
CHASTITY, } the Seven Virtues, th
INDUSTRY,   keepers of the Castle.
GENEROSITY,
PACIENCE,

CONFESSION.
PENANCE.
MERCY,
PEACE, } the Four Daughters
TRUTH,   of God.
RIGHTEOUSNESS,
DEATH.
GOD THE FATHER.]

[HERE BEGINNETH THE PLAY OF THE CASTLE OF PERSEVERANCE.]

[*On the scaffold of the World.*]

WORLD. Worthy wytis [1] in al this wer[l]d
      wyde,
    Be wylde wode wonys [2] and euery weye-
      went, [3]
Precyous in prise, prekyd [4] in pride,
    Thorwe [5] this propyr pleyn place, [6] in pes
      be ye bent!   160
Buske [7] you, bolde bacheleris, vnder my
      baner to a-byde,
    Where bryth basnetis [8] be bateryd, and
      backys ar schent.
Ye, syrys semly, all same syttyth on
      syde,
    For bothe be see and be londe my sondis [9]
      I haue sent;   164
      Al the Werld myn nam[e] is ment;
      Al a-bowtyn my bane [10] is blowe;
    In euery cost I am knowe;
      I do men rawyn on ryche rowe [11]
        Tyl thei be dyth to dethys
        dent. [12] ...   169

[*On the scaffold of the Devil. Belial, Pride,
      Envy, and Wrath.*]

BELYAL. Now I sytte, Satanas, in my sad
      synne,
    As deuyl dowty, in draf as a drake! [13]

I champe and I chase, I chocke on my
      chynne,
    I am boystows [1] and bold, as Belyal the
      blake.   199
What folk that I grope, [2] thei gapyn and
      grenne.
I-wys, fro Carlylle in-to Kent my carp-
      ynge [3] thei take!
Bothe the bak and the buttoke brestyth al
      on brenne; [4]
    With werkys of wreche, [5] I werke hem
      mykyl wrake; [6]   203
      In woo is al my wenne. [7]
      In care I am cloyed
      And fowle I am a-noyed
      But Mankynde be stroyed
        Be dykes and be denne. ...   208

[*On the scaffold of the Flesh. Flesh, Glut-
      tony, Sloth, and Lechery.*]

FLESH. I byde, as a brod brustun gutte,
      a-bouyn [8] on these touris!
    Euery body is the beter that to myn byd-
      dynge is bent.
I am Mankyndis fayre Flesch, florchyd in
      flowris;
    My lyfe is with lustys and lykynge
      i-lent;   238
With tapytys [9] of tafata I tymbyr [10] my
      towris;

---

[1] Persons.   [2] Dwellings.
[3] Cross-road.   [4] Set.
[5] Through.   [6] Playing place?
[7] Prepare.   [8] Helmets.
[9] Messengers.   [10] Proclamation.
[11] Ravin (or array) in a rich row (in vast numbers)?
[12] Ordained to Death's blow.
[13] In draff as a dragon.

[1] Boisterous.   [2] Tear.
[3] Talk.   [4] Bursteth all on burning.
[5] Vengeance.
[6] Harm.   [7] Delight.
[8] As a broad burst-gut, aloft.
[9] Hangings.   [10] Cover, decorate.

In myrthe and in melodye my mende is
    i-ment;
Thou I be clay and clad, clappyd vndir
    clowris,[1]
Yit wolde I that my wyll in the werld
    went   242
    Ful trew, I you be-hyth.
    I loue wel myn ese,
    In lustis me to plese;
    Thou [2] synne my sowle sese,[3]
    1 geue not a myth.[4] . . .   247

[*On the platea. Enter Mankind, attended
by the Good Angel on his right and the
Bad Angel on his left.*]

MANKIND. Aftyr oure forme faderis kende,[5]
    This nyth I was of my moder born.
Fro my moder I walke, I wende.[6]
    Ful feynt and febyl I fare [7] you be-
    forn.   278
I am nakyd of lym and lende,[8]
    As mankynde is schapyn and schorn.
I not wedyr [9] to gon ne to lende,
    To helpe my-self mydday nyn morn. 282
    For schame I stonde and schende.[10]
    I was born this nyth in blody ble;
    And nakyd I am, as ye may se.
    A! Lord God in Trinite,
    Whow Mankende is vnthende! [11] 287

Where-to I was to this werld browth,
    I ne wot; but to woo and wepynge
I am born, and haue ryth nowth
    To helpe my self in no doynge.   291
I stonde and stodye, al ful of thowth.
    Bare and pore is my clothynge;
A sely crysme,[12] myn hed hath cawth,
    That I tok at myn crystenynge: 295
    Certis, I haue no more.
    Of erthe I cam, I wot ryth wele;
    And as erthe I stande this sele; [13]
    Of mankende it is gret dele.[14]
    Lord God, I crye thyne ore! [15]   300

Ij aungels bene a-synyd to me.
    The ton techyth me to goode;

On my ryth syde ye may hym se,   303
    He cam fro Criste that deyed on rode.
A-nother is ordeynyd her to be,
    That is my foo be fen and flode;
He is a-bout, in euery degre,
    To drawe me to tho dewylys wode,[1] 308
    That in helle ben thycke.
    Swyche to [2] hath euery man on lyue,
    To rewlyn hym and hys wyttis fyue:
    Whanne man doth ewyl, the ton wolde
    schryue; [3]
    The tother drawyth to wycke.   313

But syn these aungelys be to me falle,
    Lord Jhesu! to you I bydde a bone,[4]
That I may folwe, be strete and stalle,
    The aungyl that cam fro heuene trone.
Now, Lord Jhesu in heuene halle,   318
    Here, whane I make my mone!
Coryows [5] Criste, to you I calle!
    As a grysly gost I grucche and grone, 321
    I wene, ryth ful of thowth.
    A! Lord Jhesu! wedyr may I goo?
    A crysyme I haue, and no moo.
    Alas! men may be wondyr woo   325
    Whanne thei be fyrst forth browth!

GOOD ANGEL. Ya, forsothe, and that is
    wel sene:
    Of woful wo man may synge,
For iche creature helpith hym-self be-
    dene,[6]
    Saue only man, at hys comynge.   330
Neuyr-the-lesse, turne thee fro tene,[7]
    And seruë Jhesu, heuene kynge,
And thou schalt, be greuys grene,[8]
    Farë wel in allë thynge.   334
    That Lord thi lyfe hath lante;
    Haue hym alway in thi mynde,
    That deyed on rodë for mankynde;
    And serue hym to thi lyfës ende; 338
    And sertis thou schalt not wante!

BAD ANGEL. Pes, aungel! Thi wordis are
    not wyse!
    Thou counselyst hym not a-ryth.
He schal hym drawyn to the Wer[l]dis
    seruyse,

---

[1] Turfs.   [2] Though.   [3] Seize.   [4] Mite.
[5] First father's fashion.   [6] Go.
[7] Walk, go.   [8] Loin.
[9] I know not whither.   [10] Am stupefied.
[11] Miserable, unthriving.
[12] Chrisom, a head cloth with which the chrism was
covered up when the child was baptized.
[13] Season, time.   [14] Pity, grief.   [15] Mercy.

---

[1] Mad.   [2] Such two.
[3] Shrive, administer absolution to.
[4] Ask a boon.
[5] Careful (caring for sinners).
[6] At once.   [7] Harm.   [8] A metrical tag.

To dwelle with caysere,[1] kynge, and
   knyth,   343
That in londe be hym non lyche.[2]
Cum on with me, stylle as ston!
Thou and I to the Wer[l]d schul goon,
And thannë thou schalt sen a-non
   Whow[3] sone thou schalt be
   ryche. . . .   348

MANKIND.   Whom to folwe, wetyn I ne
   may!
I stonde in stodye, and gynne to raue.
I wolde be ryche in gret a-ray,
   And fayn I wolde my sowlë saue!   379
     As wynde in watyr I wave.
Thou woldyst to the Werld I me toke;
And he wolde that I it for-soke.
Now, so God me helpe, and the holy
   boke,
   I not wyche I may haue!   384

BAD ANGEL.   Cum on, man! Where-of
   hast thou care?
Go we to the Werld, I rede thee, blyue;[4]
For ther thou schalt mow[5] ryth wel fare,
   In case if thou thynke for to thryue; 388
     No lord schal be thee lyche.
Take the Werld to thine entent,
And late thi loue be ther-on lent;
With gold and syluyr, and ryche rent,
   A-none thou schalt be ryche.   393

MANKIND.   Now, syn thou hast be-hetyn[6]
   me so,
I wyl go with thee and a-say;
I ne lette for frende ner fo,
   But with the Werld I wyl go play, 397
     Certis, a lytyl throwe.[7]
In this World is al my trust,
To lyuyn in lykyng and in lust.
Haue he and I onys cust,[8]
   We schal not part, I trowe.   402

GOOD ANGEL.   A! nay, man! For Cristis
   blod,
Cum a-gayn be strete and style!
The Werld is wyckyd, and ful wod,[9]
   And thou schalt leuyn but a whyle. 406
   What coueytyst thou to wynne?

Man, thynke on thyn endynge day
Whanne thou schalt be closyd vnder
   clay!
And if thou thenke of that a-ray,
   Certis thou schalt not synne.   411
Homo, memento finis! et in eternum non
   peccabis.

BAD ANGEL.   Ya, on thi sowle thou schalt
   thynke al be-tyme.[1]
Cum forth, man, and take non hede!
Cum on, and thou schalt holdyn hym inne.
   Thi flesch thou schalt foster and fede 416
     With lofly lyuys fode.[2]
   With the Werld thou mayst be bold
   Tyl thou be sexty wynter hold.[3]
Wanne thi nosë waxit cold,
   Thanne mayst thou drawe to
   goode.   421

MANKIND.   I vow to God, and so I may
Make mery a ful gret throwe!
I may leuyn many a day;
   I am but yongë, as I trowe,   425
     For to do that I schulde.
Myth I ryde be sompe and syke,[4]
And be ryche, and lord [i-]lyke,
   Certis thanne schulde I be fryke,[5]
   And a mery man on molde.[6] . . . 430

*[The Bad Angel leads Mankind away, and
   the Good Angel, left behind, laments.]*

GOOD ANGEL.   I weyle, and wrynge, and
   makë mone!
This man with woo schal be pylt.[7]
I syë sore, and grysly grone,
   For hys folye schal make hym spylt! 452
   I not weder to gone.
Mankynde hath forsakyn me!
Alas, man, for loue of the!
Ya, for this gamyn and this gle, 456
   Thou schalt grocchyn and grone.
                 [Exit.]
       Pipe vp music.

[On the scaffold of the World. World
boasts that he is lord of king, knight, and
kaiser, and cares not for God. He orders
his attendants, Lust (also called Lyking)

---

[1] Kaiser.   [2] Like.   [3] How.
[4] Quickly.   [5] Be able to.   [6] Promised.
[7] Time.   [8] Kissed.   [9] Mad.

[1] In time enough.   [2] Food.
[3] Old.   [4] By swamp and rill.
[5] Joyful.   [6] On the earth.   [7] Tortured.

and Folly, to "cry all about" if any man will serve the World. They descend into the *platea* and address the audience, urging all men to serve the World. In the meanwhile, the Bad Angel, leading Mankind, salutes them.]

BAD ANGEL. How, Lust! Lykyng and Folye!
   Take to me good entent!
I haue browth, be downys drye,[1]
   To the Werld a gret present!   533
I haue gylyd [2] hym ful qweyntly;
   For, syn he was born, I haue hym blent.[3]
He schal be serwaunt good and try;
   A-monge you his wyl is lent;   537
     To the Werld he wyl hym take;
For, syn he cowde wyt,[4] I vndirstonde,
   I haue hym tysyd [5] in euery londe.
   Hys Goode Aungel, be strete and st[r]onde,
     I haue don [6] hym forsake. . . .   542

FOLLY. With ryche rentys I schal hym blynde
Wyth the werld tyl he be pytte;[7]
And thanne schal I, longe or his ende,
   Make that caytyfe to be knytte   564
     On the werld whanne he is set s[ore].

[*Addressing Mankind.*]

   Cum on, Man! Thou schalt not rewe;
   For thou wylt be to vs trewe
   Thou schalt be clad in clothis newe,
     And be ryche euere-more.   569

MANKIND. Mary, felaw, gramercy!
I wolde be ryche and of gret renoun.
[Of God] I geue no tale trewly,
   So that I be lord of toure and toun, 573
     Be buskys and bankys broun.[8]
   Syn that thou wylt makë me
   Bothë ryche of gold and fee,
   Goo forthe! for I wyl folow thee
     Be dale and euery towne.   578

---

[1] By downs dreary, or distant (a metrical tag).
[2] Beguiled.
[3] Blinded.
[4] Know (reached the age of intelligence).
[5] Enticed, tempted to sin.
[6] Made.
[7] Buried.
[8] By bushes and banks brown (a metrical tag).

Trumpe vp. Then Lust and Folly, the Bad Angel and Mankind will go to [*the scaffold of*] *the World, and let* [*Lust*] *say:* [1]

LUST. How, lord! loke owt! for we haue browth
   A serwant of nobyl fame!

[*Presents Mankind.*]

Of worldly good is al his thouth;
   Of lust and folye he hath no schame; 582
     He wolde be gret of name;
     He wolde be at gret honour,
     For to rewlë town and toure;
   He wolde haue to his paramoure
     Sum louely dyngë dame.[2]   587

WORLD [*to Mankind*]. Welcum, syr, semly in syth!
Thou art welcum to worthy wede,[3]
For thou wylt be my serwaunt day and nyth,
   With my seruyse I schal thee foster and fede;   591
Thi bak schal be betyn with besawntis [4] bryth;
   Thou schalt haue byggyngys be bankis brede; [5]
To thi cors schal knele kayser and knyth,
   And ladys louely on lere,[6]   595
     Where that thou walke, be sty or be strete.
   But Goddys seruyse thou must forsake,
   And holy to the Werld thee take,
   And thanne a man I schal thee make
     That non schal be thi pere.   600

MANKIND. Yis, Werld, and ther-to here myn honde,
   To forsake God and hys seruyse.
To medys [7] thou geue me howse and londe
   That I regne rychely at myn enprise.[8] 604
So that I fare wel be strete and stronde
   Whil I dwelle here in werldly wyse,
I reeke neuere of heuene wonde,[9]
   Nor of Jhesu, that jentyl justyse.   608

---

[1] MS. trumpe vp. *Tunc ibunt Voluptas et Stulticia, Malus Angelus et Humanum Genus, ad Mundum, et dicat.*
[2] Wortny lady.   [3] Clothes.
[4] Bezants, gold coins.
[5] Buildings by banks broad.   [6] In face.
[7] For rewards.   [8] Will.   [9] Chastisement.

Of my sowle I haue non rewthe.
What schulde I recknen of domysday,
So that I be ryche, and of gret a-ray?
I schal make mery whyl I may.
And ther-to here my trewthe. 613

WORLD. Now sertis, syr, thou seyst wel!
I holde thee trewe ffro top to the too.
But thou were ryche, it were gret del,[1]
And all men that wyl farë soo. 617
Cum up, my serwaunt trew as stel!

Then Mankind ascends to the World.[2]

Thou schalt be ryche where so thou goo;
Men schul seruyn thee at mel[3]
With mynstralsye and bemys blo,[4] 621
With metis and drynkis trye;[5]
Lust and lykynge schal be thin ese;
Louely ladys thee schal plese;
Who-so do thee any disesse,
He schal ben hangyn hye! 626

Lykynge, be-lyue
Late clothe hym swythe[6]
In robys ryve[7]
With ryche a-ray. 630
Folye, thou fonde,[8]
Be strete and stronde,
Serue hym at honde
Bothe nyth and day. . . . 634

[*Lust and Folly take Mankind aside to array
him.*]

[*On the platea. Enter Backbiter.*]

BACKBITER. All thyngis I crye a-gayn the
pes
To knyt and knaue. This is my kende.[9]
Ya! dyngne dukis on her des,[10]
In bytter balys I hem bynde; 654
Cryinge and care, chydynge and ches,[11]
And sad sorwe, to hem I sende.
Ya! lowdë lesyngis lachyd in les,[12]
Of talys vn-trewe is al my mende. 658
Mannys bane[13] a-bowtyn I bere,
I wyl that ye wetyn, all tho that ben
here;

For I am knowyn fer and nere;
I am the Werldys messengere;
My name is Bacbytere. . . . 663

Ther-fore I am mad massenger
To lepyn ouer londis leye,[1]
Thorwe all the world, fer and ner,
Vnsayd sawys for to seye.[2] 693
In this holte I huntë here
For to spye a preuy pley;[3]
For whanne Mankynde is clothyd clere,
Thanne schal I techyn hym the wey 697
To the dedly synnys seuene.
Here I schal a-bydyn with my pese,
The wronge to do hym for to chese,[4]
For I thynke that he schal lese
The lyth of hey heuene. 702

[*On the scaffold of the World. Lust and
Folly leap forward Mankind gorgeously
arrayed.*]

LUST. Worthy World, in welthys wonde,
Here is Mankynde ful fare in folde![5]
In bryth besauntys he is bownde, 705
And bon[6] to bowe to you so bolde. . . .

FOLLY. Dysplese thee, he wyl for no
man; 716
On me, Folye, is al hys thowth. . . .

WORLD. Now, Folye, fayre thee be-fall!
And Lustë, blyssyd be thou ay!
Ye han browth Mankynde to myn hall
Sertis in a nobyl a-ray! 732
With Werldys welthys with-inne these
wall,
I schal hym feffe of that I may.
Welcum, Mankynde, to thee I call!
Clenner clothyd thanne any clay, 736
Be downë, dale, and dyche.
Mankynde, I redë that thou reste
With me, the Werld, as it is beste.
Loke thou holde myn hendë[7] feste,
And euere thou schalt be ryche. 741

MANKIND. Whou[8] schul I but I thi hestis
helde?
Thou werkyst with me holy my wyll;
Thou feffyst me with fen and felde,

---

[1] Pity.
[2] MS. *Tunc ascendit Humanum Genus ad Mundum.*
[3] Meal.   [4] Blowing of trumpets.
[5] Delicate.   [6] Quickly.   [7] Abundant.
[8] Fool.   [9] Nature.
[10] Worshipful dukes on their thrones.   [11] Strife.
[12] Loud lyings bound in leash?   [13] Sorrow.

[1] Untilled lands.   [2] Unsaid-sayings to say.
[3] Play, trick.   [4] Choose.
[5] In rich garments.   [6] Bound; ready.
[7] Hands.   [8] How.

And hyë hall be holtis and hyll;   745
In werldly wele my wytte I welde;[1]
In joye I jette[2] with juelys jentyll;
On blysful banke my boure is bylde;
   In veynglorye I stondë styll;   749
     I am kene as a knyt.
   Who-so a-geyn the Werld wyl speke,
   Mankynde schal on hym be wreke;
   In stronge presun[3] I schal hym steke,
     Be it wronge or ryth!   754

WORLD.   A, Mankynde, wel thee be-tyde,
   That thi loue on me is sette!
In my bowris thou schalt a-byde,
   And yit fare makyl the bette.[4]   758
I feffe thee in all my wonys wyde,
   In dalc of dros[5] tyl thou be deth.[6]
I make thee lord of mekyl pryde,
   Syr, at thyn owyn mowthis mette.[7] 762
     I fynde in thee no tresun.
   In all this worlde, be se and sonde,
   Parkis, placis, lawnde and londe,
   Here I gyfe thee with myn hondc,
     Syr, an opyn sesun.   767

Go to my tresorer, Syr Couetouse!
Loke thou tell hym as I seye!
Bydde hym make thee mayster in his house,
With penys and powndis for to pleye. 771
Loke thou geuë not a lous
Of the day that thou schalt deye.

     [He calls Backbiter.]

Messenger, do now thyne vse!
   Bakbytere, teche hym the weye!   775
     Thou art swetter thanne mede.[8]
   Mankynde, take with thee Bakbyt-
     ynge!
   Lefe hym for no maner thynge!
   Flepergebet[9] with hys flaterynge
     Standith mankynde in stede.   780

BACKBITER.   Bakbytynge and Detraccion
Schal goo with thee fro toun to toun.
Haue don, Mankynde, and cum doun!

     [Mankind descends.]

I am thyne owyn page.   784
I schal bere thee wyttnesse with my myth,
Whanne my lord, the Werlde, it behyth.[1]

   [He points to the scaffold of Covetousness.]

   Lo, where syr Coueytyse sytt,
     And bydith us[2] in his stage. . . .

   [Backbiter leads Mankind up to the scaffold
     of Covetousness.]

BACKBITER.   Syr Coueytyse, God thee
     saue,
   Thi pens and thi poundys all!
I, Bakbytere, thyn owyn knaue,
   Haue browt Mankynde vn-to thine
     hall.   820
The Worlde bad thou schuldyst hym haue,
   And feffyn hym, what-so be-fall.
In grene gres tyl he be graue,[3]
   Putte hym in thi precyous pall,   824
     Coueytyse! it were all rewthe.
   Whyl he walkyth in worldly wolde,
   I, Bakbytcr, am with hym holde;[4]
   Lust and Folye, tho barouns bolde,
     To hem · he hath plyth hys
     trewthe.   829

COVETOUSNESS.   Ow, Mankynde! blyssyd
     mote thou be!
I haue louyd thee derworthly many a
     day;
And so I wot wel that thou dost me.
   Cum up and se my ryche a-ray!   833

     [Mankind ascends the scaffold
     of Covetousness.]

It were a gret poynte of pyte
But Coueytyse were to thi pay.[5]
Sit up ryth here in this se;[6]
   I schal thee lere[7] of werldiys lay,   837
     That fadyth as a flode.
   With good i-now[8] I schal thee store;
   And yit oure gamë is but lore[9]
   But thou coueyth mekyl more   841
     Thanne euere schal do thee goode.

Thou muste gyfe thee to symonye,
   Extorsion, and false asyse;[10]

---

[1] In worldly happiness my mind I rule.
[2] Strut.   [3] Prison.
[4] Much the better.
[5] In the grave.   [6] Put.
[7] Mouth's might (at command).
[8] Mead, a sweet drink made from honey.
[9] Flibbertigibbet, one of the names of Backbiter.

[1] Commands.   [2] Waits for us.
[3] Buried.   [4] Gracious, friendly.
[5] Liking, satisfaction.   [6] Seat.
[7] Teach.   [8] Wealth enough.
[9] Lost.   [10] Measure.

Helpe no man but thou haue why; [1]
  Pay not thi serwauntys here serwyse; 846
Thi neyborys, loke thou dystroye;
  Tythe not on non wyse;
Here no begger, thou he crye —
  And thanne schalt thou ful sonë ryse. 850
    And whanne thou vsyste marchaun-
      dyse,
  Loke that thou be sotel of sleytys;
  And also swere al be deseytys;
  Bye and sell be fals weytys;
    For that is kyndë coueytyse.[2] ...855

MANKIND.   A, Auaryce! wel thou spede!
  Of werldly wytte thou canst,[3] i-wys.
Thou woldyst not I haddë nede,
  And schuldyst be wrothe if I ferd
    a-mys.   873
I schal neuere begger bede [4]
  Mete nyn drynke, be heuene blys;
Rather or I schulde hym clothe or fede,
  He schulde sterue and stynke, i-wys. 877
    Coueytyse, as thou wylt, I wyl do.
  Where-so that I fare, be fenne or flod,
  I make a-vow, be Goddys blod,
  Of Mankynde getyth no man no good,
    But if he synge " si dedero." ... 882

[Covetousness calls aloud:]

Prydë, Wrathë, and Envye,
  Com forthe, the deuelys chyldryn thre!
Lechery, Slawth, and Glotonye,
  To mans flesch ye are fendis fre!   899
Dryuyth downne ouer dalys drye!
  Beth [5] now blythe as any be!
Ouer hyll and holtys ye you hyghe
  To com to Mankynde and to me   903
    Fro youre dowty dennys!
  As dukys dowty, ye you dresse!
  Whanne ye sex be comme, I gesse,
  Thanne be we seuene, and no lesse,
    Of the dedly synnys. ... 908

[On the scaffold of the Devil, Pride,
Wrath, and Envy hear the call, and take
farewell of Belial. Belial urges them to do
their best to bring Mankind to hell. On
the scaffold of the Flesh, Gluttony, Lechery, and Sloth likewise hear the call, and
take a farewell of their master.   Flesh

gives them his blessing, and exhorts them
to use every means to keep Mankind from
the bliss of heaven.]

*Then Pride, Wrath, Envy, Gluttony,
Lechery, and Sloth will go to [the scaffold
of] Covetousness; and let Pride say:* [1]

PRIDE.   What is thi wyll, Syr Coveytyse?
  Why hast thou afftyr vs sent?
Whanne thou creydyst, we ganne a-gryse,[2]
  And come to thee now par asent.   1016
    Oure loue is on thee lent.
  I, Pryde, Wrath, and Envye,
  Gloton, Slawth, and Lechery,
  We arn cum all sex for thi crye,
    To be at thi commaundement. 1021

COVETOUSNESS.   Welcum be ye, bretheryn
    all,
  And my sy[s]tyr, swete Lecherye!
Wytte ye why I gan to call?
  For ye must me helpe, and that in
    hy.[3]   1025
Mankynde is now com to myn hall
  With me to dwell, be downys dry;
Therfore ye must, what so be-ffall,
  Feffyn hym with youre foly;   1029
    And ellis ye don hym wronge,
  For whanne Mankynde is kendly
    koueytous,[4]
  He is provd, wrathful, and envyous;
  Glotons, slaw,[5] and lecherous,   1033
    Thei arn other whyle amonge. ...

PRIDE.   In gle and game I growë glad!
  Mankynde, take good hed,
And do as Coveytyse thee bad!   1050
  Take me in thyn hert, precyous Pride;
Loke thou be not ouer-lad;[6]
  Late no bacheler thee mysbede;[7]
Do thee [8] to be dowtyd and drad;
  Bete boyes tyl they blede;   1055
    Kast hem in careful kettis;[9]
  Frende, fadyr, and moder dere,[10]
  Bowe hem not in non manere;
  And hold no maner man thi pere;
    And vsë these new iettis: [11]   1060

---

[1] MS. *Tunc ibunt Superbia, Ira, Invidia, Gula,
Luxuria, et Accidia ad Auariciam; et dicat Superbia.*
[2] Tremble.   [3] In haste.
[4] Naturally covetous.   [5] Slothful.
[6] Lorded over.   [7] Ill use.   [8] Make thyself.
[9] Grievous troubles.
[10] Injure.   [11] Fashions.

---

[1] Reason therefor.   [2] Natural covetousness.
[3] Hast knowledge.   [4] Offer.   [5] Be.

Loke thou blowë mekyl bost,
  With longe crakows on thi schos;[1]
Jagge thi clothis in euery cost,[2]
  And ellis men schul lete [3] thee but a
    goos.   1064
It is thus, Man, wel thou wost;
  Therfore do as no man dos;
And euery man sette at a thost;[4]
  And of thi-self make gret ros;[5]   1068
    Now se thi-self on euery syde.
    Euery man thou schalt schende and
      schelfe;[6]
    And holde no man betyr thanne thi
      selfe;
    Tyl dethys dynt thi body delfe,[7]
      Put holy thyn hert in Pride. ...1073

WRATH.   Be also wroth as thou were wode!
  Make thee be dred be dalys derne!
Who so thee wrethe, be fen or flode,
  Loke thou be a-vengyd yerne![8]   1094
Be redy to spylle mans blod!
  Loke thou hem ferc,[9] be feldis ferne![10]
Alway, Man, be ful of mod![11]
  My lothly lawys loke thou lerne,   1098
    I rede,[12] for any thynge.
    A-non take veniaunce, Man, I rede;
    And thanne schal no man thee ouerlede,
    But of thee they schul haue drede,
      And bowe to thi byddynge.   1103

MANKIND.   Wrethë, for thi councel hende
  Haue thou Goddis blyssynge and myn!
What caytyf of al my kende
  Wyl not bowe, he schal a-byn;[13]   1107
With myn veniaunce I schal hym schende,[14]
  And wrekyn [15] me, be Goddis yne.[16] ...

ENVY.   Envye with Wrathe muste dryve
  To haunte Mankynde al-so.
Whanne any of thy neyboris wyl thryve,
  Loke thou haue Envye ther-to. ...1124

MANKIND.   Envye! thou art bothe good
    and hende,
  And schalt be of my counsel chefe. ...

---

[1] Pointed and curved toes on thy shoes.
[2] Way, manner.   [3] Reckon.
[4] A piece of dung.   [5] Esteem.
[6] Injure and shove aside.   [7] Bury.
[8] Thoroughly.   [9] Frighten.
[10] By fields distant (a metrical tag).
[11] Anger.   [12] Advise.   [13] Suffer.
[14] Injure.   [15] Avenge.   [16] Eyes.

GLUTTONY.   In gay glotony a game thou
    be-gynne!
  Ordeyn thee mete and drynkis goode.
Loke that no tresour thee part a-twynne,
  But thee feffe and fede with al kynnys
    fode.[1]   1154
With fastynge schal man neuere heuene
    wynne:
  These grete fasteris, I hold hem wode.
Thou thou ete and drynke, it is no synne.
  Fast no day, I rede, be the rode. ... 1158

MANKIND.   A, Glotony! wel I thee grete!
  Soth and sad it is, thy sawe.
I am no day wel, be sty nor strete,
  Tyl I haue wel fyllyd my mawe.   1167
Fastynge is fellyd vnder fete. ...

LECHERY.   Ya whanne thi flesche is fayrë
    fed,
  Thanne schal I, louely Lecherye,
Be bobbyd with thee in [thi] bed;
  Here-of serue mete and drynkis trye.[2]
In louë thi lyf schal be led;   1185
  Be a lechour tyl thou dye! ...

MANKIND.   A, Lechery, wel thee be!
  Mans sed in thee is sowe;
Fewe men wyl forsakë thee
  In any cuntre that I knowe. ...   1197

SLOTH.   Ya! whanne ye be in bedde
    browth bothe,
  Wappyd wel in worthy wede,
Thanne I, Slawthë, wyl be wrothe
  But ij brothelys [3] I may brede.   1214
Whanne the messë-bellë goth,[4]
  Lye stylle, man, and take non hede! ...

MANKIND.   Owe, Slawthe, thou seyst m(
    skylle!   1224
  Men vse thee mekyl,[5] God it wot. ...

[*Having accepted the Seven Deadly Sins,*
    Mankind rejoices.]

MANKIND.   "Mankynde" I am callyd be
    kynde,
  With curssydnesse in costis knet,
In sowre swettenesse my syth I sende,

---

[1] Food.   [2] Rich, delicate.
[3] Worthless persons, scoundrels.
[4] Mass-bell rings (calling to church).
[5] Much.

With seuene synnys sadde be-set. 1244
Mekyl myrthe I moue in mynde,
With melody at my mowthis met.[1]
My prowd pouer schal I not pende [2]
Tyl I be putte in peynys pyt, 1248
To hellë hent [3] fro hens.
In dale of dole tyl we are downe,
We schul be clad in a gay gowne.
I se no man but they vse somme
Of these vij dedly synnys. . . . 1253

[On the *platea*, the Good Angel sorely mourns. Shrift and Penance come to him, and ask why he laments. The Good Angel answers that he is lamenting for Mankind, whose ruin is near, and begs Shrift to help. Shrift promises to do what he can.]

Then they will go to Mankind [who is still on the scaffold of Covetousness]; and let Shrift say: [4]

SHRIFT. What, Mankynde! Whou [5] goth this?
What dost thou with these deuelys seuene?
Alas, alas! man, al a-mys!
Blysse in the mane [6] of God in heuene,
I rede, so haue I rest. 1344
These lotly lordeynys [7] awey thou lyfte,
And cum doun and speke with Schryfte,
And drawe thee yernë to sum thryfte!
Trewly it is the best. 1348

MANKIND. A, Schryfte! thou art wel be-note [8]
Here to Slawthe, that syttyth here-inne.
He seyth thou mytyst a com to mannys cote [9]
On Palme-Sunday al be tyme. 1352
Thou art com al to sone!
Therfore, Schryfte, be thi fay,
Goo forthe tyl on Good Fryday!
Tente [10] to thee thanne wel I may;
I haue now ellys to done. . . . 1357

[1] Mouth's might (at command).
[2] Limit. [3] Carried off, snatched.
[4] MS. *Tunc ibunt ad Humanum Genus; et dicat Confessio.*
[5] How. [6] Rejoice in the power.
[7] Loathsome rascals. [8] Beknown?
[9] Dwelling. [10] Listen.

[Shrift bids Mankind confess, if he wishes for bliss. Penance, too, urges him to repent. At last Mankind sighs for his sins, and cries to God for mercy.]

MANKIND. Nay, sertis, that schal I not do!
Schryfte, thou schalte the sothë se;
For thow Mankynde be wonte ther-to,
I wyl now al a-mendë me. 1448
I com to thee, Schryfte, al holy, lo!

Then he descends [from the scaffold of Covetous] to Shrift.[1]

I forsake you, synnys, and fro you fle!
Ye schapyn to man a sory scho! [2]
Whanne he is be-gylyd in this degre, 1452
Ye bleykyn al hys ble.[3]
Synne, thou art a sory store! . . .

[Mankind confesses his misdeeds, and Shrift grants him absolution from all his sins. Mankind then requests to be placed where he will be free from the attacks of the Seven Deadly Sins.]

SHRIFT. To swyche a place I schal thee kenne,[4]
Ther thou mayst dwelle with-outyn dystaunsce [5]
And al-wey kepë thee fro synne —
In-to the Castel of Perseueraunce. 1552
If thou wylt to heuene wynne,
And kepe thee fro werldyly dystaunce,
Goo [to] yone Castel, and kepe thee ther-inne,
For [it] is strenger thanne any in Fraunce. 1556
To yone castel I thee seende.
That castel is a precyous place,
Ful of vertu and of grace:
Who-so leuyth there his lyuys space,
No synne schal hym schende.[6] . . .

[Shrift then leads him up to the Castle. Before he is allowed to enter, he is addressed by the ladies who keep the Castle — the Seven Moral Virtues: Meekness, Patience, Charity, Abstinence, Chastity,

[1] MS. *Tunc descendit ad Confessionem.*
[2] Shoe. [3] Bleach all his color.
[4] Direct, guide.
[5] Dissension, enmity. [6] Injure.

Industry, and Generosity — each giving
him good advice. Mankind promises that
he will follow their instructions.]

MANKIND.   Ladys in lond, louely and
        lyt,[1]   1670
  Lykynge lelys, ye be my leche![2] . . .

MEEKNESS.   Mercy may mende al thi
        mone.   1696
  Cum in here at thynne owyn wylle!

[*She opens the gate, and Mankind enters,
while the Virtues sing "Cum sancto
sanctus eris," et cetera.*][3]

We schul thee fendë fro thi fon[4]
If thou kepe thee in this castel stylle.
Stonde here-inne as stylle as ston,
  Thanne schal no dedly synne thee
        spylle:
Whether that synnys cumme or gon, 1702
  Thou schalt with us thi bouris bylle;[5]
    With vertuse we schul thee vaunce.[6]
    This Castel is of so qweynt a gynne,[7]
    That who-so-euere holde hym ther-
        inne,
  He schal neuere fallyn in dedly synne:
  It is the Castel of Perseueranse. 1708
Qui perseuerauerit usque in finem, hic
saluus erit.[8] . . .

Then they sing "Eterne Rex altissime," etc.[9]

[*On the platea.*]

BAD ANGEL.   Nay! be Belyals bryth
        bonys,
  Ther schal he no whyle dwelle!
He schal be wonne fro these wonys,[10]
  With the Werld, the Flesch, and the
        Deuyl of hell!   1721
    Thei schul my wyl a-wreke.
  The synnys seuene, the kyngis thre,
  To Mankynde haue enmyte;
  Scharpely thei schul helpyn me,
    This Castel for to breke.   1726

[1] Gentle.
[2] Amiable fair ones, ye be my physician.
[3] The MS. has written in the margin: *Cum sancto
sanctus eris & cetera.*
[4] Protect from thy foes.
[5] Dwelling build.   [6] Advance.   [7] Device.
[8] Matthew xxiv, 13: "But he that shall endure
unto the end, the same shall be saved."
[9] MS. *Tunc cantabunt "Eterne Rex altissime, &c."*
[10] Dwellings.

Howe! Flypyrgebet Bakbytere!
  Yerne [1] oure message loke thou make!
Blythe a-bowt loke thou bere!
  Sey, Mankynde his synnys hath for-
        sake.   1730
With yene wenchys he wyl hym were;[2]
  Al to holynesse he hath hym take.
In myn hert it doth me dere;[3]
  The bost that tho moderis crake[4] 1734
    My galle gynnyth to grynde.
    Flepyrgebet, ronne up-on a rasche![5]
  Byd the Werld, the Fend, and the
        Flesche
  That they com to fytyn fresche,[6]
    To wynne a-geyn Mankynde. 1739

BACKBITER.   I go! I go, on groundë
        glad!
  Swyfter thannë schyp with rodyr!
I makë men masyd and mad,
  And euery man to kyllyn odyr   1743
    With a sory chere.
  I am glad, be Seynt Jamys of Galys,
  Of schrewdnes to tellyn talys   1746
  Bothyn in Ingelond and in Walys;
    And feyth I haue many a fere.[7]

Then they will go to Belial.[8]

[*On the scaffold of the Devil.*]

[BACKBITER.] Heyl, set in thyn selle! [9]
Heyl, dynge deuyl in thi delle!
Heyl, lowe in helle!
I cum to thee, talys to telle.   1752

BELYAL.   Bakbyter, boy, alwey be holtis
        and hethe,
Sey now, I sey, what tydyngis? Telle me
        the sothe!   1754

BACKBITER.   Teneful [10] talys I may thee
        sey,
  To thee no good, as I gesse!
Mankynde is gon now a-wey
  In-to the Castel of Goodnesse!   1758
Ther he wyl bothe lyuyn and deye,
  In dale of dros tyl deth hym dresse.
Hathe thee forsakyn, forsothe I sey,

[1] Swift.   [2] Guard.   [3] Injure.
[4] Those mothers brag.   [5] Haste.
[6] Fight vigorously.   [7] Companion.
[8] MS. *Tunc ibu[nt] ad Belial.*   [9] Throne.
[10] Painful, distressing.

And all thi werkis, more and lesse! 1762
    To yone Castel he gan to crepe.
Yone modyr, Meknes, sothe to sayn,
And all yene maydnys on yone playn,
For to fytyn thei be ful fayn,
    Mankynde for to kepe.   1767

[*Belial calls for Pride, Envy, and Wrath.*]

Then Pride, Envy, and Wrath turn them-
    selves about.[1]

PRIDE. Syr kynge, what wytte?[2]
We be redy throtis to kytte.[3]   1769
BELYAL. Sey, gadelyngis, haue ye harde
    grace![4]
And euyl deth mote ye deye!
Why lete ye Mankynde fro you pase
In-to yene Castel, fro us a-weye?   1773
    With tene I schal you tey![5]
    Harlotis! at onys
    Fro this wonys![6]
    Be Belyals bonys,[7]
    Ye schul a-beye![8]   1778

And he will beat them to the ground.[9]

[*On the scaffold of the Flesh. Enter Back-*
    biter, running.]

BACKBITER. Heyle, kynge I-calle!
Heyl, prinse, proude prekyd in palle![10]
Heyl, hende in halle!
Heyl, syr kynge! Fayre thee be-falle! 1795

FLESH. Roy Bakbytynge,
Ful redy in robys to rynge,[11]
Ful glad tydynge,   1798
Be Belyalys bonys, I trow thow brynge.

BACKBITER. Ya, for God! owt I crye
On thi too sonys and thi dowtyr yinge!
Glotoun, Slawthe, and Lechery
    Hath put me in gret mornynge.   1803
They let Mankynde gon up hye
In-to yene castel at hys lykynge,
Ther-in for to leue and dye,
    With tho ladys to make endynge,   1807

The flouris fayre and fresche.
He is in the Castel of Perseuerauns,
And put hys body to penauns.
Of hard happe is now thi chauns,
    Syr kynge, mankyndys Flesche.1812

Then the Flesh will call aloud to Gluttony,
    Sloth and Lechery, [*who enter*].[1]

[Flesh abuses them for letting Mankind
slip away, and then administers to them a
sound flogging. Backbiting chuckles at
their misfortune, then rushes away to inform the World.]

[*On the scaffold of the World. Enter*
Backbiter, who, after informing the World
of the loss of Mankind, urges that venge-
ance be taken on the head of Covetousness.]

BACKBITER. Lo, syr Werld, ye moun
    a-gryse[2]
That ye be seruyd on this wyse!
Go pley you with syr Coueytyse
    Tyl his crownë crake!   1853

Then they will blow a horn for Covetousness,
    [*who, hearing it, enters*].[3]

COVETOUSNESS. Syr bolnynge bowde,[4]
Tell me why blowe ye so lowde?   1855

WORLD. Lowde, losel! The deuel thee
    brenne![5]
I prey God geue thee a fowl hap!
Sey, why letyst thou Mankynde
In-to yene castel for to skape?   1859
    I trow thou gynnyst to raue.
    Now, for Mankynde is went,
    Al oure game is schent:[6]
Therfore, a sore dryuynge dent,[7]
    Harlot, thou schalt haue!   1864

Then they will beat him.[8]

COVETOUSNESS. Mercy! mercy! I wyl
    no more!
Thou hast me rappyd with rewly rowtis![9]
I snowre![10] I sobbe! I syë sore! 1867
Myn hed is clateryd al to clowtis![11]. . .

---

[1] MS. *Tunc vertunt Superbia, Inuidia, & Ira.*
[2] What is your mind?
[3] Throats to cut.   [4] Plague take you.
[5] With pain I shall you punish.
[6] Dwellings.   [7] By Belial's bones!
[8] Suffer for it.
[9] MS. *& verberabit eos super terram.*
[10] Proud set in rich clothes.   [11] Reign.

[1] MS. *Tunc Caro clamabit ad Gulam, Accidiam,*
  & Luxuriam.
[2] Be horrified.
[3] MS. *Tunc buccinabunt cornuo ad Auariciam.*
[4] Swelling bold one. [5] Burn. [6] Ruined. [7] Blow.
[8] MS. *Tunc verberant eum.* [9] Pitiful blows.
[10] Scowl, frown. [11] Shaken all to pieces (rags).

[After much boasting, the World, the Flesh, and the Devil severally prepare to attack the Castle of Perseverance and take Mankind thence. Meekness appeals to her sister Virtues to defend Mankind.]

MEEKNESS. Now, my seuene systerys swete,
This day fallyth on us the lot
Mankynde for to schylde and schete [1]
Fro dedly synne and schamely schot. [2]
Hys enmys strayen in the strete   2052
    To spyllë man with spetows spot; [3]
Therfor oure flouris lete now flete, [4]
And kepe we hym, as we haue het, [5] 2055
    Amonge vs in this halle.
Therfor, vij systeris swote,
Lete oure vertus reyne on rote! [6]
This day we wyl be mans bote [7]
A-geyns these deuelys alle.   2060

[Belial first leads his followers, Pride, Wrath, and Envy, against the Castle of Perseverance. Pride, Wrath, and Envy, with foul language, defy in turn Meekness, Patience, and Charity, and are appropriately answered by those Virtues. At last Belial calls upon his followers to stop talking, and assault the Castle.]

BELYAL. What, for Belyalys bonys!
Where a-bowtyn chydë ye?
Haue don, ye boyes, al at onys!   2189
    Lasche don [8] these moderys, allë thre!
Werkë wrakë to this wonys! [9]
The vaunward is grauntyd me.
Do these moderys [10] to makyn monys!
Youre dowty dedys [11] now lete se! 2194
    Dasche hem al to daggys! [12]
Haue do, boyës blo and blake!
Wirke these wenchys wo and wrake!
Claryouns cryith up at a krake, [13]
And blowe your brodë baggys! [14] 2199

Then they will assault the Castle. He that schal pleyc Belyal, loke that he haue gunne-

---

: Shield and guard.
[2] Shame-bringing shot (assault).
[8] Despitous (vexing) disgrace.
[4] Fly (the Virtues throw flowers at the attackers).
[5] Promised.   [6] Reign (or prevail) in a troop.
[7] Help, salvation.   [8] Beat down.
[9] Dwellings.   [10] Make these mothers.
[11] Doughty deeds.   [12] Tatters, rags.
[13] Clarions cry up loudly.   [14] Bag-pipes.

powder brennyn[ge] in pyps in his hands and in his eris and in his ers, whanne he gothe to bat[tel]. [1]

[The Virtues beat them back with roses, emblematic of Christ's passion. With many exclamations of pain, Belial and his followers depart, confessing themselves utterly defeated. Next Flesh assembles his warriors, Gluttony, Sloth, and Lechery, and leads them to an assault upon the Castle. Gluttony abuses Abstinence, Lechery defies Chastity, and Sloth threatens Industry. The Virtues make suitable replies. At last Flesh orders his followers to stop talking and fight.]

FLESH. Ey, for B[e]lyalys bonys, the kynge,
Where-a-bowte stonde ye al day!
Caytyuys! lete be your kakelynge,
And rappe at rowtis of a-ray! [2]   2369
Glotony, thou fowle gadlynge,
Sle [3] Abstynens, if thou may!
Lechery, with thi werkynge,
To Chastyte make a wyckyd a-ray 2372
    A lytyl throwe. [4]
And whyl we fyth
For owre ryth,
In bemys bryth [5]
    Late blastis blowe!   2378

[They assault the Castle, [6] but are beaten back in utter discomfort. Then the World assumes the task of overcoming Mankind. He appeals to Covetousness to "work in the best wise" and make Mankind come away "from yon Virtues all." Covetousness advances alone to the Castle, and addresses Mankind.]

COVETOUSNESS. How, Mankynde! I am a-tenyde [7]
For thou art there so in that holde.
Cum and speke with thi best frende,
    Syr Coueytyse! Thou knowyst me of olde.   2431

---

[1] MS. has merely *Tunc pugnabunt domini.* I have added the stage-direction from the plan of the staging (see p. 264).
[2] Strike at crowds in martial array.
[2] Kill.   [4] Time, while.
[5] Trumpets bright.
[6] MS. *Tunc pugnabunt domini.*   [7] Vexed.

What deuyl! schalt thou ther lenger
   lende [1]
With grete penaunce in that castel
   colde!
In-to the werld, if thou wylt, wende
   A-monge men to bere thee bolde, 2435
   I redë,[2] be seynt Gyle.
How, Mankynde! I thee say,
Com to Coueytyse, I thee prey.
We to schul to-gedyr pley,
   If thou wylt, a whyle. . . .   2440

MANKIND. Coueytyse, whedyr schuld I
   wende?
What wey woldyst that I sulde holde?
To what place woldyst thou me sende?
I gynne to waxyn hory and colde; 2483
My bake gynnyth to bowe and bende;
I crulle [3] and crepe, and wax al colde.
Age makyth man ful vnthende,[4]
   Body and bonys, and al vnwolde.[5] 2487
   My bonys are febyl and sore;
   I am arayed in a sloppe;[6]
   As a yonge man, I may not hoppe;
   My nose is colde, and gynnyth to
      droppe;
   Myn her [7] waxit al hore.   2492

COVETOUSNESS. Petyr! thou hast the
   morë nede
To hauë sum good [8] in thyn age —
Markys,[9] poundys, londys and lede, 2495
   Howsys and homys, castell and cage!
Therfor do as I thee rede!
To Coueytyse cast thi parage! [10]
Cum, and I schal thyne erdyn bede; [11]
   The werthi World schal geue thee
      wage,   2500
   Certis not a lyth. [¹²]
   Com on, olde man! It is no reprefe
   That Coueytysë be thee lefe.[13] . . .

MANKIND. I wyl not do these ladys dys-
   pyt
To forsakyn hem for so lyt.
To dwellyn here is my delyt;
Here arn my best frendis.   2518

COVETOUSNESS. Ya! up and doun thou
   take the wey
Thorwe this werld to walkyn and wende,
And thou schalt fyndë, soth to sey,
   Thi purs schal be thi best[ë] frende. 2522
Thou thou syt al day and prey,
   No man schal com to thee, nor sende;
But if thou haue a peny to pey,
   Men schul to thee thanne lystyn and
      lende,   2526
   And kelyn [1] al thi care.
   Therfore to me thou hange and helde,[2]
   And be coueytous whylys thou may
      thee welde.[3]
   If thou be pore, and nedy, and elde,
   Thou schalt oftyn euyl fare.   2531

MANKIND. Coueytyse, thou seyst a good
   skyl.[4]
So gretë god [5] me [wyl] a-vaunce,
Al thi byddynge don I wyl.
I forsake the Castel of Perseuer-
   aunce;   2535
In Coueytyse I wyl me hyle,[6]
For to gete sum sustynaunce.

Then Mankind descends to Covetousness.[7]

[The Virtues plead with Mankind not to
leave the Castle of Perseverance, pointing
out to him the folly of trusting to worldly
wealth. But the Bad Angel interrupts
them, and says to Mankind:]

BAD ANGEL. Ya! go forthe, and lete the
   qwenys cakle!
Ther wymmen arn are many wordys.
Lete hem gone hoppyn with here hakle! [8]
Ther ges syttyn are many tordys. 2652
With Coueytyse thou renne on rakle,[9]
   And hange thyne hert up on his hordis.
Thou schalt be schakyn in myn schakle; [10]
   Vnbynde thi baggys on his bordis,
      On hys benchys a-boue.   2657
   Parde, thou gost owt of mankynde
   But Coueytyse be in thi mende;

---

[1] Remain.   [2] Advise.   [3] Crawl.
[4] Miserable.   [5] Unwieldy, stiff.
[6] A loose gown.   [7] Hair.   [8] Riches.
[9] A denomination of money, 13*s*., 4*d*.
[10] Lineage; kinship?   [11] Message present.
[¹²] Little.   [13] Be to thee dear.

[1] Cool.   [2] Hold.
[3] Rule, govern.   [4] Sayest a good reason.
[5] Great riches.   [6] Hide.
[7] MS. *Tunc descendit ad Auariciam Humanum
Genus.*
[8] Hopping with their mantles (cf. the stage direction at line 3130).
[9] In haste.   [10] Shackle.

If euere thou thynkë to be thende,[1]
On hym thou ley thi loue.   2661

[Mankind makes his decision, and goes
away with Covetousness, while the Good
Angel laments sorely.]

[*On the scaffold of the World.*]

WORLD.   A, A! This game goth as I wolde.
. Mankynde wyl neuere the Werld for-
sake!
Tyl he be ded, and vndyr molde,
Holy to me he wyl hym take.   2691
To Coveytyse he hath hym yolde;[2]
With my wele [3] he wyl a-wake.
For a thousende pounde I nolde
But Coveytysë were Mans make,[4]   2695
Certys, on euery wyse.
All these gamys he schal be-wayle,
For I, the Werld, am of this entayle;[5]
In hys moste nede I schal hym fayle,
And al for Coveytyse.   2700

[Covetousness leads Mankind to a
"bower" under the Castle, where a bed
and a cupboard are prepared.[6]]

COVETOUSNESS.   Now, Mankynde, be war
of this:
Thou art a party wele in age;
I woldë not thou ferdyst a-mys;
Go we now knowe my castel cage.   2704
In this bowre I schal thee blys;
Worldly wele schal be thi wage;
More mucke thanne is thyne, i-wys,
Take thou in this trost terage,[7]   2708
And loke that thou do wronge.
Coveytyse, it is no sore,
He wyl thee feffen ful of store,
And alwey, alwey, sey "more and
more";
And that schal be thi songe.   2713

MANKIND.   A, Coveytyse, haue thou good
grace!
Certys thou beryst a trewe tonge:
"More and more," in many a place,
Certys, that song is oftyn songe.   2717

---

[1] Prosperous.   [2] Yielded.
[3] Wealth, happiness.   [4] Mate.
[5] Entail; fashion, quality.
[6] See the instructions on page 264.
[7] Trust payment.

I wyste neuere man, be bankis bace,[1]
So seyn, in clay tyl he were clonge: [2]
"I-now, i-now" [3] hadde neuere space;
That ful songe was neuere songe,   2721
Nor I wyl not begynne.
Goode Coveytysë, I thee prey
That I myth with thee pley!
Geue me good inow or that I dey,
To wonne in werldys wynne.[4]   2726

COVETOUSNESS.   Haue here, Mankynde, a
thousend marke!
I, Coveytyse, haue thee this gote.
Thou mayst purchase ther-with bothe
ponde and parke,
And do ther-with mekyl note.   2730
Lene no man here-of, for no karke,[5]
Thou he schuld hangë be the throte,
Monke nor frerë, prest nor clerke;
Ne helpë ther-with chyrche nor
cote,[6]   2734
Tyl deth thi body delue.
Thou he schuld sterue in a caue,
Lete no pore man ther-of haue;
In grene gres tyl thou be graue,
Kepe sum-what for thi selue.   2739

MANKIND.   I vow to God, it is gret hus-
bondry:
Of thee I take these noblys [7] rownde.
I schal me rapyn,[8] and that in hye,
To hyde this gold vnder the grownde.
Ther schal it ly tyl that I dye;   2744
It may be kepte ther saue and sownde.
Thou my neygbore schuld be hangyn
hye,
Ther-of getyth he neythyr peny nor
pownde.   2747
Yit am I not wel at ese;
Now wolde I haue castel wallys,
Strongë stedys and styf in stallys.
With hey holtys [9] and hey hallys,   2751
Coveytyse, thou must me sese.[10]

[Exit Covetousness. Mankind declares
that the burden of his song shall be "more
and more" wealth, and that if he can dwell
in prosperity, he is willing "never to comyn
in hevene."]

---

[1] A metrical tag.   [2] Till he were buried.
[3] "Enough, enough."   [4] Joy, pleasure.
[5] Distress.   [6] Cottage.   [7] A coin.
[8] Hasten.   [9] Woods.   [10] Endow.

[Enter Death with a dart.]

DEATH.   Ow! now it is tyme hye
  To castyn Mankynde to dethys dynt! [1]
In all hys werkis he is vnslye; [2]   2781
  Mekyl of hys lyf he hath myspent.
To Mankynde I ney ny. [3]
  With rewly [4] rappys he schal be rent.
Whanne I com, iche man drede forthi,
  But yit is ther no geyn [i]-went, [5]   2786
    Hey hyl, holte, nyn hethe. [6]
  Ye schul me drede, euery-chone; [7]
  Whanne I come, ye schul grone!
  My name in londe is lefte a-lone:
    I hatte [8] " Drery Dethe." . . .   2791

To Mankynde now wyl I reche; [9]
  He hathe hole hys hert on Coveytyse.
A newe lessun I wyl hym teche,
  That he schal bothe grwcchyn and
    gryse! [10]   2834
No lyf [11] in londe schal ben his leche; [12]
  I schal hym proue of myn empryse; [13]
With this poynt I schal hym breche,
  And wappyn [14] hym in a woful wyse; 2838
    No body schal ben hys bote. [15]

[Goes to Mankind.]

  I schal thee schapyn a schenful
    schappe: [16]
  Now I kylle thee with myn knappe! [17]
  I reche to thee, Mankynde, a rappe
    To thyne hertë rote!   2843

[He strikes him with his dart.]

MANKIND.   A, Deth, Deth! Drye is thi
    dryfte! [18]
Ded is my desteny!
Myn hed is cleuyn al in a clyfte!
  For clappe of carë now I crye;   2847
Myn eye-ledys may I not lyfte;
  Myn braynys waxyn al emptye;
I may not onys myn hod up schyfte. [19]
  With Dethys dynt[ë] now I dey!   2851

---

1 Blow.   2 Unskilful, foolish.
3 Approach near.   4 Pitiful.
5 No help hoped for.
6 High hill, holt, nor heath.   7 Everyone.
8 I am called.   9 Proceed, go
10 Complain and tremble.   11 Person, one.
12 Physician.   13 Prowess.
14 Bewilder, strike.   15 Help.
16 Shape an infamous shape.   17 Blow.
18 Dreary is thy driving.
19 My hood (*qy.* head) up shift (move).

Syr Werld, I am hent!
Werld! Werld! haue me in mende!
Goode syr Werld! helpe now Man-
  kende!
But thou me helpe, Deth schal me
  schende;
  He hat dyth to me a dynt! [1]   2856

Werld! my wyt waxyt wronge;
  I chaunge, bothe hyde and hewe;
Myn eye-ledys waxyn al outewronge; [2]
  But thou me helpe sore it schal me
    rewe!   2860
Now holde that thou haste be-hete [3] me
  longe!
For all felechepys olde and newe,
Lesse me of my peynys stronge!
  Sum bote of balë [4] thou me brewe, 2864
    That I may of thee yelpe! [5]
Werld, for oldë aqweyntawns,
  Helpe me fro this sory chawns!
  Deth hathe lacchyd [6] me with his
    launce!
    I deye but thou me helpe.   2869

WORLD.   Owe, Mankynde, hathe Dethe
    with thee spoke?
A-geyns hym helpyth no wage! [7]
I wold thou were in the erthe be-loke, [8]
  And a-nother hadde thyne erytage! 2873
Oure bonde of loue schal sone be broke;
  In coldë clay schal be thy cage.
Now schal the World on thee be wroke, [9]
  For thou hast don so gret outrage; 2877
    Thi good [10] thou schalt for-goo.
Werldlys good thou hast for-gon,
  And with tottys [11] thou schalt be torn.
Thus haue I seruyd here be-forn,
  A hundryd thousand moo!   2882

MANKIND.   Ow, Werld! Werld! euere
    worthe wo! [12]
And thou, synful Coveytyse,   2884
Whanne that a man schal fro you go,
  Ye werke with hym on a wonder wyse!
The wytte of this werld is sorwe and wo.
  Be ware, good men, of this gyse!

---

1 Given to me a blow.
2 Outwrung (flowing with tears).
3 Promised.   4 Relief from harm.
5 Speak (in praise).   6 Struck.
7 Challenge to fight.   8 Enclosed.
9 Avenged.   10 Goods, riches.
11 Fools.   12 Woe befall thee ever.

Thus hathe he seruyd many on mo.
  In sorwe slakyth al his a-syse; [1]   2890
    He beryth a tenynge [2] tungge!
    Whyl I leyd with hym my lott,
    Ye seyn whou fayre he me be-hett; [3]
    And now he wolde I were a clott
    In colde cley for to clynge. . . . 2895

[After much lamentation, Mankind lies down upon his bed to die.]

Now, alas, my lyf is lak!
  Bitter balys I gynne to brewe!
Certis, a vers that Dauid spak
  I the Sawter,[4] I fynde it trewe: 2986
*Tesaurizat, et ignorat cui congregabit
ea.*[5]
Tresor, tresor, it hathe no tak; [6]
  It is other mens, olde and newe.
Ow, ow! my good gothe al to wrak!
  Sorë may Mankyndë rewe!   2990
    God kepe me fro dyspayr!
    Al my good, with-out[en] fayle,
  I haue gadryd with gret trauayle,
  The Werld hathe ordeynyd of his
    entayle;   2994
  I wot neuere who to be myn eyr.

Now, good men, takythe example at
  me!
  Do for youre self whyl ye han spase!
For many men thus seruyd be
  Thorwe the Werld in dyuerse place.
I bolne and bleyke in blody ble,[7]   3000
  And as a flour fadyth my face.
To helle I schal bothe fare and fle,[8]
  But God me grauntë of his grace.   3003
    I deyë certeynly.
    Now my lyfe I hauë lore.[9]
    Myn hert brekyth. I syhë sore.
  A word may I speke no more.   3007
    I putte me in Godys mercy. [*Dies.*]

[*Mankind's Soul crawls from beneath the*

bed.[1]   *Enter the Good Angel and the Bad
Angel.*]

SOUL.   "Mercy!"   This was my last
  tale
  That euere my body was a-bowth.
But Mercy helpe me in this vale,
  Of dampnynge drynke sore I me
    doute.   3012

[*The Soul goes to the bed and addresses the
Body.*]

Body! thou dedyst brew a byttyr bale,
  To thi lustys whanne gannyst loute! [2]
Thi sely [3] sowle schal ben a-kale.[4]   3015
  I beye thi dedys with rewly rowte; [5]
    And al it is for gyle.
    Euere thou hast be coueytows,
    Falsly to getyn londe and hows;
    To me thou hast brewyn a byttyr
      jows; [6]
      So welaway the whyle!   3021

[*The Soul turns for aid to the Good Angel.*]

Now, swet aungel, what is thi red? [7]
  The ryth red thou me reche!
Now my body is dressyd to ded,
  Helpe now me, and be my leche!   3025
Dyth [8] thou me fro deuelys drede!
  Thy worthy weyë thou me teche!
I hope that God wyl helpyn and be myn
  hed,[9]
    For "Mercy" was my lastë speche:
    Thus made my body his ende. 3030

[*   *   *   *   *   *] [10]

[BAD ANGEL.]   Wyttnesse of al that ben
  a-bowte,
  Syr Coueytyse he had hym owte;
Therfor he schal, with-outyn dowte,
  With me to hellë pytt.   3034

---

[1] See the diagram of the stage, page 264: "Man-kynde-is bed schal be vnder the Castel, and there schal the Sowle lye vnder the bed tyl he schal ryse and pleye."
[2] Bow to, submit to.
[3] Poor, deserving of pity.
[4] Frozen (overwhelmed in suffering).
[5] I pay for thy deeds with pitiful blows (of suffering).
[6] Brewed a bitter juice. E.E.T.S. prints *brokyn*, but the MS. clearly has *brewyn.*
[7] Advice.
[8] Put.
[9] Heed (one who cares for).
[10] A page in the manuscript is here lost, containing, doubtless, the reply of the Good Angel.

[1] Assize, fashion, judgment.
[2] Harm-inflicting.
[3] How fair he promised me.
[4] Psalter.
[5] Psalm xxxviii, 7 (in the Vulgate), xxxix, 6 (in the Authorized Version): "He heapeth up riches, and knoweth not who shall gather them."
[6] Endurance.
[7] I swell and become pale in bloody color.
[8] Go and flee.
[9] Lost.

GOOD ANGEL. Ye, a-las! and welawo!
A-geyns Coueytyse can I not telle.
Resun wyl I fro thee goo;
    For, wrechyd sowle, thou muste to
      helle! 3038
Coueytyse, he was thi fo;
    He hathe thee schapyn a schameful
    schelle.[1]
Thus hathë seruyd many on mo,
    Tyl thei be dyth to dethys delle, 3042
      To byttyr balys bowre.
    Thou muste to peyne, be ryth resun.
    With Coveytyse, for he is chesun,[2]
    Thou art trappyd ful of tresun, 3046
    But Mercy be thi socowre.[3] . . .
                  [Exit.]

[The Soul calls upon Mercy.]

SOUL. Alas, Mercy! thou art to longe!
Of sadde sorwe now may I synge!
Holy Wryt it is ful wronge,
    But Mercy pasë allë thynge. 3064
I am ordeynyd to peynys stronge;
    In wo is dressyd myn wonnynge;[4]
In helle on hokys I schal honge;
    But Mercy fro a wellë sprynge, 3068
      This deuyl wyl haue me a-way.
    Weleaway! I was ful wod
    That I forsoke myn Aungyl Good,
    And with Coueytysë stod
      Tyl that day that I schuld dey. 3073

BAD ANGEL. Ya! why woldyst thou be
    coueytous,
And drawe thee a-gayn to synne?
I schal thee brewe a byttyr jous![5]
    In bolnynnge bondys[6] thou schalt
    brenne; 3077
In hyë helle schal be thyne hous;
    In pycke and ter to grone and grenne,[7]
Thou schalt lye drenkelyd[8] as a movs;
    Ther may no man ther-fro thee werne[9]
    For that ilkë wyll.[10] 3082
    That day the ladys thou for-soke,
    And to my counsel thou thee toke,
    Thou were betyr an-hangyn on hoke
      Up on a jebet hyll. . . . 3086

Now dagge[1] we hens a doggë trot; 3100
    In my dongion I schal thee dere.[2] . . .

Lo! synful tydynge,
Boy, on thi bak I brynge.
Spedely thou sprynge;[3]
Thi *placebo* I schal synge! 3125
    To deuelys delle
    I schal thee bere to helle.
    I wyl not dwelle.

[To the audience.]

Haue good day! I goo to helle! 3129

[He takes the Soul on his back to hell.]

*[On the platea enter the Four Daughters of
God: Mercy, Truth, Righteousness, and
Peace. " The iiij dowteris shul be clad
in mentelys; Merci in wyth, Rythwysnesse in red, al to-gedyr; Trewth in sad
grene, and Pes al in blake." [4]]*

MERCY. A mone I herd of "mercy" meve,[5]
And to me, Mercy, gan crye and call;
But if[6] it haue mercy, sore it schal me
    greve,
    For ellis it schal to hellë fall. 3133
Rythwysnes,[7] my syster cheve,[8]
    Thys ye herde: so dyde we all;
For we were mad frendis leve[9]
    Whanne the Jevys proferyd Criste
    eysyl[10] and gall 3137
      On the Good Fryday.
    God graunted that remission,
    Mercy, and absolicion,
    Thorwe vertu of his passion,
      To no man schuld be seyd
      "nay." 3142

Therfore, my systers, Rytwysnes,
Pes, and Trewthe, to you I tell, —
Whanne man crieth "mercy," and wyl not
    ses, 3145
    Mercy schal be his waschynge well:
    Wytnesse of holy kyrke.

---

[1] Hut, shanty.   [2] The cause.   [3] Succor.
[4] Prepared my dwelling.   [5] Juice.
[6] In swelling bonds.   [7] Groan and grin.
[8] Drowned.   [9] Defend.
[10] Very fiend? While (time)? The MS. may be
kyll (furnace), for its *K* and *w* are much alike.

[1] Jog.   [2] Vex, do harm to.
[3] The text here may be confused. We should expect the fiend to order the lost soul to spring on his
back.
[4] See the instructions accompanying the plan for
staging the play (page 264).
[5] Solicit, beg.   [6] Unless.
[7] Righteousness.   [8] Chief.
[9] Dear friends.   [10] Vinegar.

For the leste drope of blode
  That God bledde on the rode,
  It hadde ben satysfaccion goode
For al Mankyndys werke.... 3151

RIGHTEOUSNESS. Lete hym a-bye his mys-
  dede!
For, thou he lye in hell and stynke,
It schal me neuere ouer-thynke.[1]
As he hath browyn,[2] lete hym drynke! 3163
  The devyl schal qwyte hym his mede.
  Vnus-quisque suum honus portabit.[3] ...

TRUTH. Rytwysnes, my syster fre,
  Your jugement is good and trewe.
In good fayth so thynkit me;
  Late hym his owyn dedis rewe!... 3181

PEACE. Pes, my syster Verite!
  I preye you, Rytwysnes, be stylle!
Lete no man be you dampnyd be,
  Nor demë ye no man to helle. 3207
IIe is on kyn tyl vs thre,[4]
  Thow he haue now not al his wylle.
For his loue, that deyed on tre,
  Late saue Mankynde fro al peryle.... 3211

Rytwysnes and Trewthe, do be my red!
And Mercy, go we to yone hey place!

    [*Points to God's scaffold.*]

We schal enforme the hey Godhed,
  And pray hym to deme[5] this case. 3220
Ye schal tell hym youre entent
  Of Trewthe and of Rytwysnesse;
And we schal pray that his jugement
  May pase be vs,[6] Mercy and Pes. 3224
    All foure, now go we hens
    Wytly[7] to the Trinite;
And, ther schal we sonë se
  What that his jugëment schal be,
    With-owtyn any deffens.[8] 3229

*Then all the Daughters of God ascend to the
  Father; and Truth says:*[9]

TRUTH. Heyl, God al-myth!

---

[1] Trouble.   [2] Brewed.
[3] Galatians vi, 5· "For every man shall bear his
own burden."
[4] He is of one kin to us three.   [5] Judge.
[6] Be rendered by us.   [7] Quickly.
[8] Without remedy or help.
[9] MS. *Tunc ascende[n]t ad Patrem omnes paritores;
et dixit Verita[s].*

We cum, thi dowteris in syth,
Trewth, Mercy, and Ryth,
And Pes, pesyble in fyth.[1]   3233

MERCY. We cum to preve,
If Man, that was thee ful leve,[2]
If he schal cheve[3]
To hell or heuene, be thi leve.   3237

RIGHTEOUSNESS. I, Rytwysnes,
Thi dowtyr, as I ges,
Let me, neuere-the-lesse,
At thi dom[4] putte me in pres.   3241

PEACE. Pesyble kynge!
I, Pes, thi dowtyr yinge,
Here my preyinge
Whanne I pray thee, Lord, of a thynge.3245

GOD. Welcum, in fere,[5]
Bryther thanne blossum on brere,
My dowteris dere!
Cum forth, and stande ye me nere!   3249

TRUTH. Lord, as thou art Kyng of kyngis,
  crownyd with crowne,
    As thou lovyste me, Trewthe, thi
    dowtyr dere,
Lete neuere me, Trewthe, to fall a-downe,
  My feythfful Fadyr, saunz[6] pere! 3253
    Quia veritatem dilexisti.
For in all trewthe standit thi renowne,
  Thi feyth, thi hope, and thi powere.
Lete it be sene, Lord, now, at thi dome,
  That I may haue my trewe prayere 3257
    To do trewthe to Mankynde.
    For if Mankynde be dempte be ryth,
    And not be mercy, most of myth,
    Here my threwthe, Lord, I thee plyth,
    In presun man schal be pynyde.[7]

Lord! whov schuld Mankynde be savyde,
Syn he dyed in dedly synne,
And all thi comaundementis he depravyde,
  And of fals covetyse he wolde neuere
  blyne?[8]...   3266

I pray thee, Lord, as I haue space,
  Late Mankynde haue dew dystresse,

---

[1] Fight.   [2] To thee full dear.   [3] Go.
[4] Judgment.   [5] Together.   [6] Without.
[7] Tormented.   [8] Cease.

In helle fere to be brent.   3310
In peyne loke he be stylle,
Lord, if it be thi wylle,
Or ellys I haue no skylle
Be thi trew jugëment.   3314

MERCY. *O pater maxime, et Deus tocius
consolacionis, qui consolatur nos in
omni tribulacione nostra!* [1]
O thou Fadyr, of mytys moste,
Mercyful God in Trinite!
I am thi dowter, wel thou woste, [2]
And Mercy fro heuene thou browtyst
fre.   3318
Schew me thi grace in euery coste! [3]
In this cas my counforte be!
Lete me, Lord, neuere be loste
At thi jugement, whov-so it be,   3322
Of Mankynde.
Ne had mans synne neuere cum in cas,
I, Mercy, schuld neuere in erthe had
plas;
Therfore graunte me, Lord, thi grace,
That Mankynde may me fynde; 3327

And mercy, Lord, haue on this man,
Aftyr thi mercy, that mekyl [4] is;
Vn-to thi grace that he be tan; [5]
Of thi mercy that he not mys!... 3331

Lord, thou[gh] that man hathe don more
mysse thanne good,
If he dey in very contricioun,
Lord, the lest drope of thi blod   3369
For hys synne makyth satisfaccioun.
As thou deydyst, Lord, on the rode,
Graunt me my peticioun!
Lete me, Mercy, be hys fode, [6]
And graunte hym thi saluacion,   3374
Quia dixisti "misericordiam amabo."
Mercy schal I synge and say,
And *"miserere"* schal I pray
For Mankynde euere and ay;
*Misericordias domini in eternum
cantabo.*   3379

RIGHTEOUSNESS. Rythwys kynge, Lord
God almyth!

I am thi dowter Rythwysnesse.
Thou hast louyd me euere, day and nyth,
As wel as other, as I gesse: 3383
Justicias Dominus justicia dilexit.
Iff thou Mans-kynde fro peyne a-quite,
Thou dost a-geyns thyne owyn processe.
Lete hym in prison to be pyth [1]
For his synne and wyckydnesse!   3387
Of a bone [2] I thee pray:
Ful oftyn he hathe thee, Lord, for-sake,
And to the devyl he hathe hym take;
Lete hym lyn in hellë lake,
Dampnyd for eure and ay!   3392
Quia Deum, qui se genuit, dereliquit....

For if thou take mans sowle to thee
A-geyns thi rythwysnesse,
Thou dost wronge, Lorde, to Trewth and
me,
And puttis us fro oure devnesse. [3]   3435
Lord, lete vs neuere fro thee fle,
Ner streyne vs neuere in stresse,
But late thi dom be by vs thre,
Mankynde in hell to presse,   3439
Lord, I thee be-seche!
For Rythwynes dwellis euere sure
To deme man aftyr his deseruiture;
For, to be dampnyd, it is his vre; [4]
On man I crie wreche. [5]   3444
Letabitur justus cum viderit vindictam. [6]...

PEACE. Pesible kyng in maieste!
I, Pes, thi dowter, aske thee a bone
Of Man, whou-so it be.   3486
Lord, graunte me myn askynge sone,
That I may euermore dwelle with thee,
As I haue euere yit done,
And lat me neuere fro thee fle,
Specialy at thi dome   3491
Of Man, thi creature.
Thou my systers, Ryth and Trewthe,
Of Mankynde haue non rewthe,
Mercy and I ful sore vs mewythe [7]
To cacche hym to our cure. [8] ...3496

Lord, for thi pyte, and that pes
Thou sufferyst in thi pascioun —

---

[1] II Corinthians i, 4: "O greatest Father, and the
God of all comfort, who comforteth us in all our trib-
ulation."
[2] Knowest.   [3] Way, region (a metrical tag).
[4] Great.   [5] Taken.   [6] Food.

[1] Set, put.   [2] Boon, favor.   [3] Right.
[4] Destiny? hour?   [5] Vengeance.
[6] Psalm lvii, 11 (in the Vulgate), lviii, 10 (in the
Authorized Version): "The righteous shall rejoice
when he seeth the vengeance."
[7] Move.   [8] To take him to our charge.

Boundyn and betyn, with-out les,[1]
  Fro the fote to the croun,   3552
Tanquam ouis ductus es.
Whanne *gutte sangu[in]is* ran adoun,
Yit the Jves wolde not ses,   3555
But on thyn hed thei thryst a croun,
  And on the cros thee naylyd —
As petously as thou were pynyd,[2]
  Haue mercy of Mankynde,
  So that he may fynde
  Oure prayer may hym a-vayle! 3561

THE FATHER (*sitting in his throne*).[3] *Ego cogito cogitaciones pacis, non affliccionis.*[4]

Fayre falle thee, Pes, my dowter dere!
  On thee I thynke, and on Mercy.
Syn ye a-cordyd beth all in fere,
  My jugement I wyl geue you by,   3565
Not aftyr deseruynge, to do reddere,[5]
  To dampne Mankynde to turmentry,
But brynge hym to my blysse ful clere,
  In heuene to dwelle endelesly,   3569
  At your prayere for-thi.
To make my blysse perfyth,
  I menge[6] with my most myth,
Alle pes, sum treuthe, and sum ryth,
  And most of my mercy.   3574

   Let him say to the Daughters:[7]

Misericordia Domini plena est terra. *Amen!*
My dowters hende,
Lufly and lusti to lende,[8]
Goo to yone fende,
And fro hym take Mankynde!   3578
  Brynge hym to me!
  And set hym here be my kne,
  In heuene to be,
  In blysse with gamyn and gle.[9]   3582

TRUTH. We schal fulfylle
Thin hestis,[10] as resun and skylle,[11]
Fro yone gost grylle,[12]
Mankynde to brynge thee tylle.   3586

Then all the Daughters of God ascend to the

Bad Angel [on the scaffold of Hell]; and let Peace say:[1]

PEACE. A, thou foule wyth![2]
Lete go that soule so tyth![3]
In he[ue]ne lyth
Mankynde sone schal be pyth.[4]   3590

RIGHTEOUSNESS. Go thou to helle,
Thou devyl bold as a belle,
Ther-in to dwelle,
In bras and brimston to welle![5]   3594

Then [leading the Soul of Mankind] they shall ascend to the throne [of God].[6]

MERCY. Lo here Mankynde,
Lyter thanne lef is on lynde!
That hath ben pynyd,[7]
Thi mercy, Lord, lete hym fynde!   3598

THE FATHER (*sitting in judgment*).[8] *Sicut sintille in medio maris.*

My mercy, Mankynde, geue I thee.
  Cum, syt at my rth honde!
Ful wel haue I louyd thee,
  Vnkynde thow I thee fonde.   3602
As a sparke of fyre in the se,
  My mercy is synne quenchande.[9]
Thou hast cause to love me
  A-bovyn al thynge in lande,   3606
    And kepe my comaundement.
  If thou me loue and drede,
  Heuene schal be thi mede;
  My face thee schal fede.
  This is myn Jugèment.   3611
Ego occidam, et viuificabo; percuciam et sanabo; et nemo est qui de manu mea possit eruere.[10]

Kyng, kayser, knyt and kampyoun,[11]
Pope, patriark, prest, and prelat in pes,
Duke dowtyest in dede be dale and be doun,   3614
Lytyl and mekyl, the more and the les,

---

[1] Without lie, in truth.   [2] Tormented.
[3] MS. *Pater sedens in trono.*
[4] Jeremiah xxix, 11: "I think thoughts of peace, not of evil." The verse is not quoted exactly.
[5] Harshness.   [6] Mix.
[7] MS. *Dicat filiabus.*
[8] To dwell (a metrical tag).
[9] Mirth and joy.   [10] Commands.
[1] As is right and proper.   [12] Horrid.

---

[1] MS. *Tunc ascendent ad Malum Angelum omnes paritores; et dicat Pax.*
[2] Wight.   [3] Quickly.
[4] Set, put.   [5] Boil.
[6] MS. *Tunc ascendant ad tronum.*
[7] Imprisoned; tortured.
[8] MS. *Pater sedens in Judi[cio].*
[9] Quenching.
[10] Deuteronomy xxxii, 39: "I kill, and I make alive; I wound and I heal; neither is there any that can deliver out of my hand."
[11] Champion.

All the statis of the werld, is at myn renoun;[1]
  To me schal thei geue a-compt at my
    dygne des.[2]
Whanne Myhel[3] his horn blowith at my
  dred dom,
  The count of here conscience schal put-
    ten hem in pres   3619
    And yelde a reknynge
  Of here space whou they han spent;
  And of here trew talent,
    At my gret Jugëment,
    An answere schal me brynge. 3624

Ecce! requiram gregem meum de manu
pastorum.

And I schal inquire of my flok and of here
  pasture,
  Whou they haue leuyd, and led here
    peple soiet.[4]
The goode, on the ryde syd schal stond ful
  sure;
  The badde on the lyfte syd, ther schal I
    set.   3628
The vij dedis of mercy, who-so hadde vre
  To fylle [5] — the hungry for to geue mete;
Or drynke to thrysty; the nakyd, vesture;
  The pore or the pylgrym, hom for to
    fette;   3632
    Thi neybour that hath nede;
  Who-so doth mercy to his myth,

To the seke,[1] or in presun pyth,[2]
  He doth to me — I schal hym
    qvyth:[3]
  Heuene blys schal be his mede. 3637

Et qui bona egerunt, ibunt in vitam
eternam: qui vero mala, in ignem
eternum.

And thei that wel do in this werld here,
  welthe schal a-wake;[4]
  In heuene thei schal heynyd [5] [be] in
    bounte and [in] blys;
And thei that evyl do, thei schul to hellë
  lake,
  In bytter balys to be brent: my jugë-
    ment it is.   3641
My vertus in heuene thanne schal thei
  qwake:
  Ther is no wyth [6] in this werld that may
    skape this!
All men example here-at may take,
  To mayntein the goode, and mendyn
    here mys.   3645

    [To the audience.]

  Thus endyth oure gamys!
  To saue you fro synnynge,
  Evyr at the begynnynge
  Thynke on youre last endynge!
    Te, Deum, laudamus!   3650

---

[1] Under my control.   [2] Worthy throne.
[3] Michael.   [4] Subject.
[5] Was accustomed to perform.

[1] Sick.   [2] Those in prison put.
[3] Reward.   [4] Well-being, bliss, shall awake.
[5] Exalted.   [6] Wight, being.

[The end.]

Hec sunt nomina ludorum.

In primis, II VEXILLATORES.
MUNDUS, *et cum eo,* VOLUPTAS, STULTICIA,
  et GARCIO.
BELYAL, *et cum eo* SUPERBIA, IRA, *et* INVIDIA.
CARO, *et cum eo* GULA, LUXURIA, *et* AC-
  CIDI[A].
HUMANUM GENUS, *et cum eo* BONUS
  ANGELUS *et* MALUS ANGELUS.
AUARICIA.
DETRACCIO.
CONFESSIO.
PENITENTIA.
HUMILITAS.

PACIENCIA.
CARITAS.
ABSTINENCIA.
CASTITAS.
SOLICITUDO.
LARGITAS.
MORS.
ANIMA.
MISERICORDIA.
VERITAS.
JUSTICIA.
PAX.
PATER, *sedens in trono.*

Summa, xxxvj *ludores.*[1]

[1] Only thirty-five players are mentioned.

EVERYMAN [1]

[DRAMATIS PERSONÆ

GOD.	GOOD DEEDS.
EVERYMAN.	KNOWLEDGE.
DEATH.	CONFESSION.
GOOD FELLOWSHIP.	BEAUTY.
KINDRED.	STRENGTH.
COUSIN.	DISCRETION.
GOODS.	FIVE WITS.

MESSENGER.
ANGEL.
DOCTOR.]

HERE BEGYNNETH A TREATYSE HOW YE HYE FADER OF HEUEN SENDETH
DETHE TO SOMON EUERY CREATURE TO COME AND GYUE
ACOUNTE OF THEYR LYUES IN THIS WORLDE,
AND IS IN MANER OF A MORALL
PLAYE.

[Enter a Messenger as a Prologue.]

MESSENGER.   I pray you all gyue your
    audyence,
And here this mater with reuerence,
By fygure [1] a morall playe.
"The Somonynge of Eueryman" called it is,
That of our lyues and endynge shewes   5
How transytory we be all daye.
This mater is wonder[ou]s precyous;
But the entent [2] of it is more gracyous,
And swete to bere awaye.
The story sayth: — Man, in the begyn-
    nynge   10
Loke well, and take good heed to the en-
    dynge,
Be you neuer so gay!

[1] In form.   [2] Meaning, import (moral lesson).

Ye thynke synne in the begynnynge full
    swete,
Whiche in the ende causeth the soule to wepe
Whan the body lyeth in claye.   15
Here shall you se how Falawshyp, and
    Iolyte,
Bothe Strengthe, Pleasure, and Beaute,
Wyll fade from the as floure in Maye;
For ye shall here how our Heuen Kynge
Calleth Eueryman to a generall reken-
    ynge.   20
Gyue audyence, and here what he doth
    saye.   [Exit.]

God speketh [from above]. [1]

GOD.   I perceyue, here in my maieste,

[1] Probably he did not come upon the stage, but
spoke from a high place.

---

[1] *Everyman*, the finest of the moralities, is doubtless derived from the Dutch *Elckerlijk*, though some scholars maintain that both plays go back to a common source.   In spite of its foreign origin, it is thoroughly English in spirit, and had a vogue with English audiences and early English readers — the fact that four different
editions are extant, all appearing shortly after 1500, is sufficient evidence of its popularity — that justifies its
inclusion in this volume.   The date of its composition is a matter of conjecture; yet we may safely assume
that the play was written before the close of the fifteenth century.

Four copies are preserved, two perfect and two fragmentary, of four separate editions, no one of which is
dated; bibliographical evidence, however, indicates that they were all printed after 1508, and, at the latest
before 1537.   I have based the present text on the Britwell copy (B) as reprinted by W. W. Greg in the *Materialien* Series, 1904 (*corrigenda* in *Materialien*, 1910), which seems to give, on the whole, the most satisfac-
tory text; but I have carefully compared this with the Huth copy (H), the British Museum fragment (M),
and the Douce fragment (D), and have introduced what seemed to me better readings when such appeared.
All changes in the text are recorded in footnotes.   A full bibliographical and textual study of the play may be
found in Greg's *Everyman*, in the *Materialien* Series, 1910.   I have inserted my own punctuation and stage-
directions, and have normalized the catch-names of the speakers.

How that all creatures be to me vnkynde,
Lyuynge without drede in worldely pros-
    peryte.
Of ghostly syght [1] the people be so blynde,
Drowned in synne, they know me not for
    theyr God. 26
In worldely ryches is all theyr mynde;
They fere not my ryghtwysnes, the sharpe
    rod; [2]
My lowe [3] that I shewed whan I for them
    dyed
They forgete clene, and shedynge of my
    blode rede; 30
I hanged bytwene two, it can not be de-
    nyed;
To gete them lyfe I suffred to be deed;
I heled theyr fete, with thornes hurt was
    my heed.
I coude do no more than I dyde, truely;
And nowe I se the people do clene forsake
    me. 35
They vse the seuen deedly synnes damp-
    nable.
As pryde, coueytyse, wrathe, and lechery
Now in the worlde be made commendable;
And thus they leue of aungelles, ye heuenly
    company.
Euery man lyueth so after his owne pleas-
    ure, 40
And of theyr lyfe they be nothynge sure.
I se the more that I them forbere
The worse they be fro [4] yere to yere;
All that lyueth appayreth [5] faste.
Therefore I wyll, in all the haste, 45
Haue a rekenynge of euery mannes per-
    sone;
For, and I leue the people thus alone
In theyr lyfe and wycked tempestes,
Veryly they wyll become moche worse
    than beestes;
For now one wolde by enuy another vp
    ete; 50
Charyte they do all clene forgete.
I hoped well that euery man
In my glory shulde make his mansyon;
And thereto I had them all electe.
But now I se, lyke traytours deiecte, 55
They thanke me not for ye pleasure that I
    to them ment,

Nor yet for theyr beynge [1] that I them
    haue lent.
I profered the people grete multytude of
    mercy,
And fewe there be that asketh it hertly. 59
They be so combred with worldly ryches
That nedes on them I must do iustyce,
On euery man lyuynge, without fere.
Where art thou Deth, thou myghty mes-
    sengere?

[Enter Death.]

DEATH. Almyghty God, I am here at your
    wyll,
Your commaundement to fulfyll. 65
GOD. Go thou to Eueryman,
And shewe hym, in my name,
A pylgrymage he must on hym take,
Which he in no wyse may escape;
And that he brynge with hym a sure reken-
    ynge, 70
Without delay or ony taryenge.

[God withdraws.]

DEATH. Lorde, I wyll in the worlde go
    renne [2] ouer all,
And cruelly out-serche bothe grete and
    small.
Euery man wyll I beset that lyueth beestly
Out of Goddes lawes, and dredeth not
    foly. 75
He that loueth rychesse I wyll stryke with
    my darte,
His syght to blynde, and fro heuen to de-
    parte [3] —
Excepte that almes be his good frende —
In hell for to dwell, worlde without ende.

[Enter Everyman at a distance.]

Loo, yonder I se Eueryman walkynge. 80
Full lytell he thynketh on my comynge;
His mynde is on flesshely lustes, and his
    treasure;
And grete payne it shall cause hym to en-
    dure
Before the Lorde, heuen['s] Kynge.

[Death halts Everyman.]

Eueryman, stande styll! Whyder arte
    thou goynge 85
Thus gayly? Hast thou thy maker forgete?

---

[1] Spiritual insight.   [2] H. *rod;* B. *rood.*
[3] Love. B. and H. *lawe.*
[4] From. (So frequently.)   [5] Becometh worse.

[1] Being, life.   [2] Run.   [3] Sunder.

EVERYMAN. Why askest thou?
Woldest thou wete? [1]
DEATH. Ye, syr; I wyll shewe you:
In grete hast I am sende to the   90
Fro God out of his Mageste.
EVERYMAN. What! sente to me?
DEATH. Ye, certaynly.
Thoughe thou haue forgete hym here,
He thynketh on the in the heuenly spere,[2]
As, or we departe, thou shalte knowe!   96
EVERYMAN. What desyreth God of me?
DEATH. That shall I shewe thee:
A rekenynge he wyll nedes haue
Without ony lenger [3] respyte.   100
EVERYMAN. To gyue a rekenynge longer
layser [4] I craue.
This blynde mater troubleth my wytte.
DEATH. On the thou must take a longe
iourney;
Therfore thy boke of counte with the thou
brynge,   104
For turne agayne thou can not by no waye.
And loke thou be sure of thy rekenynge,
For before God thou shalte answere and
shewe
Thy many badde dedes, and good but a fewe,
How thou hast spente thy lyfe, and in what
wyse,
Before the Chefe Lorde of paradyse.   110
Haue ado that [5] we were in that waye,
For wete thou well thou shalte make none
attournay.[6]
EVERYMAN. Full vnredy I am suche rek-
enynge to gyue.
I knowe the not. What messenger arte
thou?
DEATH. I am Dethe, that no man dred-
eth;[7]   115
For euery man I rest,[8] and no man spareth;
For it is Goddes commaundement
That all to me sholde be obedyent.
EVERYMAN. O Deth! thou comest whan I
had ye leest in mynde!
In thy power it lyeth me to saue;   120
Yet of my good [9] wyl I gyue ye, yf thou wyl
be kynde;
Ye, a thousande pounde shalte thou haue,
And [thou] dyfferre this mater tyll an other
daye.

DEATH. Eueryman, it may not be, by no
waye!
I set not by golde, syluer, nor ryoh-
esse,   125
Ne by pope, emperour, kynge, duke, ne
prynces;
For, and I wolde receyue gyftes grete,
All the worlde I myght gete;
But my custome is clene contrary.
I gyue the no respyte. Come hens, and not
tary!   130
EVERYMAN. Alas! shall I haue no lenger
respyte?
I may saye Deth geueth no warnynge!
To thynke on the it maketh my herte seke,
For all vnredy is my boke of rekenynge.
But twelue yere and I myght haue abyd-
ynge,   135
My countynge-boke I wolde make so clere
That my rekenynge I sholde not nede to
fere.
Wherfore, Deth, I praye the, for Goddes
mercy,
Spare me tyll I be prouyded of remedy!
DEATH. The auayleth not to crye, wepe,
and praye;   140
But hast the lyghtly that thou wert [1] gone
that iournaye!
And preue thy frendes, yf thou can;
For wete thou well the tyde abydeth no
man;
And in the worlde eche lyuynge creature
For Adams synne must dye of nature.[2] 145
EVERYMAN. Dethe, yf I sholde this pyl-
grymage take,
And my rekenynge suerly make,
Shewe me, for Saynt Charyte,
Sholde I not come agayne shortly?
DEATH. No, Eueryman; and thou be ones
there,   150
Thou mayst neuer more come here,
Trust me veryly.
EVERYMAN. O gracyous God in the hye
sete celestyall,
Haue mercy on me in this moost nede!
Shall I haue no company fro this vale teres-
tryall   155
Of myne acqueyn[taun]ce that way me to
lede?
DEATH. Ye, yf ony be so hardy

---

[1] Know.   [2] Sphere.   [3] Longer.
[4] Leisure.   [5] B. *Haue I do we;* I follow H.
[6] Attorney.   [7] That respecteth no man.
[8] Arrest.   [9] Goods, riches.

[1] B. H. *were.*
[2] By course of nature (i.e. without escape).

That wolde go with the and bere the company.

Hye the that thou wert [1] gone to Goddes magnyfycence,

Thy rekenynge to gyue before his presence.   160

What! wenest thou thy lyue is gyuen the,

And thy worldely gooddes also?

EVERYMAN.   I had wende so, veryle.

DEATH.   Nay, nay; it was but lende the;

For, as soone as thou arte go,   165

Another a whyle shall haue it, and than go therfro,

Euen as thou hast done.

Eueryman, thou arte mad! [2]   Thou hast thy wyttes fyue,

And here on erthe wyll not amende thy lyue;

For sodeynly I do come.   170

EVERYMAN.   O wretched caytyfe! wheder shall I flee

That I myght scape this endles sorowe?

Now, gentyll Deth, spare me tyll to-morowe,

That I may amende me

With good aduysement.   175

DEATH.   Naye; therto I wyll not consent,

Nor no man wyll l respyte;

But to the herte sodeynly I shall smyte

Without ony aduysement.

And now out of thy syght I wyll me hy.

Se thou make the redy shortely,   181

For thou mayst saye this is the daye

That no man lyuynge may scape awaye.

[*Exit Death.*]

EVERYMAN.   Alas! I may well wepe with syghes depe!

Now haue I no maner of company   185

To helpe me in my iourney and me to kepe;

And also my wrytynge is full vnredy.

How shall I do now for to excuse me?

I wolde to God I had neuer be gete! [3]   189

To my soule a full grete profyte it had be;

For now I fere paynes huge and grete.

The tyme passeth.   Lorde, helpe, that all wrought!

For though I mourne it auayleth nought;

The day passeth, and is almoost ago. [4]

I wote not well what for to do.   195

[1] B. H. *were.*   [2] B. *made;* H. *mad.*
[3] Been born.   [4] Gone by.

To whome were I best my complaynt to make?

What and [1] I to Felawshyp therof spake,

And shewed hym of this sodeyne chaunce?

For in hym is all myne affyaunce, [2]

We haue in the worlde so many a daye

Be good frendes in sporte and playe.   201

I se hym yonder certaynely.

I trust that he wyll bere me company,

Therfore to hym wyll I speke to ese my sorowe.

Well mette, Good Felawshyp! and good morowe!   205

Felawshyp speketh.

FELLOWSHIP.   Eueryman, good morowe, by this daye!

Syr, why lokest thou so pyteously?

If ony thynge be amysse, I praye the me saye,

That I may helpe to remedy.

EVERYMAN.   Ye, Good Felawshyp, ye;

I am in greate ieoparde.   211

FELLOWSHIP.   My true frende, shewe to me your mynde;

I wyll not forsake the to my lyues ende

In the waye of good company.

EVERYMAN.   That was well spoken, and louyngly!   215

FELLOWSHIP.   Syr, I must nedes knowe your heuynesse;

I haue pyte to se you in ony dystresse.

If ony haue you wronged, ye shall reuenged be,

Thoughe I on the grounde be slayne for the,

Though that I knowe before that I sholde dye!   220

EVERYMAN.   Veryly, Felawshyp, gramercy.

FELLOWSHIP.   Tusshe! by thy thankes I set not a strawe!

Shewe me your grefe, and saye no more.

EVERYMAN.   If I my herte sholde to you breke,

And than you to tourne your mynde fro me   225

And wolde not me comforte whan ye here me speke,

Than sholde I ten tymes soryer be.

FELLOWSHIP.   Syr, I saye as I wyll do, indede.

[1] If. (So frequently.)   [2] Trust.

EVERYMAN.   Than be you a good frende at
    nede!
I haue founde you true here before.   230
FELLOWSHIP.   And so ye shall euermore;
For, in fayth, and thou go to hell
I wyll not forsake the by the waye.
EVERYMAN.   Ye speke lyke a good frende!
    I byleue you well.
I shall deserue it, and I may.   235
FELLOWSHIP.   I speke of no deseruynge,
    by this daye!
For he that wyll saye, and nothynge do,
Is not worthy with good company to go.
Therfore shewe me the grefe of your
    mynde,
As to your frende mooste louynge and
    kynde.   240
EVERYMAN.   I shall shewe you how it is:
Commaunded I am to go a iournaye —
A longe waye, harde, and daungerous —
And gyue a strayte counte, without delaye,
Before the hye Iuge, Adonay.[1]   245
Wherfore, I pray you, bere me company,
As ye haue promysed, in this iournaye.
FELLOWSHIP.   That is mater indede!
    Promyse is duty;
But, and I sholde take suche a vyage on
    me,
I knowe it well, it shulde be to my payne.
Also it make[th] me aferde, certayne.   251
But let vs take counsell here, as well as we
    can;
For your wordes wolde fere [2] a stronge
    man.
EVERYMAN.   Why, ye sayd yf I had nede
Ye wolde me neuer forsake, quycke ne
    deed,[3]   255
Thoughe it were to hell, truely.
FELLOWSHIP.   So I sayd, certaynely!
But suche pleasures be set asyde, the sothe
    to saye.
And also, yf we toke suche a iournaye,
Whan sholde we come agayne? [4]   260
EVERYMAN.   Naye, neuer agayne, tyll the
    daye of dome!
FELLOWSHIP.   In fayth! than wyll not I
    come there!

---

[1] One of the names given in the Old Testament to
God.
[2] Frighten.
[3] Alive nor dead.
[4] Possibly for the rhyme this should be *agayne
come.*

Who hath you these tydynges brought?
EVERYMAN.   Indede, Deth was with me
    here.
FELLOWSHIP.   Now, by God, that all
    hathe bought,   265
If Dethe were the messenger,
For no man that is lyuynge to-daye
I wyll not go that lothe [1] iournaye —
Not for the fader that bygate me!
EVERYMAN.   Ye promysed otherwyse,
    parde.   270
FELLOWSHIP.   I wote well I sayd [2] so,
    truely.
And yet, yf thou wylte ete, and drynke,
    and make good chere,
Or haunt to women the lusty company,
I wolde not forsake you whyle the daye is
    clere,
Truste me, veryly.   275
EVERYMAN.   Ye, therto ye wolde be
    redy!
To go to myrthe, solas, and playe,
Your mynde wyll soner apply,
Than to bere me company in my longe
    iournaye.
FELLOWSHIP.   Now, in good fayth, I wyll
    not that waye.   280
But and thou wylte [3] murder, or ony man
    kyll,
In that I wyll helpe the with a good wyll.
EVERYMAN.   O, that is a symple aduyse,
    indede.
Gentyll Felaw[ship]e, helpe me in my neces-
    syte!
We haue loued longe, and now I nede;
And now, gentyll Felawshyp, remenbre
    me!   286
FELLOWSHIP.   Wheder ye haue loued me
    or no,
By Saynt Iohan, I wyll not with the go!
EVERYMAN.   Yet, I pray the, take ye la-
    bour, and do so moche for me
To brynge me forwarde,[4] for Saynt Char-
    yte,   290
And comforte me tyll I come without the
    towne.
FELLOWSHIP.   Nay, and thou wolde gyue
    me a newe gowne,
I wyll not a fote with the go!

---

[1] H. *lothesome.*   [2] B. *say;* H. *sayd.*
[3] B. *wyll;* H. *wylte.*
[4] Accompany me, escort me.

But, and thou had taryed, I wolde not haue
    lefte the so.
And as now God spede the in thy iour-
    naye! 295
For from the I wyll departe as fast as I
    maye.
EVERYMAN. Wheder awaye, Felawshyp?
    Wyll you forsake me?
FELLOWSHIP. Ye, by my faye! To God I
    betake [1] the.
EVERYMAN. Farewell, Good Falawshyp!
    for ye my herte is sore.
Adewe for euer! I shall se the no more!
FELLOWSHIP. In fayth, Eueryman, fare
    well now at the ende! 301
For you I wyll remembre that partynge is
    mournynge.

[Exit Fellowship.]

EVERYMAN. Alacke! shall we thus [2] de-
    parte indede
(A, Lady helpe!) without ony more com-
    forte?
Lo, Felawshyp forsaketh me in my moost
    nede. 305
For helpe in this worlde wheder [3] shall I re-
    sorte?
Felawshyp here before with me wolde mery
    make,
And now lytell sorowe for me dooth he
    take.
It is sayd, "In prosperyte men frendes may
    fynde, 309
Whiche in aduersyte be full vnkynde."
Now wheder [3] for socoure shall I flee,
Syth that Felawshyp hath forsaken me?
To my kynnesmen I wyll, truely,
Prayenge them to helpe me in my neces-
    syte.
I byleue that they wyll do so, 315
For "kynde wyll crepe where it may not
    go."
I wyll go saye,[4] for yonder I se them go.
Where be ye now, my frendes and kynnes-
    men?

[Enter Kindred and Cousin.]

KINDRED. Here be we now, at your com-
    maudement.
Cosyn, I praye you shewe vs your entent

In ony wyse, and do not [1] spare. 321
COUSIN. Ye, Eueryman, and to vs declare
Yf ye be dysposed to go ony whyder;
For, wete you well, we [2] wyll lyue and dye
    togyder.
KINDRED. In welth and wo we wyll with
    you holde,[3] 325
For ouer his kynne a man may be bolde.
EVERYMAN. Gramercy, my frendes and
    kynnesmen kynde.
Now shall I shewe you the grefe of my
    mynde.
I was commaunded by a messenger
That is a hye kynges chefe offycer; 330
He bad me go a pylgrymage, to my payne;
And I knowe well I shall neuer come
    agayne:
Also I must gyue a rekenynge strayte,
For I haue a grete enemy that hath me in
    wayte,
Whiche entendeth me for to hynder. 335
KINDRED. What a[c]counte is that whiche
    ye must render?
That wolde I knowe.
EVERYMAN. Of all my workes I must
    shewe
How I haue lyued, and my dayes spent;
Also of yll dedes that I haue vsed 340
In my tyme syth lyfe was me lent,
And of all vertues that I haue refused.
Therfore, I praye you, go thyder with me
To helpe to make myn accounte, for Saynt
    Charyte.
COUSIN. What! to go thydr? Is that
    the mater? 345
Nay, Eueryman, I had leuer fast brede and
    water [4]
All this fyue yere and more.
EVERYMAN. Alas, that euer I was bore!
For now shall I neuer be mery,
If that you forsake me. 350
KINDRED. A, syr, what! ye be a mery
    man!
Take good herte to you, and make no
    mone.
But one thynge, I warne you, by Saynt
    Anne —

---

[1] B. *and not;* M. *and nat;* H. *and do not.*
[2] *We* added in H. and M.
[3] B. exchanges the rhyme-words *holde* and *bolde;*
correct in H. and M.
[4] A proverbial phrase, meaning to abstain from
all food save bread and water.

---

[1] Hand over, commit.   [2] B. *this;* H. *thus.*
[3] Whither.   [4] Assay, put it to trial.

As for me, ye shall go alone!

EVERYMAN.   My Cosyn, wyll you not
with me go?   355

COUSIN.   No, by Our Lady!   I haue the
crampe in my to[e].

Trust not to me; for, so God me spede,
I wyll deceyue you in your moost nede.

KINDRED.   It auayleth not vs to-tyse.[1]
Ye shall haue my mayde with all my
herte;   360
She loueth to go to feestes, there to be
nyse,
And to daunce, and abrode to sterte:[2]
I wyll gyue her leue to helpe you in that
iourney,
If that you and she may agree.

EVERYMAN.   Now, shewe me the very effecte of your mynde;   365
Wyll you go with me, or abyde behynde?

KINDRED.   Abyde behynde? ye, that wyll
I, and I maye!
Therfore farewell tyll another daye.

[Exit Kindred.]

EVERYMAN.   Howe sholde I be mery or
gladde?
For fayre promyses men to me make,   370
But whan I haue moost nede they me for-
sake.
I am deceyued; that maketh me sadde.

COUSIN.   Cosyn Eueryman, farewell now;
For veryly I wyll not go with you.
Also of myne owne lyfe [3] an vnredy reken-
ynge   375
I haue to accounte; therfore I make tary-
enge.
Now God kepe the, for now I go.

[Exit Cousin.]

EVERYMAN.   A Iesus! is all come hereto?
Lo, fayre wordes maketh fooles fayne;
They promyse, and nothynge wyll do cer-
tayne.   380
My kynnesmen promysed me faythfully
For to abyde with me stedfastly;
And now fast awaye do they flee.
Euen so Felawshyp promysed me.   384
What frende were best me of to prouyde?
I lose my tyme here longer to abyde;

Yet in my mynde a thynge there is:
All my lyfe I haue loued ryches;
If that my Good now helpe me myght
He wolde make my herte full lyght.   390
I wyll speke to hym in this dystresse.
Where arte thou, my Gooddes and ryches?

GOODS *[within].*   Who calleth me? Euery-
man?   What! hast thou haste?
I lye here in corners, trussed and pyled so
hye,
And in chestes I am locked so fast, 395
Also sacked in bagges — thou mayst se
with thyn eye —
I can not styre.   In packes, lowe, I lye.
What wolde ye haue? lyghtly me saye.

EVERYMAN.   Come hyder, Good, in al the
hast thou may;
For of counseyll I must desyre the. 400

[Enter Goods.]

GOODS.   Syr, and ye in the worlde haue
sorowe or aduersyte,
That can I helpe you to remedy shortly.

EVERYMAN.   It is another dysease [1] that
greueth me;
In this worlde it is not, I tell the so;
I am sent for an other way to go,   405
To gyue a strayte counte generall
Before the hyest Iupyter of all;
And all my lyfe I haue had ioye and pleas-
ure in the,
Therfore, I pray the, go with me;
For, parauenture, thou mayst before God
Almyghty   410
My rekenynge helpe to clene and puryfye;
For it is sayd euer amonge
That "money maketh all ryght that is
wronge."

GOODS.   Nay, Eueryman; I synge an
other songe!
I folowe no man in suche vyages;   415
For, and I wente with the,
Thou sholdes fare much the worse for
me;
For bycause on me thou dyd set thy
mynde,
Thy rekenynge I haue made blotted and
blynde,
That thyne accounte thou can not mak
truly —   420
And that hast thou for the loue of me!

---

[1] To induce by the offer of advantage.
[2] Rush.
[3] *Lyfe* added in M.; omitted in B. and H.

[1] Annoyance, trouble.

EVERYMAN. That wolde greue me full
  sere, [1]
Whan I sholde come to that ferefull an-
  swere.
Vp, let vs go thyder to gyder.
GOODS. Nay, not so! I am to brytell; I
  may not endure. 425
I wyll folowe no [2] man one fote, be ye sure.
EVERYMAN. Alas! I haue the loued, and
  had grete pleasure
All my lyfe-dayes on good and treasure.
GOODS. That is to thy dampnacyon,
  without lesynge!
For my loue is contrary to the loue euer-
  lastynge. 430
But yf thou had me loued moderately dur-
  ynge
As to the poore to [3] gyue parte of me,
Than sholdest thou not in this dolour be,
Nor in this grete sorowe and care.
EVERYMAN. Lo! now was I deceyued or I
  was ware; 435
And all, I may wyte, my[s]spendynge of
  tyme.
GOODS. What! wenest thou that I am
  thyne?
EVERYMAN. I had went so.
GOODS. Naye, Eueryman; I saye no.
As for a whyle I was lente the; 440
A season thou hast had me in prosperyte.
My condycyon is mannes soule to kyll;
Yf I saue one, a thousande I do spyll.
Wenest thou that I wyll folowe the
From this worlde? nay, veryle. [4] 445
EVERYMAN. I had wende otherwyse.
GOODS. Therfore to thy soule Good is a
  thefe;
For whan thou arte deed, this is my
  gyse —
Another to deceyue in this same wyse
As I haue done the, and all to his soules re-
  prefe. 450
EVERYMAN. O false Good! cursed may [5]
  thou be,
Thou traytour to God, that hast deceyued
  me

And caugh[t] me in thy snare!
GOODS. Mary! thou brought thy selfe in
  care!
Wherof I am right [1] gladde. 455
I must nedes laugh; I can not be sadde.
EVERYMAN. A, Good! thou hast had longe
  my hertely loue;
I gaue the that which sholde be the Lordes
  aboue.
But wylte thou not go with me indede?
I praye the trouth to saye. 460
GOODS. No, so God me spede!
Therfore farewell, and haue good daye!

  [Exit Goods.]

EVERYMAN. O, to whome shall I make my
  mone
For to go with me in that heuy iournaye?
Fyrst Felawshyp sayd he wolde with me
  gone — 465
His wordes were very plesaunte and
  gaye;
But afterwarde he lefte me alone.
Than spake I to my kynnesmen, all in de-
  spayre,
An[d] also they gaue me wordes fayre —
They lacked no fayre spekynge! 470
But all forsoke [2] me in the endynge.
Than wente I to my Goodes, that I loued
  best,
In hope to haue comforte; but there had I
  leest,
For my Goodes sharpely dyd me tell
That he bryngeth many into hell. 475
Than of my selfe I was ashamed;
And so I am worthy to be blamed.
Thus may I well my selfe hate.
Of whom shall I now counseyll take?
I thynke that I shall neuer spede 480
Tyll that I go to my Good Dede.
But, alas! she is so weke
That she can nother go nor speke.
Yet wyll I venter on her now.
My Good Dedes, where be you? 485

  [Good Deeds speaks up from the ground.]

GOOD DEEDS. Here I lye, colde in the
  grounde.
Thy synnes hath me sore bounde,
That I can not stere.

---

[1] Sore. B. has sore; I have changed for the sake of
the rhyme.
[2] No omitted in B., added in H. and M.
[3] To omitted in B. and M., added in H.
[4] B. Nay fro this worlde not veryle; M. Nay nat fro
this worlde verely. I have adopted the reading of H.,
though the reading of M. is equally good.
[5] May omitted in B. and H., added in M.

[1] Right omitted in B. and H., added in M.
[2] B. H. forsake; M. forsoke.

EVERYMAN. O Good Dedes! I stande in
    fere!
I must you pray of counseyll,   490
For helpe now sholde come ryght well.
GOOD DEEDS. Eueryman, I haue vnder-
    standynge
That ye be somoned a[c]counte to make
Before Myssyas, of Iherusalem Kynge;
And you do by me,[1] that iournay with you
    wyll I take.   495
EVERYMAN. Therfore I come to you my
    moone to make.
I praye you that ye wyll go with me.
GOOD DEEDS. I wolde full fayne, but I
    can not stande, veryly.
EVERYMAN. Why, is there ony thynge on
    you fall?
GOOD DEEDS. Ye, syr, I may thanke you
    of all!   500
Yf ye had parfytely chered me,
Your boke of counte full redy had be.

[*Good Deeds shows him his Book of Account.*]

Loke, the bokes of your workes and dedes
    eke!
Behold [2] how they lye vnder the fete
To your soules heuynes.   505
EVERYMAN. Our Lorde Iesus helpe me!
For one letter here I can not se.
GOOD DEEDS. There [3] is a blynde reken-
    ynge in tyme of dystres!
EVERYMAN. Good Dedes, I praye you
    helpe me in this nede,   509
Or elles I am for euer dampned indede!
Therfore helpe me to make my [4] rekenynge
Before the Redemer of all thynge,
That Kynge is, and was, and euer shall.
GOOD DEEDS. Eueryman, I am sory of
    your fall;
And fayne wolde I helpe you, and I were
    able.   515
EVERYMAN. Good Dedes, your counseyll
    I pray you gyue me.
GOOD DEEDS. That shall I do veryly.
Thoughe that on my fete I may not go,
I haue a syster that shall with you also,
Called Knowlege, whiche shall with you
    abyde   520

---

[1] According to my advice.
[2] B. M. *Ase* (*Qy.* A! see); H. *Behold.*
[3] M. *Here;* but Everyman has the book in his
hands.
[4] *My* omitted in B., added in H. and M.

To helpe you to make that dredefull reken-
    ynge.

[*Enter Knowledge.*]

KNOWLEDGE. Eueryman, I wyll go with
    the, and be thy gyde,
In thy moost nede to go by thy syde.
EVERYMAN. In good condycyon I am now
    in euery thynge,
And am hole [1] content with this good
    thynge,   525
Thanked be [2] God my createre! [3]
GOOD DEEDS. And whan he hath
    brought you there
Where thou shalte hele the of thy smarte,
Than go you with your rekenynge and your
    Good Dedes togyder
For to make you ioyfull at herte   530
Before the Blessyd Trynyte.
EVERYMAN. My Good Dedes, gramercy!
I am well content, certaynly,
With your wordes swete.
KNOWLEDGE. Now go we togyder lou-
    yngly   535
To Confessyon, that clensyng ryuere.
EVERYMAN. For ioy I wepe! I wolde we
    were there!
But, I pray you, gyue me cognycyon
Where dwelleth that holy man, Confes-
    syon?
KNOWLEDGE. In the house of saluacyon;
We shall fynde hym in that place,   541
That shall vs comforte, by Goddes grace.

[*Knowledge leads Everyman to Confession.*]

Lo, this is Confessyon. Knele downe, and
    aske mercy;
For he is in good conceyte [4] with God Al-
    myghty.   544
EVERYMAN [*kneeling*]. O gloryous fou-
    tayne, that all vnclennes doth clar-
    yfy,
Wasshe fro me the spottes of vyce vnclene
That on me no synne may be sene.
I come, with Knowlege, for my redemp
    cyon,
Redempte with herte and full contrycyon
For I am commaunded a pylgrymage to
    take,   550
And grete accountes before God to make.

---

[1] Wholly. H. M. *holy.*   [2] B. M. *by;* H. *be.*
[3] B. H. M. *creature.* I have changed for the rhyme
[4] High esteem.

Now I praye you, Shryfte, moder of saluacyon,
Helpe my Good Dedes for my pyteous exclamacyon.
CONFESSION.   I knowe your sorowe well, Eueryman.
Bycause with Knowlege ye come to me,
I wyll you comforte as well as I can;   556
And a precyous iewell I wyll gyue the,
Called penaunce, voyder [1] of aduersyte;
Therwith shall your body chastysed be
With abstynence, and perseueraunce in Goddes seruyce.   560

[Gives Everyman a scourge.]

Here shall you receyue that scourge of me,
Whiche is penaunce stronge that ye must endure
To remembre thy Sauyour was scourged for the
With sharpe scourges, and suffred it pacyently;
So must thou, or thou scape that paynful pylgrymage.   565
Knowlege, kepe hym in this vyage,[2]
And by that tyme Good Dedes wyll be with the.
But in ony wyse be seker [3] of mercy,
For your tyme draweth fast; and [4] ye wyll saued be,
Aske God mercy, and he wyll graunte truely.   570
Whan with the scourge of penaunce man doth hym bynde,
The oyle of forgyuenes than shall he fynde.
EVERYMAN.   Thanked be God for his gracyous werke!
For now I wyll my penaunce begyn;
This hath reioysed and lyghted my herte,
Though the knottes be paynfull and harde within.   576
KNOWLEDGE.   Eueryman, loke your penaunce that ye fulfyll,
What payne that euer it to you be;
And Knowlege shall gyue you counseyll at wyll
How your accounte ye shall make clerely.

[1] B. *voyce voyder;* H. and M. omit *voyce.*
[2] Course.
[3] B. M. *seker;* H. *sure.* The meaning is probably "seeker."
[4] If.

[Everyman kneels in Prayer.]

EVERYMAN.   O eternal God! O heuenly fygure!   581
O way of ryghtwysnes! O goodly vysyon!
Whiche descended downe in a vyrgyn pure
Because he wolde euery man redeme,
Whiche Adam forfayted by his dysobedyence!   585
O blessyd Godheed! electe and hye deuyne!
Forgyue me [1] my greuous offence.
Here I crye the mercy in this presence.
O ghostly treasure! O raunsomer and redemer!   589
Of all the worlde hope and conduyter! [2]
Myrrour of ioye! foundatour [3] of mercy,
Whiche enlumyneth heuen and erth therby!
Here my clamorous complaynt, though it late be.
Receyue my prayers, vnworthy of thy benygnytye.[4]
Though I be a synner moost abhomynable,   595
Yet let my name be wryten in Moyses table.
O Mary! praye to the Maker of all thynge
Me for to helpe at my endynge,
And saue me fro the power of my enemy;
For Deth assayleth me strongly.   600
And, Lady, that I may by meane of thy prayer
Of your Sones glory to be partynere
By the meanes of his passyon, I it craue.
I beseche you helpe my soule to saue.

[He rises.]

Knowlege, gyue me the scourge of penaunce.   605
My fleshe therwith shall gyue aquytaunce.[5]
I wyll now begyn, yf God gyue me grace.
KNOWLEDGE.   Eueryman, God gyue you tyme and space!
Thus I bequeth you in ye handes of our Sauyour.
Now may you make your rekenynge sure.   610

[1] *Me* omitted in B., added in H. and M.
[2] Guide.   H. *conductor;* M. *conduiter.*
[3] Founder.   H. *and founder;* M. *foundacion.*
[4] B. M. *in this heuy lyfe.*   I have adopted the reading in H.
[5] B. *acqueyntaunce;* M. *aquaintaunce.*   I have adopted the reading in H.

EVERYMAN.   In the name of the Holy Trynyte
My body sore punysshyd shall be.

[*He begins to scourge himself.*]

Take this, body, for the synne of the
flesshe!
Also thou delytest to go gay and fresshe,
And in the way of dampnacyon thou dyd
me brynge;   615
Therfore suffre now strokes of punyssh-
ynge!
Now of penaunce I wyll wade the water
clere,
To saue me from purgatory, that sharpe
fyre.

[*Good Deeds rises from the floor.*]

GOOD DEEDS.   I thanke God, now I can
walke and go,
And am delyuered of my sykenesse and
wo.   620
Therfore with Eueryman I wyll go, and not
spare;
His good workes I wyll helpe hym to de-
clare.
KNOWLEDGE.   Now, Eueryman, be mery
and glad!
Your Good Dedes cometh now, ye may not
be sad.
Now is your Good Dedes hole and
sounde,   625
Goynge vpryght vpon the grounde.
EVERYMAN.   My herte is lyght, and shalbe
euermore.
Now wyll I smyte faster than I dyde be-
fore.
GOOD DEEDS.   Eueryman, pylgryme, my
specyall frende,
Blessyd be thou without ende!   630
For the is preparate the eternall glory!
Ye haue me made hole and sounde,
Therfore I wyll byde by the in euery
stounde.[1]
EVERYMAN.   Welcome, my Good Dedes!
Now I here thy voyce
I wepe for very swetenes of loue.   635
KNOWLEDGE.   Be no more sad, but euer
reioyce;
God seeth thy lyuynge in his trone aboue.
Put on this garment to thy behoue,

Whiche is wette with your teres,   639
Or elles before God you may it mysse,
Whan ye to your iourneys ende come
shall.
EVERYMAN.   Gentyll Knowlege, what do
ye it call?
KNOWLEDGE.   It is the [1] garmente of sor-
owe;
Fro payne it wyll you borowe;
Contrycyon it is   645
That getteth forgyuenes,
It [2] pleaseth God passynge well.
GOOD DEEDS.   Eueryman, wyll you were it
for your hele?

[*Everyman puts on the robe of contrition.*]

EVERYMAN.   Now blessyd be Iesu, Maryes
sone,
For now haue I on true contrycyon.   650
And lette vs go now without taryenge.
Good Dedes, haue we clere our rekenynge?
GOOD DEEDS.   Ye, indede, I haue here.
EVERYMAN.   Than I trust we nede not
fere.   654
Now, frendes, let vs not parte in twayne.
KNOWLEDGE.[3]   Nay, Eueryman, that wyll
we not, certayne.
GOOD DEEDS.   Yet must thou le[a]d with
the
Thre persones of grete myght.
EVERYMAN.   Who sholde they be?
GOOD DEEDS.   Dyscrecyon and Strength
they hyght,   660
And thy Beaute may not abyde be-
hynde.
KNOWLEDGE.   Also ye must call to mynde
Your Fyue Wyttes as for your counsey-
lours.
GOOD DEEDS.   You must haue them redy
at all houres.
EVERYMAN.   Howe shall I gette them
hyder?   665
KINDRED.   You must call them all togy-
der,
And they wyll here you incontynent.
EVERYMAN.   My frendes, come hyder and
be present,
Dyscrecyon, Strengthe, my Fyue Wyttes,
and Beaute!

---

[1] B. *a;* H. M. *the.*   [2] B. M. *He;* H. *It.*
[3] B. H. M. *all,* in error, assign this speech to Kindred; but Kindred left the stage at line 368.

[1] In every attack (or, always).

[*Enter Discretion, Strength, Five Wits, and Beauty.*]

BEAUTY.   Here at your wyll we be all
    redy.   670
What wyll ye that we sholde do?
GOOD DEEDS.   That ye wolde with Euery-
    man go
And helpe hym in his pylgrymage.
Aduyse you; wyll ye with him or not in
    that vyage?
STRENGTH.   We wyll brynge hym all
    thyder,   675
To his helpe and comforte, ye may beleue
    me.
DISCRETION.   So wyll we go with hym all
    togyder.
EVERYMAN.   Almyghty God, loued may [1]
    thou be!
I gyue the laude that I haue hyder brought
Strength, Dyscrecyon, Beaute and Five
    Wyttes. Lacke I nought.   680
And my Good Dedes, with Knowlege
    clere,
All be in [2] company at my wyll here.
I desyre no more to my besynes.[3]
STRENGTH.   And I, Strength, wyll by you
    stande in dystres,
Though thou wolde in batayle fyght on the
    grounde.   .685
FIVE WITS.   And though it were thrugh
    the worlde rounde,
We wyll not departe for swete ne soure.
BEAUTY.   No more wyll I, vnto dethes
    houre,
What so euer therof befall.
DISCRETION.   Eueryman, aduyse you
    fyrst of all;   690
Go with a good aduysement and delybera-
    cyon.
We all gyue you vertuous monycyon [4]
That all shall be well.
EVERYMAN.   My frendes, harken what I
    wyll tell —
I praye God rewarde you in his heuenly [5]
    spere —   695
Now herken all that be here,
For I wyll make my testament
Here before you all present:

    [1] B. *myght*; H. M. *may*.
    [2] B. *in my*; H. M. *in*.
    [3] Business.   [4] Admonition.
    [5] B. *heuen*; H. M. D. *heuenly*.

In almes halfe my good I wyll gyue with
    my handes twayne
In the way of charyte with good en-
    tent,   700
And the other halfe styll shall remayne,
In queth [1] to be retourned there it ought to
    be.
This I do in despyte of the fende of hell,
To go quyte out of his perell
Euer after and this daye.   705
KNOWLEDGE.   Eueryman, herken what I
    saye:
Go to Presthode, I you aduyse,
And receyue of hym, in ony wyse,
The holy sacrament and oyntement togy-
    der;
Than shortly se ye tourne agayne hy-
    der;   710
We wyll all abyde you here.
FIVE WITS.   Ye, Eueryman, hye you that
    ye redy were.
There is no emperour, kinge, duke, ne
    baron,
That of God hath commycyon
As hath the leest preest in the worlde be-
    ynge;   715
For of the blessyd sacramentes pure and
    benygne
He bereth the keyes, and therof hath the
    cure
For mannes redempcyon — it is euer sure —
Whiche God for our soules medycyne 719
Gaue vs out of his herte with grete payne,
Here in this transytory lyfe for the and me.
The blessyd sacramentes seuen there be —
Baptym, confyrmacyon, with preesthode
    good,
And ye sacrament of Goddes precyous
    flesshe and blod,
Maryage, the holy extreme vnccyon, and
    penaunce.   725
These seuen be good to haue in remem-
    braunce,
Gracyous sacramentes of hye deuynyte.
EVERYMAN.   Fayne wolde I receyue that
    holy body,
And mekely to my ghostly fader [2] I wyll go.
FIVE WITS.   Eueryman, that is the best
    that ye can do.   730
God wyll you to saluacyon brynge,

    [1] *Bequest;* H. *In quyet;* M. D. *I it bequethe.*
    [2] Spiritual father.

For preesthode excedeth all other thynge:
To vs holy scripture they do teche,
And conuerteth man fro synne heuen to
   reche;
God hath to them more power gyuen   735
Than to ony aungell that is in heuen.
With fiue wordes he may consecrate
Goddes body in flesshe and blode to
   make, ·
And handeleth his Maker bytwene his
   hande[s].
The preest byndeth and vnbyndeth all
   bandes,   740
Both in erthe and in heuen.
Thou mynystres all the sacramentes seuen;
Though we kyst [1] thy fete, thou wert [2]
   worthy;
Thou arte the [3] surgyon that cureth synne
   deedly;
No remedy we fynde vnder God   745
But all onely preesthode.
Eueryman, God gaue preest[s] that dygnyte
And setteth them in his stede amonge vs to
   be.
Thus be they aboue aungelles in degree.

[*Exit Everyman to receive from the priest the
   Sacrament and extreme unction. Knowledge and the rest remain.*]

KNOWLEDGE.   If preestes be good, it is so,
   suerly.[4]   750;
But whan Iesu hanged on ye crosse with
   grete smarte,
There he gaue out of his blessyd herte
The same sacrament in grete tourment.
He solde them not to vs, that Lorde om-
   nypotent;
Therefore Saynt Peter the Apostell dothe
   saye   755
That Iesus curse hath all they
Whiche God theyr Sauyour do by or sell,
Or they for ony money do take or tell.
Synfull preests gyueth the synners example
   bad;
Theyr chyldren sytteth by other mennes
   fyres, I haue harde;   760
And some haunteth womens company
With vnclen lyfe, as lustes of lechery.
These be with synne made blynde.

---

[1] B. H. *kysse;* M. *kyst.*   [2] B. H. M. *were.*
[3] B. H. omit *thee;* added in M.
[4] I.e., that they are above the angels (see preceding line).

FIVE WITS.   I trust to God no suche may
   we fynde.
Therfore let vs preesthode honour,   765
And folowe theyr doctryne for our soules
   socoure.
We be theyr shepe, and they shepeherdes
   be,
By whome we all be kepte in suerte.
Peas! for yonder I se Eueryman come, 769
Whiche hath made true satysfaccyon.
GOOD DEEDS.   Methynke it is he indede.

[*Re-enter Everyman.*]

EVERYMAN.   Now Iesu be your alder
   spede! [1]
I haue receyued the sacrament for my re-
   dempcyon,
And than myne extreme vnccyon.[2]
Blessyd be all they that counseyled me to
   take it!   775
And now, frendes, let vs go without longer
   respyte.
I thanke God that ye haue taryed so longe.
Now set eche of you on this rodde your
   honde,
An shortely folowe me.
I go before there I wolde be.   God be our [3]
   gyde!   780
STRENGTH.   Eueryman, we wyll not fro
   you go
Tyll ye haue done this vyage longe.
DISCRETION.   I, Dyscrecyon, wyll byde by
   you also.
KNOWLEDGE.   And though this pylgrym-
   age be neuer so stronge,
I wyll neuer parte you fro.   785
Eueryman, I wyll be as sure by the
As euer I dyde by Iudas Machabee.[4]

[*They proceed together to the grave.*]

EVERYMAN.   Alas!   I am so faynt I may
   not stande!
My lymmes vnder me doth folde!
Frendes, let vs not tourne agayne to this
   lande,   790
Not for all the worldes golde;
For into this caue must I crepe
And tourne to erth,[5] and there to slepe.

---

[1] Now Jesus be the one who gives prosperity to all
of you.
[2] Unction.   [3] B. *your;* H. M. D. *our.*
[4] See in the Apocrypha, I Maccabees, chap. iii.
[5] B. M. D. *the earth.*

BEAUTY. What! into this graue? Alas!

EVERYMAN. Ye, there shall ye consume,
more and lesse.[1]   795

BEAUTY. And what! sholde I smoder
here?

EVERYMAN. Ye, by my fayth, and neuer
more appere.

In this worlde lyue no more we shall,

But in heuen before the hyest Lorde of
all.

BEAUTY. I crosse out all this! Adewe, by
Saynt Iohan!   800

I take my cap[2] in my lappe, and am
gone.

EVERYMAN. What, Beaute! whyder wyll
ye?

BEAUTY. Peas! I am defe. I loke not
behynde me,

Not and thou woldest gyue me all ye golde
in thy chest!   [Exit Beauty.]

EVERYMAN. Alas! wherto may I truste?

Beaute gothe fast awaye fro me!   806

She promysed with me to lyue and dye.

STRENGTH. Eueryman, I wyll the also forsake and denye.

Thy game lyketh me not at all.

EVERYMAN. Why than, ye wyll forsake
me all?   810

Swete Strength, tary a lytell space.

STRENGTH. Nay, syr, by the rode[3] of
grace!

I wyll hye me from the fast,

Though thou wepe tyll[4] thy herte tobrast.[5]

EVERYMAN. Ye wolde euer byde by me,
ye sayd.   815

STRENGTH. Ye, I haue you ferre ynoughe
conueyde!

Ye be olde ynoughe, I vnderstande,

Your pylgrymage to take on hande.

I repent me that I hyder came.

EVERYMAN. Strength, you to dysplease I
am to blame,   820

Yet promise is dette, this ye well wot.[6]

STRENGTH. In fayth, I care not!

[1] Great persons, and persons of little fame.
[2] B. M. *tappe* (*Qy.* tape); H. *cap.* "I doff my cap
(so deep that it comes) into my lap." Logeman.
[3] Rood, cross.
[4] B. *to;* H. M. D. *tyll.*
[5] Burst into pieces.
[6] B. H. D. *Wyll ye breke promyse that is dette.* I
have adopted the reading of M., which is justified by
the rhyme.

Thou arte but a foole to complayne.

You spende your speche, and wast your
brayne.

Gc, thryst the into the grounde!   825

[Exit Strength.]

EVERYMAN. I had wende surer I shulde
you haue founde.

He that trusteth in his Strength

She hym deceyueth at the length.

Bothe Strength and Beaute forsaketh
me;

Yet they promysed me fayre and louyngly.   830

DISCRETION. Eueryman, I will after
Strength be gone.

As for me, I will leue you alone.

EVERYMAN. Why Dyscrecyon! wyll ye
forsake me?

DISCRETION. Ye, in fayth, I wyll go fro
the;

For whan Strength goth before   835

I folowe after euer more.

EVERYMAN. Yet, I pray the, for the loue
of the Trynyte,

Loke in my graue ones pyteously.

DISCRETION. Nay, so nye wyll I not
come.

Fare well euerychone!

[Exit Discretion.]

EVERYMAN. O, all thynge fayleth, saue
God alone —   841

Beaute, Strength, and Dyscrecyon;

For whan Deth bloweth his blast

They all renne fro me full fast.

FIVE WITS. Eueryman, my leue now of
the I take.   845

I wyll folowe the other, for here I the forsake.

EVERYMAN. Alas! than may I wayle and
wepe,

For I toke you for my best frende.

FIVE WITS. I wyll no lenger the kepe.

Now farewell, and there an ende!   850

[Exit Five Wits.]

EVERYMAN. O Iesu, helpe! All hath forsaken me!

GOOD DEEDS. Nay, Eueryman; I wyll
byde with the.

I wyll not forsake the indede;

Thou shalte fynde me a good frende at
    nede.
EVERYMAN.   Gramercy, Good Dedes!
    Now may I true frendes se.   855
They haue forsaken me, euerychone;
I loued them better than my Good Dedes
    alone.
Knowlege, wyll ye forsake me also?
KNOWLEDGE.   Ye, Eueryman, whan ye to
    Deth shall go;
But not yet, for no maner of daunger. 860
EVERYMAN.   Gramercy, Knowlege, with
    all my herte!
KNOWLEDGE.   Nay, yet I wyll not from
    hens departe
Tyll I se where ye shall be come.
EVERYMAN.   Methynke, alas, that I must
    be gone
To make my rekenynge, and my dettes
    paye;   865
For I se my tyme is nye spent awaye.
Take example, all ye that this do here or
    se,
How they that I loued [1] best do forsake
    me,
Excepte my Good Dedes that bydeth
    truely.
GOOD DEEDS.   All erthly thynges is but
    vanyte.   870
Beaute, Strength, and Dyscrecyon do man
    forsake,
Folysshe frendes, and kynnesmen, that
    fayre spake, —
All fleeth saue Good Dedes, and that am I.
EVERYMAN.   Haue mercy on me, God
    moost myghty,
And stande by me, thou moder and mayde,
    Holy Mary!   875
GOOD DEEDS.   Fere not; I wyll speke for
    the.

       [1] B. *loue*; H. M. D. *loued*.

EVERYMAN.   Here I crye God mercy!
GOOD DEEDS.   Shorte oure ende, **and**
    mynysshe [1] our payne.
Let vs go, and neuer come agayne.
EVERYMAN.   Into thy handes, Lorde, **my**
    soule I commende.   880
Receyue it, Lorde, that it be not lost.
As thou me boughtest, so me defende,
And saue me from the fendes boost,
That I may appere with that blessyd
    hoost
That shall be saued at the day of dome. 885
In manus tuas, [2] of myghtes moost
For euer, *commendo spiritum meum!* [3]

[*Everyman and Good Deeds descend into the
    grave.*]

KNOWLEDGE.   Now hath he suffred that
    we all shall endure.
The Good Dedes shall make all sure.
Now hath he made endynge.   890
Methynketh that I here aungelles synge,
And make grete ioy and melody
Where Euerymannes soule receyued shall
    be.
ANGEL [*within*].   Come, excellente electe
    spouse to Iesu!
Here aboue thou shalte go,   895
Bycause of thy synguler vertue.
Now the soule is taken the body fro,
Thy rekenynge is crystall clere.
Now shalte thou in to the heuenly spere;
Vnto the whiche all ye shall come   900
That lyueth well before the daye or
    dome.

       [*Exit Knowledge.*]

    [1] Lessen.
    [2] "Into thy hands."
    [3] "I commit my spirit."

[Enter the Doctor as an Epilogue.]

DOCTOR.   This morall men may haue in mynde.
Ye herers, take it of worth,[1] olde and yonge!
And forsake Pryde, for he deceyueth you in the ende.
And remembre Beaute, Five Wyttes, Strength, and Dy[s]crecyon,   905
They all at the last do euery man forsake,
Saue his Good Dedes there dothe he take —
But beware, and they be small
Before God he hath no helpe at all.
None excuse may be there for euery man.   910
Alas, how shall he do, than?
For, after dethe, amendes may no man make;
For than mercy and pyte doth hym forsake.
If his rekenynge be not clere whan he doth come
God wyll saye: *"Ite, maledicti, in ignem eternum!"*   915
And he that hath his accounte hole and sounde,
Hye in heuen he shall be crounde.
Vnto whiche place God brynge vs all thyder,
That we may lyue body and soule togyder.
Therto helpe, the Trynyte!   920
Amen, saye ye, for Saynt Charyte.

[1] Prize it highly.

FINIS.

Thus endeth this morall playe of Eueryman.
Imprynted at London in Poules
Chyrche yarde by me
Johan Skot.

MANKIND [1]

[DRAMATIS PERSONÆ

MANKIND.
MERCY.
TITIVILLUS.

NOUGHT.]

MISCHIEF.
NEW-GYSE.
NOW-A-DAYS.

[*Enter Mercy.*]

MERCY.   The very fownder and begynner
of owur fyrst creacion,
A-monge ws synfull wrechys he oweth
to be magnyfyede,
That for owur dysobedyenc[e] he hade non
indygnacion
To sende hys own Son to be torn and
crucyfyede.   4
Owur obsequyouse [1] seruyce to hym
xulde be aplyede
Where he was lorde of all and made all
thynge of nought,
For the synfull synner, to hade [2] hym
revyuyde,[3]
And, for hys redempcyon, sett hys
own Son at nought.   8

That may be seyde, and veryfyede, mankynde was dere bought;
By the pytuose deth of Jhesu he hade
hys remedye; [4]
He was purgyde of hys defawte, that
wrechydly hade wrought,

By hys gloryus passyon, that blyssyde
lauatorye.[1]   12
O souerence,[2] I be-seche yow yowur condycions to rectyfye,
Ande with humylite and reuerence to
haue a remocyon [3]
To this blyssyde Prynce that owur
nature doth gloryfye,
That ye may be partycypable of hys
retribucyon.[4]   16

I haue be [5] the very mene for yowur res-
tytucyon.   17
Mercy ys my name, that mornyth for
yowur offence.
Dyverte not yowur sylffe [6] in tyme of
temtacyon,
That ye may be acceptable to Gode at
yowur goynge hence.   20
The grett mercy of Gode, that ys of most
preemmynence,
Be medyacyon [7] of Owur Lady, that
ys euer habundante

----

[1] Dutiful.   [2] Hold.
[3] Revived.   [4] Salvation.

----

[1] Washing (from sin).
[2] Masters (i.e. the audience).   [3] Change.
[4] Retribution (for men's sins in his passion).
[5] Been.   [6] Self.
[7] MS. *medytacyon;* corr. by M.

[1] This play was written about 1475; and, as numerous allusions in the text show, it is to be assigned to the neighborhood of Cambridge. Its chief interest lies in the fact that it illustrates the beginning of professionalism in the drama. It was acted by a company of apparently six players (the parts of Mercy and of Titivillus could easily be assumed by one man), who gave their performance in a public inn-yard (cf. ll. 29, 554, 722, 725) for gain—at one point, ll. 448–65, they halt the play in order to collect money from the audience. The properties they were required to carry are negligible — little more than their costumes; and possibly they limited their dramatic activities, as did the plowboy morris-dancers, to the Christmas holiday season (cf. ll. 54, 62, 316, 325, 381, 539). The result of thus professionalizing the drama is readily apparent in the text: the moral element is reduced to a minimum, and even the sole representative of good, Mercy, is deliberately made fun of with his ponderous Latinistic diction and his saccharine talk; the humor becomes at times exceedingly vulgar; and the literary skill of the writer is unusually poor. Possibly the author merely reworked an earlier and more serious morality, eliminating the moral element, and accentuating in his own way the comic features.

The manuscript is found in the collection of moralities formerly in the possession of the Rev. Cox Macro (see page 265, note 1). I have based the present text on that in *The Macro Plays,* edited by F. J. Furnivall and A. W. Pollard, for the Early English Text Society, 1904; but I have checked doubtful readings with the photographic facsimile of the manuscript issued by J. S. Farmer, and I have made use of the edition by Manly, *Specimens,* 1896. I have noted the principal, but not all the minor, emendations adopted from Manly (M.). All additions to the manuscript are set in square brackets, and changes duly recorded in foot-notes. The punctuation, the use of capitals, and the stage-directions are my own.

To the synfull creature that wyll repent
    hys neclygence.[1]
I prey Gode, at yowur most nede, that
    Mercy be yowur defendawnte.   24

In goode werkys I a-wyse[2] yow, souer-
    ence, to be perseuerante
To puryfye yowur sowlys that thei be
    not corupte;
For yowur gostly enmy[3] wyll make hys
    a-vaunte,[4]
    Yowur goode condycions yf he may
      interrupte.   28
O ye souerens that sytt, and ye brothern
    that stonde ryght wppe,[5]
    Pryke[6] not yowur felycytes in
      thyngis transytorye!
Be-holde not the erth, but lyfte yowur
    ey wppe!
    Se how the hede the members dayly
      do magnyfye.   32

Who ys the hede, forsoth, I xall yow
    certyfye:
I mene owur Sauyowur, that was lykyn-
    nyde[7] to a lambe;
Ande hys sayntis be the members that
    dayly he doth satysfye
With the precyose reuer that runnyth
    from hys wombe.[8]   36

Ther ys non such foode, be watur nor by
    londe,
So precyouse, so gloryouse, so nedefull
    to owur entent![9]
For yt hath dyssoluyde mankynde from
    the bittur bonde
Of the mortall enmye, that vemynousse[10]
    serpente;   40
From the wyche Gode preserue yow all
    at the last Iugement!
For sekyrly ther xall be a strerat[11]
    examynacyon;

The corn xall be sauyde, the chaffe xall
    be brente.
I be-sech yow hertyly, haue this
    premedytacyon.   44

[Enter Mischief.]

MYSCHEFFE. I be-seche yow hertyly, leue
    yowur calcacyon!   45
Leue yowur chaffe! leue yowur corn! leue
    yowur dalyacyon!
Yowur wytt ys lytyll, yowur hede ys
    mekyll![1] ye are full of predycacyon.[2]
But, ser, I prey [yow] this questyon to
    claryfye: —   48
Dryff-draff, mysse-masche,
Sume was corn, and sume was chaffe;
My dame seyde my name was Raffe;
    On-schett yowur lokke,[3] and take an
    halpenye.   52

MERCY. Why come ye hethyr, brother?
    Ye were not dysyryde.   53
MYSCHEFF. For a wyntur corn-threscher,
    ser, I haue hyryde;
Ande ye sayde the corn xulde be sauyde,
    and the chaffe xulde be feryde;
Ande he prouyth nay, as yt schewth be
    this werse:[4]   56
    " Corn seruit bredibus, chaffe horsibus,
    straw fyrybusque," [5]
Thys ys as moche to say to yowur leude[6]
    wndyrstondynge,
As the corn xall serue to brede at the nexte
    bakynge,
    " Chaff horsybus," *et reliqua*,[7]   60
The chaff, to horse xall be goode produce;
When a man ys for-colde,[8] this straw may
    be brent.
And so forth, *et cetera*.   63

MERCY. A-voyde, goode brother! Ye ben
    culpable   64
To interrupte thus my talkynge delectable.
MYSCHEFF. Ser, I haue nother horse nor
    sadyll;
Therfor I may not ryde.   67
MERCY. Hye yow forthe on fote, brother,
    in Godis name!

---

[1] Sinning.   [2] Advise.
[3] Enemy.   [4] Boast.
[5] The better classes, seated in the galleries sur-
rounding the inn-yard, are respectfully addressed as
"sovereigns," the rabble, standing in the yard, as
"brethren." Note also the familiar way in which
the ctors in coming in and going out address those
standing about the stage.
[6] Set.   [7] Likened.
[8] Side (into which the spear was thrust).
[9] Purpose.
[10] Venomous.   [11] Strict.

[1] Big.   [2] Preaching.
[3] Open your lock.   [4] Verse.
[5] Dog Latin: "Corn serves for bread, chaff for
horses, and straw for fires."
[6] Ignorant.   [7] MS. *reliqud.*   [8] Very cold.

MYSCHEFF. I say, ser, I am cumme hedyr
    to make yow game; [1]
Yet bade ye me not go out in the deullys
    name,
    Ande I wyll a-byde.   71
[MERCY [2] . . . .

. . . .

*Enter New-gyse, Now-a-days, and Nought,
    with minstrels.*

NEW-GYSE . . . .
NOW-A-DAYS . . . .
NOUGHT . . . .
NEW-GYSE. [2]] Ande how, mynstrellys!
    pley the comyn trace! [3]   72
Ley on with thi ballys [4] tyll hys bely
    breste!

NOUGHT. I put case I breke my neke:
    how than?
NEW-GYSE. I gyff no force, by Sent
    Tanne! [5]
NOW-A-DAYS. Leppe a-bout lyuely! Thou
    art a wyght [6] man.
    Lett ws be mery wyll we be here!   77
NOUGHT. Xall I breke my neke to schow
    yow sporte?
NOW-A-DAYS. Therfor euer be-ware of
    thi reporte.
NOUGHT. I be-schrew ye all! her ys a
    schrewde sorte! [7]   80
    Haue ther att them with a mery chere!

Her thei daunce. Mercy seyth:

[MERCY.] Do wey! Do wey this reuell,
    sers! Do wey!   82
NOW-A-DAYS. Do wey, goode Adam? do
    wey?
Thys ys no parte of thi pley.
NOUGHT. Yis, mary, I prey yow, for I
    loue not this rewelynge. [8]
Cum forth, goode fader, I yow prey!
Be a lytyll ye may assay. [9]
A-non, of with yowur clothes, yf ye wyll
    pray!
    Go to! for I haue hade a praty
    scottlynge. [10]   89

MERCY. Nay, brother, I wyll not daunce.
NEW-GYSE. Yf ye wyll, ser, my brother
    wyll make yow to prawnce.
NOW-A-DAYS. With all my herte, ser, yf I
    may yow a-vaunce. [1]
    Ye may assay be a lytyll trace.   93
NOUGHT. Ye, ser, wyll ye do well?
Trace not with them, be my cownsell;
For I haue tracyed sumwhat to fell! [2]
    I tell [yow] [3] yt ys a narow space.   97

But, ser, I trow, of ws thre I herde you
    speke.   98
NEW-GYSE. Crystis curse had [y]e [4]
    therfor; for I was in slepe.
NOW-A-DAYS. A[nd] I hade the cuppe redy
    in my honde, redy to goo to met. [5]
    Therfor, ser, curtly [6] grett yow well. 101
MERCY. Few wordis! Few and well sett!
NEW-GYSE. Ser, yt ys the new gyse and
    the new jett. [7]
Many wordis, and schortely sett:
    Thys ys the new gyse, euery dele. [8] 105

MERCY. Lady, helpe! How wrechys
    delyte in ther sympull weys!
NOW-A-DAYS. Say not a-geyn the new
    gyse now-a-days!
Thou xall fynde ws sch[r]ewys at all
    assays.
    Be ware! Ye, may son lyke [9] a bofett.
MERCY. He was well occupyede that
    browte yow brethern!   110
NOUGHT. I harde yow call "New-gyse,
    Now-a-days, Nought," all thes thre
    to-gether.
Yf ye sey that I lye, I xall make yow to
    slyther! [10]
    Lo, take yow here a trepett! [11]   113

MERCY. Say me yowur namys! I know
    yow not.   114
NEW-GYSE. New-gyse, I.
[NOW-A-DAYS.]   Now-a-days, [I].
[NOUGHT.]   I, Nought.
MERCY. Be Jhesu Cryst, that me dere
    bowte,

---

[1] Advance.
[2] Vigorously. MS. *fylde fell;* apparently the first
word was written in error.
[3] Added by M.   [4] MS. *hade.*   [5] Meat.
[6] Briefly.   [7] Fashion.   [8] Bit.
[9] Taste.   [10] Slide.
[11] Trip (he tries to trip him up).

---

[1] Fun.   [2] A page lost from the MS.
[3] Dance.   [4] Bellows (of bagpipe?).
[5] Saint Anne.   [6] Active, agile.
[7] Bad lot.   [8] Reveling.
[9] You may try a little dance.
[10] Running with hurried steps (here, a dance).

Ye be-tray many men. 117

NEW-GYSE. Be-tray? nay, nay, ser! nay,
nay!

We make them both fresch and gay.

But of yowur name, ser, I yow prey,

That we may yow ken. 121

MERCY. Mercy ys my name and my
denomynacyon.

I conseyue ye haue but a lytyll faus [1] in my
communycacyon.

NEW-GYSE. Ey, ey! yowur body ys full of
Englysch Laten!

NOW-A-DAYS. I prey yow hertyly, worschypp[f]ull clerke — 125

I haue etun a dysch full of curdis,

Ande I haue . . . . [2]

Now opyn yowur sachell with Laten
wordis, 128

Ande sey me this in clerycall [3] manere!

Also I haue a wyf; her name ys Rachell;

Betwyx her and me was a gret batell;

Ande fayn of yow I wolde here tell

Who was the most mastur. 133

NOUGHT. Thy wyf Rachell, I dare ley
xx[ti] lyse.[4] 134

NOW-A-DAYS. Who spake to thee, foll?
Thou art not wyse!

Go and do that longyth to thin offyce —
Osculare fundamentum! 137

NOUGHT. Lo, mastur! lo! here ys a pardon
bely mett; [5]

Yt ys grawntyde of Pope Pokett.

Yf ye wyll putt yowur nose . . . . [6]

Ye xall haue xl[ty] days of pardon. 141

MERCY. Thys ydyll language ye xall
repent! 142

Out of this place I wolde ye went.

NEW-GYSE. Goo we hens all thre with on
assent!

My fadyr ys yrke [7] of owur eloquence;

Therfor I wyll no lenger tary. 146

Gode brynge yow, master, and blyssyde
Mary,

To the numbur of the demonycall frayry! [1]

[. . . . .] [2]

NOW-A-DAYS. Cum wynde, cum reyn, 149

Thow I cumme neuer a-geyn!

The deull put out both yowur eyn! [3]

Felouse, go we hens tyght! [4] 152

NOUGHT. Go we hens, a deull wey!

Here ys the dore, her ys the wey!

[*To Mercy.*]

Farwell, jentyll Jaffrey!

I prey Gode gyf yow goode nyght! 156

Let them go out in silence. [5]

MERCY. Thankyde be Gode, we haue a
fayer dylyuerance 157

Of thes iij onthryfty gestis!

They know full lytyll what ys ther ordynance.

I preue, by reson, thei be wers then
bestis: 160

A best doth after hys naturall instytu-
cyon; [6]

Ye may conseyue by there dysporte and
be-hauour

Ther joy ande delyte ys in derysyon 163

Of her [7] owyn Cryste, to his dyshonur.

Thys condycyon of leuynge, yt ys preiudy-
cyall.

Be-ware therof! Yt ys wers than ony
felony or treson.

How may yt be excusyde be-for the Iustyce
of all,

When for euery ydyll worde we must
yelde a reson? 168

They haue grett ease; ther-for thei wyll
take no thought.

But how then, when the angell of hewyn
xall blow the trumpe,

Ande sey to the transgressors that wyk-
kydly hath wrought,

"Cum forth on-to yowur juge, and yelde
yowur a-cownte!" 172

---

[1] Force?
[2] Omitted because of obscenity.
[3] Clerk-like, learned.
[4] Lice.
[5] *Qy.* be lymett (by limit) M.
[6] The language is unprintable.
[7] Tired.

[1] Friary, a society of friars.
[2] Apparently a line missing in MS.
[3] Eyes.   [4] Quickly.
[5] MS. *Exiant silentio.*
[6] The established order by which a thing is regu-
lated (here, nature).
[7] Their.

Then xall I, Mercy, be-gyn sor to wepe;
    Nother comfort nor cownsell ther xall
        non be hade;
But such as thei haue sowyn, such xall thei
    repe.
    Thei be wanton [1] now, but then xall thei
        be sade.   176

The goode new-gyse now-a-days I wyll
    not dysalow;
    I dyscomende the vycyouse gyse.   I
        prey haue me excusyde,
I nede not to speke of yt; yowur reson
    wyll tell it yow.
    Take that ys to be takyn, and leue that
        ys to be refusyde!   180

[Enter Mankind with a spade.]

MANKYNDE.   Of the erth and of the cley
    we haue owur propagacyon;   181
    By the prouydens of Gode thus be we
        deryvatt,[2]
To whos mercy I recomende this holl
    congrygacyon.
    I hope, on-to hys blysse ye be all pre-
        destynatt!   184
Euery man, for hys degre, I trust xall
    be partycypatt,
Yf we wyll mortyfye owur carnall con-
    dycyon
Ande owur voluntarye dysyres, that
    euer be pervercionatt,[3]
To renunce thes and yelde ws wndur Godis
    provycyon.   188

My name ys Mankynde.   I haue my com-
    posycyon   189
Of a body and of a soull, of condycyon
    contrarye:
Be-twyx the tweyn ys a grett dyvisyon.
    He that xulde be s[u]biecte, now he hath
        the victory.   192
    Thys ys to me a lamentable story,
    To se my flesch, of my soull to haue
        gouernance.
    Wher the goode wyff ys master, the
        goode-man may be sory.
        A-lasse! what was thi fortune and thi
            chaunce   196
        To be assocyat with my flesch, that
            stynkyng dunge-hyll!

[1] Jovial.   [2] Derived.   [3] Perverted.

Lady, helpe!   Souerens, yt doth my soull
    myche yll   198
    To se the flesch prosperouse, and the
        soull trodyn wndur fote.
I xall go to yondyr man, and a-say hym I
    wyll.
    I trust of gostly solace he wyll be my
        bote.[1]   201

[He goes to Mercy, and kneels.]

All heyll, semely father!   Ye be welcome
    to this house!
    Of the very wysdam ye haue partycy-
        pacyon.
My body with my soull ys euer querulose.[2]
    I prey yow, for sent charyte, of yowur
        supportacyon!   205

I be-seche yow hertyly of yowur gostly [3]
    comforte!
    I am onstedfast in lywynge; [4] my name
        ys Mankynde.
My gostly enmy, the deull, wyil haue a
    grett dysporte,
    In sympull gydynge yf he may se me
        ende.   .   209

MERCY.   Cryst sende yow goode comforte!
    Ye be welcum, my frende!
    Stonde wppe on yowur fete!   I prey
        yow aryse!
My name ys Mercy: ye be to me full hende.[5]
    To eschew vyce I wyll yow a-vyse.   213

MANKYNDE.   O Mercy! of all grace and
    vertu ye are the well! [6]
    I haue herde tell of ryght worschyppfull
        clerkis
Ye be approxymatt to Gode, and nere of
    hys consell;
    He hat instytut [7] you a-boue all hys
        werkis.   217

O! yowur louely words [8] to my soull are
    swetere then hony!
MERCY.   The temtacyon of the flesch ye
    must resyst lyke a man,
For ther ys euer a batell betwyx the soull
    and the body;   220
    Vita hominis est milicia super terram.[9]

[1] Help.   [2] Quarrelsome.   [3] Spiritual.   [4] Living.
[5] Gracious.   [6] Spring.   [7] Established.
[8] E.E.T.S. *workis;* but the MS. is clearly *words.*
[9] "The life of man is a warfare on the earth."

Oppresse [1] yowur gostly enmy, and be
    Crystis own knyght!
Be neuer a cowarde a-geyn [2] yowur
    aduersary!
Yf ye wyll be crownyde ye must nedis fyght.
Intende well, and Gode wyll be yow
    adiutory. [3]   225

Remembur, my frende, the tyme of con-
    tynuance! [4]   226
So helpe me Gode, yt ys but a chery
    tyme! [5]
Spende yt well! Serue Gode with hertis
    affyance.
Dystempure not yowur brayn with
    goode ale nor with wyn.

"Mesure ys tresure"; Y for-byde yow not
    the vse.   230
Mesure yowur sylf euer; be-ware of
    excesse!
The superfluouse gyse [6] I wyll that ye
    refuse;
When nature ys suffysyde, a-non that
    ye sese. [7]   233

Yf a man haue an hors, and kepe hym not
    to hye,
He may then reull hym at hys own
    dysyere;
Yf he be fede ouer well he wyll dysobey,
Ande in happe cast his master in the
    myre.   237

[*New-gyse speaks from behind.*]

NEW-GYSE. Ye sey trew, ser; ye are no
    faytour! [8]   238
I haue fede my wyff so well tyll sche ys
    my master!
I haue a grett wonde on my hede, lo!
    and ther-on leyth a playster;
Ande a-nother ther I pysse my
    peson. [9]   241
Ande [10] my wyf were yowur hors sche wolde
    yow all to-samne. [11]
Ye fede yowur hors in mesure; ye are a
    wyse man!

---

[1] Overcome.   [2] In the face of.
[3] To you helpful.
[4] The duration (brevity) of life.
[5] Brief, as the cherry season (or cherry blossoms).
[6] The fashion of immoderation.
[7] Cease.   [8] Liar.   [9] Peas.
[10] If.   [11] Exceedingly disgrace.

I trow, and ye were the kyngis palfrey-
    man,
A goode horse xulde be geason. [1]   245

MANKYNDE. Wher spekys this felow?
    Wyll he not come nere?
MERCY. All to sone, my brother, I fere
    me, for yow.
He was here ryght now (by hym that
    bowte me dere!) [2]
With other of hys felouse. Thei kan [3]
    moche sorow.   249

They wyll be here ryght sone, yf I owt
    departe.
Thynke on my doctryne! yt xall be
    yowur defence.
Lerne wyll [4] I am here! Sett my wordis in
    herte!
With-in a schorte space I must nedis
    hens.   253

[*Now-a-days speaks from behind.*]

NOW-A-DAYS. The sonner the leuer, and
    yt be ewyn a-non! [5]   254
I trow yowur name ys "Do-lytyll"; ye
    be so longe fro hom.
Yf ye wolde go hens we xall cum euery-
    chon, [6]
Mo then a goode sorte.   257
Ye haue leve, I dare well say;
To hem ye wyll go forth yowur wey.
Men haue lytyll deynte [7] of yowur pley,
Be-cause ye make no sporte.   261

[*Nought speaks from behind.*]

NOUGHT. Yowur potage xall be for-colde,
    ser: when wyll ye go dyne?   262
I haue sene a man lost xx[ti] noblys [8] in as
    lytyll tyme —
Yet yt was not I, be Sent Qisyntyn!
For I was neuer worth a pottfull a
    wortis [9] sythyn I was borne.
My name ys Nought, I loue well to
    make mery;   266
I haue be sethen [10] with ye comyn tapster
    of Bury;

---

[1] Scarce. MS. *gesumme*, which does not rhyme.
Emend. by M.
[2] Dear.   [3] Know.   [4] While.
[5] The sooner the better, if it be even at once.
[6] Everyone.   [7] Pleasure.
[8] Gold coins.   [9] Roots.   [10] Since.

I pleyde so longe the foll that I am ewyn
    wery wery; [1]
Yit xall I be ther ageyn to-morow!   269

MERCY [to Mankind].   I haue moche care
    for yow, my own frende.
Yowur enmys wyll be here a-non; thei
    made ther avaunte.
Thynke well in yowur hert yowur name ys
    "Mankynde";
Be not wnkynde to Gode, I prey yow!
    Be hys seruante!
Be stedefast in condycyon!   Se ye be
    not varyant!   274
    Lose not thorow foly that ys sowte so
    dere!
Gode wyll proue yow sone; ande yf that
    ye be constant,
    Of hys blysse perpetuall ye xall be
    partener.   277

Ye may not haue yowur intent at yowur
    fyrst dysyer.
Se the grett pacyence of Iob and trib-
    ulacyon:
Lyke as the smyth trieth ern in the
    feer,[2]
ı So was he triede by Godis vysytacyon.[3]

He was of yowur nature and of yowur
    fragylyte:[4]   282
    Folow the steppys of hym, my own
    swete son,
Ande sey, as he seyde, in yowur trobyll and
    aduersyte:
Dominus dedit, Dominus abstulit, sicut
    sibi placuit; sit nomen Domini
    benedictum![5]   285

More-ouer, in specyall I gyue yow in
    charge, —
    Be-ware of New-gyse, Now-a-days, and
    Nought!
Nyse in ther a-ray, in language thei be
    large.
    To perverte thi [6] condycyouns all ther
    menys [7] xall be sowte.   289

Gode son, intyrmyse [1] yowur sylff not in
    ther cumpeny!   290
Thei harde not a masse thi[s] twel-
    monyth, I dare well say!
Gyff them non audyence; thei wyll tell
    yow many a lye.
Do truly yowur labure, and kepe yowur
    haly day.   293

Be-ware of Tytivillus [2] (fo[r] he lesyth no
    wey),
    That goth in-vysybull and wyll not be
    sen;
He wyll ronde [3] in yowur ere, and cast a
    nett [4] be-for yowur eyn.
    He ys worst of them all!   Gode let hym
    neuer then! [5]   297

Yf ye dysples Gode, aske mercy a-non,
    Ellys Myscheff wyll be redy to brace [6]
    yow in hys brydyll.
Kysse me now, my dere darlynge!   Gode
    sche[l]de yow from yowur fon!
    Do truly yowur labure, and be neuer
    ydyll!   301
The blyssynge of Gode be with yow, —
    and with all thes worchypp[f]ull
    men!   [Exit.]
MANKYNDE.   Amen! for Sent Charyte,
    amen!   303

Now, blyssyde be Ihesu, my soull ys well
    sacyatt
    With the mellyfluose doctryne of this
    worschyppfull man!
The rebellyn of my flesch, now yt ys
    superatt,[7]
    Thankynge be [to] Gode of the con-
    nynge that I kan.[8]   307

Her wyll I sytt, and tytyll [9] in this papyr
    The incomparable astat of my promy-
    cyon.[10]   [He writes.]

[To the audience.]

Worschypfull souerence, I haue wretyn
    here

---

[1] Very weary.   [2] Iron in the fire.
[3] Affliction.   [4] Frailty.
[5] Job i, 21: "The Lord gave, and the Lord hath
taken away, as it was pleasing to him; blessed be
the name of the Lord."
[6] MS. ther.   [7] Means.

[1] Mix.
[2] A common name in early plays for a devil.
[3] Whisper.
[4] Supposed to render him invisible.
[5] Thrive.   [6] Fasten.
[7] Conquered.   [8] The skill that I have.
[9] Write down.   [10] Promotion?

The gloryuse remembrance of my
   nobyll condycyon,   311

To haue remo[r]s and memory of my sylff.
   Thus wretyn yt ys
To defende me from all superstycyus
   charmys:
*Memento, homo, quod cinis es, et in cinerem
   reuerteris.*[1]
Lo!   I ber on my bryst the bagge [2] of
   myn armys.   315

[Enter New-gyse.]

NEW-GYSE.   The wether ys colde! Gode
   sende ws goode ferys! [3]
*Cum sancto sanctus eris, et cum peruerso,
   peruerteris.*[4]
Ecce quam bonum et quam jocundum,
   quod the deull to the frerys.
Habitare fratres in vnum.[5]   319

MANKYNDE.   I her a felow speke. With
   hym I wyll not mell.[6]
Thys erth with my spade I xall assay to
   delffe;
To eschew ydullnes I do yt myn own selffe.
   I prey Gode sende yt hys fusyon! [7]   323

*[He begins to dig. Enter Now-a-days and
Nought, shouting to the audience.]*

NOW-A-DAYS.   Make rom, sers, for we
   haue be longe! [8]
We wyll cum gyf yow a Crystemes songe.

NOUGHT.   Now I prey all the yemandry [9]
   that ys here
To synge with ws with a mery chere.

*[He sings a line at a time, which New-gyse
and Now-a-days, leading the audience,
sing after him.]*

Yt ys wretyn with a coll,[10] *yt ys wretyn
   with a cole.*   328

---

[1] "Remember, O man, that thou art ashes, and to
  ashes thou shalt return." Cf. Job xxxiv, 15.
[2] Badge.   [3] Fires.
[4] Psalms xviii, 26 (Authorized Version): "With
  he pure thou wilt show thyself pure; and with the
  roward thou wilt shew thyself froward."
[5] Psalms cxxxiii, 1 (Authorized Version): "Behold
  ow good and how pleasant it is for brethren to dwell
  ogether in unity!"
[6] Speak.   [7] Fruition.
[8] Apparently the actors have to pass through the
  udience to reach their platform.
[9] Yeomen, folk.   [10] Coal.

NEW-GYSE AND NOW-A-DAYS.   *Yt ys
wretyn with a colle, yt ys wretyn
[with a cole].*

. . . .
. . . .[1]

All sing.[2]

*Hoylyke, holyke, holyke! holyke, holyke,
   holyke!*   336

NEW-GYSE.   Ey, Mankynde, Gode spede
   yow with yowur spade!
I xall tell yow of a maryage:
I wolde . . . .[3]
   Wer maryede junctly to-gether.   340
MANKYNDE.   Hey yow hens, felouse, with
   bredynge! [4]
Leue yowur derysyon and yowur jap-
   ynge! [5]
I must nedis labure; yt ys my lyvynge.
NOW-A-DAYS.   What, ser? we came but
   lat hethyr.   344

Xall all this corn grow here
That ye xall haue the nexte yer?
Yf yt be so, corn hade nede be dere,
   Ellys ye xall haue a pore lyffe.   348
NOUGHT.   A-lasse, goode fadere, this labor
   fretyth [6] yow to the bone!
But for yowur croppe I take grett mone:
Ye xall neuer spende yt a-lonne:
   I xall assay to geett yow a wyffe.   352

How many acres suppose ye here by
   estymacyon?
NEW-GYSE.   Ey, how ye turne the erth
   wppe and down!
I haue be in my days in many goode
   town,
   Yett saw I neuer such a-nother tyllynge!
MANKYNDE.   Why stonde ye ydyll? Yt
   ys pety that ye were born!   357
NOW-A-DAYS.   We xall bargen with yow,
   and nother moke [7] nor scorne:
Take a goode carte in herwest, and lode yt
   with yowur corne,
   Ande what xall we gyf yow for the
   levynge?   360

---

[1] The song is unprintable.
[2] MS. *Cantant omnes.*
[3] Unprintable.   [4] Politeness.
[5] Mocking.   [6] Consumeth.   [7] Mock.

NOUGHT. He ys a goode starke [1] laburrer!
He wolde fayn do well!
He hath mett with the goode man Mercy
in a schroude sell.[2]
For all this, he may haue many a hungry
mele.
Yit, woll ye se, he ys polytyke: 364
Here xall be goode corn; he may not mysse
yt;
Yf he wyll haue reyn,[3] he may ouer-pysse
yt;
Ande yf he wyll haue compass[t]e,[4] he may
ouer-blysse yt
A lytyll with hys ers lyke. 368

MANKYNDE. Go and do yowur labur!
Gode lett yow neuer the! [5]
Or with my spade I xall yow dynge,[6] by
the Holy Trinyte!
Haue ye non other man to moke but euer
me?
Ye wolde haue me of yowur sett? 372
Hye yow forth lyuely, for hens I wyll yow
dryffe!

[He beats them with his spade.]

NEW-GYSE. A-las, my jewelles! I xall
be schent [7] of my wyff!
NOW-A-DAYS. A-lasse! and I am lyke
neuer for to thryue,
I haue such a buffett. 376

MANKYNDE. Hens I sey, New-gyse,
Now-a-days, and Nowte!
Yt was seyde be-forn all the menys xull[d]
be sought
To peruerte my condycions and brynge me
to nought.
Hens, thevys! Ye haue made many a
lesynge.[8] 380
NOUGHT. Marryde [9] I was for colde, but
now am I warme!
Ye are ewyll avysyde, ser, for ye haue done
harme.
By cokkys body sakyrde,[10] I haue such a
peyn in my arme 383
I may not chonge a man a ferthynge.

[New-gyse, Now-a-days, and Nought
start out.]

[1] Strong.   [2] A bad time.   [3] Rain.   [4] Compost.
[5] Thrive.   [6] Beat.   [7] Punished.   [8] Lie.
[9] Marred.   [10] By God's body consecrated.

MANKYNDE [kneels]. Now I thanke Gode,
knelynge on my kne —
Blyssyde be hys name! he ys of hye
degre —
By the ayde [1] of hys grace that he hath
sente me
iij of myn enmys I haue putt to flyght.

[Holds up his spade.]

Yit this instrument, souerens, ys not
made to defende. 389
Dauide seyth, nec in hasta, nec in gladio,
saluat Dominus.[2]
NOUGHT [over his shoulder]. No, mary, I
be-schrew yow, yt ys in spadibus!
Therfor Crystis curse cum on yowur
hedybus 392
To sende yow lesse myght! [Exiant.

MANKYNDE. I promytt yow thes felouse
wyll no more cum here,
For summe of them, certenly, were summe-
what to nere.
My fadyr Mercy a-vysyde me to be of a
goode chere,
Ande a-gayn my enmys manly for to
fyght. 397

I xall convycte [3] them, I hope, euerychon!
Yet I say amysse; I do yt not a-lone:
With the helpe of the grace of Gode I resyst
my fon [4]
Ande ther malycyuse herte. 401
With my spade I wyll departe, my wor-
schypp[f]ull souerence,
Ande lyue euer with labure, to corecte my
insolence.
I xall go fett corn for my londe. I prey
yow of pacyence;
Ryght sone I xall reverte.[5] 405

[He goes out to get corn to plant.]

[Enter Myschief.]

MYSCHEFF. A-las, a-lasse! that euer I
was wrought!
A-lasse the whyll, I [am] wers then nought!

[1] MS. sysyde, the first two, or possibly three, letters crossed through.
[2] "The Lord saveth neither with the spear, nor
with the sword." Quoted, but incorrectly, from the
Vulgate, Regum i, 47.
[3] Conquer.   [4] Foes.   [5] Return.

Sythyn I was here, by hym that me bought,
   I am wtterly on-don!   409
I, Myscheff, was here at the begynnynge of
   the game,
Ande arguyde with Mercy — Gode gyff
   hym schame!
He hath taught Mankynde, wyll I haue be
   vane,[1]
   To fyght manly a-geyn hys fon.   413

For with hys spade, that was hys wepyn,
New-gyse, Now-a-days, Nought, hath [he]
   all to-beten.
I haue grett pyte to se them wepyn.
   Wyll ye lyst? I here them crye.   417

They cry,[2] [*and Myschief calls to them.*]

A-lasse! a-lasse! Cum hether! I xall be
   yowur borow.[3]
A-lac, a-lac! vene, vene![4] cum hethere
   with sorowe!

[*Enter New-gyse, Now-a-days, and Nought,
   crying.*]

Pesse, fayer babys! Ye xall haue a
   nappyll [5] — to-morow.
   Why grete ye so, why?   421

NEW-GYSE. A-lasse, master! a-lasse, my
   privyte!
MYSCHEFF. A! wher? A-lake![6] fayer
   babe, ba me!
Abyde to sone; [7] I xall yt se.
NOW-A-DAYS. Here, here! se my hede,
   goode master!   425
MYSCHEFF. Lady, helpe! Sely [8] darlynge,
   vene, vene!
I xall helpe the of thi peyn;
I xall smytt of thi hede, and sett yt on
   agayn.
NOUGHT. By Owur Lady, ser, a fayer
   playster!   429

Wyll ye of with hys hede? Yt ys a schreude
   charme!
As for me, I haue non harme.
I were loth to for-bere myn arme.   432
   Ye, pley! *In nomine patris,*[9] choppe!

NEW-GYSE. Ye xall not choppe my
   jewellys, and I may!
NOW-A-DAYS. Ye, Cristis crose! wyll ye
   smyght my hede a-wey?
Ther, wher, on and on? Oute! ye xall not
   assay!
   I myght well be callyde a foppe.   437

MYSCHEFF. I kan choppe yt of and make
   yt a-gayn.
NEW-GYSE. I hade a schreude recumben-
   tibus,[1] but I fele no peyn.   439
NOW-A-DAYS. Ande my hede ys all saue
   and holl agayn. —
Now, towchynge the mater of Mankynde,
Lett ws haue an interleccyon,[2] sythen ye be
   cum hethere.
   Yt were goode to haue an ende.   443

MYSCHEFF. How, how! a mynstrell!
   Know ye ony out? [3]
NOUGHT. I kan pype in a Walsyngham
   wystyll, I, Nought, Nought.   445
MYSCHEFF. Blow a-pase, and thou xall
   brynge hym in with a flewte.

[*There is an explosion of powder, and
   Titivillus shouts within.*]

TYTIVILLUS. I com, with my leggis vndur me!
MYSCHEFF. How, New-gyse, Now-a-days!
   herke or I goo!
When owur hedis wer to-gethere I spake of
   si dedero.[4]
NEW-GYSE. Ye! go thi wey! We xall
   gather mony on-to —
   Ellys ther xall no man hym se.   451

[*To the audience.*]

Now gostly to owur purpos, worschypfull
   souerence,
We intende to gather mony, yf yt plesse
   yowur neclygence,
For a man with a hede that [is] of grett
   omnipotens —
NOW-A-DAYS. Kepe yowur tayll, in goodnes, I prey yow, goode brother!
He ys a worschypp[f]ull man, sers, sauynge
   yowur reuerens!   456

----

[1] Been idle.   [2] MS. *Clamant.*
[3] Protector.   [4] Come.
[5] An apple.   [6] Alack!
[7] Wait a moment.   [8] Pitiful, poor.
[9] "In the name of the Father.".

[1] A knockdown blow.
[2] Consultation.   [3] Aught.
[4] "If I paid" (i.e. spoke of a collection of money).

He louyth no grotis, nor pens, or to-pens:
Gyf ws rede reyallys,[1] yf ye wyll se hys
abhomynabull presens!
NEW-GYSE. Not so! Ye that mow[2]
not pay the ton, pay the tother!

[*They descend, and begin to take up a
collection.*]

At the goode man of this house[3] fyrst we
wyll assay. 460
Gode blysse yow, master! Ye say as yll,
yet ye wyll not sey "nay."
Lett ws go by and by. And do them pay!
Ye pay all a-lyke. Well mut ye fare!

[*The collecting of money over, they return
to the stage.*]

NOUGH[T]. I sey, New-gyse, Now-a-days,
estis vos pecuniatus?[4] 464
I haue cryede a fayer wyll, I beschrew
yowur patus![5]

[*Now-a-days turns to call in Titivillus.*]

NOW-A-DAYS. *Ita vere, magister!*[6] cumme
forth now yowur gatus![7]
He ys a goodly man, sers: make space!
and be ware! 467

[*Enter Titivillus, horribly arrayed like a
devil, with a net in his hand.*]

TITIVILLUS. *Ego sum dominancium dominus,*[8] and my name ys Titivillus.
Ye that haue goode hors, to yow I sey,
caueatis![9]
Here ys an abyll felyschyppe to tryse hym
out at yowur gatis.[10]

He speaks to New-gyse.[11]

Ego probo sic.[12] Ser New-gys, lende me a
peny. 471
NEW-GYSE. I haue a grett purse, ser, but
I haue no monay;
By the masse, I fayll ij farthyngis of an
halpeny;
Yit hade I ten pounds[13] this nyght that
was.

He speaks to Now-a-days.[1]

TITYUILLUS. What ys in thi purse? thou
art a stout felow. 475

NOW-A-DAYS. The deull haue [the][2]
qwyll![3] I am a clen jentyllman.
I prey Gode I be neuer wers storyde[4] then
I am.
Yt xall be otherwyse, I hope, or this
nyght passe. 478

He speaks to Nought.[5]

TYTIVILLUS. Herke now! I say thou hast
many a peny?
NOUGHT. *No[n] nobis, dominie; non nobis,*[6] by Sent Denny!
The deull may daunce in my purse for ony
peny;
Yt ys as clen as a byrdis ars. 482

TITIVILLUS. Now I sey yet a-geyn
caueatis! 483
Her ys an abyll felyschyppe to tryse hem
out of yowur gatis.
Now I sey, New-gyse, Now-a-days, and
Nought,
Go and serche the contre! anon that [yt][7]
be sowghte,
Summe here, summe ther, what yf ye may
cache owghte.[8] 487

Yf ye fayll of hors, take what ye may
ellys!
NEW-GYSE. Then speke to Mankynde for
the recumbentibus[9] of my jewellys.
NOW-A-DAYS. Remembre my brokyn hede
in the worschyppe of the v. vow-
ellys.[10]
NOUGHT. Ye, goode ser, and the sytyca[11]
in my arme! 491
TITYUILLUS. I know full well what Mankynde dyde to yow;
Myschyff hat informyde [me] of all the
matere thorow.

---

[1] Royals, gold coins. [2] May.
[3] Apparently the host of the inn.
[4] "Are you monied?"
[5] Pate, head. [6] "Yea truly, Master."
[7] Gate, door. [8] "I am the lord of lords."
[9] Beware. [10] To snatch them out at your gates.
[11] MS. *Loquitur ad New-gyse.*
[12] "I will try him this way." [13] MS. X*li*.

[1] MS. *Loquitur ad Now-a-days.*
[2] Added by M.
[3] Lot, set? (E.E.T.S.) *Qy.* qwytt.
[4] Stored (with money).
[5] MS. *Loquitur ad Nought.*
[6] "Not unto us, O lord, not unto us."
[7] Added by M. [8] Catch (steal) anything.
[9] Knockdown blow.
[10] The five vowels. [11] Sciatica.

I xall venge yowur quarell, I made Gode
a-vow.

    Forth! and espye were ye may do
      harme! 495
    Take W[illiam] Fyde,[1] yf ye wyll haue
      ony mo.
    I sey, New-gyse, wether art thou
      avysyde to go? 497

NEV-GYSE.   Fyrst I xall be-gyn at M[aster]
    Huntyngton of Sanston;
Fro thens I xall go to Wylliam Thurlay of
    Hanston,
Ande so forth to Pycharde of Trumpyngton:
    I wyll kepe me to thes iij. 501

NOW-A-DAYS.   I xall goo to Wyllyham
    Baker of Walton,
To Rycherde Bollman of Gayton,
I xall spare master Woode of Fullburn;
    He ys a *noli me tangere!* [2] 505

NOUGHT.   I xall goo to Wyllyam Patryke
    of Massyngham;
I xall spare master Alyngton of Botysam,
Ande Hamonde of Soffeham.

    Felous, cum forth! and go we hens
      to-gethyr, 509
    For drede of *in manus tuas*, qweke.[3]
NEU-GYSE.   Syth we xall go, lett ws se
    well ware and wether;
    Yf we may be take, we com no more
      hethyr. 512
    Lett ws con well owur neke verse,[4]
    that we have not a cheke.

TITYVILLUS.   Goo yowur wey, a deull
    wey! Go yowur wey, all!
I blysse yow with my lyfte honde! [5] Foull
    yow be-fall!
Com a-gayn, I werne, as sone as I yow
    call,
    A[nd] brynge yowur a-vantage in-to this
    place. 517

[*Exeunt Mischief, New-gyse, Now-a-days,
    and Nought.*]

To speke with Mankynde I wyll tary here
    this tyde,
Ande assay hys goode purpose for to sett
    a-syde.
The goode man Mercy xall no lenger be
    hys gyde;
    I xall make hym to dawnce a-nother
      trace! [1] 521

Euer I go invysybull — yt ys my jett; [2]
Ande be-for hys ey, thus I wyll hange my
    nett
To blench hys syght. I hope to haue hys
    fote mett,[3]
    To yrke [4] hym of hys labur I xall make a
      frame: [5] 525
Thys borde xall be hyde wndur the erth
    preuely;
Hys spade xall entur, I hope, ouer redyly; [6]
Be then [7] he hath assayde, he xall be very
    angry, 528
Ande lose hys pacyens, peyn of schame.

[*He puts a board under the earth that Man-
    kind is tilling.*]

I xall menge [8] hys corne with drawk and
    with durnell; [9]
Yt xall not be lyke to sow nor to sell.
Yondyr he commyth. I prey of cownsell.
He xall wene grace were wane.[10] 533

[*Enter Mankind with a sack of corn.*]

MANKYNDE.   Now Gode, of hys mercy,
    sende ws of hys sonde! [11]
I haue brought seed her to sow with my
    londe;
Qwyll I ouer dylew yt,[12] here yt xall stonde.

[*He sets the corn down, and Titivillus goes
out with it. Mankind takes up his spade.*]

*In nomine Patris et Filii et Spiritus
    Sancti,*[13] now I wyll be-gyn. 537

---

[1] This and the following allusions are doubtless
"local hits." All the towns mentioned lie within a
short distance from Cambridge.
[2] "Touch me not," an irascible fellow.
[3] "Into thy hands" quick. Possibly the allusion
is to the hands of the sheriff.
[4] Neck-verse, the first verse of the fifty-first Psalm,
by citing which a person condemned to death might
claim right of clergy in order to avoid the gallows.
[5] Left hand. Devils and witches were supposed to
use the left hand, especially in incantations and
"blessings."

[1] Dance.   [2] Fashion.
[3] Caught (E.E.T.S.). Manly prints *wett*, which
seems correct.
[4] Disgust.   [5] A frame of wood.
[6] Manly emends *on-readily*.
[7] By the time that.   [8] Mix.
[9] The names of certain weeds; the "thorns and
thistles" of Genesis iii,18.
[10] Think grace were lacking.   [11] Message.
[12] While I dig it over?
[13] "In the name of the Father, and of the Son, and
of the Holy Spirit."

[Tries to dig; his spade strikes the board.]

Thys londe ys so harde yt makyth wn-
    lusty and yrke.[1]
I xall sow my corn at wyntur and lett Gode
    werke.

[He turns to get his sack of corn.]

A-lasse! my corn ys lost! Here ys a foull
    werke!   540
  I se well, by tyllynge lytyll xall I wyn.

[He throws his spade down in anger.]

Here I gyf wppe my spade, for now and
    for euer!
To occupye my body I wyll not put me in
    deuer![2]

Here Titivillus goth out with the spade.

I wyll here my ewynsonge[3] here or I
    dysseuer.[4]   544
Thys place I assynge as for my kyrke;[5]
Here, in my kerke, I knell on my kneys.

[He kneels, and with his beads begins to say
the Lord's Prayer.]

Pater noster, qui es in celis, [etc.]   547

[Re-enter Titivillus.]

TYTYVILLUS.   I promes yow I haue no
    lede on my helys!
  I am here a-geyn to make this felow
    yrke.   549

Qwyst![6] pesse! I xall go to hys ere, and
    tytyll[7] ther-in.

[He approaches Mankind, and whispers
in his ear.]

" A schorte preyere thyrlyth hewyn.[8]
Of thi preyere blyn.[9]
Thou art holyer then euer was ony of thi
    kyn.
  A-ryse and avent thee! nature com-
    pellys."   553

[Mankind rises, and addresses the audience.]

MANKYNDE.   I wyll in-to thi yerde,
    souerens, and cum a-geyn sone;

---

[1] Troublesome.   [2] Hardship.
[3] Evensong.   [4] Depart.   [5] Church.
[6] Whist (be silent)!   [7] Whisper.
[8] Pierces heaven.   [9] Cease.

For drede of the colyke and eke of the
    ston
I wyll go do that nedis must be don.
  My bedis xall be here for who-summ
    euer wyll cumme.   *[Exiat.* 557

TITYUILLUS.   Mankynde was besy in hys
    prayere, yet I dyde hym aryse;
He is conveyde (be Cryst!) from hys dyvyn
    seruyce.
Whether ys he, trow ye? I-wysse I am
    wondur wyse!
  I haue sent hym forth to schyte les-
    ynges.   561
Yff ye haue ony syluer, in happe pure
    brasse,
Take a lytyll pow[d]er of Parysch[1] and cast
    ouer hys[2] face,
Ande ewyn in the howll-flyght[3] let hym
    passe.
Titivillus kan lerne yow many praty
    thyngis!   565

I trow Mankynde wyll cum a-geyn son,
Or ellys, I fer me, ewynsonge wyll be
    don.
Hys bedis xall be trysyde[4] a-syde, and
    that a-non.
  Ye xall [se][5] a goode sport, yf ye wyll
    a-byde.   569
Mankynde cummyth a-geyn: well fare he!
I xall answere hym *ad omnia quare;*[6]
Ther xall be sett a-broche a clerycall
    mater;
  I hope, of hys purpose to sett hym
    a-syde.   573

[Re-enter Mankind.]

MANKYNDE.   Ewynsonge hath be in the
    saynge, I trow, a fayer wyll!
I am yrke of yt: yt ys to longe be on myle.
Do wey! I wyll no more so oft on the
    chyrche-style;[7]
Be as be may, I xall do a-nother.   577
Of labure and preyer, I am nere yrke of
    both;
I wyll no more of yt, thow Mercy be
    wroth!
My hede ys very heuy, I tell yow for soth;

---

[1] Paris powder.   [2] Its (the coin's).
[3] Owl-flight (the dark).   [4] Thrown.
[5] Added by M.   [6] " At every why."
[7] Stile in the churchyard.

I xall slepe full my bely,[1] and he were my
   brother.   581

[*Goes to sleep and snores.*]

TITYVILLUS [*to the audience*].   Ande euer
   ye dyde, for me kepe now yowur
   sylence!
Not a worde, I charge yow, peyn of xl
   pens!
A praty game xall be scheude yow, or ye go
   hens.
   Ye may here hym snore; he ys sade
      a-slepe!   585
Qwyst! pesse! the Deull ys dede!   I xall
   goo ronde [2] in hys ere.

[*He approaches Mankynde, and whispers in
   his ear.*]

"A-lasse, Mankynde! a-lasse!   Mercy
   stown a mere! [3]
He ys runn a-way fro hys master, ther wot
   no man where.
   More-ouer, he stale both a hors and a
      nete.[4]   589

But yet I herde sey he brake hys neke as he
   rode in Fraunce;
But I thynke he rydyth ouer the galous [5]
   to lern for to daunce,
By-cause of hys theft.   That ys hys
   gouernance!
   Trust no more on hym; he ys a marryde
      man!   593
Mekyll sorow with thi spade be-forn thou
   hast wrought.
A-ryse, and aske mercy of Neu-gyse, Now-
   a-days, and Nought!
Thei cum.   A-vyse thee for the best.   Lett
   ther goode wyll be sought.
   Ande thi own wyff [be]brethell,[6] and
      take thee a lemman." [7]   597

[*To the audience.*]

For well, euerychon! for I haue don my
   game,
For I haue brought Mankynde to myscheff
   and to schame.

---

[1] My belly full.   [2] Whisper.
[3] Hath stolen a mare.   [4] Ox.
[5] Gallows.
[6] Be-brothel, put to the brothel?
[7] Sweetheart, mistress.

[*Exit Titivillus.   Mankind awakes.*]

MANKYNDE.   Whope! who!   Mercy hath
   brokyn hys nekekycher,[1] a-vows!
Or he hangyth by the neke hye wpp on the
   gallouse!
A-dew, fayer mastere!   I wyll hast me to
   the ale-house,
   Ande speke with New-gyse, Now-a-days
      and Nought,   603
A[nd] geett me a lemman with a smat-
   trynge [2] face.

[*Enter New-gyse running, with a broken rope
   about his neck.*]

NEW-GYSE.   Make space! for Cokkes
   body sakyrde, make space!
A ha! well on ron!   Gode gyff hym ewyll
   grace!
   We were nere Sent Patrykes wey, by hym
      that me bought;   607

I was twychyde [3] by the neke; the game
   was be-gunne;
A grace was, the halter brast asondur —
   Ecce signum!

[*He holds up the broken rope.*]

The halff ys a-bowte my neke.   We hade a
   nere rune!
"Be-ware," quod the goode wyff when
   sche smot of here husbondis hede,
   "be-ware!"   611
Myscheff ys a convicte, for he coude [4] hys
   neke-verse,
My body gaff a swynge when I hynge
   wpp-on the casse.[5]
A-lasse! he wyll hange such a lygh[t]ly [6]
   man, and a fers,
   For stelynge of an horse!   I prey Gode
      gyf hym care!   615

Do wey [7] this halter!   What deull doth
   Mankynde here, with sorow!
A-lasse, how my neke ys sore!   I make
   a-vowe!
M[ANKYNDE].   Ye be welcom, New-gyse!
   Ser, what chere with yow?

---

[1] Neckerchief (i.e. neck).
[2] Ready for kissing? (*N.E.D.*)
[3] Twitched.   [4] Knew.
[5] Frame of the gibbet?
[6] Likely.   [7] Take off.

NEW-GYSE. Well, ser; I haue no cause to
       morn!   619
M[ANKYNDE].   What was ther abowte
       yowur neke, so Gode yow a-mende?
NEW-GYSE.   In feyth, Sent Audrys holy
       bende.[1]
I haue a lytyll dyshes,[2] as yt plesse Gode to
       sende,
   With a runnynge rynge-worme.[3]   623

[Enter Now-a-days laden with church plate.]

NOW-A-DAYS.   Stonde a rom, I prey the,
       brother myn!
I haue laburyde all this nyght; wen xall we
       go dyn?
A chyrche her be-syde xall pay for ale,
       brede, and wyn.
   Lo, here ys stoff wyll serue!   627
NEW-GYSE.   Now, by the holy Mary, thou
       art bettur marchande then I!

[Enter Nought.]

NOUGHT.   A-vante, knawys! lett me go by!
   I kan not geet, and I xulde sterue.[4] 630
[.   .   .   .   .
   .   .   .   .[5]]

[Enter Mischief running, with broken fetters
       on his arms.]

MYSCHEFF.   Here cummyth a man of
       armys! Why stonde ye so styll?
Of murdur and man-slawter I haue my
       bely fyll.
NOW-A-DAYS.   What, Myscheff, haue ye
       bene in presun, and yt be yowur
       wyll?
Me semyth ye haue scoryde[6] a peyr of
       fetters.   634
MYSCHEFF.   I was chenyde by the armys
       — lo! I haue them here —
The chenys I brast asundyr, and kyllyde
       the jaylere,
Ye, ande hys fayer wyff halsyde[7] in a
       cornere.
   A! how swetly I kyssyde tho swete
       mowth of hers!   638

When I hade do, I was myn owghun bottler;

[1] Band (rope).   [2] Disease.
[3] Ring-worm (alluding to his sore neck).
[4] Get, if I should starve.
[5] Apparently a lacuna in the MS.
[6] Scoured, polished (by wearing).   [7] Embraced.

I brought a-wey with me both dysch and
       dublere.[1]
Here ys a-now for me; be of goode chere!
   Yet well fare the new chesance![2]   642
MANKYNDE.   I aske mercy of New-gyse,
       Now-a-days, and Nought.
Onys with my spade I remembur that I
       faught:
I wyll make yow a-mendis yf I hurt yow
       ought,
   Or dyde ony grevaunce.   646

NEW-GYSE.   What a deull lykyth[3] thee
       to be of this dysposycyon?
MANKYNDE.   I drempt Mercy was hange
       — this was my vysyon —
Ande that to yow iij I xulde haue recors
       and remocyon.[4]
   Now I prey yow hertyly of yowur goode
       wyll.   650
I crye you mercy of all that I dyde
       a-mysse.
NOW-A-DAYS [aside].   I sey, New-gys,
       Nought! Tytivillus made all this:
As sekyr[5] as Gode ys in hewyn, so yt ys!
NOUGHT.   Stonde wppe on yowur feet!
   why stonde ye so styll?

NEW-GYSE.   Master Myscheff, we wyll
       yow exort   655
Mankyndis name in yowur bok for to re-
       port.
MYSCHEFF.   I wyll not so; I wyll sett a
       corte.
   A! do yt forma jurys, dasarde![6]

Now-a-days, mak proclamacyon.

NOW-A-DAYS.   "Oy-yt! Oy-yit! Oyet![7]
   All maner of men and comun women,
To the cort of Myschyff othere cum or sen!
Mankynde xall retorn; he ys one of owur
       men."
MYSCHEFF.   Nought, cum forth! Thou
       xall be stewerde.[8]   663

NEW-GYSE.   Master Myscheff, hys syde
       gown may be solde;

[1] Dish and plate.
[2] Bargain.   [3] Pleaseth.
[4] Removing.   [5] Sure.
[6] Do it in legal form, fool!   [7] Oyes.
[8] Steward of the Manor. The scene is a parody on
the proceedings in a manor-court.

He may haue a jakett ther-of, and mony
   tolde.[1]

MANKYNDE.   I wyll do for the best, so I
   haue no colde.   666

[He takes off his gown.]

Holde, I prey yow, and take yt with yow;
Ande let me haue yt a-geyn in ony wyse!

Nought is busy writing.[2]

NEW-GYSE.   I promytt yow a fresch
   jakett after the new gyse.

MANKYNDE.   Go and do that longyth to
   yowur offyce;
A[nd] spare that ye may!   671

*[New-gyse goes out with Mankind's coat.
Nought hands what he has written to
Mischief.]*

NOUGHT.   Holde, master Myscheff, and
   rede this!

MYSCHEFF.   Here ys — "*blottybus in blottis,
Blottorum blottibus istis.*"
   I be-schrew yowur erys, a [3] fayer hande!

NOW-A-DAYS.   Ye! yt ys a goode renny[n]ge
   fyst;   676
Such an hande may not be myst.

NOUGHT.   I xulde haue don bettur, hade I
   wyst.

MYSCHEFF.   Take hede, sers, yt stonde
   you on hande!   679

[He reads the document.]

" *Curia tenta generalis,*" [4]
In a place ther goode ale ys,
" *Anno regni regitalis
   Edwardi millateni.*" [5]
On yestern day, in Feuerere, the yere
   passyth fully.
As Nought hath wrytyn; here ys owur
   tulli,[6]
   "*Anno regni regis nulli.*" [7]   686

NOW-A-DAYS.   What, how, New-gyse!
   Thou makyst moche [taryynge].[8]
That jakett xall not be worth a ferthynge.

[1] Counted.   [2] MS. *Nought scri.*   [3] MS. &.
[4] "The general heading of the record of Manorial-
Court proceedings." J. Herbert. (E.E.T.S.)
[5] "In the regnal year of King Edward, one thousand."
[6] Quarrel, brawl?
[7] "In the regnal year of King Nobody."
[8] Added by M.

*[Re-enter New-gyse with Mankind's gown
   much abbreviated.]*

NEW-GYSE.   Out of my wey, sers, for drede
   of fyghtynge!
Lo! here ys a feet tayll,[1] lyght to leppe
   a-bowte!   690

NOUGHT.   Yt ys not schapyn worth a
   morsell of brede!
Ther ys to moche cloth; yt weys as ony
   lede.
I xall goo and mende yt, ellys I wyll lose
   my hede.
Make space, sers! lett me go owte!   694

[Nought goes out with the gown.]

MYSCHEFF.   Mankynde, cum hether!
   God sende yow the gowte!
Ye xall goo to all the goode felouse in the
   cuntre a-boute;
On-to the goode wyff, when the goode man
   ys owte.
   "I wyll," say ye!

MANKYNDE.   I wyll, ser.   698

NEW-GYSE.   There arn but sex dedly
   synnys: lechery ys non,
As yt may be verefyede be ws brethellys
   euerychon.[2]
Ye xall goo robbe, stell, and kyll, as fast as
   ye may gon.
   "I wyll," sey ye!

M[ANKYNDE].   I wyll, ser.   702

NOW-A-DAYS.   On Sundays, on the morow,
   erly be tyme,
Ye xall with ws to the alle-house erly to go
   dyne,
A[nd] for-ber masse and matens, owres and
   prime.[3]
   "I wyll," sey ye!

M[ANKYNDE].   I wyll, ser.   706

MYSCHEFF.   Ye must haue be yowur syde
   a longe *da pacem,*[4]
As trew men ryde be the wey, for to on-
   brace [5] them;
Take ther money, kytt ther throtes! thus
   ouer-face [6] them.
   "I wyll," sey ye!

MANKYNDE.   I wyll, ser.   710

[1] Fine tail.   [2] Everyone.
[3] Church services.
[4] "Give-peace," a dagger.
[5] Unbrace.   [6] Overcome.

[*Re-enter Nought, with Mankind's gown cut into a ridiculously short jacket.*]

NOUGHT.   Here ys a joly jakett! How sey ye?

NEW-GYSE.   Yt ys a goode jake[t] of fence [1] for a mannys body!

[*They put it on Mankind.*]

HAY, doog! [2] hay, whoppe! whoo! go yowur wey lyghtly!
Ye are well made for to ren.   714

[*Enter Mercy at a distance.*]

MYSCHEFF.   Tydyngis, tydyngis! I haue a-spyede on!
Hens with yowur stuff! Fast we were gon!
I be-schrew the last xall com to hys hom!

Let all say: [3]

[ALL.]   Amen!

MERCY.   What, how, Mankynde! Fle that felyschyppe, I yow prey!

MANKYNDE.   I xall speke with [thee] a-nother tyme; to morn, or the next day.
We xall goo forth to-gether to kepe my faders yer-day. [4]
A tapster! a tapster! stow, statt, stow!

MYSCHEFF.   A myscheff go with here! I haue a foull fall.   723
Hens, a-wey fro me! or I xall be-schyte yow all.

NEW-GYSE.   What, how! ostler, hostler! lende ws a foot-ball!
Whoppe, whow! a-now, a-now, a-now, a-now!   726

[*Exeunt all, including Mankind.*]

MERCY.   My mynde ys dyspersyde! My body tir-trymmelyth as the aspen leffe!
The terys xuld trekyll down by my chekys, were not yowur reuerrence.
Yt were to me solace, the cruell vysyta-cyon of deth.
With-out rude be-hauer I kan [not] [5] expresse this inconvenyens;

Wepynge, sythynge, and sobbynge, were my suffycyens; [1]   731
All naturall nutriment to me as caren ys odybull; [2]
My inwarde afflixcyon yeldyth me tedy-ouse wn-to yowur presens;
I kan not bere yt ewynly, that man-kynde ys so flexibull.   734

Man, on-kynde wher-euer thou be! for all this world was not apprehensyble
To dyscharge thin orygynall offence, thraldam, and captyuyte,
Tyll Godis own welbelouyde Son was obedient and passyble.
Euery droppe of his bloode was schede to purge thin iniquite.
I dyscomende and dysalow this oftyn imutabylyte;   739
To euery creature thou art dyspect-uose and odyble. [3]
Why art thou so on-curtess, so inconsyd-eratt? A-lasse! who [4] ys me!
As the fane [5] that turnyth with the wynde, so thou art conuerty-ble. [6]

In trust ys treson; this promes ys not credyble;   743
Thys peruersyose ingratytude I can not rehers.
To go ouer to all the holy corte of hewyn thou art despectyble,
As a nobyll versyfyer makyth mencyon in this verse:
Lex et natura, Christus et omnia iura
Damnant in-gratum; lugetur eum fore natum. [7]   748

O goode Lady and Mother of Mercy, haue pety and compassyon
Of the wrechydnes of Mankynde that ys so wanton and so frayll!
Lett Mercy excede Justice, dere Mother!
A[d]mytt this supplycacyon —
Equyte to be leyde ouer party, [8] and Mercy to prevayll.   752

---

[1] Coat of mail (or of defence against the cold?).
[2] A corruption of "God," used as a vulgar oath.
[3] MS. *dicant omnes.*
[4] Anniversary (usually a service for the dead).
[5] Ad[d]ed by M.

[1] Sustenance, food.   [2] Carrion is hateful.
[3] Contemptible and odious.
[4] Woe.   [5] Weather-vane.
[6] Changeable.
[7] "Law and nature, Christ and all justice con-demn the ingrate; he will be sorry that he was born."
[8] To be overcome somewhat?

To sensuall lyvynge ys reprouable that ys
  now-a-days,
  As be the comprehence of this mater yt
  may be specyfyede.
New-gyse, Now-a-days, Nought, with ther
  allectuose [1] ways
  They haue pervertyde Mankynde, my
  swet sun, I haue well espyede.   756

A! with thes cursyde caytyfs, and I may,
  he xall not long indure.
  I, Mercy, hys father gostly,[2] wyll procede forth, and do my propyrte.[3]
Lady, helpe! This maner of lyvynge ys a
  detestabull plesure;   759
Vanitas vanitatum, all ys but a vanyte.

Mercy xall neuer be convicte of his on-
  curtes condycyon;
  With wepynge terys, be nyghte and be
  day, I wyll goo, and neuer sesse.
Xall I not fynde hym? Yes, I hope. Now
  Gode be my proteccyon!

  [He calls aloud.]

My predylecte son, wher be ye? Mankynde! *vbi es?* [4]   764

*Exit Mercy crying "Ubi es?" Enter Mis-
  chief.]*

MYSCHEFF. My prepotent father, when
  ye sowpe,[5] sowpe owt yowur messe.
Ye are all to-gloryede [6] in yowur termys;
  ye make many a lesse.[7]
Wyll ye here? He cryeth euer "Mankynde, *vbi es?*"   767

Enter New-gyse, Now-a-days, and Nought.]

NEW-GYSE. Hic, hyc! hic, hic! hic, hic!
  hic, hic! [8]
That ys to say, here! here! here! ny dede in
  the cryke.[9]
Yf ye wyll haue hym, goo and syke, syke,
  syke! [10]
  Syke not ouer longe, for losynge of
  yowur mynde!   771
Now-a-days. Yf ye wyll haue Mankynde
  — how, *domine, domine, domine!* —

Ye must speke to the schryue [1] for a
  cepe coppus,[2]
Ellys ye must be fayn to retorn with
  non est inventus.[3]
  How say ye, ser? my bolte ys
  schott.   775
NOUGHT. I am doynge of my nedyngis:
  be ware how ye schott!
Fy, fy, fy! I haue fowll a-rayde my fote.
Be wyse for schotynge with yowur takyllys,[4]
  for, Gode wott,
  My fote ys fowly ouer-schett.   779

MYSCHEFF. A parlement! a parlement! [5]
  Cum forth, Nought, be-hynde!
A cownsell be-lyue! [6] I am a-ferde Mercy
  wyll hym fynde.
How say ye? and what sey ye? How xall we
  do with Mankynde?
NEU-GYSE. Tysche! a flyes weynge! [7]
  Wyll ye do well?   783
He wenyth [8] Mercy were honge for stelynge
  of a mere.
Myscheff, go sey to hym that Mercy
  sekyth euerywere;
He wyll honge hym selff, I wndyrtake, for
  fere.
MYSCHEFF. I assent ther-to; yt ys
  wyttyly seyde, and well.

NOW-A-DAYS. I-wyppe yt in thi cote;[9]
  a-non yt wer don.
Now, Sent Gabryellis modyr saue the
  clothes of thi schon! [10]
All the bokys in the worlde, yf thei hade be
  wndon,
  Kowde not a cownselde ws bett.   791

Here [11] *exit Myscheff. [He returns
  leading Mankind, now a victim of despair.]*
MYSCHEFF. How, Mankynde! cumm and
  speke with Mercy! He ys here fast
  by.
MANKYNDE. A roppe! a rope! a rope! I
  am not worthy!

---

[1] Alluring.   [2] Spiritual.   [3] Peculiar task.
[4] "Where art thou?"   [5] Sup.
[6] Exceedingly glorified. Manly emends to *to-glos-
ede.*
[7] Lying.   [8] Here.   [9] Creek.   [10] Seek.

[1] Sheriff.   [2] "Take his body," a legal phrase.
[3] "He is not found," a legal phrase.
[4] Tackles (bow and arrows, E.E.T.S.); but possibly an obscene pun.
[5] Consultation.   [6] Quickly.
[7] A fly's weight (a trifle).   [8] Thinketh.
[9] Put it quickly in thy coat (i.e. hide the rope?).
[10] Shoes.   [11] MS. *hic.*

MYSCHEFF. A-non, a-non, a-non! I haue
 yt here redy;
 With a tre also that I haue gett. 795

[They produce a rope, and also a gallows-
tree.]

Holde the tre, Now-a-days! Nought, take
 hede, and be wyse!
NEU-GYSE. Lo, Mankynde, do as I do.
 This ys thi new gyse.[1]
Gyff [2] the roppe just to thy [3] neke: this
 ys myn a-vyse.

[New-gyse adjusts the rope about his own
neck. Mercy enters at a distance.]

MYSCHEFF. Helpe thi sylff, Nought!
 lo, Mercy ys here! 799
He skaryth ws with a bales; [4] we may no
 lengere tary.

[They run away. New-gyse, in his haste
forgetting the rope, hangs himself.]

NEW-GYSE. Qweke, qweke, qweke! [5]
 A-lass, my thrott! I beschrew
 yow, mary!
A, Mercy! Crystis coppyde [6] curse go
 with yow, and Sent Dauy!

[They return and release him.]

A-lasse, my wesant! [7] Ye wer sumwhat
 to nere. 803

Exiant [all save Mankind, who falls in
despair on the floor. Mercy ascends the
stage, and addresses him.]

MERCY. A-ryse, my precyose redempt
 son! Ye be to me full dere.
He ys so tymerouse; me semyth hys
 vytall spryt doth expy[re].
MANKYNDE. Alasse! I haue be so bes-
 tyally dysposyde I dare not a-pere.
To se yowur solaycyose [8] face I am not
 worthy to dysyer. 807

MERCY. Yowur crymynose [9] compleynt
 wondyth my hert as a lance!
Dyspose yowur sylff mekly to aske mercy,
 and I wyll assent.

Yelde me nethyr golde nor tresure, but
 yowur humbyll obeysyance,
The voluntary subieccyon of yowur hert,
 and I am content. 811

MANKYNDE. What! aske mercy yet onys
 a-gayn? Alas, yt were a wyld
 petycyn!
Ewyr to offend and euer to aske mercy,
 that ys a puerilite.
Yt ys so abhomminabell to rehers my werst
 transgrescion;
I am not worthy to hawe mercy, be no
 possibilite! 815

MERCY. O Mankend, my singler solas,
 this is a lamentabyll excuse.
The dolorus feris [1] of my hert, how thei
 begyn to a-mownte!
O blyssed [2] Ihesu, help thou this synfull
 synner to redeme!
Nam hec est mutacio dextre Excelsi: vertit
Impios, et non sunt. [3]

A-ryse and aske mercy, Mankend, and be
 associat to me! 820
 Thy deth schall be my hewynesse: alas!
 tys pety yt schuld be thus.
Thy obstinacy wyll exclude [thee] fro the
 glorius perpetuite.
 Yet, for my lofe, ope thy lyppys, and sey
 "*miserere mei, Deus!*" [4]

MANKEND. The egall justyse of God wyll
 not permytte sych a synfull wrech
To be rewyvyd and restoryd a-geyn. Yt
 were impossibyll!
MERCY. The justice of God wyll as I
 wyll, as hym sylfe doth precyse: [5]
Nolo mortem peccatoris, inquit,[6] and yff
 he wyll [be] [7] reducyble. 827

MANKEND. Than mercy, good Mercy!
 What ys a man wyth-owte mercy?

---

[1] New-gyse attempts to show him the latest fashion in suicide by hanging.
[2] Adjust. [3] MS. *pye;* corr. by M.
[4] A scourge. [5] Queak (sound of choking).
[6] Huge. [7] Throat.
[8] Solace-giving. [9] Marked by crime.

[1] Fires.
[2] MS. *pirssie;* emend. by M.
[3] "For this is the change of the right hand of the
Most High: he overthrows the wicked, and they are
not." Cf. in the Vulgate, Psalmi lxxvi, 11, and Pro-
verbia xii, 7.
[4] "Have mercy on me, O God." Psalms lxi, i.
[5] Precisely determine.
[6] "I do not wish the death of sinners, he said."
Cf. Ezekiel xxxiii, 11.
[7] Added by M.

Lytyll ys our parte of paradyse were
   mercy ne were.[1]
Good Mercy, excuse the ineuytabyll ob-
   ieccion of my gostly enmy:
The prowerbe seyth "the trewth tryith
   the sylfe." Alas! I hawe mech
   care.[2]   831

MERCY. God wyll not make yow preuy on-
   to hys last iugement.
Justyce and equite xall be fortyfyid, I
   wyll not denye.
Trowthe may not so cruelly procede in hys
   streyt [3] argument,
But that Mercy schall rewle the mater
   with-owte controuersye.

Aryse now, and go with me in thys deam-
   bulatorye! [4]
Inclyne yowyr capacite! My doctrine
   ys conuenient.
Synne not in hope of mercy! That ys a
   cryme notary; [5]
To truste ouermoche in a prince, yt ys
   not expedient.   839

In hope, when ye syn, ye thynke to
   haue mercy: be-ware of that awen-
   ture! [6]
The good Lord seyd to the lecherus
   woman of Chanane,[7] —
The holy gospell ys the awtorite, as we
   rede in scrypture, —
"*Vade! etiam amplius noli peccare.*"[8] 843

Cryst preseruyd this synfull woman takyn
   in a-wowtry:[9]
He seyde to here theis wordis, "Go, and
   syn no more!"
So to yow: "Go, and syn no more!" Be-
   ware of weyn [10] confidens of mercy;
Offend not a prince on trust of hys
   fauour, as I [11] seyd before.   847
Yf ye fele your sylfe trappyd in the snare of
   your gostly enmy,
Aske mercy a-non; be-ware of the con-
   tynnance! [12]

Whyll a wond [1] ys fresch, yt ys prowyd
   curabyll be surgery,   850
That, yf yt procede ouyrlonge, yt ys
   cawse of gret grewance.

MANKEND. To aske mercy and to haue,
   this ys a lyberall possescion.
Schall this expedycius petycion euer be
   alowyd, as ye hawe in syght?
MERCY. In this present lyfe mercy ys plente,
   tyll deth makyth hys dywysion;
But, whan ye be go, *vsque ad minimum
   quadrantem* [2] ye scha[ll] rekyn this
   ryght.   855

Aske mercy, and hawe, whyll the body
   with the sow[l]e hath hys annexion;
Yf ye tary tyll your dyscesse, ye may hap
   of your desyre to mysse.
Be repentant here! Trust not the owur of
   deth! Thynke on this lessun:
"*Ecce nunc tempus acceptabile! ecce nunc
   dies salutis!*" [3]   859

All the wertu in the wor[l]d yf ye myght
   comprehend,
Your merytis were not premyabyll [4] to
   the blys a-bowe.
Not to the holest [5] [is] joy of hewyn, of
   your proper efforte to ascend;
With Mercy ye may, I tell yow no fabyll,
   scrypture doth prewe.   863

MANKEND. O Mercy, my suatius [6] solas
   and synguler recreatory,[7]
My predilecte specyall! ye are worthy to
   hawe my lowe; [8]
For, wyth-owte deserte, and menys sup-
   plicatorie,
Ye be compacient [9] to my inexcusabyll
   reprowe.   867

A! yt swemyth [10] my hert to thynk how on-
   wysely I hawe wroght.
Tytiuilly, that goth invisibele, hynge hys
   nett be-fore my eye,

---

[1] No protection (or no where, lacking).
[2] Much care.   [3] Strict.
[4] Place to walk in.   [5] A notable crime.
[6] Peril.   [7] Canaan?
[8] "Go! and now sin no more." John viii, 11.
[9] Adultery.   [10] Vain.
[11] MS. *he;* corr. by M.   [12] Continuance in it.

[1] Wound.
[2] "Up to the last farthing."
[3] "Behold, now is the accepted time! behold, now is the day of salvation!" II Corinthians vi, 2.
[4] Deserving of reward.   [5] The most perfect.
[6] Sweet.   [7] Source of comfort.
[8] Have my love.   [9] Compassionate
[10] Maketh to swim.

And by hys fantasticall visionys sedo-
ciusly [1] sowght,
Be New-gyse, Now-a-dayis, Nowght,
causyd me to obey. 871

MERCY. Mankend, ye were obliuyows of
my doctrine manyterye! [2]
I seyd be-fore Titiuilly wold a-say yow
a bronte. [3]
Be-ware fro hens-forth of hys fablys delu-
sory!
The prowerbe seyth *"Jacula prefata mi-
nus ledunt."* [4] 875

Ye hawe iij aduersaryis, he ys master of
hem all, —
That ys to sey, the World, the Flesch and
the Fell; [5]
The New-gyse, Now-a-dayis, Nowgth, the
"world" we may hem call;
And propy[r]lly Titiuilly syngnyfyes the
fend of helle; 879

The Flesch — that ys the vnclene concup-
iscens of your body.
These be your iij gostly enmyis, in whom
ye haue put your confidens. 881
Thei browt yow to Myscheffe to conclude
your temperall glory,
As yt hath be schewyd [6] before this
worschypp[f]yll audiens.

Remembyr how redy I was to help yow:
fro swheche [7] I was not dangerus;
Wherfore, good sunne, absteyne fro syn
euer-more after this!
Ye may both saue and spyll [8] yowur sowle
that ys so precyus;
Libere welle, libere welle! [9] God may
not deny, i-wys. 887

Beware of Titiuilly with hys net, and of all
his enuyus will,

[1] Sedulously?
[2] Admonitory.
[3] Brunt, attack.
[4] "A dart fore-announced wounds less."
[5] Devil. MS. *"the Dewell, the World, the Flesh, and the Fell."* Apparently the scribe wrote *Dewell* (Devil) in error, and forgot to erase it.
[6] Showed.
[7] From such.
[8] Destroy.
[9] "Freely wish."

Of your synfull delectacion that grewyth
your gostly substans.
Your body ys your enmy; let hym not
haue hys wyll!
Take your lewe [1] whan ye wyll! God
send yow good perseuerans! 891

[MANKYNDE.] Syth I schall departe,
blyse me, fader, her! Then I go.
God send ws all plente of hys gret
mercy!

[He kneels, and Mercy blesses him.]

MERCY. *Dominus custodi[a]t te [2] ab omni
malo!* [3]
*In nomine Patris, et Filij, et Spiritus
Sancti. Amen!* 895

Here Mankind goes out. [4]

Wyrschep[f]yll sofereyns, I hawe do my
propirte:
Mankynd ys deliueryd by my suuerall
patrocynye. [5]
God preserue hym fro all wyckyd captiu-
ite,
And send hym grace hys sensuall condicions to mortifye! 899

Now, for hys lowe that for vs receywyd hys
humanite,
Serche your condicyons with dew exam-
innacion!
Thynke and remembyr, the world ys but a
wanite, [6]
As yt ys prowyd daly by d[i]uerse
transmutacyon. [7] 903

Mankend ys wrechyd; he hath sufficyent
prowe;
There-fore God [kepe] [8] yow all *per suam
misericordiam.* [9]
That ye may be pleyseris [10] with the an-
gellis a-bowe,
And hawe to your porcyon *vitam eternam.* [11] Amen! 907

Fynis.

[1] Leave.   [2] MS. *custodit se;* corr. by M.
[3] "May the Lord preserve thee from all evil."
[4] MS. *hic exit Mankende.*
[5] Individual patronage.   [6] Vanity.
[7] Changes.   [8] Added by M. (*qy.* save)
[9] "Through his mercy."
[10] Sharers in pleasure?   [11] "Life everlasting."

WYT AND SCIENCE [1]

[DRAMATIS PERSONÆ

WYT, a student.
LADY SCIENCE, whom he seeks to wed.
REASON, her father.
EXPERIENCE, her mother.
INSTRUCTION.
STUDY.
DYLYGENCE.
HONEST RECREATION.
CONFYDENCE.

TEDIOUSNESS.
IDLENESS.
IGNORANCE.
SHAME.
CUMFORT.
QUYCKNES.
STRENGTH.
FAME.
RYCHES.
FAVOR.

WOORSHYP.]

[The manuscript is defective at the beginning. Wyt has asked the hand of Lady Science from her father, Reason. Reason has given his consent to the match, on certain conditions, namely that he overcome Tediousness, and that he make a journey to Mount Parnassus. In conclusion Reason presented Wyt with the Glass of Reason.]

[WYT. . . . .
. . . .]

REASON. Then in remembrance of Reson hold yee —
A glas of Reson, wherein beholde yee
Youre-sealfe to youre-selfe. Namely when ye
Cum neere my dowghter, Science, then see
That all thynges be cleane and trycke abowte ye, 5
Least of sum sloogyshnes she myght dowte ye.
Thys glas of Reason shall show ye all;
Whyle ye have that, ye have me, and shall.
Get ye foorth, now! Instruccion, farewell!

INSTR.[1] Syr, God keepe ye!
REASON. And ye all from parell! 10

Heere all go out save Resone.

If anye man now marvell that I
Woolde bestowe my dowghter thus baselye,
Of truth I, Reson, am of thys mynde:
Where partyes together be enclynde
By gyftes of graces to love ech other, 15
There let them joyne the tone wyth the toother.
Thys Wyt such gyftes of graces hath in hym
That makth my dowghter to wysh to wyn hym:
Yoong, paynefull, tractable and capax,[2] —
Thes be Wytes gyftes whych Science doth axe. 20
And as for her, as soone as Wyt sees her,
For all the world he woold not then leese her.
Wherfore, syns they both be so meete matches

[1] The manuscript gives in the margins the names of each speaker in full and variously spelled. I follow Manly's use of abbreviated catch-names.
[2] Capable.

---

[1] *Wyt and Science* is an example of the morality adapted in later times to other themes than the salvation of man, and to performance in halls before small and select audiences. Of such allegorical "interludes" there is a notable group dealing with topics of school interest; I have chosen the present play as, on the whole, the best and most representative of its type. The author, John Redford, was Master of the singing boys at St. Paul's Cathedral in London, and it is quite likely that he wrote the play to be acted by his boys. The date of its composition cannot be definitely fixed; it was certainly written before the death of Queen Katherine Parr, 1548 (see line 1098), and probably we should not be far wrong if we guessed 1530.

The manuscript is found in a commonplace-book (now the property of the British Museum) containing in addition to this play some musical sketches, numerous poems and songs by various authors, and brief fragments of two other unnamed moralities. I have based the present text on Halliwell's careful edition prepared for the Shakespeare Society, 1848, compared with the photographic facsimile of the manuscript issued by J. S. Farmer. I have also made use of Manly's edition, *Specimens*, 1896, based on Halliwell, and of Farmer's edition in "*Lost*" *Tudor Plays*, 1907. I have, of course, modernized the punctuation, and added, in brackets, stage directions. Unfortunately the manuscript has lost a page or more at the beginning.

To love ech other, strawe for the patches
Of worldly mucke! Syence hath inowghe 25
For them both to lyve.   Yf Wyt be
        throwhe [1]
Stryken in love, as he synes [2] hath showde,
I dowte not my dowghter well bestowde.
Thende of hys jornay wyll aprove all.
Yf Wyt hold owte, no more proofe can
        fall;   30
And that the better hold out he [3] may,
To refresh my soone, Wyt, now by the way
Sum solas for hym I wyll provyde.
An honest woman dwellth here besyde,
Whose name is cald Honest Recreacion. 35
As men report, for Wytes consolacion
She hath no peere; yf Wyt were halfe deade,
She cowld revyve hym, — thus is yt sed.
Wherfore, yf monye or love can hyre her,
To hye after Wyt I wyll desyre her.
                                    [*Exit.*]

Confydence cumth in with a pycture of Wyt.

[CONF.] Ah! syr, what tyme of day yst,
        who can tell?   41
The day ys not far past, I wot well,
For I have gone fast, and yet I see
I am far from where as I wold be.
Well, I have day inowgh yet, I spye; 45
Wherfore, or I pas hens, now must I
See thys same token heere, a playne case,
What Wyt hath sent to my ladyes grace.

[*Holds the picture up to the audience.*]

Now wyll ye see? a goodly pycture
Of Wyt hymselfe, hys owne image
        sure, —   50
Face, bodye, armes, legges, both lym and
        joynt, —
As lyke hym as can be, in every poynt:
Yt lakth but lyfe.   Well I can hym thanke,
Thys token in-deede shall make sum
        cranke; [4]
For, what wyth thys pycture so well
        faverde,   55
And what wyth those sweete woordes so
        well saverd
Dystyllyng from the mowth of Confy-
        dence, —
Shall not thys apese the hart of Science?
Yes, I thanke God, I am of that nature

Able to compas thys matter sure,   60
As ye shall see now, who lyst to marke yt,
How neately and feately [1] I shall warke yt.
                                    [*Exit.*]

*Wyt cumth in without Instruccion, with
        Study, &c.*

[WYT.] Now, syrs, cum on.   Whyche is the
        way now?
Thys way or that way?   Studye, how say
        you?

[*Study ponders.*]

Speake, Dylygence, whyle he hath be-
        thowghte hym.   65
DYL. [*points*].   That way, belyke; most
        usage hath wrowht hym. [2]
STUD. Ye, hold your pease!   Best we here
        now stay
For Instruccion.   I lyke not that waye.
WYT. Instruccion, Studye!   I weene we
        have lost hym.

Instruccion cumth in.

[INSTR.] Indeade, full gently abowte ye
        have tost hym!   70
What mene you, Wyt, styll to delyghte
Runnynge before thus, styll owt of syghte,
And therby out of your way now quyghte?
What doo ye here, excepte ye woold
        fyghte?
Cum back agayne, Wyt, for I must choose
        ye   75
An esyer way then thys, or ells loose
        ye.
WYT. What ayleth thys way?   Parell [3]
        here is none.
INSTR. But as much as your lyfe standth
        upon!
Youre enmye, man, lyeth heere before
        ye, —
Tedyousnes, to brayne or to gore ye! 80
WYT. Tedyousnes?   Doth that tyran[t]
        rest
In my way now?   Lord, how am I blest
That occacion so nere me sturres
For my dere hartes sake to wynne m[y]
        spurres!
Ser, woold ye fere me with that fowl
        theeafe,   8[
Wyth whome to mete my desyre is cheafe[

---

[1] Through.   [2] Signs, indications.
[3] MS. *ye*; corr. by M.   [4] Merry, sprightly.

[1] Finely.   [2] It, the way.   [3] Peril.

INSTR.   And what woold ye doo, — you havyng nowghte
For your defence? For thowgh ye have cawghte [1]
Garmentes of Science upon your backe,
Yet wepons of Science ye do lak.   90
WYT.   What wepons of Science shuld I have?
INSTR.   Such as all lovers of ther looves crave, —
A token from Ladye Science, wherbye
Hope of her favor may spryng, and therbye
Comforte, whych is the weapon dowteles 95
That must serve youe agaynst Tedyousnes.
WYT.   Yf Hope or Comfort may be my weapen,
Then never with Tedyousnes mee threten;
For, as for hope of my deere hartes faver —
And therby comfort — inowghe I gather.
INSTR.   Wyt, here me! Tyll I see Confydence   101
Have browght sum token from Ladye Science,
That I may feele that she favorth you,
Ye pas not thys way, I tell you trew.
WYT.   Whych way than?
INSTR.   A playner way, I told ye,   105
Out of danger from youre foe to hold ye.
WYT.   Instruccion, here me! Or [2] my swete hart
Shall here that Wyt from that wreche shall start
One foote, thys bodye and all shall cracke!
Foorth I wyll, sure, what-ever I lacke! 110
DYL.   Yf ye lacke weapon, syr, here is one.
WYT.   Well sayde, Dylygence, thowe art alone!
How say ye, syr; is not here weapon?
INSTR.   Wyth that weapon your enmy never threton,   114
For wythowt the returne of Confydence
Ye may be slayne, sure, for all Dylygence.
DYL.   God, syr! and Dylygence, I tell you playne,
Wyll play the man or [2] my master be slayne!
INSTR.   Ye; but what! sayth Studye no wurde to thys?
WYT.   No, syr. Ye knowe Studyes ofyce is   120

Meete for the chamber, not for the feeld.
But tell me, Studye, wylt thow now yeid?
STUD.   My hed akth sore; I wold wee returne!
WYT.   Thy hed ake now? I wold it were burne!
Cum on! Walkyng may hap to ese the. 125
INSTR.   And wyll ye be gone, then, wythout mee?
WYT.   Ye, by my fayth; except ye hy ye after,
Reson shall know yee are but an hafter.[1]

Exceat Wyt, Study, and Dylygence.

INSTR.   Well, go your way! Whan your father Reson   129
Heerth how ye obay me at thys season,
I thynke he wyll thynke hys dowghter now
May mary another man for you.
When wytes stand so in ther owne conceite,
Best let them go, tyll pryde at hys heyghte
Turne and cast them downe hedlong agayne,   135
As ye shall see provyd by thys Wyt playne.
Yf Reson hap not to cum the rather,[2]
Hys owne dystruccion he wyll sure gather.
Wherefore to Reson wyll I now get me,
Levyng that charge whereabowt he set mee.   140

Exceat Instruccion.   Tedyousnes cumth in with a vyser over hys hed, [and a club in his hand].

[TEDY.]   Oh the body of me!
What kaytyves be those
That wyll not once flee
From Tediousnes nose,
But thus dysese [3] me   145
Out of my nest,
When I shoold ese mee
Thys body to rest!
That Wyt, that vylayne,
That wrech, — a shame take hym! — 150
Yt is he playne
That thus bold doth make hym,
Wythowt my lycence
To stalke by my doore
To that drab, Syence,   155
To wed that whore!

---

[1] Received, got.   [2] Ere.

[1] Wrangler, dodger.
[2] More quickly.   [3] Disturb.

But I defye her.[1]
  And for that drabes sake,
Or Wyt cum ny her,
  The knaves hed shall ake!   160
Thes bones, this mall,[2]
  Shall bete hym to dust
Or that drab shall
  Once quench that knaves lust!
But, hah! mee thynkes   165
  I am not halfe lustye;
Thes jo[y]ntes, thes lynkes,[3]
  Be ruffe[4] and halfe rustye;
I must go shake them,
  Supple to make them!   170

[He swings his club.]

Stand back, ye wrechys!
  Beware the fechys[5]
Of Tediousnes,
  Thes kaytyves to bles!
Make roome, I say!   175
  Rownd evry way!
Thys way! That way!
  What care I[6] what way?
Before me, behynd me,
  Rownd abowt wynd me!   180
Now I begyn
  To swete in my skin.
Now am I nemble
  To make them tremble.
Pash[7] hed! pash brayne!   185
  The knaves are slayne,
All that I hyt!
  Where art thow, Wyt?
Thow art but deade!
  Of goth thy hed   190
A[t] the fyrst blow!
  Ho, ho! ho, ho!   *[Sits down.]*

Wyt spekyth at the doore.

[Wyt.] Studye!
Stud.   Here, syr!
Wyt.   How? doth thy hed ake?
Stud. Ye, God wot, syr, much payne I do
  take!
Wyt. Dylygens!
Dyl.   Here, syr! here!

---

1 MS. *here*; corr. by M.   2 Club.
3 Joints of the body.   4 Rough.
5 *N.E.D.* defines as "stratagems"; but apparently the meaning is "strokes," "sweeps."
6 So the MS. H. prints *What cares what*; M. suggests *What care I*, or *Who cares.*
7 Dash to pieces.

Wyt.   How dost thow?   195
Doth thy stomak[1] serve the to fyght now?
Dyl. Ye, syr, wyth yonder wrech, — a
  vengans on hym! —
That thretneth you thus. Set evyn upon
  hym!
Stud. Upon hym, Dylygence? Better
  nay!
Dyl. Better nay, Studye? Why shoold
  we fray?[2]   200
Stud. For I am wery; my hed akth sore.[3]
Dyl. Why, folysh Studye, thow shalt doo
  no more
But ayde my master wyth thy presens.
Wyt. No more shalt thow nether, Dyly-
  gence.
Ayde me wyth your presence, both you
  twayne,   205
And, for my love, myselfe shall take payne!
Stud. Syr, we be redye to ayde you so.
Wyt. I axe no more, Studye. Cum then;
  goe!

[They advance.]

Tedyiousnes rysyth up.

[Tedy.] Why, art thow cum?
Wyt.   Ye, wrech, to thy payne!
Tedi. Then have at the!
Wyt.   Have at the, agayne!   210

Here Wyt fallyth downe and dyeth.

Tedi. Lye thow there! Now have at ye,
  kaytyves!

[Study and Diligence flee.]

Do ye fle, ifayth? A! horeson theves!
By Mahowndes[4] bones, had the wreches
  taryd,
Ther neckes wythowt hedes they showld
  have caryd!
Ye, by Mahowndes nose, myght I have
  patted[5] them,   215
In twenty gobbetes[6] I showld have
  squatted[7] them,
To teche the knaves to cum neere the
  snowte
Of Tediousnes! Walke furder abowte

---

1 Courage, inclination.   2 Be frightened.
3 This, and the two preceding lines, heavily crossed through in the MS.
4 Mahomet's.   5 Struck (with his club).
6 Pieces of raw flesh.   7 Smashed, squashed.

I trow now they wyll!   And as for thee,
Thow wy\`lt no-more now troble mee.   220
Yet, lest the knave be not safe inowghe,
The horeson shall bere me another kuffe.

[*Strikes him with his club.*]

Now ly styll, kaytyv, and take thy rest,
Whyle I take myne in myne owne nest. 224

Exceat Tedy[ousnes].

Here cumth in Honest Recreacion, Cum-
fort, Quyckknes, and Strenght, and go and
knele abowt Wyt, [singing as follows]: [1]

When travelles grete [2] *in matters thycke* 225
Have duld your wyttes and made them
   sycke,
What medson than [3] *your wyttes to quycke?* [4]
Yf ye wyll know, the best phisycke
   Is to geve place to Honest Recreacion.
   Gyve place, we say, now for thy consola-
      cion!   230

Where is that Wyt that we seeke than?
Alas, he lyeth here pale and wan!
Helpe hym at once now, yf we can.
O Wyt, how doest thow?   Looke up, man!
   O Wyt, geve place to Honest Recreacion.
   Gyve place, we say, now for thy consola-
      cion!   236

After place gyvyn, let eare obay.
Gyve an eare, O Wyt, now we the pray;
Gyve eare to that we syng and say;
Gyve an eare, and healp wyll cum strayghte-
   way;
   Gyve an eare to Honest Recreacion.
   Gyve an ere, now, for thy consolacion! 242

After eare gyvyn, now gyve an eye.
Behold thy freendes abowte the lye:
Recreacion I, and Comfort I,
Quicknes am I, and Strength herebye.
   Gyve an eye to Honest Recreacion;
   Gyve an eye, now, for thy consolacion!   247

After eye gyvyn, an hand gyve ye.
Gyve an hand, O Wyt, feele that ye see;
Recreacion feele, feele Comfort fre,
Feele Quicknes here, feale Strength to the!
   Gyve an hand to Honest Recreacion;   253
   Gyve an hand, now, for thy consolacion!

Upon his feete woold God he were!
To rayse hym now we neede not fere.
Stay you hys handes, whyle we hym [1] *bere.*
Now all at once upryght him rere!
   O Wyt, gyve place to Honest Recreation;
   Gyve place, we say, now for thy consola-
      cion!   260

And at the last verce reysyth hym up upon
hys feete, and so make an end.   And
than Honest Recreacion sayth as folow-
yth: [2]

HON. REC.   Now, Wyt, how do ye?   Wyll
      ye be lustye?
WYT.   The lustier for you needes be must
      I.
HON. REC.   Be ye all hole yet after your
      fall?
WYT.   As ever I was, thankes to you all.

Reson cummth in, and sayth as folowyth:

[RESON.]   Ye myght thanke Reson that
      sent them to ye;   265
But syns the[y] have done [3] that the[y]
      shoold do ye,
Send them home, soonne, and get ye for-
      warde.
WYT.   Oh father Reson, I have had an
      hard
Chance synce ye saw me!
RESON. [4]   I wot well that.
The more to blame ye, when ye wold
      not   270
Obay Instruccion, as Reson wyld ye.
What marvell thowgh Tedyousness had
      kyld ye?
But let pas now, synce ye ar well agayne.
Set forward agayne Syence to attayne!
WYT.   Good father Reson, be not to
      hastye.   275

---

[1] The song is found, with two others, in the same
MS. volume, but quite apart from the play.   It is
labeled: "The fyrst song in the play of Science."   I
have inserted it here, where it obviously belongs, although to do so I have had to break the stage direction into two parts.   H. and M. treat the title-head-
ing of the song as, apparently, a part of the text of
the song.
[2] Labors great.   [3] Then.   [4] Enliven.

[1] MS. *here;* corr. by M.
[2] This is a part of the stage-direction which pre-
cedes the song here inserted.
[3] The MS. has the word *done,* though H. omits it,
and M. supplies in brackets *do.*
[4] In the margin below this word the MS. has *cumth
in.*

In honest cumpany no tyme wast I.
I shall to youre dowghter all at leyser.
RESON.   Ye, Wyt, is that the grete love ye
    rayse [1] her?
I say, yf ye love my dowghter Science,
Get ye foorth at once, and get ye hence. 280

Here Comfort, Quiknes and Strength go out. [2]

WYT.   Nay, by Saynt George, they go not
    all yet!
RESON.   No?   Wyll ye dysobey Reson,
    Wyt?
WYT.   Father Reson, I pray ye content ye,
For we parte not yet.
RESON.   Well, Wyt, I went [3] ye
Had bene no such man as now I see.   285
Fare-well!   *Exceat.*
HON. REC.   He ys angry.
WYT.   Ye, let hym be!
I doo not passe! [4]
Cum now, a basse! [5]
HON. REC.   Nay, syr, as for bassys,
From hence none passys   290
But as in gage
Of mary-age.
WYT.   Mary, evyn so.
A bargayne, lo!
HON. REC.   What! wythout lycence
Of Ladye Science?   296
WYT.   Shall I tell you trothe?
I never lovde her.
HON. REC.   The common voyce goth
    That mariage ye movd her.   300
WYT.   Promyse hath she none.
Yf we shalbe wone,
    Wythout mo wurdes grawnt! [6]
HON. REC.   What! upon this soodayne?
Then myghte ye playne
    Byd me avawnt!   306
Nay, let me see
In honeste
    What ye can doo
To wyn Recreacion.
Upon that probacion
    I grawnt therto.   312
WYT.   Small be my dooinges,
But apt to all thynges
    I am, I trust.

HON. REC.   Can ye dawnce than?
WYT.   Evyn as I can,
    Prove me ye must.   318
HON. REC.   Then for a whyle
Ye must excyle [1]
    This garment cumbryng. [2]
WYT.   In-deede, as ye say,
This cumbrus aray
    Woold make Wyt slumbryng.   324
HON. REC.   Yt is gay geere. [3]
Of Science cleere,
    Yt seemth her aray.
WYT.   Whose-ever it were,
Yt lythe now there! [*Throws off his gown.*]
HON. REC.   Go to, my men, play!   330

*Here they dawnce; and in the mene-whyle
Idellnes cumth in and sytth downe; and
when the galyard [4] is doone, Wyt sayth as
folowyth, and so falyth downe in Idellnes
'ap.*

WYT.   Sweete hart, gramercys!
HON. REC.   Why, whether now?   Have ye
    doone, synce?
WYT.   Ye, in fayth, with wery bones ye
    have possest me;
Among thes damselles now wyll I rest me.
HON. REC.   What, there?
WYT.   Ye, here; I wylbe so bold.   335
IDLE.   Ye, and wellcum, by hym that God
    sold!
HON. REC.   Yt ys an harlot, may ye not
    see?
IDLE.   As honest a woman as ye be!
HON. REC.   Her name is Idlenes.   Wyt,
    what mene you?
IDLE.   Nay, what meane you to scolde
    thus, you quene, you?   340
WYT.   Ther, go to!   Lo now, for the best
    game!
Whille I take my ese, youre toonges now
    frame!
HON. REC.   Ye, Wyt; by youre fayth, is
    that youre facion?
Wyll ye leave me, Honest Recreacion,
For that common strumpet, Idellnes,   345
The verye roote of all vyciousnes?

---

[1] Bear?
[2] The scribe first wrote *Al go out save Honest*, then
squeezed in below the stage-direction as here printed.
[3] Thought.   [4] Care.
[5] Kiss.   [6] Grant.

[1] Get rid of.
[2] H. prints *cum bryng*, but MS. has *cumbryng*.
[3] Apparel.
[4] A quick lively dance. The first allusion recorded
in *N.E.D.* is dated 1533; but the passage indicates
that the dance was then well known.

Wyt. She sayth she is as honest as ye.
Declare yourselves both now as ye be!
Hon. Rec. What woolde ye more for my
 declaracion
Then evyn my name, Honest Recrea-
 cion? 350
And what wold ye more her to expres
Then evyn her name, to, Idlenes —
Dystruccion of all that wyth her tarye?
Wherfore cum away, Wyt; she wyll mar ye!
Idel. Wyll I mar hym, drabb, thow
 calat,[1] thow, 355
When thow hast mard hym all-redye now?
Cawlyst thow thysealfe Honest Recreacion,
Ordryng a poore man after thys facion,
To lame hym thus and make his lymmes
 fayle
Evyn wyth the swyngyng there of thy
 tayle? 360
The dyvyll set fyre one the! for now must
 I,
Idlenes, hele hym agayne, I spye.
I must now lull hym, rock hym, and frame
 hym
To hys lust agayne, where thow dydst lame
 hym.
Am I the roote, sayst thow, of vycious-
 nes? 365
Nay, thow art roote of all vyce dowteles!
Thow art occacion, lo! of more evyll
Then I, poore gerle, — nay, more then the
 dyvyll!
The dyvyll and hys dam can not devyse
More devlyshnes then by the[e] doth
 ryse. 370
Under the name of Honest Recreacion,
She, lo! bryngth in her abhominacion!
Mark her dawnsyng, her maskyng, and
 mummyng.
Where more concupyscence then ther cum-
 myng?
Her cardyng,[2] her dycyng, dayly and
 nyghtlye — 375
Where fynd ye more falcehod then there?
 Not lyghtly!
Wyth lyeng and sweryng by no poppetes,[3]
But teryng God in a thowsand gobbetes.
As for her syngyng, pypyng and fydlyng,
What unthryftynes therin is twydlyng![4]
Serche the tavernes and ye shall here cleere

Such bawdry as bestes wold spue to heere.
And yet thys is kald Honest Recreacion,
And I, poore Idlenes, abhomynacion!
But whych is wurst of us twayne, now judg,
 Wyt. 385
Wyt. Byrladye, not thow, wench, I judge
 yet.

*[While Honest Recreation appeals to him,
Wyt falls asleep in the lap of Idleness.]*

Hon. Rec. No? Ys youre judgment such
 then that ye
Can neyther pe[r]seve that best, how she
Goth abowte to dyceve you, nor yet
Remembre how I savyd youre lyfe, Wyt?
Thynke you her meete wyth mee to com-
 pare 391
By whome so manye wytes curyd are?
When wyll she doo such an act as I dyd,
Savynge your lyfe when I you revyved?
And as I savyd you, so save I all 395
That in lyke jeoperdy chance to fall.
When Tediousnes to grownd hath smytten
 them,
Honest Recreacion up doth quyken them
Wyth such honest pastymes, sportes or
 games
As unto myne honest nature frames, 400
And not, as she sayth, with pastymes suche
As be abusyd lytell or muche;
For where honest pastymes be abusyd,
Honest Recreacion is refused;
Honest Recreacion is present never 405
But where honest pastymes be well usyd
 ever.
But in-deede Idlenes, she is cawse
Of all such abuses; she, lo! drawes
Her sort to abuse myne honest games,
And therby full falsly my name defames.
Under the name of Honest Recreacion 411
She bryngth in all her abhomynacion,
Dystroyng all wytes that her imbrace,
As youre-selfe shall see wythin short space.
She wyll bryng you to shamefull end,
 Wyt,
Except the sooner from her ye flyt. 416
Wherefore cum away, Wyt, out of her
 pawse!
Hence, drabb! Let hym go out of thy
 clawse!
Idle. Wyll ye get ye hence? or, by the
 mace,

---

[1] Strumpet.   [2] Card-playing.
[3] Idols.   [4] Being busy about trifles.

Thes clawes shall clawe you by youre
   drabbes face!   420
Hon. Rec. Ye shall not neade. Syns
   Wyt lyethe as wone
That neyther heerth nor seeth, I am gone.
                Exceat.
Idle. Ye, so? fare-well! And well fare
   thow, toonge!
Of a short pele this pele was well roong, —
To ryng her hence, and hym fast asleepe
As full of sloth as the knave can kreepe!
How, Wyt! awake! How doth my babye?
Neque vox neque sensus,[1] byr Ladye!
A meete man for Idlenes, no dowte.
Hark my pygg! How the knave dooth
   rowte![2]   430
Well, whyle he sleepth in Idlenes lappe,
Idlenes marke on hym shall I clappe.
Sum say that Idlenes can not warke;[3]
But those that so say, now let them
   marke!
I trowe they shall see that Idlenes 435
Can set hersealfe abowt sum busynes;
Or, at the lest, ye shall see her tryde,
Nother idle nor well ocupyde.

        [She blackens his face.][4]

Lo! syr, yet ye lak another toye!
Wher is my whystell to call my boye? 440

   Here she whystleth, and Ingnorance cumth
   in, [dressed in a fool's coat, and a cap with
   large ears and a coxcomb.]

[Ingn.] I cum! I cum!
Idle.   Coomme on, ye foole!
All thys day or ye can cum to scoole?
Ingn. Um! mother wyll not let me cum.
Idle. I woold thy mother had kyst thy
   bum!
She wyll never let the thryve, I trow. 445
Cum on, goose! Now, lo! men shall know
That Idlenes can do sumwhat; ye,
And play the scoolemystres, to, yf neade
   bee.
Mark what doctryne by Idlenes cummes!
Say thy lesson, foole.
Ingn.   Upon my thummes? 450
Idel. Ye, upon thy thummes. Ys not
   there thy name?
Ingn. Yeas.

Idle. Go to, than; spell me that same.
Where was thou borne?[1]
Ingn. Chwas i-bore in Ingland, mother
   sed.
Idle. In Ingland?   455
Ingn. Yea.
Idle. And whats half "Ingland"?

   [Pointing to her thumb and first finger.]

Heeres "ing," and heeres "land." Whats
   tys?
Ingn. Whats tys?
Idel. Whats tys, horeson? whats tys? 460
Heeres "ing," and heeres "land." Whats
   tys?
Ingn. Tys my thum.
Idel. Thy thum? "Yng," horeson,
   "ing," "ing"!
Ingn. Yng, yng, yng, yng.
Idel. Foorth! Shall I bete thy narse,
   now?   465
Ingn. Um-m-m-m —
Idel. Shall I not bete thy narse, now?
Ingn. Um-m-m —
Idel. Say "no," foole, say "no."
Ingn. Noo, noo, noo, noo, noo! 470
Idel. Go to, put together: "yng."
Ingn. "Yng."
Idel. "No."
Ingn. "Noo."
Idel. Forth now! What sayth the
   dog?   475
Ingn. Dog barke.
Idle. Dog barke? Dog ran, horeson, dog
   ran!
Ingn. Dog ran, horson, dog ran, dog
   ran.
Idel. Put together: "ing."
Ingn. "Yng."   480
Idel. "No."
Ingn. "Noo."
Idel. "Ran."
Ingn. "Ran."
Idle. Foorth now; what seyth the
   goose?   485
Ingn. Lag! lag!
Idle. "Hys," horson, "hys"!
Ing[n]. Hys, hys-s-s-s-s.

---

1 "Neither voice nor feeling."   2 Snore.
3 Work.   4 Cf. lines 802–20.

1 From this point to line 542 I have not tried
treat the text as verse, but have set it exactly as
appears in the MS. It seems to me to be intende
as prose. I have made the line numbering confor
to the lines in the manuscript.

IDLE. Go to, put together: "Ing."
INGN. "Ing."   490
IDLE. "No."
INGN. "Noo."
IDLE. "Ran."
INGN. "Ran."
IDLE. "Hys."   495
ING[N]. "Hys-s-s-s-s-s-s."
IDLE. No[w], who is a good boy?
INGN. I, I, I, I, I, I.
IDLE. Go to, put together: "Ing."
INGN. "Ing."   500
IDLE. "No."
INGN. "Noo."
IDEL. "Ran."
INGN. "Ran."
IDEL. "His."   505
INGN. "Hys-s-s-s-s."
IDEL. "I."
INGN. "I."
IDEL. "Ing-no-ran-his-I."
INGN. "Ing-no-ran-hys-s-s-s."   510
IDLE. "I."
INGN. "I."
IDEL. "Ing."
INGN. "Ing."
IDEL. Foorth!   515
INGN. "Hys-s-s-s."
IDEL. Ye! "No," horeson, "no"!
INGN. "Noo, noo, noo, noo"!
IDLE. "Ing-no."
INGN. "Ing-noo."   520
IDLE. Forth now!
INGN. "Hys-s-s-s-s."
IDEL. Yet agayne! "Ran," horeson, "ran," "ran."
INGN. "Ran, horson, ran, ran."
IDLE. "Ran," say!   525
INGN. "Ran-say."
IDLE. "Ran," horson!
INGN. "Ran, horson!"
IDLE. "Ran"!
INGN. "Ran."   530
IDLE. "Ing-no-ran."
INGN. "Ing-no-ran."
IDEL. Foorth, now. What sayd the goose?
INGN. Dog barke.
IDLE. Dog barke? "Hys," horson, "hys-s-s-s-s-s."   535
INGN. "Hys-s-s-s-s-s-s."
IDLE. "I."

INGN. "I." [1]
IDLE. "Ing-no-ran-hys-I."
INGN. "Ing-no-ran-hys-s-s-s-s." [2]   540
IDLE. "I."
INGN. "I."
IDLE. How sayst, now, foole? Is not there thy name?
INGN. Yea.
IDLE. Well than; can [3] me that same! What hast thow lernd?
INGN. Ich can not tell.   545
IDLE. "Ich can not tell"? thou sayst evyn very well,
For yf thow cowldst tell then had not I well
Towght the thy lesson which must be tawghte, —
To tell all when thow canst tell ryghte noght.
INGN. Ich can my lesson.
IDLE. Ye; and therfore   550
Shalt have a new cote, by God I swore!
INGN. A new cote?
IDLE. Ye, a new cote by-and-by. [4]
Of wyth thys old cote; "a new cote" crye!
INGN. [shouting]. A new cote! A new cote! A new cote!
IDLE. Pease, horson foole!
Wylt thow wake hym now? Unbuttun thy cote, foole!   555
Canst thow do nothyng? [5]
INGN. I note [6] how choold be.
IDLE. "I note how choold be"! A foole betyde the!
So wysly hyt spekyth. Cum on now. Whan!
Put bak thyne arme, foole!
INGN. Put backe?

[*She takes the fool's coat from Ignorance's back.*]

IDLE. So, lo! Now let me see how thys geere   560

---

[1] H. omits this line; but though it is faint in the MS. it can be clearly read in Farmer's photographic facsimile. Since it is necessary to the sense, I have restored it to the printed text.
[2] Originally the scribe wrote *Ing-no-ran-hys-I-sss*, but corrected to the form printed above. H. ignored the correction, though it is clearly necessary to the sense.
[3] Study by repetition.   [4] At once.
[5] MS. has the speech of Idleness as two lines; corr. by M.
[6] Know not.

Wyll trym this jentel-man that lyeth
    heere, —
Ah! God save hyt, so sweetly hyt doth
    sleepe! —
Whyle on your back thys gay cote can
    creepe,
As feete [1] as can be for this one arme.
INGN. Oh! cham a-cold.

[Puts Wyt's gown of learning on Ingnorance.]

IDLE.   Hold, foole! keepe the warme.
And cum hyther; hold this hed here.
    Softe now, for wakyng!   566
Ye shall see wone here browght in such
    takynge
That he shall soone scantlye knowe hym-
    sealfe.
Heere is a cote as fyt for this elfe   569
As it had bene made evyn for thys bodye.

[Puts Ingnorance's coat on Wyt.]

So! It begynth to looke lyke a noddye!
INGN. Um-m-m-m —
IDLE.   What aylest now, foole?
INGN.   New cote is gone!
IDLE. And why is it gone?
INGN.   'Twool not byde on.
IDLE. "Twool not byde on?" 'Twoold,
    if it cowlde!   574
But marvell it were that byde it shoold, —
Sciens garment on Ingnorance bak!

[Looking at Wit.]

But now lets se, syr; what do ye lak?
Nothyng but evin to bukell heere this
    throte,
So well this Wyt becumthe a fooles cote!
INGN. He is I now!
IDLE.   Ye; how lykste hym now?   580
Is he not a foole as well as thow?
INGN. Yeas.
IDLE. Well, than, won foole keepe another!
Geve me this, and take thow that brother.

[Sets Ignorance's cap on Wit's head.]

INGN. Um-m —
IDLE.   Pyke the home, go!
INGN. Chyll go tell my moother!
IDLE.   Yea, doo!   585

[Exit Ignorance.]

[1] Fine.

But yet to take my leve of my deere, lo!
Wyth a skyp or twayne, heere lo! and heer
    lo!
And heere agayne! and now this heele
To bles his weake brayne! Now are ye
    weele,
By vertu of Idellnes blessyng toole,   590
Conjurd from Wyt unto a starke foole!
    [Exit.]

*Confydence cumth in with a swoord by his
    syde, and sayth as folowyth:*

[CONF.] I seake and seake, as won on no
    grownde
Can rest, but lyke a masterles hownde
Wandryng all abowt seakyng his master.
Alas! jentle Wyt, I feare the fasster   595
That [1] my tru servyce clevth unto thee,
The slacker thy mynd cleevth unto mee!
I have doone thye message in such sorte
That I not onlye, for thy comfort
To vanquishe thyne enmy have browght
    heere   600
A swoord of comfort from thy love deere,
But also, furder, I have so enclynd her
That upon my wurdes she hath assynd
    her
In her owne parson [2] half-way to meete
    thee,
And hytherward she came for to greete
    thee.   605
And sure, except she be turned agayne,
Hyther wyll she cum or [3] be long, playne,
To seake to meate the heere in this cost.[4]
But now, alas! thy-selfe thow hast lost,   609
Or, at the least, thow wylt not be fownd.
Alas! jentle Wyt, how doost thow woonde
Thy trusty and tru servant, Confydence,
To lease my credence to Ladye Science!
Thow lesyst me, to; for yf I can not
Fynd the shortly, lenger lyve I ma not, 615
But shortly get me evyn into a corner
And dye for sorowe throwhe such a scorner!
    Exceat.

Here the[y] cum in with vyols.

FAME. Cum syrs, let us not dysdayne to
    do
That the World hath apoynted us too.

[1] H. prints *Thy;* M. changes to *That* in text, but
observes in a footnote "perhaps it would be better to
read *Thys.*" The MS. clearly reads *That.*
[2] Person.   [3] Ere.   [4] Place.

FAVOR. Syns to serve Science the World
    hath sent us,   620
As the World wylth ¹ us, let us content us.
RYCHES. Content us we may, synce we
    be assynde
To the fayrest lady that lyvth, in my mynde!
WOORSHYP. Then let us not stay here
    muet and mum,
But tast we thes instrumentes tyll she
    cum.   625

Here the[y] syng " Excedynge Mesure." ²

Exceedyng mesure, wyth paynes continewall,
Langueshyng in absens, alas! what shall I
    doe,
Infortunate wretch, devoyde of joyes all,
    Syghes upon syghes redoublyng my woe,
    And teares downe fallyng fro myne eyes
    toe?
Bewty wyth truth so doth me constrayne
Ever to serve where I may not attayne! 632

Truth byndyth me ever to be true,
    How-so-that fortune faverth my chance.
Duryng my lyfe none other but you
    Of my tru hart shall have the governance!
O good swete hart, have you remembrance
Now of your owne, whych for no smart
Exyle shall yow fro my tru hart!   639

[*During the song, Experyence and Science*
    have entered.]

EXPER. Dowghter, what meanyth that ye
    dyd not syng?
SCIENCE. Oh mother, for heere remaynth
    a thynge!
Freendes, we thanke you for thes your
    plesures,
Takyn on us as chance to us measures.
WOORSHYPPE. Ladye, thes our plesures,
    and parsons too,
Ar sente to you, you servyce to doo. 645
FAME. Ladye Science, to set foorth your
    name,
The World to wayte on you hath sent me,
    Fame.
FAVOR. Ladye Science, for your vertues
    most plentye,

---

¹ Commands.
² The song is not given in the play, but appears
with the other songs in another part of the manuscript volume. It is labeled "The ij Song." I
have inserted it here in its proper place.

The World, to cherysh you, Favor hath
    sent ye.
RYCHES. Lady Science, for youre bene-
    fytes knowne,   650
The World, to mayntayne you, Ryches
    hath thrown.
WOORSHYP. And, as the World hath sent
    you thes three,
So he sendth mee, Woorshypp, to avawnce
    your degre.
SCIENCE. I thank the World; but cheefly
    God be praysed,
That in the World such love to Science
    hath raysed!   655
But yet, to tell you playne, ye iiij ar suche
As Science lookth for lytell nor muche;
For beyng, as I am, a lone wooman,
Neede of your servyce I nether have nor
    can.
But, thankyng the World, and you for your
    payn,   660
I send ye to the World evyn now agayne.
WOORSHYPPE. Why, ladye, set ye no
    more store by mee,
Woorshypp? Ye set nowght by yourselfe,
    I se!
FAME. She setthe nowght by Fame;
    wherby I spye her, —
She carethe not what the World sayth by
    her.   665
FAVOR. She setthe nowght by Favor;
    wherby I trye her, —
She caryth not what the World sayth or
    dooth by her.
RYCHES. She setth nowght by Ryches;
    whych dooth showe
She careth not for the World. Cum, let us
    goe!

[*Exeunt Woorship, Fame, Favor, and*
    Ryches.]

SCIENCE. In-deede, smalle cawse gevyn to
    care for the Worldes favering, 670
Seeyng the wyttes of Worlde be so waver-
    yng.
EXPER. What is the matter, dowghter,
    that ye
Be so sad? Open your mynd to mee.
SCIENCE. My marvell is no les, my good
    moother,
Then my greefe is greate, to see, of all
    other,   675

The prowde scorne of Wyt, soone to Dame
    Nature,
Who sent me a pycture of hys stature
Wyth all the shape of hymselfe there open-
    yng,
Hys amorous love therby betokenyng,
Borne toward me in abundant facion; 680
And also, furder, to make ryght relacion
Of this hys love, he put in commyshion
Such a messenger as no suspicion
Cowld growe in mee of hym, — Confy-
    dence.
EXPER. Um!
SYENCE.   Who, I ensure ye, wyth such
    vehemence,   685
And faythfull behavoure in hys movynge,
Set foorth the pyth [1] of hys masters lov-
    ynge
That no lyvyng creature cowld conjecte
But that pure love dyd that Wyt dyrect.
EXPER. So?
SCIENCE. Now, this beinge synce the space
Of three tymes sendyng from place to place
Betwene Wyt and hys man, I here no more
Nether of Wyt, nor his love so sore.
How thynk you by thys, my nowne deere
    mother?
EXPER. Dowghter, in this I can thynke
    none oother   695
But that it is true — thys proverbe old:
"Hastye love is soone hot and soone cold!"
Take hede, dowghter, how you put youre
    trust
To lyght lovers to hot at the furst. 699
For had this love of Wyt bene growndyd,
And on a sure fowndashyon fowndyd,
Lytell voyde tyme wold have bene be-
    twene ye
But that this Wyt wolde have sent or seene
    ye.
SCIENCE. I thynke so.
EXPER.   Ye, thynke ye so or no,
Youre mother, Experience, proofe shall
    showe   705
That Wyt hath set hys love — I dare say
And make ye warrantyse — another way.

*Wyt cumth before [in his fool's coat and cox-
comb, and with his face blackened.]*

[WYT.] But your warrantyse warrant no
    trothe!

[1] Vigor, force.

Fayre ladye, I praye you be not wrothe
Tyll you here more; for, deere Ladye Sci-
    ence,   710
Had your lover, Wyt, — ye[a], or Confy-
    dence,
Hys man, — bene in helth all this tyme
    spent,
Long or this tyme Wyt had cumme or sent.
But the trothe is they have bene both
    sykke,
Wyt and hys man, ye and wyth paynes
    thycke   715
Bothe stayde by the way, so that your
    lover
Could neyther cum [1] nor send by none
    other.
Wherefore, blame not hym, but chance of
    syknes.
SCIENCE. Who is this?
EXPER.   Ingnorance, or his lykenes.
SCIENCE. What! the common foole?
EXPER.   Yt is much lyke hym. 720
SCIENCE. By my soothe, his toong servth
    him now trym!
What sayst thow, Ingnorance? Speak
    agayn!
WYT. Nay, ladye, I am not Ingnorance,
    playne,
But I am your owne deere lover, Wytt,
That hath long lovd you, and lovth you
    yet.   725
Wherefore, I pray the now, my nowne
    swetyng,
Let me have a kys at this our meetyng.

[Tries to kiss her.]

SCIENCE. Ye, so ye shall anone, but not
    yet!
Ah, syr, this foole here hath got sum wyt!
Fall you to kyssyng, syr, now-a-dayes? 730
Your mother shall charme you. Go your
    wayes!
WYT. What nedth all this, my love of long
    growne?
Wyll ye be so strang to me, your owne?
Youre aquayntance to me was thowht
    esye; [2]
But now your woordes make my harte all
    quesye,   735

[1] H. says the MS. has *cumne*, but the reading is
clearly *cum*.
[2] Easy, conducive to pleasure.

Youre dartes at me so strangely be shott.
SCIENCE. Heere ye what termes this foole
here hath got?
WYT. Well I perseve my foolyshnes now;
Indeede, ladyes no dasterdes alowe.
I wylbe bolde wyth my nowne darlyng!
Cum now, a bas, my nowne proper sparl-
yng!   741

[*Tries again to kiss her.*]

SCIENCE. What wylt thow, arrand foole?
WYT.   Nay, by the mas,
I wyll have a bas or I hence pas!
SCIENCE. What wylt thow, arrande foole?
Hence, foole, I say!
WYT. What! nothyng but "foole" and
"foole" all this day?   745
By the mas, madam, ye can no good.
SCIENCE. Art a-sweryng, to? Now, by
my hood,
Youre foolyshe knaves breeche vj strypes
shall bere!
WYT. Ye, Godes bones! "foole" and
"knave," to? Be ye there?
By the mas, call me foole once agayne, 750
And thow shalt sure call a blo or twayne.[1]
EXPER. Cum away, dowghter; the foole is
mad.
WYT. Nay, nor yet nether hence ye shall
gad!
We wyll gre better, or ye pas hence.
I praye the now, good swete Ladye Sci-
ence,   755
All this strange maner now hyde and cover,
And play the goodfelowe wyth thy lover!
SCIENCE. What goodfelowshyppe wold ye
of me,
Whome ye knowe not, nether yet I knowe
ye?
WYT. Know ye not me?
SCIENCE. No; how shoold I know ye? 760
WYT. Dooth not my pycture my parson
shoow ye?
SCIENCE. Your pycture?
WYT.   Ye, my picture, ladye,
That ye spake of. Who sent it but I?
SCIENCE. Yf that be youre pycture, then
shall we
Soone se how you and your pycture
agree.   765
Lo, here! the pycture that I named is this.

SCIENCE. Heere ye what termes this foole
here hath got?

WYT. Ye, mary, myne owne lykenes this
is.
You havyng this, ladye, and so lothe
To knowe me, whych this so playne
showthe!
SCIENCE. Why, you are nothyng lyke, in
myne eie.   770
WYT. No? [*To Experience.*] How say
ye?
EXPER.   As she sayth, so say I.
WYT. By the mas, than are ye both
starke blynde!
What dyference betwene this and this can
ye fynd?
EXPER. Marye, this is fayer, plesant, and
goodlye,
And ye are fowle, dysplesant, and ug-
lye.   775
WYT. Mary, avawnt, thow fowle ugly
whoore!
SCIENCE. So, lo! now I perseve ye more
and more.
WYT. What! perseve you me, — as ye
wold make me, —
A naturall foole?
SCIENCE.   Nay, ye mystake me;
I take ye for no foole naturall,   780
But I take ye thus, — shall I tell all?
WYT. Ye, marye, tell me youre mynd, I
pray ye,
Wherto I shall trust. No more delay ye.
SCIENCE. I take ye for no naturall foole,
Browght up among the innocentes scoole,
But for a nawgty vycious foole,   786
Browght up wyth Idellnes in her scoole.
Of all arrogant fooles thow art one!
WYT. Ye! Goges bodye!
EXPER.   Cum, let us be gone!

[*Exeunt Experyence and Science.*]

WYT. My swerd! Is yt gone? A venge-
ance on them!   790
Be they gone, to, and ther hedes upon
them?
But, prowde quenes, the dyvyll go wyth
you both!
Not one poynt of curtesye in them gothe.
A man is well at ease by sute to payne him
For such a drab, that so doth dysdayne
hym!   795
So mokte, so lowted,[1] so made a sot,

---

[1] Call (upon your head) a blow or two.

[1] Flouted, mocked.

Never was I erst synce I was begot!
Am I so fowle as those drabes wold make
  me?
Where is my glas that Reson dyd take [1]
  me?
Now shall this glas of Reson soone trye
  me   800
As fayre as those drabes that so doth belye
  me.

        [He looks in the glass.]

Hah! Goges sowle! What have we here?
  A dyvyll?
This glas, I se well, hath bene kept evyll.

    [Cleans the glass, and looks again.]

Goges sowle! a foole! a foole, by the mas!
What a very vengeance aylth this glas? 805
Other this glas is shamefully spotted,
Or els am I to shamefully blotted!
Nay, by Goges armes, I am so, no dowte!
How loke ther facis heere rownd abowte?

  [He holds the glass up to the audience.]

All fayre and cleere they, evrychone; 810
And I, by the mas, a foole alone,
Deckt, by Goges bones, lyke a very asse!
Ingnorance cote, hoode, eares, — ye, by
  the masse,
Kokescome and all. I lack but a bable! [2]
And as for this face, [it] is abhominable, 815
As black as the devyll! God, for his pas-
  sion!
Where have I bene rayde [3] affter this fas-
  syon?
This same is Idlenes, — a shame take her!
This same is her wurke, — the devill in hell
  rake her!
The whoore hath shamd me for-ever, I
  trow!   820
I trow? Nay verely, I knowe!
Now it is so — the stark foole I playe
Before all people. Now see it I maye.
Evrye man I se lawhe [4] me to scorne.
Alas, alas, that ever I was borne! 825
Yt was not for nowght, now well I se,
That those too ladyes dysdayned me.
Alas! Ladye Science, of all oother —
How have I rayled on her and her moother!
Alas! that lady I have now lost 830
Whome all the world lovth and honoryth
  most!

    [1] Give.   [2] Bauble.   [3] Arrayed.   [4] Laugh.

Alas! from Reson had I not varyd.
Ladye Science or this I had maryd!
And those fower gyftes which the World
  gave her
I had woon, to, had I kept her favor; 835
Where now, in-stede of that lady bryght
Wyth all those gallantes seene in my
  syght, —
Favor, Ryches, ye, Worshyp and Fame, —
I have woone Hatred, Beggry and Open
  Shame.

*Shame cumth in wyth a whyppe, [followed by
  Reason.]*

Wʏᴛ. Out upon the, Shame! What doost
  thowe heere?   840
Rᴇsᴏɴ. Mary, I, Reason, bad hym heere
  appeere.
Upon hym, Shame! wyth stryppes inow
  smitten,
While I reherce his fawtes herein wrytten:

      [He reads from a paper.]

Fyrst, he hath broken his promyse formerly
Made to me, Reson, my dowghter to
  marye;   845
Nexte, he hath broken his promyse prom-
  isyd
To obay Instruccion, and him dyspised;
Thurdlye, my dowghter Science to re-
  prove,
Upon Idlenes he hath set his love; 849
Forthlye, he hath folowed Idellnes scoole
Tyll she hath made him a verye stark foole;
Lastlye, offendyng both God and man,
Sweryng grete othes as any man can,
He hath abused himselfe, to the grete
  shame
Of all his kynred and los of his good name.
Wherfore, spare him not, Shame! Bete
  him well there!   856
He hath deservyd more then he can beare.

      Wyt knelith downe.

[Wʏᴛ.] Oh father Reson, be good unto
  me!
Alas, thes strypes of Shame will undo me!
Rᴇsᴏɴ. Be still a while, Shame! Wyt,
  what sayst thow?   860
Wʏᴛ. Oh syr, forgeve me, I beseech you!
Rᴇsᴏɴ. Yf I forgeve the thy ponyshment,
Wylt thow than folow thy fyrst entent

And promyse made, my dowghter to
    marye?

WYT.   Oh syr, I am not woorthy to
    carye   865
The dust out where your dowghter shoold
    syt.

RESON. I wot well that! But yf I admyt
The, unwoorthy, agayne to her wooer,
Wylt thow then folow thy sewte unto her?

WYT. Ye, syr, I promyse you, while lyfe
    enduryth.   870

RESON.   Cum neere, masters; heere is
    wone ensuryth [1]
In woordes to becum an honest man!

Here cumth Instruccion, Studye, and
Diligens in.

Take him, Instruccion; do what ye can.

INSTR. What! to the purpose he went be-
    fore?

RESON. Ye, to my dowghter prove him
    once more.   875
Take him, and trym hym in new aparell,
And geve that to Shame there to his fare-
    well. [2]

INSTR. Cum on your way, Wyt. Be of
    good cheere!
After stormy clowdes cumth wether clere!

Instrucion, Study, Wyt, and Dyligens go out.

RESON. Who lyst to marke now this
    chance heere doon,   880
May se what Wyt is wythout Reson.
What was this Wyt better then an asse
Being from Reson strayde as he was?
But let pas now, synce he is well poon-
    yshyd,
And thereby, I trust, meetely well mon-
    yshyd. [3]   885
Ye, and I lyke him never the wurs, I,
Thowgh Shame hath handled hym shame-
    fullye;
For, lyke as, yf Wyt had prowdly bent hym
To resyst Shame to make Shame absent
    hym, [4]
I wold have thowght than that Wyt had
    bene —   890
As the sayeng is, and daylye seene —
"Past shame once, and past all amend-
    ment":

[1] Pledgeth himself.   [2] Payment on leaving?
[3] Admonished.   [4] Withdraw himself.

So, contra[r]ye, syns he dyd relent
To Shame when Shame ponysht him evyn
    yll,
I have, I say, good hope in him styll. 895
I thynke, as I thowght, — yf joyne thei
    can, —
My dowghter wel bestowd on this man.
But all the dowte now is to thynke how
My dowghter takth this. For, I may tell
    yow,   899
I thynk she knew this Wyt, evyn as weele
As she seemd heere to know him no deele;
For lak of knoledge in Science there is
    none;
Wherfore, she knew him; and therupon
His mysbehavor perchance evyn strykyng
Her hart agaynst him, [1] she now myslyk-
    yng, —   905
As women oft-tymes wylbe hard-hartyd, —
Wylbe the stranger to be revertyd. [2]
This must I helpe. Reson must now walke,
On Wytes part wyth my Science to talke.
A neere way to her know I, wherebye 910
My soonnes cummyng prevent now must I.
Perchance I may bryng my dowghter
    hyther;
Yf so, I dowght not to joyne them together.

Exceat Reson.   Confydence cumth in.

[CONF.] I thanke God, yet at last I have
    fownd hym!
I was afrayde sum myschance had drownd
    him, —   915
My master, Wyt, wyth whome I have
    spoken,
Ye, and deliverd token for token,
And have anoother to Science agayne, —
A hart of gold, syngnifyeng playne
That Science hath wun Wytes hart for-
    ever.   920
Whereby I trust, by my good endever
To that good ladye, so sweete and so
    sortly, [3]
A maryage betwene them ye shall see
    shortlye.

Confydens exceat.   Instruccion cumth in
wyth Wyt, Study, and Dylygence.

[INSTR.] Lo! syr, now ye be entryd agayne

[1] Causing her heart to turn against him.
[2] The harder to be made to return (after estrangement).
[3] Appropriate (*N.E.D.*).

Toward that passage where dooth re-
   mayne 925
Tedyousnes, your mortall enmy.
Now may ye choose whether ye wyll trye
Your handes agayne on that tyrant stowte,
Or els, walkyng a lytell abowte —
WYT. Nay; for Godes pashion, syr, let me
   meete him! 930
Ye se I am able now for to greete him.
This sword of cumfort, sent fro my love,
Upon her enmy needes must I proove!
INSTR. Then foorth there; and turne on
   your ryght hand
Up that mownt before ye shall see stand.
But heere ye! Yf your enmye chance to
   ryse, 936
Folowe my cowncell in anye wyse:
Let Studye and Dyligence flee ther
   towche,[1] —
The stroke of Tediousnes, — and then
   cowche
Themselves, as I told ye, — ye wot
   how.[2] 940
WYT. Ye, syr, for that how, marke the
   proofe now!

[*Wyt, with drawn sword, and attended by
Study and Dylygence, proceeds to the
Mount.*]

INSTR. To mark it, indeede, here wyll I
   abyde,
To see what chance of them wyll betyde;
For heere cumth the pyth,[3] lo! of this
   iornaye.
That mowntayne, before which they must
   assaye, 945
Is cald in Laten *Mons Pernassus;*
Which mowntayne, as old auctors dyscus,
Who attaynth ones[4] to sleepe on that
   mownt,
Ladye Science his owne he may cownt.
But, or he cum there, ye shall see fowght 950
A fyght with no les polycye wrowght
Then strenghth, I trow, — if that may be
   praysed.
TEDI. [*within.*] Oh! ho! ho!
INSTR. Hark!
TEDI. [*entering.*] Out, ye kaytyves!
INSTR. The feend is raysyd!

---

[1] Blow.
[2] Instruction has devised some "polycye" by
means of which Wyt is to overcome Tediousness.
[3] Important part.   [4] Once.

TEDI. Out, ye vilaynes! Be ye cum
   agayne?
Have at ye, wretches! [*Rushes at them.*]
WYT [*aside*]. Fle, syrs, ye twayne! 953
   [*Study and Dylygence flee.*]
TEDI. Thei fle not far hens!
[*Tediousness pursues them, but is attacked
   by Wyt.*]
DYLI. Turne agayne, Studye!
STUDYE. Now, Dylygence!
INSTR. Well sayde! Hold fast now!
STUDYE. He fleeth!
DYLI. Then folowe!
[*Tediousness flees, beaten in by Wyt; Study
   and Dylygence follow.*]
INSTR. Wyth his owne weapon now wurke
   him sorow!
Wyt lyth at reseyte![1]
TEDI. [*within.*] Oh! ho! ho! *Dyeth.*
INSTR. Hark! he dyeth! 960
Where strength lakth, policye ssupplieth.
*Heere Wyt cumth in and bryngth in the hed
upon his swoorde, and sayth as folowyth:*
WYT. I can ye thanke, syrs; this was well
   doone!
STUDYE. Nay, yours is the deede!
DYLI. To you is the thank!
INSTR. I can ye thank, all; this was well
   doone!
WYT. How say ye, man? Is this feelde
   well woonne? 965
   Confydence cumth running in.
[CONF.] Ye, by my fayth, so sayth your
   deere hart.
WYT. Why where is she, that here now
   thow art?
CONF. Upon yonder mowntayne, on hye,
She saw ye strike that hed from the bodye;
Wherby ye have woonne her, bodye and
   all! 970
In token whereof reseve heere ye shall
A gowne of knoledge, wherin you must
Reseve her here strayght.
WYT. But sayst thow just?
[CONF.][2] So just I say that, except ye
   hye ye,

---

[1] A hunting term. To take up a position waiting
for hunted game.
[2] Though the MS. indicates another speaker, no
name is prefixed. Supplied by H.

Or ye be redye she wylbe by ye. 975

WYT. Holde! Present unto her this hed heere,

And gyve me warning when she cumth nere.

[*Exit Confidence.*]

Instruccion, wyll ye helpe to devyse
To trim this geere now in the best wyse?

INSTR. Geve me that gowne, and cum wyth me, all! 980

DYLI. Oh, how this gere to the purpose dooth fall!

Confidens cumth running in.

[CONF.] How, master, master! Where be ye now?

WYT. Here, Confydence; what tydynges bryngst thow?

CONF. My ladye at hand heere dooth abyde ye. 984

Byd her wellcum! What! do ye hide ye?

Here Wyt, Instruccion, Studye, and Dili-gence syng "Wellcum, my nowne," and Syence, Experience, Reson and Confidence cum in at l[eft], and answer evre second verse: [1]

WYT AND HIS CUMPANE:
 O ladye deere,
 Be ye so neere
  To be knowne?
 My hart yow cheere
 Your voyce to here.
  Wellcum, myne owne! / 991

SCIENCE AND HIR CUMPANYE:
 As ye rejoyse
 To here my voyce
  Fro me thus blowne,
 So in my choyce
 I show my voyce
  To be your owne. 997

WYT AND HIS CUMPANYE:
 Then drawe we neere
 To see and heere
  My love long growne!
 Where is my deere?
 Here I apeere
  To see myne owne. 1003

[1] The song is not given in the play, but is found with the other two songs in another part of the manu-script volume. It is labeled "The thyrd song," and has the title "Wellcum, myne owne, Welleum myne owne." M., following H., prints this title in two lines and, apparently, as a part of the song itself.

SCIENCE AND HIR CUMPANYE:
 To se and try
 Your love truly
  Till deth be flowne,
 Lo! here am I,
 That ye may spie
  I am your owne. 1009

WYT AND HIS CUMPANYE:
 Then let us meete,
 My love so sweete,
  Halfe-way heere throwne! 1012

SIENS AND HIR CUMPANYE:
 I wyll not sleete [1]
 My love to greete.
  Wellcum, myne owne! 1015

WYT AND HIS CUMPANYE:
 Wellcum, myne owne!

ALL *sing:*
  Wellcum, myne owne! 1017

And when the song is doone, Reson send-yth Instruccion, Studye, and Dyligence, and Confidens out; and then, standyng in the myddell of the place, Wyt sayth as folowyth:

WYT. Wellcum, myne owne, wyth all my hole harte,

Whych shalbe your owne till deth us de-part! [2]

I trust, ladye, this knot evyn syns knyt.

SCIENCE. I trust the same; for syns ye have smitt 1021

Downe my grete enmye, Tedyousnes,

Ye have woon me for-ever, dowghtles, —

Althowgh ye have woon a clogg [3] wyth-all!

WYT. A clogg, sweete hart? What?

SCIENCE.   Such as doth fall 1025

To all men that joyne themselves in mariage, —

In kepyng ther wyves. A carefull cariage!

WYT. Careful? Nay, ladye, that care shall imploye

No clogg, but a key of my most joye.

To kepe you, swete hart, as shall be fyt, 1030

Shalbe no care, but most joy to Wyt!

SCIENCE. Well, yet I say, — marke well what I saye! —

[1] Slight?
[2] Separate (an echo of the marriage ceremony).
[3] Encumbrance.

My presence brynghth you a clogg, no naye,
Not in the kepynge of me onelye,
But in the use of Science cheeflye;   1035
For I, Science, am in this degree, —
As all, or most part, of woomen bee:
Yf ye use me well, in a good sorte,
Then shall I be youre joy and comfort;
But yf ye use me not well, then dowt me,
For, sure, ye were better then wythout me!
WYT.   Why, ladye, thinke you me such a
          wyt,
As being avansyd by you, and yet
Wold mysuse ye?   Nay, yf ye dowt that,
Heere is wone lovth thee more then sum-
          what, —   1045
Yf Wyt mysuse ye at any season,
Correct me then your owne father, Reson.
RESON.   Ho, dowghter, can ye desyre any
          more?
What neede thes dowtes?   Avoyde them,
          therfore!
EXPER.   Byrlakyn, syr, but, under your
          favor,   1050
This dowgt our dowghter doth well to gather
For a good warnyng now at begynnynge
What Wyt in the end shall looke for in
          wynning;
Whych shalbe this, syr: yf Science here,
Whych is Godes gyft, be usyd meere 1055
Unto Godes honor, and profyt both
Of you and your neybowre,[1] — whych goth
In her, of kynd,[2] to do good to all, —
This seene to, Experience, I, shall
Set you forth, Wyt, by her to imploye 1060
Doble encrece to your doble joye;
But yf you use her contrarywyse
To her good nature, and so devyse
To evyll effectes to wrest and to wry her,
Ye, and cast her of, and set nowght by
          her,   1065
Be sure I, Experience, shall than
Declare you so before God and man
That thys talent[3] from you shalbe taken
And you ponysht for your gayne forsaken.
WYT.   "Once warnd,[4] half-armd," folk
          say, namely whan   1070
Experience shall warne a man, than
Tyme to take heede!   Mother Experience,
Towchyng youre dowghter, my deere hart,
          S[c]iens,

As I am sertayne that to abuse her
I brede myne owne sorow, and well to use
          her   1075
I encrece my joy; and so to make yt
Godes grace is redye yf I wyll take yt.
Then, but[1] ye cownt me no wyt at all,
Let never thes dowtes into your hed fall;
But, as yourself, Experience, cleryng 1080
All dowtes at lenght, so, tyll tyme aperyng,
Trust ye wyth me in God.   And, swete hart,
Whyle your father Reson takth wyth[2] parte,
To reseve Godes grace as God shall send it,
Dowte ye not our joy, tyll lyves end end[3]
          yt!   1085
SCIENCE.   Well, than, for the end of all
          dowtes past,
And to that end whiche ye spake of last:
Among our weddyng matters heere rend-
          ryng,
Thend of our lyves wold be in remembryng;
Which remembrance, Wyt, shall sure de-
          fend ye   1090
From the mysuse of Science, and send ye[4]
The gayne my mother to mynd did call, —
Joy wythout end.   That wysh I to all!

RESON.   Well sayd!   And as ye, dowghter,
          wyshe it,
That joy to all folke in generall,   1095
So wysh I, Reson, the same.   But yet
Fyrst in this lyfe wysh I here to fall
To our most noble Kyng and Quene in
          especiall,
To ther honorable Cowncell, and then to
          all the rest,
Such joy as long may rejoyse them all
          best![5]   1100
          All say Amen.

*Heere cumth in fowre wyth violes and syng,
"Remembre me,"[6] and at the last quere all
make cur[t]sye, and so goe forth syngyng.*

*Thus endyth the Play of Wyt and Science,
made by Master Jhon Redford.*

Finis.

[1] Neighbor.   [2] By nature.
[3] The reference is to the parable of the talents.
[4] H. *warne;* M. *warne[d]*.   The MS. is clearly
warnd.

[1] Unless.   [2] With.
[3] In MS., but crossed through, obviously by mistake.
[4] MS. *you;* corr. by M.
[5] It was customary for actors at the end of a play
to utter a prayer for the sovereign and his council.
[6] The song is not given in the MS.

VIII
FOLK PLAYS

ROBIN HOOD AND THE SHERIFF OF NOTTINGHAM [1]

[SCENE I.]

[*Enter Sir Guy of Gisborne and the Sheriff of Nottingham.*]

[SIR GUY.] Syr Sheryffe, for thy sake
Robyn Hode wull Y take.
[SHERIFF.] I wyll the gyffe golde and fee [1]
This be-heste [2] thou holde me.

[SCENE II.]

[*Sir Guy approaches Robin Hood.*]

[SIR GUY.] Robyn Hode, ffayre and fre, 5
Vndre this lynde [3] shote we.
[ROBIN.] With the shote Y wyll
Alle thy lustes to full-fyll.
[SIR GUY.] [*Shoots.*] Have at the pryke! [4]
[ROBIN.] [*Shoots.*] And Y cleue the
styke! 10

[*Robin Hood wins.*]

[SIR GUY.] Late vs caste the stone.
[ROBIN.] I graunte well, be Seynt Iohn!

[*They cast the stone, and again Robin Hood wins.*]

[SIR GUY.] Late vs caste the exaltre.
[ROBIN.] Have a foote be-fore the!

[*They wrestle; Robin throws the knight.*]

[ROBIN.] Syr Knyght, ye haue a falle! 15
[SIR GUY.] And I the, Robyn, qwyte [5]
shall.
Owte on the! I blowe myn horne!

[*Sir Guy starts to blow his horn, but Robin Hood halts him.*]

[ROBIN.] Hit ware better be vn-borne!
Lat vs fyght at ottraunce. [1]
[SIR GUY.] He that fleth, God gyf hym
myschaunce! 20

[*They fight with swords. At last Robin Hood slays Sir Guy.*]

[ROBIN.] Now I haue the maystry here!
Off I smyte this sory swyre. [2]
This knyghtys clothis wolle I were,
And in my hode his hede woll bere. 24

[*Robin disguises himself in Sir Guy's clothes, and, taking with him the severed head, goes out.*]

[SCENE III.]

[*The Sheriff has attacked Robin Hood's men with success. Little John, hurrying towards the scene of the conflict, meets Scarlet.*]

[LITTLE JOHN.] Welle mete, felowe myn!
What herst thou of gode Robyn?
[SCARLET.] Robyn Hode and his menye [3]
With the Sheryffe takyn be.
[LITTLE JOHN.] Sette on foote with gode
wyll,
And the Sheryffe wull we kyll. 30

[*They stand together, watching the fight.*]

[SCARLET.] Be-holde wele Frere Tuke
Howe he dothe his bowe pluke!

---

[1] Money. [2] Promise. [3] Linden tree.
[4] Target. [5] Pay back.

[1] To the death. [2] Neck. [3] Followers.

---

[1] This fragment of a Robin Hood play (the earliest text we have preserved) is found on the upper half of a leaf originally pasted at the end of some folio volume. On the verso of the leaf are accounts of quarterly payments for house rent extending, apparently, from May, 1475, to August, 1476 (one is dated November 7, 1475). It is likely that the text of the Robin Hood play was written at a still earlier date; but even if the record of house-rent payments preceded, the handwritings on the two sides of the leaf, as Greg observes, are obviously contemporary, and the entries can hardly be separated by more than a few years." The history of the manuscript makes it probable that the leaf was once in the possession of William Paston, second Earl of Yarmouth; and in one of the Paston letters, April 16, 1473, we discover that Sir John Paston had a certain man named Woode in his employ "thys iij yer to pleye Seynt Jorge [George], and Robyn Hod and the Sheriff off Notyngham." Greg, agreeing with Child and Chambers, writes: "There can be little question . . . that this last piece is none other than the play to which our fragment belongs."

I have reproduced the text from that issued by Greg, with facsimile, in The Malone Society's *Collections*, 117, and have taken advantage of both Manly's and Greg's dramatic reconstruction, though the punctuation and the stage-directions are my own. The fragment ends before the climax of the play has been reached; but the story is well-known in the ballad of Guy of Gisborne. I have added, with some changes, Greg's completion based on the ballad.

[*The Sheriff and his men overcome the outlaws, and bind Friar Tuck and the rest. Entering with the prisoners, they spy Little John and Scarlet.*]

[SHERIFF.]   Yeld yow, syrs, to the Sheryffe,
Or elles shall your bowes clyffe.   34

[*Little John and Scarlet yield, and are bound.*]

[LITTLE JOHN.]   Now we be bownden alle in same!
Frere [T]uke, this is no game.[1]
[SHERIFF.]   Co[m]e thou forth, thou fals outlawe;
Thou shall [be] hangyde and y-drawe!
[FRIAR TUCK.]   Now[e], allas, what shall we doo?
We [m]oste to the prysone goo.   40
[SHERIFF.]   Opy[n] the yatis[2] faste anon,
An[d la[te] theis thevys ynne gon.[3]

[*Robin enters disguised as Sir Guy.*]

[ROBIN.]   Holde[4] thou here, syr Sheryffe,
Robyns hede, by my lyffe!   44

[*He presents the severed head.*]

---
[1] Jest.   [2] Doors.
[3] At this point the fragment ends.
[4] Take, receive.

[SHERIFF.]   Now, take thou golde and fee!
Syr Gwye, wellcume mote thou be!
[ROBIN.]   Golde and fee wylle I none,
But yon outlawe alone.

[*He points to Little John.*]

[SHERIFF.]   Take hym lyghtlie to thy wylle,
Thogh thou hys lyffe spille.   50

[*Robin goes to Little John, reveals himself to him, cuts his bonds, and, thrusting a bow into his hands, whispers:*]

[ROBIN.]   Now haue this bow intill thy honde.
By thy syde I take my stonde!

[*They draw upon the Sheriff.*]

[SHERIFF.]   Owt alas! we be fordone![1]
Robin Hode is vs vpon!   54

[*The Sheriff and his men start to run away.*]

[LITTLE JOHN.]   Now do they runne for drede.
Syr Sheryffe, thou art but dede!

[*Little John shoots; the Sheriff falls.*]

[FRIAR TUCK.]   By Chryst, this was welle wroght.
Gode Robyn hath his menye boght![2]   58

---
[1] Ruined.   [2] Followers saved.

ROBIN HOOD AND THE FRIAR[1]

Here beginnethe the playe of Robyn Hoode, verye proper to be played in Maye games.

[Scene I.]

[*Enter Robin Hood and his men, dressed in Kendal green.*]

Robyn Hode. Now stand ye forth, my
    mery men all,
And harke what I shall say!
Of an adventure I shal you tell,
The which befell this other day:
As I went by the hygh-way,   5
With a stoute frere I met,
And a quarter-staffe in his hande;
Lyghtely to me he lept,
And styll he bade me stande.
There were strypes two or three,   10
But I can not tell who had the worse;
But well I wote the horeson lepte within
    me,
And fro me he toke my purse.
Is there any of my mery men all
That to that frere wyll go,   15
And bryng him to me forth-withall,
Whether he wyll or no?
Lytell Iohn. Yes, mayster, I make God
    avowe,
To that frere wyll I go,
And bryng him to you,   20
Whether he wyl or no.   [*Exeunt.*]

[Scene II.]

[*Enter Friar Tucke in a long coat, leading three dogs by a string.*]

Fryer Tucke. Deus hic! Deus hic!
    God be here!
Is not this a holy worde for a frere?
God save all this company!
But am not I a iolly fryer?   25
For I can shote both farre and nere,
And handle the sworde and buckler —

And this quarter-staffe also.
If I mete with a gentylman or yeman,
I am not afrayde to loke hym upon,   30
Nor boldly with him to carpe;
If he speake any wordes to me,
He shall have strypes two or thre
That shal make his body smarte!
But, maister[s], to shew you the matter 35
Wherfore and why I am come hither,
In fayth, I wyl not spare:
I am come to seke a good yeman,
In Bernisdale men sai is his habitacion,
His name is Robyn Hode.   40
And if that he be better man than I,
His servaunt wyll I be, and serve him
    truely;
But if that I be better man than he,
By my truth, my knave shall he be,
And leade these dogges all three!   45

[*Robin enters and seizes him by the throat.*]

Robyn Hode. Yelde the, fryer in thy long
    cote!
Fryer Tucke. I beshrew thy hart,
    knave! Thou hurtest my throt[e].

[*Shakes him off.*]

Robyn Hode. I trowe, fryer, thou begin-
    nest to dote!
Who made the so malapert and so bolde
To come into this forest here   50
Amonge my falowe-dere?
Fryer. Go louse the, ragged knave!
If thou make mani wordes, I will geve the
    on the eare,
Though I be but a poore fryer,
To seke Robyn Hode I am com here,   55
And to him my hart to breke.
Robyn Hode. Thou lousy frer, what
    wouldest thou with hym?

[1] Appended to *Gest of Robin Hood*, printed by William Copland, without date, but apparently between 1553 and 1569. I have based the text on the careful reprint by W. W. Greg in The Malone Society's *Collections*, 1909, i, 125, and have compared this with Manly's reprint, *Specimens*, 1896. Copland gives two texts carelessly run together as one; the second text, dealing with Robin Hood and the Potter, is a mere fragment, breaking off in the middle of the action, a fact which led Greg plausibly to suggest "that Copland (or some predecessor) printed from a copy of an earlier edition which had lost a leaf or more at the end." I have omitted the fragment.

He never loved fryer, nor none of freiers kyn.

FRYER. Avaunt, ye ragged knave,
Or ye shall have on the skynne! 60
ROBYN HODE. Of all the men in the morning thou art the worst;
To mete with the I have no lust,
For he that meteth a frere, or a fox, in the morning,
To spede ill that day he standeth in ieoperdy:[1]
Therfore I had lever[2] mete with the devil of hell — 65
Fryer, I tell the as I thinke —
Then mete with a fryer, or a fox,
In a mornyng or I drynke.
FRYER. Avaunt, thou ragged knave! this is but a mock.
If you make mani words, you shal have a knock. 70
ROBYN HODE. Harke, frere, what I say here:
Over this water thou shalt me bere, —
The brydge is borne away.
FRYER. To say naye I wyll not —
To let the of thine oth it were great pitie and sin — 75
But, up on a fryers backe, and have even in!
ROBYN HODE. Nay, have over!

[*Robin Hood gets on Friar Tuck's back; the Friar wades into the stream, and stops.*]

FRYER. Now am I, frere, within, and thou, Robin, without.
To lay the here I have no great doubt.

[*He drops him in the water, and wades out.*]

Now am I, frere, without, and thou, Robyn, within![3] 80
Lye ther, knave! Chose whether thou wilte sinke or swym.
ROBYN HODE. Why, thou lowsy frere! what hast thou done?
FRYER. Mary, set a knave over the shone.[4]
ROBYN HODE. Therfore thou [shalt] abye.[5]

[*Robin Hood draws, and rushes at the Friar.*]

FRYER. Why, wylt thou fyght a plucke?[1]
ROBYN HODE. And God send me good lucke! 86
FRYER. Than have a stroke for Fryer Tucke!

[*They fight. Robin Hood is unable to get the better of the Friar.*]

ROBYN HODE. Holde thy hande, frere, and here me speke!
FRYER. Say on, ragged knave!
Me semeth ye begyn to swete. 90
ROBYN HODE. In this forest I have a hounde,
I wyl not give him for a hundreth pound;
Geve me leve my horne to blowe,
That my hounde may knowe.
FRYER. Blowe on, ragged knave, without any doubte, 95
Untyll bothe thyne eyes starte out!

[*Robin Hood blows his horn, and his men rush in.*]

Here be a sorte of ragged knaves come in,
Clothed all in Kendale grene;
And to the they take their way nowe.
ROBYN HODE. Peradventure they do so. 100
FRYER. I gave the leve to blowe at thy wyll,
Now give me leve to whistell my fyll.
ROBIN HODE. Whystell, frere, evyl mote thou fare!
Untyll bothe thyne eyes stare.[2]

[*The Friar whistles, and his men rush in.*]

FRYER. Now, Cut and Bause! 105
Breng forth the clubbes and staves,
And downe with those ragged knaves!

[*They fight with clubs and staves. Robin Hood and his men are unable to overcome Friar Tuck and his men.*]

ROBYN HODE. How sayest thou, frere?
Wylt thou be my man,
To do me the best servyse thou can?
Thou shalt have both golde and fee; 110

---

[1] An old proverb.   [2] Rather.
[3] The original text reads: "Now art thou, Robyn, without, and I, frere, within." I follow Child's correction.
[4] Shoes.   [5] Pay for.

[1] Bout.
[2] Original text reads "starte"; corrected by Manly.

[He leads forward Maid Marian.]

And also here is a lady free;
I wyll geve her unto the,
And her chapplayn I the make
To serve her for my sake.

[The Friar throws his arms about her.]

FRYER.   Here is an huckle-duckle   115
An inch above the buckle!
She is a trul of trust

To serve a frier . . . .

. . . .[1]   120

[Turning to his men.]

Go home, ye knaves, and lay crabbes in the
fyre,
For my lady and I will daunce in the myre
For veri pure ioye!   123

[1] Lines omitted by the present editor.

SHETLAND SWORD DANCE [1]

PERSONÆ DRAMATIS [2]

[ST. GEORGE, OF ENGLAND, the master.
ST. JAMES, OF SPAIN.
ST. DENIS, OF FRANCE.
ST. DAVID, OF WALES.

ST. PATRICK, OF IRELAND.
ST. ANTHONY, OF ITALY.
ST. ANDREW, OF SCOTLAND.]

WORDS USED AS A PRELUDE TO THE SWORD-DANCE.

*Enter Master, in the character of
Saint George.*

Brave gentles all within this boor,[1]
If ye delight in any sport,
Come see me dance upon this floor,
Which to you all shall yield comfort.
Then shall I dance in such a sort   5
As possible I may or can.
You minstrel man, play me a Porte,[2]
That I on this floor may prove a man.

He bows, and dances in a line.

Now have I danced with heart and hand,
Brave gentles all, as you may see,   10
For I have been tried in many a land,
As yet the truth can testify;
In England, Scotland, Ireland, France,
    Italy, and Spain,
Have I been tried with that good sword of
    steel.

Draws, and flourishes.

Yet I deny that ever a man did make me
    yield;   15
For in my body there is strength,
As by my manhood may be seen;
And I, with that good sword of length,
Have oftentimes in perils been;
And over champions I was king;   20
And by the strength of this right hand

Once on a day I kill'd fifteen,
And left them dead upon the land.
Therefore, brave minstrel, do not care,
But play me a Porte most light,   25
That I no longer do forbear,
But dance in all these gentles' sight.
Although my strength makes you abased,
Brave gentles all, be not afraid,
For here are six champions with me,
    staid;   30
All by my manhood I have raised.

He dances.

Since I have danced, I think it best
To call my brethren in your sight,
That I may have a little rest;   34
And they may dance with all their might,
With heart and hand, as they are knights,
And shake their swords of steel so bright,
And show their main strength on this floor.
For we shall have another bout
Before we pass out of this boor.   40
Therefore, brave minstrel, do not care
To play to me a Porte most light,
That I no longer do forbear,
But dance in all these gentles' sight.

*He dances; and then introduces his Knights as
under:*

Stout James of Spain, both tried and
    stour,   45

---

[1] Bower.	[2] A lively tune.

[1] From a note inserted in Scott's *The Pirate*, 1821, and reprinted, with other material, by E. K. Chambers, *The Mediæval Stage*, ii, 271. It is stated that "the manuscript from which the above was copied was transcribed from *a very old* one, by Mr. William Henderson, jun., of Papa Stour, in Zetland. Mr. Henderson's copy is not dated, but bears his own signature, and, from various circumstances, it is known to have been written about the year 1788." The date of the original manuscript is not indicated. In Sir Walter Scott's *Diary* for August 7, 1814, we read: "At Scalloway my curiosity was gratified by an account of the sword-dance, now almost lost, but still practised in the Island of Papa, belonging to Mr. Scott. . . . Some rude couplets are spoken (in *English* not *Norse*), containing a sort of panegyric upon each champion as he is presented. They then dance a sort of cotillion, as the ladies described it, going through a number of evolutions with their swords."

[2] Though this heading appears in the manuscript, the names are omitted, possibly because they were those of the famous Seven Champions of Christendom.

Thine acts are known full well indeed;
[*St. James advances.*]
And champion Dennis, a French knight,
Who stout and bold is to be seen;
[*St. Denis advances.*]
And David, a Welshman born,
Who is come of noble blood; 50
[*St. David advances.*]
And Patrick also, who blew the horn,
An Irish knight, amongst the wood;
[*St. Patrick advances.*]
Of Italy brave Anthony the good,
And Andrew of Scotland king.
[*St. Anthony and St. Andrew advance.*]

[SAINT JAMES.[1]] Saint George of England,
    brave indeed, 55
Who to the Jews wrought muckle tinte,[2]
Away with this! Let us come to sport,
Since that ye have a mind to war.
Since that ye have this bargain sought,
Come, let us fight, and do not fear. 60
[SAINT GEORGE.] Therefore, brave min-
    strel, do not care
To play to me a Porte most light,
That I no longer do forbear,
But dance in all these gentles' sight.

He dances, and advances to James of Spain.

[SAINT GEORGE.] Stout James of Spain,
    both tried and stour, 65
Thine acts are known full well indeed.
Present thyself within our sight,
Without either fear or dread.
Count not for favour or for feid,[3]
Since of thy acts thou hast been sure. 70
Brave James of Spain, I will thee lead
To prove thy manhood on this floor.

James dances.

[SAINT GEORGE.] Brave champion Dennis,
    a French knight,
Who stout and bold is to be seen,

Present thyself here in our sight, 75
Thou brave French knight,
Who bold hast been;
Since thou such valiant acts hast done,
Come let us see some of them now.
With courtesy, thou brave French knight,
Draw out thy sword of noble hue. 81

Dennis dances, while the others retire to a side.

[SAINT GEORGE.] Brave David a bow must
    string, and with awe
Set up a wand upon a stand,
And that brave David will cleave in twa.[1]

David dances solus.

[SAINT GEORGE.] Here is, I think, an
    Irish knight, 85
Who does not fear, or does not fright.
To prove thyself a valiant man,
As thou hast done full often bright,
Brave Patrick dance, if that thou can.

He dances.

[SAINT GEORGE.] Thou stout Italian, come
    thou here! 90
Thy name is Anthony, most stout.
Draw out thy sword that is most clear,
And do thou fight without any doubt;
Thy leg thou shake, thy neck thou lout,[2]
And show some courtesy on this floor. 95
For we shall have another bout
Before we pass out of this boor.

[*He dances.*]

[SAINT GEORGE.] Thou kindly Scotsman,
    come thou here!
Thy name is Andrew of Fair Scotland.
Draw out thy sword that is most clear; 100
Fight for thy king with thy right hand;
And aye as long as thou canst stand
Fight for thy king with all thy heart,
And then, for to confirm his band,
Make all his enemies for to smart. 105

He dances. Music begins.

---

[1] No speaker's name is indicated in the manuscript.
[2] Much harm. [3] Feud, enmity.

[1] Two. [2] Bend.

FIGUIR.

The six stand in rank, with their swords reclining on their shoulders.

The Master (Saint George) dances, and then strikes the sword of James of Spain, who follows George, then dances, strikes the sword of Dennis, who follows behind James. In like manner the rest — the music playing — swords as before.

After the six are brought out of rank, they and the Master form a circle, and hold the swords point and hilt. This circle is danced round twice.

The whole, headed by the Master, pass under the swords held in a vaulted manner. They jump over the swords. This naturally places the swords across, which they disentangle by passing under their right sword.

They take up the seven swords, and form a circle, in which they dance round.

The Master runs under the sword opposite, which he jumps over backwards. The others do the same. He then passes under the right-hand sword, which the others follow, in which position they dance, until commanded by the Master, when they form into a circle, and dance round as before.

They then jump over the right-hand sword, by which means their backs are to the circle, and their hands across their backs. They dance round in that form, until the Master calls "Loose!" when they pass under the right sword, and are in a perfect circle.

The Master lays down his sword, and lays hold of the point of James's sword. He then turns himself, James, and the others, into a clew. When so formed, he passes under out of the midst of the circle; the others follow. They vault, as before. After several other evolutions, they throw themselves into a circle, with their arms across the breast.

They afterwards form such figures as to form a shield of their swords,[1] and the shield is so compact that the Master and his knights dance alternately with this shield upon their heads. It is then laid down upon the floor. Each knight lays hold of their former points and hilts with their hands across, which disentangle by figuirs directly contrary to those that formed the shield.

This finishes the ballet.

[1] This is called a "glass" in the Revesby Sword Play; see p. 358.

EPILOGUE.

Mars does rule; he bends his brows;
He makes us all agast.
After the few hours that we stay here
Venus will rule at last.
Farewell, farewell, brave gentles all,
That herein do remain!
I wish you health and happiness
Till we return again.

Exeunt.

OXFORDSHIRE ST. GEORGE PLAY [1]

DRAMATIS PERSONÆ

St. George of England.
King Alfred.
King Alfred's Queen.
King William.
Old King Cole, with a wooden leg.
Giant Blunderbore.

Little Jack.
The Old Dragon.
Old Doctor Ball.
Father Christmas.
The Merry Andrew.
Morres-men.

*All the mummers come in singing, and
walk round the place in a circle, and then
stand on one side.*

*Enter King Alfred and his Queen, arm
in arm.*

I am King Alfred, and this here is my bride.
I've a crown on my pate and a sword by
 my side.   *Stands apart.*

Enter King Cole.

I am King Cole, and I carry my stump.
Hurrah for King Charles! Down with old
 Noll's Rump! [1] *Stands apart.*

Enter King William.

I am King William of blessed me-mo-ry,
Who came and pulled down the high gal-
 lows-tree,   6
And brought us all peace and pros-pe-
 ri-ty.   *Stands apart.*

Enter Giant Blunderbore.

I am Giant Blunderbore, fee, fi, fum!
Ready to fight ye all, — so I says, "Come!"

Enter Little Jack [a small boy].

And this here is my little man Jack. 10

---

[1] Apparently an allusion to Oliver Cromwell and
the Rump Parliament.

A thump on his rump, and a whack on his
 back!   *Strikes him twice.*
I'll fight King Alfred, I'll fight King Cole,
I'm ready to fight any mortal soul!
So here I, Blunderbore, takes my stand,
With this little devil, Jack, at my right
 hand,   15
Ready to fight for mortal life. Fee, fi, fum!
 The Giant and Little Jack stand apart.

Enter St. George [the leader of the dance].

I am St. George of Merry Eng-land.
Bring in the morres-men, bring in our
 band.

*Morres-men come forward and dance to a
tune from fife and drum. The dance being
ended, St. George continues:*

These are our tricks, — ho! men, ho!
These are our sticks, — whack men so! 20
*Strikes the Dragon, who roars, and comes
 forward.*

The Dragon speaks.

Stand on head, stand on feet!
Meat, meat, meat for to eat!

Tries to bite King Alfred.

I am the Dragon, — here are my jaws!
I am the Dragon, — here are my claws!

---

[1] Printed by F. G. Lee in *Notes and Queries*, 5 Series (1874), ii, 503, with the following comment: "The text
of the play was taken down by myself from the lips of one of the performers in 1853.   I first saw it acted in
the Hall of the old Vicarage House at Thame, in the year 1839, by those whose custom it had been, from time
immemorial, to perform it at the houses of the gentle-people of that neighborhood at Christmas, between St.
Thomas's Day [December 21] and Old Christmas Eve, January 5.   These performers (now long scattered,
and all dead but one, as I am informed) claimed to be the 'true and legitimate successors' of the mummers
who, in the previous centuries, constantly performed at the 'Whitsun' and 'Christmas Church Ales.' . . .
The man from whom I took down the following in my Note-book had performed at Brill, in the year 1807, and
his father had done the same at Thame Park in the previous century." In *Harper's Monthly Magazine*, 1907,
Max Beerbohm gives a delightful account of an Oxfordshire Morris he had recently witnessed by chance "in
a tiny village near Oxford."   The text of a Worcestershire St. George Play may be found in *Notes and Queries*,
2 Series (1860), xi, 271, and of a Middlesex play, *Ibid.*, x, 466.

Meat, meat, meat for to eat! 25
Stand on my head, stand on my feet!

Turns a summersault, and stands aside.

All sing, several times repeated:

> Ho! ho! ho!
> Whack men so!

The drum and fife sound. They all fight, and after general disorder, fall down.

Enter Old Dr. Ball.

I am the Doctor, and I cure all ills,
Only gullup my portions,[1] and swallow my
    pills; 30
I can cure the itch, the stitch, the pox, the
    palsy, and the gout,
All pains within, and all pains without.
Up from the floor, Giant Blunderbore!

Gives him a pill, and he rises at once.

Get up, King! get up, Bride!
Get up, Fool! and stand aside. 35

Gives them each a pill, and they rise.

Get up, King Cole, and tell the gentlefolks
    all
There never was a doctor like Mr. Doctor
    Ball.
Get up, St. George, old England's knight!

Gives him a pill.

You have wounded the Dragon and fin-
    ished the fight.

All stand aside but the Dragon, who lies in convulsions on the floor.

Now kill the Dragon, and poison old
    Nick; 40
At Yule-tyde, both o' ye, cut your stick!

The Doctor forces a large pill down the

[1] A vulgarism for "potions."

Dragon's throat, who thereupon roars, and dies in convulsions.

Then enter Father Christmas.

I am Father Christmas! Hold, men, hold!

[*Addressing the audience.*]

Be there loaf in your locker, and sheep in
    your fold,
A fire on the hearth, and good luck for your
    lot,
Money in your pocket, and a pudding in
    the pot! 45

He sings:

> Hold, men, hold!
> Put up your sticks;
> End all your tricks;
> Hold, men, hold!

Chorus (all sing, while one goes round with a hat for gifts).

> Hold, men, hold! 50
> We are very cold,
> Inside and outside,
> We are very cold.
> If you don't give us silver,
> Then give us gold 55
From the money in your pockets —

Some of the performers show signs of fighting again.

Hold, men, hold! [*etc.*]

Song and chorus.

God A'mighty bless your hearth and fold,
Shut out the wolf, and keep out the cold!
You gev' us silver, keep you the gold, 60
For 'tis money in your pocket. — Hold,
    men, hold!

Repeat in chorus.

God A'mighty bless, &c.

Exeunt omnes.

LEICESTERSHIRE ST. GEORGE PLAY [1]

DRAMATIS PERSONÆ

1. **Captain Slasher,** *in military costume, with sword and pistol.*
2. **King of England,** *in robes, wearing the crown.*
3. **Prince George,** *King's son, in robes, and sword by his side.*
4. **Turkish Champion,** *in military attire, with sword and pistol.*
5. **A Noble Doctor.**
6. **Beelzebub.**
7. **A Clown.**

Enter Captain Slasher.

[Capt. S.] I beg your pardon for being so
    bold;
I enter your house, the weather's so cold.
Room! a room! brave gallants, give us
    room to sport;
For in this house we do resort,
Resort, resort, for many a day.   5
Step in, the King of England,
And boldly clear the way!

Enter King of England.

[King of E.] I am the King of England,
    that boldly does appear.
I come to seek my only son, — my only son
    is here.

Enter Prince George.

[Prince G.] I am Prince George, a
    worthy knight.   10
I'll spend my blood for England's right;
England's right I will maintain;
I'll fight for old England once again.

Enter Turkish Knight.

Turk. Kn.] I am the Turkish Cham-
    pion.[1]
From Turkey's land I come;   15
I come to fight the King of England
And all his noble men.

    [1] Probably an echo from the Crusades.

Captain Slasher.

[Capt. S.] In comes Captain Slasher.
Captain Slasher is my name,
With sword and pistol by my side.   20
I hope to win the game.

King of E. I am the King of England,
As you may plainly see.
These are my soldiers standing by me;
They stand by me your life to end;   25
On them doth my life depend.

Prince G. I am Prince George, the cham-
    pion bold,
And with my sword I won three crowns of
    gold;
I slew the fiery dragon and brought him to
    the slaughter,
And won the King of Egypt's only daugh-
    ter.   30

Turk. Kn. [*sneeringly*]. As I was going
    by St. Francis' School,
I heard a lady cry, "A fool! a fool!"
"A fool!" was every word.
"That man's a fool,
Who wears a wooden sword!"   35

    [*Points to Prince George's sword.*]

Prince G. A wooden sword, you dirty
    dog!

[1] Printed by William Kelly, *Notices Illustrative of the Drama and Other Popular Amusements*, 1865, p. 53. Kelly writes: "Among the most vivid of our boyish recollections some five and thirty years ago, is that of seeing parties of Mummers going about the town, from house to house, some of them wearing high conical caps of pasteboard, decorated with ribbons and gilt paper, and carrying wooden swords, a club, frying-pan. etc."; and he adds: "As the last traces of this ancient custom will be inevitably swept away in a very few years, we gladly avail ourselves of the opportunity of placing before our readers the 'Mummers' Play' as performed in some villages near Lutterworth, at Christmas, 1863." One may find a vivid description of a very similar play, with Captain Slasher, Prince George, the Turkish Knight, and other characters, in Thomas Hardy's *The Return of the Native*, book ii, chapters iv and v.

My sword is made of the best of metal
free.
If you would like to taste of it,
I'll give it unto thee.

[He draws his sword.]

Stand off! stand off! you dirty dog!   40
Or by my sword you'll die!
I'll cut you down the middle,
And make your blood to fly.

*They fight; Prince George falls, mortally
wounded.*

KING OF E.   Oh horrible! terrible!   What
hast thou done?
Thou hast ruin'd me! ruin'd me!   45
By killing of my only son!
Oh, is there ever a noble doctor to be
found,
To cure this English champion
Of his deep and deadly wound?

Enter Noble Doctor.

[DOCTOR.]   Oh yes, there is a noble doctor
to be found,   50
To cure this English champion
Of his deep and deadly wound.

KING OF E.   And pray what is your
practice?
DOCTOR.   I boast not of my practice;
neither do I study in the practice of
physic.   57
KING OF E.   What can you cure?
DOCTOR.   All sorts of diseases,
Whatever you pleases: 60
I can cure the itch, the pitch,
The phthisic, the palsy, and the gout;
And if the devil's in the man,
I can fetch him out.
My wisdom lies in my wig.   65
I torture not my patients with excations

Such as pills, boluses, solutions, and em-
brocations;
But by the word of command
I can make this mighty prince to stand.

KING.   What is your fee?   70
DOCTOR.   Ten pounds, is true.
KING.   Proceed, noble doctor;
You shall have your due.

DOCTOR.   Arise! arise! most noble prince,
arise,
And no more dormant lay!   75
And with thy sword
Make all thy foes obey.

The Prince arises.

PRINCE G.   My head is made of iron,
My body is made of steel,
My legs are made of crooked bones   80
To force you all to yield!

Enter Beelzebub.

BEEL.   In comes I, old Beelzebub;
Over my shoulder I carry my club,
And in my hand a frying-pan,
Pleased to get all the money I can.   85

Enter Clown.

CLOWN.   In comes I, who's never been yet,
With my great head and little wit:
My head is great, my wit is small,
I'll do my best to please you all.

*[The Clown turns somersaults, etc., while
Beelzebub collects money in his frying-pan.]*

Song, all join.

And now we are done, and must be gone,
    No longer will we stay here;
But, if you please, before we go,
    We'll taste your Christmas beer.
           Exeunt omnes.

THE REVESBY SWORD PLAY [1]

Acted by a set of Plow Boys or Morris Dancers, in riband dresses, with swords, on October 20th, 1779, at Revesby Abbey, in Lincolnshire, the seat of the Right Hon. Sir Joseph Banks, Bart., P.R.S. [2]

DRAMATIS PERSONÆ

Men.

THE FOOL	John Johnson.
PICKLE HERRING	Richd. Johnson.
BLUE BREECHES	Henry Johnson.
PEPPER BREECHES	John Tomlinson.
GINGER BREECHES	Chas. Hodgson.
MR. ALLSPICE	Thos. Harness.

Women.

CICELY	John Fisher.
FIDLER, *or* MR. MUSICK MAN	John Johnson, jun[r].

THE PLOUGH BOYS, OR MORRIS DANCERS.

Enter Fool. [1]

You gentle lords of honour,
　Of high and low, I say,
We all desire your favour
　For to see our pleasant play.　　4

Our play it is the best, kind sirs,
　That you would like to know;
And we will do our best, sirs,
　And think it well bestowd.　　8

Tho some of us be little,
　And some of a middle sort,
We all desire your favour
　To see our pleasant sport.　　12

You must not look on our actions;
　Our wits they are all to seek;
So I pray take no exceptions
　At what I am a-going to speak.　　16

We are come over the mire and moss;
We dance an Hobby Horse; [1]
A Dragon [2] you shall see,
And a wild Worm [3] for to flee.
　Still we are all brave, jovial boys,
　And takes delight in Christmas toys. [4]　22

We are come both for bread and beer,
And hope for better cheer,
And something out of your purse, [5] sir,
Which I hope you will be never the worse, sir.
　Still we are all brave, jovial boys,
　And takes delight in Christmas toys.　28

[1] The plow boys, in their enthusiasm, have combined several plays into one long performance; the first may be called the Morris Dance of the Hobby Horse, with a prologue, lines 1–28, and an epilogue, lines 60–65, in itself a complete text.

[1] The figure of a horse, usually made of canvas, fastened round the waist of the dancer, his own legs going through the body of the horse and enabling him to walk. This amusing device was nearly always employed in the morris dance.
[2] Possibly suggesting the dragon killed by St. George, in which case the rider of the Hobby Horse may be regarded as St. George himself.
[3] Dragon.
[4] Several references in this composite play show that certain of its elements were designed for performance at Christmas.
[5] For the custom of taking a collection, see pages 354, 356.

---

[1] Printed by T. Fairman Ordish in *The Folk-Lore Journal*, vii (1889), 338, from a manuscript apparently written down at the time of the performance; John Brand, *Popular Antiquities*, 1813, i, 573, speaks of having "a copy" before him, and quotes some of the lines. Ordish calls the play *Morrice Dancers at Revesby;* I have adopted the title devised by Manly, and have also, for the most part, retained Manly's arrangement of certain lines as verse which appear as prose in the original. All additions to the manuscript as reproduced by Ordish I have set in square brackets.　　[2] Brand, *Popular Antiquities*, i, 573.

[Turning to the Fiddler.]

Come now, Mr. Musick Man, play me my
delight.

FIDLER.   What is that, old father?   31

FOOL.   Ah! boy, times is hard!   "I love to
have money in both pockets." [1]

FID.   You shall have it, old father.

FOOL.   Let me see it.   35

*The Fool then calls in his five sons; first
Pickle Herring, then Blue Britches, then
Ginger Britches, Pepper Britches, and last
calls out:*

Come now, you Mr. Allspice!

*They foot it once round the room, and the
man that is to ride the Hobby Horse goes
out, and the rest sing the following song:*

[ALL.] Come in, come in, thou Hobby Horse,
And bring thy old fool at thy arse!
Sing tanter[a]day, sing tanter[a]day,
Sing heigh down, down, with a derry
          down a!   40

[Enter the Hobby Horse.]

*Then The Fool and the Horse fights about
the room, whilst the following song is singing by the rest:*

[ALL.]   Come in, come in, thou bonny wild
          Worm!
For thou hast ta'en many a lucky turn.
Sing tanteraday, sing tanteraday,
Sing heigh down, down, with a derry
          down [a]!   44

[Enter the Wild Worm.]

*The wild Worm is only sprung three or
four times, as the man walks round the
room, and then goes out; and the Horse and
The Fool fights again, whilst the following
song is sung:*

[ALL.]   Come in, come in, thou Dragon
          stout,[2]
And take thy compass round about!
Sing tanteraday, sing tanteraday,

Sing heigh down, down, with a derry
          down [a]!   48

Now you shall see a full fair fight
Between our old Fool and his right.
Sing tanteraday, sing tanteraday,
Sing heigh down, down, with a derry
          down [a]!   52

Now our scrimage is almost done;
Then you shall see more sport soon.
Sing tanteraday, sing tanteraday,
Sing heigh down, down, with a derry
          down [a]!   56

FOOL.   Up well hart,[1] and up well hind!
Let every man then to his own kind.
Sing tanteraday, sing tanteraday,
Sing heigh down, down, with a derry
          down [a]!   60

Come, follow me, merry men all!
Tho' we have made bold for to call,[2]
It is only once by the year
That we are so merry here.
     Still we are all brave, jovial boys,
     And takes delight in Christmas toys. 66

*Then they all foot it round the room and
          follows The Fool out.*

*They all re-enter, and lock their swords to
     make the glass;[3] The Fool running
     about the room.*

PICKLE HERRING.   What is the matter
now, father?

FOOL.   Why, I tell the[e] what, Pickle
Herring.   As a I was a-looking round
about me through my wooden spectacles
made of a great, huge, little, tiney bit of
leather, placed right behind me, even
before me, I thought I saw a feat [4]
thing —   75

P. H.   You thought you saw a feat thing?
What might this feat thing be, think
you, father?

---

[1] A popular old song, referred to in the sixteenth
century.

[2] The manuscript does not note that a Dragon enters, although the Prologue seems to promise "A
Dragon you shall see," as well as "a wild Worm."
Probably the "Worm" and the "Dragon" are identical.

[1] Ordish *hark;* corrected by Manly.

[2] Clearly this stanza marks the end of the first
text.

[3] See the *Shetland Sword Dance,* p. 352.   The
swords were locked together so that all might be
lifted by the hilt of one.

[4] Fine.

FOOL. How can I tell, boy, except I see it again? 80

P. H. Would you know it if you see it again?

FOOL. I cannot tell thee, boy. Let me get it looked at.

Pickle Herring, holding up the glass, says:

[P. H.] Is this it, father? 85

The Fool, looking round, says:

[FOOL.] Why, I protest, Pickle Herring, the very same thing! But what might thou call this very pretty thing?

P. H. What might you call it? You are older than I am. 90

FOOL. How can that be, boy, when I was born before you?

P. H. That is the reason that makes you older.

FOOL. Well, what dost thou call this very pretty thing? 96

P. H. Why, I call it a fine large looking-glass.

FOOL. Let me see what I can see in this fine large looking-glass. Here's a hole through it. [*Looking through at Pickle Herring.*] I see, I see, and I see! 102

P. H. You see, and you see? And what do you see?

FOOL. Marry, e'en a fool, just like the[e]!

P. H. It is only your own face in the glass. 107

FOOL. Why, a fool may be mistain sometimes, Pickle Herring. But what might this fine large looking-glass cost the[e]?

P. H. That fine large looking-glass cost me a guinea.[1]

FOOL. A guinea, boy? Why, I could have bought as good a one at my own door for three half-pence. 115

P. H. Why, fools and cuckolds has always the best luck!

FOOL. That is as much to say thy father is one?

P. H. Why, you pass for one! 120

The Fool, keeping the glass all the while in his hands, says:

FOOL. Why was thou such a ninnie,[2] boy, to go to ware[3] a guinea, to look for thy

---

beauty where it never was? But I will shew thee, boy, how foolish thou hast wared a deal of good money.[1] 125

Then The Fool flings the glass upon the floor, jumps upon it; then the dancers every one drawing out his own sword [from the glass], and The Fool dancing about the room; Pickle Herring takes him by the collar and says:

[P. H.] Father, father, you are so merrylly disposed this good time there is no talking to you! Here is very bad news.

FOOL. Very good news? I am glad to hear it! I do not hear good news every day. 131

P. H. It is very bad news!

FOOL. Why, what is the matter now, boy? 134

P. H. We have all concluded to cut off your head.

FOOL. Be mercyfull to me, a sinner![2] If you should do as you have said, there is no such thing. I would not lose my son Pickle Herring for fifty pounds. 140

P. H. It is your son Pickle Herring that must lose you. It is your head we desire to take off.

FOOL. My head? I never had my head taken off in all my life! 145

P. H. You both must and shall.

FOOL. Hold, hold, boy! Thou seem'st to be in good earnest! But I'll tell thee where I'll be buryed. 149

P. H. Why, where will you be buried but in the churchyard, where other people are buried?

FOOL. Churchyard! I never was buried there in all my life! 154

P. H. Why, where will you be buried?

FOOL. Ah, boy! I am often dry; I will be buried in Mr. Mirfin's ale-celler.[3]

P. H. It is such a place as I never heard talk off in all my life.

FOOL. No, nor nobody else, boy. 160

P. H. What is your fancy to be buried there?

FOOL. Ah, boy! I am oftens dry; and, when they come to fill the quart, I'll

---

[1] One pound one shilling.
[2] Fool. [3] Invest, spend.

[1] This seems to be broken-down verse.
[2] A Biblical echo, the prayer of the publican, Luke xviii. 13.
[3] Probably a local allusion.

drink it off, and they will wonder what
is the matter.   166
P. H.   How can you do so when you will be
dead?   We shall take your head from
your body; and you will be dead.
FOOL.   If I must die, I will dye with my
face to the light, for all you!   171

*Then The Fool, kneeling down, with the
swords round his neck, says [to the audi-
ence]:*

[FOOL.] Now, gentlemen, you see how un-
gratefull my children is grown! When
I had them all at home, small, about as
big as I am, I put them out to good
learning: I put them to Coxcomb Col-
ledge, and then to the University of
Loggerheads; and I took them home
again this good time of Christmas,[1] and
I examin'd them all one by one, all together [2] for shortness.   And now they
are grown so proud and so presumptious
they are a-going to kill their old father
for his little means.   So I must dye for
all this?   185
P. H.   You must dye, father.
FOOL.   And I will die for all the tother.
But I have a little something; I will give
it amongst you as far as it goes, and then
I shall dye quietly.   190
P. H.   I hope you will.
FOOL.   So, to my first son, Pickle Herring, —
I'll give him the roaned nag,
And that will make the rogue brag. 195
And to my second son, —
I'll give him the brindled cow.
. . . .[3]
And to my third son, —
I'll give him the sanded sow;
And hope I shall please you all enow.
And to my fourth son, —
I'll give him the great ruff dog, 202
For he always lives like a hog.
And to my fifth son, —
I'll give him the ram,
And I'll dye like a lamb.

*Then they draw their swords, and The
Fool falls on the floor [as dead], and the
dancers walk once round The Fool; and
Pickle Herring stamps with his foot and
The Fool rises on his knees again; and
Pickle Herring says:*

[P. H.] How now, father?   207
FOOL.   How now, then, boy? I have an-
other squeak for my life?
P. H.   You have a many.

*Then, the dancers puting their swords round
The Fool's neck again,*

FOOL.   So I must dye?
P. H.   You must dye, father.[1]   212
FOOL.   Hold! I have yet a little some-
thing more to leave amongst you, and
then I hope I shall dye quietly.   So, to
my first son, Pickle Herring, —
I'll give him my cap and my coat, — 217
A very good sute, boy.
And to my second son, —
I'll give him my purse and apparel,
But be sure, boys, you do not quarrel.
As to my other three,   222
My executors they shall be.

*Then, Pickle Herring, puting his hand
to his sword,*

FOOL.   Hold, hold, boy! Now I submit
my soul to God.
P. H.   A very good thought, old father!
FOOL.   Mareham churchyard,[2] I hope,
shall have my bones.   228

[The Fool falls to the floor as dead.]

*Then the dancers walk round The Fool
with their swords in their hands; and
Pickle Herring stamps with his foot and
says:*

[P. H.] Heigh, old father!
FOOL.   Why, boy, since I have been out of
this troublesome world I have heard so
much musick of fiddles playing and bells
ringing that I have a great fancy to go
away singing.   So, prithee, Pickle Her-

---

[1] The allusion points to a Christmas performance.
Possibly the appearance of the plow boys at Revesby
on October 20 was induced by some special occasion.
[2] Ordish *altogether*; corrected by Manly.
[3] A line seems to be lost.

[1] Apparently the dancers have run in a portion of
the text of another play, thus necessitating a second
killing of the Fool.
[2] This constitutes further evidence of a second
text; cf. lines 148–60.

ring, let me have one of thy best
songs.[1] 236

. H. You shall have it, old father.

'OOL. Let me see it.

[*The dancers again put their swords about
the Fool's neck.*]

They sing.

)ONS.] Good people all, I pray you now
behold,

'ur old Fool's bracelet is not made of
gold,

)ut it is made of iron and good steel,

,nd unto death we'll make this old Fool
yield. 242

[*The Fool sings.*]

'OOL. I pray forbear, my children small;

'or, as I am lost as parent to you all,

•, let me live a while your sport for to advance,

'hat I may rise again and with you have a
dance. 246

The Sons sing.

)ONS.] Now, old father, that you know
our will,

'hat for your estate we do your body kill,

)oon after death the bell for you shall toll,

,nd wish the Lord he may receive your
soul! 250

*Then The Fool falls down; and the dancers,
with their swords in their hands, sings the
following song:*

)ONS.] Good people all, you see what we
have done:

Ve have cut down our father like the evening sun!

,nd here he lies all in his purple gore,

,nd we are afraid he never will dance [no]
more. 254

Fool rises from the floor and says:

'OOL.] No, no, my children! By chance
you are all mistaen!

'or here I find myself, I am not slain;

)ut I will rise, your sport then to advance,

,nd with you all, brave boys, I'll have a
dance. 258

[1] Possibly a portion of a third text is here intro-
,ced, necessitating the third death of the Fool.

*Then the Foreman and Cicely dances
down, and the other two couple stand their
ground. After a short dance called "Jack,
the brisk young Drummer," they all go out
but The Fool, Fidler, and Cicely.*[1]

FOOL. Hear you, do you please to hear the
sport of a fool?

CICELY. A fool? for why?

FOOL. Because I can neither leap, skip,
nor dance, but cut a caper thus high.

[*He cuts capers while the dancers are
changing costume.*]

Sound, music! I must be gon; the Lord
of Pool draws nigh. 265

Enter Pickle Herring.

P. H. I am the Lord of Pool,
And here begins my measure,
And after me a fool,
To dance a while for pleasure
In Cupid's school. 270

FOOL. A fool, a fool, a fool,
A fool I heard thou say,
But more the other way,
For here I have a tool
Will make a maid to play,
Although in Cupid's school.
Come all away! [*Exit the Fool.*] 277

Enter Blue Britches.

BLUE B. I am the Knight of Lee,
And here I have a dagger,
Offended not to be.
Come in, thou needy beggar,
And follow me! 282

Enter Ginger Britches.

GINGER B. Behold, behold, behold
A man of poor estate!
Not one penny to infold! 285
. . . .[2]

[1] This, possibly, ends the second play, a sword
play, the chief episode of which is the death of the
Fool. The next play, beginning at line 266, is preceded by "capers" with which the Fool amuses the
spectators while the dancers make a change of costume.

[2] A line seems to be lost. Possibly Ginger Britches
and Pepper Britches originally appeared as Lazarus
and Dives. The speech of Pepper Britches has been
reduced to one line, doubtless through faulty memory.

Enter Pepper Britches.

PEPPER B.   My money is out at use, or
    else I would.

Enter Mr. Allspice.

ALLSPICE.   With a hack, a hack, a hack,
    See how I will skip and dance
        For joys that we have found!
    Let each man take his chance,
        And we will all dance round.   292

*Then they dance the sword dance which
is called "Nelly's Gig." Then they run
under their swords, which is called "Run-
ing Battle." Then three dancers dances
with three swords, and the Foreman jump-
ing over the swords. Then The Fool goes
up to Cicely.*

FOOL [*rushing in.*]   Here comes I that
        never come yet,
    Since last time, lovy!
    I have a great head but little wit.
    Tho' my head be great and my wits be small,
    I can play the fool for a while as well as
        [the] best of ye all.   297

    My name is noble Anthony;
    I am as meloncholly as a mantle-tree.
    I am come to show you a little sport and
        activity,
        And soon, too!
    Make room for noble Anthony
    And all his good company!   303

    Drive out all these proud rogues, and let
        my lady and I have a parl!¹

[*He drives out all the dancers, and remains
        with Cicely.*]²

CICELY.   O, ye clown! what makes you
    drive out my men so soon?³   309

FOOL.   O, pardon, madam, pardon! and I
    Will never offend you more.
    I will make your men come in as fast
        As ever they did before.   311

    ¹ Conversation.
    ² This, possibly, marks the end of the third play,
a sword play, in which the text has largely disap-
peared.
    ³ This scene between the two clowns has the pur-
pose of enabling the dancers to rest, or to change costume.

CICELY.   I pray you at my sight,
    And drive it not till night,
That I may see them dance once more
    So lovely in my sight.   315

FOOL.   A-faith, madam, and so I will!
    I will play the man
And make them come in
    As fast as ever I can. —   319

But hold, gip, Mrs. Clagars!
    How do you sell geese?
CICELY.   Go, look, Mister Midgecock!
    Twelve pence apiece.   323

FOOL.   Oh, the pretty pardon!
CICELY.   A gip for a frown!
FOOL.   An ale-wife for an apparitor!
CICELY.   A rope for a clown!
FOOL.   Why, all the devise in the country
    Cannot pull this down!   329

I am a valiant knight just come from [over]
        the seas:
    You do know me, do you?
I can kill you ten thousand, tho' they be
        but fleas.
I can kill you a man for an ounce of mus-
        tard,
Or I can kill you ten thousand for a good
        custard.
    I have an old sheep skin,
        And I lap it well in,
Sword and buckler by my side, all read[y]
        for to fight!   33[.]

Come out, you whores and gluttons all! fo[r]
    had it not been in this country, I shoul[d]
    not have shewen my valour amongs[t]
    you.   But sound, music! for I must b[e]
    gone.   [*Exit the Fool.*] 34[.]

Enter Pickle Herring.

P. H.   In, first and formost, do I come,
    All for to lead this race,¹
Seeking the country far and near
    So fair a lady to embrace.   3[.]

[*He advances to Cicely.*]

So fair a lady did I never see,
    So comely in my sight,

    ¹ Dance; *qy. trace.*

Drest in her gaudy gold
   And silver shining bright. 350

She has fingers long, and rings
   Of honor of beaten gold:
   My masters all, behold!
It is now for some pretty dancing time,
And we will foot it fine. 355

[He dances once round with Cicely.]

[Enter Blue Britches.]

BLUE B.   I am a youth of jollitree!
Where is there one like unto me?
My hair is bush'd very thick;
My body is like an hasel stick; 359

My legs they quaver like an eel;
My arms become my body weel;
My fingers they are long and small:
Am not I a jolly youth, proper and tall? 363

Therefore, Mister Musick Man,
   Whatsoever may be my chance,
It is for my ladie's love and mine,
   Strike up the morris dance. 367

Then they foot it once round.

[Enter Ginger Britches.]

GINGER B.   I am a jolly young man of
   flesh, blood and bone;
Give eare, my masters all, each one, 369

And especially you, my lady dear!
   I hope you like me well.
Of all the gallants here
   It is I that doth so well. 373

Therefore, Mister Musick Man,
   Whatsoever may be my chance,
It is for my ladie's love and mine,
   Strike up the morris dance. 377

Then they foot it round.

[Enter Pepper Britches.]

PEPPER B.   I am my father's eldest son,
   And heir of all his land[s],
And in a short time, I hope,
   It will fall into my hands. 381

was brought up at Lindsey Court

All the days of my life.
Here stands a fair lady,
   I wish she was my wife. 385

I love her at my heart,
   And from her I will never start.
Therefore, Mr. Musick Man, play up my
   part.
FOOL *[rushing in].*   And mine, too! 389

*Enter Allspice, and they foot it round.
Pickle Herring, suter to Cicely, takes
her by the hand, and walks about the
room.*

P. H.   Sweet Ciss, if thou wilt be my love,
A thousand pounds I will give thee.
CICELY.   No, you're too old, sir, and I am
   too young;
And alas! old man, that must not be! 393

P. H.   I'll buy the[e] a gown of violet blue,
A petticoat imbroidered to thy knee;
Likewise my love to thee shall be true.
CICELY.   But alas! old man, that must not
   be! 397

P. H.   Thou shalt walk at thy pleasure,
   love, all the day,
If at night thou wilt but come home to me;
And in my house bear all the sway.
CICELY.   Your children they'll find fault
   with me. 401

P. H.   I'll turn my children out of doors.
CICELY.   And so, I fear, you will do me.
P. H.   Nay, then, sweet Ciss, ne'er trust
   me more,
   For I never loved lass like the[e] be-
   fore.[1] 405

Enter Fool.

FOOL.   No, nor behind, neither.
Well met, sweet Cis! Well over-ta'en!
CICELY.   You are kindly wellcome, sir, to
   me.
FOOL.   I'll wipe my eyes, and I'll look
   again! 409
   Methinks, sweet Cis, I now the[e] see!

[1] Manly adopts Kittredge's emendation "before
like thee"; and this may have been the original form
of the line; but the plow boys doubtless altered the
verse for the sake of the Fool's witticism in the line
that follows.

CICELY. Raf, what has thou to pleasure me?

FOOL. Why, this, my dear, I will give the[e],
And all I have it shall be thine.

CICELY. Kind sir, I thank you heart-
elly.   414

P. H. [*to the Fool*]. Stand back! stand
back, thou silly old swain!
This girl shall go with none but me.

FOOL. I will not!

P. H. Stand back! stand back! or I'll
cleave thy brain!

Then Pickle Herring goes up to Cis, and says:

O, now, sweet Cis, I am come to thee! 419

CICELY. You are as wellcome as the rest,
Wherein you brag so lustilly.

FOOL. For a thousand pounds she loves
me best!
I can see by the twinkling of her ee.[1] 423

P. H. I have store of gold, whereon I boast;
Likewise my sword, love, shall fight for
the[e];
When all is done, love, I'll scour the coast,
And bring in gold for thee and me. 427

CICELY. Your gold may gain as good as I,
But by no means it shall tempt me;
For youthfull years and frozen age
Cannot in any wise agree. 431

Then Blue Britches goes up to her, and says:

[BLUE B.] Sweet mistress, be advised by me:
Do not let this old man be denyed,
But love him for his gold in store;
Himself may serve for a cloak, be-
side. 435

CICELY. Yes, sir, but you are not in the
right.
Stand back! and do not council me!
For I love a lad that will make me laugh
In a secret place, to pleasure me.

FOOL. Good wench! 440

PICKLE HERRING. Love, I have a beard as
white as milk.[2]

[1] Eye.
[2] An echo of the old Elizabethan song: "His head
as white as milk"?

CICELY. Ne'er better for that, thou silly
old man!

P. H. Besides, my skin, love, is soft as silk.

FOOL. And thy face shines like a dripping
pan. 444

P. H. Rafe, what has thou to pleasure her?

FOOL. Why a great deal more, boy, than
there's in the[e].

P. H. Nay then, old rogue, I thee defye.

CICELY. I pray, dear friends, fall not out
for me! 548

P. H. Once I could skip, leap, dance, and
sing;
Why will you not give place to me?

FOOL. Nay, then, old rogue, I thee defye;
For thy nose stands like a Maypole
tree. 552

*Then goes up Ginger Breeches to Cisley and
says:*

[GINGER B.] Sweet mistress, mind what
this man doth say,
For he speaks nothing but the truth:
Look on the soldier, now I pray;
See, is not he a handsome youth? 556

CICELY. Sir, I am engaged to one I love,
And ever constant I will be,
There is nothing that I prize above.

P. H. For a thousand pounds, she's gone
from me!

FOOL. Thou may lay two! 561

CICELY [*to Pickle Herring*]. Old father, for
your reverend years,
Stand you the next man unto me;
Then, he that doth the weapon bear;
For I will have the hind man of the
three! 565

FOOL [*to Pickle Herring*]. Old father, a fig
for your old gold!
The soldier, he shall bear no sway!
But you shall see, and so shall we,
'Tis I that carries the lass away! 56[...]

*Then the dancers takes hold of thei[r]
swords, and foots it round the room; the[n]
every man makes his obeisance to th[e]
master of the house, and the whole concludes*

FINIS.

IX
FARCES

THE PLAYE CALLED THE FOURE PP.[1]

· A Newe and a Very Mery Enterlude [2] of

A Palmer.[3]	A Potycary.[5]
A Pardoner.[4]	A Pedler.

Made by JOHAN HEEWOOD.

[*Enter the Palmer, with a palm leaf in his hand.*]

PALMER. Nowe God be here! Who kepeth this place?
Now, by my fayth, I crye you mercy!
Of reason I must sew for grace,
My rewdnes sheweth me no[w] so homely.[1]
Wherof your pardon axt, and wonne,   5
I sew you, as curtesy doth me bynde,
To tell thys whiche shalbe begonne
In order as may come beste in mynde.[2]
I am a palmer, as ye se,   9
Whiche of my lyfe much part hath spent
In many a fayre and farre countre,
As pylgrymes do of good intent.
At Hierusalem haue I bene
Before Chrystes blessed sepulture;
The Mount of Caluery haue I sene, —   15
A holy place, ye may be sure;
To Iosophat and Olyuete
On fote, God wote, I wente ryght bare, —
Many a salt tere dyde I swete
Before thys carkes coulde come there;   20
Yet haue I bene at Rome, also,
And gone the stacions all arow,[3]
Saynt Peters Shryne, and many mo
Then, yf I tolde, all ye do know, —
Except that there be any suche   25

That hath ben there and diligently
Hath taken hede and marked muche,
Then can they speke as muche as I.
Then at the Rodes also I was,
And rounde about to Amyas;   30
At Saynt Toncomber; and Saynt Tronion;
At Saynt Bothulph; and Saynt Anne of Buckston;
On the hylles of Armony,[1] where I see Noes arke;
With holy Iob; and Saynt George in Suthwarke;
At Waltam; and at Walsyngam;   35
And at the good Rood [2] of Dagnam;
At Saynt Cornelys; at Saynt Iames in Gales;
And at Saynt Wynefrydes Well in Walles;
At Our Lady of Boston; at Saynt Edmundes-byry;
And streyght to Saynt Patrykes Purgatory;   40
At Rydybone; and at the Blood of Hayles,
Where pylgrymes paynes ryght muche auayles;
At Saynt Dauys; and at Saynt Denis;
At Saynt Mathew; and Saynt Marke in Venis;
At Mayster Iohan Shorne; at Canterbury;   45

---

[1] Lacking in refinement.
[2] M. *myndy.*   [3] In succession.

[1] Armenia.   [2] Cross.

---

[1] The author, John Heywood, was born about 1497, was for a time a musician in the employ of the court, and later became master of an organization of singing boys, probably those connected with St. Paul's Cathedral. The boys of Pauls, we know, were very active in presenting plays; but whether Heywood wrote his farces for them (which seems likely) or for some troupe connected with the court we cannot say. The date of *The Four PP.* is about 1521–25; *Johan Johan,* and *The Weather* were written a little later.
   I have reproduced the text from the earliest edition (M.) printed by Wyllyam Myddlyton about 1545 (photographic facsimile by J. S. Farmer, 1908). With this I have collated Manly's careful reprint in *Specimens,* 1896, from which I have taken a few emendations (recorded in footnotes), and have derived aid in my effort to modernize the punctuation and equip the play with stage-directions.
   [2] Used at this time in the sense of "play," generally implying an amusing performance.
   [3] One who spent his time traveling from shrine to shrine; having visited the Holy Land, he carried, as a sign thereof, a palm leaf in his hand.
   [4] One licensed to sell papal pardons and indulgences. He was usually provided also with a stock of holy relics.
   [5] Obviously in this case an itinerant vendor of medicines.

The Graet God of Katewade; at Kynge
   Henry;
At Saynt Sauyours; at Our Lady of South-
   well;
At Crome; at Wylsdome; and at Muswell;
At Saynt Rycharde; and at Saynt Roke;
And at Our Lady that standeth in the
   Oke.   50
To these, with other many one,
Deuoutly haue I prayed and gone,
Prayeng to them to pray for me
Unto the Blessed Trynyte;
By whose prayers and my dayly payne 55
I truste the soner to obtay[n]e
For my saluacyon grace and mercy.
For, be ye sure, I thynke surely
Who seketh sayntes for Crystes sake —
And namely suche as payne do take   60
On fote to punyshe their [1] frayle body —
Shall therby meryte more hyely
Then by any thynge done by man.

[*The Pardoner with his packet of pardons
and relics has entered while the Palmer is
speaking.*]

PARDONER. And when ye haue gone as
   farre as ye can,
For all your labour and gostely entente 65
Yet welcome home as wyse as ye wente!
PALMER. Why, sir, dyspyse ye pylgrym-
   age?
PARDONER. Nay, for God, syr! Then
   dyd I rage!
I thynke ye ryght well occupyed
To seke these sayntes on euery syde. 70
Also your payne I nat disprayse it;
But yet I discomende your wit;
And, or [2] we go, euen so shall ye,
If ye in this wyl answere me:
I pray you, shew what the cause is   75
Ye wente al these pylgrymages.
PALMER. Forsoth, this lyfe I dyd begyn
To rydde the bondage of my syn;
For whiche these sayntes, rehersed or this,
I haue both sought and sene, i-wys, 80
Besechynge them to be recorde
Of all my payne vnto the Lorde
That gyueth all remyssyon
Upon eche mans contricyon.
And by theyr good mediacyon,   85
Upon myne humble submyssion,

[1] M. *thy.*   [2] Ere.

I trust to haue in very dede
For my soule helth the better spede.
PARDONAR. Nowe is your owne confes-
   syon lyckely
To make your-selfe a fole quyckely! 90
For I perceyue ye wolde obtayne
No nother thynge for all your payne
But onely grace your soule to saue.
Nowe, marke in this what wyt ye haue
To seke so farre, and helpe so nye! 95
Euen here at home is remedy,
For at your dore my-selfe doth dwell,
Who coulde haue saued your soule as well
As all your wyde wandrynge shall do,
Though ye wente thryes to Iericho. 100
Nowe, syns ye myght haue spedde at
   home,
What haue ye wone by ronnyng at Rome?
PALMER. If this be true that ye haue
   moued,[1]
Then is my wyt in-dede reproued!
But let vs here fyrste what ye are. 105
PARDONAR. Truly, I am a pardoner.
PALMER. Truely a pardoner, — that may
   be true,
But a true pardoner doth nat ensew!
Ryght selde [2] is it sene, or neuer,
That treuth and pardoners dwell to-
   gether;   110
For, be your pardons neuer so great,
Yet them to enlarge [3] ye wyll nat let [4]
With suche lyes that oftymes, Cryste wot,
Ye seme to haue that ye haue nat.
Wherfore I went my-selfe to the selfe
   thynge [5]   115
In euery place, and, without faynynge,[6]
Had as muche pardon there assuredly
As ye can promyse me here doutefully.
Howe-be-it, I thynke ye do but scoffe.[7]
But yf ye hadde all the pardon ye speke [8]
   of,   120
And no whyt of pardon graunted
In any place where I haue haunted,
Yet of my labour I nothynge repent.
God hathe respect how eche tyme is spent
And, as in his knowledge all is regarded, 125
So by his goodnes all is rewarded.
PARDONAR. By the fyrste parte of this
   laste tale

[1] Brought forward, propounded.
[2] Seldom.   [3] Magnify.
[4] Desist, forbear.   [5] Thing itself.
[6] Unfeignedly.   [7] M. *scofte.*   [8] M. *Kepe.*

It semeth you come late from the ale!
For reason on your syde so farre doth
    fayle
That ye leue [re]sonyng and begyn to
    rayle;   130
Wherin ye forget your owne parte clerely,
For ye be as vntrue as I;
And in one poynte ye are beyonde me,
For ye may lye by aucthoryte, —
And all that hath wandred so farre   135
That no man can be theyr controller.[1]
And, where ye esteme your labour so
    muche,
I say yet agayne my pardons be suche
That, yf there were a thousande soules on a
    hepe,
I wolde brynge them all to heuen as good
    chepe [2]   140
As ye haue brought your-selfe on pylgrym-
    age
In the leste quarter of your vyage, —
Whiche is farre a thys syde heuen, by God!
There your labour and pardon is od,[3]
With smale cost, and without any payne,
These pardons bryngeth them to heuen
    playne.   146
Geue me but a peny, or two pens,
And as sone as the soule departeth hens,
In halfe an houre — or thre quarters at
    moste —
The soule is in heuen with the Holy
    Ghost!   150

[*The Potycary with his packet of medicines
has entered during the Pardonar's speech.*]

POTYCARY. Sende ye any soules to heuen
    by water?
PARDONER. If we dyd, syr, what is the
    mater?
POTYCARY. By God, I haue a drye soule
    shulde thyther!
I praye you let our soules go to heuen to-
    gyther.
So bysy you twayne be in soules helth, 155
May nat a potycary come in by stelth?
Yes, that I wyll, by Saynt Antony!
And, by the leue of thys company,
Proue ye false knaues bothe, or we goo,
In parte of your sayenges, as thys, lo: [4]

Thou by thy trauayle thynkest heuen to
    gete;   161
         [*To the Pardoner.*]
And thou by pardons and relyques count-
    est no lete
To sende thyne owne soule to heuen sure,
And all other whome thou lyste to procure.
If I toke an accyon,[1] then were they
    blanke;   165
For, lyke theues, the knaues rob away my
    thanke.
All soules in heuen hauynge relefe,
Shall they thanke your craftes? Nay,
    thanke myn, chefe!
No soule, ye knowe, entreth heuen gate
Tyll from the bodye he be separate; 170
And whome haue ye knowen dye ho[ne]st-
    lye
Without helpe of the potycary?
Nay, all that commeth to our handlynge, —
Except ye happe to come to hangynge —
That way, perchaunce, ye shall nat
    myster [2]   175
To go to heuen without a glyster! [3]
But, be ye sure, I wolde be wo
If ye shulde chaunce [4] to begyle me so.
As good to lye with me a-nyght
As hange abrode in the mone lyght! 180
There is no choyse to fle my hande
But, as I sayd, into the bande.[5]
Syns of our soules the multitude
I sende to heuen, when all is vewed,
Who shulde but I, then, all-togyther 185
Haue thanke of all theyr commynge
    thyther?
PARDONER. If ye kylde a thousande in an
    houre space,
When come they to heuen dyenge from
    state of grace?
POTYCARY. If a thousande pardons about
    your neckes were teyd,
When come they to heuen yf they neuer
    dyed?   190
PALMER. Longe lyfe after good workes,
    in-dede,
Doth hynder mannes receyt of mede,[6]
And deth before one dewty done

---

[1] Tester as to facts; see lines 454-55.
[2] At as good a bargain.   [3] Different,
  Manly in error states that M. has *so*.

[1] Instituted legal proceedings.   [2] Need.
[3] Purge.   [4] M. *chaunge*.
[5] Hangman's rope.   [6] Reward.

May make vs thynke we dye to[o] sone.
Yet better tary a thynge, then haue it, 195
Then go to[o] sone and vaynly craue it.
PARDONER.   The longer ye dwell in com-
   municacion,
The lesse shall you lyke thys ymagynacyon;
For ye may perceyue euen at the fyrst chop
Your tale is trapt in such a stop   200
That, at the leste, ye seme worse then we.
POTYCARY.   By the masse, I holde vs
   nought, all thre!

[*The Pedler with his pack on his back has
   entered in time to hear the last speech.*]

PEDLER.   By Our Lady, then haue I gone
   wronge!
And yet to be here I thought longe.
POTYCARY.   Brother, ye haue gone wronge
   no w[h]yt.   205
I prayse your fortune and your wyt
That can dyrecte you so discretely
To plante you in this company:
Thou [a] palmer, and thou a pardoner,
I a potycary.
PEDLER.   And I a pedler!   210
POTYCARY.   Nowe, on my fayth, full well
   matched! [1]
Were the deuyll were we foure hatched?
PEDLER.   That maketh no mater, syns we
   be matched.
I coulde be mery yf that I catchyd
Some money for parte of the ware in my
   packe.   215
POTYCARY.   What the deuyll hast thou
   there at thy backe?
PEDLER.   Why, dost thou nat knowe that
   every pedler [2]
In euery tryfull must be a medler?
Specyally in womens tryflynges, —
Those vse we chefe aboue all thynges.   220
Whiche thynges to se, yf ye be disposed,
Beholde what ware here is disclosed.

[*He opens his pack.*]

Thys gere sheweth it-selfe in suche bewte
That eche man thynketh it sayth: "Come,
   bye me!"
Loke, were your-selfe can lyke to be
   chooser,   225
Your-selfe shall make pryce, though I be
   looser!

   [1] M. *watched*.   [2] M. *pedled*.

Is here nothynge for my father Palmer?
Haue ye nat a wanton in a corner
For your walkyng to holy places?
By Cryste, I haue herde of as straunge
   cases!   230
Who lyueth in loue, or loue wolde wynne,
Euen at this packe he must begynne,
Where is ryght many a proper token,
Of whiche by name parte shall be spoken:
Gloues, pynnes, combes, glasses vn-
   spottyd,   235
Pomanders, hookes, and lasses [1] knotted,
Broches, rynges, and all maner bedes,
Lace, rounde and flat, for womens hedes,
Nedyls, threde, thymbell[s], shers, and all
   suche knackes, —
Where louers be, no suche thynges
   lackes, —   240
Sypers,[2] swathbondes, rybandes, and sleue-
   laces,
Gyrdyls, knyues, purses, and pyncases.
POTYCARY.   Do women bye theyr pyn-
   cases of you?
PEDLER.   Ye, that they do, I make God
   a-vow!
POTYCARY.   So mot I thryue, then for my
   parte,   245
I be-shrewe thy knaues nakyd herte
For makynge my wyfeys pyncase so wyde!
The pynnes fall out; they can nat abyde.
Great pynnes must she haue, one or other;
Yf she lese one, she wyll fynde an-other!
Wherin I fynde cause to complayne, — 251
New pynnes to her pleasure, and my
   payne!
PARDONER.   Syr, ye seme well sene in
   womens causes.
I praye you, tell me what causeth this,
That women, after theyr arysynge,   255
Be so longe in theyr apparelynge?
PEDLER.   Forsoth, women haue many
   lettes,[3]
And they be masked in many nettes,
As frontlettes, fyllettes, par[t]lettes and
   barcelettes;
And then theyr bonettes, and theyr poy-
   nettes.   260
By these lettes and nettes the lette is suche
That spede is small whan haste is muche.

   [1] Laces.
   [2] Kerchiefs, hat-bands, etc., of cypress satin.
   [3] Hindrances.

POTYCARY.   An-other cause why they
        come nat forwarde,
Whiche maketh them dayly to drawe back-
        warde,
And yet is a thynge they can nat for-
        bere —   265
The trymmynge and pynnynge vp theyr
        gere,
Specyally theyr fydlyng with the tayle-
        pyn;
And, when they wolde haue it prycke in,
If it chaunce to double in the clothe
Then be they wode [1] and swereth an
        othe;   270
Tyll it stande ryght, they wyll nat forsake
        it.
Thus, though it may nat, yet wolde they
        make it.
But be ye sure they do but defarre [2] it,
For, when they wolde make it, ofte tymes
        marre it.
But prycke them and pynne them as
        myche [3] as ye wyll,   275
And yet wyll they loke for pynnynge styll!
So that I durste holde [4] you a ioynt [5]
Ye shall neuer haue them at a full [6] poynt.
PEDLER.   Let womens maters passe, and
        marke myne!
What-euer theyr poyntes be, these poyntes
        be fyne.   280
Wherfore, yf ye be wyllynge to bye,
Ley downe money!   Come of quyckely!
PALMER.   Nay, by my trouth, we be lyke
        fryers:
We are but beggers, we be no byers.
PARDONER.   Syr, ye maye showe your
        ware for your mynde,   285
But I thynke ye shall no profyte fynde.
PEDLER.   Well, though thys iourney [7]
        acquyte no coste, [8]
Yet thynke I nat my labour loste;
For, by the fayth of my body,
I lyke full well thys company.   290
Up shall this packe, for it is playne
I came not hyther al for gayne.
Who may nat play one day in a weke,
May thynke hys thryfte is farre to seke!
Deuyse what pastyme ye thynke beste, 295

And make ye sure to fynde me prest. [1]
POTYCARY.   Why, be ye so vnyuersall
That you can do what-so-euer ye shall?
PEDLER.   Syr, yf ye lyste to appose [2] me,
What I can do then shall ye se.   300
POTYCARY.   Than tell me thys: be ye
        perfyt in drynkynge?
PEDLER.   Perfyt in drynkynge as may be
        wysht by thynkyng!
POTYCARY.   Then after your drynkyng,
        how? fall ye to wynkyng?
PEDLER.   Syr, after drynkynge, whyle the
        shot [3] is tynkynge,
Some hedes be swynkynge, [4] but myne wyl be
        synkynge,   305
And vpon drynkynge myne eyse wyll be
        pynkynge, [5]
For wynkynge [6] to drynkynge is alway
        lynkynge. [7]
POTYCARY.   Then drynke and slepe ye can
        well do.
But, yf ye were desyred therto,
I pray you, tell me, can you synge?   310
PEDLER.   Syr, I haue some syght [8] in syng-
        ynge.
POTYCARY.   But is your brest any-thynge
        swete?
PEDLER.   What-euer my breste be, my
        voyce is mete.
POTYCARY.   That answere sheweth you a
        ryght syngynge man!
Now what is your wyll, good father,
        than?   315
PALMER.   What helpeth wyll where is no
        skyll?
PARDONER.   And what helpeth skyll
        where is no wyll? [9]
POTYCARY.   For wyll or skyll, what help-
        eth it
Where frowarde knaues be lackynge
        wyt? [10]
Leue of thys curyosytie; [11]   320
And who that lyste, synge after me!

Here they synge. [12]

PEDLER.   Thys lyketh [13] me well, so mot I
        the! [14]

---

[1] Mad.   [2] Defer.   [3] M. *nyche.*
[4] Wager.   [5] M. *soynt* (or *loynt*).   [6] M. *fall.*
[7] M. *yourney,* which is a variant spelling for *journey.*
[8] Produce no profit.

[1] Ready.   [2] Interrogate.
[3] Reckoning, bill.   [4] M. *swymmyng.*
[5] Blinking.   [6] Sleeping.
[7] Linking (associated with).   [8] Skill.
[9] M. *Wyt.*   [10] M. *Wyll.*
[11] Subtlety.   [12] No song is given.
[13] Pleaseth.   [14] So may I thrive.

PARDONER.   So helpe me God, it lyketh
    nat me!
Where company is met and well agreed,
Good pastyme doth ryght well in-dede; 325
But who can set [1] in dalyaunce
Men set [2] in suche a variaunce
As we were set or ye came in?
Whiche stryfe thys man dyd fyrst begynne,

[*Points to the Palmer.*]

Allegynge that suche man as vse,   330
For loue of God, and nat [3] refuse,
On fot to goo from place to place
A pylgrymage, callynge for grace,
Shall in that payne with penitence
Obtayne discharge of conscyence, —   335
Comparynge that lyfe for the beste
Enduccyon [4] to our endles reste.
Upon these wordes our mater grewe;
For, yf he coulde auow them true,
As good to be a gardener   340
As for to be a pardoner.
But, when I harde hym so farre wyde,
I then aproched and replyed,
Sayenge this: that this indulgence,
Hauyng the forsayd penitence,   345
Dyschargeth man of all offence
With muche more profyt then this pre-
    tence.
I aske but two pens at the moste, —
I-wys, this is nat very great coste, — 349
And from all payne, without dyspayre, —
My soule for his, — kepe euen his chayre,[5]
And when he dyeth he may be sure
To come to heuen, euen at pleasure.
And more then heuen he can nat get,
How farre so-euer he lyste to iet.[6] 355
Then is hys payne more then hys wit
To wa[l]ke to heuen, syns he may syt!
Syr, as we were in this contencion,
In came thys daw [7] with hys inuencyon,

[*Points to the Potycary.*]

Reuilynge [8] vs, hym-selfe auauntynge, 360
That all the soules to heuen assendynge
Are most bounde to the potycary,
Bycause he helpeth most men to dye;

---

[1] M. *syt.* Manly suggests *fet* (fetch).
[2] M. *syt;* emend. suggested by Manly.
[3] M. *God nat and.*
[4] Induction, that which leads on to.
[5] Sit at ease.   [6] Strut, walk.
[7] Fool.   [8] M. *reuelynge.*

Before whiche deth he sayeth, in-dede,
No soule in heuen can haue hys mede. 365
PEDLER.   Why, do potycaries kyll men?
POTYCARY.   By God, men say so now and
    then!
PEDLER.   And I thought ye wolde nat
    haue myst
To make men lyue as longe as ye lyste.
POTYCARY.   As longe as we lyste? nay,
    longe as they can!   370
PEDLER.   So myght we lyue without you
    than.
POTYCARY.   Ye, but yet it is necessary
For to haue a potycary;
For when ye fele your conscyens redy,
I can sende you to heuen quyckly.   375
Wherfore, concernynge our mater here,
Aboue these twayne I am best, clere.
And, yf ye [1] lyste to take me so,
I am content you, and no mo,
Shall be our iudge as in thys case,   380
Whiche of vs thre shall take the best place.
PEDLER.   I neyther wyll iudge the beste
    nor worste;
For, be ye bleste or be ye curste,
Ye know it is no whyt my sleyght [2]
To be a iudge in maters of weyght.   385
It behoueth no pedlers nor proctours [3]
To take on them iudgemente as doctours.
But yf your myndes be onely set
To worke for soule helthe, ye be well met,
For eche of you somwhat doth showe 390
That soules towarde heuen by you do
    growe.
Then, yf ye can so well agree
To contynue togyther all thre,
And all you thre obey on wyll,
Then all your myndes ye may fulfyll: 395
As, yf ye came all to one man
Who shulde goo pylgrymage more then he
    can,

[*To the Palmer.*]

In that ye, palmer, as debite,
May clerely dyscharge [4] hym, parde;

[*To the Pardoner.*]

And for all other syns, ones had contrys-
    syon,   400
Your pardons geueth hym full remyssyon;

---

[1] M. *he.*
[2] M. may have *fleyght,* but the heavy inking makes
certainty impossible.
[3] Minor university officials.   [4] M. *dyscharde.*

[*To the Potycary.*]

And then ye, mayster potycary,
May sende hym to heuen by-and-by.[1]

POTYCARY.   Yf he taste this boxe nye
aboute the pryme,[2]
By the masse, he is in heuen or euensonge
tyme!   405
My craft is suche that I can ryght well
Sende my fryndes to heuen — and my-
selfe to hell.

But, syrs, marke this man, for he is wyse
Who [3] coulde deuyse suche a deuyce;
For yf we thre may be as one,   410
Then be we Lordes [4] euerychone, —
Betwene vs all coulde nat be myste
To saue the soules of whome we lyste.
But, for good order, at a worde,   414
Twayne of vs must wayte on the thyrde;
And vnto that I do agree,
For bothe you twayne shall wayt on me!

PARDONER.   What chaunce is this that
suche an elfe
Commaund two knaues, besyde hym-
selfe? [5]   419
Nay, nay, my frende, that wyll nat be;
I am to good to wayt on the!

PALMER.   By Our Lady, and I wolde be
loth
To wayt on the better on [6] you both!

PEDLER.   Yet be ye sewer, for all thys
dout,   424
Thys waytynge must be brought about.
Men can nat prosper, wylfully ledde;
All thynge decayeth [7] where is no hedde.
Wherfore, doutlesse, marke what I say:
To one of you thre, twayne must obey;
And, synnes ye can nat agree in voyce 430
Who shall be hed, there is no choyse
But to deuyse some maner thynge
Wherin ye all be lyke [8] connynge;
And in the same who can do beste,   434
The other twayne to make them preste
In euery thynge of hys entente
Holly to be at commaundement.
And now haue I founde one mastry

[1] Immediately.
[2] The first hour of the day, beginning about six
o'clock.
[3] M. *How.*   [4] Alluding to the Trinity.
[5] M. assigns this and the preceding line to the
Potycary, and gives the reading *Commaunded two
knaues be, beside hym selfe.* I follow Dodsley's reading.
[6] Of.   [7] M. *decayed.*   [8] Equally.

That ye can do in-dyfferently,
And is nother sellynge nor byenge,   440
But euyn only very lyenge!
And all ye thre can lye as well
As can the falsest deuyll in hell.
And, though afore ye harde me grudge
In greater maters to be your iudge,   445
Yet in lyeng I can [1] some skyll;
And, yf I shall be iudge, I wyll.
And, be ye sure, without flatery,
Where my consciens fyndeth the mastrye,
Ther shall my iudgement strayt be
founde,   450
Though I myght wynne a thousande
pounde.

PALMER.   Syr, for lyeng, though I can do
it,
Yet am I loth for to goo to it.

PEDLER [*to the Palmer*].   Ye haue nat cause
to feare to be bolde,
For ye may be here vncontrolled.[2]   455

[*To the Pardoner.*]

And ye in this haue good auauntage,
For lyeng is your comen vsage.

[*To the Potycary.*]

And you in lyenge be well spedde,
For all your craft doth stande in falshed.

[*To all three.*]

Ye nede nat care who shall begyn,   460
For eche of you may hope to wyn.
Now speke, all thre, euyn as ye fynde:
Be ye agreed to folowe my mynde?

PALMER.   Ye, by my trouth, I am con-
tente.

PARDONER.   Now, in good fayth, and I
assente.   465

POTYCARY.   If I denyed, I were a nody,
For all is myne, by Goddes body!

Here the Potycary hoppeth.

PALMER.   Here were a hopper to hop for
the rynge!
But, syr, thys gere goth nat by hoppynge.

POTYCARY.   Syr, in this hopynge I wyll
hop so well   470
That my tonge shall hop as well as my hele;
Upon whiche hoppynge I hope, and nat
doute it,
To hope so that ye shall hope without
[it].

[1] Have.   [2] Untested as to facts.

PALMER.   Syr, I wyll neyther boste ne
    brawll,[1]
But take suche fortune as may fall;   475
And, yf ye wynne this maystry,
I wyll obaye you quietly.
And sure I thynke that quietnesse
In any man is great rychesse,
In any maner company,   480
To rule or be ruled indifferently.
PARDONER.   By that bost thou semest a
    begger in-dede.
What can thy quyetnesse helpe vs at nede?
Yf we shulde starue, thou hast nat, I
    thynke,   484
One peny to bye vs one potte of drynke.
Nay, yf rychesse mygh[t]e rule the roste,[2]
Beholde what cause I haue to boste!

[*He opens his pack.*]

Lo, here be pardons halfe a dosyn.
For gostely [3] ryches they haue no cosyn;
And, more-ouer, to me they brynge   490
Sufficient succour for my lyuynge.
And here be relykes of suche a kynde
As in this worlde no man can fynde.
Knele downe, all thre, and, when ye leue
    kyssynge,
Who lyste to offer shall haue my blys-
    synge!   495

[*He holds up a relic.*]

Frendes, here shall ye se euyn anone
Of All-Hallows the blessyd iaw-bone, —
Kys it hardely, with good deuocion!
POTYCARY.   This kysse shall brynge vs
    muche promocyon. —
Fogh! by Saynt Sauyour, I neuer kyst a
    wars!   500
Ye were as good kysse All-Hallows ars!
For, by All-Halows, me thynketh
That All-Halows breth stynkith.
PALMER.   Ye iudge All-Halows breth vn-
    knowen;
Yf any breth stynke, it is your owne.   505
POTYCARY.   I knowe myne owne breth
    from All-Halows,
Or els it were tyme to kysse the galows.

[*He holds up another relic.*]

PARDONER.   Nay, syrs, beholde, here may
    ye se

The great-toe of the Trinite.
Who to thys toe any money voweth,   510
And ones may role it in his moueth,
All hys lyfe after, I vndertake,
He shall be ryd of the toth-ake.
POTYCARY.   I praye you, torne that relyke
    aboute!
Other the Trinite had the goute,   515
Or elles, bycause it is iii toes in one,
God made it muche as thre toes alone.
PARDONER.[1]   Well, lette that passe, and
    loke vpon thys; —

[*He holds up another relic.*]

Here is a relyke that doth nat mys
To helpe the leste as well as the moste.   520
This is a buttocke-bone of Pentecoste!
POTYCARY.   By Chryste, and yet, for all
    your boste,
Thys relyke hath be-shyten the roste!

[*Takes out another relic.*]

PARDONER.   Marke well thys relyke, —
    here is a whipper! [2]
My frendes, vnfayned,[3] here is a slyp-
    per   525
Of one of the Seuen Slepers,[4] be sure.
Doutlesse thys kys shall do you great pleas-
    ure,
For all these two dayes it shall so ease
    you
That none other sauours shall displease
    you.
POTYCARY.   All these two dayes! nay, all
    thys two yere!   530
For all the sauours that may come here
Can be no worse; for, at a worde,
One of the Seuen Slepers trode in a torde.
PEDLER.   Syr, me thynketh your deuocion
    is but smal.
PARDONER.   Small? mary, me thynketh he
    hath none at all!   535
POTYCARY.   What the deuyll care I what
    ye thynke?
Shall I prayse relykes when they stynke?

[*Takes out another.*]

PARDONER.   Here is an eye-toth of the
    Great Turke.

---

[1] Manly states in error that M. has *drawll*.
[2] Have full authority.   [3] Spiritual.

[1] M. assigns this speech to the Potycary.
[2] A thing that surpasses all others.
[3] Without feigning.   [4] M. *ssepers.*

Whose eyes be ones sette on thys pece of
worke 539
May happely lese parte of his eye-syght,
But nat all tyll he be blynde out-ryght.
POTYCARY. What-so-euer any other man
seeth,
I haue no deuocion [1] to Turkes teeth;
For, all-though I neuer sawe a greter,
Yet me thynketh I haue sene many better.

[*The Pardoner takes out a box.*]

PARDONER. Here is a box full of humble-
bees 546
That stonge Eue as she sat on her knees
Tastynge the frute to her forbydden.
Who kysseth the bees within this hydden
Shall haue as muche pardon, of ryght, 550
As for any relyke he kyst thys nyght.
PALMER. Syr, I wyll kysse them, with all
my herte.
POTYCARY. Kysse them agayne, and take
my parte,
For I am nat worthy, — nay, lette be!
Those bees that stonge Eue shall nat stynge
me! 555

[*The Pardoner holds up a flask.*]

PARDONER. Good frendes, I haue yet here
in thys glas,
Whiche on the drynke at the weddynge
was
Of Adam and Eue vndoutedly.
If ye honor this relyke deuoutly, 559
All-though ye thurste no whyt the lesse,
Yet shall ye drynke the more, doutlesse, —
After whiche drynkynge ye shall be as
mete
To stande on your hede as on your fete.
POTYCARY. Ye, mary, now I can [2] ye
thanke!
In presents of thys the reste be blanke. 565
Wolde God this relyke had come rather! [3]
Kysse that relyke well, good father!
Suche is the payne that ye palmers take
To kysse the pardon-bowle for the drynke
sake.

[*He prays.*]

"O holy yeste, [4] that loketh full sowr and
stale, 570
For Goddes body helpe me to a cuppe of
ale!

[1] M. *devacion*   [2] Give.   [3] Sooner.   [4] Yeast.

The more I be-holde the, the more I
thurste;
The oftener I kysse the, more lyke to
burste!
But syns I kysse the so deuoutely,
Hyre me, and helpe me with drynke till I
dye!" 575
What, so muche prayenge and so lytell
spede?
PARDONER. Ye, for God knoweth whan it
is nede
To sende folkes drynke; but, by Saynt
Antony,
I wene he hath sent you to muche all-redy.
POTYCARY. If I haue neuer the more for
the, 580
Then be the relykes no ryches to me,
Nor to thy-selfe, excepte they be
More benefycyall then I can se.

[*He opens his packet of medicines.*]

Rycher is one boxe of [t]his tryacle [1]
Then all thy relykes that do no myra-
kell. 585
If thou haddest prayed but halfe so muche
to me
As I haue prayed to thy relykes and the,
Nothynge concernynge myne occupacion
But streyght shulde haue wrought in opera-
cyon.
And, as in value, I pas you an ace. 590

[*He takes out a box.*]

Here lyeth muche rychesse in lytell
space, —
I haue a boxe of rebarb here,
Whiche is as deynty as it is dere.
So helpe me God and hollydam,
Of this I wolde nat geue a dram [2] 595
To the beste frende I haue in Englandes
grounde,
Though he wolde geue me xx pounde;
For, though the stomake do it abhor,
It pourget[h] you clene from the color, [3]
And maketh your stomake sore to wal-
ter, [4] 600
That ye shall neuer come to the halter.
PEDLER. Then is that medycyn a sou-
erayn thynge
To preserue a man from hangynge.

[1] Treacle, a salve.   [2] M. *deam.*
[3] Choler, bile.   [4] Be upset.

[He takes out another.]

POTYCARY.   If ye wyll taste but thys
    crome that ye se,
If euer ye be hanged, neuer truste me!   605

[He holds up an ointment.]

Here haue I diapompholicus, —
A speciall oyntement, as doctours discuse;
For a fistela or a canker
Thys oyntement is euen shot-anker,[1]   609
For this medecyn helpeth one and other,
Or bryngeth them in case that they nede
    no other.

[Holds up a vial of syrup.]

Here is syrapus de Byzansis, —
A lytell thynge is i-nough of this,
For euen the weyght of one scryppull[2]
Shall make you stronge as a cryppull.   615

[Displays the rest.]

Here be other: as, diosfialios,
Diagalanga, and sticados,
Blanka manna, diospoliticon,
Mercury sublyme, and metridaticon,
Pelitory, and arsefetita,   620
Cassy, and colloquintita.
These be the thynges that breke all stryfe
Betwene mannes sycknes and his lyfe.
From all payne these shall you deleuer,
And set you euen at reste for-euer!   625
Here is a medecyn — no mo lyke the same
Whiche comenly is called thus by name
Alikakabus or alkakengy, —
A goodly thynge for dogges that be mangy.
Suche be these medycynes that I can   630
Helpe a dogge as well as a man.
Nat one thynge here partycularly
But worketh vniuersally, —
For it doth me as muche good when I sell it
As all the byers that taste it or smell it.   635
Now, syns my medycyns be so specyall,
And in operacion so generall,
And redy to worke when-so-euer they
    shall,
So that in ryches I am principall,
Yf any rewarde may entreat ye,   640
I besech your mashyp[3] be good to me,
And ye shall haue a boxe of marmelade

---

[1] The chief and last reliance.
[2] Scruple.   [3] Mastership.

So fyne that ye may dyg it with a spade.
PEDLER.   Syr, I thanke you; but your re-
    warde
Is nat the thynge that I regarde.   645
I muste, and wyll, be indifferent:
Wherfore procede in your intente.
POTYCARY.   Nowe, yf I wyst[1] thys wysh
    no synne,
I wolde to God I myght begynne!
PARDONER.   I am content that thou lye
    fyrste.   650
PALMER.   Euen so am I; and say thy
    worste!
Now let vs here of all thy lyes
The greatest lye thou mayst deuyse,
And in the fewyst wordes thou can.
POTYCARY.   Forsoth, ye be an honest
    man.   655
PALMER.   There sayde ye muche! but yet
    no lye.
PARDONER.   Now lye ye bothe, by Our
    Lady!
Thou lyest in bost of hys honestie,
And he hath lyed in affyrmynge the.
POTYCARY.   Yf we both lye, and ye say
    true,   660
Then of these lyes your parte adew!
And yf ye wyn, make none auaunt;
For ye are sure of one yll seruaunte.

[To the Palmer.]

Ye may perceyue by the wordes he gaue
He taketh your mashyp but for a knaue.
But who tolde true, or lyed in-dede,   666
That wyll I knowe or we procede.
Syr, after that I fyrste began
To prayse you for an honest man,
When ye affyrmed it for no lye, —   670
Now, by our fayth, speke euen truely, —
Thought ye your affyrmacion true?
PALMER.   Ye, mary, I! for I wolde ye
    knewe
I thynke my-selfe an honest man.
POTYCARY.   What, thought ye in the con-
    trary than?   675
PARDONER.   In that I sayde the contrary,
I thynke from trouth I dyd nat vary.
POTYCARY.   And what of my wordes?
PARDONER.   I thought ye lyed.
POTYCARY.   And so thought I, by God
    that dyed!

---

[1] Knew.

Nowe haue you twayne eche for hym-selfe
    layde   680
That none hath lyed ou[gh]t, but both
    truesayd;
And of vs twayne none hath denyed,
But both affyrmed, that I haue lyed:
Now syns [ye] both your trouth confes,
And that we both my lye so witnes   685
That twayne of vs thre in one agree, —
And that the lyer the wynner must be, —
Who coulde prouyde suche euydens
As I haue done in this pretens?

[To the Pedler.]

Me thynketh this mater sufficient   690
To cause you to gyue iudgement,
And to giue me the mastrye,
For ye perceyue these knaues can nat lye.
PALMER.   Though nother of vs as yet had
    lyed,
Yet what we can do is vntryed;   695
For yet we haue deuysed nothynge,
But answered you and geuen hyrynge.
PEDLER.   Therfore I haue deuysed one
    waye
Wherby all thre your myndes may saye:
For eche of you one tale shall tell;   700
And whiche of you telleth most meruell [1]
And most vnlyke to be true,
Shall most preuayle, what-euer ensew.
POTYCARY.   If ye be set in mervalynge,
Then shall ye here a meruaylouse
    thynge;   705
And though, in-dede, all be nat true,
Yet suer the most parte shall be new.

[He begins his lie.]

I dyd a cure, no lenger a-go
But *Anno Domini millesimo,*
On a woman, yonge and so fayre   710
That neuer haue I sene a gayre.
God saue all women from that lyknes!
This wanton had the fallen-syknes, —
Whiche by dissent came lynyally,
For her mother had it naturally.   715
Wherfore, this woman to recure
It was more harde ye may be sure.
But, though I boste my crafte is suche
That in suche thynges I can do muche,
How ofte she fell were muche to re-
    porte;   720

[1] Marvelous.

But her hed so gydy and her helys [1] so
    shorte
That, with the twynglynge of an eye,
Downe wolde she falle euyn by-and-by.
But, or she wolde aryse agayne,
I shewed muche practyse, muche to my
    payne;   725
For the tallest [2] man within this towne
Shulde nat with ease haue broken her
    sowne. [3]
All-though for lyfe I dyd nat doute her,
Yet dyd I take more payne about her
Then I wolde take with my owne syster.730
Syr, at the last I gaue her a glyster, —
I thrust a tampyon [4] in her tewell
And bad her kepe it for a iewell.
But I knewe it so heuy to cary
That I was sure it wolde nat tary;   735
For where gonpouder is ones fyerd
The tampyon wyll no lenger be hyerd.
Whiche was well sene in tyme of thys
    chaunce;
For, when I had charged this ordynaunce,
Sodeynly, as it had thonderd,   740
Euen at a clap losed her bumberd.
Now marke, for here begynneth the reuell: [5]
This tampion [6] flew x longe myle leuell,
To a fayre castell of lyme and stone, —
For strength I knowe nat suche a one,—745
Whiche stode vpon an hyll full hye,
At fote wherof a ryuer ranne bye,
So depe, tyll chaunce had it forbyden,
Well myght the Regent [7] there haue ryden.
But when this tampyon on this castell
    lyght,   750
It put the castels so farre to flyght
That downe they came eche vpon other,
No stone lefte standynge, by Goddes
    Mother!
But rolled downe so faste the hyll
In suche a nomber, and so dyd fyll,   755
From botom to bryme, from shore to
    shore,
Thys forsayd ryuer, so depe before,
That who lyste nowe to walke therto,
May wade it ouer and wet no shoo.
So was thys castell layd wyde open   760
That euery man myght se the token.

[1] Heels.   [2] Stoutest, bravest.
[3] Swoon.   [4] M. *thampyon.*
[5] Merry-making.
[6] Manly states in error that M. has *tampton.*
[7] The name of a ship?

But — in a good houre maye these wordes
    be spoken! —
After the tampyon on the walles was
    wroken,[1]
And pece by pece in peces broken,
And she delyuered with suche violens 765
Of all her inconueniens,
I left her in good helth and luste.
And so she doth contynew, I truste!
PEDLER.   Syr, in your cure I can nothynge
    tell;
But to our purpose ye haue sayd well. 770
PARDONER.   Well, syr, then marke what I
    can say!

[He begins his lie.]

I haue ben a pardoner many a day,
And done greater cures gostely
Then euer he dyd bodely;
Namely, thys one whiche ye shall here, 775
Of one departed within thys seuen yere, —
A frende of myne, and lykewyse I
To her agayne was as frendly, —
Who fell so syke so sodeynly
That dede she was euen by-and-by,[2] 780
And neuer spake with preste nor clerke,
Nor had no whyt of thys holy warke,
For I was thens, it coulde nat be;
Yet harde I say she asked for me.
But when I bethought me howe thys
    chaunced, 785
And that I haue to heuen auaunced
So many soules to me but straungers
And coude nat kepe my frende from
    daungers,
But she to dy so daungerously,
For her soule helth especyally, — 790
That was the thynge that greued me soo
That nothynge coulde release my woo
Tyll I had tryed euen out of hande[3]
In what estate her soule dyd stande.
For whiche tryall, shorte tale to make, 795
I toke thys iourney for her sake, —
Geue eare, for here begynneth the story! —
From hens I went to purgatory,
And toke with me thys gere in my fyste,
Wherby I may do there what I lyste. 800
I knocked, and was let in quyckly;
But, Lorde, how lowe the soules made
    curtesy!
And I to euery soule agayne

Dyd gyue a beck them to retayne,
And axed them thys question than: 805
Yf that the soule of suche a woman
Dyd late amonge them there appere.
Wherto they sayd she came nat here.
Then ferd I muche it was nat well.
Alas! thought I, she is in hell! 810
For with her lyfe I was so acqueynted
That sure I thought she was nat saynted.
With thys it chaunced me to snese;
"Christe helpe!" quoth a soule that ley for
    his fees.
"Those wordes," quoth I, "thou shalt nat
    lees!"[1] 815
Then with these pardons of all degrees
I payed hys tole, and set hym so quyght[2]
That strayt to heuen he toke his flyght.
And I from thens to hell that nyght,
To help this woman, yf I myght, 820
Nat as who sayth by authorite,[3]
But by the waye of entreate.
And fyrst [to] the deuyll that kept the gate
I came, and spake after this rate:
"All hayle, syr deuyll!" and made lowe
    curtesy. 825
"Welcome!" quoth he, thys smillyngly.
He knew me well. And I at laste
Remembred hym syns longe tyme paste,
For, as good happe wolde haue it chaunce,
Thys deuyll and I were of olde acqueynt-
    aunce, 830
For oft in the play of Corpus Cristi
He hath[4] played the deuyll at Couentry.
By his acqueyntaunce and my behauoure
He shewed to me ryght frendly fauoure.
And — to make my returne the shorter —
I sayd to this deuyll: "Good mayster
    porter, 836
For all olde loue, yf it lye in your power,
Helpe me to speke with my lorde and
    your."
"Be sure," quoth he, "no tongue can tell
What tyme thou coudest haue come so
    well, 840
For thys daye Lucyfer fell, —
Whiche is our festyuall in hell.
Nothynge vnreasonable craued thys day
That shall in hell haue any nay.
But yet be-ware thou come nat in 845
Tyll tyme thou may thy pasporte wyn.

---

[1] Avenged.   [2] Immediately.   [3] At once.

[1] Lose (without reward).   [2] Free.
[3] M. *outhorite.*   [4] Manly has *had.*

Wherfore stande styll, and I wyll wyt [1]
Yf I can get thy saue-condyt."
He taryed nat, but shortely gat it,
Under seale, and the deuyls hande at it, 850
In ample wyse, as ye shall here.
Thus it began: "Lucyfere,
By the power of God chyefe deuyll of hell,
To all the deuyls that there do dwell,
And euery of them, we sende gretynge, 855
Under streyght [2] charge and commaund-
ynge,
That they aydynge and assystent be
To suche a pardoner," — and named [3]
me, —
"So that he may at lybertie
Passe saue without hys ieopardy 860
Tyll that he be from vs extyncte [4]
And clerely out of helles precincte.
And, hys pardons to kepe sauegarde,
We wyll they lye in the porters warde.
Geuyn in the fornes of our palys, [5] 865
In our hye courte of maters of malys,
Suche a day and yere of our reyne."
"God saue the deuyll!" quoth I, "for
playne, [6]
I truste thys wrytynge to be sure."
"Then put thy truste," quoth he, "in
euer, [7] 870
Syns thou art sure to take no harme."
Thys deuyll and I walket arme in arme,
So farre tyll he had brought me thyther
Where all the deuyls of hell togyther
Stode in a-ray in suche apparell 875
As for that day there metely fell:
Theyr hornes well gylt, theyr clowes [8] full
clene,
Theyr taylles well kempt, [9] and, as I wene,
With sothery [10] butter theyr bodyes
anoynted, —
I neuer sawe deuyls so well appoynted. 880
The mayster deuyll sat in his iacket,
And all the soules were playnge at racket.
None other rackettes they hadde in hande
Saue euery soule a good fyre-brande;
Wherwith they played so pretely 885
That Lucyfer laughed merely,
And all the resedew of the fendes [11]

Dyd laugh full well togytther lyke frendes.
But of my frende I sawe no whyt,
Nor durst nat axe for her as yet. 890
Anone all this rout was brought in silens,
And I by an vsher brought in presens.
Then to Lucyfer low as I coude
I knelyd. Whiche he so well alowde
That thus he beckte; and, by Saynt
Antony, 895
He smyled on me well-fauoredly,
Bendynge hys browes, as brode as barne-
durres,
Shakynge hys eares, as ruged as burres,
Rolynge hys yes, [1] as rounde as two bushels,
Flastynge [2] the fyre out of his nose-
thryls, 900
Gnashynge hys teeth so vaynglorousely
That me thought tyme to fall to flatery.
Wherwith I tolde, as I shall tell:
"O plesant pycture! O prince of hell!
Feutred [3] in fashyon abominable! 905
And syns that [it] is inestimable
For me to prayse the worthyly,
I leue of prays, vnworthy
To geue the prays, besechynge the
To heare my sewte, and then to be 910
So good to graunt the thynge I craue.
And, to be shorte, thys wolde I haue, —
The soule of one whiche hyther is flytted
Deliuered hens, and to me remitted.
And in thys doynge, though al be nat quyt,
Yet some parte I shall deserue it — 916
As thus: I am a pardoner,
And ouer soules, as a controller,
Thorough-out the erth my power doth
stande,
Where many a soule lyeth on my hande,
That spede in maters as I vse them, 921
As I receyue them or refuse them;
Wherby, what tyme thy pleasure is,
Ye [4] shall requyre any part of thys, —
The leste deuyll here that can come
thyther 925
Shall chose a soule and brynge hym
hyther."
"Nowe," quoth the deuyll, "we are well
pleased!
What is hys name thou woldest haue
eased?"
"Nay," quoth I, "be it good or euyll,

My comynge is for a she deuyll."   930
"What calste her?" quoth he, "thou
      horson!" [1]
"Forsoth," quoth I, "Margery Coorson."
"Now, by our honour," sayd Lucyfer,
"No deuyll in hell shall witholde her!
And yf thou woldest haue twenty mo, 935
Were nat for iustyce, they shulde goo.
For all we deuyls within thys den
Haue more to do with two women
Then with all the charge we haue besyde.
Wherfore, yf thou our frende wyll be
      tryed,   940
Aply thy pardons to women so
That vnto vs there come no mo."
To do my beste I promysed by othe.
Whiche I haue kepte; for, as the fayth
      goth,
At these [2] dayes to heuen I do procure 945
Ten women to one man, be sure.
Then of Lucyfer my leue I toke,
And streyght vnto the mayster coke.
I was hadde into the kechyn,
For Margaryes offyce was ther-in.   950
All thynge handled there discretely, —
For euery soule bereth offyce metely, —
Whiche myght be sene to se her syt
So bysely turnynge of the spyt;
For many a spyt here hath she turned, 955
And many a good spyt hath she burned,
And many a spyt full hot [3] hath tosted
Before the meat coulde be halfe rosted.
And, or the meate were halfe rosted in-
      dede,   959
I toke her then fro the spyt for spede.
But when she sawe thys brought to pas,
To tell the ioy wherin she was,
And of all the deuyls, for ioy how they
Dyd rore at her delyuery,   964
And how the cheymes [4] in hell dyd rynge,
And how all the soules therin dyd synge,
And how we were brought to the gate,
And how we toke our leue therat, —
Be suer lacke of tyme sufferyth nat
To reherse the xx parte of that!   970
Wherfore, thys tale to conclude breuely,
Thys woman thanked me chyefly
That she was ryd of thys endles deth;
And so we departed on New-Market Heth.
And yf that any man do mynde her,   975

Who lyste to seke her, there shall he fynde
      her!
PEDLER.   Syr, ye haue sought her wonders
      well;
And, where ye founde her, as ye tell,
To here the chaunce ye founde in hell,
I fynde ye were in great parell.[1]   980

      [The Palmer begins his lie.]

PALMER.   His tale is all muche parellous;
But parte is muche more meruaylous.
As where he sayde the deuyls complayne
That women put them to suche payne
By theyr condicions so croked and crab-
      bed,   985
Frowardly fashonde, so waywarde and
      wrabbed,
So farre in deuision, and sturrynge suche
      stryfe,
That all the deuyls be wery of theyr lyfe!
This in effect he tolde for trueth;[2] 989
Wherby muche maruell [3] to me ensueth,
That women in hell suche shrewes can
      be,
And here so gentyll, as farre as I se.
Yet haue I sene many a myle,
And many a woman in the whyle, —
Nat one good cytye, towne, nor borough
In Cristendom but I haue ben th[o]r-
      ough, —   996
And this I wolde ye shulde vnderstande:
I haue sene women v hundred thousande
[Wives and widows, maids and maryed,]
And oft with them haue longe tyme
      taryed,[4]   1000
Yet in all places where I haue ben,
Of all the women that I haue sene,
I neuer sawe, nor knewe, in my consyens,
Any one woman out of paciens.
POTYCARY.   By the masse, there is a great
      lye!   1005
PARDONER.   I neuer harde a greater, by
      Our Lady!
PEDLER.   A greater? nay, knowe ye any so
      great?
PALMER.   Syr, whether that I lose or get,
For my parte, iudgement shall be prayed.[5]

---

[1] M. *horyson*.   [2] M. *thys*.   [3] M. *hoth*.
[4] M. *cheynes*, which may be correct

[1] Peril.   [2] M. *ttueth*.   [3] M. *muruell*.
[4] M. *maryed*; Collier cites Allde's edition, 1569, as
having *taried*. Obviously a line is missing; Manly
plausibly suggests *Wives and widows, maid and married*, which would explain the printer's error of *maryed*. I have inserted Manly's suggestion in the text
[5] Asked for.

PARDONER. And I desyer as he hath
   sayd. 1010
POTYCARY. Procede, and ye shall be
   obeyed.
PEDLER. Then shall nat iudgement be de-
   layd.
Of all these thre, yf eche mannes tale
In Poules Churche-yarde [1] were set on sale
In some mannes hande that hath the
   sleyghte,[2] 1015
He shulde sure sell these tales by weyght.
For, as they wey, so be they worth.
But whiche weyth beste? to that now forth!

[To the Potycary.]

Syr, all the tale that ye dyd tell
I bere in mynde; [to the Pardoner] and yours
   as well; 1020
And, as ye sawe the mater metely,
So lyed ye bothe well and discretely.
Yet were your lyes with the lest, truste me!

[To the Potycary.]

For, yf ye had sayd ye had made fle
Ten tampyons, out of ten womens tayles,
Ten tymes ten myle, to ten castels or
   iayles, 1026
And fyll ten ryuers, ten tymes so depe
As ten of that whiche your castell stones
   dyde kepe,[3] —

[To the Pardoner.]

Or yf ye ten tymes had bodely
Fet ten soules out of purgatory, 1030
And ten tymes so many out of hell, —
Yet, by these ten bonnes,[4] I could ryght
   well
Ten tymes sonner all that haue beleued
Then the tenth parte of that he hath
   meued.[5]
POTYCARY. Two knaues before i lacketh ii
   knaues of fyue; 1035
Then one, and then one, and bothe knaues
   a-lyue;
Then two, and then two, and thre at a
   cast;[6]
Thou knaue, and thou knaue, and thou
   knaue, at laste!
Nay, knaue, yf ye try me by nomber,

I wyll as knauyshly you accomber.[1] 1040
Your mynde is all on your pryuy tythe,[2]
For all in ten me thynketh your wit
   lythe.[3]
Now ten tymes I beseche Hym that hye
   syttes
Thy wyfes x commaundementes [4] may
   serch thy v wittes;
Then ten of my tordes in ten of thy
   teth, 1045
And ten on [5] thy nose — whiche euery man
   seth.
And twenty tymes ten this wyshe I
   wolde, —
That thou haddest ben hanged at ten yere
   olde!
For thou goest about to make me a
   slaue.
I wyll thou knowe yt [6] I am a gentylman,
   knaue! 1050

[Points to the Pardoner.]

And here is an other shall take my parte.
PARDONER. Nay, fyrste I be-shrew your
   knaues herte
Or I take parte in your knauery!
I wyll speke fayre, by Our [7] Lady!
Syr, I beseche your mashyp to be 1055
As good as ye can be to me.
PEDLER. I wolde be glade to do you good,
And hym also, be he neuer so wood.[8]
But dout you nat I wyll now do 1059
The thynge my consciens ledeth me to.
Both your tales I take farre impossyble,
Yet take I his fa[r]ther incredyble.
Nat only the thynge it-selfe alloweth it,
But also the boldenes therof auoweth it.

[To the Potycary.]

I knowe nat where your tale to trye,[9] 1065

[To the Pardoner.]

Nor yours, but in hell or purgatorye;
But hys boldnes hath faced a lye
That may be tryed euyn in thys companye,
As, yf ye lyste, to take thys order:

[He points to the audience.]

---

[1] Overwhelm.
[2] Tithe (tenth) which he expected from the Palmer
by way of reward.
[3] Lyeth.   [4] Finger-nails, claws.
[5] M. *of.*   [6] M. *yf.*   [7] M. *one.*
[8] Mad.   [9] M. *trye* (Manly says *crye*).

Amonge the women in thys border, 1070
Take thre of the yongest and thre of the
    oldest,
Thre of the hotest and thre of the coldest,
Thre of the wysest and thre of the shrewd-
    est,
Thre of the chastest and thre of the lewd-
    est,[1]
Thre of the lowest and thre of the hy-
    est, 1075
Thre of the farthest and thre of the nyest,
Thre of the fayrest and thre of the mad-
    dest,
Thre of the fowlest and thre of the sad-
    dest, —
And when all these threes be had a-sonder,
Of eche thre, two, iustly by nomber, 1080
Shall be founde shrewes — excepte thys fall,
That ye hap to fynde them shrewes all!
Hym-selfe for trouth all this doth knowe,
And oft hath tryed some of thys rowe;
And yet he swereth, by his consciens, 1085
He neuer saw woman breke paciens!
Wherfore, consydered with true entente,
Hys lye to be so euident,
And to appere so euydently
That both you affyrmed it a ly, 1090
And that my consciens so depely
So depe hath sought thys thynge to try,
And tryed it with mynde indyfferent,
Thus I awarde, by way of iudgement, —
Of all the lyes ye all haue spent 1095
Hys lye to be most excellent.

PALMER.   Syr, though ye were bounde of
    equyte
To do as ye haue done to me,
Yet do I thanke you of your payne,
And wyll requyte some parte agayne. 1100

PARDONER.   Mary, syr, ye can no les do
But thanke hym as muche as it cometh to.
And so wyll I do for my parte:
Now a vengeaunce on thy knaues harte!
I neuer knewe pedler a iudge before, 1105
Nor neuer wyll truste pedlynge-knaue
    more!

[*The Potycary, as though to fulfill the agreement of the wager, begins to courtesy to the
Palmer.*]

What doest thou there, thou horson nody?

POTYCARY.   By the masse, lerne to make
    curtesy!
Curtesy before, and curtesy behynde hym,
And then on eche syde — the deuyll blynde
    hym! 1110
Nay, when I haue it perfytly,
Ye shall haue the deuyll and all of curtesy!
But it is nat sone lerned, brother,
One knaue to make curtesy to another.
Yet, when I am angry, that is the worste,
I shall call my mayster knaue at the fyrste.

PALMER.   Then wolde some mayster per-
    happes clowt [1] ye!
But, as for me, ye nede nat doute ye;
For I had leuer be without ye
Then haue suche besynesse aboute ye. 1120

PARDONER.   So helpe me God, so were ye
    better!
What, shulde a begger be a ietter? [2]
It were no whyt your honestie
To haue vs twayne iet after ye.

POTYCARY.   Syr, be ye sure he telleth you
    true. 1125
Yf we shulde wayte,[3] thys wolde ensew:
It wolde be sayd — truste me at a worde —
Two knaues made curtesy to the [4] thyrde.

PEDLER [*to the Palmer*].   Now, by my trouth,
    to speke my mynde, —
Syns they be so loth to be assyned,[5] 1130
To let them lose I thynke it beste,
And so shall ye lyue beste in rest.

PALMER.   Syr, I am nat on them so fonde [6]
To compell them to kepe theyr bonde.

[*To the Potycary and Palmer.*]

And, syns ye lyste nat to wayte on me, 1135
I clerely of waytynge dyscharge ye.

PARDONER.   Mary, syr, I hertely thanke
    you!

POTYCARY.   And I lyke-wyse, I make God
    auowe!

PEDLER.   Now be ye all euyn as ye begoon;
No man hath loste, nor no man hath
    woon. 1140
Yet in the debate wherwith ye began,
By waye of aduyse I wyll speke as I can:

[*To the Palmer.*]

---

[1] This line is missing in M.; supplied by Collier from Allde's edition, 1569.

[1] Cuff heavily.   [2] Swaggerer, strutter.
[3] Attend as followers.   [4] Manly has *a*.
[5] Appointed (to the office of attending on the Palmer).
[6] Infatuated.

I do perceyue that pylgrymage
Is chyefe the thynge ye haue in vsage;
Wherto, in effecte, for loue of Chryst 1145
Ye haue, or shulde haue, bene entyst.
And who so doth, with suche entent,
Doth well declare hys tyme well spent.

[*To the Pardoner.*]

And so do ye in your pretence,
If ye procure thus indulgence   1150
Unto your neyghbours charytably
For loue of them in God onely. —
All thys may be ryght well applyed
To shew [1] you both well occupyed;
For, though ye walke nat bothe one
        waye,   1155
Yet, walkynge thus, thys dare I saye:
That bothe your walkes come to one ende.
And so for all that do pretende,
By ayde of Goddes grace, to ensewe [2]
Any maner kynde of vertue: 1160
As, some great almyse for to gyue,
Some in wyllfull pouertie to lyue,
Some to make hye-wayes and suche other
        warkes,
And some to mayntayne prestes and
        clarkes   1164
To synge and praye for soule departed, —
These, with all other vertues well marked,
All-though they be of sondry kyndes,
Yet be they nat vsed with sondry myndes;
But, as God only doth all those moue,
So euery man, onely for His loue,   1170
With loue and dred obediently
Worketh in these vertues vnyformely.
Thus euery vertue, yf we lyste to scan,
Is pleasaunt to God and thankfull to man;
And who that by grace of the Holy Goste
To any one vertue is moued moste,   1176
That man, by that grace, that one apply,
And therin serue God most plentyfully!
Yet nat that one so farre wyde to wreste,
So lykynge the same to myslyke the
        reste;   1180
For who so wresteth hys worke is in vayne.
And euen in that case I perceyue you
        twayne,
Lykynge your vertue in suche wyse
That eche others vertue you do dyspyse.
Who walketh thys way for God wolde
        fynde hym,   1185

[1] M. *shewell.*   [2] Follow.

The farther they seke hym, the farther be-
        hynde hym.
One kynde of vertue to dyspyse another
Is lyke as the syster myght hange the
        brother.
POTYCARY.   For fere lest suche parels to
        me myght fall,
I thanke God I vse no vertue at all! 1190
PEDLER.   That is of all the very worste
        waye!
For more harde it is, as I haue harde
        saye,
To begynne vertue where none is pre-
        tendyd
Then, where it is begonne, the abuse to be
        mended.
How-be-it, ye be nat all to begynne; 1195
One syne [1] of vertue ye are entred in:
As thys, I suppose ye dyd saye true,
In that ye sayd ye vse no vertue;
In the whiche wordes, I dare well reporte,
Ye are well be-loued of all thys sorte, 1200
By your raylynge here openly
At pardons ond relyques so leudly.
POTYCARY.   In that I thynke my faute nat
        great;
For all that he hath I knowe conterfete.
PEDLER.   For his, and all other that ye
        knowe fayned,   1205
Ye be nother counceled nor constrayned
To any suche thynge in any suche case
To gyue any reuerence in any suche place;
But where ye dout the truthe, nat know-
        ynge,
Beleuynge the beste, good may be grow-
        ynge.   1210
In iudgynge the beste, no harme at the
        leste,
In iudgynge the worste, no good at the
        beste.
But beste in these thynges, it semeth to
        me,
To take [2] no iudgement vpon ye;
But, as the Churche doth iudge or take
        them,   1215
So do ye receyue or forsake them;
And so, be sure, ye can nat erre,
But may be a frutfull folower.
POTYCARY.   Go ye before, and, as I am
        true man,
I wyll folow as faste as I can.   1220

[1] Sign.   [2] M. *make;* emend. b* Manly.

PARDONER.　And so wyll I; for he hath
　　sayd so well,
Reason wolde we shulde folowe hys counsell.

[*The Palmer addresses the audience by way
　　of Epilogue.*]

PALMER.　Then to our reason God gyue vs
　　his grace,
That we may folowe with fayth so fermely
His commaundementes, that we maye pur-
　　chace　　　　　　　　　　　　　　1225
Hys loue, and so consequently
To byleue hys Churche faste and fayth-
　　fully;

So that we may, accordynge to his prom-
　　yse,
Be kepte out of errour in any wyse.
And all that hath scapet vs here by negly-
　　gence,　　　　　　　　　　　　　1230
We clerely reuoke and forsake it.
To passe the tyme in thys without of-
　　fence,
Was the cause why the maker dyd make
　　it;
And so we humbly beseche you take it;
Besechynge Our Lorde to prosper you
　　all　　　　　　　　　　　　　　1235
In the fayth of hys Churche Vniuersall!

FINIS.

Imprynted at London in Fletestrete at
the sygne of the George by Wyllyam
Myddylton.

A MERY PLAY BETWENE JOHAN JOHAN, THE HUSBANDE, TYB, HIS WYFE, AND SYR JOHAN, THE PREEST [1]

[DRAMATIS PERSONÆ

JOHAN JOHAN, the husband.
TYB, his wife.
SYR JOHAN, the priest.]

Johan Johan, the Husbande.

God spede you, maysters, everychone!
Wote ye not whyther my wyfe is gone?
I pray God the dyvell take her!
For all that I do I can not make her
But she wyll go a gaddynge, very myche 5
Lyke an Anthony pyg, with an olde wyche [1]
Whiche ledeth her about hyther and
    thyther;
But, by Our Lady, I wote not whyther.
But, by goggis [2] blod, were she come home
Unto this, my house, by our lady of Crome,
I wolde bete her or that I drynke.   11
Bete her, quod a? yea, that she shall
    stynke!
And at every stroke lay her on the grounde,
And trayne her by the here [3] about the
    house rounde.
I am evyn mad that I bete her not nowe.
But I shall rewarde her hardly [4] well
    ynowe;   16
There is never a wyfe betwene heven and hell
Whiche was ever beten halfe so well.
    Beten, quod a?   Yea, but what and she
        therof dye?   19

[1] Witch.   St. Anthony was the patron saint of
swineherds, and was usually pictured with a pig for
his page.
[2] God's.   [3] Drag her by the hair.
[4] With energy.

Then I may chaunce to be hanged shortly.
And whan I have beten her tyll she smoke,
And gyven her many a C [1] stroke,
Thynke ye that she wyll amende yet?
Nay, by Our Lady, the devyll spede whyt!
Therfore I wyll not bete her at all.   25
    And shall I not bete her?   No shall?
Whan she offendeth and doth a-mys,
And kepeth not her house, as her duetie is?
Shall I not bete her, if she do so?
Yes, by cokkis [2] blood, that shall I do! 30
I shall bete her, and thwak her, I trow,
That she shall beshyte the house for very
    wo.
    But yet I thynk what my neybour wyll
        say than.
He wyll say thus: "Whom chydest thou,
    Johan Johan?"
"Mary!" wyll I say, "I chyde my curst
    wyfe,   35
The veryest drab that ever bare lyfe,
Whiche doth nothying but go and come,
And I can not make her kepe her at home."
Than I thynke he wyll say by and by: [3]
"Walke her cote, [4] Johan Johan! and bete
    her hardely!"   40
But than unto hym myn answere shal be:
"The more I bete her, the worse is she:

[1] A hundred.   [2] God's.
[3] At once.   [4] Give her a beating.

[1] Scholars have generally assigned this play to John Heywood, and internal evidence of style supports the
attribution.   There is no external evidence, however, to connect his name with the production, and one
should not ignore the possibility of its having been written by some other member of the minstrel-playwright
class.
    I have reproduced the copy in the Pepys Collection, Magdalene College, Cambridge, of the earliest edi-
tion, printed by William Rastell, 1533.   Charles Whittington edited the play for the Chiswick Press, about
1830, from a copy of the same edition in the Ashmolean Museum, Oxford.   Mr. A. W. Pollard, in *Representative English Comedies*, 1903, reproduced the Chiswick text corrected by the copy in the Pepys Collection. Pollard's
reprint is not quite as accurate as modern scholars could wish; I have not been able to see the Ashmolean
copy.   I have modernized the punctuation, the use of capitals, the use of the letters u, v, i, j, and have added
in brackets stage-directions to help the reader in following the action.

And wors and wors make her I shall!"
   He wyll say than: "Bete her not at all."
"And why?" shall I say; "this wolde be
   wyst,[1]   45
Is she not myne to chastice as I lyst?"
   But this is another poynt worst of all, —
The folkis wyll mocke me whan they here
   me brall.
But, for all that, shall I let [2] therfore
To chastyce my wyfe ever the more,   50
And to make her at home for to tary?
Is not that well done? Yes, by Saynt
   Mary!
That is a poynt of an honest man
For to bete his wyfe well nowe and than.
   Therfore I shall bete her, have ye no
   drede!   55
And I ought to bete her, tyll she be starke
   dede.
And why? By God, bicause it is my
   pleasure!
And if I shulde suffre her, I make you sure,
Nought shulde prevayle [3] me, nother staffe
   nor waster; [4]
Within a whyle she wolde be my mayster.
   Therfore I shall bete her, by cokkes
   mother,   61
Both on the tone syde and on the tother,
Before and behynde — nought shall be her
   bote — [5]
From the top of the heed to the sole of the
   fote.
   But, masters, for Goddis sake, do not
   entrete   65
For her whan that she shal be bete;
But, for Goddis passion, let me alone,
And I shall thwak her that she shall grone:
Wherfore I beseche you, and hartely you
   pray,
And I beseche you say me not nay,   70
But that I may beate her for this ones.
And I shall beate her, by cokkes bones,
That she shall stynke lyke a pole-kat!
But yet, by goggis body, that nede nat,
For she wyll stynke without any betyng; 75
For every nyght, ones she gyveth me an
   hetyng,[6]
From her issueth suche a stynkyng smoke
That the savour therof almost doth me
   choke.

But I shall bete her nowe, without fayle;
I shall bete her toppe and tayle,   80
Heed, shulders, armes, legges, and all,
I shall bete her, I trowe; that I shall!
And, by goggis boddy, I tell you trewe,
I shall bete her tyll she be blacke and
   blewe.
   But where the dyvell trowe ye she is
   gon?   85
I holde a noble [1] she is with Syr Johan.
I fere I am begyled alway;
But yet, in fayth, I hope well nay.
Yet I almost enrage that I ne can
Se the behavour of our gentylwoman. 90
And yet, I thynke, thyther as she doth go,
Many an honest wyfe goth thyther also,
For to make some pastyme and sporte.
But than my wyfe so ofte doth thyther
   resorte
That I fere she wyll make me weare a
   fether.   95
But yet I nede not for to fere nether,
For he is her gossyp, that is he.
   But abyde a whyle! yet let me se!
Where the dyvell hath our gyssypry [2]
   begon?
My wyfe had never chylde, doughter nor
   son.   100
Nowe if I forbede her that she go no more,
Yet wyll she go as she dyd before;
Or els wyll she chuse some other place,
And then the matter is in as yll case.
   But, in fayth, all these wordes be in
   wast,   105
For I thynke the matter is done and past.
And whan she cometh home she wyll
   begyn to chyde;
But she shall have her payment-styk [3] by
   her syde!
For I shall order her, for all her brawlyng,
That she shall repent to go a catter-
   wawlyng.[4]   110

[*Tyb has entered during this speech.*]

TYB. Why, whom wylt thou beate, I say,
   thou knave?
JOHAN. Who, I, Tyb? None, so God me
   save.

---

[1] I wager a noble (a coin, 6*s*. 8*d*.).
[2] Gossipry, spiritual relationship, here referring to
sponsorship at the baptism of a child.
[3] Beating.
[4] Go, like cats, on amorous expeditions.

Known.   [2] Desist.   [3] Avail.
Club.   [5] Remedy, help.   [6] Heating.

TYB. Yes, I harde the say thou woldest one bete.

JOHAN. Mary, wyfe, it was stokfysshe[1] in Temmes Strete,

Whiche wyll be good meate agaynst Lent.

Why, Tyb, what haddest thou thought that I had ment? 116

TYB. Mary, me-thought I harde the bawlyng.

Wylt thou never leve this wawlyng?[2]

Howe the dyvell dost thou thy selfe behave?

Shall we ever have this worke, thou knave? 120

JOHAN. What! wyfe, howe sayst thou? was it well gest of me,

That thou woldest be come home in safete

As sone as I had kendled a fyre?

Come warme the, swete Tyb, I the requyre.

TYB. O, Johan, Johan, I am afrayd, by this lyght, 125

That I shalbe sore syk this nyght.

JOHAN [aside]. By cokkis soule, nowe, I dare lay a swan

That she comes nowe streyght fro Syr Johan!

For ever whan she hath fatched of hym a lyk,[3]

Than she comes home, and sayth she is syk. 130

TYB. What sayst thou?

JOHAN.   Mary, I say

It is mete for a woman to go play

Abrode in the towne for an houre or two.

TYB. Well, gentylman, go to, go to!

JOHAN. Well, let us have no more debate. 135

TYB [aside]. If he do not fyght, chyde, and rate,

Braule, and fare as one that were frantyke,

There is nothyng that may hym lyke.[4]

JOHAN [aside]. If that the parysshe preest, Syr Johan,

Dyd not se her nowe and than, 140

And gyve her absolution upon a bed,

For wo and payne she wolde sone be deed.

TYB. For goddis sake, Johan Johan, do the not displease;

Many a tyme I am yll at ease.

What thynkest nowe, am not I somwhat syk? 145

JOHAN [aside]. Nowe wolde to God, and swete Saynt Dyryk,

That thou warte in the water up to the throte,

Or in a burnyng oven red hote,

To se and I wolde pull the out!

TYB. Nowe, Johan Johan, to put the out of dout, 150

Imagyn thou where that I was

Before I came home.

JOHAN.   My percase,[1]

Thou wast prayenge in the Churche of Poules

Upon thy knees for all Chrysten soules.

TYB. Nay.

JOHAN. Than if thou wast not so holy,

Shewe me where thou wast, and make no lye? 156

TYB. Truely, Johan Johan, we made a pye,

I and my gossyp Margery,

And our gossyp the preest, Syr Johan,

And my neybours yongest doughter An.

The preest payde for the stuffe and the makyng, 161

And Margery she payde for the bakyng.

JOHAN [aside]. By cokkis lylly woundis,[2] that same is she

That is the most bawde hens to Coventre.

TYB. What say you?

JOHAN. Mary, answere me to this: 165

Is not Syr Johan a good man?

[TYB.]   Yes, that he is.

JOHAN. Ha, Tyb, if I shulde not greve the,

I have somwhat wherof I wolde meve[3] the.

TYB. Well, husbande, nowe I do conject

That thou hast me somwhat in suspect. 170

But, by my soule, I never go to Syr Johan

But I fynde hym lyke an holy man;

For eyther he is sayenge his devotion,

Or els he is goynge in processyon.

JOHAN [aside]. Yea, rounde about the bed doth he go, 175

You two together, and no mo;

And for to fynysshe the processyon,

He lepeth up, and thou lyest downe.

---

[1] Dried fish, too hard to be cooked without beating.

[2] Squalling, noise-making.

[3] Pleasure.   [4] Compare to.

[1] Maybe (guess).   [2] By God's lovely wounds.

[3] Exhort, request.

Tyb. What sayst thou?
Johan.   Mary, I say he doth well;
For so ought a shepherde to do, as I harde
    tell,   180
For the salvation of all his folde.
Tyb. Johan Johan!
[Johan].   What is it that thou wolde?
Tyb. By my soule I love thee too too! [1]
And I shall tell the, or I further go,
The pye that was made, I have it nowe
    here,   185
And therwith I trust we shall make good
    chere.
Johan. By kokkis body, that is very
    happy!
Tyb. But wotest who gave it?
Johan.   What the dyvel rek [2] I?
Tyb. By my fayth, and I shall say trewe,
    than:
The Dyvell take me and it were not Syr
    Johan.   190
Johan. O, holde the peas, wyfe, and
    swere no more!
[Aside.] But I beshrewe both your hartes
    therfore.
Tyb. Yet peradventure, thou hast sus-
    pection
Of that that was never thought nor done.
Johan. Tusshe, wyfe, let all suche mat-
    ters be.   195
I love thee well, though thou love not me.
But this pye doth nowe catche harme;
Let us set it upon the harth to warme.
Tyb. Than let us eate it as fast as we can.
But bycause Syr Johan is so honest a
    man,   200
I wolde that he shulde therof eate his part.
Johan. That were reason, I thee ensure.
Tyb. Than, syns that it is thy pleasure,
I pray the than go to hym ryght,   204
And pray hym come sup with us to nyght.
Johan [aside]. Shall he cum hyther?
By kokkis soule, I was a-curst
Whan that I graunted to that worde furst!
But syns I have sayd it I dare not say nay,
For than my wyfe and I shulde make a
    fray;
But whan he is come, I swere by goddis
    mother,   210
I wold gyve the dyvell the tone to cary
    away the tother!

[1] Exceedingly, overmuch.   [2] Care.

Tyb. What sayst?
Johan.   Mary, he is my curate, I say,
My confessour, and my frende alway.
Therfore go thou and seke hym by and by,
And tyll thou come agayne, I wyll kepe the
    pye.   215
Tyb. Shall I go for him! Nay, I shrewe
    me than!
Go thou, and seke, as fast as thou can,
And tell hym it.
Johan.   Shall I do so?
In fayth, it is not mete for me to go.
Tyb. But thou shalte go tell hym, for all
    that.   220
Johan.   Than shall I tell hym, wotest
    [thou] [1] what?
That thou desyrest hym to come make
    some chere.
Tyb. Nay, that thou desyrest hym to
    come sup here.
Johan. Nay, by the rode, wyfe, thou
    shalt have the worshyp
And the thankes of thy gest that is thy
    gossyp.   225
Tyb [aside]. Full ofte, I se, my husbande
    wyll me rate
For this hether commyng of our gentyll
    curate.
Johan. What sayst, Tyb? Let me here
    that agayne.
Tyb. Mary, I perceyve very playne
That thou hast Syr Johan somwhat in
    suspect;   230
But, by my soule, as far as I conject,
He is vertuouse and full of charyte.
Johan [aside].   In fayth, all the towne
    knoweth better — that he
Is a hore-monger, a haunter of the stewes,
An ypocrite, a knave that all men re-
    fuse,   235
A lyer, a wretche, a maker of stryfe —
Better than they knowe that thou art my
    good wyfe.
Tyb. What is that that thou hast sayde?
Johan. Mary, I wolde have the table set
    and layde,
In this place or that, I care not whether.
Tyb. Than go to, brynge the trestles [2]
    hyther.   241

[1] Supplied by P.
[2] The table was a board set on trestles; when not
in use, board and trestles were placed out of the
way.

JOHAN. [1]   Abyde a whyle, let me put of
  my gown!
But yet I am afrayde to lay it down,
For I fere it shal be sone stolen.
And yet it may lye safe ynough un-
  stolen.   245
It may lye well here, and I lyst, —
But, by cokkis soule, here hath a dogge
  pyst!
And if I shulde lay it on the harth bare,
It myght hap to be burned or I were ware.

[To one of the audience.]

Therfore I pray you take ye the payne
To kepe my gowne tyll I come agayne.

[Snatches it back.]

  But yet he shall not have it, by my fay;
He is so nere the dore he myght ron away.

[To another one of the audience.]

But bycause that ye be trusty and sure,
Ye shall kepe it, and it be your pleas-
  ure;   255
And bycause it is arrayde [2] at the skyrt,
Whyle ye do nothyng, skrape of the dyrt.

[He turns to his wife.]

Lo, nowe am I redy to go to Syr Johan,
And byd hym come as fast as he can.
[TYB.]   Ye, do so without ony taryeng.

[As he reaches the door she calls him back.]

But, I say, harke! thou hast forgot one
  thyng: 261
Set up the table, and that by and by.[3]

*[Johan returns and sets the boards on the
  trestles.]*

Nowe go thy ways.
JOHAN.   I go shortly;
But se your candelstykkis be not out of the
  way.
TYB [*as he reaches the door*]. Come agayne,
  and lay the table I say.   265

[He returns and lays the table.]

---

[1] R. assigns this speech to Johan, rightly, as it
seems to me.   Pollard assigns it to Tyb   What has
happened is that the marginal catch-names at lines
260 and 263 have been carelessly set by a printer
confused by the paragraph signs.
[2] Soiled with dirt.   [3] Instantly.

What! me thynkis, ye have sone don!
JOHAN.   Nowe I pray God that his malediction
Lyght on my wyfe, and on the baulde [1]
  preest!
TYB.   Nowe go thy ways, and hye the!
  seest?

[Johan starts out.]

JOHAN.   I pray to Christ, if my wyshe be
  no synne,   270
That the preest may breke his neck whan
  he comes in.
TYB [*as he reaches the door*]. Now cum
  agayn!
JOHAN.   What a myschefe wylt thou, fole!
TYB.   Mary, I say, brynge hether yender
  stole.
JOHAN.   Nowe go to!   A lyttell wolde
  make me
For to say thus: "A vengaunce take
  the!"   275

[He brings her the stool.]

TYB.   Nowe go to hym, and tell hym
  playn
That tyll thou brynge hym thou wylt not
  come agayn.
JOHAN.   This pye doth borne here as it
  doth stande.

[He starts out.]

TYB [*as he reaches the door*]. Go, washe
  me these two cuppes in my hande.

[He washes the cups, and brings them to her.]

JOHAN.   I go, with "a myschyefe lyght on
  thy face!"   280
TYB.   Go, and byd hym hye hym a-pace;
And the whyle I shall all thynges amende.
JOHAN.   This pye burneth here at this ende.
Understandest thou?
TYB.   Go thy ways, I say!
JOHAN.   I wyll go nowe, as fast as I may.

[Johan starts out.]

TYB [*as he reaches the door*]. How! come
  ones agayne: I had forgot.   286
Loke, and there be ony ale in the pot.
JOHAN.   Nowe, a vengaunce and a very
  myschyefe

---

[1] Bald (with shaven crown).

Lyght on the pylde [1] preest, and on my
    wyfe,
On the pot, the ale, and on the table, 290
The candyll, the pye, and all the rable,
On the trystels, and on the stole!
It is moche ado to please a curst fole.

[*He fills the pot with ale.*]

Tyb. Go thy ways nowe; and tary no
    more,
For I am a-hungred very sore. 295
Johan. Mary, I go.
Tyb [*as he reaches the door*]. But come ones
    agayne yet!
Brynge hyther that breade, lest I forget it.

[*He brings the bread.*]

Johan. I-wys, it were tyme for to torne
The pye; for, y-wys, it doth borne.
Tyb. Lorde! how my husbande nowe doth
    patter, 300
And of the pye styl doth clatter.
Go nowe, and byd hym come away;
I have byd the an hundred tymes to day.
Johan. I wyll not gyve a strawe, I tell
    you playne,
If that the pye waxe cold agayne — 305
Tyb. What! art thou not gone yet out of
    this place?
I had went [2] thou haddest ben come agayne
    in the space!
But, by cokkis soule, and I shulde do the
    ryght,
I shulde breke thy knaves heed to nyght.
Johan. Nay, than, if my wyfe be set a
    chydyng, 310
It is tyme for me to go at her byddyng.
There is a proverbe, whiche trewe nowe
    preveth:
" He must nedes go that the dyvell dry-
    veth."

[*He arrives at the Priest's house.*]

How, mayster curate, may I come in 314
At your chamber dore without ony syn?

Syr Johan, the preest.

Who is there nowe that wolde have
    me?
What! Johan Johan! What newes with
    the?

[1] Bald, shaven.   [2] Thought.

Johan. Mary, Syr, to tell you shortly,
My wyfe and I pray you hartely,
And eke desyre you wyth all our myght,
That ye wolde come and sup with us to
    nyght. 321
Syr J. Ye must pardon me; in fayth I ne
    can.
Johan. Yes, I desyre you, good Syr
    Johan,
Take payne this ones. And, yet at the
    lest,
If ye wyll do nought at my request, 325
Yet do somwhat for the love of my wyfe.
Syr J. I wyll not go, for makyng of stryfe.
But I shall tell the what thou shalte do, —
Thou shalt tary, and sup with me or thou
    go.
Johan. Wyll ye not go than? Why
    so? 330
I pray you tell me, is there any dysdayne,
Or ony enmyte, betwene you twayne?
Syr J. In fayth, to tell the, betwene the
    and me,
She is as wyse a woman as any may be.
I know it well; for I have had the charge
Of her soule, and serchyd her conscyens at
    large. 336
I never knew her but honest and wyse,
Without any yvyll or any vyce,
Save one faut — I know in her no more —
And because I rebuke her now and then
    therfore, 340
She is angre with me, and hath me in hate.
And yet that that I do, I do it for your
    welth.[1]
Johan. Now God yeld it yow,[2] god mas-
    ter curate,
And as ye do, so send you your helth.
Ywys, I am bound to you a plesure. 345
Syr J. Yet thou thynkyst amys, perad-
    venture,
That of her body she shuld not be a good
    woman.
But I shall tell the what I have done,
    Johan,
For that matter; she and I be somtyme
    aloft,
And I do lye uppon her many a tyme and
    oft 350
To prove her; yet could I never espy
That ever any dyd worse with her than I.

[1] Profit, advantage.   [2] Reward you for it.

JOHAN. Syr, that is the lest care I have of
nyne,
Thankyd be God, and your good doctryne.
But, yf it please you, tell me the mat-
ter, 355
And the debate [1] betwene you and her.
SYR J. I shall tell the; but thou must kepe
secret.
JOHAN. As for that, Syr, I shall not let. [2]
SYR J. I shall tell the now the matter
playn:
She is angry with me, and hath me in
dysdayn, 360
Because that I do her oft intyce
To do some penaunce, after myne advyse,
Because she wyll never leve her wrawlyng, [3]
But alway with the she is chydyng and
brawlyng.
And therfore, I knowe, she hatyth my [4]
presens. 365
JOHAN. Nay, in good feyth, savyng your
reverens.
SYR J. I know very well she hath me in
hate.
JOHAN. Nay, I dare swere for her, master
curate.
[*Aside.*] But, was I not a very knave!
I thought surely, so God me save, 370
That he had lovyd my wyfe for to deseyve
me.
And now he quytyth [5] hym-self; and here
I se
He doth as much as he may, for his lyfe,
To stynte [6] the debate betwene me and my
wyfe.
SYR J. If ever she dyd, or though[t] me
any yll, 375
Now I forgyve her with my [7] fre wyll.
Therfore, Johan Johan, now get the home;
And thank thy wyfe, and say, I wyll not
come.
JOHAN. Yet let me know now, good Syr
Johan,
Where ye wyll go to supper than. 380
SYR J. I care nat greatly and I tell the.
On Saterday last I and ii or thre
Of my frendes made an appoyntement,
And agaynst this nyght we dyd assent
That in a place we wolde sup together. 385

And one of them sayd, [s]he wolde brynge
thether
Ale and bread; and for my parte, I
Sayd that I wolde gyve them a pye, —
And there I gave them money for the
makynge;
And an-other sayd, she wolde pay for the
bakyng; 390
And so we purpose to make good chere
For to dryve away care and thought.
JOHAN. Than I pray you, Syr, tell me
here,
Whyther shulde all this geare be brought?
SYR J. By my fayth, and I shulde not
lye, 395
It shulde be delyvered to thy wyfe, the pye.
JOHAN. By God! it is at my house stand-
yng by the fyre.
SYR J. Who bespake that pye? I the
requyre.
JOHAN. By my feyth, and I shall not lye:
It was my wyfe, and her gossyp Mar-
gerye, 400
And your good masshyp callyd Syr Johan,
And my neybours yongest doughter An;
Your masshyp payde for the stuffe and
makyng,
And Margery she payde for the bakyng.
SYR J. If thou wylte have me nowe, in
faithe I wyll go. 405
JOHAN. Ye, mary, I beseche your masshyp
do so.
My wyfe taryeth for none but us twayne;
She thynketh longe or I come agayne.
SYR J. Well nowe, if she chyde me in thy
presens 409
I wylbe content, and take [it] [1] in pacyens.
JOHAN. By cokkis soule, and she ones
chyde,
Or frowne, or loure, or loke asyde,
I shall brynge you a staffe, as myche as I
may heve. [2]
Than bete her, and spare not! I gyve you
good leve
To chastyce her for her shreude varyeng. [3]

[*They return to Johan's house.*] [4]

TYB. The devyll take the for thy long
taryeng! 416
Here is not a whyt of water, by my gowne,

[1] Contention, quarrel.
[3] Squalling (in quarrels).
[5] Freeth.
[6] R. *stynk.*
[2] Omit to do.
[4] R. *me.*
[7] R. *me.*

[1] Supplied by P.
[2] As big as I may lift.
[3] Wicked quarreling.
[4] Added by P.

To washe our handis that we myght syt
    downe.[1]
Go, and hye the as fast as a snayle,   419
And with fayre water fyll me this payle.
JOHAN.   I thanke our Lorde of his good
    grace
That I can not rest longe in a place!
TYB.   Go, fetche water, I say, at a worde,
For it is tyme the pye were on the borde;
And go with a vengeance, and say thou art
    prayde.   425

[*Johan takes the pail and starts out.*]

SYR J.   A, good gossyp! is that well sayde?
TYB.   Welcome, myn owne swete harte!
We shall make some chere or we departe.[2]
JOHAN.   Cokkis soule, loke howe he ap-
    procheth nere
Unto my wyfe!   This abateth my chere.

[*Exit Johan with the pail.*]

SYR J.   By God, I wolde ye had harde the
    tryfyls,   431
The toys, the mokkes, the fables, and the
    nyfyls,[3]
That I made thy husbande to beleve and
    thynke!
Thou myghtest as well into the erthe synke,
As thou coudest forbeare laughyng any
    whyle.   435
TYB.   I pray the, let me here parte of that
    wyle.[4]
SYR J.   Mary, I shall tell the as fast as I
    can —
But peas! no more; yonder cometh thy
    good man.

[*Re-enter Johan.*]

JOHAN.   Cokkis soule, what have we
    here!
As far as I sawe, he drewe very nere   440
Unto my wyfe.
TYB.   What, art come so sone?
Gyve us water to wasshe nowe; have
    done.

Than he bryngeth the payle empty.

JOHAN.   By kockes soule, it was even
    nowe full to the brynk,

---

[1] It was customary to wash the hands immediately before eating.
[2] Separate.   [3] Fictitious tales
[4] Wile, stratagem.

But it was out agayne or I coude thynke;
Wherof I marveled, by God Almyght.
And than I loked betwene me and the
    lyght,   446
And I spyed a clyfte, bothe large and
    wyde.
Lo, wyfe! here it is on the tone syde.
TYB.   Why dost not stop it?
JOHAN.   Why, howe shall I do it?
TYB.   Take a lytle wax.
JOHAN.   Howe shal I come to it?   450
SYR J.   Mary, here be ii wax candyls, I
    say,
Whiche my gossyp Margery gave me
    yesterday.
TYB.   Tusshe, let hym alone; for, by the
    rode,
It is pyte to helpe hym, or do hym
    good.
SYR J.   What! Johan Johan, canst thou
    make no shyfte?   455
Take this waxe, and stop therwith the
    clyfte.
JOHAN.   This waxe is as harde as any
    wyre.
TYB.   Thou must chafe it a lytle at the
    fyre.
JOHAN.   She that boughte the these waxe
    candelles twayne,
She is a good companyon certayn!   460

[*Johan goes to the fire to mend the pail.*]

TYB.   What, was it not my gossyp
    Margery?
SYR J.   Yes; she is a blessed woman,
    surely.
TYB.   Nowe wolde God I were as good as
    she,
For she is vertuous, and full of charyte.
JOHAN [*aside*].   Nowe, so God helpe me,
    and by my holydome,[1]   465
She is the erranst baud betwene this and
    Rome.
TYB.   What sayst?
JOHAN.   Mary, I chafe the wax,
And I chafe it so hard that my fyngers
    krakks.
But take up this py that I here torne;
And it stand long, y-wys, it wyll borne.
TYB [*removing the pie*].   Ye, but thou must
    chafe the wax, I say.   471

---

[1] Anything sacred; much used in oaths.

[*Johan approaches the table.*]

JOHAN. Byd hym syt down, I the pray —
Syt down, good Syr Johan, I you requyre.
TYB. Go, I say, and chafe the wax by the
fyre,
Whyle that we sup, Syr Johan and I. 475
JOHAN. And how now! what wyll ye do
with the py?
Shall I not ete therof a morsell?
TYB. Go, and chafe the wax whyle thou
art well!
And let us have no more pratyng thus.

[*Syr Johan starts to say grace.*]

SYR J. Benedicite —
JOHAN [*approaching*]. Dominus. 480
TYB. Now go chafe the wax, with a
myschyfe!
JOHAN. What! I come to blysse the
bord, swete wyfe.
It is my custome now and than.
Mych good do it you, Master Syr Johan.
TYB. Go chafe the wax, and here no
lenger tary. 485

[*Johan returns to the fire.*]

JOHAN [*aside*]. And is not this a very
purgatory —
To se folkis ete, and may not ete a byt?
By kokkis soule, I am a very wodcok.
This payle here, now a vengaunce take it!
Now my wyfe gyveth me a proud mok! 490
TYB [*eating*]. What dost?
JOHAN. Mary, I chafe the wax here,
And I ymagyn to make you good chere —
[*Aside.*] That a vengaunce take you both
as ye syt;
For I know well I shall not ete a byt.
But yet, in feyth, yf I myght ete one
morsell, 495
I wold thynk the matter went very well.
SYR J. [*eating*]. Gossyp Johan Johan, now
"mych good do it you!"
What chere make you, there by the fyre?
JOHAN. Master parson, I thank yow now,
I fare well inow after myne own desyre.
SYR J. What dost, Johan Johan, I the
requyre? 501
JOHAN. I chafe the wax here by the fyre.
TYB. Here is good drynk! and here is a
good py!

SYR J. We fare very well, thankyd be Our
Lady.
TYB. Loke how the kokold chafyth the
wax that is hard, 505
And, for his lyfe, daryth not loke hether-
ward.
SYR J. [*to Johan*]. What doth my gossyp?
JOHAN. I chafe the wax —
[*Aside.*] And I chafe it so hard that my
fyngers krakks;
And eke the smoke puttyth out my eyes
two:
I burne my face, and ray my clothys also,
And yet I dare not say one word; 511
And they syt laughyng yender at the bord.
TYB. Now, by my trouth, it is a prety
jape,[1]
For a wyfe to make her husband her ape.
Loke of Johan Johan, which maketh hard
shyft 515
To chafe the wax, to stop therwith the
clyft!
JOHAN [*aside*]. Ye, that a vengeaunce take
ye both two,
Both hym and the, and the and hym, also!
And that ye may choke with the same
mete
At the furst mursell that ye do ete. 520
TYB. Of what thyng now dost thou clat-
ter,[2]
Johan Johan? or whereof dost thou patter?
JOHAN. I chafe the wax, and make hard
shyft
To stopt her-with of the payll the ryft.
SYR J. So must he do, Johan Johan, by
my father kyn, 525
That is bound of wedlok in the yoke.
JOHAN [*aside*]. Loke how the pyld preest
crammyth in;
That wold to God he myght therwith
choke!
TYB. Now, Master Parson, pleasyth your
goodnes
To tell us some tale of myrth or sadnes 530
For our pastyme, in way of communyca-
cyon?
SYR J. I am content to do it for our recre-
acyon;
And of iii myracles I shall to you say.

[1] Jest.
[2] R. misprints *clatier;* at line 523 *thafe* for *chafe;* at
line 600 *notwithstankyng;* and at line 661 *nonght.*

JOHAN. What! must I chafe the wax all day,
And stond here, rostyng by the fyre? 535
SYR J. Thou must do somwhat at thy wyves desyre.
I know a man whych weddyd had a wyfe, —
As fayre a woman as ever bare lyfe, —
And within a senyght after, ryght sone,
He went beyond se, and left her alone, 540
And taryed there about a vii yere.
And as he cam homeward he had a hevy chere,
For it was told hym that she was in heven.
But when that he comen home agayn was,
He found his wyfe, and with her chyldren seven, 545
Whiche she had had in the mene space —
Yet had she not had so many by thre
Yf she had not had the help of me.
Is not this a myracle, yf ever were any,
That this good wyfe shuld have chyldren so many 550
Here in this town, whyle her husband shuld be
Beyond the se, in a farre contre?
JOHAN [aside]. Now, in good soth, this is a wonderous myracle!
But for your labour, I wolde that your tacle
Were in a skaldyng water well sod.[1] 555
TYB. Peace, I say; thou lettest the worde of God.
SIR J. An other myracle eke I shall you say,
Of a woman whiche that many a day
Had ben wedded, and in all that season
She had no chylde, nother doughter nor son. 560
Wherfore to Saynt Modwin she went on pilgrimage,
And offered there a lyve pyg, as is the usage
Of the wyves that in London dwell;
And through the vertue therof, truly to tell,
Within a moneth after, ryght shortly, 565
She was delyvered of a chylde as moche as I.
How say you, is not this myracle wonderous?
JOHAN. Yes, in good soth, syr, it is marvelous.

But surely, after myn opynyon,
That chylde was nother doughter nor son.
For certaynly, and I be not begylde, 571
She was delyvered of a knave [1] chylde.
TYB. Peas, I say, for Goddis passyon!
Thou lettest Syr Johans communication.
SIR J. The thyrde myracle also is this:
I knewe another woman eke, y-wys, 576
Whiche was wedded, and within v monthis after
She was delyvered of a fayre doughter,
As well formed in every membre and joynt,
And as perfyte in every poynt, 580
As though she had gone v monthis full to th' ende.
Lo! here is v monthis of advantage.
JOHAN. A wonderous myracle, so God me mende!
I wolde eche wyfe that is bounde in maryage,
And that is wedded here within this place,
Myght have as quicke spede in every suche case. 586
TYB. Forsoth, Syr Johan, yet for all that
I have sene the day that pus, my cat,
Hath had in a yere kytlyns eyghtene.
JOHAN. Ye, Tyb my wyfe, and that have I sene. 590
But howe say you, Syr Johan, was it good, your pye?
The dyvell the morsell that therof eate I.
By the good Lorde, this is a pyteous warke.
But nowe I se well the olde proverbe is treu:
"The parysshe preest forgetteth that ever he was clarke!" 595
But, Syr Johan, doth not remembre you
How I was your clerke, and holpe you masse to syng,
And hylde the basyn alway at the offryng?
Ye [2] never had halfe so good a clarke as I!
But, notwithstandyng all this, nowe our pye 600
Is eaten up, there is not lefte a byt;
And you two together there do syt,
Eatynge and drynkynge at your owne desyre,
And I am Johan Johan, whiche must stande by the fyre
Chafyng the wax, and dare none other wyse do. 6c5

---

[1] Boiled.

[1] Male (with pun).   [2] P. prints He.

Syr J. And shall we alway syt here styll,
    we two?
That were to mych.
Tyb.   Then ryse we out of this place.
Syr J. And kys me than in the stede of
    grace.[1]
And farewell, leman,[2] and my love so dere.
Johan. Cokkis body, this waxe it waxte
    colde agayn here.   610
But what! shall I anone go to bed,
And eate nothyng, nother meate nor brede?
I have not be wont to have suche fare.
Tyb. Why! were ye not served there as ye
    are,
Chafyng the waxe, standyyng by the
    fyre?   615
Johan. Why, what mete gave ye me, I
    you requyre?
Sir J. Wast thou not served, I pray the
    hartely,
Both with the brede, the ale, and the pye?
Johan. No, syr, I had none of that fare.
Tyb. Why! were ye not served there as ye
    are,   620
Standyng by the fyre chafyng the waxe?
Johan [aside]. Lo, here be many tryfyls
    and knakks —
By kokkis soule, they wene I am other
    dronke or mad!
Tyb. And had ye no meate, Johan Johan?
    no had?
Johan. No, Tyb my wyfe, I had not a
    whyt.   625
Tyb. What, not a morsel?
Johan.   No, not one byt.
For honger, I trowe, I shall fall in a sowne.[3]
Sir J. O, that were pyte, I swere by my
    crowne.
Tyb. But is it trewe?
Johan.   Ye, for a surete.
Tyb. Dost thou ly?
Johan.   No, so mote I the![4] 630
Tyb. Hast thou had nothyng?
Johan.   No, not a byt.
Tyb. Hast thou not dronke?
Johan.   No, not a whyt.
Tyb. Where wast thou?
Johan.   By the fyre I dyd stande.
Tyb. What dydyst?

Johan.   I chafed this waxe in my hande,
Where-as I knewe of wedded men the
    payne   635
That they have, and yet dare not com-
    playne;
For the smoke put out my eyes two,
I burned my face, and rayde my clothes
    also,
Mendyng the payle, whiche is so rotten and
    olde   639
That it wyll not skant together holde.
And syth it is so, and syns that ye twayn
Wold gyve me no meate for my suffys-
    aunce,
By kokis soule, I wyll take no lenger
    payn!
Ye shall do all your-self, with a very
    vengaunce,
For me. And take thou there thy payle
    now,   645
And yf thou canst mend it, let me se how.

[Hurls the pail to the floor.]

Tyb. A! horson knave! hast thou brok
    my payll?
Thou shalt repent, by kokis lylly nayll.[1]
Rech me my dystaf, or my clyppyng-
    sherys!
I shall make the blood ronne about his
    erys.   650

[Johan takes up a shovel full of coals.]

Johan. Nay, stand styll, drab, I say, and
    come no nere;
For, by kokkis blood, yf thou come here,
Or yf thou onys styr toward this place,
I shall throw this shovyll full of colys in thy
    face.
Tyb. Ye! horson dryvyll! get the out of
    my dore!   655
Johan. Nay! get thou [2] out of my house,
    thou prestis hore!
Sir J. Thou lyest, horson kokold, evyn to
    thy face!
Johan. And thou lyest, pyld preest, with
    an evyll grace!
Tyb. And thou lyest!
Johan.   And thou lyest!
Syr J.   And thou lyest agayn!

---

[1] The grace at the end of the meal.
[2] Sweetheart.   [3] Swoon.
[4] May I thrive.

---

[1] By God's lovely nail (alluding either to the nails
used in the crucifixion, or to the fingers).
[2] R. *thy.* P. prints *thou* without note.

JOHAN. By kokkis soule, horson preest,
thou shalt be slayn. 660
Thou hast eate our pye, and gyve me
nought.
By kokkes blod, it shalbe full derely
bought!
TYB. At hym, Syr Johan, or els God gyve
the sorow.
JOHAN. And have at you,[1] hore and thefe,
Saynt George to borrow! [2]

*Here they fyght by the erys a whyle, and
than the preest and the wyfe go out of the
place.*

JOHAN. A! syrs! I have payd some of
them even as I lyst. 665
They have borne many a blow with my
fyst.

[1] R. *your.*   [2] Saint George speed me!

I thank God, I have walkyd them well,
And dryven them hens. But yet, can ye
tell
Whether they be go? For, by God, I fere
me
That they be gon together, he and she, 670
Unto his chamber; and perhappys she
wyll,
Spyte of my hart, tary there styll;
And, peradventure, there he and she
Wyll make me cokold, evyn to anger me.
And then had I a pyg in the woyrs pan-
yer! [1] 675
Therfore, by God, I wyll hye me thyder
To se yf they do me any vylany.
And thus, fare well this noble company!
[*Exit Johan Johan after his wife and the
priest.*]

[1] In the worse basket.

FINIS

Impryntyd by Wyllyam Rastell the xii day
of February the yere of our Lord
MCCCCC and XXXIII.
Cum privilegio.

THE PLAY OF THE WETHER [1]

A NEW AND A VERY MERY ENTERLUDE OF ALL MANER WETHERS

Made by JOHN HEYWOOD

THE PLAYERS NAMES

IUPITER, a god.	THE WATER-MYLLER.
MERY-REPORTE, the vyce.	THE WYNDE-MYLLER.
THE GENTYLMAN.	THE GENTYLWOMAN.
THE MARCHAUNT.	THE LAUNDER.
THE RANGER.	A BOY, the lest that can play.

[*Jupyter speaks from his throne.*]

JUPYTER. Ryght farre to longe, as now,
were to recyte
The [1] auncyent estate wherein our selfe
hath reyned,
What honour, what laude, gyven us of very
ryght,
What glory we have had, dewly unfayned,
Of eche creature, whych dewty hath con-
strayned. 5
For above all goddes, syns our fathers
fale, [2]
We, Iupiter, were ever pryncypale.

If we so have ben — as treuth yt is in-
dede —
Beyond the compas of all comparyson,
Who coulde presume to shew, for any
mede, [3] 10

So that yt myght appere to humayne
reason
The hye renowme we stande in at this
season?
For, syns that heven [1] and erth were fyrste
create,
Stode we never in suche tryumphaunt
estate 14

As we now do. Whereof we woll reporte
Suche parte as we se mete for tyme present,
Chyefely concernynge your perpetuall con-
forte,
As the thynge selfe shall prove in expery-
ment;
Whyche hyely shall bynde you, on knees
lowly bent,
Soolly to honour oure hyenes, day by
day. 20
And now to the mater gyve eare, and we
shall say:

[1] A. *That.*   [2] The fall of Saturn.
[3] Reward, recompense.

[1] R. *heueu.*

---

[1] For a notice of the author, and date, see page 367, note 1.
The first edition was issued by William Rastell in 1533. The printer seems to have had excellent copy (possibly the author's own manuscript), and his text is unusually good. An undated edition, attributed to Robert Wyer, was printed from Rastell's edition; and another, by Anthony Kytson (without date, but between 1549 and 1579) was printed from Wyer. These two later editions have no textual value. In 1906 there was discovered in Ireland still another edition, printed by John Awdeley (without date, but between 1559 and 1575). My collation shows this to be perhaps the poorest of all the editions; innumerable errors are introduced by a slovenly type-setter, and at times whole lines are dropped.
I have reproduced Rastell's edition of 1533 (R.). Mr. A. W. Pollard's reprint (P.) of the same copy of this edition, in *Representative English Comedies*, 1903, is very unsatisfactory, due, probably, to the initial troubles he had in securing copy, and to the difficulty of reading proof in a book printed across the ocean. Only occasionally have I noted readings from the edition by Awdeley (A.). I have modernized the punctuation, and the use of the letters u and v; and I have normalized the catch-names of the speakers.

Before our presens, in our hye parlyament,
Both goddes and goddeses of all degrees
Hath late assembled, by comen assent,
For the redres of certayne enormytees, 25
Bred amonge them thorow extremytees
Abusyd in eche to other of them all;
Namely, to purpose, in these moste spe-
    cyall:

Our forsayde father Saturne, and Phebus,
Eolus, and Phebe, these four [1] by name,
Whose natures not onely so farre contrary-
    ous, 31
But also of malyce eche other to defame,
Have longe tyme abused, ryght farre out of
    frame,
The dew course of all theyr constellacyons,
To the great damage of all yerthly na-
    cyons. 35

Whyche was debated in place sayde be-
    fore;
And fyrste (as became), our father, moste
    auncyent,
With berde whyte as snow, his lockes both
    colde and hore,
Hath entred [2] such mater as served his en-
    tent,[3]
Laudynge his frosty mansyon in the fyrma-
    ment, 40
To ayre and yerth as thynge moste pre-
    cyous,
Pourgynge all humours that are conta-
    gyous.

How-be-yt, he alledgeth that of longe tyme
    past
Lyttell hath prevayled his great dylygens.
Full oft uppon yerth his fayre frost he hath
    cast, 45
All thynges hurtfull to banysh out of
    presens;
But Phebus, entendynge to kepe hym in
    sylens,
When he hath labored all nyght in his
    powres,[4]
His glarynge beamys maryth all in two
    howres.

Phebus to this made no maner answer-
    ynge. 50
Whereuppon they both then Phebe defyed.
Eche for his parte leyd in her reprovynge
That by her showres superfluous they have
    tryed [1]
In all that she may theyr powres be de-
    nyed.
Wherunto Phebe made answere no more
Then Phebus to Saturne hadde made be-
    fore. 56

Anone uppon Eolus all these dyd fle,
Complaynynge theyr causes, eche one
    arow,[2]
And sayd, to compare none was so evyll as
    he;
For, when he is dysposed his blastes to
    blow, 60
He suffereth neyther sone-shyne, rayne,
    nor snow.
They eche agaynste other, and he agaynste
    all thre —
Thus can these iiii in no maner agre!

Whyche sene in themselfe, and further con-
    syderynge,
The same to redres was cause of theyr as-
    semble. 65
And also — that we evermore beynge,
Besyde our puysaunt power of deite,
Of wysedome and nature so noble and so
    fre,
From all extremytees the meane devyd-
    ynge,
To pease and plente eche thynge attemper-
    ynge — 70

They have, in conclusyon, holly surrendryd
Into our handes, as mych as concernynge
All maner wethers by them engendryd,
The full of theyr powrs, for terme everlast-
    ynge,
To set suche order as standyth wyth our
    pleasynge; 75
Whyche thynge, as of our parte no parte re-
    quyred,
But of all theyr partys ryght humbly de-
    syred

To take uppon us; wherto we dyd assente.

---

[1] Representing cold, heat, wind, and rain respectively.
[2] Introduced (entered upon record).
[3] Purpose.
[4] Powers (i.e. spreading frost and snow).

[1] Found by experience.   [2] In turn.

And so in all thynges, wyth one voyce agre-
able,
We have clerely fynyshed our foresayd
parleament, 80
To your great welth,[1] whyche shall be
fyrme and stable,
And to our honour farre inestymable;
For syns theyr powers, as ours, addyd to
our owne,
Who can, we say, know us as we shulde be
knowne?

But now, for fyne,[2] the rest of our entent
Wherfore, as now, we hyther are dy-
scendyd 86
Is onely to satysfye and content
All maner people whyche have ben of-
fendyd
By any wether mete to be amendyd;
Uppon whose complayntes, declarynge
theyr grefe, 90
We shall shape remedy for theyr relefe.

And to gyve knowledge for theyr hyther
resorte
We wolde thys afore proclaymed to be
To all our people, by some one of thys
sorte,[3]
Whom we lyste to choyse here amongest
all ye. 95
Wherfore eche man avaunce, and we shal
se
Whyche of you is moste mete to be our
cryer.

Here entreth Mery-reporte.[4]

MERY-REPORTE. Brother, holde up your
torche a lytell hyer![5]
Now, I beseche you, my lorde, loke on me
furste.
I truste your lordshyp shall not fynde me
the wurste. 100
JUPYTER. Why! what arte thou that ap-
prochyst so ny?
MERY-REPORTE. Forsothe, and please
your lordshyppe, it is I.
JUPYTER. All that we knowe very well;
but what I?

MERY-REPORTE. What I? Some saye I
am I perse I.[1]
But, what maner I so ever be I, 105
I assure your good lordshyp, I am I.
JUPYTER. What maner man arte thou,
shewe quyckely!
MERY-REPORTE. By god! a poore gentyl-
man, dwellyth here by.
JUPYTER. A gentylman! Thyselfe bryng-
eth wytnes naye,
Bothe in thy lyght behavour and araye.110
But what arte thou called where thou dost
resorte?
MERY-REPORTE. Forsoth, my lorde,
Mayster Mery-reporte.
JUPYTER. Thou arte no mete man in our
bysynes,
For thyne apparence ys of to mych lyght-
nes.
MERY-REPORTE. Why, can not your lord-
shyp lyke my maner, 115
Myne apparell, nor my name nother?
JUPYTER. To nother of all we have devo-
cyon.
MERY-REPORTE. A proper lycklyhod of
promocyon!
Well, than, as wyse as ye seme to be,
Yet can ye se no wysdome in me. 120
But syns ye dysprayse me for so lyghte an
elfe,
I praye you gyve me leve to prayse my-
selfe.
And, for the fyrste parte, I wyll begyn
In my behavour at my commynge in;
Wherin I thynke I have lytell offendyd, 125
For, sewer, my curtesy coulde not be
amendyd!
And, as for my sewt your servaunt to be,
Myghte yll have bene myst for your hon-
este;
For, as I be saved, yf I shall not lye,
I saw no man sew for the offyce but I! 130
Wherfore yf ye take me not or I go,
Ye must anone whether ye wyll or no.
And syns your entent is but for the wethers,
What skyls[2] our apparell to be fryse[3] or
fethers?
I thynke it wysdome, syns no man for-bad
it, 135

Wyth thys to spare a better — yf I had it!
And, for my name: reportyng alwaye
    trewly,
What hurte to reporte a sad mater merely?
As, by occasyon, for the same entent,
To a serteyne wedow thys daye was I
    sent,   140
Whose husbande departyd wythout her
    wyttynge,[1] —
A specyall good lover, and she hys owne
    swettynge! [2]
To whome, at my commyng, I caste suche
    a fygure,
Mynglynge the mater accordynge to my
    nature,
That when we departyd,[3] above al other
    thynges   145
She thanked me hartely for my mery tyd-
    ynges!
And yf I had not handled yt meryly,
Perchaunce she myght have take[n] yt
    hevely;
But in suche facyon I coniured and bounde
    her,
That I left her meryer then I founde
    her!   150
What man may compare to shew the lyke
    comforte
That dayly is shewed by me, Mery-reporte?
And, for your purpose at this tyme ment,
For all wethers I am so indyfferent,[4]
Without affeccyon, standynge so up-
    ryght,[5]   155
Son-lyght, mone-lyght, ster-lyght, twy-
    lyght, torch-light,
Cold, hete, moyst, drye, hayle, rayne,
    frost, snow, lightnyng, thunder,
Cloudy, mysty, wyndy, fayre, fowle above
    hed or under,
Temperate, or dystemperate, what-ever yt
    be,
I promyse your lordshyp, all is one to
    me.   160

JUPYTER.   Well, sonne, consydrynge thyne
    indyfferency,
And partely the rest of thy declaracyon,
We make the our servaunte. And immedy-
    ately

We [1] woll thou departe and cause procla-
    macyon,
Publyshynge our pleasure to every na-
    cyon;   165
Whyche thynge ons done, wyth all dyly-
    gens
Make thy returne agayne to this presens,

Here to receyve all sewters of eche degre;
And suche as to the may seme moste
    metely,
We wyll thow brynge them before our
    maieste;   170
And for the rest, that be not so worthy,
Make thou reporte to us effectually,
So that we may heare eche maner sewte at
    large.
Thus se thow departe, and loke uppon thy
    charge!

MERY-REPORTE.   Now, good my lorde
    god, Our Lady be wyth ye!   175

    [To the audience.]

Frendes, a fellyshyppe,[2] let me go by ye!
Thynke ye I may stand thrustyng amonge
    you there?
Nay, by god, I muste thrust about other
    gere!

Mery-reporte goth out [to make proclama-
    tion].

At thende of this staf [3] the god hath a song
    played in his trone or Mery-report come in.

JUPYTER.   Now, syns we have thus farre
    set forth our purpose,
A whyle we woll wythdraw our godly pres-
    ens,   180
To enbold all such more playnely to dys-
    close,
As here wyll attende, in our foresayde
    pretens.
And now, accordynge to your obedyens,
Reioyce ye in us wyth ioy most ioyfully,
And we our-selfe shall ioy in our owne
    glory!   185

    [Jupyter draws a curtain about his throne,
    thus concealing himself from the audience;
    thereafter the song is played.]

---

[1] Knowing it.   [2] Sweeting, darling.
[3] Separated   [4] Impartial.
[5] This line omitted in A.

[1] R. Well; A. We.
[2] Out of friendly feeling   [5] Stanza

Mery-report cometh in.

MERY-REPORTE. Now, syrs, take hede!
for here cometh goddes servaunt!
Avaunte! carte[r]ly [1] keytyfs, avaunt!
Why, ye dronken horesons, wyll yt not be?
By your fayth, have ye nother cap nor kne?
Not one of you that wyll make curtsy 190
To me, that am squyre for goddes precyous
body?
Regarde ye nothynge myne authoryte?
No "Welcome home!" nor "Where have
ye be?'
How-be-yt, yf ye axyd, I coulde not well
tell;
But suer I thynke a thousande myle from
hell, 195
And, on my fayth, I thynke, in my con-
scyens,
I have ben from hevyn as farre as heven is
hens —
At Lovyn, at London, and in Lombardy,
At Baldock, at Barfolde, and in Barbary,
At Canturbery, at Coventre, at Colches-
ter, 200
At Wansworth, and Welbecke, at West-
chester,
At Fullam, at Faleborne, and at Fenlow,
At Wallyngford, at Wakefeld, and at Wal-
tamstow,
At Tawnton, at Typtre, and at Totnam,
At Glouceter, at Gylford, and at Gotham,
At Hartforde, at Harwyche, at Harowe on
the Hyll, 206
At Sudbery, Suthhampton, at Shoters
Hyll,
At Walsyngham, at Wyttam, and at Wer-
wycke,
At Boston, at Brystow, and at Berwycke,
At Gravelyn, at Gravesend, and at Glas-
tynbery, 210
Ynge Gyngiang Iayberd, the paryshe of
Butsbery —
The devyll hym-selfe, wythout more lea-
sure,
Coulde not have gone halfe thus myche, I
am sure!
But, now I have warned [2] them, let them
even chose;
For, in fayth, I care not who wynne or
lose. 215

[1] Rude. (A. *carterly.*) [2] Given them notice.

*Here the gentylman before he cometh in blow-
eth his horne.*

MERY-REPORTE. Now, by my trouth, this
was a goodly hearyng!
I went [1] yt had ben the gentylwomens
blowynge;
But yt is not so, as I now suppose,
For womens hornes sounde more in a man-
nys nose.
GENTYLMAN. Stande ye mery, my
frendes, everychone. 220
MERY-REPORTE. Say that to me and let
the reste alone!
Syr, ye be welcome, and all your meyny. [2]
GENTYLMAN. Now, in good sooth, my
frende, god a mercy!
And syns that I mete the here thus by
chaunce,
I shall requyre the of further acqueynt-
aunce; 225
And brevely to shew the, this is the mater:
I come to sew to the great god Iupyter
For helpe of thynges concernynge my rec-
reacyon,
Accordynge to his late proclamacyon.
MERY-REPORTE. Mary, and I am he that
this must spede. 230
But fyrste tell me, what be ye in-dede?
GENTYLMAN. Forsoth, good frende, I am
a gentylman.
MERY-REPORTE. A goodly occupacyon,
by Seynt Anne!
On my fayth, your mashyp [3] hath a mery
lyfe.
But who maketh all these hornes, your self
or your wife? [4] 235
Nay, even in earnest I aske you this ques-
tyon.
GENTYLMAN. Now, by my trouth, thou
art a mery one!
MERY-REPORTE. In fayth, of us both I
thynke never one sad,
For I am not so mery but ye seme as
mad!
But stande ye styll and take a lyttell
payne; 240
I wyll come to you, by and by, agayne.

[1] Thought.
[2] Attendants. Possibly the Gentylman was attended by hunters leadïng dogs.
[3] Mastership.
[4] Alluding to the horns of the cuckold.

[He approches Jupyter's throne.]

Now, gracyous god, yf your wyll so be,
I pray ye let me speke a worde wyth ye.
JUPYTER.   My sonne, say on! Let us here
      thy mynde.
MERY-REPORTE.   My lord, there standeth
      a sewter even here behynde,   245
A Gentylman, in yonder corner;
And, as I thynke, his name is Mayster
      Horner.
A hunter he is, and comyth to make you
      sporte.
He wolde hunte a sow or twayne out of
      thys sorte.[1]

Here he poynteth to the women.

JUPYTER.   What-so-ever his mynde be, let
      hym appere.   250
MERY-REPORTE.   Now, good Mayster
      Horner, I pray you come nere.
GENTYLMAN.   I am no horner,[2] knave! I
      wyll thou know yt.
MERY-REPORTE.   I thought ye had [been],
      for when ye dyd blow yt,
Harde I never horeson make horne so
      goo.
As lefe ye kyste myne ars as blow my hole
      soo!   255
Come on your way, before the God Iupy-
      ter,
And there for your selfe ye shall be
      sewter.

[He leads him to the throne of Jupyter.]

GENTYLMAN.   Most myghty prynce, and
      god of every nacyon,
Pleasyth your hyghnes to vouchsave the
      herynge
Of me, whyche, accordynge to [y]our[3]
      proclamacyon,   260
Doth make apparaunce, in way of besech-
      ynge
Not sole for my-self, but generally
For all come of noble and auncyent stock,
Whych sorte above all doth most thank-
      fully
Dayly take payne for welth of the comen
      flocke,[4]   265

With dylygent study alway devysynge
To kepe them in order and unyte,
In peace to labour the encrees of theyr lyv-
      ynge,
Wherby eche man may prosper in plente.
Wherfore, good god, this is our hole desyr-
      ynge,   270
That for ease of our paynes, at tymes
      vacaunt,[1]
In our recreacyon, whyche chyefely is
      huntynge,
It may please you to sende us wether pleas-
      aunt,
Drye and not mysty, the wynde calme and
      styll,
That after our houndes yournynge[2] so
      meryly,   275
Chasynge the dere over dale and hyll,
In herynge we may folow and to-comfort
      the cry.
JUPYTER.   Ryght well we do perceyve
      your hole request,
Whyche shall not fayle to reste in mem-
      ory.
Wherfore we wyll ye set your-selfe at
      rest,   280
Tyll we have herde eche man indyfferently;
And we shall take suche order, unyversally,
As best may stande to our honour infynyte,
For welth in commune and ech mannys
      synguler profyte.
GENTYLMAN.   In heven and yerth hon-
      oured be the name   285
Of Iupyter, who[3] of his godly goodnes
Hath set this mater in so goodly frame
That every wyght shall have his desyre,
      doutles.
And fyrst for us nobles and gentylmen, 289
I doute not, in his wysedome, to provyde
Suche wether as in our huntynge, now and
      then,
We may both teyse[4] and receyve[5] on
      every syde.
Whyche thynge ones had, for our seyd rec-
      reacyon,
Shall greatly prevayle[6] you in preferrynge
      our helth.
For what thynge more nedefull then our
      preservacyon,   295

---

[1] I.e., the audience   [2] Cuckold.
[3] R. *our*; A. *your*.
[4] The common people as opposed to the gentry.

[1] Idle; leisure time.   [2] Running.
[3] R. *whome*.   [4] Drive, chase
[5] Bring down the game.   [6] Avail, profit.

Beynge the weale and heddes of all comen-
        welth?

MERY-REPORTE. Now I besech your
        mashyp, whose hed be you?

GENTYLMAN. Whose hed am I? Thy
        hed! What seyst thou now?

MERY-REPORTE. Nay, I thynke yt very
        trew, so god me helpe! 299

For I have ever ben, of a lyttell whelpe,
So full of fansyes, and in so many fyttes,
So many smale reasons, and in so many
        wyttes,
That, even as I stande, I pray god I be dede
If ever I thought them all mete for one
        hede. 304

But syns I have one hed more then I knew,
Blame not my reioycynge, — I love all
        thynges new.

And suer yt is a treasour of heddes to have
        store.

One feate can I now that I never coude be-
        fore.

GENTYLMAN. What is that?

MERY-REPORTE. By god, syns ye came
        hyther, 309

can set my hedde and my tayle to-gyther!
This hed shall save mony, by Saynt Mary;
From hens-forth I wyll no potycary;
For at al tymys, when suche thynges shall
        myster,[1]
My new hed shall geve myne olde tayle a
        glyster.[2]

And, after all this, then shall my hedde
        wayte 315

Uppon my tayle, and there stande at
        receyte.

Syr, for the reste I wyll not now move you;
But yf we lyve, ye shall smell how I love
        yow.

And, syr, touchyng your sewt here, depart
        when it please you;

For, be ye suer, as I can I wyll ease you. 320

GENTYLMAN. Then gyve me thy hande!
        That promyse I take.

And yf for my sake any sewt thou do make,
promyse thy payne to be requyted
More largely than now shall be recyted.

[Exit the Gentylman.]

MERY-REPORTE. Alas, my necke! God-
        des pyty, where is my hed? 325

[1] Be necessary. [2] Purge.

By Saynt Yve, I feare me I shall be ded!
And yf I were, me-thynke yt were no
        wonder,
Syns my hed and my body is so farre
        asonder.

Entreth the Marchaunt.

Mayster person,[1] now welcome, by my
        lyfe!
I pray you, how doth my mastres, your
        wyfe?[2] 330

MARCHAUNT. Syr, for the presthod, and
        wyfe that ye alledge,
I se ye speke more of dotage then knowl-
        edge.

But let pas, syr. I wolde to you be sewter
To brynge me, yf ye can, before Iupiter.

[MERY-REPORTE.] Yes, mary, can I; and
        wyll do yt, in-dede. 335

Tary, and I shall make wey for your spede.

[Goes to the throne of Jupyter.]

In fayth, good lord, yf it please your gra-
        cyous godshyp,
I muste have a worde or twayne wyth your
        lordshyp!
Syr, yonder is a nother man in place,
Who maketh great sewt to speke wyth your
        grace. 340

Your pleasure ones knowen, he commeth
        by and by.[3]

JUPYTER. Bryng hym before our presens,
        sone, hardely.

MERY-REPORTE. Why! where be you?
        Shall I not fynde ye?
Come a-way! I pray god, the devyll
        blynde ye!

[He leads him to the throne.]

MARCHAUNT. Moste myghty prynce, and
        lorde of lordes all, 345

Ryght humbly besecheth your maieste
Your marchaunt-men thorow the worlde
        all,
That yt may please you, of your benyg-
        nyte,
In the dayly daunger of our goodes and
        lyfe,

[1] Parson; perhaps suggested by the merchant's
long cloak.
[2] The clergy were supposed to be celibate, hence
the witticism.
[3] At once.

Fyrste to consyder the desert of our request,   350
What welth we bryng the rest, to our great
care and stryfe,
And then to rewarde us as ye shall thynke
best.
What were the surplysage of eche com-
modyte [1]
Whyche groweth and encreaseth in every
lande,   354
Excepte exchaunge by suche men as we be,
By wey of entercours, that lyeth on our
hande! [2]
We fraught [3] from home thynges wherof
there is plente,
And home we brynge such thynges as
there be scant.
Who sholde afore us marchauntes ac-
compted be?
For were not we, the worlde shuld wyshe
and want   360
In many thynges, whych now shall lack re-
hersall.
And, brevely to conclude, we beseche your
hyghnes
That of the benefyte proclaymed in gen-
erall
We may be parte-takers, for comen
encres,
Stablyshynge wether thus, pleasynge your
grace;   365
Stormy nor mysty, the wynde mesurable,
That savely we may passe from place to
place,
Berynge our seylys for spede moste vayle-
able. [4]
And also the wynde to chaunge, and to
turne
Eest, West, North, and South, as best may
be set;   370
In any one place not to longe to soiourne,
For the length of our vyage may lese our
market.
JUPYTER. Ryght well have ye sayde; and
we accept yt so,
And so shall we rewarde you ere we go
hens.
But ye muste take pacyens tyll we have
harde mo, [5]   375

---

[1] The over-abundance of each article of commerce.
[2] That we are unable to dispose of.
[3] Freight, convey as freight.
[4] Advantageous.   [5] Heard more suitors.

That we may indyfferently gyve sentens;
There may passe by us no spot of negly-
gence,
But iustely to iudge eche thynge so up-
ryghte
That ech mans parte maye shyne in the
selfe ryghte. [1]
MERY-REPORTE. Now, syr, by your fayth,
yf ye shulde be sworne,   380
Harde ye ever god speke so, syns ye were
borne?
So wysely, so gentylly hys wordes be
showd!
MARCHAUNT. I thanke hys grace. My
sewte is well bestowd.
MERY-REPORTE. Syr, what vyage entende
ye nexte to go?
MARCHAUNT. I truste or myd-lente to be
to Syo. [2]   385
MERY-REPORTE. Ha, ha! Is it your
mynde to sayle at Syo?
Nay, then, when ye wyll, byr lady, ye
maye go.
And let me alone with thys; be of good chere!
Ye maye truste me at Syo as well as here.
For though ye were fro me a thousande
myle space,   390
I wolde do as myche as ye were here in
place;
For, syns that from hens it is so farre
thyther,
I care not though ye never come agayne
hyther.
MARCHAUNT. Syr, yf ye remember me
when tyme shall come,
Though I requyte not all, I shall deserve
some.   395

Exeat Marchaunt.

MERY-REPORTE. Now, farre ye well, and
god thanke you, by Saynt Anne!
I pray you, marke the fasshyon of thys
honeste manne;
He putteth me in more truste at thys met-
ynge here,
Then he shall fynde cause why thys twenty
yere.

Here entreth the Ranger.

RANGER. God be here! Now Cryst kepe
thys company!   400

---

[1] Same equitable treatment.   [2] Chios.

MERY-REPORTE. In fayth, ye be welcome
evyn very skantely!
Syr, for your comynge what is the mater?
RANGER. I wolde fayne speke with the
god Iupyter.
MERY-REPORTE. That wyll not be. But
ye may do thys — 404
Tell me your mynde; I am an offycer of hys.
RANGER. Be ye so? Mary, I crye you
marcy!
Your maystershyp may say I am homely.[1]
But syns your mynde is to have reportyd
The cause wherfore I am now resortyd,
Pleasyth your maystershyp it is so: 410
I come for my-selfe and suche other mo,
Rangers [2] and kepers of certayne places,
As forestes, parkes, purlews, and chasys,[3]
Where we be chargyd with all maner game.
Smale is our profyte, and great is our
blame. 415
Alas! For our wages, what be we the
nere? [4]
What is forty shyllynges, or fyve marke, a
yere!
Many tymes and oft, where we be flyttynge,
We spende forty pens a pece at a syt-
tynge!
Now for our vauntage, whyche chefely is
wyndefale,[5] 420
That is ryght nought; there blowyth no
wynde at all.
Whyche is the thynge wherin we fynde
most grefe,
And cause for my commynge to sew for re-
lefe,
That the god, of pyty, all thys thynge
knowynge,
May sende us good rage of blustryng and
blowynge; 425
And yf I can not get god to do some good,
I wolde hyer the devyll to runne thorow the
wood,
The rootes to turne up, the toppys to
brynge under.
A myschyefe upon them, and a wylde
thunder!
MERY-REPORTE. Very well sayd! I set by
your charyte 430

As mych, in a maner, as by your honeste.
I shall set you somwhat in ease anone;
Ye shall putte on your cappe, when I am
gone.
For, I se, ye care not who wyn or lese,
So ye maye fynde meanys to wyn your
fees.[1] 435
RANGER. Syr, as in that, ye speke as it
please ye.
But let me speke wyth the god, yf it maye
be.

[*He tries to approach the throne.*]

I pray you, lette me passe ye.
MERY-REPORTE. Why, nay, syr! By the
masse, ye —
RANGER. Then wyll I leve you evyn as I
founde ye. 440
MERY-REPORTE. Go when ye wyll! No
man here hath bounde ye.

*Here entreth the Water Myller, and the
Ranger goth out.*

WATER MYLLER. What the devyll shold
skyl [2] though all the world were dum,
Syns in all our spekynge we never be
harde?
We crye out for rayne — the devyll sped
drop wyll cum! 444
We water myllers be nothynge in regarde.[3]
No water have we to grynde at any
stynt;
The wynde is so stronge the rayne cannot
fall,[4]
Whyche kepeth our myldams as drye as a
flynt.
We are undone! We grynde nothynge at
all! 449
The greter is the pyte, as thynketh me.
For what avayleth to eche man hys corne
Tyll it be grounde by such men as we be?
There is the losse, yf we be forborne.[5]
For, touchynge our-selfes, we are but
drudgys, 454
And very beggers — save onely our tole,
Whiche is ryght smale, and yet many
grudges
For gryste of a busshell to gyve a quarte
bole.[6]

---

[1] Rude, unmannerly.   [2] Keepers of forests.
[3] Hunting-grounds.
[4] Near our purpose, wishes.
[5] Trees blown down by the wind, which rangers
could sell for fuel.

---

[1] Perquisites.   [2] Matter.   [3] Estimation.
[4] This line omitted in A.
[5] Dispensed with.   [6] Quart bowl.

Yet, were not reparacyons,[1] we myght do
    wele:
Our mylstons, our whele with her kogges,
    and our trindill [2]
Our floodgate, our mylpooll, our water
    whele,   460
Our hopper, our extre,[3] our yren spynd-
    yll, —
In this, and mych more, so great is our
    charge
That we wolde not recke though no water
    ware;
Save onely it toucheth eche man so
    large,
And ech for our neyghbour Cryste byddeth
    us care.   465
Wherfore my conscyence hath prycked me
    hyther,
In thys to sewe, accordynge to the cry,[4]
For plente of rayne to the god Iupiter.
To whose presence I wyll go evyn boldely!

[*Mery-reporte bars his way.*]

MERY-REPORTE.   Sir, I dowt nothynge
    your audacyte,   470
But I feare me ye lacke capacyte;
For, yf ye were wyse, ye myghte well espye
How rudely ye erre from rewls of courtesye.
What! ye come in revelynge and reheyt-
    ynge,[5]
Evyn as a knave myght go to a beare-
    beytynge!   475
WATER MYLLER.   All you bere recorde
    what favour I have!
Herke, howe famylyerly he calleth me
    knave!
Dowtles the gentylman is universall!
But marke thys lesson, syr: You shulde
    never call
Your felow [6] knave, nor your brother hore-
    son;   480
For nought can ye get by it when ye have
    done.
MERY-REPORTE.   Thou arte nother brother
    nor felowe to me,
For I am goddes servaunt, mayst thou not
    se?
Wolde ye presume to speke wyth the great
    god?   484

Nay! dyscrecyon and you be to farre od!
Byr lady, these knavys must be tye
    shorter! [2]
Syr, who let you in?   Spake ye wyth th
    porter?
WATER MYLLER.   Nay, by my trouth; no
    wyth no nother man,
Yet I saw you well when I fyrst began. 48
How-be-it, so helpe me god and holydam,
I toke you but for a knave, as I am.
But, mary! now, syns I knowe what ye be
I muste, and wyll, obey your authoryte.
And yf I maye not speke wyth Iupiter,
I beseche you be my solycyter.   49
MERY-REPORTE.   As in that, I wyl be you
    well-wyller.
I perceyve you be a water myller;
And your hole desyre, as I take the mater
Is plente of rayne for encres of water. 49
The let [4] wherof, ye affyrme determynately
Is onely the wynde, your mortall enemy.
WATER MYLLER.   Trouth it is; for it blow
    yth so alofte,
We never have rayne, or, at the most, no
    ofte.
Wherfore, I praye you, put the god i
    mynde
Clerely for ever to banysh the wynde. 50

Here entreth the Wynd Myller.

WYNDE MYLLER.   How! Is all the wethe
    gone or I come?
For the passyon of god, helpe me to som
I am a wynd myller, as many mo be.
No wretch in wretchydnes so wrechyd a
    we!
The hole sorte [5] of my crafte be all mard a
    onys!   51
The wynde is so weyke it sturryth not ou
    stonys,
Nor skantely can shatter [6] the shyttyn say
That hangeth shatterynge [7] at a woma
    tayle.
The rayne never resteth, so longe be th
    showres,
From tyme of begynnyng tyll foure an
    twenty howres;   51
And, ende when it shall, at nyght or a
    none,

---

[1] Repairs.   [2] Lantern-wheel.
[3] Axletree of a wheel.   [4] Proclamation.
[5] Scolding.   [6] Equal.

[1] Separated.   [2] Restrained.
[3] Things sacred.   [4] Prevention, hindranc
[5] Particular class, order.
[6] Wave to and fro.   [7] Waving.

An-other begynneth as soone as that is done.

Such revell of rayne, ye knowe well inough,

Destroyeth the wynde, be it never so rough;

Wherby, syns our myllys be come to styll standynge,   520

Now maye we wynd myllers go evyn to hangynge.

A myller! Wyth a moryn [1] and a mys-chyefe!

Who wolde be a myller? As good be a thefe!

Yet in tyme past, when gryndynge was plente,   524

Who were so lyke goddys felows as we?

As faste as god made corne, we myllers made meale.

Whyche myght be best forborne [2] for comyn-weale?

But let that gere [3] passe; for I feare our pryde

Is cause of the care whyche god doth us provyde.   529

Wherfore I submyt me, entendynge to se

What comforte may come by humylyte.

And, now, at thys tyme, they sayd in the crye,

The god is come downe to shape remedye.

MERY-REPORTE. No doute he is here, even in yonder trone;   534

But in your mater he trusteth me alone.

Wherein, I do perceyve by your com-playnte,

Oppressyon of rayne doth make the wynde so faynte

That ye wynde myllers be clene caste away.

WYNDE MYLLER. If Iupyter helpe not, yt is as ye say.

But, in few wordes to tell you my mynde rounde;   540

Uppon this condycyon I wolde be bounde

Day by day to say Our Ladyes sauter [4] —

That in this world were no drope of water,

Nor never rayne, but wynde contynuall.

Then shold we wynde myllers be lordes over all!   545

MERY-REPORTE. Come on, and assay how you twayne can agre —

A brother of yours, a myller, as ye be!

WATER MYLLER. By meane of our craft we may be brothers,

But whyles we lyve shall we never be lovers.   549

We be of one crafte, but not of one kynde—

I lyve by water and he by the wynde.

Here Mery-report goth out.

And, syr, as ye desyre wynde contynuall,

So wolde I have rayne ever-more to fall;

Whyche two, in experyence ryght well ye se,

Ryght selde or never to-gether can be. 555

For as longe as the wynde rewleth, yt is playne,

Twenty to one ye get no drop of rayne;

And when the element is to farre opprest,

Downe commeth the rayne and setteth the wynde at rest.   559

By this, ye se, we can not both obtayne;

For ye must lacke wynde, or I must lacke rayne.

Wherfore I thynke good, before this audy-ens,

Eche for our selfe to say, or we go hens;

And whom is thought weykest, when we have fynysht,

Leve of[f] his sewt and content to be banysht.   565

WYNDE MYLLER. In fayth, agreed! But then, by your lycens,

Our mylles for a tyme shall hange in sus-pens.

Syns water and wynde is chyefely our sewt,

Whyche best may be spared we woll fyrst dyspute.

Wherfore to the see my reason shall re-sorte,   570

Where shyppes by meane of wynd try from port to port,

From lande to lande, in dystaunce many a myle, —

Great is the passage and smale is the whyle.

So great is the profyte, as to me doth seme,

That no mans wysdome the welth can ex-teme.[1]   575

And syns the wynde is conveyer of all

Who but the wynde shulde have thanke above all?

---

[1] Plague. [2] Spared, done away with.

[3] Matter. [4] Psalter.

[1] Value.

WATER MYLLER.   Amytte [1] in thys place
   a tree here to growe,
And therat the wynde in great rage to
   blowe;
When it hath all blowen, thys is a clere
   case,   580
The tre removyth no here-bred [2] from hys
   place.
No more wolde the shyppys, blow the best
   it cowde!
All-though it wolde blow downe both mast
   and shrowde,
Except the shyppe flete [3] uppon the water
The wynde can ryght nought do, — a
   playne mater.   585
Yet maye ye on water, wythout any
   wynde,
Row forth your vessell where men wyll
   have her synde.[4]
Nothynge more reioyceth the maryner
Then meane coolys [5] of wynde and plente
   of water;   589
For commenly the cause of every wracke
Is excesse of wynde where water doth lacke.
In rage of these stormys the perell is suche
That better were no wynde then so farre to
   muche.
WYNDE MYLLER.   Well, yf my reason in
   thys may not stande,   594
I wyll forsake the see and lepe to lande.
In every chyrche where goddys servyce is,
The organs beare brunt of halfe the quere,
   i-wys.
Whyche causyth the sounde, or [6] water or
   wynde?
More-over, for wynde thys thynge I
   fynde —   599
For the most parte all maner mynstrelsy,
By wynde they delyver theyr sound chefly.
Fyll me a bagpype of your water full,
As swetly shall it sounde as it were stuffyd
   with wull!
WATER MYLLER.   On my fayth, I thynke
   the moone be at the full!
For frantyke fansyes be then most plente-
   full,   605
Whych are at the pryde of theyr sprynge [7]
   in your hed,
So farre from our matter he is now fled.

As for the wynde in any instrument,
It is no percell [1] of our argument;   609
We spake of wynde that comyth naturally,
And that is wynde forcyd artyfycyally —
Whyche is not to purpose.   But, yf it were,
And water, in-dede, ryght nought coulde
   do there,
Yet I thynke organs no suche commod-
   yte [2]   614
Wherby the water shulde banyshed be.
And for your bagpypes, I take them as
   nyfuls.[3]
Your mater is all in fansyes and tryfuls.
WYNDE MYLLER.   By god, but ye shall
   not tryfull me of[f] so!
Yf these thynges serve not, I wyll reherse
   mo.
And now to mynde there is one olde prov-
   erbe come,   620
"One bushell of Marche dust is worth a
   kynges raunsome."
What is a hundreth thousande bushels
   worth than?
WATER MYLLER.   Not one myte, for the
   thynge selfe, to no man.
WYNDE MYLLER.   Why, shall wynde
   every-where thus be obiecte? [4]   624
Nay, in the hye-wayes he shall take effecte,
Where-as the rayne doth never good, but
   hurt;
For wynde maketh but dust, and water
   maketh durt.
Powder, or syrop, syrs, whyche lycke ye
   beste?
Who lycketh not the tone maye lycke up
   the rest.
But, sure, who-so-ever hath assayed such
   syppes   630
Had lever have dusty eyes then durty
   lyppes.
And it is sayd syns afore [5] we were borne
That "drought doth never make derth of
   corne."
And well it is knowen to the most foole
   here
How rayne hath pryced corne within this
   vii yere.[6]   635
WATER MYLLER.   Syr, I pray the, spare
   me a lytyll season,

---

[1] Admit.   [2] Hair-bredth.
[3] Float.   [4] Sent.   [5] Moderate breezes.
[6] R. of.   [7] Springtime.

[1] Part.   [2] Advantage.   [3] Trifles.
[4] Objected to.   [5] Before.
[6] Pollard notes the dearth and high price of corn
in 1523 and 1528.

And I shall brevely conclude [1] the wyth
    reason.

Put case on[e] somers daye wythout wynde
    to be,

And ragyous wynde in wynter dayes two or
    thre;

Mych more shall dry that one calme daye
    in somer,   640

Then shall those thre wyndy dayes in
    wynter.

Whom shall we thanke for thys, when all is
    done?

The thanke to wynde? Nay! Thanke
    chyefely the sone.

And so for drought, yf corne therby
    encres,

The sone doth comfort and rype all dowt-
    les.   645

And oft the wynde so leyth the corne, god
    wot,

That never after can it rype, but rot.

Yf drought toke place, as ye say, yet maye
    ye se,

Lytell helpeth the wynde in thys com-
    modyte.   649

But, now, syr, I deny your pryncypyll.

Yf drought ever were, it were impossybyll

To have ony grayne; for, or it can grow,

Ye must plow your lande, harrow, and
    sow, —

Whyche wyll not be, except ye maye have
    rayne   654

To temper the grounde; and after agayne,

For spryngynge and plumpyng [2] all maner
    corne,

Yet muste ye have water, or all is forlorne. [3]

Yf ye take water for no commodyte,

Yet must ye take it for thynge of neces-
    syte.

For washynge, for skowrynge, all fylth
    clensynge,   660

Where water lacketh what bestely beynge!

In brewyng, in bakynge, in dressynge of
    meate,

Yf ye lacke water what coulde ye drynke or
    eate?

Wythout water coulde lyve neyther man
    nor best,   664

For water preservyth both moste and lest.

For water coulde I say a thousande thynges
    mo,

Savynge as now the tyme wyll not serve so.

And as for that wynde that you do sew
    fore,

Is good for your wyndemyll, and for no
    more!   669

Syr, syth all thys in experyence is tryde,

I say thys mater standeth clere on my
    syde.

WYNDE MYLLER.   Well, syns thys wyll
    not serve, I wyll alledge the reste.

Syr, for our myllys, I saye myne is the
    beste.

My wyndmyll shall grynd more corne in
    one our

Then thy water-myll shall in thre or
    foure —   675

Ye, more then thyne shulde in a hole yere,

Yf thou myghtest have as thou hast
    wyshyd here.

For thou desyrest to have excesse of rayne,

Whych thyng to the[e] were the worst thou
    couldyst obtayne.

For, yf thou dydyst, it were a playne induc-
    cyon [1]   680

To make thyne owne desyer thyne owne
    destruccyon.

For in excesse of rayne at any flood

Your myllys must stande styll; they can do
    no good.

And whan the wynde doth blow the utter-
    most

Our wyndmylles walke a-mayne [2] in every
    cost. [3]   685

For, as we se the wynde in hys estate, [4]

We moder [5] our saylys after the same rate.

Syns our myllys grynde so farre faster then
    yours,

And also they may grynde all tymes and
    howrs,

I say we nede no watermylles at all,   690

For wyndmylles be suffycyent to serve all.

WATER MYLLER.   Thou spekest of "all"
    and consyderest not halfe!

In boste [6] of thy gryste thou art wyse as a
    calfe!

For, though above us your mylles grynde
    farre faster,

---

[1] Confute
[2] For causing to spring up and grow plump.
[3] Utterly lost.

---

[1] Initial step.   [2] Go with full force.   [3] Place
[4] State (blowing strongly or weakly).
[5] Adjust.   [6] Boast, praise.

What helpe to those from whome ye be
    myche farther?   695
And, of two sortes, yf the tone shold be
    conserved,[1]
I thynke yt mete the moste nomber be
    served.
In vales and weldes,[2] where moste com-
    modyte is,
There is most people; ye must graunte me
    this.
On hylles and downes, whyche partes are
    moste barayne,   700
There muste be few; yt can no mo sus-
    tayne.
I darre well say, yf yt were tryed even now,
That there is ten of us to one of you.
And where shuld chyefely all necessaryes
    be,   704
But there as people are moste in plente?
More reason that you come vii myle to
    myll
Then all we of the vale sholde clyme the
    hyll.
If rayne came reasonable, as I requyre yt,
We sholde of your wyndemylles have nede
    no whyt.

Entreth Mery-reporte.

MERY-REPORTE.   Stop, folysh knaves! for
    your reasonynge is suche,   710
That ye have resoned even ynough, and to
    much.
I hard all the wordes that ye both have
    hadde.
So helpe me god, the knaves be more then
    madde!
Nother of them both that hath wyt nor
    grace
To perceyve that both myllys may serve in
    place.   715
Betwene water and wynde there is no suche
    let
But eche myll may have tyme to use his
    fet.[3]
Whyche thynge I can tell by experyens;
For I have, of myne owne, not farre from
    hens,   719
In a corner to-gether, a couple of myllys,
Standynge in a marres[4] betwene two
    hyllys —

Not of inherytaunce, but by my wyfe;
She is feofed in the tayle for terme of her
    lyfe,
The one for wynde, the other for water.
And of them both, I thanke god, there
    standeth [1] nother;   725
For, in a good hour be yt spoken,
The water gate is no soner open,
But clap, sayth the wyndmyll, even
    strayght behynde!
There is good spedde the devyll and all
    they grynde!
But whether that the hopper be dusty, 730
Or that the mylstonys be sumwhat rusty,
By the mas, the meale is myschevous
    musty!
And yf ye thynke my tale be not trusty,
I make ye trew promyse: come, when ye
    lyst,
We shall fynde meane ye shall taste of the
    gryst.   735
WATER MYLLER.   The corne at recey&#t
    happely is not good.
MERY-REPORTE.   There can be no sweeter,
    by the sweet rood! [2]
Another thynge yet, whyche shall not be
    cloked,[3]
My watermyll many tymes is choked.
WATER MYLLER.   So wyll she be, though
    ye shuld burste your bones,   740
Except ye be perfyt in settynge your
    stones.
Fere not the lydger,[4] beware your ron-
    ner.[5]
Yet this for the lydger, or ye have wonne
    her —
Parchaunce your lydger doth lacke good
    peckyng.
MERY-REPORTE.   So sayth my wyfe; and
    that maketh all our checkyng.[6] 745
She wolde have the myll peckt, peckt,
    peckt, every day!
But, by god, myllers muste pecke when
    they may!
So oft have we peckt that our stones wax
    right thyn,
And all our other gere not worth a pyn;
For wyth peckynge and peckyng I have so
    wrought,   750

---

[1] Kept.   [2] Wealds.
[3] Its feat, its customary action.   [4] Marsh.

[1] Standeth idle.   [2] Cross.   [3] Concealed.
[4] The nether, and fixed, millstone.
[5] The upper, and moving, millstone.
[6] Quarreling.

That I have peckt a good peckynge-yron
    to nought.
How-be-yt, yf I stycke no better tyll her,
My wyfe sayth she wyll have a new myller.
But let yt passe! And now to our mater:
I say my myllys lacke nother wynde nor
    water;   755
No more do yours, as farre as nede doth re-
    quyre.
But, syns ye can not agree, I wyll desyre
Iupyter to set you both in suche rest
As to your welth and his honour may
    stande best.
WATER MYLLER.   I praye you hertely re-
    member me!   760
WYNDE MYLLER.   Let not me be forgotten,
    I beseche ye!

Both Myllers goth forth.

MERY-REPORTE.   If I remember you not
    both a-lyke
I wolde ye were over the eares in the dyke.
Now be we ryd of two knaves at one
    chaunce!
By Saynte Thomas, yt is a knavyshe ryd-
    daunce.   765

The Gentylwoman entreth.

GENTYLWOMAN.   Now, good god! what a
    foly is this?
What sholde I do where so mych people is?
I know not how to passe in to the god
    now.
MERY-REPORTE.   No, but ye know how he
    may passe into you.
GENTYLWOMAN.   I pray you let me in at
    the backe syde.   770
MERY-REPORTE.   Ye, shall I so and your
    foresyde so wyde?
Nay, not yet! But syns ye love to be
    alone,
We twayne wyll into a corner anone.
But fyrste, I pray you, come your way
    hyther,   774
And let us twayne chat a whyle to-gyther.
GENTYLWOMAN.   Syr, as to you I have
    lyttell mater.
My commynge is to speke wyth Iupiter.
MERY-REPORTE.   Stande ye styll a whyle,
    and I wyll go prove
Whether that the god wyll be brought in
    love.   779

[He goes to Jupyter's throne.]

My lorde, how nowe! Loke uppe lustely!
Here is a derlynge come, by Saynt Antony!
And yf yt be your pleasure to mary,
Speke quyckly, for she may not tary.
In fayth, I thynke ye may wynne her
    anone,[1]
For she wolde speke wyth your lordshyp
    alone.   785
JUPYTER.   Sonne, that is not the thynge at
    this tyme ment.
If her sewt concerne no cause of our hyther
    resorte,
Sende her out of place; but yf she be bent
To that purpose, heare her and make us re-
    porte.
MERY-REPORTE.   I count women lost, yf
    we love them not well,   790
For ye se god loveth them never a dele!
Maystres ye can not speake wyth the
    god.
GENTYLWOMAN.   No! why?
MERY-REPORTE.   By my fayth, for his
    lordshyp is ryght besy
Wyth a pece of worke that nedes must be
    doone.   794
Even now is he makynge of a new moone.
He sayth your olde moones be so farre
    tasted [2]
That all the goodnes of them is wasted;
Whyche of the great wete [3] hath ben moste
    mater,
For olde moones be leake; [4] they can holde
    no water.
But for this new mone, I durst lay my
    gowne,   800
Except a few droppes at her goyng downe,
Ye get no rayne tyll her arysynge —
Wythout yt nede, and then no mans devys-
    ynge
Coulde wyshe the fashyon of rayne to be so
    good;
Not gushynge out lyke gutters of Noyes
    flood,   805
But small droppes sprynklyng softly on the
    grounde;
Though they fell on a sponge they wold
    gyve no sounde.

[1] At once, quickly.
[2] Tried by tasting, or eating.
[3] Flood.   [4] Leaky.

This new moone shall make a thing spryng
  more in this while
Then a olde moone shal while a man may
  go a mile.
By that tyme the god hath all made an
  ende,   810
Ye shall se how the wether wyll amende.
By Saynt Anne, he goeth to worke even
  boldely!
I thynke hym wyse ynough; for he loketh
  oldely!
Wherfore, maystres, be ye now of good
  chere;
For though in his presens ye can not ap-
  pere,   815
Tell me your mater and let me alone;
May-happe I wyll thynke on you when you
  be gone.
GENTYLWOMAN.   Forsoth, the cause of my
  commynge is this:
I am a woman ryght fayre, as ye se;   819
In no creature more beauty then in me is.
And, syns I am fayre, fayre wolde I kepe
  me;
But the sonne in somer so sore doth burne
  me,
In wynter the wynde on every syde me,
No parte of the yere wote I where to turne
  me,
But even in my house am I fayne to hyde
  me.   825
And so do all other that beuty have.
In whose name at this tyme this sewt I
  make,
Besechynge Iupyter to graunt that I
  crave;
Whyche is this: that yt may please hym,
  for our sake,   829
To sende us wether close and temperate,
No sonne-shyne, no frost, nor no wynde to
  blow.
Then wolde we get [1] the stretes trym as a
  parate. [2]
Ye shold se how we wolde set our-selfe to
  show!
MERY-REPORTE.   Iet where ye wyll, I
  swere, by Saynte Quintyne,
Ye passe them all, both in your owne con-
  ceyt and myne.   835
GENTYLWOMAN.   If we had wether to
  walke at our pleasure,

[1] Jet, strut up and down.   [2] Parrot.

Our lyves wolde be mery out of measure:
One part of the day for our apparellynge,
A nother parte for eatynge and drynk-
  ynge,   839
And all the reste in stretes to be walkynge,
Or in the house to passe tyme wyth talk-
  ynge.
MERY-REPORTE.   When serve ye God?
GENTYLWOMAN.   Who bosteth in vertue
  are but daws. [1]
MERY-REPORTE.   Ye do the better, namely
  syns there is no cause.
How spende ye the nyght?
GENTYLWOMAN.   In daunsynge and
  syngynge   844
Tyll mydnyght, and then fall to slepynge.
MERY-REPORTE.   Why, swete herte! by
  your false fayth, can ye syng?
GENTYLWOMAN.   Nay, nay, but I love yt
  above all thynge.
MERY-REPORTE.   Now, by my trouth, for
  the love that I owe you,
You shall here what pleasure I can shew
  you.   849
One songe have I for you, suche as yt is,
And yf yt were better ye should have yt, by
  gys. [2]
GENTYLWOMAN.   Mary, syr, I thanke you
  even hartely.
MERY-REPORTE.   Come on, syrs! [3]   But
  now let us synge lust[e]ly.

Here they synge. [4]

GENTYLWOMAN.   Syr, this is well done!   I
  hertely thanke you.
Ye have done me pleasure, I make God
  a-vowe.   855
Ones in a nyght I longe for suche a fyt; [5]
For longe tyme have I bene brought up in
  yt.
MERY-REPORTE.   Oft tyme yt is sene, both
  in court and towne,
Longe be women a bryngyng up, and sone
  brought down!
So fete [6] yt is, so nete yt is, so nyse yt
  is,   860
So trycke [7] yt is, so quycke yt is, so wyse yt
  is!

[1] Fools.   [2] By Jesus.
[3] Possibly addressed to the musicians.
[4] The song is not given.
[5] Strain of music; song.
[6] Fine.   [7] Tricked out.

I fere my selfe, excepte I may entreat her,
I am so farre in love I shall forget her.
Now, good maystres, I pray you, let me kys
ye.
GENTYLWOMAN.   Kys me, quoth a!   Why,
        nay, syr, I wys ye.   865
MERY-REPORTE.   What! yes, hardely!
Kys me ons and no more.
I never desyred to kys you before.

Here the Launder cometh in.

LAUNDER.   Why! have ye alway kyst her
        behynde?
In fayth, good inough, yf yt be your
        mynde.   869
And yf your appetyte serve you so to do,
Byr lady, I wolde ye had kyst myne ars,
        to!
MERY-REPORTE.   To whom dost thou
        speke, foule hore? canst thou tell?
LAUNDER.   Nay, by my trouth, syr,[1] not
        very well;
But by coniecture this ges I have,   874
That I do speke to an olde baudy knave!
I saw you dally with your symper de cok-
        ket.[2]
I rede[3] you beware she pyck not your pok-
        ket.
Such ydyll huswyfes do now and than
Thynke all well wonne that they pyck from
        a man.
Yet such of some men shall have more
        favour   880
Then we, that for them dayly toyle and
        labour.
But I trust the god wyll be so indyfferent
That she shall fayle some parte of her en-
        tent.
MERY-REPORTE.   No dout he wyll deale so
        gracyously   884
That all folke shall be served indyfferently.
How-be-yt, I tell the trewth, my offyce is
        suche
That I muste reporte eche sewt, lyttell or
        muche.
Wherfore, wyth the god syns thou canst
        not speke,
Trust me wyth thy sewt; I wyll not fayle yt
        to breke.[4]

LAUNDER.   Then leane not to myche to
        yonder gyglet,[1]   890
For her desyre contrary to myne is set.
I herde by her tale she wolde banyshe the
        sonne,
And then were we pore launders all un-
        donne.
Excepte the sonne shyne that our clothes
        may dry,   894
We can do ryght nought in our laundry.
A nother maner losse, yf we sholde mys,
Then of suche nycebyceters[2] as she is.
GENTYLWOMAN.   I thynke yt better that
        thou envy me,
Then I sholde stande at rewarde[3] of thy
        pytte.
It is the guyse of such grose queynes as
        thou art   900
Wyth such as I am evermore to thwart.
Bycause that no beauty ye can obtayne
Therfore ye have us that be fayre in dys-
        dayne.
LAUNDER.   When I was as yonge as thou
        art now,
I was wythin lyttel as fayre as thou; 905
And so myght have kept me, yf I hadde
        wolde;
And as derely my youth I myght have
        solde
As the tryckest and fayrest of you all.
But I feared parels[4] that after myght
        fall.   909
Wherfore some besynes I dyd me provyde,
Lest vyce myght enter on every syde,
Whyche hath fre entre where ydylnesse
        doth reyne.
It is not thy beauty that I dysdeyne,
But thyne ydyll lyfe that thou hast re-
        hersed,
Whych any good womans hert wolde have
        perced.[5]   915
For I perceyve in daunsynge and syngynge,
In eatyng and drynkynge, and thyne ap-
        parellynge,
Is all the ioye wherin thy herte is set.
But nought of all this doth thyne owne
    •   labour get;
For haddest thou nothyng but of thyne
        owne travayle[6]   920

---

[1] R. has "*trouth I syr*"; the Awdeley edition has
"*Now, by my trouth, syr, I wot not very well.*"
[2] Mlle. Simper de Coquette.
[3] Advise.   [4] Disclose, deliver.

[1] Wanton.   [2] Nicely decked out girls.
[3] As the object of. (Pollard.)
[4] Perils (to the soul).
[5] Penetrated with grief.   [6] Labor.

Thou myghtest go as naked as my nayle.
Me-thynke thou shuldest abhorre suche
    ydylnes,
And passe thy tyme in some honest besy-
    nes.
Better to lese some parte of thy beaute 924
Then so ofte to ieoberd all thyne honeste.[1]
But I thynke, rather then thou woldest so
    do,
Thou haddest lever have us lyve ydylly to.
And so, no doute, we shulde, yf thou
    myghtest have
The clere sone banysht, as thou dost
    crave!
Then were we launders marde; and unto
    the   930
Thyne owne request were smale com-
    modyte.
For of these twayne I thynke yt farre bet-
    ter
Thy face were sone-burned, and thy clothis
    the swetter,[2]
Then that the sonne from shynynge sholde
    be smytten,
To kepe thy face fayre and thy smocke
    beshytten.   935
Syr, howe lycke ye my reason in her case?
MERY-REPORTE.   Such a raylynge hore, by
    the holy mas,
I never herde, in all my lyfe, tyll now!
In-dede, I love ryght well the ton of you;
But, or I wolde kepe you both, by goddes
    mother,   940
The devyll shall have the tone to fet[3] the
    tother!
LAUNDER.   Promise me to speke that the
    sone may shyne bryght,
And I wyll be gone quyckly for all nyght.
MERY-REPORTE.   Get you both hens, I
    pray you hartely.
Your sewtes I perceyve, and wyll reporte
    them trewly   945
Unto Iupyter at the next leysure,
And, in the same, desyre to know his pleas-
    ure;
Whyche knowledge hadde, even as he doth
    show yt,
Feare ye not, tyme inough ye shall know
    yt.
GENTYLWOMAN.   Syr, yf ye medyll, re-
    member me fyrste   950

[1] Virtue.   [2] Sweeter, cleaner.   [3] Fetch.

LAUNDER.   Then in this medlynge my
    parte shalbe the wurst.
MERY-REPORTE.   Now, I beseche our
    lorde, the devyll the burst!
Who medlyth wyth many I hold hym ac-
    curst,
Thou hore, can I medyl wyth you both at
    ones?

Here the Gentylwoman goth forth.

LAUNDER.   By the mas, knave, I wold I
    had both thy stones   955
In my purs, yf thou medyl not indyfferently,
That both our maters in yssew may be
    lyckly.
MERY-REPORTE.   Many wordes, lyttell
    mater, and to no purpose —
Suche is the effect that thou dost dys-
    close.   959
The more ye byb,[1] the more ye babyll;
The more ye babyll, the more ye fabyll;
The more ye fabyll, the more unstabyll;
The more unstabyll, the more unabyll
In any maner thynge to do any good.
No hurt though ye were hanged, by the
    holy rood!   965
LAUNDER.   The les your sylence, the lesse
    your credence;
The les your credens, the les your honeste;
The les your honeste, the les your as-
    systens;
The les your assystens, the les abylyte
In you to do ought.   Wherfore, so god me
    save,   970
No hurte in hangynge such a raylynge
    knave!
MERY-REPORTE.   What monster is this! I
    never harde none suche!
For loke how myche more I have made her
    to myche;
And so farre, at lest, she hath made me to
    lyttell.
Wher be ye, Launder?   I thynke in some
    spyttell.[2]   975
Ye shall washe me no gere, for feare of fret-
    ynge.[3]
I love no launders that shrynke my gere in
    wettynge.
I praye the go hens, and let me be in rest.
I wyll do thyne erand as I thynke best.

[1] Chatter.   [2] Lazar-house.
[3] Destruction by hard rubbing.

Launder. Now wolde I take my leve, yf
 I wyste how.   980
The lenger I lyve the more knave you!
Mery-reporte. The lenger thou lyvest
 the pyte the gretter,
The soner thou be ryd, the tydynges the
 better!

[Exit the Launder.]

Is not this a swete offyce that I have, 984
When every drab shall prove me a knave?
Every man knoweth not what goddes serv-
 yce is;
Nor I my selfe knewe yt not before this.
I thynke goddes servauntes may lyve
 holyly,
But the devyls servauntes lyve more
 meryly.
I know not what god geveth in standynges
 fees,   990
But the devyls servauntes have cas-
 weltees [1]
A hundred tymes mo then goddes serv-
 auntes have.
For, though ye be never so starke a knave,
If ye lacke money the devyll wyll do no
 wurse
But brynge you strayght to a nother mans
 purse.   995
Then wyll the devyll promote you here in
 this world,
As unto suche ryche [2] yt doth moste accord.
Fyrste *pater noster qui es in celis,* [3]
And then ye shall sens [4] the shryfe wyth
 your helys.
The greatest frende ye have in felde or
 towne,   1000
Standynge a-typ-to, shall not reche your
 crowne.

The Boy comyth in, the lest that can play.

Boy. This same is even he, by al lycklyhod.
Syr, I pray you, be not you master god?
Mery-reporte. No, in good fayth,
 sonne. But I may say to the
I am suche a man that god may not mysse
 me.   1005

Wherfore wyth the god yf thou woldest
 have ought done,
Tell me thy mynde, and I shall shew yt,
 sone.
Boy. Forsothe, syr, my mynde is thys, at
 few wordes:
All my pleasure is in catchynge of byrdes,
And makynge of snow-ballys and throwyng
 the same;   1010
For the whyche purpose to have set in
 frame,[1]
Wyth my godfather god I wolde fayne have
 spoken,
Desyrynge hym to have sent me by some
 token
Where I myghte have had great frost for
 my pytfallys,
And plente of snow to make my snow-
 ballys.   1015
This onys [2] had, boyes lyvis be such as no
 man leddys.
O, to se my snow-ballys lyght on my fel-
 owes heddys!
And to here the byrdes how they flycker
 theyr wynges
In the pytfale! I say yt passeth all
 thynges.
Syr, yf ye be goddes servaunt, or his kyns-
 man,   1020
I pray you helpe me in this yf ye can.
Mery-reporte. Alas, pore boy, who sent
 the hether?
Boy. A hundred boys that stode to-
 gether,
Where they herde one say in a cry
That my godfather, god almyghty, 1025
Was come from heven, by his owne ac-
 corde,
This nyght to suppe here wyth my lorde;[3]
And farther he sayde, come whoso [4] wull,
They shall sure have theyr bellyes full
Of all wethers, who lyste to crave, 1030
Eche sorte suche wether as they lyste to
 have.
And when my felowes thought this wolde
 be had,
And saw me so prety a pratelynge lad,
Uppon agrement, wyth a great noys,
"Sende lyttell Dycke!" cryed all the boys.

---

[1] Perquisites.   [2] Mighty person.
[3] First you say the Lord's Prayer (before execution).
[4] Swing your heels, like censers, over the head of
the sheriff who hangs you.

---

[1] Order, definite form. [2] Once.
[3] A compliment to the person in whose house the
play was acted.
[4] R. *whose.*

By whose assent I am purveyd [1]   1036
To sew for the wether afore-seyd.
Wherin I pray you to be good, as thus,
To helpe that god may geve yt us.
MERY-REPORTE. Gyve boys wether, quoth
    a? nonny, nonny! [2]   1040
BOY. Yf god of his wether wyll gyve
    nonny,
I pray you, wyll he sell ony?
Or lend us a bushell of snow, or twayne,
And poynt us a day to pay hym agayne?
MERY-REPORTE. I can not tell; for, by
    thys lyght,   1045
I chept [3] nor borowed none of hym this
    nyght.
But by suche shyfte as I wyll make
Thou shalte se soone what waye he wyll
    take.
BOY. Syr, I thanke you. Then I may de-
    parte?

The Boye goth forth.

MERY-REPORTE. Ye, farewell, good sonne,
    wyth all my harte!   1050
Now suche an other sorte [4] as here hath
    bene
In all the dayes of my lyfe I have not sene!
No sewters now but women, knavys, and
    boys;
And all theyr sewtys are in fansyes and
    toys!   1054
Yf that there come no wyser after thys cry
I wyll to the god and make an ende
    quyckely.

[*He makes a proclamation to the audience.*]

Oyes! yf that any knave here
Be wyllynge to appere,
For wether fowle or clere,
Come in before thys flocke;   1060
And be he hole or syckly,
Come shew hys mynde quyckly;
And yf hys tale be not lyckly [5]
Ye shall lycke my tayle in the nocke.

[*He pauses; no one advances.*]

All thys tyme, I perceyve, is spent in wast
To wayte for mo sewters. I se none make
    hast.   1066

---

[1] Provided, prepared.
[2] A meaningless exclamation.
[3] P. *chept not, nor.*   [4] Crowd.   [5] Likely.

Wherfore I wyll shew the god all thys
    procys,[1]
And be delyvered of my symple [2] offys.

[*He goes to the throne of Jupyter.*]

Now, lorde, accordynge to your com-
    maundement,   1069
Attendynge sewters I have ben dylygent.
And, at begynnyng as your wyll was I
    sholde,
I come now at ende to shewe what eche
    man wolde.
The fyrst sewter before your selfe dyd ap-
    pere, —
A gentylman desyrynge wether clere, 1074
Clowdy nor mysty, nor no wynde to blow,
For hurt in hys huntynge. And then, as
    ye know,
The marchaunt sewde for all of that kynde,
For wether clere, and mesurable wynde,
As they maye best bere theyr saylys to
    make spede.
And streyght after thys there came to me,
    in-dede,   1080
An other man, who namyd hym-selfe a
    ranger,
And sayd all of hys crafte be farre brought
    in daunger
For lacke of lyvynge, whyche chefely ys
    wynde-fall:
But he playnely sayth there bloweth no
    wynde at al;
Wherfore he desyreth, for encrease of theyr
    fleesys,[3]   1085
Extreme rage of wynde, trees to tere in
    peces.
Then came a water-myller, and he cryed
    out
For water, and sayde the wynde was so
    stout
The rayne could not fale; wherfore he made
    request
For plenty of rayne to set the wynde at
    rest.   1090
And then, syr, there came a wyndemyller
    in,
Who sayde for the rayne he could no
    wynde wyn;
The water he wysht to be banysht all,
Besechynge your grace of wynde contynu-
    all.

---

[1] Procedure, story.   [2] Humble.   [3] Plunder.

Then came there an other that wolde ban-
  ysh all this —   1095
A goodly dame, an ydyll thynge iwys!
Wynde, rayne, nor froste, nor sonshyne,
  wold she have,
But fayre close wether, her beautye to save.
Then came there a nother that lyveth by
  laundry,
Who muste have wether hote and clere
  here clothys to dry.   1100
Then came there a boy for froste and snow
  contynuall,
Snow to make snowballys, and frost for his
  pytfale;
For whyche, god wote, he seweth full
  gredely!
Your fyrst man wold have wether clere and
  not wyndy;
The seconde the same, save cooles to blow
  meanly; [1]   1105
The thyrd desyred stormes and wynde
  moste extremely;
The fourth all in water, and wolde have no
  wynde;
The fyft no water, but al wynde to grynde;
The syxt wold have none of all these, nor
  no bright son;
The seventh extremely the hote son wold
  have wonne;   1110
The eyght, and the last, for frost and snow
  he prayd.
Byr lady, we shall take shame, I am
  a-frayd!
Who marketh in what maner this sort is led
May thynke yt impossyble all to be sped.
This nomber is smale — there lacketh
  twayne of ten —   1115
And yet, by the masse, amonge ten
  thousand men
No one thynge could stand more wyde
  from the tother!
Not one of theyr sewtes agreeth wyth an
  other.
I promyse you, here is a shrewed pece of
  warke!   1119
This gere wyll trye wether ye be a clarke.
Yf ye trust to me, yt is a great foly;
For yt passeth my braynes, by goddes
  body!
JUPYTER. Son, thou haste ben dylygent,
  and done so well

That thy labour is ryght myche thanke-
  worthy.
But be thou suer we nede no whyt thy
  counsell;   1125
For in our-selfe we have foresene remedy,
Whyche thou shalt se. But fyrste, de-
  parte hence quyckly
To the gentylman and all other sewters
  here,
And commaunde them all before us to ap-
  pere.
MERY-REPORTE. That shall be no lenger
  in doynge   1130
Then I am in commynge and goynge.

Mery-report goth out.

JUPYTER. Suche debate as from above [1]
  ye have harde,
Suche debate beneth amonge your selfes ye
  se.
As longe as heddes from temperaunce be
  deferd,   1134
So longe the bodyes in dystemperaunce be:
This perceyve ye all, but none can helpe
  save we.
But as we there have made peace con-
  cordantly,
So woll we here now gyve you remedy.

Mery-reporte and al the sewters entreth.

MERY-REPORTE. If I hadde caught them
Or ever I raught [2] them,   1140
I wolde have taught them
  To be nere me.
Full dere have I bought them, [3]
Lorde, so I sought them;
Yet have I brought them,   1145
  Suche as they be!
GENTYLMAN. Pleaseth yt your maieste,
  lorde, so yt is,
We, as your subiectes and humble sewters
  all,
Accordynge as we here your pleasure is,
Are presyd [4] to your presens, beynge pryn-
  cypall   1150
Hed and governour of all in every place.
Who ioyeth not in your syght, no ioy can
  have.
Wherfore we all commyt us to your grace

---

[1] In heaven; cf. ll. 22–63.   [2] Reached.
[3] I have paid dear for them (i.e. the search was tedious).
[4] Hurried.

[1] Breezes to blow moderately.

As lorde of lordes us to peryshe [1] or
save.

JUPYTER.   As longe as dyscrecyon so well
doth you gyde   1155
Obedyently to use your dewte,
Dout ye not we shall your savete provyde.
Your grevys we have harde; wherfore we
sent for ye
To receyve answere, eche man in his
degre.   1159
And fyrst to content, most reason yt is,
The fyrste man that sewde; wherfore
marke ye this:

Oft shall ye have the wether clere and styll
To hunt in for recompens of your payne.
Also you marchauntes shall have myche
your wyll;
For oft-tymes, when no wynde on lande
doth remayne,   1165
Yet on the see pleasaunt cooles you shall
obtayne.
And syns your huntynge maye reste in the
nyght,
Oft shall the wynde then ryse, and before
day-lyght.

It shall ratyll downe the wood in suche
case   1169
That all ye rangers the better lyve may.
And ye water-myllers shall obteyne this
grace —
Many tymes the rayne to fall in the valey,
When at the selfe tymes on hyllys we shall
purvey
Fayre wether for your wyndmilles, with
such coolys of wynde
As in one instant both kyndes of mylles
may grynde.   1175

And for ye fayre women that close wether
wold have,
We shall provyde that ye may suffycyently
Have tyme to walke in, and your beauty
save.
And yet shall ye have, that lyveth by
laundry,
The hote sonne oft ynough your clothes to
dry.   1180
Also ye, praty chylde, shall have both frost
and snow.

[1] Destroy.

Now marke this conclusyon, we charge you
arow: [1]
Myche better have we now devysed for ye
all
Then ye all can perceyve, or coude desyre.
Eche of you sewd to have contynuall 1185
Suche wether as his crafte onely doth re-
quyre.
All wethers in all places yf men all tymes
myght hyer,
Who could lyve by other?   What is this
neglygens
Us to atempt in suche inconvenyens!

Now, on the tother syde, yf we had
graunted   1190
The full of some one sewt, and no mo,
And from all the rest the wether had for-
byd,
Yet who so hadde obtayned had wonne his
owne wo.
There is no one craft can preserve man so,
But by other craftes, of necessyte,   1195
He muste have myche parte of his com-
modyte.

All to serve at ones, and one destroy a
nother,
Or ellys to serve one and destroy all the
rest, —
Nother wyll we do the tone nor the
tother,
But serve as many, or as few, as we thynke
best.   1200
And where, or what tyme, to serve moste or
lest,
The dyreccyon of that doutles shall stande
Perpetually in the power of our hande.

Wherfore we wyll the hole worlde to at-
tende
Eche sorte on suche wether as for them
doth fall,   1205
Now one, now other, as lyketh us to sende.
Who that hath yt, ply [2] it; and suer we
shall
So gyde the wether in course to you all,
That eche wyth other ye shall hole [3] re-
mayne   1209
In pleasure and plentyfull welth, certayne.

[1] In a row.   [2] Make use of it.
[3] Whole, hale, sound.

GENTYLMAN. Blessyd was the tyme wherin we were borne!
Fyrst for the blysfull chaunce of your godly presens,
Next for our sewt. Was there never man beforne
That ever harde so excellent a sentens 1214
As your grace hath gevyn to us all arow?
Wherin your hyghnes hath so bountyfully
Dystrybuted my parte that your grace shall know
Your selfe sooll [1] possessed of hertes of all chyvalry.
MARCHAUNT. Lyke-wyse we marchauntes shall yeld us holy,[2]
Onely to laude the name of Iupyter 1220
As god of all goddes, you to serve soolly;
For of every thynge, I se, you are norysher.
RANGER. No dout yt is so, for so we now fynde.
Wherin your grace us rangers so doth bynde,
That we shall gyve you our hertes with one accorde, 1225
For knowledge to know you as our onely lorde.
WATER MYLLER. Well, I can no more, but — for our water
We shall geve your lordshyp Our Ladyes sauter.
WYNDE MYLLER. Myche have ye bounde us; for, as I be saved,
We have all obteyned better then we craved. 1230
GENTYLWOMAN. That is trew; wherfore your grace shal trewly
The hertes of such as I am have surely.
LAUNDER. And suche as I am — who be as good as you! —

¹ Solely.　　² Wholly.

His hyghnes shall be suer on, I make a vow.
BOY. Godfather god, I wyll do somwhat for you agayne. 1235
By Cryste, ye may happe to have a byrd or twayne!
And I promyse you, yf any snow come,
When I make my snow-ballys ye shall have some.
MERY-REPORTE. God thanke your lord-shyp. Lo, how this is brought to pas!
Syrs, now shall ye have the wether even as yt was. 1240

JUPYTER. We nede no whyte our selfe any farther to bost,
For our dedes declare us apparauntly.
Not onely here on yerth, in every cost,
But also above in the hevynly company, 1244
Our prudens hath made peace unyversally;
Whyche thynge, we sey, recordeth us as pryncypall
God and governour of heven, yerth, and all.

Now unto that heven we woll make retourne,
Where we be gloryfyed most tryumphantly. 1249
Also we woll all ye that on yerth soiourne,
Syns cause gyveth cause, to know us your lord onely,
And now here to synge moste ioyfully,
Reioycynge in us. And in meane-tyme we shall
Ascende into our trone celestyall. 1254

[*While they sing, Jupyter withdraws.*]

FINIS

Prynted by W. Rastell.
1533.
Cum privilegio.

X
SCHOOL PLAYS

The Comicall Scene

ROISTER DOISTER[1]

By NICHOLAS UDALL

[DRAMATIS PERSONÆ

RALPH ROYSTER DOYSTER, a braggart.

MATHEWE MERYGREEKE, the fun-maker.

GAWIN GOODLUCKE, a London merchant, affianced to the wealthy widow Custance.

TRISTRAM TRUSTY, an old friend to Goodlucke and Custance.

DOBINET DOUGHTIE, a boy, servant to Royster.

TOM TRUPENIE, a boy, servant to Custance.

SYM SURESBY, loyal servant to Goodlucke.

HARPAX, servant to Royster.

SCRIVENER.

MUSICIANS.

SERVANTS.

CHRISTIAN CUSTANCE, a wealthy widow, affianced to Goodlucke.

MADGE MUMBLECRUST, an old woman, nurse to Custance.

TIBET TALK-A-PACE ⎰
ANNOT ALYFACE ⎱ maids to Custance.

The place, LONDON.]

[1] In the first quarter of the sixteenth century the scholars of England came under the influence of the great neo-classical revival of Roman plays inaugurated by the Italian academies, and English high schools and colleges began to present before school audiences (and occasionally, by invitation, before the Court and before persons of eminence) the comedies of Terence and Plautus. Though at first the students acted the original plays of the Roman dramatists, very soon they began to compose and present plays modeled after the classical masterpieces. some in Latin and some in English. The earliest of the English adaptations of Roman comedy that has come down to us is *Roister Doister*, written by Nicholas Udall, and, in all probability, while he was headmaster of Eton, 1534–41. The importance of the academic drama in calling attention to the technique of the classical drama (act- and scene-divisions, coherence of plot, the unities of time and place, the careful motivation of entrances and exits, etc.) is obvious. And in still another way, perhaps, the efforts of the scholars to revive the drama of the ancients exerted an influence upon the English drama. The great revival of interest in Roman plays led, especially in Italy, to a revival of interest in the classical mode of stage representation. With hints derived from Vitruvius, and under the inspiration of enthusiastic Italian scholars, the architects and painters began to develop theatres and stage-scenery for presenting plays in "the manner of the ancients." The scenery devised consisted usually of canvas stretched over wooden frames (called "players' houses"), and painted in perspective to represent a street. There were entrances at either side into the houses of the chief personages, and a passage or door at the end of the street, leading, as it were, into the town. The figure entitled "The Comicall Scene," here reproduced from Serlio's *The Second Book of Architecture*, illustrates a rather elaborate setting for a comedy; in the English plays, no doubt, the setting was much simpler. The actors of *Roister Doister*, we may suppose, placed on one side the house of Dame Custance, on the other side the house of Roister, with a street in perspective between; and all the performers came in or went out at the doors of these two houses, or at the rear end of the street.

Only one copy of the play is extant (now preserved at Eton, and referred to hereafter as E.), and that lacks the title-page. The play, however, was licensed to Thomas Hacket in 1566/67, and was presumably issued shortly afterwards. I have based the text on Arber's reprint, with the corrections noted by Gayley (*Representative English Comedies*, 1903) as a result of his careful collation of this reprint with the unique copy at Eton. The punctuation and the bracketed stage-directions are mine.

THE PROLOGUE

What creature is in health, eyther yong or olde,
  But som mirth with modestie wil be glad to vse —
As we in thys enterlude shall now vnfolde?
  Wherin all scurilitie we vtterly refuse;
  Auoiding such mirth wherin is abuse;
Knowing nothing more comendable for a mans recreation
Than mirth which is vsed in an honest fashion.   7

For myrth prolongeth lyfe, and causeth health;
  Mirth recreates our spirites, and voydeth pensiuenesse;
Mirth increaseth amitie, not hindring our wealth;
  Mirth is to be vsed both of more and lesse,[1]
  Being mixed with vertue in decent comlynesse —
As we trust no good nature can gainsay the same.
Which mirth we intende to vse, auoidyng all blame.   14

The wyse poets long time heretofore
  Vnder merrie comedies secretes did declare,
Wherein was contained very vertuous lore,
  With mysteries and forewarnings very rare.
  Suche to write neither *Plautus* nor *Terence* dyd spare,
Whiche among the learned at this day beares the bell.[2]
These with such other therein dyd excell.   21

Our comedie, or enterlude, which we intende to play
  Is named "Royster Doyster," in-deede,
Which against the vayne-glorious doth inuey,
  Whose humour the roysting sort continually doth feede.
  Thus, by your pacience, we intende to proceede
In this our enterlude, by Gods leaue and grace.
And here I take my leaue for a certaine space.   28

[1] Persons of great and of small importance.   [2] Are ranked foremost.

FINIS.

ACTUS I. SCÆNA I

MATHEWE MERYGREEKE.[1] *He entreth singing.*

[M. MERY.] As long lyueth the mery man,
  they say,
As doth the sory man, and longer by a day;
Yet the grassehopper, for all his sommer
  pipyng,
Sterueth in winter wyth hungrie gripyng.
Therefore an-other sayd sawe[2] doth men
  aduise   5

[1] The word regularly means "a merry fellow."
[2] Spoken sententious passage.

That they be together both mery and wise.
Thys lesson must I practise, or else ere long
Wyth mee, Mathew Merygreeke, it will be
  wrong.
In-deede, men so call me; for, by Him that
  vs bought,
What-euer chaunce betide, I can take no
  thought.   10
Yet wisedome woulde that I did my-selfe
  bethinke
Where to be prouided this day of meate
  and drinke;
For knowe ye, that, for all this merie note
  of mine,

He might appose [1] me now that should
    aske where I dine.
My lyuing lieth heere, and there, of Gods
    grace: —   15
Sometime wyth this good man, sometyme
    in that place;
Sometime Lewis Loytrer biddeth me come
    neere;
Somewhyles Watkin Waster maketh vs
    good cheere;
Sometime Dauy Diceplayer, when he hath
    well cast,
Keepeth reuell-route as long as it will
    last;   20
Sometime Tom Titiuile maketh vs a feast;
Sometime with Sir Hugh Pye I am a bidden
    gueast;
Sometime at Nichol Neuerthriues I get a
    soppe;
Sometime I am feasted with Bryan Blink-
    insoppe;
Sometime I hang on Hankyn Hoddydodies
    sleeue —   25
But thys day, on Ralph Royster Doysters,
    by hys leeue!
For truely of all men he is my chiefe
    banker,
Both for meate and money, and my chiefe
    shootanker. [2]
For, sooth [3] Roister Doister in that he doth
    say,
And require what ye will; ye shall haue no
    nay.   30
But now of Roister Doister somewhat to
    expresse,
That ye may esteeme him after hys worthi-
    nesse:
In these twentie townes, and seke them
    throughout,
Is not the like stocke whereon to graffe a
    loute.
All the day long is he facing and crak-
    ing [4]   35
Of his great actes in fighting and fray-
    making;
But, when Roister Doister is put to his
    proofe,
To keepe the Queenes [5] peace is more for
    his behoofe.

[1] Pose, put to a nonplus.   [2] Last reliance.
[3] Support, flatter by assenting to.
[4] Swaggering and boasting
[5] Doubtless originally *Kings*.

If any woman smyle, or cast on hym an
    eye,
Vp is he to the harde eares in loue by-and-
    by! [1]   40
And in all the hotte haste must she be hys
    wife,
Else farewell hys good days, and farewell
    his life!
Maister Raufe Royster Doister is but dead
    and gon
Excepte she on hym take some compassion.
Then chiefe of counsell must be Mathew
    Merygreeke.   45
"What if I for mariage to suche an one
    seeke?"
Then must I sooth it, what-euer it is;
For what he sayth or doth can not be
    amisse.
Holde vp his yea and nay, be his nowne
    white sonne; [2]
Prayse and rouse [3] him well, and ye haue
    his heart wonne;   50
For so well liketh he his owne fonde [4]
    fashions
That he taketh pride of false commenda-
    tions.
But such sporte haue I with him as I would
    not leese
Though I should be bounde to lyue with
    bread and cheese.
For exalt hym, and haue hym as ye lust,
    in-deede —   55
Yea, to hold his finger in a hole for a
    neede.
I can, with a worde, make him fayne or
    loth;
I can, with as much, make him pleased or
    wroth;
I can, when I will, make him mery and
    glad;
I can, when me lust, make him sory and
    sad;   60
I can set him in hope, and eke in dis-
    paire;
I can make him speake rough, and make
    him speake faire.
But I maruell I see hym not all thys same
    day.
I wyll seeke him out. — But, loe! he com-
    meth thys way!

[1] Immediately.   [2] Darling, boon friend.
[3] Encourage.   [4] Ridiculous, foolish.

I haue yond espied hym sadly comming, — 65
And in loue, for twentie pounde, by hys
glommyng! [1]

ACTUS I. SCÆNA II

[*Enter*] *Rafe Roister Doister. Mathew
Merygreeke* [*remains*].

R. ROYSTER. Come, death, when thou
wilt! I am weary of my life!
M. MERY. I tolde you, I, we should wowe
another wife!
R. ROYSTER. Why did God make me
suche a goodly person?
M. MERY. He is in by the weke. We
shall haue sport anon.
R. ROYSTER. And where is my trustie
friende, Mathew Merygreeke? 5
M. MERY. I wyll make as I sawe him not.
He doth me seeke.
R. ROISTER. I haue hym espyed, me
thinketh; yond is hee.
Hough, Mathew Merygreeke, my friend!
a worde with thee!
M. MERY. I wyll not heare him, but make
as I had haste.

[*Pretending to go.*]

Farewell, all my good friendes! the tyme
away dothe waste; 10
And the tide, they say, tarieth for no man!
R. ROISTER. Thou must with thy good
counsell helpe me if thou can.
M. MERY. God keepe thee, worshypfull
Maister Roister Doister!
And fare-well the[e], lustie Maister Roister
Doister!

[*As he starts away, Roister Doister
holds him.*]

R. ROYSTER. I muste needes speake with
thee a worde or twaine. 15
M. MERY. Within a month or two I will
be here againe.
Negligence in greate affaires, ye knowe,
may marre all.
R. ROISTER. Attende vpon me now, and
well rewarde thee I shall.
M. MERY. I haue take my leaue, and the
tide is well spent.

[1] Scowling.

R. ROISTER. I die except thou helpe! I
pray thee, be content. 20
Doe thy parte wel, nowe, and aske what
thou wilt;
For without thy aide my matter is all spilt.
M. MERY. Then, to serue your turne, I
will some paines take,
And let all myne owne affaires alone — for
your sake.
R. ROYSTER. My whole hope and trust
resteth onely in thee. 25
M. MERY. Then can ye not doe amisse,
what-euer it bee.
R. ROYSTER. Gramercies, Merygreeke!
most bounde to thee I am.
M. MERY. But vp with that heart, and
speake out like a ramme!
Ye speake like a capon that had the cough
now.
Bee of good cheere! Anon ye shall doe
well ynow. 30
R. ROYSTER. Vpon thy comforte I will all
things well handle.
M. MERY. So, loe, that is a breast to
blowe out a candle!
But what is this great matter, I woulde
faine knowe?
We shall fynde remedie therefore, I trowe.
Doe ye lacke money? Ye knowe myne
olde offers; 35
Ye haue always a key to my purse and
coffers.
R. ROYSTER. I thanke thee! Had euer
man suche a frende?
M. MERY. Ye gyue vnto me; I must
needes to you lende.
R. ROYSTER. Nay, I haue money plentie
all things to discharge.
M. MERY. [*aside*]. That knewe I ryght
well when I made offer so large. 40
R. ROYSTER.[1] But it is no suche matter.
M. MERY. What is it, than?
Are ye in daunger of debte to any man?
If ye be, take no thought, nor be not
afraide;
Let them hardly take thought how they
shall be paide.
R. ROYSTER. Tut! I owe nought!
M. MERY. What then? Fear ye im-
prisonment? 45
R. ROYSTER. No.

[1] Omitted in E.; supplied by Cooper.

M. Mery.   No, i-wist, ye offende not so to be shent.[1]

But if ye [2] had, the Toure [3] coulde not you so holde

But to breake out at all times ye would be bolde.

What is it? Hath any man threatned you to beate?

R. Royster.   What is he that durst haue put me in that heate?   50

He that beateth me — by His armes! — shall well fynde

That I will not be farre from him, nor runne behinde.[4]

M. Mery.   That thing knowe all men euer since ye ouerthrewe

The fellow of the lion which Hercules slewe.

But what is it, than?

R. Royster.   Of loue I make my mone

M. Mery.   Ah, this foolishe a loue! Wilt neare let vs alone?   56

But, bicause ye were refused the last day,[5]

Ye sayd ye woulde nere more be intangled that way.

I would medle no more, since I fynde all so vnkinde.

R. Royster.   Yea, but I can not so put loue out of my minde.   60

Math. Mer.   But is your loue — tell me first, in any wise —

In the way of mariage, or of merchandise? [6]

If it may otherwise than lawfull be founde,

Ye get none of my helpe for a hundred pounde.

R. Royster.   No, by my trouth; I would haue hir to my wife.   65

M. Mery.   Then are ye a good man, and God saue your life!

And what, or who, is she with whome ye are in loue?

R. Royster.   A woman, whome I knowe not by what meanes to moue.

M. Mery.   Who is it?

R. Royster.   A woman, yond!

[He points to Custance's house]

M. Mery.   What is hir name?

R. Royster.   Hir, yonder.

[1] Blamed.   [2] E. *he.*
[3] The Tower of London.
[4] The reader should observe the numerous *double entendres.*
[5] Yesterday.   [6] I.e., illicit love.

M. Mery.   Whom?

R. Royster.   Mistresse — ah —

M. Mery.   Fy, fy, for shame!   70

Loue ye, and know not whome, but "hir yonde," "a woman"?

We shall then get you a wyfe I can not tell whan!

R. Royster.   The faire woman that supped wyth vs yesternyght;

And I hearde hir name twice or thrice, and had it ryght.

M. Mery.   Yea, ye may see ye nere take me to good cheere with you;   75

If ye had, I coulde haue tolde you hir name now.

R. Royster.   I was to blame in-deede; but the nexte tyme, perchaunce —

And she dwelleth in this house.

M. Mery.   What! Christian Custance?

R. Royster.   Except I haue hir to my wife, I shall runne madde.

M. Mery.   Nay, vnwise perhaps, but I warrant you for madde!   80

R. Royster.   I am vtterly dead vnlesse I haue my desire.

M. Mery.   Where be the bellowes that blewe this sodeine fire?

R. Royster.   I heare she is worthe a thousande pounde and more.

M. Mery.   Yea, but learne this one lesson of me afore:

An hundred pounde of marriage-money, doubtlesse,   85

Is euer thirtie pounde sterlyng, or somewhat lesse.

So that hir thousande pounde, yf she be thriftie,

Is muche neere about two hundred and fiftie.

Howebeit, wowers and widowes are neuer poore!

R. Royster.   Is she a widowe? I loue hir better therefore.   90

M. Mery.   But I heare she hath made promise to another.

R. Royster.   He shall goe without hir, and [1] he were my brother!

M. Mery.   I haue hearde say — I am right well aduised —

That she hath to Gawyn Goodlucke promised.

[1] If.

R. ROYSTER.   What is that Gawyn Good-
    lucke?
M. MERY.   A merchant man.   95
R. ROYSTER.   Shall he speede afore me?
    Nay, sir, by sweete Sainct Anne!
Ah, sir, "Backare," [1] quod Mortimer to his
    sowe.
I wyll haue hir myne owne selfe, I make
    God a-vow —
For, I tell thee, she is worthe a thousande
    pounde!
M. MERY.   Yet a fitter wife for your
    maship might be founde.   100
Suche a goodly man as you might get one
    wyth lande,
Besides poundes of golde a thousande, and
    a thousande,
And a thousande, and a thousande, and a
    thousande,
And so to the summe of twentie hundred
    thousande.
Your most goodly personage is worthie of
    no lesse.   105
R. ROYSTER.   I am sorie God made me so
    comely, doubtlesse;
For that maketh me eche-where so highly
    fauoured,
And all women on me so enamoured.
M. MERY.   "Enamoured," quod you?
    Haue ye spied out that?
Ah, sir, mary, nowe I see you know what is
    what.   110
"Enamoured," ka?   Mary, sir, say that
    againe!
But I thought not ye had marked it so
    plaine.
R. ROYSTER.   Yes, eche-where they gaze
    all vpon me, and stare.
M. MERY.   Yea, Malkyn, I warrant you,
    as muche as they dare.
And ye will not beleue what they say in the
    streete   115
When your mashyp passeth by, all such as
    I meete,
That sometimes I can scarce finde what
    aunswere to make.
"Who is this?" sayth one, "Sir Launcelot
    du Lake?"
"Who is this?   Greate Guy [2] of War-
    wike?" sayth an-other.

"No," say I, "it is the thirtenth Hercules
    brother."   120
"Who is this?   Noble Hector of Troy?"
    sayth the thirde.
"No, but of the same nest," say I, "it is a
    birde."
"Who is this?   Greate Goliah, Sampson,
    or Colbrande?"
"No," say I, "but it is a brute of the Alie [1]
    Lande."
"Who is this?   Greate Alexander? or
    Charle le Maigne?"   125
"No, it is the tenth Worthie," say I to
    them agayne.
I knowe not if I sayd well?
R. ROYSTER.   Yes; for so I am.
M. MERY.   Yea, for there were but nine
    Worthies before ye came.
To some others, the thirde Cato I doe you
    call.
And so, as well as I can, I aunswere them
    all.   130
"Sir, I pray you, what lorde, or great
    gentleman, is this?"
"Maister Ralph Roister Doister, dame,"
    say I, ywis.
"O Lorde!" sayth she than, "what a
    goodly man it is!
Woulde Christ I had such a husbande as he
    is!"
"O Lorde," say some, "that the sight of
    his face we lacke!"   135
"It is inough for you," say I, "to see his
    backe;
His face is for ladies of high and noble
    parages. [2]
With whome he hardly scapeth great mar-
    iages";
With muche more than this — and much
    otherwise.
R. ROYSTER.   I can [3] thee thanke that
    thou canst suche answeres deuise.
But I perceyue thou doste me throughly
    knowe.   141
M. MERY.   I marke your maners for myne
    owne learnyng, I trowe.
But suche is your beautie, and suche are
    your actes,
Suche is your personage, and suche are
    your factes, [4]

That all women, faire and fowle, more and
    lesse, 145
They [1] eye you, they lubbe you, they talke
    of you doubtlesse.
Your p[l]easant looke maketh them all
    merie;
Ye passe not by but they laugh till they be
    werie;
Yea, and money coulde I haue, the truthe
    to tell,
Of many, to bryng you that way where
    they dwell. 150
R. ROYSTER. Merygreeke, for this thy
    reporting well of mee —
M. MERY. What shoulde I else, sir? It
    is my duetie, pardee!
R. ROYSTER. I promise thou shalt not
    lacke, while I haue a grote.
M. MERY. Faith, sir, and I nere had more
    nede of a newe cote.
R. ROYSTER. Thou shalte haue one to-
    morowe, and golde for to spende. 155
M. MERY. Then I trust to bring the day
    to a good ende;
For, as for mine owne parte, hauing money
    inowe,
I could lyue onely with the remembrance of
    you.
But nowe to your widowe, whome you loue
    so hotte.
R. ROYSTER. By Cocke, thou sayest
    truthe! I had almost forgotte. 160
M. MERY. What if Christian Custance
    will not haue you? what?
R. ROISTER. Haue me? yes, I warrant
    you, neuer doubt of that!
I knowe she loueth me, but she dare not
    speake.
M. MERY. In-deede, meete it were some-
    body should it breake.[2]
R. ROISTER. She looked on me twentie
    tymes yesternight, 165
And laughed so —
M. MERY. That she coulde not sitte
    vpright?
R. ROISTER. No, faith, coulde she not.
M. MERY. No, euen such a thing I
    cast.[3]
R. ROYSTER. But, for wowyng, thou
    knowest, women are shamefast.

But, and she knewe my minde, I knowe she
    would be glad,
And thinke it the best chaunce that euer
    she had. 170
M. MERY. Too hir, then, like a man, and
    be bolde forth to starte!
Wowers neuer speede well that haue a
    false harte.
R. ROISTER. What may I best doe?
M. MERY. Sir, remaine ye a while [here];[1]
Ere long one or other of hir house will ap-
    pere.
Ye knowe my minde.
R. ROYSTER. Yea, now, hardly, lette
    me alone! 175
M. MERY. In the meane-time, sir, if you
    please, I wyll home
And call your musitians; for in this your case
It would sette you forth, and all your wow-
    yng grace;
Ye may not lacke your instrumentes to
    play and sing.
R. ROYSTER. Thou knowest I can doe that.
M. MERY. As well as any-thing. 180
Shall I go call your folkes, that ye may
    shewe a cast? [2]
R. ROYSTER. Yea, runne, I beseeche thee,
    in all possible haste.
M. MERY. I goe. *Exeat.*
R. ROYSTER. Yea, for I loue singyng
    out of measure;
It comforteth my spirites, and doth me
    great pleasure.
But who commeth forth yond from my
    swete hearte Custance? 185
My matter frameth well; thys is a luckie
    chaunce.

ACTUS I. SCÆNA III

[*Enter*] *Mage Mumble-crust,*[3] *spinning on
the distaffe, Tibet Talk-apace, sowyng;
[later enter] Annot Alyface, knittyng.
R. Roister [remains].*

M. MUMBL. If thys distaffe were spoonne,
    Margerie Mumblecrust —

[*Seating herself on the bench.*]

TIB. TALK. Where good stale ale is, will
    drinke no water, I trust.

---

[1] Arber misprints *that.*   [2] Divulge.
[3] Forecasted, anticipated.

[1] Not in E.; added by Cooper.   [2] Specimen.
[3] One who mumbles her crusts with toothless gums.

M. Mumbl.   Dame Custance hath promised vs good ale and white bread —

Tib. Talk.   If she kepe not promise I will
beshrewe hir head!

But it will be starke nyght before I shall
haue done.   5

R. Royster.   I will stande here a-while,
and talke with them anon.

I heare them speake of Custance, which
doth my heart good;

To heare hir name spoken doth euen comfort my blood.

M. Mumbl.   Sit downe to your worke,
Tibet, like a good girle.

Tib. Talk.   Nourse, medle you with your
spyndle and your whirle!   10

No haste but good, Madge Mumblecrust;
for, whip and whurre,

The olde prouerbe doth say, neuer made
good furre.

M. Mumbl.   Well, ye wyll sitte downe to
your worke anon, I trust.

Tib. Talk.   Soft fire maketh sweete
malte, good Madge Mumblecrust.

M. Mumbl.   And sweete malte maketh ioly
good ale for the nones.   15

Tib. Talk.   Whiche will slide downe the
lane without any bones.

She sings: [1]

Old browne bread crustes must haue much
good mumblyng,

But good ale downe your throte hath good
easie tumbling.

R. Royster.   The iolyest wenche that ere
I hearde! little mouse!

May I not reioyce that she shall dwell in
my house?   20

[Tibet seats herself.]

Tib. Talk.   So, sirrha,[2] nowe this geare
beginneth for to frame.

M. Mumbl.   Thanks to God, though your
work stand stil, your tong is not lame!

Tib. Talk.   And, though your teeth be
gone, both so sharpe and so fine,

Yet your tongue can renne on patins [3] as
well as mine.

---

[1] E. *Cantet.*

[2] Formerly used in addressing women as well as men.

[3] Make a great clatter (as the feet do in pattens, or wooden shoes).

M. Mumbl.   Ye were not for nought
named Tyb Talke-apace.   25

Tib. Talk.   Doth my talke grieue you?
Alack, God saue your grace!

M. Mumbl.   I holde [1] a grote ye will
drinke anon for this geare.

Tib. Talk.   And I wyll pray you the
stripes for me to beare.

M. Mumbl.   I holde a penny, ye will
drink without a cup.

Tib. Talk.   Wherein-so-ere ye drinke, I
wote ye drinke all vp.   30

[Enter Annot Alyface knitting.]

An. Alyface.   By Cock! [2] and well
sowed, my good Tibet Talke-apace!

Tib. Talk.   And een as well knitte, my
nowne Annot Alyface!

R. Royster.   See what a sort [3] she kepeth
that must be my wife!

Shall not I, when I haue hir, leade a merrie
life?

Tib. Talk.   Welcome, my good wenche,
and sitte here by me iust!   35

An. Alyface.   And howe doth our old
beldame here, Mage Mumblecrust?

Tib. Talk.   Chyde, and finde faultes, and
threaten to complaine.

An. Alyface.   To make vs poore girles
shent, to hir is small gaine.

M. Mumbl.   I dyd neyther chyde, nor
complaine, nor threaten.

R. Royster.   It woulde grieue my heart
to see one of them beaten.   40

M. Mumbl.   I dyd nothyng but byd hir
worke, and holde hir peace.

Tib. Talk.   So would I, if you coulde your
clattering ceasse;

But the deuill can not make olde trotte [4]
holde hir tong.

An. Alyface.   Let all these matters
passe, and we three sing a song!

So shall we pleasantly bothe the tyme beguile now   45

And eke dispatche all our workes ere we
can tell how.

Tib. Talk.   I shrew them that say nay,
and that shall not be I!

M. Mumbl.   And I am well content.

Tib. Talk.   Sing on, then, by-and-by.

---

[1] Wager.   [2] God.

[3] Retinue.   [4] Hag.

R. ROYSTER. And I will not away, but listen to their song.
Yet Merygreeke and my folkes tary very long. 50

Tib, An, and Margerie, doe singe here.

Pipe, mery Annot, etc.[1]
Trilla, trilla, trillarie!
Worke, Tibet; worke, Annot; worke, Margerie!
Sewe, Tibet; knitte, Annot; spinne, Margerie!
Let vs see who shall winne the victorie. 55

TIB. TALK. This sleue is not willyng to be sewed, I trowe.
A small thing might make me all in the grounde to throwe!

Then they sing agayne.

Pipe, merrie Annot, etc.
Trilla, trilla, trillarie!
What, Tibet? what, Annot? what, Margerie? 60
Ye sleepe, but we doe not, that shall we trie.
Your fingers be nombde, our worke will not lie.

TIB. TALK. If ye doe so againe, well, I would aduise you nay.
In good sooth, one stoppe more, and I make holy-day.

They singe the thirde tyme.

Pipe, mery Annot, etc. 65
Trilla, trilla, trillarie!
Nowe, Tibbet; now, Annot; nowe, Margerie!
Nowe whippet apace for the maystrie!
But it will not be, our mouth is so drie.

TIB. TALK. Ah, eche finger is a thombe to-day, me thinke! 70
I care not to let all alone, choose it swimme or sinke!

They sing the fourth tyme.

Pipe, mery Annot, etc.
Trilla, trilla, trillarie!

[1] *I suppose* etc. *is to be expanded as* Pipe, Tibet; pipe, Margerie! — Manly.

When, Tibet? when, Annot? when, Margerie?
I will not! I can not! No more can I! 75
Then giue we all ouer, and there let it lye!

Lette hir [Tibet] caste downe hir vvorke.

TIB. TALK. There it lieth! The worste is but a curried cote.[1]
Tut, I am vsed therto; I care not a grote!
AN. ALYFACE. Haue we done singyng since? Then will I in againe.
Here I founde you, and here I leaue both twaine. *Exeat.* 80
M. MUMBL. And I will not be long after.
[*She spies Roister.*] Tib Talke-apace!
TIB. TALK. What is the matter?
M. MUMB. Yond stode a man al this space,
And hath hearde all that euer we spake to-gyther.
TIB. TALK. Mary! the more loute he for his comming hither!
And the lesse good he can, to listen maidens talke! 85
I care not and I go byd him hence for to walke.
It were well done to knowe what he maketh here-away.
R. ROYSTER. Nowe myght I speake to them, if I wist what to say.
M. MUMBL. Nay, we will go both off, and see what he is.

[*They approach him.*] [2]

R. ROYSTER. One that hath hearde all your talke and singyng, ywis. 90
TIB. TALK. The more to blame you! A good thriftie husbande [3]
Woulde elsewhere haue had some better matters in hande.
R. ROYSTER. I dyd it for no harme, but for good loue I beare
To your dame, Mistresse Custance, I did your talke heare.
And, mistresse nource, I will kisse you for acquaintance. 95
M. MUMBL. I come anon,[4] sir.

[1] A beating.   [2] Added by Manly.
[3] One who manages his affairs with care.
[4] At once, without delay.

Tib. Talk.　Faith, I would our dame
Custance
Sawe this geare!

M. Mumbl.　I must first wipe al cleane,
yea, I must!

[*She wipes her mouth with her apron.*]

Tib. Talk.　Ill chieue [1] it, dotyng foole,
but it must be cust!

[*Roister kisses Madge.*]

M. Mumbl.　God yelde [2] you, sir! Chad
not so much ichotte [3] not whan,
Nere since chwas bore, chwine, of such a
gay gentleman!　100

R. Royster.　I will kisse you, too,
mayden, for the good will I beare
you.

Tib. Talk.　No, forsoth, by your leaue, ye
shall not kisse me!

R. Royster.　Yes; be not afearde; I doe
not disdayne you a whit.

Tib. Talk.　Why shoulde I feare you? I
haue not so little wit.
Ye are but a man, I knowe very well.

R. Royster.　Why, then?　105

Tib. Talk.　Forsooth, for I wyll not. I
vse not to kisse men.

R. Royster.　I would faine kisse you too,
good maiden, if I myght.

Tib. Talk.　What shold that neede?

R. Royster.　But to honor you, by this
light!
I vse to kisse all them that I loue, to God I
vowe.

Tib. Talk.　Yea, sir, I pray you, when
dyd ye last kisse your cowe?　110

R. Royster.　Ye might be proude to kisse
me, if ye were wise.

Tib. Talk.　What promotion were therein?

R. Royster.　Nourse is not so nice.

Tib. Talk.　Well, I haue not bene taught
to kissing and licking.

R. Royster.　Yet I thanke you, mistresse
nourse, ye made no sticking.

M. Mumbl.　I will not sticke for a kosse
with such a man as you!　115

[1] Succeed.　　[2] Reward.
[3] Ich wott, I know.　The pronominal form *ich*
and its compounds (ich had, chad; ich was, chwas;
ich ween, chwine; etc.) was the stage dialect of the
rustic.

Tib. Talk.　They that lust! I will againe
to my sewyng now.

[*Re-enter Annot Alyface.*]

An. Alyfac[e].　Tidings, hough! tidings!
Dame Custance greeteth you well!

R. Royster.　Whome? me?

An. Alyface.　You, sir? no, sir; I do no
suche tale tell.

R. Royster.　But, and she knewe me
here —

An. Alyface.　Tybet Talke-apace,
Your mistresse, Custance, and mine, must
speake with your grace.　120

Tib. Talk.　With me?

An. Alyface.　Ye muste come in to hir,
out of all doutes.

Tib. Talk.　And my work not half done!
A mischief on all loutes!

*Ex[eant] am[bae. Roister and Madge Mum-
blecrust are left alone].*

R. Royster.　Ah, good, sweet nourse!

M. Mumb.　A, good, sweete gentleman!

R. Royster.　What?

M. Mumbl.　Nay, I can not tel, sir; but
what thing would you?

R. Royster.　Howe dothe sweete Custance, my heart of gold, tell me
how?　125

M. Mumbl.　She dothe very well, sir, and
commaunde me [1] to you.

R. Royster.　To me?

M. Mumbl.　Yea, to you, sir.

R. Royster　To me? Nurse, tel
me plain, —
To me?

M. Mumb.　Ye.

R. Royster.　That word maketh me
aliue again!

M. Mumbl.　She commaunde me to one
last day, who-ere it was.

R. Royster.　That was een to me and
none other, by the masse!　130

M. Mumbl.　I can not tell you surely, but
one it was.

R. Royster.　It was I and none other.
This commeth to good passe!
I promise thee, nourse, I fauour hir.

M. Mumb.　Een so, sir.

R. Royster.　Bid hir sue to me for mariage.

[1] Presents her kind regards to you.

M. Mumbl.   Een so, sir.

R. Royster.   And surely, for thy sake, she shall speede.

M. Mumb.   Een so, sir.   135

R. Royster.   I shall be contented to take hir.

M. Mumb.   Een so, sir.

R. Royster.   But at thy request, and for thy sake.

M. Mumb.   Een so, sir.

R. Royster.   And, come hearke in thine eare what to say.

M. Mumb.   Een so, sir.

Here lette him tell hir a great long tale in hir eare.

ACTUS I. SCÆNA IIII

[Enter at a distance] Mathew Merygreeke, Dobinet Doughtie, Harpax [and Musicians]. Ralph Royster [and] Margerie Mumblecrust [remain whispering].

M. Mery.   Come on, sirs, apace; and quite your-selues like men.

Your pains shalbe rewarded.

D. Dou.   But I wot not when.

M. Mery.   Do your maister worship as ye haue done in time past.

D. Dough.   Speake to them; of mine office he shall haue a cast.

M. Mery.   Harpax, looke that thou doe well, too, and thy fellow.   5

Harpax.   I warrant, if he will myne example folowe.

M. Mery.   Curtsie, whooresons; douke you and crouche at euery worde!

D. Dough.   Yes, whether our maister speake earnest or borde.[1]

M. Mery.   For this lieth vpon[2] his preferment indeede.

D. Dough.   Oft is hee a wower, but neuer doth he speede.   10

M. Mery.   But with whome is he nowe so sadly roundyng[3] yond?

D. Dough.   With *Nobs nicebecetur miserere*[4] fonde.

[Merygreeke advances and pretends to think Mumblecrust Roister's bride.]

[1] Jest.   [2] Is necessary to.
[3] Whispering.
[4] Dear dainty-girl, have mercy!

[M.] Mery.   God be at your wedding! Be ye spedde alredie?

I did not suppose that your loue was so greedie.

I perceiue nowe ye haue chose of deuotion;   15

And ioy haue ye, ladie, of your promotion!

R. Royster.   Tushe, foole, thou art deceiued; this is not she.

M. Mery.   Well, mocke muche of hir, and keepe hir well, I vise ye;

I will take no charge of such a faire piece keeping.

M. Mumbl.   What ayleth thys fellowe? He driueth me to weeping.   20

M. Mery.   What! weepe on the weddyng day? Be merrie, woman!

Though I say it, ye haue chose a good gentleman.

R. Royster.   Kocks nownes![1] what meanest thou man? tut a whistle!

[M. Mery.][2]   Ah, sir, be good to hir; she is but a gristle!

Ah, sweete lambe and coney![3]

R. Royster.   Tut, thou art deceiued! 25

M. Mery.   Weepe no more, lady; ye shall be well receiued.

[To the musicians.]

Vp wyth some mery noyse, sirs, to bring home the bride!

R. Royster.   Gogs armes, knaue! Art thou madde? I tel thee thou art wide.

M. Mery.   Then ye entende by nyght to haue hir home brought?

R. Royster.   I tel thee, no!

M. Mery.   How then?

R. Royster.   Tis neither ment ne thought.   30

M. Mery.   What shall we then doe with hir?

R. Royster.   Ah, foolish harebraine! This is not she!

M. Mery.   No is? Why then, vnsayde againe!

And what yong girle is this with your mashyp so bolde?

R. Royster.   A girle?

[1] God's wounds. [2] E. assigns this speech to Roister.
[3] Rabbit, a term of endearment.

M. Mery.   Yea; I dare say scarce yet
three-score yere old.

R. Royster.   This same is the faire widowes nourse of whome ye wotte. 35

M. Mery.   Is she but a nourse of a house?
Hence home, olde trotte! [1]
Hence at once!

R. Royster.   No! no!

M. Mery.   What! an please your
maship

A nourse talke so homely [2] with one of your
worship?

R. Royster.   I will haue it so: it is my
pleasure and will.

M. Mery.   Then I am content. Nourse,
come againe; tarry still.   40

R. Royster.   What! she will helpe forward this my sute for hir part.

M. Mery.   Then ist mine owne pygs-nie,[3]
and blessing on my hart!

R. Royster.   This is our best friend, man!

M. Mery.   Then teach hir what to say.

M. Mumbl.   I am taught alreadie.

M. Mery.   Then go, make no delay!

R. Royster.   Yet hark one word in thine
eare. [He begins again to whisper.]

M. Mery.   Back, sirs from his taile! 45

[Merygreek pushes the musicians on Roister.]

R. Royster.   Backe vilaynes! Will ye
be priuie of my counsaile?

M. Mery.   Backe, sirs! so! I tolde you
afore ye woulde be shent!

[He pushes them away from Roister.]

R. Royster.   She shall haue the first day
a whole pecke of argent.

M. Mumbl.   A pecke! Nomine Patris!
haue ye so much spare?

R. Royster.   Yea, and a carte-lode therto,
or else were it bare,[4]   50
Besides other mouables, housholde stuffe
and lande.

M. Mumbl.   Haue ye lands too?

R. Royster.   An hundred marks.

M. Mery.   Yea, a thousand!

M. Mumbl.   And haue ye cattell too? and
sheepe too?

R. Royster.   Yea, a fewe.

[1] Hag.   [2] Intimately.
[3] Pig's eye, a term of endearment.
[4] Perhaps this speech should be assigned to Merygreeke.

M. Mery.   He is ashamed the numbre of
them to shewe.

Een rounde about him as many thousande
sheepe goes   55
As he and thou and I too haue fingers and
toes.

M. Mumbl.   And how many yeares olde
be you?

R. Royster.   Fortie at lest.

M. Mery.   Yea, and thrice fortie to them!

R. Royster.   Nay, now thou dost iest:
I am not so olde; thou misreckonest my
yeares.

M. Mery.   I know that; but my minde
was on bullockes and steeres.   60

M. Mumbl.   And what shall I shewe hir
your masterships name is?

R. Royster.   Nay, she shall make sute
ere she know that, ywis!

M. Mumbl.   Yet let me somewhat knowe.

M. Mery.   This is hee, vnderstand,
That killed the Blewe Spider in Blanche-
pouder Lande.

M. Mumbl.   Yea, Iesus! William! Zee
law! Dyd he zo? Law!   65

M. Mery.   Yea, and the last elephant
that euer he sawe;
As the beast passed by, he start out of a
buske,
And een with pure strength of armes pluckt
out his great tuske.

M. Mumbl.   Iesus! Nomine Patris! what a
thing was that!

R. Roister.   Yea, but, Merygreke, one
thing thou hast forgot.   70

M. Mery.   What?

R. Royster.   Of thother elephant.

M. Mery.   Oh, hym that fledde away?

R. Royster.   Yea.

M. Mery.   Yea! he knew that his
match was in place that day.
Tut, he bet the King of Crickets on
Christmasse-day,
That he crept in a hole, and not a worde to
say!

M. Mumbl.   A sore [1] man, by zembletee!

M. Mery.   Why, he wrong a club 75
Once, in a fray, out of the hande of Belze-
bub.

R. Royster.   And how when Mumfision?

M. Mery.   Oh, your coustrelyng [2]

[1] Strong, bold, fierce.   [2] Groom, lad.

Bore the lanterne a-fielde so before the gozelyng —
Nay, that is to long a matter now to be tolde!
Neuer aske his name, nurse! I warrant thee, be bolde.   80
He conquered in one day from Rome to Naples,
And woonne townes, nourse, as fast as thou canst make apples.
M. MUMBL. O Lorde! My heart quaketh for feare! He is to sore!
R. ROYSTER. Thou makest hir to much afearde. Merygreeke, no more!
This tale woulde feare my sweete heart Custance right euill.   85
M. MERY. Nay, let hir take him, nurse — and feare not the deuill!
But thus is our song dasht. Sirs, ye may home againe.
R. ROYSTER. No, shall they not! I charge you all here to remaine.
The villaine slaues! a whole day ere they can be founde!
M. MERY. Couche! On your marybones, whooresons! Down to the ground!

[*They kneel before Roister.*]

Was it meete he should tarie so long in one place   91
Without harmonie of musike, or some solace?
Who-so hath suche bees as your maister in hys head
Had neede to haue his spirites with musike to be fed.
By your maisterships licence!

[*Picks something from his coat.*]

R. ROYSTER.   What is that? a moate?
M. MERY. No; it was a fooles feather had light on your coate.   96
R. ROISTER. I was nigh no feathers since I came from my bed.
M. MERY. No, sir, it was a haire that was fall from your hed.
R. ROYSTER. My men com when it plese them. —
M. MERY.   By your leue!

[*Brushes something from his gown.*]

R. ROYSTER.   What is that?

M. MERY. Your gown was foule spotted with the foot of a gnat.   100
R. ROISTER. Their maister to offende they are nothing afearde.

[*Merygreeke picks something from Roister's doublet.*]

What now?
M. MERY. A lousy haire from your masterships beard.
ALL SERVANTS.[1] And, sir, for nurses sake, pardon this one offence.
We shall not after this shew the like negligence.
R. ROYSTER. I pardon you this once; and come sing nere the wurse!   105
M. MERY. How like you the goodnesse of this gentleman, nurse?
M. MUMBL. God saue his maistership that so can his men forgeue!
And I wyll heare them sing ere I go, by his leaue.
R. ROYSTER. Mary, and thou shalt, wenche! Come, we two will daunce!
M. MUMBL. Nay, I will by myne owne selfe foote the song perchaunce.
R. ROYSTER. Go to it, sirs, lustily!
M. MUMBL.   Pipe vp a mery note.
Let me heare it playde, I will foote it, for a grote!   112

[*They sing,[2] while Mumblecrust foots it.*]

Who-so to marry a minion wife
    Hath hadde good chaunce and happe,
Must loue hir and cherishe hir all his life,
    And dandle hir in his lappe.   116

If she will fare well, yf she wyll go gay,
    A good husbande euer styll,
What-euer she lust to doe or to say,
    Must lette hir haue hir owne will.   120

About what affaires so-euer he goe,
    He must shewe hir all his mynde;
None of hys counsell she may be kept froe,[3]
    Else is he a man vnkynde.   124

R. ROYSTER [*producing a letter*]. Now, nurse, take thys same letter here to thy mistresse;

[1] E. *Omnes famulae.*
[2] E. *Cantent.* The song is printed at the end of the play, and entitled "The Seconde Song."
[3] E. *free;* corr. by Cooper.

And, as my trust is in thee, plie my businesse.

M. MUMBL. It shalbe done.

M. MERY. Who made it?

R. ROYSTER. I wrote it, ech whit.

M. MERY. Then nedes it no mending.

R. ROYSTER. No, no!

M. MERY. No; I know your wit;
I warrant it wel.

M. MUMBL. It shal be deliuered.
But, if ye speede, shall I be considered? 130

M. MERY. Whough! dost thou doubt of
that?

MADGE. What shal I haue?

M. MERY. An hundred times more than
thou canst deuise to craue.

M. MUMBL. Shall I haue some newe
geare? [1] for my olde is all spent.

M. MERY. The worst kitchen wench shall
goe in ladies rayment.

M. MUMBL. Yea?

M. MERY. And the worst drudge in the
house shal go better 135
Than your mistresse doth now.

M. MUMBL.[2] Then I trudge with your
letter.

[Exit Mumblecrust into the house.]

R. ROYSTER. Now may I repose me,
Custance is mine owne.
Let vs sing and play homeward, that it may
be knowne.

M. MERY. But are you sure that your
letter is well enough?

R. ROYSTER. I wrote it my-selfe!

M. MERY. Then sing we to dinner! 140

Here they sing, and go out singing.

ACTUS I. SCÆNA V

*[Enter] Christian Custance [with the letter,
unopened; followed by] Margerie Mumblecrust.*

C. CUSTANCE. Who tooke [3] thee thys
letter, Margerie Mumblecrust?

M. MUMBL. A lustie gay bacheler tooke
it me of trust;
And if ye seeke to him, he will lowe [4] your
doing.

[1] Clothes.   [2] E. *Mar.* (i.e. Margery).
[3] Gave.   [4] Allow.

C. CUSTANCE. Yea, but where learned he
that manner of wowing?

M. MUMBL. If to sue to hym you will any
paines take, 5
He will haue you to his wife, he sayth, for
my sake.

C. CUSTANCE. Some wise gentleman, belike! I am bespoken; [1]
And I thought, verily, thys had bene some
token
From my dere spouse, Gawin Goodluck;
whom, when him please,
God luckily sende home to both our
heartes ease! 10

M. MUMBL. A ioyly man it is, I wote well
by report,
And would haue you to him for marriage
resort.
Best open the writing, and see what it doth
speake.

C. CUSTANCE. At thys time, nourse, I will
neither reade ne breake.

M. MUMBL. He promised to giue you a
whole pecke of golde. 15

C. CUSTANCE. Perchaunce lacke of a
pynte, when it shall be all tolde!

M. MUMBL. I would take a gay, riche
husbande, and I were you.

C. CUSTANCE. In good sooth, Madge, een
so would I, if I were thou.
But no more of this fond talke now; let vs
go in.
And see thou no more moue me folly to
begin, 20
Nor bring mee no mo letters for no mans
pleasure,
But thou know from whom.

M. MUMBL. I warrant ye, shall be
sure!

[Exeunt into the house.]

ACTUS II. SCÆNA I

[Enter] Dobinet Doughtie [Roister's page].[1]

D. DOUGH. Where is the house I goe to?
before or behinde?
I know not where, nor when, nor how, I
shal it finde.
If I had ten mens bodies and legs and
strength,

[1] Promised, engaged.

This trotting that I haue must needes lame
  me at length.
And nowe that my maister is new set on
  wowyng,   5
I trust there shall none of vs finde lacke of
  doyng.
Two paire of shoes a day will nowe be too
  litle
To serue me, I must trotte to and fro so
  mickle.
"Go beare me thys token!" "Carrie me
  this letter!"
"Nowe this is the best way"; "nowe that
  way is better!"   10
"Vp before day, sirs, I charge you, an
  houre or twaine!"
"Trudge!" "Do me thys message, and
  bring worde quicke againe!"
If one misse but a minute, then: "His
  armes and woundes,
I woulde not haue slacked for ten thousand
  poundes!
Nay, see, I beseeche you, if my most
  trustie page   15
Goe not nowe aboute to hinder my mar-
  iage!"
So feruent hotte wowyng, and so farre
  from wiuing,
I trowe neuer was any creature liuyng.
With euery woman is he in some loues pang.
Then vp to our lute at midnight, twangle-
  dome twang;   20
Then twang with our sonets, and twang
  with our dumps,[1]
And heyhough from our heart, as heauie as
  lead lumpes;
Then to our recorder,[2] with toodleloodle
  poope,
As the howlet out of an yuie bushe should
  hoope;
Anon to our gitterne,[3] thrumpledum,
  thrumpledum thrum,   25
Thrumpledum, thrumpledum, thrumple-
  dum, thrumpledum thrum!
Of songs and balades also he is a maker,
And that can he as finely doe as Iacke
  Raker;[4]
Yea, and *extempore* will he dities com-
  pose, —

[1] Mournful songs.
[2] A wind instrument like the flute.
[3] A stringed instrument like the guitar.
[4] Proverbial as a writer of bad verse.

Foolishe Marsias nere made the like, I suppose!   30
Yet must we sing them; as good stuffe, I
  vndertake,
As for such a pen-man is well-fittyng to
  make.
"Ah, for these long nights! heyhow! when
  will it be day?
I feare, ere I come, she will be wowed
  away."
Then, when aunswere is made that it may
  not bee,   35
"O death, why commest thou not by-and-
  by?" sayth he.
But then, from his heart to put away sor-
  owe,
He is as farre in with some newe loue next
  morowe.
But in the meane season we trudge and we
  trot;
From dayspring to midnyght I sit not nor
  rest not.   40
And now am I sent to Dame Christian
  Custance;
But I feare it will ende with a mocke for
  pastance.
I bring hir a ring, with a token in a cloute;[1]
And, by all gesse,[2] this same is hir house
  out of doute.
I knowe it nowe perfect, I am in my right
  way.   45
And loe yond the olde nourse that was
  wyth vs last day!

ACTUS II. SCÆNA II

*[Enter hurriedly] Mage Mumblecrust. Dobi-
  net Doughtie [remains].*

M. MUMBL. I was nere so shoke vp afore
  since I was borne!
That our mistresse coulde not haue chid, I
  wold haue sworne;
And I pray God I die if I ment any harme.
But, for my life-time, this shall be to me a
  charme![3]
D. DOUGH. God you saue and see, nurse!
  And howe is it with you?   5
M. MUMBL. Mary, a great deale the
  worse it is, for suche as thou!

[1] Cloth.   [2] Guess.
[3] An enchantment, warning her against such conduct in the future.

D. Dough. For me? Why so?

M. Mumb.   Why, wer not thou one of them, say,

That song and playde here with the gentleman last day?

D. Dough. Yes; and he would know if you haue for him spoken;

And prayes you to deliuer this ring and token.   10

M. Mumbl. Nowe, by the token that God tokened, brother,

I will deliuer no token, one nor other!

I haue once ben so shent for your maisters pleasure

As I will not be agayne for all hys treasure.

D. Dough. He will thank you, woman.

M. Mumbl. I will none of his thanke.

Ex[it into the house].

D. Dough. I weene I am a prophete! this geare will proue blanke!   16

But what! should I home againe without answere go?

It were better go to Rome on my head than so.

I will tary here this moneth but some of the house

Shall take it of me; and then I care not a louse.   20

But yonder commeth forth a wenche — or, a ladde;

If he haue not one Lumbardes touche,[1] my lucke is bad.

ACTUS II. SCÆNA III

*[Enter] Truepenie. D. Dough[tie remains].
Tibet T[alk-apace and] Anot Al[yface
enter later].*

Trupeny. I am cleane lost for lacke of mery companie!

We gree not halfe well within, our wenches and I.

They will commaunde like mistresses; they will forbyd;

If they be not serued, Trupeny must be chyd.

Let them be as mery nowe as ye can de-
sire,   5

[1] Coin of Lombardy, with a pun on the meaning of Lombard, a pawnbroker.

With turnyng of a hande our mirth lieth in the mire!

I can not skill of such chaungeable mettle;

There is nothing with them but "in docke, out nettle!"

D. Dough. Whether is it better that I speake to him furst,

Or he first to me? It is good to cast the wurst.   10

If I beginne first he will smell all my purpose;

Otherwise, I shall not neede any-thing to disclose.

Trupeny. What boy haue we yonder? I will see what he is.

D. Dough. He commeth to me. [*Pre-
tends to be looking for a house.*] It is hereabout, ywis.

Trupeny. Wouldest thou ought, friende, that thou lookest so about?   15

D. Dough. Yea; but whether ye can helpe me or no, I dout.

I seeke to one Mistresse Custance house, here dwellyng.

Trupenie. It is my mistresse ye seeke too, by your telling.

D. Dough. Is there any of that name heere but shee?

Trupenie. Not one in all the whole towne that I knowe, pardee.   20

D. Dough. A widowe she is, I trowe?

Trupenie.   And what and she be?

D. Dough. But ensured to an husbande?

Trupenie.   Yea, so thinke we.

D. Dough. And I dwell with hir husbande that trusteth to be.

Trupenie. In faith, then must thou needes be welcome to me.

Let vs for acquaintance shake handes to-
gither;   25

And, what-ere thou be, heartily welcome hither!

[Enter Tibet and Anot.]

Tib. Talk. Well, Trupenie, neuer but flinging?[1]

An. Alyface.   And frisking?

Trupenie. Well, Tibet and Annot, still swingyng and whiskyng?

Tib. Talk. But ye roile[2] abroade.

An. Alyface. In the streete, euerewhere.

[1] Running about.   [2] Gad about.

TRUPIENE. Where are ye twaine, in chambers, when ye mete me there? [1]   30
But come hither, fooles; I haue one nowe by the hande,
Seruant to hym that must be our mistresse husbande.
Byd him welcome.
AN. ALYFACE.   To me, truly, is he welcome!
TIB. TALK. Forsooth, and as I may say, heartily welcome!
D. DOUGH. I thank you, mistresse maides.
AN. ALYFACE. I hope we shal better know.   35
TIB. TALK. And when wil our new master come?
D. DOUGH.   Shortly, I trow.
TIB. TALK. I would it were to-morow; for, till he resorte,
Our mistresse, being a widow, hath small comforte.
And I hearde our nourse speake of an husbande to-day
Ready for our mistresse, a riche man and a gay;   40
And we shall go in our Frenche hoodes euery day,
In our silke cassocks, I warrant you, freshe and gay,
In our tricke ferdegews [2] and billiments [3] of golde,
Braue [4] in our sutes of chaunge seuen double folde.
Then shall ye see Tibet, sirs, treade the mosse so trimme, —
Nay, why sayd I treade? ye shall see hir glide and swimme,   46
Not lumperdee clumperdee like our spaniell Rig.

[*She struts like a grand lady.*]

TRUPENY. Mary, then, prickmedaintie,[5] come toste me a fig!
Who shall then know our Tib Talke-apace, trow ye?

AN. ALYFACE. And why not Annot Alyface as fyne as she?   50
TRUPENY. And what! had Tom Trupeny a father, or none?
AN. ALYFACE.   Then our prety newecome man will looke to be one.
TRUPENY. We foure, I trust, shall be a ioily, mery knot! [1]
Shall we sing a fitte to welcome our friende, Annot?
AN. ALYFACE. Perchaunce he can not sing.
D. DOUGH.   I am at all assayes.[2]
TIB. TALK. By Cocke, and the better welcome to vs alwayes!   56

Here they sing:

A thing very fitte
For them that haue witte,
And are felowes knitte,
    Seruants in one house to bee,
Is fast [3] for to sitte,
And not oft to flitte,
Nor varie a whitte,
    But louingly to agree.   64

No man complainyng,
Nor other disdayning,
For losse or for gainyng,
    But felowes or friends to bee;
No grudge remainyng,
No worke refrainyng,
Nor helpe restrainyng,
    But louingly to agree.   72

No man for despite
By worde or by write
His felowe to twite,[4]
    But further in honestie;
No good turnes entwite,[5]
Nor olde sores recite,
But let all goe quite,
    And louingly to agree.   80

After drudgerie,
When they be werie,
Then to be merie,
    To laugh and sing they be free;
With chip and cherie

---

[1] I.e. "Are you two in-doors when you meet me in the street?"
[2] Trim farthingales.
[3] Head-dresses.   [4] Handsome.
[5] One who is ridiculously finical in matters of dress.

[1] Group.   [2] Attempts.
[3] E. *Ts fast fast*
[4] Blame.   [5] Rebuke.

Heigh derie derie,
Trill on the berie,[1]
And louingly to agree.   88

Finis.

TIB. TALK.   Wyll you now in with vs vnto
our mistresse go?
D. DOUGH.   I haue first for my maister an
errand or two.
But I haue here from him a token and a
ring;
They shall haue moste thanke of hir that
first doth it bring.
TIB. TALK. [*snatching*].   Mary, that will I!
TRUPENY.   See and Tibet snatch not
now!
TIB. TALK.   And why may not I, sir, get
thanks as well as you?

Exeat [*Tibet hastily into the house*].

AN. ALYFACE.   Yet get ye not all; we will
go with you both,   95
And haue part of your thanks, be ye neuer
so loth!

Exeant omnes [*in haste after Tibet*].

D. DOUGH.   So my handes are ridde of it,
I care for no more.
I may now return home; so durst I not
afore.   *Exeat.*

ACTUS II. SCÆNA IIII

[*Enter*] *C. Custance, Tibet, Annot Alyface,*
[*and*] *Trupeny.*

C. CUSTANCE.   Nay, come forth all three!
and come hither, pretie mayde!
Will not so many forewarnings make you
afrayde?
TIB. TALK.   Yes, forsoth.
C. CUSTANCE.   But stil be a runner vp
and downe?
Still be a bringer of tidings and tokens to
towne?
TIB. TALK.   No, forsoth, mistresse.
C. CUSTANCE.   Is all your delite and
ioy   5
In whiskyng and ramping abroade like a
tom-boy?
TIB. TALK.   Forsoth, these were there
too, — Annot and Trupenie.

[1] Whirl (dance) on the hillock.

TRUPENIE.   Yea, but ye alone tooke it, ye
can not denie.
ANNOT ALY.   Yea, that ye did!
TIBET.   But if I had not, ye twaine
would.
C. CUSTANCE.   You great calfe! ye should
haue more witte, so ye should!   10
But why shoulde any of you take such
things in hande?
TIBET.   Because it came from him that
must be your husbande.
C. CUSTANCE.   How do ye know that?
TIBET.   Forsoth, the boy did say so.
C. CUSTANCE.   What was his name?
AN. ALYFACE.   We asked not.
C. CUSTANCE.   No did?
AN. ALIFACE.   He is not farre gone, of
likelyhod.
TRUPENY.   I will see.   15
C. CUSTANCE.   If thou canst finde him in
the streete, bring him to me.
TRUPENIE.   Yes.   *Exeat.*
C. CUSTANCE.   Well, ye naughty girles,
if euer I perceiue
That henceforth you do letters or tokens
receiue
To bring vnto me from any person or
place,
Except ye first shewe me the partie face to
face,   20
Eyther thou, or thou, full truly abye thou
shalt.
TIBET.   Pardon this, and the next tyme
pouder [1] me in salt!
C. CUSTANCE.   I shall make all girles by
you twaine to beware.
TIBET.   If euer I offende againe, do not me
spare.
But if euer I see that false boy any more,
By your mistreshyps licence, I tell you
afore,   26
I will rather haue my cote twentie times
swinged
Than on the naughtie wag not to be
auenged.
C. CUSTANCE.   Good wenches would not
so rampe abrode ydelly,
But keepe within doores, and plie their
work earnestly.   30
If one would speake with me that is a man
likely,

[1] Preserve.

Ye shall haue right good thanke to bring
    me worde quickly;
But otherwyse with messages to come in
    post,
From henceforth, I promise you, shall be to
    your cost.
Get you in to your work!
TIB. AN.   Yes, forsooth.
C. CUSTANCE.   Hence, both twaine; 35
And let me see you play me such a part
    againe!

[Exeunt Tibet and Annot. Re-enter
Trupeny.]

TRUPENY.   Maistresse, I haue runne past
    the farre ende of the streete,
Yet can I not yonder craftie boy see nor
    meete.
C. CUSTANCE.   No?
TRUPENY.   Yet I looked as farre be-
    yonde the people
As one may see out of the toppe of Paules
    steeple.   40
C. CUSTANCE.   Hence in at doores, and let
    me no more be vext!
TRUPENY.   Forgeue me this one fault, and
    lay on for the next!   *[Exeat.]*
C. CUSTANCE.   Now will I in too; for I
    thinke, so God me mende,
This will proue some foolishe matter in the
    ende!   *Exeat.*

ACTUS [I]II. SCÆNA I

[Enter] Mathewe Merygreeke.

M. MERY.   Nowe say thys againe: — he
    hath somewhat to dooing
Which followeth the trace [1] of one that is
    wowing,
Specially that hath no more wit in his hedde
Than my cousin Roister Doister withall is
    ledde.
I am sent in all haste to espie and to
    marke   5
How our letters and tokens are likely to
    warke.
Maister Roister Doister must haue aun-
    swere in haste,
For he loueth not to spende much labour in
    waste.

[1] Path, way.

Nowe, as for Christian Custance, by this
    light,
Though she had not hir trouth to Gawin
    Goodluck plight,   10
Yet rather than with such a loutishe dolte
    to marie,
I dare say, woulde lyue a poore lyfe soli-
    tarie.
But fayne would I speake with Custance, if
    I wist how,
To laugh at the matter. Yond commeth
    one forth now!

ACTUS III. SCÆNA II

[Enter] Tibet. M. Merygreeke [remains].
Christian Custance [enters later].

TIB. TALK.   Ah, that I might but once in
    my life haue a sight
Of him that made vs all so yll-shent, by
    this light!
He should neuer escape if I had him by the
    eare,
But euen from his head I would it bite or
    teare;
Yea, and if one of them were not inowe, 5
I would bite them both off, I make God
    auow!
M. MERY.   What is he whome this little
    mouse doth so threaten?
TIB. TALK.   I woulde teache him, I trow,
    to make girles shent or beaten!
M. MERY.   I will call her. Maide, with
    whome are ye so hastie?
TIB. TALK.   Not with you, sir, but with a
    little wagpastie,   10
A deceiuer of folkes by subtill craft and
    guile.
M. MERY. *[aside].*   I knowe where she is;
    Dobinet hath wrought some wile.
TIB. TALK.   He brought a ring and token
    which he sayd was sent
From our dames husbande; but I wot well I
    was shent!
For it liked hir as well, to tell you no
    lies,   15
As water in hir shyppe, or salt cast in hir
    eies.
And yet whence it came neyther we nor she
    can tell.
M. MERY. *[aside].*   We shall haue sport
    anone; I like this very well! —

And dwell ye here with Mistresse Custance,
    faire maide?
TIB. TALK.   Yea, mary, doe I, sir.   What
    would ye haue sayd?   20
M. MERY.   A little message vnto hir by
    worde of mouth.
TIB. TALK.   No messages, by your leaue,
    nor tokens, forsoth!
M. MERY.   Then help me to speke with hir.
TIBET.   With a good wil that.
Here she commeth forth.   Now speake —
    ye know best what.

[Enter Custance.]

C. CUSTANCE.   None other life with you,
    maide, but abrode to skip?   25
TIB. TALK.   Forsoth, here is one would
    speake with your mistresship.
C. CUSTANCE.   Ah, haue ye ben learning
    of mo messages now?
TIB. TALK.   I would not heare his minde,
    but bad him shewe it to you.
C. CUSTANCE.   In at dores!
TIB. TALK.   I am gon.   *Ex[eat]*.
M. MERY.   Dame Custance, God ye
    saue!
C. CUSTANCE.   Welcome, friend Mery-
    greeke!   And what thing wold ye
    haue?   30
M. MERY.   I am come to you a little mat-
    ter to breake.
C. CUSTANCE.   But see it be honest, else
    better not to speake.
M. MERY.   Howe feele ye your-selfe af-
    fected here of late?
C. CUSTANCE.   I feele no maner chaunge,
    but after the olde rate.
But wherby do ye meane?
M. MERY.   Concerning mariage.   35
Doth not loue lade [1] you?
C. CUSTANCE.   I feele no such cariage.[2]
M. MERY.   Doe ye feele no pangues of
    dotage? aunswere me right.
C. CUSTANCE.   I dote so that I make but
    one sleepe all the night.
But what neede all these wordes?
M. MERY.   Oh Iesus! will ye see
What dissemblyng creatures these same
    women be?   40
The gentleman ye wote of, whome ye doe
    so loue

That ye woulde fayne marrie him, yf ye
    durst it moue,
Emong other riche widowes, which are of
    him glad,
Lest ye for lesing of him perchaunce might
    runne mad,
Is nowe contented that, vpon your sute
    making,   45
Ye be as one in election of taking.
C. CUSTANCE.   What a tale is this!   That
    I wote of?   Whome I loue?
M. MERY.   Yea, and he is as louing a
    worme, againe, as a doue.
Een of very pitie he is willyng you to take
Bicause ye shall not destroy your-selfe fo
    his sake.   50
C. CUSTANCE.   Mary, God yelde [1] hi
    mashyp!   What-euer he be,
It is gentmanly spoken!
M. MERY.   Is it not, trowe ye?
If ye haue the grace now to offer your-self
    ye speede.
C. CUSTANCE.   As muche as though I did
    this time it shall not neede.
But what gentman is it, I pray you tell m
    plaine,   5
That woweth so finely?
M. MERY.   Lo where ye be againe,
As though ye knewe him not!
C. CUSTANCE.   Tush, ye speake in iest
M. MERY.   Nay, sure, the partie is in goo
    knacking earnest;
And haue you he will, he sayth, and hau
    you he must.
C. CUSTANCE.   I am promised duryng m
    life; that is iust.   6
M. MERY.   Mary, so thinketh he, vnt
    him alone.
C. CUSTANCE.   No creature hath my fait
    and trouth but one, —
That is Gawin Goodlucke; and, if it be ne
    hee,
He hath no title this way, what-euer he b
Nor I know none to whome I haue suc
    worde spoken.   6
M. MERY.   Ye, knowe him not you by h
    letter and token?
C. CUSTANCE.   In-dede, true it is that
    letter I haue;
But I neuer reade it yet, as God m
    saue!

---

[1] Load.   [2] Burden.

[1] Reward.

M. MERY. Ye a woman, and your letter
so long vnredde?

C. CUSTANCE. Ye may therby know what
hast I haue to wedde.   70

But now who it is for my hande, I knowe by
gesse.

M. MERY. Ah well, I say!

C. CUSTANCE.   It is Roister Doister,
doubtlesse.

M. MERY. Will ye neuer leaue this dis-
simulation?

Ye know hym not?

C. CUSTANCE.   But by imagination;

For no man there is but a very dolt and
loute   75

That to wowe a widowe woulde so go
about.

He shall neuer haue me hys wife while he
doe liue.

M. MERY. Then will he haue you if he
may, so mote I thriue!

And he biddeth you sende him worde by me

That ye humbly beseech him ye may his
wife be,   80

And that there shall be no let in you, nor
mistrust,

But to be wedded on Sunday next, if he lust;

And biddeth you to looke for him.

C. CUSTANCE.   Doth he byd so?

M. MERY. When he commeth, aske hym
whether he dyd or no.

C. CUSTANCE. Goe, say that I bid him
keepe him warme at home!   85

For, if he come abroade, he shall cough me
a mome.[1]

My mynde was vexed, I shrew his head!
Sottish dolt!

M. MERY. He hath in his head —

C. CUSTANCE.   As much braine as a
burbolt!

M. MERY. Well, Dame Custance, if he
heare you thus play choploge [2] —

C. CUSTANCE. What will he?

M. MERY. Play the deuill in the horo-
loge.[3]   90

C. CUSTANCE. I defye him, loute!

M. MERY. Shall I tell hym what ye say?

C. CUSTANCE. Yea; and adde what-so-
euer thou canst, I thee pray,

[1] Prove himself a fool.
[2] Chop-logic, contentious argument.
[3] The devil in the clock, playing havoc with its
works, creating confusion.

And I will auouche it, what-so-euer it bee.

M. MERY.   Then let me alone! we will
laugh well, ye shall see.

It will not be long ere he will hither resorte.   95

C. CUSTANCE. Let hym come when hym
lust, I wishe no better sport.

Fare ye well. I will in and read my great
letter;

I shall to my wower make answere the
better.   *Exeat.*

ACTUS III. SCÆNA III

*Mathew Merygreeke [remains; enter] Roister
Doister [later].*

M. MERY. Nowe that the whole answere
in my deuise doth rest,

I shall paint out our wower in colours of the
best;

And all that I say shall be on Custances
mouth;

She is author of all that I shall speake, forsoth.

But yond commeth Roister Doister nowe,
in a traunce.   5

[Enter Roister.]

R. ROYSTER. Iuno sende me this day
good lucke and good chaunce!

I can not but come see how Merygreeke
doth speede.

M. MERY. I will not see him, but giue
him a iutte, in-deede.

[Runs into him.]

I crie your mastershyp mercie!

R. ROYSTER.   And whither now?

M. MERY. As fast as I could runne, sir, in
poste against you.   10

But why speake ye so faintly? or why are
ye so sad?

R. ROYSTER. Thou knowest the prouerbe
— bycause I can not be had.

Hast thou spoken with this woman?

M. MERY.   Yea, that I haue!

R. ROYSTER. And what, will this geare
be?

M. MERY.   No, so God me saue!

R. ROYSTER. Hast thou a flat answer?

M. MERY.   Nay, a sharp answer!

R. ROYSTER.   What?   15

M. MERY.   Ye shall not, she sayth, by hir
  will marry hir cat!
Ye are such a calfe! such an asse! such a
  blocke!
Such a lilburne! such a hoball! such a lob-
  cocke!
And, bicause ye shoulde come to hir at no
  season,
She despised your maship out of all rea-
  son.   20
"Bawawe ¹ what ye say," ko I, "of such a
  ientman!"
"Nay, I feare him not," ko she, "doe the
  best he can.
He vaunteth him-selfe for a man of prow-
  esse greate,
Where-as a good gander, I dare say, may
  him beate.
And, where he is louted, and laughed to
  skorne,   25
For the veriest dolte that euer was
  borne,
And veriest lubber, slouen, and beast
Liuing in this worlde from the west to the
  east,
Yet of himselfe hath he suche opinion
That in all the worlde is not the like min-
  ion.   30
He thinketh eche woman to be brought in
  dotage
With the onely sight of his goodly per-
  sonage;
Yet none that will haue hym.   We do hym
  loute and flocke,
And make him among vs our common
  sporting-stocke.
And so would I now," ko she, "saue onely
  bicause" —   35
"Better nay," ko I, — "I lust not medle
  with dawes."
"Ye are happy," ko I, "that ye are a
  woman!
This would cost you your life in case ye
  were a man."
R. ROYSTER.   Yea, an hundred thousand
  pound should not saue hir life!
M. MERY.   No, but that ye wowe hir to
  haue hir to your wife.   40
But I coulde not stoppe hir mouth.
R. ROYSTER [*sinking on a bench*].   Heigh
  how, alas!

  ¹ Beware?

M. MERY.   Be of good cheere, man, and
  let the worlde passe!
R. ROYSTER.   What shall I doe, or say,
  nowe that it will not bee?
M. MERY.   Ye shall haue choise of a thou-
  sande as good as shee.
And ye must pardon hir; it is for lacke of
  witte.   45
R. ROYSTER.   Yea, for were not I an hus-
  bande for hir fitte?
Well, what should I now doe?
M. MERY.   In faith, I can not tell.
R. ROYSTER.   I will go home and die!
M. MERY.   Then shall I bidde toll the
  bell?
R. ROYSTER.   No.
M. MERY.   God haue mercie on your
  soule! Ah, good gentleman,
That er ye shuld th[u]s dye for an vnkinde
  woman!   50
Will ye drinke once ere ye goe? ¹
R. ROYSTER.   No, no, I will none.
M. MERY.   How feele your soule to God?
R. ROYSTER.   I am nigh gone.
M. MERY.   And shall we hence streight?
R. ROYSTER.   Yea.
M. MERY.   *Placebo dilexi:* ²
Maister [R]oister Doister will streight go
  home and die.³
Our Lorde Iesus Christ his soule haue
  mercie vpon: 55
Thus you see to day a man, to morrow
  Iohn.
Yet sauing for a womans extreeme cru-
  eltie,
He might haue lyued yet a moneth or two
  or three.
R. ROYSTER.   Heigh how, alas, the pangs
  of death my hearte do breake!
M. MERY.   Holde your peace!   For
  shame, sir! a dead man may not
  speake!   60
Nequando: What mourners and what
  torches shall we haue?
R. ROYSTER   None.
M. MERY.   *Dirige:* He will go darklyng
  to his graue, —

  ¹ It was customary to offer those who were to be
executed something to drink.
  ² What follows is an amusing parody on the Catho-
lic service for the dead.
  ³ E. adds *ut infra.* I have inserted the four lines,
55–58, from the mock requiem as printed after the
songs at the end of the play.

Neque lux, neque crux, neque mourners, *neque* clinke;[1]

He will steale to heauen vnknowing to God, I thinke,

A porta inferi. Who shall your goodes possesse? 65

R. ROYSTER. Thou shalt be my sectour,[2] and haue all, more and lesse.

M. MERY. *Requiem æternam!* Now God reward your mastershyp!

And I will crie halfepenie-doale for your worshyp.

Come forth, sirs, heare the dolefull newes I shall you tell!

He calls in Roister's servants.[3]

Our good maister here will no longer with vs dwell. 70

But, in spite of Custance, which hath hym weried,

Let vs see his mashyp solemnely buried;

And, while some piece of his soule is yet hym within,

Some part of his funeralls let vs here begin.

Audiui vocem: All men, take heede by this one gentleman 75

Howe you sette your loue vpon an vnkinde woman!

For these women be all suche madde, pieuishe elues,

They will not be wonne except it please them-selues.

But, in fayth, Custance, if euer ye come in hell,

Maister Roister Doister shall serue you as well. 80

And will ye needes go from vs thus, in very deede?

R. ROYSTER. Yea, in good sadnesse.

M. MERY. Now Iesus Christ be your speede!

Good night, Roger, olde knaue! farewell, Roger, olde knaue!

Good night, Roger, old knaue! knaue, knap!

---

[1] The clinking of the bell, supposed to drive away evil spirits. In the mock requiem printed at the end of the play we find this variant reading:

Neque lux, neque crux, neque, nisi solum clinke.
Neuer gentman so went toward heauen I thinke.
Yet sirs, as ye wyll the blisse of heauen win,
When he commeth to the graue lay hym softly in.

The last two lines probably should follow line 74.
[2] Executor.　　[3] E. *Evocat seruos militis.*

Nequando. Audiui vocem. Requiem æternam.[1] 85

Pray for the late Maister Roister Doisters soule!

And come forth, parish clarke, let the passing bell toll. [*Enter Parish Clerk.*]

To Roister's servants.[2]

Pray for your mayster, sirs, and for hym ring a peale;

He was your right good maister while he was in heale.

THE PEALE OF BELLES RONG BY THE PARISH CLERK AND ROISTER DOISTERS FOURE MEN.[3]

The first Bell a Triple.
When dyed he? When dyed he? 90
The seconde.
We haue hym! We haue hym!
The thirde.
Royster Doyster! Royster Doyster!
The fourth Bell.
He commeth! He commeth!
The greate Bell.
Our owne! Our owne!

M. MERY. *Qui Lazarum.*

R. ROYSTER. Heigh how!

M. MERY. Dead men go not so fast 95 *In Paradisum.*

R. ROYSTER. Heihow!

M. MERY. Soft, heare what I haue cast!

R. ROYSTER. I will heare nothing, I am past.[4]

M. MERY. Whough, wellaway! Ye may tarie one houre, and heare what I shall say.

Ye were best, sir, for a-while to reuiue againe

And quite[5] them er ye go.

R. ROYSTER. Trowest thou so?

M. MERY. Ye, plain. 100

R. ROYSTER. How may I reuiue, being nowe so farre past?

---

[1] E. *ut infra.* I have added the line from the text of the mock requiem as printed at the end of the play.
[2] E. *Ad Seruos Militis.*
[3] The Peale I have added from the text of the mock requiem at the end of the play.
[4] Dead.　　[5] Requite, get even with.

M. Mery. I will rubbe your temples, and fette you againe at last.

R. Royster. It will not be possible.

M. Mery. Yes, for twentie pounde.

[*Rubs his head roughly.*]

R. Royster [*leaping up angrily*]. Armes! what dost thou?

M. Mery. Fet you again out of your sound.

By this crosse, ye were nigh gone in-deede! I might feele 105
Your soule departing within an inche of your heele.
Now folow my counsell.

R. Royster. What is it?

M. Mery. If I wer you,
Custance should eft[1] seeke to me ere I woulde bowe.

R. Royster. Well, as thou wilt haue me, euen so will I doe.

M. Mery. Then shall ye reuiue againe for an houre or two? 110

R. Royster. As thou wilt; I am content, for a little space.

M. Mery. Good happe is not hastie; yet in space com[e]th grace.
To speake with Custance your-selfe shoulde be very well;
What good therof may come, nor I nor you can tell.
But, now the matter standeth vpon your mariage, 115
Ye must now take vnto you a lustie courage.
Ye may not speake with a faint heart to Custance,
But with a lusty breast and countenance,
That she may knowe she hath to answere to a man.

R. Royster. Yes, I can do that as well as any can. 120

M. Mery. Then, bicause ye must Custance face to face wowe,
Let vs see how to behaue your-selfe ye can doe.
Ye must haue a portely bragge,[2] after your estate.[3]

R. Roister. Tushe, I can handle that after the best rate.

[He struts back and forth.]

M. Mery. Well done! So loe! Vp, man, with your head and chin! 125
Vp with that snoute, man! So loe! nowe ye begin!
So! that is somewhat like! But, prankie cote,[1] nay, whan!
That is a lustie brute! Handes vnder your side, man!
So loe! Now is it euen as it shoulde bee!
That is somewhat like for a man of your degree! 130
Then must ye stately goe, ietting[2] vp and downe.
Tut! can ye no better shake the taile of your gowne?
There, loe! suche a lustie bragge it is ye must make!

R. Royster. To come behind and make curtsie, thou must som pains take.

M. Mery. Else were I much to blame, I thanke your mastershyp. 135

[*Making curtsy.*]

The Lorde one day all to-begrime you with worshyp!

[*Shoving imaginary persons out of the way.*]

Backe, sir sauce! let gentlefolkes haue elbowe roome!
Voyde, sirs! see ye not Maister Roister Doister come?
Make place, my maisters!

[*He bumps hard into Roister.*]

R. Royster. Thou iustlest nowe to nigh.

M. Mery. Back, al rude loutes!

[*Bumps him again.*]

R. Royster. Tush!

M. Mery. I crie your maship mercy! 140
Hoighdagh! if faire, fine Mistresse Custance sawe you now,
Ralph Royster Doister were hir owne, I warrant you.

R. Royster. Neare an M by your girdle?[3]

M. Mery. Your Good Mastershyps

---

[1] A second time.
[2] Pompous demeanor. [3] State, rank.

[1] Set your coat in order. (But *N.E.D.*, citing this passage, defines *prankie* as "full of pranks.")
[2] Strutting.
[3] A proverbial phrase: have you no respectful terms of address to employ towards me?

Maistershyp were hir owne Mistreshyps
    Mistreshyps!
Ye were take vp for haukes,[1] ye were gone,
    ye were gone!   145
But now one other thing more yet I thinke
    vpon.
R. ROYSTER.   Shewe what it is.
M. MERY.   A wower be he neuer so
    poore,
Must play and sing before his bestbeloues
    doore;
How much more, than, you!
R. ROYSTER.   Thou speakest wel, out of
    dout.
M. MERY.   And perchaunce that woulde
    make hir the sooner come out.   150
R. ROYSTER.   Goe call my musitians;
    bydde them high apace.
M. MERY.   I wyll be here with them ere
    ye can say trey ace.   *Exeat.*
R. ROYSTER.   This was well sayde of
    Merygreeke! I lowe hys wit.
Before my sweete hearts dore we will haue
    a fit,
That, if my loue come forth that I may
    with hir talke,   155
I doubt not but this geare shall on my side
    walke.
But lo, how well Merygreeke is returned
    sence!

[Re-enter Merygreeke with Musicians.]

M. MERY.   There hath grown no grasse on
    my heele since I went hence!
Lo, here haue I brought that shall make
    you pastance.
R. ROYSTER.   Come, sirs, let vs sing, to
    winne my deare loue Custance!   160

[They sing.] [2]

I mun be maried a Sunday;
I mun be maried a Sunday;
Who-soeuer shall come that way,
    I mun be maried a Sunday.   164

Royster Doyster is my name,
Royster Doyster is my name;
A lustie brute, I am the same.
    I mun be maried a Sunday.   168

[1] Hawks, used of officers of the law who pounced
on criminals.
[2] E.   *Cantent.*   The song, entitled "The fourth
Song," is printed at the end of the play.

Christian Custance haue I founde,
Christian Custance haue I founde,
A wydowe worthe a thousande pounde.
    I mun be maried a Sunday.   172

Custance is as sweete as honey,
Custance is as sweete as honey;
I hir lambe and she my coney.
    I mun be maried a Sunday.   176

When we shall make our weddyng-feast,
When we shall make our weddyng-feast,
There shall bee cheere for man and beast.
    I mun be maried a Sunday.
        I mun be maried a Sunday, etc.   181

M. MERY.   Lo, where she commeth!
    Some countenaunce to hir make,
And ye shall heare me be plaine with hir
    for your sake.

ACTUS III. SCÆNA IIII

*[Enter] Custance. Merygreeke [and] Roister
Doister [remain].*

C. CUSTANCE.   What gaudyng and fool-
    yng is this afore my doore?
M. MERY.   May not folks be honest, pray
    you, though they be pore?
C. CUSTANCE.   As that thing may be true,
    so rich folks may be fooles!
R. ROYSTER.   Hir talke is as fine as she
    had learned in scholes.   4
M. MERY. *[aside to Roister].* Looke partly
    towarde hir, and drawe a little nere.
C. CUSTANCE.   Get ye home, idle folkes!
M. MERY.   Why, may not we be here?
Nay, and ye will haze,[1] haze; otherwise, I
    tell you plaine,
And ye will not haze, then giue vs our geare
    againe.
C. CUSTANCE.   In-deede I haue of yours
    much gay things, God saue all!
R. ROYSTER *[aside to Merygreeke].* Speake
    gently vnto hir, and let hir take all.
M. MERY.   Ye are to tender-hearted;
    shall she make vs dawes?   11
Nay, dame, I will be plaine with you in my
    friends cause.
R. ROYSTER.   Let all this passe, sweete
    heart, and accept my seruice!

[1] Have us.

C. Custance.   I will not be serued with a
    foole, in no wise;
When I choose an husbande, I hope to take
    a man.   15
M. Mery.   And where will ye finde one
    which can doe that he can?
Now, thys man towarde you being so
    kinde,
You not to make him an answere some-
    what to his minde!
C. Custance.   I sent him a full answere
    by you, dyd I not?
M. Mery.   And I reported it.
C. Custance.   Nay, I must speake it
    againe.   20
R. Royster.   No, no! he tolde it all.
M. Mery.   Was I not metely plaine?
R. Royster.   Yes.
M. Mery.   But I would not tell all;
    for, faith, if I had,
With you, Dame Custance, ere this houre
    it had been bad;
And not without cause, for this goodly per-
    sonage
Ment no lesse than to ioyne with you in
    mariage.   25
C. Custance.   Let him wast no more
    labour nor sute about me.
M. Mery.   Ye know not where your pre-
    ferment lieth, I see,
He sending you such a token, ring and
    letter.
C. Custance.   Mary, here it is.   Ye
    neuer sawe a better!
M. Mery.   Let vs see your letter.
C. Custance.   Holde;[1] reade it, if ye can, 30
And see what letter it is to winne a woman!

[*He reads the superscription on the outside.*]

M. Mery.   "To mine owne deare coney,[2]
    birde, swete-heart, and pigsny,[3]
Good Mistresse Custance, present these by
    and by."
Of this superscription do ye blame the stile?
C. Custance.   With the rest as good
    stuffe as ye redde a great while! 35

[*He opens the letter, and reads.*]

M. Mery.   "Sweete mistresse, where as I
    loue you nothing at all,

---
[1] Take.   [2] Rabbit, a term of endearment.
[3] Pig's eye, a term of endearment.

Regarding your substance and richesse
    chiefe of all,
For your personage, beautie, demeanour
    and wit,
I commende me vnto you neuer a whit.
Sorie to heare report of your good wel-
    fare.   40
For (as I heare say) suche your conditions
    are
That ye be worthie fauour of no liuing man.
To be abhorred of euery honest man;
To be taken for a woman enclined to vice;
Nothing at all to vertue gyuing hir due
    price.   45
Wherfore concerning mariage, ye are
    thought
Suche a fine paragon, as nere honest man
    bought.
And nowe by these presentes I do you ad-
    uertise
That I am minded to marrie you in no wise.
For your goodes and substance, I coulde
    bee content   50
To take you as ye are.   If ye mynde to bee
    my wyfe,
Ye shall be assured for the tyme of my lyfe
I will keepe ye ryght well from good ray-
    ment and fare;
Ye shall not be kepte but in sorowe and
    care.
Ye shall in no wyse lyue at your owne lib-
    ertie;   55
Doe and say what ye lust, ye shall neuer
    please me;
But when ye are mery, I will be all sadde,
When ye are sory, I will be very gladde;
When ye seeke your heartes ease, I will be
    vnkinde;
At no tyme, in me shall ye muche gentle-
    nesse finde.   60
But all things contrary to your will and
    minde
Shall be done: otherwise I wyll not be be-
    hinde
To speake.   And as for all them that
    woulde do you wrong
I will so helpe and mainteyne, ye shall not
    lyue long.
Nor any foolishe dolte shall cumbre you
    but I.   65
I, who ere say nay, wyll sticke by you tyll I
    die.

Thus good mistresse Custance, the Lorde
  you saue and kepe
From me Roister Doister, whether I wake
  or slepe.
Who fauoureth you no lesse (ye may be
  bolde)
Than this letter purporteth, which ye haue
  vnfolde." 70
C. CUSTANCE. Howe by this letter of
  loue? is it not fine?
R. ROYSTER. By the armes of Caleys, it is
  none of myne!
M. MERY. Fie! you are fowle to blame!
  This is your owne hand!
C. CUSTANCE. Might not a woman be
  proude of such an husbande?
M. MERY. Ah, that ye would in a letter
  shew such despite! 75
R. ROYSTER. Oh, I would I had hym
  here, the which did it endite!
M. MERY. Why, ye made it your-selfe, ye
  tolde me, by this light!
R. ROYSTER. Yea, I ment I wrote it myne
  owne selfe, yesternight.
C. CUSTANCE. Ywis, sir, I would not haue
  sent you such a mocke.
R. ROYSTER. Ye may so take it, but I
  ment it not so, by Cocke! 80
M. MERY. Who can blame this woman to
  fume, and frette, and rage?
Tut, tut! your-selfe nowe haue marde your
  owne marriage.
Well, yet, Mistresse Custance, if ye can
  this remitte,
This gentleman other-wise may your loue
  requitte.
C. CUSTANCE. No! God be with you
  both, and seeke no more to me. 85

Exeat [Custance].

R. ROYSTER. Wough! she is gone for-
  euer! I shall hir no more see!

[*He begins to weep.*]

M. MERY. What, weepe? fye, for shame!
  and blubber? For manhods sake,
Neuer lette your foe so muche pleasure of
  you take!
Rather play the mans parte, and doe loue
  refraine.
If she despise you, een despise ye hir
  againe! 90

R. ROYSTER. By Gosse, and for thy sake
  I defye hir, indeede!
M. MERY. Yea, and perchaunce that way
  ye shall much sooner speede;
For one madde propretie these women
  haue, in fey:
When ye will, they will not; will not ye,
  then will they.
Ah, foolishe woman! Ah, moste vnluckie
  Custance! 95
Ah, vnfortunate woman! Ah, pieuishe
  Custance!
Art thou to thine harmes so obstinately bent
That thou canst not see where lieth thine
  high preferment?
Canst thou not lub dis man, which coulde
  lub dee so well? 90
Art thou so much thine own foe?
R. ROYSTER. Thou dost the truth tell.
M. MERY. Wel, I lament —
R. ROYSTER. So do I.
M. MERY. Wherfor?
R. ROYSTER. For this thing:
Bicause she is gone.
M. MERY. I mourne for an-other thing.
R. ROYSTER. What is it, Merygreeke,
  wherfore thou dost griefe take?
M. MERY. That I am not a woman my-
  selfe, for your sake.
I would haue you my-selfe, and a strawe
  for yond Gill! 105
And mocke much of you, though it were
  against my will.
I would not, I warrant you, fall in such a
  rage
As so to refuse suche a goodly personage.
R. ROYSTER. In faith, I heartily thanke
  thee, Merygreeke.
M. MERY. And I were a woman —
R. ROYSTER. Thou wouldest to me
  seeke. 110
M. MERY. For, though I say it, a goodly
  person ye bee.
R. ROYSTER. No, no.
M. MERY. Yes, a goodly man as ere I
  dyd see.
R. ROYSTER. No, I am a poore homely
  man, as God made mee.
M. MERY. By the faith that I owe to
  God, sir, but ye bee!
Woulde I might, for your sake, spende a
  thousande pound land. 115

R. Royster.   I dare say thou wouldest
     haue me to thy husbande.
M. Mery.   Yea; and I were the fairest
     lady in the shiere,
And knewe you as I know you, and see you
     nowe here —
Well, I say no more!
R. Royster. Gramercies, with all my hart!
M. Mery.   But, since that can not be,
     will ye play a wise parte?   120
R. Royster.   How should I?
M. Mery.   Refraine from Custance
     a-while now,
And I warrant hir soone right glad to seeke
     to you;
Ye shall see hir anon come on hir knees
     creeping,
And pray you to be good to hir, salte teares
     weeping.
R. Royster.   But what and she come not?
M. Mery.   In faith, then, farewel
     she!   125
Or else, if ye be wroth, ye may auenged be.
R. Royster.   By Cocks precious pot-
     sticke,[1] and een so I shall!
I wyll vtterly destroy hir, and house, and
     all!
But I woulde be auenged, in the meane
     space,
On that vile scribler,[2] that did my wowyng
     disgrace.   130
M. Mery. "Scribler," ko you? in-deede,
     he is worthy no lesse!
I will call hym to you and ye bidde me,
     doubtlesse.
R. Royster.   Yes, for although he had as
     many liues
As a thousande widowes, and a thousande
     wiues,
As a thousande lyons, and a thousand
     rattes,   135
A thousande wolues, and a thousande
     cattes,
A thousande bulles, and a thousande calues,
And a thousand legions diuided in halues,
He shall neuer scape death on my swordes
     point —
Though I shoulde be torne therfore ioynt
     by ioynt!   140

[1] By God's precious stick for stirring the pot; a
meaningless oath.
[2] Roister means "scrivener."

M. Mery.   Nay, if ye will kyll him, I will
     not fette him;
I will not in so muche extremitie sette him.
He may yet amende, sir, and be an honest
     man.
Therfore pardon him, good soule, as muche
     as ye can.
R. Royster.   Well, for thy sake, this once
     with his lyfe he shall passe.   145
But I wyll hewe hym all to pieces, by the
     masse!
M. Mery.   Nay, fayth, ye shall promise
     that he shall no harme haue,
Else I will not fet him.
R. Royster.   I shall, so God me saue!
But I may chide him a good?
M. Mery.   Yea, that do, hardely.
R. Royster.   Go, then.
M. Mery.   I returne, and bring him to
     you by-and-by.[1]   Ex[eat]. 150

ACTUS III. SCÆNA V

*Roister Doister [remains. Later] Mathewe
     Merygreeke [enters with the] Scriuener.*

R. Royster.   What is a gentleman but his
     worde and his promise?
I must nowe saue this vilaines lyfe in any
     wise;
And yet at hym already my handes doe
     tickle.
I shall vneth [2] holde them, they wyll be so
     fickle.
But lo and Merygreeke haue not brought
     him sens!   5

[*Enter at a distance Merygreeke and the
     Scrivener, talking angrily.*]

M. Mery.   Nay, I woulde I had of my
     purse payde fortie pens!
Scriuener.   So woulde I, too; but it
     needed not that stounde.[3]
M. Mery.   But the ientman had rather
     spent fiue thousande pounde;
For it disgraced him at least fiue tymes so
     muche.
Scriuener.   He disgraced hym-selfe, his
     loutishnesse is suche.   10
R. Royster.   Howe long they stande
     prating!   Why comst thou not
     away?

[1] Immediately.   [2] With difficulty.   [3] Time.

M. Mery. Come nowe to hymselfe, and hearke what he will say.

Scriuener. I am not afrayde in his presence to appeere.

[*They approach Roister.*]

R. Royster. Arte thou come, felow?

Scriuener. How thinke you? am I not here?

R. Royster. What hindrance hast thou done me, and what villanie? 15

Scriuener. It hath come of thy-selfe, if thou hast had any.

R. Royster. All the stocke thou comest of, later or rather,[1]

From thy fyrst fathers grandfathers fathers father,

Nor all that shall come of thee, to the worldes ende,

Though to three-score generations they descende, 20

Can be able to make me a iust recompense

For this trespasse of thine and this one offense!

Scriuener. Wherin?

R. Royster. Did not you make me a letter, brother?

Scriuener. Pay the like hire, I will make you suche another.

R. Royster. Nay, see and these whooreson Phariseys and Scribes 25

Doe not get their liuyng by polling[2] and bribes!

If it were not for shame —

[*Drawing back to strike.*]

Scriuener. Nay, holde thy hands still!

M. Mery. Why, did ye not promise that ye would not him spill?[3]

Scriuener. Let him not spare me.

R. Royster. Why, wilt thou strike me again?

Scriuener. Ye shall haue as good as ye bring, of me; that is plaine! 30

M. Mery. I can not blame him, sir, though your blowes wold him greue,

For he knoweth present death to ensue of all ye geue.

R. Royster. Well, this man for once hath purchased thy pardon.

¹ Sooner.　² Extortion.　³ Destroy, kill.

Scriuener. And what say ye to me? or else I will be gon.

R. Royster. I say the letter thou madest me was not good. 35

Scriuener. Then did ye wrong copy it, of likelyhood.

R. Royster. Yes, out of thy copy worde for worde I wrote.

[*Roister produces his copy of the letter, and also the Scrivener's original draft.*]

Scriuener. Then was it as ye prayed to haue it, I wote.

But in reading and pointyng there was made some faulte.

R. Royster. I wote not; but it made all my matter to haulte. 40

Scriuener. Howe say you, is this mine originall or no?

R. Royster. The selfe-same that I wrote out of,[1] so mote I go!

Scriuener. Loke you on your owne fist,[2] and I will looke on this,

And let this man be iudge whether I reade amisse.

[*Reads the superscription.*]

"To myne owne dere coney, birde, sweeteheart, and pigsny, 45

Good mistresse Custance, present these by and by."

How now? doth not this superscription agree?

R. Royster. Reade that is within, and there ye shall the fault see.

[*The Scrivener opens the letter and reads.*]

Scriuener. " Sweete mistresse, where as I loue you — nothing at all

Regarding your richesse and substance, chiefe of all 50

For your personage, beautie, demeanour and witte —

I commende me vnto you. Neuer a whitte

Sory to heare reporte of your good welfare;

For (as I heare say) suche your conditions are

That ye be worthie fauour; of no liuing man 55

To be abhorred; of euery honest man

To be taken for a woman enclined to vice

¹ Copied.　² The copy in your own writing

Nothing at all; to vertue giuing hir due price.
Wherfore, concerning mariage, ye are
    thought
Suche a fine paragon as nere honest man
    bought.   60
And nowe by these presents I doe you ad-
    uertise
That I am minded to marrie you — in no
    wyse
For your goodes and substance; I can be
    content
To take you as you are.   Yf ye will be my
    wife,
Ye shall be assured for the time of my
    life   65
I wyll keepe you right well.   From good
    raiment and fare,
Ye shall not be kept; but in sorowe and
    care
Ye shall in no wyse lyue; at your owne lib-
    ertie
Doe and say what ye lust; ye shall neuer
    please me
But when ye are merrie; I will bee all
    sadde   70
When ye are sorie; I wyll be very gladde
When ye seeke your heartes ease; I will be
    vnkinde
At no time; in me shall ye muche gentle-
    nesse finde.
But all things contrary to your will and
    minde
Shall be done otherwise; I wyl not be be-
    hynde   75
To speake.   And as for all they that woulde
    do you wrong
(I wyll so helpe and maintayne ye), shall
    not lyue long.
Nor any foolishe dolte shall cumber you;
    but I —
I, who ere say nay — wyll sticke by you tyll
    I die.
Thus, good mistresse Custance, the Lorde
    you saue and kepe.   80
From me, Roister Doister, whether I wake
    or slepe,
Who fauoureth you no lesse (ye may be
    bolde)
Than this letter purporteth, which ye haue
    vnfolde."
Now, sir, what default can ye finde in this
    letter?

R. ROYSTER.   Of truth, in my mynde
    there can not be a better.   85
SCRIUENER.   Then was the fault in read-
    yng, and not in writyng, —
No, nor, I dare say, in the fourme of endit-
    yng.
But who read this letter, that it sounded so
    nought?
M. MERY.   I redde it, in-deede.
SCRIUENER.   Ye red it not as ye ought.

[*Roister draws back as though to strike Mery-
    greeke.*]

R. ROYSTER.   Why, thou wretched vil-
    laine! was all this same fault in
    thee?   90
M. MERY.   I knocke your costarde if ye
    offer to strike me!

[*Strikes him.*]

R. ROYSTER.   Strikest thou in-deede? and
    I offer but in iest.
M. MERY.   Yea, and rappe you againe,
    except ye can sit in rest.
And I will no longer tarie here, me beleue.
R. ROYSTER.   What! wilt thou be angry,
    and I do thee forgeue?   95
Fare ye well, scribler.   I crie thee mercie,[1]
    indeede!
SCRIUENER.   Fare ye well, bibbler, and
    worthily may ye speede!

[*Exit the Scrivener.*]

R. ROYSTER.   If it were an-other but thou,
    it were a knaue.
M. MERY.   Ye are an-other your-selfe, sir,
    the Lorde vs both saue!
Albeit, in this matter I must your pardon
    craue.   100
Alas! woulde ye wyshe in me the witte that
    ye haue?
But, as for my fault, I can quickely
    amende;
I will shewe Custance it was I that did of-
    fende.
R. ROYSTER.   By so doing, hir anger may
    be reformed.
M. MERY.   But, if by no entreatie she will
    be turned,   105
Then sette lyght by hir, and bee as testie as
    shee,

---

[1] I beg your pardon.

And doe your force vpon hir with extremitie.

R. ROISTER. Come on, therefore, lette vs
go home, in sadnesse.

M. MERY. That if force shall neede, all
may be in a readinesse.

And, as for thys letter, hardely let all
go; 110

We wyll know where she refuse you for that
or no. *Exeant am[bo].*

ACTUS IIII. SCÆNA I

[*Enter*] *Sym Suresby* [*servant to Gawin
Goodluck*].

SIM SURE. Is there any man but I, Sym
Suresby, alone,

That would haue taken such an enterprise
him vpon,

In suche an outragious tempest as this was,

Suche a daungerous gulfe of the sea to passe?

I thinke verily Neptunes mightie godshyp 5

Was angry with some that was in our shyp;

And, but for the honestie which in me he
founde,

I thinke for the others sake we had bene
drownde.

But fye on that seruant which for his
maisters wealth

Will sticke[1] for to hazarde both his lyfe
and his health! 10

My maister, Gawyn Goodlucke, after me a
day,

Bicause of the weather, thought best hys
shyppe to stay.

And now that I haue the rough sourges so
well past,

God graunt I may finde all things safe here
at last!

Then will I thinke all my trauaile well
spent. 15

Nowe the first poynt wherfore my maister
hath me sent

Is to salute Dame Christian Custance, his
wife

Espoused, whome he tendreth[2] no lesse
than his life.

I must see how it is with hir, well or wrong,

And whether for him she doth not now
thinke long. 20

[1] Hesitate.   [2] Esteemeth.

Then to other friendes I haue a message or
tway;

And then so to returne and mete him on
the way.

Now wyll I goe knocke, that I may dispatche with speede —

But loe, forth commeth hir-selfe, happily,
in-deede!

ACTUS IIII. SCÆNA II

[*Enter*] *Christian Custance. Sim Suresby
*[*remains*].

C. CUSTANCE. I come to see if any more
stirryng be here.

But what straunger is this which doth to
me appere?

SYM SURS. I will speake to hir. Dame,
the Lorde you saue and see!

C. CUSTANCE. What! friende Sym Suresby? Forsoth, right welcome ye be!

Howe doth mine owne Gawyn Goodlucke?
I pray the tell. 5

S. SURESBY. When he knoweth of your
health, he will be perfect well.

C. CUSTANCE. If he haue perfect helth, I
am as I would be.

SIM SURE. Suche newes will please him
well; this is as it should be.

C. CUSTANCE. I thinke now long for him.

SYM SURE.   And he as long for you.

C. CUSTANCE. When wil he be at home?

SYM SURE.   His heart is here een now; 10
His body commeth after.

C. CUSTANCE.   I woulde see that faine.

SIM SURE. As fast as wynde and sayle can
cary it a-maine. —

But what two men are yonde comming
hitherwarde?

C. CUSTANCE. Now, I shrew their best
Christmasse chekes, both togeth-
erward!

ACTUS IIII. SCÆNA III

Christian Custance [*and*] *Sym Suresby* [*remain. At a distance enter*] *Ralph Roister
*[*and*] *Mathew Merygreke. Trupenj
*[*enters later*].

C. CUSTANCE [*aside*]. What meane these
lewde felowes thus to trouble me
stil?

Sym Suresby here, perchance, shal therof
    deme som yll,
And shall su[s]pect in me some point of
    naughtinesse,
And ¹ they come hitherward.
Sym Sure.   What is their businesse?
C. Custance. I haue nought to them, nor
    they ci to me, in sadnesse.   5
Sim Sure. Let vs hearken them. [Aside.]
    Somewhat there is, I feare it.
R. Royster.   I will speake out aloude;
    best that she may heare it.
M. Mery. Nay, alas, ye may so feare hir
    out of hir wit!
R. Royster. By the crosse of my swarde,
    I will hurt hir no whit!
M. Mery. Will ye doe no harme,
    indeede?   Shall I trust your
    worde?   10
R. Royster. By Roister Doisters fayth, I
    will speake but in borde! ²
Sim Sure. Let vs hearken them. [Aside.]
    Somwhat there is, I feare it.
R. Royster. I will speake out aloude, I
    care not who heare it!

[He pretends to speak to his servants within.]

Sirs, see that my harnesse, my tergat, and
    my shield
Be made as bright now as when I was last
    in fielde,   15
As white as I shoulde to warre againe to-
    morrowe;
For sicke shall I be but I worke some folke
    sorow.
Therfore see that all shine as bright as
    Sainct George,
Or as doth a key newly come from the
    smiths forge.
I woulde haue my sworde and harnesse to
    shine so bright   20
That I might therwith dimme mine enimies
    sight;
I would haue it cast beames as fast, I tell
    you playne,
As doth the glittryng grasse after a showre
    of raine.
And see that, in case I shoulde neede to
    come to arming,
All things may be ready at a minutes
    warning!   25

¹ If.   ² Jest.

For such chaunce may chaunce in an
    houre, do ye heare?
M. Mery. As perchance shall not chaunce
    againe in seuen yeare.
R. Royster. Now draw we neare to hir,
    and here what shall be sayde.
M. Mery. But I woulde not haue you
    make hir too muche afrayde.

[They advance to Custance.]

R. Royster. Well founde, sweete wife, I
    trust, for al this your soure looke!
C. Custance. Wife! why cal ye me wife?
Sim Sure. [aside].   Wife! this gear goth
    acrook!   31
M. Mery. Nay, Mistresse Custance, I
    warrant you, our letter
Is not as we redde een nowe, but much
    better;
And, where ye halfe stomaked ¹ this gentle-
    man afore
For this same letter, ye wyll loue hym now
    therefore.   35
Nor it is not this letter, though ye were a
    queene,
That shoulde breake marriage betweene
    you twaine, I weene.
C. Custance. I did not refuse hym for
    the letters sake.
R. Royster. Then ye are content me for
    your husbande to take?
C. Custance. You for my husbande to
    take? nothing lesse, truely!   40
R. Royster. Yea, say so, sweete spouse,
    afore straungers hardly!
M. Mery. And, though I haue here his
    letter of loue with me,
Yet his ryng and tokens he sent keepe safe
    with ye.
C. Custance. A mischiefe take his tok-
    ens! and him, and thee too!
But what prate I with fooles? Haue I
    nought else to doo?   45
Come in with me, Sym Suresby, to take
    some repast.
Sim Sure. I must, ere I drinke, by your
    leaue, goe in all hast
To a place or two with earnest letters of his.
C. Custance. Then come drink here with
    me.
Sim Sure.   I thank you.

¹ Were offended at.

C. Custance. Do not misse!
You shall haue a token to your maister
with you. 50
Sym Sure. No tokens this time, gramercies! God be with you! *Exeat.*
C. Custance. Surely this fellowe mis-
deemeth some yll in me;
Which thing, but God helpe, will go neere
to spill me.

[*Roister calls after Sim Suresby:*]

R. Royster. Yea, farewell, fellow! And
tell thy maister, Goodlucke,
That he commeth to late of thys blossome
to plucke! 55
Let him keepe him there still, or, at least-
wise, make no hast;
As for his labour hither, he shall spende in
wast:
His betters be in place nowe!
M. Mery. [*aside*]. As long as it will
hold.
C. Custance. I will be euen with thee,
thou beast, thou mayst be bolde! [1]
R. Royster. Will ye haue vs, then?
C. Custance. I will neuer haue thee! 60
R. Royster. Then will I haue you.
C. Custance. No, the deuill shal haue
thee!
I haue gotten this houre more shame and
harme by thee
Then all thy life-days thou canst do me
honestie.
M. Mery. Why, nowe may ye see what it
comth too in the ende
To make a deadly foe of your most louing
frende! 65
And, ywis, this letter, if ye woulde heare it
now —
C. Custance. I will heare none of it!
M. Mery. In faith, would rauishe you.
C. Custance. He hath stained my name
for-euer, this is cleare.
R. Royster. I can make all as well in an
houre.
M. Mery. As ten yeare.
How say ye? Wil ye haue him?
C. Custance. No.
M. Mery. Wil ye take him? 70
C. Custance. I defie him.
M. Mery. At my word? [2]

C. Custance. A shame take him!
Waste no more wynde, for it will neuer
bee.
M. Mery. This one faulte with twaine
shall be mended, ye shall see.
Gentle Mistresse Custance now, good
Mistresse Custance,
Honey Mistresse Custance now, sweete
Mistresse Custance, 75
Golden Mistresse Custance now, white [1]
Mistresse Custance,
Silken Mistresse Custance now, faire Mis-
tresse Custance —
C. Custance. Faith, rather than to mary
with suche a doltishe loute,
I woulde matche my-selfe with a begger,
out of doute!
M. Mery. Then I can say no more. [*To
Roister.*] To speede we are not
like, 80
Except ye rappe out a ragge of your rhet-
orike.
C. Custance. Speake not of winnyng me;
for it shall neuer be so.
R. Royster. Yes, dame! I will haue
you, whether ye will or no.
I commaunde you to loue me! Wherfore
shoulde ye not?
Is not my loue to you chafing and burning
hot? 85
M. Mery. Too hir! That is well sayd!
R. Royster. Shall I so breake my
braine
To dote vpon you, and ye not loue vs
againe?
M. Mery. Wel sayd yet!
C. Custance. Go to, you goose!
R. Royster. I say, Kit Custance,
In case ye will not haze,[2] — well, better
yes, perchaunce!
C. Custance. Auaunt, lozell! Picke
thee hence!
M. Mery. Wel, sir, ye perceiue, 90
For all your kinde offer, she will not you
receiue.
R. Royster. Then a strawe for hir! And
a strawe for hir, againe!
She shall not be my wife, woulde she neuer
so faine!
No, and though she would be at ten thou-
sand pounde cost!

---

[1] Certain, confident.   [2] On my assurance.

[1] A term of endearment.   [2] Have us.

M. MERY. Lo, dame, ye may see what an
    husbande ye haue lost! 95
C. CUSTANCE. Yea, no force;[1] a iewell
    muche better lost than founde!
M. MERY. Ah, ye will not beleue how this
    doth my heart wounde!
How shoulde a mariage betwene you be
    towarde
If both parties drawe backe and become so
    frowarde?
R. ROYSTER. Nay, dame, I will fire thee
    out of thy house, 100
And destroy thee and all thine, and that
    by-and-by.[2]
M. MERY. Nay, for the passion of God,
    sir, do not so!
R. ROYSTER. Yes, except she will say yea
    to that she sayde no.
C. CUSTANCE. And what! be there no
    officers, trow we, in towne
To checke idle loytrers braggyng vp and
    downe? 105
Where be they by whome vacabunds
    shoulde be represt,
That poore sillie[3] widowes might liue in
    peace and rest?
Shall I neuer ridde thee out of my companie?
I will call for helpe. What, hough! Come
    forth, Trupenie!
TRUPENIE [within]. Anon. [Entering.]
    What is your will, mistresse? Dyd
    ye call me? 110
C. CUSTANCE. Yea; go runne apace, and,
    as fast as may be,
Pray Tristram Trusty, my moste assured
    frende,
To be here by-and-by, that he may me de-
    fende.
TRUPENIE. That message so quickly shall
    be done, by Gods grace,
That at my returne ye shall say I went
    apace. Exeat. 115
C. CUSTANCE. Then shall we see, I trowe,
    whether ye shall do me harme!
R. ROYSTER. Yes, in faith, Kitte, I shall
    thee and thine so charme[4]
That all women incarnate by thee may be-
    ware.
C. CUSTANCE. Nay, as for charming me,
    come hither if thou dare!

I shall cloute[1] thee tyll thou stinke, both
    thee and thy traine, 120
And coyle[2] thee mine owne handes, and
    sende thee home againe.
R. ROYSTER. Yea, sayst thou me that,
    dame? Dost thou me threaten?
Goe we, I will[3] see whether I shall be
    beaten.
M. MERY. Nay, for the paishe of God, let
    me now treate peace;
For bloudshed will there be, in case this
    strife increace. 125
Ah, good Dame Custance, take better way
    with you!
C. CUSTANCE. Let him do his worst!

[Roister Doister advances on Custance; she
    beats him.]

M. MERY.   Yeld in time.
R. ROYSTER [to Merygreeke].   Come
    hence, thou!

Exeant Roister et Mery.

ACTUS IIII. SCÆNA IIII

Christian Custance [remains. Later enter]
Anot Alyface, Tibet T., M. Mumblecrust.

C. CUSTANCE. So, sirra! If I should not
    with hym take this way,
I should not be ridde of him, I thinke, till
    doomes-day.
I will call forth my folkes, that, without
    any mockes,
If he come agayne, we may giue him rappes
    and knockes.
Mage Mumblecrust, come forth! and Tibet
    Talke-apace! 5
Yea, and come forth, too, Mistresse Annot
    Alyface!
ANNOT ALY. [entering]. I come.
TIBET [entering].   And I am here.
M. MUMB. [entering].   And I am here
    too at length.
C. CUSTANCE. Like warriers, if nede bee,
    ye must shew your strength.
The man that this day hath thus begiled you
Is Ralph Roister Doister, whome ye know
    well inowe,[4] 10

---

[1] It does not matter.   [2] At once.
[3] Defenceless.   [4] Overcome.

[1] Beat.   [2] Thrash.
[3] E. *still;* corrected by Cooper.
[4] E. *mowe;* corrected by Cooper.

The moste loute and dastarde that euer on
    grounde trode.
Tib. Talk.   I see all folke mocke hym
    when he goth abrode.
C. Custance.   What, pretie maide! will
    ye talke when I speake?
Tib. Talk.   No, forsooth, good mistresse.
C. Custance.   Will ye my tale breake?
He threatneth to come hither with all his
    force to fight;   15
I charge you, if he come, on him with all
    your might!
M. Mumbl.   I with my distaffe will reache
    hym one rappe!
Tib. Talk.   And I with my newe broome
    will sweepe hym one swappe,
And then with our greate clubbe I will
    reache hym one rappe!
An. Aliface.   And I with our skimmer [1]
    will fling him one flappe!   20
Tib. Talk.   Then Trupenies fireforke [2]
    will him shrewdly fray,[3]
And you with the spitte may driue him
    quite away.
C. Custance.   Go make all ready, that it
    may be een so.
Tib. Talk.   For my parte, I shrewe [4]
    them that last about it go!

Exeant [the Servants].

ACTUS IIII. SCÆNA V

*Christian Custance [remains].   Trupenie
[and] Tristram Trusty [enter later].*

C. Custance.   Trupenie dyd promise me
    to runne a great pace,
My friend Tristram Trusty to fet into this
    place.
In-deede he dwelleth hence a good stert,[5] I
    confesse;
But yet a quicke messanger might twice
    since, as I gesse,
Haue gone and come againe.   Ah, yond I
    spie him now!   5

[Enter Trupeny and Trusty.]

Trupeny.   Ye are a slow goer, sir, I make
    God auow;

[1] A kitchen utensil for skimming liquids.
[2] An iron fork for stirring the fire.
[3] Frighten, assault.
[4] Curse.   [5] Distance.

My Mistresse Custance will in me put all
    the blame.
Your leggs be longer than myne; come
    apace, for shame!
C. Custance.   I can thee thanke, Tru-
    penie; thou hast done right wele.
Trupeny.   Maistresse, since I went, no
    grasse hath growne on my hele;   10
But Maister Tristram Trustie here maketh
    no speede.
C. Custance.   That he came at all, I
    thanke him in very deede,
For now haue I neede of the helpe of some
    wise man.
T. Trusty.   Then may I be gone againe,
    for none such I [a]m.
Trupenie.   Ye may bee, by your going; [1]
    for no alderman   15
Can goe, I dare say, a sadder pace than ye
    can.
C. Custance.   Trupenie, get thee in.
    Thou shalt among them knowe
How to vse thy-selfe like a propre man, I
    trowe.
Trupeny.   I go.   *Ex[eat].*
C. Custance.   Now, Tristram Trusty,
    I thank you right much;
For, at my first sending, to come ye neuer
    grutch.   20
T. Trusty.   Dame Custance, God ye
    saue! and, while my life shall last,
For my friende Goodlucks sake ye shall not
    sende in wast.
C. Custance.   He shal giue you thanks.
T. Trusty.   I will do much for his sake.
C. Custance.   But, alack, I feare, great
    displeasure shall be take!
T. Trusty.   Wherfore?
C. Custance.   For a foolish matter.
T. Trusty.   What is your cause?   25
C. Custance.   I am yll accombred with a
    couple of dawes.
T. Trusty.   Nay, weepe not, woman, but
    tell me what your cause is.
As concerning my friende is any thing
    amisse?
C. Custance.   No, not on my part; but
    here was Sym Suresby —
T. Trustie.   He was with me and told me
    so.
C. Custance.   And he stoode by 30

[1] Walking, pace.

While Ralph Roister Doister, with helpe of
    Merygreeke,
For promise of mariage dyd vnto me seeke.
T. Trusty. And had ye made any prom-
    ise before them twaine?
C. Custance. No; I had rather be torne
    in pieces and slaine!
No man hath my faith and trouth but
    Gawyn Goodlucke,   35
And that before Suresby dyd I say, and
    there stucke.
But of certaine letters there were suche
    words spoken —
T. Trustie. He tolde me that too.
C. Custance.   And of a ring, and
    token,
That Suresby, I spied, dyd more than halfe
    suspect
That I my faith to Gawyn Goodlucke dyd
    reiect.   40
T. Trusty. But there was no such mat-
    ter, Dame Custance, in-deede?
C. Custance. If euer my head thought it,
    God sende me y!l speede!
Wherfore I beseech you with me to be a
    witnesse
That in all my lyfe I neuer intended thing
    lesse.
And what a brainsicke foole Ralph Roister
    Doister is   45
Your-selfe know well enough.
T. Trusty.   Ye say full true, ywis!
C. Custance. Bicause to bee his wife I ne
    graunt nor apply,[1]
Hither will he com, he sweareth, by-and-by,
To kill both me and myne, and beate
    downe my house flat.
Therfore I pray your aide.
T. Trustie.   I warrant you that. 50
C. Custance. Haue I so many yeres liued
    a sobre life,
And shewed my-selfe honest, mayde, wid-
    owe, and wyfe,
And nowe to be abused in such a vile
    sorte?
Ye see howe poore widowes lyue, all voyde
    of comfort!
T. Trusty. I warrant hym do you no
    harme nor wrong at all.   55
C. Custance. No; but Mathew Mery-
    greeke doth me most appall,

      [1] Think of it.

That he woulde ioyne hym-selfe with suche
    a wretched loute.
T. Trusty. He doth it for a iest; I knowe
    hym out of doubte.
And here cometh Merygreke.
C. Custance.   Then shal we here his
    mind.

ACTUS IIII. SCÆNA VI

*[Enter] Merygreke [to] Christian Custance
[and] Trist. Trusty.*

M. Mery. Custance and Trustie both, I
    doe you here well finde.
C. Custance. Ah, Mathew Merygreeke,
    ye haue vsed me well!
M. Mery. Nowe for altogether [1] ye must
    your answere tell:
Will ye haue this man, woman? or else, will
    ye not?
Else will he come — neuer bore so brymme [2]
    nor tost so hot.   5
Tris. and Cu. But why ioyn ye with
    him?
T. Trusty.   For mirth?
C. Custance.   Or else in sadnesse?
M. Mery. The more fond of you both!
    hardly the mater gesse.
Tristram. Lo, how say ye, dame?
M. Mery.   Why, do ye thinke, Dame
    Custance,
That in this wowyng I haue ment ought
    but pastance?
C. Custance. Much things ye spake, I
    wote, to maintaine his dotage.   10
M. Mery. But well might ye iudge I
    spake it all in mockage.
For-why, is Roister Doister a fitte husband
    for you?
T. Trusty. I dare say ye neuer thought
    it.
M. Mery.   No; to God I vow!
And dyd not I knowe afore of the insurance
Betweene Gawyn Goodlucke and Christian
    Custance?   15
And dyd not I, for the nonce, by my con-
    ueyance,
Reade his letter in a wrong sense for dali-
    ance,
That, if you coulde haue take it vp at the
    first bounde,

      [1] Definitely.   [2] Furious.

We should therat such a sporte and pastime haue founde
That all the whole towne should haue ben the merier? 20
C. CUSTANCE. Ill ake your heades both! I was neuer werier,
Nor neuer more vexte, since the first day I was borne!
T. TRUSTY. But very well I wist he here did all in scorne.
C. CUSTANCE. But I feared therof to take dishonestie.[1]
M. MERY. This should both haue made sport and shewed your honestie; 25
And Goodlucke, I dare sweare, your witte therin would low.[2]
T. TRUSTY. Yea, being no worse than we know it to be now.
M. MERY. And nothing yet to late; for, when I come to him,
Hither will he repaire with a sheepes looke full grim,
By plaine force and violence to driue you to yelde. 30
C. CUSTANCE. If ye two bidde me, we will with him pitche a fielde,
I and my maides together.
M. MERY. Let vs see! be bolde!
C. CUSTANCE. Ye shall see womens warre!
T. TRUSTY. That fight wil I behold.
M. MERY. If occasion serue, takyng his parte full brim,[3]
I will strike at you, but the rappe shall light on him. 35
When we first appeare —
C. CUSTANCE. Then will I runne away
As though I were afeard.
T. TRUSTY. Do you that part wel play;
And I wil sue for peace.
M. MERY. And I wil set him on.
Then will he looke as fierce as a Cottsold lyon.[4]
T. TRUSTY. But when gost thou for him?
M. MERY. That do I very nowe. 40
C. CUSTANCE. Ye shal find vs here.
M. MERY. Wel, God haue mercy on you! *Ex[eat].*
T. TRUSTY. There is no cause of feare. The least boy in the streete —

C. CUSTANCE. Nay, the least girle I haue will make him take his feete.

[*The sound of a drum is heard within.*]

But hearke! me-thinke they make preparation.
T. TRUSTY. No force,[1] it will be a good recreation. 45
C. CUSTANCE. I will stand within, and steppe forth speedily,
And so make as though I ranne away dreadfully.

[*Exeunt Custance and Trusty.*]

ACTUS IIII. SCÆNA VII

[*Enter*] R. Royster [*and*] M. Merygreeke [*with Roister's servants in martial array*]. C. Custance, D. Doughtie, Harpax, [*and*] Tristram Trusty [*enter later*].

R. ROYSTER. Nowe, sirs, keepe your ray; and see your heartes be stoute!
But where be these caitifes? me-think they dare not route![2]
How sayst thou, Merygreeke? What doth Kit Custance say?
M. MERY. I am loth to tell you.
R. ROYSTER. Tushe, speake, man! yea or nay?
M. MERY. Forsooth, sir, I haue spoken for you all that I can. 5
But, if ye winne hir, ye must een play the man;
Een to fight it out ye must a mans heart take.
R. ROYSTER. Yes, they shall know, and thou knowest, I haue a stomacke.[3]
[M. MERY.] "A stomacke," quod you? yea, as good as ere man had.
R. ROYSTER. I trowe they shall finde and feele that I am a lad. 10
M. MERY. By this crosse, I haue seene you eate your meate as well
As any that ere I haue seene of or heard tell!
"A stomacke," quod you? He that will that denie,

I know was neuer at dynner in your companie!

R. ROYSTER.   Nay, the stomacke of a man
it is that I meane!   15

M. MERY.   Nay, the stomacke of a horse,
or a dogge, I weene.

R. ROYSTER.   Nay, a mans stomacke with
a weapon, meane I.

M. MERY.   Ten men can scarce match you
with a spoone in a pie.

R. ROYSTER.   Nay, the stomake of a man
to trie in strife.

M. MERY.   I neuer sawe your stomacke
cloyed yet in my lyfe.   20

R. ROYSTER.   Tushe! I meane in strife or
fighting to trie.

M. MERY.   We shall see how ye will strike
nowe, being angry.

R. ROYSTER.   Haue at thy pate, then!
and saue thy head if thou may!
                [*Strikes at him.*]

M. MERY.   Nay, then, haue at your pate
agayne, by this day! [*Strikes back.*]

R. ROYSTER.   Nay, thou mayst not strike
at me againe, in no wise.   25

M. MERY.   I can not in fight make to you
such warrantise.

But, as for your foes here, let them the
bargaine bie.

R. ROYSTER.   Nay, as for they, shall euery
mothers childe die!

And in this my fume [1] a little thing might
make me

To beate downe house and all, and else the
deuill take me!   30

M. MERY.   If I were as ye be, by Gogs
deare mother,

I woulde not leaue one stone vpon an-other,

Though she woulde redeeme it with
twentie thousand poundes!

R. ROYSTER.   It shall be euen so, by His
lily [2] woundes!

M. MERY.   Bee not at one [3] with hir vpon
any amendes.   35

R. ROYSTER.   No, though she make to me
neuer so many frendes,

Nor if all the worlde for hir woulde vndertake; [4]

No, not God hymselfe, neither, shal not hir
peace make!

     [1] Fit of anger.   [2] Lovely.
     [3] Reconciled.   [4] Intercede.

[*To his servants.*]

On, therfore! Marche forwarde! Soft!
stay a-whyle yet!

M. MERY.   On!

R. ROYSTER.   Tary!

M. MERY.   Forth!

R. ROYSTER.   Back!

M. MERY.   On!

R. ROYSTER.   Soft! Now forward set!

[*Custance enters.*]

C. CUSTANCE.   What businesse haue we
here? Out! alas! alas!   41

[*She flees, as if in terror.*]

R. ROYSTER.   Ha, ha, ha, ha, ha!

Dydst thou see that, Merygreeke? how
afrayde she was?

Dydst thou see how she fledde apace out of
my sight?

Ah, good sweete Custance! I pitie hir, by
this light!   45

M. MERY.   That tender heart of yours
wyll marre altogether.

Thus will ye be turned with waggyng of a
fether?

R. ROYSTER.   On, sirs! keepe your ray!

M. MERY.   On! Forth, while this
geare is hot!

R. ROYSTER.   Soft! The armes of Caleys!
I haue one thing forgot.

M. MERY.   What lacke we now?

R. ROYSTER.   Retire! or else we be all
slain!   50

M. MERY.   Backe! for the pashe of God,
backe, sirs! backe againe!

What is the great mater?

R. ROYSTER.   This hastie forth-goyng

Had almost brought vs all to vtter vndo-
ing!

It made me forget a thing most necessarie!

M. MERY.   Well remembred of a captaine
by Sainct Marie!   55

R. ROYSTER.   It is a thing must be had.

M. MERY.   Let vs haue it, then.

R. ROYSTER.   But I wote not where, nor
how.

M. MERY.   Then wote not I when.
But what is it?

R. ROYSTER.   Of a chiefe thing I am
to seeke.

M. MERY.   Tut! so will ye be when ye
    haue studied a weke.
But tell me what it is.
R. ROYSTER.   I lacke yet an hedpiece.[1]
M. MERY.   The kitchen collocauit [2] — the
    best hennes to Grece!   61
Runne fet it, Dobinet, and come at once
    withall.
And bryng with thee my potgunne [3] hang-
    yng by the wall!

    [Exit Dobinet.]

I haue seene your head with it full many a
    tyme
Couered as safe as it had bene with a
    skrine; [4]   65
And I warrant it saue your head from any
    stroke,
Except perchaunce to be amased [5] with the
    smoke; [6]
I warrant your head therwith — except for
    the mist —
As safe as if it were fast locked vp in a chist.
And loe, here our Dobinet commeth with
    it nowe!   70

    [Re-enter Dobinet.]

D. DOUGH.   It will couer me to the shoul-
    ders well inow.
M. MERY.   Let me see it on.

    [He sets it on Roister's head.]

R. ROYSTER.   In fayth, it doth metely well.
M. MERY.   There can be no fitter thing.
    Now ye must vs tell
What to do.
R. ROYSTER.   Now forth in ray, sirs! and
    stoppe no more!
M. MERY.   Now Sainct George to borow! [7]
    Drum, dubbe-a-dubbe afore!   75

    [The drum sounds.   Enter Trusty.]

T. TRUSTY.   What meane you to do, sir?
    committe manslaughter?
R. ROYSTER.   To kyll fortie such is a mat-
    ter of laughter.
T. TRUSTY.   And who is it, sir, whome ye
    intende thus to spill?

R. ROYSTER.   Foolishe Custance, here,
    forceth me against my will.
T. TRUSTY.   And is there no meane your
    extreme wrath to slake?   80
She shall some amendes vnto your good
    mashyp make.
R. ROYSTER.   I will none amendes.
T. TRUSTY.   Is hir offence so sore?
M. MERY.   And he were a loute, she
    coulde haue done no more.
She hath calde him foole, and dressed [1] him
    like a foole,
Mocked hym lyke a foole, vsed him like a
    foole.   85
T. TRUSTY.   Well, yet the sheriffe, the
    iustice, or constable,
Hir misdemeanour to punishe might be able.
R. ROYSTER.   No, sir! I mine owne selfe
    will in this present cause
Be sheriffe, and iustice, and whole iudge of
    the lawes.
This matter to amende, all officers be I
    shall —   90
Constable, bailiffe, sergeant —
M. MERY.   And hangman and all.
T. TRUSTY.   Yet a noble courage, and the
    hearte of a man,
Should more honour winne by bearyng
    with a woman.
Therfore, take the lawe, and lette hir aun-
    swere therto.
R. ROYSTER.   Merygreeke, the best way
    were euen so to do.   95
What honour should it be with a woman to
    fight?
M. MERY.   And what then! will ye thus
    forgo and lese your right?
R. ROYSTER.   Nay, I will take the lawe on
    hir withouten grace.
T. TRUSTY.   Or, yf your mashyp coulde
    pardon this one trespace,   99
I pray you forgiue hir.
R. ROYSTER.   Hoh! [2]
M. MERY.   Tushe! tushe, sir, do not!
[T. TRUSTY.]   Be good, maister, to hir.
R. ROYSTER.   Hoh!
M. MERY.   Tush, I say, do not!
And what! shall your people here returne
    streight home?
R. ROYSTER.   Yea; leuie the campe, sirs,
    and hence againe, eche one!

But be still in readinesse if I happe to
   call;
I can not tell what sodaine chaunce may
   befall.[1]   105
M. MERY.   Do not off your harnesse,[2]
   sirs, I you aduise,
At the least for this fortnight, in no maner
   wise;
Perchaunce in an houre when all ye thinke
   least,
Our maisters appetite to fight will be best.
But soft! Ere ye go, haue once at Custance house!   110

[*He aims his harquebus at Custance's door.*]

R. ROYSTER.   Soft! what wilt thou do?
M. MERY.   Once discharge my harque-
   bouse;
And, for my heartes ease, haue once more
   with my potgoon.
R. ROYSTER.   Holde thy handes! else is all
   our purpose cleane fordoone.
M. MERY.   And it cost me my life!
R. ROYSTER.   I say thou shalt not!
M. MERY.   By the matte,[3] but I will!
   [*Shoots the harquebus.*]   Haue once
   more with haile-shot!
                  [*Shoots the potgun.*]
I will haue some penyworth! I will not
   leese all!

ACTUS IIII. SCÆNA VIII

M. Merygreeke. C. Custance. R. Roister.
Tib. T. An. Alyface. M. Mumblecrust.
Trupenie. Dobinet Doughtie. Harpax.
Two drummes with their ensignes.[4]

C. CUSTANCE [*rushing out*]. What caitifes
   are those that so shake my house-
   wall?
M. MERY. Ah, sirrha! now, Custance, if
   ye had so muche wit,
I woulde see you aske pardon, and your-
   selues submit.
C. CUSTANCE. Haue I still this adoe with
   a couple of fooles?
M. MERY. Here ye what she saith?
C. CUSTANCE.   Maidens, come forth
   with your tooles!   5

[1] E. attributes lines 104–05 to T. Trustie.
[2] Armour.   [3] Mass.
[4] One drum with ensign (flag) was borne by
Roister's forces, and one by Custance's army.

[*Enter the maids, armed, and Truepenny
with drum and ensign.*]

R. ROYSTER.   In a-ray!
M. MERY.   Dubba-dub, sirrha!
R. ROYSTER.   In a-ray!
They come sodainly on vs.
M. MERY.   Dubbadub!
R. ROYSTER.   In a-ray!
That euer I was borne! We are taken
   tardie!
M. MERY.   Now, sirs, quite our-selues
   like tall [1] men and hardie.
C. CUSTANCE.   On afore, Truepenie!
   Holde thyne owne, Annot!   10
On towarde them, Tibet! for scape vs they
   can not.
Come forth, Madge Mumblecrust! So!
   stand fast togither!
M. MERY.   God sende vs a faire day.
R. ROYSTER.   See, they marche on hither![1]
TIB. TALK.   But, mistresse!
C. CUSTANCE.   What sayst thou? [2]
TIB. [TALK.]   Shall I go fet our goose?[1]
C. CUSTANCE.   What to do?
TIB. [TALK.]   To yonder captain I wil,
   turne hir loose: 15
And she gape and hisse at him, as she doth
   at me,
I durst ieoparde my hande she wyll make
   him flee.

[*Custance and her forces advance to the fray.*]

C. CUSTANCE.   On! Forward!
R. ROYSTER.   They com!
M. MERY.   Stand!
R. ROYSTER.   Hold!
M. MERY.   Kepe!
R. ROYSTER.   There!
M. MERY.   Strike!
R. ROYSTER.   Take heede!
C. CUSTANCE.   Wel sayd, Truepeny!
TRUPENY.   Ah, whooresons!
C. CUSTANCE.   Wel don, in-deede,
M. MERY.   Hold thine owne, Harpax!
   Downe with them, Dobinet!   20
C. CUSTANCE.   Now, Madge! There,
   Annot! Now, sticke them, Tibet!
TIB. TALK. [*singling out Dobinet*]. All my
   chiefe quarell is to this same little
   knaue

[1] Valiant.   [2] E. *you.*

That begyled me last day. Nothyng shall him saue!

D. DOUGH. Downe with this litle queane that hath at me such spite!
Saue you from hir, maister; it is a very sprite! 25

C. CUSTANCE. I my-selfe will Mounsire Graunde Captaine vndertake!

R. ROYSTER. They win grounde!

M. MERY. Saue your-selfe, sir, for Gods sake!

[*Merygreeke lands a blow on Roister's "helmet."*]

R. ROYSTER. Out! alas, I am slaine! helpe!

M. MERY. Saue your-self!

R. ROYSTER. Alas!

M. MERY. Nay, then, haue at you, mistresse!

[*Pretending to strike at Custance he hits Roister.*]

R. ROYSTER. Thou hittest me, alas!

M. MERY. I wil strike at Custance here.

[*Hits him again.*]

R. ROYSTER. Thou hittest me!

M. MERY. So I wil! 30
Nay, Mistresse Custance!

[*Hits him again.*]

R. ROYSTER. Alas, thou hittest me still! Hold!

M. MERY. Saue your-self, sir.

[*Hits him again.*]

R. ROYSTER. Help! out! alas, I am slain!

M. MERY. Truce! hold your hands! truce for a pissing-while or twaine!

[*All cease fighting.*]

Nay, how say you, Custance? For sauing of your life,
Will ye yelde, and graunt to be this gentmans wife? 35

C. CUSTANCE. Ye tolde me he loued me. Call ye this loue?

M. MERY. He loued a-while, euen like a turtle-doue.

C. CUSTANCE. Gay loue, God saue it, so soone hotte, so soone colde!

M. MERY. I am sory for you. He could loue you yet, so he coulde.

R. ROYSTER. Nay, by Cocks precious, she shall be none of mine! 40

M. MERY. Why so?

R. ROYSTER. Come away. By the matte, she is mankine! [1]
I durst aduenture the losse of my right hande
If shee dyd not slee hir other husbande.
And see, if she prepare not againe to fight!

M. MERY. What then? Sainct George to borow, our Ladies knight! 45

R. ROYSTER. Slee else whom she will, by Gog, she shall not slee mee!

M. MERY. How then?

R. ROYSTER. Rather than to be slaine, I will flee.

C. CUSTANCE. Too it againe, my knightesses! Downe with them all!

[*The fight is resumed.*]

R. ROYSTER. Away! away! away! She will else kyll vs all!

M. MERY. Nay, sticke to it, like an hardie man and a tall. 50

[*Hits him.*]

R. ROYSTER. Oh, bones! thou hittest me! Away! or else die we shall!

M. MERY. Away, for the pashe of our sweete Lord Iesus Christ!

C. CUSTANCE. Away, loute and lubber! or I shall be thy priest!

[*Roister flees, followed by all his men.*] [2]

So this fielde is ours! We haue driuen them all away!

TIB. TALK. Thankes to God, mistresse, ye haue had a faire day! 55

C. CUSTANCE. Well, nowe goe ye in, and make your-selfe some good cheere.

ALL. [3] We goe.

[*Exeunt the maids and Truepenny.*]

T. TRUST. Ah, sir, what a field we haue had heere!

C. CUSTANCE. Friend Tristram, I pray you, be a witnesse with me.

---

[1] Infuriated. [2] E. *Exeant om.*
[3] E. *Omnes pariter.*

T. Trusty. Dame Custance, I shall depose [1] for your honestie.
And nowe fare ye well, except some-thing
else ye wolde. 60
C. Custance. Not now; but, when I nede
to sende, I will be bolde.

Exeat [Tristram].

I thanke you for these paines. And now I
wyll get me in.
Now Roister Doister will no more wowyng
begin! *Ex[eat].*

ACTUS V. SCÆNA I

[*Enter] Gawyn Goodlucke [and] Sym Suresby
[in front of Custance's house].*

[G. Goodl.] Sym Suresby, my trustie
man, nowe aduise thee well,
And see that no false surmises thou me tell:
Was there such adoe about Custance, of a
truth?
Sim Sure. To reporte that I hearde and
sawe, to me is ruth,
But both my duetie and name and prop-
retie 5
Warneth me to you to shewe fidelitie.
It may be well enough, and I wyshe it so to
be;
She may hir-selfe discharge, and trie [2] hir
honestie.
Yet their clayme to hir, me-thought, was
very large,[3]
For with letters, rings and tokens they dyd
hir charge; 10
Which when I hearde and sawe, I would
none to you bring.[4]
G. Goodl. No, by Sainct Marie! I allowe
thee in that thing!
Ah, sirra, nowe I see truthe in the prouerbe
olde:
All things that shineth is not by-and-by
pure golde.
If any doe lyue a woman of honestie, 15
I would haue sworne Christian Custance
had bene shee.
Sim Sure. Sir, though I to you be a seruant true and iust,

---

[1] Give evidence under oath.
[2] Prove. [3] Ample, great.
[4] I.e. no token; cf. Act IV, Sc. iii, lines 50–51.

Yet doe not ye therfore your faithfull
spouse mystrust;
But examine the matter, and if ye shall it
finde
To be all well, be not ye for my wordes vn-
kinde. 20
G. Goodl. I shall do that is right, and as
I see cause why.
But here commeth Custance forth; we shal
know by-and-by.

ACTUS V. SCÆNA II

[*Enter] C. Custance. Gawyn Goodlucke
[and] Sym Suresby [remain].*

C. Custance. I come forth to see and
hearken for newes good,
For about this houre is the tyme, of likely-
hood,
That Gawyn Goodlucke, by the sayings of
Suresby,
Would be at home. And lo, yond I see
hym, I!

[*She runs to him.*]

What, Gawyn Goodlucke, the onely hope
of my life, 5
Welcome home! and kysse me, your true
espoused wife!
Ga. Good. Nay, soft, Dame Custance!
I must first, by your licence,
See whether all things be cleere in your
conscience.
I heare of your doings, to me very straunge.
C. Custance. What, feare ye that my
faith towardes you should chaunge?
Ga. Good. I must needes mistrust ye be
elsewhere entangled, 11
For I heare that certaine men with you haue
wrangled
About the promise of mariage by you to
them made.
C. Custance. Coulde any mans reporte
your minde therein persuade?
Ga. Good. Well, ye must therin declare
your-selfe to stande cleere, 15
Else I and you, Dame Custance, may not
ioyne this yere.
C. Custance. Then woulde I were dead,
and faire layd in my graue!
Ah, Suresby! is this the honestie that ye
haue,

To hurt me with your report, not knowyng
the thing?

SIM SURE. If ye be honest, my wordes can
hurt you nothing; 20

But what I hearde and sawe, I might not
but report.

C. CUSTANCE. Ah, Lorde, helpe poore
widowes, destitute of comfort!

Truly, most deare spouse, nought was done
but for pastance.

G. GOOD. But such kynde of sporting is
homely [1] daliance.

C. CUSTANCE. If ye knewe the truthe, ye
would take all in good parte. 25

GA. GOOD. By your leaue, I am not halfe-
well skilled in that arte.

C. CUSTANCE. It was none but Roister
Doister, that foolishe mome.[2]

GA. GOOD. Yea, Custance, "Better," they
say, "a badde scuse than none."

C. CUSTANCE. Why, Tristram Trustie,
sir, your true and faithfull frende,

Was priuie bothe to the beginning and the
ende. 30

Let him be the iudge and for me testifie.

GA. GOOD. I will the more credite that he
shall verifie.

And, bicause I will the truthe know een as it
is,

I will to him my-selfe, and know all without
misse.

Come on, Sym Suresby, that before my
friend thou may 35

Auouch the same wordes which thou dydst
to me say.

Exeant [*Goodluck and Suresby*].

ACTUS V. SCÆNA III

Christian Custance [*remains*].

C. CUSTANCE. O Lorde! howe necessarie
it is nowe-of-dayes

That eche bodie liue vprightly all maner
wayes;

For lette neuer so little a gappe be open,

And be sure of this: — the worst shall be
spoken!

Howe innocent stande I in this for deede or
thought! 5

And yet see what mistrust towardes me it
hath wrought!

¹ Uncomely, rude.   ² Dolt.

But thou, Lorde, knowest all folkes
thoughts and eke intents;

And thou arte the deliuerer of all innocentes.

Thou didst helpe the aduoutresse [1] that she
might be amended;

Much more, then, helpe, Lorde, that neuer
yll intended! 10

Thou didst helpe Susanna, wrongfully accused,

And no lesse dost thou see, Lorde, how I
am now abused.

Thou didst helpe Hester when she should
haue died,

Helpe also, good Lorde, that my truth may
be tried!

Yet, if Gawin Goodlucke with Tristram
Trusty speake, 15

I trust of yll report the force shall be but
weake.

And loe! yond they come, sadly talking togither.

I wyll abyde, and not shrinke for their
comming hither.

ACTUS V. SCÆNA IIII

[*Enter at a distance*] *Gawyn Goodlucke* [*and*]
Tristram Trustie [*walking towards*] *C.
Custance. Sym Suresby* [*accompany-
ing them*].

GA. GOOD. And was it none other than ye
to me reporte?

TRISTRAM. No; and here were ye wished
to haue seene the sporte.

GA. GOOD. Woulde I had, rather than
halfe of that in my purse!

SIM SURE. And I doe muche reioyce the
matter was no wurse.

And, like as to open it I was to you faithfull, 5

So of Dame Custance honest truth I am
ioyfull;

For God forfende that I shoulde hurt hir by
false reporte.

GA. GOOD. Well, I will no longer holde hir
in discomforte.

C. CUSTANCE. Nowe come they hitherwarde. I trust all shall be well.

GA. GOOD. Sweete Custance, neither
heart can thinke nor tongue tell 10

¹ Adulteress.

Howe much I ioy in your constant fidelitie.
Come nowe, kisse me, the pearle of perfect
    honestie!
C. Custance.   God lette me no longer to
    continue in lyfe
Than I shall towardes you continue a true
    wyfe!
Ga. Goodl.   Well now, to make you for
    this some parte of amendes,   15
I shall desire first you, and then suche of
    our frendes
As shall to you seeme best, to suppe at
    home with me,
Where at your fought fielde we shall laugh
    and mery be.
Sim Sure.   And, mistresse, I beseech you,
    take with me no greefe;
I did a true mans part, not wishyng you re-
    preefe.   20
C. Custance.   Though hastie reportes
    through surmises growyng
May of poore innocentes be vtter ouer-
    throwyng,
Yet, bicause to thy maister thou hast a
    true hart,
And I know mine owne truth, I forgiue
    thee for my part.
Ga. Goodl.   Go we all to my house.   And
    of this geare no more!   25
Goe prepare all things, Sym Suresby;
    hence, runne afore!
Sim Sure.   I goe.   *Ex[eat]*.
G. Good.   But who commeth yond?
    M. Merygreeke?
C. Custance.   Roister Doisters cham-
    pion; I shrewe his best cheeke!
T. Trusty.   Roister Doister selfe, your
    wower, is with him, too.
Surely some-thing there is with vs they
    haue to doe.   30

ACTUS V. SCÆNA V

[*Enter at a distance*] *M. Merygreeke* [*and*]
    *Ralph Roister.   Gawyn Goodlucke,
    Tristram Trustie* [*and*] *C. Custance*
    [*remain*].

M. Mery.   Yond I see Gawyn Goodlucke,
    to whom lyeth my message.
I will first salute him after his long voyage,
And then make all thing well concerning
    your behalfe.

R. Royster.   Yea, for the pashe of God!
M. Mery.   Hence out of sight, ye calfe,
Till I haue spoke with them, and then I
    will you fet.[1]   5
R. Royster.   In Gods name!

[*Roister retires.*]

M. Mery. [*advancing*].   What, Master
    Gawin Goodluck, wel met!
And from your long voyage I bid you right
    welcome home.
Ga. Good.   I thanke you.
M. Mery.   I come to you from an hon-
    est mome.[2]
Ga. Good.   Who is that?
M. Mery.   Roister Doister, that dough-
    tie kite.
C. Custance.   Fye!   I can scarce abide
    ye shoulde his name recite.   10
M. Mery.   Ye must take him to fauour,
    and pardon all past.
He heareth of your returne, and is full yll
    agast.
Ga. Good.   I am ryght well content he
    haue with vs some chere.
C. Custance.   Fye vpon him, beast!
    Then wyll not I be there!
Ga. Good.   Why, Custance! do ye hate
    hym more than ye loue me?   15
C. Custance.   But for your mynde, sir,
    where he were would I not be!
T. Trusty.   He woulde make vs al
    laugh.
M. Mery.   Ye nere had better sport.
Ga. Good.   I pray you, sweete Custance,
    let him to vs resort.
C. Custance.   To your will I assent.
M. Mery.   Why, suche a foole it is
As no man for good pastime would forgoe
    or misse.   20
G. Goodl.   Fet him to go wyth vs.
M. Mery.   He will be a glad man.

Ex[eat Merygreeke].

T. Trusty.   We must, to make vs mirth,
    maintaine [3] hym all we can.
And loe, yond he commeth, and Mery-
    greeke with him!
C. Custance.   At his first entrance ye
    shall see I wyll him trim!

---

[1] Fetch.   [2] Fool.
[3] Back him up (with flattery and encouragement).

But first let vs hearken the gentlemans
    wise talke. 25
T. Trusty. I pray you marke if euer ye
    sawe crane so stalke.

ACTUS V. SCÆNA VI

[*Enter at a distance*] *R. Roister* [*and*] *M.*
Merygreeke. C. Custance, G. Goodlucke,
T. Trustie [*remain*]. *D. Doughtie*
[*and*] *Harpax* [*enter later*].

R. Royster. May I then be bolde?
M. Mery. I warrant you, on my worde.
They say they shall be sicke but ye be at
    theyr borde.
R. Royster. Thei wer not angry, then?
M. Mery. Yes, at first, and made strange;
But, when I sayd your anger to fauour
    shoulde change,
And therewith had commended you ac-
    cordingly, 5
They were all in loue with your mashyp
    by-and-by,
And cried you mercy that they had done
    you wrong.
R. Royster. For-why no man, woman,
    nor childe can hate me long?
M. Mery. "We feare," quod they, "he
    will be auenged one day;
Then for a peny giue all our liues we
    may!" 10
R. Royster. Sayd they so in-deede?
M. Mery. Did they? yea, euen with
    one voice.
"He will forgiue all," quod I. Oh, how
    they did reioyce!
R. Royster. Ha, ha, ha!
M. Mery. "Goe fette hym," say they,
    "while he is in good moode,
For, haue his anger who lust, we will not,
    by the roode!" 15
R. Royster. I pray God that it be all
    true that thou hast me tolde —
And that she fight no more.
M. Mery. I warrant you, be bolde.
Too them, and salute them!
R. Royster [*advancing*]. Sirs, I greete
    you all well!
Omnes. Your maistership is welcom!
C. Custance. Sauyng my quarell,
For, sure, I will put you vp into the
    Eschequer — 20

M. Mery. Why so? better nay. Wherfore?
C. Custance. For an vsurer.
R. Royster. I am no vsurer, good mis-
    tresse, by His armes!
M. Mery. When tooke he gaine of money
    to any mans harmes?
C. Custance. Yes, a fowle vsurer he is,
    ye shall see els, —
R. Royster. Didst not thou promise she
    would picke no mo quarels? 25
C. Custance. He will lende no blowes
    but he haue in recompence
Fiftene for one: whiche is to muche, of
    conscience!
R. Royster. Ah, dame, by the auncient
    lawe of armes, a man
Hath no honour to foile [1] his handes on a
    woman.
C. Custance. And, where other vsurers
    take their gaines yerely, 30
This man is angry but he haue his by-
    and-by.
Ga. Goodl. Sir, doe not for hir sake beare
    me your displeasure.
M. Mery. Well, he shall with you talke
    therof more at leasure.
Vpon your good vsage, he will now shake
    your hande.
R. Royster. And much heartily welcome
    from a straunge lande! 35
M. Mery. Be not afearde, Gawyn, to let
    him shake your fyst!
Ga. Goodl. Oh, the moste honeste
    gentleman that ere I wist! [2]

[*They shake hands.*]

I beseeche your mashyp to take payne to
    suppe with vs!
M. Mery. He shall not say you nay; and
    I too, by Iesus!
Bicause ye shall be friends, and let all
    quarels passe. 40
R. Royster. I wyll be as good friends
    with them as ere I was.
M. Mery. Then let me fet your quier
    that we may haue a song.
R. Royster. Goe.

[*Exit Merygreeke.*]

G. Goodluck. I haue hearde no mel-
    odie all this yeare long.

---

[1] Foul, defile.   [2] Knew.

[Re-enter Merygreeke with the musicians.]

M. MERY. Come on, sirs, quickly!
R. ROYSTER.   Sing on, sirs, for my
    frends sake!
D. DOUGH. Cal ye these your frends?
R. ROYSTER.   Sing on, and no mo
    words make!   45

Here they sing.[1]

[After the song, the actors all kneel.]

GA. GOOD. The Lord preserue our most
    noble Queene of renowne,
And hir virtues rewarde with the heauenly
    crowne.
C. CUSTANCE. The Lorde strengthen hir
    most excellent Maiestie,
Long to reigne ouer vs in all prosperitie.

    [1] The song is not given.

T. TRUSTY. That hir godly proceedings
    the faith to defende   50
He may stablishe and maintaine through to
    the ende.
M. MERY.   God graunt hir, as she doth,
    the Gospell to protect,
Learning and vertue to aduaunce, and vice
    to correct.
R. ROYSTER. God graunt hir louyng sub-
    iects both the minde and grace
Hir most godly procedyngs worthily to
    imbrace.   55
HARPAX. Hir Highnesse most worthy
    counsellers God prosper
With honour and loue of all men to minister.
OMNES. God graunt the Nobilitie hir to
    serue and loue,
With all the whole Commontie,[1] as doth
    them behoue.

          Amen.

    [1] Commons.

FINIS.

A RYGHT
PITHY, PLEASAUNT AND MERIE COMEDIE: INTYTULED

GAMMER GURTONS NEDLE [1]

PLAYED ON STAGE, NOT LONGE AGO IN CHRISTES COLLEDGE IN CAMBRIDGE

Made by MR. S. MR. OF ART

Imprented at London in Fleetestreat beneth the Conduit at the signe
of S. John Euangelist by Thomas Colwell.

THE NAMES OF THE SPEAKERS IN THIS COMEDIE

DICCON, the Bedlem. [2]
HODGE, Gammer Gurtons seruante.
TYB, Gammer Gurtons mayde.
GAMMER GURTON.
COCKE, [3] Gammer Gurtons boye.

DAME CHATTE.
DOCTOR RAT, the Curate.
MAYSTER BAYLYE.
DOLL, Dame Chattes mayde.
SCAPETHRYFT, [4] Mayst[er] Beylies seruante.

Mutes.

[The place: A village in England.]

GOD SAUE THE QUEENE!

---

[1] Professor Henry Bradley has presented evidence rendering it highly probable that this play was written by William Stevenson, Fellow of Christ's College, Cambridge, and acted by the students in Christ's College in 1553–54, and revived in 1559–60, possibly with the assistance of John Bridges. The play was entered by Thomas Colwell in the Stationers' Registers, 1563, as *Dyccon of Bedlam*, *etc.*, and he may then, or shortly after, have issued an edition. The only edition of which we know, however, bears the date 1575.

I have based the present text on the copy of the 1575 edition (A.) in the British Museum. In modernizing the punctuation and stage directions, as well as in other details, I have derived some assistance from the editions by Manly, *Specimens*, 1896, and Bradley, in *Representative English Comedies*, 1903.

[2] A discharged patient from the Bethlehem Hospital for the insane, who was licensed to travel about the country as a beggar.

[3] A. *Docke*.

[4] Manly's scribe in error reads *Scapethryk*.

THE PROLOGUE

As Gammer Gurton with manye a wyde styche
Sat pesynge [1] and patching of Hodg her mans briche,
By chance, or misfortune, as shee her geare [2] tost,
In Hodge lether bryches her needle shee lost.
When Diccon the bedlem had hard by report   5
That good Gammer Gurton was robde in thys sorte,
He quyetly perswaded with her in that stound [3]
Dame Chat, her deare gossyp, [4] this needle had found.
Yet knew shee no more of this matter, alas,
Then knoeth Tom, our clarke, what the priest saith at masse!   10
Here-of there ensued so fearfull a fraye
Mas Doctor was sent for these gossyps to staye,
Because he was Curate, and estemed full wyse;
Who found that he sought not, [5] by Diccons deuice.
When all thinges were tombled and cleane out of fassion,   15
Whether it were by fortune or some other constellacion,
Sodenlye the neele Hodge found by the prickynge,
And drew it out of his bottocke where he felt it stickynge.
Theyr hartes then at rest with perfect securytie,
With a pot of good nale [6] they stroake vp theyr plauditie.   20

[1] Mending.   [2] Stuff.   [3] Time.   [4] Friend, chum.
[5] Found what he was not expecting.   [6] Ale.

THE FYRST ACTE

The fyrst Sceane

[*A village street in perspective. Gammer Gurton's house on one side, Dame Chat's ale-house on the other.   The time, Saturday evening after sun-down.*]

[*Enter*] Diccon [*out of Gammer Gurton's house*].

DICCON.   Many a myle haue I walked diuers and sundry waies,
And many a good mans house haue I bin at in my daies,
Many a gossips cup in my tyme haue I tasted,
And many a broche and spyt haue I both turned and basted,
Many a peece of bacon haue I had out of thir balkes [1]   5
In ronnyng ouer the countrey with long and were walkes —
Yet came my foote neuer within those doore-cheekes,
To seeke flesh, or fysh, garlyke, onyons, or leekes,

[1] Tie-beams in houses.

That euer I saw a sorte [1] in such a plyght
As here within this house appereth to my syght!   10
There is howlynge and scowlyng, all cast in a dumpe; [2]
With whewling and pewling, as though they had lost a trump;
Syghing and sobbing they weepe and they wayle.
I maruell in my mynd what the deuill they ayle.
The olde trot [3] syts groning, with "alas!" and "alas!"   15
And Tib wringes her hands, and takes on in worse case,
With poore Cocke, theyr boye.   They be dryuen in such fyts
I feare mee the folkes be not well in theyr wyts.
Aske them what they ayle, or who brought them in this staye,
They aunswer not at all but "alacke!" and "welaway!"   20
Whan I saw it booted not, out at doores I hyed mee,

[1] Crowd, company.   [2] Fit of sadness.   [3] Hag.

And caught a slyp of bacon, when I saw
that none spyed mee;
Which I intend not far hence, vnles my
purpose fayle,
Shall serue for a shoinghorne [1] to draw on
two pots of ale.

[*He starts over towards Dame Chat's ale-*
house.]

THE FYRST ACTE

The second Sceane

[*Enter, as from the fields*] Hodge [*to*] Diccon.

HODGE.   See! So cham [2] arayed with
dablynge in the durt!

[*Points to the dirt on his breeches.*]

She that set me to ditchinge, ich wold she
had the squrt!
Was neuer poore soule that such a life had!
Gogs bones, thys vylthy glaye hase drest [3]
mee to bad!
Gods soule, see how this stuffe teares!   5

[*Shows the torn state of his breeches.*]

Iche were better to bee a bearward and set
to keepe beares!
By the masse, here is a gasshe! a shamefull
hole in-deade!
And one stytch teare furder, a man may
thruste in his heade.
DICCON.   By my fathers soule, Hodge, if I
shulde now be sworne
I can not chuse but say thy breech is foule
be-torne!   10
But the next remedye in such a case and hap
Is to plaunche [4] on a piece as brode as thy
cap.
HODGE.   Gogs soule, man, tis not yet two
dayes fully ended
Synce my dame Gurton, chem sure, these
breches amended!
But cham made such [5] a drudge, to trudge
at euery neede,   15
Chwold rend it though it were stitched
wath [6] sturdy pacthreede.

---

[1] The *N.E.D.* defines as "an appetizer." It possibly means here that Diccon will exchange the bacon for two pots of ale.
[2] The southern dialect (ich = I, icham = cham = I am, chaue = I have, etc.) early became the conventional stage dialect for rustics.
[3] Spoiled.   [4] Clap.
[5] A *suce,* possibly intentionally.   [6] A. *what.*

DICCON.   Hoge, let thy breeches go, and
speake and tell mee soone
What deuill ayleth Gammer Gurton and
Tib, her mayd, to frowne.
HODGE.   Tush, man, thart deceyued! Tys
theyr dayly looke;
They coure [1] so ouer the coles theyr eyes be
bleard with smooke.   20
DICCON.   Nay, by the masse! I perfectly
perceiued, as I came hether,
That eyther Tib and her dame hath ben by
the eares together,
Or els as great a matter — as thou shalt
shortly see.
HODGE.   Now iche beseeche our Lord they
neuer better agree!
DICCON.   By Gogs soule, there they syt as
still as stones in the streite,   25
As though they had ben taken [2] with
fairies, or els with some il sprite.
HODGE.   Gogs hart! I durst haue layd
my cap to a crowne
Chwould lerne of some prancome [3] as sone
as ich came [4] to town!
DICCON.   Why, Hodge, art thou inspyred?
or dedst thou therof here?
HODGE.   Nay; but ich saw such a wonder
as ich saw nat this vii yere.   30
Tome Tannkards cow — be Gogs bones! —
she set me vp her saile,
And flynging about his halfe-aker, fysking
with her taile,
As though there had ben in her ars a
swarme of bees —
And chad not cryed, "Tphrowh, hoore!"
shead lept out of his lees.[5]
DICCON.   Why, Hodg! lies the connyng in
Tom Tankards cowes taile?   35
HODGE.   Well, ich chaue hard some say
such tokens do not fayle.
But ca[n]st thou not tell,[6] in faith, Diccon,
why she frownes, or wher-at?
Hath no man stolne her ducks, or henes, or
gelded Gyb, her cat?
DICCON.   What deuyll can I tell, man? I
cold not haue one word;
They gaue no more hede to my talk then
thou woldst to a lorde.   40
HODGE.   Iche cannot styll but muse what
meruaylous thinge it is!

---

[1] Cower.   [2] Bewitched.   [3] Unusual occurrence.
[4] Manly *come.*   [5] Pastures.   [6] A. *till.*

Chyll in, and know my-selfe what matters
    are amys.

DICCON.   Then farewell, Hodge, a-while,
    synce thou doest inward hast,

For I will into the good-wyfe Chats, to
    feele how the ale dooth taste.

[*Exit Diccon into Dame Chat's ale-house.*]

THE FYRST ACTE

THE THYRD SCEANE

Hodge [*remains.   Later enter*] *Tyb.*

HODGE.   Cham agast, by the masse! Ich
    wot not what to do.

Chad nede blesse me well before ich go
    them to!   [*Crosses himself.*]

Perchaunce some felon sprit may haunt our
    house indeed,

And then chwere but a [1] noddy to venter
    where cha no neede!

[*While he stands, afraid to enter, Tyb comes
    out of the house.*]

TIB.   Cham worse then mad, by the masse,
    to be at this staye! [2]   5

Cham chyd, cham blamd, and beaton all
    thoures on the daye,

Lamed, and hunger-storued, prycked vp
    all in iagges,

Hauyng no patch to hyde my backe saue a
    few rotten ragges!

HODGE.   I say, Tyb, — if thou be Tyb, as
    I trow sure thou bee, —

What deuyll make-a-doe is this betweene
    our dame and thee?   10

TYB.   Gogs breade, Hodg, thou had a good
    turne thou warte not here [this
    while!] [3]

It had ben better for some of vs to haue ben
    hence a myle!

My gammer is so out of course and fran-
    tyke all at ones

That Cocke, our boy, and I, poore wench,
    haue felt it on our bones.

HODGE.   What is the matter — say
    on, Tib — wherat she taketh so
    on?   15

TYB.   She is vndone, she sayth! Alas, her
    ioye and life is gone!

---

[1] A. *at.*   [2] State of affairs, condition.
[3] Added by Dodsley.

If shee here not of some comfort, she is,
    sayth, but dead;

Shall neuer come within her lyps one inch
    of meate ne bread!

HODGE.   Byr Ladie, cham not very glad to
    see her in this dumpe.

Cholde a noble [1] her stole hath fallen and
    shee hath broke her rumpe!   20

TYB.   Nay, and that were the worst we
    wold not greatly care,

For bursting of her huckle-bone, or break-
    yng of her chaire;

But greatter, greater, is her grief! as,
    Hodge, we shall all feele.

HODGE.   Gogs woundes, Tyb! my gammer
    has neuer lost her — neele? [2]

TYB.   Her neele!

HODGE.   Her neele?

TIB.   Her neele!   25

By him that made me, it is true, Hodge, I
    tell thee.

HODGE.   Gogs sacrament, I would she had
    lost tharte [3] out of her bellie!

The deuill, or els his dame, they ought [4]
    her, sure, a shame!

How a murryon came this chaunce — say,
    Tib — vnto our dame?

TYB.   My gammer sat her downe on
    her pes,[5] and bad [6] me reach thy
    breeches;   30

And by-and-by, — a vengeance in it! — or
    she had take two stitches

To clap a clout vpon thine ars, by chaunce
    a-syde she leares,

And Gyb, our cat, in the milke-pan she
    spied ouer head and eares.

"Ah, hore!   Out, thefe!" she cryed aloud,
    and swapt the breches downe.

Up went her staffe, and out leapt Gyb at
    doors into the towne.   35

And synce that time was neuer wyght cold
    set their eies vpon it.

Gogs malison [7] chaue Cocke and I byd
    twenty times light on it.

HODGE.   And is not, then, my breches
    sewid vp, to-morow that I shuld
    were? [8]

---

[1] I wager a noble.   [2] Needle.   [3] The heart
[4] Owed.   [5] Stool.   [6] Manly *had.*   [7] Curse.
[8] Hodge's anxiety about his breeches is explained
by the fact that he was eager to go to church on the
morrow to see Kirstian Clack, a young lady who
smiled at him last Sunday. See II, i, 61–64.

Tyb.   No, in faith, Hodge. Thy breeches lie, for al this, neuer the nere.[1]

Hodge.   Now a vengeance light on al the sort, that better shold haue kept it, —   40
The cat, the house, and Tib our maid that better shold haue swept it!

[*He spies Gammer coming out.*]

Se where she commeth crawling! Come on, in twenty deuils way!
Ye haue made a fayre daies worke, haue you not? pray you say!

THE FYREST ACTE

The IIII Sceane

[*Enter from her house*] Gammer.   Hodge [*and*] Tyb [*remain*].   Cocke [*enters later*].

Gammer.   Alas, Hoge! Alas! I may well cursse and ban
This daie, that euer I saw it, with Gyb and the mylke-pan!
For these, and ill lucke to-gather, as knoweth Cocke, my boye,
Haue stacke[2] away my deare neele, and robd me of my ioye, —
My fayre, longe, strayght neele, that was myne onely treasure!   5
The fyrst day of my sorow is, and last end of my pleasure!

Hodge.   Might ha kept it when ye had it! But fooles will be fooles styll!
Lose that is vast in your handes? — ye neede not; but ye will!

Gammer.   Go hie thee, Tib, and run, thou hoore, to thend here of the towne![3]
Didst cary out dust in thy lap; seeke wher thou porest it downe;[4]   10
And, as thou sawest me roking[5] in the asshes where I morned,[6]
So see in all the heape[7] of dust thou leaue no straw vnturned.

Tyb.   That chal, Gammer, swythe and tyte,[8] and sone be here agayne!

Gammer.   Tib, stoope, and loke downe to the ground! To it, and take some paine!   [*Exit Tyb.*]

Hodge.   Here is a pretty matter! To see this gere how it goes!   15
By Gogs soule, I thenk you wold loes your ars and it were loose!
Your neele lost? It is a pitie you shold lack care and endlesse sorow!
Gogs deth, how shall my breches be sewid? Shall I go thus to-morow?[1]

Gammer.   Ah, Hodg, Hodg! if that ich cold find my neele, by the reed,[2]
Chould sow thy breches, ich promise thee[3] with full good double threed,   20
And set a patch on either knee shuld last this monethes twaine.
Now God and good Saint Sithe I praye to send it home againe!

Hodge.   Wherto serued your hands and eies but this your neele to kepe?
What deuill had you els to do? Ye kept, ich wot, no sheepe!
Cham faine a-brode to dyg and delue, in water, myre, and claye,   25
Sossing and possing in the durte styll[4] from day to daye;
A hundred thinges that be abrode, cham set to see them weele, —
And foure of you syt idle at home, and can not keepe a neele!

Gammer.   My neele, alas! Ich lost it, Hodge, what time ich me vphasted
To saue the milke set vp for the, which Gib our cat hath wasted.   30

Hodge.   The deuill he burst both Gib and Tib, with all the rest!
Cham alwayes sure of the worst end, who-euer haue the best!
Where ha you ben fidging[5] abrode since you your neele lost?

Gammer.   Within the house, and at the dore sitting by this same post,
Wher I was loking a long howre before these folks came here.   35
But, welaway! all was in vayne; my neele is neuer the nere!

Hodge.   Set me a candle; let me seeke and grope where-euer it bee.

---

[1] No better off.   [2] Stuck.
[3] The yard attached to a house.
[4] A. *dowde;* corr. by Dodsley, the first editor of the play, who has made various other obvious corrections.
[5] Possibly *raking.*   [6] Mourned?
[7] Manly *heaps.*   [8] Quickly and speedily.

[1] Sunday. At church Hodge expects to see a certain young lady, Kirstian Clack. Cf. II, i, 61–64.
[2] Cross.   [3] A. has *yt.*
[4] Continuously.   [5] Moving about uneasily.

Gogs hart, ye be so folish, ich thinke you
    knowe it not when you it see!

GAMMER. Come hether, Cocke! What,
    Cocke, I say!

[*Enter from the house Gammer's boy, Cocke.*]

COCKE.   Howe, Gammer!

GAMMER.   Goe hye the soone,
And grope behynd the old brasse pan;
    whych thing when thou hast done,
Ther shalt thou fynd an old shooe; wher-in,
    if thou looke well,   41
Thou shalt fynd lyeng an inche of a whyte
    tallow-candell.[1]

Lyght it, and brynge it tite awaye.

COCKE.   That shalbe done anone.

[*Exit Cocke into the house.*]

GAMMER. Nay, tary, Hodg, til thou hast
    light, and then weele seke ech one.

HODGE. Cum away, ye horson boy! Are
    ye a slepe? Ye must haue a
    crier![2]   45

COCKE. Ich cannot get the candel light;
    here is almost no fier.[3]

HODGE. Chil hold the a peny chil make
    the come if that ich may catch thine
    eares!

Art deffe, thou horson boy? Cocke, I say,
    why, canst not heares?

GAMMER. Beate hym not, Hodge, but help
    the boy, and come you two together.

[*Hodge rushes into the house.*]

THE I ACTE
THE V SCEANE

Gammer [*remains. Enter*] *Tyb. Cocke*
[*and*] *Hodge* [*enter later*].

GAMMER. How now, Tyb? Quycke, lets
    here what newes thou hast brought
    hether!

TYB. Chaue tost and tumbled yender
    heap ou[e]r and ouer againe,
And winowed it through my fingers as men
    wold winow grain;
Not so much as a hens turd but in pieces I
    tare it,

---

[1] I have adopted Manly's division of lines 39–42.
[2] One to summon you by formal proclamation.
[3] Cocke was attempting to light the candle from
the coals in the fire-place.

Or what-so-euer clod or clay I found, I did
    not spare it,   5
Lokyng within, and eke without, to fynd
    your neele, alas!
But all in vaine, and without help. Your
    neele is where it was!

GAMMER. Alas, my neele! We shall
    neuer meete! Adue! Adue, for
    aye!

TYB. Not so, Gammer; we myght it fynd
    if we knew where it laye.

[*Enter Cocke from the house, laughing.*]

COCKE. Gogs crosse, Gammer! if ye will
    laugh, looke in but at the doore,   10
And see how Hodg lieth tomblynge and
    tossing amids the floure!
Rakyng there some fyre to find amonge the
    asshes dead, —
Where there is not one sparke so byg as a
    pyns head, —
At last in a darke corner two sparkes he
    thought he sees,
Whiche were,[1] indede, nought els but Gyb
    our cats two eyes.   15
"Puffe!" quod Hodg, thinking therby to
    haue fyre without doubt;
With that Gyb shut her two eyes, and so
    the fyre was out.
And by-and-by them opened, euen as they
    were before;
With that the sparkes appered, euen as
    they had done of yore.
And euen as Hodge blew the fire, as he did
    thincke,   20
Gyb, as she felt the blast, strayght-way be-
    gan to wyncke.
Tyll Hodge fell of swering, as came best to
    his turne,
The fier was sure bewicht, and therfore
    wold not burne.
At last Gyb vp the stayers among the old
    postes and pinnes;
And Hodge he hied him after till broke
    were both his shinnes, —   25
Cursynge and swering othes were neuer of
    his makyng,
That Gyb wold fyre the house if that shee
    were not taken.

GAMMER. See! here is all the thought that
    the foolysh urchyn taketh!

---

[1] A. *where.*

And Tyb, me thinke, at his elbowe almost
as mery maketh!
This is all the wyt ye haue, when others
make their mone. 30
Come downe, Hodge! Where art thou?
And let the cat alone!

HODGE [*within*]. Gogs harte, helpe and
come vp! Gyb in her tayle hath fyre,
And is like to burne all if shee get a lytle
hier!
"Cum downe," quoth you? nay, then you
might count me a patch!
The house cometh downe on your heads if
it take ons the thatch.[1] 35

GAMMER. It is the cats eyes, foole, that
shineth in the darke!

HODGE [*within*]. Hath the cat, do you
thinke, in euery eye a sparke?

GAMMER. No, but they shyne as lyke fyre
as euer man see.

HODGE [*within*]. By the masse, and she
burne all, yoush beare the blame for
mee!

GAMMER. Cum downe, and help to seeke
here our neele, that it were found. 40
Downe, Tyb, on thy[2] knees, I say!
Downe, Cocke, to the ground!
To God I make a-vowe, and so to good
Saint Anne,
A candell shall they haue a-peece, get it
where I can,
If I may my neele find in one place or in
other.

[*Enter Hodge.*]

HODGE. Now a vengeaunce on Gib lyght,
on Gyb and Gybs mother, 45
And all the generacyon of cats both far and
nere!
Looke on the ground, horson? Thinks
then the neele is here?

COCKE. By my trouth, Gammer, me
thought your neele here I saw,
But, when my fyngers toucht it, I felt it
was a straw.

TYB. See, Hodge! whats tys? May it not
be within it? 50

HODGE. Breake it, foole, with thy hand,
and see and thou canst fynde it.

TYB. Nay, breake it you, Hodge, accordyng to your word.

HODGE. Gogs sydes! fye, it styncks! It
is a cats tourd!
It were well done to make thee eate it, by
the masse!

GAMMER. This matter amendeth not; my
neele is still where it wasse; 55
Our candle is at an ende: let vs all in
quight,
And come another tyme, when we haue
more lyght!

[*They go into the house.*]

THE II ACTE

Fyrste a songe:[1]

Backe and syde, go bare, go bare;
 Booth foote and hande, go colde:
But, bellye, God sende thee good ale ynoughe,
 Whether it be newe or olde! 4

I can not eate but lytle meate,
 My stomacke is not good;
But, sure, I thinke that I can dry[n]cke
 With him that weares a hood.
Thoughe I go bare, take ye no care,
 I am nothinge a-colde,
I stuffe my skyn so full within
 Of ioly good ale and olde. 12

Backe and syde, go bare, go bare;
 Booth foote and hand, go colde:
But, belly, God send the good ale inoughe,
 Whether it be new or olde! 16

I loue no[2] rost, but a nut-browne toste[3]
 And a crab[4] layde in the fyre;
A lytle bread shall do me stead,
 Much breade I not desyre.
No froste nor snow, no winde, I trowe,
 Can hurte mee if I wolde,
I am so wrapt and throwly lapt
 Of ioly good ale and olde. 24

Backe and syde, go bare, &c.

And Tyb, my wyfe, that as her lyfe
 Loueth well good ale to seeke,

---

[1] In the academic drama we find evidence that
the acts were separated by music; cf. II, v, 11–12.
[2] Manly incorrectly gives the reading of A. as *to*.
[3] A piece of toasted bread, soaked in the ale.
[4] Crab-apple, roasted at the fire and dropped into
the pot of ale.

[1] The grass roof of the house. [2] A. *tho.*

Full ofte drynkes shee tyll ye may see
   The teares run downe her cheeke; [1]
Then dooth she trowle to mee the bowle,
   Euen as a mault-worme shuld,
And sayth, "Sweete hart, I tooke my part
   Of this ioly good ale and olde."   32

Backe and syde, go bare, &c.

Now let them drynke tyll they nod and
   winke,
   Euen as good felowes shoulde doe;
They shall not mysse to haue the blisse
   Good ale doth bringe men to.
And all poore soules that haue scowred
   boules
   Or haue them lustely trolde,
God saue the lyues of them and theyr
   wyues,
   Whether they be yonge or olde!   40

Backe and syde, go bare, &c.

The Fyrst Sceane

[*Enter*] *Diccon* [*from Dame Chat's ale-house,
with a pot of ale in his hand*]. *Hodge*
[*enters later*].

DICCON. Well done, be Gogs malt! Well
   songe, and well sayde!
Come on, mother Chat, as thou art true
   mayde!
One fresh pot of ale lets see, to make an
   ende,
Agaynst this colde wether my naked armes
   to defende!

[*Dame Chat gives him a fresh pot of ale,
which he drinks off.*]

This gere it warms the soule! Now, wind,
   blow on thy [2] worst!   5
And let vs drink and swill till that our
   bellies burste!
Now were he a wyse man by cunnynge
   colde defyne
Which way my iourney lyeth, or where
   Dyccon will dyne.
But one good turne I haue: be it by nyght,
   or daye,
South, east, north, or west, I am neuer out
   of my waye!   10

[*Enter from Gammer's house Hodge with a*

[1] A. *cheekes.*   [2] A. *the.*

*piece of barley bread in one hand, and
an empty milk pan in the other.*]

HODGE. Chym goodly rewarded, cham I
   not, do you thyncke?
Chad a goodly dynner for all my sweate
   and swyncke!
Neyther butter, cheese, mylke, onyons,
   fleshe, nor fyshe,
Saue thys poor pece of barly bread, — tis a
   pleasant costly dishe!
DICCON. Haile, fellow Hodge, and will [1] to
   fare with thy meat — if thou haue
   any!   15
But by thy words, as I them smelled, thy
   daintrels [2] be not manye.
HODGE. Daintrels, Diccon? Gogs soule,
   man, saue this pece of dry horsbred,
Cha byt no byt this lyue-longe daie; no
   crome come in my hed;
My gutts they yawle-crawle, and all my
   belly rumbleth;
The puddynges [3] can not lye still, ech one
   ouer other tumbleth.   20
By Gogs harte, cham so vexte and in my
   belly pende
Chould one peece were at the spittlehouse,
   another at the castels ende!
DICCON. Why, Hodge, was there none at
   home thy dinner for to set?
HODGE. Godgs bread, Diccon, ich came to
   late; was nothing ther to get!
Gib — a fowle feind might on her light! —
   lickt the milke-pan so clene, —   25
See, Diccon, twas not so well washt this vii
   yere, as ich wene!
A pestilence lyght on all ill lucke! Chad
   thought yet, for all thys,
Of a morsell of bacon behynde the dore at
   worst shuld not misse;
But when ich sought a slyp to cut, as ich
   was wont to do,
Gogs soule, Diccon, Gyb, our cat, had eate
   the bacon to!   30

*Which bacon Diccon stole, as is declared
before.*

DICCON. Ill [4] luck, quod he? mary, swere
   it, Hodg! This day, the trueth to tel,
Thou rose not on thy right syde, or els blest
   thee not wel.

[1] Well.   [2] Dainties.   [3] Entrails.
[4] Manly incorrectly states that A. reads *All.*

Thy mylk slopt vp, thy bacon filtched, —
    that was to bad luck, Hodg!

HODGE. Nay, nay, ther was a fowler fault:
    my gammer ga me the dodge! [1]

Seest not how cham rent and torn — my
    heels, my knees, and my breech? 35

Chad thought as ich sat by the fire, help
    here and there a stitch;

But there ich was powpte [2] indeede!

DICCON. Why, Hodge?

HODGE. Bootes not, [3] man, to tell.

Cham so drest [4] amonst a sorte of fooles
    chad better be in hell!

My gammer, cham ashamed to say, by
    God, serued me not weele!

DICCON. How so, Hodge?

HODGE. Hase she not gone, trowest
    now, and lost her neele? 40

DICCON. Her eele, Hodge? Who fysht of
    late? That was a dainty dysh!

HODGE. Tush, tush, her neele! her neele!
    her neele, man! Tys neyther flesh
    nor fysh.

A lytle thing, with an hole in the end, as
    bright as any syller,

Small, longe, sharpe at the poynt, and
    straight as any pyller.

DICCON. I know not what a deuil thou
    menest. Thou bringst me more in
    doubt! 45

HODGE. Knowest not with what Tom
    Tailers man sits broching througe
    a clout?

A neele! neele! a neele! my gammers neele
    is gone!

DICCON. Her neele, Hodge? Now I smel
    thee! That was a chaunce alone!

By the masse, thou hadst a shamefull losse
    and it wer but for thy breches!

HODGE. Gogs soule, man, chould giue a
    crown [5] chad it but iii stitches! 50

DICCON. How sayest thou, Hodg? What
    shuld he haue, again thy neele
    got?

HODGE. Bem vathers soule, [6] and chad it,
    chould giue him a new grot!

DICCON. Canst thou keepe counsaile in
    this case?

[1] The "slip." A. misprints *dogde*.
[2] Cheated, befooled.   [3] It avails nothing.
[4] Spoiled, undone.
[5] A coin of the value of five shillings.
[6] By my father's soul.

HODGE. Els chwold my tonge [1] were
    out.

DICCON. Do thou [2] but then by my ad-
    uise, and I will fetch it without
    doubt.

HODGE. Chyll runne, chyll ryde, chyll
    dygge, chyl delue, chill toyle, chill
    trudge, shalt see; 55

Chill hold, chil drawe, chil pull, chill
    pynche, chill kneele on my bare
    knee;

Chill scrape, chill scratche, chill syfte, chyll
    seeke, chill bowe, chill bende, chill
    sweate,

Chil stoop, chil stur, chil cap, chil knele,
    chil crepe on hands and feete;

Chil be thy bondman, Diccon, ich sweare
    by sunne and moone.

And channot sum-what to stop this gap,
    cham vtterly vndone! 60

Pointing behind to his torne breeches. [3]

DICCON. Why, is ther any special cause
    thou takest hereat such sorow?

HODGE. Kirstian Clack, Tom Simsons
    maid, bi the masse, coms hether to-
    morow!

Chamnot able to say, betweene vs what
    may hap, —

She smyled on me the last Sonday when ich
    put of my cap.

DICCON. Well, Hodge, this is a matter of
    weight, and must be kept close; 65

It might els turne to both our costes, as the
    world now gose.

Shalt sware to be no blab, Hodge!

HODGE. Chyll, Diccon!

DICCON. Then, go to!

Lay thine hand here; say after me as thou
    shalt here me do.

Haste no booke?

HODGE. Cha no booke, I!

DICCON. Then needes must force
    vs both

Upon my breech to lay thine hand, and
    there to take thine othe. 70

[*Hodge places his hand on Diccon's breech,
and recites the oath after Diccon line by
line.*]

HODGE. **I, Hodge, breechelesse,**

[1] A. *thonge*.   [2] A. *than*.   [3] A *kreche*.

Sweare to Diccon, rechelesse,[1]
    By the crosse that I shall kysse,
To kepe his counsaile close,
And alwayes me to dispose
    To worke that his pleasure is.   76

    Here he kysseth [2] Diccons breeche.

DICCON.   Now, Hodge, see thou take
        heede
And do as I thee byd.
    For so I iudge it meete
This nedle againe to win, —
There is no shift therin
    But coniure vp a spreete.   82

HODGE.   What! the great deuill? Diccon,
        I saye!
DICCON.   Yea, in good faith, that is the
        waye, —
    Fet with some prety charme.

*[Diccon begins to draw a magician's circle
        on the floor.]*

HODGE. Softe, Diccon! Be not to hasty yet,
    By the masse, for ich begyn to sweat!
    Cham afrayde of some [3] harme!   88
DICCON.   Come hether then, and sturre
        the nat
One inche out of this cyrcle plat,
    But stande as I thee teache.

    [Places him in a small circle.]

HODGE.   And shall ich be here safe from
        theyr clawes?
DICCON.   The mayster deuill with his
        longe pawes
Here to thee can not reache.   94

Now will I settle me to this geare.

    *[Takes his place in a larger circle, and
        prepares to conjure.]*

HODGE.   I saye, Diccon!   Heare me,
        heare!
    Go softely to thys matter!
DICCON. What deuyll, man! art afraide of
        nought?
HODGE.   Canst not tarrye a lytle thought
    Tyll ich make a curtesie of water?   100

    [1] Careless.
    [2] Manly gives the reading of A. as *kessech;* it is
kyssech.
    [3] A. *syme.*

DICCON.   Stand still to it!   Why shuldest
        thou feare hym?

    [Resumes his conjuring.]

HODGE.   Gogs sydes, Diccon, me thinke
        ich heare him!
    And tarrye, chal mare all!
DICCON.   The matter is no worse than I
        tolde it.
HODGE.   By the masse, cham able no
        longer to holde it!
    To bad! iche must beraye the hall!   106

DICCON.   Stand to it, Hodge!   Sture not,
        you horson!
What deuyll!   be thine ars-strynges
        brusten?
    Thy-selfe a-while but staye;
The deuill — I smell hym — wyll be here
        anone.
HODGE.   Hold him fast, Diccon!   Cham
        gone! Cham gone!
    Chyll not be at that fraye!   112

    [Exit Hodge running.]

THE II ACTE

THE II SCEANE

*Diccon [remains].   [Dame] Chat [enters
        later].*

DICCON.   Fy, shytten knaue! and out vpon
        thee!
Aboue all other loutes fye on thee!
    Is not here a clenly prancke?
But thy matter was no better,
Nor thy presence here no sweter,
    To flye I can the thanke.   6

Here is a matter worthy glosynge [1]
Of Gammer Gurtons nedle losynge,
    And a foule peece of warke!
A man, I thyncke, myght make a playe,
And nede no worde to this they saye,
    Being but halfe a clarke.   12

Softe, let me alone! I will take the charge
This matter further to enlarge
    Within a tyme shorte.
If ye will marke my toyes, and note,
I will geue ye leaue to cut my throte
    If I make not good sporte.   18

    [1] Making glosses on; editing with commentaries

[*Advances to Dame Chat's door.*]

Dame Chat, I say! Where be ye? within?

[*Enter Dame Chat, with cards in her hand.*]

CHAT. Who haue we there maketh such a
  din?

DICCON. Here is a good fellow maketh no
  great daunger.

CHAT. What? Diccon? Come nere; ye
  be no straunger!

We be fast set at trumpe, man, hard by the
  fyre.

Thou shalt set on the king, if thou come a
  litle nyer.

DICCON. Nay, nay, there is no tarying; I
  must be gone againe.   25

But, first, for you in councel I haue a word
  or twaine.

CHAT. Come hether, Dol! [*Enter Dol.*]
  Dol, sit downe and play this game,

And, as thou sawest me do, see thou do
  euen the same.

There is five trumps beside the queene, —
  the hindmost thou shalt finde her.

Take hede of Sim Glouers wife; she hath an
  eie behind her!   [*Exit Dol.*]   30

Now, Diccon, say your will.

DICCON.   Nay, softe a litle yet!

I wold not tel it my sister, the matter is so
  great.

There I wil haue you sweare by our dere
  Lady of Bullaine,

S. Dunstone, and S. Donnyke, with the
  three Kinges of Kullaine,

That ye shal keepe it secret.

CHAT.   Gogs bread, that will I doo! 35
As secret as mine owne thought, by God,
  and the deuil two! [1]

DICCON. Here is Gammer Gurton, your
  neighbour, a sad and heuy wight, —

Her goodly faire red cock at home was
  stole this last night.

CHAT. Gogs soule! her cock with the
  yelow legs, that nightly crowed so
  iust? [2]

DICCON. That cocke is stollen.

CHAT. What! was he fet out of the hens
  ruste?   40

DICCON. I can not tel where the deuil he
  was kept, vnder key or locke;

But Tib hath tykled [1] in Gammers eare
  that you shoulde steale the cocke.

CHAT. Haue I, stronge hoore? By bread
  and salte —

DICCON.   What, softe, I say! be styl!
Say not one word for all this geare.

CHAT.   By the masse, that I wyl!
I wil haue the yong hore by the head and
  the old trot by the throte!   45

DICCON. Not one word, Dame Chat, I
  say! Not one word, for my cote!

CHAT. Shall such a begars brawle [2] as
  that, thinkest thou, make me a
  theefe?

The pocks light on her hores sydes! a
  pestlence and a mischeefe!

[*Starts towards Gammer Gurton's.*]

Come out, thou hungry, nedy bytche! O
  that my nails be short!

[*Diccon restrains her.*]

DICCON. Gogs bred, woman, hold your
  peace! this gere wil els passe sport!

I wold not for an hundred pound this matter shuld be knowen,   51

That I am auctour of this tale or haue
  abrode it blowen!

Did ye not sweare ye wold be ruled, before
  the tale I tolde?

I said ye must all secret keepe, and ye said
  sure ye wolde.

CHAT. Wolde you suffer, your-selfe, Diccon, such a sort to reuile you,   55

With slaunderous words to blot your name,
  and so to defile you?

DICCON. No, goodwife Chat; I wold be loth
  such drabs shulde blot my name;

But yet ye must so order all that Diccon
  beare no blame.

CHAT. Go to, then! What is your rede? [3]
  Say on your minde; ye shall mee
  rule herein.

DICCON. Godamercye to Dame Chat! In
  faith, thou must the gere begin.   60

It is twenty pound to a goose-turd my
  Gammer will not tary,

But hetherward she comes as fast as her
  legs can her cary

To brawle with you about her cocke. For
  well I hard Tib say

---

[1] Too.   [2] So accurately on the hour.

[1] Whispered.   [2] Brat.   [3] Advice.

The cocke was rosted in your house to
    breafast yesterday;
And, when ye had the carcas eaten, the
    fethers ye out flunge;   65
And Doll, your maid, the legs she hid a
    foote depe in the dunge.

CHAT.   Oh gracyous God! my harte is
    bursted! [1]

DICCON.   Well, rule your-selfe a space!
And Gammer Gurton, when she commeth
    anon into thys place —
Then to the queane! Lets see! Tell her
    your mynd, and spare not!
So shall Diccon blamelesse bee; and then,
    go to, I care not!   70

CHAT.   Then hoore, beware her throte! I
    can abide no longer! [2]
In faith, old witch, it shalbe seene which of
    vs two be stronger!
And, Diccon, but at your request, I wold
    not stay one howre.

DICCON.   Well, keepe it in till she be here,
    and then — out let it powre!
In the meane-while get you in, and make
    no wordes of this.   75
More of this matter with-in this howre to
    here you shall not misse.
Because I knew you are my freind, hide it
    I cold not, doubtles.
Ye know your harm; see ye be wise about
    your owne busines!
So fare ye will!

CHAT.   Nay, soft, Diccon, and drynke!
    What, Doll, I say!
Bringe here a cup of the best ale; lets see!
    come quicly a-waye!   80

[*Doll serves him with a cup of ale.*]

THE II ACTT

THE III SCEANE

Hodge [*later enters*]. *Diccon* [*remains*].

DICCON.   Ye see, masters, the one end
    tapt of this my short deuise!
Now must we broche tother,[3] to, before the
    smoke arise.
And, by the time they haue a-while run, I
    trust ye need not craue it,

[1] A. *burstes.*
[2] A. *lenger,* and its rhyme mate seems to be
strenger; but the ink is blurred.
[3] A. *thoter.*

But, loke, what lieth in both their harts, ye
    ar like, sure, to haue it.

[*Hodge sticks his head through the door of
Gammer's house.*]

HODGE.   Yea, Gogs soule, art aliue yet?
    What, Diccon, dare ich come?   5

DICCON.   A man is wel hied [1] to trust to
    thee! I wil say nothing but mum.
But, and ye come any nearer, I pray you
    see all be sweete!

[*Hodge advances, wearing his other breeches
which Gammer had been mending.*]

HODGE.   Tush, man! Is Gammers neele
    found? That chould gladly weete! [2]

DICCON.   She may thanke thee it is not
    found; for if thou had kept thy
    standing,
The deuil he wold haue fet it out, euen,
    Hodg, at thy commaunding.   10

HODGE.   Gogs hart! and cold he tel noth-
    ing wher the neele might be found?

DICCON.   Ye folysh dolt, ye were to seek
    ear we had got our ground;
Therfore his tale so doubtfull was that I
    cold not perceiue it.

HODGE.   Then ich se wel somthing was
    said. Chope one day yet to haue it.
But, Diccon, Diccon, did not the deuill cry
    "ho! ho! ho"?   15

DICCON.   If thou hadst taryed where thou
    stoodst, thou woldest haue said so.

HODGE.   Durst swere of a boke, chard [3]
    him rore, streight after ich was
    gon!
But tel me, Diccon, what said the knaue?
    let me here it anon.

DICCON.   The horson talked to mee I
    know not well of what:
One whyle his tonge it ran and paltered of a
    cat;   20
Another whyle he stamered styll vppon a
    rat;
Last of all, there was nothing but euery
    word "chat!" "chat!"
But this I well perceyued, before I wolde
    him rid,
Betweene "chat" and the "rat" and the
    "cat", the nedle is hyd.

[1] Manly suggests *paied,* rewarded.
[2] Know.   [3] I heard.

Now, wether Gyb, our cat, haue eate it in
   her mawe,   25
Or Doctor Rat, our curat, haue found it in
   the straw,
Or this Dame Chat, your neighbour, haue
   stollen it, God hee knoweth!
But by the morow at this time we shal
   learn how the matter goeth.
HODGE.   Canst not learn to-night, man?
   Seest not what is here?

Pointyng behind to his torne breeches.

DICCON.   Tys not possyble to make it
   sooner appere.   30
HODGE.   Alas, Diccon, then chaue no
   shyft but — least ich tary to
   longe —
Hye me to Sym Glouers shop, theare to
   seeke for a thonge,
Ther-with this breech to tatche and tye as
   ich may.
DICCON.   To-morow, Hodg, if we chaunce
   to meete, shalt see what I will say.

[*Exit Hodge down the street.*]

THE II ACTE

THE IIII SCEANE

Diccon [*remains*].   *Gammer* [*enters later*].

DICCON.   Now this gere must forward goe,
   for here my gammer commeth.
Be still a-while, and say nothing; make
   here a litle romth![1]

[*Enter from her house Gammer Gurton.*]

GAMMER.   Good Lord, shall neuer be my
   lucke my neele agayne to spye!
Alas the whyle, tys past my helpe! Where
   tis, still it must lye!
DICCON.   Now Iesus, Gammer Gurton,
   what driueth you to this sadnes? 5
I feare me, by my conscience, you will sure
   fall to madnes.
GAMMER.   Who is that? What, Diccon?
   Cham lost, man, fye! fye!
DICCON.   Mary, fy on them that be
   worthy! But what shuld be your
   troble?
GAMMER.   Alas, the more ich thinke on it,
   my sorow it waxeth doble!

My goodly tossing sporyars[1] neele, chaue
   lost, ich wot not where.   10
DICCON.   Your neele! Whan?
GAMMER.   My neele! Alas, ich myght
   full ill it spare!
As God him-selfe he knoweth, nere one be-
   syde chaue.
DICCON.   If this be all, good Gammer, I
   warrant you all is saue.
GAMMER.   Why, know you any tydings
   which way my neele is gone?
DICCON.   Yea, that I do, doubtlesse, as ye
   shall here anone.   15
A[2] see a thing this matter toucheth, within
   these xx howres,
Euen at this gate,[3] before my face, by a
   neyghbour of yours:
She stooped me downe, and vp she toke a
   nedle or a pyn.
I durst be sworne it was euen yours, by all
   my mothers kyn.
GAMMER.   It was my neele, Diccon, ich
   wot;[4] for here, euen by this poste, 20
Ich sat, what time as ich vp-starte, and so
   my neele it loste.
Who was it, leiue[5] son? Speke, ich pray
   the, and quickly tell me that!
DICCON.   A suttle queane as any in thys
   towne! your neyghboure here, Dame
   Chat.
GAMMER.   Dame Chat, Diccon? Let me
   be gone! Chil thyther in post-
   haste.

[*Starting toward Dame Chat's.*]

DICCON.   Take my councell yet or ye go,
   for feare ye walke in wast!   25
It is a murrion crafty drab, and froward to
   be pleased;
And ye take not the better way, our nedle
   yet ye lese[6] it.
For when she tooke it vp, euen here before
   your doores,
"What, soft, Dame Chat," quoth I, "that
   same is none of yours!"
"Auant," quoth she, "syr knaue! What
   pratest thou of that I fynd?   30
I wold thou hadst kist me I wot whear," —
   she ment, I know, behind.

---

[1] Excellent spurrier's (harness-maker's).
[2] I.   [3] Door.   [4] I know.
[5] Dear.   [6] A. *lose;* corr. by Manly.

---

[1] Space.

And home she went as brag [1] as it had ben a
    bodelouce,[2]
And I after as bold as it had ben the good-
    man of the house.
But there and ye had hard her how she
    began to scolde —
The tonge it went on patins,[3] by hym that
    Iudas solde!   35
Ech other worde I was a knaue, and you a
    hore of hores,
Because I spake in your behalfe and sayde
    the neele was yours.

GAMMER.   Gogs bread! and thinks the
    callet thus to kepe my neele me fro?
DICCON.   Let her alone, and she minds non
    other but euen to dresse you so!
GAMMER.   By the masse, chil rather spend
    the cote that is on my backe!   40
Thinks the false quean by such a slyght [4]
    that chill my neele lacke?
DICCON.   Slepe [5] not you[r] gere, I counsell
    you, but of this take good hede:
Let not be knowen I told you of it, how well
    soeuer ye spede!
GAMMER.   Chil in, Diccon, a cleene aperne
    to take and set before me;
And ich may my neele once see, chil, sure,
    remember the!   45

[*Exit Gammer Gurton into her house.*]

THE II ACTE
THE v SCEANE

Diccon [remains].

DICCON.   Here will the sporte begin! If
    these two once may meete,
Their chere,[6] durst lay money, will proue
    scarsly sweete!
My gammer, sure, entends to be vppon her
    bones
With staues or with clubs or els with coble-
    stones.
Dame Chat, on the other syde, if she be far
    behynde,   5
I am right far deceiued; she is geuen to it of
    kynde.[7]
He that may tarry by it a-whyle, and that
    but shorte,

---

[1] Valiant, briskly.   [2] Body-louse.
[3] Noisily, as a person wearing pattens, or wooden
shoes.
[4] A. *slygh.*   [5] Slip.   [6] Cheer.   [7] By nature.

I warrant hym — trust to it — he shall see
    all the sporte.
Into the towne will I, my frendes to vysit
    there,
And hether straight againe to see thend of
    this gere.   10
In the meane-time, felowes, pype vpp your
    fiddles! I saie, take them,
And let your freyndes here such mirth as ye
    can make them! [1]

[*Exit Diccon down the street.*]

THE III ACTE
THE i SCEANE

[*Enter*] *Hodge* [*with thongs and awl, returning from Sym Glover's*].

HODGE.   Sym Glouer, yet gramercy! cham
    meetlye well-sped now.
Thart euen as good a felow as euer kyste a
    cowe!
Here is a thonge [2] in-dede; by the masse,
    though ich speake it,
Tom Tankards great bald curtal,[3] I thinke,
    could not breake it!
And when he spyed my neede to be so
    straight and hard,   5
Hays lent me here his naull [4] to set the gyb
    forward.[5]
As for my gammers neele, the flyenge feynd
    go weete! [6]
Chill not now go to the doore againe with it
    to meete.
Chould make shyfte good inough and chad
    a candels ende.
The cheefe hole in my breeche with these
    two chil amende.   10

THE III ACTE
THE ii SCEANE

Gammer [meets] Hodge [at the door].

GAMMER.   How, Hodge! mayst nowe be
    glade! Cha newes to tell thee:
Ich knowe who hais my neele; ich trust
    soone shalt it see.

---

[1] See page 475, note 1.   [2] A. *thynge.*
[3] A horse with its tail cut short.   [4] Awl.
[5] To help matters.   [6] With it.

HODGE. The deuyll thou does! Hast hard, Gammer, indeede, or doest but iest?

GAMMER. Tys as true as steele, Hodge.

HODGE. Why, knowest well where dydst leese it?

GAMMER. Ich know who found it, and tooke it vp; shalt see, or it be longe. 5

HODGE. Gods Mother dere, if that be true, far-wel both naule an thong! But who hais it, Gammer? say on! Chould faine here it disclosed.

GAMMER. That false fixen,[1] that same Dame Chat, that counts her-selfe so honest!

HODGE. Who tolde you so?

GAMMER. That same did Diccon the bedlam, which saw it done.

HODGE. Diccon? It is a vengeable knaue, Gammer! Tis a bo[m]nable horson! 10

Can do mo things then that, els cham de-ceyued euill.

By the masse, ich saw him of late cal vp a great blacke deuill!

O, the knaue cryed "ho! ho!" He roared, and he thundred.

And yead bene here, cham sure yould mur-renly ha wondred!

GAMMER. Was not thou afraide, Hodge, to see him in this place? 15

HODGE. No! And chad come to me, chould haue laid him on the face! Chould haue! promised him!

GAMMER. But, Hodge, had he no hornes to pushe?

HODGE. As long as your two armes! Saw ye neuer Fryer Rushe

Painted on a cloth,[2] with a side long cowes tayle,

And crooked clouen feete, and many a hoked nayle? 20

For al the world, if I shuld iudg, chould recken him his brother.

Loke, euen what face Frier Rush had, the deuil had such another!

GAMMER. Now[3] Iesus! mercy! Hodg! did Diccon in him bring?

HODGE. Nay, Gammer, heare me speke! Chil tel you a greater thing:

The deuil, when Diccon had him, — ich hard him wondrous weel, — 25

Sayd plainly here before vs that Dame Chat had your neele.

GAMMER. Then let vs go and aske her wherfore she minds to kepe it! Seing we know so much, tware a madnes now to slepe it.

HODGE. Go to her, Gammer. See ye not where she stands in her doores? Byd her geue you the neele. Tys none of hers but yours! 30

THE III ACTE

THE III SCEANE

Gammer [advances to Dame] Chat. Hodge [keeps at a safe distance].

GAMMER. Dame Chat, cholde praye the fair, let me haue that is mine! Chil not this twenty yeres take one fart that is thyne.

Therfore giue me mine owne, and let me liue besyde the!

CHAT. Why! art thou crept from home hether to mine own doores to chide me?

Hence, doting drab! auaunt, or I shall set the further! 5

Intends thou and that knaue mee in my house to murther?

GAMMER. Tush, gape not so on[1] me, woman! Shalt not yet eate mee! Nor all the frends thou hast in this shall not intreate mee!

Mine owne goods I will haue, and aske the on beleue.[2]

What, woman! pore folks must haue right, though the thing you agreue. 10

CHAT. Giue thee thy right, and hang thee vp, with al thy baggers[3] broode! What, wilt thou make me a theefe, and say I stole thy good?

GAMMER. Chil say nothing, ich warrant thee, but that ich can proue it well. Thou fet[4] my good euen from my doore, cham able this to tel!

---

[1] Vixen
[2] The painted cloths used to adorn the homes of the middle classes.
[3] A. *New.*

[1] A. *no.*
[2] Ask thee for quickly.
[3] Beggar's
[4] Fetched, took.

CHAT. Dyd I, olde witche, steale oft [1] was
thine? How should that thing be
knowen?   15
GAMMER. Ich can not tel; but vp thou
tokest it, as though it had ben thine
owne.
CHAT. Mary, fy on thee, thou old gyb,[2]
with al my very hart!
GAMMER. Nay, fy on thee, thou rampe,[3]
thou ryg,[4] with al that take thy
parte!
CHAT. A vengeaunce on those lips that
laieth such things to my charge!
GAMMER. A vengeance on those callats[5]
hips whose conscience is so large! 20
CHAT. Come out, hogge!
GAMMER.   Come out, hogge! and let me
haue[6] right!
CHAT. Thou arrant witche!
GAMMER.   Thou bawdie bitche, chil
make thee cursse this night!
CHAT. A bag and a wallet!
GAMMER.   A carte for a callet!
CHAT.   Why, wenest thou thus to pre-
uaile?
I hold thee a grote I shall patche thy coate!
GAMMER.   Thou warte as good kysse
my tayle!
Thou slut! thou kut! thou rakes! thou
iakes! will not shame make thee[7]
hide?   25
CHAT. Thou skald! thou bald! thou rot-
ten! thou glotton! I will no lenger
chyd![8]
But I will teache the to kepe home.
GAMMER. Wylt thou, drunken beaste?

[They fight.]

HODGE *[at a distance]*. Sticke to her,
Gammer! Take her by the head!
Chil warrant you thys feast!
Smyte, I saye, Gammer! Byte, I say,
Gammer! I trow ye wyll be
keene!
Where be your nayls? claw her by the
iawes! Pull me out bothe her
eyen!   30

[1] Aught.
[2] A cat; used as a term of reproach for an old
woman.
[3] A vulgar woman.   [4] A wanton woman.
[5] Whore's.   [6] A. *let haue me.*
[7] Manly states, incorrectly, that A. reads *y*[u].
[8] A. *chyd the.*

[Dame Chat gets Gammer down.]

Gogs bones, Gammer, holde vp your head!
CHAT.   I trow, drab, I shall dresse thee.

[To Hodge.]

Tary, thou knaue, I hold the a grote I shall
make these hands blesse thee!

*[Exit Hodge. Dame Chat gives Gammer a
sound beating.]*

Take thou this, old hore, for a-mends, and
lerne thy tonge well to tame,
And say thou met at this bickering, not
thy[1] fellow, but thy dame!

*[Exit Dame Chat. Hodge enters with a
heavy club.]*

HODGE. Where is the strong stued hore?
Chil geare[2] a hores marke!   35
Stand out ones way that ich kyll none in
the darke!
Up, Gammer, and ye be alyue! Chil
feygh[t] now for vs bothe.

[Dame Chat re-appears at her door.]

Come no nere me, thou scalde callet! To
kyll the ich wer loth.
CHAT. Art here agayne, thou hoddy-peke!
What, Doll, bryng me out my
spitte!
HODGE.   Chill broche thee wyth this!
Bim father soule, chyll coniure that
foule sprete!   40

[Over his shoulder to Cocke:]

Let dore stand, Cock! *[To Dame Chat:]*
Why coms in-deede? *[To Cocke:]*
Kepe dore, thou horson boy!
CHAT. Stand to it, thou dastard, for thine
eares! Ise teche the, a sluttish toyel!

[Dame Chat advances towards Hodge.]

HODGE. Gogs woundes, hore, chil make
the auaunte! *[Hodge flees into the
house.]* Take heede, Cocke, pull in
the latche!
CHAT. I faith, sir loose-breche, had ye
taried, ye shold haue found your
match!

[1] Manly incorrectly states that A. repeats *thy.*
[2] Give her.

[*While Dame Chat stands at the door threatening Hodge, Gammer rises and attacks her from behind.*]

GAMMER. Now ware thy throte, losell! Thouse pay [1] for al!

[*Gets Dame Chat down and gives her a sound beating.*]

HODGE [*from the door*]. Well said, Gammer, by my soule! 45
Hoyse her! souse her! bounce her! trounce her! pull out her throte-boule!

CHAT. Comst behynd me, thou withered witch? And I get once on foote,
Thouse pay for all, thou old tarlether! Ile teach the what longs to it!

[*Dame Chat gets Gammer down and beats her again.*]

Take the this to make vp thy mouth til time thou come by more!

[*Exit Dame Chat in triumph. After a time Hodge cautiously advances.*]

HODGE. Up, Gammer! Stand on your feete. Where is the old hore? 50
Faith, woulde chad her by the face! choulde cracke her callet crowne!

GAMMER. A, Hodg, Hodg, where was thy help, when fixen [2] had me downe?

HODGE. By the masse, Gammer, but for my staffe, Chat had gone nye to spyl you!
Ich think the harlot had not cared, and chad not com, to kill you.
But shall we loose our neele thus?

GAMMER. No, Hodge, chwarde [3] lothe doo soo. 55
Thinkest thou chill take that at her hand? No, Hodg, ich tell the, no!

HODGE. Chold yet this fray wer wel take vp, and our own neele at home.
Twill be my chaunce els some to kil, whereuer it be, or whome!

GAMMER. We haue a parson, Hodge, thou knoes, a man estemed wise,
Mast[er] Doctor Rat; chil for hym send, and let me here his aduise. 60
He will her shriue for all this gere, and geue her penaunce strait;

¹ A. *pray.*   ² Vixen.   ³ Ich ware, I would be.

Wese [1] haue our neele, els Dame Chat comes nere with-in heauen gate!

HODGE. Ye, mary, Gammer, that ich think best. Wyll you now for him send?
The sooner Doctor Rat be here, the soner wese ha an ende.
And here, Gammer! Dyccons deuill, as iche remember well, 65
Of cat, and Chat and Doctor Rat a felloneus tale dyd tell.
Chold [2] you forty pound that is the way your neele to get againe!

GAMMER. Chil ha him strait! Call out the boy; wese make him take the payn.

HODGE. What, Coke, I saye! Come out! What deuill! canst not here?

COCKE [3] [*entering*]. How now, Hodg? How does, Gammer? Is yet the wether cleare? 70
What wold chaue me to doo?

GAMMER. Come hether, Cocke, anon!
Hence swythe [4] to Doctor Rat, hye the that thou were gone!
And pray hym come speke with me; cham not well at ease.
Shalt haue him at his chamber, or [5] els at Mother Bees; [6]
Els seeke him at Hob Fylchers shop, for, as charde it reported, 75
There is the best ale in al the towne, and now is most resorted.

COCKE. And shall ich brynge hym with me, Gammer?

GAMMER. Yea, by-and-by,[7] good Cocke.

COCKE. Shalt see that shalbe here anone, els let me haue on [8] the docke! [9]

[*Exit Cocke down the street.*]

HODGE.[10] Now, Gammer, shal we two go in, and tary for hys commynge?
What deuill, woman! plucke vp your hart, and leue of al this glomming! 80
Though she were stronger at the first, as ich thinke ye did find her,
Yet there ye drest the dronken sow what time ye cam behinde her.

¹ We shall.   ² I wager.
³ A. incorrectly assigns to Gammer.
⁴ Quickly.   ⁵ A. *of.*   ⁶ An ale house.
⁷ At once.   ⁸ A. *one.*   ⁹ Tail.
¹⁰ In A. this and the three preceding speakers' names are elevated one line in the margin above their correct place.

GAMMER. Nay, nay, cham sure she lost
not all; for, set thend to the beginning,
And ich doubt not but she will make small
bost of her winning.

[*They start to go in.*]

THE III ACTE

THE IIII SCEANE

Tyb [*entering hurriedly, meets*] *Hodge* [*and*]
Gammer. Cocke [*enters later*].

TYB. See, Gammer, Gammer, Gib, our
cat! Cham afraid what she ayleth!
She standes me gasping behind the doore,
as though her winde her faileth.
Now let ich doubt what Gib shuld mean,
that now she doth so dote.
HODGE. Hold hether! [1] Ichould twenty
pound your neele is in her throte!

[*Hodge takes the cat.*]

Grope [2] her, ich say! Me thinkes ich feele
it. Does not pricke your hand? 5
GAMMER. Ich can feele nothing.
HODGE. No? Ich know thars not
within this land
A muryner [3] cat then Gyb is, betwixt the
Tems and Tyne;
Shase as much wyt in her head almost as
chaue in mine!
TYB. Faith, shase eaten some-thing that
wil not easely downe.
Whether she gat it at home or abrode in the
towne 10
Iche can not tell.
GAMMER. Alas, ich feare it be some
croked pyn!
And then, farewell Gyb! she is vndone, and
lost — al saue the skyn.
HODGE. Tys [4] your neele, woman, I lay!
Gogs soule, geue me a knyfe,
And chil haue it out of her mawe, or els chal
lose my lyfe!
GAMMER. What! Nay, Hodg, fy! Kil
not our cat. Tis al the cats we ha
now! 15

---

[1] Hand her hither.   [2] Feel, probe.
[3] A more curse[d].   [4] A. *Tyb.*

HODGE. By the masse, Dame Chat hays
me so moued iche care not what I
kyll, ma[k] God a-vowe!
Go to, then, Tyb! to this geare! Holde vp
har tayle, and take her!
Chil see what deuil is in her guts! Chil
take the [1] paines to rake [2] her!
GAMMER. Rake a cat, Hodge? what
woldst thou do?
HODGE. What! thinckst that cham not
able?
Did not Tom Tankard rake his curtal
toore [3] day, standing in the stable?

[*Enter Cocke from down the street.*]

GAMMER. Soft, be content; lets here what
newes Cocke bringeth from Mais-
t[er] Rat! 21
COCKE. Gammer, chaue ben ther-as you
bad, you wot wel about what.
Twill not be long before he come, ich durst
sweare of a booke.
He byds you see ye be at home, and there
for him to looke.
GAMMER. Where didst thou find him,
boy? Was he not wher I told
thee? 25
COCKE. Yes, yes, euen at Hob Filchers
house, by him that [4] bought and
solde me;
A cup of ale had in his hand, and a crab lay
in the fyer.
Chad much a-do to go and come, al was so
ful of myer.
And, Gammer, one thing I can tel: Hob
Filchers naule was loste,
And Doctor Rat found it againe, hard be-
side the doore-poste. 30
I chould a penny can say something your
neele againe to fet.
GAMMER. Cham glad to heare so much,
Cocke. Then trust he wil not let
To helpe vs herein best he can; therfore, tyl
time he come,
Let vs go in. If there be aught to get, thou
shalt haue some.

[*They go into the house.*]

---

[1] A. *thou.*
[2] Scrape clean.
[3] The other. Manly prints *toure.*
[4] Manly's scribe reads A. as *y*ᵃ; to me it is clearly
*y*ᵗ.

THE IIII ACTE

THE I SCEANE [1]

[*Enter*] *Doctor Rat.* *Gammer Gurton* [*enters later*].

D. RAT. A man were better twenty times be a bandog and barke,
Then here among such a sort be parish-priest or clarke,
Where he shal neuer be at rest one pissing-while a day,
But he must trudge about the towne this way and that way,
Here to a drab, there to a theefe, his shoes to teare and rent,　5
And, that which is worst of al, at euery knaues commaundement!
I had not sit the space to drinke two pots of ale
But Gammer Gurtons sory boy was straite-way at my taile,
And she was sicke, and I must come — to do I wot not what!
If once her fingers-end but ake, "Trudge! Call for Doctor Rat!"　10
And when I come not at their call, I only therby loose;
For I am sure to lacke therfore a tythe-pyg or a goose.
I warrant you, when truth is knowen, and told they haue their tale,
The matter where-about I come is not worth a half-peny-worth of ale!
Yet must I talke so sage and smothe as though I were a glosier,[2]　15
Els, or the yere come at an end, I shalbe sure the loser.

[*He sees Gammer Gurton working in her house.*]

What! worke ye, Gammer Gurton! Hoow, here is your frend M[aster] Rat!
GAMMER [*entering*]. A, good M[aster] Doctor, cha trobled, cha trobled you, chwot wel that!
D. RAT. How do ye, woman? Be ye lustie, or be ye not wel at ease?
GAMMER. By Gys, master, cham not sick,[1] but yet chaue a disease.　20
Chad a foule turne now of late; chill tell it you, by Gigs!
D. RAT. Hath your browne cow cast hir calfe, or your sandy sowe her pigs?
GAMMER. No; but chad ben as good they had as this, ich wot weel.
D. RAT. What is the matter?
GAMMER. Alas! alas! cha lost my good neele!
My neele, I say! And, wot ye what? a drab came by and spied it,　25
And, when I asked hir for the same, the filth flatly denied it.
D. RAT. What was she that —
GAMMER. A dame, ich warrant you! She began to scold and brawle —
Alas, alas! Come hether, Hodge! This wr[e]tche can tell you all.

THE IIII ACTE

THE II SCEANE

[*Enter*] *Hodge* [*to*] *Doctor Rat* [*and*] *Gammer. Diccon* [*enters later*].[2]

HODGE. God morow, Gaffer Vicar!
D. RAT.[3] Come on, fellow; let vs heare.
Thy dame hath sayd to me thou knowest of all this geare;
Lets see what thou canst saie.
HODGE. Bym fay, sir, that ye shall!
What matter so-euer here was done, ich can tell your maship [all].
My Gammer Gurton heare — see now?　5
Sat her downe at this doore — see now?
And, as she began to stirre her — see now?
Her neele fell in the floore — see now?
And while her staffe shee tooke — see now?
At Gyb her cat, to flynge — see now?　10
Her neele was lost in the floore — see now?
Is not this a wondrous thing — see now?
Then came the queane, Dame Chat — see now?
To aske for hir blacke cup — see now?

[1] A. gives this as Act II scene iv, obviously in error; cf. the following scene.
[2] Flatterer.

[1] A. *sich*.
[2] A. adds the name of Chat. But the author begins a new scene with the entrance of a new character creating a new situation. I have adopted Manly's scene division.
[3] Manly says not in A. His copyist was mistaken.

Anð euen here at this gate — see now? 15
  She tooke that neele vp — see now?
My gammer then she yeede [1] — see
    now?
  Hir neele againe to bring — see now?
And was caught by the head — see now?
  Is not this a wondrous thing — see
    now? 20
She tare my gammers cote — see now?
  And scratched hir by the face — see
    now?
Chad thought shad stopt hir throte — see
    now?
  Is not this a wondrous case — see
    now?
When ich saw this, ich was wrothe [2] — see
    now? 25
  And start betwene them twaine — see
    now?
Els, ich durst take a booke-othe — see
    now?
  My gammer had bene slaine — see
    now?
GAMMER. This is euen the whole matter,
    as Hodge has plainly tolde.
And chould faine be quiet, for my part,
    that chould. 30
But helpe vs, good master, — beseech ye
    that ye doo, —
Els shall [3] we both be beaten, and lose our
    neele too.
D. RAT. What wold ye haue me to doo?
    Tel me, that I were gone.
I will do the best that I can to set you both
    at one.
But be ye sure Dame Chat hath this your
    neele founde? 35
GAMMER. Here comes the man that see
    hir take it vp of the ground;
Aske him your-selfe, Master Rat, if ye be-
    leue not me.
And helpe me to my neele, for Gods sake
    and Saint Charitie!

[*Enter Diccon from down the street.*]

D. RAT. Come nere, Diccon, and let vs
    heare what thou can expresse.
Wilt thou be sworne thou seest Dame Chat
    this womans neele haue? 40

DICCON. Nay, by S. Benit, wil I not!
    Then might ye thinke me raue.
GAMMER. Why, didst not thou tel me so
    euen here? Canst thou for shame
    deny it?
DICCON. I, mary, Gammer; but I said I
    wold not abide by it.
D. RAT. Will you say a thing, and not
    sticke to it to trie it?
DICCON. "Stick to it," quoth you, Master
    Rat? mary, sir, I defy it! 45
Nay, there is many an honest man, when
    he suche blastes hath blowne
In his freindes eares, he woulde be loth the
    same by him were knowne.
If such a toy be vsed oft among the hon-
    estie,
It may be-seme a simple man of [1] your and
    my degree.
D. RAT. Then we be neuer the nearer for
    all that you can tell? 50
DICCON. Yes, mary, sir, if ye will do by
    mine aduise and counsaile.
If Mother Chat se al vs here, she knoweth
    how the matter goes;
Therfore I red you three go hence, and
    within keepe close;
And I will into Dame Chats house, and so
    the matter vse
That, or you cold go twise to church, I war-
    ant you here news. 55
She shall looke wel about hir, but, I durst
    lay a pledge,
Ye shal of Gammers neele haue shortly bet-
    ter knowledge.
GAMMER. Now, gentle Diccon, do so; and,
    good sir, let vs trudge.
D. RAT. By the masse, I may not tarry so
    long to be your iudge.
DICCON. Tys but a litle while, man.
    What! take so much paine! 60
If I here no newes of it, I will come sooner
    againe.
HODGE. Tary so much, good Mastei
    Doctor, of your gentlenes!
D. RAT. Then let vs hie vs inward; and,
    Diccon, speede thy busines!

[*Dr. Rat, Gammer, and Hodge go into the
    house.*]

---

[1] Went.
[2] Angered. A. misprints *worthe*.
[3] A. *shalt*, or the final *l* may be merely broken.

[1] A. *if.*

[THE IIII ACT

The iii Sceane] [1]

[Diccon remains.]

DICCON. Now, sirs, do you no more but
kepe my counsaile iuste,
And Docter Rat shall thus catch some
good, I trust.
But Mother Chat, my gossop, talke first
with-all I must,
For she must be chiefe captaine to lay the
Rat in the dust.

*[Diccon walks towards Dame Chat's house,
and meets her coming out.]*

God deuen, Dame Chat, in faith, and wel
met in this place!   5
CHAT. God deuen, my friend Diccon.
Whether walke ye this pace?
DICCON. By my truth, euen to you, to
learne how the world goeth.
Hard ye no more of the other matter, say
me now, by your troth!
CHAT. O yes, Diccon. Here the olde
hoore, and Hodge, that great
knaue —
But, in faith, I would thou hadst sene! —
O Lord, I drest them braue!   10
She bare me two or three souses behind in
the nape of the necke,
Till I made hir olde wesen [2] to answere
againe, "kecke"! [3]
And Hodge, that dirty dastard that at hir
elbow standes, —
If one paire of legs had not bene worthe
two paire of hands,
He had had his bearde shauen if my nayles
wold haue serued!   15
And not without a cause, for the knaue it
well deserued.
DICCON. By the masse, I can the thank,
wench, thou didst so wel acquite
the!
CHAT. And thodst seene him, Diccon, it
wold haue made the beshite the
For laughter. The horsen dolt at last
caught vp a club

As though he would haue slaine the master-
deuil, Belsabub;   20
But I set him soone inward.
DICCON. O Lorde, there is the thing
That Hodge is so offended! That makes
him starte and flyng!
CHAT. Why, makes the knaue any moyl-
ing, as ye haue sene or hard?
DICCON. Euen now I sawe him last. Like
a mad-man he farde, [1]
And sware by heauen and hell he would
a-wreake [2] his sorowe,   25
And leue you neuer a hen on-liue by viii of
the clock to-morow.
Therfore marke what I say, and my
wordes see that ye trust:
Your hens be as good as dead if ye leaue
them on the ruste!
CHAT. The knaue dare as wel [3] go hang
himself as go vpon my ground!
DICCON. Wel, yet take hede, I say! I
must tel you my tale round.   30
Haue you not about your house, behind
your furnace or leade, [4]
A hole where a crafty knaue may crepe in
for neade? [5]
CHAT. Yes, by the masse, a hole broke
down euen within these ii dayes.
DICCON. Hodge he intendes this same
night to slip in there-a-wayes.
CHAT. O Christ, that I were sure of it!
In faith, he shuld haue his mede!   35
DICCON. Watch wel, for the knaue wil be
there as sure as is your crede.
I wold spend my-selfe a shilling to haue
him swinged well.
CHAT. I am as glad as a woman can be of
this thing to here tell.
By Gogs bones, when he commeth, now
that I know the matter,
He shal sure at the first skip to leape in
scalding water, —   40
With a worse turne besides! When he will,
let him come!
DICCON. I tell you as my sister. [6] You
know what meaneth "mum"!

[Exit Dame Chat into her house.]

---

[1] Manly begins a new scene at this point, correctly,
think. Hazlitt would begin the scene five lines
 later.
[2] Throat.
[3] A. *kicke*(?), corr. by Dodsley.

[1] Walked about, behaved.
[2] Avenge.
[3] A. *wol*, which may be Chat's pronunciation of
"well."
[4] Pot used for brewing ale.   [5] A. *neades*.
[6] In strict confidence.

[THE IIII ACT

The IIII Sceane] [1]

[Diccon remains.]

[Diccon.]   Now lacke I but my doctor to
play his part againe.
And lo,[2] where he commeth towards, — peraduenture, to his paine!

[Enter Dr. Rat from Gammer's house.]

D. Rat.   What good newes, Diccon, fel-
low?   Is Mother Chat at home?
Diccon.   She is, syr, and she is not, but it
please her to whome.
Yet dyd I take her tardy, as subtle as she
was!   5
D. Rat.   The thing that thou wentst for,
hast thou brought it to passe?
Diccon.   I haue done that I haue done, be
it worse, be it better!
And Dame Chat at her wyts ende I haue
almost set her.
D. Rat.   Why, hast thou spied the neele?
Quickly, I pray thee, tell!
Diccon.   I haue spyed it, in faith, sir, I
handled my-selfe so well.   10
And yet the crafty queane had almost take
my trumpe.
But, or all came to an ende, I set her in a
dumpe!
D. Rat.   How so, I pray thee, Diccon?
Diccon.   Mary, syr, will ye heare?
She was clapt downe on the backside, by
Cocks Mother dere,
And there she sat sewing a halter, or a
bande,   15
With no other thing saue Gammers nedle
in her hande.
As soone as any knocke, if the filth be in
doubte,
She needes but once puffe, and her candle
is out.
Now I, sir, knowing of euery doore the
pin,
Came nycely, and said no worde till time I
was within;   20
And there I sawe the neele, euen with thes
two eyes.

Who-euer say the contrary, I will sweare he
lyes!
D. Rat.   O Diccon, that I was not there
then in thy steade!
Diccon.   Well, if ye will be ordred and do
by my reade,[1]
I will bring you to a place, as the house
standes,   25
Where ye shall take the drab with the
neele in hir handes.
D. Rat.   For Gods sake, do so, Diccon,
and I will gage my gowne
To geue thee a full pot of the best ale in the
towne!
Diccon.   Follow me but a litle, and marke
what I will say.
Lay downe your gown beside you.

[Dr. Rat lays aside his clerical gown.]

                     Go to, come on your way!   30
Se ye not what is here? — a hole wherin ye
may creepe
Into the house, and sodenly vnwares
among them leape.
There shal ye finde the bitchfox and the
neele together.
Do as I bid you, man; come on your wayes
hether!
D. Rat.   Art thou sure, Diccon, the swil-
tub standes not here-aboute?   35
Diccon.   I was within my-selfe, man, euen
now, there is no doubt.
Go softly, make no noyse.   Giue me your
foote, sir John! [2]

[Diccon helps him up.]

Here will I waite vpon you tyl you come
out anone.

*[Doctor Rat climbs into the house.   Dame
Chat and her maids fall upon him with
clubs.]*

D. Rat.   Helpe, Diccon!   Out, alas!   I
shal be slaine among them!
Diccon.   If they giue you not the nedle,
tel them that ye will hang them.   40
Ware that!   Hoow, my wenches! haue ye
caught the foxe
That vsed to make reuel among your
hennes and cocks?

---

[1] The scene division added by Manly.
[2] A. *to*, but inking is heavy, and the reading may
be *lo.*

[1] Advice.
[2] The conventional name for a parson.

Saue his life yet for his order, though he
    susteine some paine.
Gogs bread, I am afraide, they wil beate
    out his braine!

[*Exit Diccon down the street. Enter Doctor
Rat through the hole, wet and torn.*]

D. RAT. Wo worth the houre that I came
    heare!   45
And wo worth him that wrought this geare!
A sort of drabs and queanes haue me blest!
Was euer creature halfe so euill drest?
Who-euer it wrought and first did inuent it,
He shall, I warrant him, erre long repent
    it!   50
I will spend all I haue, without my skinne,[1]
But he shall be brought to the plight I am
    in!
Master Bayly,[2] I trow, and he be worth his
    eares,
Will snaffle these murderers and all that
    them beares.[3]
I will surely neither byte nor suppe   55
Till I fetch him hether, this matter to take
    vp.

[*Exit down the street.*]

THE V ACTE

THE I SCEANE

Enter] *Master Bayly* [*led in by*] *Doctor Rat.*
[*Scapethryft attending.*]

BAILIE. I can perceiue none other, I speke
    it from my hart,
But either ye ar in al the fault, or els in the
    greatest part.
D. RAT. If it be counted his fault, besides
    all his greeues,
When a poore man is spoyled and beaten
    among theeues,
Then I confesse my fault herein at this
    season;   5
But I hope you wil not iudge so much
    against reason.
BAILY. And me thinkes, by your owne
    tale, of all that ye name,
f any plaid the theefe, you were the very
    same.

[1] Except my skin.   [2] Bailiff.
[3] Support, uphold.

The women they did nothing, as your
    words make probation,
But stoutly withstood your forcible inua-
    sion.   10
If that a theefe at your window to enter
    should begin,
Wold you hold forth your hand and helpe
    to pull him in?
Or wold you [1] kepe him out? I pray you,
    answere me.
D. RAT. Mary, kepe him out, and a good
    cause why!
But I am no theefe, sir, but an honest,
    learned clarke.   15
BAILY. Yea, but who knoweth that when
    he meets you in the darke.
I am sure your learning shines not out at
    your nose.
Was it any maruaile though the poore
    woman arose
And start vp, being afraide of that was in
    her purse?
Me thinke you may be glad that you[r]
    lucke was no worse.   20
D. RAT. Is not this euill ynough, I pray
    you, as you thinke?

Showing his broken head.

BAILY. Yea, but a man in the darke, if [2]
    chaunces do wincke,
As soone he smites his father as any other
    man,
Because for lacke of light discerne him he
    ne can.
Might it not haue ben your lucke with a
    spit to haue ben slaine?   25
D. RAT. I thinke I am litle better — my
    scalpe is clouen to the braine!
If there be all the remedy, I know who
    beares the k[n]ockes.
BAILY. By my troth, and well worthy be-
    sides to kisse the stockes.
To come in on the backe-side, when ye
    might go about!
I know non such, vnles they long to haue
    their braines knockt out.   30
D. RAT. Well, wil you be so good, sir, as
    talke with Dame Chat,
And know what she intended? I aske no
    more but that.

[1] A. *you wold;* like many other obvious corrections
in the text; this was first noted by Dodsley.
[2] A. *of.*

BAYLY.   Let her be called, fellow, because of Master Doctor.

[*Scapethryft goes to Dame Chat's house.*]

I warrant in this case she wil be hir owne proctor;
She will tel hir owne tale, in metter or in prose,   35
And byd you seeke your remedy, and so go wype your nose!

THE V ACTE

THE II SCEANE

[*To*] *M. Bayly* [*Scapethrift leads in Dame Chat. D. Rat* [*remains*]. *Gammer, Hodge,* [*and*] *Diccon* [*enter later*]].

BAYLY.   Dame Chat, Master Doctor vpon you here complained
That you and your maides shuld him much misorder,
And taketh many an oth that no word he fained,
Laying to your charge how you thought him to murder;
And, on his part againe, that same man saith furder
He neuer offended you in word nor intent.
To heare you answer hereto, we haue now for you sent.   7
CHAT.   That I wold haue murdered him? Fye on him, wretch!
And euil mought he thee [1] for it, our Lord I besech.
I will swere on al the bookes that opens and shuttes,
He faineth this tale out of his owne guttes!
For this seuen weekes with me, I am sure, he sat not downe.
Nay, ye haue other minions, in the other end of the towne,
Where ye were liker to catch such a blow
Then any-where els, as farre as I know!   15
BAILY.   Be-like then, Master Doctor, you[r] stripe there ye got not!
D. RAT.   Thinke you I am so mad that where I was bet I wot not?
Will ye beleue this queane before she hath tryd [2] it?

----

¹ Thrive.   ² Put it to proof.

It is not the first dede she hath done and afterward denide it.
CHAT.   What, man, will you say I broke your head?   20
D. RAT.   How canst thou proue the contrary?
CHAT.   Nay, how prouest thou that I did the deade?
D. RAT.   To plainly, by S. Mary!
This profe, I trow, may serue though I no word spoke!

Showing his broken head.

CHAT.   Bicause thy head is broken, was it I that it broke?   25
I saw thee, Rat, I tel thee, not once within this fortnight.
D. RAT.   No, mary, thou sawest me not, for-why thou hadst no light;
But I felt thee, for al the darke, beshrew thy smothe cheekes!
And thou groped me — this wil declare any day this six weekes.

Showing his heade.

BAILY.   Answere me to this, M[aster] Rat: when caught you this harme of yours?   30
D. RAT.   A-while a-go, sir, God he knoweth, with-in les then these ii houres.
BAILY.   Dame Chat, was there none with you — confesse, i-faith — about that season?
What, woman! let it be what it wil, tis neither felony nor treason.
CHAT.   Yes, by my faith, Master Bayly, there was a knaue not farre
Who caught one good philup on the brow with a dore-barre, —   35
And well was he worthy, as it semed to mee.
But what is that to this man, since this was not hee?
BAILY.   Who was it then? Lets here!
D. RAT.   Alas! sir, aske you that?
Is it not made plain inough by the owne mouth of Dame Chat?
The time agreeth, my head is broken, her tong can not lye;   40
Onely vpon a bare nay she saith it was not I.
CHAT.   No, mary, was it not, indeede. Ye shal here by this one thing:

This after-noone a frend of mine for good
    wil gaue me warning,
And bad me wel loke to my ruste [1] and al
    my capons pennes,
For, if I toke not better heede, a knaue
    wold haue my hennes.   45
Then I, to saue my goods, toke so much
    pains as him to watch;
And, as good fortune serued me, it was my
    chaunce him for to catch.
What strokes he bare away, or other what
    was his gaines,
I wot not — but sure I am he had some-
    thing for his paines!
BAILY.   Yet telles thou not who it was.
CHAT.   Who it was?   A false theefe, 50
That came like a false foxe my pullaine [2] to
    kil and mischeefe!
BAILY.   But knowest thou not his name?
CHAT.   I know it.   But what than?
It was that crafty cullyon,[3] Hodge, my
    Gammer Gurtons man.
BAILIE.   Call me the knaue hether.   He
    shal sure kysse the stockes.
I shall teach him a lesson for filching hens
    or cocks!   55

[*Exit Scapethryft into Gammer's house.*]

D. RAT.[4]   I maruaile, Master Bayly, so
    bleared be your eyes!
An egge is not so ful of meate as she is ful of
    lyes.
When she hath playd this pranke to excuse
    al this geare,
She layeth the fault in such a one as I know
    was not there.
CHAT.   Was he not thear?   Loke on his
    pate!   That shalbe his witnes!   60
D. RAT.   I wold my head were half so hole,
    I wold seeke no redresse!

[*Enter Gammer Gurton.*]

BAILY.   God blesse you, Gammer Gurton!
GAMMER.   God dylde you, master mine!
BAILY.   Thou hast a knaue with-in thy
    ho[u]se, — Hodge, a seruant of
    thine.
They tel me that busy knaue is such a filch-
    ing one

[1] Roost.   [2] Poultry, hens.   [3] Rascal.
[4] A. inserts this name before the preceding line;
but the ¶ mark clearly shows that it was misplaced
by printer's error.

That hen, pig, goose, or capon thy neigh-
    bour can haue none.   65
GAMMER.   By God, cham much ameued to
    heare any such reporte!
Hodge was not wont, ich trow, to haue [1]
    him in that sort.
CHAT.   A theeuisher knaue is not on-liue,
    more filching nor more false!
Many a truer man then he hase hanged vp
    by the halse.[2]
And thou, his dame, of al his theft thou art
    the sole receauer.   70
For Hodge to catch and thou to kepe I
    neuer knew none better.
GAMMER.   Sir reuerence of your master-
    dome, and you were out a-doore,
Chold be so bolde, for al hir brags, to cal
    hir arrant whoore!
And ich knew Hodge so bad as tow,[3] ich
    wish me endlesse sorow
And chould [4] not take the pains to hang
    him vp before to-morow!   75
CHAT.   What haue I stolne from the or
    thine, thou il-fauored olde trot?
GAMMER.   A great deale more, by Gods
    blest, then cheuer by the got!
That thou knowest wel, I neade not say it.
BAILY.   Stoppe there, I say!
And tel me here, I pray you, this matter by
    the way:
How chaunce Hodge is not here?   Him
    wol[d]e I faine haue had.   80
GAMMER.   Alas, sir, heel be here anon; ha
    be handled to bad!
CHAT.   Master Bayly, sir, ye be not such a
    foole, wel I know,
But ye perceiue by this lingring there is a
    pad [5] in the straw.

*Thinking that Hodg his head was broke,
and that Gammer wold not let him come
before them.*

GAMMER.   Chil shew you his face, ich war-
    rant the, — lo now where he is!

[*Scapethryft leads in Hodge.*]

BAILIE.   Come on, fellow!   It is tolde me
    thou art a shrew, i-wysse.   85
Thy neighbours hens thou takest, and
    playes the two-legged foxe;

[1] Behave.   [2] Neck.   [3] As thou.   [4] If I would.
[5] Toad; a proverbial saying — something hidden.

Their chikens and their capons to, and now
and then their cocks.

HODGE. Ich defy them al that dare it say!
Cham as true as the best!

BAILY. Wart not thou take within this
houre in Dame Chats hens nest?

HODGE. Take there? No, master.
Chold not do't for a house-ful of
gold! 90

CHAT. Thou, or the deuil in thy cote!
sweare this I dare be bold.

D. RAT. Sweare me no swearing, quean!
The deuill he geue the sorow!

Al is not worth a gnat thou canst sweare
till to-morow.

Where is the harme he hath? Shew it, by
Gods bread!

Ye beat him, with a witnes, but the stripes
light on my head! 95

HODGE. Bet me? Gogs blessed body,
chold first, ich trow, haue burst the.

Ich thinke, and chad my hands loose, callet, chould haue crust the!

CHAT. Thou shitten knaue, I trow thou
knowest the ful weight of my fist!

I am fowly deceiued onles thy head and my
doore-bar kyste!

HODGE. Hold thy chat, whore. Thou cri-
est so loude can no man els be
hard. 100

CHAT. Well, knaue, and I had the alone, I
wold surely rap thy costard!

BAYLY. Sir, answer me to this: is thy head
whole or broken?

CHAT. Yea, Master Bayly, blest be euery
good token!

HODGE. Is my head whole? Ich warrant
you tis neither scuruy nor scald!

What, you foule beast, does think tis either
pild [1] or bald? 105

Nay, ich thanke God, chil not, for al that
thou maist spend,

That chad one scab on my narse as brode as
thy fingers end.

BAYLY. Come nearer heare!

HODGE. Yes, that iche dare.

[*The bailiff examines Hodge's head.*]

PAYLY. By Our Lady, here is no harme.
Hodges head is hole ynough, for al Dame
Chats charme.

¹ Shorn.

CHAT. By Gogs blest, how-euer the thing
he clockes [1] or smolders, 110

I know the blowes he bare away either
with head or shoulders.

Camest thou not, knaue, within this houre
creping into my pens,

And there was caught within my hous
groping among my hens?

HODGE. A plage both on thy hens and the!
A carte, whore! a carte! [2]

Chould I were hanged as hie as a tree and
chware as false as thou art! 115

Geue my Gammer again her washical [3]
thou stole away in thy lap!

GAMMER. Yea, Maister Baily, there is
a thing you know not on, may-
hap:

This drab she kepes away my good — the
deuil he might her snare!

Ich pray you that ich might haue a right
action on her.

CHAT. Haue I thy good, old filth, or any
such, old sowes? [4] 120

I am as true, I wold thou knew, as skin betwene thy browes!

GAMMER. Many a truer hath ben hanged,
though you escape the daunger!

CHAT. Thou shalt answer, by Gods pity,
for this thy foule slaunder!

BAILY. Why, what can ye charge hir
withal? To say so ye do not well.

GAMMER. Mary, a vengeance to hir
hart, the whore hase stoln my
neele! 125

CHAT. Thy nedle, old witch? How so?
It were almes thy scul to knock!

So didst thou say the other day that I had
stolne thy cock,

And rosted him to my breakfast, — which
shal not be forgotten.

The deuil pul out thy lying tong and teeth
that be so rotten!

GAMMER. Geue me my neele! As for my
Cocke, chould be very loth 130

That chuld here tel he shuld hang on thy
false faith and troth.

BAILY. Your talke is such I can scarse
learne who shuld be most in fault.

¹ Cloaks, conceals.
² Whores were carted through the streets.
³ What-you-call-it.
⁴ A term of abuse, sometimes, as here, used in the
plural of a single person.

GAMMER. Yet shal ye find no other wight
saue she, by bred and salt!

BAILY. Kepe ye content a-while; se that
your tonges ye holde;

Me thinkes you shuld remembre this is no
place to scolde. 135

How knowest thou, Gammer Gurton,
Dame Chat thy nedle had?

GAMMER. To name you, sir, the party,
chould not be very glad.

BAILY. Yea, but we must nedes heare it,
and therfore say it boldly.

GAMMER. Such one as told the tale full
soberly and coldly,

Euen he that loked on — wil sweare on a
booke — 140

What time this drunken gossip my faire
long neele vp tooke:

Diccon, Master, the bedlam. Cham very
sure ye know him.

BAILIE. A false knaue, by Gods pitie! Ye
were but a foole to trow [1] him.

I durst auenture wel the price of my best
cap

That when the end is knowen all wil turne
to a iape.[2] 145

Tolde he not you that, besides, she stole
your cocke that tyde? [3]

GAMMER. No, master, no indede; for then
he shuld haue lyed!

My cocke is, I thanke Christ, safe and wel
a-fine.

CHAT. Yea, but that ragged colt, that
whore, that Tyb of thine,

Said plainly thy cocke was stolne, and in
my house was eaten. 150

That lying cut [4] is lost that she is not
swinged and beaten, —

And yet for al my good name it were a
small amendes!

I picke not this geare, hearst thou, out of
my fingers endes;

But he that hard it told me, who thou of
late-didst name, —

Diccon, whom al men knowes, — it was the
very same. 155

BAILY. This is the case: you lost your
nedle about the dores,

And she answeres againe she hase no cocke
of yours;

Thus, in you[r] talke and action, from that
you do intend

She is whole fiue mile wide from that she
doth defend.

Will you saie she hath your cocke?

GAMMER. No, mary,[1] sir, that chil
not! 160

BAYLY. Will you confesse hir neele?

CHAT. Will I? no, sir, will I not!

BAYLY. Then there lieth all the matter.

GAMMER. Soft, master, by the way!

Ye know she could do litle and she cold
not say nay.

BAYLY. Yea, but he that made one lie
about your cock-stealing,

Wil not sticke to make another, what time
lies be in dealing. 165

I weene the ende wil proue this brawle did
first arise

Upon no other ground but only Diccons
lyes.

CHAT. Though some be lyes, as you belike
haue espyed them,

Yet other some be true — by proof I haue
wel tryed them.

BAYLY. What other thing beside this,
Dame Chat.

CHAT. Mary, syr, euen this: 170

The tale I tolde before, the selfe-same tale
it was his;

He gaue me, like a frende, warning against
my losse,

Els had my hens be stolne eche one, by
Gods crosse!

He tolde me Hodge wold come, and in he
came indeede;

But, as the matter chaunsed, with greater
hast then speede. 175

This truth was said, and true was found, as
truly I report.

BAYLY. If Doctor Rat be not deceiued, it
was of another sort.

D. RAT. By Gods Mother, thou and he be
a cople of suttle foxes!

Betweene you and Hodge I beare away the
boxes.

Did not Diccon apoynt the place wher thou
shuldst stand to mete him? 180

CHAT. Yes, by the masse; and, if he
came, bad me not sticke to speet [2]
hym.

---

[1] Trust. [2] Jest. [3] Time.
[4] A term of abuse.

[1] A. mery. [2] Spit.

D. RAT.   Gods sacrament, the villain
　　knaue hath drest vs round about!
He is the cause of all this brawle, that
　　dyrty, shitten loute!
When Gammer Gurton here complained,
　　and made a ruful mone,
I heard him sweare that you had gotten hir
　　nedle that was gone;   185
And this to try, he furder said, he was ful
　　loth; how-be-it
He was content with small adoe to bring
　　me where to see it.
And where ye sat, he said ful certain, if I
　　wold folow his read,
Into your house a priuy way he wold me
　　guide and leade,
And where ye had it in your hands, sewing
　　about a clowte;   190
And set me in the backe-hole, therby to
　　finde you oute.
And, whiles I sought a quietnes, creping
　　vpon my knees,
I found the weight of your dore-bar for my
　　reward and fees.
Such is the lucke that some men gets while
　　they begin to mel
In setting at one such as were out, minding
　　to make al wel.   195
HODGE.   Was not wel blest, Gammer, to
　　scape that stoure? [1] And chad ben
　　there,
Then chad ben drest,[2] be-like, as ill, by the
　　masse, as Gaffar Vicar.
BAYLY.   Mary, sir, here is a sport alone.
I loked for such an end.
If Diccon had not playd the knaue, this had
　　ben sone amend.
My Gammer here he made a foole, and
　　drest hir as she was;   200
And goodwife Chat he set to scole, till both
　　partes cried "alas";
And D[octor] Rat was not behind, whiles
　　Chat his crown did pare;
I wold the knaue had ben starke blind, if
　　Hodg had not his share!
HODGE.   Cham meetly wel-sped alredy
　　amongs; cham drest like a coult!
And chad not had the better wit, chad bene
　　made a doult.   205
BAYLY.   Sir knaue, make hast Diccon were
　　here; fetch him where-euer he bee!

[*Exit Scapethryft.*]

CHAT.   Fie on the villaine! fie! fie! that
　　makes vs thus agree!
GAMMER.   Fie on him knaue, with al my
　　hart! now fie! and fie againe!
D. RAT.   Now fie on him! may I best say,
　　whom he hath almost slaine.

[*Scapethryft leads in Diccon.*]

BAYLY.   Lo where he commeth at hand.
　　Belike he was not fare!   210
Diccon, heare be two or three thy company
　　can not spare.
DICCON.   God blesse you — and [1] you may
　　be blest so many al at once!
CHAT.   Come, knaue, it were a good deed
　　to geld the, by Cockes bones!
Seest not thy handiwarke? Sir Rat, can ye
　　forbeare him?
DICCON.   A vengeance on those hands
　　lite! for my hands cam not nere
　　hym.   215
The horsen priest hath lift the pot in some
　　of these alewyues chayres,
That his head wolde not serue him, belyke,
　　to come downe the stayres.
BAILY.   Nay, soft! thou maist not play the
　　knaue and haue this language to!
If thou thy tong bridle a-while, the better
　　maist thou do.
Confesse the truth, as I shall aske, and
　　cease a-while to fable;   220
And for thy fault, I promise the, thy han-
　　dling shalbe reasonable.
Hast thou not made a lie or two to set these
　　two by the eares?
DICCON.   What if I haue? Fiue hundred
　　such haue I seene within these seuen
　　yeares.
I am sory for nothing else but that I see not
　　the sport
Which was betwene them when they met,
　　as they them-selues report.   225
BAYLY.   The greatest thing [*pointing to Dr.
　　Rat*] — Master Rat! Ye se how he is
　　drest! [2]
DICCON.   What deuil nede he be groping so
　　depe in goodwife Chats hens nest?
BAYLY.   Yea, but it was thy drift to bring
　　him into the briars.

Diccon. Gods bread! hath not such an
old foole wit to saue his eares?
He showeth himselfe herein, ye see, so very
a coxe,[1]   230
The cat was not so madly alured by the foxe
To run into the snares was set for him,
doubtlesse;
For he leapt in for myce, and this sir John [2]
for madnes.
D. Rat. Well, and ye shift no better, ye
losel, lyther and lasye,[3]
I will go neare, for this, to make ye leape at
a dasye.[4]   235
In the kings [5] name, Master Bayly, I
charge you set him fast!
Diccon. What? fast at cardes, or fast on-
slepe? It is the thing I did last.
D. Rat. Nay, fast in fetters, false varlet,
according to thy deedes!
Bayly. Master doctor, ther is no remedy,
I must intreat you, needes,
Some other kinde of punishment.
D. Rat. Nay, by all halowes!   240
His punishment, if I may iudg, shalbe
naught els but the gallous.
Bayly. That ware to sore. A spiritual
man to be so extreame!
D. Rat. Is he worthy any better, sir?
How do ye iudge and deame?
Bayly. I graunt him wort[h]ie punish-
ment, but in no wise so great.
Gammer. It is a shame, ich tel you plaine,
for such false knaues intreat!   245
He has almost vndone vs al; that is as true
as steele.
And ye[t] for al this great ado cham neuer
the nere my neele!
Bayly. Canst thou not say any-thing to
that, Diccon, with least or most?
Diccon. Yea, mary, sir, thus much I can
say: — wel, the nedle is lost!
Bayly. Nay, canst not thou tel which
way that nedle may be found?   250
Diccon. No, by my fay, sir, though I
might haue an hundred pound.
Hodge. Thou lier, lickdish! didst not say
the neele wold be gitten?

1 Fool.   2 Parson.
3 Ye scoundrel, base and lazy.
4 Be hanged.
5 This indicates that the play was written while a
king was upon the throne. Professor Bradley has
shown that the date of the original presentation of the
play fell in the last year of Edward's reign.

Diccon. No, Hodge, by the same token
you were [1] that time beshittene
For feare of Hobgobling, — you wot wel
what I meane;
As long as it is sence, I feare me yet ye be
scarce cleane.   255
Bayly. Wel, Master Rat, you must both
learne and teach vs to forgeue.
Since Diccon hath confession made and is
so cleane shreue,[2]
If ye to me consent, to amend this heauie
chaunce
I wil inioyne him here some open kind of
penaunce, —
Of this condition: where ye know my fee is
twenty pence   260
For the bloodshed, I am agreed with you
here to dispence, —
Ye shal go quite,[3] so that ye graunt the
matter now to run
To end with mirth among vs al, euen as it
was begun.
Chat. Say yea, Master Vicar, and he shal
sure confes to be your detter,
And al we that be heare present wil loue
you much the better.   265
D. Rat. My part is the worst; but, since
you al here-on agree,
Go euen to, Master Bayly, — let it be so
for mee!
Bayly. How saiest thou, Diccon? art content this shal on me depend?
Diccon. Go to, M[aster] Bayly, say on
your mind. I know ye are my frend.
Bayly. Then marke ye wel: to recompence this thy former action,   270
Because thou hast offended al, to make
them satisfaction,
Before their faces here kneele downe, and,
as I shal the teach, —
For thou shalt take on othe of Hodges
leather breache:
First, for Master Doctor, vpon paine of his
cursse,
Where he wil pay for al thou neuer draw
thy pursse,   275
And when ye meete at one pot, he shall
haue the first pull,
And thou shalt neuer offer him the cup but
it be full;

1 A. where.   2 Shriven.
3 Freed from the sum due me.

To goodwife Chat thou shalt be sworne,
    euen on the same wyse,
If she refuse thy money once, neuer to offer
    it twise, —
Thou shalt be bound by the same here, as
    thou dost take it,   280
When thou maist drinke of free cost, thou
    neuer forsake it;
For Gammer Gurtons sake, againe sworne
    shalt thou bee,
To helpe hir to hir nedle againe, if it do lie
    in thee, —
And likewise be bound by the vertue of that
To be of good abering to Gib, hir great
    cat;   285
Last of al, for Hodge, the othe to scanne,
Thou shalt neuer take him for fine gentle-
    man.

HODGE [*stooping over*]. Come on, fellow
    Diccon! Chalbe euen with thee
    now!
BAYLY. Thou wilt not sticke to do this,
    Diccon, I trow?
DICCON. No, by my fathers skin, my hand
    downe I lay it!   290
Loke! as I haue promised, I wil not denay
    it.
But, Hodge, take good heede now thou do
    not beshite me!

And gaue him a good blow on the buttocke.

HODGE [*leaping up*]. Gogs hart! Thou
    false villaine, dost thou bite mee?
BAYLY. What, Hodge! doth he hurt the or
    euer he begin?
HODGE. He thrust me into the buttocke
    with a bodkin or a pin!   295

[*He draws out the needle.*]

I saie, Gammer! Gammer!
GAMMER. How now, Hodge? how now?
HODGE. Gods malt, Gammer Gurton!
GAMMER.   Thou art mad, ich trow!
HODGE. Will you see! The deuil, Gam-
    mer!
GAMMER.   The deuil, sonne? God
    blesse vs!
HODGE. Chould iche were hanged, Gam-
    mer!
GAMMER.   Mary, so [1] ye might
    dresse vs.

    [1] A. *se;* emend. suggested by Manly.

HODGE. Chaue it, by the masse, Gammer!
GAMMER.   What? Not my neele,
    Hodge?   300
HODGE. Your neele, Gammer! your neele!
GAMMER.   No, fie, dost but dodge!
HODGE. Cha found your neele, Gammer!
    Here in my hand be it!
GAMMER. For al the loues on earth,
    Hodge, let me see it!
HODGE. Soft, Gammer!
GAMMER.   Good Hodge!
HODGE.   Soft, ich say; tarie a while!
GAMMER. Nay, sweete Hodge, say truth,
    and do not me begile!   305
HODGE. Cham sure on it, ich warrant you
    it goes no more a-stray.
GAMMER. Hodge, when I speake so faire,
    wilt stil say me nay?
HODGE. Go neare the light, Gammer.
    This wel! In faith, good lucke!
Chwas almost vndone, twas so far in my
    buttocke!
GAMMER. Tis min owne deare neele,
    Hodge, sykerly I wot!   310
HODGE. Cham I not a good sonne, Gam-
    mer! cham I not?
GAMMER. Christs blessing light on thee!
    hast made me for-euer!
HODGE. Ich knew that ich must finde it,
    els choud a had it neuer!
CHAT. By my troth, Gossyp Gurton, I am
    euen as glad
As though I mine owne selfe as good a
    turne had!   315
BAYLY. And I, by my concience, to see it
    so come forth,
Reioyce so much at it as three nedles be
    worth!
D. RAT. I am no whit sory to see you so
    reioyce!
DICCON. Nor I much the gladder for al
    this noyce!
Yet say, "Gramercy, Diccon," for spring-
    ing of the game.   320
GAMMER. Gramercy, Diccon, twenty
    times! O how glad cham!
If that chould do so much, your master-
    dome to come hether,
Master Rat, goodwife Chat, and Diccon,
    together, —
Cha but one halfpeny, as far as iche know
    it,

And chil not rest this night till ich bestow
    it.   325
If euer ye loue me, let vs go in and drinke!
BAYLY.   I am content, if the rest thinke as
    I thinke.
Master Rat, it shalbe best for you if we so
    doo;
Then shall you warme you and dresse your-
    self too.
DICCON.   Soft, syrs, take vs with you; the
    company shalbe the more!   330

As proude coms behinde, they say, as any
    goes before!

               [*To the audience.*]

But now, my good masters, since we must
    be gone
And leaue you behinde vs here, all alone, —
Since at our last ending thus mery we
    bee,
For Gammer Gurtons nedle sake let vs
    haue a plaudytie!   335

FINIS, GURTON. PERUSED AND ALOWED, &C.

*Imprinted at London
in Fleetestreate beneath the Conduite
at the signe of S. John Euangelist, by
Thomas Colwell.*
1575.

XI
INNS OF COURT PLAYS

THE TRAGIDIE OF
[GORBODUC; OR OF] FERREX AND PORREX [1]

SET FORTH WITHOUT ADDITION OR ALTERATION BUT ALTOGETHER AS
THE SAME WAS SHEWED ON STAGE BEFORE THE QUEENES MAIESTIE,
ABOUT NINE YEARES PAST, VZ.,THE XVIIJ DAY OF IANUARIE 1561.
BY THE GENTLEMEN OF THE INNER TEMPLE.

Seen and allowed, &c.

Imprinted at London by Iohn Daye, dwelling ouer Aldersgate.

THE P[RINTER] TO THE READER

Where this tragedie was for furniture of part of the grand Christmasse in the Inner
Temple first written about nine yeares agoe by the Right Honourable Thomas, now
Lorde Buckherst, and by T. Norton, and after shewed before her Maiestie, and neuer
intended by the authors therof to be published; yet one W. G.[2] getting a copie therof at
some yongmans hand that lacked a litle money and much discretion, in the last great
plage, an[no] 1565, about v yeares past, while the said lord was out of England, and T.
Norton farre out of London, and neither of them both made priuie, put it forth exceedingly
corrupted, — euen as if by meanes of a broker, for hire, he should haue entised into his
house a faire maide and done her villanie, and after all-to-bescratched her face, torne her
apparell, berayed and disfigured her, and then thrust her out of dores dishonested. In
such plight, after long wandring, she came at length home to the sight of her frendes, who
scant knew her but by a few tokens and markes remayning. They — the authors, I
meane — though they were very much displeased that she so ranne abroad without leaue,
whereby she caught her shame, as many wantons do, yet seing the case, as it is, remedi-
lesse, haue, for common honestie and shamefastnesse, new apparelled, trimmed, and
attired her in such forme as she was before. In which better forme since she hath come

---

[1] The Inns of Court Plays, following the models of the classical drama, are closely akin to the School
Plays; but they were performed by gallants of fashion (many of them young noblemen), in the highest
circles of London society, and as products of fashionable society, they show the marked influence of the
contemporary Italian drama. *Gorboduc*, famous as the first regular English tragedy, was composed by
Thomas Sackville (later Earl of Dorset and Lord High Treasurer) and Thomas Norton (whose brilliant
career as a lawyer and courtier was cut short by his early death). It was acted by the young gentlemen of
the Inner Temple in 1561–62 on the occasion of their annual Christmas festival, and was repeated by them
before Queen Elizabeth on January 18, 1561–62, at Whitehall Palace. Though the play was ultimately
modeled on Seneca, the authors drew much of their inspiration from contemporary Italian tragedy (itself
an adaptation of Seneca); for instance, blank verse, now first used in the English drama, they took over
from the Italians; and the dumb shows they derived from the Italian *intermedii*. But Sackville and Norton
were not slavish imitators either of Seneca or of the Italian writers of tragedy.
    A surreptitious and very corrupt edition (A.) was published by William Griffith in 1565, with the title:
*The Tragedie of Gorboduc, wherof three Actes were wrytten by Thomas Nortone, and the two laste by Thomas
Sackuyle.* The authors, apparently, were offended at the corrupt text of this edition, and gave an authorized
text to John Day, who published it about 1570 (B.). A third edition (C.) was issued by Edward Alde in 1590,
but this was merely a reprint of the first, and corrupt, edition, and has no special value. I have based the
present text on a copy of the second and authorized edition (B.) in the British Museum. In a few cases I
have adopted readings from the other editions; these are properly recorded in the footnotes. I have, of
course, modernized the punctuation; and I have abbreviated the catch-names, and supplied stage-directions
in place of the bare list of speakers with which each scene is headed.
[2] William Griffith.

to me, I haue harbored her for her frendes sake, and her owne; and I do not dout her
parentes, the authors, will not now be discontent that she goe abroad among you, good
readers, so it be in honest companie.   For she is by my encouragement, and others, somewhat lesse ashamed of the dishonestie done to her, because it was by fraude and force.
If she be welcome among you, and gently enterteined, in fauor of the house from whense
she is descended and of her owne nature courteously disposed to offend no man, her
frendes will thanke you for it.   If not, but that she shall be still reproched with her
former missehap, or quarelled at by enuious persons, she, poore gentlewoman, will
surely play Lucreces part, and of her-self die for shame; and I shall wishe that she had
taried still at home with me, where she was welcome, for she did neuer put me to more
charge but this one poore blacke gowne lined with white that I haue now geuen her to
goe abroad among you withall.

THE ARGUMENT OF THE TRAGEDIE [1]

Gorboduc, king of Brittaine, diuided his realme in his lifetime to his sonnes, Ferrex
and Porrex; the sonnes fell to discention; the yonger killed the elder; the mother, that
more dearely loued the elder, for reuenge killed the yonger; the people, moued with the
crueltie of the fact, rose in rebellion and slew both father and mother; the nobilitie
assembled and most terribly destroyed the rebels; and afterwardes, for want of issue of
the prince, whereby the succession of the crowne became vncertaine, they fell to ciuill
warre, in which both they and many of their issues were slaine, and the land for a long
time almost desolate and miserably wasted.

THE NAMES OF THE SPEAKERS

GORBODUC, king of Great Brittaine.
VIDENA, queene, and wife to king Gorboduc.
FERREX, elder sonne to king Gorboduc.
PORREX, yonger sonne to king Gorboduc.
CLOTYN,[2] duke of Cornewall.
FERGUS, duke of Albanye.
MANDUD, duke of Loegris.
GWENARD, duke of Cumberland.
EUBULUS, secretarie to the king.
AROSTUS, a counsellor to the king.
DORDAN, a counsellor assigned by the king to his eldest sonne, Ferrex.
PHILANDER, a counsellor assigned by the king to his yongest sonne, Porrex.
          Both being of the olde kinges counsell before.
HERMON, a parasite remaining with Ferrex.
TYNDAR, a parasite remaining with Porrex.
NUNTIUS, a messenger of the elder brothers death.
NUNTIUS, a messenger of Duke Fergus rising in armes.
MARCELLA, a lady of the queenes priuie-chamber.
CHORUS, foure auncient and sage men of Brittaine.

[THE SCENE: Britain.]

---

[1] In B. this argument is printed on the back of the title-page.   [2] B. *Cloyton.*

[GORBODUC; OR, FERREX AND PORREX.]

THE ORDER OF THE DOMME SHEW BEFORE
THE FIRST ACT, AND THE SIGNIFICA-
TION THEREOF.

First the musicke of violenze began to play, during
which came in vpon the stage sixe wilde men clothed
n leaues; of whom the first bare in his necke a fagot
of small stickes, which they all, both seuerally and
together, assayed with all their strengthes to breake;
but it could not be broken by them. At the length,
one of them plucked out one of the stickes and brake
t; and the rest plucking out all the other stickes one
after an-other did easely breake them, the same be-
ng seuered, which, being conioyned, they had before
attempted in vaine. After they had this done, they
departed the stage, and the musicke ceased. Hereby
was signified that a state knit in vnitie doth continue
strong against all force, but being diuided is easely
destroyed; as befell vpon Duke Gorboduc diuiding his
and to his two sonnes, which he before held in
nonarchie, and vpon the discention of the brethren
to whom it was diuided.

ACTUS PRIMUS

SCENA PRIMA.

*The palace of King Gorboduc. Enter Queen
Videna and her eldest son Ferrex.]* [1]

VID. The silent night, that bringes the
     quiet pawse
From painefull trauailes of the wearie day,
Prolonges my carefull thoughtes, and
     makes me blame
The slowe Aurore, that so for loue or shame
Doth long delay to shewe her blushing
     face;   5
And now the day renewes my grieefull
     plaint.
FERR. My gracious lady and my mother
     deare,
Pardon my griefe for your so grieued
     minde
To aske what cause tormenteth so your
     hart.
VID. So great a wrong, and so vniust de-
     spite,   10
Without all cause, against all course of
     kinde!
FERR. Such causelesse wrong, and so vn-
     iust despite,

[1] In the old editions each scene is headed with a
ist of all the speakers without indication as to when
hey entered.

May haue redresse, or, at the least, re-
     uenge.
VID. Neither, my sonne; such is the
     froward will,
The person such, such my missehappe and
     thine.   15
FERR. Mine know I none but grief for
     your distresse.
VID. Yes, mine for thine, my sonne. A
     father? No;
In kinde [1] a father, not in kindliness.
FERR. My father? Why, I know nothing
     at all   19
Wherein I haue misdone vnto his Grace.
VID. Therefore the more vnkinde to thee
     and mee!
For, knowing well, my sonne, the tender loue
That I haue euer borne and beare to thee,
He, greued thereat, is not content alone
To spoile thee of my sight,[2] my chiefest
     ioye;   25
But thee of thy birthright and heritage,
Causelesse, vnkindly, and in wrongfull wise
Against all lawe and right, he will bereaue.
Halfe of his kingdome he will geue away.
FERR. To whom?
VID. Euen to Porrex, his yonger sonne; 30
Whose growing pride I do so sore suspect
That, being raised to equall rule with thee,
Mee thinkes I see his enuious hart to swell,
Filled with disdaine, and with ambicious
     hope.
The end the goddes do know, whose al-
     tars I   35
Full oft haue made in vaine of cattell slaine
To send the sacred smoke to Heauens
     throne
For thee, my sonne, if thinges do so suc-
     cede [3]
As now my ielous mind misdemeth sore.
FERR. Madam, leaue care and carefull
     plaint for me.   40
Just hath my father bene to euery wight;
His first vniustice he will not extend
To me, I trust, that geue no cause therof

[1] Nature.
[2] Manly suggests *To spoile me of thy sight.*
[3] Come to pass.

My brothers pride shall hurt him-selfe, not
  me.
VID.   So graunt the goddes! But yet thy
  father so   45
Hath firmely fixed his vnmoued minde
That plaintes and prayers can no whit
  auaile, —
For those haue I assaied,—but euen this day
He will endeuour to procure assent
Of all his counsell to his fonde [1] deuise. 50
FERR.   Their ancestors from race to race
  haue borne
True fayth to my forefathers and their
  seede;
I trust they eke will beare the like to me.
VID.   There resteth all. But if they faile
  thereof,
And if the end bring forth an ill successe, 55
On them and theirs the mischiefe shall befall;
And so I pray the goddes requite it them, —
And so they will, for so is wont to be.
When lordes, and trusted rulers vnder
  kinges,   59
To please the present fancie of the prince,
With wrong transpose the course of gou-
  ernance,
Murders, mischiefe, or ciuill sword at
  length,
Or mutuall treason, or a iust reuenge
When right-succeding line returnes againe,
By Ioues iust iudgement and deserued
  wrath   65
Bringes them to cruell and reprochfull
  death,
And rootes their names and kindredes from
  the earth.
FERR.   Mother, content you; you shall see
  the end.
VID.   The end? Thy end, I feare! Ioue
  end me first!   [Exeunt.]

ACTUS PRIMUS

SCENA SECUNDA

[The Court of King Gorboduc.   Enter King
  Gorboduc, with his Counsellors Arostus
  and Philander, and his Secretary,
  Eubulus.]

GORB.   My lords, whose graue aduise and
  faithful aide

[1] Foolish

Haue long vpheld my honour and my
  realme,
And brought me to this age from tender
  yeres,
Guidyng so great estate with great re-
  nowme,
Nowe more importeth mee than erst to
  vse   5
Your fayth and wisedome, — whereby yet
  I reigne, —
That when by death my life and rule shall
  cease
The kingdome yet may with vnbroken
  course
Haue certayne prince, by whose vndoubted
  right
Your wealth and peace may stand in quiet
  stay; [1]   10
And eke that they, whome nature hath pre-
  parde
In time to take my place in princely seate,
While in their fathers tyme their pliant
  youth
Yeldes to the frame of skilfull gouernance
Maye so be taught and trayned in noble
  artes   15
As, what their fathers which haue reigned
  before
Haue with great fame deriued downe to
  them,
With honour they may leaue vnto their
  seede;
And not be thought, for their vnworthy life
And for their lawlesse swaruynge out of
  kinde,   20
Worthy to lose what lawe and kind them
  gaue;
But that they may preserue the common
  peace —
The cause that first began and still main-
  teines
The lyneall course of kinges inheritance —
For me, for myne, for you, and for the
  state,   25
Whereof both I and you haue charge and
  care.
Thus do I meane to vse youre wonted fayth
To me and myne, and to your natiu
  lande.
My lordes, be playne, without all wrie re-
  spect

[1] Condition.

Or poysonous craft to speake in pleasyng
wise; 30
Lest, as the blame of yll-succedyng thinges
Shall light on you, so light the harmes
also.

AROS.   Your good acceptance so, most
noble king,
Of suche our faithfulnesse as heretofore
We haue employed in dueties to your
Grace 35
And to this realme, whose worthy head you
are,
Well proues that neyther you mistrust at
all,
Nor we shall neede in boasting wise to
shewe
Our trueth to you, nor yet our wakefull
care
For you, for yours, and for our natiue
lande. 40
Wherefore, O kyng, — I speake as one for
all,
Sithe all as one do beare you egall faith, —
Doubt not to vse our counsells and our
aides,
Whose honours, goods, and lyues are whole
auowed
To serue, to ayde and to defende your
Grace. 45

GORB.   My lordes, I thanke you all! This
is the case:
Ye know, the gods — who haue the sou-
eraigne care
For kings, for kingdomes, and for common-
weales —
Gaue me two sonnes in my more lusty age,
Who nowe in my decayeng yeres are
growen 50
Well towards ryper state of minde and
strength
To take in hande some greater princely
charge.
As yet they lyue and spende [their] [1] hope-
full daies
With me and with their mother here in
courte.
Their age nowe asketh other place and
trade, 55
And myne also doth aske an-other chaunge:
Theirs to more trauaile,[2] myne to greater
ease.

Whan fatall death shall ende my mortall
life,
My purpose is to leaue vnto them twaine
The realme diuided in two [1] sondry
partes: 60
The one Ferrex, myne elder sonne, shall
haue;
The other shall the yonger, Porrex, rule.
That both my purpose may more firmely
stande,
And eke that they may better rule their
charge,
I meane forthwith to place them in the
same, 65
That in my life they may both learne to
rule,
And I may ioy to see their ruling well.
This is, in summe, what I woulde haue ye
wey:
First, whether ye allowe my whole deuise
And thinke it good for me, for them, for
you, 70
And for our countrey, mother of vs all;
And, if ye lyke it and allowe it well,
Then, for their guydinge and their gou-
ernaunce,
Shew forth such meanes of circumstance
As ye thinke meete to be both knowne and
kept. 75
Loe, this is all.   Now tell me your aduise.

AROS.   And this is much! and asketh great
aduise.
But, for my part, my soueraigne lord and
kyng,
This do I thinke: your Maiestie doth know
How, vnder you, in iustice and in peace 80
Great wealth and honour long we haue en-
ioyed,
So as we can not seeme with gredie mindes
To wisshe for change of prince or gouer-
naunce;
But, if we lyke your purpose and deuise,
Our lyking must be deemed to proceede 85
Of rightfull reason, and of heedefull care
Not for ourselues but for the common
state,
Sithe our owne state doth neede no better
change.
I thinke in all as erst your Grace hath saide.
Firste, when you shall vnlode your aged
mynde 90

<hr>

[2] B. omits *their*.   [3] Labor.

[1] A. B. *into two;* corr. by Manly.

Of heuye care and troubles manifolde,
And laye the same vpon my lordes your
    sonnes,
Whose growing yeres may beare the burden
    long, —
And long I pray the goddes to graunt it
    so! —
And in your life while you shall so be-
    holde   95
Their rule, their vertues, and their noble
    deedes,
Suche as their kinde behighteth [1] to vs all,
Great be the profites that shall growe
    therof:
Your age in quiet shall the longer last;
Your lasting age shalbe their longer stay;
For cares of kynges that rule — as you
    haue ruled —   101
For publique wealth and not for priuate
    ioye
Do wast mannes lyfe, and hasten crooked
    age
With furrowed face and with enfeebled
    lymmes
To draw on creepyng death a swifter
    pace.   105
They two yet yong shall beare the parted
    reigne
With greater ease than one, nowe olde,
    alone
Can welde the whole, for whom muche
    harder is
With lessened strength the double weight
    to beare.
Your eye, your counsell, and the graue re-
    garde   110
Of fathers [2] — yea, of such a fathers —
    name,
Nowe at beginning of their sondred reigne,
When is the hazarde of their whole suc-
    cesse,
Shall bridle so their force of youthfull
    heates,
And so restreine the rage of insolence, 115
Whiche most assailes the yonge and noble
    minds,
And so shall guide and traine in tempred
    stay
Their yet greene, bending wittes with reu-
    erent awe,

As — now inured with vertues at the
    first, —
Custome, O king, shall bring delightful-
    nesse;   120
By vse of vertue, vice shall growe in hate.
But if you so dispose it that the daye
Which endes your life shall first begin their
    reigne,
Great is the perill what will be the ende,
When such beginning of such liberties, 125
Voide of suche stayes as in your life do
    lye,
Shall leaue them free to randon of their
    will,
An open praie to traiterous flatterie, —
The greatest pestilence of noble youthe;
Whiche perill shalbe past, if in your life 130
Their tempred youthe with aged fathers
    awe
Be brought in vre [1] of skilfull stayednesse;
And in your life their liues disposed so,
Shall length your noble life in ioyfulnesse.
Thus thinke I that your Grace hath wisely
    thought,   135
And that your tender care of common
    weale
Hath bred this thought, so to diuide your
    lande
And plant your sonnes to beare the present
    rule
While you yet liue to see their rulinge well
That you may longer lyue by ioye therein.
What furder meanes behouefull are and
    meete,   141
At greater leisure may your Grace deuise,
When all haue said, and when we be agreed
If this be best to part the realme in twaine
And place your sonnes in present gouerne-
    ment.   145
Whereof, as I haue plainely said my mynde
So woulde I here the rest of all my lordes
PHIL.   In part I thinke as hath bene said
    before,
In parte, agayne, my minde is otherwise.
As for diuiding of this realme in twaine, 150
And lotting out the same in egall partes
To either of my lordes your Graces sonnes
That thinke I best for this your realme
    behofe,
For profite and aduauncement of your
    sonnes,

---

[1] Their nature promises.
[2] B. *father;* I follow the reading of A.

[1] Practice.

And for your comforte and your honour
eke.   155
But so to place them while your life do last
To yelde to them your royall gouernaunce,
To be aboue them onely in the name
Of father not in kingly state also,
I thinke not good for you, for them, nor
vs.   160
This kingdome, since the bloudie ciuill
fielde
Where Morgan-slaine did yeld his con-
quered parte
Unto his cosins sworde in Camberland,
Conteineth all that whilome did suffice
Three noble sonnes of your forefather
Brute.   165
So your two sonnes it maye suffice also.
The moe [1] the stronger, if they gree in one.
The smaller compasse that the realme doth
holde
The easier is the swey thereof to welde,
The nearer iustice to the wronged poore,
The smaller charge, — and yet ynoughe
for one.   171
And, whan the region is diuided so
That brethren be the lordes of either parte,
Such strength doth Nature knit betwene
them both
In sondrie bodies by conioyned loue   175
That, not as two, but one of doubled force,
Eche is to other as a sure defence;
The noblenesse and glory of the one
Doth sharpe the courage of the others
mynde
With vertuous enuie to contende for
praise.   180
And suche an egalnesse [2] hath Nature
made
Betwene the brethren of one fathers seede
As an vnkindly wrong it seemes to bee
To throwe the brother subiect vnder feete
Of him whose peere hc is by course of
kinde.   185
And Nature, that did make this egalnesse,
Ofte so repineth at so great a wrong
That ofte she rayseth vp a grudginge griefe
In yonger brethren at the elders state,
Wherby both townes and kingdomes haue
ben rased,   190
And famous stockes of royall bloud de-
stroied:

[1] More.   [2] Equalness.

The brother, that shoulde be the brothers
aide
And haue a wakefull care for his defence,
Gapes for his death, and blames the lynger-
ing yeres
That draw not forth his ende with faster
course;   195
And oft, impacient of so longe delayes,
With hatefull slaughter he preuentes the
Fates,
And heapes a iust rewarde for brothers
bloode,
With endlesse vengeaunce on his stocke for
aye.
Suche mischiefes here are wisely mette
withall,   200
If egall state maye nourishe egall loue,
Where none hath cause to grudge at others
good.
But nowe the head to stoupe beneth them
bothe,
Ne kind, ne reason, ne good ordre beares.
And oft it hath ben seene, where Natures
course   205
Hath ben peruerted in disordered wise,
When fathers cease to know that they
should rule,
The children cease to know they should
obey;
And often ouerkindly tendernesse
Is mother of vnkindly stubbornenesse. 210
I speake not this in enuie or reproche,
As if I grudged the glorie of your sonnes, —
Whose honour I besech the goddes en-
crease! —
Nor yet as if I thought there did remaine
So filthie cankers in their noble brestes, 215
Whom I esteeme — which is their greatest
praise —
Undoubted children of so good a kyng;
Onelie I meane to shewe, by certeine rules
Whiche Kinde hath graft within the mind
of man,
That Nature hath her ordre and her
course,   220
Which being broken doth corrupt the state
Of myndes and thinges, euen in the best of
all.
My lordes your sonnes may learne to rule
of you;
Your owne example in your noble courte
Is fittest guyder of their youthfull yeares.

If you desire to see some present ioye 226
By sight of their well rulynge in your lyfe,
See them obey, so shall you see them rule:
Who-so obeyeth not with humblenesse
Will rule with outrage and with inso-
   lence.   230
Longe maye they rule, I do beseche the
   goddes!
But longe may they learne, ere they begyn
   to rule!
If Kinde and Fates woulde suffre, I would
   wisshe
Them aged princes, and immortall kinges.
Wherfore, most noble kynge, I well as-
   sent   235
Betwene your sonnes that you diuide your
   realme,
And, as in kinde, so match them in degree.
But, while the goddes prolong your royall
   life,
Prolong your reigne! For therto lyue you
   here,
And therfore haue the goddes so long for-
   borne   240
To ioyne you to them-selues, that still you
   might
Be prince and father of our common-weale.
They, when they see your children ripe to
   rule,
Will make them roume, and will remoue
   you hence,
That yours, in right ensuynge of your
   life,   245
Maye rightly honour your immortall name.
Eub.   Your wonted true regarde of faith-
   full hartes
Makes me, O kinge, the bolder to presume
To speake what I conceiue within my brest,
Although the same do not agree at all 250
With that which other here my lordes haue
   said,
Nor which yourselfe haue seemed best to
   lyke.
Pardon I craue, and that my wordes be
   demed
To flowe from hartie zeale vnto your Grace,
And to the safetie of your common-
   weale.   255
To parte your realme vnto my lordes your
   sonnes
I thinke not good for you, ne yet for them,
But worste of all for this our natiue lande.

Within one land one single rule is best:
Diuided reignes do make diuided hartes,
But peace preserues the countrey and the
   prince.   261
Suche is in man the gredy minde to reigne,
So great is his desire to climbe alofte,
In worldly stage the stateliest partes to
   beare,
That faith and iustice and all kindly
   loue   265
Do yelde vnto desire of soueraignitie
Where egall state doth raise an egall hope
To winne the thing that either wold at-
   taine.
Your Grace remembreth how in passed
   yeres
The mightie Brute, first prince of all this
   lande,   270
Possessed the same and ruled it well in one;
He, thinking that the compasse did suffice
For his three sonnes three kingdoms eke to
   make,
Cut it in three, as you would now in twaine;
But how much Brittish bloud hath since
   bene spilt   275
To ioyne againe the sondred vnitie,
What princes slaine before their timely
   houre,
What wast of townes and people in the
   lande,
What treasons heaped on murders and on
   spoiles
Whose iust reuenge even yet is scarcely
   ceased,   280
Ruthefull remembraunce is yet rawe in
   minde!
The gods forbyd the like to chaunce againe!
And you, O king, geue not the cause therof!
My lord Ferrex, your elder sonne, per-
   happes,
Whome kinde and custome geues a right-
   full hope   285
To be your heire and to succeede your
   reigne,
Shall thinke that he doth suffre greater
   wrong
Than he perchaunce will beare, if power
   serue.
Porrex, the younger, so vpraised in state,
Perhappes in courage will be raysed
   also.   290
If flatterie, then, which fayles not to assaile

The tendre mindes of yet vnskilfull youth,
In one shall kindle and encrease disdaine,
And enuie in the others harte enflame,
This fire shall waste their loue, their liues,
    their land,   295
And ruthefull ruine shall destroy them
    both.
I wishe not this, O kyng, so to befall,
But feare the thing that I do most abhorre.
Geue no beginning to so dreadfull ende!
Kepe them in order and obedience,   300
And let them both, by now obeying you,
Learne such behauiour as beseemes their
    state, —
The elder, myldenesse in his gouernaunce,
The yonger, a yelding contentednesse.
And kepe them neare vnto your presence
    still,   305
That they, restreyned by the awe of you,
May liue in compasse of well tempred
    staye,
And passe the perilles of their youthfull
    yeares.
Your aged life drawes on to febler tyme,
Wherin you shall lesse able be to beare 310
The trauailes that in youth you haue sus-
    teyned
Both in your persones and your realmes de-
    fence.
If planting now your sonnes in furder
    partes
You sende them furder from your present
    reach,
Lesse shall you know how they them-selues
    demeane;   315
Traiterous corrupters of their plyant youth
Shall haue, vnspied, a muche more free ac-
    cesse;
And if ambition and inflamed disdaine
Shall arme the one, the other, or them
    both,
To ciuill warre or to vsurping pride,   320
Late shall you rue that you ne recked be-
    fore.
Good is, I graunt, of all to hope the best,
But not to liue still dreadlesse of the worst;
So truste the one that the other be forsene.
Arme not vnskilfulnesse with princely
    power;   325
But you, that long haue wisely ruled the
    reignes
Of royaltie within your noble realme,

So holde them, while the gods for our
    auayles
Shall stretch the thred of your prolonged
    daies.
To soone he clambe into the flaming
    carre   330
Whose want of skill did set the earth on
    fire.
Time, and example of your noble Grace,
Shall teach your sonnes both to obey and
    rule.
When time hath taught them, time shal
    make them place, —
The place that now is full: and so, I
    pray,   335
Long it remaine, to comforte of vs all!
GORB. I take your faithful harts in thank-
    ful part.
But sithe I see no cause to draw my minde
To feare the nature of my louing sonnes,
Or to misdeme that enuie or disdaine 340
Can there worke hate where nature plant-
    eth loue,
In one selfe purpose do I still abide.
My loue extendeth egally to both;
My lande suffiseth for them both also.
Humber shall parte the marches [1] of theyr
    realmes: 345
The sotherne part the elder shall possesse;
The no[r]therne shall Porrex, the yonger,
    rule.
In quiet I will passe mine aged dayes,
Free from the trauaile and the painefull
    cares
That hasten age vpon the worthiest
    kinges.   350
But, lest the fraude that ye do seeme to
    feare
Of flattering tongues corrupt their tender
    youth
And wrythe them to the wayes of youthfull
    lust,
To climyng pride, or to reuenging hate,
Or to neglecting of their carefull charge,
Lewdely to lyue in wanton recklessnesse,
Or to oppressing of the rightfull cause,
Or not to wreke the wronges done to the
    poore,   358
To treade downe truth, or fauour false de-
    ceite,
I meane to ioyne to eyther of my sonnes

[1] Boundaries.

Some one of those whose long approued
    faith   361
And wisdome tryed may well assure my
    harte
That mynyng fraude shall finde no way to
    crepe
Into their fensed eares with graue aduise.
This is the ende.   And so I pray you all
To beare my sonnes the loue and loyaltie
That I haue founde within your faithfull
    brestes.   367
AROS.   You, nor your sonnes, our sou-
    eraign lord, shal want
Our faith and seruice while our liues do
    last!   [*Exeunt.*]

CHORUS.

When settled stay doth holde the royall
    throne
    In stedfast place by knowen and doubt-
      les right,
And chiefely when discent on one alone
    Makes single and vnparted reigne to
      light,
Eche chaunge of course vnioynts the whole
    estate
And yeldes it thrall to ruyne by debate.[1] 6

The strength that, knit by faste accorde in
    one,
    Against all forrein power of mightie foes
Could of it-selfe defende it-selfe alone,
    Disioyned once, the former force doth
      lose.
The stickes that, sondred, brake so soone in
    twaine,
In faggot bounde attempted were in
    vain.   12

Oft tender minde, that leades the parciall eye
    Of erring parentes in their childrens loue,
Destroyes the wrongly loued childe
    thereby.
    This doth the proude sonne of Apollo
    proue,
Who, rasshely set in chariot of his sire,
Inflamed the parched earth with heauens
    fire.   18

And this great king, that doth deuide his
    land,

And chaunge the course of his discending
    crowne,
And yeldes the reigne into his childrens
    hande,
    From blisfull state of ioye and great re-
    nowne
A myrrour shall become to princes all
To learne to shunne the cause of suche a
    fall.   24

THE ORDER AND SIGNIFICATION OF THE
DOMME SHEW BEFORE THE SECOND
ACTE.

First, the musicke of cornettes began to playe, during which came in vpon the stage a king accompanied
with a nombre of his nobilitie and gentlemen.   And,
after he had placed him-self in a chaire of estate prepared for him, there came and kneled before him a
graue and aged gentleman, and offred vp a cuppe
vnto him of wyne in a glasse, which the king refused;
after him commes a braue [1] and lustie yong gentleman
and presentes the king with a cup of golde filled with
poyson, which the king accepted, and, drinking the
same, immediatly fell downe dead vpon the stage,
and so was carried thence away by his lordes and
gentelmen.   And then the musicke ceased.   Hereby
was signified, that, as glasse by nature holdeth no
poyson, but is clere and may easely be seen through,
ne boweth [2] by any arte, so a faythfull counsellour
holdeth no treason, but is playne and open, ne yeld-
eth to any vndiscrete affection, but geueth holsome
counsell, which the yll-aduised prince refuseth.   The
delightfull golde filled with poyson betokeneth flattery, which vnder faire seeming of pleasaunt wordes
beareth deadly poyson, which destroieth [3] the prince
that receyueth it; as befell in the two brethren,
Ferrex and Porrex, who, refusing the holsome aduise
of graue counsellours, credited these yong paracites,
and brought to them-selues death and destruction
therby.

ACTUS SECUNDUS

SCENA PRIMA.

[*The court of Ferrex.   Enter Ferrex attended
by the parasite Hermon and the wise Counsellor Dordan.*]

FERR.   I meruaile much what reason ledde
    the king,
My father, thus without all my desert,
To reue [4] me halfe the kingdome, which by
    course
Of law and nature should remayne to me.
HER.   If you with stubborne and vntamed
    pryde   5
Had stood against him in rebelling wise,
Or if with grudging minde you had enuied

---

[1] Strife.

[1] Handsomely dressed.   [2] Bendeth.
[3] B. *destroyed;* A. *destroieth.*   [4] Rob.

So slow a slidyng of his aged yeres,
Or sought before your time to haste the
     course
Of fatall death vpon his royall head,   10
Or stained your stocke with murder of your
     kyn,
Some face of reason might perhaps haue
     seemed
To yelde some likely cause to spoyl ye thus.
FERR.   The wrekeful [1] gods powre on my
     cursed head
Eternall plagues and neuer-dying woes, 15
The hellish prince adiudge my dampned
     ghost
To Tantales thirste, or proude Ixions
     wheele,
Or cruell gripe to gnaw my growing harte,
To during tormentes and vnquenched
     flames,
If euer I conceyued so foule a thought   20
To wisshe his ende of life, or yet of reigne!
DOR.   Ne yet your father, O most noble
     prince,
Did euer thinke so fowle a thing of you;
For he, with more than fathers tendre
     loue,
While yet the Fates do lende him life to
     rule, —   25
Who long might lyue to see your ruling
     well, —
To you, my lorde, and to his other sonne,
Lo, he resignes his realme and royaltie:
Which neuer would so wise a prince haue
     done,
If he had once misdemed that in your
     harte   30
There euer lodged so vnkinde a thought.
But tendre loue, my lorde, and setled
     truste
Of your good nature and your noble minde
Made him to place you thus in royall
     throne,
And now to geue you half his realme to
     guide, —   35
Yea, and that halfe which in abounding
     store
Of things that serue to make a welthy
     realme,
In stately cities, and in frutefull soyle,
In temperate breathing of the milder
     heauen,

----

[1] Avenging.

In thinges of nedefull vse which frendly
     sea   40
Transportes by traffike from the forreine
     partes,
In flowing wealth, in honour, and in force,
Doth passe the double value of the parte
That Porrex hath allotted to his reigne.
Such is your case; such is your fathers
     loue.   45
FERR.   Ah loue, my frendes? loue wrongs
     not whom he loues!
DOR.   Ne yet he wrongeth you, that geu-
     eth you
So large a reigne ere that the course of
     time
Bring you to kingdome by discended right;
Which time, perhaps, might end your time
     before.   50
FERR.   Is this no wrong, say you, to reaue
     from me
My natiue right of halfe so great a realme,
And thus to matche his yonger sonne with
     me
In egall power and in as great degree?
Yea, and what sonne?   The sonne whose
     swelling pride   55
Woulde neuer yelde one poinct of reuerence
Whan I, the elder and apparaunt heire,
Stoode in the likelihode to possesse the
     whole;
Yea, and that sonne which from his child-
     ish age
Enuieth myne honour and doth hate my
     life.   60
What will he now do, when his pride, his
     rage,
The mindefull malice of his grudging harte,
Is armed with force, with wealth, and
     kingly state?
HER.   Was this not wrong, — yea, yll-
     aduised wrong,
To giue so mad a man so sharpe a
     sworde?   65
To so great perill of so great missehappe
Wide open thus to set so large a waye?
DOR.   Alas, my lord, what griefull thing is
     this,
That of your brother you can thinke so ill?
I neuer saw him vtter likelie signe   70
Whereby a man might see or once misdeme
Such hate of you ne such unyelding pride.
Ill is their counsell, shamefull be their ende.

That, raysing such mistrustfull feare in
          you,
Sowing the seede of such vnkindly hate, 75
Trauaile [1] by treason to destroy you both.
Wise is your brother, and of noble hope,
Worthie to welde a large and mightie
          realme:
So much a stronger frende haue you therby,
Whose strength is your strength, if you
          gree in one.   80
HER.   If Nature and the goddes had
          pinched so
Their flowing bountie and their noble
          giftes
Of princelie qualities from you, my lorde,
And powrde them all at ones in wastfull
          wise
Upon your fathers yonger sonne alone, 85
Perhappes there be that in your preiudice
Would say that birth should yeld to worth-
          inesse.
But sithe in eche good gift and princelie
          arte
Ye are his matche, and, in the chiefe of
          all, —
In mildenesse and in sobre gouer-
          naunce, —   90
Ye farre surmount; and sith there is in you
Sufficing skill and hopefull towardnesse
To weld the whole and match your elders
          prayse,
I see no cause why ye should loose the
          halfe.
Ne would I wisshe you yelde to such a
          losse,   95
Lest your milde sufferaunce of so great a
          wronge
Be deemed cowardishe and simple dreade,
Which shall geue courage to the fierie head
Of your yonge brother to inuade the whole.
While yet, therfore, stickes in the peoples
          minde   100
The lothed wrong of your disheritaunce;
And ere your brother haue, by settled
          power,
By guilefull cloke of an alluring showe,
Got him some force and fauour in the
          realme;
And while the noble queene, your mother,
          lyues   105
To worke and practise all for your auaile,—

Attempt redresse by armes, and wreake
          your-self
Upon his life that gayneth by your losse,
Who nowe, to shame of you, and griefe of
          vs,
In your owne kingdome triumphes ouer
          you.   110
Shew now your courage meete for kingly
          state,
That they which haue auowed to spend
          theyr goods,
Their landes, their liues and honours in
          your cause,
May be the bolder to mainteyne your
          parte,
When they do see that cowarde feare in
          you   115
Shall not betray ne faile their faithfull
          hartes.
If once the death of Porrex ende the strife,
And pay the price of his vsurped reigne,
Your mother shall perswade the angry
          kyng.
The lords, your frends, eke shall appease
          his rage;   120
For they be wise, and well they can forsee
That ere longe time your aged fathers
          death
Will bryng a time when you shall well re-
          quite
Their frendlie fauour, or their hatefull
          spite,
Yea, or their slackenesse to auaunce your
          cause.   125
"Wise men do not so hang on passing state
"Of present princes, chiefely in their age,
"But they will further cast their reaching
          eye
"To viewe and weye the times and reignes
          to come." [1]
Ne is it likely, though the kyng be wrothe,
That he yet will or that the realme will
          beare   131
Extreme reuenge vpon his onely sonne;
Or, if he woulde, what one is he that dare
Be minister to such an enterprise?
And here you be now placed in your
          owne,   135
Amyd your frendes, your vassalles, and
          your strength.

----

[1] Labor.

[1] Quotation marks were used in the sixteenth century to emphasize sententious passages.

We shall defende and kepe your person
    safe,
Till either counsell turne his tender minde,
Or age or sorrow end his werie dayes.
But, if the feare of goddes and secrete
    grudge   140
Of Natures law, repining at the fact,
Withholde your courage from so great at-
    tempt,
Know ye that lust of kingdomes hath no
    law:
The goddes do beare and well allow in
    kinges
The thinges [that] they abhorre in rascall
    routes.   145
"When kinges on slender quarrells runne to
    warres,
"And then, in cruell and vnkindely wise,
"Commaund theftes, rapes, murders of
    innocentes,
"The spoile of townes, ruines of mighty
    realmes, —
"Thinke you such princes do suppose
    them-selues   150
"Subiect to lawes of Kinde and feare of
    gods?"
Murders and violent theftes in priuate men
Are hainous crimes, and full of foule re-
    proch;
Yet none offence, but deckt with glorious
    name
Of noble conquestes, in the handes of
    kinges.   155
But, if you like not yet so hote deuise,
Ne list to take such vauntage of the time,
But, though with perill of your owne es-
    tate,
You will not be the first that shall inuade,
Assemble yet your force for your de-
    fence,   160
And, for your safetie, stand vpon your
    garde.
Dor.   O Heauen! was there euer heard or
    knowen
So wicked counsell to a noble prince?
Let me, my lorde, disclose vnto your Grace
This hainous tale, what mischiefe it con-
    taines: —   165
Your fathers death, your brothers, and
    your owne,
Your present murder and eternall shame.
Heare me, O king, and suffer not to sinke

So high a treason in your princely brest!
Ferr.   The mightie goddes forbid that
    euer I   170
Should once conceaue such mischiefe in my
    hart!
Although my brother hath bereft my
    realme,
And beare, perhappes, to me an hatefull
    minde,
Shall I reuenge it with his death, therefore?
Or shall I so destroy my fathers life   175
That gaue me life? The gods forbid, I
    say!
Cease you to speake so any more to me.
Ne you, my frend, with answere once re-
    peate
So foule a tale, — in silence let it die!
What lord or subiect shall haue hope at
    all   180
That vnder me they safely shall enioye
Their goods, their honours, landes, and lib-
    erties,
With whom neither one onely brother
    deare,
Ne father dearer, could enioye their liues?
But, sith I feare my yonger brothers
    rage,   185
And sith perhappes some other man may
    geue
Some like aduise to moue his grudging head
At mine estate, — which counsell may per-
    chaunce
Take greater force with him than this with
    me, —
I will in secrete so prepare myselfe   190
As, if his malice or his lust to reigne
Breake forth in armes or sodeine violence,
I may withstand his rage and keepe mine
    owne.

[*Exeunt Ferrex with the parasite Hermon.*]

Dor.   I feare the fatall time now draweth
    on
When ciuil hate shall end the noble line   195
Of famous Brute and of his royall seede.
Great Ioue, defend the mischiefes now at
    hand!
O that the Secretaries wise aduise
Had erst bene heard, when he besought the
    king
Not to diuide his land, nor send his
    sonnes   200

To further partes from presence of his court,
Ne yet to yelde to them his gouernaunce.
Lo, such are they now in the royall throne
As was rashe Phaeton in Phœbus carre;
Ne then the fiery stedes did draw the
   flame   205
With wilder randon through the kindled
   skies
Than traitorous counsell now will whirle
   about
The youthfull heades of these vnskilfull
   kinges!
But I hereof their father will enforme.
The reuerence of him perhappes shall
   stay   210
The growing mischiefes while they yet are
   greene.
If this helpe not, then woe vnto them-
   selues,
The prince, the people, the diuided land!

                  [*Exit.*]

ACTUS SECUNDUS

Scena Secunda.

[*The court of Porrex. Enter Porrex attended
by the parasite Tyndar and the wise
Counsellor Philander.*]

Porr. And is it thus? And doth he so
   prepare
Against his brother as his mortall foe?
And now while yet his aged father liues?
Neither regardes he him, nor feares he me?
Warre would he haue? And he shall haue
   it so!   5
Tynd. I saw myselfe the great prepared
   store
Of horse, of armour, and of weapon there;
Ne bring I to my lorde reported tales
Without the ground of seen and searched
   trouth.
Loe, secrete quarrels runne about his
   court   10
To bring the name of you, my lorde, in
   hate.
Ech man almost can now debate the cause
And aske a reason of so great a wrong: —
Why he, so noble and so wise a prince,
Is, as vnworthy, reft his heritage;   15
And why the king, misseledde by craftie
   meancs,

Diuided thus his land from course of right.
The wiser sort holde downe their griefull
   heades.
Eche man withdrawes from talke and com-
   pany
Of those that haue bene knowne to fauour
   you.   20
To hide the mischiefe of their meaning
   there,
Rumours are spread of your preparing
   here.
The rascall numbers of [the][1] vnskilfull sort
Are filled with monstrous tales of you and
   yours.   24
In secrete I was counselled by my frendes
To hast me thence, and brought you, as
   you know,
Letters from those that both can truely tell
And would not write vnlesse they knew it
   well.
Phil. My lord, yet ere you moue vn-
   kindly warre,
Send to your brother to demaund the
   cause.   30
Perhappes some traitorous tales haue filled
   his eares
With false reportes against your noble
   Grace,
Which once disclosed shall end the growing
   strife,
That els, not stayed with wise foresight in
   time,
Shall hazarde both your kingdomes and
   your liues.   35
Send to your father eke. He shall appease
Your kindled mindes, and rid you of this
   feare.
Porr. Ridde me of feare? I feare him
   not at all!
Ne will to him, ne to my father, send.
If danger were for one to tary there,   40
Thinke ye it safetie to returne againe?
In mischiefes such as Ferrex now intendes
The wonted courteous lawes to messengers
Are not obserued, which in iust warre they
   vse.
Shall I so hazard any one of mine?   45
Shall I betray my trusty frendes to him,
That haue disclosed his treason vnto me?
Let him entreate that feares! I feare him
   not!

    [1] The reading of A.; omitted in B.

Or shall I to the king, my father, send?
Yea, and send now while such a mother
    liues,   50
That loues my brother and that hateth me?
Shall I geue leasure, by my fonde delayes,
To Ferrex to oppresse me all vnware?
I will not. But I will inuade his realme,
And seeke the traitour prince within his
    court!   55
Mischiefe for mischiefe is a due reward.
His wretched head shall pay the worthy
    price
Of this his treason and his hate to me.
Shall I abide, and treate, and send, and
    pray,
And holde my yelden throate to traitours
    knife,   60
While I, with valiant minde and conquer-
    ing force,
Might rid myselfe of foes and winne a
    realme?
Yet rather, when I haue the wretches head,
Then to the king, my father, will I send!
The bootelesse case may yet appease his
    wrath;   65
If not, I will defend me as I may.

[Exeunt Porrex with the parasite Tyndar.]

PHIL. Lo, here the end of these two
    youthful kings,
The fathers death, the ruine of their
    realmes!
"O most vnhappy state of counsellers
"That light on so vnhappy lordes and
    times   70
"That neither can their good aduise be
    heard,
"Yet must they beare the blames of ill suc-
    cesse."
But I will to the king, their father, haste,
Ere this mischiefe come to the likely end,
That, — if the mindfull wrath of wrekefull
    gods,   75
Since mightie Ilions fall not yet appeased
With these poore remnantes of the Troian
    name,[1]
Haue not determined by vnmoued fate
Out of this realme to rase the Brittishe
    line, —
By good aduise, by awe of fathers name, 80

[1] The royal family of Britain traced its pedigree
back to Brutus, a grandson of Æneas of Troy.

By force of wiser lordes, this kindled hate
May yet be quenched ere it consume us
    all.   *[Exit.]*

CHORUS.

When youth, not bridled with a guiding
    stay,
  Is left to randon of their owne delight
And welds whole realmes by force of sou-
    eraign sway,
    Great is the daunger of vnmaistred
      might,
Lest skillesse rage throwe downe with
    headlong fall
Their lands, their states, their liues, them-
    selues, and al.   6

When growing pride doth fill the swelling
    brest,
  And gredy lust doth rayse the climbing
    minde,
Oh hardlie maye the perill be represt:
  Ne feare of angrie goddes, ne lawes
    kinde,
  Ne countries care can fiered hartes re-
    strayne,
Whan force hath armed enuie and dis-
    daine.   12

When kinges of foresette [1] will neglect the
    rede [2]
Of best aduise, and yelde to pleasing tales
That do their fansies noysome humour
    feede,
  Ne reason nor regarde of right auailes:
Succeding heapes of plagues shall teach, to
    late,
To learne the mischiefes of misguided
    state.   18

Fowle fall the traitour false that vnder-
    mines
  The loue of brethren to destroye them
    both!
Wo to the prince that pliant eare enclynes,
  And yeldes his mind to poysonous tale
    that floweth
From flattering mouth! And woe to
    wretched land
That wastes it-selfe with ciuil sworde in
    hand!   24

[1] Fore-determined.   [2] Advice.

Loe, thus it is, poyson in golde to take,
And holsome drinke in homely cuppe for-
    sake.

THE ORDER AND SIGNIFICATION OF THE
DOMME SHEWE BEFORE THE THIRDE ACT.

Firste the musicke of flutes began to playe, during
which came in vpon the stage a company of mourners
all clad in blacke, betokening death and sorowe to
ensue vpon the ill-aduised misgouernement and
discention of bretherne: as befell vpon the murder [1]
of Ferrex by his yonger brother.   After the mourners
had passed thryse about the stage, they departed;
and than the musicke ceased.

ACTUS TERTIUS

SCENA PRIMA.

[*The court of King Gorboduc.   Enter King
    Gorboduc with his Secretary, Eubulus, and
    his Counsellor, Arostus.*]

GORB.   O cruel Fates! O mindful wrath
        of goddes!
Whose vengeance neither Simois stayned
    streames
Flowing with bloud of Troian princes
    slaine,
Nor Phrygian fieldes made ranck with
    corpses dead
Of Asian kynges and lordes, can yet ap-
    pease!   5
Ne slaughter of vnhappie Pryams race,
Nor Ilions fall made leuell with the soile,
Can yet suffice! but still-continued rage
Pursues our lynes, and from the farthest
    seas   9
Doth chase the issues of destroyed Troye.
"Oh, no man happie till his ende be seene."
If any flowing wealth and seemyng ioye
In present yeres might make a happy
    wight,
Happie was Hecuba, the wofullest wretch
That euer lyued to make a myrrour of; 15
And happie Pryam with his noble sonnes;
And happie I, till nowe, alas, I see
And feele my most vnhappye wretched-
    nesse!
Beholde, my lordes! read ye this letter
    here!
Loe, it conteins the ruine of our realme, 20
If timelie speede prouide not hastie helpe.
Yet, C ye goddes, if euer wofull kyng

Might moue ye, kings of kinges, wreke it on
    me
And on my sonnes, not on this giltlesse
    realme!
Send down your wasting flames from
    wrathful skies   25
Te reue me and my sonnes the hatefull
    breath!
Read, read, my lordes! This is the matter
    why
I called ye nowe to haue your good aduyse.

*The letter from Dordan, the Counsellour of
    the elder prince.*

Eubulus readeth the letter:

"My Soueraigne Lord: what I am loth to
    write,
But lothest am to see, that I am forced 30
By letters nowe to make you vnderstande.
My lord Ferrex, your eldest sonne, mis-
    ledde
By traitorous fraude of yong vntempred
    wittes,
Assembleth force agaynst your yonger
    sonne;
Ne can my counsell yet withdrawe the
    heate   35
And furyous panges of hys enflamed head.
Disdaine, sayth he, of his disheritance
Armes him to wreke the great pretended
    wrong
With ciuyll sword vpon his brothers life.
If present helpe do not restraine this
    rage,   40
This flame will wast your sonnes, your
    land, and you.

        *Your Maiesties faithfull and most
            humble subiect,*
                DORDAN."

AROS.   O king, appease your griefe and
        stay your plaint!
Great is the matter, and a wofull case;
But timely knowledge may bring timely
    helpe.
Sende for them both vnto your presence
    here: 45
The reuerence of your honour, age and state,
Your graue aduice, the awe of fathers
    name,
Shall quicklie knit agayne this broken
    peace.

And if in either of my lordes your sonnes
Be suche vntamed and vnyelding pride 50
As will not bende vnto your noble hestes, —
If Ferrex, the elder sonne, can beare no
   peere,
Or Porrex, not content, aspires to more
Than you him gaue aboue his natiue
   right, —
Ioyne with the iuster side. So shall you
   force   55
Them to agree, and holde the lande in stay.
EUB. What meaneth this? Loe, yonder
   comes in hast
Philander from my lord your yonger sonne.

[*Enter Philander, the Counsellor of the
   younger prince.*]

GORB. The goddes sende ioyfull newes!
PHIL.   The mightie Ioue
Preserue your Maiestie, O noble king! 60
GORB. Philander, welcome! But how
   doth my sonne?
PHIL. Your sonne, sir, lyues, and healthie
   I him left.
But yet, O king, the want of lustfull health
Could not be halfe so griefefull to your
   Grace
As these most wretched tidynges that I
   bryng.   65
GORB. O heauens, yet more? no [1] ende of
   woes to me?
PHIL. Tyndar, O king, came lately from
   the court
Of Ferrex to my lord your yonger sonne,
And made reporte of great prepared store
For warre, and sayth that it is wholly
   ment   70
Agaynst Porrex, for high disdayne that he
Lyues now a king, and egall in degree
With him that claimeth to succede the
   whole
As by due title of discending right.
Porrex is nowe so set on flaming fire, 75
Partely with kindled rage of cruell wrath,
Partely with hope to gaine a realme
   thereby,
That he in hast prepareth to inuade
His brothers land, and with vnkindely
   warre
Threatens the murder of your elder
   sonne;   80

[1] The reading of A.; B. has *not*.

Ne could I him perswade that first he
   should
Send to his brother to demaunde the cause,
Nor yet to you to staie this hatefull
   strife.
Wherfore, sithe there no more I can be
   hearde,
I come my-selfe now to enforme your
   Grace,   85
And to beseche you, as you loue the life
And safetie of your children and your
   realme,
Now to employ your wisdome and your
   force
To stay this mischiefe ere it be to late.
GORB. Are they in armes? Would he not
   sende to me?   90
Is this the honour of a fathers name?
In vaine we trauaile to asswage their
   mindes,
As if their hartes, whome neither brothers
   loue,
Nor fathers awe, nor kingdomes cares, can
   moue,
Our counsels could withdraw from raging
   heat.   95
Ioue slay them both and end the cursed
   line!
For, though perhappes feare of such
   mightie force
As I, my lordes, ioyned with your noble
   aides,
Maye yet raise shall represse their present
   heate,
The secret grudge and malice will re-
   mayne.   100
The fire, not quenched, but kept in close
   restraint,
Fedde still within, breakes forth with
   double flame.
Their death and myne must peaze [1] the
   angrie gods.
PHIL. Yelde not, O king, so much to
   weake dispeire!
Your sonnes yet lyue, and long, I trust,
   they shall.   105
If Fates had taken you from earthly life
Before beginning of this ciuyll strife,
Perhaps your sonnes in their vnmaistered
   youth,
Loose from regarde of any lyuing wight,

[1] Appease.

Would runne on headlong with vnbridled
    race   110
To their owne death and ruine of this
    realme;
But, sith the gods — that haue the care for
    kinges,
Of thinges, and times — dispose the order
    so
That in your life this kindled flame breakes
    forth,
While yet your lyfe, your wisdome, and
    your power   115
May stay the growing mischiefe and re-
    presse
The fierie blaze of their inkindled heate,
It seemes — and so ye ought to deeme
    thereof —
That louyng Ioue hath tempred so the
    time
Of this debate to happen in your dayes 120
That you yet lyuing may the same appeaze
And adde it to the glory of your latter age,
And they, your [1] sonnes, may learne to liue
    in peace.
Beware, O king, the greatest harme of
    all —
Lest by your waylefull plaints your has-
    tened death   125
Yelde larger roume vnto their growing
    rage.
Preserue your life, the onely hope of stay.
And, if your Highnes herein list to vse
Wisdome, or force, counsell, or knightly
    aide,
Loe, we, our persons, powers, and lyues,
    are yours.   130
Use us tyll death, O king! We are your
    owne.
EUB. Loe, here the perill that was erst
    foresene,
When you, O king, did first deuide your
    lande
And yelde your present reigne vnto your
    sonnes!
But now, O noble prince, now is no
    time   135
To waile and plaine, and wast your wofull
    life.
Now is the time for present good aduise.
Sorow doth darke the iudgement of the
    wytte.

        [1] A. B. *our:* C. *uour.*

"The hart vnbroken, and the courage free
"From feble faintnesse of bootelesse de-
    speire,   140
"Doth either ryse to safetie or renowme
"By noble valure of vnuanquisht minde,
"Or yet doth perishe in more happy sort."
Your Grace may send to either of your
    sonnes
Some one both wise and noble person-
    age,   145
Which with good counsell and with
    weightie name
Of father shall present before their eyes
Your hest, your life, your safetie, and their
    owne,
The present mischiefe of their deadly
    strife.
And, in the while, assemble you the
    force   150
Which your commaundement and the
    spedy hast
Of all my lordes here present can prepare.
The terrour of your mightie power shall
    stay
The rage of both, or yet of one at lest.

        [Enter Nuntius.]

NUNT. O king, the greatest griefe that
    euer prince dyd heare,   155
That euer wofull messenger did tell,
That euer wretched lande hath sene before,
I bryng to you! Porrex, your yonger
    sonne,
With soden force inuaded hath the lande
That you to Ferrex did allotte to rule,
And with his owne most bloudy hand he
    hath   161
His brother slaine, and doth possesse his
    realme.
GORB. O Heauens, send down the flames
    of your reuenge!
Destroy, I say, with flash of wrekefull fier
The traitour sonne, and then the wretched
    sire!   165
But let vs go, that yet perhappes I may
Die with reuenge, and peaze the hatefull
    gods.   *[Exeunt.]*

CHORUS.

The lust of kingdome knowes no sacred
    faith,
    No rule of reason, no regarde of right.

No kindely loue, no feare of heauens
    wrath;
    But with contempt of goddes, and mans
        despite,   4
Tnrough blodie slaughter doth prepare the
    waies
To fatall scepter and accursed reigne!
The sonne so lothes the fathers lingering
    daies,
    Ne dreades his hand in brothers blode to
        staine.   8
O wretched prince, ne doest thou yet re-
    corde
    The yet fresh murthers done within the
        lande
Of thy forefathers, when the cruell sworde
    Bereft Morgan his life with cosyns
        hand?   12
Thus fatall plagues pursue the giltie race
    Whose murderous hand, imbrued with
        giltlesse blood,
Askes vengeaunce still before the heauens
    face,
    With endlesse mischiefes on the cursed
        broode!   16
The wicked childe thus bringes to wofull
    sire
    The mournefull plaintes, to wast his very
        life.
Thus do the cruell flames of ciuyll fier
Destroy the parted reigne with hatefull
    strife;
And hence doth spring the well from which
    doth flow
The dead black streames of mourning,
    plaints, and woe!   22

The Order and Signification of the Domme Shew before the Fourth Act.

First the musick of howboies [1] began to plaie,
during which there came from vnder the stage, as
hough out of hell, three Furies, Alecto, Megera and
Ctesiphone, clad in black garmentes sprinkled with
loud and flames, their bodies girt with snakes, their
eds spred with serpentes in stead of heare; the one
earing in her hand a snake, the other a whip, and the
hird a burning firebrand; ech driuing before them a
ing and a queene, which, moued by furies, vn-
aturally had slaine their owne children: the names
f the kings and queenes were these: Tantalus, Me-
ea, Athamas, Ino, Cambises, Althea. After that the
uries and these had passed about the stage thrise,

----

[1] A double-reed wind instrument of high pitch.

they departed; and than the musicke ceased. Hereby
was signified the vnnaturall murders to follow, that
is to say, Porrex slaine by his owne mother, and of
King Gorboduc and Queene Viden, killed by their
owne subiectes.

ACTUS QUARTUS
Scena Prima.

[King Gorboduc's palace. Enter Queen Videna.]

Vid.   Why should I lyue, and linger forth
    my time
In longer life to double my distresse?
O me, most wofull wight, whom no mis-
    happe
Long ere this day could haue bereued
    hence!
Mought not these handes by fortune or by
    fate   5
Haue perst this brest, and life with iron
    reft?
Or in this palace here, where I so long
Haue spent my daies, could not that happie
    houre
Once, once haue hapt in which these hugie
    frames
With death by fall might haue oppressed
    me?   10
Or should not this most hard and cruell
    soile,
So oft where I haue prest my wretched
    steps,
Sometime had ruthe of myne accursed life
To rende in twayne [and] [1] swallow me
    therin?   14
So had my bones possessed now in peace
Their happie graue within the closed
    grounde,
And greadie wormes had gnawen this
    pyned [2] hart
Without my feeling payne; so should not
    now
This lyuing brest remayne the ruthefull
    tombe
Wherin my hart yelden to death is
    graued,   20
Nor driery thoughts, with panges of pining
    griefe,
My dolefull minde had not afflicted thus.

----

[1] Omitted in B., supplied from A.
[2] Wasted by suffering.

O my beloued sonne! O my swete childe!
My deare Ferrex, my ioye, my lyues de-
    lyght!   24
Is my beloued sonne, is my sweete childe,
My deare Ferrex, my ioye, my lyues de-
    light,
Murdered with cruell death? O hatefull
    wretch!
O heynous traitour both to heauen and
    earth!
Thou, Porrex, thou this damned dede hast
    wrought!
Thou, Porrex, thou shalt dearely bye the
    same!   30
Traitour to kinne and kinde, to sire and me,
To thine owne fleshe, and traitour to thy-
    selfe,
The gods on thee in hell shall wreke their
    wrath,
And here in earth this hand shall take re-
    uenge
On thee, Porrex, thou false and caitife
    wight!   35
If after bloud so eigre [1] were thy thirst,
And murderous minde had so possessed
    thee,
If such hard hart of rocke and stonie flint
Liued in thy brest that nothing els could
    like [2]
Thy cruell tyrantes thought but death and
    bloud,   40
Wilde sauage beasts, mought not their
    slaughter serue
To fede thy gredie will, and in the middest
Of their entrailes to staine thy deadly
    handes
With bloud deserued, and drinke thereof
    thy fill?
Or, if nought els but death and bloud of
    man   45
Mought please thy lust, could none in
    Brittaine land,
Whose hart betorne out of his panting
    brest
With thine owne hand, or worke what
    death thou wouldest,
Suffice to make a sacrifice to peaze [3]
That deadly minde and murderous thought
    in thee,   50
But he who in the selfesame wombe was
    wrapped

Where thou in dismall hower receiuedst
    life?
Or, if nedes, nedes, thy hand must slaugh-
    ter make,
Moughtest thou not haue reached a mor-
    tall wound,
And with thy sword haue pearsed this
    cursed wombe   55
That the accursed Porrex brought to
    light,
And geuen me a iust reward therefore?
So Ferrex yet sweete life mought haue en-
    ioyed,
And to his aged father comfort brought
With some yong sonne, in whom they both
    might liue.   60
But whereunto waste I this ruthfull speche
To thee that hast thy brothers bloud thus
    shed?
Shall I still thinke that from this wombe
    thou sprong?
That I thee bare? Or take thee for my
    sonne?
No, traitour, no! I thee refuse for
    mine!   65
Murderer, I thee renounce; thou art not
    mine.
Neuer, O wretch, this wombe conceiued
    thee,
Nor neuer bode I painfull throwes for
    thee!
Changeling to me thou art, and not my
    childe,
Nor to no wight that sparke of pitie
    knew.   70
Ruthelesse, vnkinde, monster of natures
    worke,
Thou neuer suckt the milke of womans
    brest,
But from thy birth the cruell tigers teates
Haue nursed thee! Nor yet of fleshe and
    bloud
Formde is thy hart, but of hard iron
    wrought;   75
And wilde and desert woods bredde thee to
    life!
But canst thou hope to scape my iust re-
    uenge?
Or that these handes will not be wrooke on
    thee?
Doest thou not know that Ferrex mother
    liues,

---

[1] Sharp.   [2] Please.   [3] Appease.

That loued him more dearly than her-
selfe? 80
And doth she liue, and is not venged on
thee? [*Exit.*]

ACTUS QUARTUS
Scena Secunda.

*The court of King Gorboduc. Enter King
Gorboduc attended by his Counsellor
Arostus.*]

GORB. We maruell much wherto this lin-
gring stay
Falles out so long. Porrex vnto our court
By order of our letters is returned,
And Eubulus receaued from vs by hest
At his arriuall here to geue him charge 5
Before our presence straight to make re-
paire, —
And yet we haue no worde whereof he
stayes.

AROS. Lo, where he commes and Eubulus
with him.

*Enter the King's Secretary, Eubulus, leading
in Porrex.*]

EUB. According to your Highnesse hest to
me,
Here haue I Porrex brought, euen in such
sort 10
As from his weried horse he did alight,
For that your Grace did will such hast
therein.

GORB. We like and praise this spedy will
in you
To worke the thing that to your charge we
gaue.
Porrex, if we so farre should swarue from
kinde 15
And from those boundes which lawe of
nature sets
As thou hast done by vile and wretched
deede
In cruell murder of thy brothers life,
Our present hand could stay no longer
time,
But straight should bathe this blade in
bloud of thee 20
As iust reuenge of thy detested crime.
So, we should not offend the lawe of
kinde

If now this sworde of ours did slay thee
here;
For thou hast murdered him whose heinous
death
Euen natures force doth moue vs to re-
uenge 25
By bloud againe, and iustice forceth vs
To measure death for death, thy due de-
sert.
Yet, sithens thou art our childe, and sith as
yet
In this hard case what worde thou canst
alledge
For thy defence by vs hath not bene
heard, 30
We are content to staye our will for that
Which iustice biddes vs presently to worke,
And geue thee leaue to vse thy speche at
full,
If ought thou haue to lay for thine excuse.

PORR. Neither, O king, I can or will
denie 35
But that this hand from Ferrex life hath
reft, —
Which fact how much my dolefull hart
doth waile,
Oh would it mought as full appeare to sight
As inward griefe doth poure it forth to me!
So yet, perhappes, if euer ruthefull hart 40
Melting in teares within a manly brest
Through depe repentance of his bloudy
fact,
If euer griefe, if euer wofull man
Might moue regreite with sorrowe of his
fault,
I thinke the torment of my mournefull
case, 45
Knowen to your Grace as I do feele the
same,
Would force euen Wrath her-selfe to pitie
me.
But, as the water troubled with the mudde
Shewes not the face which els the eye
should see,
Euen so your irefull minde with stirred
thought 50
Cannot so perfectly discerne my cause.
But this vnhappe, amongest so many
happes,[1]
I must content me with — most wretched
man —

[1] B. *heapes.*

That to my-selfe I must reserue my woe
In pining thoughtes of mine accursed
    fact,   55
Since I may not shewe here my smallest
    griefe
Such as it is, and as my brest endures.
Which I esteeme the greatest miserie
Of all missehappes that fortune now can
    send:
Not that I rest in hope with plaint and
    teares   60
To purchase life; for to the goddes I clepe [1]
For true recorde of this my faithfull
    speche: —
Neuer this hart shall haue the thoughtfull
    dread
To die the death that by your Graces dome,
By iust desert, shall be pronounced to
    me,   65
Nor neuer shall this tongue once spend the
    speche
Pardon to craue, or seeke by sute to liue.
I meane not this as though I were not
    touchde
With care of dreadfull death, or that I helde
Life in contempt, but that I know the
    minde   70
Stoupes to no dread, although the fleshe be
    fraile.
And, for my gilt, I yelde the same so great
As in my-selfe I finde a feare to sue
For graunt of life.
GORB.   In vaine, O wretch, thou shewest
A wofull hart!   Ferrex now lies in graue, 75
Slaine by thy hand.
PORR.   Yet this, O father, heare;
And then I end.   Your Maiestie well
    knowes
That when my brother Ferrex and my-selfe
By your owne hest were ioyned in gouer-
    nance
Of this your Graces realme of Brittaine
    land,   80
I neuer sought nor trauailled for the same,
Nor by my-selfe, nor by no frend I wrought,
But from your Highnesse will alone it
    sprong,
Of your most gracious goodnesse bent to
    me.
But how my brothers hart euen then re-
    pined   85

With swollen disdaine against mine egall
    rule,
Seing that realme, which by discent should
    grow
Wholly to him, allotted halfe to me,
Euen in your Highnesse court he now re-
    maines,
(And with my brother then in nearest
    place),   90
Who can recorde what proofe thereof was
    shewde,
And how my brothers enuious hart ap-
    pearde.
Yet I, that iudged it my part to seeke
His fauour and good will, and loth to make
Your Highnesse know the thing which
    should haue brought   95
Grief to your Grace, and your offence to
    him,
Hoping my earnest sute should soone haue
    wonne
A louing hart within a brothers brest,
Wrought in that sort that for a pledge of
    loue
And faithfull hart he gaue to me his hand
This made me thinke that he had banisht
    quite   100
All rancour from his thought, and bare to
    me
Such hartie loue as I did owe to him.
But, after once we left your Graces court
And from your Highness presence liued
    apart,   105
This egall rule still, still, did grudge him so
That now those enuious sparkes which erst
    lay raked
In liuing cinders of dissembling brest
Kindled so farre within his hart disdaine
That longer could he not refraine from
    proofe   110
Of secrete practise to depriue me life
By poysons force; and had bereft me so,
If mine owne seruant, hired to this fact,
And moued by trouth with hate to worke
    the same,
In time had not bewrayed it vnto me.   115
Whan thus I sawe the knot of loue vn-
    knitte,
All honest league and faithfull promis
    broke,
The law of kinde and trouth thus rent in
    twaine,

---

[1] Cry, appeal.

His hart on mischiefe set, and in his brest
Blacke treason hid, then, then did I de-
   speire 120
That euer time could winne him frend to
   me!
Then saw I how he smiled with slaying
   knife
Wrapped vnder cloke! Then saw I depe
   deceite
Lurke in his face and death prepared for
   me!
Euen nature moued me than to holde my
   life 125
More deare to me than his, and bad this
   hand, —
Since by his life my death must nedes en-
   sue,
And by his death my life to be pre-
   serued, —
To shed his bloud, and seeke my safetie so;
And wisedome willed me without pro-
   tract 130
In spedie wise to put the same in vre.
Thus haue I tolde the cause that moued me
To worke my brothers death. And so I
   yeld
My life, my death, to iudgement of your
   Grace.
GORB. Oh cruell wight! should any cause
   preuaile 135
To make thee staine thy hands with
   brothers bloud?
But what of thee we will resolue to doe
Shall yet remaine vnknowen. Thou in the
   meane
Shalt from our royall presence banisht be
Untill our princely pleasure furder shall
To thee be shewed. Depart therefore our
   sight, 141
Accursed childe!

[Exit Porrex.]

What cruell destenie,
What froward fate hath sorted vs this
   chaunce,
That euen in those where we should com-
   fort find,
Where our delight now in our aged
   dayes 145
Should rest and be, euen there our onely
   griefe
And depest sorrowes to abridge our life,

Most pyning cares and deadly thoughts do
   grow?
AROS. Your Grace should now in these
   graue yeres of yours
Haue found ere this the price of mortall
   ioyes, 150
How short they be, how fading here in
   earth,
How full of chaunge, how brittle our estate,
Of nothing sure saue onely of the death,
To whom both man and all the world doth
   owe
Their end at last. Neither should natures
   power 155
In other sort against your hart preuaile
Than as the naked hand whose stroke as-
   sayes
The armed brest, where force doth light in
   vaine.
GORB. Many can yelde right sage and
   graue aduise
Of pacient sprite to others wrapped in
   woe, 160
And can in speche both rule and conquere
   kinde,
Who, if by proofe they might feele natures
   force,
Would shew them-selues men, as they are
   in-dede,
Which now wil nedes be gods. But what
   doth meane
The sory chere of her that here doth
   come? 165

*[Enter Marcella, a lady of the Queen's privy-
chamber.]*

MARC. Oh where is ruth? or where is pitie
   now?
Whether is gentle hart and mercy fled?
Are they exiled out of our stony brestes
Neuer to make returne? Is all the world
Drowned in bloud and soncke in cru-
   eltie? 170
If not in women mercy may be found,
If not, alas! within the mothers brest
To her owne childe, to her owne fleshe and
   bloud,
If ruthe be banished thence, if pitie there
May haue no place, if there no gentle
   hart 175
Do liue and dwell, where should we seeke it
   then?

GORB. Madame, alas, what meanes your
    woful tale?

MARC. O sillie woman I, why to this houre
Haue Kinde and Fortune thus deferred my
    breath
That I should liue to see this dolefull
    day?   180
Will euer wight beleue that such hard hart
Could rest within the cruell mothers brest
With her owne hand to slay her onely
    sonne?
But out! alas! these eyes behelde the same!
They saw the driery sight, and are be-
    come   185
Most ruthfull recordes of the bloudy fact!
Porrex, alas, is by his mother slaine,
And with her hand — a wofull thing to
    tell! —
While slumbring on his carefull bed he
    restes,
His hart, stabde in with knife, is reft of
    life!   190

GORB. O Eubulus! oh draw this sword of
    ours
And pearce this hart with speed! O hate-
    full light!
O lothsome life! O sweete and welcome
    death!
Deare Eubulus, worke this, we thee besech.

EUB. Pacient your Grace. Perhappes he
    liueth yet,   195
With wound receaued, but not of certaine
    death.

GORB. O let us then repayre vnto the
    place,
And see if Porrex liue, or thus be slaine.

[Exeunt Gorboduc and Eubulus.]

MARC. Alas, he liueth not! It is to true
That, with these eyes, of him, a perelesse
    prince,   200
Sonne to a king, and in the flower of youth,
Euen with a twinke a senselesse stocke I
    saw.

AROS. O damned deede!

MARC.   But heare hys ruthefull end!
The noble prince, pearst with the sodeine
    wound,
Out of his wretched slumber hastely
    start,   205
Whose strength now fayling, straight he
    ouerthrew, —

When in the fall his eyes, euen new vn-
    closed,
Behelde the queene, and cryed to her for
    helpe.
We then, alas! the ladies which that time
Did there attend, seing that heynous
    deede,   210
And hearing him oft call the wretched
    name
Of mother, and to crye to her for aide
Whose direfull hand gaue him the mortall
    wound,
Pitying, alas! — for nought els could we
    do, —
His ruthefull end, ranne to the wofull
    bedde,   215
Dispoyled straight his brest, and, all we
    might,
Wiped in vaine with napkins next at hand
The sodeine streames of bloud that flushed
    fast
Out of the gaping wound. O what a looke,
O what a ruthefull stedfast eye, me
    thought,   220
He fixt vpon my face, which to my death
Will neuer part fro me, when with a braide
A deepe-fet sigh he gaue, and therewithall
Clasping his handes, to heauen he cast his
    sight!
And straight — pale death pressing within
    his face —   225
The flying ghost his mortall corpes for-
    sooke.

AROS. Neuer did age bring forth so vile a
    fact!

MARC. O hard and cruell happe, that thus
    assigned
Unto so worthy a wight so wretched end!
But most hard, cruell hart, that could con-
    sent   230
To lend the hatefull destenies that hand
By which, alas, so heynous crime was
    wrought!
O queene of adamant, O marble brest,
If not the fauour of his comely face,
If not his princely chere and counte-
    nance,   235
His valiant actiue armes, his manly brest
If not his faire and seemely personage,
His noble limmes in such proportion cast
As would have wrapt a sillie woman
    thought,

If this mought not haue moued thy bloudy
hart   240
And that most cruell hand the wretched
weapon
Euen to let fall, and kiste him in the face,
With teares for ruthe to reaue such one by
death, —
Should nature yet consent to slay her
sonne?
O mother, thou to murder thus thy
childe!   245
Euen Ioue with iustice must with lightning
flames
From heauen send downe some strange re-
uenge on thee.
Ah, noble prince, how oft haue I beholde
Thee mounted on thy fierce and traump-
ling stede,   249
Shining in armour bright before the tilt,
And with thy mistresse sleue tied on thy
helme,
And charge thy staffe to please thy ladies
eye,
That bowed the head-peece of thy frendly
foe!
How oft in armes on horse to bend the
mace!
How oft in armes on foote to breake the
sworde!   255
Which neuer now these eyes may see againe.
Aros.   Madame, alas, in vaine these
plaints are shed!
Rather with me depart, and helpe to swage
The thoughtfull griefes that in the aged
king
Must needes by nature growe, by death of
this   260
His onely sonne, whom he did holde so
deare.
Marc.   What wight is that which saw that
I did see,
And could refraine to waile with plaint and
teares?
Not I, alas!   That hart is not in me.
But let vs goe, for I am greued anew   265
To call to minde the wretched fathers woe.
[*Exeunt.*]

Chorus.

Whan greedy lust in royall seate to reigne
  Hath reft all care of goddes and eke of
  men,

And cruell hart, wrath, treason, and disdaine
  Within ambicious brest are lodged, then
Beholde how mischiefe wide her-selfe dis-
playes,
  And with the brothers hand the brother
  slayes.   6

When bloud thus shed doth staine the
  heauens face,
  Crying to Ioue for vengeance of the
  deede,
The mightie God euen moueth from his
  place,
  With wrath to wreke.   Then sendes he
  forth with spede
The dreadfull Furies, daughters of the
  night,
  With serpentes girt, carying the whip of
  ire,
With heare of stinging snakes, and shining
  bright
  With flames and bloud, and with a brand
  of fire.
These, for reuenge of wretched murder done,
Do make the mother kill her onely sonne.16

Blood asketh blood, and death must death
  requite:
  Ioue by his iust and euerlasting dome
Iustly hath euer so requited it.
  The times before recorde, and times to
  come
Shall finde it true, and so doth present
  proofe
Present before our eyes for our behoofe. 22

O happy wight that suffres not the snare
  Of murderous minde to tangle him in
  blood!
And happy he that can in time beware
  By others harmes, and turne it to his
  good!
But wo to him that, fearing not to offend,
Doth serue his lust, and will not see the
  end.   28

The Order and Signification of the
Domme Shew before the Fifth Act.

First the drommes and fluites began to sound, during which there came forth vpon the stage a company
of hargabusiers and of armed men all in order of

battaile. These, after their peeces discharged, and that the armed men had three times marched about the stage, departed; and then the drommes and fluits did cease. Hereby was signified tumults, rebellions, armes and ciuill warres to follow: as fell in the realme of Great Brittayne, which by the space of fiftie yeares and more continued in ciuill warre betwene the nobilitie after the death of King Gorboduc and of his issues, for want of certayne limitacion in sucèssion of the crowne, till the time of Dunwallo Molmutius, who reduced the land to monarchie.

ACTUS QUINTUS

Scena Prima.

[*The court of King Gorboduc. Enter Clotyn, Duke of Cornewall, Mandud, Duke of Loegris, Gwenard, Duke of Cumberland, Fergus, Duke of Albanye, and Eubulus, the King's Secretary.*]

CLO.　Did euer age bring forth such tirants harts?
The brother hath bereft the brothers life;
The mother she hath died her cruell handes
In bloud of her owne sonne; and now at last
The people, loe! forgetting trouth and loue,　5
Contemning quite both law and loyall hart,
Euen they haue slaine their soueraigne lord and queene.
MAND.　Shall this their traitorous crime vnpunished rest?
Euen yet they cease not, caryed on with rage,　9
In their rebellious routes to threaten still
A new bloud-shed vnto the princes kinne,
To slay them all, and to vproote the race
Both of the king and queene: so are they moued
With Porrex death, wherin they falsely charge
The giltlesse king, without desert at all,　15
And traitorously haue murdered him therfore,
And eke the queene.
GWEN.　Shall subiectes dare with force
To worke reuenge vpon their princes fact? [1]
Admit the worst that may (as sure in this
The deede was fowle, the queene to slay her sonne),　20

---

[1] Deed.

Shall yet the subiect seeke to take the sworde,
Arise agaynst his lord, and slay his king?
O wretched state, where those rebellious hartes
Are not rent out euen from their liuing breastes,
And with the body throwen vnto the foules　25
As carrion foode, for terrour of the rest!
FERG.　There can no punishment be thought to great
For this so greuous cryme. Let spede therfore
Be vsed therin, for it behoueth so.
EUB.　Ye all, my lordes, I see, consent in one,　30
And I as one consent with ye in all.
I holde it more than neede with sharpest law
To punish this tumultuous bloudy rage;
For nothing more may shake the common state
Than sufferance of vproares without redresse,　35
Wherby how some kingdomes of mightie power,
After great conquestes made, and florishing
In fame and wealth, haue ben to ruine brought,
I pray to Ioue that we may rather wayle
Such happe in them than witnesse in ourselues.　40
Eke fully with the duke my minde agrees,
[That no cause serues wherby the subiect maye
Call to accompt the doynges of his prince,
Muche lesse in bloode by sworde to worke reuenge,
No more then maye the hande cut of the heade.　45
In acte nor speache, no, not in secrete thoughte,
The subiect maye rebell against his lorde,
Or iudge of him that sittes in Ceasars seate,
With grudging minde to [1] damne those he mislikes.] [2]
Though kinges forget to gouerne as they ought,　50

---

[1] A. *do;* corr. by Manly.
[2] B. omits lines 42–49.

Yet subiectes must obey as they are
    bounde.
But now, my lordes, before ye farder wade,
Or spend your speach what sharpe reuenge
    shall fall
By iustice plague on these rebellious
    wightes,
Me thinkes ye rather should first search
    the way   55
By which in time the rage of this vproare
Mought be repressed and these great tu-
    mults ceased.
Euen yet the life of Brittayne land doth
    hang
In traitours balaunce of vnegall weight.
Thinke not, my lordes, the death of
    Gorboduc,   60
Nor yet Videnaes bloud will cease their
    rage.
Euen our owne lyues, our wiues and chil-
    dren deare,
Our countrey, dearest of all, in daunger
    standes
Now to be spoiled, now, now, made deso-
    late,
And by our-selues a conquest to ensue. 65
For geue once swey vnto the peoples lustes
To rush forth on, and stay them not in
    time,
And, as the streame that rowleth downe
    the hyll,
So will they headlong ronne with raging
    thoughtes
From bloud to bloud, from mischiefe vnto
    moe,   70
To ruine of the realme, them-selues, and all,
So giddy are the common peoples mindes,
So glad of chaunge, more wauering than
    the sea.
Ye see, my lordes, what strength these reb-
    elles haue,
What hugie nombre is assembled still; 75
For though the traiterous fact for which
    they rose
Be wrought and done, yet lodge they still
    in field;
So that how farre their furies yet will
    stretch
Great cause we haue to dreade.   That we
    may seeke
By present battaile to represse their
    power,   80

Speede must we vse to leuie force therfore;
For either they forthwith will mischiefe
    worke
Or their rebellious roares forthwith will
    cease:
These violent thinges may haue no lasting
    long.   84
Let vs therfore vse this for present helpe:—
Perswade by gentle speach, and offre grace
With gift of pardon, saue vnto the chiefe,
And that vpon condicion that forthwith
They yelde the captaines of their enter-
    prise,
To beare such guerdon of their traiterous
    fact   90
As may be both due vengeance to them-
    selues
And holsome terrour to posteritie.
This shall, I thinke, scatter the greatest
    part
That now are holden with desire of home,
Weried in field with cold of winters
    nightes,   95
And some, no doubt, striken with dread of
    law.
Whan this is once proclamed, it shall make
The captaines to mistrust the multitude,
Whose safetie biddes them to betray their
    heads, —
And so much more bycause the rascall
    routes   100
In thinges of great and perillous attemptes
Are neuer trustie to the noble race.
And, while we treate and stand on termes of
    grace,
We shall both stay their furies rage the while
And eke gaine time, whose onely helpe
    sufficeth   105
Withouten warre to vanquish rebelles
    power.
In the meane while make you in redynes
Such band of horsemen as ye may prepare.
Horsemen, you know, are not the commons
    strength,
But are the force and store of noble
    men,   110
Wherby the vnchosen and vnarmed sort
Of skillesse rebelles, whome none other
    power
But nombre makes to be of dreadfull force,
With sodeyne brunt may quickely be op-
    prest.

And if this gentle meane of proffered
grace 115
With stubborne hartes cannot so farre
auayle
As to asswage their desperate courages,
Then do I wish such slaughter to be made
As present age and eke posteritie
May be adrad with horrour of reuenge 120
That iustly then shall on these rebelles fall.
This is, my lord[s], the sum of mine aduise.
CLO. Neither this case admittes debate at
large,
And, though it did, this speach that hath
ben sayd
Hath well abridged the tale I would haue
tolde. 125
Fully with Eubulus do I consent
In all that he hath sayd. And, if the same
To you, my lordes, may seeme for best ad-
uise,
I wish that it should streight be put in vre.
MAND. My lordes, than let vs presently
depart 130
And follow this that liketh vs so well.

[*Exeunt all but Fergus, Duke of Albanye.*]

FERG. If euer time to gaine a kingdome
here
Were offred man, now it is offred mee.
The realme is reft both of their king and
queene;
The ofspring of the prince is slaine and
dead; 135
No issue now remaines, the heire vn-
knowen;
The people are in armes and mutynies;
The nobles they are busied how to cease
These great rebellious tumultes and vp-
roares;
And Brittayne land, now desert left
alone 140
Amyd these broyles, vncertayne where to
rest,
Offers her-selfe vnto that noble hart
That will, or dare, pursue to beare her
crowne.
Shall I, that am the Duke of Albanye,
Discended from that line of noble bloud 145
Which hath so long florished in worthy
fame
Of valiaunt hartes, such as in noble brestes
Of right should rest aboue the baser sort,

Refuse to venture life to winne a crowne?
Whom shall I finde enmies that will with-
stand 150
My fact herein, if I attempt by armes
To seeke the same now in these times of
broyle?
These dukes power can hardly well appease
The people that already are in armes.
But, if perhappes my force be once in
field, 155
Is not my strength in power aboue the best
Of all these lordes now left in Brittayne
land?
And though they should match me with
power of men,
Yet doubtfull is the chaunce of battailles
ioyned.
If victors of the field we may depart, 160
Ours is the scepter then of Great Brittayne;
If slayne amid the playne this body lye,
Mine enemies yet shall not deny me this,
But that I dyed geuing the noble charge
To hazarde life for conquest of a crowne.
Forthwith therefore will I in post depart
To Albanye, and raise in armour there
All power I can; and here my secret friendes
By secret practise shall sollicite still
To seeke to wynne to me the peoples
hartes. [*Exit.*] 170

ACTUS QUINTUS

SCENA SECUNDA.

[*The court. Enter Eubulus.*]

EVB. O Ioue! how are these peoples
harts abusde!
What blind fury thus headlong caries them,
That, though so many bookes, so many
rolles
Of auncient time recorde what greuous
plagues
Light on these rebelles aye, and though so
oft 5
Their eares haue heard their aged fathers
tell
What iuste reward these traitours still receyue,
Yea, though them-selues haue sene depe
death and bloud
By strangling cord and slaughter of the
sword

To such assigned, yet can they not be-
ware, 10
Yet can not stay their lewde rebellious
handes,
But, suffring, loe, fowle treason to distaine
Their wretched myndes, forget their loyall
hart,
Reiect all truth, and rise against their
prince
A ruthefull case, that those, whom duties
bond, 15
Whom grafted law by nature, truth, and
faith
Bound to preserue their countrey and their
king,
Borne to defend their common-wealth and
prince,
Euen they should geue consent thus to
subuert
Thee, Brittaine land, and from thy wombe
should spring, 20
O native soile, those that will needs destroy
And ruyne thee, and eke them-selues in
fine!
For lo, when once the dukes had offred grace
Of pardon sweete the multitude missledde
By traitorous fraude of their vngracious
heades, 25
One sort, that saw the dangerous successe
Of stubborne standing in rebellious warre
And knew the difference of princes power
From headlesse nombre of tumultuous
routes,
Whom common countreies care and priuate
feare 30
Taught to repent the errour of their rage,
Layde handes vpon the captaines of their
band
And brought them bound vnto the mightie
dukes;
And other sort, not trusting yet so well
The truth of pardon, or mistrusting more
Their owne offence than that they could
conceiue 36
Such hope of pardon for so foule misdede,
Or for that they their captaines could not
yeld,
Who, fearing to be yelded, fled before,
Stale home by silence of the secret night; 40
The thirde, vnhappy and enraged sort
Of desperate hartes, who, stained in
princes bloud,

From trayterous furour could not be with-
drawen
By loue, by law, by grace, ne yet by feare,
By proffered life, ne yet by threatned
death, 45
With mindes hopelesse of life, dreadlesse of
death,
Carelesse of countrey, and awelesse of God,
Stoode bent to fight as Furies did them
moue,
With violent death to close their traiterous
life.
These all by power of horsemen were op-
prest, 50
And with reuenging sworde slayne in the
field,
Or with the strangling cord hangd on the
tree,
Where yet their carryen carcases do preach
The fruites that rebelles reape of their vp-
roares
And of the murder of their sacred prince. 55
But loe, where do approche the noble dukes
By whom these tumults haue ben thus ap-
peasde.

[*Enter Clotyn, Duke of Cornewall, Mandud,
Duke of Loegris, Gwenard, Duke
of Cumberland, and the Counsellor,
Arostus.*]

CLO. I thinke the world will now at length
beware,
And feare to put on armes agaynst their
prince!
MAND. If not, those trayterous hartes
that dare rebell, 60
Let them beholde the wide and hugie
fieldes
With bloud and bodies spread of rebelles
slayne,
The lofty trees clothed with the corpses dead
That strangled with the corde do hang
theron!
AROS. A iust rewarde! such as all times
before 65
Haue euer lotted to those wretched folkes.
GWEN. But what meanes he that com-
meth here so fast?

[*Enter Nuntius.*]

NUNT. My lordes, as dutie and my trouth
doth moue,

And of my countrey worke a care in mee,
That, if the spending of my breath auailed
To do the seruice that my hart desires, 71
I would not shunne to imbrace a present
    death,
So haue I now, in that wherein I thought
My trauayle mought performe some good
    effect,
Ventred my life to bring these tydinges
    here. 75
Fergus, the mightie Duke of Albanye,
Is now in armes, and lodgeth in the fielde
With twentie thousand men. Hether he
    bendes
His spedy marche, and mindes to inuade
    the crowne.
Dayly he gathereth strength, and spreads
    abrode 80
That to this realme no certeine heire re-
    maines,
That Brittayne land is left without a guide,
That he the scepter seekes for nothing els
But to preserue the people and the land,
Which now remaine as ship without a
    sterne. 85
Loe, this is that which I haue here to say.
CLO. Is this his fayth? And shall he
    falsely thus
Abuse the vauntage of vnhappie times?
O wretched land, if his outragious pride,
His cruell and vntempred wilfulnesse, 90
His deepe dissembling shewes of false pre-
    tence,
Should once attaine the crowne of Brittaine
    land!
Let vs, my lordes, with timely force resist
The new attempt of this our common foe,
As we would quench the flames of common
    fire. 95
MAND. Though we remaine without a cer-
    tain prince
To weld the realme or guide the wandring
    rule,
Yet now the common mother of vs all,
Our natiue land, our countrey, that con-
    teines
Our wiues, children, kindred, our-selues,
    and all 100
That euer is or may be deare to man,
Cries vnto vs to helpe our-selues and her.
Let vs aduaunce our powers to represse
This growing foe of all our liberties.

GWEN. Yea, let vs so, my lordes, with
    hasty speede. 105
And ye, O goddes, send vs the welcome
    death,
To shed our bloud in field, and leaue us not
In lothesome life to lenger out our dayes
To see the hugie heapes of these vnhappes
That now roll downe vpon the wretched
    land, 110
Where emptie place of princely gouer-
    naunce,
No certaine stay now left of doubtlesse
    heire,
Thus leaue this guidelesse realme an open
    pray
To endlesse stormes and waste of ciuill
    warre.
AROS. That ye, my lordes, do so agree in
    one 115
To saue your countrey from the violent
    reigne
And wrongfully vsurped tyrannie
Of him that threatens conquest of you all,
To saue your realme, and in this realme
    your-selues,
From forreine thraldome of so proud a
    prince, 120
Much do I prayse; and I besech the goddes
With happy honour to requite it you.
But, O my lordes, sith now the heauens
    wrath
Hath reft this land the issue of their prince,
Sith of the body of our late soueraigne
    lorde 125
Remaines no moe since the yong kinges be
    slaine,
And of the title of discended crowne
Uncertainly the diuerse mindes do thinke
Euen of the learned sort, and more vncer-
    tainly 129
Will parciall fancie and affection deeme, —
But most vncertainly will climbing pride
And hope of reigne withdraw to sundry
    partes
The doubtfull right and hopefull lust to
    reigne, —
When once this noble seruice is atchieued
For Brittaine land, the mother of ye all,
When once ye haue with armed force re-
    prest 136
The proude attemptes of this Albanian
    prince

That threatens thraldome to your natiue
    land,
When ye shall vanquishers returne from
    field   139
And finde the princely state an open pray
To gredie lust and to vsurping power,
Then, then, my lordes, if euer kindly care
Of auncient honour of your auncesters,
Of present wealth and noblesse of your
    stockes,   144
Yea, of the liues and safetie yet to come
Of your deare wiues, your children, and
    your-selues,
Might moue your noble hartes with gentle
    ruth,
Then, then haue pitie on the torne estate,
Then helpe to salue the welneare hopelesse
    sore!
Which ye shall do, if ye your-selues with-
    holde   150
The slaying knife from your owne mothers
    throate.
Her shall you saue, and you and yours in
    her,
If ye shall all with one assent forbeare
Once to lay hand or take vnto your-selues
The crowne by colour[1] of pretended right
Or by what other meanes so-euer it be, 156
Till first by common counsell of you all
In Parliament the regall diademe
Be set in certaine place of gouernaunce.
In which your Parliament, and in your
    choise,   160
Preferre the right, my lordes, with[out] re-
    spect
Of strength, or frendes, or what-soeuer
    cause
That may set forward any others part;
For right will last, and wrong cannot en-
    dure.
Right meane I his or hers vpon whose
    name   165
The people rest by meane of natiue line
Or by the vertue of some former lawe,
Already made their title to aduaunce.
Such one, my lordes, let be your chosen
    king,
Such one, so borne within your natiue
    land,   170
Such one preferre.   And in no wise ad-
    mitte

[1] Excuse, pretence.

The heauie yoke of forreine gouernaunce!
Let forreine titles yelde to publike wealth;
And with that hart wherewith ye now pre-
    pare
Thus to withstand the proude inuading
    foe,   175
With that same hart, my lordes, keepe out
    also
Unnaturall thraldome of strangers reigne,
Ne suffer you against the rules of kinde
Your mother land to serue a forreine prince.
EUB.   Loe here the end of Brutus royall
    line!   180
And loe the entry to the wofull wracke
And vtter ruine of this noble realme!
The royall king and eke his sonnes are
    slaine,
No ruler restes within the regall seate,
The heire, to whom the scepter longes, vn-
    knowen;   185
That to eche force of forreine princes power
Whom vauntage of our wretched state may
    moue
By sodeine armes to gaine so riche a
    realme,
And to the proud and gredie minde at
    home
Whom blinded lust to reigne leades to
    aspire,   190
Loe, Brittaine realme is left an open pray,
A present spoyle by conquest to ensue!
Who seeth not now how many rising
    mindes
Do feede their thoughts with hope to reach
    a realme?
And who will not by force attempt to
    winne   195
So great a gaine, that hope perswades to
    haue?
A simple colour shall for title serue.
Who winnes the royall crowne will want no
    right,
Nor such as shall display by long discent
A lineall race to proue him lawfull king.
In the meane-while these ciuil armes shall
    rage;   201
And thus a thousand mischiefes shall vn-
    folde,
And farre and neare spread thee, O Brit-
    taine Land!
All right and lawe shall cease; and he that
    had

Nothing to-day, to-morrowe shall en-
    ioye   205
Great heapes of golde, and he that flowed
    in wealth,
Loe, he shall be bereft of life and all;
And happiest he that then possesseth least.
The wiues shall suffer rape, the maides de-
    floured;
And children fatherlesse shall weepe and
    waile;   210
With fire and sworde thy natiue folke shall
    perishe;
One kinsman shall bereaue an-others life;
The father shall vnwitting slay the sonne;
The sonne shall slay the sire, and know it
    not;
Women and maides the cruell souldiers
    sword   215
Shall perse to death; and sillie children,
    loe,
That playing [1] in the streetes and fieldes
    are found,
By violent hand shall close their latter
    day!
Whom shall the fierce and bloudy souldier
Reserue to life? Whom shall he spare
    from death?   220
Euen thou, O wretched mother, halfe aliue,
Thou shalt beholde thy deare and onely
    childe
Slaine with the sworde while he yet suckes
    thy brest.
Loe, giltlesse bloud shall thus eche-where
    be shed!
Thus shall the wasted soile yelde forth no
    fruite,   225
But dearth and famine shall possesse the
    land!
The townes shall be consumed and burnt
    with fire,
The peopled cities shall waxe desolate;
And thou, O Brittaine, whilome in re-
    nowme,
Whilome in wealth and fame, shalt thus be
    torne,   230
Dismembred thus, and thus be rent in
    twaine,
Thus wasted and defaced, spoyled and de-
    stroyed!
These be the fruites your ciuil warres will
    bring.

      [1] B. *play;* A. *playing.*

Hereto it commes when kinges will not con-
    sent
To graue aduise, but followe wilfull
    will.   235
This is the end when in fonde princes
    hartes
Flattery preuailes, and sage rede hath no
    place.
These are the plages when murder is the
    meane
To make new heires vnto the royall crowne.
Thus wreke the gods when that the moth-
    ers wrath   240
Nought but the bloud of her owne childe
    may swage.
These mischiefes spring when rebells will
    arise
To worke reuenge and iudge their princes
    fact.
This, this ensues when noble-men do faile
In loyall trouth, and subiectes will be
    kinges.   245
And this doth growe when, loe, vnto the
    prince
Whom death or sodeine happe of life be-
    reaues
No certaine heire remaines — such certaine
    heire
As not all-onely is the rightfull heire
But to the realme is so made knowen to
    be,   250
And trouth therby vested in subiectes
    hartes
To owe fayth there where right is knowen
    to rest.
Alas! in Parliament what hope can be,
When is of Parliament no hope at all,
Which, though it be assembled by con-
    sent,   255
Yet is not likely with consent to end?
While eche one for him-selfe, or for his
    frend,
Against his foe shall trauaile what he may,
While now the state, left open to the man
That shall with greatest force inuade the
    same,   260
Shall fill ambicious mindes with gaping
    hope,
When will they once with yelding hartes
    agree?
Or, in the while, how shall the realme be
    vsed?

No, no; then Parliament should haue bene
    holden,
And certeine heires appointed to the
    crowne,   265
To stay the title of established right,
And in the people plant obedience
While yet the prince did liue, whose name
    and power
By lawfull sommons and authoritie   269
Might make a Parliament to be of force,
And might haue set the state in quiet stay.

But now, O happie man whom spedie death
Depriues of life, ne is enforced to see
These hugie mischiefes, and these miseries,
These ciuil warres, these murders, and
    these wronges   275
Of iustice.   Yet must God in fine restore
This noble crowne vnto the lawfull heire;
For right will alwayes liue and rise at
    length,
But wrong can neuer take deepe roote, to
    last.

[THE END.]

SVPPOSES [1]

A COMEDIE WRITTEN IN THE ITALIAN TONGUE BY ARIOSTO

ENGLISHED BY GEORGE GASCOYGNE, OF GRAYES INNE, ESQUIRE, AND THERE PRESENTED. 1566

THE NAMES OF THE ACTORS

BALIA, the Nurse.
POLYNESTA, the yong woman.
CLEANDER, the Doctor,[2] suter to Polynesta.
PASYPHILO, the Parasite.
CARION, the Doctors man.
DVLYPO, fayned seruant, and louer of Polynesta.
EROSTRATO, fayned master, and suter to Polynesta.
DALIO & CRAPYNO } seruantes to fayned Erostrato.
SCENÆSE, a gentleman stranger.
PAQUETTO & PETRUCIO } his seruantes.
DAMON, father to Polinesta.
NEUOLA, and two other his seruants.
PSYTERIA, an olde hag in his house.
PHYLOGANO, a Scycilian gentleman, father to Erostrato.
LYTIO, his seruant.
FERRARESE, an inkeeper of Ferrara.

The comedie presented as it were in *Ferrara*.

---

[1] As the author states, this play is mainly a translation from the Italian of Ariosto's *I Suppositi*, and was presented by the young gentlemen of Grays Inn, 1566. I have based the text on R. W. Bond's exact reprint (in *Early Plays from the Italian*, 1911) of the second quarto, 1575, "corrected, perfected, and augmented by the Authour." I have modernized the punctuation and capitals, have added in brackets stage-directions, and have slightly expanded the abbreviated forms of the speakers' names from the usual two letters (as *Da.* for *Dalio*, expanded to *Dal.*, *Da.* for *Damon*, expanded to *Dam.*). I have also omitted the marginal glosses in which the author called attention to the "supposes"; these usually take the form "Another suppose," sometimes varied as "A stout suppose," "A pleasant suppose." They are of little importance, and could not conveniently be reproduced in the present edition.
[2] One skilled in law; here, a barrister.

THE PROLOGUE OR ARGUMENT

I suppose you are assembled here supposing to reape the fruite of my trauayles;[1] and, to be playne, I meane presently to presente you with a comedie called *Supposes*, the verye name wherof may peraduenture driue into euery of your heades a sundry suppose to suppose the meaning of our Supposes. Some, percase,[2] will suppose we meane to occupie your eares with sophisticall handling of subtill suppositions; some other wil [5 suppose we go about to discipher vnto you some queint conceiptes, which hitherto haue bene onely supposed, as it were, in shadowes;[3] and some I see smyling as though they supposed we would trouble you with the vaine suppose of some wanton suppose.[4] But, vnderstand, this our Suppose is nothing else but a mystaking, or imagination of one thing for an other. For you shall see the master supposed for the seruant, the seruant for [10 the master; the freeman for a slaue, and the bondslaue for a freeman; the stranger for a well knowen friend, and the familiar for a stranger. But what? I suppose that euen already you suppose me very fonde that haue so simply disclosed vnto you the subtilties of these our Supposes; where, otherwise, in-deede, I suppose you shoulde haue heard almoste the laste of our Supposes before you could haue supposed anye of them [15 arighte. Let this then suffise.

[1] Labors.   [2] Perchance.   [3] Pictures, as the *imprese*.   [4] Prostitute.

ACTUS PRIMUS
SCENA I

[*On one side, the house of Damon; on the other side, the house of the fayned Erostrato; between, a street painted in perspective, and leading into the town.*]

[*Enter*] *Balia, the Nurse,* [*calling in*] *Polynesta, the yong woman.*

[BALIA.] Here is nobody. Come foorth, Polynesta. [*Enter Polynesta.*] Let vs looke about, to be sure least any man heare our talke; for I thinke within the house the tables, the plankes, the beds, the por- [5 tals,[1] yea and the cupbords them-selues haue eares.

POLY. You might as well haue sayde, the windowes and the doores: do you not see howe they harken?   10

BAL. Well, you iest faire; but I would aduise you take heede! I haue bidden you a thousande times beware. You will be spied one day talking with Dulippo.

POLY. And why should I not talke [15 with Dulippo as well as with any other, I pray you?

BAL. I haue giuen you a wherfore for this why many times. But go too! followe

[1] Recesses.

your owne aduise till you ouerwhelme [20 vs all with soden mishappe.

POLY. A great mishappe, I promise you! Marie, Gods blessing on their heart that sette such a brouche on my cappe.

BAL. Well, looke well about you! [25 A man would thinke it were inough for you secretly to reioyce that by my helpe you haue passed so many pleasant nightes togither. And yet, by my trouth, I do it more than halfe agaynst my will, for I [30 would rather you had setled your fansie in some noble familie; yea, and it is no small griefe vnto me that (reiecting the suites of so many nobles and gentlemen) you have chosen for your darling a poore seru- [35 aunt of your fathers, by whome shame and infamie is the best dower you can looke for to attayne.

POLY. And, I pray you, whome may I thanke but gentle Nourse? that contin- [40 ually praysing him, what for his personage, his curtesie, and, aboue all, the extreme passions of his minde, — in fine, you would neuer cease till I accepted him, delighted in him, and, at length, desired him with [45 no lesse affection than he earst desired me.

BAL. I can not denie but at the beginning I did recommende him vnto you (as, in-deede, I may say that for my selfe I haue a pitiful heart) seeing the depth of his [50 vnbridled affection, and that continually he neuer ceassed to fill mine eares with lamentable complaynts.

POLY. Nay, rather that he filled your pursse with bribes and rewards, [55 Nourse!

BAL. Well, you may iudge of Nourse as you liste. In-deede, I haue thought it alwayes a deede of charitie to helpe the miserable yong men whose tender youth [60 consumeth with the furious flames of loue. But, be you sure, if I had thought you would haue passed to the termes you nowe stand in, pitie nor pencion, peny nor paternoster,[1] shoulde euer haue made Nurse [65 once to open hir mouth in the cause.

POLY. No? Of honestie, I pray you, who first brought him into my chamber? Who first taught him the way to my bed, but you? Fie, Nourse, fie! Neuer [70 speake of it for shame! You will make me tell a wise tale anone.

BAL. And haue I these thanks for my good wil? Why then, I see wel I shall be counted the cause of all mishappe. [75

POLY. Nay, rather the author of my good happe, gentle Nourse. For I would thou knewest I loue not Dulipo, nor any of so meane estate, but haue bestowed my loue more worthily than thou deemest. [80 But I will say no more at this time.

BAL. Then I am glad you haue changed your minde yet.

POLY. Nay, I neither haue changed, nor will change it.   85

BAL. Then I vnderstande you not. How sayde you?

POLY. Mary, I say that I loue not Dulipo, nor any suche as he; and yet I neither haue changed, nor wil change, my minde.   91

BAL. I can not tell. You loue to lye with Dulipo very well. This geare is Greeke to me: either it hangs not well togither, or I am very dull of vnderstanding. Speake plaine, I pray you.   96

POLY. I can speake no plainer; I haue sworne to the contrary.

BAL. Howe! Make you so deintie to tell it Nourse, least she shoulde reueale [100

it? You haue trusted me as farre as may be (I may shewe to you) in things that touche your honor if they were knowne, and make you strange to tell me this? I am sure it is but a trifle in comparison of those things wherof heretofore you haue made me priuie.   107

POLY. Well, it is of greater importance than you thinke, Nourse; yet would I tell it you — vnder condition and promise [110 that you shall not tell it agayne, nor giue any signe or token to be suspected that you know it.

BAL. I promise you, of my honestie. Say on.   115

POLY. Well, heare you me then. This yong man whome you haue alwayes taken for Dulipo is a noble-borne Sicilian, his right name Erostrato, sonne to Philogano, one of the worthiest men in that [120 countrey.

BAL. How! Erostrato? Is it not our neighbour, whiche ——?

POLY. Holde thy talking nourse, and harken to me that I may explane the [125 whole case vnto thee. The man whome to this day you haue supposed to be Dulipo is, as I say, Erostrato, a gentleman that came from Sicilia to studie in this citie and euen at his first arriuall met me in [130 the street, fel enamored of me; and of suche vehement force were the passions he suffred, that immediatly he cast aside both long gowne and bookes, and determined on me only to apply his study. And to [135 the end he might the more commodiously bothe see me and talke with me, he exchanged both name, habite, clothes, and credite with his seruant Dulipo (whom only he brought with him out of [140 Sicilia); and so, with the turning of a hand of Erostrato, a gentleman, he became Dulipo, a seruing man; and soone afte sought seruice of my father, and obteyned it.   142

BAL. Are you sure of this?

POLY. Yea, out of doubt. On the othe side Dulippo tooke vppon him the name o Erostrato his maister, the habite, the cred ite, bookes, and all things needefull to [15 a studente; and in shorte space profited ver muche, and is nowe esteemed as you see

BAL. Are there no other Sicylians heere, nor none that passe this way, which may discouer them? 155

POLY. Very fewe that passe this way, and fewe or none that tarrie heere any time.

BAL. This hath been a straunge [159 aduenture! But, I pray you, howe hang these thinges togither — that the studente, whom you say to be the seruant and not the maister, is become an earnest suter to you, and requireth you of your father [164 in mariage?

POLY. That is a pollicie deuised betweene them to put Doctor Dotipole [1] out of conceite — the olde dotarde! — he that so instantly dothe lye vpon [2] my [169 father for me. But looke where he comes — as God helpe me it is he. Out vpon him! What a luskie [3] yonker [4] is this! Yet I had rather be a noonne a thousande times than be combred with suche a coy- [174 strell. [5]

BAL. Daughter, you haue reason. But let vs go in before he come any neerer.

Polynesta goeth in, and Balya stayeth a little whyle after, speaking a worde or two to the Doctor, and then departeth.

[ACTUS I]
SCENA II

[*Enter*] *Cleander,* [*the*] *Doctor,* [*attended by*] *Pasiphilo,* [*a*] *Parasite. Balya,* [*the,*] *Nourse,* [*stands apart overhearing*].

[CLEANDER.] Were these dames heere, or did mine eyes dazil?

PASIPH. Nay, syr, heere were Polynesta and hir nourse.

CLEAN. Was my Polynesta heere? [5 Alas, I knewe hir not!

BAL. He muste haue better eyesight that shoulde marry your Polynesta — or else he may chaunce to ouersee the best poynt in his tables [6] sometimes. 10

[Exit Balia.]

---

[1] A common name for a blockhead.
[2] So insistently doth urge.   [3] Sluggish.
[4] Young man.   [5] Knave.
[6] "I.e. be made a cuckold, metaphor from black-gammon." — Bond.

PASIPH. Syr, it is no maruell; the ayre is very mistie too-day. I my selfe knew hir better by hir apparell than by hir face.

CLEAN. In good fayth, and I thanke God, I haue mine eye sighte goode and [15 perfit, — little worse than when I was but twentie yeres olde.

PASIPH. How can it be otherwise? you are but yong.

CLEAN. I am fiftie yeres olde. 20

PASIPH. [*aside*]. He telles [1] ten lesse than he is.

CLEAN. What sayst thou of ten lesse?

PASIPH. I say I woulde haue thoughte you tenne lesse; you looke like one of [25 sixe and thirtie, or seuen and thirtie at the moste.

CLEAN. I am no lesse than I tell.

PASIPH. You are like inough too liue fiftie more. Shewe me your hande. 30

CLEAN. Why, is Pasiphilo a chiromancer? [2]

PASIPH. What is not Pasiphilo? I pray you, shewe mee it a little.

CLEAN. Here it is. 35

[Holds out his palm.]

PASIPH. O how straight and infracte [3] is this line of life! You will liue to the yeeres of Melchisedech.

CLEAN. Thou wouldest say Methusalem. 40

PASIPH. Why, is it not all one?

CLEAN. I perceiue you are no very good Bibler, Pasiphilo.

PASIPH. Yes sir, an excellent good bibbeler, specially in a bottle. Oh what a [45 mounte of Venus here is! But this lighte serueth not very well. I will beholde it an other day, when the ayre is clearer, and tell you somewhat, peraduenture to your contentation. 50

CLEAN. You shal do me great pleasure. But tell me, I pray thee, Pasiphilo, whome doste thou thinke Polynesta liketh better, Erostrato or me?

PASIPH. Why you, out of doubt! [55 She is a gentlewoman of a noble minde, and maketh greater accompte of the reputation she shall haue in marrying your worship, than that poore scholer, whose birthe and

---

[1] Counts.   [2] Palmist.   [3] Unbroken.

parentage God knoweth, and very fewe [60 else.

CLEAN. Yet he taketh it vpon him brauely [1] in this countrey.

PASIPH. Yea, where no man knoweth the contrarie. But let him braue it, bost [65 his birth, and do what he can, the vertue and knowledge that is within this body of yours is worth more than all the countrey he came from. 69

CLEAN. It becommeth not a man to praise him selfe; but, indeede, I may say, and say truely, that my knowledge hath stoode me in better steade at a pinche than coulde all the goodes in the worlde. I came out of Otranto when the Turkes [75 wonne it, and first I came to Padua, after hither, where by reading,[2] counsailing, and pleading, within twentie yeares I haue gathered and gayned as good as ten thousande ducats. 80

PASIPH. Yea, mary, this is the righte knowledge! Philosophie, Poetrie, Logike, and all the rest, are but pickling [3] sciences in comparison to this.

CLEAN. But pyckling in-deede; [85 whereof we haue a verse:

The trade of lawe doth fill the boystrous [4] bagges;
They swimme in silke, when others royst [5] in ragges.

PASIPH. O excellent verse! Who made it? Virgil? 90

CLEAN. Virgil? Tushe, it is written in one of our gloses.[6]

PASIPH. Sure, who-soeuer wrote it, the morall is excellent, and worthy to be written in letters of golde. But too the [95 purpose: I thinke you shall neuer recouer the wealth that you loste at Otranto.

CLEAN. I thinke I haue dubled it, or rather made it foure times as muche! But, in-deed, I lost mine only sonne there, a [100 childe of fiue yeres old.

PASIPH. O great pitie!

CLEAN. Yea, I had rather haue lost al the goodes in the world.

PASIPH. Alas! alas! by God! And [105

grafts of suche a stocke are very gayson [1] in these dayes.

CLEAN. I know not whether he were slayne, or the Turks toke him and kept him as a bond slaue. 110

PASIPH. Alas, I could weepe for compassion! But there is no remedy but patience. You shall get many by this yong damsell, with the grace of God.

CLEAN. Yea, if I get hir. 115

PASIPH. Get hir? Why doubt you of that?

CLEAN. Why? Hir father holds me off with delayes, so that I must needes doubt.

PASIPH. Content your selfe, sir: he [121 is a wise man, and desirous to place his daughter well; he will not be too rashe in hys determination; he will thinke well of the matter. And lette him thinke! for the [126 longer he thinketh, the more good of you shall he thinke. Whose welth? whose vertue? whose skill? or whose estimation can he compare to yours in this citie?

CLEAN. And hast thou not tolde him that I would make his daughter a dower of two thousand ducates? 132

PASIPH. Why, euen now I came but from thence since.

CLEAN. What said he?

PASIPH. Nothing, but that Eros- [136 trato had profered the like.

CLEAN. Erostrato? How can he make any dower, and his father yet aliue?

PASIPH. Thinke you I did not tell him so? Yes, I warrant you, I forgot [141 nothing that may furder your cause. And doubte you not, Erostrato shal neuer haue hir — vnlesse it be in a dreame.

CLEAN. Well, gentle Pasiphilo, go thy wayes and tell Damon I require noth- [146 ing but his daughter; I wil none of his goods; I shal enrich hir of mine owne; and if this dower of two thousand ducates seem not sufficient, I wil make it fiue hundreth more, yea a thousand, or what [151 so euer he will demaund, rather then faile Go to Pasiphilo! Shew thy selfe frendly in working this feate for me; spare for no cost! Since I haue gone thus farre, I wilbe loth to be out bidden. Go. 156

[1] Ostentatiously.
[2] Lecturing.
[3] Trifling.
[4] Massive.
[5] Riot.
[6] Commentaries (written, presumably, by Cleander).

[1] Rare.

PASIPH. Where shall I come to you againe?

CLEAN. At my house.

PASIPH. When?

CLEAN. When thou wilte. 161

PASIPH. Shall I come at dinner time?

CLEAN. I would byd thee to dinner, but it is a Saincts euen, which I haue euer fasted.

PASIPH. [aside]. Faste till thou [166 famishe!

CLEAN. Harke.

PASIPH. [aside]. He speaketh of a dead mans faste.[1]

CLEAN. Thou hearest me not. 171

PASIPH. [aside]. Nor thou vnderstandest me not.

CLEAN. I dare say thou art angrie I byd the not to dinner; but come, if thou wilte; thou shalt take such as thou findest. 176

PASIPH. What! think you I know not where to dine?

CLEAN. Yes, Pasiphilo, thou art not to seeke.[2]

PASIPH. No, be you sure; there are [181 enowe will pray me.

CLEAN. That I knowe well enough, Pasiphilo. But thou canst not be better welcome in any place than to me. I will tarrie for thee. 186

PASIPH. Well, since you will needes, I will come.

CLEAN. Dispatche, then; and bring no newes but good.

PASIPH. [aside]. Better than my [191 rewarde, by the rood!

Cleander exit, Pasiphilo restat.

[ACTUS I]
SCENA IIJ

Pasiphilo [remains]. Dulipo [enters later].

[PASIPH.] O miserable, couetous wretche! He findeth an excuse by S. Nicolas fast, bicause I should not dine with him — as though I should dine at his owne dishe! He maketh goodly feasts, I [5 promise you! It is no wonder though hee thinke me bounde vnto him for my fare;

for, ouer and besides that his prouision is as skant as may be, yet there is great difference betweene his diet and mine: I [10 neuer so much as sippe of the wine that he tasteth; I feede at the bordes ende with browne bread — marie, I reach always to his owne dishe, for there are no more but that only on the table. Yet he thinks [15 that for one such dinner I am bound to do him al the seruice that I can, and thinks me sufficiently rewarded for all my trauell with one suche festiuall promotion! And yet, peraduenture, some men thinke I [20 haue great gaines vnder him; but I may say, and sweare, that this dosen yeere I haue not gayned so muche in value as the points [1] at my hose (whiche are but three, with codpeece poynt and al). He [25 thinkes that I may feede vpon his fauour and faire wordes; but if I could not otherwise prouide for one, Pasiphilo were in a wyse case. Pasiphilo hath mo pastures to passe in than one, I warrant you! I [30 am of housholde with this scholer Erostrato (his riuale), as well as with Domine Cleander: nowe with the one, and then with the other, according as I see their caters [2] prouide good cheere at the [35 market; and I finde the meanes so to handle the matter that I am welcome too bothe. If the one see me talke with the other, I make him beleeue it is to harken newes in the furtherance of his cause; [40 and thus I become a broker on bothe sides. Well, lette them bothe apply the matter as well as they can; for, in-deede, I will trauell [3] for none of them bothe, yet will I seeme to worke wonders on eche hande. [45 But is not this one of Damons seruants that commeth foorth? It is. Of him I shall vnderstand where his master is. Whither goeth this ioyly gallant?

[Enter Dulipo from Damon's house.]

DUL. I come to seeke some body [50 that may accompany my master at dinner; he is alone, and woulde fayne haue good company.

PASIPH. Seeke no further! You coulde neuer haue found one better than me. 55

---

[1] Which is absolute and eternal.
[2] Deficient (probably with a pun).

[1] Laces used to fasten certain parts of the dress.
[2] Caterers.   [3] Labor.

DUL. I haue no commission to bring so many.

PASIPH. How, many? I will come alone.

DUL. How canst thou come alone [60 that hast continually a legion of rauening wolues within thee?

PASIPH. Thou doest (as seruants commonly doe) hate al that loue to visite their maisters. 65

DUL. And why?

PASIPH. Because they haue too many teeth, as you thinke.

DUL. Nay, bicause they haue to many tongues. 70

PASIPH. Tongues? I pray you, what did my tongue euer hurt you?

DUL. I speake but merily with you, Pasiphilo. Goe in; my maister is ready to dine. 75

PASIPH. What! dineth he so earely?

DUL. He that riseth early, dineth early.

PASIPH. I would I were his man. Maister Doctor neuer dineth till noone, and how delicately then, God knoweth! I [80 wil be bolde to goe in, for I count my selfe bidden.

DUL. You were best so.

[Pasiphilo enters Damon's house.] [1]

[DUL.] Hard hap had I when I first began this vnfortunate enterprise! For [85 I supposed the readiest medicine to my miserable affects [2] had bene to change name, clothes, and credite with my seruant, and to place my selfe in Damons seruice; thinking that, as sheuering colde [90 by glowing fire, thurst by drinke, hunger by pleasant repasts, and a thousande suche like passions finde remedie by their contraries, so my restlesse desire might haue founde quiet by continuall contempla- [95 tion. But, alas! I find that only loue is vnsaciable: for, as the flie playeth with the flame till at last she is cause of hir owne decay, so the louer that thinketh with kissing and colling [3] to content his vnbrideled [100 apetite, is commonly seene the only cause of his owne consumption. Two yeeres are nowe past since (vnder the colour [4] of

Damons seruice) I haue bene a sworne seruant to Cupid — of whom I haue [105 receiued as much fauour and grace as euer man founde in his seruice. I haue free libertie at al times to behold my desired, to talke with hir, to embrace hir, yea (be it spoken in secrete) to lie with hir. I [110 reape the fruites of my desire; yet, as my ioyes abounde, euen so my paines encrease. I fare like the couetous man, that hauing all the world at will is neuer yet content: the more I haue, the more I desire. [115 Alas! what wretched estate haue I brought my selfe vnto, if in the ende of all my farre fetches she be giuen by hir father to this olde doting doctor, this buzard, this bribing villaine, that by so many meanes seek- [120 eth to obtain hir at hir fathers hands! I know she loueth me best of all others. But what may that preuaile when perforce she shalbe constrained to marie another? Alas! the pleasant tast of my sugred ioyes [125 doth yet remaine so perfect in my remembrance, that the least soppe of sorow seemeth more soure than gal in my mouth. If I had neuer knowen delight, with better contentation might I haue passed these [130 dreadful dolours. And if this olde *mumpsimus* [1] (whom the pockes consume!) should win hir, then may I say, "Farewell the pleasant talke, the kind embracings, yea, farewel the sight of my Poly- [135 nesta!" For he, like a ielouse wretch, will pen hir vp, that I thinke the birdes of the aire shall not winne the sighte of hir. I hoped to haue caste a blocke in his waie by the meanes that my seruant (who is [140 supposed to be Erostrato, and with my habite and credite is wel esteemed) should proffer himself a suter — at the least to counteruaile the doctors proffers. But my maister, knowing the wealth of the [145 one and doubting the state [2] of the other, is determined to be fed no longer with faire wordes, but to accept the doctor (whom he right well knoweth) for his sonne-in-law. Wel, my seruant promised me yester- [150 day to deuise yet againe some newe conspiracie to driue Maister Doctor out of conceite, and to laye a snare that the foxe himselfe might be caughte in! What it is, I

---

[1] Original has *Pasiphilo intrat. Dul. restat.*
[2] Desires.   [3] Embracing.   [4] Pretence.

[1] Consumptive.   [2] Estate.

knowe not, nor I saw him not since he [155
went about it. I will goe see if he be
within, that at least if he helpe me not he
maye yet prolong my life for this once.
But here commeth his lackie. Ho, Iack
pack! where is Erostrato? 160

*Here must Crapine be comming in with
a basket, and a sticke in his hand.*

[ACTUS I]
Scena IIIJ

[*Enter*] *Crapino, the Lackie,* [*to*] *Dvlipo.*

[Crapino.] Erostrato? mary, he is in
his skinne.

Dul. Ah, hooreson boy! I say, howe
shall I finde Erostrato?

Cra. Finde him? howe meane you —
by the weeke [1] or by the yeere? 6

Dul. You cracke-halter! [2] if I catche
you by the eares I shall make you answere
me directly.

Cra. In-deede? 10

Dul. Tarry me a little.

Cra. In faith, sir, I haue no leisure.

Dul. Shall we trie who can runne
fastest?

Cra. Your legges be longer than [15
mine; you should haue giuen me the ad-
uauntage.

Dul. Go to! Tell me where is Erostrato?

Cra. I left him in the streete, [20
where he gaue me this casket (this basket I
would haue sayde), and bad me beare it to
Dalio, and returne to him at the Dukes
Palace.

Dul. If thou see him, tell him I [25
must needes speake with him immediatly;
or, abide awhyle; I will go seeke him my
selfe, rather than be suspected by going to
his house.

*Crapino departeth, and Dulipo also:
after Dulipo commeth in agayne
seeking Erostrato.*

FINIS ACTUS I.

[1] Punning on the meaning of "find," to board,
support.
[2] Alluding to the gallows.

ACTUS IJ
Scena J

[*Enter*] *Dulipo* [*seeking*] *Erostrato.*

[Dulipo.] I thinke if I had as many
eyes as Argus I coulde not haue sought a
man more narrowly in euery streete and
euery by-lane! There are not many gentlemen, scholers, nor marchauntes in the [5
citie of Ferara but I haue mette with them,
excepte him. Peraduenture hee is come
home an other way. But looke where he
commeth at the last.

[*Enter Erostrato.*]

Erost. In good time haue I spied [10
my good maister!

Dul. For the loue of God call me
"Dulipo," not "master." Maintayne the
credite that thou haste hitherto kepte, and
let me alone. 15

Erost. Yet, sir, let me sometimes do
my duetie vnto you, especially where no
body heareth.

Dul. Yea, but so long the parat vseth to
crie knappe [1] in sporte, that at the last [20
she calleth hir maister knaue in earnest; so
long you will vse to call me master, that at
the last we shall be heard. What newes?

Erost. Good!

Dul. In-deede? 25

Erost. Yea, excellent. We haue as
good as won the wager!

Dul. Oh, how happie were I if this
were true! 29

Erost. Heare you me. Yesternight in
the euening I walked out, and founde Pasiphilo, and with small entreating I had him
home to supper; where by suche meanes as
I vsed he became my great friend, and [34
tolde me the whole order of our aduersaries
determination; yea, and what Damon doth
intende to do also; and hath promised me
that from time to time, what he can espie
he will bring me word of it. 39

Dul. I can not tel whether you know
him or no. He is not to trust vnto — a
very flattering and a lying knaue.

Erost. I know him very well; he can
not deceiue me. And this that he hath [44
told me I know must needes be true.

[1] Rascal.

DUL. And what was it in effect?

EROST. That Damon had purposed to giue his daughter in mariage to this doctor vpon the dower that he hath profered. 49

DUL. Are these your good newes? your excellent newes?

EROST. Stay a whyle; you will vnderstande me before you heare me.

DUL. Well, say on. 54

EROST. I answered to that, I was ready to make hir the lyke dower.

DUL. Well sayde.

EROST. Abide; you heare not the worst yet. 59

DUL. O God, is there any worsse behinde?

EROST. Worsse? why what assurance coulde you suppose that I might make without some speciall consent from Philogano, my father? 65

DUL. Nay, you can tell; you are better scholer than I.

EROST. In-deede, you haue lost your time; for the books that you tosse now a dayes treate of smal science! 70

DUL. Leaue thy iesting, and proceede.

EROST. I sayd further, that I receyued letters lately from my father, whereby I vnderstoode that he woulde be heere [74 very shortly to performe all that I had profered; therefore I required him to request Damon, on my behalf, that he would stay his promise to the doctor for a fourtnight or more. 79

DUL. This is somewhat yet; for by this meanes I shal be sure to linger and liue in hope one fourtnight longer. But, at the fourthnights ende when Philogano commeth not, how shall I then do? Yea, [84 and though he came, howe may I any way hope of his consent, when he shall see that to follow this amorous enterprise I haue set aside all studie, all remembraunce of my duetie, and all dread of shame. Alas, alas, I may go hang my selfe! 90

EROST. Comforte your selfe, man; and trust in me. There is a salue for euery sore, and doubt you not, to this mischeefe we shall finde a remedie. 94

DUL. O, friend, reuiue me, that hitherto, since I first attempted this matter, haue bene continually dying.

EROST. Well, harken a while then. This morning I tooke my horse and [99 rode into the fieldes to solace my self; and, as I passed the foorde beyonde S. Anthonies gate, I met at the foote of the hill a gentleman riding with two or three men; and, as me thought by his habite and his [104 lookes, he should be none of the wisest. He saluted me, and I him. I asked him from whence he came, and whither he would. He answered that he had come from Venice, then from Padua, nowe [109 was going to Ferrara, and so to his countrey, whiche is Scienna. As soone as I knewe him to be a Scenese,[1] sodenly lifting vp mine eyes (as it were with an admiration), I sayd vnto him, "Are you a [114 Scenese, and come to Ferrara?" "Why not?" sayde he. Quoth I (halfe and more with a trembling voyce), "Know you the daunger that should ensue if you be knowne in Ferrara to be a Scenese?" [119 He, more than halfe amased, desired me earnestly to tell him what I ment.

DUL. I vnderstande not wherto this tendeth.

EROST. I beleeue you. But harken to me. 125

DUL. Go too, then.

EROST. I answered him in this sorte: "Gentleman, bycause I haue heretofore founde very curteous entertaynement [129 in your countrey, beeing a student there, I accompt my self, as it were, bounde to a Scenese; and therefore if I knewe of any mishappe towards any of that countrey, God forbid but I should disclose it. [134 And I maruell that you knewe not of the iniurie that your countreymen offered this other day to the Embassadours of Counte Hercules."

DUL. What tales he telleth me! What appertayne these to me? 140

EROST. If you will harken a whyle, you shall finde them no tales, but that they appertayne to you more than you thinke for. 144

DUL. Foorth.

EROST. I tolde him further, these Ambassadoures of Counte Hercules had dyuers mules, waggens, and charettes,[2] laden with

_____
[1] Sienese.   [2] Carts.

diuers costly iewels, gorgeous furni- [149
ture, and other things, which they caried as
presents (passing that way) to the king of
Naples; the which were not only stayd
in Sciene by the officers whom you cal
customers, but serched, ransacked, [154
tossed, and turned, and, in the end, exacted
for tribute, as if they had bene the goods of
a meane marchaunt.

DUL. Whither the diuell wil he! Is it
possible that this geare appertaine any [159
thing to my cause? I finde neither head
nor foote in it.

EROST. O how impacient you are! I
pray you, stay a while.

DUL. Go to yet a while, then.   164

EROST. I proceeded, that vpon these
causes the Duke sent his Chauncelor to declare the case vnto the Senate there, of
whome he had the moste vncurteous answere that euer was heard; whervpon [169
he was so enraged with all of that countrey,
that for reuenge he had sworne to spoyle as
many of them as euer should come to
Ferara, and to sende them home in their
dublet and their hose.   174

DUL. And, I pray thee, how couldest
thou vpon the sudden deuise or imagine
suche a lye? and to what purpose?

EROST. You shall heare by and by a
thing as fitte for our purpose as any could
haue happened.   180

DUL. I would fayne heare you conclude.

EROST. You would fayne leape ouer the
stile before you come at the hedge. I
woulde you had heard me, and seene the
gestures that I enforced to make him [185
beleeue this!

DUL. I beleeue you; for I knowe you
can counterfet wel.   188

EROST. Further, I sayde, the Duke had
charged vpon great penalties that the in-
holders and vitlers shoulde bring worde
dayly of as many Sceneses as came to their
houses. The gentleman, beeing (as I [193
gessed at the first) a man of smal sapientia,
when he heard these newes, would haue
turned his horse an other way.

DUL. By likelyhoode he was not very
wise when hee would beleeue that of [198
his countrey, which, if it had bene true,
euery man must needes haue knowen it.

EROST. Why not — when he had not
beene in his countrey for a moneth paste,
and I tolde him this had hapned within
these seuen dayes?   204

DUL. Belike he was of small experience.

EROST. I thinke of as litle as may be.
But beste of all for our purpose, and good
aduenture it was, that I mette with such an
one. Now harken, I pray you.   209

DUL. Make an ende, I pray thee.

EROST. He, as I say, when he hard
these words, would haue turned the bridle;
and I, fayning a countenance as [213
though I were somewhat pensiue and carefull for him, paused a while, and after, with
a great sighe, saide to him: "Gentleman,
for the curtesie that (as I said) I haue found
in your countrey, and bicause your [218
affaires shall be the better dispatched, I
will finde the meanes to lodge you in my
house, and you shal say to euery man that
you are a Sicilian of Cathanea, your name
Philogano, father to me — that am in- [223
deede of that countrey and citie — called
here Erostrato. And I, to pleasure you,
will, during your abode here, do you reuerence as you were my father."   227

DUL. Out vpon me! what a grosse hed-
ded foole am I! Now I perceiue wherto
this tale tendeth.

EROST. Well, and how like you of it?

DUL. Indifferently.[1] But one thing I
doubt.   233

EROST. What is that?

DUL. Marie, that when he hath bene
here twoo or three dayes, he shal heare
of euery man that there is no such thing
betwene the Duke and the towne of
Sciene.

EROST. As for that let me alone. [240
I doe entertaine and will entertaine him so
well, that within these two or three daies I
will disclose vnto him all the whole matter,
and doubte not but to bring him in for [244
performance of as muche as I haue promised to Damon. For what hurte can it be
to him, when he shall binde a strange name
and not his owne?   248

DUL. What! thinke you he will be en-
treated to stande bounde for a dower of
two thousand ducates by the yeere?

---

[1] To some extent.

EROST. Yea, why not — if it were ten thousande — as long as he is not in-deede the man that is bound? 254

DUL. Well, if it be so, what shall we be the neerer to our purpose?

EROST. Why, when we haue done as muche as we can, how can we doe any more? 259

DUL. And where haue you left him?

EROST. At the inne, bicause of his horses. He and his men shall lie in my house.

DUL. Why brought you him not with you? 265

EROST. I thought better to vse your aduise first.

DUL. Well, goe take him home; make him all the cheere you can; spare for no cost; I will alowe it. 270

EROST. Content. Looke where he commeth.

DUL. Is this he? Goe meete him. By my trouthe, he lookes euen lyke a [274 good soule! He that fisheth for him mighte bee sure to catche a cods heade! I will rest here a while to discipher him.

Erostrato espieth the Scenese and goeth towards him: Dulipo standeth aside.

[ACTUS II]

SCENA IJ

[*Enter*] *The Scenese* [*attended by*] *Paqveito and Petrvcio, his seruants. Erostrato* [*and Dulipo stand aside*].

[SCENESE.] He that trauaileth in this worlde passeth by many perilles.

PAQ. You saye true, sir. If the boate had bene a little more laden this morning at the ferrie wee had bene all drowned; [5 for, I thinke, there are none of vs that could haue swomme.

SCEN. I speake not of that.

PAQ. O, you meane the foule waye that we had since wee came from this Padua. [10 I promise you, I was afraide twice or thrice that your mule would haue lien fast in the mire.

SCEN. Jesu, what a blockehead thou art! I speake of the perill we are in presently since we came into this citie. 16

PAQ. A great peril, I promise you! — that we were no sooner ariued but you founde a frende that brought you from the inne and lodged you in his owne house. 20

SCEN. Yea, marie, God rewarde the gentle yong man that we mette; for else we had bene in a wise case by this time. But haue done with these tales. And take you heede, and you also, sirra, take [25 heede that none of you saie we be Sceneses; and remember that you call me Philogano of Cathanea.

PAQ. Sure, I shal neuer remember these outlandish words! I could well remember Haccanea.[1] 31

SCEN. I say, Cathanea, and not Haccanea, with a vengeance!

PAQ. Let another name it, then, when neede is, for I shall neuer remember it. 35

SCEN. Then holde thy peace; and take heede thou name not Scene.[2]

PAQ. Howe say you if I faine my selfe dum, as I did once in the house of Crisobolus? 40

SCEN. Doe as thou thinkest best. [*Erostrato advances.*] But looke where commeth the gentleman whom we are so much bounde vnto.

EROST. Welcome, my deare father Philogano. 46

SCEN. Gramercie, my good sonne Erostrato.

EROST. That is well saide. Be mindefull of your toung, for these Ferareses be as craftie as the deuill of hell. 51

SCEN. No, no; be you sure we will doe as you haue bidden vs!

EROST. For if you should name Scene they would spoile you immediatly, and [55 turne you out of the towne with more shame than I woulde shoulde befall you for a thousande crownes.

SCEN. I warant you, I was giuing them warning as I came to you; and I doubt not but they will take good heede. 61

EROST. Yea, and trust not the seruauntes of my housholde to far, for they are Ferareses all, and neuer knew my father, nor came neuer in Sicilia. This is my [65

---

[1] Possibly a pun on *hackney* (*hakenai, hackenaye*), a prostitute.
[2] Siena.

house. Will it please you to goe in? I will
follow.

*They goe in. Dulipo tarieth, and espieth
the Doctor comming in with his man.*

[ACTUS II]
Scena IIJ

Dvlipo alone.

[Dulipo.] This geare hath had no euill
beginning, if it continue so and fall to happie ende. But is not this the silly Doctor
with the side bonet — the doting foole —
that dare presume to become a suter to [5
such a peerlesse paragone? O how coue-
tousnesse doth blind the common sort of
men! Damon, more desirous of the dower
than mindfull of his gentle and gallant
daughter, hath determined to make [10
him his sonne-in-law, who for his age may
be his father-in-law; and hath greater respect to the abundance of goods than to his
owne naturall childe. He beareth well in
minde to fill his owne purse, but he litle [15
remembreth that his daughters purse
shalbe continually emptie — vnlesse Maister Doctour fill it with double ducke egges.[1]
Alas, I iest, and haue no ioy! I will stand
here aside and laugh a litle at this lob-
cocke.   21

*Dulippo espieth the Doctor and his man
comming.*

[ACTUS II]
Scena IIIJ

[*Enter*] Carion, the doctors man, [*attending
his master*] Cleander. Dvlipo [*stands
aside*].

[Carion.] Maister, what the diuel
meane you to go seeke guestes at this time
of the day? The maiors officers haue dined
ere this time, which are alway the last in
the market.   5
  Clean. I come to seeke Pasiphilo, to
the ende he may dine with mee.
  Car. As though sixe mouthes, and the

cat for the seuenth, bee not sufficient to
eate an harlotrie shotterell,[1] a pennie- [10
worth of cheese, and halfe a score spurl-
ings![2] This is all the dainties you haue
dressed for you and your familie.
  Clean. Ah, greedie gut, art thou
afearde thou shalt want?   15
  Car. I am afearde in-deede! It is not
the first time I haue founde it so.
  Dul. [*aside*]. Shall I make some sporte
with this gallant? What shall I say to
him?   20
  Clean. Thou arte afearde, belike, that
he will eate thee and the rest.
  Car. Nay, rather that he will eate your
mule, both heare and hyde.
  Clean. Heare and hyde? and why not
flesh and all?   26
  Car. Bicause she hath none. If she
had any flesh, I thinke you had eaten hir
your selfe by this time.
  Clean. She may thanke you then, for
your good attendance.   31
  Car. Nay she may thanke you for your
small allowance.
  Dul. [*aside*]. In faith, now, let me
alone.   35
  Clean. Holde thy peace, drunken
knaue; and espie me Pasiphilo.
  Dul. [*aside*]. Since I can doe no better,
I will set such a staunce[3] betweene him
and Pasiphilo that all this towne shall not
make them friendes.   41
  Car. Could you not haue sent to seeke
him, but you must come your selfe?
Surely you come for some other purpose;
for if you would haue had Pasiphilo to [45
dinner, I warant you he would haue taried
here an houre since.
  Clean. Holde thy peace. Here is one
of Damons seruaunts; of him I shall vnderstand where he is. Good fellow, art not
thou one of Damons seruaunts?   51
  Dul. Yes sir, at your knamandement.[4]
  Clean. Gramercie. Tell me, then,
hath Pasiphilo bene there this day or
no?
  Dul. Yes sir, and I thinke he be there
still. Ah, ah, ah!   57
  Clean. What laughest thou?

---

[1] Pun on "duckets," and also with a further and
coarse meaning.

[1] Pike.   [2] Smelts.
[3] Distance.   [4] So all the editions; command.

Dul. At a thing — that euery man may not laugh at.

Clean. What?   61

Dul. Talke that Pasiphilo had with my master this day.

Clean. What talke, I pray thee?

Dul. I may not tell it.

Clean. Doth it concerne me?   66

Dul. Nay, I will say nothing.

Clean. Tell me.

Dul. I can say no more.

Clean. I woulde but knowe if it concerne mee. I pray thee tell mee.   71

Dul. I would tell you, if I were sure you would not tell it againe.

Clean. Beleue me, I will kepe it close. Carion, giue vs leaue a litle; goe aside.

[*Carion stands aside.*]

Dul. If my maister shoulde know [76 that it came by me, I were better die a thousand deaths!

Clean. He shall neuer know it. Say on.

Dul. Yea, but what assurance shall I haue?   82

Clean. I lay thee my faith and honestie in paune.

Dul. A pretie paune! The fulkers [1] will not lend you a farthing on it.   86

Clean. Yea, but amongst honest men it is more worth than golde.

Dul. Yea, marie sir, but where be they? But will you needes haue me tell it vnto you?   91

Clean. Yea, I pray thee, if it any thing appertaine to me.

Dul. Yes, it is of you. And I would gladly tell it you, bicause I would not haue suche a man of worship so scorned by a villaine ribaulde.   97

Clean. I pray thee tell me then.

Dul. I will tell you, so that you will sweare neuer to tell it to Pasiphilo, to my maister, nor to any other bodie.   101

Car. [*aside*]. Surely it is some toye [2] deuised to get some money of him.

Clean. I thinke I haue a booke here.

Car. [*aside*]. If he knew him as well as I, he woulde neuer goe aboute it, for he [106 may as soone get one of his teeth from his

iawes with a paire of pinchers as a pennie out of his purse with such a conceite.

Clean. Here is a letter wil serue the turne. I sweare to thee by the contents hereof neuer to disclose it to any man. 112

Dul. I will tell you, I am sorie to see how Pasiphilo doth abuse you, perswading you that alwayes he laboureth for you, where, in-deede, he lieth on [1] my [116 maister continually, as it were with tooth and naile, for a straunger, a scholer, borne in Sicilia; they call him Roscus, or Arskisse — he hathe a madde name, I can neuer hit vpon it.   121

Clean. And thou recknest it as madly; is it not Erostrato?

Dul. That same. I should neuer haue remembred it! And the villaine speaketh al the euill of you that can be deuised. 126

Clean. To whom?

Dul. To my maister; yea, and to Polynesta hirselfe sometimes.

Clean. Is it possible? Ah slaue! And what saith he?   131

Dul. More euill than I can imagine. That you are the miserablest and most nigardly man that euer was —

Clean. Sayeth Pasiphilo so by me? 135

Dul. And that as often as he commeth to your house he is like to die for hunger, you fare so well.

Clean. That the deuill take him else!

Dul. And that you are the testiest man, and moste diuers to please, in [141 the whole worlde, so that he cannot please you vnlesse he should euen kill himselfe with continuall paine.

Clean. O deuilish tong!

Dul. Furthermore, that you [146 cough continually and spit, so that a dogge cannot abide it.

Clean. I neuer spitte nor coughe more than thus, vho, vho; and that but since I caughte this murre. [2] But who is free from it?   152

Dul. You saye true, sir. Yet further he sayth, your arme holes stincke, your feete worse than they, and your breathe worst of all.   156

Clean. If I quite him not for this geare!

---

[1] Usurers.   [2] Trick.   [1] Urgeth.   [2] Catarrh.

Dul. And that you are bursten in the cods.

Clean. O villaine! He lieth! [161 And if I were not in the streete thou shouldest see them.

Dul. And he saith that you desire this yong gentlewoman as much for other mens pleasure as for your owne. 166

Clean. What meaneth he by that?

Dul. Peraduenture that by hir beautie you woulde entice many yong men to your house.

Clean. Yong men? To what purpose? 172

Dul. Nay, gesse you that.

Clean. Is it possible that Pasiphilo speaketh thus of me?

Dul. Yea, and much more. 176

Clean. And doth Damon beleeue him?

Dul. Yea, more than you would thinke; in such sort, that long ere this he woulde haue giuen you a flat repulse, but Pasiphilo intreated him to continue you a suter, for his aduantage. 183

Clean. How for his aduantage?

Dul. Marie, that during your sute he might still haue some rewarde for his great paines. 187

Clean. He shall haue a rope! and yet that is more than he deserueth. I had thought to haue giuen him these hose [1] when I had worne them a little nearer, but he shall haue a &c.[2] 192

Dul. In good faith, sir, they were but loste on him. Will you any thing else with me sir?

Clean. Nay, I haue heard to much of thee already. 197

Dul. Then I will take my leaue of you.

Clean. Farewell! But tell me, may I not know thy name?

Dul. Sir, they call me Foule-fall-you.

Clean. An ill fauored name, by my trouthe! Arte thou this countreyman? 203

Dul. No sir, I was borne by a castle men cal Scabbe-catch-you. Fare you well sir! [Exit Dulipo.]

Clean. Farewel! Oh, God, how [207

haue I bene abused! What a spokesman! what a messanger had I prouided!

Car. Why, sir, will you tarie for Pasiphilo till we die for hunger?

Clean. Trouble me not, that the deuill take you both! 213

Car. [aside]. These newes, what so euer they be, like him not.

Clean. Art thou so hungrie yet? I pray to God thou be neuer satisfied! 217

Car. By the masse, no more I shal, as long as I am your seruant.

Clean. Goe, with mischaunce!

Car. Yea, and a mischiefe to you, and to al such couetous wretches! [Exeunt.]

FINIS ACTUS 2.

ACTUS IIJ

Scena J

[Enter] Dalio, the cooke, [and] Crapine the lackie. [Later enter] Erostrato [and] Dvlipo.

[Dalio, to Crapine]. By that time we come to the house I truste that of these xx. egges in the basket we shall find but very few whole. But it is a folly to talke to him. What the deuill! wilt thou neuer lay [5 that sticke out of thy hande? He fighteth with the dogges, beateth the beares; at euery thing in the streate he findeth occasion to tarie. If he spie a slipstring[1] by the waye, such another as himself, a [10 page, a lackie, or a dwarfe, the deuill of hell cannot holde him in chaynes but he will be doing with him. I cannot goe two steppes but I muste looke backe for my yonker. Goe to, halter-sicke![2] if you breake one egge I may chance breake &c. 16

Cra. What will you breake? your nose in mine &c?

Dal. Ah, beast!

Cra. If I be a beast, yet I am no horned[3] beast. 21

Dal. Is it euen so? Is the winde in that doore? If I were vnloden I would tel you whether I be a horned beast or no.

---

[1] Breeches.
[2] Possibly the actor was supposed to fill out the sentence (with something unprintable?).

[1] A gadding boy, a truant.
[2] Ready for the gallows.
[3] Alluding to the horns of the cuckold.

CRA.   You are alway laden either with
wine or with ale.   26
DAL.   Ah, spitefull boy!   Shall I suffer
him?   [*Strikes him.*]
CRA.   Ah, cowardely beast! darest thou
strike and say neuer a woorde?   30
DAL.   Well, my maister shall know of
this geere.   Either he shall redresse it, or
he shall lose one of vs.
CRA.   Tel him the worst thou canst by
me.   35

[*Enter Erostrato unexpectedly.*] [1]

EROST.   What noise! what a rule is this!
CRA.   Marie sir, he striketh mee bicause
I tell him of his swearing.
DAL.   The villaine lieth deadly!   He
reuiles me bicause I bid him make hast. 40
EROST.   Holla! no more of this.   Dalio,
doe you make in a readinesse those pigeons,
stock doues, and also the breast of veale;
and let your vessell be as cleare as glasse
against I returne, that I may tell you [45
which I will haue roasted, and which
boyled.   [*Exit Dalio.*]   Crapine, lay downe
that basket, and followe me.   Oh that I
coulde tell where to finde Pasiphilo!

Dulipo is espied by Erostrato.

But looke where he commeth that can
tell me of him.   51
DUL.   What haue you done with Philogano your father?
EROST.   I haue left him within.   I
would faine speake with Pasiphilo; can you
tell me where he is?   56
DUL.   He dined this day with my
maister, but whether he went from thence
I know not.   What would you with
him?
EROST.   I woulde haue him goe tell [61
Damon that Philogano, my father, is come,
and ready to make assurance of as much as
he wil require.   Now shall I teach Maister
Doctor a schole point; he trauaileth to none
other end but to catche *Cornua*,[2] and [66
he shall haue them, for, as old as he is, and
as many subtilties as he hath learned in the
law, he can not goe beyond me one ace.

[1] The original edition has in the margin: *Erostra
& Du. ex improuiso.* But Dulipo enters later.
[2] An allusion to the horns of the cuckold.

DUL.   O, deere friend, goe thy wayes;
seeke Pasiphilo; finde him out; and conclude somewhat to our contentation.   72
EROST.   But where shall I finde him?
DUL.   At the feasts, if there be any; or
else in the market with the poulters or the
fishmongers.   76
EROST.   What should he doe with them?
DUL.   Mary, he watcheth whose caters
bie the best meat.   If any bie a fat capon, a
good breast of veale, fresh samon, or any
suche good dishe, he followeth to the [81
house, and either with some newes, or some
stale iest, he will be sure to make himselfe a
geast.
EROST.   In faith, and I will seeke there
for him.   86
DUL.   Then muste you needes finde
him; and when you haue done I will make
you laughe.
EROST.   Whereat?
DUL.   At certaine sport I made to day
with Master Doctor.   92
EROST.   And why not now?
DUL.   No, it asketh further leysure.   I
pray thee dispatche, and finde out Pasiphilo that honest man.   96

*Dulipo tarieth.   Erostrato [followed by
Crapino] goeth out.*

[ACTUS III]

SCENA IJ

Dvlipo, alone.

[DULIPO.]   This amorous cause that
hangeth in controuersie betwene Domine
Doctor and me may be compared to them
that play at primero: [1] of whom some one,
peraduenture, shal leese a great sum of [5
money before he win one stake, and at last,
halfe in anger, shal set vp his rest,[2] win it,
and after that another, another, and another, till at last he draw the most part of
the money to his heape, the other, by [10
litle and litle, stil diminishing his rest, til at
last he be come as neere the brinke as earst
the other was; yet again, peraduenture,
fortune smiling on him, he shal, as it were
by peece-meale, pull out the guts of his [15

[1] A favorite gambling game of cards.
[2] Stake all on one play.

fellows bags, and bring him barer than he himselfe was tofore; and so in play continue stil (fortune fauoring now this way, now that way) til at last the one of them is left with as many crosses [1] as God hath [20 brethren. O, howe often haue I thoughte my selfe sure of the vpper hande herein! — but I triumphed before the victorie. And then, how ofte againe haue I thoughte the fielde loste! Thus haue I beene tossed, [25 nowe ouer, nowe vnder, euen as fortune list to whirle the wheele, neither sure to winne, nor certayne to loose the wager. And this practise that nowe my seruaunte hath deuised, although hitherto it hath not [30 succeeded amisse, yet can I not count my selfe assured of it; for I feare still that one mischance or other wyll come and turne it topsie turuie. But looke where my mayster commeth. 35

Damon comming in, espieth Dulipo and calleth him.

[ACTUS III]
SCENA IIJ

[Enter] Damon [to] Dvlipo. [Later enter] Nevola, and two mo seruants.

[DAMON.] Dvlipo.

DUL. Here sir.

DAM. Go in and bid Neuola and his fellowes come hither, that I may tell them what they shall goe about. And go you [5 into my studie; there vpon the shelfe you shall find a roule of writings which Iohn of the Deane made to my Father when he solde him the Grange ferme, endorced with bothe their names. Bring it hither to me.

DUL. It shall be done, sir. [Exit.] 11

DAM. Go. I wil prepare other maner of writings for you than you are aware of! O fooles, that trust any man but themselues now adaies! Oh spiteful for- [15 tune! thou doest me wrong, I thinke, that from the depth of hell pitte thou haste sente mee this seruaunt to be the subuersion of me and all mine! 19

The seruants come in.

Come hither sirs, and heare what I shal say vnto you. Go into my studie, where

you shall finde Dulipo. Step to him all at once, take him, and, with a corde that I haue laide on the table for the nonce, bind him hande and foote, carie him into the [25 dungeon vnder the stayres, make faste the dore, and bring me the key — it hangeth by vpon a pin on the wall. Dispatche, and doe this geare as priuily as you can. And thou, Neuola, come hither to me againe with speede. 31

NEV. Well I shall.

[Exit Nevola and the other servants.]

DAM. Alas, how shall I be reuenged of this extreme despite? If I punishe my seruant according to his diuelishe de- [35 serts, I shall heape further cares vpon mine owne head. For to suche detestable offences no punishment can seeme sufficient but onely death; and in such cases it is not lawful for a man to be his owne caruer. [40 The lawes are ordeyned, and officers appoynted to minister iustice for the redresse of wrongs; and if to the potestates [1] I complayne me, I shall publishe mine owne reproche to the worlde. Yea, what [45 should it preuayle me to vse all the punishments that can be deuised? The thing, once done, can not be vndone. My daughter is defloured, and I vtterly dishonested. How can I then wype that blot off my [50 browe? And on whome shall I seeke reuenge? Alas, alas, I my-selfe haue bene the cause of all these cares, and haue serued to beare the punishment of all these mishappes! Alas, I should not haue [55 committed my dearest darling in custodie to so carelesse a creature as this olde Nurse! for we see by common proofe that these olde women be either peeuishe, or pitifull; either easily enclined to euill, or [60 quickly corrupted with bribes and rewards. O wife, my good wife (that nowe lyest colde in the graue), now may I well bewayle the wante of thee! and mourning nowe may I bemone that I misse thee! [65 If thou hadst liued, suche was thy gouernement of the least things that thou wouldest prudently haue prouided for the preseruation of this pearle. A costly iewell may I well accompte hir, that hath been my [70 cheefe comforte in youth, and is nowe become the corosiue of mine age! O Polynesta, full euill hast thou requited the clemencie of thy carefull father! And yet to excuse thee giltlesse before God, and to [75 condemne thee giltie before the worlde, I can count none other but my wretched selfe the caytife and causer of all my cares. For of al the dueties that are requisite in humane lyfe, onely obedience is by the [80 parents to be required of the childe: where, on the other side, the parents are bound, first to beget them, then to bring them foorth, after to nourish them, to preserue them from bodily perils in the cradle, [85 from daunger of soule by godly education, to matche them in consort[1] enclined to vertue, too banish them all ydle and wanton companie, to allow them sufficiente for their sustentation, to cut off excesse — [90 the open gate of sinne, — seldome or neuer to smile on them vnlesse it be to their encouragement in vertue, and, finally, to prouide them mariages in time conuenient, lest (neglected of vs) they learne to [95 sette either to much or to litle by themselues. Fiue years are past since I might haue maried hir, when by continuall excuses I haue prolonged it to my owne perdition. Alas, I shoulde haue considered [100 she is a collop[2] of my owne flesh. What! shold I think to make hir a princesse? Alas, alas, a poore kingdome haue I now caught to endowe hir with! It is too true, that of all sorowes this is the head source and [105 chiefe fountaine of all furies: the goods of the world are incertain, the gaines [litle][3] to be reioyced at, and the losse not greatly to be lamented; only the children, cast away, cutteth the parents throate with the [110 knife of inward care. Which knife will kill me surely, I make none other accompte.

Damons seruants come to him againe.

[ACTUS III]

Scena IIIJ

[*Re-enter*] *Nevola* [*to*] *Damon.* [*Later enter*] *Pasiphilo.*

[Nevola.] Sir, we haue done as you badde vs; and here is the key.

---

[1] Society.   [2] Slice.   [3] Added bj Bond.

Dam. Well, go then, Neuola, and seeke master Casteling, the iayler; he dwelleth by S. Antonies Gate. Desire him too lend [5 me a paire of the fetters he vseth for his prisoners; and come againe quickly.

Nev. Well, sir.

Dam. Heare you; if he aske what I would do with them, say you can not [10 tell. And tell neither him nor any other what is become of Dulipo.

Damon goeth out.

[Nev.] I warant you, sir. Fye vpon the deuill! it is a thing almost vnpossible for a man nowe a dayes to handle [15 money but the mettal will sticke on his fingers. I maruelled alway at this fellowe of mine, Dulipo, that of the wages he receiued he could maintaine himselfe so brauely apparelled; but nowe I per- [20 ceiue the cause. He had the disbursing and receit of all my masters affaires; the keys of the granarie; Dulippo here, Dulippo there; in fauoure with my maister, in fauoure with his daughter — what woulde [25 you more, he was *magister factotum*. He was as fine as the crusadoe,[1] and wee silly wretches as course as canuas. Wel, behold what it is come to in the ende! He had bin better to haue done lesse. 30

[*Pasiphilo suddenly and unexpectedly enters from Damon's house.*][2]

Pasiph. Thou saist true, Neuola! He hath done to much, in-deed.

Nev. From whence commest thou, in the deuils name? 34

Pasiph. Out of the same house thou camest from, but not out of the same dore.

Nev. We had thought thou hadst bene gone long since.

Pasiph. When I arose from the table I felte a rumbling in my belly, whiche [40 made me runne to the stable; and there I fell on sleepe vppon the strawe, and haue line there euer since. And thou — whether goest thou?

Nev. My master hath sent me on an errand in great hast. 46

---

[1] A coin bearing the figure of the cross.
[2] Original edition has in the margin: *Pasi. subito & improuiso venit.*

PASIPH. Whether, I pray thee?

NEV. Nay, I may not tell. Farewell.

[Exit Nevola down the street.]

PASIPH. As though I neede any further instructions! O God, what newes I [50 heard euen now, as I lay in the stable! O good Erostrato, and pore Cleander, that haue so earnestly strouen for this damsel! Happie is he that can get hir, I promise you! He shall be sure of mo than one [55 at a clap that catcheth hir — eyther Adam or Eue within hir belie. Oh God, how men may be deceiued in a woman! Who wold haue beleeued the contrary but that she had bin a virgin? Aske the neigh- [60 bours, and you shall heare very good report of hir; marke hir behauiors, and you would haue iudged hir very maydenly; seldome seene abroade but in place of prayer, and there very deuout; and no gaser at out- [65 warde sightes, no blaser of hir beautie aboue in the windowes, no stale[1] at the doore for the bypassers: you would haue thought hir a holy yong woman. But muche good doe it Domine Doctor! Hee shall be sure [70 to lacke no CORNE[2] in a deare yere, what-soeuer he haue with hir else. I beshrewe me if I let[3] the mariage any way. But is not this the old scabbed queane that I heard disclosing all this geere to hir [75 master as I stoode in the stable ere nowe? It is shee. Whither goeth, Psiteria?

Pasiphilo espieth Psiteria comming.

[ACTUS III]

SCENA V

[Enter] Psiteria [to] Pasiphilo.

[PSIT.] To a gossip of myne heereby.

PASIPH. What? to tattle of the goodly stirre that thou keptst concerning Polynesta.

PSIT. No, no. But how knew you of that geere? 5

PASIPH. You tolde me.

PSIT. I? When did I tell you?

PASIPH. Euen now when you tolde it to Damon. I both sawe you and heard [9 you, though you saw not me. A good parte, I promise you, to accuse the poore

wenche, kill the olde man with care, ouer and besides the daunger you haue brought Dulipo and the Nursse vnto, and many moe! Fie! fie! 15

PSIT. In-deed, I was to blame; but not so much as you think.

PASIPH. And how not so muche? Did I not heare you tell? 19

PSIT. Yes. But I will tell you how it came to passe: I haue knowen for a great while that this Dulipo and Polynesta haue lyen togither, and all by the meanes of the Nurse; yet I held my peace, and neuer [24 tolde it. Now this other day the Nursse fell on scolding with me, and twyce or thryce called me drunken olde whore, and suche names that it was too badde; and I called hir baude, and tolde hir that I [29 knew well enoughe howe often she had brought Dulipo to Polynestas bed. Yet all this while I thought not that anye body had heard me; but it befell cleane con-trarye, for my maister was on the other [34 side of the wall, and heard all our talke. Wherevpon he sent for me, and forced me to confesse all that you heard.

PASIPH. And why wouldest thou tell him? I woulde not for &c. 39

PSIT. Well, if I had thought my maister would haue taken it so, he should rather haue killed me.

PASIPH. Why, how could he take it? 43

PSIT. Alas, it pitieth me to see the poore yong woman, how she weepes, wailes, and teares hir heare, not esteming hir owne life halfe so deare as she doth poore Dulipos; and hir father, he weepes on the other side, that it would pearce an hart of stone with pitie. But I must be gone. 50

PASIPH. Go, that the gunne pouder con-sume thee, olde trotte![1]

FINIS ACTUS 3.

ACTUS IIIJ

SCENA J

[Enter] Erostrato, fained, [attended by the lackey, Crapine.]

[EROST.] What shall I doe? Alas! what remedie shall I finde for my ruefull

---

[1] Lure.   [2] A pun on "horns," in cuckoldry.
[3] Hinder.

[1] Hag.

estate? What escape or what excuse may I now deuise to shifte ouer our subtile supposes? For though to this day I haue [5 vsurped the name of my maister, and that without checke or controll of any man, now shal I be openly discyphred, and that in the sight of euery man; now shal it openly be knowen, whether I be Erostrato the [10 gentleman, or Dulipo the seruaunt. We haue hitherto played our parts in abusing others; but nowe commeth the man that wil not be abused — the right Philogano, the right father of the right Erostrato. [15 Going to seke Pasiphilo, and hearing that he was at the water gate, beholde I espied my fellowe Litio, and by and by my olde maister Philogano setting forth his first step on land. I to fuge,[1] and away [20 hither as fast as I could to bring word to the right Erostrato, of his right father Philogano, that to so sodaine a mishap some subtile shift might be vpon the sodaine deuised. But what can be imag- [25 ined to serue the turne, although we had monethes respite to beate oure braines about it, since we are commonly knowen — at the least supposed — in this towne, he for Dulipo, a slaue and seruant to [30 Damon, and I for Erostrato, a gentleman and a student? But beholde, runne, Crapine, to yonder olde woman before she get within the doores, and desire hir to call out Dulipo. But heare you — if she [35 aske who would speake with him, saye thy selfe and none other.

Erostrato espieth Psiteria comming, and sendeth his lackey to hir.

[ACTUS IV]
Scena IJ

Crapine [goes to] Psiteria. Erostrato, fained, [stands waiting].

[CRAPINE.] Honest woman! you gossip! thou rotten whore! hearest thou not, olde witche?

Psit. A rope stretche your yong bones! Either you muste liue to be as old as I, or be hanged while you are yong. 6

Cra. I pray thee, loke if Dulipo be within.

———
[1] Flee.

Psit. Yes, that he is, I warrant him!

Cra. Desire him, then, to come [10 hither and speake a word with me. He shall not tarie.

Psit. Content your selfe; he is otherwise occupied.

Cra. Yet tell him so, gentle girle. 15

Psit. I tell you, he is busie.

Cra. Why, is it such a matter to tell him so, thou crooked crone?

Psit. A rope stretche you, marie!

Cra. A pockes eate you, marie! 20

Psit. Thou wilt be hanged, I warant thee, if thou liue to it.

Cra. And thou wilt be burnt, I warant thee, if the canker consume thee not.

Psit. If I come neere you, hempstring, I will teache you to sing sol fa![1] 26

Cra. Come on! and if I get a stone I will scare crowes with you.

Psit. Goe, with a mischiefe! I thinke thou be some deuill that woulde tempte me. *[Exit Psiteria.]* 31

Erost. Crapine! Heare you? Come away. Let hir goe, with a vengeance! Why come you not? Alas! loke where my maister Philogano commeth. What [35 shall I doe? Where shall I hide me? He shall not see me in these clothes, nor before I haue spoken with the right Erostrato.

Erostrato espyeth Phylogano comming, and runneth about to hide him.

[ACTUS IV]
Scena IIJ

[Enter] Philogano, Ferrarese the Inne keper, [and] Litio, a seruant [to Philogano].

[PHILO.] Honest man, it is euen so: be you sure there is no loue to be compared like the loue of the parents towards their children. It is not long since I thought that a very waightie matter shoulde not [5 haue made me come out of Sicilia; and yet now I haue taken this tedious toyle and trauaile vpon me, only to see my sonne, and to haue him home with me. 9

Fer. By my faith, sir, it hath ben a great trauaile in-dede, and to much for one of your age.

———
[1] Scream (with pain).

PHILO. Yea, be you sure. I came in companie with certaine gentlemen of my countrey, who had affaires to dispatche [15 as far as to Ancona, from thence by water too Rauenna, and from Rauenna hither, continually against the tide.

FER. Yea, and I think that you had but homly [1] lodging by the way. 20

PHILO. The worst that euer man had. But that was nothing to the stirre that the serchers [2] kept with me when I came aborde the ship. Jesus, how often they vntrussed my male,[3] and ransaked a [25 litle capcase [4] that I had, tossed and turned al that was within it, serched my bosome, yea my breeches, that I assure you I thought they would haue flayed me to searche betwene the fell [5] and the fleshe for fardings.[6] 31

FER. Sure, I haue heard no lesse, and that the marchants bobbe [7] them somtimes; but they play the knaues still.

PHILO. Yea, be you well assured; [35 suche an office is the inheritancee of a knaue, and an honest man will not meddle with it.

FER. Wel, this passage shal seme pleasant vnto you when you shall finde your [40 childe in health and well. But, I praye you, sir, why did you not rather send for him into Sicilia than to come your selfe, specially since you had none other businesse? Peraduenture you had rather [45 endanger your selfe by this noysome [8] iourney than hazard to drawe him from his studie.

PHILO. Nay, that was not the matter, for I had rather haue him giue ouer his studie altogither and come home. 51

FER. Why, if you minded not to make him learned, to what ende did you send him hither at the first? 54

PHILO. I will tell you. When he was at home he did as most yong men doe — he played many mad prankes, and did many things that liked me not very well; and I, thinking that by that time he had sene the worlde he would learne to know him- [60

selfe better, exhorted him to studie, and put in his election what place he would go to. At the last he came hither. And I thinke he was scarce here so sone as I felt the want of him, in suche sorte as from [65 that day to this I haue passed fewe nightes without teares. I haue written to him very often that he shoulde come home, but continually he refused stil, beseching me to continue his studie, wherein he doubted not (as he said) but to profite greatly. 71

FER. In-dede, he is very much commended of al men, and specially of the best reputed studentes. 74

PHILO. I am glad he hath not lost his time; but I care not greatly for so muche knowledge. I would not be without the sighte of hym againe so long for all the learning in the worlde! I am olde nowe, and if God shoulde call me in his absence, I promise you I thinke it would driue me into disperation. 82

FER. It is commendable in a man to loue his children, but to be so tender ouer them is more womanlike. 85

PHILO. Well, I confesse it is my faulte. And yet I will tell you another cause of my comming hither, more waightie than this. Diuers of my countrey haue bene here since hee came hither, by whome I haue [90 sente vnto him, and some of them haue bene thrice, some foure or fiue times at his house, and yet could neuer speake with him. I feare he applies his studie so that he will not leese the minute of an houre [95 from his booke. What, alas! he might yet talke with his countrymen for a while! He is a yong man, tenderly brought vp, and if he fare thus continually night and day at his booke, it may be enough to driue him into a frenesie. 101

FER. In-dede, enough were as good as a feast. Loe you, sir, here is your sonne Erostratoes house. I will knocke.

PHILO. Yea, I pray you knocke. 105

[He knocks on the door.]

FER. They heare not.

PHILO. Knocke againe.

FER. I thinke they be on slepe.

LIT. If this gate were your grandefathers soule, you coulde not knocke [110

---

[1] Poor, ordinary.   [2] Customs officers.
[3] Opened up my trunk.
[4] A traveling case.   [5] Skin.
[6] Goods on which a farthing's duty was levied.
[7] Jeer at.   [8] Troublesome.

more softly. Let me come. [*He knocks violently.*] Ho, ho! Is there any body within?

Dalio commeth to the wyndowe, and there maketh them answere.

[ACTUS IV]
Scena IIIJ

Dalio, the cooke, [at the window]. Ferarese the inholder, Philogano, [and] Litio, his man, [below].

[DALIO.] What deuill of hell is there? I thinke hee will breake the gates in peeces!

LIT. Marie, sir, we had thoughte you had beene on sleepe within, and therefore we thought best to wake you. What doth Erostrato?   6

DAL. He is not within.

PHILO. Open the dore, good fellow, I pray thee.

DAL. If you thinke to lodge here, [10 you are deceiued, I tell you; for here are guestes enowe already.

PHILO. A good fellow, and much for thy maisters honesty, by our Ladie! And what guestes, I pray thee?   15

DAL. Here is Philogano, my maisters father, lately come out of Sicilia.

PHILO. Thou speakest truer than thou arte aware of. He will be, by that time thou hast opened the dore. Open, I pray thee hartily.   21

DAL. It is a small matter for me to open the dore; but here is no lodging for you, I tell you plaine; the house is full.

PHILO. Of whome?   25

DAL. I tolde you: here is Philogano, my maisters father, come from Cathanea.

PHILO. And when came he?

DAL. He came three houres since, or more. He alighted at the Aungell, and [30 left his horses there; afterwarde my maister brought him hither.

PHILO. Good fellow, I thinke thou hast good sport to mocke mee.   34

DAL. Nay, I thinke you haue good sporte to make me tary here, as though I haue nothing else to doe. I am matched with an vnrulye mate in the kitchin. I will goe looke to him another while.

PHILO. I thinke he be drunken.   40

FER. Sure he semes so; see you not how redde he is about the gilles?

PHILO. Abide, fellow. What Philogano is it whome thou talkest of?

DAL. An honest gentleman, father to Erostrato, my maister.   46

PHILO. And where is he?

DAL. Here within.

PHILO. May we see him?

DAL. I thinke you may, if you be not blind.   51

PHILO. Go to! Go tel him here is one wold speake with him.

DAL. Mary, that I will willingly doe.

Dalio draweth his hed in at the wyndowe.[1]

PHILO. I can not tell what I shoulde say to this geere. Litio, what thinkest thou of it?   57

LIT. I cannot tell you what I shoulde say, sir. The worlde is large and long; there maye be moe Philoganos and moe [60 Erostratos than one, yea and moe Ferraras, moe Sicilias, and moe Cathaneas; peraduenture this is not that Ferrara whiche you sent your sonne vnto.   64

PHILO. Peraduenture thou arte a foole, and he was another that answered vs euen now. [*To the innholder.*] But be you sure, honest man, that you mistake not the house?   69

FER. Nay, then God helpe! Thinke you I knowe not Erostratos house? Yes, and himselfe also. I sawe him here no longer since than yesterday. But here commes one that wil tell vs tydings of him. I like his counternaunce better than the others that answered at the windowe ere-while.   77

The Scenese [led by Dalio] commeth out.

[ACTUS IV]
Scena V

[*Enter the*] *Scenese* [*to*] *Philogano,* [*Ferarese, and Litio.*] *Dalio* [*accompanies the Scenese*].

[SCENESE.] Would you speake with me, sir?

---

[1] This is printed at the end of the scene.

PHILO. Yea, sir; I would faine knowe whence you are.

SCEN. Sir, I am a Sicilian, at your commaundement. 6

PHILO. What part of Sicilia?

SCEN. Of Cathanea.

PHILO. What shall I call your name?

SCEN. My name is Philogano. 10

PHILO. What trade doe you occupie?

SCEN. Marchandise.

PHILO. What marchandise brought you hither?

SCEN. None. I came onely to see a [15 sonne that I haue here whom I sawe not these two yeares.

PHILO. What call they your sonne?

SCEN. Erostrato.

PHILO. Is Erostrato your sonne? 20

SCEN. Yea verily.

PHILO. And are you Philogano?

SCEN. The same.

PHILO. And a marchant of Cathanea?

SCEN. What neede I tell you so often? I will not tell you a lye. 26

PHILO. Yes, you haue told me a false lie! and thou arte a vilaine, and no better!

SCEN. Sir, you offer me great wrong with these iniurious wordes. 31

PHILO. Nay, I will doe more than I haue yet proffered to doe, for I will proue thee a lyer and a knaue to take vpon thee that thou art not. 35

SCEN. Sir, I am Philogano of Cathanea, out of all doubte. If I were not, I would be loth to tell you so.

PHILO. Oh, see the boldnesse of this brute beast! What a brasen face he setteth on it! 41

SCEN. Well, you may beleue me if you liste. What wonder you?

PHILO. I wonder at thy impudencie; for thou, nor nature that framed thee, can euer counterfaite thee to be me, ribauld villaine and lying wretch that thou arte! 47

DAL. Shall I suffer a knaue to abuse my maisters father thus? [*Draws his sword.*] Hence villaine! Hence, or I will sheath this good fawchion in your [51 paunch! If my maister Erostrato find you prating here on this fashion to his father, I wold not be in your coate for mo conney

skins [1] than I gat these twelue monethes. Come you in againe, sir, and let this curre barke here till he burst! 57

Dalio pulleth the Scenese in ai the dores.

[ACTUS IV]
SCENA VJ

Philogano, Litio, [and] Ferarese [remain].

[PHILO.] Litio, how likest thou this geere?

LIT. Sir, I like it as euill as may be. But haue you not often heard tell of the falsehood of Ferara? and now may you see, it falleth out accordingly. 6

FER. Friend, you do not well to slaunder the citie. These man are no Ferrareses, you may know by their tong. 9

LIT. Well, there is neuer a barrell better herring beetwene you both.[2] But, indeed, your officers are most to blame, that suffer such faultes to escape vnpunished.

FER. What knowe the officers of this? Thinke you they know of euery fault? 15

LIT. Nay, I thinke they will knowe as little as may bee, specially when they haue no gaines by it; but they ought to haue their eares as open to heare of such offences, as the ingates be to receiue guests.

PHILO. Holde thy peace, foole! 21

LIT. By the masse, I am afearde that we shall be proued fooles, both two.

PHILO. Well, what shall we doe?

LIT. I would thinke best we should go seeke Erostrato him selfe. 26

FER. I will waite vpon you willingly; and either at the schooles, or at the conuocations, we shall find him. 29

PHILO. By our Lady, I am wery. I will run no longer about to seke him. I am sure hither he will come at the last.

LIT. Sure, my mind giues me that we shall find a new Erostrato ere it be long. 34

Erostrato is espied vppon the stage running about.[3]

FER. Looke where he is! Whether runnes he? Stay you awhile; I will goe tell

---

[1] Rabbit skins, which the cook saved and sold.
[2] A proverbial phrase, meaning "there is no difference between you two."
[3] Printed at the end of the scene.

him that you are here.   Erostrato!   Erostrato! ho, Erostrato!   I would speake with you!

[ACTUS IV]
Scena VIJ

Fained Erostrato [is approached by] Ferarese.   Philogano, Litio, [and] Dalio [remain].

[Erost.]   Nowe can I hide me no longer. Alas! what shall I doe?   I will set a good face on, to beare out the matter.

Fera.   O Erostrato!   Philogano, your father, is come out of Sicilia.   5

Erost.   Tell me that I knowe not.   I haue bene with him, and seene him alredy.

Fera.   Is it possible?   And it seemeth by him that you know not of his comming.

Erost.   Why, haue you spoken with him?   When saw you him, I pray you?   11

Fera.   Loke you where he standes. Why go you not too him?   Looke you, Philogano; beholde your deare son Erostrato.   14

Philo.   Erostrato?   This is not Erostrato?   Thys seemeth rather to be Dulipo — and it is Dulipo, in-deede.

Lit.   Why, doubte you of that?

Erost.   What saith this honest man?   19

Philo.   Mary, sir, in-deede you are so honorably cladde it is no maruell if you loke bigge.

Erost.   To whome speaketh he?

Philo.   What!   God helpe!   do you not know me?   25

Erost.   As farre as I remember, sir, I neuer sawe you before.

Philo.   Harke Litio, here is good geere! this honest man will not know me!   29

Erost.   Gentleman, you take your markes amisse.

Lit.   Did I not tell you of the falsehood of Ferrara, master?   Dulipo hath learned to play the knaue indifferently well since he came hither.   35

Philo.   Peace, I say.

Erost.   Friend, my name is not Dulipo. Aske you thoroughout this towne of great and small; they know me.   Aske this [39 honest man that is with you, if you wyll not beleeue me.

Ferra.   In-deede, I neuer knewe him otherwise called than Erostrato; and so they call him, as many as knowe him.   44

Lit.   Master, nowe you may see the falsehood of these fellowes: this honest man, your hoste, is of counsaile with him, and woulde face vs down that it is Erostrato. Beware of these mates!   49

Fera.   Friende, thou doest me wrong to suspect me; for sure I neuer hearde hym otherwise called than Erostrato.

Erost.   What name could you heare me called by but by my right name?   But [54 I am wise enough to stand prating here with this old man!   I thinke he be mad.

Philo.   Ah, runnagate!   ah, villaine traitour!   doest thou vse thy master thus? What hast thou done with my son, [59 villain?

[Enter Dalio and other servants.]

Dal.   Doth this dogge barke here still? And will you suffer him, master, thus to reuile you?

Erost.   Come in, come in.   What wilt thou do with thys pestil?   65

Dal.   I will rap the olde cackabed [1] on the costerd.[2]

Erost.   Away with it.   And you, sirra, lay downe these stones.   Come in at [69 dore, euery one of you.   Beare with him, for his age.   I passe not of his euill wordes.

Erostrato taketh all his seruantes in at the dores.

[ACTUS IV]
Scena VIIJ

Philogano, Ferarese, [and] Litio [remain].

[Philo.]   Alas, who shall relieue my miserable estate?   To whome shall I complaine?   since he whome I brought vp of a childe, yea and cherished him as if he had bene mine owne, doth nowe vtterly de- [5 nie to knowe me!   And you, whome I toke for an honest man and he that should haue broughte me to the sighte of my sonne, are compacte with this false wretch, and woulde face me downe that he is Eros- [10 trato.   Alas, you might haue some com-

---

[1] A term of abuse.   [2] Head (apple)

passion of mine age, to the miserie I am now in, and that I am a stranger desolate of all comforte in this countrey; or, at the least, you shoulde haue feared the [15 vengeaunce of God, the supreme iudge, whiche knoweth the secrets of all harts, in bearing this false witnesse with him, whome neauen and earth doe knowe to be Dulipo and not Erostrato. 20

LIT. If there be many such witnesses in this countrey, men may go about to proue what they wil in controuersies here.

FER. Well, sir, you may iudge of me as it pleaseth you; and how the matter [25 commeth to passe I know not; but, truly, euer since he came first hither I haue knowen him by the name of Erostrato, the sonne of Philogano a Cathanese. Nowe, whether he be so in-deede, or whether [30 he be Dulipo, as you alledge, let that be proued by them that knewe him before he came hether. But I protest before God that whiche I haue said is neither a matter compact with him, nor any other, but [35 euen as I haue hard him called and reputed of al men.

PHILO. Out and alas! he whom I sent hither with my son to be his seruaunt and to giue attendance on him, hath eyther [40 cut his throate, or by some euill meanes made him away, and hath not onely taken his garmentes, his bookes, his money, and that whiche he brought out of Sicilia with him, but vsurpeth his name also, and [45 turneth to his owne commoditie the bills of exchaunge that I haue alwayes allowed for my sonnes expences. Oh miserable Philogano! Oh vnhappie old man! Oh eternall God! Is there no iudge, no officer, no [50 higher powers whom I may complaine vnto for redresse of these wrongs?

FER. Yes sir, we haue potestates,[1] we haue iudges, and, aboue al, we haue a most iuste prince. Doubt you not but you shall haue iustice, if your cause be iust. 56

PHILO. Bring me then to the iudges, to the potestates, or to whome you thinke best; for I will disclose a packe of the greatest knauerie, a fardell of the fowlest falsehoode, that euer was heard of! 61

LIT. Sir, he that wil goe to the lawe

must be sure of foure things: first, a right and a iust cause; then, a righteous aduocate to pleade; nexte, fauour *coram iudice;* [1] and, aboue all, a good purse to procure it. 66

FER. I haue not heard that the law hath any respect to fauour; what you meane by it I cannot tell.

PHILO. Haue you no regard to his wordes; he is but a foole. 71

FER. I pray you, sir, let him tell me what is fauour.

LIT. Fauour cal I to haue a friend neere about the iudge, who may so sollicite [75 thy cause, as, if it be right, speedie sentence may ensue without any delayes; if it be not good, then to prolong it, till at the last thine aduersarie, being wearie, shal be glad to compound with thee. 80

FER. Of thus much (although I neuer heard thus muche in this countrey before) doubt you not, Philogano, I will bring you to an aduocate that shall speede you accordingly. 85

PHILO. Then shall I giue my selfe, as it were, a pray to the lawyers, whose insatiable iawes I am not able to feede although I had here all the goods and landes which I possesse in mine own countrey; much [90 lesse, being a straunger in this miserie. I know their cautels [2] of old. At the first time I come they wil so extoll my cause as though it were already won; but within a seuennight or ten daies, if I do not [95 continually feede them, as the crow doth hir brattes, twentie times in an houre, they will begin to waxe colde, and to finde cauils in my cause, saying that at the firste I did not well instructe them; till, at the [100 last, they will not onely drawe the stuffing out of my purse but the marrow out of my bones.

FER. Yea, sir; but this man that I tell you of is halfe a saincte. 105

LIT. And the other halfe a deuill, I hold [3] a pennie!

PHILO. Well sayd, Litio. In-deede I haue but smal confidence in their smothe lookes. 110

FER. Well, sir, I thinke this whom I meane is no suche manner of man. But if he were, there is such hatred and euil-wil

---

[1] Magistrates.

[1] "Before a iudge." [2] Tricks. [3] Wager.

betwene him and this gentleman (whether
he be Erostrato or Dulipo, what-so- [115
euer he be) that I warrant you he will doe
whatsoeuer he can do for you, were it but
to spite him.

PHILO.   Why, what hatred is betwixt
them?   120

FER.   They are both in loue and suters
to one gentlewoman, the daughter of a
welthie man in this citie.

PHILO.   Why, is the villeine become of
such estimation that he dare presume to be
a suter to any gentlewoman of a good
familie?   127

FER.   Yea, sir, out of all doubt.

PHILO.   How call you his aduersarie?

FER.   Cleander, one of the excellentest
doctors in our citie.   131

PHILO.   For Gods loue let vs goe to him!

FER.   Goe we, then.   [*Exeunt.*]

FINIS ACTUS 4.

ACTUS V

SCENA I

[Enter] Fayned Erostrato.

[EROST.]   What a mishappe was this!
that before I could meete with Erostrato I
haue light euen ful in the lap of Philogano!
where I was constrained to denie my name,
to denie my master, and to faine that I [5
knew him not, to contend with him, and to
reuile him in such sort that hap what hap
can, I can neuer hap well in fauour with
him againe.   Therefore, if I could come to
speake with the right Erostrato, I will [10
renounce vnto him both habite and credite,
and away as fast as I can trudge into some
strange countrey where I may neuer see
Philogano againe.   Alas, he that of a litle
childe hath brought me vp vnto this [15
day, and nourished me as if I had bene
his owne: and, in-deede (to confesse the
trouth) I haue no father to trust vnto but
him.   But looke where Pasiphilo commeth,
the fittest man in the world to goe on my
message to Erostrato.   21

*Erostrato espieth Pasiphilo comming
towards him.*

[ACTUS V]

SCENA IJ

[Enter] Pasiphilo [to Fayned] Erostrato.

[PASIPH.]   Two good newes haue I heard
to day alreadie: one, that Erostrato prepared a great feast this night; the other,
that he seeketh for me.   And I, to ease
him of his trauaile, least he shoulde [5
runne vp and downe seeking me, and bicause no man loueth better than I to haue
an erand where good cheere is, come in
post-hast euen home to his owne house.
And loke where he is.   10

EROST.   Pasiphilo, thou muste doe one
thing for me, if thou loue me.

PASIPH.   If I loue you not, who loues
you?   Commaunde me.

EROST.   Go then a litle there, to Damons
house; aske for Dulipo, and tell him — 16

PASIPH.   Wot you what?   I cannot
speake with him.   He is in prison.

EROST.   In prison!   How commeth that
to passe?   Where is he in prison?   20

PASIPH.   In a vile dungeon, there,
within his masters house.

EROST.   Canst thou tell wherefore?

PASIPH.   Be you content to know he is
in prison.   I haue told you to muche.   25

EROST.   If euer you will doe any thing
for me, tell me.

PASIPH.   I pray you, desire me not.
What were you the better if you knew?

EROST.   More than thou thinkest, Pasiphilo, by God.   31

PASIPH.   Well, and yet it standes me
vpon, more than you thinke, to keepe it
secrete.   34

EROST.   Why, Pasiphilo, is this the
trust I haue had in you?   Are these the
faire promises you haue alwayes made me?

PASIPH.   By the masse, I would I had
fasted this night with Maister Doctor,
rather than haue come hither.   40

EROST.   Wel, Pasiphilo, eyther tel me,
or at few woordes neuer thinke to be welcome to this house from hence forthe!

PASIPH.   Nay, yet I had rather leese all
the gentlemen in this towne.   But if I [45
tell you any thing that displease you, blame
no body but your selfe now.

EROST. There is nothing can greue me more than Dulipoes mishappe — no, not mine owne; and therfore I am sure thou canst tell me no worsse tidings.　51

PASIPH. Well, since you would needes haue it, I wil tell you. He was taken a bed with your beloued Polynesta.

EROST. Alas! and doth Damon knowe it?　56

PASIPH. An olde trotte in the house disclosed it to him; wherupon he tooke bothe Dulipo and the Nurse, which hath bene the broker of all this bargayne, and clapte [60 them bothe in a cage — where, I thinke they shall haue sowre soppes too their sweete meates.

EROST. Pasiphilo, go thy wayes into the kitchin, commaund the cooke to boyle [65 and roast what liketh thee best. I make thee supra visour of this supper.

PASIPH. By the masse, if you should haue studied this seuennight you could not haue appointed me an office to please [70 me better! You shall see what dishes I will deuise.

Pasiphilo goeth in, Erostrato tarieth.

[ACTUS V]
SCENA IIJ
Fayned Erostrato alone.

[EROST.] I was glad to rid him out of the way, least he shoulde see me burst out of these swelling teares, which hitherto with great payne I haue prisoned in my brest, and least he shoulde heare the [5 eccho of my doubled sighes, whiche bounce [1] from the botome of my heuy heart. O cursed I! O cruell fortune! that so many dispersed griefes, as were sufficient to subuert a legion of louers, hast sod- [10 enly assembled within my carefull carkase to freat this fearfull heart in sunder with desperation! Thou that hast kepte my master all his youthe within the realme of Sicilia, reseruing the wind and waues in [15 a temperate calme — as it were at his commaunde — nowe to conuey his aged limmes hither, neither sooner nor later, but euen in the worst time that may be! If at any time before thou haddest conducted [20

[1] Bound (or explode).

him, this enterprise had bene cut off without care in the beginning; and if neuer so little longer thou hadst lingred [1] his iorney, this happie day might then haue fully finished our drifts and deuises. But, [25 alas, thou hast brought him euen in the very worst time, to plunge vs al in the pit of perdition! Neither art thou content to entangle me alone in thy ruinous ropes, but thou must also catch the right Eros- [30 trato in thy crooked clawes, to reward vs both with open shame and rebuke. Two yeeres hast thou kept secrete our subtill supposes, euen this day to discipher them with a sorowfull successe. [2] What shall [35 I do? Alas, what shift shall I make? It is too late now to imagine any further deceite, for euery minute seemeth an houre til I find some succour for the miserable captiue Erostrato. Wel, since there is [40 no other remedie, I wil go to my master Philogano, and to him will I tell the whole truth of the matter, that at the least he may prouide in time before his sonne feele the smart of some sharpe reuenge and [45 punishment. This is the best; and thus wil I do. Yet I know that for mine owne parte I shal do bitter penance for my faults forepassed! But suche is the good will and duetie that I beare to Erostrato, as [50 euen with the losse of my life I must not sticke to aduenture any thing which may turne to his commoditie. But what shall I do? Shal I go seeke my master about the towne, or shall I tarrie his returne [55 hither? If I meete him in the streetes, he wil crie out vpon me; neither will he harken to any thing that I shall say till he haue gathered all the people wondring about me, as it were at an owle. Therefore I [60 were better to abide here. And yet, if he tarrie long, I will goe seeke him rather than prolong the time to Erostratos perill.

Pasiphilo returneth to Erostrato.

[ACTUS V]
SCENA IIIJ
[Re-enter] Pasiphilo [to] Fayned Erostrato.

[PASIPH.] *[To Dalio within.]* Yea, dresse them, but lay them not to the fire

[1] Delayed.　　　[2] Result.

till they will be ready to sit downe. [*To Erostrato.*] This geere goeth in order; but if I had not gone in, there had fallen a foule faulte. 6

EROST. And what fault, I pray thee?

PASIPH. Marie, Dalio would haue layd the shoulder of mutton and the capon bothe to the fire at once, like a foole! [10 He did not consider that the one would haue more roasting than the other.

EROST. [*aside*]. Alas, I would this were the greatest fault. 14

PASIPH. Why, and either the one should haue bene burned before the other had bene roasted; or else he muste haue drawne them off the spitte, and they would haue bene serued to the boorde either colde or rawe. 20

EROST. Thou hast reason, Pasiphilo.

PASIPH. Now, sir, if it please you I will goe into the towne and buye oranges, oliues, and caphers; for without suche sauce the supper were more than halfe lost. 26

EROST. There are within already. Doubt you not there shal lacke nothing that is necessarie. 29

Erostrato exit.

PASIPH. Since I told him these newes of Dulipo, he is cleane beside himself. He hath so many hammers in his head that his braynes are ready to burst. And let them breake. So I may suppe with him to night, what care I? But is not this *Dom-* [35 *inus noster Cleandrus* that commeth before? Well sayde. By my truth, we will teache Maister Doctor to weare a cornerd cappe [1] of a new fashion. By God, Polynesta shal be his! He shall haue hir, out of [40 doubt; for I haue tolde Erostrato such newes of hir that he will none of hir.

Cleander and Philogano come in, talking of the matter in controuersie.

[ACTUS V]
SCENA V

[*Enter*] *Cleander, Philogano,* [*and*] *Litio. Pasiphilo* [*remains*].

[CLEAND.] Yea, but howe will ye proue

that he is not Erostrato, hauing such presumptions to the contrarie? Or how shall it be thought that you are Philogano, when an other taketh vpon him this same [5 name, and for proofe bringeth him for a witnesse which hath bene euer reputed here for Erostrato?

PHILO. I will tel you, sir. Let me be kept here fast in prison, and at my [10 charges let there be some man sent into Sicilia that may bring hither with him two or three of the honestest men in Cathanea, and by them let it be proued if I, or this other, be Philogano, and whether he be [15 Erostrato, or Dulipo my seruant; and if you finde me contrarie, let me suffer death for it.

PASIPH. I will go salute Master Doctour. 20

CLEAN. It will aske great labour and great expences to proue it this way; but it is the best remedie that I can see.

PASIPH. God saue you, sir!

CLEAN. And reward you as you haue deserued. 26

PASIPH. Then shall he giue me your fauour continually.

CLEAN. He shall giue you a halter, knaue and villein that thou arte! 30

PASIPH. I knowe I am a knaue, but no villein. I am your seruaunt.

CLEAN. I neither take thee for my seruant, nor for my friend.

PASIPH. Why, wherein haue I offended you sir? 36

CLEAN. Hence to the gallowes, knaue!

PASIPH. What! softe and faire, sir, I pray you; *I præ, sequar;* [1] you are mine elder. 40

CLEAN. I will be euen with you, be you sure. Honest man —

PASIPH. Why, sir? I neuer offended you.

CLEAN. Well, I will teach you. Out of my sight, knaue! 46

PASIPH. What! I am no dogge, I would you wist.

CLEAN. Pratest thou yet, villein? I will make thee — 50

PASIPH. What will you make me? I

---

[1] "You go first, I'll follow." Quoted from Terence, *Andria*, I, i, 144.

[1] Another allusion to the horns of the cuckold.

ee wel the more a man doth suffer you, the
vorsse you are.

Clean. Ah, villein, if it were not for this
gentleman, I wold tell you what I —   55

Pasiph. Villein? Nay, I am as honest
a man as you.

Clean. Thou liest in thy throate,
knaue!   59

Philo. O, sir, stay your wisedome.

Pasiph. What! will you fight? Marie,
come on!

Clean. Well, knaue, I will meete with
you [1] another time. Goe your way.   64

Pasiph. Euen when you list sir, I will
be your man.

Clean. And if I be not euen with thee,
call me cut! [2]   68

Pasiph. Nay, by the masse, all is one.
care not, for I haue nothing. If I had
either landes or goods, peraduenture you
would pull me into the lawe.

[Exit Pasiphilo.]

Philo. Sir, I perceiue your pacience is
moued.   74

Clean. This villaine! But let him goe.
will see him punished as he hath deserued.
Now to the matter. How said you?

Philo. This fellow hath disquieted you,
sir. Peraduenture you would be loth to be
troubled any further.   80

Clean. Not a whit. [3] Say on, and let
him go — with a vengeance!

Philo. I say, let them send at my
charge to Cathanea.   84

Clean. Yea, I remember that wel; and
it is the surest way as this case requireth.
But tel me, how is he your seruant? and
how come you by him? Enforme me fully
in the matter.   89

Philo. I will tell you sir. When the
Turkes won Otranto —

Clean. Oh, you put me in remembrance of my mishappes!

Philo. How, sir?   94

Clean. For I was driuen among the rest
out of the towne (it is my natiue countrey),
and there I lost more than euer I shall recouer againe while I liue.

[1] Get even with you.
[2] Horse (a term of disparagement).
[3] In the margin: "Lawyers are neuer weary to
get money."

Philo. Alas, a pitifull case, by S. Anne!

Clean. Well, proceede.   100

Philo. At that time, as I saide, there
were certaine of our countrey that scoured
those costes vpon the seas with a good
barke, well appointed for the purpose, [104
and had espiall of a Turkey vessell that
came laden from thence with great aboundance of riches.

Clean. And peraduenture most of
mine.   109

Philo. So they boarded them, and in
the end ouercame them; and brought the
goods to Palermo, from whence they came;
and amongst other things that they had
was this villeine, my seruaunt, a boy [114
at that time, I thinke not past fiue yeeres
olde.

Clean. Alas, I lost one of that same
age there.   118

Philo. And I beyng there, and liking
the childes fauour well, proffered them
foure and twentie ducates for him, and had
him.

Clean. What! was the childe a Turke?
or had the Turkes brought him from
Otranto?   125

Philo. They saide he was a childe of
Otranto. But what is that to the matter?
Once xxiiij Ducattes he cost me — that I
wot well.   129

Clean. Alas, I speake it not for that,
sir. I woulde it were he whome I meane.

Philo. Why, whom meane you sir?

Liti. Beware sir; be not to lauish!

Clean. Was his name Dulipo then? or
had he not another name?   135

Liti. Beware what you say, sir!

Philo. What the deuill hast thou to
doe! — Dulipo? No, sir; his name was
Carino.   139

Liti. Yea, well said! Tell all, and
more to; doe!

Clean. O Lord, if it be as I thinke how
happie were I! And why did you change
his name then?   144

Philo. We called him Dulipo bycause
when he cryed, as Children doe sometimes,
he woulde alwayes cry on that name
Dulipo.   148

Clean. Well, then I see well it is my
owne onely childe, whome I loste when I

loste my countrie! He was named **Carino** after his grandfather; and this **Dulipo**, whome he alwayes remembred in his lamenting, was his foster father that nourished him and brought him vp.   155

LITI.   Sir, haue I not told you enough of the falshood of Ferara? This gentleman will not only picke your purse, but beguile you of your seruaunt also, and make you beleue he is his son.   160

CLEAN.   Well, goodfellow, I haue not **vs**ed to lie.

LITI.   Sir, no; but euery thing hath a beginning.   164

CLEAN.   Fie! Philogano, haue you not the least suspecte that may be of me?

LITI.   No, marie; but it were good he had the most suspecte that may be.   168

CLEAN.   Well, hold thou thy peace a litle, good fellow. I pray you tell me, Philogano, had the child any remembrance of his fathers name, his mothers name, or the name of his familie?   173

PHILO.   He did remember them, and could name his mother also; but sure I haue forgotten the name.

LITI.   I remember it well enough!

PHILO.   Tell it then.

LITI.   Nay, that I will not, marie! You haue tolde him too much al ready.   180

PHILO.   Tell it, I say, if thou can.

LITI.   Can? yes, by the masse, I can wel enough! But I wil haue my tong pulled out rather than tell it, vnlesse he tell [184 it first. Doe you not perceiue, sir, what he goeth about?

CLEAN.   Well, I will tell you then. My name you know alredy; my wife, his mothers, name was Sophronia; the house that I came of they call Spiagia.   190

LITI.   I neuer heard him speake of Spiagia; but, in-deede, I haue heard him say his mothers name was Sophronia. But what of that? A great matter, I promise you! [194 It is like enoughe that you two haue compact together to deceiue my maister.

CLEAN.   What nedeth me more euident tokens? This is my sonne out of doubt, [198 whom I lost eighteen yeares since; and a thousand thousand times haue I lamented for him. He shuld haue also a mould on his left shoulder.   202

LITI.   He hath a moulde there, in-deede; and an hole in an other place, to — I would your nose were in it.

CLEAN.   Faire wordes, fellow Litio. Oh, I pray you, let vs goe talke with him! O fortune, howe much am I bounde to thee if I finde my sonne!   209

PHILO.   Yea, how little am I beholden to fortune, that know not where my sonne is become, and you, whome I chose to be mine aduocate, will nowe (by the meanes of this Dulipo) become mine aduersarie! 214

CLEAN.   Sir, let vs first goe find mine; and, I warrant you, yours will be founde also ere it be long.

PHILO.   God graunt! Goe we, then.

CLEAN.   Since the dore is open I will neuer knocke nor cal, but we will be bolde to goe in.   221

LITI.   [to Philogano].   Sir, take you heede, least he leade you to some mischiefe.

PHILO.   Alas, Litio, if my sonne be loste what care I what become of me?   225

LITI.   Well. I haue tolde you my minde, Sir. Doe you as you please.

*Exeunt [into Erostrato's house]; Dam*s *and Psiteria come in.*

[ACTUS V]
SCENA VJ [1]

[Enter] Damon [and] Psiteria [in the street].

[DAMON.]   Come hither, you olde kallat! [2] you tatling huswife! — that the deuill cut oute your tong! Tell me, howe could Pasiphilo know of this geere but by you?

PSIT.   Sir, he neuer knewe it of me; he was the firste that tolde me of it.   6

DAM.   Thou liest, old drabbe! But I would aduise you tel me the truth, or I wil make those old bones rattle in your skin.

PSIT.   Sir, if you finde me contrarie, kil**t** me.   11

DAM.   Why, where should he talke with thee?

PSIT.   He talked with me of it here in the streete.   15

DAM.   What did you here?

PSIT.   I was going to the weauers for a webbe of clothe you haue there.

---
[1] Edition of 1575 has *sexta.*   [2] W**h**ore.

Dam. And what cause coulde Pasiphilo haue to talke of it, vnlesse thou began the mater first? 21

Psit. Nay, he began with me sir, reuiling me bycause I had tolde you of it. I asked him how he knewe of it, and he said he was in the stable when you examined me erewhile. 26

Dam. Alas, alas! what shall I doe then? In at dores, olde whore! I wil plucke that tong of thine out by the rootes one day. *Exit Psiteria.*] Alas, it greeueth me [30 more that Pasiphilo knoweth it than all the rest. He that will haue a thing kept secrete, let him tell it to Pasiphilo! the people shall knowe it, and as many as haue eares, and no mo. By this time he hath tolde [35 it in a hundreth places! Cleander was the firste, Erostrato the seconde; and so, from one to another, throughout the citie. Alas, what dower, what mariage shall I nowe prepare for my daughter? O poore [40 dolorous Damon, more miserable than miserie it selfe! Would God it were true that Polynesta tolde me ere while — that he who hathe defloured hir is of no seruile estate (as hitherto he hath bene sup- [45 posed in my seruice), but that he is a gentleman, borne of a good parentage in Sicilia. Alas, small riches shoulde content me if he be but of an honest familie. But I feare that he hathe deuised these [50 toyes to allure my daughtres loue. Well, I vil goe examine hir againe. My minde giueth me that I shall perceiue by hir tale whether it be true or not. But is not this Pasiphilo that commeth out of my [55 neighbours house? What the deuill ayleth him to leape and laughe so like a foole in the high way?

Pasiphilo commeth out of the house[1] *laughing.*

[ACTUS V]
SCENA VIJ[2]

[Enter] Pasiphilo [to] Damon.

[Pasiph.] O God, that I might finde Damon at home!

[1] Misprinted *towne,* but corrected in "Faults scaped."
[2] Ed. 1575, *septima.*

Dam. What the diuill would he with me?

Pasiph. That I may be the firste that shall bring him these newes! 6

Dam. What will he tell me, in the name of God?

Pasiph. O Lord, how happie am I! loke where he is. 10

Dam. What newes, Pasiphilo, that thou arte so merie?

Pasiph. Sir, I am mery to make you glad. I bring you ioyfull newes!

Dam. And that I haue nede of, Pasiphilo. 16

Pasiph. I knowe, sir, that you are a sorowfull man for this mishap that hath chaunced in your house. Peraduenture you thoughte I had not knowen of it. [20 But let it passe! Plucke vp your sprits, and reioyce! for he that hath done you this iniurie is so well borne, and hath so riche parents, that you may be glad to make him your sonne in law. 25

Dam. How knowest thou?

Pasiph. His father, Philogano, one of the worthiest men in all Cathanea, is nowe come to the citie, and is here in your neighbours house. 30

Dam. What, in Erostratos house?

Pasiph. Nay, in Dulipos house. For where you haue alwayes supposed this gentleman to be Erostrato, it is not so; but your seruaunt, whom you haue impris- [35 oned, hitherto supposed to be Dulipo, he is in-dede Erostrato, and that other is Dulipo. And thus they haue alwayes, euen since their first ariual in this citie, exchaunged names, to the ende that Erostrato, the [40 maister, vnder the name of Dulipo, a seruant, might be entertained in your house, and so winne the loue of your daughter.

Dam. Wel, then I perceiue it is euen as Polinesta told me. 45

Pasiph. Why, did she tell you so?

Dam. Yea; but I thought it but a tale.

Pasiph. Well, it is a true tale. And here they will be with you by and by — both Philogano, this worthie man, and Maister Doctor, Cleander. 51

Dam. Cleander? What to doe?

Pasiph. Cleander? Why therby lies another tale — the moste fortunate ad uenture that euer you heard! Wot you [55 what? This other Dulipo, whome all this while we supposed to be Erostrato, is founde to be the sonne of Cleander, whome he lost at the losse of Otranto, and was after solde in Sicilia too this Philogano. [60 The strangest case that euer you heard! A man might make a comedie of it. They wil come euen straight, and tell you the whole circumstance of it themselues. 64

DAM. Nay, I will first goe heare the storie of this Dulipo, be it Dulipo or Erostrato, that I haue here within, before I speake with Philogano.

PASIPH. So shall you doe well, sir. I wil goe tell them that they may stay a while. But loke where they come. 71

Damon goeth in; Scenese, Cleander and Philogano come vpon the stage.

[ACTUS V]
SCENA VIIJ

[Enter] Scenese, Cleander, [Carino, and] Philogano. [Pasiphilo remains.]

[SCENESE.] Sir, you shal not nede to excuse the matter any further. Since I haue receiued no greater iniurie than by words, let them passe like wind; I take them well in worthe, and am rather well [5 pleased than offended. For it shall bothe be a good warning to me another time howe to trust euery man at the firste sighte, yea, and I shall haue good game hereafter to tel this pleasant story another day in mine owne countrey. 11

CLEAN. Gentleman, you haue reason; and be you sure that as many as heare it will take great pleasure in it. And you, Philogano, may thinke that God in heauen [15 aboue hath ordained your comming hither at this present to the ende I might recouer my lost sonne, whom by no other meanes I coulde euer haue founde oute. 19

PHILO. Surely, sir, I thinke no lesse; for I think that not so much as a leafe falleth from the tree without the ordinance of God. But let vs goe seke Damon, for me thinketh euery day a yeare, euery [24 houre a daye, and euery minute to much, till I see my Erostrato.

CLEAN. I cannot blame you. Goe we, then. Carino, take you that gentleman home in the meane time. The fewer the better to be present at such affaires. 30

Pasiphilo stayeth their going in.

[ACTUS V]
SCENA IX

Pasiphilo [advances to] Cleander.

[PASIPH.] Maister Doctor, will you not shew me this fauour, to tell me the cause of your displeasure?

CLEAN. Gentle Pasiphilo, I muste needes confesse I haue done thee wrong, and that I beleued tales of thee, whiche, indeede, I finde now contrary. 7

PASIPH. I am glad, then, that it proceeded rather of ignorance than of malice.

CLEAN. Yea, beleue me, Pasiphilo. 10

PASIPH. O, sir, but yet you shoulde not haue giuen me suche foule wordes.

CLEAN. Well, content thy selfe, Pasiphilo. I am thy frende, as I haue alwayes bene; for proofe whereof, come suppe [15 with me to night, and from day to day this seuen night be thou my guest. But beholde, here commeth Damon out of his house.

Here they come all togither.

[ACTUS V]
SCENA X [1]

[In the street gather] Cleander, Philogano, Damon, Erostrato, Pasiphilo, [and] Polinesta. [Later enter] Nevola And other seruaunts.

[CLEAN. *addressing Damon.*] We are come vnto you, sir, to turne your sorowe into ioy and gladnesse: the sorow, we meane, that of force you haue sustained since this mishappe of late fallen in your [5 house. But be you of good comforte, sir, and assure your selfe that this yong man which youthfully and not maliciously hath committed this amorous offence, is verie well able (with consent of this worthie [10 man, his father) to make you sufficient

[1] Ed. 1575, *decima.*

amendes, being borne in Cathanea of
Sicilia, of a noble house, no way inferiour
vnto you, and of wealth (by the reporte of
suche as knowe it) farre exceeding that of
yours.   16

PHILO. And I here, in proper person,
doe presente vnto you, sir, not onely my
assured frendship and brotherhoode, but
do earnestly desire you to accepte my [20
poore childe (though vnworthy) as your
sonne-in-lawe. And for recompence of the
iniurie he hath done you, I profer my
whole lands in dower to your daughter; yea,
and more would, if more I might.   25

CLEAN. And I, sir, who haue hitherto so
earnestly desired your daughter in mariage,
doe now willingly yelde vp and quite claime
to this yong man, who, both for his yeares
and for the loue he beareth hir, is most [30
meetest to be hir husband. For wher I
was desirous of a wife by whom I might
haue yssue, to leaue that litle which God
hath sent me, now haue I litle neede, that
(thankes be to God) haue founde my [35
deerely beloued sonne, whom I loste of a
childe at the siege of Otranto.

DAM. Worthy gentleman, your friendship, your alliaunce, and the nobilitie of
your birthe are suche as I haue muche [40
more cause to desire them of you than you
to request of me that which is already
graunted. Therfore I gladly and willingly
receiue the same, and thinke my selfe
moste happie now of all my life past [45
that I haue gotten so toward a sonne-in-
lawe to my selfe, and so worthye a father-
in-lawe to my daughter. Yea, and muche

the greater is my contentation, since this
worthie gentleman, Maister Cleander, [50
doth holde himselfe satisfied. And now,
behold your sonne.

[Enter Erostrato.]

EROST. O father!

PASIPH. Beholde the naturall loue of
the childe to the father. For inwarde [55
ioye he cannot pronounce one worde, in
steade wherof he sendeth sobbes and teares
to tell the effect of his inward intention.
But why doe you abide here abrode? Wil
it please you to goe into the house sir? 60

DAM. Pasiphilo hath saide well. Will
it please you to goe in sir?

[Enter Nevola with fetters.]

NEV. Here I haue brought you, sir,
bothe fetters and boltes.

DAM. Away with them, now!   65

NEV. Yea, but what shal I doe with
them?

DAM. Marie, I will tell thee, Neuola: to
make a righte ende of our supposes, lay one
of those boltes in the fire, and make [70
thee a suppositorie [1] as long as mine arme.
God saue the sample!

[Turning to the audience.]

Nobles and gentlemen, if you suppose that
our *Supposes* haue giuen you sufficient
cause of delighte, shewe some token,
whereby we may suppose you are con-
tent.   77

Et plauserunt.

[1] A medical device, with a pun on "suppose."

FINIS.

XII
THE COURT DRAMA

THE EXCELLENT COMEDIE

OF TWO THE MOSTE FAITHFULLEST FREENDES,

DAMON AND PITHIAS[1]

Newly Imprinted, as the same was shewed before the Queenes Maiestie, by the Children of her Graces Chappell, except the Prologue that is somewhat altered for the proper vse of them that hereafter shall haue occasion to plaie it, either in Priuate, or open Audience. Made by Maister Edwards, then beynge Maister of the Children.

1571

Imprinted at London in Fleetelane by Richarde Iohnes, and are to be solde at his shop, ioyning to the Southwest doore of Paules Churche.

THE SPEAKERS' NAMES [2]

ARISTIPPUS, a Pleasant Gentleman.
CARISOPHUS, a Parasite.
DAMON, } Two Gentlemen of Greece.
PITHIAS, }
STEPHANO, Servant to Damon and Pithias.
WILL, Aristippus' Lackey.

JACK, Carisophus' Lackey.
SNAP, the Porter.
DIONYSIUS, the King.
EUBULUS, the King's Councillor.
GRONNO, the Hangman.
GRIM, the Collier.

---

[1] Richard Edwards, musician and poet, was appointed Master of the Children of the Chapel Royal in 1561, and thenceforth devoted his energies to writing plays to be acted by the boys before Elizabeth. Although he is known to have composed numerous plays for the Court, only *Damon and Pithias* was published under his name. It was probably performed during the Christmas season of 1564–65. Notable as the first tragi-comedy in England, it well illustrates the refined drama with which the child-actors were accustomed to entertain courtly audiences. Professor Wallace (*The Evolution of the English Drama up to Shakespeare*, 1912, p. 110) writes: "This fine old tale out of Syracusan history, with its tragic and comic elements happily mingled in a rising tide of suspense to the climax, as presented by Edwards, formed the high-water mark of English drama up to that time."

The earliest extant edition (A) bears the date 1571, but the title-page describes the text as "newly imprinted." Another edition appeared in 1582. I have based the present reprint on Farmer's photographic facsimile reproduction of the copy of the 1571 edition in the British Museum. All changes are recorded in footnotes, and additions set in brackets. The spelling of the original edition is so atrocious that I deemed it wise to modernize, in so far as possible, the spelling as well as the punctuation. John S. Farmer, in *Early English Dramatists*, 1906, professed to reprint the play "from the edition of 1571," but he merely reproduced the Hazlitt-Dodsley (H.) text. It has not seemed worth while to note all the errors in the exceedingly inaccurate Hazlitt-Dodsley edition; I have observed more than twenty words carelessly dropped, eight words inserted without authority, and over forty serious corruptions of the text, besides innumerable minor mistakes.

[2] In A. this is printed after the prologue.

THE PROLOGUE

On every side whereas I glance my roving eye,
Silence in all ears bent I plainly do espy.
But if your eager looks do long such toys to see
As heretofore in comical wise were wont abroad to be,
Your lust is lost, and all the pleasures that you sought   5
Is frustrate quite of toying [1] plays. A sudden change is wrought.
For lo, our author's muse, that masked in delight,
Hath forc'd his pen against his kind [2] no more such sports to write.
Muse he that lust, right worshipful, for chance hath made this change,
For that to some he seemed too much in young desires [3] to range;   10
In which, right glad to please, seeing that he did offend,
Of all he humbly pardon craves: his pen that shall amend.
And yet, worshipful audience, thus much I dare avouch:
In comedies the greatest skill is this: rightly to touch
All things to the quick, and eke to frame each person so   15
That by his common talk you may his nature rightly know.
A roister [4] ought not preach — that were too strange to hear, —
But, as from virtue he doth swerve, so ought his words appear.
The old man is sober; the young man rash; the lover triumphing in joys;
The matron grave; the harlot wild, and full of wanton toys: 20
Which all in one course they no wise do agree,
So correspondent to their kind their speeches ought to be.
Which speeches, well-pronounc'd, with action lively framed —
If this offend the lookers on, let Horace then be blamed,
Which hath our author taught at school, from whom he doth not swerve,   25
In all such kind of exercise *decorum* to observe.
Thus much for his defence (he saith), as poets earst have done,
Which heretofore in comedies the self-same race did run.
But now, for to be brief, the matter to express
Which here we shall present is this: *Damon and Pithias,*   30
A rare ensample of friendship true. It is no legend-lie,
But a thing once done, indeed, as histories do descry;
Which, done of yore in long time past, yet present shall be here
Even as it were in doing now, so lively it shall appear.
Lo, here is [5] Syracuse, th' ancient town which once the Romans won,   35
Here Dionysius palace, within whose court this thing most strange was done.
Which matter, mix'd with mirth and care, a just name to apply
As seems most fit, we have it termed a "tragical comedy." [6]
Wherein, talking of courtly toys, we do protest this flat: —
We talk of Dionysius court; we mean no court but that!   40
And that we do so mean, who wisely calleth to mind
The time, the place, the author,[7] here most plainly shall it find.
Lo, this I speak for our defence, lest of others we should be shent.[8]
But, worthy audience, we you pray, take things as they be meant.
Whose upright judgment we do crave with heedful ear and eye   45
To hear the cause and see th' effect of this new tragical comedy.   *Exit.*

---

[1] Amorously sportive.   [2] Its nature.   [3] I.e., in love.   [4] Cf. Roister Doister.
[5] A. *in.* Since the play was staged by the Office of the Revels with "players' houses," probably the speaker pointed to the "city" on one side, and to Dionysius' palace on the other side. The personages enter from Damon's lodgings in the "city," from the palace, or from the rear of the stage.
[6] Apparently the earliest occurrence of the word, earlier than any noted in *N.E.D.*
[7] A. *Authours.*   [8] Blamed.

[DAMON AND PITHIAS]

[On one side, the city of Syracuse, with the lodging of Damon and Pithias in the foreground; on the other side, the palace of King Dionysius.]

Here entereth Aristippus.

[ARISTIPPUS.]   Too [1] strange, perhaps, it
　　seems to some
That I, Aristippus, a courtier am become;
A philosopher of late, not of the meanest
　　name,
But now to the courtly behaviour my life I
　　frame.
Muse he that list.   To you of good skill 5
I say that I am a philosopher still.
Loving of wisdom is termed philosophy; [2]
Then who is a philosopher so rightly as I?
For in loving of wisdom proof doth this
　　try,
That *frustra sapit, qui non sapit sibi.* [3]   10
I am wise for myself: then tell me, of troth,
Is not that great wisdom, as the world
　　go'th?
Some philosophers in the street go ragged
　　and torn,
And feed [4] on vile roots, whom boys laugh
　　to scorn;
But I in fine silks haunt Dionysius'
　　palace,   15
Wherein with dainty fare myself I do
　　solace.
I can talk of philosophy as well as the best,
But the strait [5] kind of life I leave to the
　　rest.
And I profess now the courtly philosophy;
To crouch, to speak fair, myself I apply,   20
To feed the king's humour with pleasant
　　devices;
For which I am called *Regius canis.* [6]
But wot ye who named me first the king's
　　dog?
It was the rogue Diogenes, that vile grunt-
　　ing hog!

Let him roll in his tub to win a vain
　　praise;   25
In the court pleasantly I will spend all my
　　days.
Wherein what to do I am not to learn;
What will serve mine own turn I can
　　quickly discern.
All my time at school I have not spent
　　vainly;
I can help one!   Is not that a good point of
　　philosophy?   30

Here entereth Carisophus.

[CARISOPHUS.]   I beshrew your fine ears,
　　since you came from school
In the court you have made many a wise
　　man a fool!
And though you paint out your feigned
　　philosophy,
So God help me, it is but a plain kind of
　　flattery!
Which you use so finely in so pleasant a
　　sort   35
That none but Aristippus now makes the
　　king sport.
Ere you came hither poor I was somebody;
The king delighted in me.   Now I am but
　　a noddy. [1]
ARISTIPPUS.   In faith, Carisophus, you
　　know yourself best!
But I will not call you noddy but only in
　　jest.   40
And thus I assure you: though I came from
　　school
To serve in this court, I came not yet to be
　　the king's fool,
Or to fill his ears with servile squirrility. [2]
That office is yours!   You know it right
　　perfectly!
Of parasites and sycophants you are a
　　grave bencher; [3]   45
The king feeds you often from his own
　　trencher. [4]
I envy not your state, nor yet your great
　　favour;
Then grudge not at all if in my behaviour

---

[1] H. misprints *Tho'*.
[2] A. *Lovers of wisdom, are termed philosophie.* Emend. by Collier.
[3] "He is wise to no purpose who is not wise for himself."
[4] A. *feedes.*   [5] Abstemious.   [6] King's dog.

[1] Fool.   [2] Scurrility.
[3] Magistrate.   [4] Plate, dish.

I make the king merry with pleasant ur-
    banity,
Whom I never abused to any man's in-
    jury.   50
CARISOPHUS. By Cock,[1] sir, yet in the
    court you do best thrive —
For you get more in one day than I do in
    five.
ARISTIPPUS. Why, man, in the court do
    you not see
Rewards given for virtue to every degree?
To reward the unworthy — that world is
    done.   55
The court is changed. A good thread hath
    been spun
Of dog's wool heretofore; and why? be-
    cause it was liked,
And not for that it was best trimmed and
    picked.
But now men's ears are finer, such gross
    toys are not set by;
Therefore to a trimmer kind of mirth my-
    self I apply: 60
Wherein, though I please, it cometh not of
    my desert
But of the king's favour.
CARISOPHUS. It may so be. Yet in your
    prosperity
Despise not an old courtier. Carisophus is
    he
Which hath long time fed Dionysius' hu-
    mour.   65
Diligently to please, still at hand, there
    was never rumour
Spread in this town of any small thing but I
Brought it to the king in post by and by.[2]
Yet now I crave your friendship; which if
    I may attain,
Most sure and unfeigned friendship I prom-
    ise you again.   70
So we two, link'd in friendship, brother and
    brother,
Full well in the court may help one an-
    other.
ARISTIPPUS. By'r Lady, Carisophus,
    though you know not philosophy,
Yet surely you are a better courtier than I!
And yet I not so evil a courtier that will
    seem to despise   75
Such an old courtier as you, so expert, and
    so wise.

But where-as you crave mine, and offer
    your friendship so willingly,
With heart I give you thanks for this your
    great courtesy,
Assuring of friendship both with tooth and
    nail,
Whiles life lasteth, never to fail.   80
CARISOPHUS. A thousand thanks I give
    you. O friend Aristippus!
ARISTIPPUS. O friend Carisophus!
CARISOPHUS. How joyful am I, sith I
    have to friend Aristippus now!
ARISTIPPUS. None so glad of Carisophus'
    friendship as I, I make God a vow!
I speak as I think, believe me.   85
CARISOPHUS. Sith we are now so friendly
    joined, it seemeth to me
That one of us help each other in every
    degree.
Prefer you my cause when you are in
    presence;
To further your matters to the king let me
    alone in your absence.
ARISTIPPUS. Friend Carisophus, this shall
    be done as you would wish.   90
But, I pray you, tell me thus much by the
    way —
Whither now from this place will you take
    your journey?
CARISOPHUS. I will not dissemble — that
    were against friendship:
I go into the city some knaves to nip [1]
For talk, with their goods to increase the
    king's treasure.   95
In such kind of service I set my chief pleas-
    ure.
Farewell, friend Aristippus, now, for a
    time.   *Exit.*
ARISTIPPUS. Adieu, friend Carisophus.
    In good faith now,
Of force I must laugh at this solemn vow!
Is Aristippus link'd in friendship with
    Carisophus?   100
Quid cum tanto asino talis philosophus? [2]
They say *Morum similitudo consuit* [3] *ami-
    citias;* [4]
Then how can this friendship between us
    two come to pass?

[1] Arrest (*N.E.D.*).
[2] "What has such a philosopher in common with
such an ass."
[3] A. *consultat.*
[4] "Likeness of character cements friendships."

[1] God.   [2] At once, immediately.

We are as like in condition as Jack
　Fletcher [1] and his bolt:
I brought up in learning, but he is a very
　dolt 105
As touching good letters; but otherwise
　such a crafty knave
If you seek a whole region his like you
　cannot have;
A villain for his life; a varlet dyed in grain;
You lose money by him if you sell him for
　one knave, for he serves for twain;
A flattering parasite; a sycophant also; 110
A common accuser of men; to the good an
　open foe.
Of half a word he can make a legend of lies,
Which he will avouch with such tragical
　cries
As though all were true that comes out of
　his mouth,
Where, indeed, to be hanged by and by, 115
He cannot tell one tale but twice he must
　lie.
He spareth no man's life to get the king's
　favour;
In which kind of service he hath got such a
　savour
That he will never leave. Methink then
　that I
Have done very wisely to join in friendship
　with him, lest perhaps I 120
Coming in his way might be nipp'd; for
　such knaves in presence
We see oft times put honest men to silence.
Yet I have played with his beard [2] in
　knitting this knot;
I promis'd friendship; but you love few
　words — I spake it, but I meant it
　not.
Who marks this friendship between us
　two 125
Shall judge of the worldly friendship with-
　out any more ado;
It may be a right pattern [3] thereof. But
　true friendship, indeed,
Of nought but of virtue doth truly proceed.
But why do I now enter into philosophy
Which do profess the fine kind of cour-
　tesy? 130

I will hence to the court with all haste I
　may.
I think the king be stirring, it is now bright
　day.
To wait at a pinch still in sight I mean;
For, wot ye what? a new broom sweeps
　clean.[1]
As to high honour I mind not to climb, 135
So I mean in the court to lose no time.
Wherein, happy man be his dole,[2] I trust
　that I
Shall not speed worst, and that very
　quickly. *Exit.*

*Here entereth Damon and Pithias like
　mariners.*

[DAMON.] O Neptune, immortal be thy
　praise,
For that so safe from Greece we have
　pass'd the seas 140
To this noble city Syracuse, where we
The ancient reign of the Romans may
　see,
Whose force Greece also heretofore hath
　known,
Whose virtue the shrill trump of fame so
　far hath blown.
PITHIAS. My Damon, of right high praise
　we ought to give 145
To Neptune, and all the gods, that we
　safely did arrive.
The seas, I think, with contrary winds
　never raged so!
I am even yet so seasick that I faint as I go.
Therefore let us get some lodging quickly.
But where is Stephano? 150

Here entereth Stephano [laden with baggage].

[STEPHANO.] Not far hence! A pox take
　these mariner-knaves!
Not one would help me to carry this stuff.
　Such drunken slaves
I think be accursed of the gods' own
　mouths!
DAMON. Stephano, leave thy raging, and
　let us enter Syracuse.
We will provide lodging, and thou shalt be
　eased of thy burden by and by. 155

---

[1] A fletcher is one who makes arrows. Possibly
the allusion is to some ballad; cf. Twyne's *Patterne
of Painfull Adventures,* 1576: "No more like than
Jack Fletcher and his bolt."
[2] Deluded him.　　　[3] A. *patron.* Cf. l. 1566.

[1] An old proverb.
[2] Lot in life (a proverbial exclamation equivalent
to "Good luck!").

STEPHANO.   Good master, make haste! for
I tell you plain,
This heavy burden puts poor Stephano to
much pain.
PITHIAS.   Come on thy ways.   Thou shalt
be eased, and that anon.
*Exit [Pithias, followed by Damon and
Stephano].*

Here entereth Carisophus.

[CARISOPHUS].   It is a true saying, that oft
hath been spoken:
"The pitcher goeth so long to the water,
that it [1] cometh home broken." 160
My own proof this hath taught me; for
truly, sith I
In the city have used to walk very
slyly,
Not with one can I meet that will in talk
join with me.
And to creep into men's bosoms [2] some
talk for to snatch,
By [3] which into one trip [4] or other I might
trimly them catch,   165
And so accuse them — now not with one
can I meet
That will join in talk with me.   I am
shunn'd like a devil in the street!
My credit is crack'd where I am known.
But yet [5] I hear say
Certain strangers are arrived.   They were
a good prey.
If happily I might meet with them, I fear
not, I,   170
But in talk I should trip them, and that
very finely.
Which thing, I assure you, I do for mine
own gain, —
Or else I would not plod thus up and down,
I tell you plain.
Well, I will for a while to the court to
see
What Aristippus doth.   I would be loth in
favour he should overrun me.   175
He is a subtle child!   He flattereth so
finely that I fear me
He will lick all [6] the fat from my lips, and
so outwear [7] me.

1 A. *he;* modernized by Dodsley.
2 Confidence.   3 H. *But.*
4 Mistake.   5 H. omits.
6 H. omits.   7 Consume.   A. *outwery.*

Therefore I will not be long absent, but at
hand,
That all his fine drifts I may understand.
Exit.

Here entereth Will and Jack.

[WILL.]   I wonder what my master Aristip-
pus means now-a-days   180
That he leaveth philosophy and seeks to
please
King Dionysius with such merry toys.
In Dionysius' court now he only joys,
As trim a courtier as the best,
Ready to answer, quick in taunts, pleasant
to jest,   185
A lusty companion to devise with fine
dames,
Whose humour to feed his wily wit he
frames.
JACK.   By Cock, as you say, your master
is a minion! [1]
A foul coil he keeps in this court!   Aris-
tippus alone
Now rules the roast [2] with his pleasant de-
vices,   190
That I fear he will put out of conceit my
master Carisophus.
WILL.   Fear not that, Jack; for, like
brother and brother,
They are knit in true friendship the one
with the other.
They are fellows, you know, and honest
men both;
Therefore the one to hinder the other they
will be loth.   195
JACK.   Yea, but I have heard say there is
falsehood in fellowship.
In the court sometimes one gives another
finely the slip;
Which when it is spied, it is laugh'd out
with a scoff,
And with sporting and playing quickly [3]
shaken off.
In which kind of toying thy master hath
such a grace   200
That he will never blush; he hath a wooden
face.
But, Will, my master hath bees in his head;
If he find me here prating, I am but dead.

1 A favorite with a sovereign.
2 Has the mastery.   3 A. *quietly.*

He is still trotting in the city; there is
    somewhat in the wind;
His looks bewrays his inward troubled
    mind. 205
Therefore I will be packing to the court by
    and by.
If he be once angry, Jack shall cry, "woe
    the pie!"
WILL. By'r Lady, if I tarry long here, of
    the same sauce shall I taste!
For my master sent me on an errand, and
    bad me make haste.
Therefore we will depart together. 210
                    Exeunt.

Here entereth Stephano.

[STEPHANO.] Ofttimes I have heard, be-
    fore I came hither,
That "no man can serve two masters to-
    gether";
A sentence so true, as most men do take it,
At any time false that no man can make it.
And yet, by their leave that first have it
    spoken, 215
How that may prove false, even here I will
    open:
For I, Stephano, lo, so named by my
    father,
At this time serve two masters together,
And love them alike; the one and the other
I duly obey — I can do no other. 220
A bondman I am, so nature hath wrought
    me;
One Damon of Greece, a gentleman,
    bought me;
To him I stand bound; yet serve I another,
Whom Damon, my master, loves as his
    own brother,
A gentleman, too, and Pithias he is
    named, 225
Fraught with virtue, whom vice never de-
    famed.
These two, since at school they fell ac-
    quainted,
In mutual friendship at no time have
    fainted,
But loved so kindly and friendly each other
As though they were brothers by father
    and mother. 230
Pythagoras' learning these two have em-
    braced,

Which both are in virtue so narrowly laced
That all their whole doings do fall to this
    issue —
To have no respect but only to virtue.
All one in effect, all one in their going, 235
All one in their study, all one in their doing,
These gentlemen both, being of one condi-
    tion,
Both alike of my service have all the frui-
    tion.
Pithias is joyful if Damon be pleased;
If Pithias be [1] served, then Damon is
    eased. 240
Serve one, serve both (so near [2]), who
    would win them.
I think they have but one heart between
    them!
In travelling countries we three have con-
    trived [3]
Full many a year; and this day arrived
At Syracuse in Sicilia, that ancient town,
Where my masters are lodged; and I up
    and down 246
Go seeking to learn what news here are
    walking,
To hark of what things the people are
    talking.
I like not this soil; for as I go plodding
I mark there two, there three, their heads
    always nodding, 250
In close secret wise still whispering to-
    gether.
If I ask any question, no man doth answer,
But shaking their heads they go their ways
    speaking.
I mark how with tears their wet eyes are
    leaking.
Some strangeness there is that breedeth
    this musing! 255
Well, I will to my masters and tell of their
    using,
That they may learn, and walk wisely to-
    gether.
I fear we shall curse the time we came
    hither. *Exit.*

Here entereth Aristippus and Will.

[ARISTIPPUS.] Will, didst thou hear the
    ladies so talk of me?

---

[1] H. *is.*   [2] I.e. So near are they. — *Hazlitt.*
[3] Spent the time.

What aileth them? From their nips [1] shall
    I never be free? 260
WILL. Good faith, sir, all the ladies in the
    court do plainly report
That without mention of them you can
    make no sport.
They are your plain-song to sing descant
    upon; [2]
If they were not, your mirth were gone.
Therefore, master, jest no more with
    women in any wise. 265
If you do, by Cock, you are like to know
    the price!
ARISTIPPUS. By'r Lady, Will, this is good
    counsel! Plainly to jest
Of women, proof hath taught me, it is not
    best. [3]
I will change my copy; howbeit I care not a
    quinch;
I know the gall'd horse will soonest winch.
But learn thou secretly what [4] privily they
    talk 271
Of me in the court; among them slyly walk,
And bring me true news thereof.
WILL. I will, sir master, thereof have no
    doubt; for I,
Where they talk of you, will inform you
    perfectly. 275
ARISTIPPUS. Do so, my boy. If thou
    bring it finely to pass,
For thy good service thou shalt go in thine
    old coat at Christmas.   *Exeunt.*

Enter Damon, Pithias, Stephano.

[DAMON.] Stephano, is all this true that
    thou hast told me?
STEPHANO. Sir, for lies hitherto ye never
    controll'd me. [5]
O, that we had never set foot on this
    land, 280
Where Dionysius reigns with so bloody a
    hand!
Every day he showeth some token of cru-
    elty;
With blood he hath filled all the streets in
    the city;

I tremble to hear the people's murmuring;
I lament to see his most cruel dealing; 285
I think there is no such tyrant under the sun.
O, my dear masters, this morning what
    hath he done!
DAMON. What is that? tell us quickly.
STEPHANO. As I this morning pass'd in
    the street,
With a woful man (going to his death) did I
    meet. 290
Many people followed; and I of one se-
    cretly
Asked the cause why he was condemned to
    die;
[Who] [1] whispered in mine ear: "Nought
    hath he done but thus:
In his sleep he dreamed he had killed Di-
    onysius;
Which dream told abroad, was brought to
    the king in post; 295
By whom, condemned for suspicion, his
    life he hath lost."
Marcia was his name, as the people said.
PITHIAS. My dear friend Damon, I blame
    not Stephano
For wishing we had not come hither, seeing
    it is so
That for so small cause such cruel death
    doth ensue. 300
DAMON. My Pithias, where tyrants reign
    such cases are not new,
Which fearing their own state for great
    cruelty,
To sit fast, as they think, do execute
    speedily
All such as any light suspicion have
    tainted.
STEPHANO (*aside*). With such quick carv-
    ers I list not be acquainted! 305
DAMON. So are they never in quiet, but in
    suspicion still;
When one is made away, they take occa-
    sion another to kill;
Ever in fear, having no trusty friend, void
    of all peoples' love,
And in their own conscience a continual
    hell they prove.
PITHIAS. As things by their contraries are
    always best proved, 310
How happy then are merciful princes, of
    their people beloved!

---

[1] Sarcasms.
[2] They are your simple musical theme to which
you extemporise an accompaniment (of wit, or
censorious criticism).
[3] H. *proof hath taught me is not the best.*
[4] H. *how.*   [5] Took me to task.
[1] Added in H.

Having sure friends everywhere, no fear
    doth touch them;
They may safely spend the day pleasantly,
    at night *securè dormiunt in utranque*
    aurem.[1]
O, my Damon, if choice were offered me I
    would choose to be Pithias
As I am — Damon's friend — rather than
    to be King Dionysius. 315
STEPHANO. And good cause why: for you
    are entirely beloved of one,
And, as far as I hear, Dionysius is beloved
    of none.
DAMON. That state is most miserable!
    Thrice happy are we,
Whom true love hath joined in perfect
    amity;
Which amity first sprung — without
    vaunting be it spoken, that is
    true — 320
Of likeness of manners, took root by com-
    pany, and now is conserved by
    virtue;
Which virtue always, though [2] worldly
    things do not frame,
Yet doth she achieve to her followers im-
    mortal fame.
Whereof if men were careful, for virtue's
    sake only
They would honour friendship, and not for
    commodity. 325
But such as for profit in friendship do link,
When storms come they slide away sooner
    than a man will think.
My Pithias, the sum of my talk falls to this
    issue —
To prove no friendship is sure but that
    which is grounded on virtue.
PITHIAS. My Damon, of this thing there
    needs no proof to me. 330
The gods forbid but that Pithias with
    Damon in all things should agree.
For why is it said, *Amicus alter ipse*,[3]
But that true friends should be two in
    body, but one in mind,
As it were, one [4] transformed into another?
    Which, against kind
Though it seem, yet, in good faith, when I
    am alone 335

I forget I am Pithias, methink I am
    Damon.
STEPHANO. That could I never do, to for-
    get myself! Full well I know,
Wheresoever I go, that I am *pauper* [1]
    Stephano!
But I pray you, sir, for all your philos-
    ophy,
See that in this court you walk very
    wisely. 340
You are but newly come hither; being
    strangers, ye know,
Many eyes are bent on you in the streets as
    ye go.
Many spies are abroad; you can not be too
    circumspect.
DAMON. Stephano, because thou art care-
    ful of me, thy master, I do thee
    praise.
Yet think this for a surety: no state to dis-
    please 345
By talk or otherwise my friend and I
    intend; we will here
As men that come to see the soil and man-
    ners of all men of every degree.
Pythagoras said that this world was like a
    stage,
Whereon many play their parts; the
    lookers-on, the sage
Philosophers are, saith he, whose part is to
    learn 350
The manners of all nations, and the good
    from the bad to discern.
STEPHANO. Good faith, sir, concerning
    the people — they are not gay;
And, as far as I see, they be mummers,[2] for
    nought they say
For the most part, whatsoever you ask
    them.
The soil is such that to live here I cannot
    like. 355
DAMON. Thou speakest according to thy
    learning; but I say,
Omne solum forti [3] *patria*, a wise man may
    live everywhere.
Therefore, my dear friend Pithias,
Let us view this town in every place,
And then consider the people's manners
    also. 360

---

[1] "They sleep securely on either ear." Cf.
Terence, *Self Tormenter*, 342.
[2] A. *through*.
[3] "A friend is a second self." [4] Omitted by H.

[1] Poor.
[2] Actors in dumb-shows, or in mummings.
[3] A. *Omnis solum fortis*. "Every soil is a father-
land to a brave man.".

PITHIAS.   As you will, my Damon.   But
    how say you, Stephano?
Is it not best, ere we go further, to take
    some repast?
STEPHANO.   In faith, I like well [1] this ques-
    tion, sir!   For all your haste,
To eat somewhat I pray you think it no folly.
It is high dinner time, I know by my
    belly.   365
DAMON.   Then let us to our lodging de-
    part.   When dinner is done
We will view this city as we have begun.
                                        Exeant.

Here entereth Carisophus.

[CARISOPHUS.]   Once again in hope of good
    wind I hoise up my sail;
I go into the city to find some prey for
    mine avail.
I hunger while I may see these strangers
    that lately   370
Arrived.   I were safe if once I might meet
    them happily.
Let them bark that lust at this kind of gain,
He is a fool that for his profit will not take
    pain!
Though it be joined with other men's hurt,
    I care not at all.
For profit I will accuse any man, hap what
    shall.   375
But soft, sirs; I pray you hush!   What are
    they that comes here?
By their apparel and countenance some
    strangers they appear.
I will shroud myself secretly even here for a
    while,
To hear all their talk, that I may them
    beguile.   [*He stands aside.*]

Here entereth Damon and Stephano.

[STEPHANO.]   A short horse soon curried!
    My belly waxeth thinner;   380
I am as hungry now as when I went to
    dinner.
Your philosophical diet is so fine and small
That you may eat your dinner and supper
    at once, and not surfeit at all.
DAMON.   Stephano, much meat breeds
    heaviness; thin diet makes thee
    light.

[1] Omitted by H.

STEPHANO.   I may be lighter thereby, but
    I shall never run the faster.   385
DAMON.   I have had sufficiently; discourse
    of amity,
Which I had at dinner with Pithias, and
    his pleasant company
Hath fully satisfied me.   It doth me good
    to feed mine eyes on him.
STEPHANO.   Course or discourse, your
    course is very coarse.   For all your
    talk,
You had but one bare course, and that was
    pick, rise, and walk.   390
And surely, for all your talk of philosophy,
I never heard that a man with words could
    fill his belly.
Feed your eyes, quoth you? the reason
    from my wisdom swerveth;
I stared on you both — and yet my belly
    starveth!
DAMON.   Ah, Stephano, small diet maketh
    a fine memory.   395
STEPHANO.   I care not for your crafty
    sophistry.
You two are fine; let me be fed like a gross
    knave still.
I pray you licence me for a while to have
    my will
At home to tarry whiles you take view of
    this city.
To find some odd victuals in a corner I am
    very witty.   400
DAMON.   At your pleasure, sir; I will wait
    on myself this day.
Yet attend upon Pithias, which for a
    purpose tarrieth at home;
So doing, you wait upon me also.
STEPHANO.   With wings on my feet I go.
                                        [*Exit.*
DAMON.   Not in vain the poet saith, *Nat-
    uram furcâ expellas, tamen usque re-
    curret;* [1]   405
For train up a bondman never to so good a
    behaviour,
Yet in some point of servility he will
    savour:
As this Stephano, trusty to me his master,
    loving and kind,
Yet touching his belly a very bondman I
    him find.

[1] "Drive nature out with a pitchfork, still ever
will she return."   Horace, *Epistles*, I. 10. 24.

He is to be borne withal,[1] being so just and
true. 410
I assure you, I would not change him for no
new.
But methinks this is a pleasant city.
The seat is good,[2] and yet not strong; and
that is great pity.

CARISOPHUS (*aside*). I am safe; he is mine
own!

DAMON. The air subtle and fine; the
people should be witty 415
That dwell under this climate in so pure a
region.
A trimmer plat I have not seen in my
peregrination.
Nothing misliketh me in this country
But that I hear such muttering of cruelty.
Fame reporteth strange things of Diony-
sius. 420
But kings' matters, passing our reach, per-
tain not to us.

CARISOPHUS [*advancing*]. Dionysius, quoth
you? Since the world began,
In Sicilia never reigned so cruel a man!
A despiteful tyrant to all men! I marvel, I,
That none makes him away, and that suddenly. 425

DAMON. My friend, the gods forbid so
cruel a thing
That any man should lift up his sword
against the king,
Or seek other means by death him to pre-
vent,
Whom to rule on earth the mighty gods
have sent.
But, my friend, leave off this talk of King
Dionysius. 430

CARISOPHUS. Why, sir? He cannot hear
us.

DAMON. What, then? *An nescis longas
regibus esse manus?* [3]
It is no safe talking of them that strikes
afar off.
But, leaving kings' matters, I pray you
show me this courtesy,
To describe in few words the state of this
city. 435
A traveller I am, desirous to know

The state of each country wherever I go —
Not to the hurt of any state, but to get ex-
perience thereby.
It is not for nought that the poet doth cry,
*Dic mihi musa virum, captæ post tempore
Troyæ,* 440
Qui mores hominum multorum vidit et urbes.[1]
In which verses, as some writers do scan,
The poet describeth a perfect wise man; [2]
Even so I, being a stranger addicted to
philosophy,
To see the state of countries myself I ap-
ply. 445

CARISOPHUS. Sir, I like this intent. But
may I ask your name without
scorn?

DAMON. My name is Damon, well known
in my country, a gentleman born.

CARISOPHUS. You do wisely to search the
state of each country
To bear intelligence thereof whither you
lust. [*Aside.*] He is a spy.
Sir, I pray you have patience awhile, for I
have to do hereby. 450
View this weak part of this city as you
stand, and I very quickly
Will return to you again; and then will I
show
The state of all this country, and of the
court also. *Exit.*

DAMON. I thank you for your courtesy.
This chanceth well, that I
Met with this gentleman so happily; 455
Which, as it seemeth, misliketh something,
Else he would not talk so boldly of the
king,
And that to a stranger. But lo, where he
comes in haste.

Here entereth Carisophus and Snap.

[CARISOPHUS.] This is he, fellow Snap.
Snap him up! Away with him!

SNAP. Good fellow, thou must go with me
to the court. 460

DAMON. To the court, sir! and why?

CARISOPHUS. Well, we will dispute that

---

[1] With.   [2] The situation is good.
[3] "Know you not that kings have long hands?"
Ovid, *Heroides*, xvi [xvii], 166.

[1] A. prints the second line: *Multorum hominum
mores qui vidit et urbis.* Corrected by Collier.
"Tell me, O Muse, of the man, who, after the capture
of Troy, saw the manners and cities of many men."
From the opening lines of the Odyssey.
[2] Scholars thought that in Odysseus Homer was
attempting to portray the virtues of the ideal man
in private life.

before the king. Away with him
    quickly!
DAMON. Is this the courtesy you prom-
    ised me, and that very lately?
CARISOPHUS. Away with him, I say!
DAMON. Use no violence; I will go with
    you quietly.   465

                            Exeunt omnes

Here entereth Aristippus.

[ARISTIPPUS.] Ah, sirrah, by'r Lady,
    Aristippus likes Dionysius' court
    very well,
Which in passing joys and pleasures doth
    excel,
Where he hath *dapsiles cœnas, geniales
    lectos, et auro
Fulgentem tyranni zonam.*[1]
I have plied the harvest, and stroke when
    the iron was hot.   470
When I spied my time, I was not squeam-
    ish to crave, God wot!
But with some pleasant toy[2] I crept into
    the king's bosom,
For which Dionysius gave me *Auri talen-
    tum magnum*[3] —
A large reward for so simple services.
What, then? the king's praise standeth
    chiefly in bountifulness;   475
Which thing, though I told the king very
    pleasantly,
Yet can I prove it by good writers of great
    antiquity.
But that shall not need at this time, since
    that I have abundantly;
When I lack hereafter I will use this point
    of philosophy.
But now, whereas I have felt the king's
    liberality,   480
As princely as it came I will spend it as
    regally.
Money is current, men say, and current
    comes of *currendo;*
Then will I make money run, as his nature
    requireth, I trow.
For what becomes a philosopher best
But to despise money above the rest?   485

---

[1] A. *Dapsiæ cœnas, gemalis lectes, et auro. Ful-
gentii turgmani zoaam.* Emended in Hazlitt, and
translated: "Plentiful suppers, luxurious couches,
and the king's purse full of gold at command."
[2] A. *tyoe.*   [3] "A great talent of gold." A. *aure.*

And yet not so despise it but to have in
    store
Enough to serve his own turn, and some-
    what more.
With sundry sports and taunts yesternight
    I delighted the king,
That with his loud laughter the whole court
    did ring —
And I thought he laugh'd not merrier than
    I when I got this money!   490
But, mumbudget![1] for Carisophus I espy
In haste to come hither. I must handle the
    knave finely.
O Carisophus! my dearest friend! my
    trusty companion!
What news with you? Where have you
    been so long?

Here entereth Carisophus.

[CARISOPHUS.] My best beloved friend
    Aristippus, I am come at last.   495
I have not spent all my time in waste;
I have got a prey, and that a good one, I
    trow.
ARISTIPPUS. What prey is that? fain
    would I know.
CARISOPHUS. Such a crafty spy I have
    caught, I dare say,
As never was in Sicilia before this day! 500
Such a one as viewed every weak place in
    the city,
Surviewed the haven, and each bulwark; in
    talk very witty —
And yet by some words himself he did
    bewray.
ARISTIPPUS. I think so in good faith — as
    you did handle him.
CARISOPHUS. I handled him clerkly.[2] I
    joined in talk with him courteously;
But when we were entered, I let him speak
    his will; and I   506
Suck'd out thus much of his words, that I
    made him say plainly
He was come hither to know the state of
    the city;
And not only this, but that he would under-
    stand
The state of Dionysius' court and of the
    whole land.   510
Which words when I heard, I desired him
    to stay

---

[1] Mum's the word!   [2] Artfully.

Till I had done a little business of the way,
Promising him to return again quickly; and
    so did convey
Myself to the court for Snap the tipstaff;[1]
    which came and upsnatched him,
Brought him to the court, and in the
    porter's lodge dispatched him. 515
After I ran to Dionysius as fast as I could,
And bewrayed this matter to him which I
    have you told.
Which thing when he heard, being very
    merry before,
He suddenly fell in dump, and, foaming
    like a boar,
At last he swore in great rage that he
    should die   520
By the sword or the wheel, and that very
    shortly.
I am too shamefast; for my travail[2] and
    toil
I crave nothing of Dionysius but only his
    spoil.
Little hath he about him but a few moth-
    eaten crowns of gold.
Cha pouch'd[3] them up already — they are
    sure in hold.   525
And now I go into the city, to say sooth,
To see what he hath at his lodging to make
    up my mouth.[4]
ARISTIPPUS. My Carisophus, you have
    done good service. But what is the
    spy's name?
CARISOPHUS. He is called Damon, born in
    Greece, from whence lately he came.
ARISTIPPUS. By my troth, I will go see
    him, and speak with him too, if I
    may.   530
CARISOPHUS. Do so, I pray you. But yet,
    by the way,
As occasion serveth, commend my service
    to the king.
ARISTIPPUS. *Dictum sapienti sat est:*[5]
    friend Carisophus, shall I forget
    that thing?
No, I warrant you! Though I say little to
    your face,
I will lay on with my mouth[6] for you to
    Dionysius, when I am in place. 535

[*Aside.*] If I speak one word for such a
    knave, hang me!   *Exit.*
CARISOPHUS. Our fine philosopher, our
    trim learned elf,
Is gone to see as false a spy as himself!
Damon smatters[1] as well as he of crafty
    philosophy,
And can turn cat in the pan[2] very pret-
    tily;
But Carisophus hath given him such a
    mighty check   541
As, I think, in the end will break his
    neck.
What care I for that! Why would he then
    pry,
And learn the secret estate of our country
    and city?
He is but a stranger! By his fall let others
    be wise.   545
I care not who fall, so that I may rise!
As for fine Aristippus, I will keep in with
    him;
He is a shrewd fool to deal withal; he can
    swim.
And yet, by my troth, to speak my con-
    science plainly,
I will use his friendship to mine own com-
    modity.[3]   550
While Dionysius favoureth him, Aristippus
    shall be mine;
But if the king once frown on him, then
    good night, Tomalin![4]
He shall be as strange[5] as though I never
    saw him before.
But I tarry too long; I will prate no more.
Jack, come away!   555
JACK. At hand, sir.
CARISOPHUS. At Damon's lodging if that
    you see
Any stir to arise, be still at hand by
    me;
Rather than I will lose the spoil I will
    blade[6] it out.
        [*Exeunt Carisophus and Jack.*]

---

[1] Constable, bailiff.
[2] Labor.   [3] Pursed.
[4] Provision (especially court-provision).
[5] "A word to the wise is sufficient."
[6] A. *I wyll lay one month.* Emend. by Collier.

[1] Talks superficially.
[2] A proverbial expression meaning "to reverse the order of things so dexterously as to make them appear the very opposite of what they really are." (*N.E.D.*)
[3] Profit, advantage.
[4] Hazlitt cites this phrase in his *Proverbs.*
[5] As a stranger to me.
[6] Fight the matter out with my sword.

Here entereth Pithias and Stephano.

[PITHIAS.] What strange news are these!
 Ah, my Stephano,   560
Is my Damon in prison, as the voice doth
 go?
STEPHANO. It is true. O cruel hap! He
 is taken for a spy,
And, as they say, by Dionysius' own
 mouth condemned to die.
PITHIAS. To die! Alas! for what cause?
STEPHANO. A sycophant falsely accused
 him; other cause there is none. 565
But,[1] O Jupiter, of all wrongs the re-
 venger,
Seest thou this unjustice, and wilt thou
 stay any longer
From heaven to send down thy hot con-
 suming fire
To destroy the workers of wrong, which
 provoke thy just ire?
Alas, Master Pithias, what shall we do, 570
Being in a strange country, void of friends
 and acquaintance too?
Ah, poor Stephano, hast thou lived to see
 this day,
To see thy true master unjustly made
 away?
PITHIAS. Stephano, seeing the matter is
 come to this extremity,
Let us make virtue our friend of mere ne-
 cessity.   575
Run thou to the court, and understand
 secretly
As much as thou canst of Damon's cause;
 and I
Will make some means to entreat Aristippus.
He can do much, as I hear, with King Dionysius.
STEPHANO. I am gone, sir. Ah, I would
 to God my travail and pain   580
Might restore my master to his liberty
 again!
PITHIAS. Ah, woful Pithias, sith now I am
 alone
What way shall I first begin to make my
 moan?
What words shall I find apt for my complaint?
Damon, my friend, my joy, my life, is
 in peril! Of force I must now faint.

[1] A. *That.* Silently emended in Hazlitt.

But, O music, as in joyful times [1] thy
 merry notes I did borrow,   586
So now lend me thy yearnful tunes to utter
 my sorrow.

Here Pithias sings, and the regals [2] play.

Awake, ye woful wights
 That long have wept in woe!
Resign to me your plaints and tears,
 My hapless hap to show.
My woe no tongue can tell,
 Ne [3] pen can well descry.
  O, what a death is this to hear,
  Damon my friend must die!   595

The loss of worldly wealth
 Man's wisdom may restore;
And physic hath provided too
 A salve for every sore:
But my true friend once lost,
 No art can well supply.
  Then, what a death is this to hear,
  Damon my friend must die!   603

My mouth, refuse the food
 That should my limbs sustain.
Let sorrow sink into my breast
 And ransack every vein.
You [4] Furies, all at once
 On me your torments try.
  Why should I live, since that I hear
  Damon my friend must [5] die?   611

Gripe me, you greedy grief,
 And present pangs of death!
You sisters three with cruel hands,
 With speed now [6] stop my breath!
Shrine me in clay alive.
 Some good man stop mine eye.
  O death, come now, seeing I hear
  Damon my friend must die.   619

He speaketh this after the song.

In vain I call for death, which heareth not
 my complaint.
But what wisdom is this, in such extremity
 to faint?

[1] A. *tunes.* Emend. by Collier.
[2] Small portable organs.
[3] H. *No.*   [4] H. *Ye.*   [5] A. *should.*
[6] H. alters to *come.* At this point I cease to note
the errors in Hazlitt's text, although these errors
become more numerous and serious.

Multum juva[t] in re malâ annimus bonus.[1]
I will to the court myself to make friends,
    and that presently.
I will never forsake my friend in time of
    misery.
But do I see Stephano amazed hither to
    run? 625

Here entereth Stephano.

[STEPHANO.] O Pithias! Pithias! we are all
    undone!
Mine own ears have sucked in mine own
    sorrow!
I heard Dionysius swear that Damon
    should die to-morrow.
PITHIAS. How camest thou so near the
    presence of the king
That thou mightest hear Dionysius speak
    this thing? 630
STEPHANO. By friendship I gat into the
    court, where in great audience
I heard Dionysius with his own mouth give
    this cruel sentence
By these express words: that Damon, the
    Greek, that crafty spy,
Without further judgment to-morrow
    should die.
Believe me, Pithias, with these ears I heard
    it myself. 635
PITHIAS. Then how near is my death also!
    Ah, woe is me!
Ah my Damon, another myself, shall I
    forego thee?
STEPHANO. Sir, there is no time of lament-
    ing now. It behoveth us
To make means to them which can do
    much with Dionysius,
That he be not made away ere his cause be
    fully heard; for we see 640
By evil report things be made to princes
    far worse than they be.
But lo, yonder cometh Aristippus, in great
    favour with king Dionysius.
Entreat him to speak a good word to the
    king for us,
And in the mean season I will to your lodg-
    ing to see all things safe there. *Exit.*
PITHIAS. To that I agree. But let us slip
    aside his talk to hear.
                [*He stands aside.*]

[1] A. *annimas.* "A good spirit in misfortune helps
much." Cf. Plautus, *Captives*, 202.

Here entereth Aristippus.

[ARISTIPPUS.] Here is a sudden change,
    indeed! a strange metamorphosis!
This court is clean altered. Who would
    have thought this?
Dionysius, of late so pleasant and merry,
Is quite changed now into such melancholy
That nothing can please him. He walketh
    up and down 650
Fretting and chaffing; on every man he
    doth frown.
In so much that when I in pleasant words
    began to play,
So sternly he frowned on me, and knit me
    up so short,
I perceive it is no safe playing with lions
    but when it please them;
If you claw where it itch not, you shall
    disease [1] them — 655
And so perhaps get a clap. Mine own
    proof taught me this —
That it is very good to be merry and wise.
The only cause of this hurly-burly is
    Carisophus, that wicked man,
Which lately took Damon for a spy, a poor
    gentleman,
And hath incensed the king against him so
    despitefully 660
That Dionysius hath judged him to-
    morrow to die.
I have talk'd with Damon, whom though in
    words I found very witty,
Yet was he more curious [2] than wise in
    viewing this city.
But truly, for aught I can learn, there is no
    cause why
So suddenly and cruelly he should be con-
    demned to die. 665
Howsoever it be, this is the short and
    long —
I dare not gainsay the king, be it right or
    wrong.
I am sorry; and that is all I may or can do
    in this case.
Nought availeth persuasion where froward
    opinion taketh place.

[*Pithias advances.*]

PITHIAS. Sir, if humble suits you would
    not despise, 670

[1] Discomfort.   [2] Desirous of knowledge.

Then bow on me your pitiful eyes.
My name is Pithias, in Greece well known,
A perfect friend to that woful Damon,
Which now a poor captive in this court
    doth lie,
By the king's own mouth, as I hear, con-
    demned to die;   675
For whom I crave your mastership's good-
    ness,
To stand his friend in this his great dis-
    tress.
Nought hath he done worthy of death; but
    very fondly,[1]
Being a stranger, he viewed this city,
For no evil practices, but to feed his
    eyes.   680
But seeing Dionysius is informed other-
    wise,
My suit is to you, when you see time and
    place,
To assuage the king's anger, and to pur-
    chase his grace.
In which doing you shall not do good to one
    only,
But you shall further two, and that
    fully.   685
ARISTIPPUS. My friend, in this case I can
    do you no pleasure.
PITHIAS. Sir, you serve in the court, as
    fame doth tell.
ARISTIPPUS. I am of the court, indeed,
    but none of the Council.
PITHIAS. As I hear, none is in greater
    favour with the king than you at
    this day.
ARISTIPPUS. The more in favour, the less
    I dare say.   690
PITHIAS. It is a courtier's praise to help
    strangers in misery.
ARISTIPPUS. To help another, and hurt
    myself, it is an evil point of cour-
    tesy.
PITHIAS. You shall not hurt yourself to
    speak for the innocent.
ARISTIPPUS. He is not innocent whom the
    king judgeth nocent.
PITHIAS. Why, sir, do you think this mat-
    ter past all remedy?   695
ARISTIPPUS. So far past that Dionysius
    hath sworn Damon to-morrow shall
    die.

[1] Foolishly.

PITHIAS. This word my trembling heart
    cutteth in two.
Ah, sir, in this woful case what wist [ye] I
    best to do?
ARISTIPPUS. Best to content yourself
    when there is no remedy.
He is well relieved that foreknoweth his
    misery.   700
Yet, if any comfort be, it resteth in
    Eubulus,
The chiefest councillor about King Diony-
    sius,
Which pitieth Damon's case in this great
    extremity,
Persuading the king from all kind of cru-
    elty.
PITHIAS. The mighty gods preserve you
    for this word of comfort!   705
Taking my leave of your goodness, I will
    now resort
To Eubulus, that good councillor.
But hark! methink I hear a trumpet blow.
ARISTIPPUS. The king is at hand. Stand
    close in the prease.[1] Beware! If
    he know
You are friend to Damon, he will take you
    for a spy also.   710
Farewell; I dare not be seen with you.

Here entereth King Dionysius, Eubulus the
Councillor, and Gronno the Hangman.

DIONYSIUS. Gronno, do my command-
    ment; strike off Damon's irons by
    and by,
Then bring him forth. I myself will see
    him executed presently.[2]
GRONNO. O mighty king, your command-
    ment will I do speedily.
DIONYSIUS. Eubulus, thou hast talked in
    vain, for sure he shall die.   715
Shall I suffer my life to stand in peril of
    every spy?
EUBULUS. That he conspired against your
    person, his accuser cannot say.
He only viewed your city; and will you for
    that make him away?
DIONYSIUS. What he would have done,
    the guess is great. He minded me
    to hurt
That came so slyly to search out the secret
    estate of my court.   720

[1] Crowd, press of people.   [2] At once.

Shall I still live in fear? No, no; I will cut
    off such imps betime,
Lest that to my farther danger too high
    they climb.
EUBULUS. Yet have the mighty gods im-
    mortal fame assigned
To all worldly princes which in mercy be
    inclined.
DIONYSIUS. Let fame talk what she list,
    so I may live in safety.   725
EUBULUS. The only mean to that is to use
    mercy.
DIONYSIUS. A mild prince the people de-
    spiseth.
EUBULUS. A cruel king the people hat-
    eth.
DIONYSIUS. Let them hate me, so they
    fear me.
EUBULUS. That is not the way to live in
    safety.   730
DIONYSIUS. My sword and power shall
    purchase my quietness.
EUBULUS. That is sooner procured by
    mercy and gentleness.
DIONYSIUS. Dionysius ought to be feared.
EUBULUS. Better for him to be well be-
    loved.
DIONYSIUS. Fortune maketh all things
    subject to my power.   735
EUBULUS. Believe her not, she is a light
    goddess; she can laugh and low'r.
DIONYSIUS. A king's praise standeth in
    the revenging of his enemy.
EUBULUS. A greater praise to win him by
    clemency.
DIONYSIUS. To suffer the wicked live, it is
    no mercy.
EUBULUS. To kill the innocent, it is great
    cruelty.   740
DIONYSIUS. Is Damon innocent which so
    craftily undermined [1] Carisophus
To understand what he could of king
    Dionysius?
Which surviewed the haven, and each bul-
    wark in the city,
Where battery might be laid, what way
    best to approach? Shall I
Suffer such a one to live, that worketh me
    such despite?   745
No, he shall die! Then I am safe: a dead
    dog cannot bite.

[1] Questioned guilefully.

EUBULUS. But yet, O mighty [king,] [1] my
    duty bindeth me
To give such counsel as with your honour
    may best agree.
The strongest pillars of princely dignity
I find this — justice with mercy, and pru-
    dent liberality: 750
The one judgeth all things by upright
    equity,
The other rewardeth the worthy, flying
    each extremity.
As to spare those which offend maliciously,
It may be called no justice, but extreme
    injury;
So, upon suspicion of each thing not well-
    proved,   755
To put to death presently whom envious
    flattery accused,
It seemeth of tyranny. And upon what
    fickle ground all tyrants do stand,
Athens and Lacedemon can teach you, if it
    be rightly scann'd;
And not only these citizens, but who curi-
    ously seeks
The whole histories of all the world — not
    only of Romans and Greeks — 760
Shall well perceive of all tyrants the ruin-
    ous fall;
Their state uncertain, beloved of none, but
    hated of all.
Of merciful princes to set out the passing [2]
    felicity
I need not; enough of that even these days
    do testify.
They live devoid of fear, their sleeps are
    sound, they dread no enemy, 765
They are feared and loved. And why?
    they rule with justice and mercy —
Extending justice to such as wickedly from
    justice have swerved,
Mercy unto those who in opinion of simple-
    ness [3] have mercy deserved.
Of liberty nought I say, but only this
    thing:
Liberty upholdeth the state of a king, 770
Whose large bountifulness ought to fall to
    this issue —

[1] Supplied from the 1582 ed.
[2] Surpassing.
[3] A. *where opinion simplenesse;* emend. by Hazlitt,
who explains: "Simpleness, ignorance — i.e., who
have deserved mercy, having offended from not
knowing better."

To reward none but such as deserve it for
    virtue.
Which merciful justice, if you would fol-
    low, and provident liberality,
Neither the caterpillars of all courts, *et
    fruges consumere nati*,[1]
Parasites with wealth puff'd up, should not
    look so high;   775
Nor yet for this simple fact poor Damon
    should die.

DIONYSIUS. With pain mine ears have
    heard this vain talk of mercy.
I tell thee, fear and terror defendeth kings
    only.
Till he be gone, whom I suspect, how shall I
    live quietly,
Whose memory with chilling horror fills my
    breast day and night violently? 780
My dreadful dreams of him bereaves my
    rest; on bed I lie
Shaking and trembling, as one ready to
    yield his throat to Damon's sword.
This quaking dread nothing but Damon's
    blood can stay.
Better he die, than I to be tormented with
    fear alway.
He shall die, though Eubulus consent not
    thereto.   785
It is lawful for kings, as they list, all things
    to do.

*Here Gronno [assisted by Snap] bringeth
in Damon; and Pithias meeteth him by the
way.*

PITHIAS. O my Damon!
DAMON. O my Pithias! Seeing death
    must part us, farewell for ever!
PITHIAS. O Damon! O my sweet friend!
SNAP. Away from the prisoner! What a
    prease have we here!   790
GRONNO. As you commanded, O mighty
    king, we have brought Damon.
DIONYS[IUS]. Then, go to; make ready.
    I will not stir out of this place
Till I see his head stroken off before my face.
GRONNO. It shall be done, sir. [*To
    Damon.*] Because your eyes have
    made such a-do
I will knock down this your lantern, and
    shut up your shop-window too. 795

[1] "And born to consume the fruits of the earth."
Horace *Episll.*, 1. 2. 27.

DAMON. O mighty king, where-as no
    truth my innocent life can save,
But that so greedily you thirst [1] my guilt-
    less blood to have,
Albeit (even in thought) I had not ought
    against your person.[2]
Yet now I plead not for life, ne will I crave
    your pardon.
But seeing in Greece, my country, where
    well I am known,   800
I have worldly things fit for mine alliance [3]
    when I am gone,
To dispose them ere I die, if I might obtain
    leisure,
I would account it (O king) for a passing
    great pleasure —
Not to prolong my life thereby (for which I
    reckon not this),
But to set my things in a stay.[4] And
    surely I will not miss,   805
Upon the faith which all gentlemen ought
    to embrace,
To return again, at your time to appoint,
    to yield my body here in this place.
Grant me (O king) such time to despatch
    this inquiry,[5]
And I will not fail, when you appoint, even
    here my life to pay.[6]

DIONYSIUS. A pleasant request! as though
    I could trust him absent   810
Whom in no wise I cannot trust being
    present!
And yet, though I sware the contrary, do
    that I require —
Give me a pledge for thy return — and
    have thine own desire.
He is as near now as he was before!

DAMON. There is no surer nor greater
    pledge than the faith of a gentle-
    man.   815

DIONYSIUS. It was wont to be; but other-
    wise now the world doth stand.
Therefore do as I say, else presently yield
    thy neck to the sword.
If I might with my honour, I would recall
    my word.

[1] A. *thrust.*
[2] A. *Albeit (euen for thought) for ought against
your person.* Silently emended in Hazlitt as above.
[3] Kindred   [4] Put in order.
[5] A. *injurie*, which may be correct. Changed by
Hazlitt.
[6] The 1582 ed. has *to yeelde speedily*, which rhymes
with the preceding line.

PITHIAS [*advancing*]. Stand to your word,
    O king! for kings ought nothing say
But that they would perform in perfect
    deeds alway.   820
A pledge you did require when Damon his
    suit did meve;
For which with heart and stretched hands
    most humble thanks I give.
And that you may not say but Damon hath
    a friend
That loves him better than his own life,
    and will do, to his end,
Take me, O mighty king! My life I pawn
    for his.   825
Strike off my head, if Damon hap at his
    day to miss.
DIONYSIUS. What art thou that chargest
    me with my word so boldly here?
PITHIAS. I am Pithias, a Greek born, which
    hold Damon my friend full dear.
DIONYSIUS. Too dear, perhaps, to hazard
    thy life for him! What fondness [1]
    moveth thee?
PITHIAS. No fondness at all, but perfect
    amity.   830
DIONYSIUS. A mad kind of amity! Ad-
    vise thyself well: if Damon fail at
    his day,
Which shall be justly appointed, wilt thou
    die for him, to me his life to pay?
PITHIAS. Most willingly, O mighty king.
    If Damon fail, let Pithias die.
DIONYSIUS. Thou seemest to trust his
    words that pawnest thy life so
    frankly.
PITHIAS. What Damon saith, Pithias be-
    lieveth assuredly.   835
DIONYSIUS. Take heed! For life wordly
    men break promise in many things.
PITHIAS. Though wordly men do so, it
    never haps amongst friends.
DIONYSIUS. What callest thou friends?
    Are they not men? is not this true?
PITHIAS. Men they be, but such men as
    love one another only for virtue.
DIONYSIUS. For what virtue dost thou
    love this spy, this Damon?   840
PITHIAS. For that virtue which yet to you
    is unknown.
DIONYSIUS. Eubulus, what shall I do? I
    would despatch this Damon fain;

[1] Folly.

But this foolish fellow so chargeth me that
    I may not call back my word again.
EUBULUS. The reverent majesty of a king
    stands chiefly in keeping his prom-
    ise.
What you have said this whole court bear-
    eth witness.   845
Save your honour, whatsoever you do.
DIONYSIUS. For saving mine honour, I
    must forbear my will. Go to.
Pithias, seeing thou tookest me at my
    word, take Damon to thee;
For two months he is thine. [*To Gronno.*]
    Unbind him; I set him free.
Which time once expired, if he appear not
    the next day by noon,   850
Without further delay thou shalt lose thy
    life, and that full soon!
Whether he die by the way, or lie sick in
    his bed,
If he return not then, thou shalt either
    hang or lose thy head!
PITHIAS. For this, O mighty king, I yield
    immortal thanks! O joyful day!
DIONYSIUS. Gronno, take him to thee.
    Bind him; see him kept in safety:
If he escape, assure thyself for him thou
    shalt die.   856
Eubulus, let us depart to talk of this
    strange thing within.
EUBULUS. I follow.

*Exit [Eubulus following Dionysius and
his train. Gronno, Snap, Damon and
Pithias remain].*

GRONNO. Damon, thou servest the gods
    well to-day; be thou of comfort.
As for you, sir, I think you will be hanged
    in sport.   860
You heard what the king said; I must keep
    you safely.
By Cock, so I will! You shall rather hang
    than I!
Come on your way.
PITHIAS. My Damon, farewell! The
    gods have thee in keeping.
DAMON. O, my Pithias, my pledge, fare-
    well! I part from thee weeping. 865
But joyful at my day appointed I will re-
    turn again,
When I will deliver thee from all trouble
    and pain.

Stephano will I leave behind me to wait
upon thee in prison alone;
And I, whom fortune hath reserved to this
misery, will walk home.
Ah, my Pithias, my pledge, my life, my
friend, farewell! 870
PITHIAS. Farewell, my Damon!
DAMON. Loth I am to depart. Sith sobs
my trembling tongue doth stay,
O music, sound my doleful plaints when I
am gone my way. [*Exit Damon.*]
GRONNO. I am glad he is gone; I had
almost wept too. Come, Pithias.
So God help me, I am sorry for thy foolish
case. 875
Wilt thou venter thy life for a man so
fondly?
PITHIAS. It is no venter; my friend is just,
for whom I desire to die.
GRONNO. Here is a madman! I tell thee,
I have a wife whom I love well,
And if ich would die for her, chould ich
were in hell!
Wilt thou do more for a man than I would
for a woman? 880
PITHIAS. Yea, that I will.
GRONNO. Then, come on your ways; you
must to prison in haste.
I fear you will repent this folly at last.
PITHIAS. That shalt thou never see. But,
O music, as my Damon requested
thee,
Sound out thy doleful tunes in this time of
calamity. 885
Exit [*Pithias, led away by Gronno*].

*Here the regals play a mourning song, and
Damon cometh in in mariner's apparel
and Stephano with him.*

[DAMON.] Weep no more, Stephano; this
is but destiny.
Had not this happ'd, yet I know I am born
to die;
Where or in what place, the gods know alone
To whose judgment myself I commit.
Therefore leave off thy moan,
And wait upon Pithias in prison till I re-
turn again, 890
In whom my joy, my care, and life doth
only remain.
STEPHANO. O my dear master, let me go
with you; for my poor company

Shall be some small comfort in this time of
misery.
DAMON. O Stephano, hast thou been so
long with me,
And yet dost not know the force of true
amity? 895
I tell thee once again, my friend and I are
but one.
Wait upon Pithias, and think thou art
with Damon.
Whereof I may not now discourse, the
time passeth away;
The sooner I am gone, the shorter shall be
my journey.
Therefore farewell, Stephano! Commend
me to my friend Pithias, 900
Whom I trust to deliver in time out of this
woful case.
STEPHANO. Farewell, my dear master,
since your pleasure is so.
[*Exit Damon.*]
O cruel hap! O poor Stephano!
O cursed Carisophus, that first moved this
tragedy!
[*He hears a noise in Damon's lodging.*]
But what a noise is this? Is all well
within, trow ye? 905
I fear all be not well within; I will go see. —
[*He goes in.*]
Come out, you weasel! Are you seeking
eggs in Damon's chest?
Come out, I say! Wilt thou be packing?
By Cock, you were best!

[*Re-enter Stephano, pulling out Carisophus,
Jack following.*]

CARISOPHUS. How durst thou, villain, to
lay hands on me?
STEPHANO. Out, sir knave, or I will send
ye! 910
Art thou not content to accuse Damon
wrongfully,
But wilt thou rob him also, and that
openly?
CARISOPHUS. The king gave me the spoil;
to take mine own wilt thou let [1]
me?
STEPHANO. Thine own, villain! Where is
thine authority?
CARISOPHUS. I am authority of myself;
dost thou not know? 915

[1] Prevent, hinder.

STEPHANO. By'r Lady, that is somewhat!
But have you no more to show?

CARISOPHUS. What if I have not?

STEPHANO. Then for an earnest penny
take this blow. [*Strikes him.*]

I shall bombast you, you mocking knave!
Chill put pro [1] in my purse for this
time!

CARISOPHUS. Jack, give me my sword and
target. 920

JACK. I cannot come to you, master; this
knave doth me let. Hold, master.
[*Extending the sword.*]

STEPHANO [*to Jack*]. Away, Jackanapes,
else I will colpheg [2] you by and
by!

Ye slave, I will have my pennyworths of
thee therefore, if I die!

About, villain! [*He beats Carisophus.*]

CARISOPHUS. O citizens, help to defend
me! 925

STEPHANO. Nay, they will rather help to
hang thee.

CARISOPHUS. Good fellow, let us reason
this matter quietly; beat me no
more.

STEPHANO. Of this condition I will stay —
if thou swear, as thou art an honest
man,

Thou wilt say nothing to the king of this
when I am gone.

CARISOPHUS. I will say nothing — here is
my hand — as I am an honest
man. 930

STEPHANO. Then say on thy mind. I
have taken a wise oath on him, have
I not, trow ye,

To trust such a false knave upon his honesty?

As he is an honest man (quoth you!) he
may bewray all to the king,

And break his oath for this never a whit —
but, my franion,[3] I tell you this one
thing:

If you disclose this I will devise such a
way 935

That whilst thou livest thou shalt remember this day.

CARISOPHUS. You need not devise for
that, for this day is printed in my
memory!

1 ?   2 Cuff.   3 Gay fellow.

I warrant you I shall remember this beating till I die.

But seeing of courtesy you have granted
that we should talk quietly,

Methinks in calling me knave you do me
much injury. 940

STEPHANO. Why so, I pray thee heartily?

CARISOPHUS. Because I am the king's
man. Keeps the king any knaves?

STEPHANO. He should not; but what he
doth, it is evident by thee.

And, as far as I can learn or understand,

There is none better able to keep knaves in
all the land. 945

CARISOPHUS. O sir, I am a courtier; when
courtiers shall hear tell

How you have used me, they will not take
it well.

STEPHANO. Nay, all right courtiers will
ken [1] me thank. And wot you
why?

Because I handled a counterfeit courtier in
his kind so finely.

What, sir! all are not courtiers that have a
counterfeit show; 950

In a troop of honest men some knaves may
stand, ye know —

Such as by stealth creep in under the colour
of honesty,

Which sort under that cloak do all kinds of
villainy.

A right courtier is virtuous, gentle, and full
of urbanity,

Hurting no man, good to all, devoid of all
villainy; 955

But such as thou art, fountains of squirrility and vain delights;

Though you hang by the courts, you are
but flatt'ring parasites,

As well deserving the right name of courtesy

As the coward knight the true praise of
chivalry.

I could say more, but I will not, for that I
am your well-willer. 960

In faith, Carisophus, you are no courtier,
but a caterpillar,

A sycophant, a parasite, a flatterer, and a
knave!

Whether I will or no, these names you must
have;

1 Give.

How well you deserve this by your deeds it
    is known,
For that so unjustly thou hast accused
    poor Damon,   965
Whose woful case the gods help alone.
CARISOPHUS. Sir, are you his servant that
    you pity his case so?
STEPHANO. No, bum troth, goodman
    Grumb; his name is Stephano.
I am called Onaphets,[1] if needs you will
    know.
[*Aside.*] The knave beginneth to sift me;
    but I turn my name in and out, 970
Cretiso cum Cretense,[2] to make him a lout.[3]
CARISOPHUS. What mumble you with
    yourself, Master Onaphets?
STEPHANO. I am reckoning with myself
    how I may pay my debts.
CARISOPHUS. You have paid me more
    than you did owe me!
STEPHANO. Nay, upon a farther reckon-
    ing, I will pay you more, if I know
Either you talk of that is done, or by your
    sycophantical envy   976
You prick forth Dionysius the sooner that
    Damon may die.
I will so pay thee that thy bones shall
    rattle in thy skin.
Remember what I have said; Onaphets is
    my name.   *Exit.*
CARISOPHUS. The sturdy knave is gone;
    the devil him take!   980
He hath made my head, shoulders, arms,
    sides, and all to ache.
Thou whoreson villain boy, why didst thou
    wait no better?
As he paid me, so will I not die thy debtor.
        [*Strikes him.*]
JACK. Master, why do you fight with me?
    I am not your match, you see.
You durst not fight with him that is gone;
    and will you wreak your anger on
    me?   985
CARISOPHUS. Thou villain, by thee I have
    lost mine honour, —
Beaten with a cudgel like a slave, a vaca-
    bone,[4] or a lazy lubber,
And not given one blow again! Hast thou
    handled me well?

[1] "Stephano" spelled backwards.
[2] "I lie with the Cretan." The Cretans were
famous as liars.
[3] Fool.   [4] Vagabond.

JACK. Master, I handled you not, but who
    did handle you very handsomely,
    you can tell.
CARISOPHUS. Handsomely, thou crack-
    rope?[1]   990
JACK. Yea, sir, very handsomely! I
    hold[2] you a groat,
He handled you so handsomely that he left
    not one mote in your coat.
CARISOPHUS. O, I had firk'd him trimly,
    thou villain, if thou hadst given me
    my sword.
JACK. It is better as it is, master, believe
    me, at a word.
If he had seen your weapon he would have
    been fiercer,   995
And so perhaps beat you worse. I speak
    it with my heart,
You were never yet at the dealing of fence-
    blows[3] but you had four away for
    your part.
It is but your luck. You are man good
    enough;
But the Welsh Onaphets was a vengeance-
    knave, and rough!
Master, you were best go home and rest in
    your bed;   1000
Methinks your cap waxeth too little for
    your head.
CARISOPHUS. What! doth my head swell?
JACK. Yea, as big as a codshead, and
    bleeds too.
CARISOPHUS. I am ashamed to show my
    face with this hue.
JACK. No shame at all; men have been
    beaten far better than you.   1005
CARISOPHUS. I must go to the chirur-
    geon's. What shall I say when I
    am a-dressing?
JACK. You may say truly you met with a
    knave's blessing.[4]   *Exeunt.*

        Here entereth Aristippus.

[ARISTIPPUS.] By mine own experience I
    prove true that many men tell:
To live in court not beloved, better be in
    hell.
What crying out, what cursing is there
    within of Carisophus,   1010

[1] Rascal destined for the gallows.   [2] Wager.
[3] Fencing.   [4] A cant term for a beating.

Because he accused Damon to King Dionysius!

Even now he came whining and crying into the court for the nonce,

Showing that one Onaphets had broke his knave's sconce.

Which strange name, when they heard, every man laugh'd heartily,

And I by myself scann'd his name secretly; 1015

For well I knew it was some mad-headed child

That invented this name that the logheaded knave might be beguil'd.

In tossing it often with myself to and fro,

I found out that Onaphets backward spelled Stephano.

I smiled in my sleeve to see [1] how by turning his name he dress'd [2] him, 1020

And how for Damon his master's sake with a wooden cudgel he bless'd him.

None pitied the knave, no man nor woman; but all laugh'd him to scorn.

To be thus hated of all, better unborn!

Far better Aristippus hath provided, I trow;

For in all the court I am beloved both of high and low. 1025

I offend none; insomuch that women sing this to my great praise,

Omnis Aristippum decuit color, et locus et res.[3]

But in all this jollity one thing 'mazeth me:

The strangest thing that ever was heard or known

Is now happened in this court by that Damon 1030

Whom Carisophus accused: Damon is now at liberty,

For whose return Pithias his friend lieth in prison, alas, in great jeopardy!

To-morrow is the day; which day by noon, if Damon return not, earnestly

The king hath sworn that Pithias should die;

Whereof Pithias hath intelligence very secretly; 1035

Wishing that Damon may not return till he hath paid

His life for his friend.   Hath it been heretofore ever said

That any man for his friend would die so willingly?

O noble friendship! O perfect amity!

Thy force is here seen, and that very perfectly. 1040

The king himself museth hereat; yet is he far out of square,

That he trusteth none to come near him. Not with his own daughters will he have

Unsearch'd to enter his chamber; which he hath made barbers his beard to shave,

Not with knife or razor — for all edge-tools he fears —

But with hot burning nutshells they singe off his hairs. 1045

Was there ever man that lived in such misery?

Well, I will go in — with a heavy and pensive heart, too,

To think how Pithias, this poor gentleman, to-morrow shall die.   *Exit.*

Here entereth Jack and Will.

[JACK.]   Will, by my honesty, I will mar your monkey's face if you so fondly prate!

WILL.   Jack, by my troth, seeing you are without the court-gate, 1050

If you play Jack-napes in mocking my master and despising my face,

Even here with a pantacle [1] I will you disgrace.

And though you have a far better face than I,

Yet who is better man of us two these fists shall try,

Unless you leave your taunting. 1055

JACK.   Thou began'st first.   Didst thou not say even now

That Carisophus, my master, was no man, but a cow,

In taking so many blows, and gave never a blow again?

WILL.   I said so, indeed.   He is but a tame ruffian

That can swear by his flask and twich-box,[2] and God's precious lady, 1060

---

[1] A. *how to see.*   [2] *Deceived.*
[3] A. *docuit colore.* "Every color, place, and thing suited Aristippus."

[1] Pantofle, or slipper, symbolical of pages.
[2] Touch-box, filled with priming-powder for the musket.

And yet will be beaten with a faggot-stick!
These barking whelps were never good
    biters,
Ne yet great crakers [1] were ever great
    fighters.
But seeing you egg me so much, I will
    somewhat more recite:
I say Carisophus, thy master, is a flatt'ring
    parasite,   1065
Gleaning away the sweet from the worthy
    in all the court.
What tragedy hath he moved of late! The
    devil take him! he doth much
    hurt.
JACK.   I pray you, what is Aristippus,
    thy master? Is not he a parasite
    too,
That with scoffing and jesting in the court
    makes so much a-do?
WILL.   He is no parasite, but a pleasant
    gentleman full of courtesy.   1070
Thy master is a churlish lout, the heir of a
    dungfork; as void of honesty
As thou art of honour.
JACK.   Nay, if you will needs be prating of
    my master still,
In faith I must cool you, my friend dapper
    Will.
Take this at the beginning!   1075
                [Strikes him.]
WILL.   Praise well your winning. My
    pantacle is as ready as yours.
JACK.   By the mass, I will box you!
WILL.   By Cock, I will fox you!
JACK.   Will, was I with you?
WILL.   Jack, did I fly?   1080
JACK.   Alas, pretty cockerel, you are too
    weak!
WILL.   In faith, dutting duttell, you will
    cry creak!

Here entereth Snap.

[SNAP.]   Away, you crack-ropes! [2]   Are
    you fighting at the court-gate?
And I take you here again I will swinge you
    both; what!   *Exit.*
JACK.   I beshrew Snap the tipstaff, that
    great knave's heart, that hither did
    come!   1085

    [1] Boasters.
    [2] A term of opprobrium, usually applied to boys;
the allusion is to the hangman's rope.

Had he not been, you had cried ere this
    Victus, victa, victum. [1]
But seeing we have breathed ourselves, if
    ye list,
Let us agree like friends, and shake each
    other by the fist.
WILL.   Content am I, for I am not mali-
    cious; — but on this condition,
That you talk no more so broad of my
    master as here you have done. 1090
But who have we here? 'Tis Coals, I spy, [2]
    coming yonder.
JACK.   Will, let us slip aside and view him
    well.   [*They stand aside.*]

Here entereth Grim the Collier, whistling.

[GRIM.]   What devil! ich ween the porters
    are drunk. Will they not dup [3] the
    gate to-day?
Take in coals for the king's own mouth! [4]
    Will nobody stir, I say?
Ich might have lain tway hours longer in
    my bed;   1095
Cha tarried so long here that my teeth
    chatter in my head.
JACK.   Will, after our falling out wilt thou
    laugh merrily?
WILL.   Ay, marry, Jack, I pray thee
    heartily.
JACK.   Then follow me, and hem in a word
    now and then.   [*They advance.*]
What brawling knave is there at the court-
    gate so early?   1100
WILL.   It is some brainsick villain, I durst
    lay a penny.
JACK.   It was you, sir, that cried so loud, I
    trow,
And bid us take in coals for the king's
    mouth even now.
GRIM.   'Twas I, indeed.
JACK.   Why, sir, how dare you speak such
    petty treason?   1105
Doth the king eat coals at any season?
GRIM.   Here is a gay world! Boys now
    sets old men to school.
I said well enough. What, Jack-sauce!
    think'st cham a fool?

    [1] Conquered (mas.), conquered (fem.), con-
quered (neut.).
    [2] A. *Cobex epi.* Emended by Hazlitt.
    [3] Open.
    [4] Provision. A technical phrase in court records;
cf. *Bouche de la cour.*

At bakehouse, butt'ry-hatch, kitchen, and
    cellar,
Do they not say "for the king's mouth"?
WILL. What, then, goodman collier? 1111
GRIM. What, then! seeing without coals
    they cannot finely dress the king's
    meat,
May I not say "take in coals for the king's
    mouth," though coals he do not
    eat?
JACK. James Christe! came ever from a
    collier an answer so trim?
You are learned, are you not, father
    Grim? 1115
GRIM. Grim is my name, indeed. Cham
    not learned, and yet the king's col-
    lier;
This vorty winter cha been to the king a
    servitor.
Though I be not learned, yet cha mother-
    wit enough, whole and some.
WILL. So it seems; you have so much
    mother-wit that you lack your
    father's wisdom.
GRIM. Mass, cham well-beset! Here's a
    trim cast of murlons![1] 1120
What be you, my pretty cockerels, that ask
    me these questions?
JACK. Good faith, Master Grim, if such
    merlins on your pouch[2] may light,
They are so quick of wing that quickly
    they can carry it out of your sight;
And though we are cockerels now, we shall
    have spurs one day,
And shall be able perhaps to make you a
    capon [to your pay.[3]] 1125
But to tell you the truth, we are the
    porter's men, which early and late
Wait on such gentlemen as you, to open
    the court-gate.
GRIM. Are ye servants then?
WILL. Yea, sir; are we not pretty men?
GRIM. Pretty men, quoth you? nay, you
    are strong men, else you could not
    bear these breeches.[4] 1130
WILL. Are these great hose?
In faith, goodman collier, you see with your
    nose.

[1] Merlins, a species of very small hawks.
[2] Purse.
[3] Added by Hazlitt.
[4] Grim is sneering at the big stuffed breeches
(called "slops") then worn by men of fashion.

By mine honesty, I have but for one lining
    in one hose but seven ells of rug.[1]
GRIM. This is but a little, yet it makes
    thee seem a great bug.[2]
JACK. How say you, goodman collier, can
    you find any fault here? 1135
GRIM. Nay, you should find fau't.
    Marry, here's trim gear!
Alas, little knave, dost not sweat? Thou
    goest with great pain.
These are no hose, but water-bougets,[3] I
    tell thee plain;
Good for none but such as have no but-
    tocks.
Did you ever see two such little Robin rud-
    docks 1140
So laden with breeches? Chill say no
    more, lest I offend.
Who invented these monsters first, did it
    to a ghostly[4] end,
To have a mail[5] ready to put in other
    folks' stuff;
We see this evident by daily proof.
One preached of late not far hence, in no
    pulpit but in a wain-cart, 1145
That spake enough of this. But for my
    part,
Chill say no more; your own necessity
In the end will force you to find some
    remedy.
JACK. Will, hold this railing knave with a
    talk when I am gone;
I will fetch him his filling ale for his good
    sermon. 1150
WILL. Go thy way. [Exit Jack.] Father
    Grim, gaily well you do say.
It is but young men's folly that list to play
And mask awhile in the net of their own
    device;
When they come to your age they will be
    wise.
GRIM. Bum troth, but few such roisters
    come to my years at this day; 1155
They be cut off betimes ere they have gone
    half their journey —
I will not tell why; let them guess that can;
    I mean somewhat thereby.[6]

[1] Coarse woolen cloth.
[2] Hobgoblin, bugbear.
[3] Leather bags used, in pairs, to carry water.
[4] Spiritual, religious (used sarcastically).
[5] Bag.
[6] He means, of course, the gallows.

Enter Jack with a pot of wine, and a cup to drink on.

[JACK.] Father Grim, because you are stirring so early

I have brought you a bowl of wine to make you merry.

GRIM. Wine! marry, that is welcome to colliers! Chill swap't off by and by.[1]   1160

Chwas stirring so early that my very soul is dry.

JACK. This is stoutly done. Will you have it warmed, Father Grim?

GRIM. No, it is warm enough; it is very lousious[2] and trim.

'Tis musselden,[3] ich ween! Of fellowship let me have another spurt.

Ich can drink as easily now as if I sat in my shirt.   1165

JACK. By Cock, and you shall have it! But I will begin, and that anon:

Je bois a vous, mon compagnon![4]

GRIM. *J'ai vous pleigé, petit Zawne!*[5]

JACK. Can you speak French? Here is a trim collier, by this day!

GRIM. What, man! ich learned this when ich was a soldier;   1170

When ich was a lusty fellow, and could yerk a whip trimly —

Better than these boy-colliers that come to the court daily;

When there were not so many captious fellows as now,

That would torup[6] men for every trifle — I wot not how:

As there was one, Damon, not long since taken for a spy —   1175

How justly I know not, but he was condemned to die.

WILL [*aside*]. This wine hath warmed him. This comes well to pass;

We shall know all now, for *in vino veritas.*[7]

Father Grim, who accused this Damon to King Dionysius?

[1] At once.   [2] Luscious.
[3] Muscatel wine.
[4] A. *Jebit avow, mon companion.*
[5] A. *Ihar vow pleadge, pety Zawne.* "Zawne" seems to be used for "Zany," clown.
[6] Not in *N.E.D.* Possibly Grim means *interrupt,* or *take up.*
[7] "In wine the truth."

GRIM. A vengeance take him! 'twas a gentleman, one Master Crowsphus.

WILL. Crowsphus! You clip the king's language; you would have said Carisophus.   1181

But I perceive now either the wind is at the south,

Or else your tongue cleaveth to the roof of your mouth.

GRIM. A murrain take thi[l]k wine! It so intoxicate my brain

That, to be hanged by and by, I cannot speak plain.   1185

JACK [*aside*]. You speak knavishly plain, seeing my master you do mock.

In faith, ere you go, I will make you a lobcock.

Father Grim, what say they of this Damon abroad?

GRIM. All men are sorry for him, so help me God!

They say a false knave 'cused him to the king wrongfully;   1190

And he is gone, and should be here tomorrow to die,

Or else his fellow, which is in prison, his room shall supply.

Chill not be his half for vorty shillings, I tell you plain!

I think Damon be too wise to return again.

WILL. Will no man speak for them in this woful case?   1195

GRIM. No, chill warrant you. One Master Stippus is in place

Where he may do good; but he frames himself so,

Whatsoever Dionysius willeth, to that he will not say no.

'Tis a subtle vox! He will not tread on thorns for none!

A merry harecop[1] 'tis, and a pleasant companion,   1200

A right courtier, and can provide for one.

JACK [*aside to Will*]. Will, how like you this gear? Your master Aristippus also

At this collier's hand hath had a blow!

But, in faith, Father Grim, cannot ye colliers

Provide for yourselves far better than courtiers?   1205

[1] Hare-brain?

GRIM. Yes, I trow! Black colliers go in threadbare coats,
Yet so provide they that they have the fair white groats.
Ich may say in counsel, though all day I moil in dirt
Chill not change lives with any in Dionysius' court;
For though their apparel be never so fine, 1210
Yet sure their credit is far worse than mine.
And, by Cock, I may say, for all their high looks,
I know some sticks full deep in merchants' books;[1]
And deeper will fall in, as fame me tells,
As long as instead of money they take up hauks' hoods and bells. 1215
Whereby they fall into a swelling disease, which colliers do not know;
'T'ath a mad name! it is called, ich ween, Centum pro cento.[2]
Some other in courts make others laugh merrily,
When they wail and lament their own estate secretly.
Friendship is dead in court; hypocrisy doth reign; 1220
Who is in favour now, to-morrow is out again:
The state is so uncertain that I, by my will,
Will never be courtier but a collier still.
WILL. It seemeth that colliers have a very trim life.
GRIM. Colliers get money still; tell me, of troth, 1225
Is not that a trim life now, as the world go'th?
All day though I toil with main and might,
With money in my pouch I come home merry at night,
And sit down in my chair by my wife, fair Alison,
And turn a crab in the fire[3] as merry as Pope John. 1230
JACK. That pope was a merry fellow of whom folk talk so much.
GRIM. H'ad to be merry withal — h'ad gold enough in his hutch.

[1] Indebted to merchants.
[2] "Hundred per cent."
[3] A crab-apple roasted in the fire and dropped into a mug of ale to warm and flavor the drink.

JACK. Can gold make men merry? They say, "Who can sing so merry a note
As he that is not able to change a groat?"
GRIM. Who sings in that case sings never in tune. I know, for my part, 1235
That a heavy pouch with gold makes a light heart;
Of which I have provided for a dear year good store; [He shows his purse.]
And these benters,[1] I trow, shall anon get me more.
WILL. By serving the court with coals you gain'd all this money?
GRIM. By the court only, I assure ye. 1240
JACK. After what sort, I pray thee tell me?
GRIM. Nay, there bate an ace, quod Bolton![2] I can wear a horn and blow it not.
JACK. By'r Lady, the wiser man!
GRIM. Shall I tell you by what sleight I got all this money?
Then ich were a noddy indeed! No, no, I warrant ye! 1245
Yet in few words I tell you this one thing —
He is a very fool that cannot gain by the king.
WILL. Well said, Father Grim! you are a wily collier, and a brave.
I see now there is no knave to the old knave.
GRIM. Such knaves have money when courtiers have none. 1250
But tell me, is it true that abroad is blown?
JACK. What is that?
GRIM. Hath the king made those fair damsels, his daughters,
To become now fine and trim barbers?
JACK. Yea, truly, — to his own person.
GRIM. Good fellows, believe me, as the case now stands 1256
I would give one sack of coals to be wash'd at their hands!
If ich came so near them, for my wit should not give three chips
If ich could not steal one swap at their lips!
JACK [aside]. Will, this knave is drunk. Let us dress[3] him; 1260

[1] Debentures, vouchers given in the royal household for sums of money due.
[2] An old proverb.
[3] Play a prank upon him.

Let us rifle him so, that he have not one
    penny to bless him,
And steal away his debenters [1] too.
WILL [*aside*]. Content; invent the way,
    and I am ready.
JACK [*aside*]. Faith, and I will make him a
    noddy.
Father Grim, if you pray me well, I will
    wash you and shave you too,   1265
Even after the same fashion as the king's
    daughters do;
In all points as they handle Dionysius, I
    will dress you trim and fine.
GRIM. Chuld vain learn that! Come on,
    then; chill give thee a whole pint of
    wine
At tavern for thy labour, when 'cha money
    for my benters here.

*Here Will fetcheth a barber's bason, a pot
with water, a razor, and cloths, and a pair
of spectacles.*

JACK. Come, mine own Father Grim; sit
    down.   1270
GRIM. Mass, to begin withal, here is a
    trim chair!
JACK. What, man, I will use you like a
    prince. Sir boy, fetch me my gear.
WILL. Here, sir.
JACK. Hold up, Father Grim.
GRIM. Me-seem my head doth swim. 1275
JACK. My costly perfumes make that.
    Away with this, sir boy; be quick!

[*Hands Will the collier's purse.*]

Aloyse, aloyse,[2] how pretty it is! Is
    not here a good face?
A fine owl's eyes! a mouth like an oven!
Father, you have good butter-teeth full
    seen.
[*Aside*] You were weaned, else you would
    have been a great calf.   1280
Ah, trim lips to sweep a manger! [3] Here is
    a chin,
As soft as the hoof of an horse.
GRIM. Doth the king's daughters rub so
    hard?
JACK. Hold your head straight, man, else
    all will be marr'd.

By'r Lady, you are of a good complex-
    ion,   1285
A right Croyden sanguine,[1] beshrew me.
Hold up, Father Grim. Will, can you be-
    stir ye?
GRIM. Methinks, after a marvellous fash-
    ion you do besmear me.
JACK. It is with unguentum of Daucus
    Maucus, that is very costly;
I give not this washing-ball [2] to every-
    body.   1290
After you have been dress'd so finely at my
    hand,
You may kiss any lady's lips within this land.
Ah, you are trimly wash'd! How say you,
    is not this trim water?
GRIM. It may be wholesome, but it is
    vengeance sour!
JACK. It scours the better. Sir boy, give
    me my razor.   1295
WILL. Here at hand, sir.
GRIM. God's arms! 'tis a chopping knife!
    'tis no razor.
JACK. It is a razor, and that a very good
    one!
It came lately from Palermo; [3] it cost me
    twenty crowns alone.
Your eyes dazzle after your washing; these
    spectacles put on.   1300

[*He places spectacles, with dark lenses, on
him.*]

Now view this razor; tell me, is it not a
    good one?
GRIM. They be gay barnacles, yet I see
    never the better.
JACK. Indeed they be a young sight, and
    that is the matter.
But I warrant you this razor is very easy.
GRIM. Go to, then; since you begun, do as
    please ye.   1305
JACK. Hold up, Father Grim.
GRIM. O, your razor doth hurt my lip.
JACK. No, it scrapeth off a pimple to ease
    you of the pip.
I have done now. How say you? are you
    not well?
GRIM. Cham lighter than ich was, the
    truth to tell.   1310

---

[1] Debentures.
[2] This exclamation is not recorded in *N.E.D.*
[3] As an ass'.

[1] "'Supposed to be a kind of sallow colour'
(Nares)." — *N.E.D.*
[2] Perfumed soap.   [3] A. *Pallarrime.*

JACK. Will you sing after your shaving?

GRIM. Mass, content! But chill be poll'd[1] first, ere I sing.

JACK. Nay, that shall not need; you are poll'd[2] near enough for this time.

GRIM. Go to, then, lustily. I will sing in my man's voice;

Chave a troubling base buss.[3]

JACK. You are like to bear the bob,[4] for we will give it. 1315

Set out your bussing base, and we will quiddle[5] upon it.

Grim singeth Buss.

JACK (*sings*). *Too nidden and too nidden!*[6]

WILL (*sings*). *Too nidden and toodle toodle doo nidden!*

Is not Grim the collier most finely shaven?[7]

GRIM. Why, my fellows, think ich am a cow, that you make such toying?

JACK. Nay, by'r Lady, you are no cow, by your singing — 1321

Yet your wife told me you were an ox.[8]

GRIM. Did she so? 'tis a pestens[9] quean! she is full of such mocks.

But go to, let us sing out our song merrily

THE SONG AT THE SHAVING OF THE COLLIER

JACK. *Such barbers God send you at all times of need —* 1325

WILL. *That can dress you [so] finely, and make such quick speed.*

JACK. *Your face like an inkhorn now shineth so gay —*

WILL. *That I with your nostrils of force must needs play,*

With too nidden and too nidden!

JACK. *With too nidden and todle todle doo nidden!* 1330

Is not Grim the collier most finely shaven?

WILL. *With shaving you shine like a pestle of pork.*[10]

---

[1] Trimmed.
[2] With a pun on the sense "cheated," "fleeced."
[3] Buzz, hum.
[4] Refrain, with a pun on the meaning "bitter jest."
[5] Sing in a trifling way.
[6] A nonsense refrain.
[7] With a pun on *shaven*, cheated.
[8] The cuckold joke.
[9] Pestilent.
[10] Ham of a pig.

JACK. *Here is the trimmest hog's flesh from London to York.*

WILL. *It would be trim bacon to hang up awhile.*

JACK. *To play with this hoglin of course I must smile,* 1335

With too nidden and too nidden!

WILL. *With too nidden and todle, &c.*

GRIM. *Your shaving doth please me; I am now your debtor.*

WILL. *Your wife now will buss[1] you, because you are sweeter.*

GRIM. *Near would I be polled, as near as cham shaven.* 1340

WILL. *Then out of your jerkin[2] needs must you be shaken.*

With too nidden and too nidden, &c.

GRIM. *It is a trim thing to be wash'd in the court.*

WILL. *Their hands are so fine, that they never do hurt.*

GRIM. *Me-think ich am lighter than ever ich was.* 1345

WILL. *Our shaving in the court hath brought this to pass.*

With two nidden and two nidden!

JACK. *With too nidden and todle todle doo nidden!*

Is not Grim the collier most finely shaven?

Finis

GRIM. This is trimly done! Now chill pitch my coals not far hence, 1350

And then at the tavern chill bestow whole tway pence. [*Exit Grim.*]

JACK. Farewell, [by] Cock. Before the collier again do us seek,

Let us into the court to part the spoil, share and share [a]like. *Exit.*

WILL. Away then. [*Exit.*]

Here entereth Grim.

[GRIM.] Out, alas! where shall I make my moan? 1355

My pouch, my benters, and all is gone!

Where is that villain that did me shave?

H'ath robbed me, alas, of all that I have.

---

[1] Kiss.
[2] The outer jacket worn by men, often made of leather.

Here entereth Snap.

[SNAP.]   Who crieth so at the court-gate?

GRIM.   I, the poor collier, that was robbed
of late.   1360

SNAP.   Who robbed thee?

GRIM.   Two of the porter's men that did
shave me.

SNAP.   Why, the porter's men are no
barbers.

GRIM.   A vengeance take them, they are
quick carvers.[1]

SNAP.   What stature were they of?   1365

GRIM.   As little dapper knaves as they
trimly could scoff.

SNAP.   They were lackeys, as near as I can
guess them.

GRIM.   Such lackeys make me lack.   An
halter beswinge them!

Cham undone; they have my benters too.

SNAP.   Dost thou know them if thou seest
them?   1370

GRIM.   Yea, that I do!

SNAP.   Then come with me; we will find
them out, and that quickly.

GRIM.   I follow, Mast Tipstaff.   They be
in the court, it is likely.

SNAP.   Then cry no mcre; come away.
                                    Exeunt.

Here entereth Carisophus and Aristippus.

[CARISOPHUS.]   If ever you will show your
friendship, now is the time.   1375

Seeing the king is displeased with me of my
part without any crime.

ARISTIPPUS.   It should appear it comes of
some evil behaviour

That you so suddenly are cast out of favour.

CARISOPHUS.   Nothing have I done but
this: in talk I overthwarted Eubulus

When he lamented Pithias' case to King
Dionysius,   1380

Which to-morrow shall die, but for that
false knave Damon,

He hath left his friend in the briars, and
now is gone.

We grew so hot in talk that Eubulus protested plainly,

[1] With a pun, "cheaters," "filchers."

Which [1] held his ears open to parasitical
flattery.

And now in the king's ear like a bell he
rings,   1385

Crying that flatterers have been the de-
stroyers of kings.

Which talk in Dionysius' heart hath made
so deep impression

That he trusteth me not, as heretofore, in
no condition;

And some words brake from him, as though
that he

Began to suspect my truth and honesty.

Which you of friendship I know will defend,
how so ever the world goeth.   1391

My friend, for my honesty will you not
take an oath? [2]

ARISTIPPUS.   To swear for your honesty I
should lose mine own.

CARISOPHUS.   Should you so, indeed?   I
would that were known

Is your void friendship come thus to
pass?   1395

ARISTIPPUS.   I follow the proverb: *Amicus
usque ad aras.*[3]

CARISOPHUS.   Where can you say I ever
lost mine honesty?

ARISTIPPUS.   You never lost it — for you
never had it, as far as I know.

CARISOPHUS.   Say you so, friend Aristippus, whom I trust so well?

ARISTIPPUS.   Because you trust me, to you
the truth I tell.   1400

CARISOPHUS.   Will you not stretch one
point to bring me in favour again?

ARISTIPPUS.   I love no stretching; so, may
I breed mine own pain.

CARISOPHUS.   A friend ought to shun no
pain to stand his friend in stead.

ARISTIPPUS.   Where true friendship is, it
is so in very deed.

CARISOPHUS.   Why, sir, hath not the
chain of true friendship linked us
two together?   1405

ARISTIPPUS.   The chiefest link lacked
thereof; it must needs dissever.

CARISOPHUS.   What link is that? fain
would I know.

ARISTIPPUS.   Honesty.

[1] "I.e. Dionysius, to which Dodsley changed it"
— Hazlitt.
[2] Will you not swear to my honesty?
[3] A. *auras.*   "A friend even to the altar."

CARISOPHUS. Doth honesty knit the perfect knot in true friendship?

ARISTIPPUS. Yea, truly; and that knot so knit will never slip.   1410

CARISOPHUS. Belike, then, there is no friendship but between honest men.

ARISTIPPUS. Between the honest only; for *Amicitia inter bonos*,[1] saith a learned man.

CARISOPHUS. Yet evil men use friendship in things unhonest, where fancy doth serve.

ARISTIPPUS. That is no friendship, but a lewd liking; it lasts but a while.

CARISOPHUS. What is the perfectest friendship among men that ever grew?   1415

ARISTIPPUS. Where men love one another not for profit but for virtue.

CARISOPHUS. Are such friends both alike in joy and also in smart?

ARISTIPPUS. They must needs; for in two bodies they have but one heart.

CARISOPHUS. Friend Aristippus, deceive me not with sophistry:

Is there no perfect friendship but where is virtue and honesty?   1420

ARISTIPPUS. What a devil then meant Carisophus

To join in friendship with fine Aristippus?

In whom is as much virtue, truth, and honesty

As there are true feathers in the Three Cranes of the Vintree.[2]

Yet these feathers have the shadow [3] of lively feathers, the truth to scan,

But Carisophus hath not the shadow of an honest man.   1426

To be plain, because I know thy villainy

In abusing Dionysius to many men's injury,

Under the cloak of friendship I play'd with his head,

And sought means how thou with thine own fancy might be led.   1430

My friendship thou soughtest for thine own commodity,

As worldly men do, by profit measuring amity;

Which I perceiving, to the like myself I framed,

Wherein I know of the wise I shall not be blamed.

If you ask me, *Quare?* I answer, *Quia prudentis est multum dissimulare.*[1]

To speak more plainer, as the proverb doth go,   1436

In faith, Carisophus, *cum Cretense cretiso.*[2]

Yet a perfect friend I show myself to thee in one thing —

I do not dissemble now I say I will not speak for thee to the king.

Therefore sink in thy sorrow! I do not deceive thee;   1440

A false knave I found thee, a false knave I leave thee!   *Exit.*

CARISOPHUS. He is gone! Is this friendship, to leave his friend in the plain field?

Well, I see now I myself have beguiled

In matching with that false fox in amity,

Which hath me used to his own commodity,   1445

Which seeing me in distress, unfeignedly goes his ways.

Lo, this is the perfect friendship among men now-a-days!

Which kind of friendship toward him I used secretly;

And he with me the like hath requited me craftily.

It is the gods' judgment, I see it plainly;

For all the world may know, *Incide in foveam quam feci.*[3]   1451

Well, I must content myself. None other help I know,

Until a merrier gale of wind may hap to blow.   *Exit.*

[*Enter Eubulus.*]

EUBULUS. Who deals with kings in matters of great weight,

When froward will doth bear the chiefest sway,   1455

Must yield of force. There need no subtle sleight,

---

[1] A. *bonus.* "Friendship between the good."
[2] The sign of a well-known tavern.
[3] Likeness.

[1] "Because it is the part of a wise man to dissemble much."
[2] A. *Cretence.* "With the Cretan I lie." Cf. line 971.
[3] "I have fallen into a pit which I myself digged"

Ne painted [1] speech the matter to convey.
No prayer can move when kindled is the
  ire;
The more ye quench, the more increased is
  the fire.
This thing I prove in Pithias' woful
  case,   1460
Whose heavy hap with tears I do lament.
The day is come when he, in Damon's
  place,
Must lose his life; the time is fully spent.
Nought can my words now with the king
  prevail;
Against the wind and striving stream I
  sail —   1465
For die thou must, alas! thou seely [2] Greek.
Ah, Pithias, now come is thy doleful hour!
A perfect friend; none such, a world to
  seek!
Though bitter death shall give thee sauce
  full sour,
Yet for thy faith enroll'd shall be thy
  name   1470
Among the gods within the book of fame.
Who knoweth his case and will not melt in
  tears?
His guiltless blood shall trickle down anon.

Then the Muses sing.

[MUSES.] *Alas, what hap hast thou, poor
  Pithias, now to die!*
*Woe worth the man which [3] for his death hath
  given us cause to cry!*   1475

EUBULUS. Methink I hear, with yellow
  rented hairs,
The Muses frame their notes my state to
  moan.
Among which sort, as one that mourneth
  with heart,
In doleful tunes myself will bear a part.

MUSES. *Woe worth the man which for his
  death, &c.*   1480

EUBULUS. *With yellow rented hairs, come
  on, you Muses nine!*
*Fill now my breast with heavy tunes; to me
  your plaint resign;*
*For Pithias I bewail, which presently must
  die.*

---

[1] Feigned.   [2] Poor.   [3] A. *which man.*

*Woe worth the man which for his death hath
  given us cause, &c.*
MUSES. *Woe worth the man which for his,
  &c.*   1485

EUBULUS. *Was ever such a man, that
  would die for his friend?*
*I think even from the heavens above the gods
  did him down send*
*To show true friendship's power, which
  forc'd thee now to die.*
Woe worth the man which for thy death, &c.
MUSES. *Woe worth the man, &c.*   1490

EUBULUS. *What tiger's whelp was he that
  Damon did accuse!*
*What faith hast thou, which for thy friend
  thy death doth not refuse!*
O heavy hap hadst thou to play this tragedy!
Woe worth the man which for thy death, &c.
MUSES. *Woe worth the man, &c.*   1495

EUBULUS. *Thou young and worthy Greek,
  that showeth such perfect love,*
*The gods receive thy simple ghost into the
  heavens above!*
*Thy death we shall lament with many a
  weeping eye.*
Woe worth the man, which for his death, &c.
MUSES. *Woe worth the man, which for thy
  death hath given us cause to cry.*   1500

Finis

EUBULUS. Eternal be your fame, ye
  Muses, for that in misery
Ye did vouchsafe to strain your notes to
  walk.[1]
My heart is rent in two with this miserable
  case;
Yet am I charged by Dionysius' mouth to
  see this place
At all points ready for the execution of
  Pithias.   1505
Need hath no law; will I or nil I,[2] it must
  be done.
But lo, the bloody minister is even here at
  hand.

[Enter Gronno.]

Gronno, I came hither now to understand

---

[1] To be in motion (or *wake,* to become animated).
[2] Whether I will or not.

If all things are well appointed for the execution of Pithias.

The king himself will see it done here in
this place. 1510

GRONNO. Sir, all things are ready. Here
is the place, here is the hand, here is
the sword!

Here lacketh none but Pithias, whose head
at a word,

If he were present, I could finely strike off!

You may report that all things are ready.

EUBULUS. I go with an heavy heart to report it. Ah, woful Pithias! 1515
Full near now is thy misery. [Exit.]

GRONNO. I marvel very much under what
constellation

All hangmen are born; for they are hated of
all, beloved of none.

Which hatred is showed by this point evi-
dently —

The hangman always dwells in the vilest
place of the city. 1520

That such spite should be, I know no cause
why,

Unless it be for their office's sake, which is
cruel and bloody.

Yet some men must do it to execute
laws.

Me-think they hate me without any just
cause.

But I must look to my toil. Pithias must
lose his head at one blow, 1525

Else the boys will stone me to death in the
street as I go.

But hark, the prisoner cometh, and the
king also.

I see there is no help, Pithias his life must
forego.

*Here entereth Dionysius and Eubulus [with
courtiers and others].*

DIONYSIUS.] Bring forth Pithias, that
pleasant companion,

Which took me at my word, and became
pledge for Damon. 1530

It pricketh fast upon [1] noon. I do him no
injury

If now he lose his head, for so he requested
me,

If Damon return not, — which now in
Greece is full merry.

[1] Approaches close to.

Therefore shall Pithias pay his death, and
that by and by.

He thought, belike, if Damon were out of
the city 1535

I would not put him to death for some
foolish pity:

But seeing it was his request; I will not be
mock'd. He shall die!

Bring him forth.

*Here entereth Snap [leading in Pithias,
Stephano accompanying him].*

[SNAP.] Give place! Let the prisoner
come by! give place!

DIONYSIUS. How say you, sir? where is
Damon, your trusty friend? 1540

You have play'd a wise part, I make God a
vow!

You know what time a day it is; make you
ready.

PITHIAS. Most ready I am, mighty king,
and most ready also

For my true friend Damon this life to
forego,

Even at your pleasure. 1545

DIONYSIUS. A true friend! A false
traitor that so breaketh his oath!

Thou shalt lose thy life, though thou be
never so loth.

PITHIAS. I am not loth to do whatsoever I
said,

Ne at this present pinch of death am I dismay'd.

The gods now I know have heard my fer-
vent prayer, 1550

That they have reserved me to this passing
great honour

To die for my friend, whose faith even now
I do not mistrust.

My friend Damon is no false traitor; he is
true and just.

But sith he is no god, but a man, he must
do as he may;

The wind may be contrary, sickness may
let him,[1] or some misadventure by
the way — 1555

Which the eternal gods turn all to my glory,

That fame may resound how Pithias for
Damon did die.

He breaketh no oath which doth as much
as he can.

[1] Hinder him.

His mind is here; he hath some let; he is but
    a man.
That he might not return, of all the gods I
    did require,   1560
Which now to my joy do [1] grant my desire.
But why do I stay any longer, seeing that
    one man's death
May suffice, O king, to pacify thy wrath?
    [Turning to Gronno.]
O thou minister of justice, do thine office
    by and by.
Let not thy hand tremble, for I tremble not
    to die.   1565
Stephano, the right pattern [2] of true fidelity,
Commend me to thy master, my sweet
    Damon! and of him crave liberty
When I am dead, in my name; for thy
    trusty services
Hath well deserved a gift far better than
    this.
O my Damon, farewell now for ever! a true
    friend, to me most dear!   1570
Whiles life doth last, my mouth shall still
    talk of thee;
And when I am dead, my simple ghost,
    true witness of amity,
Shall hover about the place, wheresoever
    thou be.
DIONYSIUS.   Eubulus, this gear is strange!
    And yet, because
Damon hath fals'd his faith, Pithias shall
    have the law.   1575
Gronno, despoil [3] him, and eke dispatch
    him quickly.
GRONNO.   It shall be done.   Since you
    came into this place
I might have stroken off seven heads in
    this space.

[Gronno takes off Pithias' outer garments.]

By'r Lady, here are good garments!   These
    are mine, by the rood!
It is an evil wind that bloweth no man
    good.   1580
Now, Pithias, kneel down, ask me blessing
    like a pretty boy,
And with a trice thy head from thy shoul-
    ders I will convey.

[Pithias kneels, and Gronno lifts his sword
    to strike.]

---

[1] A. doth.   [2] A. patrone. Cf. l. 127.
[3] Strip off his outer garments.

---

*Here entereth Damon running, and stays
the sword.*

[DAMON.] Stay! stay! stay! for the king's
    advantage, stay!
O mighty king, mine appointed time is not
    yet fully pass'd;
Within the compass of mine hour, lo, here I
    come at last.   1585
A life I owe, a life I will you pay.
O my Pithias, my noble pledge, my con-
    stant friend!
Ah! woe is me! for Damon's sake how near
    were thou to thy end!
Give place to me; this room is mine; on
    this stage must I play.
Damon is the man, none ought but he to
    Dionysius his blood to pay.   1590
GRONNO. Are you come, sir? You might
    have tarried, if you had been wise.
For your hasty coming you are like to
    know the price.
PITHIAS. O thou cruel minister, why didst
    not thou thine office?
Did not I bid thee make haste in any wise?
Hast thou spared to kill me once, that I
    may die twice?   1595
Not to die for my friend is present death to
    me; and, alas!
Shall I see my sweet Damon slain before
    my face?
What double death is this! But, O mighty
    Dionysius,
Do true justice now; weigh this aright,
    thou noble Eubulus;
Let me have no wrong. As now stands the
    case   1600
Damon ought not to die, but Pithias;
By misadventure — not by his will — his
    hour is past; therefore I,
Because he came not at his just time, ought
    justly to die.
So was my promise, so was thy promise, O
    king.
All this court can bear witness of this
    thing.   1605
DAMON. Not so, O mighty king! To
    justice it is contrary
That for another man's fault the innocent
    should die:
Ne yet is my time plainly expired; it is not
    fully noon

Of this my day appointed, by all the clocks
   in the town.

PITHIAS. Believe no clock; the hour is
   past by the sun. 1610

DAMON. Ah, my Pithias, shall we now
   break the bonds of amity?

Will you now overthwart me, which heretofore so well did agree?

PITHIAS. My Damon, the gods forbid but
   we should agree!

Therefore agree to this — let me perform
   the promise I made for thee.

Let me die for thee; do me not that
   injury 1615

Both to break my promise and to suffer me
   to see thee die,

Whom so dearly I love. This small request
   grant me;

I shall never ask thee more; my desire is
   but friendly.

Do me this honour, that fame may report
   triumphantly

That Pithias for his friend Damon was contented to die. 1620

DAMON. That you were contented for me
   to die, fame cannot deny;

Yet fame shall never touch me with such a
   villainy

To report that Damon did suffer his friend
   Pithias for him guiltless to die.

Therefore content thyself; the gods requite
   thy constant faith.

None but Damon's blood can appease Dionysius' wrath. 1625

And now, O mighty king, to you my talk I
   convey.

Because you gave me leave my worldly
   things to stay,

To requite that good turn, ere I die, for
   your behalf this I say:

Although your regal state dame Fortune
   decketh so

That like a king in worldly wealth abundantly ye flow, 1630

Yet fickle is the ground whereon all tyrants
   tread!

A thousand sundry cares and fears do
   haunt their restless head!

No trusty band, no faithful friends do
   guard thy hateful state.

And why? Whom men obey for deadly
   fear, sure them they deadly hate.

That you may safely reign, by love get
   friends, whose constant faith 1635

Will never fail. This counsel gives poor
   Damon at his death.

Friends are the surest guard for kings.
   Gold in time do[es] wear away,

And other precious things do fade; friendship will never decay.

Have friends in store, therefore; so shall
   you safely sleep;

Have friends at home, of foreign foes so
   need you take no keep. 1640

Abandon flatt'ring tongues, whose clacks
   truth never tells;

Abase the ill, advance the good, in whom
   dame virtue dwells;

Let them your playfellows be. But, O you
   earthly kings,

Your sure defence and strongest guard
   stands chiefly in faithful friends!

Then get you friends by liberal deeds.
   And here I make an end. 1645

Accept this counsel, mighty king, of
   Damon, Pithias' friend.

O my Pithias! now farewell for ever! Let
   me kiss thee, ere I die.

My soul shall honour thee; thy constant
   faith above the heavens shall fly.

[*He divests himself, and kneels on the place
of execution.*]

Come, Gronno, do thine office now. Why
   is thy colour so dead?

My neck is so [1] short that thou wilt never
   have honesty in striking off this
   head? 1650

DIONYSIUS. Eubulus, my spirits are suddenly appalled; my limbs wax weak!

This strange friendship amazeth me so that
   I can scarce speak.

PITHIAS. O mighty king, let some pity
   your noble heart meve.

You require but one man's death; take
   Pithias, let Damon live.

EUBULUS. O unspeakable friendship! 1655

DAMON. Not so. He hath not offended.
   There is no cause why

My constant friend, my Pithias, for
   Damon's sake should die.

Alas, he is but young; he may do good to
   many.

[1] A. *is so is.*

Thou coward minister, why dost thou not
   let me die?

GRONNO.   My hand with sudden fear
   quivereth.   1660

PITHIAS.   O noble king, show mercy upon
   Damon; let Pithias die.

DIONYSIUS.   Stay, Gronno!   My flesh
   trembleth.   Eubulus, what shall I
   do?

Were there ever such friends on earth as
   were these two?

What heart is so cruel that would divide
   them asunder?

O noble friendship, I must yield!   At thy
   force I wonder.   1665

My heart this rare friendship hath pierc'd
   to the root,

And quenched all my fury.   This sight
   hath brought this about,

Which thy grave counsel, Eubulus, and
   learned persuasion could never do.

[To Damon and Pithias] O noble gentlemen,
   the immortal gods above

Hath made you play this tragedy, I think,
   for my behoof.   1670

Before this day I never knew what perfect
   friendship meant;

My cruel mind to bloody deeds was full and
   wholly bent;

My fearful life I thought with terror to defend.

But now I see there is no guard unto a
   faithful friend,

Which will not spare his life at time of
   present need.   1675

O happy kings, who in [1] your courts have
   two such friends indeed!

I honour friendship now; which that you
   may plainly see,

Damon, have thou thy life; from death I
   pardon thee.

For which good turn, I crave, this honour
   do me lend:

O friendly heart, let me link with you! to
   you make me the third friend!   1680

My court is yours; dwell here with me.   By
   my commission large

Myself, my realm, my wealth, my health, I
   commit to your charge.

Make me a third friend.   More shall I joy
   in that thing,

             [1] A. *within.*

Than to be called, as I am, Dionysius the
   mighty king.

DAMON.   O mighty king, first for my life
   most humble thanks I give;   1685

And next, I praise the immortal gods that
   did your heart so meve

That you would have respect to friendship's heavenly lore,

Foreseeing well he need not fear which hath
   true friends in store.

For my part, most noble king, as a third
   friend welcome to our friendly society!

But you must forget you are a king, for
   friendship stands in true equality.

DIONYSIUS.   Unequal though I be in great
   possessions,   1691

Yet full equal shall you find me in my
   changed conditions.

Tyranny, flattery, oppression, lo, here I
   cast away;

Justice, truth, love, friendship, shall be my
   joy.

True friendship will I honour unto my life's
   end;   1695

My greatest glory shall be to be counted a
   perfect friend.

PITHIAS.   For this your deed, most noble
   king, the gods advance your name.

And since to friendship's lore you list your
   princely heart to frame,

With joyful heart, O king, most welcome
   now to me!

With you will I knit the perfect knot of
   amity;   1700

Wherein I shall instruct you so, and
   Damon here your friend,

That you may know of amity the mighty
   force, and eke the joyful end,

And how that kings do stand upon a fickle
   ground

Within whose realm at time of need no
   faithful friends are found.

DIONYSIUS.   Your instruction will I follow; to you myself I do commit.1705

Eubulus, make haste to fet new apparel, fit
For my new friends.

EUBULUS.   I go with joyful heart.   O
   happy day!   *Exit.*

GRONNO.   I am glad to hear this word.
   Though their lives they do not
   lese,

It is no reason the hangman should lose his
    fees.   1710
These are mine, I am gone with a trice.

*Exit [Gronno with the discarded garments of
    Damon and Pithias].*

Here entereth Eubulus with new garments.

DIONYSIUS. Put on these garments now.
    Go in with me, the jewels of my
    court.
DAMON *and* PITHIAS. We go with joyful
    hearts.
STEPHANO. O Damon, my dear master, in
    all this joy remember me.
DIONYSIUS. My friend Damon, he asketh
    reason.[1]   1715
DAMON. Stephano, for thy good service be
    thou free.

*Exeunt Dion. [and the rest. Stephano
    remains].*

STEPHANO. O most happy, pleasant, joy-
    ful, and triumphant day!
Poor Stephano now shall live in continual
    play.[2]
Vive le roy, with Damon and Pithias, in
    perfect amity!
Vive tu, Stephano, in thy pleasant liberal-
    ity!   1720
Wherein I joy as much as he that hath a
    conquest won.
I am a free man! None so merry as I now
    under the sun.
Farewell, my lords! Now the gods grant
    you all the sum of perfect amity,
And me long to enjoy my long-desired lib-
    erty.   *Exit.*

Here entereth Eubulus beating Carisophus.

[EUBULUS.] Away, villain! Away, you
    flatt'ring parasite!   1725
Away, the plague of this court! Thy filed[3]
    tongue that forged lies
No more here shall do hurt. Away, false
    sycophant! wilt thou not?
CARISOPHUS. I am gone, sir, seeing it is
    the king's pleasure.
Why whip ye me alone? A plague take

---

[1] A. adds at the extreme right *Dam. Pithias;* apparently a printer's blunder.
[2] A. *joy:* emend. by Hazlitt.   [3] Defiled.

Damon and Pithias! Since they
    came hither
I am driven to seek relief abroad, alas! I
    know not whither.   1730
Yet, Eubulus, though I be gone, hereafter
    time shall try,
There shall be found, even in this court, as
    great flatterers as I.
Well, for a while I will forego the court,
    though to my great pain.
I doubt not but to spy a time when I may
    creep in again.   *Exit.*
EUBULUS. The serpent that eats men
    alive — flattery — with   all   her
    brood,   1735
Is whipp'd away in princes' courts, which
    yet did never good.
What force, what mighty power true
    friendship may possess,
To all the world Dionysius' court now
    plainly doth express;
Who, since to faithful friends he gave his
    willing ear,
Most safely sitteth in his seat, and sleeps
    devoid of fear.   1740
Purged is the court of vice since friendship
    ent'red in.
Tyranny quails; he studieth now with love
    each heart to win;
Virtue is had in price, and hath his just re-
    ward;
And painted speech, that gloseth for gain,
    from gifts is quite debarr'd.
One loveth another now for virtue, not for
    gain.   1745
Where virtue doth not knit the knot, there
    friendship cannot reign;
Without the which no house, no land, ne
    kingdom can endure;
As necessary for man's life as water, air,
    and fire;
Which frameth the mind of man all honest
    things to do.
Unhonest things friendship ne craveth, ne
    yet consents thereto.   1750
In wealth a double joy, in woe a present stay,
A sweet companion in each state true
    friendship is alway;
A sure defence for kings; a perfect trusty
    band;
A force to assail, a shield to defend the
    enemies' cruel hand;

A rare and yet the greatest gift that God
    can give to man; —   1755
So rare, that scarce four couple of faithful
    friends have been since the world
    began.
A gift so strange, and of such price, I wish
    all kings to have.
But chiefly yet, as duty bindeth, I humbly
    crave
True friendship and true friends, full
    fraught with constant faith,
The giver of friends, the Lord, grant her,
    most noble Queen Elizabeth!   1760

FINIS

THE LAST SONG [1]

The strongest guard that kings can have
Are constant friends their state to save.

[1] Added on the page following. Possibly it was
sung by all the actors.

True friends are constant both in word and
    deed;
True friends are present, and help at each
    need;
True friends talk truly, they glose for no gain;
When treasure consumeth, true friends will
    remain;
True friends for their true prince refuseth
    not their death.
The Lord grant her such friends, most noble
    Queen Elizabeth!   1768

Long may she govern in honour and wealth,
Void of all sickness, in most perfect health!
Which health to prolong, as true friends re-
    quire,
God grant she may have her own heart's desire,
Which friends will defend with most steadfast
    faith.
The Lord grant her such friends, most noble
    Queen Elizabeth!   1774

FINIS

CAMPASPE[1]

PLAYED BEEFORE THE QUEENES MAIESTIE

On Newyeares Day at Night, by Her Maiesties Children, and the Children of Paules

Imprinted at London for Thomas Cadman, 1584

[DRAMATIS PERSONÆ

ALEXANDER THE GREAT, King of Macedon.
HEPHAESTION, his General and Confidant.

CLITUS, } Officers.
PARMENIO, }

MILECTUS, } Soldiers.
PHRYGIUS, }

MELIPPUS, Chamberlain to Alexander.

DIOGENES, ⎫
PLATO, ⎪
ARISTOTLE, ⎪
CHRYSIPPUS, ⎬ Philosophers.
CRATES, ⎪
CLEANTHES, ⎪
ANAXARCHUS, ⎪
CRYSUS, ⎭

APELLES, a Painter.

SOLINUS, } Citizens of Athens.
SYLVIUS, }

PERIM, }
MILO, } Sons to Sylvius.
TRICO, }

GRANICHUS, Servant to Plato.
MANES, Servant to Diogenes.
PSYLLUS, Apprentice to Apelles.
Page to Alexander.
Citizens of Athens.
SOLDIERS.
POPULACE.

CAMPASPE, } Theban Captives.
TIMOCLEA, }

LAIS, a Courtezan.

THE SCENE: Athens.]

---

[1] John Lyly, who had attained great fame by his two novels, *Euphues the Anatomy of Wyt*, 1578, and *Euphues and his England*, 1580, was presented by the Earl of Oxford in the summer of 1583 with the lease of Blackfriars hall where the royal boy-choristers and the singing children of St. Paul's Cathedral were accustomed to present their plays — mainly designed for Court performance — before the general public. At once Lyly set himself to the task of writing plays, and within a few weeks had *Campaspe* ready for the stage. The comedy, after being shown to the public at Blackfriars (the performances served for dress-rehearsals), was acted at Court before Elizabeth on Newyear's Day at night.

The play was outfitted by the Office of the Revels, which supplied the customary "players' houses" of canvas painted and stretched on wooden frames. From the text it appears that on one side of the stage was placed the palace of Alexander, and on the opposite side the studio of Apelles (with a curtain that could be drawn open to reveal the interior); and between these two "houses" was an open street, or "market-place" in which was set Diogenes' tub. An entrance at the rear enabled persons to come in from the "city." The action moved freely from the palace-gate to the market-place (with its tub) and to Apelles' studio.

For the text I have used the second quarto of 1584 as reproduced by R. W. Bond in *The Complete Works of John Lyly*, 1902; but I have altered the original punctuation, and modernized the use of capital letters and italics. In brackets I have added stage-directions to enable the reader to visualize the movements of the actors on the stage peculiar to Court plays.

THE PROLOGUE AT THE BLACK-FRYERS [1]

They that feare the stinging of waspes make fannes of peacockes tailes, whose spots are like eies; and Lepidus, which coulde not sleepe for the chatting of birdes, set vp a beaste whose head was like a dragon: and we, which stande in awe of reporte, are compelled to sette beefore our owle Pallas shield,[2] thinking by her vertue to couer the others deformitie.   It was a signe of famine to Aegypte when Nilus flowed lesse then twelue cubites, or more then eighteene: and it may threaten dispaire vnto vs if we be lesse curious [3] then you looke for, or more combersome.   But, as Theseus, being promised to be brought to an eagles neast, and trauailing al the day, found but a wrenne in a hedg, yet said, "This is a bird": so, we hope, if the shower of our swelling mountaine seeme to bring foorth some eliphant, perfourme but a mouse, you will gently say, "This is a beast."   Basill softly touched yeeldeth a sweete sent, but chafed in the hand, a ranke sauour; wee feare, euen so, that our labours slylye [4] glaunced on will breede some content, but examined to the proofe, small commendation.   The haste in performing [5] shall bee our excuse.   There went two nightes to the begetting of Hercules; feathers appeare not on the Phœnix vnder seauen monethes; and the mulbery is twelue in budding: but our trauailes [6] are like the hares, who at one time bringeth foorth, nourisheth, and engendreth againe; or like the broode of Trochilus, whose egges in the same moment that they are layd become birdes.   But howsoeuer we finish our worke, we craue pardon if we offend in matter, and patience if we transgresse in manners.   We haue mixed mirth with counsell, and discipline with delight, thinking it not amisse in the same garden to sowe pot-hearbes that we set flowers.   But we hope, as harts that cast their hornes, snakes their skinnes, eagles their bils, become more fresh for any other labour: so, our charge being shaken of, we shalbe fitte for greater matters.   But least, like the Mindyans, we make our gates greater then our towne, and that our play runnes out at the preface, we here conclude: — wishing that although there bee in your precise iudgementes an vniuersall mislike, yet wee maye enioy by your woonted courtisies a general silence.

THE PROLOGUE AT THE COURT

Wee are ashamed that our birde, which fluttered by twilight [7] seeming a swan, should bee proued a batte set against the sunne.   But, as Iupiter placed Silenus asse among the starres, and Alcebiades couered his pictures, beeing owles and apes, with a courtaine embroidered with lions and eagles, so are we enforced vpon a rough discource to drawe on a smooth excuse; resembling lapidaries who thinke to hide the crake in a stone by setting it deepe in golde.   The gods supped once with poore Baucis; the Persian kings sometimes shaued stickes: our hope is Your Heighnesse wil at this time lend an eare to an idle pastime.   Appion, raising Homere from hell, demanded onely who was his father; and we, calling Alexander from his graue, seeke onely who was his loue.   Whatsoeuer we present, we wish it may be thought the daunsing of Agrippa his shadowes, who, in the moment they were seene, were of any shape one woulde conceiue; or lynces, who hauing a quicke sight to discerne, haue a short memorie to forget.   With vs it is like to fare as with these torches,[8] which, giuing light to others, consume themselues: and wee, shewing delight to others, shame our selues.

---

[1] The small private theatre in which the children were accustomed to present their plays before the better class of Londoners.
[2] Alluding to the Queen.   [3] Careful as to the standards of excellence.   [4] Without full attention.
[5] Lyly acquired Blackfriars in June or July, 1583.   He wrote *Campaspe* in great haste in order to have it ready for the Queen at the following Christmas season.
[6] Labors.
[7] Alluding to the public performances at Blackfriars.   As this clause indicates, the play was first acted at Blackfriars.
[8] Wax candles.   The stage was illuminated by candles set in "great branches" and "smaller branches" hung from wires overhead.

ʹCAMPASPE

ACTUS PRIMUS

Scæna Prima

[The street, before Alexander's Palace. Enter two officers, Clitus and Parmenio.] [1]

CLITUS. Parmenio, I cannot tel whether I should more commend in Alexanders victories courage or curtesie, in the one being a resolution without feare, in the other a liberality aboue custome. [5 Thebes is rased, the people not racked; towers throwne down, bodies not thrust aside; a conquest without conflict, and a cruell warre in a milde peace. 9

PAR. Clytus, it becommeth the sonne of Phillip to be none other then Alexander is; therfore, seeing in the father a ful perfection, who could haue doubted in the son an excellencie? For, as the moone can borrow nothing els of the sunne but light, [15 so, of a sire in whome nothing but vertue was, what coulde the childe receiue but singular? [2] It is for turkies to staine each other,[3] not for diamondes; in the one to bee made a difference in goodnes, in the other no comparison. 21

CLITUS. You mistake mee, Parmenio, if whilest I commend Alexander you imagine I call Phillip into question; vnlesse, happely, you coniecture (which none of [25 iudgment will conceiue) that because I like the fruit, therefore I heaue [4] at the tree, or coueting to kisse the child, I therfore go about to poyson the teat. 29

PAR. I [5] but, Clytus, I perceiue you are borne in the East, and neuer laugh but at the sunne-rising; which argueth, though a duetie where you ought, yet no great deuotion where you might. 34

CLITUS. We will make no controuersie of that which there ought to be no question.

Onely this shal be the opinion of vs both — that none was worthy to be the father of Alexander but Phillip, nor any meete to bee the sonne of Phillip but Alexander. 40

PAR. Soft, Clytus! behold the spoiles and prisoners! A pleasaunt sight to vs, because profit is ioyned with honour; not much paineful to them, because their captiuitie is eased by mercy. 45

[Enter soldiers with spoils, leading in as captives Timoclea, Campaspe, and other Thebans.]

TIMO. Fortune, thou didst neuer yet deceiue vertue, because vertue neuer yet did trust fortune. Sworde and fire will neuer get spoyle where wisdome and fortitude beares sway. O Thebes! thy [50 walles were raysed by the sweetnesse of the harpe, but raced [1] by the shrilnes of the trumpet! Alexander had neuer come so neere the wals had Epaminondas walkt about the walles; and yet [2] might the [55 Thebanes haue beene mery in there streetes if he had beene to watch their towers. But destinie is seldome foreseene, neuer preuented. We are here now captiues, whose neckes are yoaked by force, but whose [60 harts can not yeelde by death! Come, Campaspe and the rest; let vs not be ashamed to cast our eyes on him, on whom wee feared not to cast our dartes. 64

PAR. Madame, you neede not doubt; [3] it is Alexander that is the conquerour.

TIMO. Alex[ander] hath ouercome, not conquered.

PAR. To bring al vnder his subiection is to conquer. 70

TIMO. He cannot subdue that which is diuine.

PAR. Thebes was not.

TIMO. Vertue is. 74

CLITUS. Alexander, as he tendreth [4] vertue, so he will you. He drinketh not bloud, but thirsteth after honor; he is

[1] Razed to the ground.
[2] Up to the present time.
[3] Fear.   [4] Cherisheth.

greedy of victory, but neuer satisfied with mercy. In fight terrible, as becometh a captaine; in conqueste milde, as be- [80 seemeth a king. In al things — then which nothing can be greater — he is Alexander!

CAMP. Then, if it be such a thing to be Alexander, I hope it shalbe no miser- [85 able thing[1] to be a virgin. For if he saue our honors, it is more then to restore our goods. And rather doe I wish hee preserue our fame, then our lyues; which if he do, wee will confesse there can be no greater thing then to be Alexander. 91

[*Enter from the palace Alexander with his general, Hephestion.*]

ALEX. Clitus, are these prisoners? Of whence these spoiles?

CLITUS. Like[2] your maiesty, they are prisoners, and of Thebes. 95

ALEX. Of what calling or reputation?

CLITUS. I know not; but they seeme to be ladies of honor.

ALEX. I wil know. [*Turning to Timoclea.*] Madam, of whence you are I know; but who, I cannot tell. 101

TIMO. Alexander, I am the sister of Theagenes, who fought a battell with thy father before the city of Chyronie, where he died, I say which none can gainsay, valiantly. 106

ALEX. Lady, there seeme in your words sparkes of your brothers deedes, but woorser fortune in your life then his death. But feare not, for you shall liue with- [110 out violence, enemies, or necessitie. [*Turning to Campaspe.*] But, what are you, fayre lady? Another sister to Theagines?

CAMP. No sister to Theagines, but an humble hand-maid to Alexander; borne of a meane parentage,[3] but to extreame fortune. 117

ALEX. Well, ladies — for so your vertues shew you whatsoeuer your birthes be — you shalbe honourably en- [120 treated. Athens shall be your Thebes, and you shal not be as abiectes[4] of warre, but

as subiectes to Alexander. Permenio, conducte these honourable ladies into the citie. Charge the souldiers not so [125 much as in wordes to offer them any offence; and let all wants be supplyed so farre forth as shalbe necessary for such persons and my prisoners. 129

Exeunt Parme[nio] et captiui.

[ALEX.] Hephestion, it resteth now that we haue as great care to gouerne in peace as conquer in war; that, whilest armes cease, artes may flourish, and, ioyning letters with launces, we endeuor to be as good philosophers as soldiers, knowing it [135 no lesse praise to be wise then commendable to be vailiant.

HEP. Your Maiestie therin sheweth that you haue as great desire to rule as to subdue. And needes must that [140 common-wealth be fortunate whose captaine is a philosopher, and whose philosopher is a captaine!

Exeunt.

[ACTUS PRIMUS.] SCHÆNA SECUNDA.

[*The street. Enter Manes, Granichus, and Psyllus.*]

MANES. I serue, in-steede of a maister, a mouse, whose house is a tub, whose dinner is a crust, and whose bed is a boord.[1]

PSYLLUS. Then art thou in a state of life which philosophers commend: a [5 crumme for thy supper, an hande for thy cup, and thy clothes for thy sheetes. For *Natura paucis contenta.*[2]

GRAN. Manes, it is pittie so proper a man should be cast away vppon a [10 philosopher: but that Diogenes, that dogge,[3] should haue Manes, that dogbolt,[4] it grieeueth nature and spiteth arte, the one hauing found thee so dissolute — absolute,[5] I would say — in body, the other so single[6] — singular — in minde. 16

---

[1] Q₂ *things;* Q₃ *thing.* [2] Please.
[3] The reader should not overlook the fact that Campaspe was of middle-class birth, and hence unsuited to be the wife of Alexander.
[4] Outcasts.

[1] Diogenes affected the extremest austerity in living — his clothing was of the coarsest, his food of the plainest, and his bed was the ground or bare floor. At last he took up his residence in a tub.
[2] "Nature is content with few things."
[3] Diogenes earned this epithet by his sharp rebukes to the Athenians.
[4] Contemptible fellow. [5] Perfect. [6] Poor.

MANES. Are you mery? It is a signe, by the trip of your tongue and the toyes of your head, that you haue done that to day which I haue not done these three dayes. 20

PSYLLUS. What is that?

MANES. Dined!

GRAN. I thinke Diogenes keepes but cold cheere.

MANES. I would it were so; but hee keepeth neither hot nor cold. 26

GRAN. What, then? luke-warme? That made Manes runne from his maister last day.[1]

PSYLLUS. Manes had reason, for his name foretold as much. 31

MANES. My name? How so, sir boy?

PSYLLUS. You know that it is called *mons, à mouendo*,[2] because it standes still.

MANES. Good. 35

PSYLLUS. And thou art named *Manes, à manendo*,[3] beecause thou runst away.

MANES. Passing [4] reasons! I did not runne awaye, but retire.

PSYLLUS. To a prison, because thou woldest haue leisure to contemplate. 41

MANES. I will proue that my body was immortall beecause it was in prison.

GRAN. As how?

MANES. Didde your maisters neuer teach you that the soule is immortall? 46

GRAN. Yes.

MANES. And the body is the prison of the soule.

GRAN. True. 50

MANES. Why then, thus: to make my body immortal I put it to prison.

GRAN. Oh bad!

PSYLLUS. Excellent ill! 54

MANES. You may see how dull a fasting wit is. Therfore, Psyllus, let vs go to supper with Granichus. Plato is the best fellow of al phylosophers. Giue me him that reades in the morning in the schoole, and at noone in the kitchin! 60

PSYLLUS. And me!

GRAN. Ah sirs, my maister is a king in his parlour [5] for the body, and a god in his study for the soule. Among all his menne he commendeth one that is an excellent [65

musition; then stand I by and clap another on the shoulder, and say, "This is a passing good cooke."

MANES. It is well doone, Granichus! For giue me pleasure that goes in at the [70 mouth, not the eare; I had rather fill my guttes then my braines.

PSYLLUS. I serue Apelles, whoe feedeth mee as Diogenes doth Manes; for at dinner the one preacheth abstinence, the other [75 commendeth counterfeiting.[1] When I would eat meat, he paintes a spit, and when I thirst, "O," saith he, "is not this a faire pot?" and points to a table[2] whiche conteines The Banquet of the Gods, [80 where are many dishes to feede the eie, but not to fill the gut.

GRAN. What doost thou then?

PSYLLUS. This doeth hee then — bring in many examples that some haue liued [85 by sauours; and proueth that much easier it is to fatte by colours; and telles of birdes that haue beene fatted by painted grapes in winter; and how many haue so fed their eies with their mistresse picture that [90 they neuer desired to take food, being glutted with the delight in their fauours.[3] Then doth he shew me counterfeits [of] such as haue surfeited with their filthy and lothsome vomits, and with the riotous [95 Bacchanalles of the god Bacchus and his disorderly crew — which are painted al to the life in his shop. To conclude, I fare hardly thogh I go richly. Which maketh me, when I shuld begin to shadow [4] a [100 ladies face, to draw a lambes head — and sometime to set to the body of a maide a shoulder of mutton! [5] for *semper animus meus est in patinis.*[6] 104

MANES. Thou art a god to me! for could I see but a cookes shop painted I would make mine eyes fatte as butter. For I haue nought but sentences to fil my maw: as, *Plures occidit crapula quàm gladius; Musa ieiunantibus amica;*[7] Reple- [110 tion killeth delicately; and an old saw [8] of

---

[1] Yesterday.   [2] "Mountain, from moving."
[3] "Manes, from standing still."
[4] Excellent.   [5] Dining hall.

[1] Painting.   [2] Picture.
[3] Features.   [4] Paint.
[5] With a pun, the word "mutton" meaning a woman of ill-fame.
[6] "My mind is always in the stew-pan."
[7] "Excess kills more than the sword; the Muse is a friend to those who fast."
[8] Saying.

abstinence, Socrates': The belly is the heads graue. Thus, with sayings, not with meate, he maketh a gally-mafrey.[1]

GRAN.   But how doest thou then liue?   116

MANES.   With fine iests, sweet aire, and the dogs almes.[2]

GRAN.   Wel, for this time I will stanch thy gut; and among pots and platters thou shalt see what it is to serue Plato.   121

PSYLLUS.   For ioy of Granichus lets sing.

MANES.   My voice is as cleare in the euening as in the morning.[3]

GRAN.   Another commodity[4] of emptines.   126

SONG[5]

GRAN.   O for a bowle of fatt canary!
Rich Palermo! sparkling sherry!
Some nectar, else, from Iuno's daiery. 129
O, these draughts would make vs merry!

PSYLLUS.   O for a wench! (I deale in faces,
And in other dayntier things.)
Tickled am I with her embraces, —
Fine dancing in such fairy ringes!   134

MANES.   O for a plump fat leg of mutton!
Veale, lambe, capon, pigge, and conney!
None is happy but a glutton,
None an asse but who wants money.

CHOR.   Wines, indeed, and girles are good,
But braue victuals feast the bloud.   140
For wenches, wine, and lusty cheere,
Ioue would leape down to surfet heere!

[*Exeunt.*]

[ACTUS PRIMUS.]   SCHÆNA TERTIA.

[*The street, before Alexander's palace. Enter Melippus.*]

MELIP.   I had neuer such a doe to warne schollers to come before a king! First I cam to Crisippus, a tall leane old mad-man, willing him presently to appeare

---

[1] Hash, a hodge-podge.
[2] Blows? Scraps such as are thrown to dogs?
[3] I.e. is not interfered with by a full stomach.
[4] Profit, advantage.
[5] One should remember that the choristers of the Chapel Royal and of St. Paul's Cathedral had charming voices.

---

before Alexander. He stoode staring on [5 my face, neither mouing his eies nor his body. I vrging him to giue some answer, hee tooke vp a booke, sate downe, and saide nothing! Melissa, his maid, told me it was his manner; and that oftentimes [10 she was fain to thrust meate into his mouth, for that he wold rather starue then ceasse studie. Well, thoght I, seeing bookish men are so blockish, and so great clarkes[1] such simple courtiers, I wil neither be [15 partaker of their commons[2] nor their commendations. From thence I came to Plato and to Aristotle, and to diuerse other; none refusing to come, sauing an olde obscure fellowe, who, sitting in a tub turned [20 towardes the sunne, reade Greek to a yong boy. Him when I willed to appeare before Alexander, he answeared: "If Alexander wold faine see me, let him come to mee; if learne of me, lette him come to me; [25 whatsoeuer it be, let him come to me." "Why," said I, "he is a king!" He answered, "Why: I am a philosopher." "Why, but he is Alexander!" "I, but I am Diogenes." I was halfe angry to [30 see one, so crooked in his shape, to be so crabbed in his sayings. So, going my way, I said, "Thou shalt repent it if thou commest not to Alexander!" "Nay," smiling answered he, "Alexander may repent it [35 if he come not to Diogenes; vertue must be sought, not offered." And so, turning himself to his cel, he grunted I know not what, like a pig vnder a tub. But I must be gone, the philosophers are comming.   40

Exit [*into the palace*].

[*Enter Plato, Aristotle, Cleanthes, Anaxarchus, Crates, and Chrysippus.*]

PLATO.   It is a difficult controuersie, Aristotle, and rather to be wondred at then beleeued, how natural causes should worke supernatural effects.   44

ARIS.   I doe not so much stand vpon the apparition is seene in the moone, neither the *Demonium* of Socrates, as that I cannot by naturall reason giue any reason of the ebbing and flowing of the sea; which makes

---

[1] Scholars.
[2] Provisions, rations.

me in the depth of my studies to crye out,
O ens entium, miserere mei! [1]   51

PLATO. Cleanthes and you attribute so
muche to nature by searching for things
which are not to be found, that, whilest you
studie a cause of your owne, you omitte [55
the occasion it selfe. There is no man so
sauage in whom resteth not this diuine
particle — that there is an omnipotent,
eternal, and deuine mouer, which may be
called "God."   60

CLEANT. I am of this minde: that that
first mouer, which you tearme "God," is
the instrument of all the mouings; which
we attribute to nature. The earth, which
is masse, swimmeth on the sea. Sea- [65
sons deuided in themselues, fruits growing
in themselues, the maiestie of the skie, the
whole firmament of the world, and whatsoeuer els appeareth miraculous — what
man, almost of meane capacitie, but can
proue it naturall?   71

ANAXAR. These causes shalbe debated
at our philosophers feast, in which controuersie I wil take parte with Aristotle,
that there is *Natura naturans*,[2] and yet not
God.   76

CRATES. And I with Plato, that there is
Deus optimus maximus,[3] and not nature.

ARIS. Here commeth Alexander.   79

[*Enter from the palace Alexander and
Hephaestion.*]

ALEX. I see, Hephestion, that these
philosophers are here attending for vs.

HEP. They were not philosophers if
they knew not their dueties.

ALEX. But I much maruaile Diogenes
shoulde be so dogged.   85

HEP. I doe not think but his excuse
wilbe better then Melippus message.

ALEX. I will go see him, Hephestion,
because I long to see him that would commaund Alexander to come, to whom al [90
the world is like [4] to come. [*Turning to the
philosophers.*] Aristotle and the rest,
sithence my comming from Thebes to
Athens, from a place of conquest to a pallace of quiet, I haue resolued with my [95

---

[1] "Oh reality of realities, have mercy on me."
[2] Nature, a creative power in itself.
[3] A God, best, most powerful.
[4] Glad, pleased.

self in my court to haue as many philosophers, as I had in my camp soldiers. My
court shalbe a schole, wherein I wil haue
vsed as great doctrine in peace as I did in
warre discipline.   100

ARIS. We are al here ready to be commaunded; and glad we are that we are commaunded, for that nothing better becommeth kings then literature, which maketh
them come as neere to the gods in wisdome
as they do in dignitie.   106

ALEX. It is so, Aristotle; but yet there
is among you — yea and of your bringing
vp! — that sought to destroy Alexander:
— Calistenes, Aristotle, whose trea- [110
sons againste his prince shall not bee borne
out with the reasons of his phylosophy.

ARIS. If euer mischiefe entred into the
heart of Calistenes, let Calistenes suffer for
it; but that Aristotle euer imagined any [115
such thing of Calistenes, Aristotle doth denie.

ALEX. Well, Aristotle, kindred may
blind thee, and affection [1] mee. But in
kinges causes I will not stande to [119
schollers arguments. This meeting shalbe
for a commandement, that you all frequent
my courte. Instructe the young with
rules, confirme the olde with reasons, lette
your liues be answerable to your learnings,
leaste my proceedings be [2] contrary to my
promises.   126

HEP. You sayde you woulde aske euery
one of them a question, which yester-night
none of vs coulde aunswere.   129

ALEX. I will. Plato, of all beastes
which is the subtillest?

PLATO. That which man hetherto neuer
knew.

ALEX. Aristotle, how should a man be
thought a god?   135

ARIS. In doing a thing vnpossible for a
man.

ALEX. Crisippus, which was first, the
day or the night?   139

CHRYS. The day, by a day.

ALEX. Indeede, straunge questions
must haue straung answeres. Cleanthes,
what say you, is life or death the stronger?

CLE. Life, that suffereth so many
troubles.   145

---

[1] Personal interest.
[2] Q₂ *by*; I adopt the reading of the other editions.

ALEX.   Crates, how long should a man liue?

CRATES.   Till he thinke it better to die then liue.   149

ALEX.   Anaxarchus, whether doth the sea or the earth bring forth most creatures?

ANAX.   The earth; for the sea is but a parte of the earth.   153

ALEX.   Hephestion, me thinkes they haue aunswered all well; and in such questions I meane often to trie them.

HEP.   It is better to haue in your courte a wise man, then in your ground a golden mine.   Therefore would I leaue war to studie wisdom, were I Alexander.   160

ALEX.   So would I, were I Hephestion. But come; let vs go and giue release, as I promised, to our Theban thralles.

[*Exeunt Alexander and Hephestion.*]

PLATO.   Thou art fortunate, Aristotle, that Alexander is thy scholler.   165

ARIS.   And you happy that he is your soueraigne.

CHRYS.   I could like the man well if he could be contented to be but a man.   169

ARIS.   He seeketh to draw neere to the gods in knowledge, not to be a god.

PLATO.   Let vs question a litle with Diogenes why he went not with vs to Alexander. [*They approach Diogenes,* [174 *who is sitting in his tub.*] Diogenes, thou didst forget thy dutie that thou wentst not with vs to the king.

DIOG.   And you your profession, that you went to the king.   179

PLATO.   Thou takest as great pride to bee peeuish as others doe glory to bee vertuous.

DIOG.   And thou as great honor, being a philosopher, to bee thought courtlike, [184 as others shame, that be courtiers, to be accounted philosophers.

ARIS.   These austere maners set a side, it is wel known that thou didst counter-feate monye.   189

DIOG.   And thou thy maners, in that thou didste not counterfeite money.

ARIS.   Thou hast reason to contemn the courte, being both in body and mynde too crooked for a courtier.   194

DIOG.   As good be crooked, and en-deuour to make my self straight, from the court, as to be straight, and learne to be crooked at the court.   198

CRATES.   Thou thinkest it a grace to be opposite against Alexander.

DIOG.   And thou to be iump with [1] Alexander.

ANAX.   Let vs go; for in contemning him wee shall better please him than in won-dring at him.   [*They walk away.*]   205

ARIS.   Plato, what dost thou thinke of Diogenes?

PLATO.   To be Socrates furious.[2]   Let vs go.   209

Exeunt Philosophi.

ACTUS SECUNDUS

SCHÆNA PRIMA

[*Diogenes advances from his tub, holding up a lantern as if seeking an honest man. Enter Psyllus, Manes, and Granicus.*]

PSYLLUS.   Behold, Manes, where thy maister is, seeking either for bones for his dinner, or pinnes for his sleeues.[3]   I wil go salute him.

MANES.   Doe so; but mum! not a woord you sawe Manes.   6

GRAN.   Then stay thou behinde, and I will goe with Psyllus.

[*Granichus and Psyllus approach Diogenes.*]

PSYLLUS.   All haile, Diogenes, to your proper person!   10

DIOG.   All hate to thy peeuish condi-tions.

GRAN.   O Dogge!

PSYLLUS.   What dost thou seeke for here?   15

DIOG.   For a man, and a beast.

GRAN.   That is easie without thy light to be found; bee not all these men? [*Point-ing to the audience.*]

DIOG.   Called men.

GRAN.   What beast is it thou lookest for?   21

DIOG.   The beast my man, Manes.

PSYLLUS.   He is a beast indeede that will serue thee!

---

[1] In accord with.   [2] Mad.
[3] Because so ragged.

DIOG. So is he that begat thee.   25

GRAN. What wouldest thou do if thou shouldest find Manes?

DIOG. Giue him leaue to doo as hee hath done before.

GRAN. Whats that?   30

DIOG. To runne away.

PSYLLUS. Why, hast thou no neede of Manes?

DIOG. It were a shame for Diogenes to haue neede of Manes, and for Manes to haue no need of Diogenes.   36

GRAN. But put the case he were gone, wouldest thou entertaine [1] any of vs two?

DIOG. Vpon condition.

PSYLLUS. What?   40

DIOG. That you should tell me wherefore any of you both were good.

GRAN. Why, I am a scholler, and well seene [2] in phylosophy.

PSYLLUS. And I a prentice, and well seene in painting.   46

DIOG. Well then, Granichus, bee thou a painter to amend thine yll face; and thou, Psyllus, a phylosopher to correct thine euil manners. But who is that? Manes?   50

MANES [advancing]. I care not who I were, so I were not Manes.

GRAN. You are taken tardie.

PSYLLUS. Let vs slip aside, Granichus, to see the salutation betweene Manes and his maister.   [They stand aside.]   56

DIOG. Manes, thou knowest the last day [3] I threw away my dish to drink in my hand, because it was superfluous; now I am determined to put away my man and serue my selfe, quia non egeo tui vel te.[4]   61

MANES. Maister, you know a while a goe I ran awaye; so doe I meane to do againe, quia scio tibi non esse argentum.[5] 64

DIOG. I know I haue no mony; neither will I haue euer a man: for I was resoluied longe sithence to put away both my slaues — money and Manes.

MANES. So was I determined to shake of both my dogs — hunger and Diogenes.

PSYLLUS. O sweete consent beetweene a crowde [1] and a Iewes harp!   72

GRAN. Come, let vs reconcile them.

PSYLLUS. It shall not neede, for this is their vse. Nowe do they dine one vpon another.   76

Exit Diogenes [into his tub].

GRAN. How now, Manes? art thou gone from thy maister?

MANES. Noe, I didde but nowe bynde my selfe to him.   80

PSYLLUS. Why, you were at mortall iars!

MANES. In faith, no; we brake a bitter iest one vppon another.

GRAN. Why, thou art as dogged as he.

PSYLLUS. My father knew them both litle whelpes.   87

MANES. Well, I will hie mee after my maister.

GRAN. Why, is it supper time with Diogenes?   91

MANES. I, with him at al times when he hath meate.

PSYLLUS. Why then, euery man to his home; and lette vs steale out againe anone.

GRAN. Where shall we meete?   96

PSYLLUS. Why, at *Alæ vendibili suspensa hedera non est opus.*[2]

MANES. O Psyllus, *habeo te loco parentis,*[3] thou blessest me!   100

Exeunt.

[ACTUS SECUNDUS.]   SCHÆNA SECUNDA.

[*The street.   Enter from the palace Alexander, Hephestion, and the Page.*]

ALEX. Stand aside, sir boy, till you be called. [*The Page withdraws.*] Hephestion, how doe yee like the sweete face of Campaspe?

HEP. I cannot but commend the stoute courage of Timoclea.   6

ALEX. Without doubt Campaspe had some great man to her father.

---

[1] Accept into service.
[2] Skilled.   [3] Yesterday.
[4] An echo of William Lyly's Latin Grammar: "Egeo, or indigeo, tui *vel* te, I have need of thee"; that is, the verb is followed by either the genitive or the accusative.
[5] "Because I know you have no money." Manes takes his quip likewise from Lyly's Grammar.

---

[1] Harmony between a violin.
[2] "Good ale needs no bush," an old English proverb turned into Latin.
[3] "I have thee in place of a parent." From Lyly's Grammar.

HEP.   You know Timoclea had Theagines to her brother.   10
ALEX.   Timoclea stil in thy mouth!
Art thou not in loue?
HEP.   Not I!
ALEX.   Not with Timoclea, you meane;
wherein you resemble the lapwing, who [15
crieth most where her neast is not; and so
you lead me from espying your loue with
Campaspe, you cry Timoclea.
HEP.   Could I aswell subdue kingdomes
as I can my thoughts, or were I as [20
farre from ambition as I am from loue, al
the world wold account mee as valiant in
armes as I know my self moderate in affection.
ALEX.   Is loue a vice?   25
HEP.   It is no vertue.
ALEX.   Well, now shalt thou see what
small difference I make betweene Alexander and Hephestion.   And sith thou
haste beene alwayes partaker of my [30
triumphes, thou shalt be partaker of my
tormentes. I loue, Hephestion! I loue!
I loue Campaspe! — a thing farre vnfit for
a Macedonian, for a king, for Alexander.
Why hangest thou down thy head, [35
Hephestion? Blushing to heare that
which I am not ashamed to tell?
HEP.   Might my wordes craue pardon,
and my counsel credite, I woulde both discharge the duetie of a subiect, for so I am,
and the office of a friend, for so I will.   41
ALEX.   Speake Hephestion; for whatsoeuer is spoken, Hephestion speaketh to
Alexander.   44
HEP.   I can not tel, Alexander, whether
the reporte be more shameful to be heard,
or the cause sorrowfull to be beleeued!
What! is the sonne of Phillip, king of
Macedon, become the subiect of Campaspe, the captiue of Thebes? Is that [50
minde, whose greatnes the world could not
containe, drawn within the compasse of an
idle alluring eie? Wil you handle the
spindle with Hercules, when you should
shake the speare with Achilles? Is the [55
warlike sound of drumme and trumpe
turned to the soft noyse of lire and lute? the
neighing of barbed steeds, whose loudnes
filled the ayre with terrour, and whose
breathes dimmed the sunne with [60

smoak, conuerted to dilicate tunes and
amorous glaunces? O Alexander! that
soft and yeelding minde should not bee in
him, whose hard and vnconquered heart
hath made so many yeelde. But, you [65
loue. Ah griefe! But whom? Campaspe! Ah shame! A maide forsooth vnknowne, vnnoble;[1] and who can tell
whether immodest? whose eies are framed
by arte to inamour, and whose heart [70
was made by nature to inchaunt. I, but
she is bewtiful. Yea, but not therefore
chast. I, but she is comly in al parts of the
body. Yea, but she may be crooked in
some part of the mind. I, but she is [75
wise. Yea, but she is a woman! Bewty is
like the blackberry, which seemeth red
when it is not ripe; resembling pretious
stones that are polished with honny,
which, the smother they look, the [80
sooner they breake. It is thought wonderful among the seamen, that mugil, of all
fishes the swiftest, is found in the belly of
the bret, of al the slowest; and shall it not
seeme monstrous to wisemen that the [85
hearte of the greatest conquerour of the
worlde should be found in the handes of the
weakest creature of nature? of a woman! of
a captiue! Hermyns[2] haue faire skinnes,
but fowle liuers: sepulchres fresh [90
colours, but rotten bones; women faire
faces, but false heartes. Remember, Alexander, thou hast a campe to gouerne, not a
chamber! Fall not from the armour of
Mars to the armes of Venus, from the [95
fiery assaults of war, to the maidenly
skirmishes of loue, from displaying the
eagle in thine ensigne, to set downe the
sparow.[3] I sighe, Alexander, that where
fortune could not conquer, folly shuld [100
ouercome. But behold al the perfection
that may be in Campaspe: a hayre curling
by nature not arte; sweete alluring eies; a
faire face made in dispite of Venus, and a
stately porte in disdaine of Iuno; a [105
witte apt to conceiue and quick to answere; a skin as soft as silk, and as smooth
as iet; a longe white hand; a fine litle foote;
— to conclude, all partes answerable to the
best part. What of this? Though [110

---

[1] Not of noble birth.   [2] Ermines.
[3] The symbol of Venus.

she haue heauenly giftes, vertue and bewtie, is she not of earthly mettall, flesh and bloud? You, Alexander, that would be a god, shew your selfe in this worse then a man — so soone to be both ouer- [115 seene and ouertaken in a woman, whose false teares know their true times, whose smooth words wound deeper then sharpe swordes. There is no surfeit so dangerous as that of honney, nor anye poyson so [120 deadly as that of loue; — in the one, phisicke cannot preuaile, nor in the other counsell.

ALEX. My case were light, Hephestion, and not worthy to be called loue, if [125 reason were a remedy, or sentences could salue that sense cannot conceiue. Litle do you know — and therefore sleightly do you regarde — the dead embers in a priuate person, or liue coles in a great prince, [130 whose passions and thoughts do as far exceede others in extremitie, as their callings doe in maiestie.[1] An eclipse in the sunne is more then the falling of a starre; none can conceiue the torments of a king, [135 vnlesse hee be a king, whose desires are not inferior to their dignities. And then iudge, Hephestion, if the agonies of loue be dangerous in a subiect, whether they be not more then deadly vnto Alexander, [140 whose deep and not-to-be-conceiued sighes cleaue the hart in shiuers, whose wounded thoughtes can neither be expressed nor endured. Cease then, Hephestion, with arguments to seeke to refel[2] that [145 which, with their deitie, the gods cannot resist; and let this suffice to aunswere thee, that it is a king that loueth, and Alexander, whose affections are not to be measured by reason, being immortall — nor, I feare me, to be borne, being intollerable! 151

HEP. I must needs yeeld when neither reason nor counsell can be heard.

ALEX. Yeeld, Hephestion; for Alexander doth loue — and therefore must obtaine. 156

HEP. Suppose she loues not you? Affection commeth not by appointmente or birth; and then as good hated as enforced.

ALEX. I am a king, and will commaund. 161

HEP. You may, to yeelde to luste by force; but to consent to loue by feare, you cannot!

ALEX. Why, what is that which Alexander may not conquer as he list? 166

HEP. Why, that which you say the gods cannot resiste — loue.

ALEX. I am a conquerour, she a captiue; I as fortunate as she faire; my [170 greatnes may aunswere her wants, and the giftes of my minde the modestie of hers. Is it not likely, then, that she should loue? Is it not reasonable? 174

HEP. You say that in loue there is no reason, and therfore there can be no likelyhood.

ALEX. No more, Hephestion! In this case I wil vse mine owne counsell, and in all other thine aduice. Thou maist be a [180 good soldier, but neuer good louer. Cal my Page. [Page advances.] Sirha, goe presently to Apelles, and will him to come to me without either delay or excuse.

PAGE. I goe. 185

[Exit the Page into the studio of Apelles.]

ALEX. In the meane season, to recreate my spirits, being so neare, we will goe see Diogenes. And see where his tub is. [They cross over to Diogenes' tub.] Diogenes? 190

DIOG. [from his tub]. Who calleth?

ALEX. Alexander. How happened it that you woulde not come out of your tub to my palace? 194

DIOG. Because it was as far from my tub to your pallace as from your palace to my tub.

ALEX. Why then, doest thou ow no reuerence to kings?

DIOG. No. 200

ALEX. Why so?

DIOG. Because they be no gods.

ALEX. They be gods of the earth.

DIOG. Yea, gods of earth.

ALEX. Plato is not of thy mind. 205

DIOG. I am glad of it.

ALEX. Why?

DIOG. Because I would haue none of Diogenes minde but Diogenes. 209

---

[1] Obviously intended as a compliment to Queen Elizabeth.
[2] Refute.

ALEX. If Alexander haue any thing that may pleasure Diogenes, let me know, and take it.

DIOG. Then take not from me that you cannot giue me — the light of the world.

[*Motions him to stand aside so as not to cut off the sun-light.*]

ALEX. What doest thou want?   215
DIOG. Nothing that you haue.
ALEX. I haue the world at commaund!
DIOG. And I, in contempt.
ALEX. Thou shalt liue no longer than I will.   220
DIOG. But I will die, whether you will or no.
ALEX. How should one learn to be content?
DIOG. Vnlearn to couet.   225
ALEX. Hephestion, were I not Alexander, I wolde wishe to be Diogenes.
HEP. He is dogged, but discrete; I cannot tel how — sharpe, with a kinde of sweetenes, ful of wit, yet too too wayward.   231
ALEX. Diogenes, when I come this way again, I will both see thee, and confer with thee.
DIOG. Doe.   235

[*Enter Apelles from his studio.*]

ALEX. But here commeth Apelles. How now, Apelles, is Venus face yet finished?

APEL. Not yet. Bewty is not so soone shadowed whose perfection commeth [240 not within the compasse either of cunning or of colour.

ALEX. Well, let it rest vnperfect; and come you with me, where I wil shewe you that finished by nature that you haue beene trifling about by art.   246

[*Exeunt.*]

ACTUS TERTIUS

SCHÆNA PRIMA

[*The street, before the studio of Apelles. Enter Apelles and Campaspe, with Psyllus attending.*]

APEL. Lady, I doubt whether there bee any colour so fresh that may shadow a countenance so faire.

CAMP. Sir, I had thought you had beene commaunded to paint with your [5 hand, not to glose [1] with your tongue. But, as I haue heard, it is the hardest thing in painting to set down a hard fauour; [2] which maketh you to dispair of my face: and then shall you haue as great thanks [10 to spare your labour as to discredit your arte.

APEL. Mistresse, you neither differ from your selfe nor your sex; for, knowing your owne perfection, you seeme to [15 dispraise that which men most commend, drawing them by that meane into an admiration, [3] where, feeding them selues, they fall into an extasie; [4] your modestie being the cause of the one, and of the other, your affections. [5]   21

CAMP. I am too young to vnderstand your speache, thogh old enough to withstand your deuise: you haue bin so long vsed to colours, you can do nothing but colour. [6]   26

APEL. Indeed, the colours I see, I feare, wil alter the colour I haue! But come, madam; will you draw neere? for Alexander will be here anon. Psyllus, stay you [30 heere at the window. If anye enquire for me, aunswere, *Non lubet esse domi.* [7]

Exeunt [into studio].

[ACTUS TERTIUS.] SCHÆNA SECUNDA.

[*The same.   Psyllus remains.*]

PSYLLUS. It is alwayes my maisters fashion, when any fair gentlewoman is to be drawne within, to make mee to stay without. But if he shuld paint Iupiter like a bul, like a swan, like an eagle, then [5 must Psyllus with one hand grind colours, and with the other hold the candle. But, let him alone! The better he shadowes her face, the more will he burne his owne heart. And now, if a manne cold meet with [10

[1] Insert comments.
[2] Feature.
[3] Wonder.
[4] Madness.
[5] Bent of mind, disposition.
[6] Disguise things in fair words.
[7] "He is not pleased to be at home."

Manes, who, I dare say, lookes as leane as if Diogenes dropped out of his nose —

[Enter Manes.]

MANES. And here comes Manes, whoe hath as muche meate in his maw as thou hast honestie in thy head.   15

PSYLLUS. Then I hope thou art very hungry.

MANES. They that know thee know that.   19

PSYLLUS. But doest thou not remember that wee haue certaine licour to conferre withall.

MANES. I, but I haue busines; I must go cry [1] a thing.

PSYLLUS. Why, what hast thou lost? 25

MANES. That which I neuer had — my dinner.

PSYLLUS. Foule lubber, wilt thou crye for thy dinner?   29

MANES. I meane, I must "cry"; not as one would saye "cry," but "cry," — that is, make a noyse.

PSYLLUS. Why, foole, that is al one; for, if thou cry, thou must needes make a noise.   35

MANES. Boy, thou art deceiued. "Cry" hath diuerse significations, and may bee alluded to manye things; "knaue" but one, and can be applyed but to thee.

PSYLLUS. Profound Manes!   40

MANES. Wee Cynickes are madde fellowes. Didste thou not finde I did quip thee?

PSYLLUS. No, verely! Why, what is a quip?   45

MANES. Wee great girders [2] cal it a short saying of a sharp witte, with a bitter sense in a sweete word.

PSYLLUS. How! canst thou thus diuine, deuide, define, dispute, and all on the suddaine?   51

MANES. Wit wil haue his swing! I am bewitcht, inspird, inflamed, infected!

PSYLLUS. Well, then will not I tempt thy gybing spirite.   55

MANES. Do not, Psyllus; for thy dull head will bee but a grindstone for my quick

wit, which if thou whet with ouerthwarts,[1] *perijsti, actum est de te;* [2] I haue drawne bloud at ones braines with a bitter bob.[3] 60

PSYLLUS. Let me crosse my selfe! [4] for I die, if I crosse thee.

MANES. Let me do my busines. I my self am afraid least my wit should waxe warm — and then must it needs con- [65 sume some hard head with fine and prety iests. I am some times in such a vaine that for want of some dull pate to worke on I begin to gird [5] my selfe.   69

PSYLLUS. The Gods shield mee from such a fine fellowe, whose words melt wits like waxe!

MANES. Well then, let vs to the matter. In fayth, my maister meaneth to morrow to fly.   75

PSYLLUS. It is a iest!

MANES. Is it a iest to flye? Shouldest thou flye so, soone thou shouldest repent it in earnest.

PSYLLUS. Well, I will be the cryer. 80

Psyllus shouts the proclamation to the audience as Manes dictates.]

MANES *and* PSYLLUS (*one after an other*). O ys! O ys! O ys! — Al manner of men, — women, or children, — that will come to-morow — into the market-place — between the houres of nine and ten, — shall see Diogenes the Cynick — flye.   86

[The last word is pronounced by Manes only.]

PSYLLUS. I do not think he will flye.

MANES. Tush! say "fly."

PSYLLUS. Fly!   89

MANES. Now let vs goe; for I will not see him againe til midnight. I haue a back way into his tub.

PSYLLUS. Which way callest thou the backwaye, when euery way is open?

MANES. I meane, to come in at his back.   96

PSYLLUS. Well, let vs goe away, that wee may returne speedily.

Exeunt.

---

1 Make a formal public proclamation.
2 Persons dealing in caustic gibes at others.

1 Retorts, contradictions.
2 "You are ruined, it is all over with you!"
3 Caustic gibe.
4 With the sign of the cross.
5 Gibe.

[ACTUS TERTIUS.] SCHÆNA TERTIA.

[*The curtains to the studio of Apelles are drawn open, revealing Campaspe seated, and Apelles busily painting her portrait.*]

APEL. I shall neuer drawe your eies well, because they blind mine.

CAMP. Why then, paint me without eies, for I am blind.

APEL. Were you euer shadowed before of any? 6

CAMP. No. And would you could so now shadow me that I might not be perceiued of any! [1] 9

APEL. It were pittie but that so absolute [2] a face should furnish Venus temple amongst these pictures.

CAMP. What are these pictures?

APEL. This is Læda, whom Ioue deceiued in likenes of a swan. 15

CAMP. A fair woman, but a foule deceit.

APEL. This is Alcmena, vnto whom Iupiter came in shape of Amphitrion her husband, and begat Hercules. 20

CAMP. A famous sonne, but an infamous fact.

APEL. He might do it, because he was a god.

CAMP. Nay, therefore it was euill done, because he was a god. 26

APEL. This is Danae, into whose prison Iupiter drisled a golden shewre, and obtained his desire.

CAMP. What gold can make one yeelde to desire? 31

APEL. This is Europa, whom Iupiter rauished. This, Antiopa.

CAMP. Were al the gods like this Iupiter. 35

APEL. There were many gods in this like Iupiter.

CAMP. I thinke in those dayes loue was wel ratified among men on earth, when lust was so ful authorised by the gods in heauen. 41

APEL. Nay, you may imagine there wer women passing amiable, when there were gods exceeding amorous.

CAMP. Were women neuer so faire, men wold be false. 46

[1] Presumably by marriage. [2] Perfect.

APEL. Were women neuer so false, men wold be fond.

CAMP. What counterfeit is this, Apelles? 50

APEL. This is Venus, the goddesse of loue.

CAMP. What! be there also louing goddesses?

APEL. This is she that hath power to commaunde the very affections of the heart. 57

CAMP. How is she hired? by praier, by sacrifice, or bribs?

APEL. By praier, sacrifice, and bribes.

CAMP. What praier? 6

APEL. Vowes irreuocable.

CAMP. What sacrifice?

APEL. Heartes euer sighing, neuer dissembling. 65

CAMP. What bribes?

APEL. Roses and kisses. But were you neuer in loue?

CAMP. No; nor loue in me.

APEL. Then haue you iniuried many. 70

CAMP. How so?

APEL. Because you haue beene loued of many.

CAMP. Flattered, parchance, of some.

APEL. It is not possible that a face [75 so faire and a wit so sharpe, both without comparison, shuld not be apt to loue!

CAMP. If you begin to tip your tongue with cunning, I pray dip your pensil in colours, and fall to that you must doe, not that you would doe. 81

[*The curtains remain open.*]

[ACTUS TERTIUS.] SCHÆNA QUARTA.

[*In the street before Alexander's palace. Enter Clitus and Parmenio.*]

CLITUS. Parmenio, I cannot tel how it commeth to passe that in Alexander now-a-daies there groweth an vnpatient kinde of life: in the morning he is melancholy, at noone solomne, at all times either more sower or seuere then he was accustomed. 6

PAR. In kinges causes I rather loue to doubt then coniecture, and think it better to be ignoraunt then inquisitiue: they haue long eares and stretched armes, in [10

whose heades suspition is a proofe, and to
be accused is to be condemned.

CLITUS. Yet betweene vs there canne
be no danger to finde out the cause, for that
there is no malice to withstand it. It [15
may be an vnquenchable thirste of conquering maketh him vnquiet. It is not
vnlikly his long ease hath altred his humour. That he should bee in loue, it is not
impossible.   20

PAR. In loue, Clytus? No, no! it is as
farre from his thought as treason in ours.
He whose euer-waking eye, whose neuer-
tyred heart, whose body patient of labour,
whose mind vnsatiable of victory hath [25
alwayes bin noted, cannot so soone be
melted into the weak conceites of loue!
Aristotle told him there were many worlds;
and that he hath not conquered one that
gapeth for al, galleth Alexander. But here
he commeth.   31

[*From the palace enter Alexander and
Hephestion.*]

ALEX. Parmenio and Clitus, I would
haue you both redy to go into Persia about
an ambassage no lesse profitable to me then
to your selues honourable.   35

CLITUS. We are ready at all com-
maundes, wishing nothing els but continually to be commaunded.

ALEX. Well then, withdraw your selues
till I haue further considered of this matter.   41

Exeunt Clytus and Parmenio.

[*Alexander and Hephestion cross over
towards Apelles' studio.*]

ALEX. Now we wil see how Apelles goeth
forward. I doubt me that nature hath
ouercome arte, and her countenance his
cunning.   45

HEP. You loue, and therefore think any
thing.

ALEX. But not so far in loue with Campaspe as with Bucephalus,[1] if occasion
serue either of conflicte or of conquest. 50

HEP. Ocasion cannot want if wil doe
not.   Behold all Persia swelling in the
pride of their owne power! the Scithians
carelesse what courage or fortune can do!

---

[1] The name of Alexander's famous war-horse.

the Aegiptians dreaming in the south- [55
sayings of their Augures, and gaping ouer
the smoak of their beasts intralles!   All
these, Alexander, are to bee subdued — if
that world be not slipped out of your head,
which you haue sworne to conquere with
that hand.   61

ALEX. I confesse the labours fit for Alexander; and yet recreation necessary among
so many assaults, bloudye wounds, intollerable troubles.   Giue mee leaue a [65
litle, if not to sitte, yet to breath.   And
doubt not but Alexander can, when he wil,
throw affections as farre from him as he
can cowardise.   [*They pause to watch Diogenes.*] But behold Diogenes talking [70
with one at his tub.

CRYSUS [*at Diogenes' tub*]. One penny,
Diogenes; I am a Cynick.

DIOG. He made thee a begger that first
gaue thee any thing.   75

CRYSUS. Why, if thou wilt giue nothing,
no-body will giue thee.

DIOG. I want nothing, till the springs
dry and the earth perish.

CRYSUS. I gather for the gods.   80

DIOG. And I care not for those gods
which want money.

CRYSUS. Thou art a right Cynicke that
will giue nothing.

DIOG. Thou art not, that will beg any
thing.   86

[*Crysus approaches Alexander.*]

CRYSUS. Alexander!   King Alexander!
giue a poore Cynick a groat.

ALEX. It is not for a king to giue a groat.

CRYSUS. Then giue me a talent.   90

ALEX. It is not for a begger to aske a
talent. A-waye! [*Alexander and Hephestion proceed to Apelles' studio.*] Apelles?

APEL. Here.   94

ALEX. Now, gentlewomanne, doeth not
your beauty put the painter to his trump?

CAMP. Yes, my lorde; seeing so disordered a countenaunce he feareth he shall
shadow a deformed counterfeit.   99

ALEX. Wold he could colour the life with
the feature!   And me thinketh, Apelles,
were you as cunning as report saith you
are, you may paint flowers aswell with
sweete smels as fresh colours, obseruing in

your mixture such things as should draw neere to their sauours. 106

APEL. Your maiestie must know it is no lesse harde to paint sauours then vertues; colours can neither speake nor think.

ALEX. Where doe you first begin when you drawe any picture? 111

APEL. The proposition of the face, in iust compasse as I can.

ALEX. I would begin with the eie, as a light to all the rest. 115

APEL. If you will paint as you are a king, your Maiestie may beginne where you please; but, as you wold be a painter, you must begin with the face.

ALEX. Aurelius would in one houre colour four faces. 121

APEL. I meruaile in half an houre he did not foure.

ALEX. Why, is it so easie?

APEL. No, but he doth it so homely.[1] 125

ALEX. When will you finish Campaspe?

APEL. Neuer finishe! — for alwayes in absolute bewtie there is somwhat aboue arte.

ALEX. Why should not I, by labour, bee as cunning as Apelles? 131

APEL. God shield you should haue cause to be so cunning as Apelles!

ALEX. Me thinketh foure colours are sufficient to shadow any countenance; and so it was in the time of Phydias. 136

APEL. Then had men fewer fancies, and women not so many fauors. For now, if the haire of her eie-browes be black, yet must the haire of her head be yellowe;[2] [140 the attire of her head must be different from the habit of her body — els must the picture seeme like the blason of auncient armorie, not like the sweet delight of new-found amiablenes. For, as in garden [145 knottes[3] diuersitie of odours make a more sweet sauor, or as in musicke diuers strings cause a more delicate consent,[4] so in painting, the more colours the better counterfeit, obseruing blacke for a ground, and the rest for grace. 151

ALEX. Lend me thy pensil, Apelles. I will paint, and thou shalt iudge.

APEL. Here.

[*Alexander attempts to paint.*]

ALEX. The coale[1] breakes. 155

APEL. You leane too hard.

ALEX. Now it blackes not.

APEL. You leane too soft.

ALEX. This is awry.

APEL. Your eie goeth not with your hand. 161

ALEX. Now it is worse.

APEL. Your hand goeth not with your mind. 164

ALEX. Nay, if al be too hard or soft, so many rules and regardes that ones hand, ones eie, ones minde must all draw together, I had rather bee setting of a battell then blotting of a boord.[2] But how haue I done heere? 170

APEL. Like a king.

ALEX. I thinke so; but nothing more vnlike a painter. Wel, Apelles, Campaspe is finished as I wish. Dismisse her, and bring presently[3] her counterfeit after me.

APEL. I will. 176

[*Alexander and Hephestion withdraw from the studio, and stand without.*]

ALEX. Now, Hephestion, doth not this matter cotton[4] as I would? Campaspe looketh pleasauntlye, liberty wil encrease her bewty, and my loue shall aduaunce her honour. 181

HEP. I will not contrary your Maiestie; for time must weare out that loue hath wrought, and reason weane what appetite noursed. 185

[*Campaspe leaves the studio and passes down the street.*]

ALEX. How stately she passeth bye! yet how soberly! a sweet consent in her countenance, with a chast disdaine! desire mingled with coynesse; and — I cannot tell how to tearme it — a curst yeelding modestie! 190

HEP. Let her passe.

---

[1] Crudely.
[2] At this time, because Elizabeth had "yellow" hair, women were accustomed to dye their hair a similar color.
[3] Flower beds laid out in fanciful designs.
[4] Harmony.

---

[1] The pencil of charcoal.
[2] The panel on which pictures were painted.
[3] At once.
[4] Thrive, succeed.

ALEX. So she shall — for the fairest on the earth!

Exeunt [into the palace].

[ACTUS TERTIUS.] SCHÆNA QUINTA.

[*The street before the studio. Enter Psyllus and Manes.*]

PSYLLUS. I shalbe hanged for tarying so long.

MANES. I pray God my maister be not flowne before I come! 4

PSYLLUS. Away, Manes! my maister doth come!

[*Exit Manes.*]

[*From the studio enter Apelles with the portrait of Campaspe.*]

APEL. Where haue you bin all this while?

PSYLLUS. No where but heere.

APEL. Who was here since my comming? 11

PSYLLUS. No-body.

APEL. Vngratious wag, I perceiue you haue beene a loytering! Was Alexander no-body? 15

PSYLLUS. He was a king; I meant no meane body.

APEL. I will cogell your body for it; and then will I say it was "no-bodie," because it was no honeste body. Away! in! 20

Exit Psyllus [into the studio].

[APEL.] Vnfortunate Apelles! and iner-fore vnfortunate beecause Apelles! Hast thou by drawing her bewty broght to passe that thou canst scarse draw thine own breath? And by so much the more [25 hast thou encreased thy care, by how much the more thou hast shewed thy cunning. Was it not sufficient to behold the fire and warme thee, but with Satyrus thou must kisse the fire and burne thee? O Cam- [30 paspe! Campaspe! Arte must yeeld to nature, reason to appetite, wisdom to affection. Could Pigmalion entreate by prayer to haue his iuory turned into flesh? and cannot Apelles obtaine by plaints to [35 haue the picture of his loue chaunged to life? Is painting so farre inferiour to caru-

ing? or dost thou, Venus, more delight to be hewed with chizels then shadowed with colours? What Pigmalyon, or what [40 Pyrgoteles, or what Lysippus is hee that euer made thy face so fayre, or spread thy fame so farre as I? Vnlesse, Venus, in this thou enuiest mine arte — that in colouring my sweete Campaspe I haue left no [45 place by cunning to make thee so amiable! But, alas! she is the paramour to a prince. Alexander, the monarch of the earth, hath both her body and affection. For what is it that kinges cannot obtaine by prai- [50 ers, threates, and promises? Wil not she think it better to sit vnder a cloth of estate [1] like a queene, then in a poore shop like a huswife? and esteme it sweeter to be the concubine of the lord of the world, [55 then spouse to a painter in Athens? Yes, yes, Apelles! Thou maist swimme against the streame with the crab, and feede against the winde with the deere, and pecke against the steele with the cockatrice: [60 starres are to be looked at, not reched at; princes to bee yeelded vnto, not contended with; Campaspe to bee honored, not obtained, to be painted, not possessed of thee! [*He holds up the portrait and gazes at it.*] 65 O fair face! O vnhappy hand! And why didst thou draw it so faire a face? O bewtifull countenance! the expresse image of Venus, but somwhat fresher; the only pattern of that eternitie which Iupiter [70 dreaming of aslepe could not conceiue again waking. Blush Venus, for I am ashamed to end thee! [2] Now must I paint things vnpossible for mine arte, but agreeable with my affections: — deepe and [75 hollowe sighes, sadde and melancholye thoughtes, wounds and slaughters of conceites, a life posting to death, a death galloping from life, a wauering constancie, an vnsetled resolution, — and what not, [80 Apelles? And what but Apelles? But, as they that are shaken with a feuer are to bee warmed with clothes, not groanes, and as he that melteth in a consumption is to bee recured by colices, [3] not conceites; so [85 the feeding canker of my care, the neuer-

---

[1] A canopy over a throne.
[2] To end thy portrait? (Cf. II, ii, 157.)
[3] Nourishing broths.

dying worm of my hart, is to be killed by counsel, not cries, by applying of remedies, not by replying of reasons. And sith in cases desperat there must be vsed [90 medicines that are extreme, I wil hazard that litle life that is left to restore the greater part that is lost. And this shalbe my first practise — for wit must work, where authoritie is not: as soone as [95 Alexander hath viewed this portraiture, I will, by deuise, giue it a blemish, that by that meanes she may come again to my shop. And then, as good it were to vtter my loue and die with deniall, as conceale it and liue in despaire.   101

Song by Apelles.

Cvpid and my Campaspe playd
At cardes for kisses. Cupid payd.
He stakes his quiuer, bow, and arrows,
His mothers doues, and teeme of sparows;
Looses them too. Then, downe he throwes
The corrall of his lippe, the rose
Growing on's cheek (but none knows how);
With these, the cristall of his brow;
And then the dimple of his chinne.   110
All these did my Campaspe winne!
At last, hee set her both his eyes;
Shee won, and Cupid blind did rise.
  O Loue! has shee done this to thee?
  What shall, alas! become of mee?   115

[Exit into the palace.]

ACTUS QUARTUS

Schæna Prima.

[The street, or market-place, before Diogenes' tub. Enter Solinus, a citizen, and Psyllus and Granicus.]

Soli. This is the place, the day, the time, that Diogenes hath appointed to flye.

Psyllus. I will not loose the flight of so faire a fowle as Diogenes is though my maister cogel my "no-bodie," as he threatned.   6

Gran. What, Psyllus, will the beaste wag his winges to-day?

Psyllus. We shall heare; for here commeth Manes. Manes, will it be?   10

[Enter Manes.]

Manes. Be? He were best be as cunning as a bee, or else shortly he will not be at all.

Gran. How is he furnished to fly? Hath he feathers?   15

Manes. Thou art an asse! Capons, geese, and owles haue feathers. He hath found Dedalus old waxen wings, and hath beene peecing them this moneth, he is so broade in the shoulders. O you shall see him cut the ayre — euen like a tortoys.   21

Sol. Me thinkes so wise a man should not be so mad. His body must needes be to heauy.

Manes. Why, hee hath eaten nothing this seuennight but corke and feathers.   26

Psyllus [aside]. Tutch him, Manes!

Manes. He is so light that he can scarse keepe him from flying at midnight.   29

Populus intrat.

Manes. See, they begin to flocke! And behold, my mayster bustels himselfe to flye!

[Diogenes comes out of his tub, and addresses the assembled populace.]

Diog. Yee wicked and beewitched Atheneans, whose bodies make the earth to groane, and whose breathes infect the [35 aire with stench! Come ye to see Diogenes fly? Diogenes commeth to see you sinke! Yee call me dog: so I am, for I long to gnaw the boanes in your skins! Yee tearme me an hater of menne: no, I am a hater of [40 your maners. Your liues dissolute, not fearing death, will proue your deaths desperate, not hoping for life. What do you els in Athens but sleepe in the day and surfeite in the night? back-gods [1] in the [45 morning with pride, in the euening bellygods with gluttonie! You flatter kings, and call them gods: speake trueth of your selues, and confesse you are diuels! From the bee you haue taken not the honney [50 but the wax to make your religion, framing it to the time, not to the trueth. Your filthy luste you colour vnder a courtly

---

[1] Referring to fine clothes.

colour of loue, iniuries abroad vnder the title of pollicies at home, and secrete [55 malice creepeth vnder the name of publick iustice. You haue caused Alexander to dry vp springs and plant vines, to sow roket [1] and weede endiffe,[2] to sheare sheepe and shrine foxes.[3] Al conscience is [60 sealed at Athens. Swearing commeth of a hot mettal; lying, of a quick wit; flattery, of a flowing tongue; vndecent talk, of a mery disposition. Al things are lawfull at Athens! Either you thinke there are [65 no gods, or I must think ye are no men. You build as though you should liue for euer, and surfet as though you should die to morow. None teacheth true phylosophy but Aristotle — because he was the [70 kings schoolemaister! O times! O menne! O coruption in manners! Remember that greene grasse must turne to dry hay. When you sleep, you are not sure to wake; and when you rise, not certeine to lye [75 downe. Looke you neuer so hie, your heads must lye leuell with your feete! Thus haue I flowne ouer your disordered liues; and if you wil not amend your manners, I wil study to fly further from you, that I may be neerer to honesty.   81

SOL. Thou rauest, Diogenes, for thy life is different from thy words; did not I see thee come out of a brothel house? Was it not a shame?   85

DIOG. It was no shame to go out, but a shame to goe in.

GRAN. It were a good deede, Manes, to beate thy maister.

MANES. You were as good eate my maister.   91

ONE OF THE PEOPLE. Hast thou made vs all fooles? And wilt thou not flye?

DIOG. I tell thee, vnlesse thou be honest, I will flye.   95

PEOPLE. Dog! Dog! Take a boane!

DIOG. Thy father neede feare no dogs, but dogs thy father.

PEOPLE. We wil tel Alexander that thou reprouest him behinde his back. 100

DIOG. And I will tell him that you flatter him before his face.

PEOPLE. We wil cause al the boyes in the streete to hisse at thee.   104

DIOG. Indeede, I thinke the Athenians haue their children ready for any vice, because they be Athenians.

[Exeunt the people.]

MANES. Why maister! meane you not to flye?   109

DIOG. No, Manes; not without wings.

MANES. Euery-body will account you a lyar.

DIOG. No, I warrant you; for I will alwaies say the Athenians are mischieuous.

[Diogenes returns to his tub.]

PSYLLUS. I care not! It was sport ynogh for me to see these old huddles hit home.   117

GRAN. Nor I.

PSYLLUS. Come, let vs goe. And hereafter, when I meane to raile vpon any [120 body openly, it shall be giuen out I will flye.

Exeunt.

[ACTUS QUARTUS.] SCHÆNA SECUNDA.

[The street before Apelles' studio. Enter Campaspe on her way to the studio.]

CAMPASPE (*sola*). Campaspe, it is hard to iudge whether thy choice be more vnwise, or the chaunce vnfortunate. Doest thou preferre — ? but stay! vtter not that in woordes which maketh thine eares to [5 glow with thoughts. Tush! better thy tongue wagge then thy heart break! Hath a painter crept further into thy mind then a prince? Apelles then Alexander? Fond wench! the basenes of thy mind be- [10 wraies the meannesse of thy birth. But, alas! affection is a fyre which kindleth as well in the bramble as in the oake, and catcheth hold where it first lighteth, not where it may best burne. Larkes that [15 mount aloof in the ayre build their neastes below in the earth; and women that cast their eies vpon kinges may place their hearts vpon vassals. A needle will become thy fingers better then a lute, and a [20 distaffe is fitter for thy hand then a scepter. Ants liue safely til they haue gotten wings, and iuniper is not blowne vp till it hath gotten an hie top. The meane estate is without care as long as it continueth [25 without pride. But here commeth Apelles, — in whom I woulde there were the like affection!

[*From the studio enter Apelles.*]

APEL. Gentlewoman, the misfortune I had with your picture wil put you to [30 some paines to sitte againe to be painted.

CAMP. It is smal paines for me to sit still, but infinit for you to draw still.[1]

APEL. No, madame. To painte Venus was a pleasure, but to shadowe the sweete face of Campaspe — it is a heauen!   36

CAMP. If your tongue were made of the same flesh that your heart is, your wordes would bee as your thoughtes are: but such a common thing it is amongst you to [40 commend, that oftentimes for fashion sake you cal them beautifull whom you know black.[2]

APEL. What might men doe to be beleeued?   45

CAMP. Whet their tongues on their heartes.

APEL. So they doe, and speake as they thinke.

CAMP. I would they did!   50

APEL. I would they did not!

CAMP. Why, would you haue them dissemble?

APEL. Not in loue, but their loue. But wil you giue me leaue to aske you a question without offence?   56

CAMP. So that you wil aunswere me another without excuse.

APEL. Whom do you loue best in the world?   60

CAMP. He that made me last[3] in the world.

APEL. That was a god.

CAMP. I had thought it had beene a man. But whome do you honour most, Apelles?   66

APEL. The thing that is lykest you, Campaspe.

CAMP. My picture?   69

APEL. I dare not venture vpon your

person! But come, let vs go in; for Alexander will thinke it long till we returne.

Exeunt [into the studio].

[ACTUS QUARTUS.]   SCHÆNA TERTIA.

[*The street before the palace.   Enter Clytus and Parmenio.*]

CLITUS. We heare nothing of our embassage. A colour, belike, to bleare our eyes, or ticle our eares, or inflame our heartes. But what doth Alexander in the meane season but vse for tantara, [5 Sol-fa-la,[1] for his harde couch, downe beddes, for his handfull of water, his standinge-cup of wine?

PAR. Clytus, I mislike this new delicacie and pleasing peace. For what [10 els do we se now then a kind of softnes in euery mans mind; bees to make their hiues in soldiers helmets; our steedes furnished with foote-clothes[2] of gold in-steede of saddles of steele; more time to bee required [15 to scoure the rust of our weapons then there was woont to be in subdewing the countries of our enemies. Sithence Alexander fell from his harde armour to his softe robes, beholde the face of his [20 court: — youthes that were woont to carry deuises of victory in their shieldes engraue now posies[3] of loue in their ringes; they that were accustomed on trotting horses to charge the enimy with a launce, now in [25 easie coches ride vp and downe to court ladies, in-steede of sword and target to hazard their liues, vse pen and paper to paint their loues! Yea, such a feare and faintnes is growne in courte that they [30 wish rather to heare the blowing of a horne to hunt then the sound of a trumpet to fight! O Phillip, wert thou aliue to see this alteration — thy men turned to women, thy soldiers to louers, gloues [35 worne in veluet caps[4] in-steede of plumes in grauen helmets — thou wouldest ether die among them for sorrow, or confound them for anger.   39

---

[1] Continually.   [2] Ugly.
[3] I.e. who painted my likeness.

[1] The sound of the war-drums, the music of loue ditties.
[2] A richly ornate cloth spread over a horse.
[3] Brief verses engraved in rings.
[4] As favors from their mistresses.

CLITUS. Cease, Permenio! least in speaking what becommeth thee not, thou feele what liketh thee not. Truth is neuer without a scratcht face; whose tongue, although it cannot be cut out, yet must it be tied vp. 45

PAR. It grieueth me not a little for Hephestion, whoe thirsteth for honour, not ease; but such is his fortune and neerenesse in friendship to Alexander that he must lay a pillowe vnder his head when he [50 would put a targette in his hand. But let vs draw in, to see how well it becomes them to tread the measurs in a daunce that were wont to sette the order for a march.

Exeunt [into the palace].

[ACTUS QUARTUS.] SCHÆNA QUARTA.

[Apelles and Campaspe discovered in the studio.]

APEL. I haue now, Campaspe, almost made an ende.

CAMP. You tolde me, Apelles, you would neuer ende!

APEL. Neuer end my loue; for it shal be eternal. 6

CAMP. That is, neither to haue beginning nor ending?

APEL. You are disposed to mistake; I hope you do not mistrust. 10

CAMP. What will you saye if Alexander perceiue your loue?

APEL. I will say, it is no treason to loue.

CAMP. But how if he wil not suffer thee to see my person? 15

APEL. Then wil I gase continually on thy picture.

CAMP. That will not feede thy heart.

APEL. Yet shall it fill mine eye. Besides, the sweete thoughtes, the sure [20 hopes, thy protested faith, wil cause me to imbrace thy shadow continually in mine armes; of the which by strong imagination I will make a substaunce. 24

CAMP. Wel, I must be gon. But this assure your self, that I had rather bee in thy shop grinding colours then in Alexanders court following higher fortunes.

[She leaves the studio.]

CAMPASPE (*alone*). Foolish wensh, what hast thou done? That, alas! which [30 cannot be vndone! and therefore I feare me vndone. But content is such a lif I care not for aboundance. O Apelles, thy loue commeth from the heart, but Alexanders from the mouth! The loue of kinges is [35 like the blowinge of windes, whiche whistle sometimes gentlye amonge the leaues, and straight-wayes turne the trees vp by the rootes; or fire, which warmeth a farre off, and burneth neere-hand; or the sea, [40 which maketh men hoyse their sayles in a flattering calme, and to cut their mastes in a rough storme. They place affection by times, by pollicie, by appointment. If they frowne, who dares cal them vncon- [45 stant? if bewray secretes, who will tearme them vntrue? if fall to other loues, who trembles not if he call them vnfaithfull? In kinges there can be no loue but to queenes; for as neere must they meete in mai- [50 estie as they doe in affection. It is requisite to stande aloofe from kinges loue, Ioue. and lightening!

Exit.

[ACTUS QUARTUS.] SCHENA QUINTA.

[Apelles in the studio.]

APEL. Now, Apelles, gather thy wits together. Campaspe is no lesse wise then fayre; thy selfe must bee no lesse cunning then faithfull. It is no small matter to be riuall with Alexander! 5

[Enter the Page of Alexander.]

PAGE. Apelles, you must come away quicklye with the picture; the king thinketh that now you haue painted it you play with it.

APEL. If I would play with pictures I haue ynough at home. 11

PAGE. None, parhaps, you like so well.

APEL. It may be I haue painted none so well.

PAGE. I haue knowne many fairer faces. 16

APEL. And I many better boyes.

Exeunt [severally].

ACTUS QUINTUS

Schæna Prima

[*Diogenes in his tub, Manes attending. To
them enter Sylvius, bringing his sons,
Perim, Milo, and Trico.*]

SYLVI. I haue brought my sons, Diogenes, to be taught of thee.

DIOG. What can thy sonnes doe?

SYL. You shall see their qualities.
Daunce, sirha!   5

Then Perim daunceth.

How like you this? Doth he well?

DIOG. The better, the worser.

SYL. The musicke very good.

DIOG. The musitions very badde, who
onelye study to haue their stringes in [10
tune, neuer framing their manners to
order.

SYL. Now shall you see the other.
Tumble, sirha!   14

Milo tumbleth.

How like you this? Why do you laugh?

DIOG. To see a wagge that was born to
break his neck by distinie, to practise it by
arte.

MILO. This dogge will bite me! I will
not be with him.   20

DIOG. Feare not, boy; dogges eate no
thistles.

PERIM. I maruel what dog thou art, if
thou be a dog.

DIOG. When I am hungry, a mastyue,
and when my belly is full, a spaniell.   26

SYL. Doest thou beleeue that there are
any gods, that thou art so dogged?

DIOG. I must needs beleeue there are
gods, for I think thee an enimie to them. 30

SYL. Why so?

DIOG. Because thou hast taught one of
thy sonnes to rule his legges, and not to
follow learning; the other, to bend his body
euery way, and his minde no way.   35

PERIM. Thou doest nothing but snarle
and barke like a dogge!

DIOG. It is the next way to driue away
a theefe.

SYL. Now shall you heare the third,
who singes like a nightingall.   41

DIOG. I care not; for I haue heard a
nightingall sing her selfe.

SYL. Sing, sirha!

Trico singeth.

SONG

What bird so sings, yet so dos wayle?   45
O, 'tis the rauish'd nightingale!
"Iug, iug, iug, iug, tereu," shee cryes;
And still her woes at midnight rise.
Braue prick-song! [1] who is't now we heare?
None but the larke so shrill and cleare. 50
How at heauens gats she claps her wings,
The morne not waking till shee sings!
Heark, heark, with what a pretty throat
Poore Robin red-breast tunes his note!
Heark how the iolly cuckoes sing!   55
"Cuckoe," to welcome in the spring,
"Cuckoe," to welcome in the spring!

SYL. Loe, Diogenes! I am sure thou
canst not doe so much.

DIOG. But there is neuer a thrush but
can.   61

SYL. What hast thou taught Manes,
thy man?

DIOG. To be as vnlike as may be thy
sonnes.   65

MANES. He hath taught me to fast, lye
hard,[2] and runne away.

SYL. How sayest thou, Perim? wilte
thou bee with him?

PERIM. I — so he will teache me first to
run away.   71

DIOG. Thou needest not be taught, thy
legges are so nimble.

SYL. How sayest thou, Milo? wilte thou
bee with hym?   75

DIOG. Nay, holde your peace; he shal
not!

SYL. Why?

DIOG. There is not roome enough for
him and mee both to tumble [3] in one tub. 80

SYL. Well, Diogenes, I perceaue my
sonnes brooke not thy manners.

DIOG. I thought no lesse, when they
knewe my vertues.   84

SYL. Farewel, Diogenes. Thou need-

---

[1] Descant accompanying a simple melody.
[2] To sleep on a board.
[3] It should be noted that Milo was the tumbler.

edst not haue scraped rootes if thou wouldest haue followed Alexander.

DIOG. Nor thou haue followed Alexander, if thou hadst scraped roots.

Exeunt [Sylvius and his three sons].

[ACTUS QUINTUS.] SCHÆNA SECUNDA.

*[The street. Enter Apelles from his
studio.]*

APELLES (*alone*). I feare me, Apelles,
that thine eies haue blabbed that which thy
tongue durst not. What little regard
hadst thou! whilst Alexander viewed the
conterfeite of Campaspe, thou stoodest [5
gazing on her countenaunce! If he espie,
or but suspect, thou must needes twice
perish — with his hate, and thine owne
loue. Thy pale lookes when he blushed,
thy sadde countenaunce when hee [10
smiled, thy sighes when he questioned, may
breede in him a ielosie, perchaunce a
frenzye. O loue! I neuer before knewe
what thou wert; and nowe haste thou made
mee that I know not what my selfe am? [15
Onely this I knowe, that I must endure
intollerable passions for vnknowne pleasures. Dispute not the cause, wretch, but
yeeld to it; for better it is to melt with desire then wrastle with loue. Cast thy [20
selfe on thy carefull bedde; be content to
lyue vnknowne; and die vnfounde! O
Campaspe, I haue painted thee in my
heart! Painted? nay, contrarye to myne
arte, imprinted! — and that in suche [25
deepe characters, that nothing can rase it
out, vnlesse it rubbe my heart out.

Exit [into the studio].

[ACTUS QUINTUS.] SCHÆNA TERTIA.

*[The street, or market-place, near Diogenes'
tub. Enter two soldiers, Milectus and
Phrigius, with the courtezan Lais.]*

MIL. It shal go hard but this peace
shall bring vs some pleasure.

PHRY. Downe with armes, and vp with
legges! This is a world for the nonce! 4

LAIS. Sweete youthes, if you knew
what it were to saue your sweete bloud, you
would not so foolishly go about to spend it.
What delight can there be in gashinge, to
make foule scarres in faire faces and
crooked maimes in streight legges? as [10
though men, being borne goodlye by nature, would of purpose become deformed
by follye! And all, forsooth, for a new
found tearme called "valiant" — a word
which breedeth more quarrelles then the
sense can commendation. 16

MIL. It is true, Lays! A featherbed
hath no fellow! Good drinke makes good
bloud, and shall pelting [1] words spill it? 19

PHRY. I meane to inioy the world, and
to draw out my life at the wiredrawers, not
to curtall it off at the cutlers.

LAIS. You may talke of warre, speake
bigge, conquer worldes with great wordes;
but, stay at home — where, in-steede [25
of alarums you shall haue daunces, for hot
battailes with fierce menne, gentle skirmishes with fayre womenne. These pewter
coates canne neuer sitte so wel as satten
dublets. Beleeue mee, you cannot [30
conceaue the pleasure of peace vnlesse you
despise the rudenesse of warre.

MIL. It is so. But see Diogenes prying
ouer his tubbe. [*They advance to Diogenes'
tub.*] Diogenes, what sayest thou to [35
such a morsel? [*Points to Lais.*]

DIOG. I say, I would spit it out of my
mouth because it should not poyson my
stomack.

PHRY. Thou speakest as thou art; it is
no meate for dogges. 41

DIOG. I am a dogge, and phylosophy
rates [2] mee from carion.

LAIS. Vnciuill wretch, whose manners
are aunswerable to thy callynge, the [45
time was thou wouldest haue hadde my
company, had it not beene, as thou saidst,
too deare!

DIOG. I remember there was a thinge
that I repented me of; and now thou [50
haste told it. Indeed, it was to deare of
nothing, and thou deare to no-bodye.

LAIS. Downe, villaine! or I wil haue thy
head broken!

MIL. Will you couch? 55

[Diogenes withdraws into his tub.]

---

[1] Petty, trifling.   [2] Chides.

PHRY. Auaunt, curre! Come, sweete Lays, let vs go to some place and possesse peace. But first let vs sing. There is more pleasure in tuning of a voyce then in a volly of shotte. 60

[They sing.] [1]

MIL. Now let vs make haste, least Alexander finde vs here.

Exeunt.

[ACTUS QUINTUS.] SCHÆNA QUARTA.

[The street, before the palace. From the palace enter Alexander, Hephestion, and the Page.]

ALEX. Mee thinketh, Hephestion, you are more melancholy then you were accustomed; but I perceiue it is all for Alexander. You can neither brooke this peace, nor my pleasure. Be of good cheare; though I winke, I sleepe not. 6

HEP. Melancholy I am not, nor well content; for, I know not how, there is such a rust crept into my bones with this long ease that I feare I shal not scowre it out with infinite labours. 11

ALEX. Yes, yes; if all the trauails of conquering the world will set either thy body or mine in tune, wee will vndertake them. But what think you of Apelles? [15 Did ye euer see any so perplexed? Hee neither aunswered directly to any question, nor looked stedfastly vppon anye thing. I hold my life the painter is in loue! 19

HEP. It may be; for commonly we see it incident in artificers to be inamoured of their own workes, as Archidamus of his woodden doue, Pigmalyon of his iuorie image, Arachne of his wodden swan; — especially painters, who playing with [25 their owne conceits, now coueting to draw a glauncing eie, then a rolling, now a wincking, stil mending it, neuer ending it, til they be caught with it; and then, poore soules! they kisse the colours with their [30 lippes, with which before they were loth to taint their fingers.

ALEX. I wil finde it out. Page, goe

speedely for Apelles. Wil him to come hither; and when you see vs earnestly [35 in talke, sodenly cry out "Apelles shoppe is on fire!"

PAGE. It shalbe done.

ALEX. Forget not your lesson.

[Exit the Page.]

HEP. I maruaile what your deuice shalbe. 41

ALEX. The euent shall proue.

HEP. I pittie the poore painter if he be in loue. 44

ALEX. Pittie him not. I pray thee, that seuere grauity set aside, what do you think of loue?

HEP. As the Macedonians doe of their hearbe beet, which, loking yellow in the ground, and blacke in the hand, thinke it better seene then toucht. 51

ALEX. But what do you imagine it to be?

HEP. A word, by superstition thought a god, by vse turned to an humour, by selfwil made a flattering madnesse. 56

ALEX. You are too hard-harted to think so of loue. Let vs go to Diogenes. Diogenes, thou maist think it somwhat that Alexander commeth to thee againe so soone. 61

DIOG. If you come to learne, you could not come soone enough; if to laugh, you be come to soone.

HEP. It would better become thee to be more curteous, and frame thy selfe to please. 67

DIOG. And you better to be lesse,[1] if you durst displease.

ALEX. What dost thou think of the time we haue here? 71

DIOG. That we haue little, and lose much.

ALEX. If one be sick, what wouldest thou haue him do? 75

DIOG. Be sure that he make not his phisition his heire.

ALEX. If thou mightest haue thy wil, how much ground wouldst content thee?

DIOG. As much as you in the ende must be contented withall. 81

ALEX. What? a world?

---

[1] The song, for which the scene was mainly created, has been lost.

[1] Less courteous.

Diog. No; the length of my body.

Alex. Hephestion, shal I be a litle pleasant with him? 85

Hep. You may; but he will be very peruerse with you.

Alex. It skilleth not; I cannot be angry with him. Diogenes, I pray thee what doost thou think of loue? 90

Diog. A little worser then I can of hate.

Alex. And why?

Diog. Because it is better to hate the thinges whiche make to loue, then to loue the things which giue occasion of hate. 95

Alex. Why, bee not women the best creatures in the world?

Diog. Next men and bees.

Alex. What dost thou dislyke chiefly in a woman? 100

Diog. One thing.

Alex. What?

Diog. That she is a woman.

Alex. In mine opinion thou wert neuer born of a woman that thou thinkest [105 so hardly of women. But now commeth Apelles, who, I am sure is as far from thy thoght as thou art from his cunning. Diog[enes], I will haue thy cabin remoued nerer to my court, bicause I wilbe a philosopher. 111

Diog. And when you haue done so, I pray you remoue your court further from my cabinne, because I wil not be a courtier.

[*From the studio enter Apelles accompanied by the Page.*]

Alex. But here commeth Apelles. [115 Apelles, what peece of worke haue you in hand?

Apel. None in hand, if it like your maiestie; but I am deuising a platforme [1] in my head. 120

Alex. I think your hand put it in your head. Is it nothing about Venus?

Apel. No, but some thing aboue Venus!

Page [*shouting*]. Apelles! Apelles! looke about you! your shop is on fire! 125

Apel. Ay me! if the picture of Campaspe be burnt, I am vndone!

[*He starts to run; Alexander stops him.*]

Alex. Stay, Apelles. No hast. It is

[1] Scheme, outline, plan.

your hart is on fire, not your shop; and if Camp[aspe] hang ther, I wold she [130 were burnt! But haue you the picture of Campaspe? Belike you loue her wel that you care not thogh al be lost so she be safe.

Apel. Not loue her! — but your Maiestie knowes that painters in their last [135 works are said to excel themselues; and in this I haue so much pleased my selfe that the shadow as much delighteth mee, being an artificer, as the substaunce doth others, that are amorous. 140

Alex. You lay your colours grosely! Though I could not paint in your shop, I can spy into your excuse. Be not ashamed, Apelles; it is a gentlemans sport to be in loue. [*To the Page.*] Call hither [145 Campaspe. [*Exit the Page.*] Me thinks I might haue bin made priuie to your affection; though my counsell had not bene necessary, yet my countenance [1] might haue bin thought requisite. But [150 Apelles, forsooth, loueth vnder hand; yea, and vnder Alexanders nose! and — but I say no more.

Apel. Apelles loueth not so; but he liueth to do as Alexander will. 155

[*Enter Campaspe led in by the Page.*]

Alex. Campaspe, here is newes! Apel[les] is in loue with you!

Camp. It pleaseth your Maiestie to say so. 159

Alex [*aside*]. Hephestion, I wil trye her to. — Campas[pe], for the good qualities I know in Apelles, and the vertue I see in you, I am determined you shal enioy one the other. How say you, Campaspe? would you say "I"? 165

Camp. Your handmaid must obey, if you commaund.

Alex. Think you not, Hephestion, that she wold faine be commaunded?

Hep. I am no thought catcher, but I gesse vnhappily.[2] 171

Alex. I will not enforce mariage where I cannot compel loue.

Camp. But your Maiestie may moue a question where you be willing to haue a match. 176

[1] Consent.
[2] I.e. she would be "unhappily" commanded.

ALEX.   Beleeue me, Hephestion, these
parties are agreed!   They would haue me
both priest and witnesse!   Apelles, take
Campaspe.   Why moue ye not? [180
Campaspe, take Apelles.   Wil it not be?
If you be ashamed one of the other, by my
consent you shal neuer come togeather.
But dissemble not; Campaspe, do you loue
Apelles?   185

CAMP.   Pardon, my lord, I loue Apelles.

ALEX.   Apelles, it were a shame for you,
being loued so openly of so faire a virgin, to
say the contrary.   Doe you loue Campaspe?   190

APEL.   Onely Campaspe!

ALEX.   Two louing wormes, Hephestion!   I perceiue Alexander cannot subdue
the affections of men, though he conquer
their countries.   Loue falleth like dew [195
aswel vpon the low grasse as vpon the high
cæder.   Sparkes haue their heate, antes
their gall, flyes their splene.   Well, enioy
one an other!   I giue her thee franckly,
Apelles.   Thou shalt see that Alex- [200
ander maketh but a toye of loue, and lead-
eth affection in fetters, vsing fancy [1] as a
foole to make him sport, or a minstrell to
make him mery.   It is not the amorous
glaunce of an eie can settle an idle [205
thought in the heart.   No, no; it is childrens game; a life for seamsters and scholers: the one, pricking in cloutes,[2] haue

[1] Love.   [2] Sticking needles in cloths.

nothing els to thinke on, the other, picking
fancies out of books, haue little els to [210
meruaile at.   Go, Apelles; take with you
your Campaspe!   Alexander is cloied with
looking on that which thou wondrest at.

APEL.   Thankes to your Maiestie on
bended knee; you haue honoured Apelles!

CAMP.   Thankes, with bowed heart; you
haue blessed Campaspe!   217

Exeunt [Apelles and Campaspe].

ALEX.   Page, goe warne Clitus and Parmenio and the other lordes to be in a readines.   Let the trumpet sound! strike [220
vp the drumme! and I will presently into
Persia.   How now, Hephestion? is Alexander able to resiste loue as he list?

HEP.   The conquering of Thebes was
not so honourable as the subdueing of these
thoughts!   226

ALEX.   It were a shame Alexander
should desire to commaund the world if he
could not commaund himselfe.   But come,
let vs go.   I wil try whether I can bet- [230
ter beare my hand with my hart then I
could with mine eie.[1]   And, good Hephestion, when al the world is woone, and euery
countrey is thine and mine, either find me
out an-other to subdue, or, of my word, I
wil fall in loue!   236

Exeunt.

[1] Referring to the scene (III. iv. 160 70) in
which he attempted to draw.

THE EPILOGUE AT THE BLACKE–FRYERS

Where the rainebowe toucheth the tree, no caterpillers wil hang on the leaues; where the gloworm creepeth in the night, no addar wil goe in the day: we hope in the eares where our trauails be lodged, no carping shal harbour in those tongues. Our exercises must be as your iudgment is, resembling water, which is alwaies of the same colour into what it runneth. 5

In the Troaine horse lay couched soldiers with children; and in heapes of many words we feare diuerse vnfitte among some allowable. But, as Demosthenes with often breathing vp the hill amended his stammering, so wee hope with sundry labours against the haire [1] to correcte our studies. If the tree be blasted that blossomes, the faulte is in the wind and not in the roote; and if our pastimes be misliked that haue bin allowed,[2] you [10 must impute it to the malice of others and not our endeuour. And so wee rest in good case, if you rest well content.

THE EPILOGUE AT THE COURT

We cannot tell whether we are fallen among Diomedes birds or his horses; the one receiued some men with sweet notes, the other bitte al men with sharp teeth. But, as Homers gods conueied them into clouds whom they would haue kept from curses, and as Venus, least Adonis shuld be pricked with the stings of adders, couered his face with the winges of swans; so, we hope, being shielded with your Highnesse countenaunce, wee [5 shall, though heare the neighing, yet not feele the kicking of those iades, and receiue, though no praise (which we cannot deserue) yet a pardon, — which in all humilytie we desire. As yet we cannot tell what we should tearme our labours, yron or bullyon; only it belongeth to your Majestie to make them fitte either for the forge, or the mint, currant by the stampe, or counterfeit by the anuil. For, as nothing is to be called whit[e] [10 vnles it had bin named "white" by the firste creator, so can there be nothing thought good in the opinion of others vnlesse it be christened "good" by the iudgement of your selfe. For our selues againe, we are those torches — waxe, — of whiche, being in your highnesse handes, you may make doues or vultures, roses or nettles, lawrell for a garland, or elder for a disgrace.[3] 15

FINIS

[1] Against the grain.
[2] Possibly this phrase was added after the play had been approved in the Court performance; or the allusion may be to the allowance by the Master of the Revels.
[3] Judas was supposed to have hanged himself on an elder-tree.

XIII
PLAYS OF THE PROFESSIONAL TROUPES

A LAMENTABLE TRAGEDIE [1]

MIXED FULL OF PLESANT MIRTH, CONTAINING

THE LIFE OF CAMBISES, KING OF PERCIA

FROM THE BEGINNING OF HIS KINGDOME, VNTO HIS DEATH, HIS
ONE GOOD DEEDE OF EXECUTION, AFTER THAT MANY
WICKED DEEDES AND TYRANNOUS MURDERS, COMMITTED
BY AND THROUGH HIM, AND LAST OF ALL, HIS
ODIOUS DEATH BY GODS IUSTICE APPOINTED.
DONE IN SUCH ORDER AS FOLLOWETH.

By THOMAS PRESTON

---

[1] *Cambises*, though entered for publication in 1569, may have been written several years earlier, perhaps as early as 1560. It was obviously designed for performance by a traveling troupe of professional actors (six men and two boys), and for presentation on a bare platform-stage. I agree with Professor Manly (*The Cambridge History of English Literature*, vi, 321) that it is difficult to identify the author, Thomas Preston, with the distinguished scholar of the same name, a fellow of King's College, Cambridge, A.B. (1557), A.M. (1561), Proctor of his college (1568), and Master of Trinity Hall (1584). Our crude writer seems to have been one of the obscure poets, possibly an actor-playwright, who in the early days of the professional drama supplied troupes with manuscripts. The play, which won great and lasting favor, is interesting as showing the popular tastes in tragedy, and hence may be profitably compared with *Gorboduc*. It is also interesting for the fact that Shakespeare was familiar with its lines (possibly he acted one of its rôles), and frequently laughed at its gross absurdities

In 1569 John Alde entered the play in the Stationers' Registers, and then or shortly after published, without date, the first edition (A.); his son, Edward Alde, who succeeded to the business in 1584, issued the second edition (B.), also without date. I have reproduced the text of Edward Alde's edition from Farmer's photographic facsimile of the copy in the British Museum. I have, of course, modernized the punctuation, and I have added in brackets a few stage-directions. I do not know which copy of this edition Manly printed from, but his text shows some fifty or more different readings and spellings.

[DRAMATIS PERSONÆ

CAMBISES, King of Persia.
SMIRDIS, brother of the king.
SISAMNES, the judge.
OTIAN, his son.
PRAXASPES, a councellor.
YOUNG CHILD, his son.
LORDS,
KNIGHTS, } in attendance on the king.
QUEEN, wife of Cambises.
WAITING-MAID, attending the queen.
WIFE of Praxaspes.

SHAME.
AMBIDEXTER.
COUNCELL.
ATTENDANCE.
DILIGENCE.
PREPARATION.

SMALL HABILITY.
COMMONS CRY.
COMMONS COMPLAINT.
TRIALL.
PROOF.
EXECUTION.
CRUELTY.
MURDER.

HUF,
RUF, } ruffianly soldiers.
SNUF,
MERETRIX, their companion.
HOB,
LOB, } clownish countrymen.
MARIAN-MAY-BE-GOOD, Hob's wife.

VENUS.
CUPID.

THE SCENE: Persia.]

THE DIUISION OF THE PARTS[1]

COUNCELL
HUF
PRAXASPES
MURDER
LOB
THE THIRD LORD
} For one man.

LORD
RUF
COMMONS CRY
COMMONS COMPLAINT
LORD SMIRDIS
VENUS
} For one man.

KNIGHT
SNUF
SMALL HABILITY
PROOF
EXECUTION
ATTENDANCE
SECOND LORD
} For one man.

CAMBISES
EPILOGUS
} For one man.

PROLOGUE
SISAMNES
DILIGENCE
CRUELTIE
HOB
PREPARATION
THE I LORD
} For one man.

AMBIDEXTER
TRIALL
} For one man.

MERETRIX
SHAME
OTIAN
MOTHER
LADY
QUEENE
} For one man.

YONG CHILD
CUPID
} For one man.

---

[1] This is printed on the title-page of the original edition. Since the last two parts were for boys, it will be observed that the play is constructed so that a troupe of six men and two boys could act it.

[PROLOGUE]

The Prologue entreth.

Agathon, he whose counsail wise to princes weale [1] extended,
By good advice unto a prince three things he hath commended:
First is, that he hath government and ruleth over men;
Secondly, to rule with lawes, eke iustice, saith he, then;
Thirdly, that he must wel conceive he may not alwaies raigne.   5
Lo, thus the rule unto a prince Agathon squared plaine!
Tullie [2] the wise, whose sapience in volumes great doth tell,
Who in wisedome in that time did many men excel, —
"A prince," saith he, "is, of himselfe, a plaine and speaking law;
The law, a schoolmaister devine," — this by his rule I draw.   10
The sage and wittie Seneca his words therto did frame:
"The honest exercise of kings, men wil insue [3] the same;
But, contrariwise, if that a king abuse his kingly seat,
His ignomie and bitter shame in fine shalbe more great."
In Percia there raignd a king, who Cirus hight [4] by name,   15
Who did deserve, as I do read, the lasting blast of fame;
But he, when Sisters Three [5] had wrought to shere his vital threed,
As heire due, to take the crowne Cambises did proceed.
He in his youth was trained up by trace [6] of vertues lore;
Yet, being king, did cleane forget his perfect race before;   20
Then, cleaving more unto his wil, such vice did immitate
As one of Icarus his kind; forewarning then did hate,
Thinking that none could him dismay, ne none his fact [7] could see.
Yet at the last a fall he tooke, like Icarus to be.
Els, as the fish, which oft had take the pleasant bait from hooke,   25
In safe [8] did spring and pearce the streams when fisher fast [9] did looke
To hoist up from the watry waves unto the dried land,
Then skapte, at last by suttle bait come to the fishers hand;
Even so this King Cambises heere.   When he had wrought his wil,
Taking delight the innocent his guiltlesse blood to spil,   30
Then mighty Ione would not permit to procecute offence,
But, what mesure the king did meat, the same did Ione commence,
To bring to end with shame his race.   Two yeares he did not raign.
His cruelty we wil delate, and make the matter plaine.
Craving that this may suffice now your patience to win,   35
I take my way.   Beholde, I see the players comming in.

FINIS

---

[1] Welfare.   [2] Cicero.   [3] Follow.   [4] Was called.
[5] The three Fates, supposed to determine the length of a man's life.   [6] Course.
[7] Deed.   [8] In safety.   [9] Confidently.

[A COMEDIE OF KING CAMBISES.] [1]

First enter Cambises, the king, Knight,
[Lord], and Councell. [2]

CAMB. My Counsaile grave and sapient,
with lords of legall traine,
Attentive ears towards me bend, and mark
what shalbe sain;
So you likewise, my valiant knight, whose
manly acts doth flie
By brute of Fame, that sounding tromp
doth perce the azur sky.
My sapient words, I say, perpend,[3] and so
your skil delate!   5
You know that Mors [4] vanquished hath
Cirus, that king of state,
And I, by due inheritance, possesse that
princely crowne,
Ruling by sword of mighty force in place of
great renowne.
You knowe, and often have heard tell, my
fathers worthy facts, —
A manly Marsis [5] heart he bare, appearing
by his acts.   10
And what? shall I to ground let fall my
fathers golden praise?
No, no! I meane for to attempt this same
more large to raise.
In that, that I, his sonne, succeed his
kingly seat, as due,
Extend your councell unto me in that I
aske of you: —
I am the king of Persia, a large and fertile
soile;   15
The Egyptians against us repugne [6] as
varlets slave and vile;
Therefore I mean with Marsis hart with
wars them to frequent,
Them to subdue as captives mine, — this is
my hearts intent;
So shall I win honors delight, and praise of
me shall go.
My Councell, speake, and, lordings, eke: is
it not best do so?   20
COUNC. O puisant king, your blisful
words deserves abundant praise,

That you in this doo go about your fathers
fame to raise.
O blisful day, that king so yoong such
profit should conceive,
His fathers praise and his to win from those
that wold deceive!
Sure, my true and soveraigne king, I fall
before you prest,[1]   25
Answere to give, as dutie mine, in that your
Grace request.
If that your heart adicted be the Egyptians
to convince,[2]
Through Marsis aid the conquest wun,
then deed of hapy prince
Shall pearce the skies unto the throne of
the supernal seat,
And merite there a iust reward of Iupiter
the Great.   30
But then your Grace must not turne backe
from this pretenced will;
For to proceed in vertuous life imploy
indevour stil;
Extinguish vice, and in that cup to drinke
have no delight;
To martiall feats and kingly sport fix all
your whole delight.
KING. My Councel grave, a thousand
thanks with hart I do you render, 35
That you my case so prosperous intirely
doo tender!
I wil not swerve from those your steps
whereto you wold me train.
But now, my lord and valiant knight, with
words give answer plain:
Are you content with me to go the Marsis
games to try?
LORD. Yea, peerelesse prince! To aid
your Grace my-selfe wil live and
die.   40
KNIGHT. And I, for my hability, for feare
will not turne backe,
But, as the ship against the rocks, sustaine
and bide the wracke.
KING. O willing harts! A thousand
thanks I render unto you!
Strik up your drums with corage great.
We wil martch foorth even now!

COUNC. Permit, O king, few wordes to
heer, — my duty serves no lesse; 45
Therefore give leave to Councel thine his
mind for to expresse!
KING. Speake on, my Councel; what it be,
you shal have favor mine.
COUNC. Then wil I speake unto your
Grace as duty doth me bind.
Your Grace doth meane for to attempt of
war the manly art;
Your Grace therein may hap receive, with
others, for your part, 50
The dent of death, — in those affaires all
persons are alike, —
The heart couragious often times his detri-
ment doth seeke:
Its best therefore for to permit a ruler of
your land
To sit and iudge with equity when things
of right are skand.
KING. My Grace doth yeeld to this
your talke. To be thus now it
shall. 55
My knight, therefore prepare your-selfe
Sisamnes for to call:
A iudge he is of prudent skil; even he shal
beare the sway
In absence mine, when from the land I do
depart my way.
KNIGHT. Your knight before your Grace
even heer himself hath redy prest
With willing heart for to fulfill as your
Grace made request. 60

Exit [*Knight*].

COUNC. Pleaseth your Grace, I iudge of
him to be a man right fit;
For he is learned in the law, having the gift
of wit;
In your Graces precinct I do not view for it
a meeter man.
His learning is of good effect — bring
proofe thereof I can;
I doo not know what is his life, — his conscience hid from me; 65
I dout not but the feare of God before his
eies to be.
LORD. Report declares he is a man that to
himselfe is nie,[1]
One that favoureth much the world, and
sets to much thereby.

[1] Nigh (i.e. a man who is self-seeking).

But this I say of certainty: If hee your
Grace succeed
In your absence but for a-while, he wil be
warnd indeed 70
No iniustice for to frequent, no partiall
iudge to proove,
But rule all things with equitie, to win your
Graces love.
KING. Of that he shall a warning have my
heasts [1] for to obay;
Great punishment for his offence against
him will I lay.

[*Enter Sisamnes.*]

COUNC. Behold, I see him now agresse [2]
and enter into place! 75
SISAM. O puissant prince and mighty
king, the gods preserve your Grace!
Your Graces message came to me, your wil
purporting forth;
With grateful mind I it receiv'd according
to mine oath,
Erecting then my-selfe with speed before
your Graces eies,
The tenor of your princely wil from you for
to agnise.[3] 80
KING. Sisamnes, this the whole effect the
which for you I sent:
Our mind it is to elevate you to great pref-
erment.
My Grace, and gracious Councel eke, hath
chose you for this cause, —
In iudgement you do office beare, which
have the skil in lawes,
We thinke that you accordingly by iustice
rule wil deale, 85
That for offence none shal have cause, of
wrong you to appeale.[4]
SISAM. Abundant thankes unto your
Grace for this benignity!
To you, his Councel, in like case, with lords
of clemency!
What-so your Grace to me permits, if I
therein offend,
Such execution then commence — and use
it to this end — 90
That all other, by that my deed, example
so may take,
To admonish them to flee the same by
feare it may them make!

[1] Commands.   [2] Approach.
[3] Learn.   [4] Accuse.

KING. Then, according to your words, if you therein offend,
I assure you, even from my brest correction shall extend.
From Persia I meane to go into the Egypt land, 95
Them to convince by force of armes, and win the upper hand.
While I therefore absent shall be, I doe you full permit,
As governour in this my right, in that estate to sit,
For to detect, and eke correct, those that abuse my grace.
This is the totall of my wil. Give answere in this case! 100
SISAM. Unworthy much, O prince, am I, and for this gift unfit;
But, sith that it hath pleasd your Grace that I in it must sit,
I do avouch, unto my death, according to my skil,
With equity for to observe your Graces mind and wil,
And nought from it to swarve, indeed, but sincerely to stay — 105
Els let me tast the penalty, as I before did say.
KING. Wel then, of this authoritie I give you ful possession.
SISAM. And I will it fulfil, also, as I have made profession.
KING. My Councel. then let us depart a final stay to make;
To Egypt land now forth with speed my voyage will I take. 110
Strike up your drums, us to reioyce to hear the warlike sound.
Stay you heere, Sisamnes, iudge, and looke wel to your bound! [1]

Exeunt King, Lord, and Councell.

SISAM. Even now the king hath me extold, and set me up aloft;
Now may I weare the bordred guard,[2] and lie in downe-bed soft;
Now may I purchase house and land, and have all at my wil; 115
Now may I build a princely place, my mind for to fulfil;

[1] Bond, agreement.
[2] Ornamental borders on garments.

Now may I abrogate the law as I shall thinke it good;
If any-one me now offend, I may demaund his blood.
According to the proverbe old, my mouth I wil up-make.[1]
Now it doth lie all in my hand to leave, or els to take, 120
To deale with iustice to my [2] bound, and so to live in hope.
But oftentimes the birds be gone while one for nest doth grope.
Doo well or il, I dare avouch some evil on me wil speake.
No, truly — yet I do not meane the kings precepts to breake;
To place I meane for to returne my duty to fulfil. 125

Exit.

Enter the Vice, [Ambidexter,] with an old capcase [3] on his head, an olde paile about his hips for harnes,[4] a scummer [5] and a potlid by his side, and a rake on his shoulder.

AMB. Stand away! stand away! for the passion of God!
Harnessed I am, prepared to the field!
I would have bene content at home to have bod,
But I am sent forth with my speare and shield.
I am appointed to fight against a snaile, 130
And Wilken Wren the ancient [6] shal beare.
I dout not but against him to prevaile, —
To be a man my deeds shall declare!
If I overcome him, then a butter-flie takes his part.
His weapon must be a blew-specked hen;
But you shall see me overthrow him with a fart. 136
So, without conquest, he shal go home againe.
If I overcome him, I must fight with a flie;

[1] Please (as with something delicious); see Heywood's *Proverbs.*
[2] B. *me.* [3] Box or chest; cf. hat-box.
[4] Knightly armor.
[5] A long ladle for removing scum from boiling liquids. This served for his sword, the potlid for his buckler, and the rake for his spear.
[6] Banner.

And a blacke-pudding the flies weapon
    must be.
At the first blow on the ground he shall lie;
    I wil be sure to thrust him through the
        mouth to the knee!   141
To conquest these fellowes the man I wil
    play.
    Ha, ha, ha! now ye wil make me to smile.
. . . . 1

To see if I can all men beguile.   145
Ha! my name?   My name would ye so
    faine know?
    Yea, iwis, shal ye, and that with al
        speed! —
I have forgot it, therefore I cannot show.
 A! a! now I have it!   I have it, in-deed!
My name is Ambidexter.   I signifie one 150
    That with both hands finely can play;
Now with King Cambises, and by-and-by
    gone.
Thus doo I run this way, and that way.
For while I meane with a souldier to be,
    Then give I a leape to Sisamnes the
        iudge, —   155
I dare avouch you shall his destruction
    see!
    To all kinde of estates I meane for to
    trudge.
Ambidexter?   Nay, he is a fellow, if ye
    knew all!
Cease for a while; heereafter heare more ye
    shall!

*Enter [as if prepared for the war] three ruffins,
Huf, Ruf, and Snuf, singing.*

HUF.   Gogs flesh and his wounds, these
    warres reioyce my hart!   160
By His wounds, I hope to doo well, for my
    part!
By Gogs hart! the world shall goe hard if I
    doo not shift;
At some olde carles [2] budget I meane for to
    lift.
RUF.   By His flesh, nose, eyes, and eares,
I will venter void of all cares!   165
He is not a souldier that doth feare any
    doubt
If that he would bring his purpose about.
SNUF.   Feare that feare list, it shall not
    be I.

By Gogs wounds, I will make some necke
    stand awry!
If I loose my share, I sweare by Gogs hart,
Then let another take up my parte!   171
HUF.   Yet I hope to come the richest soul-
    dier away.
RUF.   If a man aske ye, ye may hap to
    say nay.
SNUF.   Let all men get what they can,
    not to leese I hope;
Wheresoever I goe, in eche corner I will
    grope.   175
AMB.   What and ye run in the corner of
    some prittie maide?
SNUF.   To grope there, good fellow, I will
    not be afraid.

[They spy Ambidexter.]

HUF.   Gogs wounds, what art thou that
    with us doost mel?
Thou seemest to be a souldier, the truth to
    tel;
Thou seemest to be harnessed — I cannot
    tel how;   180
I thinke he came lately from riding some
    cow.
Such a deformed slave did I never see!
Ruf, doost thou know him?   I pray thee,
    tel me!
RUF.   No, by my troth, fellow Huf, I
    never see him before!
SNUF.   As for me, I care not if I never see
    him more.   185
Come, let us run his arse against the poste!
AMB.   A, ye slaves!   I will be with you at
    oste! [1]
Ah, ye knaves!   I wil teach ye how ye shal
    me deride!

Heere let him swinge them about.

Out of my sight!   I can ye not abide!
Now, goodman poutchmouth, I am a slave
    with you?   190
Now have at ye a-fresh, againe, even now!
Mine arse against the poste you will run?
But I wil make you from that saying to
    turn!
HUF.   I beseech ye hartely to be content.
RUF.   I insure you, by mine honesty, no
    hurt we ment.   195

---

[1] A line missing.   [2] Countryman's.

[1] Lie at the same inn with you; hence, be familiar
with you.

Beside that, againe, we do not know what ye are.

Ye know that souldiers their stoutnes will declare;

Therefore, if we have any thing offended,

Pardon our rudenes, and it shalbe amended.

AMB. Yea, Gods pittie, begin ye to intreat me? 200

Have at ye once againe! By the masse, I will beat ye!

Fight againe.

HUF. Gogs hart, let us kill him! Suffer no longer!

Draw their swords.

SNUF. Thou slave, we will see if thou be the stronger!

RUF. Strike of his head at one blow!

That we be souldiers, Gogs hart, let him know! 205

AMB. O the passion of God, I have doon! by mine honestie!

I will take your part heerafter, verily.

ALL. Then come, let us agree!

AMB. Shake hands with me, I shake hands with thee.

Ye are full of curtesie, that is the best. 210

And you take great paine, ye are a man-nerly guest.

Why, maisters, doo you not know me? the truth to me tel!

ALL. No, trust us; not very well.

AMB. Why, I am Ambidexter, who[m] many souldiers doo love.

HUF. Gogs hart, to have thy company needs we must prove! 215

We must play with both hands, with our hostes and host,

Play with both hands, and score on the poste; [1]

Now and then, with our captain, for many a delay,

We wil not sticke with both hands to play.

AMB. The honester man, ye may me trust! 220

Enter Meretrix, with a staffe on her shoulder.

MER. What! is there no lads heere that hath a lust

[1] The door-post in a tavern on which was scored up the reckonings of the guests.

To have a passing trul to help at their need?

HUF. Gogs hart, she is come, indeed!

What, Mistres Meretrix, by His wounds, welcome to me!

MER. What wil ye give me? I pray you, let me see. 225

RUF. By His hart, she lookes for gifts by-and-by! [1]

MER. What? Maister Ruf? I cry you mercy!

The last time I was with you I got a broken head,

And lay in the street all night for want of a bed!

SNUF. Gogs wounds, kisse me, my trull so white! [2] 230

In thee, I sweare, is all my delight!

If thou shouldst have had a broken head for my sake,

I would have made his head to ake!

MER. What? Maister Ambidexter? Who looked for you?

AMB. Mistres Meretrix, I thought not to see you heere now. 235

There is no remedy, — at meeting I must have a kisse!

MER. What, man, I wil not sticke for that, by Gisse!

Kisse.

AMB. So now, gramercy! I pray thee be gone!

MER. Nay, soft, my freend; I meane to have one!

[She kisses him.]

Nay, soft! I sweare, and if ye were my brother, 240

Before I let go, I wil have another!

Kisse, kisse, kisse.

RUF. Gogs hart, the whore would not kisse me yet!

MER. If I be a whore, thou art a knave; then it is quit!

HUF. But hearst thou, Meretrix? With who this night wilt thou lye?

MER. With him that giveth the most money. 245

[1] Immediately. [2] Dear.

HUF.   Gogs hart, I have no money in purse, ne yet in clout! [1]

MER.   Then get thee hence and packe, like a lout!

HUF.   Adieu, like a whore!

Exit Huf.

MER.   Farwell, like a knave!

RUF.   Gogs nailes, Mistres Meretrix, now he is gone,
A match ye shall make straight with me:
I wil give thee sixpence to lye one night
    with thee.   251

MER.   Gogs hart, slave, doost thinke I am a sixpeny iug? [2]
No, wis ye, Iack, I looke a little more smug!

SNUF.   I will give her xviii pence to serve me first.

MER.   Gramercy, Snuf, thou art not the wurst!   255

RUF.   By Gogs hart, she were better be hanged, to forsake me and take thee!

SNUF.   Were she so? that shall we see!

RUF.   By Gogs hart, my dagger into her I will thrust!

SNUF.   A, ye boy, ye would doo it and ye durst!

AMB.   Peace, my maisters; ye shall not fight.   260
He that drawes first, I will him smite.

RUF.   Gogs wounds, Maister Snuf, are ye so lusty?

SNUF.   Gogs sides, Maister Ruf, are ye so crusty?

RUF.   You may happen to see!

SNUF.   Doo what thou darest to me! 265

Heer draw and fight. Heere she must lay on and coyle [3] them both; the Vice must run his way for feare; Snuf fling down his sword and buckler and run his way.

MER.   Gogs sides, knaves! seeing to fight ye be so rough,
Defend yourselves, for I will give ye both inough!
I will teach ye how ye shall fall out for me!
Yea, thou slave, Snuf! no more blowes wilt thou bide?   269
To take thy heeles a time hast thou spied?

---

[1] In my clothes.
[2] Joan, woman of light fame.   [3] Beat.

Thou villaine, seeing Snuf has gone away,
A little better I meane thee to pay!

He falleth downe; she falleth upon him, and beats him, and taketh away his weapons.

RUF.   Alas, good Mistres Meretrix, no more!
My legs, sides, and armes with beating be sore!

MER.   Thou a souldier, and loose thy weapon!   275
Goe hence, sir boy; say a woman hath thee beaten!

RUF.   Good Mistres Meretrix, my weapon let me have;
Take pittie on me, mine honestie to save!
If it be knowne this repulse I sustaine,
It will redound to my ignomy and shame.

MER.   If thou wilt be my man, and waite upon me,   281
This sword and buckler I wil give thee.

RUF.   I will doo all at your commaundement;
As servant to you I wilbe obedient.

MER.   Then let me see how before me you can goe.   285
When I speake to you, you shall doo so:
Of with your cap at place and at boord,[1] —
"Forsooth, Mistres Meretrix," at every word.
Tut! tut! in the campe such souldiers there be,
One good woman would beat away two or three!   290
Wel, I am sure customers tarry at home.
Manerly before, and let us be gone!

Exeunt [with Ruf walking in advance as a gentleman-usher].

Enter Ambidexter.

AMB.   O the passion of God! be they heer still or no?
I durst not abide to see her beat them so!
I may say to you I was [2] in such a fright,[3]
Body of me, I see the heare of my head stand upright!   296
When I saw her so hard upon them lay on,
O the passion of God! thought I, she wil be with me anon!
I made no more [4] adoo but avoided the thrust;

---

[1] Table.   [2] B. *wis.*   [3] B. *flight.*   [4] B. *mare.*

And to my legs began for to trust;   300
And fell a-laughing to my-selfe, when I was
    once gone.
It is wisdome, quoth I, by the masse, to
    save one!
Then into this place I intended to trudge,
Thinking to meete Sisamnes the iudge.
Beholde where he commeth! I will him
    meet,   305
And like a gentleman I meane him to greet.

Enter Sisamnes.

SISAM. Since that the Kings Graces Mai-
    estie in office did me set,
What abundance of wealth to me might I
    get!
Now and then some vantage I atchive;
    much more yet may I take,
But that I fear unto the king that some
    complaint will make.   310
AMB. Iesu, Maister Sisamnes, you are
    unwise!
SISAM. Why so? I pray thee let me agnise.
What, Master Ambidexter, is it you?
Now welcome to me, I make God a-vow!
AMB. Iesu, Maister Sisamnes, with me
    you are wel acquainted!   315
By me rulers may be trimly painted.
Ye are unwise if ye take not time while ye
    may;
If ye wil not now, when ye would ye shall
    have nay.
What is he that of you dare make exclama-
    tion,
Of your wrong-dealing to make explica-
    tion?   320
Can you not play with both hands? and
    turn with the winde?
SISAM. Beleeve me, your words draw
    deepe in my minde.
In collour [1] wise unto this day, to bribes I
    have inclined;
More the same for to frequent, of truth I
    am now minded.
Beholde, even now unto me suters doo
    proceed.   325

[*Enter Small Habilitie.*]

SM. HAB. I beseech you heer, good
    Maister Iudge, a poor mans cause
    to tender!

    [1] In outward appearance.

Condemne me not in wrongfull wise that
    never was offender.
You know right wel my right it is. I have
    not for to give.
You take away from me my due, that
    should my corps releeve.
The commons of you doo complaine from
    them you devocate;[1]   330
With anguish great and grevos words their
    harts do penetrate;
The right you sell unto the wrong, your
    private gain to win;
You violate the simple man, and count it
    for no sinne.
SISAM. Hold thy tung, thou pratling
    knave! and give to me reward,
Els, in this wise, I tell thee truth, thy tale
    wil not be heard.   335
Ambidexter, let us goe hence, and let the
    knave alone!
AMB. Farwell, Small Habilitie, for helpe
    now get you none;
Bribes hath corrupt him good lawes to
    polute.

Exeunt [*Sisamnes and Ambidexter*].

SM. HAB. A naughty man, that will not
    obay the kings constitute!   339
With hevy hart I wil return, til God re-
    dresse my pain.   *Exit.*

Enter Shame, with a trump blacke, [sounding
a blast].

SHAME. From among the grisly ghosts I
    come, from tirants testy train.
Unseemely Shame, of sooth, I am, pro-
    cured to make plaine
The odious facts and shameles deeds that
    Cambises king doth use.
All pietie and vertuous life he doth it cleane
    refuse;
Lechery and drunkennes he doth it much
    frequent;   345
The tigers kinde to imitate he hath given
    full consent;
He nought esteems his Counsel grave ne
    vertuous bringing-up,
But dayly stil receives the drink of damned
    Vices cup;

    [1] "Perhaps 'to make calls or demands,' if not a
misprint for *derogate*." (*N.E.D.*)

He can bide no instruction, he takes so
    great delight
In working of iniquitie for to frequent his
    spight.   350
As Fame doth sound the royal trump of
    worthy men and trim,
So Shame doth blow with strained blast the
    trump of shame on him.

Exit [blowing the trumpet].

*Enter the King, Lord, Praxaspes, and
Sisamnes.*

KING.   My Iudge, since my departure
    hence, have you used iudgement
    right?
If faithful steward I ye finde, the same I
    wil requite.
SISAM.   No doubt your Grace shal not
    once hear that I have done amis. 355
PRAX.   I much reioyce to heare so good
    newes as this.

*Enter Commons Cry running in; speake this
verse; and goe out againe hastily.*

COM. CRY.   Alas! alas! how are the com-
    mons oppressed
By that vile iudge, Sisamnes by name!
I doo not know how it should be redressed!
    To amend his life no whit he dooth
    frame.   360
We are undoone and thrown out of doore,
    His damnable dealing dooth us so tor-
    ment!
At his hand we can finde no releefe nor suc-
    cour.
God graunt him grace for to repent!

Run away crying.

KING.   What doleful cries be these, my
    l[ord], that sound do in mine eare? 365
Intelligence if you can give, unto your king
    declare.
To me it seemeth my commons al they doo
    lament and cry
Out of Sisamnes, iudge most cheefe, even
    now standing us by.
PRAX.   Even so, O king, it seemd to me, as
    you rehearsall made.
I doubt the iudge culpable be in some re-
    spect or trade.[1]   370

        ¹ Course, way.

SISAM.   Redouted king, have no mistrust!
    No whit your minde dismay!
There is not one that can me charge, or
    ought against me lay.

*Enter Commons Complaint, with Proofe and
Triall.*

COM. COMP.   Commons Complaint I rep-
    resent, with thrall of dolfull state.
My urgent cause erected foorth my greefe
    for to dilate.
Unto the king I wil prepare my miserie to
    tell,   375
To have releefe of this my greefe and fet-
    tered feet so fel.

[Kneels before Cambises.]

Redoubted prince and mighty king, myself
    I prostrat heere!
Vouchsafe, O king, with me to beare for
    this that I appeere!
With humble sute I pardon crave of your
    most Royall Grace,
To give me leave my minde to break before
    you in this place.   380
KING.   Commons Complaint, keep noth-
    ing back! Fear not thy tale to tel.
What-ere he be within this land that hath
    not used thee wel,
As princes mouth shal sentence give, he
    shal receive the same.
Unfolde the secrets of thy brest, for I extin-
    guish blame.
COM. COMP.   God preserve your Royall
    Grace, and send you blisfull daies,
That all your deeds might stil accord to
    give the god[s] the praise!   386
My complaint is, O mighty king, against
    that iudge you by,
Whose careles deeds, gain to receive, hath
    made the commons cry.
He, by taking bribes and gifts, the poore he
    doth oppresse,
Taking releefe from infants yong, widows,
    and fatherles.   390
KING [*to Sisamnes*].   Untrustfull traitor
    and corrupt iudge, how likest thou
    this complaint?
Forewarning I to thee did give of this to
    make restraint.
And hast thou doon this divelish deed mine
    ire for to augment?

I sentence give, thou Iudas iudge. Thou
    shalt thy deed repent!

SISAM. O pusant prince, it is not so! His
    complaint I deny. 395

COM. COMP. If it be not so, most mighty
    king, in place then let me dye!

Behold that I have brought with me both
    Proof and Triall true,

To stand even heere, and sentence give
    what by him did insue.

PROOF. I, Proof, do him in this appeal: [1]
    he did the commons wrong;

Uniustly he with them hath delt, his
    greedy was so strong; 400

His hart did covet in to get, he cared not
    which way;

The poor did leese their due and right, be-
    cause they want [2] to pay

Unto him for bribes, indeed, — this was his
    wanted use;

Whereas your Grace good lawes did make,
    he did the same abuse.

TRIALL. I, Triall, heer to verifie what
    Proof dooth now unfolde, 405

To stand against him in his wrong, as now
    I dare be bolde.

KING. How likest thou this, thou caitive
    vile? Canst thou the same deny?

SISAM. O noble king, forgive my fact! [3] I
    yeeld to thy mercy.

KING. Complaint [4] and Proof, redresse
    will I all this your misery.

Depart with speed from whence you came;
    and straight commaund by me 410

The execution-man to come before my
    Grace with haste.

ALL. For to fulfill this your request no
    time we meane to waste.

Exeunt they three.

KING. My lord, before my Grace goe call
    Otian, this iudges sonne,

And he shal heare and also see what his
    father hath doon.

The father he shal suffer death, the sonne
    his roome succeed; 415

And, if that he no better prove, so likewise
    shall he speed.

PRAX. As your Grace hath commaund-
    ment given, I mean for to fulfil.

[1] Accuse.   [2] Failed.
[3] Deed.   [4] B. *Complaints.*

Step aside and fetch him.

KING. Accursed iudge, couldst thou con-
    sent to do this cursed ill?

According unto thy demaund, thou shalt,
    for this thy gilt,

Receive thy death before mine eyes. Thy
    blood it shalbe spilt. 420

[Re-enter Praxaspes bringing in Otian.]

PRAX. Beholde, O king, Sisamnes sonne
    before you doth appere.

KING. Otian, this is my minde, therefore
    to me come neere:

Thy father heer for iudgment wrong pro-
    cured hath his death,

And thou, his son, shalt him succeed when
    he hath lost his breth;

And, if that thou dost once offend, as thou
    seest thy father have, 425

In like wise thou shalt suffer death. No
    mercy shal thee save!

OTIAN. O mighty king, vouchsafe your
    grace my father to remit.

Forgive his fault. His pardon I doo aske
    of you as yet.

Alas! although my father hath your
    princely hart offended,

Amends for misse he wil now make, and
    faults shalbe amended. 430

In-stead of his requested life, pleaseth your
    Grace take mine!

This offer I as tender childe, so duty doth
    me binde.

KING. Doo not intreat my grace no more,
    for he shal dye the death!

Where is the execution-man him to bereave
    of breath?

Enter Execution.

EXEC. At hand, and if it like your Grace,
    my duty to dispatch, 435

In hope that I, when deede is doone, a good
    reward shall catch.

KING. Dispatch with sword this iudges
    life; extinguish fear and cares:

So doon, draw thou his cursed skin strait
    over both his eares.

I wil see the office done, and that before
    mine eyes.

EXEC. To doo the thing my king com-
    maunds I give the enterprise. [1] 440

[1] Readiness to engage in a task.

SISAM.   Otian, my sonne, the king to death
  by law hath me condemned,
And you in roome and office mine his
  Graces wil hath placed;
Use iustice, therefore, in this case, and
  yeeld unto no wrong,
Lest thou do purchase the like death ere
  ever it be long.[1]
OTIAN.   O father deer, these words to hear,
  — that you must dye by force, —
Bedews my cheeks with stilled teares.   The
  king hath no remorce. 446
The greevous greefes and strained sighes
  my hart doth breake in twaine,
And I deplore, most woful childe, that I
  should see you slaine.
O false and fickle frowning dame, that
  turneth as the winde,
Is this the ioy in fathers age thou me as-
  signest to finde? 450
O dolefull day, unhappy houre, that loving
  childe should see
His father deer before his face thus put to
  death should be!
Yet, father, give me blessing thine, and let
  me once imbrace
Thy comely corps in foulded arms, and
  kisse thy ancient face!
SISAM.   O childe, thou makes my eyes to
  run, as rivers doo, by streame. 455
My leave I take of thee, my sonne.   Be-
  ware of this my beame![2]
KING.   Dispatch even now, thou man of
  death; no longer seem to stay!
EXEC.   Come, M[aster] Sisamnes, come on
  your way.
My office I must pay; forgive therefore my
  deed.
SISAM.   I doo forgive it thee, my freend;
  dispatch therefore with speed! 460

*Smite him in the neck with a sword to signifie
his death.*

PRAX.   Beholde, O king, how he dooth
  bleed, being of life bereft!
KING.   In this wise he shall not yet be left.
Pull his skin over his eares [3] to make his
  death more vile.

---

[1] This line omitted in B.
[2] Distress, alluding to the cross.   But cf. *N.E.D.*
beam, sb.[2]
[3] B. *eyes.*

A wretch he was, a cruell theefe, my commons to beguile!

Flea him with a false skin.

OTIAN.   What childe [1] is he of natures
  mould could bide the same to see, —
His father fleaed in this wise?   Oh, how it
  greeveth me! 466
KING.   Otian thou seest thy father dead,
  and thou art in his roome:
If thou beest proud, as he hath beene, even
  thereto shalt thou come.
OTIAN.   O king, to me this is a glasse: with
  greefe in it I view
Example that unto your Grace I doo not
  prove untrue. 470
PRAX.   Otian, convay your father hence to
  tomb where he shall lye.
OTIAN.   And if it please your lordship, it
  shall be done by-and-by.
Good execution-man, for need, helpe me
  with him away.
EXEC.   I wil fulfill, as you to me did say.

They take him away.[2]

KING.   My l[ord], now that my Grace hath
  seen that finisht is this deed, 475
To question mine give tentive eare, and
  answere make with speed:
Have not I doon a gratious deed, to redresse my commons woe?
PRAX.   Yea, truely, if it please your Grace,
  you have indeed doon so.
But now, O king, in freendly wise I counce!
  you in this, —
Certain vices for to leave that in you
  placed is: 480
The vice of drunkennes, Oh king, which
  doth you sore infect,
With other great abuses, which I wish you
  to detect.
KING.   Peace, my lord!   What needeth
  this?   Of this I will not heare!
To pallace now I will returne, and thereto
  make good cheere.
God Baccus he bestows his gifts, we have
  good store of wine, 485
And also that the ladies be both passing
  brave and fine.

---

[1] B. *thilde.*
[2] Since there were no stage-curtains, the actors
had to make some provision for removing each
"dead" player.

But stay! I see a lord now come, and eke a
    valiant knight.
What news, my lord? To see you heer my
    hart it doth delight.

Enter Lord and Knight to meet the King.

LORD. No news, O king; but of duty come
    to wait upon your Grace.
KING. I thank you, my l[ord] and loving
    knight. I pray you with me trace.[1]
My lords and knight, I pray ye tel, — I wil
    not be offended, —   491
Am I worthy of any crime once to be repre-
    hended?
PRAX. The Persians much doo praise your
    Grace, but one thing discommend,
In that to wine subiect you be, wherein you
    doo offend.
Sith that the might of wines effect doth oft
    subdue your brain,   495
My counsel is, to please their harts from it
    you would refraine.
LORD [*to Praxaspes*]. No, no, my lord! it is
    not so! For this of prince they tel,
For vertuous proofe and princely facts
    Cirus he doth excel.
By that his Grace by conquest great the
    Egiptians did convince,
Of him report abroad doth passe to be a
    worthy prince.   500
KNIGHT. In person of Cresus I answer
    make: we may not his Grace com-
    pare
In whole respect for to be like Cirus, the
    kings father,
In-so-much your Grace hath yet no childe
    as Cirus left behinde,
Even you I meane, Cambises king, in
    whom I favour finde.
KING. Cresus said well in saying so. But,
    Praxaspes, tel me why   505
That to my mouth in such a sort thou
    should avouch a lye,
Of drunkenes me thus to charge! But thou
    with speed shalt see
Whether that I a sober king or els a drunk-
    ard be.
I know thou hast a blisfull babe, wherein
    thou doost delight;
Me to revenge of these thy words I wil go
    wreke this spight: 510

[1] Proceed, go.

When I the most have tasted wine, my bow
    it shalbe bent, —
At hart of him even then to shoote is now
    my whole intent;
And, if that I his hart can hit, the king no
    drunkard is;
If hart of his I doo not kill, I yeeld to thee
    in this.
Therefore, Praxaspes, fetch to me thy
    yongest son with speed.   515
There is no way, I tell thee plaine, but I
    wil doo this deed!
PRAX. Redoubted prince, spare my sweet
    childe. He is mine only ioy!
I trust your Grace to infants hart no such
    thing will imploy.
If that his mother hear of this, she is so
    nigh her flight,
In clay her corps wil soone be shrinde to
    passe from worlds delight.   520
KING. No more adoe! Go fetch me him!
    It shalbe as I say.
And if that I doo speak the word, how dare
    ye once say nay?
PRAX. I wil go fetch him to your
    Grace; but so, I trust, it shall not
    be!
KING. For feare of my displeasure great,
    goe fetch him unto me.

[*Exit Praxaspes.*]

Is he gone? Now, by the gods, I will doo
    as I say!   525
My lord, therefore fill me some wine, I
    hartely you pray;
For I must drinke to make my braine some-
    what intoxicate.
When that the wine is in my head, O,
    trimly I can prate!
LORD. Heere is the cup, with filled wine,
    thereof to take repast.
KING. Give it me to drinke it off, and see
    no wine be wast.   530

Drink.

Once againe inlarge this cup, for I must
    tast it stil.[1]

[1] Shakespeare laughs at this scene in *I Henry IV*,
II, iv: "Give me a cup of sack to make mine eyes
look red, that it may be thought I have wept; for I
must speak in passion, and I will do it in King Cam-
byses' vein."

Drink.

By the gods, I think of plesant wine I
    cannot take my fill!
Now drink is in, give me my bow and
    arrows from sir knight;
At hart of childe I meane to shoot, hoping
    to cleve it right.
KNIGHT. Behold, O king, where he
    doth come, his infant yong in
    hand.   535

[*Re-enter Praxaspes, leading in the Child.*]

PRAX. O mighty king, your Grace behest
    with sorrow I have scand,
And brought my childe fro mothers knee
    before you to appeer,
And she thereof no whit doth know that he
    in place is heer.
KING. Set him up, my marke to be! I
    will shoot at his hart.
PRAX. I beseech your Grace not so to doo!
    Set this pretence a-part!   540
Farewel, my deer and loving babe! Come,
    kisse thy father deer!
A greevous sight to me it is to see thee
    slaine even heere.
Is this the gaine now from the king for giv-
    ing councell good, —
Before my face with such despight to spil
    my sons hart-blood?
O heavy day to me this is, and mother in
    like case!   545
YONG CHILDE. O father, father, wipe your
    face;
    I see the teares run from your eye.
My mother is at home sowing of a band.
Alas! deere father, why doo you cry?
KING. Before me as a mark now let him
    stand!   550
I wil shoot at him my minde to fulfill.
YONG CHILDE. Alas, alas, father, wil you
    me kill?
Good Master king, doo not shoot at me;
    my mother loves me best of all.

Shoot.

KING. I have despatched him! Down he
    doth fall!
As right as a line his hart I have hit.   555
Nay, thou shalt see, Praxaspes, stranger
    newes yet.

My knight, with speed his hart cut out and
    give it unto me.
KNIGHT. It shalbe doon, O mighty king,
    with all seleritie.
LORD. My lord Praxaspes, this had not
    been but your tung must be walking!
To the king of correction you must needs
    be talking!   560
PRAX. No correction, my lord, but coun-
    cel for the best.

[*The knight presents the child's heart to the
king.*]

KNIGHT. Heere is the hart, according to
    your Graces behest.
KING. Beholde, Praxaspes, thy sonnes
    owne hart! O, how well the same
    was hit!
After this wine to doo this deed I thought
    it very fit.
Esteem thou maist right well therby no
    drunkard is the king   565
That in the midst of all his cups could doo
    this valiant thing.
My lord and knight, on me attend; to
    pallace we will goe,
And leave him heer to take his son when
    we are gone him fro.
ALL. With al our harts we give consent to
    wait upon your Grace.

[*Exeunt all except Praxaspes.*]

PRAX. A wofull man, O Lord, am I, to see
    him in this case!   570
My daies, I deem, desires their end. This
    deed wil help me hence.
To have the blossoms of my feeld de-
    stroyed by violence!

Enter Mother.

[MOTHER.] Alas, alas! I doo heare tell the
    king hath kild my sonne!
If it be so, wo worth the deed that ever it
    was doone!
It is even so! My lord I see, how by him
    he dooth weepe.   575
What ment I, that from hands of him this
    childe I did not keepe?
Alas! husband and lord, what did you
    meane to fetch this childe away?
PRAX. O lady wife, I little thought for to
    have seene this day.

MOTHER. O blisful babe! O ioy of
    womb! Harts comfort and delight!
For councel given unto the king is this thy
    iust requite? 580
O hevy day and dolefull time, these mourn-
    ing tunes to make!
With blubred eies, into mine armes from
    earth I wil thee take,
And wrap thee in mine apron white.
    But, oh my heavy hart!
The spiteful pangs that it sustains wold
    make it in two to part,
The death of this my sonne to see! O hevy
    mother now, 585
That from thy sweet and sugred ioy to sor-
    row so shouldst bow!
What greef in womb did I retain before I
    did thee see!
Yet at the last, when smart was gone, what
    ioy wert thou to me!
How tender was I of thy food, for to pre-
    serve thy state!
How stilled I thy tender hart at times early
    and late! 590
With velvet paps I gave thee suck with
    issue from my brest,
And danced thee upon my knee to bring
    thee unto rest.
Is this the ioy of thee I reap? O king, of
    tigers brood!
Oh tigers whelp, hadst thou the hart to see
    this childs hart-blood?
Nature inforseth me, alas! in this wise to
    deplore, 595
To wring my hands. O welaway, that I
    should see this houre!
Thy mother yet wil kisse thy lips, silk-soft,
    and pleasant white,
With wringing hands lamenting for to see
    thee in this plight!
My lording deer, let us goe home our
    mourning to augment.
PRAX. My lady deer, with heavy hart to
    it I doo consent, 600
Between us both the childe to bere unto
    our lordly place.
    Exeunt [bearing the body].

*Enter Ambidexter. [He addresses the
    audience.]*

AMB. Indeed, as ye say, I have been ab-
    sent a long space.

But is not my cosin Cutpurse [1] with you in
    the meane-time?
To it! to it, cosin, and doo your office fine!
How like you Sisamnes for using of me? 605
He plaid with both hands, but he sped il-
    favourdly!
The king himselfe was godly up trained;
He professed vertue — but I think it was
    fained.
He plaies with both hands, good deeds and
    ill;
But it was no good deed Praxaspes sonne
    for to kill. 610
As he for the good deed on the iudge was
    commended,
For all his deeds els he is reprehended.
The most evill-disposed person that ever
    was
All the state of his life he would not let
    passe —
Some good deeds he will doo, though they
    be but few: 615
The like things this tirant Cambises doth
    shew.
No goodnes from him to none is exhibited,
But still malediction abroad is distributed;
And yet ye shall see in the rest of his race
What infamy he will work against his owne
    grace. 620
Whist! no more words! heere comes the
    kings brother.

*Enter Lord Smirdis, with Attendance and
    Diligence.*

SMIR. The kings brother by birth am I,
    issued from Cirus loynes;
A greefe to me it is to heare of this the king
    repines.[2]
I like not well of those his deeds that he
    dooth still frequent;
I wish to God that other waies his minde he
    could content. 625
Yong I am, and next to him; no moe of us
    there be.
I would be glad a quiet realme in this his
    reign to see.
ATT. My lord, your good a[nd] [3] willing
    hart the gods wil recompence,

---

[1] The audiences, crowded in the yard about the
stage, were much troubled by pickpockets, as the
early plays abundantly testify.
[2] Feels discontent. B. reads *kings repines.*
[3] Added by Manly.

In that your minde so pensive is for those
    his great offence.
My lord, his Grace shall have a time to
    paire and to amend.   630
Happy is he that can escape and not his
    Grace offend.
DIL.   If that wicked vice he could refraine,
    from wasting wine forbere,
A moderate life he would frequent, amend-
    ing this his square.
AMB.   My lord, and if your Honor it shall
    please,
I can informe you what is best for your
    ease: 635
Let him alone, of his deeds doo not talke,
Then by his side ye may quietly walke;
After his death you shalbe king,
Then may you reforme eche kinde of thing;
In the meane-time live quietly, doo not
    with him deale; —   640
So shall it redound much to your weale.
SMIR.   Thou saist true, my freend; that is
    the best.
I know not whether he love me or doo me
    detest.
ATT.   Leane from his company all that you
    may.
I, faithfull Attendance, wil your Honor
    obay;   645
If against your Honor he take any ire,
His Grace is as like to kindle his fire
To your Honors destruction as otherwise.
DIL.   Therefore, my lord, take good advise,
And I, Diligence, your case wil so tender
That to his Grace your Honor shalbe none
    offender.   651
SMIR.   I thank you both, intire freends.
    With my Honor stil remaine.
AMB.   Beholde where the king doth come
    with his train!

Enter King, and a Lord.

KING.   O lording deer and brother mine, I
    ioy your state to see,
Surmising much what is the cause you ab-
    sent thus from me.   655
SMIR.   Pleaseth your Grace, no absence I,
    but redy to fulfill,
At all assaies, my prince and king, in that
    your Grace me will.
What I can doo in true defence to you, my
    prince, aright,

In readines I alwaies am to offer foorth my
    might.
KING.   And I the like to you againe doo
    heer avouch the same.   660
ALL.   For this your good agreement heer,
    now praised be Gods name!
AMB.   [*to Smirdis*].   But heare ye, noble
    prince; harke in your eare:
It is best to doo as I did declare.
KING.   My lord and brother Smirdis, now
    this is my minde and will:
That you to court of mine returne, and
    there to tary still   665
Till my returne within short space your
    Honor for to greet.
SMIR.   At your behest so wil I doo till time
    againe we meet.
My leave I take from you, O king; even
    now I doo departe.

*Exeunt Smirdis, Attendance and
    Diligence.*

KING.   Farwel, lord and brother mine! far-
    wel with all my hart!
My lord, my brother Smerdis is of youth
    and manly might,   670
And in his sweet and pleasant face my hart
    doth take delight.
LORD.   Yea, noble prince, if that your
    Grace before his Honor dye,
He wil succeede, a vertuous king, and rule
    with equitie.
KING.   As you have said, my lord, he is
    cheefe heire next my Grace,
And, if I dye to-morrow, next he shall suc-
    ceed my place.   675
AMB.   And if it please your Grace, O king,
    I heard him say,
For your death unto the god[s] day and
    night he did pray;
He would live so vertuously and get him
    such a praise
That Fame by trump his due deserts in
    honor should upraise;
He said your Grace deserved had the curs-
    ing of all men;   680
That ye should never after him get any
    praise againe.
KING.   Did he speake thus of my Grace in
    such despightful wise?
Or els doost thou presume to fill my
    princely eares with lyes?

LORD. I cannot think it in my hart that
he would report so.

KING. How saist thou? Speake the
truth: was it so or no?   685

AMB. I thinke so, if it please your Grace,
but I cannot tell.

KING. Thou plaist with both hands, now
I perceive well!

But, for to put al doubts aside, and to make
him leese his hope,

He shall dye by dint of swoord or els by
choking rope.

Shall he succeed when I am gone, to have
more praise then I?   690

Were he father, as brother, mine, I swere
that he shal dye!

To pallaice mine I will therefore, his death
for to pursue.

Exit [King with the Lord].

AMB. Are ye gone? Straightway I will
follow you.

[Turning to the audience.]

How like ye now, my maisters? Dooth
not this geere cotten? [1]

The proverbe olde is verified: "soone ripe,
and soone rotten!"   695

He wil not be quiet til his brother be kild;

His delight is wholly to have his blood
spild.

Mary, sir, I tolde him a notable lye!

If it were to doo againe, I durst [not] doo
it, I!

Mary, when I had doon, to it I durst not
stand;   700

Thereby ye may perceive I use to play
with eche hand.

But how now, cosin Cutpursse, with whom
play you?

Take heed, for his hand is groping even
now!

Cosin, take heed, if you doo secretly grope;

If ye be taken, cosin, ye must looke through
a rope.   705

Exit.

Enter Lord Smirdis alone.

[SMIR.] I am wandring alone, heere and
there to walke;

---

[1] Prosper, succeed.

The Court is so unquiet, in it I take no
ioy.

Solitary to my-selfe now I may talke.

If I could rule, I wist what to say.

*Enter Cruelty and Murder with bloody
hands.*

CRUEL. My coequall partner, Murder,
come away;   710

From me long thou maist not stay.

MURD. Yes, from thee I may stay, but
not thou from me;

Therefore I have a prerogative above thee.

CRUEL. But in this case we must togither
abide.

Come, come! Lord Smirdis I have spide.

Lay hands on him with all festination, [1] 716

That on him we may worke our indigna-
tion!

[They lay hands upon him.]

SMIR. How now, my freends? What
have you to doo with me?

MURD. King Cambises hath sent us unto
thee,

Commaunding us straightly, without
mercy or favour,   720

Upon thee to bestow our behaviour,

With cruelty to murder you and make you
away.

SMIR. Yet pardon me, I hartely you pray!

Consider, the king is a tirant tirannious,

And all his dooings be damnable and parnitious: 725

Favour me therfore; I did him never offend.

CRUEL. No favour at all! Your life is at
an end!

Even now I strike, his body to wound.

Strike him in divers places. [2]

Beholde, now his blood springs out on the
ground!

A little bladder of vineger prickt. [3]

MURD. Now he is dead, let us present him
to the king.   730

CRUEL. Lay to your hand, away him to
bring.

Exeunt [bearing the body].

---

[1] Speed.
[2] In B. this stage direction is opposite line 723.
[3] In B. this stage direction is opposite line 727.

Enter Ambidexter.

AMB. O the passion of God, yonder is a hevy Court!

Some weepes, some wailes — and some make great sport.

Lord Smirdis by Cruelty and Murder is slaine;

But, Iesus! for want of him how some doo complaine!   735

If I should have had a thousand pound I could not forbeare weeping.

Now Iesus have his blessed soule in keeping!

Ah good Lord! to think on him, how it dooth me greeve!

I cannot forbeare weeping, ye may me beleeve.

Weep.

O my hart! how my pulses doo beate,   740

With sorrowfull lamentations I am in such a heate!

Ah, my hart, how for him it doth sorrow!

[He begins to laugh.]

Nay, I have done, in faith, now.   And God give ye good morrow!

Ha, ha! Weep? Nay, laugh, with both [1] hands to play!

The king through his cruelty hath made him away;   745

But hath not he wrought a most wicked deed,

Because king after him he should not proceed, —

His owne naturall brother, and having no more, —

To procure his death by violence sore?

In spight, because his brother should never be king,   750

His hart, being wicked, consented to this thing.

Now he hath no more brothers nor kinred alive.

If the king use this geere still, he cannot long thrive.

Enter Hob and Lob.

HOB. Gods hat, neighbour, come away! Its time to market to goe!

[1] B. *buth.*

LOB. Gods vast,[1] naybor, zay ye zo?   755

The clock hath stricken vive, ich [2] think, by Laken!

Bum vay, vrom sleep cham not very well waken!

But, naybor Hob, naybor Hob, what have ye to zel?

HOB. Bum troth, naybor Lob, to you I chil tel:

Chave two goslings, and a chine of porke —

There is no vatter between this and Yorke; —   761

Chave a pot of strawberies, and a calves head —

A zennight zince,[3] to-morrow, it hath been dead.

LOB. Chave a score of egges, and of butter a pound;

Yesterday a nest of goodly yong rabits I vound;   765

Chave vorty things mo, of more and of lesse, —

My brain is not very good them to expresse.

But, Gods hat, naybor, wotst [4] what?

HOB. No, not wel, naybor; whats that?

LOB. Bum vay, naybor, maister king is a zhrode [5] lad!   770

Zo God help me, and holidam, I think the vool [6] be mad!

Zome zay he deale cruelly: his brother he did kill,

And also a goodly yung lads hart-blood he did spill.

HOB. Vorbod of God, naybor! Has he plaid zuch a volish deed?

AMB. Goodman Hob and goodman Lob, God be your speed!   775

As you two towards market doo walke,

Of the kings cruelty I did heare you talke:

I insure you he is a king most vile and parnitious, —

His dooings and life are odious and vicious.

LOB. It were a good deed zome-body would break his head.   780

HOB. Bum vay, naybor Lob, I chuld [7] he were dead!

[1] Fist.
[2] By this time the reader has learned to identify this brogue with the stage rustic.
[3] Sennight since.
[4] Knowest.   [5] Shrewd.
[6] Fool.   [7] I would.

AMB. So would I, Lob and Hob, with all
my hart!

[*To the audience*] Now with both hands will
you see me play my parte. —

A, ye whorson traitorly knaves,

Hob and Lob, out upon you, slaves! 785

LOB. And thou calst me knave, thou art
another!

My name is Lob, and Hob my next naybor.

AMB. Hob and Lob! a, ye cuntry patches! [1]

A, ye fooles! ye have made wrong matches!

Ye have spoken treason against the kings
Grace! 790

For it I will accuse ye before his face;

Then for the same ye shalbe martered.

At the least ye shalbe hangd, drawne, and
quartered!

HOB. O gentleman, ye shal have two
peare-pyes, and tel not of me!

LOB. By God, a vat gooce [2] chil give thee.

I think no hurt, by my vathers soule I
zweare! 796

HOB. Chave lived wel all my life-time, my
naybors among;

And now chuld be loth to come to zuch
wrong —

To be hanged and quartered — the greefe
would be great!

LOB. A foule evil on thee, Hob! Who bid
thee on it treat? 800

Vor it was thou that first did him name.

HOB. Thou lyest like a varlet and thou
zaist the zame!

It was zuch a foolish Lob as thou.

LOB. Speak many words, and, by Cods
nailes [3] I vow,

Upon thy pate my staffe I will lay! 805

AMB. [*aside*]. By the masse, I will cause
them to make a fray. —

Yea, Lob, thou saist true: all came through
him.

LOB. Bum vay, thou Hob,[4] a little would
make me thee [5] trim!

Give thee a zwap on thy nose till thy hart
ake!

HOB. If thou darest, doo it! Els, man,
cry creke! [6] 810

I trust, before thou hurt me,

With my staffe chil make a Lob of thee!

*Heer let them fight with their staves, not
come neer an-other by three or foure
yardes; the Vice set them on as hard as he
can; one of their wives come out, and all
to-beat the Vice; he run away.*

*Enter Marian-may-be-good, Hobs wife, run-
ning in with a broome, and parte them.*

MARIAN. O the body of me! husband Hob,
what meane ye to fight?

For the passion of God, no more blowes
smite!

Neighbours and freends so long, and now to
fall out? 815

What! in your age to seeme so stout?

If I had not parted ye, one had kild another.

LOB. I had not cared, I swere by Gods
Mother!

MARIAN. Shake hands againe at the request of me;

As ye have been freends, so freends still be.

HOB. Bum troth, cham content and zaist
word, neighbour Lob. 821

LOB. I am content; agreed, neighbor Hob!

*Shake hands and laugh hartily one at
another.*

MARIAN. So, get you to market; no longer
stay.

And with yonder knave let me make a fray.

HOB. Content, wife Marian; chill doo as
thou doost say. 825

But busse me, ich pray thee, at going away!

Exeunt Hob, Lob.

MARIAN. Thou whorson knave, and
prickeard boy, why didst thou let
them fight?

If one had kild another heer, couldst thou
their deaths requite?

It beares a signe by this thy deed a cowardly knave thou art,

Els wouldst thou draw that weapon thine,
like a man,[1] them to parte. 830

AMB. What, Marian-may-be-good, are
you come prattling?

Ye may hap get a box on the eare with your
talking!

If they had kild one another, I had not
cared a pease.

[1] B. *knaue.*

---

[1] Fools. [2] Goose.
[3] By God's nails. [4] B. *Hod.* [5] B. *ye.*
[6] Confess yourself beaten; give up.

Heer let her swinge him in her brome; she gets him down, and he her down, — thus one on the top of another make pastime.

MARIAN.   A, villain! my-selfe on thee I
    must ease!
Give me a box on the eare? that will I try.
Who shalbe maister, thou shalt see by-and-
    by!   836
AMB.   O, no more! no more, I beseech you
    hartily!
Even now I yeeld, and give you the
    maistry.

Run his way out while she is down.

MARIAN.   A, thou knave! doost thou
    throw me down and run thy [1] way?
If he were heere againe, oh, how I would
    him pay!   840
I will after him; and, if I can him meet,
With these my nailes his face I wil greet.

[*Exit.*]

Enter Venus leading out her sonne, Cupid, blinde: he must have a bow and two shafts, one headed with golde and th' other headed with lead.

VENUS.   Come foorth, my sonne. Unto
    my words attentive eares resigne;
What I pretend, see you frequent, to force
    this game of mine.
The king a kinswoman hath, adornd with
    beauty store;   845
And I wish that Dianas gifts they twain
    shal keep no more,
But use my silver sugred game their ioyes
    for to augment.
When I doo speak, to wound his hart,
    Cupid my son, consent.
And shoot at him the shaft of love that
    beares the head of golde,
To wound his hart in lovers wise, his greefe
    for to unfolde.   850
Though kin she be unto his Grace, that
    nature me expell,
Against the course thereof he may in my
    game please me wel.
Wherfore, my sonne, doo not forget; forth-
    with pursue the deed!

               [1] B. *the.*

CUPID.   Mother, I meane for to obay as
    you have whole decreed;
But you must tel me, mother deere, when I
    shal arrow draw,   855
Els your request to be attaind wil not be
    worth a straw;
I am blinde and cannot see, but stil doo
    shoot by gesse, —
The poets wel, in places store, of my might
    doo expresse.
VENUS.   Cupid my son, when time shall
    serve that thou shalt do this deed,
Then warning I to thee wil give; but see
    thou shoot with speed.   860

Enter a Lord, a Lady, and a Waiting-maid.

LORD.   Lady deer, to king a-kin, forthwith
    let us proceed
To trace abroad the beauty feelds, as erst
    we had decreed.
The blowing buds whose savery sents our
    sence wil much delight,
The sweet smel of musk white-rose to
    please the appetite,
The chirping birds whose pleasant tunes
    therein shal hear record,[1]   865
That our great ioy we shall it finde in feeld
    to walk abroad,
On lute and cittern there to play a heav-
    enly harmony:
Our eares shall heare, hart to content, our
    sports to beautify.
LADY.   Unto your words, most comely
    lord, my-selfe submit doo I;
To trace with you in feeld so green I meane
    not to deny.   870

Heere trace up and downe playing [on the lute and cittern].

MAID.   And I, your waiting-maid, at hand
    with diligence will be,
For to fulfil with hart and hand, when you
    shal commaund me.

Enter King, Lord, and Knight.

KING.   Come on, my lord and knight;
    abroad our mirth let us imploy.
Since he is dead, this hart of mine in corps
    I feel it ioy.
Should brother mine have raigned king
    when I had yeelded breth?   875

               [1] Warble.

A thousand brothers I rather had to put
    them all to death.
But, oh beholde, where I doo see a lord and
    lady faire!
For beauty she most worthy is to sit in
    princes chaire.

VENUS. Shoot forth, my son! Now is the
    time that thou must wound his hart.

CUPID. Content you, mother; I will doo
    my parte. 880

Shoote there; and goe out, Venus and Cupid.

KING. Of truth, my lord, in eye of mine
    all ladies she doth excell.
Can none reporte what dame she is, and to
    my Grace it tell?

LORD. Redouted prince, pleaseth your
    Grace, to you she is a-kin,
Cosin-iarmin,[1] nigh of birth, by mothers
    side come in.

KNIGHT. And that her waiting-maiden is,
    attending her upon. 885
He is a lord of princes court, and wil be
    there anon.
They sport themselves in pleasant feeld, to
    former used use.

KING. My lord and knight, of truth I
    speak: my hart it cannot chuse
But with my lady I must speake and so
    expresse my minde.

[*He calls to the lady and her attendants.*]

My lord and ladyes, walking there, if you
    wil favour finde, 890
Present your-selves unto my Grace, and by
    my side come stand.

FIRST LORD. We wil fulfil, most mighty
    king, as your Grace doth com-
    maund.

KING. Lady deere, intelligence my Grace
    hath got of late,
You issued out of mothers stocke and kin
    unto my state.
According to rule of birth you are cosin-
    iarmin mine; 895
Yet do I wish that farther of this kinred I
    could finde;
For Cupid he, that eylesse boy, my hart
    hath so enflamed
With beauty you me to content the like
    cannot be named;

       [1] Cousin-german.

For, since I entred in this place and on you
    fixt mine eyes,
Most burning fits about my hart in ample
    wise did rise. 900
The heat of them such force doth yeeld, my
    corps they scorch, alas!
And burns the same with wasting heat, as
    Titan doth the gras.
And, sith this heat is kindled so and fresh in
    hart of me,
There is no way but of the same the
    quencher you must be.
My meaning is that beauty yours my hart
    with love doth wound; 905
To give me love minde to content; my hart
    hath you out found;
And you are she must be my wife, els shall
    I end my daies.
Consent to this — and be my queen, to
    weare the crown with praise!

LADY. If it please your Grace, O mighty
    king, you shall not this request.
It is a thing that Natures course doth ut-
    terly detest, 910
And high it would the god[s] displease, —
    of all that is the woorst.
To graunt your Grace to marry so, it is not
    I that durst.
Yet humble thanks I render now unto you,
    mighty king,
That you vouchsafe to great estate so
    gladly would me bring.
Were it not it were offence, I would it not
    deny, 915
But such great honor to atchive my hart I
    would apply.
Therefore, O king, with humble hart in this
    I pardon crave;
My answer is: in this request your minde
    ye may not have.

KING. May I not? Nay, then, I will! by
    all the gods I vow!
And I will mary thee as wife. This is mine
    answere now! 920
Who dare say nay what I pretend? Who
    dare the same withstand
Shal lose his head, and have reporte as
    traitor through my land.
There is no nay. I wil you have, and you
    my queene shalbe!

LADY. Then, mighty king, I crave your
    Grace to heare the words of me:

Your councel take of lordings wit, the
   lawes aright peruse;   925
If I with safe may graunt this deed, I will it
   not refuse.
KING. No, no! What I have said to you,
   I meane to have it so.
For councel theirs I mean not, I, in this
   respect to goe;
• But to my pallaice let us goe, the mariage
   to prepare;
For, to avoid my wil in this, I can it not
   forbeare.   930
LADY. O God, forgive me, if I doo amisse!
The king by compultion inforceth me
   this.
MAID. Unto the gods for your estate I
   will not cease to pray,
That you may be a happy queen, and see
   most ioyfull day.
KING. Come on, my lords; with gladsome
   harts let us reioyce with glee! 935
Your musick shew to ioy this deed at the
   request of me!
BOTH. For to obey your Graces words our
   Honors doo agree.

Exeunt.

Enter Ambidexter.

AMB. O the passion of me! Mary, as ye
   say, yonder is a royal court!
There is triumphing, and sporte upon
   sporte,
Such loyall lords, with such lordly exercise,
Frequenting such pastime as they can devise,   941
Running at tilt, iusting, with running at
   the ring,
Masking and mumming, with eche kinde of
   thing,
Such daunsing, such singing, with musicall
   harmony, —
Beleeve me, I was loth to absent their company.   945
But wil you beleeve? Iesu, what hast they
   made till they were maried!
Not for a milion of pounds one day longer
   they would have tar[i]ed!
Oh! there was a banquet royall and super-
   excellent!
Thousands and thousands at that banquet
   was spent.

I muse of nothing but how they can be
   maried so soone;   950
I care not if I be maried before to-morrow
   at noone,
If mariage be a thing that so may be had.

[*To one in the audience.*]

How say you, maid? to marry me wil ye be
   glad?
Out of doubt, I beleeve it is some excellent
   treasure, —
Els to the same belongs abundant pleasure.
Yet with mine eares I have heard some
   say: 956
"That ever I was maried, now cursed be
   the day!"
Those be they [that] [1] with curst wives be
   matched.
That husband for haukes meat [2] of them is
   up-snatched,
Head broke with a bedstaffe, face all to-be-
   scratched,   960
"Knave!" "slave!" and "villain!" a
   coylde [3] cote now and than, —
When the wife hath given it, she wil say,
   "Alas, good man!"
Such were better unmarried, my maisters,
   I trow,
Then all their life after be matched with a
   shrow.

Enter Preparation.

PREP. With speed I am sent all things to
   prepare,   965
My message to doe as the king did declare.
His Grace doth meane a banquet to make,
Meaning in this place repast for to take.
Wel, the cloth shalbe laid, and all things in
   redines,
To court to return, when doon is my busi-
   nes.   970
AMB. A proper man and also [a] [4] fit
For the kings estate to prepare a banquet!
PREP. What, Ambidexter? Thou art not
   unknowen!
A mischeefe on all good faces, so that I
   curse not mine owne!
Now, in the knaves name, shake hands
   with me.   975

---

[1] B. omits; supplied from A.
[2] Hawk's meat, something snatched up greedily.
[3] Beaten.   [4] Supplied from A.

AMB.   Wel said, goodman pouchmouth; your reverence I see.

I will teach ye, if your manners no better be!

A, ye slave! the king doth me a gentleman allow;

Therefore I looke that to me ye should bow.

Fight.

PREP.   Good Maister Ambidexter, pardon my behaviour;   980

For this your deeds you are a knave, for your labour!

AMB.   Why, ye stale counterly [1] villain, nothing but "knave"?

Fight.

PREP.   I am sorry your maistership offended I have;

Shake hands, that betweene us agreement may be.

I was over-shot with my-selfe, I doo see.

Let me have your helpe this furniture to provide.   986

The king from this place wil not long abide.

Set the fruit on the boord.

AMB.   Content; it is the thing that I would wish.

I my-selfe wil goe fetch one dish.

Let the Vice fetch a dish of nuts, and let them fall in the bringing of them in.

PREP.   Clenly, Maister Ambidexter; for faire on the ground they lye.   990

AMB.   I will have them up againe by-and-by.

PREP.   To see all in redines I will put you in trust;

There is no nay, to the court needs I must.

Exit Preparation.

AMB.   Have ye no doubt but all shalbe wel.

Mary, sir, as you say, this geer dooth excell!   995

All things is in a readines, when they come hither, —

The kings Grace and the queene both togither.

[1] Referring to the Counter (prison); jail-bird.

[To the audience.]

I beseech ye, my maisters, tell me, is it not best

That I be so bolde as to bid a guest?

He is as honest a man as ever spurd cow, —   1000

My cosin Cutpursse, I meane; I beseech ye, iudge you.

Beleeve me, cosin, if to be the kings guest ye could be taken,

I trust that offer will never be forsaken.

But, cosin, because to that office ye are not like to come,

Frequent your exercises — a horne on your thumb,[1]   1005

A quick eye, a sharpe knife, at hand a receiver.

But then take heed, cosin, ye be a clenly convayour.

Content your-selfe, cosin; for this banquet you are unfit,

When such as I at the same am unworthy to sit.

Enter King, Queene, and his traine.

KING.   My queen and lords, to take repast, let us attempt the same.   1010

Heer is the place; delay no time, but to our purpose frame.

QUEENE.   With willing harts your whole behest we minde for to obay.

ALL.   And we, the rest of princes traine, will doo as you doo say.

Sit at the banquet.

KING.   Me think mine eares doth wish the sound of musicks harmony;

Heer, for to play before my Grace, in place I would them spy.   1015

Play at the banquet.

AMB.   They be at hand, sir, with sticke and fiddle;

They can play a new daunce, called Heydiddle-diddle.

KING.   My queene, perpend.   What I pronounce, I wil not violate,

[1] A casing of horn was worn over the thumb by the cutpurse, apparently to resist the sharp edge of the knife in cutting purses.   *Horn-thumb* became a cant-term for a cutpurse.

But one thing which my hart makes glad I
    minde to explicate: [1]
You know in court uptrained is a lyon very
    yong;   1020
Of one litter two whelps [2] beside, as yet not
    very strong.
I did request one whelpe to see and this
    yong lyon fight;
But lion did the whelpe convince by
    strength of force and might.
His brother whelpe, perceiving that the
    lion was too good,
And he by force was like to see the other
    whelp his blood,   1025
With force to lyon he did run, his brother
    for to helpe.
A wonder great it was to see that freend-
    ship in a whelpe!
So then the whelps between them both the
    lyon did convince.
Which thing to see before mine eyes did
    glad the hart of prince.

At this tale tolde, let the Queene weep.

QUEENE.   These words to heare makes
    stilling teares issue from christall
    eyes.[3]   1030
KING.   What, doost thou meane, my
    spouse? to weep for losse of any
    prise?
QUEENE.   No, no, O king; but, as you see,
    freendship in brothers whelp:
When one was like to have repulse, the
    other yeelded helpe.
And was this favour shewd in dogs, to
    shame of royall king?
Alack, I wish these eares of mine had not
    once heard this thing!   1035
Even so should you, O mighty king, to
    brother beene a stay,
And not, without offence to you, in such
    wise him to slay.
In all assaies it was your part his cause to
    have defended,
And, who-so-ever had him misused, to have
    them reprehended.
But faithfull love was more in dog then it
    was in your Grace.   1040

[1] Explain, unfold.
[2] Dogs were often pitted against animals, especially bears, in England.
[3] Shakespeare gives an amusing parody of this
scene in *I Henry IV*, II, iv.

KING.   O cursed caitive, vicious and vile!
    I hate thee in this place!
This banquet [now] [1] is at an end; take all
    these things away.
Before my face thou shalt repent the words
    that thou dost say.
O wretch most vile! didst thou the cause of
    brother mine so tender
The losse of him should greeve thy hart, —
    he being none offender?   1045
It did me good his death to have — so will
    it to have thine!
What freendship he had at my hands, the
    same even thou shalt finde.
I give consent, and make a-vow, that thou
    shalt dye the death!
By Cruels sword and Murder fel even thou
    shalt lose thy breth.
Ambidexter, see with speed to Cruelty ye
    goe;   1050
Cause him hither to approche, Murder
    with him also.
AMB.   I am redy for to fulfil,
If that it be your Graces will.[2]
KING.   Then nought oblight [3] my message
    given; absent thy-selfe away.
AMB.   Then in this place I will no longer
    stay.   1055
[*whispering to the Queen*] If that I durst, I
    would mourne your case;
But, alas! I dare not, for feare of his
    Grace.   *Exit Ambidex.*

KING.   Thou cursed Iill! by all the gods I
    take an othe and sweare,
That flesh of thine these hands of mine in
    peeces small could tere!
But thou shalt dye by dent of sword: there
    is no freend ne fee   1060
Shall finde remorce at princes hand to save
    the life of thee!
QUEENE.   O mighty king and husband
    mine, vouchsafe to heare me speak,
And licence give to spouse of thine her
    patient minde to breake.
For tender love unto your Grace my words
    I did so frame;
For pure love doth hart of king me violate
    and blame.   1065

[1] Supplied by Manly.
[2] B. has lines 1052–53 as one. I follow Manly's
division.
[3] Forget.

And to your Grace is this offence that I
    should purchase death?
Then cursed time that I was queene to
    shorten this my breth!
Your Grace doth know by mariage true I
    am your wife and spouse,
And one to save anothers helth at troth-
    plight made our vowes;
Therefore, O king, let loving queen at thy
    hand finde remorse,   1070
Let pitie be a meane to quench that cruell
    raging force,
And pardon, plight from princes mouth,
    yeeld grace unto your queen,
That amity with faithfull zeal may ever be
    us between.
KING.   A, caitive vile! to pitie thee my
    hart it is not bent;
Ne yet to pardon your offence it is not mine
    intent.   1075
FIRST LORD.   Our mighty prince, with
    humble sute of your Grace this I
    crave,
That this request it may take place, your
    favour for to have.
Let mercy yet aboundantly the life of
    queen preserve,
Sith she in most obedient wise your Graces
    will doth serve.
As yet your Grace but while with her hath
    had cohabitation,   1080
And sure this is no desert [1] why to yeeld
    her indignation.
Therefore, O king, her life prolong, to ioy
    her daies in blisse!
SECOND LORD.   Your Grace shal win im-
    mortall fame in graunting unto
    this.
She is a queene whose goodly hue [2] excelles
    the royall rose,
For beauty bright Dame Nature she a large
    gift did dispose.   1085
For comelines who may compare? Of all
    she beares the bell. [3]
This should give cause to move your Grace
    to love her very wel.
Her silver brest in those your armes to sing
    the songs of love, —
Fine qualities most excellent to be in her
    you prove;

[1] Deserving.   [2] Complexion.
[3] Takes precedence.

A precious pearle of prise to prince, a iewell
    passing all!   1090
Therefore, O king, to beg remorce on both
    my knees I fall;
To graunt her grace to have her life, with
    hart I doo desire.
KING.   You villains twain! with raging
    force ye set my hart on fire!
If I consent that she shall dye, how dare ye
    crave her life?
You two to aske this at my hand dooth
    much inlarge my strife.   1095
Were it not for shame, you two should dye,
    that for her life do sue!
But favour mine from you is gone; my
    lords, I tell you true.
I sent for Cruelty of late; if he would come
    away,
I would commit her to his hands his cruell
    part to play.
Even now I see where he dooth come; it
    dooth my hart delight.   1100

Enter Cruelty and Murder.

CRUEL.   Come, Murder, come; let us goe
    foorth with might;
Once againe the kings commaundement we
    must fulfill.
MURD.   I am contented [1] to doo it with a
    good will.
KING.   Murder and Cruelty, for both of
    you I sent,
With all festination [2] your offices to fre-
    quent.   1105
Lay holde on the queene; take her to your
    power,
And make her away within this houre!
Spare for no feare; I doo you full permit.
So I from this place doo meane for to
    flit. [3]
BOTH.   With couragious harts, O king, we
    will obay.   1110
KING.   Then come, my lords, let us de-
    parte away.
BOTH THE LORDS.   With hevy harts we
    will doo all your Grace dooth say.

Exeunt King and Lord[s].

CRUEL.   Come, lady and queene; now are
    you in our handling;
In faith, with you we will use no dandling.

[1] B. *contended.*   [2] Speed.   [3] Betake myself.

MURD. With all expedition I, Murder,
will take place;   1115
Though thou be a queene, ye be under my
grace.
QUEENE. With patience I will you both
obay.[1]
CRUEL. No more woords, but goe with us
away!
QUEENE. Yet, before I dye, some psalme
to God let me sing.
BOTH. We be content to permit you that
thing.   1120
QUEENE. Farewell, you ladies of the court,
With all your masking hue!
I doo forsake these brodered gardes [2]
And all the fashions new,
The court and all the courtly train   1125
Wherin I had delight;
I banished am from happy sporte,
And all by spitefull spite;
Yet with a ioyfull hart to God
A psalme I meane to sing,   1130
Forgiving all [men] [3] and the king
Of eche kinde of thing.

Sing,[4] and exeunt.

Enter Ambidexter weeping.

AMB. A, a, a, a! I cannot chuse but
weepe for the queene!
Nothing but mourning now at the court
there is seene.
Oh, oh! my hart, my hart! O, my bum
will break!   1135
Very greefe so torments me that scarce I
can speake.
Who could but weep for the losse of such a
lady?
That cannot I doo, I sweare by mine hon-
estie.
But, Lord! so the ladies mourne, crying
"Alack!"   1139
Nothing is worne now but onely black:
I beleeve all [the] [5] cloth in Watling Street
to make gowns would not serve, —
If I make a lye, the devill let ye sterve!
All ladyes mourne, both yong and olde;

There is not one that weareth a points
woorth of golde.
There is a sorte for feare for the king doo
pray   1145
That would have him dead, by the masse, I
dare say.
What a king was he that hath used such
tiranny!
He was akin to Bishop Bonner,[1] I think
verily!
For both their delights was to shed
blood,
But never intended to doo any good. 1150
Cambises put a iudge to death, — that was
a good deed, —
But to kill the yong childe was worse to
proceed,
To murder his brother, and then his owne
wife, —
So help me God and holidom, it is pitie of
his life!
Heare ye? I will lay twenty thousand
pound   1155
That the king himselfe dooth dye by some
wound;
He hath shed so much blood that his will be
shed.
If it come to passe, in faith, then he is sped.

*Enter the King, without a gowne, a swoord
thrust up into his side, bleeding.*

KING. Out! alas! What shal I doo? My
life is finished!
Wounded I am by sodain chaunce; my
blood is minished.   1160
Gogs hart, what meanes might I make my
life to preserve?
Is there nought to be my helpe? nor is there
nought to serve?
Out upon the court, and lords that there
remaine!
To help my greefe in this my case wil none
of them take paine?
Who but I, in such a wise, his deaths
wound could have got?   1165
As I on horseback up did leap, my sword
from scabard shot,
And ran me thus into the side — as you
right well may see.

---

[1] B. interchanges this word and its rhyme-mate
away.
[2] Ornamental borders on garments.
[3] Supplied by Manly.   [4] The song is lost.
[5] Supplied by Hazlitt.

[1] Edmund Bonner, Bishop of London, who, by
his cruel persecution of Protestant martyrs during
Queen Mary's Reign, became odious.

A marvels chaunce unfortunate, that in
    this wise should be!
I feele my-selfe a-dying now; of life bereft
    am I;
And Death hath caught me with his dart,
    for want of blood I spy.   1170
Thus, gasping, heer on ground I lye; for
    nothing I doo care.
A iust reward for my misdeeds my death
    doth plaine declare.

Heere let him quake and stir.

AMB. How now, noble king? Pluck up
    your hart!
What! will you dye, and from us depart?
Speake to me and ye be alive!   1175
He cannot speak. But beholde, how with
    Death he doth strive.

[The king dies.]

Alas, good king! Alas, he is gone!
The devill take me if for him I make any
    mone.
I did prognosticate of his end, by the
    masse!   1179
Like as I did say, so is it come to passe.
I wil be gone. If I should be found heere,
That I should kill him it would appeer.
For feare with his death they doo me
    charge,
Farwell, my maisters, I will goe take barge;

I meane to be packing; now is the tide;
Farwell, my maisters, I will no longer
    abide!   .   1186

Exit Ambidexter.

Enter three Lords.

FIRST LORD. Beholde, my lord[s], it is even
    so as he to us did tell!
His Grace is dead, upon the ground, by
    dint of sword most fel.
SECOND LORD. As he in saddle would have
    lept, his sword from sheath did goe,
Goring him up into the side, — his life was
    ended so.   1190
THIRD LORD. His blood so fast did issue
    out that nought could him prolong;
Yet, before he yeelded up the ghost, his
    hart was very strong.
FIRST LORD. A iust reward for his mis-
    deeds the God above hath wrought,
For certainly the life he led was to be
    counted nought.
SECOND LORD. Yet a princely buriall he
    shall have, according to his estate;
And more of him heere at this time we have
    not to dilate.   1196
THIRD LORD. My lords, let us take him
    up, and carry him away!
BOTH. Content we are with one accord to
    doo as you doo say.

Exeunt all [bearing out the body of Cambises].

EPILOGUE

Right gentle audience, heere have you perused
    The tragicall history of this wicked king.
According to our duty, we have not refused,
    But to our best intent exprest everything.
    We trust none is offended for this our dooing.
Our author craves likewise, if he have squared amisse,
By gentle admonition to know where the fault is.   7

His good will shall not be neglected to amend the same.
    Praying all to beare, therefore, with this simple deed
Untill the time serve a better he may frame.
    Thus yeelding you thanks, to end we decreed
    That you so gently have [1] suffered us to proceed,
In such patient wise as to heare and see.
We can but thank ye therfore; we can doo no more, we!   14

As duty bindes us, for our noble Queene let us pray,
    And for her Honorable Councel, the truth that they may use,
To practise iustice and defend her Grace eche day;
    To maintain Gods woord they may not refuse,
    To correct all those that would her Grace and Graces lawes abuse;
Beseeching God over us she may raigne long,
To be guided by truth and defended from wrong.   21

        Amen, quod Thomas Preston.[2]

Imprinted at London by Edward Allde.

[1] B. *huue.*   [2] B. *Prestou.*

THE FAMOVS VICTORIES OF HENRY THE FIFTH [1]

CONTAINING THE HONOURABLE BATTELL OF AGIN-COURT: AS IT WAS PLAIDE BY THE QUEENES MAIESTIES PLAYERS

London: Printed by Thomas Creede, 1598

Enter the yoong Prince, Ned, and Tom.

HENRY THE FIFTH. Come away, Ned and Tom.

BOTH. Here, my lord.

HEN. 5. Come away, my lads. Tell me, sirs, how much gold haue you got? 5

NED. Faith, my lord, I haue got fiue hundred pound.

HEN. 5. But tell me, Tom, how much hast thou got?

TOM. Faith, my lord, some foure hundred pound. 11

HEN. 5. Foure hundred pounds! Brauely spoken, lads! But tell me, sirs, thinke you not that it was a villainous part of me to rob my fathers receiuers? [1] 15

NED. Why no, my lord; it was but a tricke of youth.

HEN. 5. Faith, Ned, thou sayest true. But tell me, sirs, whereabouts are we?

TOM. My lord, we are now about a mile off London. 21

HEN. 5. But, sirs, I maruell that Sir

[1] Officers appointed to receive money due.

Iohn Old-castle comes not away. Sounds! [1] see where he comes. 24

Enters Iockey.

How now, Iockey? what newes with thee?

IOCKEY. Faith, my lord, such newes as passeth! For the towne of Detfort is risen with hue and crie after your man, which parted from vs the last night and has set vpon and hath robd a poore carrier. [2] 30

HEN. 5. Sownes! the vilaine that was wont to spie out our booties?

IOCK. I, my lord, euen the very same.

HEN. 5. Now, base-minded rascal to rob a poore carrier! Wel, it skils not; [35 Ile saue the base vilaines life i[f] I may. But tel me, Iockey, whereabout be the receiuers?

IOC. Faith, my lord, they are hard by; but the best is we are a horse-backe and they be a-foote, so we may escape them. 41

HEN. 5. Wel, i[f] the vilaines come, let

[1] By God's wounds.
[2] One who conveyed goods and parcels on a certain route at certain times.

[1] *The Famous Victories*, written before 1588, is of importance as being our earliest extant history, or chronicle play, a type which later became exceedingly popular as a result of the victory over the Spanish Armada. It is also of interest as being the inspiration for Shakespeare's splendid trilogy, *I Henry IV, II Henry IV*, and *Henry V.* Sir John Oldcastle, sometimes called Jockey, was the original of Sir John Falstaff (whom Shakespeare first named Oldcastle); and Ned and the other "evil companions" who fore-gathered with the young Prince at "the old taverne in Eastcheape," find their counterpart in Ned, Poins, and the rest, of the famous Boar's Head. From *Tarlton's Jests* we learn that the immortal Dick Tarlton, "the lord of mirth," who died in 1588, assumed the clown's part of Dericke; possibly he created the rôle. The play must have been a favorite with theatre-goers; Nash, in *Pierce Penilesse* (1592), speaks of it in terms that imply its popularity. The text as we have it seems to have been cut down and otherwise mangled for traveling purposes; but this has not seriously affected its power to entertain.

The play was entered in the Stationers' Registers in May, 1594; our earliest edition (A.) bears the date 1598. Another edition was published in 1617. I have reproduced the text of the 1598 quarto from Farmer's photographic facsimile of the copy in the Bodleian Library. In the original many lines are set as though they were verse (as is often the case with plays printed from prompt copies); I have chosen to print these as prose. And, of course, I have modernized the punctuation and the use of capital letters, and have added, in brackets, a few stage-directions.

me alone with them! But tel me, Iockey,
how much gots thou from the knaues?
For i am sure I got something, for one [45
of the vilaines so belamed me about the
shoulders as I shal feele it this moneth.

IOCK. Faith, my lord, I haue got a
hundred pound. 49

HEN. 5. A hundred pound! Now
brauely spoken, Iockey. But come, sirs;
laie al your money before me. [*They lay
down the money.*] Now, by heauen, here is
a braue shewe! But, as I am true gentleman, I wil haue the halfe of this spent [55
to-night! But, sirs, take vp your bags,
here comes the receiuers. Let me alone.

Enters two Receiuers.

ONE. Alas, good fellow, what shal we
do? I dare neuer go home to the Court, for
I shall be hangd. But looke, here is the
yong Prince. What shal we doo? 61

HEN. 5. How now, you vilaines! What
are you?

ONE RECEI. Speake you to him.

OTHER. No, I pray speake you to him.

HEN. 5. Why, how now, you rascals!
why speak you not? 67

ONE. Forsooth, we be — pray speake
you to him.

HEN. 5. Sowns, vilains, speak, or Ile cut
off your heads! 71

OTHER. Forsooth, he can tel the tale
better then I.

ONE. Forsooth, we be your fathers receiuers. 75

HEN. 5. Are you my fathers receiuers?
Then I hope ye haue brought me some
money.

ONE. Money? Alas, sir, we be robd!

HEN. 5. Robd! How many were there
of them? 81

ONE. Marry, sir, there were foure of
them; and one of them had Sir Iohn Old-
castles bay hobbie, and your blacke nag. 84

HEN. 5. Gogs wounds! How like ycu
this, Iockey? Blood, you vilaines! my
father robd of his money abroad, and we
robd in our stables! But tell me, how
many were of them? 89

ONE RECEI. If it please you, there
were foure of them; and there was one
about the bignesse of you; — but I am sure

I so belambd him about the shoulders that
he wil feele it this month. 94

HEN. 5. Gogs wounds, you lamd them
faierly — so that they haue carried away
your money. But come, sirs, what shall
we do with the vilaines?

BOTH RECEI. I beseech your Grace, be
good to vs. 100

NED. I pray you, my lord, forgiue them
this once.

[HEN. 5.] Well, stand vp, and get you
gone. And looke that you speake not a
word of it — for, if there be, sownes! Ile
hang you, and all your kin! 106

Exit Purseuant[s].

HEN. 5. Now, sirs, how like you this?
Was not this brauely done? For now the
vilaines dare not speake a word of it, I haue
so feared them with words. Now, whither
shall we goe? 111

ALL. Why, my lord, you know our old
hostes at Feuersham.

HEN. 5. Our hostes at Feuersham!
Blood, what shal we do there? We [115
haue a thousand pound about vs, and we
shall go to a pettie ale-house? No, no.
You know the olde tauerne in Eastcheape;
there is good wine: — besides, there is a
pretie wench that can talke well; for [120
I delight as much in their toongs as any
part about them.

ALL. We are readie to waite vpon your
Grace. 124

HEN. 5. Gogs wounds, "wait"? we
will go altogither; we are all fellowes. I
tell you, sirs, and the king my father were
dead, we would be all kings. Therefore,
come away!

NED. Gogs wounds, brauely spoken,
Harry! 131

[*Exeunt omnes.*]

*Enter Iohn Cobler, Robin Pewterer, Law-
rence Costermonger, [the watch].*

IOHN COB. All is well here; all is well,
maisters.

ROBIN. How say you, neighbour Iohn
Cobler? I thinke it best that my [135
neighbour, Robin Pewterer, went to Pudding Lane End, and we will watch here at

Billinsgate Ward. How say you, neighbour Robin? how like you this?   139

ROBIN. Marry, well, neighbours; I care
not much if I goe to Pudding Lanes End.
But, neighbours, and you heare any adoe
about me, make haste; and if I heare any
ado about you, I will come to you.

Exit Robin.

LAW. Neighbor, what newes heare you
of the young Prince?   146

IOHN. Marry, neighbor, I heare say he
is a toward yoong Prince; for if he me[e]t
any by the hie-way he will not let [1] to talke
with him; — I dare not call him theefe, but
sure he is one of these taking fellowes.[2] 151

LAW. Indeed, neighbour, I heare say he
is as liuely a young Prince as euer was.

IOHN. I, and I heare say if he vse it long,
his father will cut him off from the crowne.
But, neighbour, say nothing of that! 156

LAW. No, no, neighbour, I warrant
you!

IOHN. Neighbour, me-thinkes you begin to sleepe. If you will, we will sit down;
for I thinke it is about midnight.   161

LAW. Marry, content, neighbour; let vs
sleepe.   [*They fall asleep.*]

Enter Dericke rowing.

DERICKE. Who![3] who, there! who,
there!   165

Exit Dericke. Enter Robin.

ROBIN. O neighbors, what meane you
to sleepe, and such ado in the streetes?

AMBO. How now, neighbor, whats the
matter?

Enter Dericke againe.

DERICKE. Who, there! who, there! who,
there!   171

COBLER. Why, what ailst thou? here is
no horses.[4]

DERICKE. O alas, man, I am robd!
Who there! who there!   175

ROBIN. Hold him, neighbor Cobler.

[1] Hesitate.   [2] A highwayman, thief.
[3] An exclamation to attract attention; *Isaiah*,
lv, 1: "Ho, every one that thirsteth."
[4] Compare the modern call to horses, "Whoa,
there!" and Thomas Heywood's *Fortune by Land
and Sea* (Pearson ed., 1874, vi, 384): "Come, Ile
teach ye *hayte*, and *ree*, *gee* and *whoe*."

ROBIN. Why, I see thou art a plaine
clowne.

DERICKE. Am I a clowne? Sownes,
maisters, do clownes go in silke ap- [180
parell? I am sure all we gentlemen-
clownes in Kent scant go so well. Sownes!
you know clownes very well! Heare you,
are you Maister Constable? And you be,
speake, for I will not take it at his [185
hands.

IOHN. Faith, I am not Maister Constable; but I am one of his bad officers, for
he is not here.   189

DERICKE. Is not Maister Constable
here? Well, it is no matter. Ile haue the
law at his hands.

IOHN. Nay, I pray you, do not take the
law of vs.

DER. Well, you are one of his beastly
officers.   196

IOHN. I am one of his bad officers.

DER. Why, then, I charge thee looke to
him!   199

COBLER. Nay, but heare ye, sir; you
seeme to be an honest fellow, and we are
poore men; and now tis night, and we
would be loth to haue any thing adoo;
therefore, I pray thee, put it vp.   204

DER. First, thou saiest true; I am an
honest fellow — and a proper, hansome
fellow, too! and you seeme to be poore men;
therefore I care not greatly. Nay, I am
quickly pacified. But, and you chance to
spie the theefe, I pray you laie hold on
him.   211

ROBIN. Yes, that we wil, I warrant you.

DER. [*to the audience*]. Tis a wonderful
thing to see how glad the knaue is, now I
haue forgiuen him.   215

IOHN. Neighbors, do ye looke about
you. How now, who's there?

Enter the Theefe.

THEEFE. Here is a good fellow. I pray
you, which is the way to the old tauerne in
Eastcheape?   220

DER. Whoope hollo! Now, Gads Hill,
knowest thou me?

THEEF. I know thee for an asse.

DER. And I know thee for a taking fellow vpon Gads Hill in Kent. A bots light
vpon ye!   226

THEEF.   The whorson vilaine would be knockt.

DER.   Villaine! Maisters,[1] and ye be men, stand to him, and take his weapon from him.   Let him not passe you!   231

[They lay hands on him.]

IOHN.   My friend, what make you abroad now?   It is too late to walke now.

THEEF.   It is not too late for true men to walke.   235

LAW.   We know thee not to be a true man.

THEEF.   Why, what do you meane to do with me?   Sownes, I am one of the kings liege people.   240

DER.   Heare you, sir, are you one of the kings liege people?

THEEF.   I, marry am I, sir!   What say you to it?

DER.   Marry, sir, I say you are one of the kings filching people.   246

COB.   Come, come, lets haue him away.

THEEF.   Why, what haue I done?

ROBIN.   Thou hast robd a poore fellow, and taken away his goods from him.   250

THEEFE.   I neuer sawe him before.

DER.   Maisters, who comes here?

Enter the Vintners boy.

BOY.   How now, good-man Cobler.

COB.   How now, Robin.   What makes thou abroad at this time of night?   255

BOY.   Marrie, I haue beene at the Counter;[2] I can tell such newes as neuer you heard the like!

COBLER.   What is that, Robin? what is the matter?   260

BOY.   Why, this night, about two houres ago, there came the young Prince, and three or foure more of his companions, and called for wine good store; and then they sent for a noyse [3] of musitians, and [265 were very merry for the space of an houre; then, whether their musicke liked them not, or whether they had drunke too much wine or no, I cannot tell, but our pots flue against the wals; and then they drew [270 their swordes and went into the streete and fought, and some tooke one part and some

tooke another; but for the space of halfe an houre there was such a bloodie fray as passeth!   And none coulde part them, vn- [275 till such time as the Maior and Sheriffe were sent for; and then, at the last, with much adoo, they tooke them; and so the yong Prince was carried to the Counter; and then, about one houre after, there [280 came a messenger from the Court in all haste from the king for my Lord Maior and the Sheriffe — but for what cause I know not.

COBLER.   Here is newes indeede, Robert!   286

LAW.   Marry, neighbour, this newes is strange indeede!   I thinke it best, neighbour, to rid our hands of this fellowe first.

THEEFE.   What meane you to doe with me?   291

COBLER.   We mean to carry you to the prison, and there to remaine till the sessions day.

THEEF.   Then, I pray you, let me go to the prison where my maister is.   296

COB.   Nay, thou must go to the country prison, to Newgate.   Therefore, come away.

THEEF *[to Dericke].*   I prethie, be good to me, honest fellow.   301

DER.   I, marry, will I; Ile be verie charitable to thee — for I will neuer leaue thee til I see thee on the gallowes.   304

[Exeunt omnes.]

Enter Henry the Fourth, with the Earle of Exeter, and the Lord of Oxford.

OXF.   And please your Maiestie, heere is my Lord Maior and the Sheriffe of London to speak with your Maiestie.

K. HEN. 4.   Admit them to our presence.

Enter the Maior and the Sheriffe.

Now, my good Lord Maior of London, [309 the cause of my sending for you at this time is to tel you of a matter which I haue learned of my Councell.   Herein I vnderstand that you haue committed my sonne to prison without our leaue and li- [314 cense.   What! althogh he be a rude youth, and likely to giue occasion, yet you might haue considered that he is a prince, and my

---

[1] A. *Maisters vilaine.*   [2] A prison in London.
[3] Band (of musicians).

sonne, and not to be halled to prison by
euery subiect.   319

MAIOR.   May it please your Maiestie to
giue vs leaue to tell our tale?

KING HEN. 4.   Or else God forbid!
Otherwise you might thinke me an vn-
equall iudge, hauing more affection to my
sonne then to any rightfull iudgement. 325

MAIOR.   Then I do not doubt but we
shal rather deserue commendations at your
Maiesties hands then any anger.

K. HEN. 4.   Go too, say on.   329

MAIOR.   Then, if it please your Maiestie, this night betwixt two and three of
the clocke in the morning my lord the yong
Prince, with a very disordred companie,
came to the old tauerne in Eastcheape; [334
and whether it was that their musicke
liked them not, or whether they were ouercome with wine, I know not, but they
drew their swords, and into the streete they
went; and some tooke my lord the [339
yong Princes part, and some tooke the
other; but betwixt them there was such a
bloodie fray for the space of halfe an houre
that neither watchmen [1] nor any other
could stay them; till my brother, the [344
Sheriffe of London, and I were sent for;
and, at the last, with much adoo, we staied
them.   But it was long first, which was a
great disquieting to all your louing subiects thereabouts.   And then, my [349
good lord, we knew not whether your
Grace had sent them to trie vs whether we
would doe iustice, or whether it were of
their owne voluntarie will or not, we cannot
tell.   And, therefore, in such a case, [354
we knew not what to do; but, for our own
safeguard, we sent him to ward; where he
wanteth nothing that is fit for his Grace
and your Maiesties sonne.   And thus,
most humbly beseeching your Maiestie to
thinke of our answere.   360

HEN. 4.   Stand aside vntill we haue
further deliberated on your answere.

Exit Maior [and Sheriff].

HEN. 4.   Ah, Harry! Harry! now
thrice-accursed Harry, that hath got- [364
ten a sonne which with greefe will end his
fathers dayes!   Oh, my sonne, a prince

[1] The watch.

thou art, I, a prince, indeed — and to deserue imprisonment!   And well haue they
done, and like faithfull subiects.   Discharge them, and let them go.   370

L. EXE.   I beseech your Grace, be good
to my lord the yong Prince.

HEN. 4.   Nay, nay, tis no matter; let
him alone.   374

L. OXF.   Perchance the Maior and the
Sheriffe haue bene too precise in this matter.

HEN. 4.   No, they haue done like faithfull subiects.   I will go my-selfe to discharge them and let them go.   380

Exit omnes.

Enter Lord Chiefe Iustice, Clarke of the
Office, Iayler, Iohn Cobler, Dericke, and
the Theefe.

IUDGE.   Iayler, bring the prisoner to the
barre.

DER.   Heare you, my lord; I pray you
bring the bar to the prisoner.   384

[The theefe is led to the bar.]

IUDGE.   Hold thy hand vp at the barre.

THEEFE.   Here it is, my lord.

IUDGE.   Clearke of the Office, reade his
inditement.

CLEARK.   What is thy name?   389

THEEFE.   My name was knowne before
I came here, and shall be when I am gone, I
warrant you.

IUDGE.   I, I thinke so; but we will know
it better before thou go.   394

DER.   Sownes, and you do but send to
the next iaile we are sure to know his
name; for this is not the first prison he hath
bene in, Ile warrant you.

CLEARKE.   What is thy name?   399

THEEF.   What need you to aske, and
haue it in writing?

CLEARKE.   Is not thy name Cutbert
Cutter? [1]

THEEFE.   What the diuell need you ask,
and know it so well?   405

CLEARK.   Why then, Cutbert Cutter, I
indite thee, by the name of Cutbert Cutter,
for robbing a poore carrier the 20 day of
May last past, in the fourteene yeare of [409

[1] A cutthroat, highway robber.

the raigne of our soueraigne lord King Henry the Fourth, for setting vpon a poore carrier vpon Gads Hill, in Kent, and hauing beaten and wounded the said carrier, and taken his goods from him —   414

DER. Oh, maisters, stay there! Nay, lets neuer belie the man! for he hath not beaten and wounded me also, but hee hath beaten and wounded my packe, and hath taken the great rase [1] of ginger that [419 Bouncing Besse with the iolly buttocks should haue had. That greeues me most.

IUDGE. Well, what sayest thou? Art thou guiltie, or not guiltie?

THEEFE. Not guiltie, my lord.   424

IUDGE. By whom wilt thou be tride?

THEEFE. By my lord the young Prince, or by my-selfe, whether you will.

Enter the young Prince, with Ned and Tom.

HEN. 5. Come away, my lads. Gogs wounds, ye villain! what make you [429 heere? I must goe about my businesse myselfe and you must stand loytering here?

THEEFE. Why, my lord, they haue bound me, and will not let me goe.

HEN. 5. Haue they bound thee, villain? Why, how now, my lord?   435

IUDGE. I am glad to see your Grace in good health.

HEN. 5. Why, my lord, this is my man. Tis maruell you knew him not long [439 before this. I tell you, he is a man of his hands.[2]

THEEFE. I, Gogs wounds, that I am! Try me, who dare.   443

IUDGE. Your Grace shal finde small credit by acknowledging him to be your man.

HEN. 5. Why, my lord, what hath he done?

IUD. And it please your Maiestie, he hath robbed a poore carrier.   450

DER. Heare you, sir; marry, it was one Dericke, goodman Hoblings man, of Kent.

HEN. 5. What! wast you, buttenbreech? Of my word, my lord, he did it but in iest.   455

DER. Heare you, sir, is it your mans

qualitie to rob folks in iest? In faith, he shall be hangd in earnest.[1]

HEN. 5. Well, my lord, what do you meane to do with my man?   460

IUDG. And please your Grace, the law must passe on him according to iustice; then he must be executed.[2]

HEN. 5. Why, then, belike you meane to hang my man?   465

IUDGE. I am sorie that it falles out so.

HEN. 5. Why, my lord, I pray ye, who am I?   468

IUD. And please your Grace, you are my lord the yong Prince, our king that shall be after the decease of our soueraigne lord King Henry the Fourth, whom God graunt long to raigne!

HEN. 5. You say true, my lord. And you will hang my man?   475

IUDGE. And like your Grace, I must needs do iustice.

HEN. 5. Tell me, my lord, shall I haue my man?   479

IUDGE. I cannot, my lord.

HEN. 5. But will you not let him go?

IUD. I am sorie that his case is so ill.

HEN. 5. Tush! case me no casings! Shal I haue my man?   484

IUDGE. I cannot, nor I may not, my lord.

HEN. 5. Nay, and "I shal not," say — and then I am answered!

IUDGE. No.   489

HEN. 5. No! Then I will haue him.

He giueth him a boxe on the eare.[3]

---

[1] In reality.

[2] Lines 456–63 are repeated in A., with the error of *iest* for the *earnest* of line 458.

[3] In *Tarlton's Jests* is recorded the following anecdote: "At the Bull [Inn] at Bishops-gate was a play of Henry the fift, wherein the judge was to take a box on the eare; and because he was absent that should take the blow, Tarlton himselfe, ever forward to please, tooke upon him to play the same judge, besides his owne part of the clowne: and Knel then playing Henry the fift, hit Tarlton a sound boxe indeed, which made the people laugh the more because it was he. But anon the judge goes in, and immediately Tarlton in his clownes cloathes comes out, and askes the actors, 'What newes?' 'O,' saith one, 'hadst thou been here, thou shouldest have seene Prince Henry hit the judge a terrible box on the eare.' 'What, man!' said Tarlton, 'strike a judge!' 'It is true, yfaith,' said the other. 'No other like,' said Tarlton; 'and it could not be but terrible to the judge, when the report so terrifies me that me thinkes the blow remaines still on my cheeke that it burnes againe!' The people laught at this mightily."

---

[1] Root.

[2] A man of valor (with, perhaps, a sly glance at his skill as a highwayman).

NED [*drawing his sword*]. Gogs wounds, my lord, shal I cut off his head?

HEN. 5. No; I charge you, draw not your swords; but get you hence; prouide a noyse of musitians. Away, be gone! 495

Exeunt Ned and Tom.[1]

IUDGE. Well, my lord, I am content to take it at your hands.

HEN. 5. Nay, and you be not, you shall haue more! 499

IUDGE. Why, I pray you, my lord, who am I?

HEN. 5. You! who knowes not you? Why, man, you are Lord Chiefe Iustice of England. 504

IUDGE. Your Grace hath said truth; therefore in striking me in this place you greatly abuse me; and not me onely but also your father, whose liuely person here in this place I doo represent. And [509 therefore to teach you what prerogatiues meane, I commit you to the Fleete [2] vntill we haue spoken with your father.

HEN. 5. Why, then, belike you meane to send me to the Fleete! 514

IUDGE. I, indeed; and therefore, carry him away.

Exeunt Hen. 5. with the officers.

IUDGE. Iayler, carry the prisoner to Newgate againe vntil the next sises.

IAY. At your commandement, my Lord, it shalbe done. 520

[*Exeunt omnes.*]

Enter Dericke and Iohn Cobler.

DER. Sownds, maisters, heres adoo when princes must go to prison! Why, Iohn, didst euer see the like?

IOHN. O Dericke, trust me, I neuer saw the like! 525

DER. Why, Iohn, thou maist see what princes be in choller. A iudge a boxe on the eare! Ile tel thee, Iohn, O Iohn, I would not haue done it for twentie shillings. 530

IOHN. No, nor I. There had bene no way but one with vs — we should haue bene hangde. 533

---

[1] A. *Exeunt the Theefe.*
[2] A well-known prison.

DER. Faith, Iohn, Ile tel thee what: thou shalt be my Lord Chiefe Iustice, and thou shalt sit in the chaire; and Ile be the yong Prince, and hit thee a boxe on the eare; and then thou shalt say, "To teach you what prerogatiues meane, I commit you to the Fleete." 540

IOHN. Come on; Ile be your iudge! But thou shalt not hit me hard?

DER. No, no.

[*John Cobler takes his place in the Judge's seat.*]

IOHN. What hath he done? 544

DER. Marry, he hath robd Dericke.

IOHN. Why, then, I cannot let him go.

DER. I must needs haue my man.

IOHN. You shall not haue him! 548

DER. Shall I not haue my man? Say "no," and you dare! How say you? Shall I not haue my man?

IOHN. No, marry, shall you not!

DER. Shall I not, Iohn?

IOHN. No, Dericke. 554

DER. Why, then, take you that [*boxing his ears*] till more come! Sownes, shall I not haue him?

IOHN. Well, I am content to take this at your hand. But, I pray you, who am I?

DER. Who art thou? Sownds, doost not know thy self? 561

IOHN. No.

DER. Now away, simple fellow. Why, man, thou art Iohn the Cobler. 564

IOHN. No, I am my Lord Chiefe Iustice of England.

DER. Oh, Iohn; masse! thou saist true, thou art indeed. 568

IOHN. Why, then, to teach you what prerogatiues mean, I commit you to the Fleete.

DER. Wel, I will go; but, yfaith, you gray-beard knaue, Ile course you! 573

Exit. And straight enters again.

Oh Iohn, come, come out of thy chair. Why, what a clown weart thou to let me hit thee a box on the eare! And now thou seest they will not take me to the Fleete. I thinke that thou art one of these Woren-day [1] clownes. 579

1 ?

Iohn.   But I maruell what will become
of thee.

Der.   Faith, Ile be no more a carrier.

Iohn.   What wilt thou doo, then?   583

Der.   Ile dwell with thee, and be a
cobler.

Iohn.   With me? Alasse, I am not able
to keepe thee. Why, thou wilt eate me out
of doores.   588

Der.   Oh Iohn! No, Iohn; I am none
of these great slouching fellowes that de-
uoure these great peeces of beefe and
brewes. Alasse, a trifle serues me — a
woodcocke, a chicken, or a capons legge,
or any such little thing serues me.   [594

Iohn.   A capon! Why, man, I cannot
get a capon once a yeare — except it be at
Christmas, at some other mans house; for
we coblers be glad of a dish of rootes.   598

Der.   Rootes! why, are you so good at
rooting?   Nay, cobler, weele haue you
ringde.[1]

Iohn.   But, Dericke, though we be so
           poore,   602
Yet wil we haue in store a crab in the fire,[2]
With nut-browne ale that is full stale,
Which wil a man quaile and laie in the mire.

Der.   A bots on you! and be but for
your ale, Ile dwel with you. Come, lets
away as fast as we can.   608

Exeunt.

Enter the yoong Prince, with Ned and Tom.

Hen. 5.   Come away, sirs.   Gogs
wounds, Ned! didst thou not see what a
boxe on the eare I tooke my Lord Chiefe
Iustice?   612

Tom.   By Gogs blood, it did me good to
see it. It made his teeth iarre in his head!

Enter Sir Iohn Old-Castle.

Hen. 5.   How now, Sir Iohn Old-
Castle, what newes with you?

Ioh. Old.   I am glad to see your Grace
at libertie. I was come, I, to visit you in
prison.   619

Hen. 5.   To visit me! Didst thou not
know that I am a princes son? Why, tis

[1] As pigs are ringed in the nose to keep them
from rooting.
[2] A crab apple, toasted in the fire and dropped
into a mug of ale to warm and flavor the drink.

inough for me to looke into a prison, though
I come not in my-selfe. But heres [623
such adoo now-a-dayes — heres prisoning,
heres hanging, whipping, and the diuel and
all. But I tel you, sirs, when I am king we
will haue no such things. But, my lads,
if the old king, my father, were dead, we
would be all kings.   629

Ioh. Old.   Hee is a good olde man; God
take him to his mercy the sooner!

Hen. 5.   But, Ned, so soone as I am king,
the first thing I wil do shal be to put [633
my Lord Chief Iustice out of office, and
thou shalt be my Lord Chiefe Iustice of
England.

Ned.   Shall I be Lord Chiefe Iustice?
By Gogs wounds, Ile be the brauest Lord
Chiefe Iustice that euer was in England!

Hen. 5.   Then, Ned, Ile turne all these
prisons into fence-schooles,[1] and I will en-
due [2] thee with them, with landes to maintaine them withall.   Then I wil haue [643
a bout [3] with my Lord Chiefe Iustice.
Thou shalt hang none but picke-purses,
and horse-stealers, and such base-minded
villaines; but that fellow that will stand
by the high-way side couragiously [648
with his sword and buckler and take a
purse — that fellow, giue him commendations! Beside that, send him to me, and I
will giue him an anuall pension out of my
exchequer to maintaine him all the dayes
of his life.   654

Ioh.   Nobly spoken, Harry! We shall
neuer haue a mery world til the old king
be dead.   657

Ned.   But whither are ye going now?

Hen. 5.   To the Court; for I heare say
my father lies verie sicke.

Tom.   But I doubt he wil not die.

Hen. 5.   Yet will I goe thither; for the
breath shal be no sooner out of his mouth
but I wil clap the crowne on my head.   664

Iockey.   Wil you goe to the Court with
that cloake so full of needles?

Hen. 5.   Cloake, ilat-holes, needles, and
all was of mine owne deuising; and therefore I wil weare it.   669

Tom.   I pray you, my lord, what may be
the meaning thereof?

[1] Schools of fencing.   [2] Endow.
[3] A. *about.* A fencing match.

Hen. 5. Why, man, tis a signe that I stand vpon thorns til the crowne be on my head.   674

Ioc. Or that euery needle might be a prick to their harts that repine at your doings.   677

Hen. 5. Thou saist true, Iockey. But thers some wil say the yoong Prince will be "a well toward yoong man" — and all this geare, that I had as leeue they would breake my head with a pot as to say any such thing. But we stand prating [683 here too long; I must needs speake with my father. Therfore, come away.

[*They cross over to the King's palace.*]

Porter. What a rapping keep you at the kings court-gate?

Hen. 5. Heres one that must speake with the king.   689

Por. The king is verie sick, and none must speak with him.

Hen. 5. No? You rascall, do you not know me?   693

Por. You are my lord the yong Prince.

Hen. 5. Then goe and tell my father that I must, and will, speake with him.

Ned [*drawing his sword*]. Shall I cut off his head?   698

Hen. 5. No, no. Though I would helpe you in other places, yet I haue nothing to doo here. What! you are in my fathers Court.   702

Ned. I will write him in my tables; for so soone as I am made Lord Chiefe Iustice I wil put him out of his office.

The trumpet sounds.

Hen. 5. Gogs wounds, sirs, the king comes. Lets all stand aside.   707

Enter the King, with the Lord of Exeter.

Hen. 4. And is it true, my lord, that my sonne is alreadie sent to the Fleete? Now, truly, that man is more fitter to rule the realme then I; for by no meanes could I rule my sonne, and he, by one word, hath caused him to be ruled. Oh my [713 sonne! my sonne! no sooner out of one prison but into another? I had thought once-whiles I had liued to haue seene this noble realme of England flourish by thee,

my sonne; but now I see it goes to ruine and decaie.   719

He wepeth.

Enters Lord of Oxford.

Ox. And please your Grace, here is my lord your sonne that commeth to speake with you. He saith he must, and wil, speake with you.   723

Hen. 4. Who? my sonne Harry?

Oxf. I, and please your Maiestie.

Hen. 4. I know wherefore he commeth. But looke that none come with him.[1]   728

Oxf. A verie disordered company, and such as make verie ill rule in your Maisties house.

Hen. 4. Well, let him come; but looke that none come with him.   733

He goeth.

Oxf. And please your Grace my lord the king sends for you.

Hen. 5. Come away, sirs; lets go all togither.

Oxf. And please your Grace, none must go with you.   739

Hen. 5. Why, I must needs haue them with me; otherwise I can do my father no countenance:[2] therefore, come away.

Oxf. The king your father commaunds there should none come.   744

Hen. 5. Well, sirs, then be gone — and prouide me three noyse of musitians.

Exeunt knights.

Enters the Prince, with a dagger in his hand.

Hen. 4. Come, my sonne; come on, a Gods name! I know wherefore thy [748 comming is. Oh, my sonne, my sonne! what cause hath euer bene that thou shouldst forsake me, and follow this vilde and reprobate company which abuseth youth so manifestly? Oh, my sonne, [753 thou knowest that these thy doings wil end thy fathers dayes.

He weepes.

I, so, so, my sonne, thou fearest not to ap-

---

[1] This line may be corrupt, caught by the printer from line 733. We should expect a question.
[2] Show him no dignity, proper respect.

proach the presence of thy sick father in that disguised sort. I tel thee, my sonne, [758 that there is neuer a needle in thy cloke but it is a prick to my heart, and neuer an ilat-hole but it is a hole to my soule; and wherefore thou bringest that dagger in thy hande I know not, but by coniecture. 763

He weepes.

Hen. 5. [*aside*]. My conscience accus-eth me. [*He kneels.*] Most soueraign lord, and welbeloued father, to answere first to the last point, that is, whereas you coniecture that this hand and this [768 dagger shall be armde against your life, no! Know, my beloued father, far be the thoughts of your sonne — "sonne," said I? an vnworthie sonne for so good a father! — but farre be the thoughts of any such [773 pretended mischiefe. And I most humbly render it to your Maiesties hand. And liue, my lord and soueraigne, for euer! And with your dagger-arme show like vengeance vpon the bodie of — "that, [778 your sonne," I was about say, and dare not; ah, woe is me therefore! — that, your wilde slaue. Tis not the crowne that I come for, sweete father, because I am vn-worthie. And those vilde and repro- [783 bate companions [1] — I abandon and vt-terly abolish their company for euer! Pardon, sweete father! pardon! the least thing and most desire. And this ruffianly cloake I here teare from my backe, [788 and sacrifice it to the diuel, which is maister of al mischiefe. Pardon me, sweet father! pardon me! Good my Lord of Exeter, speak for me. Pardon me! pardon, good father! Not a word? [793 Ah, he wil not speak one word! A, Harry, now thrice vnhappie Harry! But what shal I do? I wil go take me into some solitarie place, and there lament my sinfull life; and, when I haue done, I wil laie me downe and die. 799

Exit.

Hen. 4. Call him againe! Call my sonne againe!

[*Re-enter the Prince.*]

Hen. 5. And doth my father call me

[1] A. *company.*

again? Now, Harry, happie be the time that thy father calleth thee againe! 804

[*He kneels.*]

Hen. 4. Stand vp, my son; and do not think thy father but at the request of thee, my sonne, I wil pardon thee. And God blesse thee, and make thee his seruant. 808

Hen. 5. Thanks, good my lord. And no doubt but this day, euen this day, I am borne new againe.

Hen. 4. Come, my son and lords, take me by the hands. 813

Exeunt omnes.

Enter Dericke [shouting at John Cobler's wife within].

Der. Thou art a stinking whore! and a whorson stinking whore! Doest thinke Ile take it at thy hands?

Enter Iohn Cobler, running.

Iohn. Derick, D[ericke], D[ericke], hearesta? [1] Oh, [2] D[ericke], neuer [818 while thou liuest vse that! Why, what wil my neighbors say and thou go away so?

Der. Shees a narrant whore; and Ile haue the lawe on you, Iohn.

Iohn. Why, what hath she done? 823

Der. Marry, marke thou, Iohn. I wil proue it, that I wil!

Iohn. What wilt thou proue?

Der. That she cald me in to dinner — Iohn, marke the tale wel, Iohn — and [828 when I was set, she brought me a dish of rootes and a peece of barrel-butter therein. And she is a verie knaue, and thou a drab if thou take her part. 832

Iohn. Hearesta, Dericke? is this the matter? Nay, and it be no worse we wil go home againe, and all shall be amended.

Der. Oh Iohn, hearesta, Iohn? is all well?

Iohn. I, all is wel. 838

Der. Then Ile go home before, and breake all the glasse windows.

[*Exeunt Dericke and John.*]

Enter the King with his lords.

Hen. 4. Come, my lords. I see it

[1] Hearest thou. [2] A. *Do.*

bootes me not to take any phisick, for all
the phisitians in the world cannot cure [843
me; no, not one.   But, good my lords, remember my last wil and testament concerning my sonne; for truly, my lordes, I
doo not thinke but he wil proue as valiant
and victorious a king as euer raigned in
England.   849

BOTH.   Let heuen and earth be witnesse
betweene vs if we accomplish not thy wil to
the vttermost.   852

HEN. IV.   I giue you most vnfained
thanks, good my lords.   Draw the curtaines, and depart my chamber a while;
and cause some musicke to rocke me
a-sleepe.   857

He sleepeth.   Exeunt Lords.

Enter the Prince.

HEN. 5.   Ah, Harry, thrice vnhappie,
that hath neglect so long from visiting of
thy sicke father!   I wil goe.   Nay, but why
doo I not go to the chamber of my sick
father to comfort the melancholy soule of
his bodie?   [*He approaches the sleep-* [863
ing king.]   His soule, said I?   Here is his
bodie, indeed, but his soule is whereas it
needs no bodie.   Now, thrice accursed
Harry, that hath offended thy father so
much!   And could not I craue [868
pardon for all?   Oh my dying father!
Curst be the day wherin I was borne, and
accursed be the houre wherin I was be-
gotten!   But what shal I do?   If weeping
teares, which come too late, may suf- [873
fice the negligence, neglected to some, I wil
weepe day and night vntil the fountaine be
drie with weeping.

Exit [with the crown].

Enter Lord of Exeter and Oxford.

EXE.   Come easily, my lord, for waking
of the king.   878

HEN. 4. [*waking*].   Now, my lords?

OXF.   How doth your Grace feele your
selfe?

HEN. 4.   Somewhat better after my
sleepe.   But, good my lords, take off [883
my crowne.   Remoue my chaire a little
backe, and set me right.

AMBO.   And please your Grace, the
crown is taken away.   887

HEN. IV.   The crowne taken away!
Good my Lord of Oxford, go see who hath
done this deed.   No doubt tis some vilde
traitor that hath done it to depriue my
sonne.   They that would do it now would
seeke to scrape and scrawle for it after my
death.   894

Enter Lord of Oxford with the Prince.

OXF.   Here, and please your Grace, is
my lord the yong Prince with the crowne.

HEN. 4.   Why, how now, my sonne!   I
had thought the last time I had you [898
in schooling I had giuen you a lesson for all;
and do you now begin againe?   Why, tel
me, my sonne, doest thou thinke the time
so long that thou wouldest haue it before
the breath be out of my mouth?   903

HEN. 5.   Most soueraign lord and welbeloued father, I came into your chamber
to comfort the melancholy soule of your
bodie; and finding you at that time past all
recouerie, and dead, to my thinking [908
— God is my witnesse — and what should
I doo, but with weeping tears lament the
death of you, my father?   And after that,
seeing the crowne, I tooke it.   And tel me,
my father, who might better take it [913
then I, after your death?   But, seeing you
liue, I most humbly render it into your
Maiesties hands; and the happiest man
aliue that my father liue[s].   And liue,
my lord and father, for euer!   918

[He kneels.]

HEN. 4.   Stand, vp my sonne.   Thine
answere hath sounded wel in mine eares;
for I must need confesse that I was in a
very sound sleep, and altogither vnmindful
of thy comming.   But come neare, [923
my sonne, and let me put thee in possession
whilst I liue, that none depriue thee of it
after my death.

HEN. 5.   Well may I take it at your
Maiesties hands; but it shal neuer touch
my head so long as my father liues.   929

He taketh the crowne.

HEN. 4.   God giue thee ioy, my sonne!
God bless thee, and make thee his seruant,
and send thee a prosperous raigne!   For
God knowes, my sonne, how hardly I came

by it, and how hardly I haue maintained it.   935
HEN. 5. Howsoeuer you came by it I know not; but now I haue it from you, and from you I wil keepe it. And he that [938 seekes to take the crowne from my head, let him looke that his armour be thicker then mine, or I will pearce him to the heart, were it harder then brasse or bol- lion.   943
HEN. IV. Nobly spoken, and like a king! Now trust me, my lordes, I feare not but my sonne will be as warlike and victorious a prince as euer raigned in Eng- land.   948
L[ORDES] AMBO. His former life shewes no lesse.
HEN. 4. Wel, my lords, I know not whether it be for sleep, or drawing neare of drowsie summer of death, but I am [953 verie much giuen to sleepe. Therefore, good my lords, and my sonne, draw the curtaines; depart my chamber; and cause some musicke to rocke me a-sleepe.   957

Exeunt omnes.

The King dieth.

Enter the theefe.

THEEFE. Ah, God, I am now much like to a bird which hath escaped out of the cage; for so soone as my Lord Chiefe Ius- tice heard that the old king was dead he was glad to let me go for feare of my lord the yong Prince. But here comes [963 some of his companions. I wil see and I can get any thing of them for old ac- quaintance.

Enter Knights raunging.

TOM. Gogs wounds, the king is dead!
IOH. Dead! then, Gogs blood, we shall be all kings!   969
NED. Gogs wounds, I shall be Lord Chiefe Iustice of England.
TOM [*to the thief*]. Why how, are you broken out of prison?   973
NED. Gogs wounds, how the villaine stinkes! [1]

---

[1] The prisons were foul, and we have many allu- sions to the evil smell of persons confined therein.

IOC. Why, what wil become of thee now? Fie vpon him, how the rascall stinkes!   978
THEEF. Marry, I wil go and serue my maister againe.
TOM. Gogs blood, doost think that he wil haue any such scab'd knaue as thou art? What, man! he is a king now.   983
NED [*giving him money*]. Hold thee. Heres a couple of angels [1] for thee. And get thee gone, for the king wil not be long before he come this way. And hereafter I wil tel the king of thee.   988

Exit Theefe.

IOC. Oh, how it did me good to see the king when he was crowned! Me-thought his seate was like the figure of heauen, and his person like vnto a god.   992
NED. But who would haue thought that the king would haue changde his countenance so?
IOC. Did you not see with what grace he sent his embassage into France to tel the French king that Harry of England [998 hath sent for the crowne, and Harry of England wil haue it?
TOM. But twas but a litle to make the people beleeue that he was sorie for his fathers death.   1003

The Trumpet sounds.

NED. Gogs wounds, the king comes! Lets all stand aside.

Enter the King with the Archbishop and the Lord of Oxford.

IOC. How do you, my lord?
NED. How now, Harry? [*The King frowns upon him.*] Tut, my lord, put [1008 away these dumpes. You are a king, and all the realme is yours. What, man! do you not remember the old sayings? You know I must be Lord Chiefe Iustice of England. Trust me, my lord, me- [1013 thinks you are very much changed. And tis but with a litle sorrowing, to make folkes beleeue the death of your father greeues you — and tis nothing so.   1017
HEN. 5. I prethee, Ned, mend thy maners, and be more modester in thy

---

[1] Gold coins, with a value of about ten shillings.

tearmes; for my vnfeined greefe is not to
be ruled by thy flattering and dissembling
talke.   Thou saist I am changed; so I am,
indeed; and so must thou be, and [1023
that quickly, or else I must cause thee to be
chaunged.

Ioc.   Gogs wounds, how like you this?
Sownds! tis not so sweete as musicke.

Tom.   I trust we haue not offended your
Grace no way.   1029

Hen. 5.   Ah, Tom, your former life
greeues me, and makes me to abandon and
abolish your company for euer.   And therfore, not vpon pain of death to ap- [1033
proch my presence by ten miles space.
Then, if I heare wel of you, it may be I wil
do somewhat for you; otherwise looke for
no more fauour at my hands then at any
other mans.   And therefore, be [1038
gone! we haue other matters to talke on.

Exeunt knights.

Now, my good Lord Archbishop of Canterbury, what say you to our embassage into
France?   1042

Archb.   Your right to the French
crowne of France came by your great
grandmother Izabel, wife to King Edward
the Third, and sister to Charles, the
French king.   Now, if the French king
deny it, as likely inough he wil, then [1048
must you take your sword in hand and conquer the right.   Let the vsurped Frenchman
know, although your predecessors haue let
it passe, you wil not; for your countrymen
are willing with purse and men to [1053
aide you.   Then, my good lord, as it hath
bene alwaies knowne that Scotland hath
bene in league with France by a sort of pen-
sions which yearly come from thence, I
thinke it therefore best to conquere [1058
Scotland; and then I think that you may go
more easily into France.   And this is all
that I can say, my good lord.

Hen. 5.   I thanke you, my good Lord
Archbisop of Canterbury.   What say you,
my good Lord of Oxford?   1064

Oxf.   And [1] please your Maiestie, I
agree to my Lord Archbishop, sauing in
this: — "He that wil Scotland win must
first with France begin," according [1068

[1] A. *And and.*

to the old saying.   Therefore, my good
lord, I thinke it best first to inuade France;
for in conquering Scotland you conquer but
one, and conquere France, and conquere
both.   1073

Enter Lord of Exeter.

Exe.   And please your Maiestie, my
Lord Embassador is come out of France.

Hen. 5.   Now trust me, my lord, he was
the last man that we talked of.   I am glad
that he is come to resolue vs of our answere.   Commit him to our presence. 1079

Enter Duke of Yorke.

York.   God saue the life of my souer-
aign lord the king!

Hen. 5.   Now, my good lord the Duke
of Yorke, what newes from our brother the
French king?   1084

Yorke.   And please your Maiestie, I deliuered him my embassage, whereof I
tooke some deliberation.   But for the answere, he hath sent my Lord Em- [1088
bassador of Burges, the Duke of Burgony,
Monsieur le Cole, with two hundred and
fiftie horsemen to bring the embassage.

Hen. 5.   Commit my Lord Archbishop of
Burges into our presence.   [1093

Enter Archbishop of Burges.

Now, my Lord Archbishop of Burges, we do
learne by our Lord Embassador that you
haue our message to do from our brother
the French king.   Here, my good lord, [1097
according to our accustomed order, we giue
you free libertie and license to speake with
good audience.

Archb.   God saue the mightie King of
England!   My lord and maister, the [1102
most Christian King Charles the Seuenth,
the great and mightie King of France, as a
most noble and Christian king not minding
to shed innocent blood, is rather content to
yeeld somewhat to your vnreason- [1107
able demaunds — that, if fiftie thousand
crownes a yeare, with his daughter, the
said Ladie Katheren, in marriage, and
some crownes which he may wel spare not
hurting of his kingdome, he is con- [1112
tent to yeeld so far to your vnreasonable
desire.

HEN. 5.   Why then, belike your lord
and maister thinks to puffe me vp with
fifty thousand crowns a yere?   No! [1117
Tell thy lord and maister that all the
crownes in France shall not serue me, except the crowne and kingdome it selfe!
And perchance hereafter I wil haue his
daughter.   1122

ARCHB.   And it please your Maiestie,
my Lord Prince Dolphin greets you well
with this present.

He deliuereth a Tunne of Tennis-balles.[1]

HEN. 5.   What, a guilded tunne!   I
pray you, my Lord of Yorke, looke what is
in it.   1128

YORKE.   And it please your Grace, here
is a carpet, and a tunne of tennis-balles.

HEN. 5.   A tunne of tennis-balles!   I
pray you, good my Lord Archbishop, what
might the meaning thereof be?   1133

ARCHB.   And it please you, my lord, a
messenger, you know, ought to keepe close
his message — and specially an embas-
sador.   1137

HEN. 5.   But I know that you may declare your message to a king; the law of
armes allowes no lesse.

ARCHB.   My Lord [Prince Dolphin],
hearing of your wildnesse before [1142
your fathers death, sent you this, my good
lord, meaning that you are more fitter for a
tennis-court then a field, and more fitter
for a carpet then the camp.   1146

HEN. 5.   My Lord Prince Dolphin is
very pleasant with me!   But tel him that
in-steed of balles of leather we wil tosse him
balles of brasse and yron — yea, such
balles as neuer were tost in France.   The
proudest tennis-court shall rue it!   I, [1152
and thou, Prince of Burges, shall rue it!
Therefore, get thee hence; and tel him thy
message quickly, least I be there before
thee.   Away, priest! be gone!   1156

ARCHB.   I beseech your Grace to deliuer me your safe conduct vnder your
broad seale emanuel.

HEN. 5.   Priest of Burges, know that
the hand and seale of a king, and his word,
is all one.   And, in-stead of my hand [1162

---

[1] A. repeats this stage-direction before and after
the speech of the Archbishop.

and seale I will bring him my hand and
sword.   And tel thy lord and maister that
I, Harry of England, said it; and I, Harry
of England, wil performe it!   My Lord of
Yorke, deliuer him our safe conduct [1167
under our broad seale emanuel.

Exeunt Archbishop and the Duke of Yorke.

Now, my lords, to armes! to armes!   For I
vow by heauen and earth that the proudest
French-man in all France shall rue [1171
the time that euer these tennis-balles were
sent into England.   My lord, I wil that
there be prouided a great nauy of ships
with all speed at South-Hampton, for there
I meane to ship my men; for I would [1176
be there before him, if it were possible.
Therefore come — but staie; I had almost
forgot the chiefest thing of all with chafing
with this French Embassador.   Call in my
Lord Chiefe Iustice of England.   1181

Enters Lord Chiefe Iustice of England.

EXE.   Here is the king, my lord.

IUSTICE.   God preserue your Maiestie!

HEN. 5.   Why, how now, my lord? what
is the matter?

IUSTICE.   I would it were vnknowne to
your Maiestie.   1187

HEN. 5.   Why, what aile you?

IUST.   Your Maiestie knoweth my
griefe well.   1190

HEN. 5.   Oh, my lord, you remember
you sent me to the Fleete, did you not?

IUST.   I trust your Grace haue forgotten
that.

HEN. 5.   I, truly, my lord; and for re-
uengement I haue chosen you to be [1196
my Protector ouer my realme, until it shall
please God to giue me speedie returne out
of France.

IUST.   And if it please your Maiestie, I
am far vnworthie of so high a dignitie. 1201

HEN. 5.   Tut, my lord! you are not vn-
worthie, because I thinke you worthie; for
you that would not spare me, I thinke, wil
not spare another.   It must needs be so.
And therefore, come, let vs be gone, and
get our men in a readinesse.   1207

Exeunt omnes.

Enter a Captaine, Iohn Cobler and his wife.

CAP. Come, come; there's no remedie. Thou must needs serue the king.

IOHN. Good Maister Captaine, let me go. I am not able to go so farre. 1211

WIFE. I pray you, good Maister Captaine, be good to my husband.

CAP. Why, I am sure he is not too good to serue the king. 1215

IOHN. Alasse, no — but a great deale too bad; therefore, I pray you, let me go.

CAP. No, no; thou shalt go.

IOHN. Oh, sir, I haue a great many shooes at home to cobble.

WIFE. I pray you, let him go home againe. 1222

CAP. Tush, I care not. Thou shalt go.

IOHN. Oh wife, and you had beene a louing wife to me this had not bene; for I haue said many times that I would go away, and now I must go against my will. 1227

He weepeth.

Enters Dericke [with a pot-lid for a shield].

DER. How now, ho! Basillus manus [1] for an old codpeece! Maister Captaine, shall we awaye? Sownds! how now, Iohn? What, a crying? What make you [1231 and my dame there? [*To the wife:*] I maruell whose head you will throw the stooles at, now we are gone.

WIFE. Ile tell you! Come, ye clog-head! What do you with my potlid? [1236 Heare you, will you haue it rapt about your pate?

She beateth him with her potlid.

DER. Oh good dame!

Here he shakes her. [2]

And I had my dagger here I wold worie you al to peeces, that I would! 1241

WIFE. Would you so? Ile trie that.

She beateth him.

DER. Maister Captaine, will ye suffer her? Go too, dame! I wil go backe as far as I can; but, and you come againe — Ile clap the law on your backe, thats [1246

flat! Ile tell you, Maister Captaine, what you shall do: presse her for a souldier! I warrant you she will do as much good as her husband and I too.

Enters the Theefe.

Sownes! who comes yonder? 1251

CAP. How now, good fellow; doest thou want a maister?

THEEFE. I, truly, sir.

CAP. Hold thee, then. I presse thee for a souldier to serue the king in France.

DER. How now, Gads! What, doest knowes, [1] thinkest? 1258

THEEFE. I, I knew thee long ago.

DER. Heare you, Maister Captaine.

CAP. What saist thou? 1261

DER. I pray you, let me go home againe.

CAP. Why, what wouldst thou do at home? 1265

DER. Marry, I haue brought two shirts with me, and I would carry one of them home againe; for I am sure heele steale it from me, he is such a filching fellow.

CAP. I warrant thee he wil not steale it from thee. Come, lets away. 1272

DER. Come, Maister Captaine, lets away. Come, follow me.

IOHN. Come, wife, lets part louingly.

WIFE. Farewell, good husband. 1276

[They embrace.]

DER. Fie, what a kissing and crying is here! Sownes, do ye thinke he wil neuer come againe? Why, Iohn, come away! Doest thinke that we are so base-minded to die among Frenchmen? Sownes, [1281 we know not whether they will laie [2] us in their church or no. Come, M[aster] Captain, lets away.

CAP. I cannot staie no longer; therefore, come away. 1286

Exeunt omnes.

Enter the [French] King, Prince Dolphin, and Lord High Constable of France.

KING. Now, my Lord High Constable, what say you to our embassage into England?

---

[1] A common phrase, corrupted from the Spanish greeting, *besár los manos* (to kiss the hands); here used as nonsense.

[2] A. prints this as a part of Dericke's speech.

[1] Know us.   [2] Bury.

CONST. And it please your Maiestie, I can say nothing untill my Lords [1291 Embassadors be come home. But yet me-thinkes your Grace hath done well to get your men in so good a readinesse for feare of the worst. 1295

KING. I, my lord, we haue some in a readinesse; but if the king of England make against vs we must haue thrice so many moe.

DOLPHIN. Tut, my lord; although the king of England be yoong and wilde- [1301 headed, yet neuer thinke he will be so un-wise to make battell against the mightie king of France.

KING. Oh, my sonne, although the king of England be yoong and wilde- [1306 headed, yet neuer thinke but he is rulde by his wise councellors.

Enter Archbishop of Burges.

ARCH. God saue the life of my souer-aign lord, the King! 1310

KING. Now, my good Lord Archbishop of Burges, what news from our brother, the English king?

ARCHB. And please your Maiestie, he is so far from your expectation that nothing wil serue him but the crowne and [1316 kingdome it-selfe. Besides, he bad me haste quickly least he be there before me. And, so far as I heare, he hath kept prom-ise; for they say he is alreadie landed at Kidcocks in Normandie vpon the [1321 Riuer of Sene, and laid his siege to the garrison-towne of Harflew.

KING. You haue made great haste in the meanetime, haue you not?

DOLPHIN. I pray you, my lord, how did the king of England take my presents? 1327

ARCHB. Truly, my lord, in verie ill part. For these your balles of leather he will toss you balles of brasse and yron. Trust me, my lord, I was verie affraide of him, [1331 he is such a hautie and high-minded prince. He is as fierce as a lyon.

CON. Tush! we wil make him as tame as a lambe, I warrant you.

Enters a Messenger.

MESSEN. God saue the mightie King of France! 1337

KING. Now, messenger, what newes?

MESSEN. And it please your Maiestie, I come from your poore distressed towne of Harflew, which is so beset on euery [1341 side, if your Maiestie do not send present aide the towne will be yeelded to the Eng-lish king.

KING. Come, my lords, come! Shall we stand still till our country be [1346 spoyled vnder our noses? My lords, let the Normanes, Brabants, Pickardies, and Danes be sent for with all speede. And you, my Lord High Constable, I make gen-erall ouer all my whole armie; Mon- [1351 sieur le Colle, Maister of the Boas,[1] Signior Deuens, and all the rest, at your appoint-ment.

DOLP. I trust your Maiestie will be-stow some part of the battell on me. [1356 I hope not to present any otherwise then well.

KING. I tell thee, my sonne, although I should get the victory, and thou lose thy life, I should thinke my-selfe quite [1361 conquered, and the English-men to haue the victorie.

DOL. Why, my lord and father, I would haue the pettie king of England to know that I dare encounter him in any ground of the world. 1367

KING. I know well, my sonne; but at this time I will haue it thus. Therefore, come away. 1370

Exeunt omnes.

Enters Henry the Fifth, with his lords.

HEN. 5. Come, my lords of England. No doubt this good lucke of winning this towne is a signe of an honourable victorie to come. But, good my lord, go and speake to the captaines with all speed, to number the hoast of the French- [1376 men, and by that meanes we may the bet-ter know how to appoint the battell.

YORKE. And it please your Maiestie, there are many of your men sicke and dis-eased, and many of them die for want of victuals. 1382

---

[1] Qy. *bowse*, crossbows. According to Holinshed, Lord Rambures was "maister of the crosbowes," and this officer played a conspicuous part in the battle.

HEN. 5. And why did you not tell me of it before? If we cannot haue it for money we will haue it by dint of sword; the lawe of armes allow no lesse.   1386

OXF. I beseech your Grace to graunt me a boone.

HEN. 5. What is that, my good lord?

OXF. That your Grace would giue me the euantgard [1] in the battell.   1391

HEN. 5. Trust me, my Lord of Oxford, I cannot; for I haue alreadie giuen it to my vncke, the Duke of York. Yet I thanke you for your good will. *A trumpet sounds.* How now, what is that?   1396

YORKE. I thinke it be some herald of armes.

Enters a Herald.

HERALD. King of England, my Lord High Constable, and others of the noble-men of France, sends me to defie thee [1401 as open enemy to God, our countrey, and vs; and hereupon they presently bid thee battell.

HEN. 5. Herald, tell them that I defie them as open enemies to God, my [1406 countrey, and me, and as wronfull vsurpers of my right. And whereas thou saist they presently bid me battell, tell them that I thinke they know how to please me. But, I pray thee, what place hath my Lord Prince Dolphin here in battell?   1412

HERALD. And it please your Grace, my lord and king, his father, will not let him come into the field.   1415

HEN. 5. Why, then he doth me great iniurie. I thought that he and I shuld haue plaid at tennis togither; therefore I haue brought tennis-balles for him — but other maner of ones then he sent me. And, Herald, tell my Lord Prince Dolphin [1421 that I haue inured [2] my hands with other kind of weapons then tennis-balles ere this time a day, and that he shall finde it, ere it be long. And so, adue my friend. And tell my lord that I am readie when he [1426 will.

Exit Herald.

Come, my lords. I care not and I go to our captaines; and Ile see the number of

the French army my selfe. Strike up the drumme!   1431

Exeunt omnes.

Enter French Souldiers.

1. SOUL. Come away, Jack Drummer! Come away all, and me will tel you what me wil doo. Me wil tro [1] one chance on the dice who shall haue the king of England and his lords.   1436

2. SOUL. Come away, Jacke Drummer, and tro your chance; and lay downe your drumme.

Enter Drummer.

DRUM. Oh, the braue [2] apparel that the English-mans hay broth ouer! I wil tel you what me ha donne. Me ha [1442 prouided a hundreth trunkes, and all to put the fine parel of the English-mans in.

1. SOUL. What do thou meane by "trunkes"?

2. SOUL. A shest, man, a hundred shests.   1448

1. SOUL. Awee, awee, awee. [3] Me wil tel you what: me ha put fiue shildren [4] out of my house, and all too litle to put the fine apparel of the English-mans in.   1452

DRUM. Oh, the braue, the braue ap-parel that we shall haue anon! But come, and you shall see what me wil tro at the kings drummer and fife. [*He throws the dice.*] Ha! me ha no good lucke. Tro you.   1458

3. SOL. Faith, me wil tro at the Earle of Northumberland, and my Lord a Wil-lowby with his great horse, snorting, fart-ing — oh braue horse! [*He throws the dice.*]

1. SOL. Ha! Bur Ladie, you ha reason-able good lucke. Now I wil tro at the king himselfe. [*He throws the dice.*] Ha! me haue no good lucke.

Enters a Captaine.

CAP. How now! what make you here so farre from the campe?   1468

2. SOL. Shal me tel our captain what we haue done here?

DRUM. Awee, awee.   1471

Exeunt Drum[mer] and one Souldier.

---

[1] The foremost part of the army.   [2] Practised.
[3] *Oui* (yes).   [2] Magnificent.   [4] Children.

2. SOL.   I wil tel you what we [1] haue
donne. We haue bene troing our shance on
the dice; but none can win the king.

CAP. I thinke so. Why, he is left behind for me! And I haue set three or foure
chaire-makers a worke to make a [1477
new disguised chaire to set that womanly
king of England in, that all the people may
laugh and scoffe at him.

2. SOUL. Oh braue captaine!   1481

CAP. I am glad, and yet with a kinde of
pitie, to see the poore king — why, who
euer saw a more flourishing armie in
France in one day then here is? Are not
here all the peeres of France? Are not
here the Normans, with their firie [1487
hand-gunnes and flaunching [2] curtleaxes?
Are not here the barbarians, with their
bard [3] horses and lanching speares? Are
not here Pickardes, with their crosbowes
and piercing dartes? The Henues,[4] [1492
with their cutting glaues [5] and sharpe car-
buckles? [6] Are not here the lance-knights
of Burgondie? And, on the other side, a
site of poore English scabs! Why, take an
English-man out of his warme bed [1497
and his stale drinke but one moneth, and,
alas! what wil become of him? But giue
the Frenchman a reddish [7] roote, and he
wil liue with it all the dayes of his life.

Exit.

2. SOUL. Oh, the braue apparel that we
shall haue of the English-mans!   1503

Exit.

Enters the King of England and his Lords.

HEN. 5. Come, my lords and fellowes
of armes. What company is there of the
French-men?   1506

OXF. And it please your Maiestie, our
captaines haue numbred them, and, so

---

neare as they can iudge, they are about
threescore thousand horsemen and fortie
thousand footemen.   1511

HEN. 5. They threescore thousand
[horsemen], and we but two thousand!
They fortie [1] thousand footemen, and we
twelue thousand! They are a hundred
thousand, and we forteen [2] thousand!
Ten to one! My lords and louing [1517
countrymen, though we be fewe, and they
many, feare not. Your quarrel is good,
and God wil defend you. Plucke vp your
hearts, for this day we shall either haue a
valiant victorie, or a honourable [1522
death! Now, my lords, I wil that my
vncle, the Duke of Yorke, haue the auant-
gard in the battell; the Earle of Darby, the
Earle of Oxford, the Earle of Kent, the
Earle of Nottingham, the Earle of [1527
Huntington I wil haue beside the army,
that they may come fresh vpon them; and
I my-selfe, with the Duke of Bedford, the
Duke of Clarence, and the Duke of Gloster
wil be in the midst of the battell. [1532
Furthermore, I wil that my Lord of Wil-
lowby and the Earle of Northhumberland,
with their troupes of horsmen, be continually running like wings on both sides of the
army — my Lord of Northhumber- [1537
land on the left wing. Then I wil that
euery archer prouide him a stake of a tre,
and sharpe it at both endes; and, at the
first encounter of the horsemen, to pitch
their stakes downe into the ground [1542
before them, that they may gore them-
selues vpon them; and then, to recoyle
backe, and shoote wholly altogither, and so
discomfit them.   1546

OXF. And it please your Maiestie, I wil
take that in charge, if your Grace be ther-
with content.

HEN. With all my heart, my good
Lord of Oxford. And go and prouide
quickly.   1552

OXF. I thanke your Highnesse.

Exit [the Earl of Oxford].

HEN. 5. Well, my lords, our battels are
ordeined, and the French making of bon-

---

[1] A. *whe.*
[2] Flaunting? (showy, gay).
[3] Covered with bards, protective plates of armor
set with spikes.
[4] Men of Hainault.
[5] Swords, or halberts.
[6] Originally a carbuncle borne in a shield; here,
apparently, the pointed spike in the centre of the
shield.
[7] Radish.

[1] A. *threescore*, possibly caught by the printer
from the second line above.
[2] A. *fortie.*

fires, and at their bankets. But let them looke, for I meane to set vpon them. 1557

The trumpet soundes.

Soft, heres comes some other French message.

Enter Herauld.

HERALD. King of England, my Lord High Constable and other of my lords, considering the poore estate of thee and [1562 thy poore countrey-men, sends me to know what thou wilt giue for thy ransome. Perhaps thou maist agree better cheape [1] now then when thou art conquered. 1566

HEN. 5. Why then, belike, your High Constable sends to know what I wil giue for my ransome? Now trust me, Herald, not so much as a tun of tennis-bals — no, not so much as one poore tennis-ball! Rather shall my bodie lie dead in the [1572 field to feed crowes then euer England shall pay one penny ransome for my bodie.

HERALD. A kingly resolution!

HEN. 5. No, Herald; tis a kingly resolution, and the resolution of a king. Here, take this for thy paines. 1578

Exit Herald.

But stay, my lords; what time is it?

ALL. Prime,[2] my lord.

HEN. 5. Then is it good time, no doubt, for all England praieth for vs. [1582 What, my lords! me-thinks you looke cheerfully vpon mee. Why then, with one voice, and like true English hearts, with me throw vp your caps, and for England cry, "S[aint] George!" And God and S[aint] George helpe vs! 1588

Strike, Drummer.[3]   Exeunt omnes.

The French-men crie within, "S[aint] Dennis! S[aint] Dennis! Mount Ioy! S[aint] Dennis!"

The Battell [within].

Enters King of England, and his Lords.

HEN. 5. Come, my lords, come! By

[1] Make a better bargain.
[2] The first of the Day Hours of the church, beginning at 6 A.M., or at sunrise.
[3] The imperative form of the stage-directions indicate that the printer was setting up from a prompt-copy of the play.

this time our swords are almost drunke with French blood. But, my Lords, which of you can tell me how many of our army be slaine in the battell? 1593

OXF. And it please your Maiestie, there are of the French armie slaine aboue ten thousand twentie-six hundred, whereof are princes and nobles bearing ban- [1597 ners; besides, all the nobilitie of France are taken prisoners. Of your Maiesties armie are slaine none but the good Duke of Yorke, and not aboue fiue or six and twentie common souldiers. 1602

HEN. 5. For the good Duke of Yorke, my vnckle, I am heartily sorie, and greatly lament his misfortune. Yet the honourable victorie which the Lord hath giuen vs doth make me much reioyce. But, staie; here comes another French message. 1608

Sound, Trumpet.

Enters a Herald, and kneeleth.

HER. God saue the life of the most mightie conqueror, the honourable King of England! 1611

HEN. 5. Now, Herald, me-thinks the world is changed with you now. What! I am sure it is a great disgrace for a Herald to kneele to the king of England! What is thy message? 1616

HER. My lord and maister, the conquered king of France, sends thee long health, with heartie greeting.

HEN. 5. Herald, his greetings are welcome; but I thanke God for my health. Well, Herald, say on. 1622

HERALD. He hath sent me to desire your Maiestie to giue him leaue to go into the field to view his poore country-men, [and] that they may all be honourably buried. 1627

HEN. 5. Why Herald, doth thy lord and maister send to me to burie the dead? Let him bury them, a Gods name! But, I pray thee, Herald, where is my Lord Hie Constable, and those that would haue had my ransome? 1633

HERALD. And it please your Maiestie, he was slaine in the battell.

HEN. 5. Why, you may see — you will make your selues sure before the [1637 victorie be wonne. But, Herald, what castle is this so neere adioyning to our campe?

HERALD. And it please your Maiestie, tis cald the Castle of Agincourt. 1642

HEN. 5. Well then, my lords of England, for the more honour of our Englishmen, I will that this be for-euer cald The Battell of Agincourt. 1646

HERALD. And it please your Maiestie, I haue a further message to deliuer to your Maiestie.

HEN. 5. What is that, Herald? say on.

HER. And it please your Maiestie, my lord and maister craues to parly with your Maiestie. 1653

HEN. 5. With a good will — so some of my nobles view the place for feare of trecherie and treason.

HERALD. Your Grace needs not to doubt that. 1658

Exit Herald.[1]

HEN. 5. Well, tell him, then, I will come. Now, my lords, I will go into the field my-selfe to view my countreymen, and to haue them honourably buried; for [1662 the French king shall neuer surpasse me in curtesie whiles I am Harry, King of England. Come on, my lords.

Exeunt omnes.

Enters Iohn Cobler, and Robbin Pewterer.

ROBIN. Now, Iohn Cobler, didst thou see how the king did behaue himselfe? 1667

IOHN. But, Robin, didst thou see what a pollicie the king had? To see how the French-men were kild with the stakes of the trees!

ROBIN. I, Iohn, there was a braue pollicie! 1673

Enters an English souldier, roming.

SOUL. What are you, my maisters?

BOTH. Why, we be English-men.

SOUL. Are you English-men? then change your language, for the kings [1677 tents are set a fire, and all they that speake English will be kild. [*Exit soldier.*]

[1] A. prints this stage-direction a line above.

IOHN. What shal we do, Robin? Faith, Ile shift,[1] for I can speake broken French.

ROBIN. Faith, so can I. Lets heare how thou canst speake. 1683

IOHN. Commodeuales,[2] Monsieur.

ROBIN. Thats well. Come, lets be gone. [*Exeunt.*]

Drum and trumpet sounds.

Enters Dericke roming. After him a Frenchman, and takes him prisoner.

DERICKE. O, good Mounser! 1687

FRENCHMAN. Come, come, you villeaco!

DER. O, I will, sir, I will.

FRENCHMAN. Come quickly, you pesant! 1692

DER. I will, sir. What shall I giue you?

FRENCH. Marry, thou shalt giue me one, to, tre, foure hundred crownes.

DER. Nay, sir, I will giue you more; I will giue as many crowns as wil lie on your sword. 1698

FRENCH. Wilt thou giue me as many crowns as will lie on my sword?

DER. I, marrie, will I. I, but you must lay downe your sword, or else they will not lie on your sword. 1703

Here the Frenchman laies downe his sword, and the clowne takes it vp, and hurles him downe.

DER. Thou villaine! darest thou looke vp?

FRENCH. O, good Mounsier, comparteue![3] Monsieur, pardon me! 1707

DER. O, you villaine! now you lie at my mercie. Doest thou remember since thou lambst me in thy short el?[4] O, villaine! Now I will strike off thy head. 1711

Here, whiles he turnes his bucke, the Frenchman runnes his wayes.

DER. What, is he gone? Masse, I am

[1] I'll manage to get along.
[2] Does John try to say *comment-allez-vous?* Cf. line 1842.
[3] Is this based on some form of *compartir*, show compassion?
[4] "To measure with a short ell" was a proverbial phrase meaning to deal unfairly. Dericke refers to the Frenchman's sword as a short ell measuring rod.

glad of it. For, if he had staid, I was afraid he wold haue sturd again, and then I should haue beene spilt.[1] But I will away to kill more Frenchmen.   [*Exit.*]

Enters King of France, King of England, and attendants.

HEN. 5. Now, my good brother of France, my comming into this land was not to shead blood, but for the right of my countrey; which if you can deny, I am content peaceably to leaue my siege and to depart out of your land.   1722

CHARLES. What is it you demand, my louing brother of England?

HEN. 5. My secretary hath it written. Read it.   1726

SECRETARY. Item, that immediately Henry of England be crowned King of France.

CHARLES. A very hard sentence, my good brother of England.

HEN. 5. No more but right, my good brother of France!   1733

FRENCH KING. Well, read on.

SECRET. Item, that after the death of the said Henry the crowne remaine to him and his heires for-euer.   1737

FRENCH KING. Why then, you do not onely meane to dispossesse me, but also my sonne!

HEN. 5. Why, my good brother of France, you haue had it long inough. [1742 And as for Prince Dolphin, it skils not though he sit beside the saddle.[2] Thus I haue set it downe, and thus it shall be!

FRENCH KING. You are very peremptorie, my good brother of England. 1747

HEN. And you as peruerse, my good brother of France.

CHARLES. Why then, belike all that I haue here is yours!

HEN. 5. I, euen as far as the kingdom of France reaches.   1753

CHARLES. I, for by this hote beginning we shall scarce bring it to a calme ending.

HEN. 5. It is as you please. Here is my resolution.   1757

CHARLES. Well, my brother of Eng-

land, if you will giue me a coppie we will meete you againe to-morrow.

HEN. 5. With a good will, my good brother of France. Secretary, de- [1762 liuer him a coppie.

Exit King of France and all their attendants.[1]

My lords of England, go before, and I will follow you.

Exeunt Lords.

Speakes to himselfe.

HEN. 5. Ah, Harry! thrice vnhappie Harry! Hast thou now conquered [1767 the French king, and begins a fresh supply with his daughter? But with what face canst thou seeke to gaine her loue which hath sought to win her fathers crowne? Her fathers crowne, said I? No, it is mine owne.   1773
I, but I loue her, and must craue her — Nay, I loue her, and will haue her!

Enters Lady Katheren and her Ladies.

But here she comes. How now, faire Ladie Katheren of France, what newes? 1777

KATHREN. And it please your Maiestie, my father sent me to know if you will debate [2] any of these vnreasonable demands which you require.   1781

HEN. 5. Now trust me, Kate, I commend thy fathers wit greatly in this; for none in the world could sooner haue made me debate it, if it were possible. But tell me, sweete Kate, canst thou tell how to loue?   1787

KATE. I cannot hate, my good lord, therefore far vnfit were it for me to loue.

HEN. 5. Tush, Kate! but tell me in plaine termes, canst thou loue the King of England? I cannot do as these [1792 countries do that spend halfe their time in woing. Tush, wench, I am none such. But, wilt thou go ouer to England?

KATE. I would to God that I had your Maiestie as fast in loue as you haue [1797 my father in warres! I would not vouchsafe so much as one looke untill you had related [3] all these vnreasonable demands.

---

[1] Ruined, killed.
[2] "To abandon oneself to despair?" (*N.E.D.*)

[1] A. prints this stage-direction two lines above.
[2] Abate, reduce.
[3] Qy. debated, abated (cf. l. 1779).

HEN. 5. Tush, Kate! I know thou wouldst not vse me so hardly. But tell me, canst thou loue the King of England? 1803

KATE. How should I loue him that hath dealt so hardly with my father?

HEN. 5. But Ile deale as easily with thee as thy heart can imagine, or [1807 tongue can require. How saist thou? What! will it be?

KATE. If I were of my owne direction I could giue you answere; but seeing I stand at my fathers direction, I must first know his will. 1813

HEN. 5. But shal I haue thy good wil in the mean season?

KATE. Whereas I can put your Grace in no assurance, I would be loth to put you in any dispaire. 1818

HEN. 5. Now, before God, it is a sweete wench!

She goes aside, and speakes as followeth.

KAT. I may thinke my selfe the happiest in the world that is beloued of the mightie King of England! 1823

HEN. 5. Well, Kate, are you at hoast [1] with me? Sweete Kate, tel thy father from me that none in the world could sooner haue perswaded me to it then thou; and so tel thy father from me. 1828

KAT. God keepe your Maiestie in good health.

Exit Kat.

HEN. 5. Farwel, sweet Kate. In faith, it is a sweet wench! But if I knew I [1832 could not haue her fathers good wil, I would so rowse the towers ouer his eares that I would make him be glad to bring her me upon his hands and knees. 1836

Exit King.

Enters Dericke with his girdle full of shooes.

DER. How, now! Sownes, it did me good to see how I did triumph ouer the French-men!

Enters Iohn Cobler rouing, with a packe full of apparell.

IOHN. Whoope, Dericke! How doest thou?

___
[1] On friendly terms.

DER. What, Iohn! Comedeuales? aliue yet? 1843

IOHN. I promise thee, Dericke, I scapte hardly; for I was within halfe a mile when one was kild!

DER. Were you so? 1847

IOHN. I, trust me. I had like bene slaine.

DER. But, once kild — why it tis nothing. I was foure or fiue times slaine. 1850

IOHN. Foure or fiue times slaine! Why, how couldst thou haue beene aliue now?

DER. O Iohn, neuer say so! For I was cald "the bloodie souldier" amongst them all. 1855

IOHN. Why, what didst thou?

DER. Why, I will tell thee, Iohn. Euery day whan I went into the field I would take a straw and thrust it into my nose and make my nose bleed; and then I wold go into the field. And when [1861 the captaine saw me, he would say, "Peace, a bloodie souldier!" and bid me stand aside. Whereof I was glad. But marke the chance, Iohn: I went and stood behinde a tree — but marke then, Iohn — [1866 I thought I had beene safe; but on a sodaine there steps to me a lustie tall French-man; now he drew, and I drew; now I lay here, and he lay there; now I set this leg before, and turned this back- [1871 ward — and skipped quite ouer a hedge; and he saw me no more there that day! And was not this well done, Iohn?

IOHN. Masse, Dericke, thou hast a wittie head. 1876

DER. I, Iohn, thou maist see, if thou hadst taken my counsell. But what hast thou there? I thinke thou hast bene robbing the French-men. 1880

IOHN. I-faith, Dericke, I haue gotten some reparrell [1] to carry home to my wife.

DER. And I haue got some shooes; for Ile tel thee what I did: when they were dead, I would go take off all their shooes.

IOHN. I, but Dericke, how shall we get home? 1887

DER. Nay, sownds, and they take thee they wil hang thee. O, Iohn, neuer do so! If it be thy fortune to be hangd, be hangd in thy owne language, whatsoeuer thou doest! 1892

___
[1] Apparel.

IOHN. Why, Dericke, the warres is done; we may go home now.

DER. I, but you may not go before you aske the king leaue. But I know a way to go home and aske the king no leaue. 1897

IOHN. How is that, Dericke?

DER. Why, Iohn, thou knowest the Duke of Yorkes funerall must be carried into England, doest thou not? 1901

IOHN. I, that I do.

DER. Why, then, thou knowest weele go with it.

IOHN. I, but Dericke, how shall we do for to meet them? 1906

DER. Sownds, if I make not shift to meet them, hang me! Sirra, thou knowst that in euery towne there wil be ringing, and there wil be cakes and drinke. Now I wil go to the clarke and sexton, and [1911 keepe a talking and say, "O, this fellow rings well!" And thou shalt go and take a peece of cake. Then Ile ring, and thou shalt say "Oh, this fellow keepes a good stint!" And then I will go drinke [1916 to thee all the way. But I maruel what my dame wil say when we come home, because we haue not a French word to cast at a dog by the way. 1920

IOHN. Why, what shall we do, Dericke?

DER. Why, Iohn, Ile go before and call my dame whore; and thou shalt come after and set fire on the house.[1] We may do it, Iohn, for Ile proue it — because we be souldiers. 1926

The trumpets sound.

IOHN. Dericke, helpe me to carry my shooes and bootes.

[*Exeunt Dericke and John.*]

Enters King of England, Lord of Oxford and Exeter, then the King of France, Prince Dolphin, and the Duke of Burgondie, and attendants.

HEN. 5. Now, my good brother of France, I hope by this time you haue deliberated of your answere. 1931

FR. KING. I, my welbeloued brother of England. We haue viewed it ouer with

our learned councell, but cannot finde that you should be crowned king of France. 1935

HEN. 5. What! not king of France? Then nothing! I must be king. But, my louing brother of France, I can hardly forget the late iniuries offered me when I came last to parley; the French-men had better a raked the bowels out of their [1941 fathers carkasses then to haue fiered my tentes. And if I knew thy sonne, Prince Dolphin, for one, I would so rowse him as he was neuer so rowsed! 1945

FR. KING. I dare sweare for my sonnes innocencie in this matter. But if this please you, that immediately you be proclaimed and crowned Heire and Regent of France, not king, because I my-selfe was once crowned king. 1951

HEN. 5. Heire and Regent of France? That is well. But that is not all that I must haue.

FR. KING. The rest my secretary hath in writing. 195(

SECRET. [*reads*]. Item, that Henry, King of England, be crowned Heire and Regent of France during the life of King Charles; and after his death the crowne with all rights to remaine to King Henry of England, and to his heires foreuer. 1962

HEN. 5. Well, my good brother of France, there is one thing I must needs desire.

FR. KING. What is that, my good brother of England? 1967

HEN. 5. That all your nobles must be sworne to be true to me.

FR. KING. Whereas they haue not stucke with greater matters, I know [1971 they wil not sticke with such a trifle. Begin you, my Lord Duke of Burgondie.

HEN. 5. Come, my Lord of Burgondie; take your oath vpon my sword. 1975

BURGON. I, Philip, Duke of Burgondie, sweare to Henry, King of England, to be true to him, and to become his league-man; and that if I, Philip, heare of any forraigne power comming to inuade the said Henry, or his heires, then I, the said Philip, [1981 to send him word, and aide him with all the power I can make. And thereunto I take my oath.

He kisseth the sword.

---

[1] Soldiers and apprentices assumed the liberty of setting fire to houses of ill-fame.

HEN. 5.   Come, Prince Dolphin, you
must sweare too.   1986

He kisseth the sword.

HEN. 5.   Well, my brother of France,
there is one thing more I must needs require of you.

FR. KING.   Wherein is it that we may
satisfie your Maiestie?   1991

HEN. 5.   A trifle, my good brother of
France: I meane to make your daughter
Queene of England, if she be willing, and
you therewith content.   How saist thou,
Kate? canst thou loue the King of Eng-
land?   1997

KATE.   How should I loue thee, which
is my fathers enemy?

HEN. 5.   Tut! stand not vpon these
points.   Tis you must make vs [2001

friends.   I know, Kate, thou art not a
litle proud that I loue thee.   What, wench,
the King of England!

FRENCH KING.   Daughter, let nothing
stand betwixt the King of England and
thee.   Agree to it.   2007

KATE.   I had best whilst he is willing,
least when I would he will not.   I rest at
your Maiesties commaund.   2010

HEN. 5.   Welcome, sweet Kate! But,
my brother of France, what say you to it?

FRENCH KING.   With all my heart I like
it.   But when shall be your wedding day?

HEN. 5.   The first Sunday of the next
moneth, God willing.   2016

Sound Trumpets.

Exeunt omnes.

FINIS

A PLEASANT CONCEYTED COMEDIE OF

GEORGE A GREENE, THE PINNER OF WAKEFIELD [1]

AS IT WAS SUNDRY TIMES ACTED BY THE SERUANTS OF THE RIGHT HONOURABLE THE EARLE OF SUSSEX.

Imprinted at London by Simon Stafford, for Cuthbert Burby: And are to be sold at his shop neere the Royall Exchange. 1599.

[DRAMATIS PERSONÆ

EDWARD, King of England.

EARL OF WARWICK, attending King Edward.

JAMES, King of Scotland, invading English territory.

LORD HUMES, attending King James.

EARL OF KENDALL, rebelliously seeking the crown of England.

LORD BONFIELD,
SIR NICHOLAS MANNERING, } Kendall's supporters.
SIR GILBERT ARMSTRONG,

MUSGROVE, Keeper of one of King Edward's strongholds.

CUDDY, his son.

GEORGE A GREENE, the pinner of Wakefield.

JENKIN, a clown, servant to George a Greene.

WILY, a boy, servant to George a Greene.

GRIME, the father of Bettris.

WOODROFFE, the justice of Wakefield.

ROBIN HOOD, the outlaw.

SCARLET, } Robin Hood's men.
MUCH,

JOHN TAYLOR, post of King James.

NED A BARLEY, a small boy, son of Jane a Barley.

JANE A BARLEY.

BETTRIS, daughter to Grime, beloved by George a Greene.

MAID MARIAN, beloved by Robin Hood.

Townsmen, Shoemakers, Soldiers, etc.]

---

[1] Our first reference to *George a Greene* is in 1593, when Henslowe records its performance, as an old play, at the Rose by the Earl of Sussex' Men who were temporarily occupying that playhouse. The exact date of its composition is a matter of conjecture, but the year 1588 would not be far wrong. Its authorship is also a matter of conjecture. The Devonshire copy of the first quarto (now in the Huntington Library) has on the title-page two notes in early seventeenth century hands: "Written by ...... a minister, who ac[ted] the pinners part in it himself. Teste W. Shakespea[re]"; and below: "Ed. Iuby saith that the play was made by Ro. Gree[ne]." Juby was an eminent Elizabethan actor; but the two notes seem to be contradictory, for, so far as we know, Robert Greene was never a minister, and there is no evidence that he was an actor. Little faith can be put in anonymous scribblings of this character, yet there is some internal evidence supporting the attribution of the play to Greene. Unquestionably the original text has been cut down for use in provincial traveling, occasioned, we may suppose, by the plague raging from 1592 to 1594; and it may be that this mutilation explains why Greene's characteristics as a writer are not more evident in the extant version. On the other hand, the play has a virility not found in Greene.

The play was entered in the Stationers' Registers in 1595, but the earliest edition we have was issued in 1599. I have reproduced the text of this edition (A.) from The Malone Society Reprints. As a result of the mutilation of the text for traveling purposes, the verse is often corrupt, and sometimes it is hard to distinguish between the verse and prose. I have followed, in the main, the line arrangement adopted by J. C. Collins (*The Plays and Poems of Robert Greene*, 1905). I have also modernized the punctuation and the use of capital letters, and I have added, in brackets, stage-directions.

A PLEASANT CONCEYTED COMEDIE OF

GEORGE A GREENE, THE PINNER [1] OF WAKEFIELD

[*Near Bradford.*]

*Enter the Earle of Kendall, with him the
 Lord Bonfild [and] Sir Gilbert Armestrong; and [enter later] Iohn [Taylor].*

EARLE OF KENDALL. Welcome to Brad-
 ford, martiall gentlemen!
L[ord] Bonfild, and Sir Gilbert Armstrong
 both,
And all my troups, euen to my basest
 groome,
Courage and welcome, for the day is
 ours!
Our cause is good — it is for the lands
 auayle;   5
Then let vs fight, and dye for Englands
 good!
OMNES. We will, my lord!
KENDALL. As I am Henrie Momford,
 Kendals Earle,
You honour me with this assent of yours.
And here vpon my sword I make protest 10
For to relieue the poore, or dye my-selfe.
And know, my lords, that Iames, the King
 of Scots,
Warres hard vpon the borders of this land.

[*Enter John Taylor.*]

Here is his post. — Say, Iohn Taylour,
What newes with King Iames?   15
IOHN. Warre, my lord! Tall [2] and good
 newes, I trow;
For King Iam[i]e vowes to meete you the
 26 of this month,
God willing; marie, doth he, sir.
KENDALL. My friends, you see what we
 haue to winne. —
Well, Iohn, commend me to King Iames, 20
And tell him, I will meete him the 26 of
 this month,
And all the rest. And so, farewell.

Exit Iohn.

---

[1] An officer whose duty is to impound stray beasts.
[2] Seemly, excellent. A. has *tell*, and Dyce and
Collins emend to *I tell*.

Bonfild, why standst thou as a man in
 dumps?
Courage! for, if I winne, Ile make thee
 duke.
I, Henry Momford, will be king my selfe;
And I will make thee Duke of Lancaster, 26
And Gilbert Armestrong Lord of Don-
 caster.
BONFILD. Nothing, my lord, makes me
 amazde [1] at all,
But that our souldiers findes our victuals
 scant.
We must make hauocke of those countrey
 swaynes;   30
For so will the rest tremble and be afraid,
And humbly send prouision to your campe.
GILB. My Lord Bonfild giues good aduice.
They make a scorne, and stand vpon the
 king;
So what is brought is sent from them per-
 force.   35
Aske Mannering else.
KEND. What sayest thou, Mannering?
MAN. When-as I shew'd your high com-
 mission,
They made this answere —
Onely to send prouision for your horses. 40
KEND. Well, hye thee to Wakefield; bid
 the towne
To send me all prouision that I want,
Least I, like martiall Tamberlaine, lay
 waste
Their bordering countries,
And leauing none aliue that contradicts my
 commission.   45
MAN. Let me alone, my lord; Ile make
 them
Vayle their plumes! For whatsoere he be,
The proudest knight, iustice, or other, that
 gaynsayeth
Your word, Ile clap him fast, to make the
 rest to feare.
KEND. Doe so, Nick. Hye thee thither
 presently;   50

---

[1] Perplexed.

And let vs heare of thee againe tomorrowe.
MAN.   Will you not remooue, my lord?
KEND.   No; I will lye at Bradford all this
night,
And all the next. — Come, Bonfield, let vs
goe
And listen out [1] some bonny lasses here.   55

Exeunt omnes.

[*Wakefield.*]

*Enter the Iustice, a Townesman, George a
Greene, and Sir Nicholas Mannering
with his Commission.*

IUSTICE.   M[aster] Mannering, stand
aside whilest we conferre what is best to
doe.   [*Mannering stands to one side.*]
Townesmen of Wakefield, the Earle of
Kendall here hath sent for victuals; [60
and in ayding him we shewe our selues no
lesse than traytours to the King.   Therefore let me heare, townesmen, what is your
consents.
TOWNES.   Euen as you please, we are all
content.   66
IUSTICE.   Then — M[aster] Mannering,
we are resolu'd.

[*Mannering advances.*]

MAN.   As howe?   69
IUSTICE.   Marrie, sir, thus.   We will
send the Earle of Kendall no victuals, be-
cause he is a traytour to the king, and in
ayding him we shewe our selues no lesse.
MAN.   Why, men of Wakefield! are you
waxen madde,
That present danger cannot whet your
wits   75
Wisely to make prouision of your selues?
The earle is thirtie thousand men strong in
power,
And what towne soeuer him resist
He layes it flat and leuell with the ground.
Ye silly men, you seeke your owne decay!
Therefore send my lord such prouision as
he wants,   81
So he will spare your towne, and come no
neerer
Wakefield then he is.

[1] Secure tidings of.

IUSTICE.   Master Mannering, you haue
your answere.
You may be gone.   85
MAN.   Well, Woodroffe — for so I gesse
is thy name — Ile make thee curse thy
ouerthwart deniall; and all that sit vpon
the bench [1] this day shall rue the houre
they haue withstood my lord's commission.
IUSTICE.   Doe thy worst, we feare thee not.
MAN.   See you these seales?   Before you
passe the towne   92
I will haue all things [that] [2] my lord doth
want,
In spite of you!
GEORGE A GREENE.   Proud dapper Iacke,
vayle bonnet to the bench [3]   95
That represents the person of the king;
Or, sirra, Ile lay thy head before thy feete.
MAN.   Why, who art thou?
GEORGE.   Why, I am George a Greene,
True liegeman to my king,   100
Who scornes that men of such esteeme as
these
Should brooke the braues of any trayterous
squire.
You of the bench, and you, my fellowe-
friends,
Neighbours we, subiects all vnto the king,
We are English borne, and therefore Ed-
wards friends,   105
Voude vnto him euen in our mothers
wombe,
Our mindes to God, our hearts vnto our
king.
Our wealth, our homage, and our carcases,
Be all King Edwards.   Then, sirra, we
haue
Nothing left for traytours but our swordes,
Whetted to bathe them in your bloods, and
dye   111
Against you, before we send you any
victuals. [4]
IUSTICE.   Well spoken, George a Greene!
TOWNES.   Pray let George a Greene speake
for vs.
GEORGE.   Sirra, you get no victuals
here —   115

[1] The bench where persons sit in some official
capacity.
[2] Added by Collins.
[3] I follow Collins' rearrangement of lines 95–96.
[4] A. arranges lines 111–12 to end with "bloods"
and "victuals."   I follow Dyce's rearrangement.

Not if a hoofe of beefe would saue your
liues.

MAN. Fellowe, I stand amazde at thy pre-
sumption.

Why, what art thou that darest gaynsay
my lord,

Knowing his mighty puissance and his
stroke?

Why, my friend, I come not barely of my
selfe;   120

For, see, I haue a large commission.

GEORGE. Let me see it, sirra. [Takes
the Commission.] Whose seales be these?

MAN. This is the Earle of Kendals seale
at armes;

This, Lord Charnel Bonfield's;   125

And this, Sir Gilbert Armestrongs.

GEORGE. I tell thee, sirra, did good
King Edwards sonne seale a commission
against the king his father, thus would I
teare it in despite of him,   130

IIe teares the Commission.

Being traytour to my soueraigne.

MAN. What! hast thou torne my lords
commission? Thou shalt rue it — and so
shall all Wakefield.   134

GEORGE. What! are you in choler? I
will giue you pilles to coole your stomacke!
Seest thou these seales? Now, by my
fathers soule, which was a yeoman when he
was aliue, eate them, or eate my daggers
poynt, proud squire!   140

MAN. But thou doest but iest, I hope.

GEORGE. Sure that shall you see before
we two part.

MAN. Well, and there be no remedie,
so, George. [Swallows one of the seals.]
One is gone. I pray thee, no more nowe.

GEORGE. O sir, if one be good, the
others cannot hurt. [Mannering swallows
the other seals.] So, sir; nowe you may goe
tell the Earle of Kendall, although I [150
haue rent his large commission, yet of curtesie I haue sent all his seales backe againe
by you.

MAN. Well, sir, I will doe your arrant.

Exit [Mannering].

GEORGE. Nowe let him tell his lord [155
that he hath spoke with George a Greene,

right [1] pinner of merrie Wakefield towne,
that hath phisicke for a foole, pilles for a
traytour that doeth wrong his soueraigne.
Are you content with this that I haue
done?   161

IUSTICE. I,[2] content, George;

For highly hast thou honourd Wakefield
toune

In cutting of proud Mannering so short.

Come; thou shalt be my welcome ghest to-
day;   165

For well thou hast deseru'd reward and
fauour.

Exeunt omnes.

[Outside the "hold" kept by Musgrove.] [3]

*Enter olde Musgroue and yong Cuddie his
sonne.*

CUDDIE. Nowe, gentle father, list vnto
thy sonne;

And for my mothers loue,

That earst was blythe and bonny in thine
eye,

Graunt one petition that I shall demaund.

OLDE MUSGROUE. What is that, my Cud-
die?   171

CUDDIE. Father, you knowe the ancient
enmitie of late

Betweene the Musgroues and the wily
Scottes,

Whereof they haue othe

Not to leaue one aliue that strides a launce.

O, Father, you are olde, and, wanyng, age
vnto the graue.   176

Olde William Musgroue, which whilome
was thought

The brauest horseman in all Westmerland,

Is weake, and forst to stay his arme vpon a
staffe,

That earst could wield a launce.   180

Then, gentle father, resigne the hold to
me;

Giue armes to youth, and honour vnto age.

MUS. Auaunt, false hearted boy! My
ioynts doe quake

---

[1] Dyce emends to *hight.*
[2] Aye.
[3] "Handoun, or Sandon Castle, off wch Sᵣ William
Musgrave and his soon Cuddy had the keepinge." —
The Famouus Hystory off George a Greene, chap. vi.
This prose romance was apparently the source of the
play, or closely related to the source.

Euen with anguish of thy verie words!
Hath William Musgroue seene an hundred
   yeres?   185
Haue I bene feard and dreaded of the
   Scottes
That when they heard my name in any
   roade [1]
They fled away, and posted thence amaine,
And shall I dye with shame nowe in mine
   age?
No, Cuddie, no. Thus resolue I: —   190
Here haue I liu'd, and here will Musgroue
   dye.

Exeunt omnes.

[*Before Grime's house.*]

*Enter Lord Bonfild, Sir Gilbert Armestrong,
   M. Grime, and Bettris his daughter.*

Bon.   Now, gentle Grime, God a mercy
   for our good chere!
O.ar fare was royall, and our welcome
   great.
And sith so kindly thou hast entertained
   vs,
If we returne with happie victorie   195
We will deale as friendly with thee in rec-
   ompence.
Grime.   Your welcome was but dutie,
   gentle lord;
For wherefore haue we giuen vs our wealth
But to make our betters welcome when
   they come?
[*Aside.*]   O, this goes hard when traytours
   must be flattered!   200
But life is sweete, and I cannot withstand
   it.
God, I hope, will reuenge the quarrell of my
   king.
Gilb.   What said you, Grime?
Grime.   I say, Sir Gilbert, looking on my
   daughter
I curse the houre that ere I got the girle;
For, sir, she may haue many wealthy sut-
   ers,   206
And yet she disdaines them all to haue
Poore George a Greene vnto her husband.
Bonfild.   On that, good Grime, I am
   talking with thy
Daughter;   210

[1] Hostile incursion on horseback, foray.

But she in quirkes and quiddities [1] of loue
Sets me to schoole, she is so ouerwise. —
But, gentle girle, if thou wilt forsake
The pinner and be my loue, I will aduaunce
   thee high.
To dignifie those haires of amber hiew, 215
Ill grace them with a chaplet made of
   pearle,
Set with choice rubies, sparkes,[2] and dia-
   monds,
Planted vpon a veluet hood, to hide that
   head
Wherein two saphires burne like sparkling
   fire.
This will I doe, faire Bettris, and farre
   more,   220
If thou wilt loue the Lord of Doncaster.
Bettris.   Heigh ho! my heart is in a
   higher place —
Perhaps on the earle, if that be he [*point-
   ing*];
See where he comes, or angrie, or in loue,
For why [3] his colour looketh discon-
   tent.   225
Kendall [*entering*].   Come, Nick, followe
   me.

*Enter the Earle of Kendall [and] Sir Nicholas
   Mannering.*

Bonfild.   Howe nowe, my lord! what
   newes?
Kendall.   Such newes, Bonfild, as will
   make thee laugh
And fret thy fill to heare how Nick was
   vsde.   229
Why, the iustices stand on their termes.[4]
Nick, as you knowe, is hawtie in his words;
He layd the lawe vnto the iustices
With threatning braues, that one lookt on
   another
Ready to stoope, but that a churle came in,
One George a Greene, the pinner of the
   towne,   235
And with his dagger drawne layd hands on
   Nick,
And by no beggers [5] swore that we were
   traytours,
Rent our commission, and vpon a braue

[1] Verbal subtleties and quibbles.
[2] Precious stones.
[3] Because.
[4] Stipulations.
[5] A proverbial phrase, "by no mean oaths."

Made Nick to eate the seales or brooke the
    stabbe.
Poore Mannering, afraid, came posting
    hither straight.   240
BETTRIS [aside].   Oh louely George, fortune
    be still thy friend!
And as thy thoughts be high, so be thy
    minde
In all accords, euen to thy hearts desire!
BONFILD.   What sayes faire Bettris?
GRIMES.   My Lord, she is praying for
    George a Greene.   245
He is the man, and she will none but him.
BONFILD.   But him! why, looke on me, my
    girle.
Thou knowest that yesternight I courted
    thee,
And swore at my returne to wedde with
    thee.
Then tell me, loue, shall I haue all thy
    faire? [1]   250
BETTRIS.   I care not for earle, nor yet for
    knight,
Nor baron that is so bold;
For George a Greene, the merrie pinner,
He hath my heart in hold.
BONFILD.   Bootlesse, my lord, are many
    vaine replies.   255
Let vs hye vs to Wakefield, and send her
    the pinners head.
KEND.   It shall be so. — Grime, gram-
    ercie.
Shut vp thy daughter; bridle her affects;
Let me not misse her when I make returne.
Therefore looke to her as to thy life, good
    Grime.   260
GRIME.   I warrant you, my Lord.
KEN. [aside to Bettris].   And, Bettris, leaue
    a base pinner, for to loue an earle.

Ex. Grime and Bettris.[2]

Faine would I see this pinner, George a
    Greene.
It shall be thus:
Nick Mannering shall leade on the battell,
And we three will goe to Wakefield in some
    disguise.   266
But howsoeuer, Ile haue his head today!

Ex. omnes.

[1] Beauty.
[2] A. prints the stage-direction after line 261.

[*Before Sir Iohn a Barley's castle.*]

*Enter the King of Scots, Lord Humes, with
    Souldiers, and Iohnie.*

KING.   Why, Iohnie, then the Earle of
    Kendall is blithe,
And hath braue men that troupe along
    with him?
IOHNIE.   I, marie, my liege, and hath good
    men   270
That come along with him;
And vowes to meete you at Scrasblesea,
    God willing.
KING.   If good S[aint] Andrewe lend King
    Iam[i]e leaue,
I will be with him at the pointed day.
But, soft! — Whose pretie boy art thou?

Enter Iane a Barleys sonne.

NED.   Sir, I am sonne vnto Sir Iohn a
    Barley,   276
Eldest and all that ere my mother had;
Edward my name.
IAME.   And whither art thou going, pretie
    Ned?
NED.   To seeke some birdes, and kill them,
    if I can.   280
And now my scholemaster is also gone,
So haue I libertie to ply my bowe;
For when he comes, I stirre not from my
    booke.
IAMES.   Lord Humes, but marke the vis-
    age of this child!
By him I gesse the beautie of his mother;
None but Læda could breede Helena. 286
Tell me, Ned, who is within with thy
    mother?
NED.   Nought [1] but her selfe and houshold
    seruants, sir.
If you would speake with her, knocke at
    this gate.
IAMES.   Iohnie, knocke at that gate. 290

Enter Iane a Barley vpon the walles.

IANE.   O, I am betraide!   What multi-
    tudes be these?
IAMES.   Feare not, faire Iane, for all these
    men are mine —
And all thy friends, if thou be friend to
    me.
I am thy louer, Iames, the King of Scottes.

[1] A. *Not;* corrected by Nicholson.

That oft haue sued and wooed with many
  letters, 295
Painting my outward passions with my pen
When-as my inward soule did bleede for
  woe.
Little regard was giuen to my sute;
But haply thy husbands presence wrought
  it.
Therefore, sweete Iane, I fitted me to time,
And, hearing that thy husband was from
  home, 301
Am come to craue what long I haue de-
  sirde.
NED. Nay, soft you, sir! You get no
  entrance here,
That seeke to wrong Sir Iohn a Barley so,
And offer such dishonour to my mother.
IAMES. Why, what dishonour, Ned? 306
NED. Though young,
Yet often haue I heard my father say,
"No greater wrong than to be made
  cuckold."
Were I of age, or were my bodie strong, 310
Were he ten kings, I would shoote him to
  the heart
That should attempt to giue Sir Iohn the
  horne. —
Mother, let him not come in.
I will goe lie [1] at Iockie Millers house.

  [He starts away.]

IAMES. Stay him. 315
IANE. I, well said, Ned! Thou hast giuen
  the king
His answere.
For were the ghost of Cesar on the earth,
Wrapped in the wonted glorie of his hon-
  our,
He should not make me wrong my husband
  so. 320
But good King Iames is pleasant, as I gesse,
And meanes to trie what humour I am in;
Else would he neuer haue brought an hoste
  of men
To haue them witnes of his Scottish lust.
IAMES. Iane, in faith, Iane — 325
IANE. Neuer reply; for I protest by the
  highest
Holy God,
That doometh iust reuenge for things
  amisse,

  [1] Live, spend the night.

King Iames, of all men, shall not haue my
  loue.
IAMES. Then list to me: Saint Andrewe be
  my boote, 330
But Ile rase thy castle to the verie ground,
Vnlesse thou open the gate and let me in!
IANE. I feare thee not, King Iamie. Doe
  thy worst!
This castle is too strong for thee to scale;
Besides, tomorrowe will Sir Iohn come
  home. 335
IAMES. Well, Iane, since thou disdainst
  King Iame's loue,
Ile drawe thee on with sharpe and deepe
  extremes;
For, by my fathers soule, this brat of thine
Shall perish here before thine eyes, 339
Vnlesse thou open the gate and let me in.
IANE. O deepe extremes! My heart be-
  gins to breake!
My little Ned lookes pale for feare. —
Cheare thee, my boy; I will doe much for
  thee.
NED. But not so much as to dishonour me.
IANE. And if thou dyest, I cannot liue,
  sweete Ned. 345
NED. Then dye with honour, mother, dy-
  ing chaste.
IANE. I am armed.
My husbands loue, his honour, and his fame,
Ioynes victorie by vertue. Nowe, King
  Iames,
If mothers teares cannot alay thine ire, 350
Then butcher him, for I will neuer yeeld.
The sonne shall dye before I wrong the
  father.
IAMES. Why, then, he dyes.

  Allarum within. Enter a Messenger.

MESSENGER. My Lord, Musgroue is at
  hand.
IAMES. Who? Musgroue! The deuill he
  is! Come, 355
My horse!

  Exeunt omnes [below].

  [Skirmish within.]

*Enter olde Musgroue with King Iames pris-
  oner.*

MUS. Nowe, King Iames, thou art my
  prisoner.
IAMES. Not thine, but Fortunes prisoner.

Enter Cuddie.

CUDDIE. Father, the field is ours! Their colours we
Haue seyzed,   360
And Humes is slayne; I slewe him hand to hand.

MUS. God and Saint George!

CUDDIE. O father, I am sore athirst!

IANE. Come in, young Cuddie, come and drinke thy fill.
Bring in King Iame with you as a ghest;
For all this broile was cause he could not enter.   366

Exeunt omnes.

[*Near George a Greene's wheat close outside Wakefield.*]

Enter George a Greene alone.

GEORGE. The sweete content of men that liue in loue
Breedes fretting humours in a restlesse minde;
And fansie,[1] being checkt by fortunes spite,
Growes too impatient in her sweete desires; —   370
Sweete to those men whome loue leades on to blisse,
But sowre to me, whose happe is still amisse.

Enter the Clowne.

IENKIN. Marie, amen, sir!

GEORGE. Sir, what doe you crye, ⸢Amen" at?   375

IENKIN. Why, did not you talke of loue?

GEORGE. Howe doe you knowe that?

IENKIN. Well, though I say it that should not say it, there are fewe fellowes in our parish so netled with loue as I haue bene of late.   381

GEOR. Sirra, I thought no lesse when the other morning you rose so earely to goe to your wenches. Sir, I had thought you had gone about my honest busines.   385

IENKIN. Trow, you haue hit it! For, master, be it knowne to you, there is some

[1] Love.

good-will betwixt Madge, the sousewife,[1] and I. Marie, she hath another louer.

GEORGE. Canst thou brooke any riuals in thy loue?   391

IEN. A rider! no, he is a sow-gelder and goes afoote. But Madge pointed to meete me in your wheate close.

GEORGE. Well, did she meete you there?   396

IEN. Neuer make question of that! And first I saluted her with a greene gowne,[2] and after fell as hard a wooing as if the priest had bin at our backs to haue married vs.   401

GEORG. What, did she grant?

IEN. Did she graunt? Neuer make question of that! And she gaue me a shirt coler wrought ouer with no counterfet stuffe.   406

GEORG. What, was it gold?

IEN. Nay, twas better than gold.

GEORG. What was it?   409

IEN. Right Couentrie-blew. We [3] had no sooner come there but wot you who came by?

GEORG. No; who?

IEN. Clim, the sow-gelder.

GEORG. Came he by?   415

IEN. He spide Madge and I sit together. He leapt from his horse, laid his hand on his dagger, and began to sweare. Now I, seeing he had a dagger, and I nothing but this twig in my hand, I gaue [420 him faire words and said nothing. He comes to me and takes me by the bosome. "You hoorson slaue," said he, "hold my horse; and looke he take no colde in his feete." "No, marie, shall he, sir," [425 quoth I; "Ile lay my cloake vnderneath him." I tooke my cloake, spread it all along, and his horse on the midst of it.

GEORG. Thou clowne! didst thou set his horse vpon thy cloake?   430

IEN. I; but marke how I serued him. Madge and he was no sooner gone downe into the ditch, but I plucked out my knife,

[1] Souse consisted of the feet, head, and other parts of the hog ground up and made into something like a jelly. A sousewife, or seller of souse, was looked upon with disdain.
[2] Rolled her in the grass so that her gown became green; a proverbial phrase.
[3] A. *Who.*

cut foure hoales in my cloake, and made his
horse stand on the bare ground.   435

GEORG. Twas well done. Now, sir, go
and suruay my fields; if you finde any cattell in the corne, to pound [1] with them.

IEN. And if I finde any in the pound, I
shall turne them out.   440

Exit Ienkin.

*Enter the Earle of Kendal, Lord Bonfield, Sir
Gilbert, all disguised, with a traine of
men [placed in ambush].*

KEND. Now we haue put the horses in
the corne, let vs stand in some corner for to
heare what brauing tearmes the pinner will
breathe when he spies our horses in the
corne.   445

Enter Ienkin [2] blowing of his horne.

IEN. O master, where are you? We
haue a prise.

GEORG. A prise! what is it?

IEN. Three goodly horses in our wheate
close.   450

GEORGE. Three horses in our wheat
close! Whose be they?

IENKIN. Marie, thats a riddle to me.
But they are there — veluet horses,[3] and I
neuer sawe such horses before. As [455
my dutie was, I put off my cappe, and said
as followeth: "My masters, what doe you
make in our close?" One of them, hearing
me aske what he made there, held vp his
head and neighed, and, after his [460
maner, laught as heartily as if a mare had
bene tyed to his girdle. "My masters,"
said I, "it is no laughing matter; for, if my
master take you here, you goe as round as a
top to the pound." Another vnto- [465
ward iade, hearing me threaten him to the
pound and to tell you of them, cast vp both
his heeles and let such a monstrous great
fart, that was as much as in his language to
say: "A fart for the pound, and a fart [470
for George a Greene!" Nowe I, hearing
this, put on my cap, blewe my horne, called
them all iades, and came to tell you.

[1] The enclosure where strayed beasts were kept
until redeemed.
[2] A. *Iacke;* possibly the name of the actor who
assumed the rôle of Jenkin.
[3] With velvet caparisons.

GEORGE. Nowe, sir, goe and driue me
those three horses to the pound.   475

IENKIN. Doe you heare? I were best
to take a constable with me.

GEORGE. Why so?

[IENKIN.] Why, they, being gentle-
mens horses, may stand on their reputation, and will not obey me.   481

GEORGE. Goe doe as I bid you, sir.

IENKIN. Well, I may goe.

*The Earle of Kendall, the Lord Bonfild, and
Sir Gilbert Armestrong, meete them.*

KEND. Whither away, sir?

IENKIN. Whither away? I am going to
put the horses in the pound.   486

KEND. Sirra, those three horses belong
to vs, and we put them in; and they must
tarrie there, and eate their fill.   489

IENKIN. Stay, I will goe tell my master.
— Heare you, master; we haue another
prise! Those three horses be in your
wheate close still, and here be three geld-
ings more.

GEORGE. What be these?   495

IENKIN. These are the masters of the
horses.

GEORGE. Nowe, gentlemen — I know
not your degrees, but more you cannot be,[1]
vnlesse you be kings — why wrong [500
you vs of Wakefield with your horses? I
am the pinner, and before you passe you
shall make good the trespasse they haue
done.   504

KEND. Peace, saucie mate! Prate not
to vs: I tell thee, pinner, we are gentlemen.

GEORGE. Why, sir, so may I, sir, although I giue no armes.

KEND. Thou! Howe art thou a gentleman?   510

IENKIN. And such is my master, and he
may giue as good armes as euer your great
grandfather could giue.

KEND. Pray thee, let me heare howe.

IENKIN. Marie, my master may [515
giue for his armes the picture of Aprill in a
greene ierkin, with a rooke on one fist and
an horne [2] on the other: but my master
giues his armes the wrong way, for he giues
the horne on his fist; and your grand- [520

[1] More than "gentlemen."
[2] Does he refer to the cornucopia?

father, because he would not lose his
armes, weares the horne on his owne head.[1]

KEND. Well, pinner, sith our horses be
in, in spite of thee they now shall feede
their fill, and eate vntill our leasures serue
to goe.   526

GEORGE. Now, by my fathers soule,
were good King Edwards horses in the
corne, they shall amend the scath, or kisse
the pound; much more yours, sir, whatso-
ere you be!   531

KEND. Why, man, thou knowest not
vs. We do belong to Henry Momford,
Earle of Kendal; men that, before a month
be full expirde, will be King Edwards betters in the land.   536

GEORG. King Edwards better[s]! Rebell, thou liest!

George strikes him.

BONFILD. Villaine, what hast thou
done? Thou hast stroke an earle.   540

GEOR. Why, what care I? A poore
man that is true is better then an earle, if
he be false. Traitors reape no better
fauours at my hands.   544

KEND. I, so me thinks; but thou shall
deare aby[2] this blow. — Now or neuer, lay
hold on the pinner!

Enter all the ambush.

GEORG. Stay, my lords. Let vs parlie
on these broiles. "Not Hercules against
two," the prouerbe is, nor I against so [550
great a multitude. — [*Aside*] Had not
your troupes come marching as they did, I
would haue stopt your passage vnto London: but nowe Ile flie to secret policie.

KEND. What doest thou murmure,
George?   556

GEORGE. Marie, this, my lord: I muse,
if thou be Henrie Momford, Kendals Earle,
that thou wilt doe poore G[eorge] a Greene
this wrong, euer to match me with a troupe
of men.   561

KEND. Why doest thou strike me,
then?

GEOR. Why, my lord, measure me but
by your selfe: had you a man had [565
seru'd you long, and heard your foe misuse

you behinde your backe and would not
draw his sword in your defence, you would
cashere him. Much more, King Edward
is my king; and, before Ile heare him [570
so wrong'd, Ile die within this place, and
maintaine good whatsoeuer I haue said.
And, if I speake not reason in this case,
what I haue said Ile maintaine in this
place.   575

BON. A pardon, my lord, for this pinner; for, trust me, he speaketh like a man of
worth.

KEND. Well, George, wilt thou[1] leaue
Wakefielde and wend with me, Ile freely
put vp all and pardon thee.   581

GEORG. I, my lord, considering me[2]
one thing — you will leaue these armes and
follow your good king.   584

KEN. Why, George, I rise not against
King Edward, but for the poore that is opprest by wrong; and if King Edward will
redresse the same, I will not offer him disparagement, but otherwise; and so let this
suffise. Thou hear'st the reason why [590
I rise in armes; nowe, wilt thou leaue Wakefield and wend with me, Ile make thee
captaine of a hardie band, and, when I haue
my will, dubbe thee a knight.

GEORGE. Why, my lord, haue you any
hope to winne?   596

KEND. Why, there is a prophecie doeth
say that King Iames and I shall meete at
London, and make the king vaile bonnet to
vs both.[3]   600

GEO. If this were true, my lord, this
were a mighty reason.

KEN. Why, it is a miraculous proph-
ecie, and cannot faile.   604

GEORGE. Well, my lord, you haue almost turned me. — Ienkin, come hither.

IENKIN. Sir?

GEORGE. Goe your waies home, sir, and
driue me those three horses home vnto my
house; and powre them downe a bushell of
good oates.   611

IENKIN.   Well, I will.   [*Aside.*]   Must I giue these scuruie horses oates?

Exit Ienkin.

GEOR.   Will it please you to commaund your traine aside?   615
KEND.   Stand aside.

Exit the trayne.

GEORGE.   Nowe list to me: here in a wood, not farre from hence, there dwels an old man in a caue alone, that can foretell what fortunes shall befall you, for he [620 is greatly skilfull in magike arte. Go you three to him early in the morning and question him: if he saies good, why, then, my lord, I am the formost man! We will march vp with your campe to London. 625
KEND.   George, thou honourest me in this. But where shall we finde him out?
GEORGE.   My man shall conduct you to the place. But, good my lords, tell me true what the wise man saith.   630
KEND.   That will I, as I am Earle of Kendal.
GEORGE.   Why, then, to honour G[eorge] a Greene the more, vouchsafe a peece of beefe at my poore house. You shall [635 haue wafer cakes your fill, a peece of beefe hung vp since Martilmas:[1] — if that like you not, take what you bring, for me!
KEND.   Gramercies, George.

Exeunt omnes.

[*Before Grime's House.*]

Enter George a Greenes boy, Wily, disguised like a woman, to M. Grimes.

WILY.   O, what is loue! It is some mightie power,   640
Else could it neuer conquer G[eorge] a Greene.
Here dwels a churle that keepes away his loue.
I know the worst — and if I be espied,
Tis but a beating.   And if I by this meanes
Can get faire Bettris forth her fathers dore,[2]   645
It is enough.

---

[1] Martinmas, November 11.
[2] I.e. enable her to escape.

Venus, for me, and all the Gods aboue,[1]
Be aiding to my wily enterprise!

He knocks at the doore.

Enter Grime.

GRI.   How now! Who knocks there? What would you haue?
From whence came you? Where doe you dwell?   650
WILY.   I am, forsooth, a semsters maide hard by,
That hath brought worke home to your daughter.
GRIME.   Nay, are you not some craftie queane
That comes from George a Greene, that rascall,
With some letters to my daughter?   655
I will haue you searcht.
WILY.   Alas, sir, it is Hebrue vnto me
To tell me of George a Greene, or any other!
Search me, good sir,
And if you finde a letter about me,   660
Let me haue the punishment that is due.
GRIME.   Why are you mufled? I like you the worse
For that.
WILY.   I am not, sir, asham'd to shew my face,
Yet loth I am my cheekes should take the aire —   665
Not that I am charie of my beauties hue,
But that I am troubled with the tooth-ach sore.

[*He takes the handkerchief from before his mouth.*][2]

GRIME.   A pretie wench, of smiling countenance!
Olde men can like, although they cannot loue —
I,[3] and loue, though not so briefe as yong men can.   670
Well, goe in, my wench, and speake with my daughter.

---

[1] A. *and all goes alone.* Dyce and Collins read: *of all the Gods alone;* Greg suggests: *and all gods a loue.*
[2] "Holdinge her handkercher beeffore mouthes as trobled with a payne in her teethe." — *The Famouus Hystory off George a Greene,* chap. ix.
[3] Aye.

Exit [Wily].

I wonder much at the Earle of Kendall,
Being a mightie man, as still he is,
Yet for to be a traitor to his king   674
Is more then God or man will well allow.
But what a foole am I to talke of him!
My minde is more heere of the pretie lasse.
Had she brought some fortie pounds to
      towne
I could be content to make her my wife.
Yet I haue heard it in a prouerbe said, 680
"He that is olde and marries with a lasse,
Lies but at home, and prooues himselfe an
      asse."

*Enter Bettris in Wilies apparell to Grime,
[holding her handkerchief before her
mouth].*

How now, my wench! How ist? What,
      not a word? —
Alas, poore soule, the tooth-ach plagues her
      sore. —
Well, my wench, here is an angel [1] for to
      buy thee pinnes.   685
And I pray thee vse mine house;
The oftner, the more welcome. Farewell.

Exit.

BETTRIS. O blessed loue, and blessed for-
      tune both!
But, Bettris, stand not here to talke of loue,
But hye thee straight vnto thy George a
      Greene.   690
Neuer went roe-bucke swifter on the
      downes
Then I will trip it till I see my George.

[Exit Bettris.]

*[Before the cave of the old magician, near
Wakefield.]*

*Enter the Earle of Kendall, L[ord] Bonfield,
Sir Gilbert, and Ienkin the clowne.*

KEND. Come away, Ienkin.
IEN. Come; here is his house. *[Calling.]*
      Where be you, ho?
GEORG *[within]*. Who knocks there? 695
KEND. Heere are two or three poore men,
      father,

---

[1] A gold coin with a value of about ten shillings.

Would speake with you.
GEORG. Pray, giue your man leaue to
      leade me forth.
KEND. Goe, Ienkin, fetch him forth.
IEN. Come, olde man.   700

Enter George a Greene disguised.

KEND. Father, heere is three poore men
      come to question
Thee a word in secrete that concernes their
      liues.
GEORGE. Say on, my sonnes.
KEND. Father, I am sure you heare the
      newes
How that the Earle of Kendal wars against
      the king.   705
Now, father, we three are gentlemen by
      birth,
But yonger brethren that want reuenues,
And for the hope we haue to be preferd,
If that we knew that we shall winne,
We will march with him;   710
If not, we will not march a foote to London
      more.
Therefore, good father, tell vs what shall
      happen,
Whether the king or the Earle of Kendal
      shall win.
GEORGE. The king, my sonne.
KEND. Art thou sure of that?   715
GEORGE. I, as sure as thou art Henry
      Momford,
The one L[ord] Bonfild, the other Sir Gilbert.
KEND. Why this is wondrous, being
      blinde of sight,
His deepe perseuerance [1] should be such to
      know vs!
GILB. Magike is mightie, and foretelletk
      great matters.   720
In-deede, father, here is the earle come to
      see thee;
And therefore, good father, fable not with
      him.
GEORGE. Welcome is the earle to my
      poore cell.
And so are you, my lords. But let me
      counsell you
To leaue these warres against your king,
And liue in quiet.   726
KEND. Father, we come not for aduice in
      warre,

---

[1] Perceiverance, power of perceiving.

But to know whether we shall win or leese.

GEORGE. Lose, gentle lords, but not by
good King Edward;
A baser man shall giue you all the foile. 730

KEND. I, marie, father, what man is that?

GEORGE. Poore George a Greene, the pinner.

KEND. What shall he?

GEORGE. Pull all your plumes, and sore
dishonour you.

KEND. He! As how? 735

GEORG. Nay, the end tries all. But so it
will fall out.

KEND. But so it shall not, by my honor!
Christ!
Ile raise my campe, and fire Wakefield
towne,
And take that seruile pinner, George a
Greene,
And butcher him before King Edwards
face. 740

GEORGE. Good my lord, be not offended;
For I speake no more then arte reueales to
me:
And for greater proofe,
Giue your man leaue to fetch me [out] [1] my
staffe.

KEND. Ienkin, fetch him his walking
staffe. 745

[*Jenkin goes in and brings out George's staff.*]

IEN. Here is your walking staffe.

GEORGE. Ile proue it good vpon your car-
cases
A wiser wisard neuer met you yet,
Nor one that better could foredoome your
fall.
Now I haue singled you here alone, 750
I care not, [I], [2] though you be three to one.

[*Throws off his disguise.*]

KEND. Villaine, hast thou betraid vs?

GEORG. Momford, thou liest! neuer was I
traitor yet;
Onely deuis'd this guile to draw you on
For to be combatants. 755
Now conquere me, and then march on to
London!
But [it] [3] shall goe hard, but I will holde you
taske. [4]

---

[1] Added by Nicholson. [2] Added by Collins.
[3] Collins changes *But* to *It.* [4] Qy. *fasie.*

GILB. Come, my lord, cheerely. Ile kill
him hand to hand.

KEND. A thousand pound to him that
strikes that stroke!

GEORG. Then giue it me, for I will haue
the first. 760

*Here they fight. George kils Sir Gilbert, and
takes the other two prisoners.*

BONFILD. Stay, George! we doe appeale. [1]

GEORGE. To whom?

BON. Why, to the king;
For rather had we bide what he appoynts,
Then here be murthered by a seruile
groome. 765

KEND. What wilt thou doe with vs?

GEORG. Euen as Lord Bonfild wis[h]t,
You shall vnto the king;
And, for that purpose, see where the Iustice
is placed.

Enter Iustice.

IUST. Now, my Lord of Kendal, where be
al your threats? 770
Euen as the cause, so is the combat fallen,
Else one could neuer haue conquerd
three.

KEND. I pray thee, Woodroffe, doe not
twit me.
If I haue faulted, I must make amends.

GEORG. Master Woodroffe, here is not a
place for many 775
Words.
I beseech ye, sir, discharge all his souldiers,
That euery man may goe home vnto his
owne house.

IUSTICE. It shall bee so. What wilt thou
doe, George?

GEORG. Master Woodroffe, looke to your
charge; 780
Leaue me to myselfe.

IUST. Come, my Lords.

Exit all but George.

GEORG. Here sit thou, George, wearing a
willow wreath,
As one despairing of thy beautious loue.
Fie, George! No more! 785
Pine not away for that which cannot be.
I cannot ioy in any earthly blisse
So long as I doe want my Bettris.

---

[1] Appeal to a higher judge.

Enter Ienkin.

IEN. Who see a master of mine?
GEORGE. How now, sirrha! whither away?
IEN. Whither away? why, who doe you
take me to bee?   791
GEORG. Why Ienkin, my man.
IEN. I was so once, in-deede, but now the
case is altered.
GEORGE. I pray thee, as how?
IEN. Were not you a fortune-teller to day?
GEORGE. Well, what of that?   796
IEN. So sure am I become a iugler.
What will you say if I iuggle your sweete
heart?
GEORGE. Peace, prating losell! Her iel-
ous father
Doth wait ouer her with such suspitious
eyes,   800
That, if a man but dally by her feete,
He thinks it straight a witch [1] to charme
his daughter.
IEN. Well, what will you giue me if I
bring her hither?
GEORGE. A sute of greene, and twentie
crownes besides.
IEN. Well, by your leaue, giue me roome.

[*He draws a magician's circle.*]

You must giue me something that you haue
lately worne.[2]   806
GEORGE. Here is a gowne; will that serue
you?

[*Throws him the gown used in the impersona-
tion of the old man.*]

IENKIN. I, this will serue me. Keepe out
of my circle,
Least you be torne in pieces by shee deuils.
Mistres Bettris, once! twice! thrice!   810
He throwes the gowne [3] in, and she comes out.

Oh, is this no cunning?
GEORGE. Is this my loue, or is it but her
shadow?
IENKIN. I, this is the shadow, but heere is
the substance.
GEORGE. Tell mee, sweete loue, what good
fortune
Brought thee hither?   815

¹ Here, as often, masculine.
² A regular device in witchcraft.   ³ A. *ground.*

For one it was that fauoured George a
Greene.
BETTRIS. Both loue and fortune brought
me to my George,
In whose sweete sight is all my hearts con-
tent.
GEOR. Tell mee, sweete loue, how camst
thou from thy fathers?
BETTRIS. A willing minde hath many
slips in loue: 820
It was not I, but Wily, thy sweete boy.
GEOR. And where is Wily now?
BETTRIS. In my apparell, in my chamber
still.
GEOR. Ienkin, come hither. Goe to
Bradford,
And listen out [1] your fellow Wily. —   825
Come, Bettris, let vs in,
And in my cottage we will sit and talke.

Exeunt omnes.

[*London: the Court of King Edward.*]

*Enter King Edward, the King of Scots, Lord
Warwicke, yong Cuddy, and their traine.*

EDWARD. Brother of Scotland, I doe hold
it hard,
Seeing a league of truce was late confirmde
Twixt you and me, without displeasure
offered   830
You should make such inuasion in my land.
The vowes of kings should be as oracles,
Not blemisht with the staine of any breach,
Chiefly where fealtie and homage willeth it.
IAMES. Brother of England, rub not the
sore afresh;   835
My conscience grieues me for my deepe
misdeede.
I haue the worst; of thirtie thousand men,
There scapt not full fiue thousand from the
field.
EDWARD. Gramercie, Musgroue, else it
had gone hard.
Cuddie, Ile quite thee well ere we two part.
IAMES. But had not his olde father, Wil-
liam Musgroue,   841
Plaid twice the man, I had not now bene
here.
A stronger man I seldome felt before.
But one of more resolute valiance

¹ Seek information concerning.

Treads not, I thinke, vpon the English
   ground.   845
EDWARD. I wot wel, Musgroue shall not
   lose his hier.[1]
CUDDIE. And it please your Grace, my
   father was
Fiue score and three at midsommer last
   past;
Yet, had King Iamie bene as good as
   George a Greene,
Yet Billy Musgroue would haue fought
   with him.   850
EDWARD. As George a Greene! I pray
   thee, Cuddie,
Let me question thee.
Much haue I heard, since I came to my
   crowne,
Many in manner of a prouerbe [2] say,
"Were he as good as G[eorge] a Green, I
   would strike him sure."   855
I pray thee tell me, Cuddie, canst thou in-
   forme me
What is that George a Greene?
CUDDIE. Know, my lord, I neuer saw the
   man,
But mickle talke is of him in the coun-
   try.
They say he is the pinner of Wakefield
   towne;   860
But for his other qualities, I let alone.
WAR. May it please your Grace, I know
   the man too wel.
EDWARD. Too well! Why so, Warwicke?
WAR. For once he swingde me till my
   bones did ake.
EDWARD. Why, dares he strike an earle?
WARW. An earle, my lord! nay, he wil
   strike a king,   866
Be it not King Edward.
For stature he is framde
Like to the picture of stoute Hercules,
And for his carriage passeth Robin Hood.
The boldest earle or baron of your land 871
That offereth scath vnto the towne of
   Wakefield,
George will arrest his pledge vnto the
   pound;
And who-so resisteth beares away the
   blowes,
For he himselfe is good inough for three.

[1] Hire, reward.
[2] The phrase quoted was a common proverb.

EDWARD. Why, this is wondrous! My
   L[ord] of Warwicke,   876
Sore do I long to see this George a Greene.
But leauing him, what shall we do, my
   lord,
For to subdue the rebels in the north?
They are now marching vp to Doncaster.

Enter one with the Earle of Kendal prisoner.

Soft! who haue we there?   881
CUDDIE.[1] Here is a traitour, the Earle of
   Kendal.
EDWARD. Aspiring traitour! how darst
   thou once
Cast thine eyes vpon thy soueraigne
That honour'd thee with kindenes and
   with fauour?   885
But I will make thee buy this treason
   deare.
KEND. Good my lord —
EDWARD. Reply not, traitor. —
Tell me, Cuddy, whose deede of honour
Wonne the victorie against this rebell? 890
CUDDY. George a Greene, the pinner cf
   Wakefield.
EDWARD. George a Greene! Now shall I
   heare newes
Certaine what this pinner is.
Discourse it briefly, Cuddy, how it befell.
CUD. Kendall and Bonfild, with Sir Gil-
   bert Armstrong,   895
Came to Wakefield towne disguisd,
And there spoke ill of your grace;
Which George, but hearing, feld them at
   his feete;
And, had not rescue come into the place,
George had slaine them [2] in his close of
   wheate.   900
EDWARD. But, Cuddy, canst thou not tell
Where I might giue and grant some thing
That might please, and highly gratifie the
   pinners thoughts?
CUDDIE. This at their parting George did
   say to me: 904
"If the king vouchsafe of this my seruice,
Then, gentle Cuddie, kneele vpon thy knee,
And humbly craue a boone of him for me."

[1] This, with the following speeches, is inconsist-
ently put into the mouth of Cuddie, possibly as a
result of the cutting of the play and the elimination
of one actor. In the prose story we read: "Justyce
Grymes arrived lykewyse and presented, as from
George a Greene, the Earle of Kendall." In the play
it should be Justice Woodroffe.   [2] A. *him.*

EDWARD. Cuddie, what is it?
CUDDIE. It is his will your Grace would
pardon them,
And let them liue, although they haue of-
fended. 910
EDWARD. I think the man striueth to be
glorious.
Well, George hath crau'd it, and it shall be
graunted,
Which none but he in England should haue
gotten.
Liue, Kendall — but as prisoner;
So shalt thou end thy dayes within the
tower. 915
KEND. Gracious is Edward to offending
subiects.
IAMES. My Lord of Kend, you are wel-
come to the court.
EDWARD. Nay, but "ill come," as it fals
out now;
I, "ill come," in-deede, were it not for
George a Greene.

[*Edward mockingly bows to James and the
Earl of Kendall.*]

But, "gentle king" — for so you would
auerre — 920
And "Edwards betters," I salute you
both,

[*He mockingly vails bonnet to them.*] [1]

And here I vowe, by good Saint George,
You wil gaine but litle when your summes
are counted!
I sore doe long to see this George a
Greene.
And for because I neuer saw the north, 925
I will forthwith goe see it;
And for that to none I will be knowen,
We will disguise our selues and steale
downe secretly,
Thou and I, King Iames, Cuddie, and two
or three,
And make a merrie iourney for a moneth.
Away, then, conduct him to the tower. 931
Come on, King Iames, my heart must
needes be merrie,
If fortune make such hauocke of our
foes.

Ex. omnes.

<hr/>

[1] Thus fulfilling the prophecy. Cf. lines 597–600.

[*Sherwood Forest.*] [1]

*Enter Robin Hood, Mayd Marian, Scarlet,
and Much, the Millers sonne.*

ROBIN. Why is not louely Marian blithe
of cheere?
What ayles my lemman,[2] that she gins to
lowre? 935
Say, good Marian, why art thou so sad?
MARIAN. Nothing, my Robin, grieues me
to the heart
But whensoeuer I doe walke abroad
I heare no songs but all of George a Greene;
Bettris, his faire lemman, passeth me. 940
And this, my Robin, gaules my very soule.
ROBIN. Content [thee].[3] What wreakes
it vs though George a
Greene be stoute,
So long as he doth proffer vs no scath?
Enuie doth seldome hurt but to it selfe. 945
And therefore, Marian, smile vpon thy
Robin.
MARIAN. Neuer will Marian smile vpon
her Robin,
Nor lie with him vnder the green wood
shade,
Till that thou go to Wakefield on a greene,
And beate the pinner for the loue of me.
ROBIN. Content thee, Marian; I will ease
thy griefe; 951
My merrie men and I will thither stray.
And heere I vow that, for the loue of thee,
I will beate George a Greene, or he shall
beate me.
SCARLET. As I am Scarlet, next to Little
Iohn, 955
One of the boldest yeomen of the crew,
So will I wend with Robin all along,
And try this pinner what he dares [to] do.
MUCH. As I am Much, the millers sonne,
That left my mill to go with thee — 960
And nill repent that I haue done;
This pleasant life contenteth me —
In ought I may, to doe thee good,
Ile liue and die with Robin Hood.
MARIAN. And, Robin, Marian she will goe
with thee, 965
To see faire Bettris how bright she is of
blee.

<hr/>

[1] The place is stated in the prose romance, *The
Famouus Hystory off George a Greene*, chap. xii.
[2] Sweetheart. [3] Supplied by Dyce.

ROBIN. Marian, thou shalt goe with thy Robin.

[*He turns to his followers.*]

Bend vp your bowes, and see your strings be tight,
The arrowes keene, and euery thing be ready;
And each of you a good bat on his necke,
Able to lay a good man on the ground.   971
SCARLET. I will haue Frier Tuckes.
MUCH. I will haue Little Iohns.
ROBIN. I will haue one made of an ashen planke,[1]
Able to beare a bout or two. —   975
Then come on, Marian, let vs goe!
For before the sunne doth shew the morning day,
I wil be at Wakefield to see this pinner, George a Greene.

Exeunt omnes.

[*The town of Bradford.*]

Enter a Shoomaker sitting vpon the stage at worke. Ienkin to him [*with a staff on his shoulder*].

IEN. My masters, he that hath neither meate nor money,
And hath lost his credite with the alewife,
For anything I know may goe supperlesse to bed.   981
But, soft! who is heere? Here is a shoomaker.
He knowes where is the best ale. —
Shoomaker, I pray thee tell me,
Where is the best ale in the towne?   985
SHOOMAKER. Afore, afore; follow thy nose;
At the signe of the eggeshell.[2]
IENKIN. Come, shoomaker, if thou wilt,
And take thy part of a pot.
SHOOMAKER. Sirra, downe with your staffe!   990
Downe with your staffe!
IENKIN. Why, how now! is the fellow mad?
I pray thee tell me, why should I hold downe my staffe?

SHOOMA. You wil downe with him, will you not, sir?
IENKIN. Why, tell me wherefore?   995
SHOO. My friend, this is the towne of merry Bradford,[1]
And here is a custome held
That none shall passe with his staffe on his shoulders
But he must haue a bout with me;
And so shall you, sir.   1000
IENKIN. And so will I not, sir!
SHOO. That wil I try. Barking dogs bite not the sorest.
IENKIN [*aside*]. I would to God I were once well rid of him.
SHOOMA. Now, what! will you downe with your staffe?
IENKIN. Why, you are not in earnest, are you?   1005
SHOOMA. If I am not, take that.

[*Strikes him with his staff.*]

IENKIN. You whoorsen cowardly scabbe,
It is but the part of a clapperdudgeon [2]
To strike a man in the streete.
But darest thou walke to the townes end with me?   1010
SHOOMAKER. I, that I dare do! But stay till I lay in my
Tooles, and I will goe with thee to the townes end
Presently.
IENKIN [*aside*]. I would I knew how to be rid of this fellow.
SHOOM. Come, sir; wil you go to the townes end now, sir?   1015
IENKIN. I, sir; come.

[*They cross over to the other end of the stage.*]

Now we are at the townes end. What say you now?
SHOOMAKER. Marry, come let vs euen haue a bout.
IENKIN. Ha! stay a little! Hold thy hands, I pray thee!
SHOOM. Why whats the matter?   1020
IENKIN. Faith, I am vnder-pinner of a towne,
And there is an order, which if I doe not keepe,

---

[1] A. *plunke;* emend. by Mitford.
[2] The sign of the ale-house.

[1] A. *Wakefield.*
[2] A term of insult, of unknown origin.

I shall be turned out of mine office.

SHOOMAKER. What is that, sir?

IENKIN. Whensoeuer I goe to fight with
any bodie, 1025
I vse to flourish my staffe thrise about my
head
Before I strike — and then shew no fauour.

SHOOMAKER. Well, sir, and till then I will
not strike thee.

IENKIN. Wel, sir, here is once, twice: —
here is my hand;
I will neuer doe it the third time. 1030

SHOOMAKER. Why, then I see we shall not
fight.

IENKIN. Faith, no. Come, I will giue
thee two pots
Of the best ale, and be friends.

SHOOMAK. Faith, I see it is as hard to get
water out of a flint, 1035
As to get him to haue a bout with me;
Therefore I will enter into him for some
good cheere. —
My friend, I see thou art a faint-hearted
fellow,
Thou hast no stomacke to fight;
Therefore let vs go to the alehouse and
drinke.

IENKIN. Well, content. Goe thy wayes,
and say thy prayers 1040
Thou scapst my hands today.

Exeunt omnes.

[*Near George a Greene's house, Wakefield.*]

Enter George a Greene and Bettris.

GEORGE. Tell me, sweet loue: how, is thy
minde content?
What, canst thou brooke to liue with
George a Greene?

BETTRIS. Oh, George, how little pleasing
are these words! 1044
Came I from Bradford for the loue of thee
And left my father for so sweet a friend.
Here will I liue vntill my life doe end.

*Enter Robin Hood and Marian, and
his traine.*

GEORGE. Happy am I to haue so sweet a
loue. —
But what are these come trasing [1] here
along?

[1] Proceeding.

BETTRIS. Three men come striking
through the corne, 1050
My loue.

[*George runs towards the trespassers.*]

GEORGE. Backe againe, you foolish trauellers!
For you are wrong, and may not wend this
way.

ROBIN HOOD. That were great shame!
Now, by my soule, proud sir, 1055
We be three tall [1] yeomen, and thou art but
one. —
Come, we will forward in despite of him.

GEORGE. Leape the ditch, or I will make
you skip!
What, cannot the hie-way serue your turne,
But you must make a path ouer the corne?

ROBIN. Why, art thou mad? Dar'st thou
incounter three? 1061
We are no babes, man; looke vpon our
limmes.

GEO. Sirra, the biggest lims haue not the
stoutest hearts.
Were ye as good as Robin Hood and his
three mery men,
Ile driue you backe the same way that ye
came. 1065
Be ye men, ye scorne to incounter me all at
once;
But be ye cowards, set vpon me all three,
And try the pinner what he dares performe!

SCARLET. Were thou as high in deedes
As thou art haughtie in wordes, 1070
Thou well mightest be a champion for the
king;
But emptie vessels haue the loudest
sounds,
And cowards prattle more than men of
worth.

GEORGE. Sirra, darest thou trie me?

SCARLET. I, sirra, that I dare. 1075

They fight, and George a Greene beats him.

MUCH. How now! what! art thou downe?
Come, sir, I am next.

They fight, and George a Greene beates him.

ROBIN HOOD. Come, sirra, now to me.
Spare me not,

[1] Stout.

For Ile not spare thee!
GEORGE.   Make no doubt I will be as lib-
erall to thee.   1080

They fight; Robin Hood stays.

ROBIN HOOD.   Stay, George! for here I doo
protest,
Thou art the stoutest champion that euer I
layd
Handes vpon.[1]
GEORGE.   Soft you, sir! by your leaue, you
lye;
You neuer yet laid hands on me.   1085
ROBIN HOOD.   George, wilt thou forsake
Wakefield,
And go with me?
Two liueries will I giue thee euerie yeere,
And fortie crownes shall be thy fee.
GEORGE.   Why, who art thou?   1090
ROBIN HOOD.   Why, Robin Hood.
I am come hither with my Marian
And these my yeomen for to visit thee.
GEORGE.   Robin Hood!   Next to King
Edward
Art thou leefe to me.   1095
Welcome, sweet Robin!   Welcome, mayd
Marian!
And welcome, you my friends!
Will you to my poore house?
You shall haue wafer cakes your fill, 1099
A peece of beefe hung vp since martlemas,
Mutton, and veale.   If this like you not,
Take that you finde, or that you bring, for
me.
ROBIN HOOD.   Godamercies, good George;
Ile be thy ghest to day.
GEORGE.   Robin, therein thou honourest
me.   1105
Ile leade the way.

Exeunt omnes.

[*Bradford.*]

*Enter King Edward and King Iames dis-
guised, with two staues [on their shoul-
ders].*

EDWARD.   Come on, King Iames.   Now
wee are
Thus disguised,
There is none, I know, will take vs to be kings.

---

[1] Cf. the Robin Hood plays.   In the prose story
the Robin Hood legend is much further developed.

I thinke we are now in Bradford,   1110
Where all the merrie shoomakers dwell.

Enter a Shoomaker.

SHOOMAKER.   Downe with your staues,
my friends!
Downe with them!
EDWARD.   Downe with our staues?   I pray
thee, why so?
SHOOMAKER.   My friend, I see thou art a
stranger heere,   1115
Else wouldest thou not haue questiond of
the thing.
This is the towne of merrie Bradford,
And here hath beene a custome, kept of olde,
That none may beare his staffe vpon his
necke,
But traile it all along throughout the
towne,   1120
Vnlesse they meane to haue a bout with me.
EDWARD.   But heare you, sir, hath the king
Granted you this custome?
SHOOMAKER.   King or kaisar, none shall
passe this way,
Except King Edward;   1125
No, nor the stoutest groome that haunts
his court.
Therefore downe with your staues!
EDWARD.   What were we best to do?
IAMES.   Faith, my lord, they are stoute
fellowes;
And because we will see some sport,   1130
We will traile our staues.
EDWARD.   Heer'st thou, my friend?
Because we are men of peace, and trauellers,
We are content to traile our staues.
SHOOMAKER.   The way lyes before you; go
along.   1135

*Enter Robin Hood and George a Greene,
disguised.*

ROBIN HOOD.   See, George, two men are
passing
Through the towne,
Two lustie men, and yet they traile their
staues.
GEORGE.   Robin, they are some pesants
Trickt in yeomans weedes. — Hollo, you
two trauellers!   1140
EDWARD.   Call you vs, sir?
GEORGE.   I, you!   Are ye not big inough
to beare

Your bats vpon your neckes,
But you must traile them along the
    streetes?
EDWAR. Yes, sir, we are big inough; but
    here is a custome   1145
Kept, that none may passe, his staffe vpon
    his necke,
Vnless he traile it at the weapons point.
Sir, we are men of peace, and loue to sleepe
In our whole skins, and therefore quietnes
    is best.
GEORGE. Base minded pesants, worth-
    lesse to be men!   1150
What! haue you bones and limmes to
    strike a blow,
And be your hearts so faint you cannot fight?
Wert not for shame I would shrub your
    shoulders well,
And teach you manhood against another
    time.
SHOOM. Well preacht, sir Iacke! Downe
    with your staffe!   1155
EDWAR. Do you heare, my friends? and
    you be wise,
Keepe downe your staues,
For all the towne will rise vpon you.
GEORGE. Thou speakest like an honest
    quiet fellow!
But heare you me: In spite of all the
    swaines   1160
Of Bradford town, beare me your staues
    vpon your necks —
Or, to begin withall, Ile baste you both so
    well,
You were neuer better basted in your liues.
EDWARD. We will hold vp our staues.

*George a Greene fights with the Shoomakers,
    and beates them all downe.*

GEORGE. What, haue you any more? 1165
Call all your towne forth, cut and longtaile.

The Shoomakers spy George a Greene.

SHOOMAKER. What, George a Greene! is
    it you?
A plague found [1] you!
I thinke you long'd to swinge me well.
Come, George, we wil crush a pot before
    we part.   1170
GEORGE. A pot, you slaue? we will haue
    an hundred!

[1] Confound.

Heere, Will Perkins; take my purse,
Fetch me a stand [1] of ale, and set [it] in the
    market-place,
That all may drinke that are athirst this day;
For this is for a feee to welcome Robin
    Hood   1175
To Bradford towne.

*They bring out the stande of ale, and fall a
    drinking.*

Here, Robin, sit thou here; for thou art the
    best man
At the boord this day.
You that are strangers, place your selues
    where you will.
Robin, heer's a carouse to good King Ed-
    wards selfe.   1180
And they that loue him not, I would we had
The basting of them a litle!

*Enter the Earle of Warwicke with other noble
    men, bringing out the Kings garments;
    then George a Greene and the rest kneele
    downe to the King.*

EDWARD. Come, masters, all fellowes!
Nay, Robin, you are the best man at the
    boord to-day;
Rise vp, George.   1185
GEORGE. Nay, good my liege, ill-nurturd
    we were, then.
Though we Yorkeshire men be blunt of
    speech,
And litle skild in court or such quaint fash-
    ions,
Yet nature teacheth vs duetie to our king;
Therefore, I humbly beseech you, pardon
    George a Greene.   1190
ROBIN. And, good my lord, a pardon for
    poore Robin;
And for vs all a pardon, good King Ed-
    ward.
SHOOMAKER. I pray you, a pardon for the
    shoomakers.
EDWARD. I frankely grant a pardon to
    you all.
And, George a Greene, giue me thy hand!
There is none in England that shall doe
    thee wrong.   1196
Euen from my court I came to see thy selfe;
And now I see that fame speakes nought
    but trueth.

[1] Cask, barrel.

GEORGE. I humbly thanke your royall
Maiestie.
That which I did against the Earle of
Kendal, 1200
It was but a subiects duetie to his soueraigne,
And therefore little merit[s] such good words,
EDWARD. But ere I go, Ile grace thee with
good deeds.
Say what King Edward may performe,
And thou shalt haue it, being in Englands
bounds. 1205
GEORGE. I haue a louely lemman,
As bright of blee as is the siluer moone;
And olde Grimes, her father, will not let
her match
With me, because I am a pinner,
Although I loue her, and she me, dearely.
EDWARD. Where is she? 1211
GEORGE. At home at my poore house,
And vowes neuer to marrie vnlesse her
father
Giue consent; which is my great griefe, my
Lord.
EDWARD. If this be all, I will dispatch it
straight; 1215
Ile send for Grime and force him giue his
grant.
He will not denie King Edward such a sute.

Enter Ienkin, and speakes.

[IENKIN.] Ho! who saw a master of mine?
Oh, he is gotten into company — and [1] a
bodie should rake
Hell for companie. 1220
GEORGE. Peace, ye slaue! see where King
Edward is?
EDWARD. George, what is he?
GEORGE. I beseech your Grace pardon
him; he is my man.
SHOOMAKER. Sirra, the king hath bene
drinking with vs,
And did pledge vs too. 1225
IENKIN. Hath he so? Kneele; I dub you
"gentlemen."
SHOOMAKER. Beg it of the king, Ienkin.
IENKIN. I wil. — I beseech your worship
grant mee one thing.
EDWARD. What is that?
IENKIN. Hearke in your eare. 1230

He whispers the King in the eare.

[1] If.

EDWARD. Goe your wayes, and do it.
IENKIN. Come! downe on your knees! I
haue got it.
SHOOMAKER. Let vs heare what it is first.
IENKIN. Mary, because you haue
drunke with the king, and the king [1235
hath so graciously pledgd you, you shall
be no more called shoomakers, but you and
yours, to the worlds ende, shall be called
"the trade of the gentle craft."
SHOOMAKER. I beseech your Maiestie
reforme [1] this which he hath spoken. 1241
IENKIN. I beesech your worship consume this which he hath spoken.
EDWARD. Confirme it, you would say.
— Well, he hath done it for you; it is sufficient. — Come, George, we will goe to
Grime, and haue thy loue. 1247
IENKIN. I am sure your worship will
abide; for yonder is comming olde Musgroue and mad Cuddie his sonne. — [1250
Master, my fellow Wilie comes drest like a
woman, and master Grime will marrie
Wilie. Heere they come.

*Enter Musgroue and Cuddie, and master
Grime, Wilie, Mayd Marian, and
Bettris.*

EDWARD. Which is thy old father, Cud-
die? 1254
CUDDIE. This, if it please your Maiestie.
EDWARD. Ah, old Musgroue, rise [2] vp!
It fits not such gray haires to kneele.
MUSGROUE. Long liue my soueraigne!
Long and happie be his dayes!
Vouchsafe, my gracious lord, a simple gift
At Billy Musgroues hand. 1261
King Iames at Meddellom Castle gaue me
this;
This wonne the honour, and this giue I
thee.

[He hands him a sword.]

EDWARD. Godamercie, Musgroue, for
this friendly gift.
And, for thou feldst a king with this same
weapon, 1265
This blade shall here dub valiant Musgroue
knight.

[1] Re-establish, renew.
[2] A. *kneele*, possibly caught by the printer from
the line below.

Musg.   Alas, what hath your highnes
    done? I am poore.
Edw.   To mend thy liuing take thou Med-
    dellom Castle,
The hold [1] of both.   And if thou want liu-
    ing, complaine;
Thou shalt haue more to mainetaine thine
    estate.   1270
George, which is thy loue?
George.   This, if please your Maiestie.
Edward.   Art thou her aged father?
Grime.   I am, and it like your Maiestie.
Edwar.   And wilt not giue thy daughter
    vnto George?   1275
Grime.   Yes, my lord, if he will let me
    marrie
With this louely lasse.
Edward.   What sayst thou, George?
George.   With all my heart, my lord, I
    giue consent.
Grime.   Then do I giue my daughter vnto
    George.   1280
Wilie.   Then shall the mariage soone be
    at an end.

                [Throws off his disguise.]

Witnesse, my lord, if that I be a woman!
For I am Wilie, boy to George a Greene,
Who for my master wrought this subtill
    shift.
Edward.   What! is it a boy?   What sayst
    thou to this, Grime?   1285
Grime.   Mary, my lord, I thinke this boy
    hath
More knauerie than all the world besides.
Yet am I content that George shall both
    haue
My daughter and my lands.
Edward.   Now, George, it rests I gratifie
    thy worth.   1290
And therefore here I doe bequeath to thee,
In full possession, halfe that Kendal hath;
And what as Bradford holdes of me in chiefe,
I giue it frankely vnto thee for euer.
Kneele downe, George.   1295
George.   What will your Maiestie do?
Edward.   Dub thee a knight, George.

George.   I beseech your Grace, grant me
    one thing.
Edward.   What is that?
George.   Then let me liue and die a yeo-
    man still.   1300
So was my father, so must liue his sonne.
For tis more credite to men of base degree
To do great deeds, than men of dignitie.
Edward.   Well, be it so, George.
Iames.   I beseech your Grace dispatch
    with me,[1]   1305
And set downe my ransome.
Edward.   George a Greene, set downe the
    King of Scots
His ransome.
George.   I beseech your Grace pardon me;
It passeth my skill.   1310
Edward.   Do it; the honor's thine.
George.   Then let King Iames make good
Those townes which he hath burnt vpon
    the borders;
Giue a small pension to the fatherlesse,
Whose fathers he caus'd murthered in
    those warres;   1315
Put in pledge for these things to your
    Grace;
And so returne.
[Edward.] [2]   King Iames, are you con-
    tent?
Iamie.   I am content, and like [3] your Mai-
    estie,
And will leaue good castles in securitie.
Edward.   I craue no more. — Now,
    George a Greene,   1321
Ile to thy house.   And when I haue supt,
    Ile go to Aske,[4]
And see if Iane a Barley be so faire
As good King Iames reports her for to be.
And for the ancient custome of "Vaile
    Staffe," keepe it still;   1325
Clayme priuiledge from me:
If any aske a reason why, or how,
Say, English Edward vaild his staffe to
    you.

                [Exeunt omnes.]

[1] Dispose of my case.
[2] A. omits speaker's name, and runs the line into
George's speech.   Corrected by Dyce.
[3] If it please.
[4] A town in Yorkshire.

[1] I imagine that Edward appoints him to be
keeper of Meddellom Castle, as well as Handoun
(or Sandon) Castle.   The line, however, may be
corrupt.

                        FINIS.